1 MONTH OF
FREE
READING

at

www.ForgottenBooks.com

By purchasing this book you are eligible for one month membership to ForgottenBooks.com, giving you unlimited access to our entire collection of over 1,000,000 titles via our web site and mobile apps.

To claim your free month visit:

www.forgottenbooks.com/free924603

ISBN 978-0-260-05135-6
PIBN 10924603

THE

REVISED REPORTS

A REPUBLICATION OF SUCH CASES

IN THE

ENGLISH COURTS OF COMMON LAW AND EQUITY,

FROM THE YEAR 1785

AS ARE STILL OF PRACTICAL UTILITY.

EDITED BY

SIR FREDERICK POLLOCK, Bart., D.C.L., LL.D.,

OF LINCOLN'S INN,

ASSISTED BY

O. A. SAUNDERS, J. G. PEASE, and ARTHUR B. CANE,
(EQUITY CASES).   (COMMON LAW CASES).

ALL OF THE INNER TEMPLE.

VOL. LXIX.

1844–1846.

12 CLARK & FINNELLY; 2 JONES & LATOUCHE; 2 COM-
MON BENCH; 14 MEESON & WELSBY; 2 DOWLING &
LOWNDES; 8 JURIST.

SWEET AND MAXWELL, Limited, 3, CHANCERY LANE.

BOSTON:

LITTLE, BROWN & CO.

1904.

BRADBURY, AGNEW, & CO., LD., PRINTERS,
LONDON AND TONBRIDGE.

TABLE OF COMPARATIVE REFERENCE.

OLD REPORTS.	REVISED REPORTS.
CASES FROM	
Adolphus & Ellis	
12 vols.	40, 42 to 48, 50, 52 & 54
Anstruther—3 vols.	3 & 4
Arnold—2 vols.	50
Ball & Beatty—2 vols.	12
Barnewall & Adolphus—5 vols.	35 to 39
Barnewall & Alderson—5 vols.	18 to 24
Barnewall & Cresswell—10 vols.	25 to 34
Beavan—Vols. 1 to 8	49, 50, 52, 55, 59, 63, 64, 66
Bingham	
10 vols.	25, 27 to 31, 33 to 35, 38
Bingham, N.C.	
6 vols.	41 to 44, 50 & 54
Blackstone, H.—2 vols.	2 & 3
Bligh—4 vols.	20 to 22
Bligh, N. S.—Vols. 1 to 11	30 to 33, 35, 36, 38, 39, 42 & 51
Bosanquet & Puller—5 vols.	4 to 9
Broderip & Bingham—3 vols.	21 to 24
Campbell—4 vols.	10 to 16
Carrington & Marshman	66
Carrington & Payne—Vols. 1 to 9	28, 31, 33, 34, 36, 40, 48, 56, 62
Chitty—2 vols.	22 & 23
Clark & Finnelly—12 vols.	36, 37, 39, 42, 47, 49, 51, 54, 57, 59, 65, 69
Collyer, C. C.—Vol. 1	66
Common Bench—Vols. 1 & 2	68, 69
Cooper temp. Brougham	38
Cooper, C. P.	46
Cooper, G.	14
Cox—2 vols.	1 & 2
Craig & Phillips	54
Crompton & Jervis—2 vols.	35 & 37
Crompton & Meeson—2 vols.	38, 39
Crompton, Meeson & Roscoe	
2 vols.	40, 41
Daniell	18
Danson & Lloyd	34
Davison & Merivale	64
Dow—6 vols.	14 to 16 & 19
Dow & Clark—2 vols.	35
Dowling—9 vols.	36, 39, 41, 46, 49, 54, 59 & 61
Dowling, N. S.—	63, 65
Dowling & Lowndes—Vols. 1 & 2	67, 69
Dowling & Ryland's K. B.	
9 vols.	24 to 30
Dowling & Ryland's N. P.	25

OLD REPORTS.	REVISED REPORTS.
CASES FROM	
Drinkwater, C. P.	60
Drury	67
Drury & Walsh—2 vols.	56
Drury & Warren—4 vols.	58, 59, 61, 65
Durnford & East—8 vols.	1 to 5
East—16 vols.	5 to 14
Espinasse—6 vols.	5, 6, 8, 9
Forrest	5
Gale & Davison—Vols. 1 to 3	55, 57, 26
Gow	21
Haggard's Adm.—3 vols.	33, 35
Hare—Vols. 1 to 4	58, 62, 64, 67
Harrison & Wollaston—2 vols.	47
Hodges—3 vols.	42 & 43
Hogan	34
Holt	17
Horn & Hurlstone—Vol. 1	51
Hurlstone & Walmsley	58
Jacob	23
Jacob & Walker—2 vols.	20 to 22
Jones & Latouche—Vols. 1 & 2	68, 69
Jurist—Vols. 1 to 8	49, 55, 58, 62, 65, 67, 69
Keen—2 vols.	44
Knapp—3 vols.	38, 40
Law Journal, O.S.—9 vols.	25 to 31, 34
Law Journal, N. S.—Vols. 1 to 14,	36, 37, 39, 41, 42, 46, 49, 52, 56, 59, 61, 63, 66
Lloyd & Goold, temp. Sugden	46
Lloyd & Welsby	35
Maddock—6 vols.	15 to 18 & 20 to 23
Manning & Granger	
7 vols.	56, 58, 60, 61, 63, 64, 66
Manning & Ryland—5 vols.	31 to 34
Marshall—2 vols.	15 & 17
Maule & Selwyn—6 vols.	14 to 18
Meeson & Welsby—Vols. 1 to 14	46, 49, 51, 52, 55, 56, 58, 60, 62, 63, 67, 69
McCleland	28
McCleland & Younge	29
Merivale—3 vols.	15 to 17
Moody & Malkin	31
Moody & Robinson—2 vols.	42, 62
Moore, C. P.—12 vols.	19 to 29
Moore, P. C.—Vols. 1 to 4	43, 46, 50, 59
Moore & Payne—5 vols.	29 to 31, 38
Moore & Scott—4 vols.	34, 35, 38
Murphy & Hurlstone	51

OLD REPORTS.	REVISED REPORTS.	OLD REPORTS.	REVISED REPORTS.
CASES FROM		CASES FROM	
Mylne & Craig—5 vols.	43, 45, 48	Smith—3 vols.	7 & 8
Mylne & Keen—3 vols.	36, 39, 41	Starkie—3 vols.	18 to 20 & 23
Nevile & Manning—6 vols.	38 to 43	Swanston—3 vols.	18 & 19
Nevile & Perry—3 vols.	44 & 45	Tamlyn	31
Peake—2 vols.	3 & 4	Taunton—8 vols.	9 to 21
Perry & Davison—4 vols.	48, 50, 52, 54	Turner & Russell	23 & 24
Phillips—Vol. 1	65	Tyrwhitt—5 vols.	35, 37 to 40
Price—13 vols.	15 to 27	Tyrwhitt & Granger	46
Queen's Bench—Vols. 1 to 7	55, 57, 61, 62, 64, 66, 68	Vesey, Jr.—19 vols.	1 to 18
		Vesey & Beames—3 vols.	12 & 13
Russell—5 vols.	25 to 29	West, H. L.	51
Russell & Mylne—2 vols.	32, 34	Wightwick	12
Russell & Ryan	15	Willmore, Wollaston & Davison	52
Ryan & Moody	27	Willmore, Wollaston & Hodges	52
Schoales & Lefroy—2 vols.	9	Wilson, Chy.	18
Scott—8 vols.	41 to 44, 50 & 54	Wilson, Ex. Eq.	18
Scott, N. R.—8 vols.	56, 58, 60, 61, 63, 64, 66	Younge, Ex. Eq.	34
Simons—Vols. 1 to 14	27, 29, 30, 33, 35, 38, 40, 42, 47, 51, 54, 56, 60 & 65	Younge & Collyer, C. C. 2 vols.	57, 60
		Younge & Collyer, Ex. Eq. 4 vols.	41, 47, 51 & 54
Simons & Stuart—2 vols.	24 & 25	Younge & Jervis—3 vols.	30 to 32

PREFACE TO VOLUME LXIX.

In the case of *Lord Dungannon* v. *Smith*, p. 137, it has been thought right to omit a considerable proportion of the judicial opinions, and some of the judgments in the House of Lords. The points of general application actually settled by the decision, namely that the question whether a limitation is bad for remoteness or not has nothing to do with the state of external facts, and that, as the rule against remoteness has nothing to do with intention, the instrument must be construed as if the rule did not exist, "and then to the provision so construed the Rule is to be remorselessly applied" (Gray on the Rule against Perpetuities, § 629) are by this time elementary. No modern student of conveyancing reading the head-note can fail to see that the gifts in question were bad. The difficulty is to understand how such eminent judges as Parke and Patteson ever contrived to think they could be supported. Lord Lyndhurst's judgment contains the whole law of the case, and is the only one to which we can find any later judicial reference.

There is a curious observation of Lord Campbell's in *Thomson* v. *The Advocate-General*, at p. 17, that "the doctrine of domicile has sprung up in this country very recently . . . but it is a very convenient doctrine." If Lord Campbell were still with us he would perhaps modify the following statement that "it is now well understood." See the very recent case of *Winans* v. *Attorney-General* [1904] A. C. 287, where the House of Lords was not unanimous on the interpretation of the facts. Nevertheless the rival doctrine of nationality, which now prevails in Continental jurisprudence, gives rise to quite as great difficulties, especially when it is applied to individual members of a composite international unit like the British Empire, who may be under any one of several different jurisdictions with different local laws: *Re Johnson* [1903] 1 Ch. 821, a case in which the subtle and ingenious reasoning of Farwell, J. commends itself to the present writer but is not universally accepted. The same difficulty might arise with regard to Switzerland, but one may doubt whether the local laws in any three cantons are as different as those, say, of Malta, Scotland, and the Province of Quebec.

If the thoroughly sound expositions given by Lord Langdale and Lord Cottenham in *Hammersley* v. *De Biel, De Biel* v. *Thomson*, p. 18, had been clearly understood at the time, we should have been spared the vague talk about "making representations good" which not only cumbered the text-books of equity for several years but led to more than one positively wrong decision. But these erroneous views are now clearly overruled. A promise *de futuro* cannot work an estoppel. It is a contract or nothing: *Re Fickus* [1900] 1 Ch. 331, 334; *George Whitechurch, Ltd.* v. *Cavanagh* [1902] A. C. 117, 130, per Lord Macnaghten. So one of the difficulties that beset counsel in the task of giving correct advice (see Lord Campbell's deprecating remarks at p. 54 of this volume) is out of the way. If, as Lord Campbell says, persons learned in the law do not guarantee the soundness of their opinions, it is obvious that lay people cannot be presumed to know the law; and we have it on the authority of Maule, J., in *Martindale* v. *Falkner*, at p. 611, that there is really no such presumption.

Rawlins v. *Overseers of West Derby*, p. 414, teaches us what may be lawfully done on a Sunday. *Coxhead* v. *Richards*, p. 530, and other cases following it, show how difficult it may be to decide, in unusual circumstances, whether an occasion is or is not privileged so as to excuse defamatory statements. The learned reporter of *Coxhead* v. *Richards* expressed his own opinion in the notes with more freedom than is now usual. Other learned notes, those to *Brown* v. *Gill*, on manorial and customary courts may safely be ascribed to Serjeant Manning. For once he was wrong in conjecturing that the court baron is *curia baronum* (p. 636). There is no authority whatever for such a title, or for supposing that the free suitors were ever called *barones*.

Turner v. *Mason*, p. 674, gives us an authentic exposition of the familiar contract of domestic service, one of the few contracts with which the majority of the lay people have a fair working acquaintance. By way of contrast *Fivaz* v. *Nicholls*, p. 514, may be mentioned for its singularity. The present writer has never met with another case at all like it. The somewhat mysterious character of the plea of *liberum tenementum* in ejectment is judicially touched upon, not for the first time, in *Harvey* v. *Brydges*, p. 718. Elsewhere we are reminded that a generation is growing up which will not remember the compulsory stop of ten minutes at Swindon. The facts and the law of the Great Western Railway Company's improvident lease to the refreshment contractor may be found at p. 836.

Lord Lyndhurst's tribute to the memory of Chief Justice Tindal (p. 166) is a judicial utterance of a rare kind in this country, there being no regular provision for it. In America commemorative speeches are not only made in Court but recorded. Our practice may be less dignified, but at any rate it escapes any suspicion of merely formal panegyric.

Towards the end of the volume the reader will find some equity cases, not without importance, originally reported only in the *Jurist*. He would obviously not get the benefit of such cases from any reprint confined to the "authorized" reports. In preparing the Revised Reports all the contemporary reports known to exist, and to fulfil the conditions making a report admissible in Court, are accounted for.

F. P.

HIGH COURT OF CHANCERY.

1844—1846.

(7 & 8 VICT.—9 & 10 VICT.)

———•———

LORD LYNDHURST, 1841—1846 . . . ⎫
LORD COTTENHAM, 1846—1850 . . . ⎭ *Lord Chancellors.*

LORD LANGDALE, 1836—1851 . . . *Master of the Rolls.*

SIR LANCELOT SHADWELL, 1827—1850 . ⎫
SIR J. L. KNIGHT BRUCE, 1841—1851 . . ⎬ *Vice-Chancellors.*
SIR JAMES WIGRAM, 1841—1850 . . ⎭

——— —— —— • ———

COURT OF QUEEN'S BENCH.

———•———

LORD DENMAN, 1832—1850 . . . *Chief Justice.*

SIR JOHN PATTESON, 1830—1852 . . . ⎫
SIR JOHN WILLIAMS, 1834—1846 . . . ⎪
SIR JOHN T. COLERIDGE, 1835—1858 . . ⎬ *Judges.*
SIR WILLIAM WIGHTMAN, 1841—1863 . . ⎪
SIR WILLIAM ERLE, 1846—1859 . . . ⎭

LIST OF JUDGES.

COURT OF COMMON PLEAS.

SIR N. C. TINDAL, 1829—1846 . . . } *Chief Justices.*
SIR THOMAS WILDE, 1846—1850 . . }

SIR THOMAS COLTMAN, 1837—1849 . . ⎫
(1) THOMAS ERSKINE, 1839—1844 . . ⎪
SIR WILLIAM H. MAULE, 1839—1855 . . ⎪
SIR C. CRESSWELL, 1842—1858 . . } *Judges.*
SIR WILLIAM ERLE, 1844—1846 . . ⎪
SIR E. V. WILLIAMS, 1846—1865 . . ⎭

COURT OF EXCHEQUER.

LORD ABINGER, 1834—1844 . . . } *Chief Barons.*
SIR FREDERICK POLLOCK, 1844—1866 . }

SIR JOHN GURNEY, 1832—1845 . . ⎫
SIR E. H. ALDERSON, 1834—1857 . . ⎪
SIR JAMES PARKE, 1834—1856 . . } *Barons.*
SIR ROBERT M. ROLFE, 1839—1850 . . ⎪
SIR THOMAS J. PLATT, 1845—1856 . . ⎭

SIR FREDERICK POLLOCK, 1841—1844 . ⎫
SIR W. W. FOLLETT, 1844—1845 . . ⎪
SIR FREDERICK THESIGER, 1845—1846 . } *Attorneys-General.*
SIR THOMAS WILDE, 1846 . . . ⎪
SIR JOHN JERVIS, 1846—1848 . . ⎭

SIR W. W. FOLLETT, 1841—1844 . . ⎫
SIR FREDERICK THESIGER, 1844—1845 . ⎪
SIR FITZROY KELLY, 1845—1846 . . } *Solicitors-General.*
SIR JOHN JERVIS, 1846 . . . ⎪
SIR DAVID DUNDAS, 1846—1848 . . ⎭

SIR EDWARD BURTENSHAW SUGDEN . . { *Lord Chancellor of Ireland.*

(1) The description of Mr. Justice Erskine as a knight in the earlier volumes of Manning and Granger's Reports was erroneous. As a peer's son he would not have been knighted in the ordinary course; and the lists of the Judicial Committee in Moore's Privy Council Reports, and of the Benchers of Lincoln's Inn in the Law List down to 1863 (confirmed by the description of the Right Hon. Thomas Erskine in a deed of which a copy is before me), show that in fact he was not.—F. P.

TABLE OF CASES

REPRINTED FROM

12 CLARK & FINNELLY; 2 JONES & LATOUCHE; 2 COM-
MON BENCH; 14 MEESON & WELSBY; 2 DOWLING
& LOWNDES; 8 JURIST.

Note.—Where the reference is to a mere note of a case reproduced elsewhere in the Revised Reports, or omitted for special reasons, the names of
the parties are printed in italics.

ERRATA.

63 R. R.—*Tindall* v. *Bell*, p. 585, line 3 from bottom, *for* " held out" *read* " held not."

68 R. R.—*Burgess* v. *Gray*, p. 769, head-note, line 8, *for* "charged A." *read* " charged B."

Both these errors occur in the original reports.

NOTE.

The first and last pages of the original report, according to the paging by which the original reports are usually cited, are noted at the head of each case, and references to the same paging are continued in the margin of the text.

The Revised Reports.

VOL. LXIX.

IN THE HOUSE OF LORDS.

THOMSON *v.* THE ADVOCATE-GENERAL.

(12 Clark & Finnelly, 1—29; S. C. 13 Sim. 153; 9 Jur. 217.)

Personal property having no *situs* of its own, follows the domicile of its owner.

The law of the domicile of a testator or intestate decides whether his personal property is liable to legacy duty.

A British-born subject, died, domiciled in a British Colony. At the time of his death he was possessed of personal property locally situate in Scotland. Probate of his will was taken out in Scotland, for the purpose of there administering this property : and out of the fund thus obtained by the executor, legacies were paid to legatees residing in Scotland:

Held, reversing a judgment of the Court of Exchequer in Scotland, that legacy duty was not payable in respect of these legacies (1).

1842.
July 12, 19.
Aug. 4.
1845.
Feb. 17, 18.

Lord
LYNDHURST,
L.C.
TINDAL,
Ch. J.
Lord
BROUGHAM.
Lord
CAMPBELL.

[1]

JOHN GRANT, a British-born subject, and native of Scotland, made his will 1829, and died in 1837. At the time of his death he was domiciled in the British Colony of Demerara, where the law of Holland was in force. There is not any local duty in the nature of legacy duty payable in that Colony.

At the time of the death of John Grant, he was entitled to a large personal debt due to him in Scotland, which arose from money acquired by him whilst domiciled in *Demerara, and transmitted by him to Scotland for safe custody. After his death, John Thomson took out probate of his will, so far as related to the debt in Scotland, and there, from money arising from the said debt, paid in pursuance of the will, certain legacies, above the amount of

[*2]

---

(1) *A.-G.* v. *Cockerell*, 15 R. R. 707, and *A.-G.* v. *Beatson*, 21 R. R. 770, overruled.—J. G. P.

THOMSON
r.
THE
ADVOCATE-
GENERAL.

twenty pounds, and paid over the rest as part of the residue of the personal estate of John Grant.

In July, 1840, an information in debt, setting forth these facts, was filed in the Court of Exchequer in Scotland by her Majesty's *Advocate-General* against John Thomson, who appeared and put in a general demurrer, on the ground of insufficiency. Joinder in demurrer. The demurrer came on for argument upon the 29th January, 1841, before the Court of Exchequer in Scotland, and the only question raised was, whether the fact of the domicile of Grant in Demerara, prevented the legacy duty (under the 55 Geo. III. c. 184, schedule, part 3 (1)) from attaching on his personal property in Scotland.. The Court of Exchequer took time to consider, and on 10th February following, overruled the demurrer, and gave judgment for the Crown (2).

A writ of error was brought on this judgment. The case was argued in 1842, by *Mr. Pemberton* and *Mr. Anderson*, for the plaintiff in error ; and by the *Solicitor-General* (*Sir W. Follett*) and *Mr. Crompton*, for the defendant in error. It was then directed by their Lordships to be argued before the Judges by one counsel on a side.

*　　　*　　　*　　　*　　　*

[7]

This further argument took place on the 17th February, 1845, when Lord Chief Justice Tindal, Justices Maule, Coltman, and Cresswell, and Barons Parke, Rolfe, and Platt attended in the House.

1845.
Feb. 17, 18.

Mr. Kelly (with whom was *Mr. Anderson*, for the plaintiff in error) :

The domicile of the testator or intestate decides the question whether the legacy duty is or is not payable. In this case the domicile was at Demerara, where, by the law of the Colony, no legacy duty is payable. None therefore can be demanded. It will be contended for the Crown that the duty is payable because the testator was a British subject, and that the very general and extensive words employed in the statute embrace such a case as the present. It will further be argued, that as the property was in part at least locally situated in this country, the duty attaches

(1) Which declares that duty shall be payable " for every legacy, specific or pecuniary, or of any other description, of the amount of 20*l.* or upwards given by any will or testamentary instrument of any person out of his or her personal or moveable estate," &c. [And see 44 Vict. c. 12, s. 42, and 43 Vict. c. 14, s. 13.—J. G. P.]

(2) 3 Dunl. Bell, Mur. & Dona. 1309.

upon it; but it is submitted that the *situs* of the property does not in the least degree affect the question.

As to the first point, the words of the statute are confined to the wills of persons domiciled in Great Britain, and do not apply to the wills of persons domiciled either in Ireland or the Colonies, and cannot certainly apply to the wills of persons domiciled in foreign countries. The words of the statute, however extensive, are not of universal application. To make all these classes of persons subject to the duties imposed by the statute, they should have been expressly named in its provisions. That has not been done, and they cannot by mere implication be rendered liable to burdens of this sort. The decision now impeached *would, if maintained, operate as a premium on fraud. The legacy duty is claimed because it is said that the debts in Scotland due to the deceased constituted personal estate, to obtain which it was necessary to put the law in motion. Had the Scotch debtors acted honestly, they would have remitted the money to Demerara without the intervention of the law, and according to that argument, no legacy duty would then have been payable.

It cannot be said that the duty payable under this statute is payable upon legacies under wills made in Ireland, for if so, such legacies would have to pay duty twice over, since there is a separate Act of Parliament imposing a duty on legacies in Ireland. Nor can it be contended that because the testator was a British subject, his property in Demerara was liable to this duty, for that would be to levy a tax in the Colonies under the authority of an English Act of Parliament, a right to do which has been distinctly and formally disclaimed by the Crown. If the duty attaches at all in this case, it does so only upon the property in this country. But even that ground of liability cannot be insisted on. In the first place, the Act makes no distinction as to parts of the property. It does not declare that one part here shall pay, and another part, situated elsewhere, shall not pay. It makes the whole of the personal property liable together, and in respect of one and the same title. Suppose a man to die in Demerara, and to leave 40,000*l.* of personal property; that of that sum 20,000*l.* were in Demerara, and 20,000*l.* were in this country; and, suppose the executor to come to this country to realize the money here, how is the Government to apportion the duty, when the legacies are paid as much out of the Demerara as out of the English funds. The statute has not provided for any such case. The liability to

THOMSON
v.
THE
ADVOCATE-
GENERAL.

[*8]

probate duty is altogether a different matter, for no doubt wherever the party takes out a probate, he must pay the duty upon it. The cases of *Thorne* v. *Watkins* (1), and *Pipon* *v. *Pipon* (2), explain the confusion, which, upon this point, has arisen in the argument on the other side. So that on the terms of the statute itself it is contended that this duty is not payable.

Then as to the authorities: *The Attorney-General* v. *Cockerell* (3), and *The Attorney-General* v. *Beatson* (4), can no longer be considered as law. The case of *In re Ewin* (5) clearly settles that the local situation of the property does not affect the question.

(THE LORD CHANCELLOR : In the case of *Jackson* v. *Forbes* (6), the property at the time of the death of the testator was in this country; in *Ewin's* case it was in the funds of four different foreign countries, so that, putting the two cases together, the circumstances are exactly what they are here.)

That is so, and taking the cases together, they form a complete answer to the claim set up here. The words of the Act cannot apply to all persons whatever. They must be limited in some way : then how are they to be limited? The authorities show that they are to be limited by the domicile of the party at the time of his death. *In re Ewin* is a clear authority for that proposition. [He also cited *In re Bruce* (7), *Arnold* v. *Arnold* (8), *Jackson* v. *Forbes* (9), *In re Coates* (10), and *The Commissioners of Charitable Donations* v. *Devereux* (11).]

The *Solicitor-General* (*Sir F. Thesiger*), with whom was *Mr. Crompton*, for the Crown :

The question which arises in the present case has never yet been settled. Its importance and difficulty appear to have been felt by this House. The whole argument upon the other side is made to rest upon the domicile of the party. It is most remarkable that

in no other cases but those of *Ewin* and of *Bruce* were *the decisions rested on the principle of domicile. That is not the true principle

(1) 2 Ves. 35.
(2) Amb. 26.
(3) 15 R. R. 707 (1 Price, 165).
(4) 21 R. R. 770 (7 Price, 560).
(5) 1 Cr. & J. 151 ; 1 Tyr. 92.
(6) 37 R. R. 12 (2 Cr. & J. 382 ;
S. C. sub nom. A.-G. v. Forbes, 2
Cl. & Fin. 48 ; S. C. sub nom. A.-G.

v. Jackson, 8 Bligh, N. S. 15).
(7) 2 Cr. & J. 436 ; 2 Tyr. 475.
(8) 2 My. & Cr. 270.
(9) 37 R. R. 12 (2 Cr. & J. 382 ;
2 Cl. & Fin. 48 ; 8 Bligh, N. S. 15).
(10) 56 R. R. 736 (7 M. & W. 390).
(11) 13 Sim. 14 ; 6 Jur. 616.

by which the law, applicable to such a case as the present, is to be
determined.　The duty attaches here, wherever there is a person
acting in this country in execution of the will.　That is the principle
which must govern the decision, and which will alone reconcile
all the cases.

By all the statutes passed before the 36 Geo. III., the legacy duty
was payable on the receipt of the money.　If a native paid a legacy
to a foreigner, that legacy would, on the payment being made, have
been liable to the receipt stamp duty.　That shows that there was
no statutory distinction as to liability.　In passing that statute it
was not the intention of the Legislature to change the liability, and
merely to impose a higher rate of duty.　The liability remained as
before.　That liability depends on the act of administering the fund.
The question, therefore, is whether the act of administering the
fund in Scotland was the act of paying legacies, whether it was an
act done in Great Britain, so as to enable the provisions of the
statute to attach upon it; for it must be admitted that in terms this
is a statute limited to Great Britain.　No one can doubt that here
has been an act of paying legacies within Great Britain; and the
provisions of the statute do therefore attach upon it.　What are the
words of the statute 55 Geo. III. c. 184?　They are (adopting those
used in the 36 Geo. III. c. 52, s. 2) that " for every legacy, specific
or pecuniary, given by any will of any person out of his personal or
moveable estate, or out of or charged upon his real or heritable
estate," the duties imposed by that Act shall be payable.　It is
impossible to employ words more general and comprehensive, and
the burthen of showing that these legacies are not liable to the duty,
lies upon those who claim the exemption, and must be made out by
something more direct than the supposed application of a principle of
law, which, however well established, must be deemed inapplicable
to *the fiscal regulations of a country.　Here there is a British
subject " taking on himself the execution of the will," that being
the very expression used in the earliest Acts of Parliament, and
paying legacies out of the personal estate.　Where the case is so
clearly within the words of the statute, the principle of domicile
cannot apply to make those words inoperative.　The property, the
executor, and the legatees, were in this country, and the executor
was obliged to take out probate here in order to administer that very
property.　The honesty or dishonesty of the debtor does not affect
the matter.　The question is whether a probate was necessary or
not—was the unappropriated property in this country, which the

THOMSON
v.
THE
ADVOCATE-
GENERAL.

[*12]

THOMSON
v.
THE
ADVOCATE-
GENERAL.

party got possession of in his representative character,—a character with which the English law clothed him, and did he distribute it to legatees in this country? These questions must be answered in the affirmative. It may be admitted that, if after probate taken out, the money had been voluntarily paid by the bankers: the mere act of taking out probate would not of itself decide the question, whether the legacy duties were payable or not. The real question is whether the party obtained the money in his representative character under the probate, or only as the mere attorney or agent of the testator. The argument on the other side would go to relieve a party from the payment of the legacy duty, though some of the legacies were specifically payable abroad; and some specifically payable here. Now, not one of the authorities goes further than to say that where the appropriation of the fund has been made abroad, and the fund is transmitted here, and a mere act of payment by an agent under the authority of that foreign appropriation is made here, the legacy duty is not payable. No such specific appropriation was made here. So that even if the law was as thus stated, it would not exempt the party in this instance from the payment of the duty.

The domicile may fix the law of the succession; but it does not affect the payment of the legacy duty. [He referred to the cases cited above, and cited *Logan* v. *Fairlie* (1).]

[13]   (THE LORD CHANCELLOR: The last case of *Logan* v. *Fairlie*, is nothing more than this: The COURT did not decide any other question than whether there had been or not an appropriation in India.)

But Lord COTTENHAM must be taken to have admitted the rule as to the liability to duty laid down by the VICE-CHANCELLOR.

(THE LORD CHANCELLOR: Nothing was decided but the question of appropriation.)

[14]   * * The next case is that of *Arnold* v. *Arnold* (2) and though it must be admitted that that case cannot be reconciled with the cases of *The Attorney-General* v. *Cockerell*, and *The Attorney-General* v. *Beatson*, yet in delivering judgment there, Lord COTTENHAM took great care to show that it did not fall within the authority of *Logan* v. *Fairlie*.

(THE LORD CHANCELLOR: I consider that in all these cases

(1) 25 R. R. 208 (2 Sim. & St. 284).   (2) 2 My. & Cr. 256.

domicile was the basis of the whole judgment; the only question was what was the effect of the other circumstances upon the rule of domicile.)

It seems difficult to come to that conclusion, since the rule as to domicile would have rendered quite unnecessary any discussion as to the appropriation of the fund. Domicile, in some of these cases, never was argued upon, and was not made the ground of the decision. This is especially to be observed in the case of *Arnold* v. *Arnold*.

(THE LORD CHANCELLOR : In that case all the funds were sent here from India, to be administered here according to the will.)

No; they were sent for the mere purpose of being paid to the legatees. Strictly speaking, there was no administration here— that is a term of a technical nature. If the fund is sent over to be divided, it is sent over for the purpose of administration ; but if it is sent merely to be paid, the person paying it would exercise no discretion, and then there would be no administration.

If this statute does not apply to property coming from abroad to be distributed in this country, how can the probate *duty be payable ? There can be no distinction in principle between probate and legacy duty. Both are the subjects of the fiscal regulations of this country.

[*15]

(THE LORD CHANCELLOR : If a will is made by a foreigner resident abroad, and it is necessary to administer his estate in England, probate must be taken out for that purpose, and probate duty becomes payable upon the mere taking out of the probate ; but the question here is, whether under such circumstances, legacy duty will be payable.)

[He cited *In re Bruce* (1), *Doe* v. *Acklam* (2), and *In re Coales* (3).]

The Attorney-General v. *Dunn* (4) is the first case in which the question of domicile was distinctly submitted to the Court ; but, as the Court held that in fact the testator had an English domicile, that question was not decided. The last case on the subject is that of *The Commissioners of Charitable Bequests* v. *Devereux* (5), and it is impossible that the VICE-CHANCELLOR could have said what is there imputed to him, for he is made to refer to *Re Bruce*, and to say, "whether the testator there was a British subject does not

(1) 2 Cr. & J. 436.
(2) 26 R. R. 544 (2 B. & C. 779).
(3) 56 R. R. 736 (7 M. & W. 390).

(4) 6 M. & W. 511.
(5) 13 Sim. 14 ; 6 Jur. 616.

appear;" when it does most clearly appear from several parts of that case that Bruce was a foreigner.

[*16]

(THE LORD CHANCELLOR: The decision as reported in the Jurist is right, but the judgment is wrong in terms. It does not matter, *for the purpose of this argument, what are the expressions used, but what was the, point decided? According to my view of the subject, the decision there was correct, for the domicile was in France.)

THE LORD CHANCELLOR:

[*17]

The *Solicitor-General* has, in my view of the case, stated every thing that the subject *admits of. The argument has been an able one; but, notwithstanding what has fallen from him, we do not think it necessary to hear *Mr. Kelly* in reply. I propose to put the following question to the Judges: " A., a British-born subject, born in England, resided in a British Colony. He made his will, and died domiciled there. At the time of his death he had debts owing to him in England. His executors in England collected these debts, and out of the money so collected paid legacies to certain legatees in England. The question is, are such legacies liable to the payment of legacy duty?"

Lord Chief Justice TINDAL, in the name of his brethren, requested time to consider the question.

The request was acceded to, and the House was adjourned during pleasure. In about an hour the House was resumed.

LORD CHIEF JUSTICE TINDAL then delivered the unanimous opinion
of the Judges. Having read the question put to the Judges
he said :

In answer to this question I have the honour to inform your Lordships that it is the opinion of all the Judges who have heard the case argued, that such legacies are not liable to the payment of legacy duty.

It is admitted in all the decided cases, that the very general words of the statute, " every legacy given by any will or testamentary instrument of any person," must of necessity receive some limitation in their application, for they cannot in reason extend to every person, everywhere, whether subjects of this kingdom or

foreigners, and whether at the time of their death domiciled within
the realm or abroad.   And as your Lordships' question applies
only to legacies out of personal estate, strictly and properly so
called, we think such necessary limitation is, that the statute does
not extend to the will of any person who at the time of his
death was domiciled out of Great Britain, whether the assets are
locally situate within England or *not.   For we cannot consider
that any distinction can be properly made between debts due to
the testator from persons resident in the country in which the
testator is domiciled at the time of his death, and debts due to him
from debtors resident in another and different country ; but that
all such debts do equally form part of the personal property of the
testator or intestate, and must all follow the same rule, namely, the
law of the domicile of the testator or intestate.

And such principle we think may be extracted from all the later
decided cases, though sometimes attempts have been made, perhaps
ineffectually, to reconcile with them the earlier decisions.   There
is no distinction whatever between the case proposed to us and
that decided in the House of Lords, *The Attorney-General* v.
Forbes (1), except the circumstance that in the present question the
personal property is assumed to be, for the purpose of the probate,
locally situated in England, at the time of the testator's death.
But that circumstance was held to be immaterial in the case *In
re Ewin* (2), where it was decided that a British subject dying
domiciled in England, legacy duty was payable on his property in
the funds of Russia, France, Austria, and America.

And again in the case of *Arnold* v. *Arnold* (3), where the testator,
a natural-born Englishman, but domiciled in India, died there, it
was held by Lord Chancellor COTTENHAM, that the legacy duty was
not payable upon the legacies under his will, his Lordship adding :
" It is fortunate that this question which has been so long afloat is
now finally settled by an authoritative decision of the House of
Lords."

And as to the arguments at your Lordships' Bar on the part of
the Crown, that the proper distinction was, whether the estate was
administered by a person in a representative *character in this
country, and that in case of such administering, the legacy duty
was payable, we think it is a sufficient answer thereto that the
liability to legacy duty does not depend on the act of the executor

(1) 37 R. R. 12 (2 Cl. & Fin. 48).   (3) 2 My. & Cr. 256.
(2) 1 Cr. & J. 151.

THOMSON
v.
THE
ADVOCATE-
GENERAL.

in proving the will in this country, or upon his administering here; the question, as it appears to us, not being whether there be administration in England or not, but whether the will and legacy are a will and legacy within the meaning of the statute imposing the duty.

For these reasons we think the legacies described in your Lordships' question are not liable to the payment of legacy duty.

THE LORD CHANCELLOR (1):

My Lords, in consequence of something that was thrown out at your Lordships' Bar, I think it proper to state that it was not from any serious doubt or difficulty which we considered to be inherent in this question in the former argument, that we thought it right to ask the opinion of the Judges, but it was on account of its extensive nature; and, because though the question applied only to Scotland in the form in which it was presented to your Lordships' House, it did in reality and in substance apply to the whole Empire—not only to Great Britain, but in substance to Ireland, and to all the British possessions. We thought it right, therefore, in consequence of the extensive nature and operation of the question, that the case should be argued a second time; and we also thought, from the nature of the question, that it was proper to require the attendance of her Majesty's Judges upon the occasion, because we thought that the judgment of your Lordships' House being in concurrence with the opinion of the learned Judges, would possess that weight with your Lordships, and with the country, which upon all occasions it is desirable it should receive.

[*20]

My Lords, it appeared to me in the course of the argument *that the question turned, as it must necessarily turn, upon the meaning of the statute. In the very first section of the statute the operation of it is limited to Great Britain. It does not extend to Ireland. It does not extend to the Colonies. And, therefore, notwithstanding the general terms contained in the schedule, those terms must be read in connection with the first section of the Act, and it is clear, therefore, that they must receive that limited construction and interpretation, which is alone consistent with the first section of the Act. Accordingly, my Lords, it has been determined in the case that was cited at the Bar, *In re Bruce* (2), that it does not apply, notwithstanding the extensive terms in which it is framed, to the case of a foreigner residing

(1) Lord LYNDHURST.   (2) 2 Cr. & J. 436.

abroad, and a will made abroad, although the property may be in
England, although the executors may be in England, although the
legatees may be in England, and although the property may be
administered in England. That was decided expressly in the case
In re Bruce, which decision, so far as I am aware, has never been
disputed, but in which the Crown seems to have acquiesced.

Also, my Lords, it has been decided in the case of British
subjects domiciled in India, and having large possessions of
personal property, which come to be disposed of in England, that
the legacy duty imposed by the Act of Parliament does not apply
to cases of that description, although the property may have been
transmitted to this country by executors in India to executors in
this country, for the purpose of being paid to legatees here. Those
are the limitations which have been put upon the Act by judicial
decisions.

But then this distinction has been attempted to be drawn, and it
is upon this distinction that the whole question here turns. It is
said that in this case a part of the property *was in England at
the time of the death of the testator, a circumstance that did not
exist in the case of *The Attorney-General* v. *Forbes*, and which did
not exist in the case of *Arnold* v. *Arnold;* and it is supposed that
some distinction is to be drawn with respect to the construction of
the Act of Parliament arising out of that circumstance. I apprehend that that is an entire mistake, that personal property in
England follows the law of the domicile, and that it is precisely
the same as if the personal property had been in India at the time
of testator's death. That is a rule of law that has always been
considered as applicable to this subject; and accordingly the case
which has been referred to by the learned CHIEF JUSTICE, the case
of *In re Ewin* (1), was a case of this description. An Englishman
made his will in England: he had foreign stock in Russia, in
America, in France, and in Austria. The question was whether
the legacy duty attached to that foreign stock, which was given as
part of the residue, the estate being administered in England;
and it was contended, I believe, in the course of the argument by
my noble and learned friend who argued the case, in the first
place, that it was real property, but, finding that that distinction
could not be maintained, the next question was whether it came
within the operation of the Act, and although the property was all
abroad, it was decided to be within the operation of the Act as

[*21]

(1) 1 Cr. & J. 151.

personal property, on this ground, and this ground only, that as it was personal property, it must, in point of law, be considered as following the domicile of the testator, which domicile was England.

Now, my Lords, if you apply that principle, which has never been quarrelled with, which is a known principle of our law, to the present case, it decides the whole point in controversy. The property, personal property, being in this country at the time of the death, you must take the *principle laid down in the case of *In re Ewin* (1), and it must be considered as property within the domicile of the testator, which domicile was Demerara. It is admitted that if it was property within the domicile of the testator in Demerara, it cannot be subject to legacy duty. Now, my Lords, that is the principle upon which this case is to be decided. The only distinction is that to which I have referred, and which distinction is decided by the case *In re Ewin* to be immaterial.

[*22]

Now, my Lords, such being the case and the principle upon which, I think, this question should be decided, I was desirous of knowing what were the grounds of the judgment of the COURT below. I find that the judgment was delivered by two, or, rather, that the case was heard by two very learned Judges, Lord GILLIES and Lord FULLERTON. The judgment was delivered by the late Lord GILLIES. I was anxious, therefore, from the respect which I entertain for those very learned persons, to know what were the grounds upon which their judgment was rested.

The first case to which they referred, for it was principally decided upon authority, was a case decided before Sir Samuel Shepherd, Chief Baron of Scotland. That case in the judgment was very shortly stated, and I am very happy that the *Solicitor-General* gave us the particulars of that case, for it appears that the legacy was charged upon real estate, and, therefore, it would not come within the principle which I have stated ; and there might, therefore, have been a sufficient ground for the decision in that case. It is sufficient to say, that it does not apply to the case which is now before your Lordships' House.

Then the next case which was referred to was the case of *The Attorney-General* v. *Dunn* (2) ; but, my Lords, that could hardly be cited as an authority. It is true the point was argued ; but it was not necessary for the decision of *the case ; and no decision, in fact, was given upon the point. The LORD CHIEF BARON pointedly reserved his opinion, and said, that he should not express what his

[*23]

(1) 1 Cr. & J. 151.   (2) 6 M. & W. 511.

opinion was; also the learned Judge near me, Mr. Baron PARKE, expressed the same thing. It is true, that one of the learned Judges said that, at that moment, according to the impression upon his mind, he rather thought the duty would be chargeable; he expressed himself in those terms according to his immediate impression; but no decision was given upon the point, it was a mere *obiter dictum*—and surely such a *dictum* as that ought not to be cited as the foundation of a judgment of this description. Looking at the authorities, therefore, they appear to me not properly to support the judgment of the COURT below.

The third authority was that of Lord COTTENHAM. Now, Lord COTTENHAM in the case of *Arnold* v. *Arnold* (1), expressly states in terms, that the two cases, *The Attorney-General* v. *Cockerell* (2), and *The Attorney-General* v. *Beatson* (3), he considered to have been overruled. He states that in precise terms. A particular passage is selected from the judgment of Lord COTTENHAM to support the opinion of the learned Judges in the Court below, but I am quite sure when that passage is read in connection with the whole judgment of that very learned person, every person reading it with attention must be satisfied that the inference drawn from that particular passage that was cited is not consistent with the whole tenor of the judgment. It appears to me, therefore, that none of the authorities cited by the COURT below sustained the judgment; and I am of opinion, therefore, independently of the great respect which I entertain for the judgment of the learned Judges who have assisted us upon this occasion, that upon the true construction of the Act of Parliament, and applying *the known principles of the   [*24]
law to that construction, the legacy duty is not in a case of this description chargeable. I shall, therefore, move that the judgment in this case be reversed.

LORD BROUGHAM:

My Lords, I entirely agree with my noble and learned friend in the view which he takes of the construction of this statute, and of the authorities, and of the argument, so far as it is there endeavoured to distinguish this case from that of *The Attorney-General* v. *Forbes*, which must be taken with *In re Ewin*, a case that also arose in the Exchequer, and when the two cases are thus considered, no doubt can be felt upon the matter. I so entirely agree upon all

(1) 2 My. & Cr. 256.   (3) 21 R. R. 770 (7 Price, 560).
(2) 15 R. R. 707 (1 Price, 165).

those three heads with my noble and learned friend, that I do not
think it necessary for me to do more than generally to express my
concurrence.   I wish, however, also to add that my recollection
coincides perfectly with his as to the reasons for troubling the
learned Judges to attend in this case.   It was not only that it was
a case from the Scotch Exchequer, but it was a case which must
impose a construction upon the General Legacy Act, applicable to
England and to all the British Colonies, and to foreign countries ;
and, therefore, we considered that it was highly expedient to have
a general consideration of the case, and the assistance of the learned
Judges.   But we also felt this, which I am sure the recollection of
my noble and learned friend will bear me out in adding, and which
the recollection of my noble and learned friend near me, who was
also present at the former argument (Lord CAMPBELL), has entirely
confirmed, namely, that we considered this to be a case in which
there was a conflict of decisions, a conflict of authorities, which
made it highly expedient that it should be settled after the fullest
and most mature deliberation, with the valuable assistance of the

[*25]   learned Judges ; for there was *the authority of *Jackson* v. *Forbes*,
in the Exchequer, and afterwards before me in Chancery, and
ultimately before your Lordships in this House, by appeal on a
writ of error; there was that authority on the one hand, with
the decision of the Exchequer not appealed against, *In the Matter
of Ewin* on the other, and the authority of those decisions appeared
to be marked by some discrepancy at least, more apparent perhaps
than real, with the two former cases of *The Attorney-General* v.
Cockerell and *The Attorney-General* v. *Beatson*.   It became, therefore, highly expedient that we should maturely weigh the whole
matter, before we held that that decision of the House of Lords in
The Attorney-General v. *Forbes* had completely overruled those other
cases, the rather because certainly words were used in disposing
of *The Attorney-General* v. *Forbes* which seemed to intimate the
possibility of those former cases standing together with the latter
case.   Upon full consideration, however, I am clearly of opinion
with Lord COTTENHAM, who expressed that opinion very strongly in
the case of *Arnold* v. *Arnold*, that those two cases of *The Attorney-
General* v. *Cockerell*, and *The Attorney-General* v. *Beatson*, cannot
stand with the case of *The Attorney-General* v. *Forbes*.   Then, my
Lords, that last case must be considered not merely by itself, as
regards its bearing upon the facts of the present case, but it must
be taken into consideration coupled with the case of *In re Ewin*,

because otherwise ground might be supposed to exist for distinguishing the two cases, inasmuch as it might be, and has been
contended, and ably contended at the Bar, that the one case does
not apply to the other, because part of the funds were in the present
case locally situated in this country. But then take the case of
Ewin, *and your Lordships must perceive at once, as my noble and
learned friend has done, and as the learned Judges have done, that
those two cases together in fact exhaust the present case, because
what was wanting in *The Attorney-General* v. *Forbes,* is supplied
by the decision *In the Matter of Ewin;* I will not say, supplied in
terms: but in what comes to the same thing, in the argument upon
the construction of the statute, and in the legal application of the
principle, the converse was decided.   Here it is a case of money or
property brought over here and administered here, the domicile of
the testator or intestate being abroad out of the jurisdiction. There,
In the Matter of Ewin, it was the converse, administration being by
a person domiciled here, and a testator or intestate domiciled here,
and the funds locally situate abroad ; it is perfectly clear that no
difference can be made in consequence of that, because the principle,
mobilia sequntur personam, as regards their distribution and their
coming or not within the scope of this Revenue Act, must be taken
to apply to cases precisely similar ; and the rule of law, indeed, is
quite general that in such cases the domicile governs the personal
property, not the real ; but the personal property is in contemplation of the law, whatever may be the fact, supposed to be within
the domicile of the testator or intestate.

I entirely agree with my noble and learned friend in the view
which he has taken of the grounds of the decision of the COURT
below; whether that decision was before or subsequent to the
decision in the case of *The Attorney-General* v. *Forbes* and *The
Matter of Ewin* I am not informed.

THE LORD CHANCELLOR:

It was subsequent.

LORD BROUGHAM:

Then their Lordships ought clearly to have taken it into account,
and more especially if they had the additional light which is thrown
upon the subject by the case of *Arnold* v. *Arnold.*

THE LORD CHANCELLOR:

They cite *Arnold* v. *Arnold.*

LORD BROUGHAM:

That makes it still more clear that the foundation of their decision was unsound. It is to be taken into account that Lord COTTENHAM does not give his opinion in *Arnold* v. *Arnold* merely upon the authority of *The Attorney-General* v. *Forbes*, because he expressly says, and very candidly and fairly says, doing justice to the grounds of the decision of your Lordships in this House, that, independently of authorities, he is of the same opinion, and should have come to the same opinion as we did in that case, notwithstanding the conflict that appears to exist between other cases. We have, therefore, the clearest reasons for saying that if my noble and learned friend had not been unfortunately absent to-day, he would have concurred entirely in this view of the case.

Upon the whole, therefore, I entirely concur in the opinion of my noble and learned friend, and acknowledge fully, and with thanks, the assistance which we have derived from the learned Judges (giving the reasons which I have given for our wishing to have their attendance rather than from any great doubt or difficulty which we felt the case to be encumbered by) ; and, therefore, my Lords, I second my noble and learned friend's motion, that judgment be given for the plaintiff in error.

LORD CAMPBELL:

My Lords, I confess that in this case I did once entertain very considerable doubts; and I was exceedingly anxious that your Lordships should have the assistance of the Queen's Judges in a case that admitted, as it seemed to me, of great doubt, and where the decisions were directly at variance with each other. Having heard the opinion of the learned Judges, it gives me extreme satisfaction to say that I entirely concur in it, and that the doubts which I before entertained are now entirely removed. Having heard the opinion of the learned Judges, I defer to it with the greatest possible respect, as I certainly should have done under any circumstances, *though, if it had not satisfied my mind, of course I should have found it my duty to act upon the result of my own judgment; but with the assistance of the learned Judges, under the present circumstances, I am relieved from anything of that sort, because I agree with them in the result to which they have arrived, and in the reasons which they have assigned for the opinion which they have given to your Lordships.

At the same time, my Lords, I believe that if the Chancellor of the

Exchequer, who introduced this Bill into Parliament, had been asked his opinion, he would have been a good deal surprised to hear that he was not to have his legacy duty on such a fund as this, where the testator was a British-born subject, and had been domiciled in Great Britain, and had merely acquired a foreign domicile, and had left property that actually was in England or in Scotland at the time of his decease.   The truth is, my Lords, that the doctrine of domicile has sprung up in this country very recently, and that neither the Legislature nor the Judges, until within a few years thought much of it; but it is a very convenient doctrine, it is now well understood, and I think that it solves the difficulty with which this case was surrounded.   The doctrine of domicile was certainly not at all regarded in the case of *The Attorney-General* v. *Cockerell*, nor in that of *The Attorney-General* v. *Beatson*.   If it had been the criterion at that time, there would have been no difficulty at all in determining this question; but now, my Lords, when we do understand this doctrine better than it was understood formerly, I think that it gives a clue which will help us to a right solution of this question.

It is impossible that the words of the statute can be received without any limitation; foreigners must be excluded.   Then the question is what limitation is to be put upon them? and, I think, the just limitation is, the property of persons who die domiciled in Great Britain.   On such property alone, I think, can it be supposed that the *Legislature intended to impose this tax.   If a testator has died out of Great Britain with a domicile abroad, although he may have personal property that is in Great Britain at the time of his death, in contemplation of law that property is supposed to be situate where he was domiciled, and, therefore, does not come within the Act: this seems to be the most reasonable construction to be put upon the Act of Parliament; it is the most convenient, any other construction would lead to very great difficulties, and, I think, the rule which is laid down by the learned Judges may now be safely acted upon, and will prevent difficulties and doubts arising hereafter.   But I think that this caution should be introduced, that this applies only to legacy duty, not to probate duty.   With respect to the probate duty, if it is necessary to take out probate, the property being in Great Britain, for the purpose of administering that property, the property would still be considered as situate in Great Britain, and the probate duty would attach.   All the cases respecting probate duty are considered untouched; but, with respect to the legacy duty, those two cases, *The Attorney-General* v. *Cockerell*

THOMSON
v.
THE
ADVOCATE-
GENERAL.

[*29]

THOMSON
v.
THE
ADVOCATE-
GENERAL.

and *The Attorney-General* v. *Beatson*, must be considered as completely' overturned, and domicile with respect to legacy duty is hereafter to be the rule.

THE LORD CHANCELLOR:

There is no question in the case as regards the probate duty, it cannot be supposed for a moment that this affects the probate duty. Your Lordships will allow me, in your name, to tender our best thanks to the learned Judges for their attendance to this case.

Judgment of the Court below reversed.

1845.
Feb. 25.
March 3.

Rolls Court.
Lord
LANGDALE,
M.R.

On Appeal.
Lord
COTTENHAM,
L.C.

Further
Appeal.
Lord
LYNDHURST,
L.C.

Lord
BROUGHAM.

Lord
CAMPBELL.

[45]

HAMMERSLEY *v.* DE BIEL(1).

(12 Clark & Finnelly, 45—90; affg. 3 Beav. 469.)

A proposal or representation of intention made by one person for the purpose of influencing the conduct of another, and acted on by him, will in general impose a contractual obligation binding upon the person who made the representation.

Proposals of marriage written by the lady's brothers, acting by her father's authority, stated that "Mr. J. P. T. (the father) also intends to leave a further sum of 10,000*l.* in his will to Miss T., to be settled on her and her children, the disposition of which, supposing she has no children, will be prescribed by the will of her father. These are the bases of the arrangement, subject, of course, to revision; but they will be sufficient for Baron B. to act upon." Baron B., upon receiving the proposals, provided a jointure as required by them for his intended wife, and then married her. In the settlement, afterwards executed, there was no mention of this sum of 10,000*l.*; and it was not left by J. P. T. in his will:

Held, that his estate was liable to the! payment of the 10,000*l.*, with interest from the end of one year after his death.

Semble, that a letter written and signed by the father, after the marriage, admitting the terms of-the written proposals, which were not signed, was a recognition of them as his agreement, and sufficiently signed by him within the Statute of Frauds.

[*46]

THIS was an appeal from a decree of the MASTER OF THE ROLLS, and from an order of the LORD CHANCELLOR affirming it. The respondent is the son and only issue of the marriage *of Baron William Julius Augustus Henry de Biel, of Zierow, in the Grand Duchy of Mecklenburgh Schwerin, and of Sophia, late Baroness de Biel, who was one of the daughters of John Poulett Thomson, late of Waverley Abbey, in the county of Surrey, Esquire, deceased. The appellant is the only surviving executor of Mr. Thomson's will; and the object of the suit was to obtain payment out of his

(1) *Maunsell* v. *Hedges White* (1854) D. 293, 7 Q. B. Div. 174, 8 App. Ca.
4 H. L. C. 1039; *Alderson* v. *Maddison*, 467, 50 L. J. Q. B. 466; *Re Fickus*
Maddison v. *Alderson* (1880—3) 5 Ex. [1900] 1 Ch. 331, 335, 69 L. J. Ch. 161.

assets of a sum of 10,000l., with interest from the time of his death,
to which the respondent claimed to be entitled, under the provisions
of a memorandum of agreement, hereinafter stated to have been
entered into between his father and Andrew Henry Poulett Thomson,
and Charles Poulett Thomson, sons of the said J. P. Thomson, on his
behalf, previously to the said marriage. The questions for the decision
of the House were, whether any such agreement was entered into?
and if it was, then what was the construction to be put upon it?

The bill, filed in 1839 against the appellant and the said A. H.
and C. Poulett Thomson (who are both since deceased), stated that
Baron William Julius Augustus Henry de Biel, the respondent's
father, was, in the year 1825, and ever since entitled to a considerable landed estate at Zierow aforesaid, which, in the event of his
dying without leaving issue, was entailed, according to the law of
Mecklenburgh Schwerin, on his brother Baron Gottlieb de Biel:
that, in December, 1825, a marriage was in contemplation between
the said Baron de Biel and Miss Sophia Poulett Thomson, the
mother of the respondent, and daughter of the said J. P. Thomson:
that he on several previous occasions had expressed his intention
to give each of his daughters a fortune of 20,000l., and in particular
by a letter written in September, 1825, in the course of a treaty of
marriage between one of his daughters and Baron Henry de
Maltzahn, which marriage took place: that in consequence of such
declaration of his intentions by J. P. Thomson, Baron de Biel, at
the time *when he sought his consent to his marriage with the   [*47]
said Sophia P. Thomson, did expect that her fortune would be
20,000l.: that after J. P. Thomson had given his consent to the
marriage, some conversation took place between him and Baron de
Biel respecting the lady's fortune, and the settlements to be made
on the marriage, when J. P. Thomson requested the Baron to call
on his sons, the said A. H. P. Thomson and C. P. Thomson—who
were both, at that time, engaged in business as merchants in
London—and added that he would forward to them his instructions
on the subject: that he, J. P. Thomson did accordingly instruct
his said sons, and authorised them to act for him, and to enter
into the necessary agreement with Baron de Biel touching the
amount of his daughter's fortune, and the terms and conditions of
the settlement to be made on the occasion of the marriage; and
that Baron de Biel accordingly met them on the 22nd of December,
1825, at the house of C. P. Thomson, when they produced a letter
from J. P. Thomson, giving them full power to act for him in

relation to the said matters: that at this meeting, after some
conversation between A. H. and C. Poulett Thomson on the one side,
and Baron de Biel on the other, they came to an agreement, which
was reduced into writing, part by A. H. P. Thomson, and the rest
by C. P. Thomson, and the same was as follows:

"The arrangement proposed, in case of the marriage of Baron
de Biel with Miss Sophia Poulett Thomson, is as follows, viz.:

"Mr. J. P. Thomson proposes to pay down the sum of 10,000*l.*
sterl* to be secured in the British, French, or other funds that may
be agreed upon, in the names of trustees to be chosen, the interest
to belong to Baron Biel, during the joint lives of himself and Miss
Thomson, and to her in case of his death before her; the principal
to be secured to the children of the marriage, or in case of there
being no issue, the survivor to have the interest for life, and the
capital to be at the disposition of Baron Biel.

[*48]
"Baron Biel to obtain the means of settling 500*l.* per an., to be
*payable to Miss Thomson for life, secured on his estate in Meck-
lenburgh, after his death, in case of her surviving him.

"Mr. J. P. T. proposes for the present to allow his daughter
200*l.* per an. for her private use, subject to a possibility of a
reduction in that sum in case political or other circumstances
should diminish his income; and also intends to leave a further
sum of 10,000*l.* in his will to Miss Thomson, to be settled on her
and her children, the disposition of which, supposing she has no
children, will be prescribed by the will of her father.

"These are the basis of the arrangements proposed, subject of
course to revision, but they will be sufficient for Baron Biel to
act upon.

"Baron Biel should forward as early as possible a joint arrangement for himself and brother, settling 500*l.* per an. on Miss Thomson.
It is a question, tho' how far that can be given by them without the
consent of their heirs, who in case of the death of both, might
vitiate it. This point should be decided."

The bill then stated, that A. H. and C. Poulett Thomson gave
the said written agreement to Baron de Biel, who accepted the
same as binding, both on himself and on J. P. Thomson: that the
Baron then returned to Germany, and as required by the said
agreement, executed an instrument in the German language, dated
the 29th of January, 1826, by which he secured out of his said
estates to his said intended wife, in case he died before her, leaving

children, a yearly jointure of 500*l*.; and about the same time, he
prevailed on his brother, the said Baron Gottlieb de Biel, to execute
a similar instrument for securing the said jointure to Miss Thomson,
in case the Baron de Biel died before her without leaving any
children, in which case, as before mentioned, the said estates would
have devolved on the Baron Gottlieb de Biel: that these two instruments were laid before an advocate at Hamburgh, selected by A. H.
and C. Poulett Thomson, and they were settled and approved by
the said advocate on behalf of J. Poulett Thomson, and were afterwards sent over to this country, and had ever since been in the
hands of A. H. and C. Poulett Thomson: that *shortly afterwards,   [*49]
and before any formal deed of settlement was executed, the Baron
de Biel and Miss Thomson were married in Dresden, where Miss
Thomson was staying with her sister, the wife of Baron de Maltzahn:
that after their marriage they came to this country, and in consequence of communications between the Baron and A. H. and
C. Poulett Thomson, who acted in the matter on behalf of their
father, respecting the settlement which it had been agreed should
be made on the occasion of the said marriage, Messrs. Dunn
and Wordsworth, as the solicitors of the Thomson family, were
instructed by A. H. and C. Poulett Thomson to prepare an indenture
of settlement.

The bill then stated the settlement so prepared, dated the 23rd
of June, 1826, and made between J. P. Thomson of the first part,
A. H. P. Thomson and Charles Hammersley (the appellant) of the
second part, and the Baron de Biel and Sophia his wife of the
third part, whereby J. P. Thomson covenanted that he, or his heirs,
executors, &c., within twelve months after his death, would pay
A. H. P. Thomson and C. Hammersley, their executors, &c.,
10,000*l*., upon the trusts therein expressed, with interest in the
mean time.   (No mention was made of the further sum of 10,000*l*.,
which the memorandum of agreement stated that Mr. Thomson
intended to leave by his will to Miss Thomson and her children, nor
of the jointure of 500*l*. secured to her by the Baron, as before stated.)

The bill next stated that the said indenture of settlement was
duly executed by all the parties thereto, but was not previously
submitted to or settled by any person, on behalf of the Baron de
Biel and his wife: that the Baron having noticed that no mention
was made therein of the said further sum of 10,000*l*., which
J. P. Thomson was to leave by his will, applied to A. H. P. Thomson
for an explanation of such omission, when he informed the Baron

that it would not be proper in point of form, to *include the same
in the indenture : that the Baron not being acquainted with the
law of this country, nor assisted by any legal adviser, and having
no reason to doubt that the said written agreement would in all
respects be faithfully performed, acquiesced in that explanation,
and did not take any steps to obtain any further security for such
further sum of 10,000*l.*: that at the time of executing the said
indenture of settlement, Baron de Biel and his wife, at the request
of J. P. Thomson, executed a deed of release, of even date therewith, by which they released all claims on account of the share of
the Baroness as one of the children of J. P. Thomson, in a sum of
15,000*l.*, and in a certain bond executed by J. P. Thomson previous
to his marriage.

The bill stated that the allowance of 200*l.* a year mentioned in
the written agreement, was duly paid to the Baroness de Biel
during her life; that she died in September, 1827, and that her
father died in 1838, having by his will given the residue of his
personal estate to his sons, and appointed them and the appellant
his executors ; but that he did not thereby leave the further 10,000*l.*
in fulfilment of the promise contained in the said agreement, nor
make any provision for paying the same.

The bill in support of the allegations and charges contained in it,
set forth a correspondence, [which concluded with the following letter,
written to the Baron de Biel, in March, 1835, by J. P. Thomson :]

[54]

" DEAR BARON,—I sit down to answer directly the letter you put
into my hand, that you may receive it before you set out. I have
placed the whole concern in the hands of my sons, whom it regards,
as residuary legatees, more than it does me. I had forgotten all
that passed at the time of your marriage, and till you gave me this
copy (1) I had not understood the exact expression to which it refers.
I had only a vague recollection of the terms in which the second
sum of 10,000*l.* was mentioned. The impression on my mind was,
that I had left it open to revision in case of a change of circumstances. That having taken place, the only question is now, I

[*55]

conceive, what the expression used in the engagement *legally
implies, in which there appears, as my sons tell me, a considerable
difference between the lawyers consulted. It is extremely painful
to me, that such a difference should exist, but I wish to keep myself
quite clear of the decision."

(1) A copy of the proposed arrange-   sentation made to the Baron de Biel,
ment in writing containing the repre-   see *ante*, p. 40.—O. A. S.

The bill, after further allegations and charges, prayed that it might be declared that J. P. Thomson was, after the death of the Baroness de Biel, bound to leave by his will a sum of 10,000*l.* to, or in trust for, the respondent, in addition to the sum of 10,000*l.* secured by the said indenture of settlement; and that the appellant and his co-executors might be decreed to pay the said sum, with interest from the death of J. P. Thomson, out of his assets, to some proper person or persons, as trustee or trustees for the respondent.

C. P. Thomson and the appellant by their answer to the bill, (A. H. P. Thomson having died before answer,) admitted that the memorandum in question was drawn up at the meeting, as in the bill mentioned; that the annuity of 200*l.*, therein agreed to be paid by J. P. Thomson, was regularly paid by him during the life of his daughter; and that the settlement of the jointure of 500*l.* was prepared and executed as stated in the bill. They also admitted the statements in the bill respecting the will of J. P. Thomson, and admitted assets sufficient to satisfy the respondent's demand, but they rested their defence to it on three grounds: first, on the want of authority in the sons to enter into a binding agreement, to the extent of the sum in question, on behalf of their father; 2ndly, on the Statute of Frauds; and 3rdly, on the construction of the memorandum, contending that it did not, at least as to the sum in question, amount to a binding agreement.

*   *   *   *   *

The Baron proved the letters and documents stated in the bill, and also in his cross-examination admitted that he received a letter written to him by C. P. Thomson, dated the 31st of January, 1826 (1).   *   *   *

[59]

(1) This letter was in French: the following is a correct translation of so much of it as is material here:

"I have received a letter, my dear Baron, from your brother, in which he directs me to consent to do what is necessary to secure the widow's jointure of Sophia, and informs me that he has sent the necessary papers to Dresden to wait for you there: my father has since received a letter from Sophia. who informs him of your departure for Mecklenburg, so that I fear you have crossed these documents on the road, and that there will still be some delay occasioned by it; how-

ever this does not signify, for this is the way *in which my father thinks it will be best to arrange the matter, a method which I hope will put an end to every possible delay, although it is perhaps not so quick as the betrothed parties wish. One of our friends, Mr. Gossler, senator of Hamburgh, will take upon him to appoint an advocate, who will arrange with yours and your brothers the documents which are necessary to secure the widow's jointure to Sophia. For this purpose my brother has written to him to-day, and given him the required particulars. As soon as the lawyers shall have

[*60, n.]

HAMMERS-
LEY
v.
DE BIEL.
[61]

The cause [intituled *De Biel* v. *Thomson*] was heard by the MASTER OF THE ROLLS, and on the 19th of February, 1840, his Lordship [delivered judgment as reported in 3 Beav. p. 469, in which, after stating the facts, he proceeded as follows:]

1841.
———
[3 Beav.
472]

The plaintiff now claims that further sum of 10,000*l.*, which the memorandum expressed it to be the intention of Mr. John Poulett Thomson to leave by his will, to be settled on the plaintiff's mother and her children; and he insists on payment out of the assets of Mr. John Poulett Thomson.

[473]

The defendants deny that they are under any obligation to pay the same; and they allege:

First, that the sons, Mr. Andrew Henry and Mr. Charles Poulett Thomson, had no authority from their father to enter into any agreement, binding the father to leave the sum of 10,000*l.* in his will to be settled; and consequently, that if the memorandum and the subsequent events amounted, in effect, to such an agreement, it was entered into without authority, and was not binding on the father, and constitutes no obligation to be satisfied out of his assets.

Secondly, that, by the Statute of Frauds (1), an agreement, entered into in consideration of marriage, is not binding, unless the same or some memorandum or note thereof, shall be in writing, and signed by the party to be charged therewith, or some other person thereunto lawfully authorised; and that this memorandum was not signed by Mr. John Poulett Thomson or his sons, and therefore was not binding.

Thirdly, that even if it shall appear, that the sons had the father's authority, and that the agreement is not made invalid by the Statute of Frauds, still, upon the true construction of it, Mr. John Poulett Thomson was under no obligation to leave the sum of 10,000*l.* to be settled; it was left at his option to do as he pleased. A hope of bounty to that extent was all that the memorandum

arranged the necessary papers, and that they are signed, or shall be ready for it, Mr. Gossler will forward them to us here, and we shall send Sophia's marriage contract (settlement) to Dresden for your signature and hers, for this document must positively be signed by both of you before the ceremony, without this it is void according to our laws. I therefore request you to hasten the arrangement of this contract on your part and that of your brother, to whom I write by this same post to inform him what we propose to do, in order that the two advocates may have a conference as soon as possible, and in the meanwhile I shall get prepared on our side Sophia's contract, securing her fortune to you, so as to be able to forward it the moment I receive the other documents, &c."

(1) 29 Car. II. c. 3, s. 4.

meant to hold out, and the bounty might be withheld; and after
the death of the daughter, was reasonably and justly withheld.
According to the expression of the defendant's counsel, Baron de
Biel might rely on bounty, but had no right to insist on obligation.

Upon a due consideration of the facts of this case, as they appear
in the evidence and in the correspondence, it appears to me to be
sufficiently established, that Mr. Andrew Henry and Mr. Charles
Poulett Thomson were authorised, by their father, to make the
proposals expressed in the memorandum of the 22nd December,
1825; and, on the part of Mr. John Poulett Thomson, to offer
those proposals to the acceptance of Baron de Biel, and enable him
to convert them into an agreement by acceptance, and doing what
was required on his part; and considering the proposal to have been,
under the circumstances of this case, ripened into an agreement, I
am of opinion that Mr. Andrew Henry and Mr. Charles Poulett
Thomson had the authority of Mr. John Poulett Thomson to enter
into that agreement on his behalf.

Upon the question whether this agreement is invalid, by reason
of the same, or any memorandum or note thereof not being signed
by Mr. John Poulett Thomson, or any person thereunto lawfully
authorised, according to the provisions of the Statute of Frauds, it
is to be considered in what situation the parties were and what
they did.

The two sons of Mr. John Poulett Thomson were, as I think,
authorised to enter into an agreement with Baron de Biel; pursuant
to the authority which they had, they made certain proposals in
their father's name in writing. In those proposals they twice write
and use their father's name, in a manner to show, with sufficient
certainty, the whole of that which was proposed on his part; the
proposals, on his part, were accompanied by a requisition of something to be done on the part of Baron de Biel; and Baron de Biel,
on receiving the proposals, accepted them and proceeded to perform
*what was required of him; and this being performed the marriage
was solemnised.

After the marriage, and after the death of the wife, Mr. Andrew
Henry Thomson, representing himself to act with the authority of
his father, acknowledged the memorandum, though a question had
arisen upon the effect of it. And Mr. John Poulett Thomson
himself, by his letter, of the 30th April, 1830, recognises the agreement, of which a copy had been put into his hands by Baron de
Biel. In this letter Mr. Thomson, although he says that he had

forgotten all that passed at the time of the marriage, and says, that until the copy was given to him, he had not understood the exact expression to which it referred, does not repudiate the expression as unauthorised, but appears to me to admit that he had agreed to the effect proposed in the memorandum ; and admitting that, he says, that he conceives the only question to be, what the expression used in "the engagement" (for so he calls it), legally implies.

In the case of *Randall* v. *Morgan* (1), Sir Wm. GRANT expressed great doubt, whether a letter written after the marriage, referring to a parol agreement before the marriage, would be sufficient to give validity to a promise, which of itself produced no obligation ; but Lord HARCOURT, in the case of *Hodgson* v. *Hutchenson* (2), thought, that a letter after the marriage, considering the transactions before, was, in that case, sufficient. And, in this case, having regard to the transactions which took place before the marriage, it appears to me, that this letter subsequently written and signed by Mr. Thomson, referring to a copy of the memorandum, as stating

[*476] the expression or the terms of the engagement *which he had entered into before the marriage, is either a sufficient note of the agreement signed by the party to be charged, or a sufficient recognition of the use made of his name in the memorandum, and of the obligation thereby contracted ; and so thinking, it does not appear to me to be necessary to determine, whether the use of the name in the memorandum, be of itself a sufficient signature of Mr. Thomson by his agents ; or whether the provision of the jointure by Baron de Biel takes the case out of the statute ; or whether, independently of the statute, this Court, for the prevention of fraud, would compel the defendants to realise the expectations on the faith of which the marriage was contracted.

If Baron de Biel, on receiving the proposals, instead of acting upon them, on the faith of their being valid and binding if adopted, had required Mr. Thomson to sign them more formally, some objection might probably have been made ; but I conceive that any such objection would not have arisen from any notion that the proposals would not otherwise be valid, but rather from a desire to withdraw the proposals, whilst it was yet time, from the consideration and acceptance of a person, so idly jealous and suspicious of the honour and integrity of those, with whom he was dealing on such an occasion.

Upon that which Mr. John Poulett Thomson appears to me to

(1) 8 R. R. at p. 293 (12 Ves. 73).   (2) 5 Vin. Abr. 522, pl. 34.

have properly considered to be the only question, viz. the legal   DE BIEL
effect of the terms in which the engagement is expressed, I am of   THOMSON.
opinion that the plaintiff is entitled to the second sum of 10,000*l.*
which he claims.

The memorandum is entitled, " The arrangement proposed in
case of the intended marriage." It expresses *what Mr. John   [*477]
Poulett Thomson proposed to do, and what Baron de Biel was
required or expected to do. In a distinct sentence, it proposed an
annual payment, subject to possible reduction in circumstances
referred to, and then expressed the intention of Mr. John Poulett
Thomson to leave a further sum of 10,000*l.* by his will ; and so
far from providing, that the leaving of this sum was to be merely
optional on his part, or was to be subject to any reduction, it
expressly provides, that it should be at the disposition of Mr. John
Poulett Thomson in a certain event only ; viz. in the event of the
intended wife having no children. It would have been absurd to
make this provision, if the parties had meant that the gift or
settlement of this sum of 10,000*l.* was to be altogether optional.
The power of disposition would not have been expressed in one
particular case, if it was intended that at all events, and in every
case, the disposition and the option, whether to give it or settle it
at all, was to be his. The use of the word "intend," does not
appear to me to be in any way material ; the parties were expressing a part of the arrangement in case of the marriage ; and the
meaning is obvious, that he intended to leave the 10,000*l.* if the
marriage took effect, pursuant to the proposal and intention thus
expressed.

The memorandum then expressed, that the arrangements proposed were, of course, subject to revision, but would be sufficient
for Baron de Biel to act upon : and it was argued, that because the
proposed arrangements were subject to revision, they could not
constitute or end in a concluded agreement. It is true that, whilst
the proposal remained subject to revision, it could not constitute a
concluded agreement. Proposals of this nature cannot result in an
agreement all at once, or be otherwise than subject to revision.
The proposals were *an offer of some things to be done by   [*478]
Mr. Thomson, and a requisition of some things to be done by
Baron de Biel, with reference to the intended marriage. Until
Baron de Biel had performed his part, and prior to the marriage,
the whole was to be subject to revision ; but no revision took place.
The proposals and intentions, thus expressed, remained without

DE BIEL
v.
THOMSON.

any alteration whatever, up to the time of the marriage; and I am of opinion that the proposals, which up to that time had been · subject to revision, did then, by the acceptance of Baron de Biel, by his due execution of the required settlement on his part, and by the solemnisation of the marriage, with the approbation of Mr. Thomson, become an agreement which Mr. Thomson was bound specifically to perform.

I am, therefore, of opinion that the plaintiff is entitled to the relief which he prays, and that there must be a decree accordingly, with costs.

Mr. Puller:

Does your Lordship think that interest ought to be paid on this sum from the death of the testator?

THE MASTER OF THE ROLLS:

I think that interest, at 4 per cent., is payable, but only from the end of one year after the testator's death, on the footing of a legacy.

1845.

[12 Cl. & Fin. 61]

[A decree was accordingly made that] the defendants, C. P. Thomson and the appellant, as the executors of the will of J. Poulett Thomson, should pay into the Bank to the credit of the cause the sum of 10,000*l.*, together with interest thereon at the rate of 4*l.* per cent. per annum, from the end of one year after J. P. Thomson's death.

An appeal against that decree was heard by Lord COTTENHAM (Chancellor) in May, 1841, and his Lordship made an order the 6th of August, affirming the decree and dismissing the appeal with costs. The case on that appeal is not reported. The following note of the LORD CHANCELLOR's judgment was printed with the appeal case, and admitted by the counsel on both sides to be correct:

THE LORD CHANCELLOR (LORD COTTENHAM):

[*62, n.]

Of the three points *relied on by the appellants as the ground of their resistance to the claim of the plaintiff, I propose, first, to consider whether there was any such agreement previous to the marriage of the plaintiff's father and mother as was binding on the late Mr. Thomson to give an additional 10,000*l.* as the portion of his daughter. If it be supposed to be necessary for this purpose to find a contract, such as usually accompanies transactions of importance

in the pecuniary affairs of mankind, there may not be found in
the memorandum, or in the other evidence in the cause, proof
of any such contract; and this may have led to the defence set up
by the defendants; but when the authorities on this subject are
attended to, it will be found that no such formal contract is
required. A representation made by one party for the purpose of
influencing the conduct of the other party, and acted on by him,
will in general be sufficient to entitle him to the assistance of this
Court for the purpose of realising such representation. Of this,
Hodgson v. *Hutchenson* (1), *Cookes* v. *Mascall* (2), and *Wankford* v.
Fotherley (3), which last case was affirmed by the House of Lords,
afford strong instances. In *Luders* v. *Anstey* (4), a suggestion for
consideration, followed by marriage, was held to be binding. In
the present case there was communicated to the intended husband
a paper purporting to contain the arrangement proposed in case of
the marriage, part of which was, that the father intended to leave
his daughter a further sum of 10,000l. in his will, to be settled on
her and her children, and the disposition of which, supposing she
had no children, would be prescribed by the will of her father.
The same paper, as part of the arrangement proposed, states, that
the intended husband was to find the means of settling 500l. a year
on the intended wife, in the case *of her surviving her husband.
This was done, and the marriage took place, of which the plaintiff
was the only issue. Some of the subsequent letters of Mr. Andrew
Thomson suggest that the second 10,000l. was only to be paid in
the event of the daughter surviving the father, which did not
happen; but the father in his letter to the surviving husband of
his daughter puts the case on its true footing in saying "The only
question is now, I conceive, what the expression used in the engagement legally implies." I am of opinion, upon the authority of the
cases before referred to, that the expressions used in the proposed
arrangement, acted on as they were, became obligatory on the party
on whose behalf the proposition was made.

But, secondly, it was contended that the provisions of the
Statute of Frauds furnish a defence to the claim founded on this
agreement. Assuming for the present that the two brothers of the
intended wife were duly authorised by the father to enter into the
arrangement with the intended husband, the document to which I
have referred, containing the proposed arrangement, proves that

[*63, n.]

---

(1) 5 Vin. Abr. 522.   (3) 2 Vern. 322.
(2) 2 Vern. 200.   (4) 4 R. R. 276 (4 Ves. 501).

both concurred in what that paper contains ; for it is written partly
by one and partly by the other, and the father's name is in one
place written at length by one son, and in the other by initials only,
by the other son ; and as it is clearly immaterial in what place the
signature of the name is to be found, it is, in the terms of the
Statute of Frauds, an agreement made in consideration of marriage,
of which there is a memorandum or note in writing signed by a
person thereunto lawfully authorised by the party to be charged
therewith. An auctioneer, whose signature is sufficient within the
statute, signs the name of the principal. Independently, however,
of this, there is the letter of the father signed by himself, in which
he, referring to this document, says, "the only question now is, I
conceive, what the expression used in the engagement legally
implies," by which he must be understood to mean, that if the
expression used amounted to an obligation to pay the additional

[*64, *n.*]

10,000*l.*, he was *ready to perform it. I am aware that in *Randall*
v. *Morgan* (1), Sir W. GRANT suggests a doubt, whether a written
promise after marriage to perform a parol agreement made before
could be enforced ; but in *Hodgson* v. *Hutchenson* (2), *Taylor* v.
Beech (3), and *Mountacue* v. *Maxwell* (4), it was held that such a
subsequent written promise would be binding within the statute.
This case does not rest solely on that ground, for though it has been
decided that a marriage is not *per se* a part performance of a parol
agreement, so as to take the case out of the statute, there was in
the dealing between these parties an important act by the intended
husband in execution of the proposed arrangement. He was
informed by it that the arrangement proposed would be sufficient
for him to act upon, and that he should forward, as early as
possible, a joint engagement for himself and his brother, settling
500*l.* a year on the intended wife, which was done. I am, therefore,
of opinion that the Statute of Frauds does not afford any defence
against the claim of the infant.

But, thirdly, it was argued that the two brothers of the intended
wife had no authority to enter into this arrangement. In the letters
of 16th December, 1833, and 7th February, 1834, of Mr. Andrew
Thomson, in whose hands as one of his sons the father says he had
placed the whole concern, and the last of which letters the answer
admits was written after communication with and by the direction

(1) 8 R. R. see p. 293 (12 Ves. see   (3) 1 Ves. Sen. 297.
p. 73).   (4) 1 Str. 236.
(2) 5 Vin. Abr. 522.

of the father, no question is raised as to the authority of the sons; on the contrary, in the former he says "in detailing to you my father's intentions with respect to his daughter on or before your marriage, I only fulfilled his directions,"—and he speaks of the proposal with respect to the second 10,000*l.*, as the promise his father had made. But what *is conclusive on this point is the letter of the father himself, who, not disputing the authority under which the engagement was made, says the whole question depends on its construction.

HAMMERS-
LEY
v.
DE BIEL.

[*65, n.]

It was said that the settlement was silent as to this second 10,000*l.*, but it is in proof, that, on the plaintiff's father observing this, Mr. Andrew Thomson answered him, by saying "that such things could not be well introduced into the settlement."

I am for these reasons of opinion, that all the three grounds of defence fail, and that the petition of appeal must be dismissed with costs.

Soon after that *order C. P. Thomson (then recently created Lord Sydenham) died.

[62]

Against the said decree and the order affirming it, the present appeal was brought by the surviving executor and defendant.

Mr. Anderdon and *Mr. Fitzroy Kelly* for the appellant:

* * The alleged agreement is not signed by any one. The name of J. P. Thomson appears twice in the body of it, but as it was not signed by him nor by his authorised agents, it is not an agreement binding on him within the Statute of Frauds (1).

[65]

THE LORD CHANCELLOR:

What do you say to the jointure of 500*l.*? Was not that a part performance and *consideration? Was not the Baron de Biel influenced in making that provision by the representations contained in the written memorandum?

[*66]

* *

LORD CAMPBELL:

If a father says to a suitor, "If you marry my daughter, and settle so much a-year on her for her jointure, I will give so much for her portion:" would not that proposal be a good contract if the marriage takes place, and the jointure is settled?

(1) See *Caton* v. *Caton* (1867) L. R. 2 H. L. 127.

HAMMERS-
LEY
v.
DE BIEL.

LORD BROUGHAM:

A case of that sort came before Lord Eldon and myself here; it was *Logan* v. *Wienholt* (1).

[*Mr. Kelly:*

This instrument purports to be no more than a preliminary arrangement, being expressly "subject to revision."]

[73]   *Mr. G. Turner* and *Mr. Phillips* appeared for the respondent, but were not called on.

THE LORD CHANCELLOR:

We have attended most carefully to the very able arguments of the learned counsel who have addressed us, but as we have formed a clear opinion on the case, we do not think it necessary to trouble the counsel for the respondent.

Mr. Andrew Thomson and Mr. Charles Thomson, by the authority given to them by their father—which, after his letter (2), I think, cannot now be disputed—entered into an arrangement for a marriage between their sister and the Baron de Biel, the terms of which arrangement have been stated to your Lordships. It is quite impossible, after the letter to which I have referred, for a moment to consider that that arrangement was not entered into by the father's authority. But reliance had been placed—and that has been the principal argument on the part of the appellant—upon certain words in that arrangement, by which it is stated " to be subject, of course, to revision," but in the meantime that it is " sufficient for the Baron de Biel to act upon."

[*74]   Now, it is to be observed that there was no stipulation *whatever as to the time when the marriage was to take place. It, in fact, did not take place till six or seven weeks after the arrangement had been entered into. During the whole of that time no intimation was given, either on the part of the brothers or of the father, that they desired any revision of this agreement, that they desired any alteration whatever to be made in it; there was no suggestion or intimation of that kind; and, under these circumstances, after the lapse of six or seven weeks, the marriage took place.

It is stated that a letter was written by Mr. Andrew Thomson, as it is suggested, by the authority of the father, to the Baron de Biel, telling him not to celebrate the marriage until after the

(1) 36 R. R. 215 (1 Cl. & Fin. 611).   (2) *Supra*, p. 22.

settlement had been executed (1), and from that it is assumed that
it was a wrongful act on the part of the Baron de Biel and of the
daughter to celebrate that marriage before the settlement had been
actually executed. Now, when you come to consider that letter,
it amounts to nothing more than this: the writer states, "no doubt
you are very impatient to marry; you will think the interval
tedious; but you will recollect that, until the settlements are
executed, if you marry before their execution, they will, by the law
of England, be altogether void." There was no intimation whatever
in that letter that the father wished to depart from the agreement
in any particular; but the sole object of the letter was to caution
them not to marry merely upon the ground that was stated in the
letter, namely, that if they did marry, the settlements executed
afterwards would be altogether void. It turned out that he was
mistaken in point of law, and, therefore, it appears to me that the
letter amounts to nothing; it was a mere intimation directed to
a particular object, with respect to which the writer of the letter
appears *to have been mistaken. I do not, under these circum-   [*75]
stances, apprehend that that letter can possibly have any weight
in this case.

Then, after the marriage took place, did the father complain
that no opportunity had been afforded for revision? Did he
suggest that he wished any alteration to be made in the terms of
the settlement? Was there any admission of that kind? Did he
complain that the marriage had been celebrated at too early a
period? Nothing of the kind. The parties come over to this
country; they were well received by the father, and preparations were
made for executing the settlement, and it does not appear that the
slightest complaint was made during that interval as to the time
when the marriage was celebrated, or as to their having anticipated
the execution of the settlement, nor any intimation whatever that
the parties desired any change or alteration in the settlement in
pursuance of that reservation of a power of revision, upon which so
much observation has been made.

Now then as to the settlement itself, and the transaction which
took place: the draft was prepared by Mr. Wordsworth and his
partner. The parties met at the house of the solicitor, for the
purpose of approving of the draft. The parties who so met were
the Baron de Biel and Mr. Andrew Thomson. The draft was read
over, and much canvassed and considered. It related only to the

(1) *Supra*, pp. 23 and 24, note.

settlement of the first 10,000l. Attention was only directed to that subject; but after the terms had been so settled with respect to that sum, with the entire approbation of both parties, then a conversation took place between the Baron de Biel and Mr. Andrew Thomson, which has been referred to in the course of the argument. That conversation related to the 10,000l. that was to be settled by the will. The Baron de Biel said "no notice has been taken of that 10,000l." This is the distinct evidence that he has given in the cause.

[*76]
This is stated, and repeatedly *stated in the letters that he wrote upon the subject. He said that, as he was coming away from Mr. Wordsworth's, in conversation with Mr. Andrew Thomson, and having stated that there was no notice taken of the 10,000l. which was to be settled by the will, Mr. Andrew Thomson said his father's intentions were still the same, there had been no alteration of any intention, but that such a matter could not be well introduced into the settlement; and the gentleman (Baron de Biel) says that, " being unacquainted with the laws of England, he took for granted that Mr. Thomson was right, and he did not press the matter further." That accounts, therefore, for this part of the arrangement not having been introduced into the settlement. I do not find any contradiction of this statement; on the contrary, it is rather confirmed by the testimony of Mr. Wordsworth. Supposing there was a competition between the evidence of those two gentlemen, what are the circumstances of the case, and upon whose evidence would your Lordships be most disposed to rely? It is quite clear that the Baron de Biel had his attention directed to the subject; he was one of the parties to the conversation. Mr. Wordsworth says he did not hear what passed from the Baron de Biel; or, if he did hear it, he heard it so imperfectly that he can give no account of it: he recollected part of the reply made by Mr. Andrew Thomson, but he goes on and says that it made no impression upon him, and that he took no notice of it. It is quite clear, therefore, if there was a conflict of evidence, your Lordships would be disposed rather to place reliance upon the accuracy of the Baron de Biel than upon the statement of Mr. Wordsworth, so qualified, and accompanied by the circumstances to which I have referred.

It is remarkable that in this conversation, when so much reliance has been placed upon the circumstance of the parties having suddenly married, and prevented all opportunity of revision of the
[*77]
arrangement, no such complaint *was made by Mr. Andrew Thomson.

If he had thought there was some just ground of complaint of that fact, the moment the Baron de Biel had said, "the 10,000*l.* to be provided for by the will are not included in the settlement," he would have said immediately, "Why, by your marriage you have prevented the alteration that my father meant to make in the arrangement;" but no intimation of that kind was given, and I am quite satisfied, from all the circumstances of the case, that there never was any intention on the part of the father to make any alteration in the terms of the settlement, but that the settlement itself, the agreement entered into, or rather the proposition made by the two brothers, was throughout to be the basis of the settlement.

If that be so, then we are brought to the consideration of the effect of that arrangement. And what does the father say in his letter?(1). He brings it to that very point. He does not make any of those points which have been urged at the Bar, but, after considering the subject, and reviving his recollection by looking at the copy of the agreement, he says he conceives it must be settled according to the legal import of the terms that are contained in the agreement; and he puts it upon that, and he acquiesces in it. He seems disposed to assent to whatever is the legal interpretation of these expressions, and feels that he is bound by them.

Then what is the legal effect of those expressions? For myself, I cannot entertain any doubt with regard to the legal effect of them. In the first place, what does the instrument purport to be? It is not a loose arrangement, but it is an arrangement entered into apparently with much consideration. It says, " The arrangement proposed in the case of the marriage of the Baron de Biel with Miss Sophia Poulett Thomson is as follows." *Then the parties go on to state what the arrangement is to be, and they come at last to this particular: " Mr. John Poulett Thomson also intends to leave a further sum of 10,000*l.* in his will to Miss Thomson, to be settled on her and her children, the disposition of which, supposing she has no children, will be prescribed by the will of her father. These are the basis of the arrangement proposed, subject, of course, to revision, but they will be sufficient for Baron de Biel to act upon." The instrument begins by stating that these are the proposed arrangements, and, after stating the intention with respect to the will, it concludes by stating, that what has been previously

[*78]

(1) *Supra*, p. 22.

3—2

stated is the basis of the arrangements, in case of the marriage taking place.

How is it possible for a moment to consider that this was not to be regarded as a substantial part of the arrangement, that was to influence the Baron, to operate upon his mind, and to induce him to form this alliance with the daughter of Mr. Thomson? He does not say merely that he intends to settle 10,000l. by his will, but he points out the particular form of that settlement, the manner in which it is to be arranged, and eventually, in case there should be no children, that then he shall have the power by his will of disposing of the property. Does that look like a mere voluntary act, which was not at all to be obligatory upon him? Why was all that arrangement set out, if he was not to be bound by it? Why were these stipulations to be inserted in this part of the instrument? They were altogether unnecessary. Why was he to be restrained only in a certain event to have a power over this property, if it was to be considered that he was not bound to bequeath the property at all, unless he thought proper to do so? But the principle of law, at least of equity, is this—that if a party holds out inducements to another to celebrate a marriage, and holds them out deliberately and plainly, and the other party consents, and celebrates the [*79] *marriage in consequence of them, if he had good reason to expect that it was intended that he should have the benefit of the proposal which was so held out, a court of equity will take care that he is not disappointed, and will give effect to the proposal. This is stated as a part of the arrangement; it is stated as the proposal.

Under these circumstances, according to the authorities that were referred to in the judgments of the learned Judges in the Courts below, I conceive this case comes clearly and distinctly within the principle to which I have referred. It is impossible to say for a moment that it was not held out to the Baron de Biel as a part of this arrangement, that 10,000l. should be left by will for the purpose of being settled upon the children of this marriage. It is impossible to suppose for a moment that that did not operate upon the mind of the Baron, and induce him, with reference also to the other provisions contained in this instrument, to celebrate the marriage; and I am sure, under these circumstances, your Lordships will see the propriety and equity of giving effect to those expectations.

Upon these grounds, my Lords, it is that the judgment below was pronounced; and upon these grounds, I think it may satisfactorily

be rested, and therefore I recommend your Lordships to affirm
the judgment of the COURT below.

I say nothing upon the Statute of Frauds, because I understand
that that objection has been distinctly abandoned by the learned
counsel; therefore that objection being out of the way, the case
rests upon the principles which I have stated, and upon these
principles I think it ought to be decided.

LORD BROUGHAM:

I entirely agree with my noble and learned friend in the view
which he has so accurately and so luminously taken of this case.
I certainly was one of those who thought it unnecessary to trouble
the counsel *for the respondent to address us, in answer to the   [*80]
able arguments which both the learned counsel have presented
on the part of the appellant. With every anxiety that a case of
such importance should be fully considered, I thought it was not
required.

The question which was raised below, and, to a certain degree,
argued by both the learned counsel here, until very late in the
day,—as to the effect of the Statute of Frauds—is now out of the
field, which I am exceedingly glad of, as the case is relieved of a
considerable degree, rather of length than of difficulty, inasmuch
as I have no doubt whatever, upon looking into it, as to how that
point ought to be disposed of.

The case then rests entirely upon the ground upon which it is
material to consider that Mr. John Poulett Thomson himself rested
it in his letter of the 30th of April, 1835, nine years and a half
after the memorandum, amounting, as we hold, and as has been
held below, to a contract; I am, therefore, to deal with the case as
if the authority of Messrs. Andrew Henry Thomson and Charles
Poulett Thomson, were admitted, it having thus been proved by
the adoption of the father, with the memorandum or a copy of it
before him, the existence of which memorandum he had not forgotten, though he may have forgotten, as he says, the particular
expressions in it. I am to take it also as if that authority, so
proved by his recognition and adoption of that instrument to have
been by him conveyed to his two sons, had been by them executed
in *modo et formâ*, in which it was given; and I am therefore to come
to that and that only, upon which he himself rests as the only
doubt which he entertains; and I shall show your Lordships that
there cannot really be a doubt upon it, namely, the legal effect of

the expression in the instrument. All the rest being admitted by
him, he relies upon that, and I am here in a condition dealing with
this case as if I had Mr. John Poulett Thomson *himself at the
Bar, arguing his own case, and saying, " I admit the authority, I
admit the execution of that power given by me to my two sons, but
I call upon your Lordships to give judgment in my favour, upon
the legal import and effect of that instrument, which they so by
me authorized did, under my instructions, execute." That is the
point upon which we are now to consider this case—as if Mr.
Thomson were here demurring in point of law to the construction
put by the Court below upon the instrument in question, but giving
up all other objections in the case.

Now it is very much to be considered (and I the more call your
Lordships' attention to this point, because it has not yet been
brought to our attention, although we should have had it probably
from the other side), it is very much to be considered in what way
Mr. J. P. Thomson states this; for I am by no means clear that,
if the obvious mistake, into which he falls in his recollection of the
purport of the instrument, had been removed, and if his mind had
been cleared up upon that point, he would not have said there is
an end to the question. Suppose he was here, and he had just
repeated here what he says in his letter of the 30th of April, 1835;
suppose he had said, " The impression on my mind was that I had
left it open to revision." Oh! but a marriage took place, says
Mr. Kelly, (which Mr. Thomson would not have said) and that
prevented the revision. He goes on, clearly showing that he was
under a total misapprehension of what it was; he says, " The
impression on my mind was that I had left it open to revision in
case of a change of circumstances." If he had left it open to
revision " in case of a change of circumstances," a question might
arise whether he would not be right in his contention here. I do
not say how I should dispose of it, if that question might be raised;
but that is a total mistake: he had not left it open to revision, in
case of a change of circumstances. The fact is that he is confound-
[*82] ing the 10,000*l.* with *the 200*l.* a-year. If your Lordships will
observe, the allowance of 200*l.* a-year is left open to revision, " in
case of a change of circumstances," because Mr. Thomson says,
" I propose, for the present, to allow 200*l.* per annum, subject to
the possibility of a reduction in that sum in case political or other
circumstances should diminish my income." But where is there
a word to be found about any change of circumstances to affect the

disposition of the 10,000*l.*? There is nothing of the kind; it is
confined to the 200*l.* But Mr. Thomson, at a distance of nine
years afterwards, and at his age, and not having till lately seen
a copy of it, had an inaccurate recollection, nay, an inaccurate
perusal of it, (because the copy was before him); he confounded
the two; he applied the words, "change of circumstances," which,
in the instrument executed on his behalf by his sons, are confined
to the 200*l.*, which was clearly optional and only a present provision; he applied that expression to the 10,000*l.* I have looked in
vain; (I shall be glad to be corrected if I am wrong, for it weighs
very much upon my mind in disposing of this case) I have looked
in vain through that instrument of the 22nd of December, 1825, to
find any word or any reference whatever to a change of circumstances, as affecting the 10,000*l.* All that I can find with reference
to that 10,000*l.* is of a totally different nature. That sum of
10,000*l.* was to be "settled on her and her children, the disposition
of which, supposing she has no children, will be prescribed by the
will of her father." These are the basis of the arrangement proposed, "subject, of course, to revision." He does not say "in
case of any change of circumstances," but "subject to revision,"
and that is all; "but it will be sufficient," he adds, "for Baron de
Biel to act upon." Then how can I be sure that if I had Mr.
Thomson standing there, as advocate in his own cause, (which,
however, he was much too sensible a man ever to be; but still we
can suppose that he might have been here) how can I be sure that
he would not have said, *"It was a part of my arrangement that   [*83]
I was to have the benefit of a power of revision in case of a change
of circumstances." But I should say to him: "No, Mr. Thomson,
please to look at what your sons signed for you, and you will find
you are mistaken; there is not a word about change of circumstances, there is only "subject to revision." "Change of circumstances, I am sure," he would have said, "is in the instrument."
Yes, I should have replied to him; but look, you will find that you
are confounding the two parts of the instrument together, the
change of circumstances applies to the 200*l.*; but it does not apply
to the 10,000*l.* at all. "I see," he would have said, "that I have
totally mistaken: I am entirely wrong: my argument went upon
a false impression on the point. I see clearly now that there is
not a word about change of circumstances, but only subject to
revision."

My Lords, I have thought it right to state what I have stated on this point, because it is one which had not hitherto been brought to our attention: the counsel for the appellant had no interest in bringing it before us. I am now to consider whether these words, "subject, of course, to revision," would make any difference; and I am clearly of opinion with the MASTER OF THE ROLLS, and I concur in what he states upon that subject, and which is stated by him so clearly, that I prefer his language to my own. He says most accurately (1), "Until Baron de Biel had performed his part, and prior to the marriage, the whole was to be subject to revision, but no revision took place. The proposals and intention thus expressed remained without any alteration whatever up to the time of the marriage, and I am of opinion (in which I entirely agree,) that the proposals, which up to that time had been subject to revision, did then, by the acceptance of the Baron de Biel, by his due execution of the required settlement on his part,

[*84]

and by the solemnization of the marriage, *with the approbation of Mr. Thomson, become an agreement (according to all the cases), which Mr. Thomson was bound specifically to perform."

My noble and learned friend has so fully pointed out the grounds upon which this is to be taken as an agreement within all the cases, and according to the fundamental and undoubted principles on which courts of equity have always acted in this country, that I have no occasion to go further into that branch of the case, having relied more upon that point which had not been previously remarked upon. But it is to be observed that this was an act of a very formal nature, and not a loose and casual arrangement; and when we have been pressed by the learned counsel with the argument, which no doubt has its foundation in fact, I agree that these are the things which are very commonly said when suitors come for a man's daughters, or nieces, or wards, or persons under their parental care, "I will give so much," or, "I will settle so much, and, besides that, you will take into your account that she may be better off at my death." That, no doubt, is very often said, but is it common to put it into writing? On the contrary, if a suitor were to say, "Will you have the goodness just to put the last part of your kind observation down into writing," the old gentleman would say, "Oh, no! I do not mean to bind myself." But here he does bind himself—he does put it into writing, and puts it into writing in as formal a way as it is well possible to conceive; and in these words he proposes to allow so much, which I say nothing about,

(1) *Supra*, p. 27 (3 Beav. 478).

for nothing turns upon that, and also by his will to leave a further sum. The word "intends" is just as if he had said "proposes;" for he afterwards has proposed to cover that, as well as the 200*l.*; he intends to leave a further sum in his will to Miss Thomson. Then how does he go on? He goes on providing for two several and distinct events, as my noble and learned friend has stated, first, providing for the *case of her having children; and secondly, providing for the case of her not having children. In case of her having children, what is to be done with it? It is to be settled on her and her children. In case of her not having children, what is to be done with it? The disposition will be prescribed by the will of her father, so that he provides, most distinctly and clearly, first, for the event of her having children, in which case it is to be settled on her children; and secondly, for the case of her not having children. Now as to the case which was put by *Mr. Kelly*, and pressed upon us strongly, of persons saying vaguely, "I intend so and so; I do not bind myself, but I intend to do so and so;" can that be supposed to be the meaning of a man who says, "I intend to leave 10,000*l.* in my will, besides this 10,000*l.*, which I have now given; and that 10,000*l.* shall be settled upon her children, if she has any; and if she has no children, then I reserve to myself the power of disposing of it as I please." According to the supposition, there was no occasion to reserve such a power, for it was all to be revised; it was all to be subject to revision, and all subject to his own option, from the essentially ambulatory nature of the instrument. No, my Lords, this is not the meaning of the language: it is quite clear that it is a great deal more specific and more precise, and therefore more binding. For all which reasons I say that, in answer to the argument of the learned counsel, pressing us with what is no doubt the common practice of parents in these cases, if another case were to arise to-morrow, in which a parent, instead of holding out a general and vague hope, *spes* (1) *successionis*, and nothing more, holds out a promise in distinct terms; where the very sum is stated—which, by the way, is very seldom stated, it is very common to say, "You will be the better for my will, for I will leave you something;" but I never recollect any person saying, "I will give you 10,000*l.*," any more than "I will give you 10,000*l.* 3 per cent. Consolidated Bank Annuities:" when the sum is specified, it does not sound *to be only in hope but in promises, not only in intention, but in contract. Then, if a case

(1) Misprinted *opes* in original report.—F. P.

HAMMERS-
LEY
v.
DE BIEL.

arises in which a person says, not generally in loose and vague language, but specifying the very sum, which is one circumstance here, and if he adds, "I will settle in such a way on you and your children; but if you have no children, then I reserve to myself the power to dispose of it by my last will;" my answer to the case put by the counsel is, "Bring me an instance of that kind, and I shall be of the same opinion, probably, that I am with respect to this case."

Upon these grounds, therefore, I am clearly of opinion that the judgments of the COURTS below are correct and well founded. I adopt all the arguments of the Judges below—with the single exception of a little mistake, committed, in point of fact, with respect to the practice of auctioneers (1), which, however, becomes quite immaterial to take the case out of the Statute of Frauds. I am clearly of opinion with them, agreeing in all their arguments, and in addition to the arguments which they have urged, upon the reasons which have occurred to my own mind, which I have thus stated at length, as the importance of the case seemed to require, and as we have not heard the respondent's arguments. For these reasons, and upon these grounds, I entirely concur in the view of the case taken by my noble and learned friend on the woolsack, that your Lordships ought to affirm this judgment, and, of course, with costs.

LORD CAMPBELL:

I will add very few words, expressing my entire concurrence with the opinions so ably presented to your Lordships by my two noble and learned friends who have preceded me.

There was no apology required at the Bar on behalf of the representatives of Mr. Thomson, for bringing this case before your Lordships. Although there had been two concurring judgments against them, if they thought that those judgments were

[*87]

erroneous, and they were advised that *they were so, it was not only right, but it was their duty to bring them before the Court of last resort. I am sure that there is nothing that appears in this case at all derogatory to the honour of that most respectable family (the Thomsons), who have brought this appeal (2).

---

(1) Lord COTTENHAM's judgment, *supra*, p. 30.

(2) His Lordship added other observations on the integrity and ability of J. P. Thomson and his late deceased son C. P. Thomson, (Lord Sydenham,) in which Lord BROUGHAM expressed his entire concurrence, observing also, that the appellant being an executor and trustee, without any personal interest, was perfectly justified in bringing the appeal.

At the same time I am bound to say, notwithstanding the very able arguments by the two counsel on the part of the appellants, that I do not entertain the slightest doubt whatsoever on the subject; and I think that it would be a waste of the public time if we called on the counsel for the respondent to answer their arguments.

With regard to the Statute of Frauds, the learned counsel has abandoned that ground of objection, and I think he was perfectly justified in abandoning it, because I think it cannot be supported. There can be no doubt that an authority may be delegated by a principal to an agent, or to agents, to execute an agreement in this form, which would be binding on the principal; and whether the signature is proper or not, must depend upon the authority that is given. The learned counsel could not at all deny the proposition that an authority might be given by a principal to an agent to execute an instrument in this form, which would be binding on the principal. If that be so, there is the most convincing evidence here under the hand of Mr. J. P. Thomson, that he did give that authority, because having a copy of the agreement before him, he writes in April, 1835, a letter, in which in plain words he intimates that his sons had authority to enter into this agreement on his behalf, and he thus brings it merely to a question of the legal construction of the instrument. He says that as different opinions had been given by lawyers *he was then reluctant—and he was perfectly justified in being reluctant—at that time to advance this second sum of 10,000*l.*, which should be secured to the Baron de Biel's family. His daughter was dead, leaving a single child, and he reasonably thought that, looking to the expectations and interests of his descendants, he could more equitably, as he thought, dispose of that property, which it was still open to him to do, among other members of his family. That child of his daughter was sufficiently provided for by the 10,000*l.* that had been settled. But at the same time he brings it to a question merely as to the legal construction of the instrument.

[*88]

Now this instrument being to be considered as made by the authority of Mr. Thomson himself, what reasonable doubt can be entertained that he was bound by it to leave by his will the second 10,000*l.*, just as much as to settle the first 10,000*l.*?

I think that the doctrine laid down by Lord COTTENHAM is fully supported by the authorities which have been cited: " A representation made by one party for the purpose of influencing the

HAMMERS-
LEY
v.
DE BIEL.

conduct of the other party, and acted on by him, will, in general, be sufficient to entitle him to the assistance of this Court for the purpose of realizing such representation " (1). Of course, Lord COTTENHAM is here speaking of negotiations in reference to marriage; and if that were not to be considered as the doctrine of a court of equity, the most monstrous frauds would be committed. Some fraudulent father might hold out to the suitor of his daughter, that he meant to make a settlement upon his daughter and her issue. The marriage would take place in the belief that that settlement would be made; and then, after the marriage he might say, " this was only an intimation of my intention at the time—I have changed my mind, and I will not give her a shilling." That would be most unjust; and to prevent such

[*89]   frauds, *this doctrine has been laid down, and I think has been most properly laid down, and ought to be acted upon.

But there is much more here than a mere representation made by one party for the purpose of influencing the conduct of the other party, because this is really a formal instrument, both with regard to the first 10,000*l.* and with regard to the second 10,000*l.* With regard to the 200*l.* a year, that was to be entirely discretionary, but with regard to the 10,000*l.*, I see no distinction that can be made between the first 10,000*l.*, which was to be settled in Mr. Thomson's lifetime, and the second 10,000*l.*, which he was to leave by his will. They were both to be given as a provision for his daughter and for her children.

I think that *Mr. Kelly* felt that so strongly that he was driven to rely on the words that occur here, " subject, of course, to revision." Of course he did not at all pretend to say that this second 10,000*l.* was to depend on a change of circumstances, but he relied on the words " subject, of course, to revision." When was this revision to take place ? *Mr. Kelly* places great reliance on the letter of Mr. Charles Poulett Thomson (*supra*, p. 23). Upon that letter I put entirely the same construction as my noble and learned friend the LORD CHANCELLOR has put. But *Mr. Kelly* need not be at all alarmed at the idea of the doctrine being laid down by this House, that, after a conditional contract has been entered into by a father with the suitor of his daughter, with the contingency attached of his afterwards having the opportunity of revising it, or changing the conditions, the daughter and the suitor may run away next morning to Gretna Green, and so deprive him of the opportunity

(1) *Per* Lord COTTENHAM, *supra*, p. 23.

that he had of modifying the contract. There is not the smallest
pretence for saying that any such doctrine can result from our
affirming the decree of the Court of Chancery in this case. Just
observe, the conditions that were to be performed were the settlement to be made by the Baron de Biel on Miss Thomson. That
is done. The 500*l.* a year was thereby settled upon her, so that
she would *clearly be entitled to that sum if she had survived her
husband. No complaint is made of the marriage being premature,
and no complaint could have been made, because no injury accrued
either to Miss Thomson or to her relations. All has been done
by the Baron de Biel which they expected that he should do, and
that is to settle upon her this sum of 500*l.* a year.

Under these circumstances, it seems to me that the decree of
the MASTER OF THE ROLLS, affirmed by the LORD CHANCELLOR, is
perfectly according to the doctrine which has hitherto prevailed in
courts of equity, and does not at all extend it; and I think that
we should infringe on a very useful and necessary rule, if we were
not to hold in this case that the contract is binding, and that
this second sum of 10,000*l.* must now be settled on the issue of
the marriage.

As to what took place when the settlement was executed, I own
it seems to me to be rather immaterial, because we are considering
the interests of the issue. This bill is filed by the child of the
marriage, therefore the interest of that child could not at all be
prejudiced by what took place when that settlement was executed.
If there never had been any settlement on the faith of this agreement of December, 1825, that agreement alone would have been
a sufficient foundation for this bill, which is filed on the part of
the infant, that the second sum of 10,000*l.* might be settled for
his benefit.

If it were material, I should feel much more inclined to rely upon
the account given by the Baron de Biel than by Mr. Wordsworth,
but it seems to me to be quite immaterial; unless that settlement
exhausts the agreement, the child has still a clear right to come
into a court of equity, and to insist on the agreement being carried
into effect.

For all these reasons I am clearly of opinion that the decree was
right, and that the judgment of the COURT below ought to be
affirmed, with costs.

The decree and order were then affirmed, with costs.

HAMMERS-
LEY
v.
DE BIEL.

[*90]

1845.
March 10.
———
Lord
LYNDHURST,
L.C.
Lord
BROUGHAM.
Lord
CAMPBELL.

PURVES *v.* LANDELL.

(12 Clark & Finnelly, 91—108.)

An attorney or law agent is only responsible in damages to his client for gross ignorance or gross negligence in the performance of his professional services.

The law as to both these matters is the same in England and in Scotland.

[91]

THIS was a suit instituted by Landell to recover from Purves, who was a Writer to the Signet, compensation for the loss occasioned, as it was alleged, by his improperly conducting a previous suit (1), in which he had acted as law agent for Landell. The summons contained allegations to the following effect: Mark Landell, of Coldingham Hill, the uncle of the respondent, was, at the time of his death, which happened many years ago, proprietor of an estate in Jamaica and of the negroes on that estate. He left a widow, Margaret, and a daughter, Hannah Landell, him surviving. By the law of Jamaica the widow was entitled to one-third of the estate in life-rent, the fee thereof being vested in the daughter, subject to the life-rent interest of her mother. Hannah Landell died on the 13th of March, 1838, and the respondent, who was her heir-at-law, then became entitled to the estate, subject to the life-rent of the widow. The compensation payable under the Slavery Abolition Act, in respect of the negroes on the estate of Mark Landell,

[*92]

amounted to 1,000*l.*, and *William Landell, as his heir-at-law, asserted himself to be entitled to receive two-thirds of that sum, or 720*l.*, as soon as the compensation was awarded, and to have the remaining third invested for his ultimate benefit, but subject to the life-interest of the widow. The whole of the compensation money had been claimed in Jamaica by the widow, who was at the time resident there, and had been paid over to her. In July, 1836, she came to reside at the village of Ayton, in the county of Berwick; and William Landell then employed Purves as his professional agent, that he might, as such, advise and adopt what legal measures were necessary for making her amenable to the Scotch Courts, in order that he might recover from her the money, which he contended she had improperly received. Purves recommended an application for a border warrant to compel her appearance, and represented that this mode of procedure was proper and legal; and he, being a regularly licensed agent or procurator before the Sheriff Court of that county, Landell relied on the accuracy and correctness of his representations. Landell accordingly lodged the regular

(1) *Landell* v. *Landell* (1841) 16 Dunl., Bell, & M. 388.

information with the Sheriff Clerk of Berwickshire; and Purves obtained a warrant in favour of Landell, to arrest the person and goods of Mrs. Landell " until she shall find sufficient caution acted in the Sheriff Court books of Berwickshire, that the debt due to Landell shall be made forthcoming as accords, and a domicile appointed within the jurisdiction of the said county of Berwick, at which she might be cited, and that as well *de judicio sisti* as *judicatum solvi*." This warrant was signed by the Sheriff Clerk of Berwickshire. The fees usual on such warrants were paid by Landell. The warrant was executed, and Mrs. Landell gave the required caution, and appointed a domicile. Landell then instituted a suit against her in the Court of Session. She appeared thereto, and lodged, among other defences, a preliminary plea, to the effect that she, " being neither domiciled *in Scotland, nor having any property or effects in it, is not within the jurisdiction of the Court of Session, and the irregular and illegal proceedings which were adopted to force her, the said defender, within the jurisdiction of the Scotch Courts, are altogether ineffectual for that purpose." The LORD ORDINARY adopted this preliminary defence, and reported the case, with his opinion, to the Court of Session ; and the Lords there, concurring with him, pronounced the proceedings to be irregular and void, and dismissed the suit with expenses. These expenses amounted to above 121*l.*, which Landell paid to Mrs. Landell, and 69*l.*, which he paid to his own agent. Mrs. Landell afterwards brought an action of false imprisonment against both Landell and the sheriff clerk, and recovered damages, as against the former, to the amount of 500*l.*, and, as against the latter, to the amount of 300*l.* (1). The summons in the present suit therefore prayed that Purves might be declared liable to make good to Landell the sums of money which he had thus paid, or become liable to pay, in consequence of the irregularity of the warrant, together with the costs of this suit.

PURVES
v.
LANDELL.

[*93]

Purves, in addition to a defence on the merits, put in pleas in law, in which he contended that the summons did not set forth a legal cause of suit ; that it only alleged that the proceedings had been held insufficient, but did not allege that he (Purves) had exhibited gross ignorance, or want of professional skill, or had departed from any established rule, or violated any acknowledged practice of the Court, or that he had been guilty of gross neglect in the conduct of the judicial proceedings against Mrs. Landell.

(1) *Landell* v. *Landell* and *Bell*, 3 Dunl., Bell, M. & D., p. 819.

The case came before Lord COCKBURN, as the Lord Ordinary, who being of opinion that the summons did not *present a relevant case for the relief sought, dismissed it with expenses. The cause was brought by a reclaiming note before the Lords of the second division of the Court of Session, who, by a decree of 27th May, 1842, altered this interlocutor, found the summons relevant, and remitted the cause to the Lord Ordinary to proceed therein (1).

This was the decree appealed against.

The *Lord Advocate* and *Mr. Turner* for the appellant:

A solicitor is not responsible for the failure of a case entrusted to his management when he pursues the ordinary and accustomed course in the conduct of it, nor is he liable except for gross ignorance or negligence: *Baikie* v. *Chandless* (2). To make him liable there must be either a manifest want of skill, or great negligence. Neither of these is charged here. The summons here does not, upon the facts stated, raise the question of negligence, or of want of skill; yet it ought to do so, and it ought to set forth all the facts that are material to constitute the ground of action. This want of a sufficient allegation of a cause of action must have been felt in the Court below; for Lord MONCRIEFF, in his judgment, said, that if all the facts stated were found as stated, he doubted whether they would show a right to damages as against the agent (3). There is no allegation in this summons of gross negligence, nor of a want of ordinary skill.

(THE LORD CHANCELLOR: Upon that, the only question would be, whether, when a case of gross negligence is shown by the facts stated on the record, an allegation distinctly charging gross negligence is indispensable.)

Here there is no statement of facts distinctly showing gross negligence. Without facts so *stated, it is clear that a direct allegation of gross negligence is necessary. *Stuart* v. *Miller* (4), *Morrison* v. *Ure* (5), *Campbell* v. *Clason* (6), and *Donald* v. *Yeats* (7), were all cases in which such an allegation was made, or the facts

---

(1) *Landell* v. *Purves* (1842) 4 Bell, Murr. & Don., p. 1300. See also the same vol., p. 1543, on a motion for leave to appeal.

(2) 13 R. R. 738 (3 Camp. 17).

(3) 4 Bell, M. & D., p. 1304.

(4) 3 Dunl., Bell, M. & D. 255.

(5) 4 Shaw & Dunl. 656.

(6) 1 Dunl., Bell & M., p. 270; 2 *Id.*, p. 1113.

(7) 1 Dunl., Bell & M., p. 1249.

stated, raised, beyond all doubt, the charge of gross ignorance or negligence.

Mr. Kelly and *Mr. Anderson* for the respondent :

This case depends on the form of Scotch pleading ; and the question is not whether this summons discloses what in England we should call a cause of action, but whether the summons is sufficient according to the law of Scotland. The cases of *Stevenson* v. *Rowand* (1), and of *Lang* v. *Struthers* (2), show that the rules of pleading are not the same in the two countries, and that the same strictness which we require here is not necessary there.

(THE LORD CHANCELLOR : Independently of the question of pleading, I am not able to understand how the law of Scotland and of England can, upon this subject, be different from each other, when you advert to the principle stated by Lord MANSFIELD, in *Pitt* v. *Yalden* (3), namely, that " an attorney ought not to be liable in cases of reasonable doubt," as that on which his liability is to rest. Do you mean to say, that for every mistake committed by an attorney in the conduct of a cause, his client may claim damages ?)

The argument is not meant to be carried quite to that extent, but still it is clear that an attorney may be responsible even for the damage occasioned by the loss of the subject-matter of the suit, or of any other proceeding where such loss has been the result of his ignorance or *negligence: *Bulkley* v. *Wilford* (4), *Donaldson* v. *Haldane* (5). But at all events it is clear that there is a distinction between the right of a client to claim damages in respect of money which he might have obtained but for the error on the part of the attorney, and his right to recover back the costs which, as a consequence of that error, he has been compelled to pay to the opposite party. The money out of pocket he must be entitled to recover.

[*96]

(LORD BROUGHAM : That is to say, that the attorney may not be held to have guaranteed the success of the suit, but must be held to have guaranteed the costs out of pocket.

THE LORD CHANCELLOR : The injury being the same, though assuming different shapes and forms.)

(1) 53 R. R. 1 (2 Dow & Cl. 104).   (3) 4 Burr. 2060.
(2) 2 Wils. & Shaw, 563 ; Fac. Coll.,   (4) 37 R. R. 39 (2 Cl. & Fin. 102).
2 Feb., 1826.   (5) 7 Cl. & Fin. 762.

PURVES
v.
LANDELL.

That does seem to be so, but the identity is in appearance only. The two things are perfectly distinct from each other. In *Grahame* v. *Alison* (1), it was held that an agent who had mistaken his course of proceeding, but had followed the usual practice in the case which was entrusted to him, could not be held responsible for the damage occasioned by the loss of the subject-matter of the suit, but was responsible for the expenses which had been incurred. That shows that the decision here is not to be governed by the rules of English law, and establishes the distinction already contended for, because there, Mr. Alison, the attorney, though not held bound to make good the loss of the subject-matter of the suit, was held bound to restore the money which he had received. That decision was affirmed in this House (2).

(LORD CAMPBELL : But what do you say upon the point of pleading? Do you say that it is sufficient to state facts which may amount, if proved, to gross negligence, without in form alleging that there has been gross negligence ?)

The respondent is bound to maintain that argument. [They cited *Stevenson* v. *Rowand* (3), *Hart* v. *Frame* (4), and *Wood* v. *Fullarton* (5).]

[97]   LORD BROUGHAM :

My Lords, in this case I move your Lordships to proceed to reverse the interlocutor of the Court below, without hearing the learned counsel for the appellant in reply. I never saw a case which stood, in my opinion, upon clearer grounds. The learned Judges of the Court below were very much divided in opinion upon this case. It is a great mistake to represent it as one in which there was no very great difference of opinion ; Lord COCKBURN clearly expressing an opinion against this action, and the LORD *ORDINARY (Lord JEFFREY) leaning the same way. Lord MONCRIEFF, too, went a great deal further than merely expressing a doubt or an inclination of opinion, because Lord MONCRIEFF's opinion upon the very point, the main point and pivot upon which this case turns, was that the Court was wrong, and he differed with the Court, and thought that there ought to have been on the record an allegation of negligence.

[*98]

My Lords, I apprehend it to be by no means a technical question, depending upon the rules of pleading ; it is of the very essence of

(1) 9 Shaw & Dl. 130.   (4) 49 R. R. 88 (6 Cl. & Fin. 193).
(2) 6 Wils. & Shaw, 518.   (5) 1710, Nov. 28, Morr. 13960.
(3) 53 R. R. 1 (2 Dow & Cl. 104).

this kind of action that it depends, not upon the party having been advised by a solicitor or attorney in a way in which the result of the proceeding may induce the party to think he was not advised properly, and may, in fact, prove the advice to have been erroneous; not upon his having received, if I may so express it in common parlance, bad law, from the solicitor; nor upon the solicitor or attorney having taken upon himself to advise him, and, having given erroneous advice, advice which the result proved to be wrong, and in consequence of which error, the parties suing under that mistake were deprived and disappointed of receiving a benefit.   But it is of the very essence of this action that there should be a negligence of a crass description, which we call *crassa negligentia*, that there should be gross ignorance, that the man who has undertaken to perform the duty of an attorney, or of a surgeon, or an apothecary (as the case may be), should have undertaken to discharge a duty professionally, for which he was very ill qualified, or, if not ill qualified to discharge it, which he had so negligently discharged as to damnify his employer, or deprive him of the benefit which he had a right to expect from the service.   That is the very ground Lord MANSFIELD has laid down in that case (1) to which my noble and learned *friend on the woolsack has referred a little while ago, and which is also referred to in the printed papers.   It was still more expressly laid down by Lord ELLENBOROUGH in the case of *Baikie* v. *Chandless* (2), because there Lord ELLENBOROUGH uses the expression, " an attorney is only liable for *crassa negligentia;*" therefore, the record must bring before the Court a case of that kind, either by stating such facts as no man who reads it will not at once perceive, although without its being alleged in terms, to be *crassa negligentia*—something so clear that no man can doubt of it; or, if that should not be the case, then he must use the very averment that it was *crassa negligentia*.

[*99]

I will not go so far as to say that, if it were for some very gross case, such, for instance, as a man advising his client that his oldest legitimate son was not his heir-at-law,—or any other thing which, upon the face of it shows gross ignorance of the A. B. C. of his profession, and the most crass negligence in the performance of his professional duty—in such a case, it is not necessary to go so far as to say, that that would not be equivalent to that which is wanting here, namely, an averment, in terms, of impropriety, of breach of professional duty, or want of sufficient knowledge, or gross and crass

(1) *Pitt* v. *Yalden*, 4 Burr. 2060.   (2) 13 R. R. 738 (3 Camp. 17).

4—2

negligence. It is not necessary to proceed upon that supposition, nor to decide whether in England or in Scotland a declaration or a summons, in a form like the present, would or would not, in such a case, be sufficient; for aught I know, it might; but that is not the case here. It is merely set forth, that a border warrant was issued; and it is further stated, that a personal damnification took place. That is all. There is no statement of the facts, which at once explains itself, so that he who runs may read. Nor is there a statement in terms that there was gross negligence. The case is [*100] wholly a blank upon these two matters, one *or other of which ought to appear on the record, otherwise the action does not lie.

Now that being the case, I cannot go into the alarming doctrine laid down by the LORD JUSTICE CLERK (1), as to a supposed distinction between error in cases where the liberty of the subject is concerned, and cases of a different kind, which I hold to be quite erroneous, and which I think is not accurately reported. It is said it is unnecessary to allege that Mr. Purves was guilty either of want of skill or of negligence; it is enough to allege that what he had done was a nullity.

Now the mere allegation and proof of such a fact as that could never be sufficient; because, unless a great deal more is proved, you may just as well say that in every nonsuit, or every action that failed, or every case in which what is called an infructuous proceeding has taken place, even though the attorney should really be successful in the case, yet that, should there not be a beneficial result from the action, that circumstance alone would make the attorney liable. No man can possibly conceive that such is the liability of an attorney. There must be considerable mismanagement, considerable ignorance, and the absence of attentive conduct in general: unless it is gross, the law holds that it is sufficient.

It is said there are such cases here; the case in Morrison's Reports (2) and others, and the case before this House in 1838 (3), in which it is said there was no such clear averment; and it was argued that, although the negligence may not be sufficiently proved to entitle the complaining party to damages, it has been sufficiently proved to entitle him to the restitution of the money paid; that [*101] there is something different between the proceedings in *England and Scotland in those respects. That is not the case; but if it was

(1) *Landell* v. *Purves*, 4 Bell, Murr.   (3) *Hart* v. *Frame*, 49 R. R. 88
& Don. 1303.   (6 Cl. & Fin., 193).
(2) *Wood* v. *Fullarton*, Morr. 18960.

so, the argument would only go to show, that, because there is a difference in one respect, that therefore there must be a difference in the other, which is a very unsatisfactory mode of reasoning.

It is contended that Mr. Purves had notice of Lord JEFFREY's interlocutor, which was against him, and that therefore he was bound to indemnify his client from the consequences of his having advised him, in the teeth and in the face of that interlocutor, to reclaim to the Inner House. It would be his bounden duty to advise him not to rest satisfied with the first unfavourable opinion, and to see whether it was well founded. If it were not so, you might just as well say, that in every case in the Courts below where the decision is against a man, and from which he appeals here, that if it is affirmed upon appeal there is crass negligence, or at least a case entitling the party who has lost the appeal to an indemnity ; because the man who was served with the notice in the course of the business was aware that there had been a decision against his client below, and therefore he ought to have known that his client could not succeed upon appeal. Such a doctrine never could be maintained.

I am of opinion, upon all these grounds, that there is no reason to support the interlocutor of the Court below, and that it must be reversed.

Lord CAMPBELL :

My Lords, I am extremely sorry for the situation in which Mr. Landell is placed ; but we must not be carried away by feelings of compassion, we must be bound by the principles of law, and upon those principles I have no doubt at all, that Lord COCKBURN and the LORD ORDINARY took a just view of this case, and that we are bound to sustain their decision.

Now what is the action we are to determine upon? It is an action in which William Landell complains that he *having brought an action against Margaret Landell, and having retained Mr. Purves as his professional adviser, that in the proceeding of that action against Margaret Landell, Mr. Purves, his professional adviser, was guilty of misconduct, whereby an action was brought against him by Mrs. Margaret Landell, and damages and costs were recovered, which he was obliged to pay. What is necessary to maintain such an action? Most undoubtedly that the professional adviser should be guilty of some misconduct, some fraudulent proceeding, or should be chargeable with gross negligence, or with gross ignorance. It is only upon

[*102]

PURVES
v.
LANDELL.

one or other of those grounds that the client can maintain an action against the professional adviser. And thus far it is quite unnecessary here to look at the case that has been referred to, which came on in the time of Lord MANSFIELD, because there the action was to recover back money which had been paid by the client to the professional adviser. It was a totally different proceeding from that which we have now to determine upon.

In an action such as this, by the client against the professional adviser, to recover damages arising from the misconduct of the professional adviser, I apprehend there is no distinction whatever between the law of Scotland and the law of England. The law must be the same in all countries where law has been considered as a science. The professional adviser has never been supposed to guarantee the soundness of his advice. I am sure I should have been sorry when I had the honour of practising at the Bar of England, if barristers had been liable to such a responsibility. Though I was tolerably cautious in giving opinions, I have no doubt that I have repeatedly given erroneous opinions; and I think it was Mr. Justice HEATH, who said that it was a very difficult thing for a gentleman at the Bar to be called upon to give his opinion, because it was calling upon him to conjecture what twelve other persons

[*103]

would say upon some point that had never before been *determined. Well then, this may happen in all grades of the profession of the law. Against the barrister in England, and the advocate in Scotland, luckily, no action can be maintained. But against the attorney, the professional adviser, or the procurator, an action may be maintained. But it is only if he has been guilty of gross negligence, because it would be monstrous to say that he is responsible for even falling into what must be considered a mistake. You can only expect from him that he will be honest and diligent; and if there is no fault to be found either with his integrity or diligence, that is all for which he is answerable. It would be utterly impossible that you could ever have a class of men who would give a guarantee, binding themselves, in giving legal advice and conducting suits at law, to be always in the right.

Then, my Lords, as *crassa negligentia* is certainly the gist of an action of this sort, the question is, whether in this summons that negligence must not either be averred or shown? This is not any technical point in which the law of Scotland differs from the law of England. I should be very sorry to see applied, and I hope this House would be very cautious in applying, technical rules which

prevail in England to proceedings in Scotland. But I apprehend
that, in this respect, the laws of the two countries do not differ, and
that the summons ought to state, and must state, what is necessary
to maintain the action; this summons must either allege negligence, or must show facts which inevitably prove that this person
has been guilty of gross negligence. Now, here it is not at all
pretended that there is any allegation of negligence.

Then what is the fact shown from which negligence is necessarily
to be inferred? Why, there is a warrant, which was sued out by
Mr. Purves or by his advice, against Margaret Landell, while she
was living in Berwick, upon the borders of the kingdom of Scotland,
she not being domiciled in Scotland, but being domiciled in England.
*It was held, that, upon that ground, that warrant was void. It
might have been subject to other objections, for anything I know to
the contrary; but it was held void upon that ground, that she
neither had property in Scotland nor effects in it, one of which
circumstances was necessary *ad fundandam jurisdictionem ;* nor was
she domiciled in Scotland, and so was not liable to be sued in the
Courts of Scotland. It was upon these grounds that the warrant
was held to be insufficient, and that the action of Landell against
Margaret Landell failed. Was that sufficient to make a case for an
action against the attorney, when the question must be, was he
guilty of negligence? It might have been proved that she had
large property in Scotland. He might have been told that she had
been domiciled in Scotland. He might have been told that she
had been living so long away from England; that she had abandoned all thoughts of returning there, and had removed her
household gods to Scotland, and represented that as her domicile.
It is possible he might have been told that that was the fact,
although it turned out that she was not domiciled in Scotland, and
had no property in Scotland.

[*104]

How then can we inevitably infer from the simple fact of the
warrant being found bad, that Purves was guilty of gross negligence? He may have been; I know nothing one way or the other
—it is not here alleged. If it had been, and he had denied it, then
the issue would have been plain, and a trial before a jury could
have taken place; and then the evidence would have shown whether
he was guilty of negligence in suing out the warrant, or whether
he had acted with due care and caution, and the warrant had turned out
to be bad, notwithstanding all the care and caution he could exercise.

It seems to me therefore, my Lords, that, upon principles as to

which there can be no doubt, this summons is defective; because it
neither alleges what is necessary *to maintain the action, nor does
it show facts that raise a necessary inference that any gross
negligence did exist.

We were referred to a case to show, that, by the law of Scotland,
it is not at all necessary to allege in the summons that there has
been negligence. But that was where there had been a clear breach
of duty. The strongest case is that of *Stevenson* v. *Rowand* (1).
Now, when we examine that case, as set out by the appellant in his
printed papers, it appears that the ground of action was upon that
summons abundantly set out; because the action was brought for
the breach of a specific duty, which duty was set out upon the face
of the summons. There is, upon the face of the summons, an
allegation, "that Stevenson did not complete the said security in
a legal manner, by obtaining from the superior any confirmation
of the said bond and disposition in security, or of the aforesaid
instrument of sasine following thereon. That it was incumbent
upon the said Nathaniel Stevenson to procure a legal and valid
security for the said Henry Wardrop and the pursuer, so as to
render it complete and effectual against all subsequent deeds and
infeftments; and as the pursuer has sustained much loss, damage,
and expense, in consequence of the said Nathaniel Stevenson not
having drawn and completed the said heritable security in such
form and manner as would have given the same priority, but in
such form and manner as has postponed the same to a posterior
security and burden, over the said lands and others, he is bound in
law, justice, and equity, to free and relieve the pursuer from the
loss, damage, and expense thereby occasioned."

Now what does that mean? It is a plain allegation that it was
the duty of Stevenson to procure the security there stated to be
framed in a particular manner, and that he had not procured it to
be framed in that particular manner, whereby a loss had accrued to
the party who complained. *Upon this it would have been the
easiest thing in the world to frame an issue, whether it was incumbent upon Stevenson to do what was alleged, and whether he had
failed in the discharge of his duty. But upon the summons here it
would be impossible to frame any such issue; the only issue that
could be framed has been framed by the clerk who discharges that
duty. He has looked at the summons, and he has framed the best
issue that the summons would admit of, and yet upon the face of it

(1) 53 R. R. 1 (2 Dow & Cl. 104).

we find that the issue avers a finding in favour of the pursuer, which could not have been found by the special finding of the jury, for, although the warrant might have been wrong, he still might have acted with the greatest care.

There is no attempt whatever to show that in such an action by the practice of the law of Scotland, it is not necessary for a man to allege negligence, or to show facts from which negligence must inevitably be inferred. As to the distinction supposed to have been taken by the LORD JUSTICE CLERK (1) between "a warrant that affects the liberty of the subject, and any ordinary matter of business in which an agent may be employed;" it appears to me, as well as to my noble and learned friend, that that learned and most laborious Judge must have been inaccurately reported with respect to that distinction: because, if the report is accurate, it seems that upon all other actions negligence must be alleged, but that when there is any proceeding that touches the liberty of the subject, then, without any allegation of negligence, the professional adviser is liable, if there has been any mistake. Now, it is enough to say that there is no authority for that distinction in the law of Scotland, and there seems to me to be no principle to warrant it, and there being neither principle nor authority, and it having been abandoned by the counsel for the respondent, I should not say a word about it, except *that it seems to me that there must have been some mistake in the report, because, although some proceeding may have taken place, whereby the liberty of the subject may be affected in the course of a judicial proceeding, yet no one could be liable but the professional adviser; and he cannot, unless he has been guilty of some negligence, as he does not guarantee the correctness of the advice which he gives. [*107]

On these grounds, my Lords, I think the reasoning of the LORD ORDINARY, in his note, is perfectly satisfactory, and I regret that it came before the Second Division of the Inner House, and that when there Lord MONCRIEFF's doubt or opinion did not prevail. I regret that there has been this distinction attempted to be made, because the distinction does not rest upon principle or authority; and, therefore, I apprehend that this interlocutor of the Second Division must be reversed, and that the interlocutor of the LORD ORDINARY should be affirmed. And I presume that now the judgment of this House should be that Mr. Purves be assoiled from the conclusion of the summons, and the interlocutor be recalled.

1) 4 Bell, Murr. & D. 1303.

PURVES
v.
LANDELL.

THE LORD CHANCELLOR (1) :

My Lords, I am of the same opinion that has been expressed so fully and ably by my noble and learned friends in this case. It is quite unnecessary for me, after the detailed manner in which they have adverted to the particular facts of the case, to go over the same ground. I shall, therefore, state, in a very few words, the principle upon which I think this question ought to be decided, and, in fact, it is nothing more than a repetition of what has been stated by my two noble and learned friends.

It is quite clear that the summons must state a sufficient cause of action. When an action is brought against a solicitor, he is liable merely in cases where he has shown a want of reasonable skill, or where he has been guilty of *gross negligence. The summons therefore, I apprehend, must state either a case of gross negligence, or a case of breach of duty. Now it is quite clear in this case, that upon the summons, there is no positive statement of any want of reasonable skill, nor any express statement of negligence ; and I am of opinion that, upon the other facts stated in the summons, there is nothing equivalent to this averment. It follows therefore that the summons in this respect is defective, and I think that the interlocutor of the Court below ought to be reversed.

*108]

(Ordered and adjudged, That the interlocutor of the 27th May, 1842, complained of in the said appeal, be reversed ; and it is further ordered, that the case be remitted back to the Court of Session in Scotland, with directions to that Court to adhere to the interlocutor of the LORD ORDINARY, of the 19th of March, 1842, and to proceed further therein as shall be just and consistent with this judgment.)

1845.
March 11.
Lord
LYNDHURST,
L.C.
Lord
BROUGHAM.
Lord
CAMPBELL.
[109]

HAMILTON v. WATSON.

(12 Clark & Finnelly, 109—120.)

A surety is not of necessity entitled to receive, without enquiry, from the party to whom he is about to bind himself, a full disclosure of all the circumstances of the dealings between the principal and that party.

If he requires to know any particular matter, of which the party about to receive the security is informed, he must make it the subject of a distinct enquiry.

An obligation to a banker by a third party to be responsible for a cash

(1) Lord LYNDHURST.

credit to be given to one of the banker's customers, is not avoided by the HAMILTON
fact, that, immediately after the execution of the obligation, the cash credit v.
is employed to pay off an old debt due to the banker. WATSON.

If the surety intends to rely upon such a fact for his defence, as showing
that there was a previous agreement between the banker and the customer
to deal with the credit in a particular manner, to which he, if he had known
it, should not have consented, he must bring such a defence before the
Court by putting it on the record.

THIS case originated in a suspension of a charge upon a cash
credit bond for 750*l.*, granted to the Glasgow and Ship Bank by
the appellant, as cautioner or surety for the late Peter Elles,
merchant in Glasgow. The following are the circumstances of
the case :

In March, 1835, the late Peter Elles obtained a cash account for
750*l.* from the firm of Carrick, Brown, & Co., carrying on the
business of bankers in Glasgow, under the name of the Ship Bank.
A bond was then granted by Elles and by his father, with two
other cautioners or sureties, Alexander Dewar, now deceased, and
David Anderson, manufacturer in Glasgow.

The whole of the sum thus credited was drawn out by *Elles [*110]
before the end of the month, and the only other entries in the
account were those of the addition of interest at the close of the
years 1835 and 1836.

Carrick & Co., on the 29th December, 1835, wrote to Elles
announcing the death of Mr. Alexander Dewar, one of the obligants,
and requesting that the credit might either be paid up, or renewed
with additional security. This demand for a settlement was
repeatedly renewed, but without effect.

In July, 1836, a junction was formed between the Bank conducted
by Carrick & Co., and the Glasgow Bank Company. By a contract
then entered into between these parties, it was agreed, that the
banking business and firm of the Ship Bank should, from and after
the 1st July, 1836, merge in the business of the Glasgow Bank, and
be thenceforth carried on under the style and firm of "the Glasgow
and Ship Bank Company," or such other style and firm as they
might afterwards choose to adopt. It was farther stipulated, that
the proprietors of the Ship Bank should transfer and convey to the
new Company their whole establishment, and their whole property,
securities, bills, and other obligations, with certain exceptions
specified in the contract, at a certain valuation put thereon ; and
on the other hand, the Glasgow Company became bound to transfer
and make over 200 shares of original stock, estimated to be worth
32,000*l.* sterling to the partners of the Ship Bank, as part of the

HAMILTON
v
WATSON.

stipulated price and value of the subjects made over to them. There was also a stipulation in the contract, that, if the Glasgow Bank Company should decline to take over any of the bonds, bills, or other obligations due to the Ship Bank at the full value, the same should remain with Mr. Rowand or Mr. Galloway, as trustee for Carrick & Co., for the purpose of recovering the same, the amount of the said obligations, with interest, being to be accounted for to the Glasgow Bank.

[*111]

On the 12th Aug., 1836, the respondent, who was the *representative of the Glasgow and Ship Bank, wrote to require payment of the debt due from Elles, and on .the 22nd of that month, the latter sent an answer, proposing a new bond with a substitute surety instead of Dewar. The offer was declined. In March, 1837, these negociations were renewed, but it was not until October, 1837, that any arrangement was finally made. In that month a new bond was executed with the appellant, as a surety, and it was arranged that the new cash account should be opened in name of the firm of Elles, Hutcheson & Company, of which Peter Elles was then the sole partner.

This new bond contained the following statement, " that the Company carrying on business in Glasgow as bankers under the firm of ' the Glasgow and Ship Bank Company,' have agreed to allow us credit on a cash account to be kept ·in the books of the said Bank Company, at their office in Glasgow, in name of the said firm of Elles, Hutcheson & Company, to the amount of 750*l.*" The parties, therefore, bound themselves, jointly and severally, to pay to the Bank " the foresaid sum of 750*l.*, or such part or parts thereof as shall appear to be due to the said Glasgow and Ship Bank Company on the said cash account to be kept in their books in name of the said firm of Elles, Hutcheson & Company, as aforesaid, upon their drafts or orders on, or receipts to the said Glasgow and Ship Bank Company."

It did not appear that when the appellant signed this bond he was aware of any of the previous transactions between the Bank and Elles, nor was any information on that subject given to him by the respondent.

On the 13th October, 1837, being within a week after the date of the bond, the interest upon the old cash account due by Elles was calculated and added to the principal, making the whole sum due 888*l.* 7*s.* 1*d.* On the same day, Elles drew a draft upon the new account with the Glasgow and Ship Bank for 750*l.*, being the total *amount of the credit for which the appellant had become bound. No part of the sum contained in this draft was actually paid to Elles. The draft was simply handed to the teller of the Bank, who made entries in his book, debiting the new Company with the whole amount of the debt due on the old account, and crediting them with the amount of the draft. With this order, and a sum of 88*l.* 7*s.* 1*d.*, paid by Mr. Elles in cash, the account between him and Carrick & Co. was credited by an entry to this effect: " 1837, Oct. 13. By cash in full, 838*l.* 7*s.* 1*d.*"

Elles subsequently deposited several sums in his account, which were generally of small amount, and drawn out again at short intervals.

Some time afterwards Mr. Elles died in insolvent circumstances, and his estate was sequestrated. The appellant was then required by the Glasgow and Ship Bank to pay the money due on his bond, with the interest thereon, amounting in the whole to 818*l.* 7*s.* 3*d.*, and proceedings were taken by the respondent to enforce this demand.

The appellant having discovered the facts above stated, presented a suspension of this charge, first, on the ground that his suretyship was void, as all the circumstances of the dealings between the parties had not been communicated to him; and secondly, that the suretyship related only to prospective advances, and could not be made applicable to the payment of an old debt.

The LORD ORDINARY, before whom the case was heard, repelled the reasons of suspension, and found the chargers entitled to expenses. This decision was brought before the Second Division of the Court, when there was a difference of opinion on the Bench. It appeared to the LORD JUSTICE CLERK that the question raised was one proper for the determination of a jury; but the other Judges took a different view, conceiving that the cause might be decided upon the admitted facts, and the written evidence in process.

*A majority of their Lordships accordingly decided that the bond of caution was binding on the appellant, notwithstanding the circumstances under which it was obtained; the LORD JUSTICE CLERK dissenting from this judgment, and delivering his opinion, to the effect that there had been a secret agreement or understanding entered into between Elles and the Bank, which had not been communicated to the appellant, and that a fraud had thus been practised upon him, whereby his cautionary obligation had been rendered null and void (1).

(1) 5 Bell, Murray, Donaldson, and Young, 280.

HAMILTON   *Mr. Turner* and *Mr. Anderson* for the appellant:
   v.
WATSON.   There has been a concealment here, which relieves the surety
                from his responsibility.   When a Bank takes a security from a
                person becoming surety for one of its customers, the managers of
                the Bank are bound to communicate to the proposed surety every
                information which, in relation to the suretyship, it may be material
                for him to know.   If such information is not communicated, the
                surety is released.   This principle has often been recognized in the
                English authorities: *Glyn* v. *Hertel*(1) established it in the plainest
                manner.   There a guarantie, given for the sum of 5,000*l.*, was
                held not to cover money to that amount already due, but to extend
                only to future loans.   That case exactly applies to, and must
                govern the present.

                    What are the facts here?   There was an old debt of 750*l.*
                existing in March, 1835; and the money thus due, continued
                unpaid from that time till the 13th of October, 1837.   During that
                time applications were made by Carrick & Co. for payment, and
                further transactions were declined unless payment was made.

[*114]   (THE LORD CHANCELLOR: There were two or three sureties; one
                of them *died; and in consequence of that circumstance application
                was made for payment, or that another surety should be provided.)

                    No surety was at that time substituted in the place of the person
                who had died; but at length, in August, 1837, the managers of
                the Bank consented to draw out this bond of suretyship, which
                they sent to Elles to get executed by the appellant, who had been
                proposed as the new surety.   It was executed by the appellant,
                and then handed by Elles to the Bank.   The circumstances of
                the person for whom the security was given—that is to say,
                the circumstances of his dealings with the Bank—were not com-
                municated by the managers of the Bank to the proposed surety.
                It was not communicated to him that the security into which he
                was about to enter for Elles was not for a fresh cash credit to that
                person, but was in fact a mere undertaking to pay an old debt of his.
                There was therefore, as to the appellant, a material suppression of
                facts with which he was entitled to be acquainted; those facts
                were in the knowledge of the parties to whom he was to become
                bound; they were such as were likely materially to influence his
                mind in undertaking or declining the suretyship, and ought to have

                            (1) 8 Taunt. 208; 2 Moore, 134.

been communicated to him before he entered into it. [They cited [115] *Smith* v. *The Bank of Scotland* (1), *The Leith Banking Co.* v. *Bell* (2), *Pidcock* v. *Bishop* (3), and *Stone* v. *Compton* (4).] The principle of the law with regard to a surety is therefore clear : it is, that all the circumstances which affect his liability must be communicated to him.

(THE LORD CHANCELLOR : It does not seem to me that there is here any allegation of fraud or misrepresentation, or even of any secret agreement as to the way in which the money was to be applied.)

All the circumstances are stated ; and they show the probable existence of an agreement, and the concealment of it from the surety. The law will not allow such a concealment. This House has, in the recent case of *Railton* v. *Mathews* (5), acted on that rule. * * *

The *Lord Advocate* and the *Solicitor-General* (*Sir F. Thesiger*) [116] for the respondent : -

The principle of law is not disputed here ; but its applicability in the present case is denied. In all the cases cited, there was a concealment of something which affected the very nature of the contract entered into by the surety. * * No such fraud has [117] been committed here. Admitting, therefore, to the fullest extent, the authority of these cases, it is submitted that they do not apply to the present. The only fact that the bankers here could communicate was, that Elles was not able at the moment to pay his own debts, and could not get money except through the credit of a third person. But that fact was evident from the circumstance of his requiring a surety ; for had he been in flourishing circumstances, there would have been no need of a surety to obtain him a credit. The argument on the other side cannot be maintained without the appellant going the length of contending that the surety is entitled to know the specific use to which the money raised on his credit is to be applied. Information to that extent would, in most cases, be impossible ; and if any necessity to impart it could be imposed upon bankers, they must altogether refuse cash

(1) 7 Shaw & Dl. 244; 1 Dow. 272.

(2) 8 Shaw & Dl. 721; 5 Wils. & Shaw, 703.

(3) 27 R. R. 430 (3 B. & C. 605).

(4) 50 R. R. 639 (5 Bing. N. C. 142; 6 Scott, 846).

(5) 59 R. R. 308 (10 Cl. & Fin. 934).

HAMILTON
v.
WATSON.

credits to any of their customers.   The appellant has not sustained any injury from this transaction.   *   *   *

[118]   THE LORD CHANCELLOR (1):

My Lords, I have already stated during the argument, that I considered that there was no averment of any agreement as to the mode in which the money was intended to be applied; and I have stated the substance of the opinion which I entertain upon this point.   The mere circumstance of the parties supposing that the money was intended to be applied to a particular purpose, and the fact that it was intended to be so applied, do not appear to me to vitiate the transaction at all.   If there was a stipulation that it was to be so applied, and these were the conditions upon which the money was advanced, it might have affected the transaction.   But, in order to raise that question, there should have been an averment upon the record that such an agreement had been entered into. In the absence of any such averment, I think the parties are not in a condition to rest their case upon the mere implied existence of such an agreement, and, therefore, I think the judgment of the Court below ought to be sustained.

LORD BROUGHAM:

My Lords, I am of the same opinion, and I have never entertained any doubt from the beginning.   Fraud is neither averred, nor supposed to be averred, nor are the circumstances so stated as to raise the inevitable inference of fraud or deception, and the party, the real creditor—the Bank—in these circumstances was not bound to volunteer a disclosure of any transaction that passed between him and the other party.

LORD CAMPBELL:

My Lords, I am of the same opinion.   Your Lordships must particularly notice what the nature of the contract is.   It is surety- ship upon a cash account.   Now the question is, what, upon entering into such a contract, ought to be disclosed? and I will venture to say, if your Lordships were to adopt the principles laid down, and contended for by the appellant's counsel here, that you

[*119]   *would entirely knock up those transactions in Scotland of giving security upon a cash account, because no bankers would rest satisfied that they had a security for the advance they made, if, as

(1) Lord LYNDHURST.

it is contended, it is essentially necessary that every thing should be disclosed by the creditor that is material for the surety to know. If such was the rule, it would be indispensably necessary for the bankers to whom the security is to be given, to state how the account has been kept: whether the debtor was in the habit of overdrawing; whether he was punctual in his dealings; whether he performed his promises in an honourable manner ; for all these things are extremely material for the surety to know. But unless questions be particularly put by the surety to gain this information, I hold that it is quite unnecessary for the creditor, to whom the suretyship is to be given, to make any such disclosure; and I should think that this might be considered as the criterion whether the disclosure ought to be made voluntarily, namely, whether there is anything that might not naturally be expected to take place between the parties who are concerned in the transaction, that is, whether there be a contract between the debtor and the creditor, to the effect that his position shall be different from that which the surety might naturally expect; and, if so, the surety is to see whether that is disclosed to him. But if there be nothing which might not naturally take place between these parties, then, if the surety would guard against particular perils, he must put the question, and he must gain the information which he requires. Now, in this case, assuming that there had been the contract contended for, and that that had been concealed, that would have vitiated the suretyship. There is no proof, nor is there any allegation that there was any such contract. There is, therefore, neither allegation nor proof, and what then does the case rest upon ? It rests merely upon this, that at most there was a concealment by the bankers of the former debt, and *of their expectation, that if this new surety was given, it was probable that that debt would be paid off. It rests merely upon non-disclosure or concealment of a probable expectation. And if you were to say that such a concealment would vitiate the suretyship given on that account, your Lordships would utterly destroy that most beneficial mode of dealing with accounts in Scotland.

HAMILTON
v.
WATSON.

[*120]

LORD BROUGHAM :

I am not at all clear (though it is quite immaterial) that the surety would have acted differently if he had known of the matter thus said to be concealed. That has been taken for granted all the while.

Judgment affirmed, with costs.

1845.
Feb. 27, 28.
March 15.
———
Lord
BROUGHAM.
Lord
COTTENHAM.
Lord
CAMPBELL.
[121]

JOHN COOKSON v. ISAAC COOKSON AND OTHERS.

(12 Clark & Finnelly, 121—150; affg. S. C. nom. *Cookson* v. *Reay*, 5 Beav. 22.)

Where money is directed to be invested in land or other security, but the conversion has not, in fact, taken place until the whole interest—whether in land or money—has become vested absolutely in one person, whether in possession or in reversion expectant upon the death of another, any act of his, indicating an option in which character to take or dispose of it, will determine the succession as between his real and personal representatives.

Held, that even if the fund had been impressed in this case with the character of real estate—which was doubtful—it was reconverted into personalty by the subsequent acts of the party absolutely entitled.

[*122]

JOHN COOKSON, by his will, dated the 7th of March, 1774, after making a specific devise to his wife for her life, and making an appointment of a settled estate and *some specific devises and bequests in favour of his eldest son, Isaac, gave all other his lands, goods, and chattels to his wife, and appointed her sole executrix, "with the tuition and education of all every such younger children, and to provide for them with regard to their fortunes as they might deserve and merit."

The testator, at the time of making his will, also wrote a further testamentary paper, as follows: "Instructions or advice to my wife, with regard to my younger children: As to my son John, who intends for the law, I would have 250*l*. per annum paid him, until a sum of 10,000*l*. can be invested in land or some other securities, which is to be invested in trustees for his use, as to the interest of such money or produce of such lands, for his natural life; and if he marries with your consent and approbation, first obtained in writing, and not otherwise, that he make such settlement on such wife as he may marry as you may judge proper, and that the remainder shall go to such child or children he may have lawfully begotten; but in failure of these, to my eldest son Isaac and his heirs for ever. As to my son Thomas, I propose he should have the same sum, but with the same limitations as my son John. As to Joseph, I would have him brought up to business, and to give the amount in some business I am concerned, in the like manner, to prevent its being spent, to fix the like 10,000*l*. in the same manner above mentioned; my daughters, Hannah and Sarah, to have 5,000*l*. each. All the surpluses over and above your own expenses to be laid out in mortgage, or purchases for the purposes before mentioned."

The testator died in Dec., 1788, leaving his wife and three sons, Isaac, John, and Joseph, surviving; Thomas died previously, unmarried. The widow and executrix proved the will and said paper

as part thereof. John Cookson, the son, intermarried with Hannah
Jane Reed in Feb., 1784, with the approbation of his mother. By
the indenture of settlement made on that occasion, to which *the
mother was a party, after reciting the said will and testamentary
paper, among other things, it was witnessed, that, in consideration
of the intended marriage, and of the covenants of the said H. J.
Reed, thereinafter contained, the said J. Cookson covenanted that
he would, within six calendar months after the solemnization of the
then intended marriage, cause 10,000*l.* to be raised out of the assets
of the said testator, and pay or cause the same to be paid to
or vested in Henry Ulrich Reay and Thomas Lowes (parties to
the indenture), their executors, administrators, and assigns, upon
trust, that they, or the survivor, &c., should, with the approbation
of the said J. Cookson and H. J. Reed, his intended wife, or the
survivor of them, so soon as a convenient purchase or purchases
should be found, lay out and dispose of the said sum of 10,000*l.*, in
one or more purchase or purchases of freehold messuages, lands,
tenements, or hereditaments of an estate of inheritance in fee
simple in possession, in some part or parts of England, and
thereupon settle, convey, and assure, or cause and procure to be
settled, conveyed, and assured, all such messuages, lands, &c., so
to be purchased, to the use of the said J. Cookson and his assigns,
during his life, with remainder to trustees to preserve contingent
remainders, with remainder to the use of his said intended wife,
and her assigns, for her life, for her jointure, and in lieu of dower,
with remainder to the use of such child or children as the said
J. Cookson might have lawfully begotten, for such estate, and in
such manner as the said testamentary paper, so signed by the said
testator, in its true construction directs, with such limitation over
as in the said testamentary paper is mentioned. And it was by the
said indenture provided and declared, that it should be lawful for
the said Reay and Lowes, and the survivor of them, &c., with the
approbation of the said J. Cookson and H. J. Reed, his intended
wife, until such purchase or purchases should be made, or in case
by the true construction of the said will and testamentary paper
*the said sum of 10,000*l.* ought not to be laid out or invested in the
purchase of lands, to lay out and invest the said sum upon any
public or private securities, or in the purchase of any public stocks,
and from time to time to call in and receive the money so lent or
placed out on securities, or to sell and dispose of such stocks so to
be purchased, and again to lend or invest the same monies, or any

COOKSON
v.
COOKSON.

[*123]

[*124]

5—2

COOKSON
v.
COOKSON.

part thereof in manner aforesaid, as often as they should think fit
with such approbation as aforesaid. And that all the clear yearly
interests, dividends, and annual proceeds of the said monies, and of
the stocks or securities upon which the same should happen to be
invested, should from time to time be paid to such person or persons
as and to whom the rents and profits of the messuages, &c., so to be
purchased as aforesaid, if purchased and settled, would for the time
being belong, by virtue of the same indenture and of the said
testamentary paper, so made by the said testator.

John Cookson received the legacy of 10,000*l*. from his father's
executrix, and it was invested in the names of Reay and Lowes, as
to 5,000*l*. thereof, in the purchase of 5,600*l*. Navy Stock; and as to
the other 5,000*l*., on a mortgage, by J. Cookson and his wife, of an
estate to which he was entitled in her right; and the mortgage
indenture dated 24th February, 1785, noticed that no convenient
purchase having been found wherein to invest the 10,000*l*., J.
Cookson had applied to the said trustees to lend him the 5,000*l*.
A further sum of 1,000*l*. was lent to him in 1786, on the same
security, whereby the Navy Stock was reduced to the sum of
4,640*l*., which was sold out in 1791, and the proceeds were then
vested in the purchase of 5,396*l*. Four per cent. Annuities.

By an indenture, dated the 2nd August, 1792, which recited,
among other things, that the sum of 4,000*l*., the residue of the
said sum of 10,000*l*., had been laid out in the purchase of 5,396*l*.
Four per cent. Annuities, until a proper purchase of messuages,

[*125]

lands, tenements and hereditaments *could be found whereon to
invest the same upon the trusts of the will of the said testator and
of the said settlement made previous to the marriage of the said
J. Cookson, and that Reay and Lowes were desirous to be discharged
from the trusts of the settlement, and that Samuel Castell and
Charles Wren had agreed to accept the same; the mortgage
securities for the 5,000*l*. and 1,000*l*. were transferred by Reay
and Lowes to Castell and Wren, and it was declared, that Castell
and Wren should stand possessed of 5,396*l*. Four per cent. Annuities
(which sum was stated to have been on that day transferred into
their names), upon the trusts of the settlement. In fact, this stock
was not transferred to the new trustees, for the bankers of the
former trustees had, under a power given to them, previously sold
out that stock, and misapplied the proceeds.

John Cookson died in 1802, without having had issue, and left
his wife, Hannah Jane, surviving him.

By an indenture dated the 23rd of July, 1804, and made between the said Hannah Jane Cookson, widow, and the said Isaac Cookson, of the one part, and Samuel Castell, the survivor of the said new trustees, of the other part, after reciting the marriage settlement of 1784, and therein the said will and testamentary paper, and the said mortgage and further charge to secure the said sums of 5,000*l.* and 1,000*l.* to the trustees of the settlement, and the appointment of new trustees by the deed of 1792, and reciting the death of the said John Cookson, the son, without leaving issue, by reason whereof the said Isaac Cookson, or his representatives, would, upon the death of the said Hannah Jane Cookson, become entitled to the actual receipt of the said sum of 1,000*l.* trust-monies; and reciting that Castell had received payment of the said sums of 5,000*l.* and 1,000*l.*, secured upon mortgage of the hereditaments and premises before mentioned, and that the said sum of 5,396*l.* 4 per cent. Annuities was *then standing in his son's name, and reciting that the said Hannah Jane and Isaac Cookson, being the only persons then interested in the said sum of 10,000*l.* trust monies, had, with the concurrence and approbation of Castell, agreed to nominate and appoint two other persons to act in conjunction with the said Samuel Castell in the several trusts then remaining unexecuted and capable of taking effect relative to the said sum of 10,000*l.*, which were by the said indenture of appointment of 23rd February, 1784, expressed and declared concerning the same, and had in consequence requested Joseph Cookson and Anthony Surtees to accept the same trusts, and to act therein in conjunction with Castell, which they had agreed to do, the said Hannah Jane and Isaac Cookson covenanted with Castell, his executors, &c., to transfer the said sum of 5,396*l.* 4 per cent. Annuities into the joint names of the said Castell, Joseph Cookson, and Surtees; and they, Hannah Jane and Isaac Cookson thereby directed Castell to make such transfer, and also forthwith to place out and invest upon real and Government securities the said sum of 6,000*l.* so lately received by him, and then in his hands, in the joint names of the said Castell, Cookson, and Surtees; and it was thereby declared and agreed, by and between the said parties thereto, that the said sum of 5,396*l.* 4 per cent. Annuities, when so transferred, and the said sum of 6,000*l.*, when so placed out and invested, and all interest, dividends and proceeds thereof respectively, should be upon such and the same trusts, and to and for such and the same intents and purposes, and under and subject to

COOKSON
v.
COOKSON.

such and the same provisos, conditions and agreements, as were mentioned and expressed of and concerning the said sum of 10,000*l.*, in the said indenture of settlement of the 23rd February, 1784, or such of them as were then existing and capable of taking effect, and for no other purpose whatsoever.

[*127]

Then followed a proviso that the trustees should only *be chargeable with such monies as they should respectively receive; and that they should not be accountable for the insufficiency or deficiency of any securities.

Castell did not transfer the 5,396*l.* stock (which had, in fact, been previously sold and misapplied, as before mentioned), but he, together with Joseph Cookson and Surtees, lent the 6,000*l.* to Isaac Cookson, upon the security of a mortgage of an estate belonging to him, and it remained upon that security until after his death.

Some time after the discovery of the fraud about the sale of the said stock, Isaac Cookson and Hannah Jane Cookson instituted a suit in Chancery against Henry Ulrich Reay, the surviving trustee of the marriage settlement, and the representatives of the bankers who had so sold out the stock, praying to have it declared that the plaintiffs were entitled to have the said sum of 5,396*l.* stock replaced, or the produce thereof laid out upon the trusts of the said marriage settlement. This suit coming on for hearing in July, 1809, it was decreed that Isaac Cookson, by his counsel, electing to take the sum of 5,339*l.*, the money produced by the sale of the said stock, instead of having the same replaced, and Hannah Jane Cookson, by her counsel also electing to take the interest of the said sum, the defendants should pay what should be found due for interest to her, and what should be found due for principal into the Bank, to the credit of the cause; and it was ordered that the same, when paid in, should be laid out in the purchase of Bank 3 per cent. Annuities.

In pursuance of this decree and subsequent proceedings, the sum of 8,502*l.* 3*s.* 2*d.* Bank 3 per cent. Annuities, was purchased in the name of the Accountant-General, in trust in the cause; and by an order on further directions, dated the 12th January, 1811, it was ordered, that the interest and dividends thereof should be paid to Hannah Jane Cookson during her life.

[*128]

The said Isaac Cookson died in December, 1831, intestate, *leaving eight children, namely, John (the appellant), his eldest son and heir-at-law, and the respondents, Isaac, Thomas, Joseph, Elizabeth, wife of Robert Surtees, and Emma, wife of Robert Bell,

and James and Christopher, both since deceased.   Administration
of the intestate's estate and effects was granted to the appellant
and the respondent Isaac, and to another son, since deceased.
Hannah Jane Cookson, the widow of John Cookson, died in April,
1841, having received the dividends of the 8,508l. 8s. 2d. up to the
time of her death.

In 1842 the respondents, who were the only parties, except the
appellant, interested in the personal estate of the deceased Isaac
Cookson, presented a petition to the Master of the Rolls, in the
cause of *Cookson* v. *Reay* and others, praying that the said sum of
stock might be transferred to the appellant and the respondent
Isaac Cookson as the surviving administrators of the estate of their
father.   The MASTER OF THE ROLLS, after hearing that petition,
made an order on the 29th of April, 1842, directing the transfer of
the said sum of 8,508l. 8s. 2d., as prayed (1).

(1) 5 Beav. 22. The following passages from the judgment of the
MASTER OF THE ROLLS, as there
reported, may be conveniently set out
here.

[Upon the question as to the original
conversion of the money into land,
his Lordship, after stating the will
and testamentary paper left by the
testator John Cookson, said:]

Upon the authorities of *Earlom* v.
Saunders,† and *Cowley* v. *Hartstonge*‡
I incline to think that the testator
ought to be deemed to have intended
that the money should be laid out in
the purchase of land, and that the
direction to invest on some other
securities, should be considered to
have reference to the time which
might elapse before a purchase of land
could be procured. The testator has
not so expressed himself, as clearly to
show the nature of the investment he
intended, or what interests the children of John were to take, or in what
way the limitation for their benefit
was to be effected; and I think that
the difficulty which arose in that
respect had a reasonable foundation;
but it seems to me more probable, that
whatever benefit the children were to
take was to be in the form of an
interest in real estate.

[His Lordship then stated the subsequent settlement on the marriage of
John Cookson the younger and his
death in 1802 without issue, and upon
the question as to the reconversion of
the property into money, his Lordship
said:]

Mrs. Cookson, the widow, and Isaac
Cookson were now the only persons
interested in the property, whether
to be considered as land or money.
They had, together, power to do with
it what they pleased. An investment
in land might have been made by the
trustees, with the approbation of Mrs.
Cookson, as the survivor of herself
and her husband; and even if it is
considered independently of any act
done by Isaac, the money ought, for
the benefit of his heir, to be considered
as land, after the death of John; yet,
as the property was his, he had a right
to dispose of it, or treat it as money,
and any act of his showing an intention to alter its character, or to treat it
as money, would be considered sufficient to remove the character of real
estate which had previously been
impressed upon it.

In July, 1804, there was only one
trustee of the 10,000l. or of the securities on which it was invested; *and
Isaac Cookson and the widow of John,

1842.

[31]

[5 Beav. 30]

[*32]

† Amb. 240.   ‡ 14 R. R. 86 (1 Dow, 361).

The appellant, conceiving that the transfer of the stock ought to be made to himself, as heir-at-law of the said Isaac Cookson, brought this appeal against the said order.

who were the sole owners of the property, thought fit to appoint a new trustee. The occasion required consideration how the property was to be dealt with, and the question is, whether it is to be collected from the deed appointing new trustees, that Isaac Cookson intended to treat the 10,000l. as money to be invested in land, and bearing the character of land, or as money which was to remain on security, and to be received by him as money, after the death of the widow of John.

(His Lordship stated the recitals.)

Now it is to be observed, that in these recitals, it is particularly noticed, that Isaac Cookson is to become entitled to the actual receipt of the 10,000l. trust monies, upon the death of Hannah Jane Cookson; there is notice taken here, that the two sums of 5,000l. and 1,000l. in money were in the hands of the surviving trustee; and here is an intention expressed that the 10,000l. trust monies were to be in the hands of the new trustees, who were to act in conjunction with the survivor of the several trustees of the trusts then remaining unexecuted and capable of taking effect.

Those trusts were for the sole use of Mrs. Cookson for her life (as previously noticed), with the actual right to receive the money vested in Isaac when she died.

How is it then that they have disposed of this by the settlement? "This indenture witnesseth, that it shall be lawful for the surviving trustee to transfer into the names of all the trustees." What were they to do with it? "They further order, direct, and appoint *Samuel Castell, his executors or administrators forthwith, and as soon as conveniently may be, to sell out and invest upon real and Government securities the sum of 6,000l. so lately received by him, and now in his hands, in the joint names

[*33]

[*34]

of Samuel Castell, Joseph Cookson, and Anthony Surtees." There were 6,000l. in the hands of the surviving trustee, and that was to be laid out forthwith, and invested upon real or Government securities; there being, in the express words here mentioned, no reference whatever to an investment in the purchase of land; and then it was "declared and agreed between the parties to these presents, that the stock and the 6,000l. when so placed out, and all interest, dividends, and proceeds thereof respectively, in the meantime, should be upon such and the same trusts, and to and for such and the same intents and purposes, and under and subject to such and the same provisoes, conditions, covenants, and agreements, as are mentioned, expressed, and declared of and concerning the same sum of 10,000l. in the indenture of settlement; and for no other intent or purpose whatsoever." And then there was a provision that the trustees should only be charged with such monies as they should respectively actually receive; and they were not to be accountable for the insufficiency or deficiency of any securities.

Now to say that this is perfectly clear, when there is such a reference to those trusts (amongst which is the trust for laying out in the purchase of land), would, I think, be expressing an opinion which could hardly be formed upon this instrument; but seeing that all the words, directly used, tend solely to the actual receipt of the money, and the investment of the money upon real or personal security; and that the only persons who had any interest in the settlement, were then dealing with the money, I do not think that the *words which have general reference to the trusts of the settlement, are sufficient to outweigh the effect which ought to be given to the direct words; and

Mr. Kindersley and *Mr. Goodeve*, for the appellant :

There are two questions for decision, first, whether the sum of 10,000*l.*, directed by the testator to be " invested in land or some other securities," for his son John was, in equity, by the terms of the gift, impressed with the character of real estate ; and that appears to have been the opinion of the MASTER OF THE ROLLS ; secondly, whether the money, having been so converted into realty, was afterwards, by the acts of the parties interested, reconverted *into personalty ; and the MASTER OF THE ROLLS held that it was,   [*129] but he did not give a decided opinion. * * *

A limitation to one and his heirs is applicable to realty only, and it is a settled rule in equity that when money is directed to be invested in land or upon other security, the direction to invest the money in land is not matter of discretion, but is imperative ; and an investment of it in other security is to continue only until a purchase can be made of lands : *Earlom* v. *Saunders* (1), *Johnson* v. *Arnold* (2), *Cowley* v. *Hartstonge* (3).   In none of these cases was   [*130] the language directing an investment in land, &c., so strong as the will here, and the marriage settlement of John, the son. * * *

Looking at the will alone, we submit that the character of realty   [135] was thereby impressed upon this sum of 10,000*l.*, and if not by the will, then by the settlement of 1784, in pursuance of the power given by the will, and if not by both these instruments, separately or together, at all events by the subsequent deeds and acts of the parties, never indicating an intention to treat the fund otherwise than as realty ; and therefore, upon the death of Hannah, the heir of Isaac, who had previously died intestate, became entitled to the property as realty : *Symons* v. *Rutter* (4), *Lechmere* v. *Earl of Carlisle* (5), *Walker* v. *Denne* (6), *Wheldale* v. *Partridge* (7), *Thornton* v. *Hawley* (8).

Mr. Bethell and *Mr. Turner* for the respondents :

* * In order to impress the money with the quality of real

without saying that this matter is perfectly clear, it does appear to me, that
even if it were originally impressed
with the character of land, it ceased
to be so by the act of Isaac, who,
at the time he executed this deed,
had a perfect right to say that he considered it either as land or as money.

I think, therefore, that the intention

was to convert it into money.

(1) Amb. 241.
(2) 1 Ves. Sen. 169.
(3) 14 R. R. 86 (1 Dow, 361).
(4) 2 Vern. 227.
(5) 3 P. Wms. 211.
(6) 2 R. R. 185 (2 Ves. Jr. 170).
(7) 7 R. R. 37 (8 Ves. 235).
(8) 7 R. R. 359 (10 Ves. 129).

COOKSON
v.
COOKSON.

estate, it must be shown that an intention to convert it into real
estate was either expressed or necessarily inferrible from the nature
of the limitations to which the fund was subjected, as in *Cowley* v.
Hartstonge and other cases that have been cited (1). As no such
intention is expressed in this testamentary paper, those cases do
not apply: [*Walker* v. *Denne* (2), *Davies* v. *Goodhew* (3).]

[137]

Suppose the fund had previously acquired the character of realty
under the will, or the deed of 1784, it lost that character by the
subsequent dealings of the parties with it by the deeds of 1792 and
1804, treating it as a money fund. * * In the deed of 1804 there
is a clear indication of intention expressed of taking the fund, as
it then existed, in money, and it is not disputed that Isaac might

[138]

then, if he wished, declare that to be its character. * * Even if
the money had been before converted into realty in equity, the
conduct of the parties absolutely interested showing their acquiescence in continuing it, as it actually existed, determined it to be a
money fund. * * *

    Mr. Kindersley, in reply. * * *

LORD BROUGHAM:

It is unnecessary in this case to recall your Lordships' attention
to the facts, which lie within a very narrow compass, and are not
disputed, unless in so far as you may think the question, whether

[*139]

the *party has declared a certain intention or not, to be a fact: but
that is the matter for our consideration, being the ground, in truth,
upon which this question was decided in the Court below, and the
ground upon which I am prepared to advise your Lordships to
affirm the decree.

The matter in dispute being whether this fund is to be considered
as land or as money, as real or as personal estate, the first question
that arose was, whether, in the original gift—which is the original
constitution of the fund—the instructions of John Cookson, by his
will of 1774, whether those instructions accompanying that will
gave the fund in question as land, directing it to be invested in
land; and whether, taking the whole of that instrument and these
instructions together, your Lordships are called upon to say that he
had made it land.

I observe that when the MASTER OF THE ROLLS disposed of this

(1) *Supra*, p. 73.   (3) 38 R. R. 183 (6 Sim. 589).
(2) 2 R. R. 185 (2 Ves. Jr. 184).

case, he at first said (1) that he inclined to think upon the authorities of *Earlom* v. *Saunders* (2) and *Cowley* v. *Hartstonge* (8), "that whatever benefit the children were to take was to be in the form of an interest in real estate." He inclined to think that that was the object of the whole instructions, and that the alternative given of laying the money out in any other fund—namely, land or some other security, the interest of such money, or the produce of such land, to go so and so—that that was to be taken to be only while they were looking out for an investment, but that the object was to invest it in land.

Certainly, if you take the whole together, there are indications of an intention that it should go in land. The word "remainder" is used, which may mean residue only, but yet it is more technical than that; then, "in failure of those"—that is to say, of child or children lawfully begotten—it is to go " to my eldest son Isaac, and *his heirs for ever,*" which is very seldom used, and very inaccurately, except as to land. But taking the word "remainder" and the words "heirs for ever" together, that probably was the ground upon which the MASTER OF THE ROLLS, with a view to those former cases, considered that it was to be taken as land in the original intention of the party making the gift. I must say that I do not feel anything at all like a clear opinion upon that, but I rather consider that it might be maintained that it was an option given to all intents and purposes, and not merely given as a power to lay it out in money while they were looking out for an investment; for when you come to look to the cases to which his Lordship refers, and there are a great many others, but those perhaps are the two most referred to; and there is also *Johnson* v. *Arnold* (4); in these cases, and particularly in *Earlom* v. *Saunders* (2) and *Johnson* v. *Arnold*, you will find a far clearer indication of the intention to lay it out in land than anything that is to be found here; for what was *Earlom* v. *Saunders?* First, the testator had given a landed estate in Surrey, which he had devised in strict settlement, in terms that could have no possible application to anything but land. He then directs 400*l.* to be raised, not from that estate, but from his other funds unconnected with that estate, to be laid out in land, or such other security as his trustees appointed thereby should think fit or convenient. And how is it to be dealt with? To be settled to such uses and under such powers as the land

[*140]

(1) 5 Beav. 30. See p. 71, *n.* above.   (3) 14 R. R. 86 (1 Dow, 361).
(2) Amb. 241.   (4) 1 Ves. Sen. 169.

COOKSON
v.
COOKSON.

[*141]

devised; that is to say, the real estate in Surrey was settled to his first and other sons in tail male, remainder to trustees to preserve contingent remainders, remainders over, and so forth, totally inapplicable to money, but perfectly applicable to land; and Lord HARDWICKE referred to that passage—namely, the strict settlement in which was given the real estate in Surrey—and *says, " it is perfectly clear the only way to make this devise of money consistent was to suppose it was to be laid out in land, for the money was to go to such uses—namely, in strict settlement—as the land that had been devised."

Then take the other cases. To say nothing of *Cowley* v. *Hartstonge*, there is the case of *Johnson* v. *Arnold* (1), which is a very strong case indeed; for it is, that if George Jackson should be willing and desirous to have the sum raised laid out in land, then he may purchase in land, and the profits thereof to be for his life, then to his wife for life, and then to his eldest son; and there being no issue male of him, then to his other sons, then, there being no issue male, to his daughters; and if the land should not be purchased, and the money should remain as stock, then to such uses as if lands had been purchased. Really one only wonders that any doubt should have arisen there, because it seems, just as Lord HARDWICKE says, a devise of profits, as if it had been a devise of land.

Now, there are other cases of another kind, in which the Court would not hold it to be land at all; for instance, *Curling* v. *May*, cited in *Guidot* v. *Guidot* (2). In that case the interest is to be laid out in land, or put out upon good security, for H., her heirs, executors, and administrators, and Lord TALBOT held that the Court would not *in dubio* interfere; that there was here nothing to show positively what the testator's intention was. There are other cases to the same effect.

[*142]

If I were to decide this case upon this ground alone, therefore, regarding those former cases as far stronger for land than the present case in every respect, I should feel some difficulty in abiding by the decision that it was land, upon the ground of those former cases, I should feel great *doubt whether, even upon the first intention which the testator indicated—namely, in the instructions accompanying the will—I should feel a grave doubt, notwithstanding those cases, whether it was not still left free from any expressions of intention to invest it in land. However,

(1) 1 Ves. Sen. 169.   (2) 3 Atk. 265.

I admit that the word "remainder" and the words "heirs for ever" may, to a certain degree, support, I will not say the decision, that it is land, but an inclination of opinion that it is, as his Lordship, the MASTER OF THE ROLLS, expressed it; although, when you come to look at a subsequent part of his opinion, he says (1), "that even if it were originally impressed with the character of land (which is somewhat weaker than saying that such was the inclination of his opinion), he is of opinion that, at the time Isaac executed the deed, he had the right to consider it as land or money."

But now we come to that upon which really the decision of the case turns, although I thought it right to say a few words upon the former cases, because this is a case which is very often occurring, and there ought to be no more doubt than is necessary left upon the subject—we now come to the other point, which is the manner in which the party dealt with the money. When you come to look at the instrument of July, 1804, in which there was to be an appointment made of new trustees, and when you look at the latter part of the recital there, it is a very anxious and careful recital: every instrument, and every deed, and every event, that has happened is most carefully gone through in the previous part of the recital; and then there is this: "And whereas the said John Cookson (the son) some time ago departed this life, without leaving lawful issue, by reason whereof the said Isaac Cookson or his representatives will, upon the death of the said Hannah Jane Cookson, become entitled to the actual receipt *of the said sum of 10,000l.:" and then it goes on to other matters, which it is unnecessary to state. Then the witnessing part of the deed is that Hannah Jane Cookson and Isaac Cookson do hereby for themselves, &c., covenant and promise, &c., "that it shall and may be lawful to and for him or them forthwith, and as soon as conveniently may be, to transfer in the books of the Governor and Company of the Bank of England, kept for that purpose, the said sum of 5,825l. 19s. 8d. into the joint names of them the said Samuel Castell and Joseph Cookson and Anthony Surtees, and they the said Hannah Jane Cookson and Isaac Cookson do hereby direct, order, and appoint the said Samuel Castell, his executors or administrators, to make such transfer accordingly." Now Isaac at this time had an undoubted right to deal with the land, and to say that he took it as land, or to say that he took it as money.

[*143]

(1) *Supra*, p. 73, n. (5 Beav. 34).

COOKSON
v.
COOKSON.

The question is, what he does with it. "And they do also hereby further order, direct, and appoint the said Samuel Castell, his executors or administrators, forthwith, and as soon as conveniently may be, to place out and invest upon real or Government securities the said sum of 6,000l., so lately received by him and now in his hands, in the joint names of them, the said Samuel Castell, Joseph Cookson, and Anthony Surtees: and it is hereby declared and agreed by and between the said parties to these presents, that the said sum of 5,325l. 19s. 8d. Four per cent. Annuities, when so transferred, and the said sum of 6,000l., when so placed out and invested;" now observe, "and all interest, dividends, and proceeds thereof," which is dealing with it as money exactly, "respectively in the mean time shall be upon such and the same trusts, and to or for such and the same intents and purposes," and so forth, and subject to the same limitations as in the settlement of 1784.

[*144]

Now I entirely concur with the MASTER OF THE ROLLS that this is a taking of the fund, that Isaac having an *entire right so to do by this deed, takes this as money, and exercises his own discretion, and indicates his own intention. All that you want here is to know the intention: he had a right to take the money as such if he chose so to do: did he or did he not intend to take it as such? have we or have we not a sufficient indication of that intention? That is the point and the sole point, and looking at this, I think he indicates that intention.

But, my Lords, I do not think that is the whole of this case, and I think when you come to look at what subsequently took place, one might say that this intention is even more strongly stated, although it is not adverted to in the judgment of the Court below, being probably thought superfluous, and unnecessary to support the judgment. In the respondent's case we find the suit stated, and the particulars of that suit, which was instituted by Isaac and Hannah Cookson against the trustees and the bankrupt's assignees; that is, after Samuel Castell, who had the custody of the fund, had become bankrupt; and we find a decree of 14th of July, 1809, in which it is said, "the plaintiff Isaac Cookson, by his counsel, electing to take the sum of 5,339l. 6s., the money produced by the sale of the 5,325l. 19s. 8d. 4 per cent. Annuities, the trust fund in the pleadings mentioned, instead of having the same replaced, and the plaintiff Hannah Jane Cookson, by her counsel, also electing to take the interest of the said sum;" and then the trusts thereof are declared accordingly.

Now, true it is, this is a proceeding between the same parties who were the parties to that suit; but this is an indication of intention, it is a declaration of intention, and it aids the other declaration of intention, and leaves it in my humble judgment in no manner of doubt at all; that that which Isaac had the authority and power to do, he did; that he formed his own judgment, and made his own choice as to how he should take it as money, and that he *clearly indicated his intention, and has given that evidence of his intention so to do.

COOKSON
v.
COOKSON.

[*145]

I am therefore of opinion, upon these grounds—and as I agree with his Lordship the MASTER OF THE ROLLS, it is unnecessary for me to trouble your Lordships further—upon these grounds, I am of opinion that the judgment of the Court below in this case should be sustained, and I move your Lordships accordingly that it be affirmed.

LORD COTTENHAM :

If it were necessary to put a construction upon the will, I should feel that there was great difficulty in distinguishing this case from those which have been cited in support of the argument, that the character of land had been fixed upon the fund, although the terms used are less strong than in any of these cases.

In *Johnson* v. *Arnold* the facts are so imperfectly stated that it is impossible, with any degree of certainty, to extract from the observation of Lord HARDWICKE any rule applicable to other cases. In *Earlom* v. *Saunders*, land had been devised upon trust applicable only to real estate, and the money was to be held in trust with the same provisions and limitations, and the difficulty arose from the direction that the trustees should "lay out the money in the purchase of lands or any other securities as the trustees should think proper and convenient." Lord HARDWICKE thought the trusts inconsistent with the supposition that the fund was to be regarded as money, and to reconcile the different provisions he held that the direction to invest in "other securities" applied only to the investment until land could be purchased. In *Cowley* v. *Hartstonge* the trust was to "invest either in the purchase of lands of inheritance, or at interest, as my said trustee shall think fit and proper," and the beneficial interest was given in the same sentence as real estate, and in a manner applicable only to real estate. The rule upon which Lord ELDON and Lord REDESDALE acted in that case, appears to be this, that *where a discretion vested in trustees

[*146]

Cookson
v.
Cookson.

had not been exercised, the Court would put that construction upon the will which seemed best calculated to answer the testator's intention. In all these cases there was a discretion as to the purchase of land or personal securities, and in all the Court expresses a strong disinclination to give effect to any such discretion which might have the effect of altering the interest of parties : it must be expressly given : the words must be so express and clear, that the design to give an absolute uncontrolled discretion cannot be misunderstood (1).

Expressions used by Judges in many other cases that there must be a clear, manifest, and ultimate intention, that at all events the conversion should take place, must, I think, be conclusive with reference to the principle upon which these leading cases have been decided. All the cases establish this, that where the conversion has not, in fact, taken place, and the interest vests absolutely, whether in land or money, in one person, any act of his, indicating an option in which character he takes or disposes of it, will determine the succession as between his real and personal representatives ; and this appears to me to be all that is necessary to determine the present question.

The deed of 1784 I consider as material only as it is referred to by the deed of 1804, because, whatever discretion may have been given to Elizabeth Cookson by the will, I think it clear that her being a party to the deed was wholly inoperative as an act exercising such discretion. By the will it could only be exercised as to the mode of investment. She had no power to declare that the fund still existing as personalty should be invested with the descendible quality of land. The will may have such effect, but her declarations could not. Her investing the fund in the purchase of land might have had that effect, but she could not produce that effect without such an investment.

[147]   The fund, therefore, remained as money, and all parties interested in the property being dead, except the widow of John, who was entitled for her life, and Isaac, to whom the fund was ultimately given, they joined in executing the deed of the 23rd of July, 1804. These two persons had a clear right to give to the fund the character of money, whatever may be the true construction of the will. Any indication of intention would be sufficient for that purpose. What does this deed indicate ? It recites, that Isaac, or his representative, will, upon the death of Hannah Jane, become

(1) See *Cowley* v. *Hartstonge*, 14 R. R. 91, 92 (1 Dow, pp. 378—380).

entitled to the actual receipt of the 10,000*l.*, and that they two were then the only persons interested in the trust funds, and that they had agreed upon the appointment of new trustees to act in the several trusts then remaining unexecuted and capable of taking effect, which are mentioned, expressed, and declared in the deed of 1784; and, after providing for the investment of the funds, it declares, that they shall be held " to and for such and the same intents and purposes, and under and subject to such and the same provisos, conditions, covenants, and agreements as are mentioned, expressed, and declared of and concerning the said sum of 10,000*l.*, in the deed of 1784, or such of them as remain existing undetermined, and are capable of taking effect." The first trust of the deed of 1784 was to invest the fund in the purchase of land, with the good liking and approbation of John Cookson and Hannah Jane, his intended wife; but it provides for the construction of the will and testamentary paper, that the money ought not to be so laid out and invested; and, after giving estates to the husband, wife, and children, the deed refers to the will as directing the parties, who, after the expiration or failure of those estates, would be entitled.

The appellant contends that, notwithstanding the recitals before alluded to, the reference in the deed of 1804 to the deed of 1784 adopts and incorporates all its provisions, *including the trust to purchase land; and the question is, whether that be the true construction, or whether the reference to the deed of 1784 was not merely to describe the beneficial interests remaining, namely, the life estate of Hannah Jane, and the absolute interest in remainder of Isaac. This latter construction is in strict conformity with the recitals, whereas it is inconceivable that these two parties, who had the actual dominion over the fund, should create a new trust for the purpose of investing the money in the purchase of land, which they might effect themselves, and which, if effected, they might immediately defeat by selling.

[*148]

I cannot adopt this construction, and I think that to make the provisions reasonable and consistent, the reference to the deed of 1784 must be considered as confined to the estates and interests remaining, namely, of Hannah Jane for life, remainder to Isaac absolutely. Were this more doubtful, I think that the decree of the 14th of July, 1809, would be conclusive. By that decree Hannah Jane and Isaac agreed to accept a sum of money, to be invested in the purchase of Three per cent. Annuities, in the name

COOKSON
v.
COOKSON.

of the Accountant-General, and the dividends to be paid to Hannah
Jane for life, with liberty, after her death, for any persons entitled,
to apply concerning the said annuities. This was a dealing by the
parties interested with the fund as a money fund, and inconsistent
with any intention of dealing with it as land ; I think, therefore,
that whatever may have been the character of the fund under the
will, the parties to the deed of 1804 and to the decree of 1809, who
were perfectly competent to do so, have impressed upon the fund
the character of personalty, and, therefore, that the decree appealed
from is right.

LORD CAMPBELL :

I entirely agree in the view taken of this case by my two noble
and learned friends. I have attended very strictly to the case, and

[*149]

I have examined the *authorities that were referred to, and I am
clearly of opinion that the decree ought to be affirmed.

The heir-at-law of Isaac Cookson is bound to show that what
de facto is money, had the character of land impressed upon it,
and is now to be considered as land. I must say that I entertain
the greatest doubt whether, under the original will, it ever had the
character of land impressed upon it. If, looking to that instrument,
you see that it was the intention of the party that it should
ultimately be vested in land, certainly while it remains upon
personal security, it is still to be considered as land.

But I doubt very much whether this testator really meant that it
should ultimately be vested in land, or at least whether he gave
such directions as made it imperative upon the trustees to vest it in
land. He intimated no general intention to create a second family.
He had four sons, Isaac, John, Thomas, and Joseph. There was a
family estate, which he limited to Isaac. Then the younger sons
were to be sent out into the world, and to have provisions made for
them ; and there seems no probability whatever that, with regard
to the 10,000*l.*, which was to be set apart for John or for Thomas,
that it was intended that there should be a second family established,
and that, failing that second family, this minor estate should be
converted into land, and should revert to the head of the house.

Then when you look to the words that are employed, it is
impossible to put upon them the interpretation that the land was to
be merely a mortgage. But, taking the whole into consideration, I
should think it more probable that the testator intended that the
money should be laid out upon security to remain as personalty,

than that it should be converted into realty. There is certainly the
word "remainder," but that, in a popular sense, might be applied
to personalty. There are also the words "heirs for ever;" they
may mean heirs in personalty. There *are very considerable
difficulties on the other side; I think the learned counsel for the
appellant had considerable difficulty in saying what estate the child
or children of John would take in the land if it had been purchased.

Referring to the cases that were cited, I do not find that any of
those cases go the length of deciding that, where the intention of
the testator is so very doubtful, you can say that the character of
land is to be impressed upon the money, where there is to be a
provision under circumstances, such as we find here, and which we
have to consider. However, there is no necessity for us to decide
that point, because, even if upon the will this sum is to be dealt
with as land, there does not seem to be the remotest doubt that the
option, which was given that it should afterwards be taken as money,
was exercised; and if it had been once land, it had ceased to be
land, and therefore it is now to be considered as personalty, and
that therefore the next of kin of Isaac, and not the heir-at-law, are
entitled to it.

It is unnecessary that I should attempt to go over the grounds
which were gone into by both of my noble and learned friends who
have preceded me: I think upon the second point, there is no
reasonable doubt whatever, and that alone is sufficient.

The decree was then affirmed, with costs.

COOKSON
v.
COOKSON.

[*150]

STOKES *v.* HERON.

(12 Clark & Finnelly, 161—203; S. C. 9 Jur. 563.)

1845.
April 11—18.

[161]

[THIS was an appeal from a decision of Sir EDWARD SUGDEN, as
Lord Chancellor of Ireland, reported under the title of *Heron v.
Stokes*, in 2 Dr. & War. 89, reversing a previous decision by Lord
PLUNKET. A note of this appeal will be found at the end of the
report of *Heron* v. *Stokes :* see 59 R. R. at p. 662.]

1844.
April 2, 30.
May 13, 21,
27.
1845.
March 17.
June 10.
July 17, 24.
———
Lord
LYNDHURST,
L.C.
Lord
BROUGHAM.
Lord
CAMPBELL.
Lord
COTTENHAM.
[295]

IN COMMITTEE OF PRIVILEGES.

THE WHARTON PEERAGE (1).

(12 Clark & Finnelly, 295—311.)

It appeared by the Parliamentary Pawns of 36 Hen. VIII., and 1 Edw. VI., that a writ had been directed to "Thomas, Lord Wharton" for each of these Parliaments; but there was no evidence of his sitting in either of them or of the writ itself. The Journals of the House of Lords showed that he was summoned to, and sat in, the Parliament of the 2nd of Edw. VI., and subsequent Parliaments. Creation of Baronies by patent was not then unusual; but no patent or record or other trace of a patent, creating the Barony of Wharton could be found:

Held, that the said Barony was created by writ and sitting in the 2nd of Edw. VI., and was descendible to heirs general (of the body).

A decretal order in Chancery, reciting the substance of the bill and answer, is admissible, on proof of pedigree, to establish the identity of parties to the suit.

But an answer alone, though sworn but not filed, is not admissible.

Scotch wills, registered in the Court of Session, are retained there, and if it is necessary to prove any such wills in England, a certified copy is given out, and is admitted to probate in the English Ecclesiastical Courts. The Lords Committees for Privileges will not, on claims of Peerage, receive such copy, unless it is shown that the original will cannot be produced.

If a judgment of outlawry stand in the way of a claim to a Barony in abeyance, although it is clearly erroneous, the Committee of Privileges cannot overlook it or reverse it; but the claimant must apply to the proper tribunal for its reversal, and produce the judgment of reversal to the Committee.

CHARLES KEMEYS KEMEYS TYNTE, of Halswell, in the county of Somerset, Esq., presented a petition to the Queen, in February, 1843, praying her Majesty "to determine the abeyance of the Barony of Wharton in his favour, by commanding a writ of [*296] summons to Parliament *to be issued to him by the name and style of Baron Wharton."

The petition stated, in substance (2), that Sir Thomas Wharton, Knight, was summoned to Parliament as a Baron of the realm, by writ, in the 36th year of the reign of Henry VIII. (1544), and to other Parliaments, in the reigns of Edward VI., Mary, and Elizabeth, and that having sat in divers Parliaments pursuant to such writs, he acquired the dignity of a Baron of the realm to him and the heirs of his body: that, upon his death, in the year 1568, his son and heir, Thomas, became second Lord Wharton, and was

(1) Explained by BRETT, L. J., in *Palini* v. *Gray* (1879) 12 Ch. Div. 411, at p. 432; *S. C.* sub nom. *Sturla* v. *Freccia* (1880) 5 App. Cas. 623, 49 L. J. Ch. 41, 50 L. J. Ch. 86; and see the *Shrewsbury Peerage* case (1858) 7 H. L. C. 1.—J. G. P.

(2) It is printed in full in the Lords' Journ., Vol. 75, p. 389.

summoned to, and sat in Parliament in the 13th and 14th years of
the reign of Elizabeth : that, on his death in 1573, his son and
heir, Phillip, then a minor, became third Lord Wharton, and was
summoned to Parliament in the 23rd of Elizabeth, and sat in that
and divers subsequent Parliaments, until the 1st year of the reign
of Charles I. (1625), when he died, having had issue two sons—
namely, George, who died in 1609, without issue, and Sir Thomas
Wharton, who died in 1623, leaving Phillip Wharton, his son
and heir, who, being also the heir of his grandfather, the third
Lord, on his death became fourth Lord Wharton, and was summoned to Parliament in the 15th of Charles I. (1639), and sat
in that and numerous Parliaments, down to the time of his death
in 1695.

The petition further stated that the said Phillip, fourth Lord
Wharton, was thrice married, and by his first wife had issue one
child, Elizabeth, who married Lord Willoughby D'Eresby, afterwards Earl of Lindsey, and is now represented by Peter Robert,
Lord Willoughby D'Eresby, and George Horatio, Marquess of
Cholmondeley, coheirs of the Barony : that the said Phillip had,
by his second wife, five sons and five daughters, all of whom died
without issue, except Thomas, the third son—*who, on his father's
death, became fifth Lord Wharton—and Margaret, Mary, and
Philadelphia, the 2nd, 3rd, and 5th daughters : that Margaret's
issue are all extinct : that Mary's issue also, by her first husband,
are extinct, and that, by her second husband, Sir Charles Kemeys,
of Kevenmably, in the county of Glamorgan, Bart., she was the
ancestrix of this petitioner : that Philadelphia married Sir George
Lockhart, of Carnwath, in Scotland, and was the ancestrix of
Baillie Cochrane, Esq., and of Mrs. Aufrere, other coheirs of the
Barony of Wharton : that the said Phillip, fourth Lord Wharton,
had, by his third wife, one child, who died without issue in 1689.

[*297]

The petition then stated that the said Thomas, fifth Lord Wharton,
was summoned to and sat in Parliament in 1696, and that having,
in 1706, been created, by letters patent, Earl of Wharton, to him
and the heirs male of his body, and, in 1715, Marquess of Wharton
and Malmesbury, with the same limitation; he died in 1715, leaving
one son, Phillip, who succeeded to all his honours, and two daughters,
Jane and Lucy : that the said Phillip, second Earl and Marquess,
and sixth Baron Wharton, was, in 1719, created Duke of Wharton,
and died, without surviving issue, in 1731, in Tarragona, in Spain—
having been outlawed for high treason in 1729, which outlawry,

as the petitioner was advised, was informal, and did not affect the
dignities of the Peerage—that upon his death, without issue, all his
honours became extinct, except the Barony of Wharton, which then
fell into abeyance between his sisters, the said Jane (then Lady
Jane Holt) and Lucy (then Lady Lucy Morrice), and remained in
abeyance until the death of Lucy, without issue, in 1789, when it
devolved on Jane, but she did not assume the title in consequence
of its having been supposed, erroneously, that all the dignities
vested in the Duke were forfeited by the outlawry : that on Jane's
death, without issue, in 1761, the Barony fell into abeyance among
[*298]   the *heirs of the aforesaid Elizabeth, Mary, and Philadelphia,
daughters of Phillip, fourth Lord Wharton, and has continued in
abeyance ever since among their heirs.

The petitioner's descent from the said Mary was stated to this
effect ; that she had by her said husband Sir C. Kemeys, one son,
Charles, and two daughters, Jane and Mary ; Charles and Mary
died unmarried, and Jane survived them, and married Sir John
Tynte of Halswell aforesaid, Bart., and had issue three sons—who
all died without leaving surviving issue—and one daughter, Jane,
who married John Hassell, Esq., and left issue a daughter, Jane,
who married John Johnson, of Glaiston, in the county of Rutland,
Esq.—who and his issue assumed, by Royal licence, the surnames
of Kemeys Tynte—and the said Jane died in 1825, leaving the
petitioner her son and heir.

The petition was referred by her Majesty, first to the *Attorney-
General*, and afterwards, with his report thereon, to the House of
Lords, and the same were, by the House, referred to the Lords
Committees for Privileges.

In March, 1844, and before the Committee of Privileges sat to
consider the said petition, Alexander Dundas Ross Cochrane
Wishart Baillie, of Lamington, in Lanarkshire, in Scotland, presented a petition to her Majesty, praying her Majesty to determine
the abeyance of the said Barony in his favour ; and after stating
the creation and descent of the Barony to the same effect (1), as was
stated by Mr. Kemys Tynte's petition, down to the abeyance of it
among the said Elizabeth, Mary, and Philadelphia, three of the
daughters of Phillip, fourth Lord Wharton, this petitioner then
stated his descent from Philadelphia: that she had by her aforesaid
husband, Sir G. Lockhart, a son, George, who died in 1731, leaving
a son, also named George, who died in 1764, having had two sons,

(1) See Lords' Journal, Vol. 76, p. 134.

the first *of whom died *in vita patris et sine prole,* and the second, James Lockhart, assumed the name of Wishart, was a Count of the Roman Empire, and died in 1790, having been twice married, leaving two daughters, namely, Maria Theresa by the first marriage, and, by the second, Marianne Matilda, now the widow of Anthony Aufrere, late of Hoverton, in the county of Norfolk, Esq., and a coheir of the said Barony: that Maria Theresa married Lieutenant-General Sir Charles Ross, Bart., and had issue a son, who died without issue, and a daughter Matilda Ross Wishart, who married Sir Thomas Cochrane, and died in 1819, leaving this petitioner her son and heir.

This petition also was, in the usual manner, referred by her Majesty to the *Attorney-General,* and with his report thereon to the House of Lords, and by the House to the said Committee of Privileges.

At the first sitting of the Committee (in April, 1844):

The *Solicitor-General (Sir W. Follett)* and *Sir Harris Nicolas* appeared for Mr. Kemeys Tynte. *Mr. Austin* appeared for Mr. Cochrane Baillie. (The other coheirs did not claim the Barony, nor appear by counsel or agents, although they had had notice of the claims of the petitioners.) The *Attorney-General (Sir F. Pollock)* attended for the Crown.

Sir W. Follett stated the case for the first-mentioned petitioner:

This is a claim to a Barony, which must be treated as a Barony created by writ, followed by a sitting in this House. The proof on this part of the case will not be difficult. Sir T. Wharton, the first Baron, held an office of great trust under the Crown—Governor of Carlisle. It can be shown that he was addressed by the Crown under the name of Sir T. Wharton in February, 36 Henry VIII. (1544), and was designated in another public document, in *March of that year, by the name of " Baron Wharton." In the interval between these two periods the creation of the Barony took place. Proof will be given that search has been made in all the places in which the patents of that date were likely to be found, and that no trace of any patent, creating this Barony, can be discovered. Evidence will also be given that on the 26th November, 1548, being the second year of the reign of Edw. VI., Baron Wharton was summoned to, and sat in this House as a peer. Upon this evidence it is submitted that according to the authority of the cases of

THE
WHARTON
PEERAGE.

The Vaux Peerage (1), *The Braye Peerage* (2), *The Camoys Peerage* (3), and *The Hastings Peerage* (4), the Barony of Wharton must be deemed to have been a peerage created by writ, and by a sitting in Parliament, and therefore descendible to the heirs general of his body.

The pedigree will be easily proved, and the only difficulty apprehended in the way of making out the claim arises from the fact that an outlawry for treason issued against the last Baron Wharton, who had also been created Duke of Wharton, but this outlawry is in many most material respects defective, and must be set aside.

Several witnesses were then examined, and all stated that, after most diligent searches in the various repositories for the custody of public instruments, they did not discover a patent creating the Barony of Wharton, or any enrolment or other evidence of such a patent. They found many patents creating other peers in the reign of Henry VIII. Neither did they find any special writ, or enrolment of such writ of summons in that reign, to Lord Wharton; the writs of that time were not preserved; but two Parliamentary

[*301]

Pawns (5) of the 36th of Henry VIII., *and 1st Edward VI., were in existence, in each of which appeared the name of Thomas, Lord Wharton; and it appeared by the Lords' Journals that he was present among the Peers in the Parliaments of the 2nd and 6th of Edward VI., and of the 5th and 6th of Philip & Mary, and that he had leave of absence, and appointed proxies, in several other Parliaments of these reigns and the reign of Elizabeth. It further appeared, by the said Journals, that Phillip, the second Lord Wharton, sat in the House in several Parliaments of the last mentioned reign. The sitting of the succeeding Lords Wharton in the House were proved by the contemporaneous journals.

A great many parish registers, monumental inscriptions, inquisitions, wills, and grants of administrations, were produced to prove the petitioner's pedigree. No question arose on them.

(1) 47 R. R. 105 (5 Cl. & Fin. 526).
(2) 49 R. R. 174 (6 Cl. & Fin. 757).
(3) 49 R. R. 195 (6 Cl. & Fin. 789).
(4) 54 R. R. 27 (8 Cl. & Fin. 144).
(5) " It became a practice about the time of King Hen. VIII., when a Parliament was to be called, for the clerks of the Petty Bag Office in Chancery, in pursuance of a warrant from the Lord Chancellor, to prepare a schedule, in which were set down the forms of the writs to be issued to the Peers, and the names, style and title of the persons to whom such writs were to be sent, which are called Parliamentary Pawns " : Cruise on Dignities, 261.

The following points arose in the course of the evidence on the admissibility of other documents :

A decretal order in Chancery, made in 1699, in a suit between *Sir C. Kemeys* and *Dame Mary*, his wife, plaintiffs, and *Sir J. Thomas* and others, defendants, and in a cross suit between the same parties, was offered in evidence to prove the identity of Dame Mary Kemeys, and other parties, to those suits.

The LORD CHANCELLOR expressed a doubt whether the decree was admissible for that purpose, without the bills and answers being also produced.

Mr. Kelly (1) said the bills and answers were fully *recited in this decree ; it appeared to be grounded on the admissions in the answers, showing that the said Dame Mary, who is the ancestrix of the plaintiff, being a daughter of the fourth Lord Wharton, had been first married to a Mr. Thomas, and after his death she married Sir C. Kemeys.   It is submitted that a decree, containing the whole substance of the bill and answer, is, under the circumstances, admissible.

The decree was received (2).

In order to prove the relation between different members of the family of Kemeys, so as to substantiate part of the pedigree, a private Act of Parliament, enabling them to sell certain estates and describing the relationship, in the recitals, was offered in evidence.

[*302]

Mr. Kelly :

This declaration of their relation, by the act of the Legislature, is admissible as proof of the fact.

THE LORD CHANCELLOR :

It is very strong proof ; for it is the well known practice of this House not to allow the insertion of such a statement in the recitals of a private Act of Parliament, unless the truth of that statement has been previously proved to the satisfaction of the Judges, to whom the bill has been referred.

The answer was received.

(1) At and from the second sitting of the Committee, on the 30th April, 1844, *Mr. Kelly* was, with *Sir H. Nicolas*, for Col. Tynte, in place of *Sir W. Follett*, who became Attorney-General, on the promotion of *Sir F. Pollock* to the Bench ; and *Mr.*

Thesiger, being then made Solicitor-General, attended in this case on behalf of the Crown.

(2) This is not a precedent for receiving modern decrees, which do not contain full recitals.

An answer in a suit in Chancery was offered as evidence to prove
a part of the pedigree. The answer was offered as a statement by
members of the family respecting the condition of the family ; and
Mr. Berrey, clerk of Records and Writs in the Court of Chancery,
said he had searched for a bill filed in November, 1761, by Sir C.
K. Tynte and James Lockhart, but could not find it : he found the
entry of it in the Six Clerks' book, made by one of the sworn clerks

[*303]

in the Six Clerks' Office. He produced *the original answer, which
appeared to have been sworn but never filed. The parties answering
claimed to be heirs-at-law and members of the family.

THE LORD CHANCELLOR :

This is a declaration of pedigree to support an actual claim of
right, put forward by the party who makes the declaration. This
declaration, too, is in an answer which was never filed. It cannot
be received as evidence for the purpose now proposed.

The answer was rejected.

Proof was offered to be given of a will of Sir C. Ross. It was
proved that the original will, which had reference principally to
property in Scotland, had been registered there ; that a certified
copy of it had been sent to England, and that on that certified copy
probate was granted in England. The certified copy of the will
was produced from the Prerogative Office in Doctors' Commons ;
and it was proved that certified or office copies coming from
Scotland were in every way treated as originals in the Prerogative
Office. The copy now produced was of this kind, and was taken off
the file of the Prerogative Office. It was also proved that any
original will, proved in Scotland, was registered in the books of
the Court of Session, and was never given back to the parties, but
that the Court did allow it to be produced in the hands of its own
officer, whenever it was required.

On objection being made to the admission of the copy,

Mr. Kelly and *Sir H. Nicolas :*

This office copy is admissible in evidence. The Ecclesiastical
Court here, which is the tribunal having peculiar jurisdiction over
wills, has treated the certified or office copy from Scotland as an
original will, and has thus admitted its authenticity. Scotland is,
for this purpose, a foreign country ; and the refusal of the Court
of Session to allow the parties ever to have back a will which has

been once registered, must be taken to dispense with the necessity of now producing the original document.

THE LORD CHANCELLOR:

Scotland is not a foreign country as to the House of Lords. So that that reason is not sufficient for us to dispense with the production of the will. Neither a certified copy of a will, nor even an examined copy of a will, is evidence in this House (1) on a claim of peerage, unless you prove that you cannot get the original (2). The evidence here shows that it can be produced in the hands of the officer of the Court of Session. It must be produced.

The copy of the will was afterwards received *de bene esse*, the counsel undertaking to send for the original, or to produce cases, in which copies had been received in evidence.

The evidence for the claimant having been closed,

Mr. Kelly addressed the Committee on it:

This is a Barony by writ. In consequence of decisions of the House in numerous cases (3), it is now established that the evidence, as given here, of sittings in Parliament, is sufficient to support a claim to a peerage so created. The evidence as to the pedigree is complete, and, so far as the claimant knows, is not contested on the part of the Crown. That evidence proves him to be one of the coheirs of the Barony.

There are two points in the case : the first relates to the creation of the peerage by writ of summons and sitting, which, it is submitted, has been clearly established ; the other relates to the effect of an outlawry for high treason, issued in 1728, against the Duke of Wharton, the last actual possessor of the Barony.

As to the effect of that outlawry, it should be stated that the claimant traces his descent from Sir Thomas Wharton, the first Baron, and does not claim through the Duke of Wharton, and, it is submitted, that cannot be affected by *the outlawry issued against him. Still as he knew that this outlawry would be made the subject of notice, he has produced evidence of the judgment in outlawry, and the question now will be what is the effect of that

[*305]

---

(1) See *The Netterville Peerage*, 35 R. R. 107 (2 Dow & Cl. 342).

(2) See *The Fitzwalter Peerage*, 59

R. R. 320 (10 Cl. & Fin. 952).

(3) *Vide ante*, p. 88, and the references there.

judgment upon the present claim? But, before entering on that
question, there is another which may be submitted to the notice of
the Committee, and that is whether the outlawry can be sustained.
It is submitted that the outlawry is absolutely null and void, under
the statutes 81 Eliz. c. 8 (1), and 4 & 5 W. & M. c. 22, and that
consequently the mere fact of its having existed, or been irregularly
issued, can produce no effect on this claim. The question then
arises whether this Committee will itself examine the judgment of
outlawry, and act upon the opinion formed upon that examination,
or will, in the first instance, assume the outlawry to be good, and
require the claimant to go to the Court of Queen's Bench and get
it reversed. The defects are apparent on the face of the judgment,
and show it to have been pronounced in disregard of the provisions
of the statutes. The first of these statutes is the 81 Eliz. c. 8,
which regulates the proceedings in outlawry in civil actions. This
was extended by the 4 & 5 W. & M. c. 22, s. 4, to all cases of
indictments for criminal matters. The latter statute was only
passed to continue for the period of three years, but by the
7 & 8 Will. III. c. 86, s. 4, it was made perpetual. By the provisions
of the first of these statutes it is clear that there ought to be a writ
of proclamation, and three proclamations made thereon, and that
they ought to appear on the face of the record, and that unless
they are issued and recorded the judgment is *ipso facto* void:
Anonymous (2), case of *Outlawry* (3), *Anonymous* (4), (where the
reversal was, because it was not shown that proclamation was
[*306]   made at the parish church, where, &c.,) *Rex* v. *Wilkes* (5),
Barrington v. *Rex* (6), *Rex* v. *Yandell* (7). The words of the
81 Eliz. are precise, " and all outlawries had and pronounced after
the end of the next Easter Term, and no writs of proclamation
awarded and performed, according to the form of this statute,
shall be utterly void and of none effect." The objection to the
judgment of outlawry being of this very plain and unquestionable
kind, it is submitted that the Committee will not require the
claimant to bring his writ of error, but will deal summarily with
the matter. That was the course pursued in the case of *Belly* v.
Algor (8), where an outlawry was reversed without writ of error, on
account of the omission of the words " made upon three several
days, whereof one proclamation, &c."

(1) Rep. 42 & 43 Vict. c. 59.   (5) 4 Burr. 2527.
(2) Styles, 297.   (6) 3 T. R. 499.
(3) Litt. Rep. 150.   (7) 4 T. R. 521.
(4) March, Rep. 20.   (8) Dyer, 206 a.

THE LORD CHANCELLOR:

Here the outlawry has been acted on, and the party has been, for a variety of purposes, treated for a long period of time as duly outlawed. This Committee, therefore, cannot now assume the outlawry to have been utterly null. Application must be made to the Court of Queen's Bench either by motion or by writ of error, and if that Court shall be satisfied that the objections are fatal, it will reverse the outlawry. This Committee cannot do that. The Lords now present are not sitting as a House. We constitute only a Committee of the House, sitting merely for the purpose of inquiry into a matter referred to us by the Crown, and relating to privilege.

Lord BROUGHAM and Lord CAMPBELL expressed their concurrence with the opinion expressed by the LORD CHANCELLOR.

Mr. *Kelly* then applied for an adjournment of the consideration *of the claim, in order to enable him to make an application to the Court of Queen's Bench.

[*307]

The application was granted.

At the next sitting of the Committee (the 10th of June, 1845),

Mr. *Kelly*, with Sir H. *Nicolas*, stated that since this case was last before their Lordships, proceedings had been taken in the Court of Queen's Bench to reverse the judgment of outlawry passed against the Duke of Wharton, the last Baron Wharton, and it had been reversed (1). He now proposed to give in evidence the judgment of outlawry, and the judgment of that COURT reversing the same.

Mr. Bond, a clerk of a branch of the public Record Office (in Carlton Ride), brought up the two judgments, and the judgment reversing the outlawry, was read at length.

(1) 25th November, 1844.—On this day Colonel Tynte, the claimant, appeared in the Court of Queen's Bench, and as one of the coheirs of Phillip, Duke of Wharton, delivered in an assignment of errors in the matter of the outlawry of the Duke, who was the last person that had enjoyed the dignity of the Barony of Wharton, of which Colonel Tynte was a claimant.

May 3rd, 1845, Mr. *Kelly* applied to the Court to reverse the outlawry which had been issued against the Duke of Wharton; and stated that the *Solicitor-General* and Mr. *M. D. Hill*, who had been instructed on the part of the Crown, had fully considered

Mr. Kelly said the evidence being now complete, he *was ready to finish his summing up, but the further search—which was directed by the Committee at the last sitting to be made for cases, if any could be found, in which, where Baronies were supposed to have been created by patent, no patent could be found to exist—had not yet been completed.

The *Solicitor-General* said the search was proceeding with diligence in the Rolls Chapel and other offices, but further time was required to complete it.

The Committee desired that the search should be proceeded with expeditiously.

At the next sitting of the Committee (the 17th July),

The *Attorney-General (Sir F. Thesiger)* stated that he had, according to the desire expressed by their Lordships, directed that the utmost diligence be used in the search, whether there was any known instance of a peerage being created by patent, and that patent not being found ; and he could now inform their Lordships that no such instance had been discovered.

> The *Solicitor-General (Mr. Kelly)* then finally summed up the case on the part of Colonel Tynte :

The first point which, it is submitted, is established in this case, is that this peerage was created by writ, and a subsequent sitting ; the second is that the pedigree has been satisfactorily proved ; and the third is that the outlawry of the last holder of the Barony of Wharton cannot affect the claim of the present claimant and the other coheirs.

The learned gentleman having gone through the evidence on the

the question, and were of opinion that the outlawry could not be supported.

LORD DENMAN :

But we must have some reason assigned to us for reversing any judgment of this Court.

Mr. Kelly :

There does not appear to have been any writ of proclamation, nor is it stated on the face of the record that any proclamations were made according to the form of the statute.

Mr. M. D. Hill afterwards appeared on the part of the Crown, and stated that the counsel for the Crown had examined the record, and considered the objections to the outlawry assigned as errors, and were of opinion that the outlawry could not be supported.

LORD DENMAN :

Then let the judgment of outlawry be reversed.

Judgment of outlawry reversed.

two first points, addressed himself to the third. The judgment of
outlawry, dated in 1729, had been brought before their Lordships
in evidence; and although the defects, manifest upon the face of
it. left no doubt that it could not be supported, still their Lordships
thought they had no power to reverse it, or treat it as a *nullity.   [*309]
It has since been reversed upon writ of error in the Court of
Queen's Bench, and the record of the judgment of reversal has
been brought up before this Committee; and thus all further
discussion on the effect of the outlawry on the present claims
becomes unnecessary.

It appears that there were two abeyances of the Barony, the first
being, on the death of the last Baron without surviving issue in
1731, between his two sisters, Lady Jane Holt and Lady Lucy
Morrice. There is no doubt that, on the death of the latter in
1739, her surviving sister, Lady Jane Holt, had then a right to the
Barony; but, in order to revive it in a female, letters patent from
the Crown would be necessary; a trouble and expense which a lady
advanced in years and without children might not think it right to
incur; or, as there was an erroneous supposition that the dignity
was forfeited by the outlawry of the last possessor, the Barony,
for one or other of these reasons—and either was sufficient to
account for her not claiming it (1)—remained dormant until, on the
death of this lady without issue in 1761, it fell again into abeyance
among the respective heirs of the three sisters of the fourth Baron.
Lords Willoughby D'Eresby and Lord Cholmondeley are the coheirs
of the eldest of the sisters; they do not claim the dignity. Colonel
Tynte is proved to be the sole heir of the second sister, and is consequently entitled to be preferred to the heir of the third sister,
who, it is to be remembered, is not represented by a sole heir, but
by coheirs, Mrs. Aufrere and Mr. Cochrane Baillie.

THE LORD CHANCELLOR:

We cannot in our report state any preference; there is none
between females or their heirs.

Mr. Walpole, for Mr. Cochrane Baillie, only wished to make
one observation, and that was on that last point mentioned. Their
Lordships never made any distinction as to precedence in the divi-
sions of coheirship. All *coheirs were treated as equal in degree,   [*310]
and the circumstance of there being more than one coheir of the
third sister, was not of the least importance.

(1) See *The Fitzwalter Peerage*, 57 R. R. 320 (10 Cl. & Fin. 952).

THE LORD CHANCELLOR:

We have nothing to do with that, which is a matter for the consideration of the Crown.

LORD COTTENHAM:

When a peerage is in abeyance, the main question for the House to report upon to the Crown is, in whom is the dignity in abeyance.

Mr. Walpole then called a witness, who proved that **Mr.** Cochrane Baillie is the person described in Colonel Tynte's petition as Mr. Baillie Cochrane, and in his own petition as Cochrane Wishart Baillie.

The *Attorney-General* expressed himself satisfied with the proof of the pedigree. On the question whether this dignity was a Barony, created by writ or patent, he thought that there was more satisfactory evidence here than in any of the cases referred to; and it seemed to him that the search which at their Lordships' desire he had caused to be made, was strong negative proof that the dignity had been created by writ of summons.

THE LORD CHANCELLOR:

I have attended carefully to the evidence, and I think, so far as I may refer to my own impressions of it as it proceeded step by step, that the claim has been satisfactorily made out.

LORD COTTENHAM:

The Committee has a right to the assistance of the *Attorney-General's* opinion upon the evidence. He will go through the evidence, and let us know his opinion on it.

July 24.   The case having been adjourned for that purpose, the *Attorney-General* communicated to the Committee at the next sitting, that he was satisfied with the evidence.

The Committee then resolved:

" That the Barony of Wharton is a Barony created by writ and sitting on the 26th of November, 2 Edward VI., in the year 1548, and is descendible to heirs general:

[311]   " That upon the death of Phillip James, the sixth Lord Wharton,

in 1731, without issue, the said Barony fell into abeyance between his two sisters and coheirs, Lady Jane Coke and Lady Lucy Morrice:

"That Lady Lucy Morrice died without issue in the year 1739: that upon the death of Lady Jane Coke (who survived her sister,) without issue, in 1761, the said Barony fell into abeyance between the descendants of the three daughters of Phillip, fourth Lord Wharton, Elizabeth, Mary, and Philadelphia Wharton:

"That the petitioner Charles Kemeys Kemeys Tynte is one of the coheirs of the said Barony, as being descended from, and sole heir of, Mary, one of the said daughters of Phillip, fourth Lord Wharton:

"That the petitioner Alexander Dundas Ross Cochrane Wishart Baillie, with Mrs. Matilda Aufrere, are two other of the coheirs of the said Barony, as being descended from Philadelphia, the youngest daughter of Phillip, the fourth Lord Wharton:

"That the Right Honourable Peter Robert, Lord Willoughby D'Eresby, and the Most Noble George Horatio, Marquess of Cholmondeley, are two other of the coheirs of the said Barony, as being descended from Elizabeth, only daughter of the said Phillip, fourth Lord Wharton, by his first marriage:

"And consequently, the said Barony is now in abeyance between the said petitioner Charles Kemeys Kemeys Tynte, the said petitioner, Alexander Dundas Ross Cochrane Wishart Baillie, Esq., Mrs. Matilda Aufrere, the Right Honourable Peter Robert, Lord Willoughby D'Eresby, and the Most Noble George Horatio, Marquess of Cholmondeley."

These resolutions were reported to the House, and being affirmed, were afterwards reported to her Majesty.

MARGARET FISHER v. WILLIAM DIXON (1).

(12 Clark & Finnelly, 312—332; S. C. 9 Jur. 883.)

1845.
June 3, 6, 12,
26.

Lord
BROUGHAM.
Lord
CAMPBELL.
Lord
COTTENHAM.

[312]

The absolute owner of land, for the purpose of better using that land, erected upon and affixed to the freehold certain machinery:

Held, that in the absence of any disposition by him of this machinery, it would go to the heir as part of the real estate.

If the *corpus* of such machinery belongs to the heir, all that belongs to

(1) Judicially cited in *Longbottom* v. *Berry* (1869) L. R. 5 Q. B. 123, 136, 39 L. J. Q. B. 37; *Climie* v. *Wood* (1869) L. R. 4 Ex. 328, 38 L. J. Ex. 223; *Ex parte Astbury* (1869) L. R. 4 Ch. 630, 38 L. J. Bk. 9; and see *Bain* v. *Brand* (1876) 1 App. Cas. 762.—J. G. P.

  that machinery, although more or less capable of being detached from it, and more or less capable of being used in a detached state, must also be considered as belonging to the heir.

No distinction arises in the application of this rule, from the circumstance that the land did not descend to, but was purchased by the owner.

THIS was an appeal against a decree of the Court of Session, arising out of the following circumstances:

The late John Dixon was an extensive coal and iron mine owner, and was at the time of his death engaged in working mines, some of which were his freehold property, having been purchased by himself, while of the rest he was tenant under leases for various terms. A very valuable portion of his property consisted of engines employed in the business he carried on. By his will and codicils he made a provision for his daughter of a sum of 4,000l. which he vested in trustees, and directed to be applied to her sole benefit, independently of any control or right of her husband. Upon his death she declined the provision made for her in her father's will, and claim *legitim*, or child's portion, in his property. To enforce this claim she instituted a suit in the Court of Session (in which her husband joined for conformity's sake) against her brothers, who were the executors under her father's will, and the general disponees of his property. The respondent, one of those

*brothers, had become, by the death of the other, sole heir-at-law to his father. In this suit she alleged that the share of her father's personal property, to which she was entitled as *legitim*, amounted to 12,000l. The respondent in his defence declared his readiness to account for the personal or executry effects of his late father, in order that the appellant's share therein might be ascertained, but insisted that these executry effects did not include either the heritage left by the deceased, or such machinery or other articles as were *fundo annexa*. The appellant put in pleas in law, insisting that—

" The trade or employment of manufacturing iron or lime, and of digging coals to be used in these manufactories, or for sale, or, in other words, the trade of a coal-master, or iron-master, or lime-worker, is of a personal nature, and all instruments, engines, and utensils, whether fixed or loose, which are necessary and subservient to such a trade, are legally to be held and treated as personal or moveable effects or personalty; that instruments, engines, and utensils, which, taken either in part or in gross, are moveable before they are placed in a particular spot, do not lose their moveable or personal character, though affixed to an heritable subject, unless they be so affixed *perpetui usus gratia*, in contradistinction to trade, such as the windows of a mansion-house; and that the fund out of which *legitim* is payable, consists of the whole moveable or personal estate, as before described, that belonged to the deceased Mr. Dixon."

The LORD ORDINARY, before whom the cause was appointed to be heard, referred it to an officer of the Court, with instructions for him to report as to the nature and amount of the deceased's property. The referee reported that the engines, colliery utensils, and rails, were claimed by the defenders as heritable property, but that he considered it doubtful whether some of these articles came *under that description, and he therefore made a list of those which he deemed to be of a doubtful or disputable nature. The LORD ORDINARY not being satisfied with this report, remitted the cause to Mr. Smith, of Deanston, as a scientific person, to report exactly on the facts as to each part of the machinery, the nature of which was in dispute. Mr. Smith made his report, in the course of which he described all the machinery as capable of being moved and replaced, but said that the removal would be very expensive; that it would more or less deteriorate the value of the machinery; that for that reason machinery was often left by the tenant, and its value made a matter of arrangement between him and the landlord; and that some parts—such as the steam-engine for pumping the mines—must, if removed, be instantly replaced, or very serious damage would arise to the mines; that the articles which were moveable were all of them, more or less, essential to the going of the different works, though, if taken away, they could be readily supplied; that it was usual to have spare articles of most of the classes described about well regulated works, these articles being equally valuable if taken to any other work where they were wanted. He also referred to the practice of the country, and said, "that the practice at coal and iron works similar to those of the deceased, is to remove the mechanism of the engine and other machinery from one part of the premises to another as occasion may require." . . . "The practice is for the tenant at the termination of his lease to remove the whole of such engines and machinery, if not previously belonging to the landlord." . . . "And in the event of the exhaustion of the mineral field, or any permanent bar arising to the profitable working of the minerals, the whole of the engines and machinery is removed by the tenant or worker of the field, or by the proprietor (if his property), and the

[*314]

general premises dismantled *as far as it may be profitable to do so." Mr. Smith made out a list of the various articles, to which he attached the character of heritable or of moveable.

The case was further debated before the Lord Ordinary, and the appellant then put in accounts, made up from time to time, by the testator, to show the state of his affairs; and likewise inventories of purchases by himself, or by himself in conjunction with others, in all of which papers the lands and the leases of them were described as "heritable," and the steam-engines and the rails laid down were described as "moveable property." It was also submitted, on behalf of the appellant, as a proposition of law, that the principle that annexation to land converts that which is itself moveable into a fixture, could not be applied to articles used in trade and to the fittings up of collieries.

The respondent, in answer to the argument, attempted thus to be drawn from the manner in which the testator had in his accounts treated the steam-engines and rails, proved that in those same accounts houses were likewise included under his arrangement of "moveable property," from which he insisted that the deceased's mode of expressing himself in these papers was no indication of his deliberate intention, and could have no effect upon the case.

The LORD ORDINARY, thinking the point raised in the case to be one of difficulty, referred it to the Lords of the Second Division, and their Lordships determined to consult the Lords of the First Division, and the permanent Lords Ordinary. Cases were therefore prepared for their opinions, and the great majority of their Lordships finally expressed an opinion to the effect, that the machinery which was fixed to the soil, and could not be used without being so fixed, and which were necessarily so fixed for the purpose of the profitable use of the land, were heritable; but that the tools employed in the machinery, but not necessarily affixed thereto, and capable of being employed elsewhere in the same manner, and

parts of *machinery prepared for fixing, but not actually affixed, were moveable (1).

Mr. Turner and *Mr. Sandford* for the appellant:

This is not a case between heir and executor, and must not be dealt with on the same principle as a case of that sort. Both the parties here are equally in the situation of heirs, and must be so treated. The same principles which favour the rights of the heir in

(1) 5 Bell, M., D. & Y., p. 775.

his claim of the land, favour also the other children in their claim   FISHER
of *legitim*.   Or if there is any difference to be made in the principle   *v.*
on which the relative rights of these parties are to be considered,   DIXON.
that difference must be in favour of the appellant, for the respondent here is the executor of the deceased, and in that character is
contesting this suit; and in the law of Scotland an executor is a
mere volunteer claiming under the will.

(LORD CAMPBELL : The claimant of *legitim* cannot be in a better
situation than the creditors; on the contrary, if they are in
opposition to him, his claim must give way to theirs.)

It is submitted that, in such a case, his claim would be better than
theirs, because of the contract made by the law for the benefit of
the children upon the marriage of the parents.   The right to *legitim*
is a principle of law which exists in favour of children who might
otherwise be left without any provision.

Then comes the question, whether these machines are, upon the
application of the principles of construction already stated, to be
considered heritable or moveable property belonging to the deceased.
It is submitted, that the machines used by the deceased to work the
mines were machines used by him in the course of his trade, and
must, therefore, fall within the principle of law which, in favour of
trade, treats such articles as personal property.   This argument is
rendered the stronger from two important circumstances—first, that
the deceased did not inherit these lands, but came into the possession of them by purchase ; *and next, that a considerable portion of   [*317]
them consists of leaseholds.   [They cited *Lawton* v. *Lawton*(1),
Lord Dudley v. *Lord Ward* (2), *Lawton* v. *Salmon* (3), *Grymes* v.
Boweren (4), *Elwes* v. *Maw* (5), and *Trappes* v. *Harter* (6).]

  The *Lord Advocate* and *Mr. Kelly* for the respondents :   [318]

This is a case between the heir and the executor, and the rules
of law, which in such a contest favour the heir rather than the
executor, must be applied here.   The real dispute is, whether these
machines are affixed to the freehold and are therefore part of the
real estate, or whether they are part of the moveable or personal
estate, or, as it is called in Scotland, part of the executry.   The

(1) 3 Atk. 13.   (4) 31 R. R. 460 (6 Bing. 437).
(2) Amb. 113.   (5) 6 R. R. 523 (3 East, 38—53).
(3) 2 R. R. 764 (1 H. Bl. 259, n.).   (6) 2 Cr. & M. 153 ; 2 Tyr. 603.

FISHER
v.
DIXON.

[*319]

respondent is the heir of the testator, and as such is entitled by law to succeed to the testator's real estate; and the fact that *he is also the executor of the testator, does not take away from him his character of heir.   The appellant claims a share in the personalty. and is endeavouring to set in motion the power of the executor against the heir.   The rules applicable to cases of contests between heir and executor are therefore applicable here, and the appellant cannot claim any benefit from any character she may suppose herself to possess as heir of a particular kind.

If the argument of the intention of the testator, as giving a character to the machinery, is to be relied on, then it is submitted that that argument is altogether favourable to the respondent.   The mere use of words wrongly used by the testator in his own accounts, cannot be taken as decisive of his intention ; for he employed similar words with respect to property which was clearly real or heritable property, and to which no act nor expression of his could by possibility give a different character.   But if his words are not of importance, his acts are.   He was the absolute owner of much of the land on which these machines were erected.   He could not, therefore, as to those lands, have any interest adverse to the owner of the land ; and on the lands thus belonging to him he erected machines, which he affixed to the soil, and gave a permanent character which the law has not permitted to be doubtful.   He did the same upon those lands of which he was only tenant, and his acts, therefore, con-tradict the supposition that he meant to preserve to these machines the character of moveables.   They have become, by the law of Scotland, parts of the land *accessione* and *destinatione* (1) ; for they have been fixed on the land, and destined to purposes to which they could not be destined unless they were fixed in the

[*320]

soil, and which purposes are in fact those of gaining a *profit from the land.   The fact that it is possible to remove them cannot affect the matter.   [They discussed the cases cited above and *Buckland* v. *Butterfield* (2).]

[321]

The cases in which the convenience of trade is to be the principle on which the question of fixture or moveable is to be decided, are those where the erections are not made for the benefit of the better enjoyment of the land, but for the purposes of trade, where such erections are put up by persons having only a transitory interest in the land, and where they are claimed by the creditors of those

(1) Ersk., Bk. 2, tit. 2, ss. 2, 3, 14;   (2) 22 R. R. 649 (2 Brod. & B. 54).
Bell's Principles, ss. 743, 1470, 1475.

persons. In such a case the rule to encourage trade applies, and the erection, though in fact affixed to the soil, having been affixed there for a particular purpose, may be removed, and the owner of the soil will be, after the removal of the erections, in the same situation as before they were put up. No one of these circumstances exists in the present case. The erections were made by the owner of the soil for the purpose of obtaining a profit from the soil; the claimant is not a creditor, but a child *for whom he has made in his will what he deemed an ample provision, and the person who resists the claim is his heir and the universal disponee of his property.

[*322]

The English authorities, which are much more numerous than the Scotch, are clear upon this point. But the principles of the Scotch law are decisive, and the few authorities to be found applicable to a case like the present, show the ordinary course of the law in Scotland upon this subject. * * *

Mr. Turner, in reply. * * *

LORD BROUGHAM:

June 26.

[*323]

This case was gone very fully into at the Bar on both sides, and, on account of the length of the case, as well as the importance of the subject-matter involved in point of value, and also in respect of some of the principles which were mooted, and some, indeed, which were disputed in point of law, your Lordships considered that it was fit that time should be taken for considering the case before finally pronouncing judgment. That consideration has been given to it, and I am now prepared to move the judgment which it appears to me, under the circumstances of this case, it is right to pronounce. I begin by laying out of view entirely what was very much relied upon, as it appeared to me, below, and much relied upon in the argument here, for the appellant, viz., a distinction taken between this case as a case of inheritance, and a case arising between executor and heir. In this case of *legitim*, as I understood them to argue, it is not a mere question between executor and heir, but it is a question between two kinds of heirs. Now that is a sort of argument I must say, with all respect for those who urge the distinction upon our attention, than which nothing can be more groundless. It is not a question *between two kinds of heirs. In what way can you distinguish this case from the common case between heir and executor, as the argument endeavours to distinguish it? The executor is heir *in mobilibus*. That is the common expression of

[*324]

the Scotch law. The *legitim* here is due to those who are not
heirs as to real property. It is that which is due out of what is
called in Scotland the executry fund; that is to say, that which
goes not to the heir, but which goes to the executor. It is, then,
in his capacity of heir *in mobilibus* that the *legitim* goes to the
child, that the bairn's part of gear goes to the bairn, because the
bairn is heir *in mobilibus;* and, therefore, I cannot discover how
the argument gains at all by insisting on this supposed distinction.
I do not say that it loses, for it neither gains nor loses by the distinction; it is left precisely in the same state in which it was before
the distinction was attempted to be set up. It is because the fund
is executry and not heritable that the *legitim* attaches. After payment of the debts the surplus fund is divided into those parts of
heritable and executry according to the Scotch law, which was
originally, indeed, the old Saxon law of England, and is now the
law of Scotland. That being the case—having relieved it from
the embarrassment of this argument—I have not much to urge
upon this case, because, upon the fullest consideration which I
have been able to give, both to the English law authorities which
were cited, and to the Scotch authorities by which it was sought
on the one side to turn aside, and on the other side to enforce
the application of the English law cases, I entirely agree with
the Court below, and I should have arrived at the self-same
conclusion as that at which the great majority of their Lordships have arrived, had I been one of the Judges in the Court
below. There is no doubt a most respectable minority of their
Lordships on the other side, including the LORD PRESIDENT, and

[*325]   the learned chief of the other Court, and Lord MONCREIFF *(to whose
authority no person is disposed, generally speaking, to yield more
entire and implicit respect than myself), whose most able and
elaborate judgment thoroughly exhausts the whole case, not only
upon principles but upon its details. But I must say that my
mind goes not with his Lordship's judgment, but with the equally
elaborate and equally able judgment of Lord COCKBURN, who also
goes into the principles and into the details of the case. I think
Lord COCKBURN has really left me little or nothing to add; and I
am bound to say that, in my view, he and the other Judges joined
with him have come to a right and sound conclusion.

Great reliance was of course placed upon the case before Lord
Hardwicke, in our Court of Chancery here, and a similar case
which occurred more recently in the Court of Exchequer, I think

in Lord Lyndhurst's time (1). But there was an attempt made to distinguish this case in principle from that, and to show that there was another inconsistent decision in *The Cider-mill* case. Now it is a remarkable circumstance, that of that case we have only a very indistinct and unsatisfactory report. We have really nothing that can be called a record of that case. It was cited in the case before Lord Hardwicke; and I must also say, that, if *The Cider-mill* case is to be taken as it is represented to us, as regards the substance of the case, and in its result, my mind goes not at all with that decision. It is contrary, undeniably, to the general principles of our law upon the subject; and if the same question were to arise to-morrow, with the circumstances which are represented to have attended that case, it would not, in my opinion, lead to the same result. Therefore I lay it out of view. We have a most imperfect account of the circumstances, and, above all, of the most material circumstances, of how the mill was affixed to the soil. For if a cider-mill be fixed to the soil, though it is a manufactory, and erected for the purpose of a manufactory, if it is really *solo infixum*, it is perfectly immaterial whether it is for the purpose of a manufactory, or a granary, or a barn, or anything else. It is a fixture on the soil, and it becomes part of the soil. Can any man say that one of the great brewhouses would belong to the executor because it is erected for the purpose of manufacture, and wholly unconnected with the land? For a brewhouse is as much unconnected with any crops upon the land upon which it is situated as a cider-mill can be said to be; it is for the purpose of brewing beer out of malt which need not have been raised on that land, but may have been grown in Russia or in Africa. It has nothing to do with the land, as may be seen by those who will take the trouble of looking at any of the brewhouses in London, which are established in places where it would be very difficult to find a blade of grass, much less a crop of barley of which to make malt. But although it is a manufactory, nobody says it belongs to the executor, nor constitutes what the Scotch generally call an executry fund, it would go unquestionably to the heir. The Scotch law appears to me only to differ from the English law in carrying the principles of our law, as laid down in the cases, a little farther rather than falling short of them. Upon the whole, therefore, I agree with Lord COCKBURN. I do not differ from his arguments any more than I do from the conclusions to which they lead.

[*326]

(1) 2 Cr. & M. 153; 3 Tyr. 603.

FISHER
v.
DIXON.

Then I come to the applications of these principles in detail; and I must say, in the outset, of the very little that I have to add as to that detail, that I should be most unwilling to come to any conclusion which should lead to upsetting or altering in any particular this elaborate judgment, thoroughly considered below, upon the ground of my differing in opinion as to the application of this clear principle to any of the details of this machinery. There are, however, one or two articles which I do not quite think have been consistently or rightly disposed of by the Court below. I do

[*327]

not deny that; but I have carefully looked to see *whether I could put my finger upon any part which has been wrongly disposed of, in favour of the respondent and against the appellant, in the Court below. If I had found that, I might have been somewhat obstructed in coming to the conclusion at which I have arrived. But my objection is to some of those articles being given to the appellant, not to the respondent; and, if there had been a cross appeal, I should have found some difficulty in resisting the argument, that there ought to have been a reversal or alteration in respect of some of those particulars. There are one or two that, in looking over, I made a query against; they are, however, of the most trivial nature, and upon them I should never advise your Lordships to reverse or alter the judgment below in any respect. Upon these grounds, therefore, I really have no hesitation whatever—as little as I ever had in any case—in recommending your Lordships to affirm the judgment of the Court below in all its parts.

LORD COTTENHAM:

I concur in the opinion that this interlocutor ought to be affirmed; and, when we separate and distinguish the real case from some of the points which have been endeavoured to be introduced into it by way of argument, it does appear to me to be free from all doubt. The point which has been already alluded to—namely, that this is not a case between the real and personal representative, but that it is a case between two kinds of heirs—appears to me to be totally destitute of foundation. *Legitim* can only be claimed by means of showing it to be personal estate. The preliminary question is therefore, is this personal estate, or is it property attachable to the freehold, and therefore descendible to the heir? The moment we see that the *legitim* can only be claimed in consequence of the property being part of the personal estate, the question of course assumes its natural shape, is it personal estate or not? That

preliminary question, therefore, being decided, it entirely disposes
*of the ground on which this has been attempted to be distinguished
from the other cases which have arisen with respect to the claims
of heirs, and those who are interested in the personalty.   The
principal stress of the argument on the side of the appellant has
been, that this is to be protected, because it is necessary for the
encouragement of trade, that this property should be considered as
not belonging to the real estate, but as belonging to the personal
estate.   The principle upon which a departure has been made from
the old rule of law in favour of trade, appears to me to have no
application to the present case.   The individual who erected the
machinery was the owner of the land and of the personal property,
which he erected and employed in carrying on the works ; he
might have done what he liked with it ; he might have disposed of
the land; he might have disposed of the machinery; he might have
separated them again.   It was, therefore, not at all necessary, in
order to encourage him to erect those new works which are supposed
to be beneficial to the public, that any rule of that kind should be
established, because he was master of his own land.   It was quite
unnecessary, therefore, to seek to establish any such rule in favour
of trade as applicable here, the whole being entirely under the
control of the person who erected this machinery.

If therefore this be clearly a question of real or personal estate,
and if the rule, which in some cases has been acted upon, of
making a departure from the established principle in favour of
trade, has no application to the present case, what does it come
to? Of course we throw out of consideration all the cases which
have arisen between landlord and tenant, and between tenant for
life and remainder-man, because the departure which has taken
place there, in some cases, has no application to the present case.
Then the case being simply this, the absolute owner of the land,
for the purpose of better using that land, having erected upon and
affixed to the freehold, and used, for the purpose of *the beneficial
enjoyment of the real property, certain machinery, the question is,
is there any authority for saying, that, under these circumstances,
the personal representative has a right to step in and lay bare the
land, and to take away all the machinery necessary for the enjoyment of the land ?   Let us consider for a moment, if that is the
principle, to what extent is it to go.   It is put by Lord Cockburn
(and a very strong illustration it is), if the owner of the land should
dig a well, and erect machinery for the purpose of using that well,

FISHER
v.
DIXON.

is it competent to the personal representative to come and take away that machinery, and leave the well useless? He thinks it is not. Where is the distinction between the two cases? Such machinery is capable of being taken away with very little, if any, damage to the land. Although, therefore, machinery is in its nature, generally, personal property, yet, with regard to machinery, or a manufactory erected upon the freehold for the enjoyment of the freehold, nobody can suppose that that can be the rule of law; and so with respect to other erections upon land. It is not necessary to go beyond the present case, which is a case of machinery erected for the better enjoyment of the land itself. The principle probably would go a great deal farther; but it is more advisable to confine the observations I have to make to the particular circumstances of this case. There is no case whatever which has been cited in which that doctrine has been recognized except the one which has been referred to (*The Cider-mill* case), as to which we really know nothing, except that at the Worcester Assizes, a good many years ago, a cider-mill was held to belong to the personal estate. Why it was so held, under what circumstances, and whether it was a cider-mill fixed to the freehold or not, we do not know. We know nothing except that this machine, called a cider-mill, was decided to go to the personal representative. It is impossible to extract a rule of law from a case of which we know so little as that.

[*330] And, with that *exception, there is a uniform course of decisions, wherever the matter has been discussed, in favour of the right of the heir to the machinery erected, under the circumstances, in the present case; and if the *corpus* of the machinery is to be held to belong to the heir, it is hardly necessary to say, that we must hold that all that belongs to that machinery, although more or less capable of being used in a detached state from it; still, if it belongs to the machinery, and belongs to the *corpus*, the article, whatever it may be, must necessarily follow the same principle, and remain attached to the freehold. I do not go into the detail of the particular items which have been objected to. I have looked them through, and quite concur with my noble and learned friend, that if any exception were to be taken with respect to particular articles, as to whether they ought to be adjudged to one or to the other, it would have been for the respondent, and not for the appellant, to take such exception.

LORD CAMPBELL:

I have very little to add to what has been said by my noble and learned friends who have preceded me, except that I entirely concur in the view which they have taken of this case. I own I was a good deal surprised that the point was so much pressed at the Bar, that this was a case of *legitim*, and that it was not the whole question of what descends to the heir, and what goes to the executor. We all know that *legitim* is a portion of the personal property, and you must first ascertain what is the personal property before the claim to *legitim* can arise. There can be no doubt, therefore, that it is in fact the whole question, whether the property in dispute goes to the heir or the executor. I have no doubt in the world that it should go to the heir, both upon reason and upon precedent. As my noble and learned friend who has just spoken has stated, none of the arguments respecting the benefit of trade at all apply to a question as between heir and executor, in a case like this *where the owner of the fee being the absolute owner of the land, and of the machinery erected upon it, the whole of it is in him, and he may dispose of it as he shall think fit for the benefit of the family.

FISHER
v.
DIXON.

[*331]

Then with reference to the authorities by which we are bound ; whatever speculative notions we might entertain with respect to propriety and expediency, if we entertain a different opinion upon that subject, all the cases are quite uniform both in England and in Scotland to show that such property shall go to the heir. The only case the other way which has been referred to is that of *The Cider-mill*, where the essential circumstance is left entirely in doubt, whether, in fact, the mill was fixed to the freehold or not. We know that a cider-mill is not necessarily affixed to the freehold, a familiar instance of which is given in " The Vicar of Wakefield," where, when a match was proposed between one of the Misses Primrose and young Farmer Flamstead, Moses said " I hope that, if my sister marries young Farmer Flamstead, he will lend us his cider-mill." I take it that the cider-mill there was moveable, and was not affixed to the freehold, but might have been carried from the farm of Farmer Flamstead to the vicarage of the Primroses. Now, this possibility was felt to be so strong on the part of the learned and able counsel who argued for the appellant, that they were almost driven to admit, that in this case, if the freehold had belonged by hereditary descent to Mr. Dixon, the machinery would have gone to his heir ; but they said the land was purchased by him for the purposes of trade, and therefore, this introduced a new distinction. This was assuming that, if a great proprietor, such as Lord Londonderry, in the county of Durham, were to erect

FISHER
v.
DIXON.

[*332]

machinery in his coal works, that would go to the heir, and not to
the executor; but that if a person bought a piece of land for the
purpose of a colliery, and erected machinery upon it, his having
bought it would make a distinction as to the character of the
machinery. There *is not the slightest authority for any such
distinction, and it would be most mischievous if we were at all to
sanction the introduction of any such distinction. It would lead
to great mischief and infinite litigation. There are cases where, as
between partners, when land is used as part of the partnership
stock, it is considered as personalty; but in those cases the land
itself, the very soil, is by previous agreement declared to be part
of the personalty, as well as any machinery erected upon it. The
arguments that were urged in this case by the appellants would
lead to the conclusion that all the land that was purchased in fee
simple by Mr. Dixon, and belonged to him as long as grass shall
grow and water run, must all be personalty just as much as the
machinery erected upon the land. I have no doubt at all that the
principle of the decision was perfectly correct. A distinction was
attempted to be made between leasehold and freehold; but when
we bear in mind, that, by the law of Scotland, leasehold is realty,
and that it goes to the heir, that distinction entirely fails. I am of
opinion, therefore, that the interlocutor must be affirmed. I am
very glad, and I think it is creditable to the respondent, that he
did not, for any minute pot-lid or miserable chattel, bring a cross
appeal, because that would only have involved the case in fresh
difficulty, and caused unnecessary expense. I therefore entirely
agree in the motion that this interlocutor should be affirmed.

LORD BROUGHAM:

I omitted to consider the matter last mentioned from pure
inadvertence, viz., as to the leasehold, and also what my noble
and learned friend near me adverted to, as to the rule being
departed from for the benefit of trade, to which he has given a
complete answer. It does not apply to this case in the slightest
degree. The argument before Lord Hardwicke was of a totally
different description. I only mention this to show that there
is no difference of opinion between us here. I omitted it from
inadvertence.

The interlocutor was

Affirmed, with costs.

RICARDO v. GARCIAS.

(12 Clark & Finnelly, 368—401.)

[A NOTE of this appeal will be found in 65 R. R. at p. 585, at the end of the report of the case before SHADWELL, V.-C. (14 Simons, 265), whose decision on a point of pleading was here reversed.]

1844.
Nov. 5.

[368]

THE CORPORATION OF NEWCASTLE-UPON-TYNE v. THE ATTORNEY-GENERAL AND OTHERS.

(12 Clark & Finnelly, 402—424; on app. from 5 Beav. 307; 6 Jur. 789.)

The Act 39 Eliz. c. 5, enables "all and every person and persons" to found hospitals for the poor, and to incorporate them:

A municipal corporation is included in the words "every person and persons," and may exercise the powers given by the Act.

A voluntary conveyance of real estates to a charity is not defeated by a subsequent conveyance of them for valuable consideration.

Real estates conveyed to, and vested in, an hospital founded under the Act 39 Eliz. c. 5, cannot be alienated by the hospital, nor can it confirm an alienation of them by the founders.

A municipal corporation voluntarily founded an hospital under the Act 39 Eliz. c. 5, and purchased real estates, and caused them to be conveyed to the hospital, but which were kept under the control and management of the founders, who afterwards sold and conveyed them for valuable consideration, granting to the purchasers covenants for title and indemnity against the claims of the hospital. The founders applied the money produced by the sale, together with other monies of their own, in the purchase of an estate at W., and they paid annually to the hospital more than the rents and profits of the sold estates. The hospital at first concurred in that arrangement, and acquiesced in it for 120 years; after which the *Attorney-General* and the hospital, by information and bill, claimed a part of the estate at W., bearing the same proportion to the whole estate that the produce of the sale of the hospital's estates bore to the whole purchase money of the estate at W.:

Held, 1st, that the estates conveyed to the hospital were well vested in it, and could not be sold without an Act of Parliament, and therefore a decree directing the hospital to confirm the sale, was in that respect erroneous.

2nd. That if the hospital's concurrence and long acquiescence in the arrangement for the sale of its estates were held to bar its right to recover them, or a commensurate portion of the estate *of W., the *Attorney-General's* right to protect the charity still existed.

3rd. *Semble*, that though the hospital's bill should be dismissed, the *Attorney-General's* information would be retained.

1842.
July.

Rolls Court.
Lord
LANGDALE,
M.R.

On Appeal.
1845.
June 16, 17.
July 7, 8.
Aug. 1.

Lord
LYNDHURST,
L.C.
Lord
CAMPBELL.
Lord
COTTENHAM.

[402]

[*403]

PREVIOUSLY to the year 1682, the corporation of the town of Newcastle-upon-Tyne—then, and down to the passing of the Act 5 & 6 Will. IV. c. 76, styled "The Mayor and Burgesses of the town of Newcastle-upon-Tyne," consisting entirely of freemen, and governed by a Common Council, composed of a Mayor, Aldermen, Sheriff, and Common Councilmen—erected an hospital in a place called " the Mannors," in the said town for their poor freemen and their families. In January, 1682, the said common council ordered that 900l. be paid out of the town revenues for the purchase of certain lands, to be settled for the use of the hospital. And for founding and establishing the hospital, the mayor and burgesses, in pursuance of the Act 39 Eliz. c. 5 (1), (made perpetual

(1) By the first section—after reciting that by the 35 Eliz. c. 7, s. 27, it was made lawful for every person during the twenty years then next following, by feoffment, will in writing, or other assurance, to give and bequeath in fee simple, as well to the use of the poor as for maintenance of any house of correction or abiding houses, all or any part of his lands, tenements, or hereditaments, but that the said law had not taken effect by reason that no person could incorporate any hospital, house of correction, or abiding places, but her Majesty, or by her licence—it was enacted "That all and every person and persons seised in fee simple, their heirs, executors, or assigns, shall have full power, &c., at any time during the space of twenty years next ensuing, by deed enrolled in the High Court of Chancery, to erect, found, and establish one or more hospitals, Maisons de Dieu, abiding places, or houses of correction, at his or their will and pleasure, as well for the finding, sustentation, and relief of the maimed, poor, needy, or impotent people, as to set the poor to work, to have continuance for ever, and from time to time to place therein such head and members, and such number of poor as to [*404, n.] him, his *heirs and assigns, shall seem [*405, n.] convenient; and that the same hospitals or houses so founded shall be incorporated and have perpetual successions for ever, in fact, deed, and name, and of such head, members, and numbers of poor, &c., as shall be appointed, &c., by the founder or founders, his or their heirs, executors, or assigns, by any such deed enrolled :

And that such hospital, &c., and the persons therein placed, shall be incorporated, named and called by such name as the said founder or founders, his heirs, executors, or assigns shall so limit, assign, and appoint : And the same hospital, &c., so incorporated and named, shall be a body corporate and politic, and shall by that name of incorporation have full power, &c., to purchase, take, hold and enjoy, and have to them and to their successors for ever, as well goods and chattels as manors, lands, &c., being freehold, of any person or persons whatsoever ; so that they exceed not the value of 200l. above all charges and expenses, to any such abiding house, &c. : And that the same hospital, &c., and the persons so being incorporated, &c., shall have full power, &c., by the true name of incorporation, to sue and be sued, &c. ; and shall have and enjoy for ever such a common seal or seals as by the said founder or founders, his or their heirs, executors, or assigns shall be in writing under his or their hand and seal assigned, &c. ; and further shall be ordered, directed, and visited, placed, or upon just cause, displaced, by such person or persons, bodies politic or corporate, their heirs, successors, or assigns as should be nominated or assigned by the founder or founders thereof, their heirs or *assigns, according to such rules, &c., as shall be set forth, &c., by the said founder or founders, their heirs or assigns, &c."

Section 3. " Provided also, that this Act, and any thing there contained shall not extend to enable any person or persons being within age, women covert without their husbands, or of

by *21 James I. c. 1), executed a deed under their common seal, bearing date the 26th of March, 1683, and enrolled, and thereby appointed forty persons, then inmates of the hospital, to be a body corporate by the name of "The Master, Brethren, and Sisters of the Hospital of the Holy Jesus, founded in the Mannors, in the town and county of Newcastle-upon-Tyne, at the costs and charges of the mayor and burgesses of the town of Newcastle-upon-Tyne," with a common seal, and with full power to sue and be sued as a corporation ; and to purchase, take, and hold to them and their successors for ever, as well goods and chattels as lands and tenements, being freehold. And *it was by the deed provided that the said mayor, aldermen, and Common Council, for the time being, should be visitors of the hospital, and should make rules for the government thereof. By the rules, which were made soon afterwards, certain sums were to be paid annually out of the town revenues to " the master, brethren, and sisters," until lands could be purchased, which together with the lands before purchased would make up 180l. a-year for the discharge of the said annual payments.

For the purpose of endowing the hospital, and providing for its maintenance, the mayor and burgesses of Newcastle-upon-Tyne purchased divers lands and tenements, and caused the same to be conveyed to its use. Accordingly by an indenture of bargain and sale, dated the 27th of March, 1683, and duly enrolled, Sir Ralph Carr, in consideration of 710l. paid to him by the mayor and burgesses out of the town revenues, granted and conveyed, by their direction, certain premises therein described, situated in Newcastle, to "the master, brethren, and sisters of the said hospital, and their successors for ever." And by two *other indentures, dated respectively the 6th of November, 1683, and the 24th of September, 1685, two freehold estates called Etherley and Whittle, in consideration

[*405]

[*406]

---

non sanæ memoriæ, to make any such corporation, or to endow the same."

Section 4. " Provided always, that no such hospital, *maison*, &c., be erected, founded, &c., unless upon the foundation or erection thereof the same be endowed for ever with lands, tenements, or hereditaments of the clear yearly value of 10l., &c."

Section 5. " Provided also, and be it enacted, that no such incorporation to be founded by force of this Act shall

do or suffer to be done any act or thing whereby any of the lands, &c., of such incorporation shall be vested or transferred in or to any other whatsoever, contrary to the true meaning of this Act; and that such construction shall be made on this Act as shall be most beneficial and available for the maintenance of the poor, and for repressing all devises contrary to the true meaning of this Act."

of 1,610l. for the former, and 1,800l. for the latter, paid to the
vendors by the mayor and burgesses out of the said town revenues,
were by their direction and appointment conveyed to the said
master, brethren, &c., and their successors for ever. The coal
mines under these two estates, with the liberty of working them,
were excepted out of the conveyances, and reserved to the vendors;
but they afterwards became the property of the said mayor and
burgesses.   These estates, thus conveyed to the hospital, were
afterwards managed, and from time to time demised (in name of
the hospital), by the mayor and burgesses, who received the rents
and profits, and carried them, as appeared by their books, to the
general town fund, out of which all necessary payments were made
for the support of the hospital.

In the year 1714, the mayor and burgesses of Newcastle contracted for the purchase of an estate situate on the banks of the
Tyne, and called the estate of Walker, for 12,220l.; and the same
was in January, 1715, conveyed to Messrs. White and Ramsay,
their heirs and assigns, as trustees for the said mayor and burgesses,
who for the purpose of raising the said sum, entered into contracts
to sell several estates, including those of Etherley and Whittle.
The Etherley estate, which for some years yielded rents of 60l. for
the lands and 80l. for the mines, was sold to one Johnson for
2,200l.; and the Whittle estate, which yielded rents of 70l. for the
lands and 10l. for the mines, was sold to one Clutterbuck for 1,615l.
The hospitallers were not parties to these contracts; but in order
to compensate them, there was an arrangement entered into between
them and the mayor and burgesses, that an application should be
made by them jointly to Parliament for an Act to empower " the

[*407]

*master, brethren," &c., to sell the estates, and for establishing for
their use a rent-charge of 185l. a-year on part of the Walker estate,
worth 275l. a-year. Application was made to Parliament accordingly
in 1716, and repeated in 1717, in the names of both parties, for a
bill to effect these objects, but no bill was passed. Subsequent
applications were made to Parliament for the same purposes by the
mayor and burgesses alone, but without success. The mayor and
burgesses, nevertheless, conveyed the Etherley and Whittle estates,
in December, 1720, to the respective purchasers, with various
covenants for title and indemnity as against " the master, brethren,"
&c., of the hospital; and they received the purchase-monies, making
altogether 3,815l., and applied the same with other funds in part
payment of the consideration for the Walker estate; for holding

which they obtained a pardon and licence from the Crown in 1723; and in the year following an order of Common Council was made, charging that estate with a yearly payment of 185*l.* to the hospital, in lieu of the Etherley and Whittle estates, until an Act of Parliament should be obtained for the purposes before mentioned. No such Act was ever obtained. Certain yearly sums as hereinafter mentioned were paid to the hospital; and matters continued in that state down to the year 1835, when by the Act 5 & 6 Will. IV. c. 76, a change was made in the name, constitution, and government of the corporation of Newcastle-upon-Tyne.

In 1836 the respondents filed their information and bill against the appellants and their town clerk, whereby, after stating at great length the several matters before mentioned, and charging, among other things, that the said mayor and burgesses, from the year 1683 to 1769, paid the said master, brethren, &c., 162*l.* a-year; and from 1769 to 1807, 242*l.* a-year, and afterwards 322*l.* a-year, and 422*l.* until the year 1825, when the mayor and burgesses increased the hospitallers to the number *of forty-two, and increased the annual payment to 548*l.*, all which payments were made out of the Walker estate, the rents whereof had increased to 3,000*l.* a-year, and, therefore, the said payments to the hospitallers were less than they were entitled to. The information and bill prayed, among other things, that the appellants might be declared trustees in equity for the respondents, " the master, brethren," &c., of the hospital, of such a proportion, in yearly value of the said estate at Walker, as the said sum of 3,815*l.*, produced by the sale of the estates at Etherley and Whittle and applied towards the purchase of the estate at Walker aforesaid, bears to the said sum of 12,220*l.*, the purchase-money for the estate at Walker; and that the appellants might be decreed to convey such proportion as aforesaid of the last mentioned estate to the said respondents and their successors for ever; and to pay to them a like proportion of the rents and profits of the said estate, received by the appellants, since 1835, or that such other right and interest of and in the estate at Walker, as the Court might think proper, be decreed to the said respondents; and that accounts might be taken of the said rents and profits; and that the appellants might be decreed to deliver up to the said respondents the messuage and premises, the property conveyed by Sir R. Carr, and account for and pay to them a proper occupation rent for the same since 1835.

[*408]

THE COR-
PORATION OF
NEWCASTLE
v.
A.-G.

[410]

The appellants, by their answer, [raised various defences chiefly of a technical character (see argument, *post*)].

The cause was heard by the MASTER OF THE ROLLS in July, 1842, when his Lordship decreed (1) that the respondents, the master, brethren, &c., of the hospital, were entitled to such proportion of the Walker estate, as the produce of the sales of the Etherley and Whittle estates (8,815*l*.) contributed to the purchase of the Walker estate, the said sum of 8,815*l*. being subject to reduction, to the extent of any monies which the appellants could show to have been applied in the purchase of leasehold interests, subsisting in the Etherley and Whittle estates, at the time they were sold, and it was referred to the Master to inquire what monies, if any, were so applied; and it was declared that, upon a conveyance being made to the hospital of such proportion of the Walker estate as should be ascertained to belong to it, the appellants would be entitled to have the conveyances of the Etherley and Whittle estates confirmed by the hospital; and it was referred to the Master to take various consequential accounts, and also to inquire and state the particulars of the messuage and premises, conveyed by Sir R. Carr, by the indenture of the 27th March, 1683, and if he should find that the appellants were in possession of them, or in receipt of the rents and profits, it was declared that they ought to be charged a fair occupation rent from 1835, and they were to pay the respondents their costs.

The appeal was brought against that decree.

[411]

Mr. Kindersley and *Mr. Koe* (with whom was *Mr. Bates*), for the appellants:

1. * * The scope and terms of the Act [39 Eliz. c. 5] clearly show, that the power to found a corporation was given only to individuals. * * *

[412]

If this objection to the title of the hospital as a corporation prevail with the House, there is an end of the cause; for the bill in which the hospital sues as a body corporate must be dismissed, and the information filed by the *Attorney-General*, without a relator, seeking to enforce the rights of the plaintiffs as a body corporate, must be dismissed with the bill.

[413]

(LORD COTTENHAM: Strict rules of pleading are not applied to cases upon charities. Suppose the plaintiffs are not a body

(1) 5 Beav. 307.

corporate, and have no title to sue as such, is there any authority for saying that, if their bill is dismissed, the information of the Attorney-General must also be dismissed ?)

THE COR-
PORATION OF
NEWCASTLE
v.
A.-G.

It appears too plain to require authority. If a private person file a bill claiming something he has no title to, and the Attorney-General joins in an information to assist and enforce the same claim, the information must have the same fate as the bill.

(LORD COTTENHAM : The Attorney-General here sues in a distinct right. He would have a right to file an information to preserve the charity property, if the argument that there is no corporation is right; but the question now is, whether his information fails because the plaintiffs fail.)

The Attorney-General and the plaintiffs seek to enforce the title of the hospital to the property in question; he does not controvert their right, but asserts it; he seeks nothing but what his co-plaintiffs seek; he might, of course, file a new information after the present suit is dismissed.

2. In the event of the House coming to the conclusion that the hospital was duly incorporated, there is another objection to its constitution; it was not duly endowed. * * The endowment on the 27th, and incorporation on the 26th, would not be simultaneous. * * *

[414]

3. * * But suppose the two objections fail, and that the hospital was duly incorporated and endowed, the next objection to the respondents' claim is that the conveyances *to them of the Etherley and Whittle estates by the deeds of November, 1683, and September, 1685, were purely voluntary, and are therefore void under the statute of Elizabeth (1), as against the subsequent conveyances to Clutterbuck and Johnson, purchasers for valuable consideration.

[*415]

(THE LORD CHANCELLOR: Does that doctrine apply to charities founded under an Act of Parliament, the very object of which was to found charities, and to encourage the conveyance of lands to charities so founded ?) (2)

* * * * *

4. * * The decree holds that these estates were well vested in

(1) 27 Eliz. c. 4.

(2) See now Ramsay v. Gilchrist [1892] A. C. 412.

the hospital corporation, and it, in effect, affirms the right of the
hospital to alienate them, contrary to the clear and positive prohibition in the 5th section of the Act—" provided that no corporation to be founded by force of this Act shall do or suffer to be done
any act or thing whereby any of the lands, &c., of such corporation
shall be vested or transferred in or to any other whatsoever."

*   *   *   *   *

[417] 5. * * The hospital's equity for compensation for their sold
estates, was as good in 1716 as it is now.   They always received
from the corporation of Newcastle much more than the rents and
profits of the Etherley and Whittle estates.   The payments made
to them annually, increased from 180*l.* to 200*l.*, then to 400*l.*, and
latterly to 600*l.* ; whereas the rents of the two estates never exceeded
400*l.*, and do not exceed that sum now.

[*418] It is also to be remembered that the Walker estate is *vested in
the corporation of Newcastle, upon trusts, and that that corporation
having purchased the estate, and taken a license to hold it for certain
purposes, cannot apply any part of it to other and different purposes,
as the decree contemplates.

        Mr. Turner and *Mr. Purvis* (with whom was *Mr. Blunt*) for
the respondents :

[419] * * The words " person and persons " in the statute 39 Eliz.,
are applicable to corporations as well as to individuals.   That was
Lord Coke's opinion (1), and there is no contrary decision or *dictum.*

(THE LORD CHANCELLOR : That commentary of Lord Coke, which
may be said to be a contemporaneous exposition of the Act, has
never been questioned; it has been accepted all over the country
since his time, and no doubt numerous charitable corporations
depend on it.   The Act itself enumerates the classes who are excepted
as incapable of creating corporations; and it also declares, that
" such construction is to be put on the Act as shall be beneficial and
available for the maintenance of the poor " (2).   I do not think this
House would feel justified in putting a construction on the Act,
inconsistent with that commentary of Lord Coke.

LORD COTTENHAM : I concur in that view, that we are not likely
to overturn Lord Coke's opinion on this subject ; but that does not
relieve the respondents from not having made a case to support their

        (1) 2 Inst. 772.   (2) *Vide ante*, p. 113, note.

decree. The case stated in their bill proceeds on a supposed agree-   THE COR-
ment with the corporation of Newcastle in 1716, to obtain the sanction   PORATION OF
of Parliament to the sale of their estates.)   NEWCASTLE
                                                                         v.
                                                                         A.-G.

The respondents' counsel were continuing their argument, that the
hospital was legally founded and endowed.

(LORD CAMPBELL: All the Lords are clearly of opinion that you   [420]
may start from this point, that the hospital was well constituted.

THE LORD CHANCELLOR: I think we have heard all the arguments
that can be adduced on the other side as to that point. . Mr. Kindersley
argued upon the construction of the Act, upon its different clauses,
and that where a corporation was mentioned, the words adapted to
a corporation were used throughout the Act, but where founder or
founders were mentioned, words not applicable to a corporation were
used. The result of that argument amounts to nothing more than
this, that the words of the statute were brought in aid of what was
considered as the obvious meaning and object of the Act. I do not
think it is necessary for you to trouble yourself as to that part of
the case. And as to the other objection, that there was no good
endowment of the hospital, I think that argument failed in point of
evidence of the date and enrolment of the deed of March, 1688;
unless the appellants can vary the facts, they cannot establish that
objection. Then as to the point made, that the deed was voluntary;
from the very nature of the transaction it was meant to be voluntary
—it was an endowment of a charity, and an endowment for charitable objects imports, of necessity, want of pecuniary consideration;
you need not argue that point either. We have now relieved you
from a great deal. I also think you need not trouble yourself about
that part of the decree directing an inquiry as to the property purchased of Sir R. Carr. If the hospital was duly constituted, it is
admitted that that inquiry must be made.) ·

The respondents' counsel then proceeded to sustain that part of
the decree, which, in effect, affirmed the sales of the Etherley and
Whittle estates, notwithstanding the prohibition of the statute
against alienating any of the charity lands. After stating the facts,
they submitted that the corporation, in assuming the management
of the property, *became trustees or agents for the hospital, and   [*421]
sold it as such trustees. The owners, or cestui que trusts, have an
option to follow the estates, or the money produced by the sales of
them, and vested in the purchase of another estate.   *   *   *

THE COR-
PORATION OF
NEWCASTLE
v.
A.-G.
[423]
[*424]

Mr. Kindersley replied.

The LORD CHANCELLOR, in the course of the reply, suggested that it would be desirable to put an end to this *litigation, if it could be done amicably.   The corporation of Newcastle founded and endowed the hospital, and always contributed most handsomely to its support —to the amount of 500*l.* or 600*l.* a-year latterly.

Mr. Purvis:

The counsel for the hospital had all the circumstances under their consideration before the appeal was brought on, and it was their opinion that the appellants did not propose a sufficient sum.

THE LORD CHANCELLOR:

Would you accept 800*l.* a-year, to be properly settled and secured to the hospital, by way of rent-charge on the Walker estate, with the sanction of the *Attorney-General?*   The sanction of Parliament also will probably be required.

After some discussion between the Lords and the counsel for both parties, the case was ordered to stand over for judgment, on the understanding that, if the parties could agree on the terms of an arrangement, to be confirmed by Act of Parliament, the House would not be called on to give any judgment.

The appellants and respondents, some days afterwards, presented a petition to the House, stating the terms of an arrangement to which they had come by advice of their counsel, and praying that the cause might be adjourned, so as to afford time to obtain an Act of Parliament to complete the same.

———————•———————

1845.

[425]

SKINNERS' COMPANY *v.* IRISH SOCIETY.
(12 Clark & Finnelly, 425—490.)

[FOR the judgment in this case, affirming the decision of Lord LANGDALE, M. R., see the end of the report of the hearing at the Rolls Court, in 64 R. R., at p. 175.]

DARLEY *v.* THE QUEEN (1).

(12 Clark & Finnelly, 520—545.)

A proceeding by information in the nature of *quo warranto* will lie for usurping any office, whether created by charter of the Crown alone, or by the Crown with the consent of Parliament, provided the office be of a public nature and a substantive office, and not merely the function or employment of a deputy or servant held at the will and pleasure of others.

The office of treasurer of the public money of the county of the city of Dublin is an office for which an information in the nature of a *quo warranto* will lie.

1845.
May 2—7.
July 1.

1846.
May 19.

Lord
LYNDHURST,
L.C.

TINDAL,
Ch. J.

Lord
BROUGHAM

[520]

THIS was a writ of error on a judgment in the Exchequer Chamber in Ireland, affirming a judgment of the Queen's Bench there in the case of an information in the nature of a *quo warranto* filed against the holder of the office of treasurer of the county of the city of Dublin.

This office having become vacant by the death of the late treasurer, a meeting was held on the 2nd of April, 1836, for the purpose of electing a new treasurer. The plaintiff in error and William Smyth, Esq., were the only candidates. The Act 49 Geo. III. c. 20, directs that the election shall be made by the board of magistrates of the county of the city of Dublin. The magistrates of the county, prior to the enactment of the statute of 48 Geo. III. c. 140, consisted solely of the aldermen of the city of Dublin. By that Act it was directed that certain police magistrates should be appointed for the county of the city of Dublin; and it was provided, that they should be deemed and held to be justices of the peace to all intents whatsoever. *The police magistrates had not, however, claimed to vote at a prior election of a treasurer, and the Lord Mayor who held the meeting for this election, did not convene or summon any magistrates save the aldermen. Five out of the eight police magistrates, however, attended the meeting, without being summoned, and claimed a right to vote at the election, and they respectively tendered their votes for the plaintiff in error. The Lord Mayor refused to receive their votes, and Mr. Smyth having a majority of the votes of the aldermen, was declared by the Lord Mayor to be duly elected, and immediately entered into the required recognizances. The plaintiff in error, conceiving himself aggrieved by the Lord Mayor's decision as to the right of the police magistrates to vote, applied for, and obtained an information in the nature of a *quo warranto* to be

[*521]

---

(1) Followed in *Reg.* v. *Guardians of St. Martin's-in-the-Fields* (1851) 17 Q. B. 149, 20 L. J. Q. B. 4; *Reg.* v. *Burrows* [1892] 1 Q. B. 399; 61 L. J. Q. B. 88.—J. G. P.

DARLEY
r.
REG.

exhibited on behalf of the Queen, and at the relation of the plaintiff in error, in the Court of Queen's Bench of Ireland, on the 7th of May, 1836, and on the 26th of November, 1888, that Court, being of opinion that the votes of the police magistrates had been improperly refused by the Lord Mayor, pronounced judgment of ouster against Mr. Smyth (1). On the 31st of January following, the plaintiff in error applied to the Court for a rule to show cause why a writ of *mandamus* should not issue to the Lord Mayor of Dublin, to command him to convene the board of magistrates, as directed by the 49 Geo. III. c. 20, and declare the plaintiff in error treasurer (2). The Lord Mayor showed cause against the writ, and set forth the proceedings which had taken place at the meeting held on the 2nd of April, 1886, and, in addition to another point (not now necessary to be adverted to), showed, as cause against the conditional *mandamus*, the meeting of that day had not been duly convened, for that the three police magistrates who were absent from the said meeting, were then living, and notwithstanding, *had not been summoned or convened, but he neglected to add that they were within summons. In consequence of this neglect, the COURT, considering the other reason insufficient, held the return bad, and issued a peremptory *mandamus* to the Lord Mayor, directing him to convene the board of magistrates, and thereat to declare the plaintiff in error treasurer of the public money of the city of Dublin, and to accept his recognizances; but the COURT in awarding the peremptory *mandamus* expressly declared that it did not thereby mean to conclude the rights of Mr. Smyth (who had been, as before mentioned, ousted), in case he should be advised to make an application for a *quo warranto* against the plaintiff in error (3). A meeting of the board of magistrates was accordingly convened and met upon the 22nd day of June, 1839, and the plaintiff in error was then and there declared treasurer, and afterwards entered into the required securities.

[*522]

On the 16th November following, *Mr. Kinahan*, the relator in the present information, obtained a rule for leave to file an information in the nature of a *quo warranto* against the plaintiff in error. On the 28th day of January, 1840, the plaintiff in error showed cause against the rule, and the COURT, after a lengthened argument on behalf of the plaintiff in error, made the rule absolute (4); and on the 27th of May in that year the present information was filed by the defendant in error.

(1) 1 Jebb & Syme, 164.   (3) 1 Jebb & Syme, 164.
(2) *Ibid.*, p. 468.   (4) 2 Jebb & Syme, 239.

To this information the plaintiff in error pleaded seven pleas. The five first pleas alleged matters to which it is not necessary to advert as the judgment of the House proceeded entirely on the question raised by the sixth plea. That plea alleged in effect that the office of treasurer of public money of the county of the city of Dublin is not an office for usurpation of which the said *information in the nature of a *quo warranto* ought to have been brought or could be sustained. To the sixth and seventh pleas the defendant in error demurred.

DABLEY
v.
REG.

[*523]

Previously to the 33 Geo. II., treasurers of the public money in Ireland appear to have been elected or appointed by the justices of the peace of the respective counties and counties of cities, and such authority to elect and the mode of election were derived from usage, and not from any legislative provision. A statute was passed in the last-mentioned year (33 Geo. II. c. 13), which, after reciting "that doubts had arisen concerning the manner of appointment of treasurers of counties," provided that whenever a vacancy should happen by death, misbehaviour, or resignation of a county treasurer, the justices of the county in which such vacancy should occur, should appoint a proper person to be treasurer, and that the person so appointed should enter into a recognizance for 1,000*l.*, and procure two sufficient sureties, who should bind themselves in 500*l.* each for his good conduct in the office, and his justly accounting for all public monies received by him." The provisions of this statute were varied by the Act 13 & 14 Geo. III. c. 18, which confined the right of voting on the election of treasurers to justices of the peace having a freehold estate of 100*l.* a year, and directed that seven justices so qualified should be present at every election. The latter Act also provided that if any treasurer should be convicted either by indictment or presentment of any of the several frauds, neglects, or offences particularly specified in the Act, he should be fined and dismissed from his office, and be rendered incapable of being again appointed treasurer for any county in Ireland. It also raised the amount in which the treasurer and his two sureties were to be bound from 1,000*l.* to 10,000*l.* for the treasurer, and from 500*l.* to 5,000*l.* for each surety, and further provided that the Court of Queen's Bench in Dublin, and the *Judges of assize in the other counties should, if so required by the grand jury of any county in Ireland, examine the treasurer of that county as to the continued solvency of his sureties, and if the treasurer should refuse to be examined, or upon being so required, fail or neglect to procure other sureties,

[*524]

DARLEY
v.
REG.

or another surety, the Judge who required him to answer or to
procure the other sureties or surety, should dismiss him from his
office of treasurer.

The last-mentioned Act was the legislative provision in force for
the appointment of county treasurers in Ireland, and the regulation
of the office, when the herein-after mentioned statute of 49 Geo. III.
c. xx. was passed for "the better regulation of the mode of election
and office of treasurer of the public money of the county of the city
of Dublin."

The corporation of the city of Dublin is a corporation by prescription, and the only justices of the peace for that city or for the
county of the city of Dublin, until the Act of 48 Geo. III. c. 140,
was passed (which provided for the appointment of magistrates of
police), were members of the corporation. A charter of the 1 Geo. II.
had provided that all the aldermen who had been Lord Mayors of
the city should be justices of the peace for the county of the city,
and the Act 33 Geo. II. c. 16, s. 18, added to the number of
magistrates by providing that all the aldermen and the sheriffs
of the city should be justices of the peace for the county of
the city.

The treasurer of the public money appears at all times to have
been elected by the justices of the county of the city, and consequently solely by the aldermen, or aldermen and sheriffs, and
his recognizance and the bonds executed by his sureties were
passed to the Lord Mayor; and that officer also presided at the
election of the treasurer. The duties to be performed by the
treasurer were solely within the district over which the jurisdic-
[*525]   tion of *the corporation extended, and the treasurer appears to have
been in every respect identified with the corporation, and to have
derived his authority solely from that body.

The first statute which expressly refers to the election of the
treasurer of the public money of the county of the city of Dublin
is the 13 & 14 Geo. III. c. 84, which provides, that if the grand jury
of the county of the city of Dublin and the Court of King's Bench
shall not approve of the security given by the treasurer at Quarter
Sessions, or if no security shall have been there given, the treasurer
shall, at the Term for the city following his election, bind himself
by recognizance in the sum of 10,000l., and procure two sureties,
to be approved of by the grand jury and Court of King's Bench,
who shall bind themselves jointly and severally in the same sum,
the condition of such recognizances being that the treasurer shall

well and truly execute his office of treasurer of the public money,   DARLEY
and truly account for all sums which shall come to his hands: and   *v.*
the Act further provides, that, in case the treasurer shall neglect to   REG.
give the recognizances, or procure the sureties, he shall, by such
neglect or omission, vacate his office; and that the justices of the
peace for the said county, at the next Quarter Sessions, shall proceed
to the election of a new treasurer.   The Act of the 26 Geo. III. c. 14,
s. 67, reduced the amount in which the treasurer and his sureties
were respectively to bind themselves from 10,000*l.* to 2,000*l.*   The
subsequent statute of 38 Geo. III. c. 56, contains various provisions
in relation to the duties of the treasurer, and particularly directs,
by the fourth section, that he shall applot and assess on the several
parishes in the said city and the county thereof, such public money
as shall, from time to time, be presented, to be raised by the grand
juries, and insert in warrants the said applotment and assessment,
and the uses for which the sums of money are respectively raised;
and the Lord Mayor is required and directed to sign the said
warrants, and cause *the same to be delivered to the church-   [*526]
wardens of the several parishes of the said city "as has been
from time immemorial accustomed;" but the Act contains no
provision for the election, appointment, or dismission of the
treasurer.

The last-mentioned Act was followed by the statute 49 Geo. III.
c. xx., which is the regulating statute as to the appointment and
office of treasurer of the public money of the county of the city
of Dublin.

This Act (sect. 2) recited that doubts had arisen whether the
treasurer should not be elected in the manner prescribed by the
hereinbefore mentioned Act of the 13 & 14 Geo. III. c. 18, and
number of justices of the peace for the said county, and of the
several persons who had served as Lord Mayor, being usually
persons in trade, it could scarcely happen that a sufficient
number of persons, qualified as directed by that Act, confirmed
the election theretofore made by the magistrates of the said city
of the then treasurer.

The third section thus provides for the election of the treasurer:
"Whenever the treasurership of the city of Dublin shall be vacant
by the death, resignation, removal, or dismission of the present or
any future treasurer, the Lord Mayor of the said city, for the time
being, shall, within twenty-one days after such vacancy, convene the
board of magistrates of the county of the said city of Dublin, to

DARLEY
v.
REG.

meet at the Sessions Court in the said city, between the hours of twelve in the forenoon and two in the afternoon, and then and there, by the majority of votes of such magistrates as shall be present (notwithstanding any want of qualification mentioned in the said recited Act, made in the thirteenth and fourteenth years of the reign of his present Majesty), shall proceed to elect a fit and sufficient person to be treasurer of the said city of Dublin, and at such meeting, the said Lord Mayor, or, in his absence, the senior

[*527]

magistrate present shall preside as *chairman, and shall take the votes of the other magistrates, and shall not himself give his vote, except in the case of equality of voices." It then declared that the treasurer should enter into his own recognizance for 5,000l., and procure two sureties, who should severally bind themselves in half that sum, the condition of such recognizance being, that the treasurer should duly account in the manner provided in the Act, and duly and faithfully discharge the duties of his said office. It provided that unless the sureties should make the affidavit as to solvency required by the Act, the election should be void, and a subsequent one be had. Power was given to the Judges of the Court of King's Bench, in case the Court should be required by the grand jury of the county, or otherwise, on sufficient cause, to examine the treasurer or any other person or persons as to the continued solvency of the sureties, and generally as to any act relative to the said office; and if the said Court apprehended that either or both the sureties was or were dead, or insufficient, and the treasurer did not procure some other surety or sureties in the place of the one or both objected to by the Court, or if the Court should otherwise see sufficient cause, it was directed and required to dismiss the treasurer from his office. The Act subsequently fixed the amount of salary of the treasurer, and provided for his making oath before one of the Judges of the Court of King's Bench, at each Term, as to the amount of public money received by him, and made certain provisions for the collection of public monies, and the application of certain sums for particular purposes.

There were several questions argued before the Court of Queen's Bench, and afterwards, on error, before the Court of Exchequer Chamber, and all of them were raised for discussion on the writ of error brought to this House. The case was twice argued before this House, but the first argument was not completely heard, as the

[*528]

Lords *intimated a wish that the case should be argued in the presence of the Judges. Their Lordships, at the same time, desired ɪat the arguments should be confined to the question whether the ffice of treasurer of the public money for the county of the city of ʰublin was an office for which an information in the nature of a *uₒ warranto* would lie.

The Judges who attended the hearing of the case were Lord ʰief Justice Tindal; Justices Patteson, Williams, Coleridge, ᴄoltman, Maule, Wightman, and Cresswell; and Barons Parke, ᴀlderson, and Platt.

Mr. Serjt. Manning and *Mr. J. Henderson* for the plaintiff in error :

The question is, whether the office of treasurer of the county of ᴛhe city of Dublin is such an office as that an information in the ɴature of *quo warranto* will lie for it? If not, the judgment of the Court below must be reversed.

The office of treasurer of the city of Dublin is not a corporate office, nor is it an office invested with a public trust or with the exercise of any Royal authority, and if so, no *quo warranto* will lie. * * The true rule as to cases in which this proceeding is maintainable, is laid down by Lord KENYON in *Rex* v. *Shepherd* (1), where it was said, " this was not a usurpation on the rights or prerogatives of the Crown, for which only the old writ of *quo warranto* lay; and an information in the nature of a *quo warranto* could only be granted in such cases." The office is not one which is invested with any public trust or authority.

[529]

(LORD BROUGHAM: But is the rule as to offices in respect of which an information in the nature of a *quo warranto* will lie, so confined? Do not offices relating to the administration of justice, to the exercise of any rights of the Crown, or of any corporation authority, or those of making returns in the cases of elections of members of Parliament, likewise come within the class of cases subject to these informations?)

They may do so, but this office does not fall within any one of those descriptions. * * The peculiar purpose of the process is to vindicate the rights of the Crown. The relator here does not show that he is entitled to this process.

[530]

(LORD BROUGHAM: In the case of the trustees of Whitehaven Harbour, *Rex* v. *Nicholson* (2), those persons were held liable to

(1) 2 R. R. 416 (4 T. R. 381).   (2) Str. 299.

DARLEY
v.
REG.

a *quo warranto*, because their office related to the exercise of a public trust. That case is in accordance with the doctrine as laid down in Comyns (1).)

[*531]

* * The general principle here contended for on behalf of the plaintiff in error is, that an information in the nature *of a *quo warranto* will not lie, except for some franchise usurped upon the Crown, or for the usurpation of some franchise which can only lawfully be enjoyed by grant from the Crown. * * *

Mr. Napier and *Mr. Fleming* for the defendant in error:

This is an important public office; and if a *quo warranto* will not lie, then the party who is unjustly excluded from the office would be without a remedy. That itself is a strong reason in favour of allowing the information. * * *

[532]

(LORD BROUGHAM: But may not the party complaining in a case of this kind bring an action for intrusion?)

He may if the other has been elected to the office, but that will not advance him in his own claim to the office. In every respect this is an office of public trust and emolument, and it is in its nature permanent. It therefore comes within the description of those offices in which, for the protection of the interests of the public, the Court of Queen's Bench will interfere by way of information.

There is a great distinction between a writ of *quo warranto*, and an information in the nature of a *quo warranto*. The latter was not for the protection of the franchises of the Crown, for they were protected by the prerogative information which could at any time be filed by the *Attorney-General* in virtue of his office; but they were allowed for the purpose of protecting the interests of the public. * * If it can be truly alleged that an office is an office which concerns the public interest, and involves the discharge of a public trust and of public duties, the minute nature of those duties can only raise the question whether the circumstances are sufficient to justify the issuing of an information in the nature of a *quo warranto* against any one who usurps the office, but the right to issue the information cannot be doubted: *Wilkes* v. *Rex* (2), *Rex* v. *The Duke of Bedford* (3), *Rex* v. *Boyles* (4).

[533]

(1) Dig. tit. Quo Warranto.
(2) Wilmot's Notes, 326.
(3) 1 Barnardiston, 282, cited in *Rex* v. *Attwood*, 38 R. R. 290 (4 B. &
Ad. 494).
(4) 2 Ld. Ray. 1559; Str. 836; Fitzg. 82.

(LORD BROUGHAM : But in each of those cases, the parties applying to the Court for leave to file the information show the office to be one which concerns the administration of public justice.)

The minute nature of the duties of a public office may raise the question of the propriety of the Court granting leave to file such an information in the particular case; but there can be no doubt that the Court has the power to grant it. In *Rex* v. *Beedle* (1), it was granted in the case of Commissioners for paving under a local Act. There the Commissioners were elected by the inhabitants; and that case must be considered as having overruled *Rex* v. *Hanley* (2).

(LORD BROUGHAM : Yet *Rex* v. *Hanley* was quoted and relied on in *Rex* v. *Ramsden* (3), where it was held that, in a case of that kind, an information *would not lie.)

That case can hardly be treated as a positive decision. It cannot be supported on principle. In *Rex* v. *Francis* (4), it was said that an information in the nature of a *quo warranto* was a proceeding of a civil nature, and therefore the Court granted a rule for a new trial in it.

In all the cases in which the application has been refused, it has been so solely upon the ground that, in the discretion of the Court, its interference in that particular case was not necessary. * * The *Anonymous* case in Barnardiston (5) is to that effect. And it is always refused where a party is the servant of another. ,

(LORD CAMPBELL : Because he has not an estate in his office.)

Here the treasurer is not the servant of any body, and he cannot, like the county treasurer, be dismissed by the justices. He is amenable only to the Court of Queen's Bench. * * *

Mr. Serjt. Manning, in reply. * * *

[The following cases were cited in argument: *R.* v. *Justices of Hereford* (6), *R.* v. *Hulston* (7), *R.* v. *Aston Union* (8), *R.* v. *Neal* (9), *R.* v. *Highmore* (10), *R.* v. *Howell* (11), *R.* v. *Cann* (12), *R.* v. *Corporation*

(1) 42 R. R. 437 (3 Ad. & El. 467).	(7) Str. 621.
(2) 42 R. R. 434 (3 Ad. & El. 463, n.).	(8) 6 Ad. & El. 784.
(3) 42 R. R. 431 (3 Ad. & El. 456).	(9) Cas. temp. Hard. 106.
(4) 2 T. R. 484.	(10) 5 B. & Ald. 771.
(5) 1 Barnardiston, 279.	(11) Cas. temp. Hard. 248.
(6) 22 R. R. 830 (1 Chit. 700).	(12) 2 T. R. 484.

DARLEY
v.
REG.

of Bedford Level (1), R. v. The Mayor and Aldermen of Hertford (2), R. v. The Mayor of Colchester (3), and R. v. Bingham (4).]

[536]   LORD BROUGHAM :

We all feel that there have been conflicting decisions on this subject. The case in Lord Raymond (5) is not clear at all; for though the Court talks of its "concerning the public government and the administration of public justice," yet that general mode of putting the matter would let in most cases now excluded by the rigorous principles held applicable to a *quo warranto*. Then, again, the case before Lord Hardwicke (6) is certainly not reconcileable with the cases of *Rex* v. *Ramsden* (7), and *Rex* v. *The Aston Union* (8).

The LORD CHANCELLOR framed a question for the Judges, which their Lordships requested time to consider.

1846.
May 19.
———

LORD CHIEF JUSTICE TINDAL :

My Lords, in this case your Lordships have put the following question to her Majesty's Judges, viz.: "An information, in the nature of a *quo warranto*, having been granted for usurping the office of treasurer of the public money of the county of *the city of Dublin, and a judgment having been awarded by the Court thereon, is such judgment, regard being had to the nature of the office, erroneous?" And, in answer to this question, I beg to state that it is the opinion of all the Judges who heard the argument at your Lordships' Bar, that such judgment is not erroneous.

[*537]

The mode of proceeding by information, in the nature of *quo warranto*, came, no doubt, in the place of the ancient writ of *quo warranto*. This writ was brought for property of, or franchises derived from, the Crown. The earliest is to be found in the 9 Richard [I.] (Abbreviatio Placitorum, p. 21), and is against the incumbent of a church, calling on him to show *quo warranto* he holds the church. Then follow many others, in the time of John, Henry II., and Edward I., for lands, for view of frankpledge, for return of writs, holding of pleas, free warren, plein-age and prisage (Abbreviatio Brevium, p. 210; 14 Edw. I.), emendation of assize of

---

(1) 6 East, 356.
(2) 1 Salk. 374; 1 Ld. Ray. 426.
(3) 1 R. R. 480 (2 T. R. 259).
(4) 2 East, 308.
(5) *Rex* v. *Boyles*, 1 Ld. Ray. 1559;

Str. 836; Fitzgib. 82.
(6) *Rex* v. *Neal*, Cas. temp. Hard. 106.
(7) 42 R. R. 431 (3 Ad. & El. 456).
(8) 6 Ad. & El. 784.

bread and beer, pillory, and tumbril, and gallows. Some of these are offices, or in the nature of offices, as in the instances of returns of writs and holding of Courts.

The practice of filing informations of this sort by the *Attorney-General*, in lieu of these writs, is very ancient; and in Coke's Entries are many precedents of such informations against persons for usurping the same sorts of franchises, as claiming to be a corporation, to have waifs, strays, holding a court leet, court baron, pillory and tumbril, markets, prison, or for usurping a public office, as conservator of the Thames, and coal and corn meter.

It is only in more modern times that informations have been exhibited by the King's coroner and attorney. The first reported case is that of *Rex* v. *Mayor of Hertford* (1), in 10 Will. III. And it is a mistake to suppose that these informations were founded on the statute of 9 Anne, *Rex* v. *Gregory* (2), and *Rex* v. *Williams* (3), where the right to file an information at common law, by the coroner and attorney, against a person for holding a criminal court of record, was recognized.

After the statute of 4 & 5 W. & M., which restrained the filings of informations by the coroner and attorney, the sanction of the Court was required, and after that statute and the 9 Anne, it exercised a discretion to grant or refuse them to private prosecutors, according to the nature of the case.

It has uniformly done so in cases under the statute 9 Anne, c. 20, *Rex* v. *Stacey* (4), and *Rex* v. *Trevenen* (5), by virtue of the words requiring the leave of the Court. In the case of the bailiff of a court leet, the Court granted leave to file an information expressing, however, a doubt whether the office was of sufficient importance; and in that of a petty constable (6), where the right to elect was in dispute between the inhabitants and the lord of the manor, the COURT refused it, saying—"no doubt the King has a right to call any one to account by his writ of *quo warranto* for exercising any public office, be it ever so small; yet we do not use to grant informations in the nature of *quo warranto* for such inferior offices."

Since the Courts have exercised a discretion under the statute of William & Mary, and the statute of Anne, the cases in which

[*588]

(1) 1 Ld. Ray. 426.
(2) 2 R. R. 371, n. (4 T. R. 240, n.).
(3) 1 Burr. 402.
(4) 3 T. R. 2.

(5) 21 R. R. 364 (2 B. & Ald. 479).
(6) *Anonymous*, 1 Barnardiston, K. B. 279.

DARLEY
v.
REG.

there has been a refusal to allow an information to be filed are not necessarily authorities against the validity of an information when filed, because in the cases of refusal the Courts may have proceeded on the ground that the circumstances were not such as to call for their interference.

[539]

On the other hand, those in which informations have been granted, are authorities in favour of their validity. That an information of this nature will lie for offices granted by charter, is a matter beyond dispute; and the authorities are numerous that the same remedy is available against intruders into offices of a public nature, which are supposed to be immediately or mediately derived from the Crown, and existing at common law, though of a very subordinate character : as bailiff of a court leet, *Rex* v. *Bingham* (1) ; or of a borough, *Rex* v. *Highmore* (2) ; a constable, *Rex* v. *Goudge* (3), *Rex* v. *Franchard* (4) ; the steward of a court leet, *Rex* v. *Hulston* (5) ; and registrar and clerk of a court of requests, *Rex* v. *Hall* (6). The cases of overseers, in which the Court has refused the liberty to proceed in this way, may be possibly explained, on the ground that it did not think fit to interfere with respect to officers whose functions were merely temporary ; so also as to churchwardens, *Rex* v. *Dawbeny* (7) ; though Lord KENYON expresses his opinion as to the case of the latter, that for such an office an information in the nature of a *quo warranto* would not lie, for that it lay only where the old writ of *quo warranto* could have lain, and that would not lie except for a usurpation on the rights and prerogatives of the Crown : *Rex* v. *Shepherd* (8).

But supposing that this proceeding is applicable only where rights of the Crown, as in the instances of offices derived from the Crown, are concerned, it is not confined to such as are created by charter, or which may be presumed to have been originally so created. It has been held *to apply to offices constituted by Parliament; nor can any good reason be assigned why it should lie, where the Crown alone creates the office by its prerogative, and not lie where it creates it with the advice and consent of the Lords and Commons. Accordingly an information has been held to lie for a corporate office created, not by charter, but by Act of Parliament : *Rex* v. *The Duke of Bedford* and others (9);

[*540]

(1) 2 East, 308.

(2) 1 Dowl. & By. 438 ; 5 B. & Ald. 771.

(3) 2 Str. 1213.

(4) *Id.* 1149.

(5) 1 Str. 621.

(6) 25 R. R. 321 (1 B. & C. 123).

(7) 2 Str. 1196.

(8) 2 R. R. 416 (4 T. R. 381).

(9) 1 Barnard. K. B. 242.

so for the office of Commissioners for paving under a local Act, *Rex* v. *Badcock* (1); and for the office of trustees of a harbour, *Rex* v. *Nicholson* (2), though constituted by a private Act, their duties being public; and the COURT said, that informations have been constantly granted when any new jurisdiction or public trust is exercised without authority, and the argument that these informations were granted only where the Crown alone could have granted the franchise, was expressly overruled. The answer attempted to be given to the last mentioned case, when cited as an authority in the present, is, that this office concerned the franchise of a port; but this was not satisfactory, for the information was not for the franchise, but for the office, which was clearly created by Parliament, and the reference by the Court to the circumstances of this office concerning a port, is only to show it was a public office.

The more modern authorities are conflicting, informations having been granted and also refused for the usurpation of offices created by statute. They were granted against a person claiming to act as guardian of the poor in Exeter, under 28 Geo. III. c. 76, in Hilary Term, 1816, against Paving Commissioners of the city of Exeter, in the year 1834: *Rex* v. *Beedle* (3). In *1830, in the case of *Rex* v. *Hanley* (4), Lord TENTERDEN, and TAUNTON and PATTESON, Justices, were against granting an information against a trustee for paving and lighting under a private Act. Mr. Justice JAMES PARKE was in favour of it, and the matter was terminated without any judgment being delivered.

[*541]

An information was refused against a Commissioner of the poor, and for watching, under a local Act, by the opinion of TAUNTON and PATTESON, Justices, who held that the information would not lie, Lord DENMAN doubting: *Rex* v. *Ramsden* (5); and the same course was followed in *Re The Aston Union* (6), the Judges there holding themselves bound by the former decision to refuse a *quo warranto* to decide the question of the validity of an election of a guardian of the poor under 4 & 5 Will. IV. c. 76. Whether, in the former case or the latter, the Court decided on the ground that the office was not public in such a sense as to make it the subject of that proceeding, or that, being created by Act of Parliament, and not by charter, the remedy by information was

(1) 6 East, 359.
(2) Str. 299.
(3) 42 R. R. 437 (3 Ad. & El. 467, n.).

(4) 42 R. R. 434 (3 Ad. & El. 463, n.).
(5) 42 R. R. 431 (3 Ad. & El. 456).
(6) 6 Ad. & El. 785.

DARLEY
v.
REG.

improper, we are not told in the short report of the judgment in that case.

On whatever ground these two last cases were decided, we cannot consider them as authorities to establish the position that a *quo warranto* information will not lie for usurping an office created by Act of Parliament, when that office is clearly of a public nature. And after the consideration of all the cases and *dicta* on this subject, the result appears to be, that this proceeding by information in the nature of *quo warranto* will lie for usurping any office, whether created by charter alone, or by the Crown, with the consent of Parliament,

[*542] provided the office be of a *public nature, and a substantive office, not merely the function or employment of a deputy or servant held at the will and pleasure of others; for, with respect to such an employment, the Court certainly will not interfere, and the information will not properly lie. The case of the Registrar of the Bedford Level, *Rex v. Corporation of Bedford Level* (1), and that of a county treasurer, who is the mere servant of the justices in England, *Rex v. Justices of Herefordshire* (2), are instances of this latter sort.

There are then only two questions in respect to this office. Was it public? and was the treasurer a mere servant of the Dublin magistrates?

The functions of the treasurer were clearly of a public nature: he was to applot the assessment, receive and hold the money for a time, keep it subject to his order on the Bank, pay the expense of public prosecutions, and pay other public monies. It is clearly, therefore, of a public nature, and it is equally clear that, though appointed by the magistrate [*sic*], he is not removeable at their pleasure, and must, we think, be treated not as their servant, but as an independent officer.

If the Crown had established this office with precisely the same functions, the person filling it being removeable in the same way as an officer of a corporation created by charter, there could be no doubt that an information would lie, and the circumstance that the Crown has enacted that there should be such an office, with the consent of the two other branches of the Legislature, has been shown to make no difference.

We think for these reasons that the nature of the office held by the plaintiff in error was such for which an information in the nature of a *quo warranto* may be sustained, and that the judgment thereon is not erroneous.

(1) 5 East, 356.   (2) 22 R. R. 830 (1 Chit. 700).

The Lord Chancellor:

My Lords, I entirely agree in the opinion which has been expressed on the part of the learned Judges. Adverting to the provisions of the Act of Parliament, I am clearly of opinion that the office of treasurer of the county of the city of Dublin is a public office, the officer having important public duties to discharge ; and that the office is also of an independent character. It is clear, therefore, that if this office had been created by charter, an information in the nature of a *quo warranto* would have lain for its usurpation. But the matter of doubt and controversy has been, whether, when an office is created, not by charter but by Act of Parliament, an information of this kind can be sustained. There is a conflict of authority upon this subject. For my own part, I have long since come to the conclusion that, in this respect, there is no difference between the circumstance of an office being created by charter and being created by Act of Parliament. In both cases the assent of the Sovereign is necessary. Whether this is given by charter, or whether it is given by assent to an Act of Parliament passed by both branches of the Legislature, I think is altogether immaterial. Recurring, therefore, to the opinion expressed by the learned Judges in reply to your Lordship's question, I move your Lordships to affirm the judgment of the Court below.

Lord Brougham:

My Lords, this case was originally heard before me, when I presided in the absence of my noble and learned friend, and it appeared to be of such importance, and there appeared to be such a considerable conflict of authorities, that I, with the concurrence of my noble and learned friends who assisted me upon the occasion, recommended that it should be argued a second time by one counsel on a side in the presence of the learned Judges, and when my noble and learned friend on the woolsack could attend. It was accordingly so argued. A question *was put upon the motion of my noble and learned friend to the learned Judges. They have taken time to consider, and they have now given in their very learned and elaborate opinion, in which they all concur, including my excellent and learned friend who was a dissentient upon the subject, but who is satisfied, upon the view of the case now taken, that there is no ground for that opinion. The opinion of my learned friend in so dissenting, had mainly weighed with me in entertaining the doubts which I entertained.

There was also some conflict upon the cases. Those cases have
been examined. That you can, upon any view of the subject, or by
having recourse to the consideration of the cases altogether, reconcile them, is what I will not take upon me to affirm. I think it is
always much better when the Court is laying down a general rule
for the future upon a most important question, as this is, if there
is a conflict of cases, to admit at once that some cases are one way,
the majority of cases being the other way, and to say that the
balance of authority is on the side upon which you incline to give
your own opinion, rather than to attempt by refinement and
subtility to reconcile cases which in themselves really are in
conflict, and are not capable of being reconciled. It is the honestest,
it is the fairest, it is the most correct course in such cases. Judges,
like other men, may be fallible, and there may be better decisions
given recently after full consideration than were given at a former
period. It is better to admit that fairly and openly, and to say
that we join in giving the weight of our authority to the side to which
we think there is the balance of authorities in the Court below, than
to make unavailing and unsatisfactory attempts to reconcile them.

My Lords, I have one very material consideration, which inclines
my mind, independently of the balance of authority, being, as I
think with the learned CHIEF JUSTICE *it is, in favour of the judgment of the Court below—in favour of the defendant in error. I
mean, that if there is not this remedy, there really is no other. It
is necessary that there should be this remedy, or else a case like
the present would be remediless. It must be considered, however,
that this judgment is confined entirely to offices of a public nature,
and so far of a public nature that they must be of a substantive
nature, and that they are independent in their title. Within both
those descriptions the present office appears to come, and I do not
think it necessary now-a-days to show, that because a *quo warranto*
was formerly only held to lie where there was an usurpation of
franchise, or of a Royal franchise, or of a matter proceeding from
the prerogative of the Crown, therefore, an information in the
nature of a *quo warranto*, which, generally speaking, follows the
same rule, is to be confined within the same strict rules. I think
if you take the whole weight of the authorities, the balance is much
in favour of the extension, which this appears to be, beyond that
limit. I, therefore, agree with my noble and learned friend, that
your Lordships will do well to give judgment for the defendant in
error in this case.

[*545]

Mr. Fleming submitted that as this was an information at the elation of a private party, and as this appeal had been brought against the decision of the Court of Queen's Bench and Exchequer Chamber in Ireland, costs ought to be given to the defendant in error.

LORD BROUGHAM :

But there is a conflict of cases, and we have thought it necessary to have two arguments.

The judgment was affirmed, without costs.

DARLEY
v.
REG.

LORD DUNGANNON *v.* SMITH (1).

(12 Clark & Finnelly, 546—640 ; S. C. 10 Jur. 721.)

A testator being entitled to leasehold premises for terms of years, bequeathed them to trustees, on trust to permit his grandson, B., to take the profits thereof during his life, and after his decease to permit such person, who for the time being would take by descent as heir male of the body of the said B., his grandson, to take the profits thereof until some such person should attain the age of twenty-one years, and then to convey the same to such person so attaining that age, his executors, administrators, and assigns ; but if no such person should live to attain the age of twenty-one, then in trust to permit such person and persons successively, who for the time being would take by descent as heirs male of the body of the testator's son (father of B.), to take the profits of the same leasehold premises until one of them should attain the age of twenty-one, and then to convey the same to such heir male first attaining that age, his executors, administrators, and assigns.

At the death of B., the grandson, his son and heir, A., had attained the age of twenty-one, and entered into possession of the leasehold premises. Upon a bill filed against him by the next of kin of the testator :

Held that A. had not a good title to the leaseholds ; that the bequest to the heir male of the grandson attaining twenty-one was void for remoteness, and, therefore, that the next of kin of the testator, at his death, became entitled to their distributive shares of the property on the death of the grandson.

1846.
April 8.
May 19, 20.
June 23, 24.
1846.
May 26.
June 8.

Lord
LYNDHURST.
L.C.
Lord
BROUGHAM,
Lord
COTTENHAM.
Lord
CAMPBELL.
TINDAL,
Ch. J.
CRESSWELL,
J.
WIGHTMAN,
J.
MAULE, J.
COLTMAN, J.
WILLIAMS, J.
PATTESON, J.
PLATT, B.
PARKE, B.
ROLFE, B.
ALDERSON, B.
[546]

ARTHUR, first Viscount Dungannon, being possessed of the lands of Magennis, otherwise the Island Magee, under a lease for ninety-nine years from the 17th of July, 1769, and of other valuable leasehold property held under the sees of Down and Dromore in Ireland, and being also seised of considerable freehold estates in England *and Ireland, duly made and published his will, dated the 19th of June, 1770, and thereby gave and bequeathed his said leasehold lands and premises, and all other chattels, leasehold

[*547]

(1) Cited by Lord CAIRNS, *Countess of Harrington* v. *Earl of Harrington* (1871) L. R. 5 H. L. 87, 105.

lands and tenements, which he should die possessed of, to his wife
and other persons therein described, their executors and administrators, upon trust out of the yearly rents, issues, and profits
thereof, to pay an annuity of 300l. a-year to his wife for her life,
and subject thereto to pay and apply certain sums yearly for the
maintenance and education of the testator's grandson, Arthur
Trevor, until he attained age; and after he should attain his age
of twenty-one years, subject to the testator's debts, annuities, and
legacies, he gave and bequeathed the said leasehold and chattel
interests to the trustees, upon the trust, and in the words following:

"In trust to permit my said grandson Arthur Trevor and his
assigns to take the profits of the same leasehold premises for and
during the term of his natural life, and from and after his decease
to permit such person who for the time being would take by descent
as heir male of the body of the said Arthur Trevor, my grandson,
to take the profits thereof until some such person shall attain the
age of twenty-one years, and then to convey the same unto such
person so attaining the age of twenty-one years, his executors,
administrators, and assigns; but if no such person shall live to
attain the age of twenty-one years, then in trust to permit such
person and persons successively who for the time being would take
by descent as heirs male of the body of the said Arthur Trevor, my
son (father of Arthur the grandson), to take the profits of the same
leasehold premises until one of them shall attain the age of twenty-
one years, and then to convey the same to such heir male first
attaining that age, his executors, administrators, and assigns; and
if all the persons who shall respectively and successively be heirs
[*548] male of the body of the said Arthur Trevor, my son, *shall die under
the age of twenty-one years, or if there shall not be any heir male
of the body of the said Arthur Trevor, my son, living at the death
of the said Arthur Trevor, my grandson, or who shall be afterwards
born, then in trust for the only daughter of my said son Arthur
Trevor, living at his decease, if he shall have but one then living,
until he shall attain the age of twenty-one years, or be married,
which shall first happen, and then to assign the same to such only
daughter, her executors, administrators, and assigns, or in such
manner as shall be agreed upon previous to her marriage." Then
followed various other trusts to take effect in events which have
not happened.

The testator subsequently executed several codicils to his will,
but they did not in any way affect the bequest in the will of the

leasehold interests. He died on the 30th of January, 1771, leaving his wife Anne, Viscountess Dungannon, and two daughters Anne, Countess of Mornington, and Penelope Prudence Leslie, and his said grandson, Arthur Trevor, who were his only next of kin, surviving him. The Viscountess was barred by her marriage settlement from taking any interest to which she might otherwise be entitled in the personal estate. Arthur Trevor, father of the said Arthur Trevor, the grandson, was living at the date of the will, but died soon afterwards, in his father's (the testator's) life-time. The will and codicils were duly proved by the testator's widow and another of the executors, and they paid the testator's debts and legacies.

On the testator's death, his said grandson succeeded to the title of Viscount Dungannon ; and having soon afterwards attained his age of twenty-one years, he entered into possession of all the said leasehold estates, with the assent of the trustees and executors, and he enjoyed the *same down to the time of his death, having regu- [*549] larly obtained renewals of the leases. By his will, dated the 24th of August, 1829, he devised his fee simple estates to the Marquis of Downshire and the Earl of Clare, upon trust for his eldest son (the appellant) for life, with remainder to his first and other sons in tail ; and he gave to the same trustees his leaseholds upon such trusts as, allowing for the different natures of the estates, would best correspond with the trusts of the fee simple estates.

Arthur, the grandson, second Viscount Dungannon, died in December, 1837, and thereupon the appellant, his only child and next of kin, succeeded to the title as the third Viscount. Having attained his age of twenty-one years in 1819, he entered imme-diately after his father's death into possession of the rents and profits of the said leasehold estates bequeathed by the will of the first Lord Viscount Dungannon, and continued in the enjoyment thereof. In June, 1841, he obtained administration, with the will annexed, of the goods and chattels unadministered of the first Viscount, and became his personal representative. He also about the same time obtained a conveyance of the legal estate in the devised premises from the administrator of the last surviving trustee of the will.

In December, 1841, the respondents, as the personal representa-tives of the said Anne, Countess of Mornington, and Penelope Prudence Leslie, daughters, and two of the next of kin of the first Viscount Dungannon, filed their bill in the Court of Chancery in

Ireland against the appellant and others (who were made defendants for form's sake), charging that the bequest of the leaseholds,
in the will of the first Viscount was void for remoteness ; and that
accordingly on the death of Arthur Trevor, that testator's grandson (the second Viscount), the said leasehold premises became
distributable among the next of kin of the said testator ; and that
the respondents, as personal representatives of two of such next of
[*550]   kin, were entitled to *two-thirds thereof, the appellant being, as the
other next of kin, entitled to the other one-third.

To that bill the appellant put in a general demurrer for want of
equity.

The cause was heard before Sir MICHAEL O'LOUGHLIN, late Master
of the Rolls, who, by an order made in May, 1842, overruled the
demurrer.

There was an appeal from that decision to Sir EDWARD SUGDEN,
then Lord Chancellor of Ireland, who suggested that it would be
better for the parties to appeal to this House at once. This
appeal was then presented against the order of the MASTER OF THE
ROLLS.

Mr. *Hodgson* and Mr. *Napier* (of the Irish Bar) for the
appellant. * * *

[556]   Mr. *Turner* and Mr. *Butt* (of the Irish Bar), with whom were
Mr. *Malins* and Mr. *Rendall*, for the respondents. * * *

[559]   Mr. *Napier* replied. * * *

[The arguments of counsel and the cases cited by them sufficiently
appear from the following opinions of the Judges :]

[560]   The LORD CHANCELLOR informed Mr. *Napier* that it was the
opinion of all the noble and learned Lords present, that the case
was extremely well argued by the learned counsel—by the learned
counsel on both sides.

His Lordship then, after conferring with the other Lords, proposed the following question to the learned Judges (who obtained
time to consider their answer) :

" The testator, being entitled to certain leasehold premises for
years, bequeathed the same to trustees, in trust to permit his
grandson B. and his assigns to take the profits of the same leasehold premises for and during the term of his natural life, and from
and after his decease to permit such person who for the time being

ld take by descent as heir male of the body of the said B., his
dson, to take the profits thereof until some such person should
the age of twenty-one years, and then to convey the same
) such person so attaining the age of twenty-one years, his
utors, administrators, or assigns; but if no such person should
to attain the *age of twenty-one years, then in trust to permit
uch person and persons successively who for the time being would
ake by descent as heirs male of the body of his (the testator's) son
o take the profits of the same leasehold premises until one of them
hould attain the age of twenty-one years, and then to convey the
ame to such heir male first attaining that age, his executors,
administrators, or assigns.

[*561]

"At the death of B., the grandson, his eldest son A. had attained
he age of twenty-one years, and afterwards, with the consent of
he trustees, but without that of the next of kin of the testator,
articled to sell the said leaseholds to a purchaser.

"Was he (A.) capable to making a good title to them?"

The learned Judges attended this day, and as they differed in
their opinions, they delivered them *seriatim.*

1846.
May 26.

PLATT, B. :

I think he (A.) was not capable of making a good title to the
purchaser.

The testator, in pointing out the object of his bounty expectant
on the death of his grandson, describes that object as "such person
who for the time being would take by descent as heir male of the
body of his grandson," and directs that such person should be
permitted to take the profits until some such person should attain
the age of twenty-one years, to whom the trustees were then to
convey. If, therefore, the first heir male of the grandson did not
attain twenty-one, the period during which the persons who in
succession might be heirs male of the body of the grandson for the
time being were designed to take the profits, and at the expiration
of which the trustees were directed to convey, might extend to half
a century. But the rule of law required that the event upon which
the estate was to be conveyed to the heir male of the body of the
grandson should happen within twenty-one years, *and the period
of gestation next, after the death of the grandson. And when a
gift is infected with the vice of its possibly exceeding the prescribed
limit, it is at once and altogether void, both at law and in equity.

[*562]

And even if in its actual event it should fall greatly within such limit, yet it is still as absolutely void as if the event, which would have taken it beyond the boundary, had occurred. The case of *Ibbetson* v. *Ibbetson* (1) appears to me to have been properly decided, and to be directly in point.

For these reasons I think the disposition too remote, and that A. was incapable to make a title to the proposed purchaser.

CRESSWELL, J.:

As a large majority of the Judges to whom your Lordships' question was proposed are agreed as to the answer to be given to it, I shall state as briefly as possible the reasons upon which my opinion is founded, well knowing that your Lordships will hear the same opinion much better maintained by many of my learned brethren. The question depends upon the effect to be given to the words "and from and after his (the grandson B.'s) decease to permit such person (who for the time being would take by descent as heir male of the body of the said B., his grandson) to take the profits thereof until some such person should attain the age of twenty-one years, and then to convey the same unto such person so attaining the age of twenty-one years, his executors, adminis- trators, or assigns;" for those are the words under which the vendor must derive his title. Now those words dispose of the estate, previously limited to B., by way of executory devise, not in favour of any individual, but in favour of such person filling the

[*563] character of heir male of the body of B., the grandson, as *should first attain the age of twenty-one years. It is a general rule, too firmly established to be controverted, that an executory devise to be valid must be so framed that the estate devised must vest, if at all, within a life or lives in being and twenty-one years after; it is not sufficient that it may vest within that period; it must be good in its creation; and unless it is created in such terms that it cannot vest after the expiration of a life or lives in being, and twenty-one years, and the period allowed for gestation, it is not valid, and subsequent events cannot make it so. [On this point his Lordship referred to *Jee* v. *Audley* (2), *Leake* v. *Robinson* (3), *Lord Southampton* v. *The Marquis of Hertford* (4), and *Ware* v.

[564] *Polhill* (5), and observed:] The doctrine, that an executory devise,

(1) 51 R. R. 304 (10 Sim. 495; 5 My. & Cr. 26).
(2) 1 R. R. 46 (1 Cox, 324).
(3) 16 R. R. 168 (2 Mer. 363).
(4) 13 R. R. 18 (2 V. & B. 54).
(5) 8 R. R. 144 (11 Ves. 257).

too remote as to some persons who would take under it, is altogether void, was propounded as a matter beyond all dispute. Upon these cases it was observed in argument, that they clearly related to classes, and that, if the whole class could not take, no part of it could ; but that the bequest in question is in favour of an individual, and not a class. It is not, however, in favour of any particular individual; there might be several persons in succession filling the character of heir male of the body of B., the grandson ; and the testator gave no preference to any one of them over the others, simply as heir male of the body, but preferred him who should first attain the age of twenty-one. *This bequest then was in favour of one of a class, it being quite uncertain who that would be, or when he would be ascertained. [After referring to *Tollemache* v. *Lord Coventry* (1) and *Ibbetson* v. *Ibbetson* (2), and observing that the reasoning of Lord BROUGHAM in *Tollemache* v. *Lord Coventry* showed that the real decision in that case was not that the bequest was good as to the third Lord Vere, but that it was bad as to the fourth Lord Vere, the learned Judge concluded by saying :] Upon the whole, then, it appears to me, that the general rule by which executory devises are to be judged of, and express authority equally call upon me to say, in answer to your Lordships' question, that A., the eldest son of the grandson B., was not, without the concurrence of the next of kin of the testator, capable of making a good title to the leaseholds which he articled to sell.

[Mr. Justice WIGHTMAN (p. 567), Mr. Baron ROLFE (p. 571), Mr. Justice MAULE (p. 577), Mr. Justice COLTMAN (p. 580), Mr. Justice WILLIAMS (p. 584), Mr. Baron ALDERSON (p. 595), and Lord Chief Justice TINDAL (p. 612) delivered opinions to the same effect. Mr. Justice PATTESON (p. 588), and Mr. Baron PARKE (p. 599) expressed opinions to the contrary effect. The following passage from the opinion of Mr. Baron PARKE explains the ground upon which their opinions were based :]

It is clear that, according to the true construction of the words of this conjoint bequest of both profits and *corpus*, reading them at the testator's death, some benefit would belong to the person who should be at the death of B., heir male of the body, in whatever degree of descent he may be such, and would necessarily take effect within the limits, for that heir must have either the rents

(1) 37 R. R. 260 (2 Cl. & Fin. 611).   (2) 51 R. R. 304 (10 Sim. 495 ; and
5 My. & Cr. 26).

Margin notes:
LORD DUNGANNON v. SMITH.

[*565]

[567]

[603]

and profits, or the estate, at the death of B. The heir male of the
body then in existence, would, if a minor, take the profits instantly,
and would, if he attained twenty-one, take the *corpus*, or if already
twenty-one, would take the *corpus* (for surely the testator's words
are not to be construed to mean, that to take any benefit at all he
must be a minor when B. dies) ; so that, though each of the two
limitations, if it had stood alone, would be void, because it could
not be predicated of it, that it would ever take effect, if at all,
within the prescribed period, yet, taken together as one bequest
of both, they must have effect in some way, and within the limits ;
they cannot be separated without defeating the testator's intention
as expressed in the bequest ; and the first heir male must take,
and within the proper limits, either one or the other of the benefits
given by the testator.

[*604]   Immediately on the death of the tenant for life the *trustees
must do something with the profits or estate ; if the heir be a
minor, they must give the profits, if a major, convey the *corpus*.
There is no interval, no suspense of enjoyment of the estate for
a moment, and no uncertainty, except as to the amount of the
benefit, which also must be determined within the proper time.
In the cases of a separate bequest of the profits alone, and a
separate bequest of the *corpus* alone, no heir male of the body can
take, except as fulfilling the condition of being heir male minor in
one case, and heir male major in he other, neither of which conditions will be necessarily fulfilled within the limits ; but under
the bequest in question, of both, he who fills the character of heir
male of the body at the death of B., be he the son, grandson, or
other more remote descendant of B., must, as such heir of the
body, and simply because he is heir of the body at the time of the
death of B., necessarily take, and, take then either the profits or
the *corpus*, that is the inevitable result of the words used ; and,
therefore, the case is the same in effect, as if the testator had so
said, and had expressly directed the trustees, at the death of B.,
to give the profits to the heir male then in being, if a minor, and
the estate, if he should be a major ; and if he should die under
twenty-one, then to the next, if a minor, and the estate if a major,
and if that heir should die under twenty-one, then to the next,
and so on, in a series of consecutive limitations, as suggested by
Mr. Napier.

A direction to give, after the death of B., to the first heir male
who should be a minor, the profits, and the first heir male who

should attain twenty-one, the *corpus*, in effect is the same thing as a direction to give the first heir male living at the death of B., either the one or the other, according as he was a minor or major; and a bequest in these terms would be, not indeed, a bequest to an individual defined, but a bequest to an undefined one, who required no other condition to take it, than fulfilling the *character of heir of the body in existence at the death of B. There is a trust for the person who should fill that character, under all possible circumstances.

Under this limitation, it is to be observed, that the testator does not give the annual rents as an accessary to the bequest of the *corpus*, for the rents are not given to, nor to accumulate for the benefit of, the person who being heir male should attain twenty-one, a description, which no one might answer within the limits, and which bequest would be therefore void; but there is a bequest, uncertain in amount, to the heir male of the body, minor or not, in existence at the death of B., the profits if a minor, the *corpus* if a major, and a series of contingent subsequent bequests to other heirs of the body, which may or may not arise. As to the first member of the series, nothing is wanting to enable him to take that bequest, except that he should be heir male in existence at the death of B., and that condition must be fulfilled, if ever it is fulfilled, at the death of B., and in that respect he differs from every subsequent member of the series; with respect to them, the bequest may or may not take effect within the limits, and is therefore void.

I come, therefore, to the conclusion, that this is a bequest to a succession or series of persons, of whom the first taker must be *in esse* at the death of the tenant for life—must, if a minor, take the rents, and if a major, the estate; and if this view of the case be correct, and the interpretation of the testator's words faithful, I do not think there is any difficulty in holding the first limitation to be good, just the same as if that were the only limitation, though the rest are bad.

The last proposition seems to me to admit of no doubt. If this be a series of bequests, and if the first differs from all the others, and would be good if it stood alone, it cannot be made bad because other subsequent limitations are so; it must stand or fall by itself. And this bequest *to a succession or series differs entirely from a bequest to a class, or number of persons to take together, which bequest is altogether void if it is in suspense at the death of the testator, and that suspense may continue for longer than the

[*606]

LORD
DUNGANNON
v.
SMITH.

prescribed limits; for the *quantum* each is to take depends upon the number of the class, and if the class cannot be ascertained within the limits, neither can the *quantum* to be claimed by any one; therefore the whole is void.   *   *   *

[621]

The LORD CHANCELLOR expressed the thanks of the House to the learned Judges, and moved that their opinions be printed. Agreed to.

June 8.

THE LORD CHANCELLOR :

[*622]

After the elaborate opinion of the learned Judges contained in the papers on your Lordships' *table, I shall not occupy any considerable portion of your time in stating the view which I entertain on this subject, and the grounds upon which I shall propose that the judgment of the COURT below be affirmed.

The question arises out of the will of Lord Dungannon, which was made as far back as the year 1770. By that will he bequeathed certain leasehold estates to trustees in trust to pay the rents and profits to his grandson, Arthur Trevor, during his life, and after his death, in trust to permit the person who for the time being should take by descent, as heir male of the body of the grandson, to take the rents and profits until the time that some one of such persons should attain the age of twenty-one years, and then to convey the premises to that person, or in default of such person attaining the age of twenty-one years, then in trust for the descendants of the son of Arthur Trevor, subject to similar limitations. The question is, whether the son of Arthur Trevor, the grandson, who was twenty-one years of age at his father's death, was entitled to take these leasehold premises; whether he had a right to call for a conveyance.

Now the disposition of these leasehold premises, of the *corpus*, was to be a person answering two descriptions. He was to be heir male of the body taking by descent from Arthur Trevor, the grandson, and he was to be of the age of twenty-one years. It is quite obvious that those two circumstances might not combine for many generations, and indeed it is possible that they might never combine. It is obvious, therefore, that this disposition of the property is void for remoteness; for, as everybody knows, property of this description must vest, if at all, within a life or lives in being, and twenty-one years afterwards; and, to speak with perfect correctness, a few months for gestation.

It is wholly immaterial in this case, that there was a person twenty-one years of age answering the description *at the time; that is, to make use of a phrase of a noble and learned Lord in the case of *Tollemache* v. *The Earl of Coventry* (1), that was a pure accident; it might or might not have happened. Unless it is absolutely certain that the event must happen within the period prescribed, it is quite clear that the rule of remoteness applies to the case, and the devise becomes altogether void. It is quite unnecessary to refer to the several cases which are mentioned in the papers upon your Lordships' table in support of this position. It is admitted on all hands, and it is a point so certain and so clear, that it does not admit of dispute.

But, my Lords, it is supposed that this gift of the *corpus* of the estate is operated upon in some degree by the disposition of the intermediate rents and profits. The disposition of the intermediate rents and profits is to the person who for the time being should take by descent as heir male of the body of the grandson, until some such person shall have attained the age of twenty-one years. Now the disposition of the *corpus* of the estate is to a party answering two descriptions or qualities. The intermediate rents and profits are taken by a person or persons who answer one of those descriptions.

It appears to me, that the dispositions can exist entirely unconnected with each other, that they have no necessary relation to each other, and that the disposition of the rents and profits to particular individuals under this will, no more affects the disposition of the *corpus* of the estate, than if that disposition had been to mere strangers. On that point I concur with the opinion expressed by several of the Judges in the course of the argument, which they have addressed to your Lordships.

But then an attempt to obviate these conclusions, and to decide this question in favour of the appellant, has *been made by putting or endeavouring to put a particular construction upon this will, or rather by endeavouring to translate the will into another form, and then upon that translated form to put the construction to which I am adverting. The course that is pursued is this: it is said, that it was the intention of the testator,—or that you may infer from that disposition that such would have been the intention of the testator,—to create successive estates; that the first estate would, under the circumstances that have taken place, not be a

[*624]

(1) 37 R. R. 260 (2 Cl. & Fin. 611). .

void estate for remoteness, but would take effect, and although the
subsequent estates become void from remoteness, that would not
affect the first estate, to which that defect would not apply.

Several cases were cited for the purpose of leading to that conclusion. I do not refer to those cases, because I do not think the
principle can be disputed, that if the first estate in the order of
succession is not void for remoteness; if it is a good estate, it
would not be affected by the fact of the successive estates being
void on that account. It is a principle conceded, and I need cite
no authority for that purpose. Then what is the estate created,
or that is supposed to be created? It is of this description: The
testator intended the rents and profits to be enjoyed by the first
descendant answering the description, until such person shall
attain the age of twenty-one years, and then to convey the estate
to that person: If the first taker should not attain the age of
twenty-one years, then he intended, upon the death of the first
taker, that it should go to the next descendant in the order of
succession: If he should attain the age of twenty-one years, then
the *corpus* of the estate was to be conveyed to him, and if he did
not attain the age of twenty-one years, the rents and profits were to
be enjoyed by the intermediate person in succession, and so on; in
fact, that there was to be a succession of estates of the nature I have
described, and then it was insisted, that the first *estate so created
should not be void for remoteness, although the subsequent estates
should be void; that would not affect the original first estate.

[*625]

Now, as it appears to me, looking at this will, the testator had
one single object, which was to point out some individual at some
future period answering a particular description, who should take
this estate. He had not in contemplation the granting of successive estates in the terms which I have stated, and which are stated
in the arguments of two of the learned Judges; he had no such
idea in his contemplation; and if we were to adopt this construction for the purpose of getting out of the difficulty arising out of
the law of perpetuities, we should be, in fact, as I consider, making
a perfectly new will for the testator. We should be, in the first
instance, translating the actual will into a new form, and we should
be putting upon that will a construction which, I admit, if the will
had been in that form, would have been the true and just construction. I never can lend myself to a measure of this kind, to
the process of altering the frame of a will and the phraseology of
a will, for the purpose of framing, as it were, a new will, in order

to put a construction upon it to obviate the difficulties arising out of the law against perpetuities.

There is another difficulty in this case; a difficulty adverted to by many of the learned Judges; if you can apply such a process in this case, you could have applied it in almost every case where there was a decision that the estate was void in consequence of remoteness. I will take, for instance, the case which was referred to by many of the learned Judges, the case of *Jee* v. *Audley* (1). What was the case? A bequest of 1,000*l.* to the children of John and Elizabeth Jee, upon Mary Hall's dying without issue, or upon failure of the issue of Mary Hall. *At the time of the testator's death there were four daughters. When the case came before the MASTER OF THE ROLLS, Lord Kenyon, he decided that that bequest was void on this ground, that, in fact, after the death of the testator, another daughter might be born, it would be void as to her, and therefore void as to the whole set. On that ground the principle of the case was decided; and the case has never been questioned from that time to this: but apply to that case the process which has been suggested in the present case (and it would equally apply), and see what the effect would be to the existing daughters who should be living at the time of the event happening; if there were no other daughters born in the mean time, and if there were another daughter born in the mean time, then to the existing daughters and that daughter, what would be the result? As far as relates to the last disposition, it would be void: as far as relates to the first disposition, it would be perfectly good. And the same principle would apply to almost every case in which the Court has decided against the validity of a bequest in respect of its remoteness. What would be the effect, then, of introducing a new principle of this kind? It would break down all the decisions upon this subject. It would remove all those landmarks of the law which have been now for some time considered as firmly established; and I protest, therefore, against the doctrine which has been attempted, for the first time, to be introduced into this case.

[His Lordship then referred to the authorities, and concluded by proposing that the judgment of the COURT below should be affirmed.

Lord BROUGHAM (p. 628), Lord COTTENHAM (p. 636), and Lord CAMPBELL (p. 638) delivered judgments to the same effect.]

(1) 1 R. R. 46 (1 Cox, 324).

LORD
DUNGANNON
v.
SMITH.

[*626]

1845.
July 1, 5.
1846.
May 19, 26.
June 22, 23.
July 7.
———
Lord
LYNDHURST,
L.C.
Lord
BROUGHAM.

[641]

THE IRISH SOCIETY *v.* THE BISHOP OF DERRY AND RAPHOE.

(12 Clark & Finnelly, 641—676.)

In a *quare impedit,* where the Bishop of Derry claimed the right of patronage of a living in the county of Londonderry, which was within the diocese of Derry, a surrender made by a former Bishop to the Crown, of all the livings in that county, was tendered in evidence. This surrender was coupled with a grant by the Crown, dated two days afterwards, of the livings which had been so surrendered. Taken together, these documents were held to be admissible in evidence; and as the grant recited that all the livings in the county had anciently belonged to the See, such evidence was, for the purpose of proving the title of the Bishop, received as an admission by the Crown of that fact.

The value of such evidence was still open to dispute.

Before the date of the grant, the Crown had entered into articles of agreement with persons now represented by the Governor and Assistants of the Irish Society, to grant to them the livings in the county of which the living in question was named as one.

Held, that this agreement did not prevent the grant from being receivable in evidence, however its value might be thereby affected.

Two letters from the Crown to two successive Bishops of Derry, directing them to perform the covenants and directions contained in the grant, were tendered in evidence as recognitions by the Crown of its previous grant.

Held, that they were admissible for this purpose.

Entries in the books kept at the First Fruits' Office are admissible to show the fact of a collation to a living made by the Bishop at a particular time.

[*642]

Returns made by the Bishop, in obedience to writs from the Exchequer, requiring him to state the vacancies of and presentations *and collations to the livings in his diocese, are admissible in evidence as statements made by a public officer in the discharge of a public duty.

Though such returns may contain statements of a kind unusual in such documents, which statements were in favour of the right of the Bishop who made them, they are nevertheless admissible, provided that the statements are within the scope of the enquiry in the writ.

An original collation from the registry of the Bishopric, and appearing on the face of it to be *pleno jure,* is admissible to show that the right claimed has in fact been exercised.

An objection was taken that certain documents tendered in evidence were not admissible for a particular purpose. The COURT decided that they were admissible. An exception was taken to this decision.

Held, that if the documents were admissible on any ground, the exception could not be sustained.

In such a case a court of error can only look at the record, and decide upon the propriety of the ruling, as therein stated.

THIS was an action of *quare impedit,* brought by the plaintiffs in the Court of Common Pleas in Ireland, to recover the advowson of the church of Camus in the city and county of Londonderry in Ireland. The declaration contained eight counts; to each of those counts several pleas were pleaded by the defendant the Bishop of Derry; on those pleas respectively issue was joined by the plaintiffs.

The action was tried at Bar, in the Court of Common Pleas, by a
jury of the city and county of Londonderry, when a verdict was found for the defendant. In the course of the trial, several documents were produced and read in evidence by the defendant's counsel, to the admission of which the plaintiff's counsel objected, and upon the Court receiving them, tendered a bill of exceptions. This bill of exceptions having been signed by the Judges, the record was removed into the Court of Exchequer Chamber; and on the 21st of April, 1842, the judgment *of that COURT (nine [*643] Judges being present, the Lord Chief Justice PENNEFEATHER declining to take any part from his having been the leading counsel of the plaintiffs, and Barons FOSTER and LEFROY being absent) was delivered by the LORD CHIEF JUSTICE of the Common Pleas, affirming in general terms the reception of the said evidence. To reverse this judgment the present writ of error was brought.

The plaintiffs in this case were incorporated by King James I., by the name of "The Governor and Assistants, London, of the new plantation in Ulster, within the realm of Ireland."

In the year 1608, the greatest part of six counties in the province of Ulster, had, upon the attainder of the Roman Catholics involved in the then recent rebellion, been escheated to King James I., in right of his Crown; and about that year the King, with the advice of his Privy Council, became desirous of planting a settlement or colony of his Protestant subjects on the escheated lands. With that view, his Majesty proposed to make grants of portions of the escheated lands to such of his Protestant subjects as might be willing to undertake the planting and settling them, upon certain terms and conditions.

The citizens of London, among others, accordingly advanced large sums of money for the above purpose, and received letters patent, incorporating them by the name before-mentioned, and granting them very extensive tracts of land, and also various advowsons, of which the plaintiffs contend, that Camus, the living in question, is one.

The course of evidence at the trial was as follows: The plaintiffs to maintain and prove their right to the advowson of the church of Camus, as derived by them through the Crown, gave in evidence the following documents: *First, letters patent, bearing date the [*644] 14th of February, in the thirty-eighth year of the reign of King Henry III., whereby the King granted and confirmed to his eldest son, Edward, and his heirs, the kingdom of Ireland, except certain places and parts as therein excepted: secondly, letters patent,

bearing date the 20th day of July, in the thirty-eighth of
Henry III., whereby the King granted and confirmed to his
said son and his heirs, the cities of Dublin and Limerick, and
other possessions which had been excepted out of the said former
grant : thirdly, letters patent from Prince Edward to Lord Walter
de Burgo, whereby the Prince granted and confirmed to Lord
Walter and his heirs, the province of Ulster in Ireland, except as
therein is excepted : (And the plaintiffs further proved, that Lord
Walter de Burgo having died, he was succeeded in his estates and
properties by his eldest son Richard de Burgo, who, after the death
of his father, became Earl of Ulster, in Ireland) : fourthly, the
record of a judgment *in quare impedit* had in the Court of Common
Pleas in Ireland, in the twenty-seventh Edward I., in which the
said Earl of Ulster was plaintiff, and Galfridus, then Bishop of
Derry, was defendant ; whereby the Earl recovered the advowson
of Drumcose, in the said diocese of Derry, and also a judgment in
another suit of *quare impedit* of the same year, and between the
same parties, whereby the Earl was adjudged to be entitled to
present a fit and proper person as clerk to the church of Camus, in
the diocese of Derry : fifthly, a writ of *levari facias*, directed to
the sheriff therein mentioned, in the twenty-seventh Edward I.,
and the return of the sheriff thereto, by which writ the sheriff was
commanded to levy the damages in these two actions : sixthly, the
plaintiffs proved, that the Earldom of Ulster and the possessions
thereof, regularly descended through several persons successively
entitled thereto, until the same became vested in Edward IV.

[*645]   They then proved *an Act passed in the tenth year of the reign of
King Henry VII., enacting (*inter alia*) that the said King should
present to the advowsons which formerly belonged to the Earls of
Ulster, and as being then annexed to the Crown. The plaintiffs
further gave in evidence a certain commission, bearing date the
21st day of July, 1609, issued by King James I., and enrolled in
the Court of Chancery in Ireland. This commission appears to
have been directed, among others, to George, then Bishop of Derry,
appointing those persons Commissioners, with full power and
authority to inquire and determine what hereditaments of various
kinds, including advowsons in the several counties of Armagh,
Coleraine (now Londonderry), Tyrone, Donegal, Fermanagh, or
Cavan, belonged to the Crown. The plaintiffs further gave in
evidence certain articles of instruction annexed to this commission,
and enrolled in the Court of Chancery, in Ireland.

The plaintiffs further gave in evidence from the Rolls of Chancery, in Ireland, a certain inquisition taken under the authority of the commission above-mentioned at Lymavaddy, in the county of Coleraine, on the 30th day of August, 1609. By this inquisition, which appears to have been signed by George, then Bishop of Derry, it is found among other things, that there was in the said county of Coleraine, (now Londonderry), the parish of Camus, wherein were both a parson and vicar, and it is thereby also expressly found that all presentations, rights of patronage, and advowsons of churches within the said county of Coleraine, did then of right belong and appertain to the King's Majesty, in right of his Imperial Crown; but that the Bishop of Derry might and did, until the statute of the eleventh of Elizabeth therein referred to, place a clerk in any parsonage or vicarage, being void, until the King either presented or bestowed the advowson upon the Bishop or some other person.

The plaintiffs further gave in evidence articles of *agreement, dated 28th January, 1609, enrolled in the Court of Chancery in Ireland, and made between the Right Honourable the Lords of his then Majesty's most honourable Privy Council in England, on the King's Majesty's behalf of the one part, and the Committees appointed by act of Common Council, on behalf of the Mayor and Commonalty of the City of London, of the other part, concerning a plantation in part of the province of Ulster. By the ninth clause of the articles it was agreed that the City of London should have the patronage of all the churches, as well within the city of the Derry and town of Coleraine, as in all lands to be undertaken by them. The plaintiffs further gave in evidence a letter from the King, also enrolled in the Court of Chancery, in Ireland, dated 4th February, 1609, addressed from the Court at Whitehall, to Sir Arthur Chichester, then Lord Deputy of Ireland, announcing that the work of the plantation of Ulster, undertaken by the City of London, had been at last resolved on, and that articles of agreement had been absolutely concluded between his Majesty and the said City; and letters patent of James I., dated 29th March, 1613, which appeared to be enrolled in Ireland, and by which the undertakers were incorporated. And by the same letters patent the advowsons, donations, free disposals and rights of patronage of all and singular churches, vicarages, and chapels, of and in the said city of Londonderry, and of all and singular churches, vicarages, and chapels of and in the village or town of Coleraine, and also the

advowsons, donations, free disposals and rights of patronage of all
and singular the rectories and churches of Towlaght, Finleggan,
Tawlaghtard, Aulowe, Bonacher, Boyvanny and Boydafeigh, in the
barony of Kennaught, and also the advowsons, donations, free disposals and rights of patronage of all and singular the rectories and
churches of Dunboe, Temple Errigal, Temple Desert, Itowhill, Camus

[*647] and Killowen, in the barony of Coleraine, *in the county of Coleraine,
and also of the rectory and church of Faughenvale, in the barony
of Annaght, in the said county, were all expressly given and
granted to the Governor and Assistants and their successors; To
have, hold, and enjoy the same, and all and singular other the
premises by the said letters patent granted or mentioned to be
granted, with the rights, members and appurtenances, to the
Governor and Assistants and their successors, to their sole and
proper use and behoof for ever.   The plaintiffs also proved a
presentation by the King upon lapse of Alexander Spicer, clerk, to
the rectory of Camus, within the diocese of Derry, and that Spicer
was duly instituted to the living.   The plaintiffs also gave in
evidence an entry contained in a book kept as of record in the
First Fruits' Office in Ireland, from which it appeared by the
certificate of John, then Bishop of Derry, that one Thomas Vesey
was in the year 1684 admitted to the said rectory of Camus, in the
county of Londonderry.   And an entry in another book kept as of
record in the First Fruits' Office in Ireland, from which it appeared
by the certificate of Robert, then Bishop of Derry, dated 28th October,
1672, that one Jonathan Edwards, was instituted and inducted to
the rectory of Camus, on the 1st May, 1672.   The value of the
living was proved to be about 850*l.* a year.

The counsel for the defendant, to support his case, tendered in
evidence several documents, all of which were objected to by the
plaintiffs, but were received in evidence, and their admission formed
the twelve heads of the bill of exceptions.   The first was a document dated the 1st August, 1610, the original of which had been
enrolled in England, but not in Ireland, and had not been confirmed by the Dean and Chapter of Derry.   This was produced for
the purpose of showing an admission on the part of King James I.,
that the advowson of the church of Camus did anciently belong to
the Bishopric of Derry.   It purported to be a surrender by George

[*648] Montgomery, *then Bishop of Derry, Raphoe and Clogher, into the
hands of James I., of several hereditaments therein mentioned,
and amongst others of the rectory and parsonage of the Derry,

formerly appropriate to that See for the maintenance of his table;
and also of all parsonages, vicarages, impropriations, advowsons,
patronages, nominations, presentations of churches, chapels or
parishes, as well within the diocese of Derry and county of
Coleraine, as within all other counties and baronies within the
several dioceses of Derry, Raphoe, and Clogher, in the realm of
Ireland, (except in the county of Monaghan), which did belong or
appertain, or were parcel or part of the said Bishoprics or any of
them, or whereto, he the said George, had or ought to have any
right of presentation.

The second was a document which had also been enrolled in
England, but not in Ireland, dated 3rd August, 1610, which was
offered, not for the purpose of proving title in the defendant, but
for that of proving an admission on the part of King James I.,
that the advowson of the church of Camus anciently belonged to
the Bishopric of Derry. This document purported to be a grant
from the King to George Montgomery, then Bishop of Derry, and
his successors for ever, of a great variety of lands, tenements, and
hereditaments therein particularly mentioned and described; and a
grant also of the advowsons, donations, free disposals, and rights of
patronage, of all and singular the rectories, churches, vicarages,
chapels, and other ecclesiastical benefices whatsoever to the premises
therein before granted, or to any part or parcel thereof belonging,
appertaining, appendant, or incumbent, and to the same Bishopric
of right belonging and appertaining, and to which the Bishops of
Derry and their successors were accustomed to present or collate, as
by the survey thereof, then lately taken in Ireland, and under the
Great Seal of Ireland, then lately exemplified at Dublin, the 26th
January, 1609, appeared. The survey itself was not *given in
evidence. Out of this grant, were excepted nine advowsons out of
the number of fifteen advowsons within the county of Coleraine,
which, it was stated in the grant, were by the mutual consent of the
then late Bishop of Derry and citizens of London, to be transferred
from the said Bishop of Derry and his successors to the said citizens;
and in the said document it was further stated, that the said George
Montgomery, then Bishop of Derry, did thereby for himself and
his successors, covenant with the said King James, his heirs, &c.,
that he the Bishop of Derry, with the consent of the chapter of the
said Bishop, should make and execute such assurances, acts, things,
and devises as should in that behalf be required concerning the
conveyance and assurance of the advowsons, and other the premises,

[*649]

in the said presents excepted, to the said King, his heirs or successors, or any other persons, bodies politic and corporate, according to the appointment and requisition of the said King, or the Deputy and others of the Privy Council of Ireland, as therein to be done in that behalf; and it was recited, that the King had been informed that there were in the county of Coleraine, and within the said diocese of Derry fifteen advowsons of churches, rectories, and other ecclesiastical benefices, anciently belonging to the Bishopric of Derry, and that by mutual consent and agreement between George Montgomery, then Bishop of Derry, and certain citizens of London, who lately undertook the planting and inhabiting of certain lands in the province of Ulster in Ireland, it was then lately concluded and agreed upon, that the then Bishop of Derry, and his successors, should have only six advowsons of the fifteen advowsons; and the document purported to point out and direct the manner in which the said fifteen advowsons were to be chosen by and divided between the Bishop and the citizens respectively, so as to give six to the Bishop, and the other nine to the citizens for ever.

[*650]   The third document was a copy, duly attested and *compared, of a certain instrument enrolled from the Rolls Office of the Court of Chancery in Ireland, dated 11th August, 1610. This instrument purported to be an appointment by King James I., of one Bruite Babington, D.D., to the Bishopric of Derry, then vacant by the resignation of George Montgomery, and giving him the mesne profits appertaining to the Bishopric, since the 2nd day of May then last, and it purported to enjoin Sir Arthur Chichester, then Deputy-Governor of Ireland, &c., to cause Babington, and the dean and clergy of the diocese of Derry, to execute and perform such covenants and directions as were comprised in the letters patent of George Montgomery on the part of the Bishop of Derry, and his successors, to be performed.

The fourth was a document of a similar kind, being the appointment of Christopher Hampton to the Bishopric on the 21st December, 1811. It contained the same injunction as the former appointment.

The fifth piece of evidence tendered and received was an entry appearing in a book produced from the First Fruits' Office in Ireland, from which book the plaintiffs' counsel had read on behalf of the plaintiffs an entry respecting the admission of Thomas Vesey to the rectory of Camus, in the year 1684. The entry proposed to be read, and read on the part of the said defendant, purported to be an entry of admissions, returned in Easter Term, 1680, and stating that one John Freeman was collated and admitted on the 7th day of October, 1629, to the rectory of Camus.

The sixth piece of evidence was another entry, appearing in another book produced from the First Fruits' Office in Ireland, and purporting to be an entry of admissions returned as of Easter Term, 1686; and stating from the certificate of Ezekiel, then Bishop of Derry, that one Walter Forest, clerk, was collated on the 25th day of March, 1686, to the rectory of Camus.

The seventh piece of evidence tendered and received was an [651] entry contained in a triennial Visitation Book of the Archdiocese of Armagh in Ireland, of the year 1664, which entry purported to state, that one Brian Roche, Master of Arts, rector, was admonished to exhibit letters of orders or to procure a certificate in two months, that he exhibited his collation and institution to the rectory of Camus M'Cosquin, dated the 17th June, 1661, with a mandate to induct the same day.

The eighth, ninth, tenth, and eleventh documents tendered and received were writs produced from the First Fruits' Office, and purporting to be issued from the Court of Exchequer in Ireland, on the 12th February, 1716, the 5th May, 1787, the 12th February, 1797, and the 11th July, 1821, and directed to the successive Bishops of Derry, commanding them respectively to make a return to the Barons of the Exchequer, of the dignities, benefices, offices, or promotions spiritual therein mentioned, which, from certain dates in the said writs respectively mentioned, had become void, and what rectors, vicars, or other beneficed clergymen had been admitted, instituted, collated, or inducted thereto. To each of these writs was appended the return made thereto, and each stated the collation of a rector to the rectory of Camus.

Lastly, the counsel for the defendant produced and offered in evidence a document found among the records of the diocese of Derry, purporting to be a collation of the Reverend Thomas Richardson to the rectory of Camus, by William, then Bishop of Derry, which recited, that the rectory of Camus, being then vacant, did belong to his collation and free disposal, in full right.

The Court of Common Pleas having given judgment for the defendant on every one of these twelve grounds of exception, the record was removed into the Court of *Exchequer Chamber, where [*652] the judgment of the Court of Common Pleas was affirmed.

This writ of error was then brought.

The Judges were summoned: and Lord Chief Justice Tindal, Justices Patteson, Williams, Coltman, Maule, Cresswell, and Wightman, and Barons Parke, Rolfe, and Platt, attended at the argument.

> *Sir T. Wilde* and *Mr. Boyd* (*Mr. James Wilde* was with them) for the plaintiffs in error:

* * As to the grant, that instrument is void, for it is founded on a void surrender.

[653]   (THE LORD CHANCELLOR (1): There is no recital that it was in consideration of the surrender.)

There is not.

(THE LORD CHANCELLOR: It was a re-grant.)

It was not intended to be so. It does no more than confirm the title of the Bishop and of some other clergymen. * * *

[654]   There is another objection to the admissibility of this grant. It is founded on information which was not true. * * *

[656]   Then again this grant is inadmissible to prove a title in the Bishop, for it is wholly uncertain. It does not state which of the fifteen livings are to belong to the Bishop and which to the citizens of London. And finally, this rectory cannot come within the grant, for the words of the grant are " rectories, &c., belonging, appertaining, appendant, or incumbent." This is a living in gross, and the words of the grant do not apply to it. Nor is it shown by the supposed grant that at the time of making it the Crown had any existing interest to be affected by it; that alone would render it invalid. Now the grant was tendered in evidence for the specific purpose of showing an admission by the Crown in favour of the Bishop; viewed in any way whatever it does not show any thing of the kind, and therefore it is not admissible.

[*657]   (THE LORD *CHANCELLOR: Counsel may insist on the admissibility or non-admissibility of documents for a particular purpose, but that will not necessarily govern the opinion of the Judge, who is not bound to say that it is or not admissible for the particular purpose for which it is offered, but who may yet think it admissible.)

But here the Court expressly admitted this evidence on the specific

(1) Lord LYNDHURST.

ound on which it was tendered,—if it is not admissible on that
ound, the judgment must be reversed. * * *

The *Solicitor-General* and *Mr. Serjt. Channell* (*Mr. Vaughan
Williams* was with them) for the defendant in error :

The only real question here is, whether these documents were
imissible in evidence. The purpose for which they were offered
innot now be the subject of discussion. [659]

(Lord Brougham : The purpose for which a document is tendered
ı evidence cannot enter into the question of its admissibility.)

ı cannot. And in this *case there is no exception taken to the
ıanner in which the evidence was left to the jury. * * * [*660]

Sir T. Wilde replied. [663]

The Lord Chancellor put the following question to the Judges :
'Adverting to the record and proceedings in this case, ought the
xceptions therein stated, or any, and which of them, to have been
llowed ? ''

Lord Chief Justice Tindal, on behalf of the Judges, asked for
ime to consider the question, which was granted.

1846.
July 7.

Lord Chief Justice Tindal died on the day before the Judges
rere called in to deliver their opinions.

Mr. Baron Parke, therefore, as senior Judge, delivered their
opinion, which was as follows :

The question proposed by your Lordships is, whether, adverting
ιo the record and proceedings in this case, the exceptions therein
stated, or any and which of them, ought to have been allowed. In
answer to that question, I have to state that the unanimous
opinion of the Judges who heard the argument at your Lordship's
Bar is, that none of the exceptions was valid in law.

These exceptions, twelve in number, were all made to the
admissibility of evidence on the trial of a *quare impedit* for the
rectory of Camus, in the county of Londonderry. The declaration
contained several counts, stating the title of the plaintiffs in
different ways. There were several pleas, and it is immaterial to
notice them or the counts in detail. The important issue was,
whether the plaintiffs were seised of the advowson of the rectory of

Camus as an advowson in gross: and the evidence which is
questioned, was offered by the defendant as applicable to that issue.
The plaintiffs gave many documents in evidence in support of their
title; the most important were an inquisition, and articles of agreement, and a grant from King James I. The inquisition was taken
in *obedience to a Royal commission directed to the Bishop of
Derry, amongst others, on the 80th August, 1609, at Lymavaddy,
and it was thereby found, that the patronage of all advowsons of
churches in the county of Coleraine (afterwards Londonderry), of
right belonged to the King in right of his Crown. The articles of
agreement were dated 16th January, 1809, and were between the
Lords of the Privy Council of King James I. and the citizens of
London, for a plantation in the province of Ulster, whereby the
citizens agreed to advance money and to undertake the plantation,
and on behalf of the Crown it was agreed that they should have
the patronage of all the churches in Derry, and the town of
Coleraine, and in all the lands to be undertaken by them.

[*664]

The letters patent were dated the 29th March, 1618. They
granted to the plaintiffs several different estates, and, *inter alia*, the
patronage of all the churches in the city of Derry and village of
Coleraine, and the advowsons of several places named, including
that of Camus.

The defendants, in support of their case, offered in evidence:
first, a surrender (unconfirmed by the dean and chapter) by Bishop
Montgomery to King James I., of the rectory of Derry, all parsonages in the county of Coleraine, and the ferry at Derry, to be
disposed of at the King's good will and pleasure. This surrender
was dated the 1st August, 1610.

This document was objected to, but received; and its reception
forms the subject of the first exception.

If this evidence had stood alone, and had not been followed up
by that of a grant on the 3rd of August, 1610, from King James
the First to Bishop Montgomery, it would have been, to say the
least, doubtful whether it was properly admitted; but in connexion
with that grant we think it was admissible, for a reason which
applies to both.

The second exception was to this grant. It was a grant under
the Great Seal of England to Bishop Montgomery *of various
lands, including lands in Camus, of all the advowsons belonging
and appertaining to them, and to the same Bishopric belonging and
appertaining, as to which the Bishops were heretofore accustomed

[*665]

to collate, as appeared by the survey then lately exemplified, which
exemplification is dated at Dublin the 26th January, 1609, except
certain advowsons particularly named, not including that of Camus,
and excepting nine out of fifteen in the county of Coleraine, which, by
mutual consent of the citizens of London and of the Bishop, were to be
transferred from the Bishop to the citizens, and a provision is made
how the nine should be selected.   The patent contains a covenant
by the Bishop of Derry, that, with the consent of the chapter,
he should make further assurances to the Crown of the excepted
premises, and amongst others of the ferry and water of Derry.

To the admission of this document the second exception was
made.   The document was offered, as showing an admission on the
part of King James the First, that the living of Camus did
anciently belong to the Bishop of Derry: it was objected to, that
it was not admissible for the purpose aforesaid; and the COURT
decided, as stated on the record, that the document so offered for
the purpose aforesaid, was legally admissible.

According to the strict construction of the decision of the Court,
so stated, it was not ruled that the document was admissible for
that purpose, but only that it was admissible; and if admissible on
any ground, the exception must be overruled.   A court of error can
only look at the record, and decide upon the propriety of the ruling
of the Judge or Court below, as therein stated.

We are all of opinion that the two documents, the surrender of
August 1st, 1610, and the patent of August 3rd, 1610, were
admissible.   The proximity of the dates, the circumstance that the
surrender is of the advowsons to be at the disposal of the Crown,
that the Crown grants all *advowsons belonging to the lands, and   [*666]
to the Bishopric belonging and appertaining, the reference in the
grant to the ferry mentioned in the surrender, are all circumstances
tending to show the connexion between the two instruments; and if
the jury should find them to be connected, the grant founded on
the surrender, and made in pursuance of it, is an act of the Crown
at variance and inconsistent with the finding in the inquisition of
Lymavaddy (which is the main foundation of the plaintiffs' case),
that all the advowsons in the county of Coleraine then of right
belonged to the Crown; and consequently is matter for the consideration of the jury to disprove that finding; for the finding is
evidence merely, but not conclusive, of the fact so found.   The
implied acceptance of the surrender by the Crown of advowsons in
the county of Coleraine as belonging to the See of Derry, and the

making a bargain with the Bishop touching advowsons, in consequence of it, by a proper instrument binding on the Crown, (for the patent is put on the footing of a patent under the Great Seal of Ireland, by the Irish statute 35 Geo. III. c. 39,) is an act of the Crown, leading to the inference that it had no prior title of its own to all the livings in Coleraine, and like every other act or conduct of the Crown, raising an inference material to the issue, is receivable in evidence against the Crown, and all who claim under it by a subsequent conveyance, and who therefore have only such title as the King had when he made that conveyance.

We are not called upon to decide whether the recital in the grant, that the Crown had been informed that there were fifteen advowsons in Coleraine, anciently belonging to the Bishop, was evidence against the Crown, as an admission of the truth of the fact; because we cannot collect from the record that the Court so decided. All we are bound to determine is, whether the documents were [*667]   admissible. We think they were; indeed the act done by *the Crown, being in the nature of an admission that some of the livings in the county of Londonderry had belonged to the See, and Camus being a living in that county, may be said to have been receivable in evidence for the purpose of proving an admission of King James, that Camus anciently belonged to the Crown : the purpose for which it was offered.

But it is said that at the time of this transaction, the Crown had already bargained for a valuable consideration, by the articles of January, 1609, to give these advowsons to the City of London; and that any admission of the Crown of a subsequent date, by conduct or otherwise, would not be admissible, as the Crown was, after the articles, only in the nature of a trustee. Supposing that the objection was well founded (upon which it is unnecessary to give any opinion), and that the declarations of a trustee who has only the legal estate, the whole beneficial interest being in another, are not admissible against a person claiming that estate under him, it would not apply to this case. The King was not, and could not be a trustee, nor had he covenanted to convey anything, nor the Lords of Council agreed to convey the living of Camus in particular, or all the advowsons in the county of Coleraine, but only that of Derry, and those in the town of Coleraine, and those in the lands to be undertaken by the City; and whether the lands in which Camus was were undertaken before the grant of 3rd of August, 1610, does not appear. We are therefore clearly of opinion, that

the articles of agreement do not prevent the subsequent act of the   <small>THE IRISH
SOCIETY
v.</small>
Crown from being receivable in evidence.

The third and fourth exceptions were to the admissibility of two   <small>THE BISHOP
OF DERRY.</small>
letters under the Privy Seal, discharging two of the succeeding
Bishops of Derry from first-fruits, and directing the Bishop and
dean and clergy to perform the covenants and directions in the
former letters patent mentioned on the part of the Bishop of Derry.
These are *both admissible, on the same ground as the letters patent,   [*668]
and as recognising the bargain with the Bishop therein contained.

The fifth exception related to an entry in one of the books of
the First Fruits' Office, of the collation and admission of John
Freeman to the rectory of Camus. Writs were issued from the
Court of Exchequer to the Bishops, to ascertain the value of the
first-fruits and twentieths, and returns were made by the Bishops.
Search for the writs and returns was made, and the book was
offered as secondary evidence of returns.

We think the entry was properly received (1). The writs related
to a public matter, the revenue of the Crown, and the Bishops, in
making the return, discharged a public duty, and faith is given
that they would perform their duty correctly : the return is therefore admissible, on the same principle on which other public
documents are received. It was contended that the Bishop could
not be permitted to make evidence for himself, and therefore that
the entry, though admissible between other parties, was not to be
received for the Bishop ; and the case was compared to an entry
in the book of a union, of a surgeon's attendance : *Merrick* v.
Wakley (2), and the receipt of a certificate in a parish book : *Rex*
v. *Debenham* (3), which have been rightly held to be inadmissible for
the surgeon in one case, or the parish keeping the book in the other.

But neither of these was an entry of a public nature, in the
the proper sense of that word ; the former was a memorandum,
intended to operate as a sort of check to the surgeon, the latter a
memorandum for the parish officer, concerning merely the particular
parish and its rights, with relation to another.

In public documents, made for the information of the Crown, or
all the King's subjects who may require the *information they   [*669]
contain, the entry by a public officer is presumed to be true when
it is made, and is for that reason receivable in all cases, whether

---

<small>(1) Cited with approval by Lord   (2) 47 R. R. 540 (8 Ad. & El. 170).
BLACKBURN in *Sturla* v. *Freccia*, 5   (3) 20 R. R. 401 (2 B. & Ald. 187).
App. Cas. 623, at p. 642.—J. G. P.</small>

the officer or his successor may be concerned in such cases or not. A marriage or burial register would certainly be admissible to prove a marriage or death, in suits to which the clergyman who made it might happen afterwards to be a party, though he had a pecuniary interest in the particular marriage or death at the time. The observation, that it might have been fabricated to advance the interests of the officer, affects the value of the evidence, not its admissibility; and may be offered with more or less effect, according to the degree of interest in the officer, and the proximity of time between the entry and the suit, and other circumstances.

The same observation which I have made on the fifth, applies to the sixth and seventh exceptions.

The eight exception was to the admissibility of part or the whole of the return of a writ from the Exchequer, returned into the office of the First Fruits.

The return stated the vacancy of Camus by the death of Walter Forrest, and the collation of one Breviter on September 4th, 1716; the cession by Breviter, and collation of Daniel; and the institution of Faning and another to other rectories in the county of Derry, and the collation of others.

It was objected that no part of this return was admissible. The part relating to Camus was, however, clearly so; for it showed two collations to that rectory. It was then objected that the remainder was not receivable; but it was answered that the whole was one official act, and the jury might look at the whole in order to explain and authenticate the part relating to Camus. And we think this was rightly done. The value of the return as an accurate document must depend upon looking at the whole of it; and the context shows that the term "collation" was used in its proper sense.

[670]   The ninth exception stands on precisely the same footing.

The tenth was somewhat different.

A First Fruits' writ of the 38 Geo. III. was offered, directed to the Bishop of Derry, by which the King requires to be certified what deans, &c., rectors and vicars, have been admitted, instituted, collated, or inducted to dignities, benefices, &c., and by what names; together with the day and year of the institution or collation of each, and the county where the dignities, &c., are situate; and the command of the writ was, that the Bishop having searched his registry and archives touching the premises, whatever he should then find he should return into the Court of Exchequer on archment, reduced into proper form, without any omission whatever.

The return by the Bishop was, that having searched the registry of Derry, and the archives thereof, he found " all whose names are in the schedule written to have been collated and instituted ; " and the schedule stated seven collations to different livings (one to Camus, and that was said to have been made on the 2nd of June, 1797, in the room of a former incumbent, who held the same for ten years and twenty-seven days from the 5th of May, 1787, and vacated the same by resignation on or about the 2nd June aforesaid) ; and similar statements were made as to the others ; and the objection to this return was the same as to the others, with this addition, that the former state of the living was not inquired into by the writ, and therefore that part of the return was not an authentic official act pursuant to the writ, and so was inadmissible ; that it was a very material part, as it showed the collation to have been made immediately after the vacancy, and consequently that it was not made by lapse, but *pleno jure* ; and it was argued that as the Court admitted the whole of the return, and held that the whole ought to be taken into consideration by the jury, the ruling was erroneous.

Supposing that the Judges had held these parts of the *return, as to the former state of the living to be admissible as proof of the truth of those facts (which it does not appear that they did), it is enough to state that we think that the answers of the Bishop in this respect were within the scope of the inquiry of the writ ; for it asks for what is contained in the registry and archives, and it is to be inferred from the return, that all the matters therein stated were in the registry and archives. This exception was therefore properly overruled.

[*671]

The eleventh exception stands on precisely the same footing as the tenth.

The twelfth was an exception to the receipt of the original collation, produced from the registry of Derry, of Thomas Richardson to the living of Camus, dated 23rd June, 1841, and made *pleno jure*.

No valid objection can certainly be made to this part of the evidence. The original document was produced, and was the best evidence of it, and proved an act of possession of the advowson on the part of the Bishop, and was consequently evidence on the question of the plaintiff's title.

I have therefore humbly to state to your Lordships, that the

THE IRISH
SOCIETY
v.
THE BISHOP
OF DERBY.
July 8.

Judges are all of opinion that none of the exceptions ought to have been allowed.

LORD LYNDHURST:

My Lords, in moving the judgment in this case, I cannot help recalling to your recollection, that you were assisted in the argument by the then Chief Justice of the Common Pleas, Sir NICHOLAS TINDAL. We have this morning received information of the death of that most excellent and eminent individual. A more upright, learned, and able Judge never adorned the seat of justice. A more able and excellent individual in all the relations of life never existed. I should have done injustice to my own feelings, if I had not upon this occasion *paid this passing and very inadequate tribute to the memory of this excellent and most eminent Judge; and I am sure your Lordships will excuse me in doing this when you recollect that I was for several years the colleague of the learned Judge, and have during a course of long public life been intimately connected with him, both in public and in private.

[*672]

I pass from this sad subject to the question which is now before this House. I attended the whole of this argument, and had an opportunity of communicating with the learned Judges, during the progress of it, upon the various points that occurred. I prepared the question for the consideration of the Judges, which was adopted by the House. The opinion which has now been given by their Lordships exhausts the whole of this subject; and I beg leave to state, that I entirely concur, after much consideration, in the view that they have taken; and I shall, therefore, with your Lordships' consent, propose that the judgment of the Court of Exchequer in Ireland, affirming the judgment of the Court of Common Pleas there, be affirmed, and with costs.

LORD BROUGHAM:

I entirely agree with my noble and learned friend in the view he takes of this case, and my mind goes along entirely (as it did during the able argument of the counsel at the Bar) with the conclusion to which the learned Judges have come, in the very judicious and satisfactory opinion which we have now heard, and which conclusion I had indeed arrived at during the course of the argument at the Bar.

The main error which ran through the argument of the very learned and ingenious counsel, who zealously defended the claims of the plaintiffs in error against the judgment of the Exchequer Chamber and the Court of Common Pleas, affirmed in the Exchequer Chamber—the main error really was that they seemed to confound the purpose *for which evidence was tendered and admitted, with the admissibility of that evidence. The evidence tendered to prove any point may be perfectly inadequate to prove that point. It may be such that if the learned Judge put it to the jury, as sufficient proof, his direction to them upon that point might well be a subject of exception. Yet the same evidence might be perfectly well admitted and received for such purposes to which it was strictly and correctly applicable.

Now that applies to many of the arguments that were urged upon several of those exceptions; it applies to the eighth as well as to others of the exceptions, in this way, that, for instance, the eighth exception goes to the admissibility of a document. Now it was admissible past all doubt as to the living in question,—Camus. Then suppose that admissibility had not opened the door to receiving that document generally in the case, but that it was to be confined to showing other matters for which it had not been produced, or in respect to which it might not be received in evidence; still if the document is to be received in evidence as to Camus, it is past all doubt,—as the learned Judges have by their opinion given us to understand to be their view, and justly,—it is past all doubt that the whole matter might well go before the jurors in order to make up their minds upon its effect after the evidence should be so received. Here, again, is to a certain degree, the same error of confounding the use to be made of the evidence, or its applicability to the purposes for which it is produced, with the admissibility of the evidence itself. Suppose that in a cause at Nisi Prius, the defendant produces a letter under my hand; that letter is received in evidence, though it may be very true it does not prove the fact for which purpose the defendant put it in. If the Judge refuses to receive it, his direction is liable to be excepted against for that refusal. If he receives and states erroneously to the jury that it proves the point which it *does not, his direction is liable to be excepted against upon another ground. But still it may be properly receivable in evidence, though it does not prove the matter, to prove which it was offered in evidence.

With respect to the argument raised upon another part of the case, upon the trust, certainly it had escaped me that at the Bar they ever made a point upon that, though most certainly they must have done so, otherwise the learned Judges would not have directed their attention to it. It is to be considered, that the Crown cannot be a trustee. It is laid down as one of the first principles of the prerogative law of this country, that the Crown cannot be a trustee for any parties. So much so is that the law, that it is laid down in Comyns' Digest (to show how strongly that is the principle of law), under the head Roy, D., it is laid down, that "if a party is attainted of treason, the Crown, by the attainder, takes that whereof the attainted person was trustee," but how? "takes it not as a trustee, but takes it discharged of the trust." That is undoubtedly the law.

I, therefore, upon the whole, entirely agree with the view of the case which has been given by the learned Judges in their very able and satisfactory opinion ; and I entirely concur, therefore, in the view taken by my noble and learned friend, namely, that the judgment for the plaintiffs in error ought to be affirmed ; that judgment ought to be pronounced here for the defendant in error, which, of course, affirms the decision substantially in favour of the defendant in error by the Exchequer Chamber, and with costs.

I wish I could close the subject without adverting to the most painful and sad circumstance, to which your Lordships' attention has been so properly and so feelingly directed, by my noble and learned friend. A more enlightened Judge than the great magistrate whom we have just lost, and a more just Judge, or, in private life, a more *amiable, honourable, and virtuous individual, I never knew. I never had the good fortune to be connected, as my noble and learned friend was, with him in official life, but I had the great honour and advantage, which might have been turned to more account by me, but which I still deem a high privilege, and which now leaves only a painful recollection,—I had the honour and singular advantage of having been one of his pupils before I was called to the Bar, when he was an eminent special pleader. I cannot trust myself to say anything more.

[*675]

Sir Fitzroy Kelly, on behalf of the defendant, [asked for a certificate for costs under 8 & 9 Vict. c. 51 (1)].

Judgment affirmed with costs.

(1) Repealed by S. L. R. Act (No. 2), 1893.—J. G. P.

THOMAS ROGERS *v.* THOMAS SPENCE (1).

(12 Clark & Finnelly, 700—721.)

1846.
July 16, 20.

Lord
COTTENHAM,
L.C.

[700]

A declaration in trespass stated a breaking and entering, damaging the doors, hinges, and locks; spoiling the grass and fruit trees; and exposing the plaintiff's goods to sale on his premises; by means of which, &c., the plaintiff was not only disturbed in the possession of his house, but prevented from carrying on his business, and deprived of the enjoyment of his goods. The defendant pleaded that, before the action brought, the plaintiff became a bankrupt. Held, on general demurrer (affirming the judgment of the COURT below), that as there were some causes of action included in the declaration which would not pass to the assignees, the plea which embraced the whole, and was not addressed to any particular portion of the declaration, was insufficient, and bad.

THIS was an action of trespass, originally brought by Spence in the Court of Exchequer against two defendants, Rogers and Hennis. The question raised in the present writ of error, depended entirely on the form of the pleadings, as between Spence and Rogers.

The declaration in the Court below, which was dated 24th October, 1842, alleged that Rogers, on the 16th August, 1842, broke and entered the dwelling-house and garden of Spence, and made a great noise and disturbance therein, and stayed and continued therein making such noise and disturbance for a long space of time, to wit, &c., *and forced and broke open, broke to pieces, and damaged divers, to wit, ten doors of Spence, of and belonging to the said dwelling-house with the appurtenances, and broke to pieces, damaged, and spoiled divers, to wit, fifty locks, &c., of great value, &c., and trod down and spoiled the grass and herbage of Spence, of great value, &c., and tore up and spoiled the fruit trees and shrubs of Spence, of great value, &c., and seized the goods of Spence, to wit, of great value, &c., and wrongfully exposed the same for sale, in and upon the dwelling-house of Spence, without the permission, licence, or authority of Spence, whereby, and by means of which several premises, Spence was not only disturbed, &c., in the possession of his house, but prevented from carrying on his lawful affairs and business, and deprived of the use and enjoyment of his goods and chattels.

[*701]

Rogers, by a plea dated 8th December, 1842, pleaded that Spence ought not further to maintain his action, because, heretofore, and after the 11th November, 1842, Spence was a trader, and was indebted to Rogers, and absented himself from his dwelling-house,

(1) See *Morgan* v. *Steble* (1872) L. R. 7 Q. B. 611, 47 L. J. Q. B. 260; *Baxendale* v. *Great Eastern Railway Co.* (1869)   L. R. 4 Q. B. 244, 38 L. J. Q. B. 137; *Rose* v. *Buckett* [1901] 2 K. B. 449, 455, 70 L. J. K. B. 736.—J. G. P.

ROGERS
v.
SPENCE.

and that a *fiat* in bankruptcy issued against him upon the petition
of Rogers, and that on the 3rd December he was declared a bankrupt,
and that one William Pennell was appointed official assignee of his
estate, and accepted and took upon himself the burden thereof; by
virtue of which said appointment and acceptance as aforesaid, and
by force of the statutes in such case made and provided (1), the
causes of action in the declaration mentioned, became and were,

[*702]

and each and every of them, became and was absolutely *vested in
and transferred to Pennell, as such official assignee, under the said
fiat, &c.   Verification.

Spence put in a general demurrer to this plea, and the paper book
stated the ground of the demurrer to be, that the declaration upon
the face of it disclosed a variety of causes of action, which did not,
according to law, pass to or vest in his assignees.   Rogers joined in
demurrer.

Judgment was given by the Court of Exchequer against the plea (2),
and the case was then carried to the Exchequer Chamber, where
that judgment was affirmed (3).

Mr. George Atkinson for the plaintiff in error:

The Courts below decided this case on the authority of *Clark* v.
Calvert (4).   The true grounds of that decision were—1st, That the
assignees had not interposed to divest the bankrupt of his leasehold
interest (for want of which averment the plea was substantially
defective: *Copeland* v. *Stephens* (5), *Williams* v. *Bosanquet* (6)) ; and,
2ndly, That no one can maintain trespass *quare clausum fregit*, but
he who is in actual possession of the *locus in quo* when the injury is
done.   This latter ground alone affects the present case.   The case

[*703]

of *Clark* v. *Calvert* is, at best, *one of doubtful authority.   *   *   *

[704]

What is the cause of action here?   It is simply the breaking and
entering—the rest is mere matter of aggravation.   The whole
fallacy of the arguments in the Courts below consists in the supposition that other matters are involved in this issue.   If there was
an attempt to apply the plea more extensively, it would fail, or the
plea itself would be bad upon demurrer.   The plaintiff had, perhaps,

(1) 6 Geo. IV. c. 16, ss. 63 and 64
(repealed by 12 & 13 Vict. c. 106, s. 1),
and 1 & 2 Will. IV. c. 56, ss. 25 and 26
(repealed by 32 & 33 Vict. c. 83, s. 20),
and see now the Bankruptcy Act, 1883
(46 & 47 Vict. c. 52), s. 44.—J. G. P.
(2) 63 R. R. 575 (11 M. & W. 191).

(3) 67 R. R. 736 (13 M. & W. 571).
(4) 21 R. R. 528 (3 Moore, 96; 8
Taunt. 742).
(5) 1 B. & Ald. 593.
(6) 21 R. R. 585 (1 Brod. & B. 238;
3 Moore, 500).

the power to make what is here alleged as aggravation of the principal trespass, a distinct cause of action in a separate count, and to that the defendant might have pleaded differently. As it now stands, the defendant could have adopted no other form of pleading than that which he has now used. *Chamberlain* v. *Greenfield* (1), *Bennett* v. *Allcott* (2), *Taylor* v. *Cole* (3), *Bracegirdle* v. *Orford* (4), *Cubitt* v. *Porter* (5), *Kavanagh* v. **Gudge* (6), distinctly establish the proposition that the breaking and entering is the gist of the action, and all the rest of the declaration mere matter of aggravation, which could not be pleaded to, or involved in the issue. * * *

[*705]

A chose in action of this sort does pass to the assignees. There is no case directly in point, but there are numerous authorities affirming the principle: [*Smith* v. *Coffin* (7), *Mitchell* v. *Hughes*, *Hancock* v. *Caffyn*, *Wright* v. *Fairfield*, *Drake* v. *Beckham*. An action of trespass *quare clausum fregit* is a chose in action—it is personal estate—it is an injury to the land, which passes to the assignees for the benefit of creditors.]

(LORD CAMPBELL: It is an injury to the possession, and not to the land.)

No: it is an injury to the land, of which possession is evidence of title: for an injury to possession (if there could be such a thing), the form of remedy would be case, and not trespass. The pleas of right of way, leave and license, Statute of Limitations, and the like, show that it is an injury to something real and substantial, and not to a thing incorporeal. * * *

If the bankrupt here had died, his executors would have been entitled to sue for the injury which his real estate had suffered.

[706]

(LORD CAMPBELL: Assuming that the breaking is the gist of the action, how does it appear that the property was injured? The bankrupt can maintain the action, because his possession was disturbed.)

The right of *action vests, because the land has been injured by the trespass. * * *

[*707]

In the Court below Mr. Baron ALDERSON asked whether there were any damages here which the bankrupt could recover, and the

(1) 3 Wils. 292.
(2) 2 T. R. 166. See 31 R. R. 667, n.
(3) 1 R. R. 706 (3 T. R. 292).
(4) 2 M. & S. 77.
(5) 32 R. R. 374 (8 B. & C. 257).
(6) 7 Scott, N. R. 1025.
(7) 3 R. R. 435 (2 H. Bl. 451).

ROGERS
v.
SPENCE.

assignees could not. That question supposed something of an entirely personal nature in the declaration, which would not give the right to the assignees to ask for damages at all. But the test thus proposed is fallacious, since, according to the form of the declaration, the *breaking and entering constituted the essence of the action, and the other matters were merely matters of aggravation.

(LORD CAMPBELL: Could the assignees recover for the mere personal suffering of the bankrupt, and his wounded feelings ?)

They could, and for this simple reason ; the cause of action, as it appears on the face of the declaration, is the simple breaking and entering—all the matters of aggravation arise out of and constitute the character of that trespass, a trespass to the real estate ; and if there was a personal wounding of the occupier, or even of a stranger in the premises at the time, the assignees could prove it, to show the character of the trespass.

(THE LORD CHANCELLOR: When the right of action passes to and may be maintained by the assignees, the right of the bankrupt is gone. The cases, however, speak of the bankrupt bringing an action for the assignees, and holding the damages as in trust for them.)

From the 4 Edw. I. to the present time, assignees have declared in trover for the possession of the bankrupt, a fact which shows that actual possession was never necessary to give them the right of action. The cause of action here passed by operation of law, and it is sufficiently alleged in the plea that it did pass. It was not, therefore, necessary to allege that this particular estate passed, since it was alleged that the right of action passed. If the right is distinct from the title to the real estate, then it passed under the 63rd section of the Bankrupt Act, and the judgment ought to be reversed.

Mr. Peacock for the defendant in error :

The action in its present form can only be maintained by virtue of actual or constructive possession. In this case there was neither actual nor constructive possession in the assignee at the time of the trespass committed. Yet one or other is absolutely necessary, in order to enable assignees to maintain an action of this kind.

This is not an action to *recover damages for an injury done to the   ROGERS
property by which its value has been lessened, but to recover   *v.*
damages for a disturbance of the bankrupt's possession and enjoy-   SPENCE.
ment of the premises. This single consideration disposes of the   [*709]
whole objection. The judgment of the COURT below must be
affirmed.   *   *   *

   It must be admitted that every chose in action does not pass to   [710]
the assignees ; one instance of which is an action against a surgeon
for negligence in the discharge of the duties of his profession. Yet
the bankrupt's estate might be seriously affected by his continued
ill-health, or by his being disabled. Nor will a right of action on
every sort of contract pass to assignees, *Beckham* v. *Drake* (1).

   (LORD CAMPBELL : It must be a contract in respect of property.)

Raymond v. *Fitch* (2) is to the same effect. * * *Brewer* v.   [711]
Dew (3) is directly in point here. * * And in *Chamberlain* v.   [712]
Williamson (4) it was held that the executor of a woman could not
sue for damages for breach of a promise to marry, the declaration
not stating any ground of injury to the personal estate. Nor can
the personal representative sue a medical practitioner for not using
proper skill and attention to a patient, for this is a cause of injury
to the person only.

   (LORD CAMPBELL : The great practical difficulty is this. Suppose
that by one and the same act some substantial injury is done to the
estate, and this is seriously aggravated by a hurt inflicted on the
person of a man who afterwards becomes bankrupt, how would you
remedy that ?)

There might be an action for the injury to the estate, and the other
matter might be given in evidence in aggravation of damages, or
there might be one action for the damage to the person, and
another for the damage to the estate. Suppose a carriage was
taken in execution when a man was going in it to a dinner party ;
that would be a great annoyance to him ; but the right of action
for that annoyance would not pass to his assignees ; and if the
assignees brought an action for the taking of the carriage, they
could not get damages for the personal annoyance to the person
who was riding in it when it was seized.

(1) 8 M. & W. 846.   (3) 63 R. R. 690 (11 M. & W. 625).
(2) 41 R. R. 797 (2 Cr. M. & R. 588).   (4) 15 R. R. 295 (2 M. & S. 408).

(LORD COTTENHAM (Lord Chancellor) : Suppose a ship belonging to the bankrupt to be run down, while he is on board, and he is thrown into the water, and he afterwards becomes bankrupt, who must bring the action ?)

The right to do so would vest in him.

(LORD CAMPBELL : But suppose the ship went to the bottom, but he escaped ?)

Still the bankrupt might maintain the action in respect of the personal trespass.

[*713]   (THE LORD CHANCELLOR : That might *involve a strange consequence ; it might put the whole of his property into his possession again.)

In such circumstances the assignees would not be excluded from likewise bringing an action for the injury to the property ; but if they did not, he might. There are cases in which actions for trespass to goods have been brought, where the jury did not give damages for the goods themselves, and actions have afterwards been brought to recover the value of them.

But, at all events, in order to set up the right of the assignees, it must be shown that the property itself was deteriorated. That is not shown here ; and the plea only answers the injury alleged to have been sustained by the bankrupt and his family.

(THE LORD CHANCELLOR : The only ground in such a case, where the assignees would have a right to interfere, would be either that the property did not come to them at all, or came in a deteriorated state.)

Nothing of that kind is alleged here.

[He argued that the plea was bad because it alleged a mere conclusion of law, not traversable according to the rules of pleading.]

[714]   Suppose that, in *Bennett* v. *Allcott* (1), the defendant had pleaded that the plaintiff had become bankrupt, could he, by so pleading, have prevented the plaintiff from maintaining the action?

(THE LORD CHANCELLOR : In that case there were two distinct causes of action, here there is but one.)

(1) 2 T. R. 166.

But the plaintiff here does not seek to recover the value of the goods. Now, *Lacon* v. *Barnard* (1) shows that trover may be maintained for goods after a verdict in trespass for taking them. * * There more than one cause of action arose from one and the same act.

(LORD CAMPBELL : But it would be difficult to say here that no injury was alleged to the personal estate, for it is stated that there was a breaking of the hinges and doors, and a rooting up of the trees and shrubs.)

Still the plea does not state that it was the estate so injured which came to the assignees.

(LORD CAMPBELL : But the property belonging to the bankrupt is alleged to have been thereby deteriorated, and that brings it within the case which was put some time ago of the ship run down at sea. Suppose a *mine, with a right to take minerals, and long before the bankruptcy a stranger entered and carried away the minerals from the pit's mouth, could not the assignees bring an action for that, though the land itself never came to and vested in them ? If the bankrupt had received the value of these minerals, he would have been richer, and the carrying them away was an injury to his personal estate. This shows that you cannot look merely to the circumstance of the land coming or not coming to the assignees.)

But the plea does not show that the injury to the estate was the cause of action, or that it was the estate so injured which passed to the assignees. The action was brought in respect of a wrong done to the possession. The bankrupt might have maintained such an action, if he had only been let into possession for a month. The declaration does not show that the bankrupt was forced to expend any part of his estate to repair any injury to the premises. There is nothing in it which proves the action to have been brought for an injury to the personal estate; and if there had been, then the defendant ought to have shown by the plea that it was that matter which passed to the assignees, and in respect of which the plea set up the right of the assignees as against the bankrupt. * * *

(1) Cro. Car. 35.

ROGERS
v.
SPENCE.

[*715]

Mr. Atkinson, in reply :

It is not correct to assume that there is no distinction between actual and constructive possession. The distinction between them is considerable : constructive possession would enable the assignees to maintain this action. The cause of action here is the injury to the land, of which the possession is the mere evidence of title.

(LORD CAMPBELL : The reversioner has the title, but not the possession. He could not maintain trespass.)

Lord Coke (1) speaks of all actions personal dying with the person. That meant at that time all actions wherein damages only could be recovered for the plaintiff. That was the law under the 4 Edw. III. Soon after that statute was passed, a question arose whether an action for slanderous words fell within its provisions. It was decided that it did not, and the distinction was clearly drawn between injuries affecting the person and personal property, and those affecting the land. In *Russell's* case (2) it was decided that trespass would lie at the suit of the executors for an injury done to the personal estate.

(LORD CAMPBELL : Would the declaration be good if it merely said, that the defendant on a certain day broke and entered this close ?)

It would. * * Any injury to the personal estate creates a right of action, which must pass to the assignees.

(THE LORD CHANCELLOR : Suppose this had been an injury to property which never could come to the assignees, as for instance, property occupied by the bankrupt for a month, and the trespass committed during that occupation.)

Then the plaintiff should have new assigned. * * *

THE LORD CHANCELLOR (3) :

It appears to me, that the judgment of the Court below is right, and right upon a ground which makes it unnecessary to go into a great deal of the matter which has been discussed, raising some questions of very considerable difficulty, to which it is scarcely possible to give a satisfactory answer. For here the declaration

(1) Co. Litt. 288.   (3) Lord COTTENHAM.
(2) 5 Co. Rep. 27.

states the fact of the breaking and entering on the 20th of August,
1842, and the injury to property, breaking locks and taking goods,
which were afterwards sold, and then states the special inconvenience and injury to the plaintiff, which he sustained by means
of this breaking and entering, and so dealing with his property.

The defendant pleads the bankruptcy, and all the circumstances
connected with the bankruptcy, and the appointment of the official
assignee, and then he states this : " Which said appointment and
the trusts thereof the said William Pennell " (that is, the official
assignee) " then accepted, and took upon himself the burthen of
the execution thereof. By virtue of which said appointment and
acceptance as aforesaid, and by force of the statutes in such case
made and provided, the causes of action in the declaration mentioned, and each and every of them, became and were, and each
and every of them became and was absolutely vested in and transferred to the said William Pennell, as such official assignee."

It seems, in the opinion of one of the learned Judges of the
Court below, to have been considered that that was an averment
of a fact, and that, therefore, unless the cause of action was one
which could not pass to the *assignees in point of law, that it must   [*718]
be considered to have passed, and did in fact pass. I confess that
I cannot so understand it. It seems to me, that that is merely a
conclusion of law, which the pleader submits to the consideration
of the Court, and that it is not at all an averment of fact. On the
contrary, it is the averment of a construction of the statute, and
refers to the statute in support of that which it avers.

As I do not consider that averment to amount to any averment
of fact, but merely to be a conclusion of law, I look to the declaration to see whether that alleges a cause of action which from its
nature must absolutely and necessarily pass to the assignees, and
I there find a mere statement of the breaking and entering of the
house, and the conduct which is alleged in that declaration.

Now it certainly does not follow that that cause of action
must necessarily pass to the assignees. It may be, that there
are circumstances connected with that transaction which would
give a right of action that would pass to the assignees; and
there may be causes of action that would certainly pass to them.
If therefore the plea merely raises, as it seems to me it does, a
defence which may or may not apply to the cause of action, it
does not cover the complaint, and does not therefore necessarily
meet the case, and consequently is no answer to the action. It is

ROGERS
v.
SPENCE.

impossible, after the argument which we have heard at the Bar, to say that there may not be a cause of action arising previous to the bankruptcy, which may be a good cause of complaint by the bankrupt himself, notwithstanding his bankruptcy, but of which the assignees could not take advantage. If that be the case (and it is possible that it might be the case), it is quite clear that the plea does not cover any such cause of action, and therefore that the plea is no answer to the action, and is, consequently, bad.

LORD CAMPBELL:

[*719]   My Lords, I am likewise of opinion *that this judgment ought to be affirmed. The plea is pleaded to the whole declaration ; and it is incumbent on the defendant below to show that all the causes of action that are set out in the declaration passed to the assignees, and that none of them can be maintained by the bankrupt ; for if any of them can be maintained by the bankrupt notwithstanding his bankruptcy, the plea is bad.

Now, if your Lordships look to the declaration, and see the causes of action that are there specified, certainly there are several of these that the assignees could not maintain. They could not be entitled to recover damages for the injury done personally to the bankrupt, as that injury is alleged in this declaration, from the taking possession of the house, and the remaining in it, and the disturbing the plaintiff in the possession of his dwelling-house. It is quite clear, that such a cause of action would not pass to the assignees under the statute 6 Geo. IV. c. 16.

But then it is said very powerfully by *Mr. Atkinson* that this action must be supposed to be brought merely for the breaking and entering, and that all the rest is mere aggravation, and that there ought to have been a new assignment. But there can be no new assignment for a cause of action which is not involved in that declaration. A new assignment is not for a new cause of action. A new assignment only informs the defendant of that which he has specified in his plea. It informs him that he is mistaken in supposing that that is the cause of action upon which the plaintiff relies, that there is another cause of action that he has specified in his declaration, and that that is what he means to rely upon. But still it is a cause of action that was specified in the declaration. Otherwise, the new assignment would clearly be bad.

Any cause of action which might be made the subject of a
[*720]   new assignment is, therefore, a cause of action that is *already

in the declaration, and for which the action must be supposed to be brought. If that be so, this plea is clearly insufficient. It is admitted that it would not be sufficient if there was a new assignment, stating that the plaintiff relies upon the defendant having remained in the dwelling-house, and disturbed his family, and done a personal injury to himself; for such a cause of action is confessed to be too purely personal to pass to the assignees. It is avowed that the bankruptcy could not be pleaded to such a new assignment. And that seems to me to show that here there is a cause of action, which is specified in the declaration, and which would not pass to the assignee, and that therefore the plea is bad.

Then, if you are to take it merely that the action is brought for the breaking and entering, I very much doubt whether this simple act of breaking and entering would be sufficient to enable the assignee to maintain an action, because there may well be a breaking and entering without any injury whatsoever to the personal estate of the bankrupt, and without his creditors being in the slightest degree prejudiced by that act. I therefore think that in any mode in which this case is to be considered the plea is bad.

It is quite unnecessary to enter into the other points that have been discussed. There is no doubt that a cause of action which is exclusively confined to injury to property will pass to the assignees. In that case there is no difficulty. The difficulty is where there is (as in the case which has been put during the argument) a mixed case of injury to the person and injury to the property. There has been no case as yet, which has decided what, under such circumstances, is to happen. It may possibly be that the law will give an action to the bankrupt for the personal injury which has been sustained by him, and will give an action to the assignees for the injury which has been done to the property; as, for example, in the case *which has been put during the arguments, of the owner of a ship being on board, and the ship being run down on the high seas, and the ship going to the bottom, and the owner escaping and afterwards becoming bankrupt: it is possible that he may maintain an action for the personal injury done to him, and that the assignees may maintain an action for the injury done to the property. But it is not necessary at all in this case to enter into the consideration of such questions. All that we have to see is, whether this plea shows that all the causes of action which are specified in the declaration pass from the bankrupt to the assignees.

ROGERS *v.* SPENCE.

[*721]

12—2

ROGERS
r.
SPENCE.

I think that it does not. I think that it has not that effect, and
therefore that the plea is bad, and the judgment ought to be
affirmed.

Judgment affirmed, with costs.

1846.
July 14, 23.
—
Lord
COTTENHAM,
L.C.

[722]

THE NORTH BRITISH RAILWAY COMPANY *v.*
JOHN TOD.

(12 Clark & Finnelly, 722—739 ; S. C. 10 Jur. 975.)

Notices given and plans and sections of an intended railway deposited, in
pursuance of the Standing Orders of the Houses of Parliament, previous to
an application for an Act, are not to be regarded in construing that Act
afterwards, unless they are so referred to as to be incorporated therewith.

A vertical deviation of the level of a railway, not exceeding five feet,
calculated with reference to the *datum* line shown on the plans and sections
deposited in pursuance of the Standing Orders of the Houses of Parliament,
is within the powers of deviation conferred by the Railway Clauses Consolidation Act for Scotland (8 & 9 Vict. c. 33, s. 11) (1), although the
deviation may exceed five feet, calculated with reference to the surface line
shown on the said plans and sections.

THIS was an appeal from an order of the Court of Session in
Scotland, and the question raised in it was whether the appellants,
if allowed to construct their railway in the manner proposed by
them, would be exceeding their statutory powers in regard to the
property of the respondent. The appellants, before obtaining their
Act, proposed to carry their railway across the approach to the
respondent's residence by means of a cutting of fifteen feet four
inches below the surface, and to throw a bridge across the cutting,
the extreme height of which should be two feet above the present
level of the approach. After they obtained their Act, they proposed to carry the railway across the approach by a cutting of two
feet eleven inches, and to throw a bridge across the cutting, the
height of which would be about seventeen feet above the present
level of the approach. As soon as the respondent got notice of the

[*723]

intentions of the appellants, he presented *a note of suspension and
interdict to the Court of Session, on the ground that the appellants
were exceeding their statutory powers; and the COURT granted
interim interdict. The appeal was brought against the interlocutor
granting that interdict.

The facts were these : On the 10th of December, 1844, the agent
of the appellants served notice on the respondent, that application

(1) Compare the Railway Clauses Consolidation Act, 1845 (8 & 9 Vict. c. 20)
(E. & I.), s. 11.—J. G. P.

was intended to be made to Parliament in the then ensuing Session, for an Act to make and maintain a railway, to be called the Edinburgh and Hawick Railway; that the property mentioned in the annexed schedule, or some part thereof, in which the respondent was interested, would be required for the purposes of the undertaking, according to the line thereof as then laid out, under the usual powers of deviation to the extent of one hundred yards on either side of the said line; and that a plan and section of the said undertaking, with a book of reference thereto, had been duly deposited at the proper offices.

The schedule annexed to the notice was entitled, " Schedule referred to in the foregoing notice, and which is intended to show the property therein alluded to, and the manner in which the line of the deposited section will affect the same." The column of the schedule which described the manner in which the respondent's property was to be affected by the railway, was headed thus: " Description of the section of the line deposited, and of the greatest height of embankment, and depth of cutting;" and in the column were inserted the words, " Cutting, fifteen feet four inches; Bridge."

The notice and the schedule were in accordance with the forms prescribed by the Standing Order of this House of the 16th of August, 1838, No. 220, sec. 4.

By the Parliamentary plan deposited in the sheriff-clerk's office, it was shown, according to the horizontal scale given on the plan, that the railway would intersect *the respondent's approach at a point about 520 feet distant from his lodge; and in the Parliamentary section deposited in the same office, the railway was represented, according to the vertical scale given thereon, as intersecting the respondent's approach at a depth of fifteen feet four inches below the surface. The depth of the line below the surface was also marked in figures on the section; and it was farther stated, that the respondent's approach was to be raised two feet, and that the railway was to pass under. The Parliamentary section farther referred to a corresponding cross-section, on which cross-section the level of the rail was represented, according to the vertical scale, as being fifteen feet four inches below the surface of the approach; and the height of the bridge which was proposed to be constructed over this cutting of fifteen feet four inches, was represented as being two feet above the present level of the approach.

THE NORTH BRITISH RAILWAY COMPANY v. TOD.

[*724]

The plan and sections were in accordance with the Standing
Orders of August, 1838, No. 228, sections 3 and 5, and No. 227,
sections 4 and 6.

The respondent, relying on those representations (contained in
the notice, schedule, and Parliamentary plan and sections), as to
the manner in which the proposed railway would affect his property,
abstained from opposing the appellants' bill in Parliament.

That bill, by the first section of which it was declared that the
Railway Clauses and Land Clauses Consolidation Acts (Scotland),
should be incorporated therewith, received the Royal assent in
July, 1845. In the month of December of the same year, a
notice, with plan and section, was served upon the respondent,
from which it appeared that the appellants intended to carry their
railway across his approach in a totally different manner from that
described in their Parliamentary plan and sections, and in the
schedule annexed to the original notice. *Instead of a cutting of
fifteen feet four inches, they proposed to make a cutting of only
two feet ten inches; and instead of constructing a bridge, the
height of which should be two feet only above the level of the
respondent's approach, it was proposed to construct a bridge, the
height of which should be about seventeen feet above it. It was
also proposed to deviate laterally from the line of railway delineated
on the Parliamentary plan, to the extent of sixty-two feet farther
from the lodge, and nearer to the house. The respondent then
applied to the Court of Session for an interdict, which was granted,
after a full hearing both in the Outer and the Inner House.

[*725]

The question submitted to the House was, Whether or not the
vertical deviation proposed by the appellants was within the limits
of deviation allowed by the Act 8 & 9 Vict. c. 33. The respondent
did not dispute their power to deviate laterally to the extent of
100 yards, according to the fifteenth section of that Act. The
point in dispute related solely to the extent of vertical deviation
claimed by the appellants. They insisted that, by the eleventh
section of that Act, they had the power to deviate vertically to the
extent claimed.

By the 11th section it is enacted, that " In making the railway,
it shall not be lawful for the Company to deviate from the levels of
the railway, as referred to the common *datum* line described in the
section approved of by Parliament, and as marked on the same, to
any extent exceeding in any place five feet; or, in passing through
a town, village, street, or land continuously built upon, two feet;

without the previous consent, in writing, of the owners and occu- THE NORTH
piers of the land in which such deviation is intended to be made, &c. BRITISH
RAILWAY
Provided always, that it shall be lawful for the Company to deviate COMPANY
from the said levels to a farther extent without such consent as v.
TOD.
aforesaid, by lowering solid embankments or viaducts, provided
that the requisite height of headway, as prescribed by Act of
*Parliament, be left for roads, streets, or canals passing under the [*726]
same," &c.

The 15th section of that Act provided for lateral deviations, which
are not in question here.

By the 16th section of the appellants' Railway Act, after reciting
that plans and sections, showing the line and levels thereof, and
also books of reference, &c., had been deposited with the sheriff-
clerks of the counties through which it was to pass, it was "enacted
that, subject to the provisions in this and the said recited Acts
contained, it shall be lawful for the said Company to make and
maintain the said railway and works in the line and upon the lands
delineated upon the said plans, and described in the said books of
reference, and to enter upon, take, and use such of the lands as
shall be necessary for the purpose."

Mr. Stuart and *Mr. Bethell* for the appellants. * * *

Sir Fitzroy Kelly and *Mr. Rolt* for the respondent. * * * [728]

THE LORD CHANCELLOR (Lord COTTENHAM) : *July 23.*

This is a case of very great importance, as affecting the rights of [730]
the parties. The first question to be considered is, what is the rule
in respect to applications for interdicts in Scotland, or for injunc-
tions in England, as applicable to cases of this kind? the case on
the part of the respondent being, that a plan was exhibited to him
and to the public previous to the passing of the Act under which
the railway in question was intended to be made, which plan represented that the railway would pass over his land in a cutting of
something more than 15 feet from the surface.

The respondent alleges that, giving faith to these representations,
he had, as he naturally might, come to the conclusion as to what
course he was to pursue with reference to the supposed state of
circumstances, as represented upon that plan ; and that now the
Railway Company have not only deviated, which they had a right
to do, by another line within the prescribed distance, which is 100
yards, but they also propose to deviate beyond 5 feet vertically,

which is the limit of the vertical deviation imposed by the Act of Parliament; that they propose to come nearer the surface by a space exceeding the 5 feet.

The Railway Company say that they do not dispute that they are actually coming nearer the surface to a much greater extent than the 5 feet, but they say they are still within the prescribed deviation from the *datum* line, as laid down for the formation of the railway; the *datum* line being an imaginary line, taking its commencement from some given point at a certain elevation, and then that line is supposed to run in a perfectly horizontal direction, and

[*731]
the inclination of the railway is measured *with reference to that *datum* line. They say they are within the distance, that is, within the 5 feet of the line laid down upon those plans, measured with reference to the *datum* line, and they contend, therefore, that they are within the provisions of the Act of Parliament, and that they are not deviating beyond what that Act authorises.

Now, as to the effect of plans exhibited previous to the contract being made, or previous to the Act of Parliament being obtained, it does seem, from cases which have occurred both in Scotland and in this country, that the rule of the Courts in the one country and in the other is no longer a matter of any doubt or dispute. If a contract or an Act of Parliament refer to a plan, to the extent that the Act refers to the plan, and for the purpose for which the Act or contract refers to the plan, undoubtedly it is part of the contract or part of the Act; about that there is no dispute. A contract or an Act of Parliament either does not refer to a plan at all, or it refers to it for a particular purpose. It has been contended, both in Scotland, and in England, that the defendants in the suit, or those who claim the benefit of the provisions of an Act of Parliament, previous to the enactment being made or the contract being concluded, have represented that the works are to be carried on in a particular mode, upon a plan shown previous to the powers being obtained under the Act, or the contract being concluded, and that the party obtaining the Act, or obtaining the contract, is bound by such representation.

There was a case very much considered in Scotland, the case of *The Feoffees of Heriot's Hospital* v. *Gibson* (1), and several cases have occurred in the courts of equity in this country. It was my fortune to have to consider the matter very minutely in the case of *Squire* v. *Campbell* (2), in which I thought it my duty to review all

(1) 14 R. R. 164 (2 Dow, 301).   (2) 43 R. R. 231 (1 My. & Cr. 459).

THE NORTH
BRITISH
RAILWAY
COMPANY
v.
TOD.
[*782]

*the cases that had occurred in the one country and in the other, for the purpose, if possible, of establishing a rule which might be a guide on future occasions when similar cases should occur, and I found that certainly, what had been very much the opinion of the profession in this country, namely, that the parties were bound by the exhibition of such plans, had met with a very wholesome correction by the doctrine laid down by Lord ELDON and Lord REDESDALE in the case of *Heriot's Hospital*, a case coming from the Court of Session, and decided by this House. Under the authority of that case, where the point was very distinctly raised and deliberately decided upon by those two very learned Lords, I came to the conclusion that there was no ground for equitable interposition.

Now, my Lords, not relying upon the authority of *Squire v. Campbell*, but relying, as we are bound to do, upon the case of *The Feoffees of Heriot's Hospital*, that being a decision of this House, I consider that this is the rule to which the Courts of this country, and the Courts of Session in Scotland, and this House, must hereafter adhere. Taking that then to be the rule, in examining the facts of this case, and the Act of Parliament upon which the question turns, we are not to look at what was represented upon the plan, except so far as its representation is incorporated in and made part of the Act of Parliament; and the real question, therefore, turns upon this, whether the Act of Parliament does or does not make the *datum* line and line of railway, with reference to that *datum* line, the subject-matter of these enactments, and the rule by which the rights of the parties are to be regulated; or whether it also includes the surfaces—which, in this instance, accidentally no doubt, had been very much misrepresented upon the plan.

We are first of all, then, to refer to the Act of Parliament under which this railway is to be carried into effect, and the enactment is in the 16th section. I may here *observe, before I refer to that section, that every thing which is out of the Act is to be found in the Standing Orders of the one House or the other, and the plans which are required to be exhibited by those Standing Orders, except so far as they are made part of this Act, are, as I apprehend, entirely out of the question; because though it may be very inconvenient that Standing Orders of this or of the other House should require plans to be exhibited, containing matters which are not binding between the parties; but still when we are looking to what the rights of the parties are, we can only look to the Act of

Parliament by which those rights are regulated. Plans or proceedings previous to the enactment, can have no effect upon the enactments themselves.

Now the 16th section of the Act of Parliament says, "And whereas plans and sections of the railway, showing the line and levels thereof, and also books of reference containing the names of the owners and lessees, and occupiers of the land through which the same is intended to pass, have been deposited with the sheriff-clerks of the counties of Edinburgh, Selkirk, and Roxburgh; be it enacted, that, subject to the provisions in this and the said recited Acts contained, it shall be lawful for the said Company to make and maintain the said railway and works on the line and upon the lands delineated in the said plans, and described in the said books of reference, and to enter upon, take, and use such of the said lands as shall be necessary for such purpose." There is a Parliamentary authority, which of course cannot be disputed, that the parties are to be at liberty to make "the railway and works on the line and upon the lands delineated on the said plans." We have therefore to look only to what is the meaning of the word "line" as used in this Act of Parliament. The reciting part of that section speaks of "line" and "levels." It is, therefore, necessary to look to other

[*734] Acts—the general Acts being required to be incorporated *and made part of this Act—to see what is the meaning of those terms used in this section; because this is a power under which the Railway Company are to act; and if they bring themselves within the meaning of the enactment, explained by provisions and sections to be found in other Acts of Parliament, beyond all doubt they are then performing the powers which the Legislature intended to vest in them.

In the Act 8 & 9 Vict. c. 33, for consolidating in one Act certain provisions usually inserted in Acts authorizing the making of railways in Scotland, we have several sections to which it appears to me to be necessary to refer; the 7th and 8th I only refer to for the purpose of observing that the plans, which are there referred to, are in cases, where, after the original plans have been deposited, it has been found that they contain certain errors; and then they define the means by which the parties are to correct those errors, and to make their plans correct. But the 11th section contains this provision: "In making the railway it shall not be lawful for the Company to deviate from the levels of the railway, as referred to the common *datum* line, described in the section approved of by

Parliament, and as marked on the same, to any extent exceeding in
any place five feet, without the previous consent in writing of the
owners and occupiers," &c.   It then provides for the case of passing
through a town, as to which other provisions are introduced.   The
description, therefore, of the levels, when it speaks of the levels of a
railway, is in very distinct terms.   It describes the levels of the
railway, as referring to the common *datum* line described in the
sections approved of by Parliament.   Then come other clauses to
which I need not particularly refer.   The 15th provides for a lateral
deviation, which is not in question in the present case.   The power
which is given by that section has been acted upon, and it is not
contended that the lateral deviation does exceed *that power.
Then come the enactments of the 16th section of the local Act:
" That, subject to the provisions in this and the said recited Acts
contained, it shall be lawful for the said Company to make and
maintain the said railway and works in the line and upon the lands
delineated in the said plans."   And then it goes on to enumerate
the works which the Company is to be authorized to make.

The North
British,
Railway
Company
v.
Tod.

[*785]

Now, taking these enactments—because I do not find that the
other Acts contain any provisions which are very material to be
attended to—taking those two enactments together, it appears to
me to be quite plain, that the Legislature intended, in speaking of
lines and in speaking of levels of the intended railway, to confine
those provisions, and to refer them to the *datum* line, and not to any
other representation.   Although great convenience may arise from
the plans and sections required by the Standing Orders to be exhibited previous to the application to Parliament for powers to make
the railway, representing the surface as well as the *datum* line, and
the intended line with reference to that *datum* line, yet if any difficulty should arise as to the construction to be put upon the sections
to which I have referred, we must recollect that Parliament must
be supposed to have had before it not only the line as explained in
these sections, but also the other surface line which is exhibited in
the plan.   But the enactment totally disregards the surface line,
and is confined in terms to the *datum* line, and to the line of railway to be measured and ascertained with reference to its distance
from that *datum* line.

I say then, my Lords, that a case does arise upon these provisions of the Acts in which the plan indeed is referred to, but the
plan referred to is in the terms of the Act of Parliament referred to,
only to ascertain the line of the railway with reference to the *datum*

THE NORTH
BRITISH
RAILWAY
COMPANY
v.
TOD.
[*736]

line. It is not referred to with reference to any surface level. The plan, therefore, is entirely out of the enactment, and is not to be referred to for the purpose of construing the enactment *as to any part of it, except so far as it is referred to and incorporated in the Act.

Arriving at that construction of the rule upon the provisions of the two Acts to which I have referred, and then applying to it the principle which has been established in Scotland and by this House, in the case of *The Feoffees of Heriot's Hospital*, and acted upon in the Court of Chancery in the case of *Squire* v. *Campbell*, we have no difficulty in coming to the conclusion that the application of that principle will necessarily lead to the construction of the clauses to which I have referred. The plan is binding to the extent of the *datum* line, and the line of railway measured with reference to that *datum* line, but it is not to be referred to for the purpose of surface levels, because the Act does not apply it for that purpose, but cautiously confines the enactment to the other lines to which I have already referred. Acting, therefore, upon the principle so established, and with reference to the construction which I conceive to be the construction to be put upon these sections—although we cannot but greatly lament the hardship which, in all probability, these circumstances have imposed upon the respondent, in having his land interfered with in a manner which he did not at all anticipate,—yet when we are called upon to consider whether the Court of Session is correct or not in suspending the further acts of the Company, with reference to the mode in which they were to pass his land, we are bound to look to see what are the powers which these Acts vest in the Company, and, according to the opinion which I have formed, for the reason which I have already explained, I come to the conclusion, that the Company have not exceeded those powers, and do not propose to exceed those powers in the plans that they have formed, and therefore that the Court of Session has been in error in granting the interdict against this Company.

LORD CAMPBELL:

I must admit, that, in this case, I felt *very considerable doubts as the argument proceeded, and I acknowledge that I come to the conclusion at which I have arrived with very great reluctance. It seems to me to be a case of very great hardship upon Mr. Tod. He, looking to the plans lodged under the Standing Orders of the House of Commons, and also of this House, had every reason to believe that there was no danger of the railroad passing his approach, in a manner that could seriously affect the convenience or amenity of his place of residence, and he might very reasonably abstain from offering any opposition to the bill before Parliament, upon that representation. But, when we come to consider what the law upon the subject is, I feel bound to concur in the opinion which has been expressed by my noble and learned friend.

The first question, as it seems to me, to be considered is this: What is the legal construction of the Acts of Parliament? Does the Company, or does it not, propose to exceed the powers which the Acts of Parliament confer upon it? Now, it is admitted that, if the deviation is to be calculated from the *datum* line alone, they (the Company) have not, because neither vertically nor laterally do they exceed the powers of deviation which are conferred upon them by the Acts of Parliament. Well then, that raises the question whether those powers of deviation are to be calculated from the *datum* line alone, or whether the surface line is to be taken into consideration? and my opinion is (and I have no doubt at all about this—I never had much doubt about it) that the Act of Parliament does refer every thing to the *datum* line. I think it is evident that the 11th section of the 8 & 9 Vict. c. 88, clearly makes this *datum* line alone that which is to be regarded.

The word " levels " in the plural number really does not, in my opinion, at all include the surface levels. It means merely the levels on the *datum* line, which point out the course the railway is to go. If that be so, the *Company do not propose to do any thing that they are not authorized to do according to the letter of the Act of Parliament. [*788]

Now, there certainly was a representation made here on the part of the Company, when they proposed to bring in an Act of Parliament, by which they intimated that at that time the intention was that the railway should be fifteen feet four inches below the surface of Mr. Tod's property, at the point of intersection; and that the bridge, by which his approach would pass over the railway, would not be more than three feet. But this was entirely an intimation on the part of the Company that such was their intention. An Act of Parliament of this sort has, by Lord ELDON, and by all other Judges who have considered the subject, been considered as a contract. Well then, this was a negotiation: it was a contract. We must disregard what took place; we must look to see what the contract was. The contract is to be gathered from the words of the

Act of Parliament; and that brings us to the question that I first considered—What is the construction of the Act of Parliament? That Act of Parliament must be considered as overruling and doing away with every thing that had taken place prior to the time when the Act of Parliament passed, and renders the representation or proposal of the Company pending the Act of Parliament of no avail. Many cases have occurred in the courts of common law, in which it has been held that every thing that takes place before a written contract signed by the parties, is entirely to be disregarded in construing the contract by which they are bound.

Now, if Mr. Tod had been cautious, he would have done what I would strongly recommend to all gentlemen hereafter to do under similar circumstances, which is to have a special clause introduced into the Act of Parliament to protect his rights. I do not believe there is any Committee either in the House of Commons or in the House of Lords, who, if he had asked for a clause providing *that the railroad passing his approach should be fifteen feet four inches (with a power of vertical deviation, perhaps)—that it should be of that depth in crossing his approach, and he should be able to pass it by a bridge not more than three feet—would not have acceded to such a clause as a matter of course ; for it is only reasonable that his property should be protected in this manner, and that he should be saved from such a deformity being erected in the sight of his dwelling-house, which would for all time to come be a great nuisance there, and might diminish its value.   But he abstained from introducing any such clause, and therefore he must be considered as having acceded to the Company having all the powers which the Act of Parliament confers upon them. The Act of Parliament confers on them the powers of deviating a hundred yards laterally, and five feet vertically, without any qualifications whatever.   The Company do not propose to deviate to a greater extent: they are, therefore, within the powers; they are not exceeding the powers which are conferred upon them ; they are acting according to the contract that must be supposed to be entered into by them with Mr. Tod.

[*739]

I have read with great attention the case of *The Feoffees of Heriot's Hospital*, and also the admirable judgment of the LORD CHANCELLOR in *Squire* v. *Campbell*, in which all the cases upon this subject are reviewed ; and these cases remove all doubt from my mind, and induce me now, I may say without hesitation—although, I again repeat, with very great reluctance—to come to the conclusion, that, neither upon the construction of the Act of Parliament, nor upon the

ground of the representation that was made, is there any sufficient
reason for supporting this interdict.   I therefore agree in the judgment which has been expressed by my noble and learned friend.

It was then ordered that the interlocutors be reversed, and the
cause remitted to the Court below.

MURRAY *v.* PINKETT (1).

(12 Clark & Finnelly, 784—786; affg. S. C. nom. *Pinkett* v. *Wright*, 2 Hare,
120; 12 L. J. Ch. 119; 6 Jur. 1102.)

1846.
Feb. 20, 27.
Aug. 13.

Lord
COTTENHAM,
L.C.
Lord
BROUGHAM.
Lord
CAMPBELL.
[764]

Trust-funds were invested in the purchase of transferable shares in a
Banking Company in the name of one of the trustees, who was also a holder
of shares in his own right in the same Company, and afterwards made
various sales and purchases of shares therein.   There was no distinguishing
mark by which the shares could be traced, the same being in the nature of
capital, expressed by quantity.   The trustee agreed to assign some of the
shares standing in his name to the Banking Company, as security for repayment of advances which had been made to him, but no transfer was made.
He afterwards became bankrupt, without having shares sufficient to satisfy
the trusts, and his agreement to assign:

Held, 1st, that the Banking Company had no lien on any of the shares
which had been held in trust.

2nd. That although the shares held in trust might have been changed by
sale and re-purchase, the trustee must still be considered as holding, for
the purposes of the trust, the same number of shares out of a larger number
that were standing in his name at the time of his bankruptcy.

3rd. That as no shares were transferred in pursuance of the agreement,
no question as to whether the Bank directors were purchasers with or without notice could arise; and of the two equities, for the cestuis que trust
and for the Bank, the former must be preferred.

THIS appeal was brought against two decrees of Vice-Chancellor
Sir J. WIGRAM, hereinafter stated.

The appellant is the registered public officer of the Provincial
Bank of Ireland, a co-partnership formed in 1825, for carrying on
the business of bankers, under the provisions of Acts of Parliament
passed in the fifth and *sixth years of Geo. IV.; with a capital of
2,000,000*l.* in 20,000 shares of 100*l.* each, of which 25*l.* only were
paid up.   The shares were not distinguishable by any marks, but were
in the nature of capital expressed by quantity only.   The capital
was increased, in 1836, by 20,000 additional shares of 10*l.* each,
resembling the original shares in all respects except the amount.
John Wright, who carried on the business of a banker, in partnership
with Henry Robinson and others, under the firm of Wright & Co.,

[*765]

(1) Considered by Romilly, M.R., *Clack* v. *Holland* (1854) 19 Beav. at pp.
274—277.

was an original proprietor and director in the Provincial Bank of
Ireland, and continued to be so until his bankruptcy in 1840.

By a deed of settlement, dated the 3rd of April, 1828, Francis
Johnson vested certain French stocks in John Wright and Henry
Robinson, upon trusts, under which the said Edward Pinkett, and
others of the respondents, became beneficially interested. The
French stocks were sold by Wright and Robinson, at Johnson's
request, in March, 1830, and in the month of April following the
produce was applied in the purchase of 21,000l. English Consols,
which were transferred to Wright and Robinson. They, in May,
1830, at the instance of Johnson, sold out 5,000l. Consols, part of
the 21,000l., and Johnson, who was himself a broker, with the
proceeds of the sale, and 82l. 5s. added by himself, purchased 160
shares of 100l. each, in the capital of the Provincial Bank of
Ireland, in the name of John Wright alone, the Bank rules requiring that shares should stand in the name of one person only. The
certificates of the shares were delivered to Wright with this indorsement on one of them : " 160 Irish Provincial Bank shares certificates
—Name of John Wright, Esq., in trust for F. Johnson." These
certificates were afterwards deposited with, and remained in the
possession of one of the cestuis que trust. In July, 1830, Johnson,
Wright, and Robinson executed a deed poll, indorsed on the settlement of April, 1828, declaring that Wright *and Robinson, as to
the sum of 16,000l. Consols, residue of the 21,000l. Consols, and
Wright, as to the said 160 shares in the Provincial Bank of Ireland,
were trustees upon the trusts of the said settlement.

[*766]

Francis Johnson died in 1833, and his two daughters, Caroline
and Louisa, and a Mr. Reynolds, became his personal representatives. Caroline afterwards married the respondent, Edward Pinkett,
and Louisa married Charles Plumley. These and their children
are the only parties interested under the trusts of the settlement of
April, 1828, and the dividends on the shares were paid to their use
by Wright from the time of Johnson's death to the time of his own
bankruptcy.

From the time when the 160 shares in the Provincial Bank of
Ireland were purchased, down to October, 1837, the number of
original shares standing in Wright's name from time to time, varied
from 750 to 225 (1), but no change appeared to have been made in

---

(1) It appeared that 125 of these 225
had been transferred to a Mr. Muspratt in 1836, and were by him re-

transferred in 1837. (See the Master's
report, infra, pp. 195—196.)

the latter number after 1837. On the creation of the additional shares in 1836, one of these was allotted as a bonus to every holder of five original shares, so that Wright, as holder of the 160 shares declared to be held by him in trust, would be likewise entitled to 32 of the additional shares; it appeared that 55 additional shares were standing in his name in 1840.

In February, 1840, Wright, being indebted to the Provincial Bank of Ireland, wrote a letter to the directors, as follows:

" SIRS,—As collateral security for the loan of 4,000*l*. from the Provincial Bank of Ireland, I hereby oblige myself to transfer unto the name of any one of your number, whenever you shall require me, one hundred of *the shares of 100*l*. each, of the stock of the Provincial Bank of Ireland, now standing in my name.

[*767]

"JOHN WRIGHT."

In November, 1840, after Wright & Co. had stopped payment, the solicitor of Edward Pinkett gave the Provincial Bank notice, that the parties interested under the settlement of April, 1828, claimed 160 original and 32 additional shares, and that the same were held by Wright in trust. The solicitors for the Bank replied, that part of the shares held by Wright were pledged to the Bank as a security for money they had advanced to him, and the remainder the directors considered themselves entitled to retain, to cover the balance due to them from Wright & Co., who were their bankers in London, adding that the directors had no previous intimation of any claim on Wright's shares, except by themselves, or that any part of them were held in trust by him. In December, 1840, Wright, Robinson, and their co-partners, were declared bankrupts.

In January, 1841, a notice, on behalf of Walter Blount, was served on the Provincial Bank, claiming twenty shares of 100*l*. each, and four shares of 10*l*. each, of those standing in Wright's name in the Bank register. The grounds of this claim were, that, in 1825, Wright & Co., being Blount's bankers, purchased the said twenty shares with his money, by his directions, and thereby became a trustee thereof for him, and afterwards regularly gave him credit for the dividends on such shares in his banking accounts.

The assignees of Wright & Co., under their bankruptcy, claimed all the shares that stood in Wright's name at the time of his bankruptcy, as being in his power and disposition within the bankrupt laws, and part of his estate, distributable among his general creditors.

In January, 1841, a bill was filed by Edward Pinkett, and other parties interested under the settlement of 1828, against Wright and Robinson, as trustees thereof, *against the appellant, as representing the Provincial Bank of Ireland, and against the other' claimants to the shares in that Bank standing in Wright's name. The bill prayed that Wright and Robinson might be removed, and new trustees of the said settlement appointed; and that the said 160 and 32 shares standing in Wright's name, might be transferred to them (subject to the provisions contained in the deed under which the Provincial Bank was constituted), and that the said shares, when so transferred, might be sold, and if the produce should not be sufficient to purchase 5,000l. Consols, that Wright and Robinson might be charged with the deficiency.

John Wright, in the answer put in by him and Robinson, stated that none of the shares standing in his name at the time of his bankruptcy belonged to him, but that he was trustee of them for the different claimants.   The assignees under the bankruptcy, the appellant, as representing the Provincial Bank of Ireland, and Blount, by their respective answers, set forth their claims to the effect before stated (1).

The cause came to be heard before Vice-Chancellor Sir J. Wigram in November and December, 1842 (2), when his Honour made a decree whereby he declared that 160 original shares of 100l. each, and 32 additional shares of 10l. each, in the Provincial Bank of Ireland, part of the shares standing in the name of Wright in the books of the said Bank at the time of his bankruptcy, were held by him on the trusts of the settlement and deed poll in the pleadings mentioned.   But that declaration was to be without prejudice to the claim of Blount to twenty *original and four additional shares, further parts of such shares, standing in Wright's name in the books of said Bank at the time of his bankruptcy; and without prejudice to any claim which the said Bank and the assignees of Wright might have on the shares standing in his name at the time of his bankruptcy, by reason of any interest Robert John Bunyon formerly had in forty-five of the original shares standing in Wright's name in the Bank books at the time of his bankruptcy, or by reason of 125 original shares alleged to have been transferred

[*769]

(1) R. J. Bunyon, a defendant, had claimed to be the owner of forty-five original shares and a proportional part of additional shares, but in consequence of an arrangement with the Provincial Bank, he, by his answer, disclaimed all interest in them. (See Master's report, next page.)
(2) 2 Hare, 120.

by Wright to John Petty Muspratt in August, 1836; and for the purpose of enabling the Court to decide on such claims, it was referred to the Master to make various inquiries specified in the decree (1).

The Master by his report, dated the 6th of July, 1843, found that 225 original shares, of 100*l.* each, in the Provincial Bank of Ireland, and 55 additional shares, of 10*l.* each, were standing in the Bank books in the name of John Wright at the time of his bankruptcy, and that there was then due, for dividends on said shares, the sum of 1,482*l.*

And he found that for many years previous to 1825, and thenceforth down to the time of Wright's bankruptcy, Walter Blount kept a banking account with Wright & Co., and Wright, by his direction in 1825, purchased for him twenty original shares in the said Bank, which shares Wright caused to be entered in his own name in the Bank books, without the knowledge of Blount; and the purchase-money and subsequent calls were paid by Wright out of Blount's monies in the hands of Wright and partners; that in 1836, four additional shares were allotted to Wright in respect of the twenty original shares, and that these twenty and four additional shares formed part of the 225 original and fifty-five additional shares standing in Wright's name in the books of said Bank at the time *of his bankruptcy, and were held by him in trust for Blount.

[*770]

And the Master found, that in August, 1825, Robert John Bunyon, being holder of scrip receipts for 95 shares of 100*l.* each in the Provincial Bank, applied to Wright & Co. to advance him 5,000*l.*, to which they agreed, on a deposit of the said scrip receipts and having the same registered in Wright's name in the Bank books as security for the 5,000*l.*, and for any balance that might be due from Bunyon. And he found that the said agreement was carried into effect, and that in 1836, 19 additional shares of 10*l.* each were allotted to Wright in respect of the said 95 shares; that 50 of the 95 shares were subsequently sold by Wright, and that since his bankruptcy an account was settled between Bunyon and the assignees of Wright & Co., whereby the assignees gave Bunyon credit for the whole value of the said 95 and 19 shares, and the dividends thereon, down to Midsummer, 1842, and that Bunyon agreed to release and assign to them all his interest in the said shares.

(1) 2 Hare, p. 138.

MURRAY
v.
PINKETT.

The Master further found, that the number of original shares standing in Wright's name were not, from 1830 to the time of his bankruptcy, less than 225, independently of the transfer of 125 shares to John Petty Muspratt, which he found to have been made in 1836, in consideration of a loan of 5,000l. made to Wright by the directors of the Provincial Bank, which loan was repaid by Wright in February, 1837, and then the said 125 shares were re-transferred to Wright, and he found that they were the same shares that had been before transferred by Wright, and that the dividends which accrued due on them in the mean time were paid to Wright.

And he found that Wright paid the dividends on the 160 original and 32 additional shares to the parties from time to time interested under the said trust settlement (of 1828) ; and that he regularly

[*771]

paid Blount the dividends *on the twenty original and four additional shares, and paid Bunyon the dividends on the said 45 original and 19 additional shares down to the time of his (Wright's) bankruptcy. The Master appointed Reynolds, before mentioned, and another person, to be trustees of the said settlement, in place of Wright and Robinson.

The report was not excepted to, and it was confirmed absolutely by an order of Court.

The cause having come on for hearing for further directions, the VICE-CHANCELLOR (Sir J. WIGRAM), made a final decree, dated the 7th of November, 1843, and thereby ordered that Wright and the Provincial Bank of Ireland should transfer 160 of the 225 shares of 100l. each, and 32 of the 55 shares of 10l. each, standing in Wright's name in the books of the said Bank at the time of his bankruptcy, and that the Bank should pay the dividends due thereon to the said Reynolds and his co-trustee, to be applied on the trusts of the said settlement, and should transfer 20 of such original and 4 of such additional shares to Blount, and pay him the dividends due thereon, and the remaining 45 original and 19 additional shares, with the dividends thereon, to the official assignee under the bankruptcy of Wright & Co.

The Provincial Bank of Ireland, by the public officer, appealed against both the decrees.

Mr. J. Russell and *Mr. J. Parker* (with whom were *Mr. Elmsley* and *Mr. V. Neale*) for the appellant:

[772]   * * The letter [of February, 1840, see *ante*, p. 193] was a

complete equitable assignment of the 100 shares out of all the   MURRAY
shares standing in Wright's name.   The Bank directors had a   *v.*
right to select the 100 out of all his shares.   They could not have   PINKETT.
any knowledge of any secret trusts, and no such trust ought to be
allowed to defeat *bonâ fide* transactions with third parties, *Ex parte
Watkins* (1).   Johnson, the author of the settlement, placed confidence in Wright personally.   The Bank directors placed no such
confidence in him, but had actual possession of the property : so,
between the two parties, the maxim, *potior est conditio possidentis*,
must be applied, in addition to the other maxim, that he who
allows the ownership of his property to appear to be in another
person, under a secret trust, has no right to be preferred to him
who deals *bonâ fide* with the ostensible owner.   *   *   *

(Lord COTTENHAM, after stating the principle of the case of   [773]
Dearle v. *Hall* (2), asked if there was any case in which the
dealing of a trustee was held to affect the right of the cestui
que trust.)

There is no case expressly on that point.   Why should not they
be held bound to have given notice of the trust to the Bank
directors ?   Neglecting to give such notice, they have no right
to complain that the directors dealt with the ostensible owner
as they did with all other owners of shares.   Had Wright contracted to pledge the shares to a stranger, and the stranger
applied to the Bank, as would be his duty, he would be informed
that they were already pledged.   But to whom would the Bank
apply for information ?   By their books Wright appeared to be
the owner ; they knew of no other owner ; and they were themselves in possession of the shares.   There was no proof that any
of the shares standing in Wright's name, at the time of the bankruptcy, were the shares purchased with the trust funds.   It was
found by the Master, and not disputed, that ninety at least of the
original shares, and a proportional part of the additional shares,
were not any of those purchased with the trust funds.   *   *   *

Mr. Bethell, for the respondents entitled under the trust settle-   [774]
ment (of 1828), and for the assignees of Wright & Co. (3) :

*   *   Whether Wright was trustee, or agent, or mortgagee, in   [777]

(1) 2 Mont. & Ayr. 348.   first set of respondents, and *Mr. J. A.*
(2) 27 R. R. 1 (3 Russ. 1).   *Cooke*, for the assignees.
(3) *Mr. Wood* was with him for the

MURRAY
v.
PINKETT.

respect of those shares, his agreement to pledge shares to the Provincial Bank could not pass any interest to that Bank, in shares which belonged to Bunyon. That agreement could not amount to an actual transfer of the legal interest in any shares, and could only operate in equity to the extent of affecting such beneficial ownership as Wright might have. And it is clear from the facts of the transaction, as found by the Master, that Wright had no beneficial interest in those shares that he could lawfully dispose of. These shares, however, were in the order and disposition of Wright at the time of his bankruptcy, within the bankruptcy laws (1). * * *

It is submitted that both decrees are unimpeachable in all respects, and ought to be affirmed.

> *Mr. Purvis*, with whom was *Mr. F. Riddell*, for the respondent Blount :

It was found by the Master's report, not excepted to, that Wright in 1825 purchased twenty original shares in the Provincial Bank—and which were standing in his name at the time of his bankruptcy—with the monies and by the direction of Walter Blount, and thereupon became a trustee of such shares for Blount, and accounted with him for the dividends which he received on the said shares, from the time of the purchase up to a short time

[*778] previous to his bankruptcy. The letter or contract by *Wright in 1840, in virtue of which the appellants claim an equitable title to 100 shares out of all that were standing in Wright's name at his bankruptcy, being long subsequent to the purchase of twenty shares in trust, cannot under any circumstances, be held to deprive Blount of the benefit of his priority of title. * * *

[779]   *Mr. J. Russell* replied.

Aug. 13.   LORD BROUGHAM :

My Lords, this is a case of very considerable importance in point of amount to the parties, but certainly not one of any difficulty in the argument. Mr. Wright, a well known banker, and who became a bankrupt towards the latter end of the year 1840, had, while he was a banker and solvent, as trustee under a settlement, joined with others in the purchase of 160 shares of a trading concern, called

---

(1) Their Lordships held that this last point could not be raised on this appeal ; see *post*, p. 200.—O. A. S.

the Provincial Bank of Ireland. This purchase was made by the
trustees at the instance of one of the cestuis que trust ; they sold
out 5,000*l.* stock, which was part of the trust funds ; and with the
proceeds of the sale, and other monies which were added by one of
the cestuis que trust, Johnston, or one acting for the other cestuis que
trust, they purchased the 160 shares of 100*l.* each. There could be no
doubt whatever that the purchase was made by Wright as trustee ;
it was equally clear that, having so purchased, he held the shares
as trustee, even if nothing further had been done in the matter
than what I have now stated. But to make it still clearer, if
possible, the certificates of the shares were, indorsed with the words
"160 Irish Provincial Bank share certificates, name,"—that is, in
the name of "John Wright, Esq., in trust for F. Johnson. June 8th,
1840." The certificates were deposited with and remained in the
possession of one of the cestuis que trust, *and there was subse-   [*780]
quently to that a declaration of trust executed by an indorsement
on the trust deed. Anything, therefore, more absolutely certain
than that this was trust property, cannot possibly be imagined.
To which I must add, that a bonus was afterwards added of ten
pound shares, which gave rise to thirty-two auxiliary or additional
shares, which, it is admitted on all hands—and I do not think it
was denied at the Bar in argument—must follow the fate of the
160, as an accessory follows the fate of his principal ; for these were
only additional shares, by way of bonus, or accession to the original
trust shares, and consequently it must be taken as if there were
the 160, *plus* the thirty-two, and whatever equities apply to the
160, must, of course, apply to the thirty-two additional shares.

Now, after this, came the bankruptcy of Mr. Wright ; he stopped
payment late in November, 1840, and afterwards a *fiat* in bankruptcy was taken out against him. But I ought to mention that,
previously to that, namely, on the 1st of January, 1840, while he
was still a banker and solvent, he had, in security of a debt contracted by him with the said Provincial Bank, agreed to assign
100 shares to that Bank ; and accordingly a memorandum, directed
by him to the directors of the Bank, is in evidence : "As security
for the sum of 4,000*l.*, held by me on loan from the Bank, I hereby
oblige myself to transfer into the name of any one of your number,
whenever you shall desire it, 100 shares, of 100*l.* each, of the stock
of the Provincial Bank of Ireland, now standing in my name."
The only question that could arise with respect to that memorandum of agreement, would relate to so many of those 100*l.*

[*781]

shares as Mr. Wright was beneficially entitled to.   Supposing that the question is decided against the Bank, and against his assignees, representing him since his bankruptcy, as to the shares, which he only held on trust under the settlement ; but as regards the shares in which *he was beneficially interested, that agreement may be argued, and has been argued, and has indeed been decided, to raise an equity in favour of the Bank in security of their loan to him of 4,000*l.*, as against the assignees under his bankruptcy.

Now, I may dispose first of that last matter which I have mentioned, because it is taken out of the cause altogether.   The learned VICE-CHANCELLOR in giving his judgment says, that the opinion which he expressed with respect to these 160 shares, and 82 additional accruing shares, he gives on the ground that that being trust property is not liable so and so, saving, he says, any question that may be raised on the ground of those shares by the assignees in respect of their contending possibly that they were in the order and disposition of the bankrupt; says he, " If that question is to be raised I must hear it argued, which I have not hitherto done."

I have enquired at the Bar, and I find that that question never could arise here ; for the assignees have acquiesced in the judgment which was given against them, and accordingly we had not that argument maintained at the Bar here.   But it is also satisfactory to know—as clearing up any doubt that might remain upon that part of the judgment of the learned Judge below— that it was argued before the VICE-CHANCELLOR, and he disposed of the question after the decree to which reference is made in the report from which I have read that passage; he disposed of that question after having heard it argued, and disposed of it against the assignees, and undoubtedly the assignees acquiesced in that decision, and so acquiescing did not raise the point at all before your Lordships.

My Lords, there came to be a question with respect to a gentle-man, Mr. Blount, who claimed twenty shares, alleging that Wright & Company, being his bankers, purchased them with money in their hands belonging to *him, and consequently he claimed those twenty shares as cestui que trust of Wright, as against the assignees and the Provincial Bank also.   The decree of the VICE-CHANCELLOR has directed an enquiry in respect of those shares, the result of which, if it be found, as Mr. Blount has alleged, that they were purchased with his monies, would of course entitle him to recover according to the tenor of the other parts of the decree ;

[*782]

supposing that to be well founded, which I think it is, defeating the
claim on the one hand of the assignees representing Wright, on the
other hand of the Provincial Bank of Ireland, between whom and
the cestuis que trust of John Wright the main contention in this
case has arisen.

MURRAY
v.
PINKETT.

Now with respect to the ground of the contention on the part of
the Provincial Bank of Ireland, I hope I may be permitted, with all
due courtesy towards those parties, to express my great wonder that
that should ever have been held to be an argueable point. Here is
a trustee, purchasing as such, without any doubt, holding as such,
acknowledged as such. Then to say, in the first place, that they
can pass by the assignment to the assignees under the *fiat* is
monstrous. But that is given up; they were not in the order and
disposition of the bankrupt, or anything of the kind. Then what
claim has the Provincial Bank of Ireland? Now here I ask to
keep entirely out of view the whole of the argument resting upon
notice. It is said, that Wright being a shareholder in the Bank,
had notice—of course he had notice as a trustee acting as such—
and that through him the Bank had notice. Now I lay that
entirely out of view. It is a perfectly debateable point on either
side. I do not deny that something may be said in support of the
point of constructive notice, and a good deal more, perhaps, in my
opinion against it; but at all events it is wholly unnecessary, it is
totally superfluous. I do not say it is beside the question; for if
the case laboured in other *points it might keep it; but I do not
see the necessity of it to support this judgment of the learned
VICE-CHANCELLOR at all; because the case stands perfectly clear
without saying one word of notice, either actual, or implied and
constructive. What is the ground of that extraordinary contention
of these parties? In the first place, we were desired to look into
the various parts of the deed of settlement of the Provincial Bank
under which they act, and we did look into them, and a minute
examination of them tended, at every step we took, to defeat the
claim of the Bank. But what is the sum and substance of their
contention? It was, that they had a general lien over Mr. Wright's
shares, and that general lien arose from his being a partner, and
that he being such partner as aforesaid, was indebted to them, or
would be found to be indebted to them upon the winding up and
balancing of the accounts, and that being so indebted to the Bank,
they had such a lien as gave them a right to retain his shares.
But even that is not sufficient; for, at the very outside, that

[*783]

argument and that statement of the case could only extend to the
right to retain, by virtue of their lien, the shares belonging to John
Wright beneficially.   But did that lien give them a right to retain
shares which were not his, John Wright's, but F. Johnson's
shares, and which had been deposited with a memorandum of
trust indorsed, and upon which shares John Wright had executed
a declaration of trust, divesting him of all beneficial interest, and
confessing that he held them as trustee for the benefit of another ?
What is said about the lien that partners have in a concern, must
be taken with very great allowance even in the ordinary case of a
beneficial interest, and supposing he had not been a trustee;
because in the case of a partnership there must be a winding up
and a dissolution before you can tell what one partner owes to
another.   In this case of a joint stock Bank, the very object of the
[*784] concern is to enable a person to cut out *and come in, as it were,
without any winding up of the concern, and when you cannot tell
how the account may stand between the parties.   That of itself is
sufficient to dispose of the main ground of their contention.

But the principal point on which I rely, and which cannot leave
a doubt in any man's mind, is, that that could never extend by
possibility to give them a lien over shares which were not John
Wright's shares at all, and therefore not the partner's shares,
supposing it were a case of common partnership, but which were
the shares of the cestuis que trust, who alone were beneficially
interested.   Without, therefore, going further into this case, as
I am moving your Lordships to affirm the judgment, I only remind
you how very clear we held this to be, from time to time, in the
course of the argument.

I will therefore simply content myself with moving, that the
judgment of the learned VICE-CHANCELLOR be affirmed, and also,
undoubtedly, with costs.

THE LORD CHANCELLOR:

If the grounds upon which the appellant has endeavoured to
support his case were to be countenanced by this House, it appears
to me that there would be a greater inroad made thereby on the
security of property held in trust than by any decision which has
ever been come to in any court of justice.   For, what is the case?
Of the fact of these shares being held in trust, there is no doubt;
the only doubt that has ever been suggested has been that, although
it is clear that the 160 shares were originally the property of the

family, yet that those were sold and changed, and other shares were
re-purchased by the trustee. Now a party who is a trustee cannot
divest himself of his trust in that way. If he commits a breach of
trust by selling the trust property, and re-purchases it, and re-invests
it again, is he not a trustee of the property so re-purchased? Is
he to say, " No, I have sold 10,000*l.* stock of yours, it is true, but
*I have sold it, and bought with the money 10,000*l.* other stock,
and I am not liable to you as a trustee." He may have changed
it from time to time, but as he is found, at the time of his bankruptcy, to be in possession of certain shares which he was bound
to have as trustee for this family, of those shares, beyond all doubt,
he must be considered, as against every person, as a trustee.

MURRAY
v.
PINKETT.

[*785]

Then what is the claim of the Bank? The Bank say, " You are
a shareholder in this concern in respect of these shares, but we have
advanced you money, not as a shareholder, not as a partner, but as
a person borrowing money of the Bank; and because you owe us
money, we insist upon retaining these shares standing in your
name, to repay the balance which is due from you to the Bank."
Whether that might or might not prevail if these shares belonged
to him individually is another matter; but is that to prevail on the
assumed fact, which is now established, that he had not these shares
beneficially, but that he was a trustee of them for others? The
doctrine would be this, that if property be vested in a person in
trust, if that property in any way comes under the controul of
persons to whom he is indebted, those persons can pay the trustee's
debt out of the trust money!

The next proposition is—and which was thought so extravagant
that it was not mentioned in the argument, though it stands in the
printed case as one of the grounds brought forward for the consideration of the House, and one of the grounds argued below—the
next proposition is one that is equally extravagant. They say you
have in terms pledged these shares. Now if this property had been
property in which the trustee had the legal estate, and the trustee
had, in breach of trust, transferred the legal estate to other persons,
the question then would have arisen as to whether they were or
were not purchasers without notice. But no such case occurs here.
The shares never have been transferred at all; they *remain in the
name of John Wright. He is trustee of those shares so standing in
his name; and all that he has done has been an attempt to commit
a breach of trust, and a fraud undoubtedly on the Bank, by saying,
" I will pledge these shares so standing in my name for the purpose

[*786]

of securing the debt which I owe to you." Then here are two
equities, that is to say, here is a trustee of the property which he
held for the benefit of the cestuis que trust, endeavouring to create
an equity upon that property to secure his own debt. Which of
those two equities is to prevail? Undoubtedly the former.

That is the whole case which has been the subject of the
argument below, and of the appeal to this House.

LORD CAMPBELL:

I entirely concur in the well considered judgment of the learned
VICE-CHANCELLOR in this case; and I do think that the parties
ought to have been satisfied with it.

The decree was affirmed, with costs.[1]

———————•———————

1846.
Feb. 25,
March 3, 9,
10.
Aug. 28.
———
Lord
LYNDHURST,
L.C.
Lord
BROUGHAM.
Lord
CAMPBELL.
[787]

BRANDAO v. BARNETT AND OTHERS (1).

(12 Clark & Finnelly, 787—811 ; S. C. 3 C. B. 519.)

The general lien of bankers is part of the law merchant, and is to be
judicially noticed, like the negotiability of bills of exchange.

A banker's lien does not arise on securities deposited with him for a
special purpose, as where Exchequer bills are placed in his hands to get
interest on them, and to get them exchanged for new bills. Such a special
purpose is inconsistent with the existence of a general lien.

Where a person who is in reality the agent of another, deposits Exchequer
bills with his own bankers, without informing them whose property these
bills are, the bankers may be held entitled to consider these bills as the
depositor's property, and to hold them as security for any money due to
them from him, if the mode of deposit, or the circumstances attending it,
give them a lien on the bills as against him.

A. was the London agent of B., a Portuguese merchant, and in that
character purchased Exchequer bills for him, received interest on them, and
at proper intervals got them exchanged for others. He acted in the same
manner for several other foreign customers. A. kept an account with C.,
as his banker, and at C.'s banking-house had several tin boxes, in which
he deposited these Exchequer bills, and of which he kept the keys. On the
1st December, 1836, A. took out of a tin box several Exchequer bills, which
he delivered to C., requesting C. to get the interest due on them, and to get
the Exchequer bills exchanged for others. C. did so. Before A. came to
take back the Exchequer bills, acceptances of his beyond the amount of his
cash-credit account, were presented at C.'s Bank, and paid. A. afterwards
became bankrupt:

Held that C. had not a lien on the Exchequer bills in his hands for the
balance due to him on A.'s account.

THIS was a writ of error brought upon a judgment of the Court
[*788] of Exchequer Chamber, reversing, upon writ of *error a judgment

(1) Followed in *London Chartered Bank of Australia* v. *White* (1879) 4 App.
Cas. 413, 48 L. J. C. P. 75.—J. G. P.

given for the plaintiff by the Court of Common Pleas, in an action of trover.

The declaration was in the usual form of trover, for converting Exchequer bills. The pleas were, 1st, Not guilty ; 2ndly, a denial of the plaintiff's property in the Exchequer bills ; and, 3rdly, a special plea, in which the defendants, as bankers, set up a claim, by way of lien, to retain the Exchequer bills to secure the balance due to them from a firm called James Burn & Co.

The Exchequer bills sought to be recovered were twenty-one in number, and amounted to the sum of 10,100l. The balance of James Burn & Co., in respect of which the lien was claimed, amounted to 3,211l. 19s. 7d.

The plaintiff was a Portuguese merchant, who, up to the year 1834, resided at Rio de Janeiro, but in that year returned to Portugal, where he has since resided.

The defendants are bankers in London.

Edward Burn, who for many years carried on business as a merchant in London, and traded under the firm of James Burn & Co., kept an ordinary banking account with them, drawing cheques upon them, and making bills payable at their Bank : and such cheques and bills were paid by the defendants out of the funds held by them on Burn's account, which was always in cash to meet them.

Burn was the agent and correspondent of the plaintiff, who from time to time remitted bills of exchange and money to Burn, and employed him upon commission to invest the proceeds in Exchequer bills. Burn was employed in the same manner by other foreign correspondents.

Burn kept at his bankers, in separate tin boxes, under his own lock, the Exchequer bills purchased for his different correspondents, except when it became necessary to receive the interest and exchange the bills.

Upon some of those occasions Burn took the plaintiff's *Exchequer bills from the tin box, and delivered them to the defendants, with a request that they would receive the interest and exchange the bills ; and after the defendants had so done, Burn obtained the new bills from them when he next called at the banking-house, which generally happened within a week or fortnight after the receipt of the bills by the defendants ; and when he so obtained them, he locked them in the tin box, as before, where they remained till wanted.

[*789]

BRANDAO
v.
BARNETT.

Prior to December, 1836, Burn had sold, by express order of the plaintiff, so much of the plaintiff's Exchequer bills as reduced the amount to 10,100*l.*, and on 1st December, 1836, the remaining Exchequer bills of the plaintiff (to that amount) were locked up in the private tin box, as before described. The usual advertisement by the Government for the payment of the interest and exchanging the Exchequer bills appeared about that time ; and on or about 1st December, Burn went to the banking-house of the defendants, and took from his private tin box the last mentioned Exchequer bills, and delivered them to one of the defendants, saying, " will you have the kindness to get these bills exchanged for me ? " The defendants counted the bills, repeated the number to Burn, who said, " Right ; " and no further conversation passed upon the occasion.

The following is the form of one of the Exchequer bills :

" No. 8,551. 1,000*l.* By virtue of an Act, 6th & 7th Gulielm IV., Regis, for raising the sum of 14,007,950*l.*, by Exchequer bills, for the service of the year 1836-7, this bill entitles ———, or order, to one thousand pounds, and interest after the rate of twopence halfpenny per centum per diem, payable out of the first aids or supplies to be granted in the next session of Parliament, and this bill is to be current and pass in any of the public revenues, aids,

[*790]

taxes, or supplies, or to the account of his Majesty's *Exchequer at the Bank of England, after the 5th day of April, 1837. Dated at the Exchequer this 19th day of December, 1836. If the blank is not filled up, this bill will be paid to bearer. The cheques must not be cut off.—J. NEWPORT."

The blanks in the Exchequer bills delivered out by Burn had not been filled up, and they were therefore negotiable securities, payable to bearer, and transferable by delivery.

The defendants, on the 20th of the same month of December, delivered up the bills so received from Burn at the proper office, receiving the interest due upon them, which they carried, as usual, to the account of Burn, and obtained in exchange the new Exchequer bills, which formed the subject of this action. The defendants had no notice, until the failure of Burn, that the bills were not his property ; nor were the names of Burn's bankers ever communicated to the plaintiff.

At the time Burn delivered the Exchequer bills to the defendants, on 1st December, he was unwell, and he was unable to come to

town on business, as usual, from that time until after his failure in
business, which happened on the 23rd day of January, 1837, and
he had no communication with his bankers (the defendants) further
than that in the interval he had desired his clerk to procure from
the defendants the particulars of the Exchequer bills received
in exchange for those delivered by him to be exchanged ; and
the defendants furnished to the clerk a paper containing such
particulars.

On the morning of the 21st January, 1837, the balance of Burn's
account was in his favour to the amount of 1,596*l.* 11*s.* But in the
course of that day, bills accepted by Burn, and made payable at the
defendants, were presented for payment, and the defendants paid
them to the amount of 4,808*l.* 10*s.* 7*d.* These bills had been accepted
at periods prior to the delivery of the exchequer bills to the defendants. These payments by the defendants absorbed the balance to
the credit of Burn's account, *and made him a debtor to the
defendants to the amount of 3,211*l.* 19*s.* 7*d.* For this amount the
defendants held the plaintiff's Exchequer bills, and in consequence
of such detention this action was brought.

At the trial of the cause before the Lord Chief Justice Tindal, at
the sittings after Michaelmas Term, 1837, a verdict was found for
the plaintiff, subject to the opinion of the Court of Common Pleas
upon a special case, with liberty to either party to turn the case
into a special verdict, which was afterwards done.

In Michaelmas Term, 1840, the COURT, after taking time to
consider, gave judgment in favour of the plaintiff (1). This judgment was afterwards reversed in the Exchequer Chamber (2).

Sir T. Wilde and *Mr. Montagu Smith* for the plaintiff in error :

It is admitted that bankers may, as a general rule, have a lien
on property deposited with them by their customer, if at the time
of such deposit their customer is actually indebted to them. But
that lien can only arise on such property as may come into their
hands in the way of their trade as bankers. The first thing, therefore, for the bankers to establish in this case is, that the Exchequer
bills were put into their hands by the customer in the course of
their trade. It cannot be said that that is the case here. The
facts of this case show that the Exchequer bills were delivered to
the bankers, not in the ordinary way of their trade, but only for a
special purpose. In such a case no general lien can arise. * * *

[*791]

BRANDAO
v.
BARNETT.

(1) 1 Man. & G. 908 ; Scott, N. R. 96.   (2) 6 Man. & G. 630.

BRANDAO
v.
BARNETT.

[792]

As a general rule, it is clear that no two persons can, by
agreement between themselves, create a lien in favour of one of
them against the goods of a third person, *Leuckhart* v. *Cooper* (1),
Rushforth v. *Hadfield* (2), *Oppenheim* v. *Russell* (3), *Lucas* v. *Dorrien* (4),
lay down that principle in a clear and positive manner.

No doubt, it is stated here, that it is the custom of bankers to
receive Exchequer bills from their customers, and in the course of
their business to receive the interest on the bills, and to get those
bills exchanged at the proper time for others ; but the case here
goes on expressly to say, that these bills were received under the
special circumstances which the verdict sets forth. This very mode
of stating how the bankers became possessed of these bills, takes
this particular case out of the general custom ; so that, supposing
the custom to be what the defendants say, the verdict here shows
that that custom does not attach on these bills. • • •

[793]

The bills are, beyond all question, the property of the plaintiff.
It lies on the bankers to show the facts which have taken out of
the plaintiff the right to dispose of this property. They have not
shown any such facts, and such facts cannot be implied. [They
cited *Withams* v. *Lewis* (5) ; *Holderness* v. *Collinson* (6) ; *Hewinson*
v. *Guthrie* (7) ; and *Scarfe* v. *Morgan* (8) ; and contended that,
assuming that any lien was created, the defendants ought to have
pleaded the particular facts on which they alleged it to arise.]

[795]

In the course of the argument in this very case in the Court
below, Mr. Baron PARKE expressed his opinion as to the necessity
of putting this claim of lien on the record. He said (9) : " where
the custom is set out upon the record, the Court can see the extent
of it, whether it extends to all negociable securities, for whatever
purpose deposited, or whether it is limited to deposits made with
the banker in the course of business." He must of course have
changed that opinion when he concurred in this judgment, since
the supposed custom, and the circumstances out of which it is said
to arise are not here set forth ; but it is submitted, with much
confidence, that his first impression was the correct one. The
special verdict here is defective in two respects, first, because

[*796]

nothing is stated as to what is the general custom of *merchants

(1) 43 R. R. 602 (3 Bing. N. C. 99).
(2) 8 R. R. 520 (7 East, 224).
(3) 6 R. R. 604 (3 Bos. & P. 42).
(4) 18 R. R. 480 (7 Taunt. 278 ; 1
Moo. 29).
(5) 1 Wills. 55. See also *Duncombe*

v. *Wingfield*, Hob. 263.
(6) 31 R. R. 174 (7 B. & C. 212).
(7) 42 R. R. 720 (2 Bing. N. C. 755).
(8) 4 M. & W. 485.
(9) 6 Man. & G. 660.

as to lien, and, secondly, because what is now claimed exceeds anything that has been usual. On both these grounds the judgment
of the Court below is defective.

(LORD CAMPBELL : If a general lien is once established, it surely
then becomes matter of law: whether it exists or not may be
matter of fact, but when it exists the extent of it must be matter
of law.)

That is not so in the first instance; for the circumstances from
which it arises, and the extent to which in any particular place or
trade the lien exists must first be ascertained by evidence. But
assuming that bankers have a general lien, and that that is such
settled matter of law as not to require to be stated in the special
verdict, then it is submitted that the facts here shown on the record
do not bring this case within that general rule. The leaving of
these Exchequer bills in the hands of the bankers was like leaving
plate with them. The property continued in the owner. The
general right of the plaintiff is clear; the defendants must, by
facts, take themselves out of the operation of that clear right. No
such facts are shown here. The deposit of the bills was like the
deposit of plate, an act done for a special purpose, but not falling
within the description of an act done in the ordinary course of their
business as bankers.

[They also cited *Collins* v. *Martin* (1), *Kruger* v. *Wilcox* (2),
Drinkwater v. *Goodwin* (8), and *Naylor* v. *Mangles* (4).]

The *Solicitor-General* (*Sir F. Kelly*) and *Mr. Martin*, for the
defendants in error :

It is perfectly clear that with respect to the general lien of
certain classes of persons, a banker, a wharfinger and a factor, the
right to lien is now matter of law. The general right of lien of a
factor, and the right of stoppage *in transitu* are instances of this
sort. This latter right is of extremely modern origin; yet it is
stated by Lord Tenterden, in his book upon shipping (5), to be
matter of law. No Judge would require it to be pleaded, nor any
one allow it to be proved. * * The right is a general right; it
is for the other party to show that his is a case of exception.

[797]

If Exchequer bills are placed in the hands of bankers to do the

(1) 4 R. R. 752 (1 Bos. & P. 648).   (4) 5 R. R. 722 (1 Esp. 109).
(2) Amb. 252.   (5) Ch. xi., Shee's ed. 511.
(3) Cowp. 251.

BRANDAO
v.
BARNETT.

particular business with respect to them, which it is the business of a banker to perform, the lien at once attaches. A case of this kind marks, in the plainest manner, the distinction between the cases of the deposit of plate with a banker and the deposit with him of bills of exchange, with a direction to him to get in the money as it becomes due on those bills. In the latter case there

[*798]

is no *doubt that the lien would attach, and so it will in the case of the Exchequer bill deposited with the banker to get interest upon and then to get exchanged. The case of *Davis* v. *Bowsher* (1), shows what is the general right of a banker to lien upon securities of the customer placed in his hands. * * *

(LORD CAMPBELL: You admit that the lien did not exist while the bills were locked up in the boxes in the bankers' strong room. Now, suppose Burn had told the bankers to get these bills exchanged and to return them to the boxes, and the bankers had promised to do so by twelve o'clock on a particular day, would they have obtained a lien upon them by the fact that at ten o'clock on that day the balance was turned in their favour?)

They would not, if it was shown that there was any positive contract to return the bills, at all events at twelve o'clock; but they would get the lien if there had been a mere delivery of the bills to get them exchanged, without any such contract being made as to their return at a particular time.

(LORD BROUGHAM: But is it not the same thing if a man says, "take the bill and get it exchanged in the usual way?" Does not the taking of the bills, under such circumstances, amount to an undertaking on the part of the bankers to return the bills as soon as the particular thing for which the bills were entrusted to them has been performed?)

[*799]

It is not the same thing. In one case the *general right to lien would arise: in the other it would be excluded by the particular terms of the contract. In the present case the transaction was one so completely in the ordinary business of bankers, and so free from the influence of any particular contract, that the lien arose as of course, and for the plaintiff to make out an exemption from its operation it is necessary for him to show that the deposit was made upon a contract, that though the balance should be against the customer, the lien of the banker should not attach.

(1) 2 R. R. 650 (5 T. R. 488).

(LORD CAMPBELL : But was it not a part of the contract that the new bills were to be restored ?)

In all cases whatever, where property is entrusted by one man to another, it is on an implied contract that it is to be returned on request, and so far as that implied contract is concerned, there is not a shadow of distinction between property put into the hands of a person in the ordinary course of his business and for a special purpose.

(LORD CAMPBELL : You may argue that there is no distinction in law, but there is plainly a distinction in fact.

LORD BROUGHAM : Thus : if I put money into the hands of my banker, he is my debtor to the amount of the money; but that is not so with respect to a bill of exchange put into a box in his house.)

If a bill of exchange and an Exchequer bill were put into the hands of a banker on the same day, he would be bound to deal with both as the property of the person depositing them, and to restore both on demand.

(THE LORD CHANCELLOR (LORD LYNDHURST): It seems to have been thought in the Court of Common Pleas that no representation was here made that the customer had a right to deal with them as his property.)

The absence of any distinct representation of that sort will not affect the case, if the deposit of the bills can be treated as a deposit for the purpose of their being used by the bankers in their character of bankers. The purpose for which the deposit was made here established that fact. It is supposed, on the other side, that these particular securities were delivered *to the bankers under an implied promise that they should be delivered back whenever the customer might think proper to ask for them. To a certain extent that is true. But that will not prevent the lien from attaching, for all deposits of property are impliedly subject to that condition.   [*800]

(THE LORD CHANCELLOR : The proposition to support your argument should be qualified thus : shall be returned when demanded, provided that the balance shall not be against the depositor.

LORD CAMPBELL : That would apply to all negotiable securities

14—2

BRANDAO
v.
BARNETT.

deposited with a banker.   You say that there is no distinction between the deposit of an Exchequer bill and other negotiable security to be locked up, and negotiable securities which remain with the banker.)

The qualification " to be locked up," is not to be introduced here; that would be matter of special direction.   The act, which takes place after the return to the customer, must not be mixed up with the return itself.

The contract with the bankers is, that they will receive the bills, and take care of them.   The moment it is shown that Exchequer bills pass by delivery, and that it is the custom of bankers, in the course of their business, as such to change them, the right to lien for a general balance is established: [*Davis* v. *Bowsher* (1), *Jourdain* v. *Lefevre* (2), *Bosanquet* v. *Dudman* (3), and *Wookey* v. *Pole* (4)].

[802]

(THE LORD CHANCELLOR : In that case there was an express pledge.)

That is so; but the case shows, by being decided on the ground of such instruments passing by delivery, that though the circumstances may not be the same, the principle is.

(THE LORD CHANCELLOR : The question here seems to be, whether, for all purposes, a party, who is in possession of a negotiable instrument, is to be considered as the owner of it.   He may pledge it, provided that all is done *bonâ fide* in making the pledge : but are the circumstances here such as are equivalent to an express pledge ?)

They must be so considered in virtue of the ordinary business of a banker, and of his established right of lien over securities deposited in his hand in the way of his business.

(THE LORD CHANCELLOR : Suppose a man goes to a banker with 1,000*l.* in bank notes, and says, I want to send this money into the country, will you get these notes changed for a Bank post bill, and the banker says that he will; but when the man goes again to get the Bank post bill, the banker says, I shall retain these notes, or this bill, until you pay the balance which I now discover to be against you.)

That is either a case *idem per idem* with the present, or the answer

(1) 2 R. R. 650 (5 T. R. 488).   (3) 1 Stark. 1.
(2) 1 Esp. 65.   (4) 22 R. R. 594 (4 B. & Ald. 1).

to it is, that what the banker undertakes to do is not in the ordinary way of his business.

(The Lords intimated that it was in the ordinary way of the banker's business.)

Then it is matter of particular contract.

(LORD BROUGHAM : In the case supposed, the banker ought to say, I take the notes subject to my right of lien ; otherwise, he waives it.)

But here the banker had not merely to change the bills, but to receive money on them, and he placed that money to the credit of the customer.   That was completely in the ordinary way of his business, and no special contract intervened to affect the transaction.   It is admitted that a special contract may affect the general right : [see *Vanderzee* v. *Willis* (1) and *Lucas* v. *Dorrien* (2)]. *Sterenson* v. *Blakelock* (3) shows that the rule of law is, that where a right to general lien exists in any person, it is not taken out of him by the fact that a particular thing coming into his hands is received for a special purpose : if it comes into his hands in the ordinary way of business, the right to lien attaches.

[803]

(THE LORD CHANCELLOR : Was it not the attorney's duty there to receive the lease ?)

It was no more his duty to receive the lease than it was the duty of these bankers to receive the Exchequer bills,—it was a mere ordinary transaction in the way of business, and so Lord ELLENBOROUGH describes it. * * *

The bills were received in the ordinary course of business, and were in the hands of the bankers to be dealt with in discharge of their ordinary duty as bankers, and consequently the right to lien attached, and the judgment of the Court below must be affirmed.

[804]

Sir T. Wilde replied.

LORD CAMPBELL :

Aug. 28.

The first question that arises upon this record is, whether judicial notice is to be taken of the general lien of bankers on the securities of their customers in their hands ?   The Exchequer bills, for which this action is brought, are found to be the property of the plaintiff,

(1) 3 Br. C. C. 21.   Moore, 29).
(2) 18 R. R. 480 (7 Taunt. 278 ; 1   (3) 14 R. R. 525 (1 M. & S. 535).

BRANDAO
v.
BARNETT.
[*805]

and the defendants rest their defence on their *second plea, that they were not possessed, &c., relying on the lien claimed for the balance due to them from Edward Burn.

The usage of trade by which bankers are entitled to a general lien, is not found by the special verdict, and unless we are to take judicial notice of it, the plaintiff is at once entitled to judgment. But, my Lords, I am of opinion that the general lien of bankers is part of the law-merchant, and is to be judicially noticed—like the negotiability of bills of exchange, or the days of grace allowed for their payment. When a general usage has been judicially ascertained and established, it becomes a part of the law-merchant, which courts of justice are bound to know and recognize. Such has been the invariable understanding and practice in Westminster Hall for a great many years ; there is no decision or *dictum* to the contrary, and justice could not be administered if evidence were required to be given *toties quoties* to support such usages, and issue might be joined upon them in each particular case.

It is hardly disputed that, under the plea of "not possessed," a lien, where it exists, may be made available as a defence ; and, therefore, if this special verdict sets forth facts which show that by the law-merchant the defendants have a lien upon these Exchequer bills, the judgment in their favour ought to be affirmed. But I am humbly of opinion that, upon the facts found, there was no lien, and that the judgment ought to be reversed.

I do not, however, proceed upon the ground taken by the Court of Common Pleas,—that these Exchequer bills being the property of Brandao, there was no lien as against him, although there might have been as against Burn. I think that the defendants were entitled to consider the Exchequer bills as the property of Burn, without any express representation by him to that effect. Exchequer bills are negotiable securities passing by delivery. The

[*806]

holder of negotiable securities is to be assumed to be *the owner, and third parties acting *bonâ fide* may treat with him as owner. It is admitted that Burn might have effectually sold these Exchequer bills, or pledged them by an express contract, without any representation that they were his own property. But the right acquired by a general lien is an implied pledge, and where it would arise (supposing the securities to be the property of the apparent owner), I think it equally exists if the party claiming it has acted with good faith, although the subject of that lien should turn out to be the property of a stranger. I think that the just view was taken of this point by the Judges in the Exchequer Chamber, and that they were right in holding the reasoning of the Judges in the Court of Common Pleas upon this point to be untenable.

But I must confess that, after much anxious consideration, I have come to the conclusion that the Judges in the Exchequer Chamber have erroneously decided the question on which the Court of Common Pleas expressed no opinion, and that the facts found by the special verdict would not have entitled the defendants to a lien, if the Exchequer bills had been the property of Burn.

Bankers most undoubtedly have a general lien on all securities deposited with them, as bankers, by a customer, unless there be an express contract, or circumstances that show an implied contract, inconsistent with lien. Lord KENYON says, in *Davis* v. *Bowsher* (1), "bankers have a general lien on all securities in their hands for their general balance, unless there be evidence to show that any particular security was received under special circumstances, which would take it out of the common rule." And Lord DENMAN, in pronouncing this very judgment in the Exchequer Chamber, says (2), "If indeed there had been an agreement, express or implied, inconsistent *with a right of lien, as to return them absolutely, at all events, to the depositor, the case would have been different."

Now it seems to me, that, in the present case, there was an implied agreement on the part of the defendants, inconsistent with the right of lien which they claim. It should be recollected that the Exchequer bills for which the action is brought, are the new Exchequer bills, which the defendants obtained for the express and only purpose of being delivered by them to Burn, that he might deposit them in the tin box, of which he kept the key. They not only were not entered in any account between Burn and the defendants, but they were not to remain in the possession of the defendants; and the defendants, in respect of them, were employed merely to carry and hold till the deposit in the tin box could be conveniently accomplished. Whether this deposit was to be made in the same hour in which the securities were obtained from the Government, without ever being placed in a drawer belonging to the defendants, or after the lapse of some days, seems to me quite immaterial, bearing in mind the purpose for which they were obtained, and for which they remained in the defendants' possession. Nor can it make any difference that, on the particular

[*807]

(1) 2 R. R. 652 (5 T. R. 491).   (2) 6 Man. & G. 670.

occasion out of which this action originated, from the illness of
Burn, so long a time elapsed from the obtaining of the securities,
without their being demanded by him, for the purpose of being
locked up in the tin box; for if the defendants had not a right of
lien upon them the moment they obtained them, the actual lien
clearly could not afterwards be claimed when his account had
been overdrawn. Nor, I presume, can any weight be attached to
the circumstance that the tin box, in which the Exchequer bills
were to be locked up, and of which Burn kept the key, remained
in the house of the defendants. Were not these Exchequer bills
obtained by the defendants to be delivered to Burn who was him-

[*808]   self *to be the depositary and custodian of them? Bankers have
a lien on all securities deposited with them as bankers; but these
Exchequer bills cannot be considered to have been deposited with
the defendants as bankers.

During the argument in the Exchequer Chamber it was very
properly admitted by *Sir Fitzroy Kelly*, that "if bills of exchange
were delivered to a banker, merely for the purpose of being
deposited in a box, there could be no lien." Does it signify
whether the defendants were to deposit the securities in the box
themselves, or to deliver them to Burn for that purpose? I think,
that, under such circumstances, bankers acquire no lien, either
upon the bills to be exchanged or the bills received in exchange.
It is hardly denied that if there had been an express undertaking
by the defendants to exchange the bills and to return the new ones
as soon as obtained to Burn, that he might lock them up, no lien
would have been acquired. But the special verdict shows the
course of dealing between them, and raises an implied promise on
their part which operates as if it was express. This seems to me
to be like the case put of bank notes given to a banker to procure
a Bank post-bill for a customer, or a promise by a purchaser to
pay ready money, which excludes set-off; there could be no implied
right inconsistent with a positive obligation.

It certainly would be most inconvenient if a lien could be claimed
under such circumstances, for then an agent, holding Exchequer
bills for another, could not, although he kept them carefully
guarded under lock and key, employ a person who happened
to be a banker to get them exchanged; for if he did—without
being aware that he was acting improperly—he might commit
a crime for which he would be liable to very serious punishment.

Much stress was laid upon the finding that " it is the custom of bankers, in the course of their trade as such, to receive the interest upon Exchequer bills for their customers, *and to exchange the Exchequer bills when such interest is paid," but there is no finding that the Exchequer bills for which this action is brought and on which the lien is claimed were in the possession of the defendants in the course of their trade as bankers, or that it was their duty as bankers to perform these offices. I think that the transaction is very much like the deposit of plate in locked chests at a banker's. A special verdict might find that it is the custom of bankers, in the course of their trade as such, to receive such deposits from their customers, but I do not think that from that finding a general lien could be claimed on the plate chests. In both cases a charge might be made by the bankers if they were not otherwise remunerated for their trouble.

I further beg leave to observe, that, in a course of dealing like this, where the old Exchequer bills are immediately to be delivered to the Government, and the new Exchequer bills to be locked up in the box of the customer, it can hardly be supposed that the bankers will accept or pay bills of exchange for their customer on the credit of securities that in the usual course of dealing are for so short a time to be in their custody.

No reliance, I think, can be placed on the circumstance of the interest received on the old Exchequer bills going to the credit of the account of the customer; for while he gives the bankers the interest to keep for him with one hand, he locks up the new Exchequer bills in his tin box with the other.

Upon the whole, my Lords, I should humbly advise your Lordships to give judgment for the plaintiff in error. This judgment will leave untouched the rule that bankers have a general lien on securities deposited with them as bankers, but will prevent them from successfully claiming a lien on securities delivered to them for a special purpose inconsistent with the existence of the lien claimed.

I move your Lordships that the judgment of the Court of Exchequer Chamber be reversed.

LORD LYNDHURST:

My Lords, I entirely concur in the opinion which has been so clearly and so fully expressed by my noble and learned friend.

With respect to some of the points in this case, no doubt whatever can be, I think, for a moment entertained. There is no question that, by the law-merchant, a banker has a lien for his

BRANDAO
v.
BARNETT.
[*809]

[810]

general balance on securities deposited with him. I consider this
as part of the established law of the country, and that the Courts
will take notice of it: it is not necessary that it should be pleaded,
nor is it necessary that it should be given in evidence in this
particular instance: therefore, as to that part of the case, I think
it is entirely free from doubt.

The only question, therefore, which remains to be considered is,
whether the facts of this case bring this deposit within the general
rule. I think that the reasoning of my noble and learned friend
is decisive upon that subject, and that the circumstances of the
case are not within the general rule: the deposit in this instance
was not such, under all the circumstances, as to give the banker
a lien upon the Exchequer bills; they were deposited in a box,
they were kept under lock and key, the key was not kept by the
banker, but it was kept by the party, Mr. Burn. From time to
time he called, for the purpose of taking the Exchequer bills out
of the box, in order that he might receive the interest upon them;
or if the bills were called in by the Government, in order that they
might be exchanged for others. He himself attended upon those
occasions, took the bills out, and delivered them for that special
purpose to the banker. They were always returned almost
immediately: the first time that he applied at the Bank after a
transaction of this kind, they were delivered to him, and were
[*811] replaced under *lock and key in the same place of deposit. It is
impossible, considering how this business was carried on, that we
can come to any other conclusion than this,—that it was an
understanding between the parties that the new bills were to be
returned after the interest was received, or after the old bills had
been exchanged. If so—if that was the understanding—or if that
was the fair inference from the transaction, it is quite clear that
there could be no lien; that it does not come within the general
rule; and what my noble and learned friend has stated, I think
is perfectly correct, that although from the accidental circumstance
of the illness of Mr. Burn these particular bills happened to remain
for a longer period in the hands of the bankers than was usual,
that accidental circumstance alone will not vary the case, nor give
the bankers a lien, if under other circumstances that lien would
not attach.

I therefore entirely concur in the judgment of my noble and
learned friend.

Judgment of the Court below reversed.

CHANCERY COURT IN IRELAND.

TAYLOR v. HUGHES (1).

(2 Jo. & Lat. 24—57; S. C. 7 Ir. Eq. R. 529.)

Where a transfer of shares is made by a shareholder to the Company, the latter may, as between the parties to the transfer, dispense with the machinery which the Legislature has rendered necessary to transfers in general; and the Company cannot afterwards, as between themselves and the shareholder with whom they contracted, impeach the transaction.

1844.
Nov. 18, 19,
20, 21.
Dec. 2.

Sir Edward
Sugden,
L.C.

[24]

[*25]

In the year 1834, the Agricultural and Commercial Bank of Ireland, consisting of branch Banks in various parts of Ireland with a central office in Dublin, was established, in pursuance *and under the regulations of the 6 Geo. IV. c. 42, and 1 Will. IV. c. 32. The capital stock of the Bank was divided into shares, payable by instalments. The Irish shares were, for the most part, of the amount of 5*l.* each, payable by instalments of 1*l.* each. Many persons became members of the Company. In March, 1835, proposals were published by the Bank for a person to fill the office of cashier in Dublin; and it was required by those proposals that the person to be appointed should deposit 2,000*l.* in the establishment, on which he was to receive interest; part of which was to be appropriated to the purchase of 300 shares (on which the first instalment only was then payable); and the person to be appointed was to receive a salary of 200*l.* per year for his services. The plaintiff, Despard Taylor, having complied with the terms of the proposal, was appointed cashier; the duties of which office he continued to discharge until the 31st of May, 1836, when he was elected one of the Board of Directors or Consulting Committee, who, in conjunction with James Dwyer, the managing Director, conducted the affairs of the Bank. At this time, in consequence of the very great irregularity with which the books of the Company were kept, the affairs of the Bank appeared, and were believed to be, in a very flourishing state; and, at a meeting of the shareholders, on the 17th of October, 1836, a statement of accounts was submitted, whereby it appeared that the amount of paid-up capital was 375,029*l.*, and of private deposits, 366,182*l.* Shortly afterwards, on the 14th of November, 1836, in consequence of a panic, and of a sudden demand for large sums of money, made on the Agricultural and Commercial Bank by the Provincial Bank and the Bank of Ireland, the Agricultural Bank

---

(1) *Bargate* v. *Shortridge* (1855) 5 H. L. C. 297; *Spackman* v. *Evans* (1868) L. R. 3 H. L. 171, 37 L. J. Ch. 752, 19 L. T. 151.

suspended payments ; and, upon the 17th of the same month, the Board *of Directors passed a resolution, which was entered on the minute-book of their proceedings, " That no transfer of stock be sanctioned by the Board until the resumption of business by the Company ; " which resolution was not at any time afterwards altered or rescinded. Mr. Taylor, in conjunction with his co-directors and others, exerted himself to procure funds to discharge the pressing liabilities of the Bank.   In consequence of those exertions, and by means of the Directors pledging the assets of the Bank, and personally guaranteeing their payment, the immediate pressure on the Company was removed, and the credit of the Bank, in some degree, restored. Mr. Dwyer, and some of the shareholders, then became desirous that the business of the Bank should be resumed ; to which others of the shareholders objected. Before the 16th of October, 1837, some steps were taken by the Directors towards the resumption of business, from which it did not appear that Mr. Taylor dissented ; and on that day, at the half-yearly meeting of the Company, a resolution was adopted by the majority of the shareholders, that the business of the Bank should be resumed ; in consequence of which Mr. Taylor, as he alleged, resolved to with-draw from the Company, and to discontinue his connexion therewith. On the 6th of November, 1837, he ceased to be a Director of the Company.

There were two classes of shares standing in the books of the Company in the name of Mr. Taylor, which were the subject of different consideration in this suit. The first class consisted of 1,100 shares, and the dealings with respect to them were the following: Upon the 24th of March, 1835, Mr. Taylor became the purchaser of 300 of those shares, as before mentioned : and on the 11th of August, 1836, *he became the purchaser of 150 other shares.   On the 22nd of April, 1837, A. C. Chadwick, in consideration of the sum of 30l., transferred to the plaintiff 300 other shares, upon which one instalment only had been paid up ; and the same were entered in the stock ledger of the Company, pursuant to an order in the handwriting of Mr. Taylor, and signed by three of the Directors, as reduced or made equivalent to 150 shares, upon which two instalments had been paid ; and on the 22nd of September, 1837, 500 other shares were transferred to Mr. Taylor by Mr. Hime, under the circumstances after mentioned.

The other class consisted of 8,000 shares, and was thus circum-stanced. The Directors, for the purpose of selling the shares of

the Company, and thereby extending the proprietary, in the months
of March and April, 1836, allotted about 20,000 shares amongst
themselves and others of the officers of the Company, to be disposed
of by them for the benefit of the Bank; and the transaction took this
shape: The Director or officer made a written application for shares to
the Board of Directors, who acceded to it; and thereupon the number
of shares applied for was allotted, in the books of the Company, to
the party applying, who accepted a bill as a security for the amount
of the shares so allotted to him, at par, and one shilling per share,
in addition, which was called outfit: the person to whom the shares
were so allotted then disposed of them in the market, and any profit
which he could make on the transaction was to belong to him, as a
remuneration for his trouble. Accordingly, on the 4th of April,
1836, the plaintiff, then being the cashier of the Bank, made a
written application to the Manager for 3,000 shares of the stock;
and the Board of Directors having acceded thereto, the stock was
allotted *to him; and, on the 15th of April, 1836, the plaintiff
accepted a bill (entitled in the books of the Company No. 516), at
twelve months, for 3,150l. being the amount of the value of 3,000
shares at par, and outfit. The dealing with these 3,000 shares
appeared, from entries in the cash and other books of the Company.
The plaintiff transferred 500 of them to J. R. Hime, on the 15th of
April, 1836; 500 of them to Peter Jones, on the 19th of April,
1836; 100 of them to Mr. Currie, on the 21st of April, 1836, and
100 of them to Henry Campion, on the same day. The application
by Peter Jones was made by him to the Directors; but, when
approved of by them, the shares were transferred to him by Mr.
Taylor, and not directly out of the stock of the Company. All the
shares were sold by Mr. Taylor at 1l. 6s. per share; and in June,
1836, he accounted with the Bank for the 3,000 shares, and paid
them 1,260l., being the amount of 1,200 shares, at par and outfit,
retaining the profits on the sales of the shares for his own benefit:
and an entry was made in the cash book of the Company, under
date of the 4th of June, 1836, not according to the real nature of
the transaction, but as if the 3,000 shares had been re-purchased
from Mr. Taylor by the Company, they returning to Mr. Taylor his
bill for 3,150l. The bill was, in fact, given up to Mr. Taylor; but
no transfer of the 1,800 shares, residue of the 3,000 shares, was
ever actually made by Mr. Taylor to the Company. The account,
however, which had been opened in the ledger with Mr. Taylor,
on foot of the 3,000 shares (and which was distinct from that

opened with him on foot of the other shares), was balanced by an entry of 8,000 shares re-purchased from him by the Company.

[*29]   After the Bank had stopped payment, in November, *1836. Mr. Hime commenced an action against Mr. Taylor to recover damages for alleged misrepresentations in the matter of the sale of the 500 shares to him : and Mr. Taylor, in order, as he alleged, to prevent disclosures of the affairs of the Bank, accepted a transfer of these 500 shares, at par, from Mr. Hime, as before mentioned.

In March, 1837, the Bank desired to raise money upon a bill of Mr. J. R. Pim, and it was proposed that Mr. Taylor should discount it : this he agreed to do, provided the Bank would accept a transfer of 450 of the shares belonging to him, at the price he had paid for the same, he alleging that 300 of the shares had been purchased by him to qualify himself to become cashier ; and the Directors having assented to that offer, an indenture of the 3rd of March, 1837, was executed between Despard Taylor, of the one part, and William Hodges, Philip Jones, and John Chambers, "trustees acting for and on behalf of the Agricultural and Commercial Bank of Ireland, under and by virtue, or in execution of the trusts and powers contained in an indenture or deed of settlement, dated on or about the 10th day of August, 1836," of the other part; whereby, in consideration of the sum of 450l., Despard Taylor assigned to the parties of the second part 450 shares of and in the capital stock and funds of the Bank. This deed was executed by Mr. Taylor only; and did not purport to have been approved of by any of the Directors for the time being. Under the same date entries were made in the cash-book and stock-ledger of the Company, stating the re-purchase of the 450 shares from Mr. Taylor at the price of 450l.

[*30]   In September, 1837, the Bank entered into another negotiation with Mr. Taylor for the discount of 3,000l., on *the security of certain bills of exchange then in the Bank. The following entry, taken from the minute-book of the Board of Directors, under the date of the 28th of September, 1837, will explain the nature of the transaction : "The Committee of Correspondence communicated to the Board that it would be very servicable to the Company's interests to obtain a discount of the Company's bills to the amount of, say 3,000l., so as to liquidate some claims which had been authenticated; and that Mr. Despard Taylor had consented to

obtain this discount or advance upon certain terms specified in a memorandum signed by him, and now submitted; as follows: ' Having taken a transfer from Mr. Hime, of Gardiner Street, of 500 shares, sold him, as I conceive, to benefit the Bank, in April, 1836, and Mr. Hime having commenced an action against me for the full value of the shares, stating he had a personal claim upon me, I, to prevent a publicity of Bank affairs, which Mr. Hime threatened, and for the advantage of the Bank, took a transfer back from Mr. Hime, at par: and I hold the Bank should take the half thereof; and if the Bank do, I shall procure for them, without commission, at 5*l.* per cent., a discount of 3,000*l.*   29th September, 1837. (Signed,) DESPARD TAYLOR.'   Ordered,—that the proposition of Mr. Taylor (as better terms cannot be had), be agreed to and confirmed.   The shares to be transferred, free from charge of outfit, and no dividend to be claimed on the 250 shares so transferred."   Accordingly, on the 30th of September, 1837, bills to the amount of 2,117*l.* 5*s.* 4*d.* were delivered to Mr. Taylor, and he was debited in account with the amount thereof; and on the 2nd of October, 1837, a deed of assignment was executed by Mr. Taylor alone, whereby he assigned 250 shares of the Agricultural and Commercial Bank to the same trustees, as in the former deed; and entries were *made in the books of the Bank, stating the re-purchase of the 250 shares by trustees for the Bank from Mr. Taylor, in consideration of the sum of 250*l.* This transfer appeared to have been approved of by three of the Directors.

[*31]

At the several times when this and the former transfer were made, the market price of the shares of the Company was far below par.

Mr. Taylor afterwards applied to the Directors to re-purchase the remaining 400 shares which he held; and on the 10th of November, 1837, this entry was made in the minute-book of the Board of Directors: "Upon reference by Mr. Hodges, cashier, as to Mr. Taylor's transactions, the Board are unanimously of opinion that they cannot entertain any question as to the stock transactions until his check is paid, for which he got value; then the Board will entertain all questions as they deserve."   The check referred to was for the sum of 600*l.*, the balance due by Mr. Taylor, on account of the discount transaction of the 28th of September, 1837. He afterwards paid the 600*l.*; and on the 16th of November, 1837, it was ordered by the Directors, "that Mr. Taylor's stock be taken

TAYLOR
v.
HUGHES.

[*32]

from him at 7*s.* 6*d.* per share, he re-conveying it to the trustees,
and handing over the order which he holds for the third instalment,
as also taking a bill at three months for the value." Accordingly,
by indenture of the 16th of November, 1837, Despard Taylor, in
consideration of 150*l.*, assigned to the trustees, as in the former
deeds, 400 shares in the stock and funds of the Bank; and the
re-purchase of those shares was duly entered in the books of
the Company. This transfer was also approved of by three of
the Directors of *the Company: but none of the transfers were
executed by the transferees, nor were they registered pursuant to
the 6 Geo. IV. c. 42, s. 22.

After Mr. Taylor had thus parted with his shares in the Bank,
a registry of persons who had ceased to be members of the
Company, in the form prescribed by the second schedule of the
6 Geo. IV. c. 42, was, on the 23rd of November, 1837, filed by
the Bank at the Stamp Office, stating therein that Mr. Taylor had
ceased to be a member of the Bank; and also (he having been,
during his connexion with the Bank, registered as one of the public
officers thereof), that he had ceased to be a public officer of the
Company; and from thenceforth, until May, 1843, the name of
Mr. Taylor was omitted in the annual registers of the members of
the Company filed at the Stamp Office.

It appeared from the books of the Bank, and from the reports
from time to time made by the Directors to the half-yearly meetings
of the Company, that the Directors were in the habit of accepting
transfers of shares from members to trustees for the Bank, when
the circumstances, in their opinion, rendered it a proper measure
to be adopted: and the stock so re-purchased was carried to an
account, entitled, Reverted or Re-purchased Stock. This mode of
dealing with the stock of the Company was particularly brought
under the notice of the proprietary at a general meeting held the
17th of April, 1837.

On the 2nd of March, 1837, and the 28th of June, 1837, bills
were filed in this Court by shareholders of the Company against

[*33]

Mr. Taylor and the other Directors; *the object of which suits
was, *inter alia,* to restrain the Directors levying the amount of
certain calls; and by the latter bill an injunction was prayed
to restrain the Directors from re-purchasing shares of the Company out of its funds. This latter suit continued pending until
the 12th of June, 1838, when it was dismissed by order of
the Court.

At the half-yearly meeting of the Company, held on the 16th of October, 1837, the Directors presented a report, which represented the nett assets of the Company, after providing for all the liabilities of the Bank, as amounting to the sum of 277,071*l.* At this meeting the proprietary resolved to resume business; and also passed the following resolution: " That we hereby, in addition to the powers given to the Directors by the deed of settlement, authorize and instruct the Board of Directors for the time being, as may to them seem expedient and for the interest of the proprietors, to accept transfers of, and to purchase the shares or stock of the Company for the benefit of the other co-partners, at the current or market price."

The deed of settlement did not expressly authorize or forbid the Directors to re-purchase or accept transfers of shares for the benefit of the Company: it provided, that the laws constituting the Company should not be altered, unless by the vote of two meetings specially called for that purpose; and that two successive extra-ordinary general assemblies, specially called for the purpose, in the manner therein mentioned, should have power to make new laws, or amend the existing laws of the Company. The resolution of the meeting of the 16th of October, 1837, was not passed in conformity with these provisions.

The Bank having resumed business, as before mentioned, the Directors made reports to the half-yearly meetings of the Company, which were adopted by them. These reports represented the affairs of the Company to be in a solvent state; and some of them referred to the purchase of reverted stock, as a matter beneficial to the interest of the Company.

[84]

In July, 1838, the Board of Directors entered into a negotiation with certain persons in London, to raise a sum of 50,000*l.*, for the purposes of the Bank; and with that object they issued debentures, or promissory notes, payable in three and four years after date, and transmitted them to the parties in London, by whom they were put in circulation; and Mr. Langford Lovel Hodge, one of the defendants in this suit, having advanced money on the security of some of the debentures, became thereby a creditor of the Company to a large amount.

By the official report of the debts and liabilities of the Bank, made by the Directors to the shareholders at the half-yearly meeting held on the 20th of April, 1840, it was stated that the profit on the business transacted at the branches for the last half-year was more

than double that of the preceding half-year, and that there was a
surplus of assets over liabilities of 204,932*l.* : but, notwithstanding
the prospects thus held forth, the Bank again got into difficulties ;
and on the 18th of June, 1840, it finally suspended payments. This
circumstance was next day announced to the proprietary by a circular
letter from the Board of Directors ; and on the 3rd of July, 1840,
a committee of shareholders was appointed to examine into the

[*35]   affairs of the Company. They made their report on the *28th of
August, 1843, and stated that, allowing largely for bad and doubtful
debts, with other losses, the assets appeared ample for to meet the
liabilities. At the half-yearly general meeting of the shareholders
of the Company, held on the 19th of October, 1840, it appearing
that more than one-fourth of the paid-up capital had been actually
lost, it was resolved to discontinue the Company ; and a committee
of nine persons (called the Winding-up Committee), was, in accordance with the provisions of the deed of partnership in that behalf,
duly appointed for the purpose of winding-up its affairs. A special
general meeting of the shareholders of the Company was held upon
the 6th of March, 1841, at which a report of the Directors was read,
stating that the liabilities of the Company, on the 27th of January,
1841, amounted to 103,208*l.* ; and it was resolved that a call of 5*l.*
per share should be made on the British stock, and 10*s.* per share
on the Irish stock, of the Company. In the meantime suits were
instituted in the Court of Chancery by creditors of the Company,
for payment of their demands out of the personal estate of the
Company, pursuant to the provisions of the Bankers' Act, (33 Geo. II.
c. 14), and for a receiver : and, on the 25th of June, 1841, a receiver
was appointed in the cause of *Acheson* v. *Hodges*, to collect and
receive the personal estate of the Company (1).

On the 20th of November, 1841, a meeting was held by certain
of the shareholders of the Company (but which was not convened
pursuant to any provision in the deed), at which it was resolved :
That for the purpose of protecting individuals who were willing to
join in creating an indemnity fund, certain persons therein named

[*36]   should form a *committee of shareholders, distinct from, and
independent of the Directors of the Company ; and that the shareholders be requested to contribute towards such indemnity fund
10*s.* on each 5*l.* share standing in their names, and 5*l.* on each 25*l.*
share, to be paid to the credit of three trustees therein named : and
that the said trustees be authorized to distribute the fund, from

(1) 3 Ir. Eq. Rep. 516.

time to time, under the written authority of the Committee ; it
being distinctly understood that such fund should not be applied
except in the protection of the subscribers to it, and to discharge
the necessary expenses of the trustees and Committee. The Committee (which was known by the name of the Shareholders'
Committee) accordingly addressed a circular letter to the shareholders of the Company, enclosing a copy of the above resolutions ;
stating that they were adopted because it had been found that the
creditors were proceeding at law against some of the shareholders,
notwithstanding the appointment of a receiver over the assets of
the Company ; requesting the party to pay the contribution mentioned in the resolutions ; and stating that " the Committee had
good reason to believe that the principal creditors of the Bank
would forward their views by selecting, as objects of their proceedings, those members only who did not contribute to the fund
proposed to be collected ; and that some of them had stayed their
proceedings for the present, with a view to their being continued
against the defaulting members of the Bank, and such as should
not contribute to the proposed fund."

In May, 1842, an order was made in the cause of *Acheson* v.
Hodges, whereby it was ordered, that such persons as certain of the
shareholders therein named (some of whom were members of the
Shareholders' Committee, and others of the Winding-up Committee)
should nominate in writing, should have access to the books of the
*Company, for the purpose of investigating the accounts generally   [*87]
of the Company, and ascertaining the amount and particulars of
the assets and liabilities thereof. In June, 1842, three vacancies
having occurred in the Winding-up Committee, three of the Shareholders' Committee were duly elected by the Winding-up Committee
to fill their places ; and a letter was shortly afterwards addressed
by the Shareholders' Committee to such of the shareholders as had
not subscribed to the indemnity fund, calling on them to pay their
contributions; stating to them the application of the money already
received, and informing them that three members of the Shareholders' Committee had been appointed, as above, so that the assets
of the Bank, and the winding-up of the affairs of the Company were
placed in the hands of persons in whom the shareholders might
have full confidence. From thenceforward it appeared that the
two Committees acted in unison:

On the 21st of June, 1842, the Shareholders' Committee having
paid off the demand and costs of the plaintiff in the cause of

Acheson v. *Hodges*, the bill in that cause was dismissed, and the
receiver discharged, and the books were delivered to the Winding-up
Committee. They immediately caused the accounts and transactions of the Company to be investigated : and having discovered
many transfers of shares, which they were advised were illegal, the
Committee, acting under the advice of counsel, revised the stock
ledgers of the Company, and caused entries to be made therein, in
an ink of a different colour from that in which the former entries
had been written (not obliterating or altering any original entry),
and so as thereby to show who were the members of the Company.
The result of this revision was, that the names of eighty-four

[*38]   persons, *holding several thousand shares, and who had been
considered shareholders and registered as such in the last registry
of the Company, were removed from the stock ledgers as shareholders of the Company, in consequence of their shares having
been acquired either by illegal transfers, or by hand-entries made
in the books of the Company, without any transfers having been
executed to them : and the names of 1,178 persons, holding 3,784
shares, were entered in the stock ledgers as shareholders, such
persons' names having been extracted from the branch books and
other documents of the Bank, but whose names had never been
entered in the books of the head office as shareholders : and the
names of 1,221 persons were restored to the stock ledger as shareholders, in consequence of illegal transfers, or no transfers having
been executed by them. Amongst the latter class, the name of
Mr. Taylor was inserted as the proprietor not only of the 1,100 but
also of the 3,000 shares : and on the 5th of May, 1843, a registry
of the shareholders of the Company, prepared according to the
revised stock ledger of the Company, was verified by affidavit, and
filed in the Stamp Office.

In September, 1842, Mr. Langford Lovel Hodge became pressing
for the settlement of his demand: and in that month, the Winding-
up Committee requested him to forbear pressing them for payment
of the sum due to him, and proposed that he should obtain a
judgment against the public officer of the Company for the amount
of his demand, to be used, when obtained, only against the defaulting
shareholders of the Company. This proposition was acceded to by
Mr. Langford Lovel Hodge ; without prejudice, however, to his
right to proceed as he might be advised against any of the share-

[*39]   holders, for the recovery of his *demand, if he should think it
necessary to do so: and judgment by confession was obtained by

him against William Hughes, the public officer of the Company, for the sum of 520*l.* After the revised registry of the Company had been filed, Mr. Langford Lovel Hodge applied to the secretary of the Shareholders' Committee to be furnished with the names of shareholders against whom he should proceed ; and he was given the names of several persons appearing on the revised registry, some of whom denied their liability, and all of whom were defaulting shareholders.

On the 25th of May, 1843, an order was made in the cause of *Hodge* v. *Hughes*, that the plaintiff should be at liberty to issue a *scire facias* on the judgment against several persons therein named, and, amongst others, against Mr. Taylor, upon a suggestion that he was a partner in the Company. This was followed by a letter of the 18th of December, 1843, from the solicitor of Mr. Hodge to Mr. Taylor, not disclosing the name of his client, but stating that his client had obtained a judgment for 520*l.* against the public officer of the Bank, and that he was instructed to apply to him, as one of the shareholders, for payment ; and if not paid, to proceed for the recovery of that sum. Mr. Taylor replied, denying his liability ; and on the 5th of January, 1844, he was served with a *scire facias* on the judgment obtained by Langford Lovel Hodge against the public officer of the Bank. He thereupon, on the 19th of January, 1844, filed the present bill against William Hughes, as such public officer, and Langford Lovel Hodge, praying that the Bank might be declared to have accepted the several transfers of the shares so purchased by the Bank from him, and that the Bank might be decreed to cause the necessary acts to be done for the purpose of registering and completing *the transfers : and that the [*40] list so registered at the Stamp Office by the Bank, on the 5th of May, 1843, and the entry of the plaintiff's name therein, might be declared to be fraudulent and void : and that the entries in the books, lists, and documents of the Bank, under their control, in which the plaintiff's name had been introduced as a partner thereof, since he ceased to be a shareholder, might be declared to be fraudulent and void as to the plaintiff ; and that the same might be brought into Court, and the plaintiff's name, so inserted therein, might be erased therefrom ; and that the Bank might be restrained from continuing the plaintiff's name on the said registered list as a shareholder thereof : and that the defendant, Hodge, might be restrained from producing or giving in evidence against the plaintiff in his proceedings at law, or any other proceedings to be instituted

by him against the plaintiff upon foot of his demands, the said list,
or any certificate founded thereon, or the said books and documents :
and that further proceedings on the writ of *scire facias* might
be stayed.

Mr. Hughes relied, in his answer, upon the conduct of Mr. Taylor,
as cashier, in not keeping regular accounts of the transactions of
the Bank (as to which evidence was read) ; and also upon the
unjustifiable advantage he took of the Directors and Bank, in
forcing the transfers of his shares upon them at par, at a time when
the stock of the Company was almost unsaleable in the market ;
and also upon his conduct in respect of the 8,000 shares, which he
sold at a premium and did not account for the profit to the Company,
as disentitling him to relief in equity.   He insisted that Mr. Taylor
still continued a shareholder in the Company, and liable to the
demands of Mr. Hodge, as his shares had never been legally
[*41]   transferred by him : *1, because the Directors were not authorized
to accept a transfer in trust for the Bank ; 2, because the transfers
were not executed by the transferees ; 3, because one of them was
not approved of by three of the Directors ; 4, because they had not
been registered pursuant to the 6 Geo. IV. c. 42, s. 22 ; 5, because
no transfer had ever been made by him of the 1,800 shares, the
residue of the 8,000 shares.

Mr. Langford Lovel Hodge denied unlawful collusion with the
Bank or the Shareholders' Committee ; but admitted the arrangement before mentioned, and that he was indemnified against costs.

The *Solicitor-General* (*Mr. Greene*), *Mr. Martley*, and *Mr. C.
Haig*, for the plaintiff. * * *

Mr. William Brooke, *Mr. Monahan*, and *Mr. Arthur Pakenham*,
   for the defendant William Hughes :

First, the facts show that Mr. Taylor is not, by reason of his
conduct, entitled to relief in a court of equity. Secondly, the
transfers by Mr. Taylor to the Company are illegal, informal, and
invalid. The Directors were not authorized to re-purchase stock
with the funds of the Company ; such a proceeding is contrary to
the spirit of the 6 Geo. IV. c. 42, the object of which, as especially
appearing from sections 2 and 22, was the establishment of
[*42]   co-partnerships of many members, *all of whom would be liable :
and it was not authorized by the deed of co-partnership, but was
impliedly forbidden by it. * * Here it does not even appear

that the transferees have accepted the transfers; they have not
executed them, as by the deed of partnership they are bound to do,
before they become members of the Company. Also, it is provided,
that no transfer shall take place without the consent of the
Directors; and that no transfer shall be valid unless signed by a
*Director, in testimony that the Directors have consented to such
transfer. Here, as to some of the transfers, there is no assent by
the Directors appearing on the face of the transfer. * * *

TAYLOR
v.
HUGHES.

[*43]

Mr. Pigot and *Mr. Wall* for Langford Lovel Hodge:

Admitting that Mr. Hodge has lent himself to aid the objects of
the Shareholders' Committee, that does not deprive him of his
right, as a *bonâ fide* creditor of the Bank, to sue any member of it.
The plaintiff's complaint is that his name has been improperly put
on the registry of May, 1843; but supposing it were not put there,
yet Mr. Hodge might and can show that Mr. Taylor is liable to him,
as a shareholder of the Company, who has never parted with his
shares. * * *

Mr. Martley, in reply:

[44]

* * It is stated by Mr. Dwyer, in his evidence, that the re-
purchase of the plaintiff's stock was a *bonâ fide* transaction, agreed
to by the Directors, because they thought it to be a measure con-
ducive to the welfare of the Company: and when the subject of
re-purchasing stock was brought before the meeting of the shareholders, they approved of the conduct of the Directors therein.

[45]

The assent of the Directors was only required in cases of transfers
from one individual to another; here the Directors have, on the
face of the transfers, assented to all of *them except that for 450
shares; and it appears from the minute-book of their proceedings,
that they did, in fact, assent to that transfer also. It was the duty
of the Company to have had the transfers properly registered; and
having neglected to do so, they cannot now take advantage of their
own wrong. * * *

[*46]

As to the relief prayed, even though Mr. Taylor may be liable
at law to third persons, yet he is entitled, in equity, to restrain the
Company using the names of such persons to enforce that legal
liability. He is also entitled to have the registry reformed by
having his name erased therefrom; for the registry of 1837, and
the subsequent ones, in which his name was omitted, were according
to the truth; and nothing was afterwards done to alter his liability.

TAYLOR
v.
HUGHES.

A creditor of the Company may be entitled to sue Mr. Taylor, but he can have no right to use against him the evidence afforded by this fraudulent registry.

THE LORD CHANCELLOR :

In this case the plaintiff, who was a shareholder in the Agricultural and Commercial Bank, seeks a declaration that the Bank accepted the several transfers of the shares which he held ; and [*47] that the registry of his name, in *May, 1843, as a member of the co-partnership, may be declared fraudulent ; and that certain recent entries in the books may be erased ; and that Mr. Hodge may be enjoined from using the evidence afforded by the register, and by the books as altered. The plaintiff was originally the cashier of the Company, and subsequently became a Director. He acquired two classes of shares—one to the number of 3,000, merely as an agent for the sale of them, with the profit of any premium which he could obtain. His case is, that he sold 1,200 of this class, and accounted for the price to the Bank ; that they accepted the rest as part of their stock ; and a bill which he had given for the amount of all the shares, 3,150*l.* was returned to him, and that account was balanced in the books. The other class, 1,100 in number, consisted of shares which he acquired, and which he sold to the Bank, and of which they took transfers to trustees ; and that account was also closed and the balance paid. The balance due from him as cashier was duly paid to his successor, and accounted for : and the balance of the general account must also, I think, be considered to have been finally settled and paid in 1837.

The plaintiff had, under the 6 Geo. IV. c. 42, been returned to the Stamp Office as a public officer, and also as a member of the Bank ; and in November, 1837, in compliance with the Act, his name was returned to the Stamp Office as having been removed from his office, and also as having ceased to be a member ; and for the five succeeding years, his name was kept off the returns, although returns of the actual members were regularly made.

After the difficulties of the Bank had ended in insolvency, the [*48] shareholders named a committee to investigate the concern. *They found it necessary to require a contribution from the members. A committee was appointed by the shareholders ; and the latter were requested to contribute according to certain proportions agreed upon. The Committee, by their circular of the 1st December, 1841, to the shareholders individually, while they held out hopes to the contributors that they would only have to pay a rateable proportion, stated that they had good reason to believe that the principal creditors of the Bank would forward their views by selecting, as objects of their proceedings, those members only who did not contribute to the proposed fund: and that some of the creditors had stayed their proceedings with that view. In pursuance of this plan, new Directors were appointed; the books were examined and new entries made in a different coloured ink, and with true dates, by which upwards of 2,400 persons, who had ceased by common consent to be members of the Bank, including the plaintiff who had refused to contribute to the fund, were brought forward as continuing members on various grounds; and, as far as relates to the plaintiff, upon the ground that some of the transfers of his shares were informal, and void in law. His name was thus, in 1843, again returned to the Stamp Office as a member; and the name of a purchaser of some of his shares, which had been on the register ever since his had been taken off, was actually omitted by the Committee. The Court cannot but regret that this rendered an oath necessary on the part of the officer by whom the return was made, and that the officer was induced to take it.

Mr. Hodge, the defendant, became a creditor of the Bank subsequently to the withdrawal of the plaintiff's name as a member. I shall not stop to consider the validity *of the debentures which he claims. It appears, clearly, from his answer, which has been read by the plaintiff, that the Company gave him a judgment by confession against their public officer, in order to enable him to go against a member for his demand, under the 6 Geo. IV.; and that this was by an arrangement with him, that they should select the victims from the contumacious alleged shareholders, he being indemnified against costs, and reserving his right to go against any other person in case he should be defeated. Now this was a proceeding contrary to the spirit of the Act, which gave the right of selection to the creditor; and not to the majority of the partners, to enable them to throw the burthen on the minority: and alike contrary to the letter; for the 19th section of 6 Geo. IV. expressly provides, that any person against whom execution is issued, shall be reimbursed all loss and costs out of the funds of the co-partnership; or in failure thereof, by contribution from the other members, as in the ordinary cases of co-partnership. And by the thirty-first article of the deed of settlement of 1834, it is in like manner provided, that where execution upon any such judgment is issued

[*49]

against any member, he shall be reimbursed out of the funds of the Company all his loss and expenses; and he is to have a right of action against any officer or other member of the Company for what he shall have paid. In *Const* v. *Harris* (1), Lord ELDON laid it down, that although the majority might bind the minority fairly in a partnership, yet that an agreement by a majority to overrule the minority, without reference to merits, would be rescinded by this Court. The parties must not abuse even a legal right. Here the whole was a contrivance to enforce indirectly against the plaintiff the contribution *which they did not venture directly to impose upon him. This was, I think, a fraud in the view of equity; and I feel no difficulty in declaring that Mr. Hodge cannot avail himself of it: and therefore the injunction against him must be made perpetual. He was the mere tool of the Company; and he could not, in any view of the case, claim a higher right than they possess.

[*50]

This leads me to the consideration of their case. It was argued that they stood on higher grounds than Mr. Hodge did. They insist that the plaintiff never ceased to be a member, although his name was improperly withheld from the register, from 1837 until they restored it in 1843.

The 3,000 shares, it was urged, were to be treated as the property of the plaintiff. His application for them, and the compliance of the Company with the application were proved: he sold 1,200 of them at a profit, which profit he retained for his own use; although, as to some of them, the purchaser went direct to the banking-house for them, and the plaintiff sold them across the counter: and no re-transfer was executed of the remaining 1,800 shares: therefore, it was said, he was still a member of the Company. Now the case which was proved is, that the Directors allotted 20,000 shares amongst themselves and the other officers for sale at par, with one shilling a share for outfit; and any premiums were to be for their own benefit. The parties gave bills for the amount as a security, and not as payment; and the forms of an application and acceptance of this security were gone through. 10,000 shares were allotted to Mr. Palmer, the Director; and he, not having sold any, re-transferred them all, and got his bill back: and Hughes himself, the defendant, who now seeks to fix the plaintiff with his 3,000 shares, had 5,000 *shares allotted to him; and he, in like manner, re-transferred them. The only difference between these cases and the present is, that the plaintiff sold 1,200 of the 3,000, and did not

[*51]

(1) 24 R. R. 108 (T. & R. 518).

re-transfer the rest. But he regularly paid to the Bank 1,260l. the price agreed upon for the shares which he sold; and although no actual transfer of the remaining shares was executed, yet his bill for 3,150l. was returned to him, and is regularly entered in the books as for the re-purchase from him of the 3,000 shares, and the account was regularly closed. I think it clear that this transaction cannot now be opened, but is binding in equity, notwithstanding the provisions of the Act of Parliament and of the deed of settlement. If the plaintiff, in the sale of the 1,200 shares, obtained any undue advantage which he is not at liberty to retain, that would not constitute him a partner as to those shares, or justify the attempt made to compel him to pay Mr. Hodge's demand.

I now come to the transactions as to the 1,100 shares. As to the portion of these shares bought by the plaintiff of Chadwick, it was objected that they were consolidated so as, in effect, to give a premium upon them to the plaintiff; but this objection, if well founded, cannot constitute the plaintiff a continuing member of the Company.

The 1,100 shares were purchased by the Company at three several periods: the last purchase of 400 shares was at the market price; but the two previous ones were at par, whilst the price in the market was greatly depreciated. But both these purchases were bargains regularly made in consideration of the plaintiff discounting bills for the Company; and, although the terms are alleged to be unreasonable, yet that would not justify the proceedings against the plaintiff, for which he seeks the injunction of this *Court. No actual fraud is attempted to be proved; and Mr. Dwyer, the Director, proves that all the three purchases and transfers were made *bonâ fide*. They were all, I may observe, regularly entered in the books. It was said, besides, that the purchases were made during the stoppage and insolvency of the Company. But business was resumed by the Bank; and favourable reports were made, and large amounts of surplus assets taken credit for, during the years which followed the plaintiff's retirement from the partnership. These general objections cannot, I think, prevail.

[*52]

It was then objected: 1, that the Directors had no power to purchase shares; 2, that in November, 1836, they had resolved not to make any purchases until business was resumed; 3, that if they could purchase, some of the assignments were not valid; 4, that if valid, they were not registered: from which it was concluded that the plaintiff was still a partner. All these shares were

TAYLOR
v.
HUGHES.

transferred by the plaintiff, by deeds, to three persons, who were described as trustees acting for and on behalf of the Bank, under the trusts or powers contained in the deed of settlement of 1836. In support of the first objection, it was said, that a purchase by the Company was contrary to the 6 Geo. IV. c. 42, sections 2 and 22; for all the individuals composing the co-partnership were made liable by sec. 2; and they could only discharge themselves of the liability by a transfer to another, under sec. 22 : and the assignee under that section must be a *bonâ fide* holder, and not a trustee for the Company. I think that the Act of Parliament did not prevent or interfere with the *bonâ fide* retirement from the co-partnership of any member; and, therefore, that the Company might buy out a partner notwithstanding the Act. It was said that such a

[*53]

purchase was *also struck at by the deed of settlement of 1836. It was admitted that it was not expressly forbidden; but the context of the deed was resorted to, in order to make out a case of exclusion; and the prohibition in clause 10 against any individual holding more than a limited number of shares was relied upon. After an attentive consideration of the deeds, I do not think that they prohibit the Company from buying out a partner; and the mode in which they thought fit to execute their purchases is, I think, unimportant. The prohibition in clause 10 cannot apply to the Company; and other clauses, which were referred to, show that the Company might become possessed of a much larger number of shares. The power in the 87th clause to the Directors or Consulting Committee to act, in cases unprovided for, in such manner as they should think best calculated to promote the welfare of the Company, would, I think, fully warrant the acts which they have done. Great numbers of shares were thus purchased; and the Company are not at liberty now to say that the Directors were not authorized to make the purchase. They cannot claim a privilege higher than any other co-partnership. Lord ELDON, in *Const* v. *Harris*, to which I before referred, said (1), that articles which had been agreed on to regulate a partnership, could not be altered without the consent of all the partners, but that if alterations were made by some of the partners, and acquiesced in by all, the Court would hold that to be an adoption of new terms. This, I may observe, is a rule always acted upon. Now, in this case, purchases were openly made, and regularly entered in the books; the stock accounts explain the transactions; and the purchases were adopted

(1) 24 R. R. at p. 126 (T. & R. 517).

by the Company at large after full notice. The reports which have been put in evidence *expressly refer to the extensive purchases of shares by the Company; and in 1837 a general meeting gave a direct authority to purchase without complaining of previous purchases. In 1837 a bill was filed for the express purpose of impeaching purchases by the Directors; but the plaintiff allowed that bill to be dismissed.

The second objection cannot, I think, be supported: for the resolution of November, 1836, was, that no transfer of stock should be sanctioned by the Board till the resumption of business by the Company; which did not, I think, prevent the Board itself from purchasing, but referred to transfers between party and party: at all events, the Directors were competent to rescind their resolution. The resolution of the general meeting, October, 1837, authorizing and instructing the Directors to make such purchases, is stated to be in addition to the powers given to them by the deed of settlement. But that would be correct if the deed did invest them with the power: for a direction to them to do the act was an addition to the power vested in them to execute it. This resolution, besides, was manifestly occasioned by the bill of 1837 to enjoin such purchases, and clearly proves the intention of the Company.

As to the third objection, I think that cannot prevail: for the transfer was in effect to the Company, and they thought fit, in some instances, to dispense with the machinery which the Legislature rendered necessary in such a case. This they were at liberty to do, even at law, according to *The Cheltenham Railway* case (1) ; and they cannot now, as between themselves and the partners with whom they contracted, impeach the transaction.

The fourth objection is of the same nature: but an assignment may be valid, and a member's name duly registered in lieu of the seller's, although, by the 9th sec. of 1 Will. IV., the transfer is not registered until a later period. The duty, moreover, of making a return of transfers seems, under the Act, to devolve on the Company; and if so, they cannot take advantage of their own neglect. The evidence proves that transfers were constantly accepted by the Company, and that some were defective from want of attention on the part of their officers.

In conclusion, it appears to me that, under the 6 Geo. IV., the return to be made is of the names of the partners as the same appear on the books of such Society; and consistently with the

[55]

(1) 2 Rail. Cas. 728.

TAYLOR
v.
HUGHES.

principle of the Act, and the decided cases, it may be found difficult for a person who, *de facto*, is a partner, and who appears to be so on the books of the co-partnership, and whose name is registered as such, to discharge himself of his liability to creditors by showing that the transfer to him was informally executed. And I am not satisfied that the return of the plaintiff's name in 1843 was authorized by the Act, even at law; for after he had ceased to appear as a partner on the books for seven years, and his name had been withdrawn from the register, it can hardly be maintained that new entries, made for the mere purpose of charging him, can be deemed an entry of his name " as a partner concerned in the co-partnership, as the same appears on the books ; " for by the books it appears, that for seven years he had ceased to be a partner, and that no new contract had been entered into with him, but an entry had been made, that the transfers by him were invalid, in order to create a continuing liability. But however this may be at

[*56]

law, I think that in equity this was a transaction *which cannot be maintained, and that I must consider all parties bound by the acts of the former Directors. I am bound, therefore, to give the relief prayed; and as I cannot approve of this mode of attempting to make a person, who had for so many years ceased to be a member of the co-partnership, liable for transactions to which he was no party, I think that the decree should be with costs.

Declare that the several transfers of shares by the plaintiff to the Society or co-partnership called the Agricultural and Commercial Bank of Ireland, or the trustees thereof in the pleadings mentioned, were accepted by the said Society; and declare that the list registered by the said Society on or about the 5th May, 1843, in the pleadings mentioned, is fraudulent and void as to the insertion of the plaintiff's name therein; and declare that the entries in the books, lists, and documents of the said Society or co-partnership, in which the plaintiff's name has been introduced as a shareholder thereof, since the date of the last of said transfers of shares on or about the 14th day of November, 1837, are fraudulent and void as to the plaintiff. And let all such books, lists, and documents of said Society, in their custody, possession, or control, be brought into the office of Edward Litton, Esq., one of the Masters of this Court, on oath; and let the said Master erase the plaintiff's name therefrom : and let an injunction issue to restrain the said Society or co-partnership from continuing the plaintiff's name on the registered list of the shareholders of the said Society or co-partnership: and let the said Society or co-partnership do all necessary acts remaining to be done, for the purpose of completing said transfers of shares by plaintiff, and also the registry of the several other *transfers of shares by plaintiff in the pleadings mentioned, and the registry thereof at the Stamp Office: and in case the parties differ respecting the form in which such transfers are to be completed and registered, refer it to the Master to settle the same. And let the injunction which issued in this cause to restrain the defendant, Langford Lovel Hodge, from all further proceedings on foot of the writ of *scire facias* sued out by him against the plaintiff, in the pleadings mentioned, be made perpetual. And let the defendant pay to the plaintiff his costs of this cause, when taxed and ascertained, and refer it to the Master to tax the same. And the defendant, William Hughes, so desiring, let the Master, in taxing such costs, ascertain whether the costs of the schedules to the answer of the defendant, William Hughes, were improperly or unnecessarily incurred by reason of the plaintiff's requiring such schedules; and if so, disallow to the plaintiff all such costs so improperly incurred; and in that case, let the plaintiff pay to, or set off against the defendant, William Hughes, the costs of the said defendant, caused by such unnecessary schedules.—Reg. Lib. vol. 91, p. 169.

DIMSDALE *v.* ROBERTSON (1).

(2 Jo. & Lat. 58—94 ; S. C. 7 Ir. Eq. R. 536.)

1844.
Nov. 22, 23.
Dec. 2.

SIR EDWARD
SUGDEN,
L.C.

[58]

An agreement to refer, and arbitrators named, and a covenant not to sue, and a power to examine witnesses upon oath, and to make the submission a rule of Court, prevent a party from filing a bill with the view of withdrawing the case from the arbitrators.

A party to a suit cannot set up an objection which grew out of his own conduct.

Two arbitrators were named in a submission to refer ; and they, or other the persons appointed in their place, were, before they proceeded, to appoint a third arbitrator : any two of the arbitrators for the time being, might, at any time, or from time to time, make awards or orders, provided the last of such awards should be made before the 1st of July, 1843, or before such other later time as any two of the arbitrators for the time being, should appoint : and any two of the arbitrators for the time being, might extend the time for making the last award, whether such time should have previously expired or not. And it was provided that X. should, as soon as conveniently might be, appoint an umpire ; and that if no two of the arbitrators for the time being, should be able to agree in making an award or order concerning any matter which ought to be awarded or ordered by

(1) *Cooke* v. *Cooke* (1867) L. R. 4 Eq. 77, 36 L. J. Ch. 480, 22 L. T. 570.

DIMSDALE
v.
ROBERTSON.

them, such matter should be awarded or ordered by the umpire: and if at any time before the several powers, authorities, covenants, and provisions, in the deed of submission were executed, either of the arbitrators named by the parties should refuse to act, the party whose arbitrator so refused, should appoint another in his place; and if he did not do so within fourteen days, then that the third arbitrator, and if none such, the umpire should appoint such arbitrator.

The plaintiff's arbitrator refused to act, and nothing was done in the matter of the reference before the 1st of July, 1843. The plaintiff having, after that day, refused to appoint an arbitrator, the defendant procured X. to appoint an umpire, who appointed an arbitrator on behalf of the plaintiff, and the two arbitrators appointed a third, and then the time was extended by the three arbitrators: Held, that the time was duly extended.

[THE facts of this case are sufficiently stated for the purposes of this report in the following judgment, and the cases cited by counsel are there noticed.]

[80]   *Mr. Brooke, Mr. Butt,* and *Mr. Armstrong,* for the plaintiff.   *   *   *

Mr. Moore, and *Mr. Wright,* for the defendant.

THE LORD CHANCELLOR:

Dimsdale having acquired certain interests in the slobs of Lough Foyle and Lough Swilly, in October, 1837, entered into a conditional agreement for sale of three-fourths of his interest to Robertson. Robertson was to provide funds for obtaining an Act of Parliament to enable the parties to reclaim and drain the slobs; but all such payments were to be the first charge upon all the reclaimed lands and the profits of the undertaking. Dimsdale was to be entitled to receive from Robertson 700*l.* annually for management; but the same was to be deducted by him out of the profits of the undertaking in the same manner as other advances. An Act of Parliament was obtained in 1838 for draining and embanking the lands. Dimsdale and Robertson afterwards agreed to divide the property between
[*81]   them equally; *and they acquired the shares of certain other persons who had been named in the Act of Parliament as undertakers with them.

By deed of November, 1840, the fee in the Lough Swilly slobs was conveyed, as to one moiety, to uses to bar down in favour of Dimsdale; and as to the other moiety, in like manner, in favour of Robertson: and the leasehold interest in Lough Foyle slobs was assigned to Dimsdale and Robertson, in equal shares, as tenants in common. These arrangements, of course, superseded the agreement of 1837, as to proportions; and materially affected the stipulation to allow Dimsdale 700*l.* a year for management; for as the

parties became entitled to the property equally, and that advance DIMSDALE
was made to be a charge on all the property, the only advantage ROBERTSON.
Dimsdale could obtain, if he were entitled still to manage, was the *v.*
advance of the money in the first instance, as, in the result, the
whole was to be a charge on all the property; and the agreement
of 1837 provided that all advances by Robertson should carry
interest.

In this state of circumstances the deed of the 18th of June, 1841,
was executed; which, stating the Act of Parliament, and the deeds
which had been executed—but not noticing the agreement of 1837
—stated, that Robertson had advanced and incurred payments, costs,
&c., to the amount of upwards of 16,500*l.*, and that Dimsdale had
secured 5,250*l.*, being a moiety of 10,000 guineas, part of that sum,
to Robertson, by promissory notes and judgments in England and
Ireland, and (as appears by the answer) by a mortgage, payable on
the 18th of September, 1841, with interest. The deed then recited
a claim by Dimsdale, by *virtue of an agreement between the   [*82]
parties (still avoiding any direct reference to the agreement of
1837), to the annual sum of 700*l.* for management; and that all
differences between the parties, except those agreed to be referred,
had been settled; and that Dimsdale had named Mr. Smith, of
London, his arbitrator; and Robertson had named Mr. Tite, of
the same place, his arbitrator. The deed then provided for the
allotment to Dimsdale and Robertson of portions of Lough Foyle
slobs, to be held in severalty. The evidence shows that the choice
was given to Dimsdale, who selected his lot.

The deed then proceeded to give powers and directions to the
arbitrators. The arbitrators were, as soon as conveniently might
be, and before they proceeded with the reference, to appoint a third
arbitrator; and the three for the time being, or any two of them,
were to make awards from time to time. First: any two of them
for the time being, should, as soon as conveniently might be, award
whether the whole or any part of the annual sum of 700*l.* should
cease to be payable; and award how much (if any) of the Lough
Swilly slobs should be given to Dimsdale in satisfaction of his
claims to that sum. Secondly: any two of the arbitrators were
to value the allotments of Lough Foyle; they were to be at liberty
to receive evidence of value; and they were to provide for equality
of partition out of the other lands not held in severalty; and each
party agreed that his allotment in severalty, and the allotment
to be made for equality of partition, should be accepted in full

DIMSDALE
v.
ROBERTSON.

[*83]

satisfaction of all his claims to Lough Foyle slobs. The arbitrators
were to determine as to the custody of. the title deeds; the proportions of compensation payable by each party, under the Act—a
most important *provision; and what deeds, releases, instruments,
and acts were to be executed and performed by the parties. Power
was given to them to examine witnesses on oath, and also the
parties. It is then provided, that the arbitrators for the time being,
shall, at any time thereafter, make such award, or, from time to
time, make such awards as they shall think proper; with a proviso,
that the last of such awards shall be made on or before the 1st of
July, 1843, or such other or later time as any two of the arbitrators for the time being shall appoint: and every two of the arbitrators, for the time being, shall have power, from time to time, to
enlarge or extend the time as they shall think proper; and that
whether such time shall have previously expired or not. Power is
then given to the senior Master of the Queen's Bench in England
to appoint an umpire, and to fill up the appointment; and he is to
act when no two of the arbitrators can agree. This is followed by
a proviso, that, at any time before the powers, authorities, covenants, agreements, and provisions therein contained, shall have
been fully executed and performed, each party will, in case his
arbitrator for the time being shall die, or refuse, &c., to act, appoint
another arbitrator within fourteen days; and, in case of neglect,
the third arbitrator, or, if none, the umpire, shall make the appointment. Neither party was to bring or prosecute any action at law,
or suit in equity against the other, touching the matters thereby
referred, or do any act to delay the arbitrators, or bring any action
against them. Robertson covenants to indemnify Dimsdale, upon
payment of the 5,250l., against all expenses covered by the account.
If either party fail to reclaim his allotment before the 27th of July,
1846, the other party may reclaim it and acquire the ownership of

[*84]

it. Finally, the reference may be *made a rule of the Court of
Queen's Bench of England and Ireland.

On the 21st of June, 1821, by a regular deed of partition, the
allotments of Lough Foyle slobs were vested in Dimsdale and
Robertson, in severalty. The deed recites that the partition was to
be valid, notwithstanding any inequality whatever in value; and
this is regularly provided for by the deed. Mr. Walker, the
engineer, acting for the Admiralty under the provision in section
95 of the Act, in striking the line of embankment, cut off several
thousands of acres from the allotments in severalty of Lough

Foyle slobs; but Dimsdale's allotment was lessened in quantity
upwards of 2,000 acres beyond the loss sustained by Robertson,
and several hundred acres were cut off the portions provided for
equality of partition. Dimsdale did not pay the 5,250l.

Under the circumstances, Dimsdale filed the present bill, for a
reference as to the 700l. per annum; and as to the present value
of the several allotments, and for a partition of Lough Swilly
slobs, and of the other part of Lough Foyle slobs: and if the
unallotted portion of the latter and Lough Swilly shall be insufficient for owelty of partition, then, that Robertson may make good
the deficiency out of his allotment of the Foyle, or by payment in
money. The plaintiff did not offer to pay the 5,250l.; but, after
some contest at the Bar, he offered, by his counsel, to pay that sum
at once to the defendant.

The main ground for equitable relief, beyond the agreement of
1841, is the loss sustained by the plaintiff, by the *line struck by   [*85]
Mr. Walker, although the defendant does not admit that the plaintiff's lot is, even now, of less value than his own. But I assume
that the plaintiff's allegation would prove to be correct; yet I
think that he has no such equity as he claims. For section 95 of
the Act expressly provided that no work should be made below the
ordinary high-water mark at spring tides without the assent of the
Admiralty; and the deed of partition recited that Mr. Walker had
been appointed, as well by the Admiralty as by the parties, to be
engineer, for the purpose of determining the lines of the proposed
embankment of Lough Foyle; and he was to determine any
dispute between the parties relating to the lines, or any dispute as
to the erecting any work below the high-water mark at spring tides
without the assent of the Admiralty. The parties, therefore, were
fully aware of their rights and liabilities; and with that knowledge
they allotted Lough Foyle between themselves, with a provision for
owelty of partition out of the unallotted lands, making the partition
absolutely binding. I think that they are not now at liberty to
disturb that arrangement, and that they must rest content with the
actual fund provided for equality of partition. The equity, if it
exist, is mutual. If I made a decree, I should be bound to provide
relief for the defendant or the plaintiff, whichever should prove to
be right in the allegation as to value. But the plaintiff has sold
his allotment in the Foyle to a third person who is not a party to
the cause; and, although that sale was made pending the suit, yet
the Court would not, at the prayer of the plaintiff, who is in prison

DIMSDALE
v.
ROBERTSON.

'[*86]

for debt, proceed to bind the purchaser from him in his absence. It appears to me, however, that the parties have, by contract, restricted their demands for owelty of partition to the properties not the subject of the partition; and the arbitrators *can, under the deed, give to the plaintiff all that he is entitled to, even if his allegation of value be correct; nor does it appear that there is not sufficient property to answer any demand which the plaintiff can establish.

The partition prayed of the remainder of Lough Foyle and of Lough Swilly seems rather to be with reference to the allotment for equality of partition. After the execution of the deed of arrangement of 1841, by which part of Lough Foyle alone was to be allotted, I do not think that the plaintiff is entitled to demand a partition of the remaining lands, in regard to which the partnership still subsists; but it must remain as a subject to be drained and embanked by the parties in common, subject to the directions of the Act, and of the deed of arrangement. Still the plaintiff would be entitled to the other relief prayed, viz., an account of the value of the allotments and a satisfaction out of the other properties, and an account of what is due for management, unless that right is prevented by the provisions of the deed of arrangement.

To the objection that the plaintiff had not performed his own part of the arrangement, either as to the money or management, it was said that he had been prevented by the conduct of the defendant, who had pursued him into many counties, and who ultimately arrested him, and threw him into prison, where he now lies. But this is not a sufficient answer. The arrest was justified by the neglect of the plaintiff to pay the 5,250*l.* He gave security to pay it in four months, and undertook to lay out 10,000*l.* more in a short time. He gave judgment in both countries, so that he assumed to be solvent, and gave, by contract, a ready relief against

[*87]

himself; and he cannot relieve himself *from the performance of his other obligations, because he has not performed that for payment of the money.

It was then objected that the plaintiff could not sustain the bill, as by the deed of arrangment the matters in question were agreed to be referred to arbitration; and the time, which had been enlarged, had not expired. In answer to this objection, it was insisted (1) that the time for making an award had passed, and had not been properly extended; (2) but that if the time were still open, an agreement to refer to arbitration could not be made a defence against a right to sue. It was not denied by the defendant that the suit could be maintained, if the power of the arbitrators had ceased. This is a legal question, depending upon the construction of the deed of arrangement, the particulars of which I have already adverted to: and I undertook the task of deciding upon it at the request of both parties, without which I should have directed a case to a court of law. The facts are, that at the time, viz., the 1st of July, 1843, when the last award was to be made, unless the time was enlarged, there was no person to act in the arbitration but the arbitrator of the defendant. The defendant has never been in default. After that day, an umpire was appointed; and he appointed an arbitrator for Dimsdale, under the power in the deed; and these two arbitrators appointed a third arbitrator, and all three enlarged the time. The deed expressly authorizes the time to be enlarged after the 1st July, 1843, if the arbitrators think proper.

DIMSDALE
v.
ROBERTSON.

The plaintiff insisted that the time could not be enlarged, as there were not two arbitrators in existence, nor an umpire named on the 1st of July, 1843; and that even if the *time could, under those circumstances, be enlarged, it could only be where there had been some previous award.

[*88]

The point is not without difficulty. I have fully considered it, and I think that the time has been duly enlarged. There are no express words to exclude the appointments which were made; and if the umpire and arbitrators were duly appointed, the time was, I think, duly enlarged. The deed gives various powers to the arbitrators, which would require time for their performance; and they are empowered at any time, or from time to time, to make one award or several awards; and then it is provided that the last of such awards shall be on or before the 1st of July, 1843, or before such other time as any two arbitrators "for the time being," shall appoint: and every two "for the time being," have power, from time to time, to enlarge the time, whether such time shall have expired or not. Now, as the time may be enlarged after the day named, the persons who are then arbitrators will be the arbitrators for the time being, competent to do the act; for the words "for the time being" refer, I think, to the time of doing the act, and not simply to the time when it might have been done. There is no provision confining the power to arbitrators actually appointed on the 1st of July, although, of course, such arbitrators could have enlarged the time, and are included within the terms of the deed.

DIMSDALE
v.
ROBERTSON.

The subsequent clauses show that the parties meant the arbitration to be proceeded with until the provisions of the deed were fully executed, and for that purpose enabled an arbitrator to be appointed for either party who should neglect to appoint one at any time before the provisions were executed. The intention, I think, is manifest to have arbitrators appointed while there was any act to

[*89]

be done. Now, all the acts remained *unperformed, and one of the powers was to enlarge the time. When the time was enlarged, all the powers were revived. This being the intention, and there being no sufficient expressions to prevent me from giving effect to that intention, I must declare that the time was duly enlarged. I do not think it material that no award was made before the 1st of July; for the provision in effect is, that no award shall be made after that day unless the time is enlarged. There might have been only one award, if the arbitrators had so thought fit. I may observe that the plaintiff filed his bill in 1841, when the arbitration clauses were in full force; and this suit must be deemed an interruption of the arbitration by the plaintiff himself; and, according to the doctrine in *Morse* v. *Merest* (1), the plaintiff could not set up an objection which grew out of his own conduct, and which in this case clearly did not exist when he filed his bill. *Morse* v. *Merest* applied the doctrine to a defendant; but in *Pope* v. *Lord Duncannon* (2), it was considered equally applicable to a plaintiff; and so I consider it. But I need not pursue this point.

2. It was contended for the plaintiff, that if the time was duly enlarged, yet the reference to arbitration cannot be used as a defence to this suit. As to one subject, the annual sum of 700*l.*, the plaintiff admitted he could not ask for a reference beyond the arrears, if any; for a Master could not be placed in the office of arbitrator and decide whether, having regard to the circumstances, the annuity should determine or not. As to the other relief, there would be no difficulty, if the bill can be maintained. The plaintiff

[*90]

relied upon the case of *Street* v. *Rigby* (3), *where, although it was not necessary to decide the point, Lord ELDON was of opinion that an agreement to refer to arbitration did not prevent a party from filing his bill.

It is, no doubt, clearly settled, as Lord KENYON said in *Thompson* v. *Charnock* (4), that an agreement to refer to arbitration is not sufficient to oust the courts of law or equity of their jurisdiction.

(1) 9 Mod. 56.   (3) 6 Ves. 815.
(2) 47 R. R. 202 (9 Sim. 177).   (4) 8 T. R. 140.

Lord HARDWICK so determined in *Wellington* v. *Mackintosh* (1); yet he said he would not have it understood that such an agreement might not be made and pleaded, but there should be a power to examine witnesses on oath; upon which it was observed by Lord KENYON, and by Lord ELDON, that the parties could not confer such a power. Now, in the present case, there is not only an agreement to refer, but arbitrators were actually named; and there is an express covenant not to sue, and an agreement to make the submission a rule of the Court of Queen's Bench of either England or Ireland: and the 3 & 4 Will. IV. c. 42, England, and 3 & 4 Vict. c. 105, Ireland, take away the right to revoke the submission without the leave of the Court, when the arbitrators are appointed by or in pursuance of any submission to reference, containing an agreement that such submission shall be made a rule of Court, and give power to compel the attendance of witnesses, and empower the arbitrators to administer an oath, where, as in this case, it is agreed that the witnesses shall be examined upon oath. These powers place such arbitrators on a different footing, and remove one great objection made to them by both Lord HARDWICK and Lord ELDON. In *Halfhide* v. *Fenning* (2), where the agreement was to *refer to arbitration, and that there should not be any suit at law or in equity, Lord KENYON allowed a plea to a bill before a reference. He held that arbitration should be first resorted to; and if the arbitrators could not determine it, the jurisdiction would be restored. It is said that this decision has been overruled, even by Lord KENYON himself. I think that the reasons for the decision are satisfactory, as applied to the actual case before Lord Kenyon; and I am prepared to act upon them, unless the case has been overruled.

In *Mitchell* v. *Harris* (3), where the agreement was simply to refer, and the bill was filed for a discovery in aid of an action, Lord ROSSLYN supported the bill; but in the course of the argument he distinguished the case before him from that of *Halfhide* v. *Fenning*. In that case, he said, there was an express agreement that there should be no suit at law or in equity. Parties may so agree; and it is every day's practice that, if they do, they cannot proceed contrary to the agreement. In that case the covenant would be a bar: here, he said, the only effect of it would be to give damages; but it could not be pleaded in bar of the action. In giving judgment, however, he wholly lost sight of this distinction;

DIMSDALE
v.
ROBERTSON.

[*91]

(1) 2 Atk. 569.
(2) 2 Br. C. C. 336.
(3) 4 Br. C. C. 311.

DIMSDALE
v.
ROBERTSON.

and therefore thought *Halfhide* v. *Fenning* contrary to the case in
Atkins, and quite inconsistent with the resolution of the Court of
King's Bench in Wilson, neither of which appears to me to clash
with it. The report in *Mitchell* v. *Harris* in Brown, merely makes
him say that it was unnecessary to discuss the case of *Halfhide* v.
Fenning. In *Tattersall* v. *Groote* (1), Lord ELDON, noticing the
distinction in *Halfhide* v. *Fenning*, thought he did not misconstrue
the case of *Mitchell* v. *Harris*, by stating that the opinion of

[*92]   *Lord LOUGHBOROUGH did not agree with the doctrine laid down in
that case. In *Street* v. *Rigby* (2), he again seemed to doubt the
authority of *Halfhide* v. *Fenning*, yet thought there would be
considerable difficulty upon a negative covenant not to sue, which
was the case before Lord Kenyon ; and he held that a covenant to
refer does not amount to an agreement to forbear to sue. In
Waters v. *Taylor* (3), Lord ELDON considered the opinion expressed
by Lord KENYON wrong, as there were against it the concurrent
opinions of Lord HARDWICK, Lord THURLOW, Lord ROSSLYN, and
Lord KENYON himself. " As a general proposition, therefore," he
added, " it is true, that an agreement to refer disputes to arbitration will not bind the parties, even to submit to arbitration, before
they came in Court." But this is a point which Lord KENYON did
not decide ; and I confine myself to the very point decided by him.
I am not aware of any case in which Lord KENYON doubted his own
decision. Probably what fell from him in the case in Term Reports
may have been so considered, although it is confined to a simple
covenant to refer. There is no report of any decision of Lord
THURLOW's impeaching Lord KENYON's. Upon the whole, therefore,
I think that *Halfhide* v. *Fenning* is still law ; and the objections to
it have probably been occasioned by Lord KENYON's general observations. At all events, I think that an agreement to refer, and
arbitrators named, and a covenant not to sue, and a power to
make the submission a rule of Court—particularly having regard to
the legislative provisions in such a case—do prevent a party from
filing a bill, with a view, as in this case, to withdraw the case from
the arbitrators. It does not appear to me that because a bill
cannot be filed to have arbitrators named, or to supply the place of

[*93]   an *award, it follows that a bill can be filed before an award, in
direct opposition to the plaintiff's own covenants.

In this case, like that of *Waters* v. *Taylor* (3), the parties have

(1) 2 Bos. & P. 131, 136. See 14   (2) 6 Ves. 821.
R. R. Pref. viii.   (3) 13 R. R. 91 (15 Ves. 18).

anxiously provided for the reference to arbitration of the several DIMSDALE
matters in respect to which any difficulty was likely to arise; ᵛ.
and, indeed this case goes much further.   Lord ELDON there, ROBERTSON.
upon an interlocutory application, drove the parties to a reference.   Sir WILLIAM GRANT afterwards observed, in *Gourlay* v.
Duke of Somerset (1), that in some cases, under particular circumstances, as in *Waters* v. *Taylor*, the Court has said, it will
leave the parties to the remedy which they have chalked out for
themselves ; but there it refused all interposition.   He, in that
case, substituted the Master for a referee named, as the plaintiff
filed his bill for relief, and he could not in that particular have it,
except through the machinery of the Court, and the defendant did
not raise the objection.   The case of *Morse* v. *Merest*, before Sir
John Leach, went further.   The parties had agreed for the sale of
an estate, by one to the other, for twenty-five years' purchase, on
an annual value, to be set by three persons named, before a certain
day.   The seller had prevented the valuation from being made by
the day named.   The purchaser filed his bill.   The VICE-CHAN-
CELLOR held, first, that the seller had, by his own conduct, opened
the time ; secondly, that although an agreement to sell, at a price
to be named by A., could not be enforced at any other price, yet it
appearing that the defendant refused to permit the referees to come
upon the land, the Court had jurisdiction to remove that impediment, and could decree that the defendant should permit the valuation to be made according to the contract ; and if *it were so made,   [*94]
then a supplemental bill might be filed for a specific performance
upon the terms of their valuation.   The Court, therefore, gave its
assistance to the referees to enable them to make the valuation,
upon which the right to a specific performance depended.   I may
observe, that *Waters* v. *Taylor* was ultimately disposed of in a way
which does not affect the question before me (2).

   It appears to me, after an anxious review of all the authorities,
that I am fully justified in refusing the relief to the plaintiff until
the parties have resorted, without effect, to the powers provided
by their deeds.   The Court would find it difficult to manage these
concerns ; and it is inequitable for the plaintiff to accept a benefit
under the deed of arrangement, and then attempt to evade the
rest of the obligations and file a bill for partial relief.   His object
manifestly was to evade the arbitration in London, and the expense
of it, although he had concurred in the appointment of arbitrators

(1) 13 R. R. 234 (19 Ves. 431).   (2) 13 R. R. 91 (2 V. & B. 299).

residing in the city of London, and to substitute this Court for
the arbitrators. If he had succeeded he would have obtained
time, and deferred the payment of the costs until the winding up
of the cause. But this is a purpose to which the Court cannot
be ancillary. As my opinion is against the plaintiff upon all the
points, the bill must be dismissed, with costs.

PEPPER AND WIFE v. TUCKEY.

(1 WILL. IV. c. 60.)

(2 Jo. & Lat. 95—98; S. C. 7 Ir. Eq. R. 572.)

1844.
Nov. 9.
Dec. 2.

SIR EDWARD
SUGDEN,
L.C.
[95]

A trustee in a marriage settlement, refused to join in lending the trust
monies, because he disapproved of the security. The wife, pursuant to a
power for the purpose, removed him and appointed a new trustee in his
place; and the husband and wife then presented a petition under the Act,
to compel the old trustee to transfer the funds to the new trustee. The
Court refused the application.

BY settlement of the 31st of May, 1842, executed upon the
marriage of the petitioners, two sums of money, the fortune of
the intended wife (one of which was then invested in Government
old Three-and-a-half per cent. stock, and the other formed part of
a larger sum, secured by the bond of Henry Wood), were assigned
to Charles C. Tuckey and W. J. Pepper, upon trust to permit Mrs.
Pepper to receive the dividends and interest for her sole and
separate use, but without the power of alienation or anticipation,
during her husband's life; and, after his decease, in case she
should survive him, to pay her the principal moneys, and all
interest due thereon; but, in case she should die in the lifetime
of her husband, leaving issue, upon trust to pay the principal sums
to the children of the marriage as therein directed; and in case
she should die without leaving issue, to such person as she should,
by deed or will, notwithstanding her coverture, appoint; and in
default of appointment, to her executors, &c. And it was thereby
agreed that it should be lawful for the trustees, with the consent,
in writing, of the husband and wife, during their joint lives, to
invest the trust moneys at interest in Government or private
security, and, from time to time, to call in, re-invest, and vary
the securities; provided that, if such investments be made on
private security, the same should be approved of by counsel for
the mutual benefit of all parties to the *settlement, who should be
of opinion that such change of securities, when so made, should
be safe, and valid, and good, and for the benefit and advantage

of Mrs. Pepper; and in case Charles C. Tuckey or W. J. Pepper, or any succeeding trustee, for the time being, to be appointed as thereinafter mentioned, should depart this life, or be desirous to be discharged from the trusts, or should be about to reside beyond the seas, or should refuse or neglect or become incapable to act in the trusts, before the same should be fully performed or determined, or if, for such or any other cause, during the lifetime of Mrs. Pepper, it should seem expedient to change Charles C. Tuckey or W. J. Pepper, her trustees, then, and in every such case, it should be lawful for her, by deed, to nominate and constitute some other fit and proper person or persons, to supply the place and stead of Charles C. Tuckey and W. J. Pepper, or such trustee so to be changed as aforesaid; and that immediately after such appointment should be made, all the trust-moneys and securities should be assigned and transferred in such manner that the same should be legally vested in the trustee or trustees so to be appointed, upon the trusts of the settlement.

Mrs. Pepper and her husband being desirous to invest the trust moneys upon a certain private security, applied to the trustees to invest them accordingly; and Charles C. Tuckey having declined to do so, Mrs. Pepper, by indenture of the 11th of July, 1844, appointed James Wilcocks to be a new trustee in the place of Charles C. Tuckey, and required Charles C. Tuckey, by letter of the 11th of July, 1844, to assign the money secured by the bond, and to transfer the stock to the new trustee jointly with the old trustee.

In reply to this requisition, Charles C. Tuckey, on the 19th of July, addressed a letter to Mr. Pepper, stating that a legal doubt had been raised as to whether the substitution of a new trustee would, under all the circumstances, free him from responsibility; and that until that was satisfactorily cleared up, he could not transmit the letter of attorney: and further, that he had no desire to remain trustee a day after he was assured of acquittal from all further obligation. Under these circumstances, a petition was presented by Mr. and Mrs. Pepper, praying that it might be referred to one of the Masters to inquire and report whether the deed of the 11th of July, 1844, was a good, legal, and valid deed; and if so, that Charles C. Tuckey be ordered to transfer the trust funds to the new trustee.

[97]

Mr. Thomas White, for the petitioners, relied upon the 10th and 11th sections of the 1 Will. IV. c. 60 (1).

(1) Rep. 13 & 14 Vict. c. 60, s. 1; see now Trustee Act, 1893, s. 35.

THE LORD CHANCELLOR:

The object of the petition in this matter is to obtain a transfer of certain stock under the 1 Will. IV. c. 60, s. 10, from a trustee who has declined to transfer the fund to a new trustee. The settlement contains powers of a very unusual character. The property was settled upon the wife for life, without power of anticipation; and after her decease, upon the children of the marriage: but the husband had no interest in the fund; and the trustees were empowered, with the consent of the husband and wife, to lend [*98] the trust funds upon private security, provided such *security were, according to counsel's opinion, safe and valid, and for the benefit of the wife. Then followed a very unusual power to appoint trustees, authorizing the wife to change a trustee whenever she should think proper. It appears that the husband was desirous of lending the money upon a private security, which the trustee did not approve of; and thereupon the husband and wife adopted this scheme: Mrs. Pepper exercised the power and changed the trustee, as she had a right to do; and then she and her husband presented this petition under the Act, to compel the old trustee to transfer the fund to the new trustee. The old trustee is not under any disability, nor unwilling to act in the trust: he exercised his discretion and refused to do the act required; stating, however, that he was willing to be discharged from the trust under the sanction of the Court. I do not think that this is a case within the statute. The trustee has only done his duty; he *bonâ fide* refused to lend the trust-money, because he thought the security offered was not a proper one. No order of mine would absolve him from responsibility; for the 10th section of the Act only applies to cases where the trustee really neglects to perform his duty. Here the trustee did not refuse to execute his trust. Even though I may have the power, I think I ought not to exercise it, in order to enable the parties to carry their intention into execution. The trustee has no right to call upon the Court in this summary manner to sanction his transfer of the property: but he has acted properly in not allowing the money to be lent upon any but good security. The Act was not intended to give a sanction to a trustee to resign his trust, rather than do an act which he deems improper. Such a settlement is well calculated to embarrass any trustee attentive to his duty. I refuse the application.

WALL *v.* BYRNE (1).

(2 Jo. & Lat. 118—120.)

1845.
Jan. 22, 23.

SIR EDWARD
SUGDEN,
L.C.

[118]

A lessee of lands demised to him, his heirs and assigns, *pur autre vie,*
devised all his real, freehold, and personal property to his wife and children,
share and share alike. One of the children who survived the testator, died
intestate : Held, that his heir-at-law, and not his personal representative,
was entitled to his share of the freehold lands.

LUKE WALL being entitled to the lessee's interest in certain lands,
held under a lease for lives renewable for ever, in 1831 obtained a
renewal thereof ; and thereby Robert Johnston, in whom the reversion was then vested, demised the lands to him, his heirs and assigns,
for the term of three lives therein named, with a covenant for
perpetual renewal.

In September, 1832, Luke Wall made his will, containing the
following devise, which included in it his interest in the lease : " And
as for and concerning all my real, freehold, and personal property,
which I now possess or am entitled to, I give, devise and bequeath
the same and every part thereof unto my dear wife and my children,
Margaret, Anne, Ellen, Mary, Joseph, Luke, Christopher, and
Valentine, share and share alike : " and died shortly afterwards.

Mary Wall and Christopher Wall, having survived the testator,
died intestate and unmarried.

This suit was instituted to administer the assets of Luke Wall,
and to carry the trusts of his will into execution : and under the
decree to account pronounced in it, the Master reported that the
shares of Mary Wall and Christopher Wall in the lands demised by
the lease of 1831, descended upon and were vested in Joseph Wall,
their eldest brother and heir-at-law.

To this report exceptions were taken upon behalf of *some of the   [*119]
younger children of the testator, upon the ground that the Master
should have found that, upon the death of Mary Wall, her share in
the freehold estates, which were estates *pur autre vie*, and devised
by the testator to his wife and children share and share alike,
without naming any special occupants, vested in her personal representatives. A similar exception was taken to the finding of the
Master with respect to Christopher Wall's share.

Mr. Fitzgibbon and *Mr. Connor*, in support of the exception,

(1) Distinguished *In re Sheppard*
[1897] 2 Ch. 67, 66 L. J. Ch. 445, 76
L. T. 756 ; and not followed, *In re*
Inman [1903] 1 Ch. 241, 72 L. J. Ch.
120, 88 L. T. 173.

WALL
v.
BYRNE.

cited *Doe* d. *Lewis* v. *Lewis* (1), and were proceeding to argue the case, when they were stopped by

THE LORD CHANCELLOR:

I cannot permit this exception to be argued. If ever a point was closed by decision it is this; that where a man has an estate *pur auter vie*, limited to him and his heirs, and devises that estate, by words which, without words of limitation, would pass the *quasi* inheritance—as the words here would—and the devisee dies intestate, the persons to take are the heirs and not the personal representatives of the devisee. The point was so decided in this country many years since (2); and that decision has been followed in England; and many opinions have been given on it. I must therefore decline to hear the question argued; for I will not be auxiliary to unsettle settled opinions. The case of *Doe* d. *Lewis* v. *Lewis* is distinguishable. There the devise was to a man and his assigns, which, it was held, did not mean heirs: but in this case the devise is in general

[*120]

terms, and in words *which are sufficient to pass the entire interest under the lease. If this had been a fee simple estate, it would have gone to the devisee and his heirs under the terms of this devise. The testator gives all his interest in the lands to his devisees; and both law and good sense require that they should take the same interest which he himself had. It is a settled point, and not now open to be disturbed. It was settled by a case in this country, decided upon great consideration, which has been since recognized and acted on. I shall therefore follow those authorities, and leave the error, if it be one, to be corrected elsewhere.

———

1845.
Feb. 7, 22.
———
SIR EDWARD
SUGDEN,
L.C.
[141]

CAULFIELD *v.* MAGUIRE (3).

(2 Jo. & Lat. 141—181; S. C. 8 Ir. Eq. R. 164.)

Where an estate, subject to a charge bearing interest, is limited to several persons in succession, as tenants for life, the conclusion to be drawn from the authorities appears to be, that each tenant for life is liable only for the interest, for his own time; but that to liquidate the arrears during his own time, he must furnish all the rents, if necessary, during the whole of his life.

A testator directed that a certain debt of 25,000*l.* should be deemed part of the residue of his personal estate; and he gave it, and all interest due and to grow due thereon, and the residue of his personal estate, to trustees, upon

(1) 60 R. R. 855 (9 M. & W. 662).
(2) See *Blake* v. *Jones* d. *Blake*, 1 Hud. & Bro. 227, *n.* ; *Philpot* v. *James*, 3 Doug. 425.

(3) *Honywood* v. *Honywood* [1902] 1 Ch. 347, 71 L. J. Ch. 174, 86 L. T. 214.

trust to collect, and from time to time invest same ; and to pay the interest of one third part thereof to each of his three children for their lives; and after their decease, respectively, to pay one third part of the principal to their children. After making his will, the testator by deed released to his debtor all interest which should become due on the 25,000*l.* during his life; and he agreed to postpone the payment of the principal sum and the interest to accrue due thereon, until the end of three years next after his decease; and then to accept payment of the principal sum and the interest which should have accrued due thereon during the three years, by instalments; and that the 25,000*l.* should not bear interest after the expiration of the three years, so long as the instalments were regularly paid ; but that if default should be made in payment of the instalments, the balance should be payable with interest, until the instalments, with the interest, should be paid. By a codicil, the testator declared that the execution of this deed should not revoke, prejudice, or affect, his will. Held, that the three years' interest did not form part of the capital of the residuary personal estate ; and that the legatees for life of the residue were entitled to it.

A. as principal and B. as surety joined in granting an annuity for the life of C. ; and A. assigned to trustees a policy of insurance upon his own life, upon trust to permit C. after the death of A., out of the money insured or the interest thereof, to receive the annuity. And A. and B. executed their joint and several bond conditioned to secure the punctual payment of the annuity. The executors of A. received the amount of the policy and invested it upon Government securities. The executor of B. was compelled to pay C. an arrear of the annuity. Held, that as against the general assets of A., the executor of B. was not entitled to interest on the money so paid by him : but that he was entitled, as against the sum insured and the interest thereon, to be put in the same situation as if it had been duly applied in payment of the annuity, and therefore to be repaid thereout the money advanced by him, with interest.

C. having power to appoint a money fund to all and every or any child or children of hers, and to the exclusion of any one or more of them, in such shares and payable at such times as she should appoint, and in default of appointment, to be equally divided between them, by her will, appointed different sums to several of her children : and reciting that her daughter M. had declared her intention of becoming a nun, and had retired into a convent preparatory thereto, she declared that she deemed her patrimony in that case sufficient for her maintenance ; but in case M. should change her mind and return to her family and friends, she bequeathed to trustees 1,000*l.* in trust for M. to receive the interest of the same during her life, and at her decease to be divided amongst her children, if any ; or in either case of her not leaving the convent or not leaving any issue, the 1,000*l.* to be divided amongst her three daughters therein named ; and she bequeathed to her said three daughters any residue of the fund that might be after paying the several legacies in her will mentioned. Held (1), that the power authorized an appointment to take effect upon the happening of a contingency ; (2) that the interest which should accrue on the 1,000*l.* while the contingency was undetermined, passed under the residuary bequest in the will.

WILLIAM, BARON ANNESLEY and Francis Annesley, Esq., being seised, as tenants in common, in fee, *inter alia*, of the lands of Gibbstown, Troystown, and Donaghpatrick, *by indenture of the 7th of March, 1764, demised the same to Samuel Gerrard and his heirs,

[*142]

subject to the yearly rent of 100l., payable half-yearly, on every 1st of
May and 1st of November.

In February, 1766, William, Baron Annesley borrowed a sum of
2,000l. from Elizabeth Salkeld; to secure which he executed to her
two bonds, each in the penal sum of 2,000l., conditioned for payment
of the sum of 1,000l., with interest at six per cent. Upon these
bonds judgments were obtained in Hilary Term, 1766.

By indenture of the 10th of March, 1766, it was agreed between
Elizabeth Salkeld and William, Baron Annesley, that if Samuel
Gerrard, or the occupier of the lands demised by the lease of 1764,
should pay the interest of the 2,000l., at the rate of 5l. per cent. per
annum, he should have credit for same out of his rent; and that
Elizabeth Salkeld should accept of that reduced rate of interest.

In pursuance of this arrangement, Samuel Gerrard for many
years paid his rent to Elizabeth Salkeld, in discharge of the interest
on the 2,000l.

[143]   William, Baron Annesley, having been created Viscount Glerawley,
made his will in May, 1770; and thereby devised all his real
estates to his eldest son, Francis Charles, afterwards created Earl
Annesley, for life; remainder to his first and other sons, in tail
male; remainder to his second son, Richard, afterwards Earl
Annesley, for his life; remainder to his first and other sons, in tail
male: and by his will he created a trust term in his real estates,
for payment of his debts and legacies. He died shortly afterwards.

In 1772, after the death of William Viscount Glerawley, a partition was made of the lands, of which he and Francis Annesley
were seised in common in fee: and a moiety thereof, including
Gibbstown, Troystown, and Donaghpatrick, was vested in trustees,
to the uses and for the purposes in the will of William Viscount
Glerawley mentioned; and subject, among other debts, to the two
judgments obtained by Elizabeth Salkeld.

Francis Charles Earl Annesley died in 1802, without issue male;
and was succeeded by Richard Earl Annesley; and by indenture of
the 19th May, 1808, executed on the marriage of William Richard
Viscount Glerawley, eldest son of Richard Earl Annesley, the lands
so allotted were re-settled, subject, among other debts, to Salkeld's
two judgments (which were stated to be for the principal sum
of 2,000l.), to the use of Richard Earl Annesley for life; with
remainder to William Richard Viscount Glerawley for life; with
remainder to his first and other sons in tail male.

[*144]   In 1776 the judgments were revived by Thomas Salkeld, *the

personal representative of Elizabeth Salkeld. In 1808 Samuel
Gerrard sold his interest in the lands above mentioned to John
Gerrard ; and the interest on the sum secured by the judgments
not having been otherwise paid either by the tenant of the lands
demised by the lease of 1764 or otherwise, Joseph Salkeld, the
administrator *de bonis non* of Elizabeth Salkeld, in 1818, filed a
bill against Richard Earl Annesley, William Richard Viscount
Glerawley, and others, to enforce payment of the judgment debts ;
and thereby claimed interest on the principal sums secured by the
judgments, from the year 1786, up to which time it was admitted
by the bill that all interest had been paid : and on the 9th of May,
1823, he obtained a decree for payment of the sum of 4,000*l*. (the
penal sums mentioned in the bonds), together with interest thereon,
from the 3rd of May, 1823, and also for the costs of the suit : or,
in default, a sale of the lands affected by the judgments.

While this suit was pending, an arrangement was entered into
between Richard Earl Annesley and William Richard Viscount
Glerawley, which was carried into execution by an indenture of the
1st of November, 1821 ; whereby, after reciting, *inter alia*, the
marriage settlement of the 19th of May, 1808 ; and that William
Richard Viscount Glerawley had executed his two bonds, with
warrants of attorney, dated the 1st of November, 1821, to Earl
Annesley, one of which was conditioned for the payment of 21,490*l*.,
on the 1st of November, 1822, with interest, at the rate of five per
cent. ; and the other was conditioned for the payment of 3,000*l*.,
with interest from the day of the decease of Earl Annesley, the
said principal sum and interest to be paid at the end of one year
after the decease of the Earl ; and that Viscount Glerawley was
also indebted to the Earl *in 550*l*., secured by his bond and [*145]
warrant, said three sums amounting in the whole to 25,040*l*., and
that judgments had been entered upon those several bonds. And
after further reciting that Viscount Glerawley was entitled to
several policies of insurance upon his own life, and therein specified,
for sums amounting to 24,492*l*. 6*s*. 8*d*. late currency, and that Earl
Annesley, being advanced in years, had agreed to relinquish and
give up to Viscount Glerawley the immediate possession and enjoyment of the settled estates ; it was witnessed that in consideration
(*inter alia*) of the several sums of money secured to be paid by the
Viscount Glerawley as aforesaid, Richard Earl Annesley and
William Richard Viscount Glerawley conveyed the manor of Castlewellan, and several denominations of lands, being the settled

estate (but not making mention of Gibbstown, Troystown, or
Donaghpatrick), for their lives, and the life of the survivor, to the
use of Lord Dufferin and the Rev. A. Maguire, for a term of 200
years ; and, subject thereto, to the use, that Richard Earl Annesley
should, during the joint lives of himself and his son, receive thereout an annuity of 4,000l. for his life ; and subject thereto, and to
the term of years, to the use of Viscount Glerawley, for his life ;
and after his decease, to the use of Richard Earl Annesley, for his
life : and the trusts of the term were declared to be, first, to secure
the payment of the annuity of 4,000l. ; and further, that the
trustees should, yearly, during the lives of the Earl and Viscount,
and the survivor of them, out of the rents, or by mortgage or sale,
levy and raise such yearly sums of money as should be sufficient
to pay the several annuities and annual outgoings, and the interest
payable upon the charges and incumbrances specified in the
schedule to the deed annexed ; amongst which, the debts due to the
representatives of Elizabeth Salkeld were not included : and

[*146] *further, by the means aforesaid, levy, raise and pay, to Earl
Annesley, his executors, &c., interest at the rate of five per cent.
on the said sum of 21,490l., from the 1st of November, 1821,
pursuant to the condition of the bond for the payment of the same,
passed by Viscount Glerawley to Earl Annesley : and further, to
raise and levy thereout, at the expiration of one year after the
decease of the Earl, the said sum of 3,000l., and to pay the
same, together with the interest thereof, to commence from the day
of the decease of the Earl, unto Richard Earl Annesley, his
executors, administrators or assigns, pursuant to the condition of
the before-mentioned bond : and further, to raise and levy thereout
the said sum of 550l., and to pay same and the interest thereof,
pursuant to the condition of the bond passed for securing same :
and further, to raise and pay the premiums on the said several
policies of insurance ; and to pay the residue of the rents to the
person entitled to the next immediate estate in remainder. And
Viscount Glerawley assigned the several policies of insurance to
the trustees of the term, upon trust to receive the several sums of
money secured by the policies, and apply same towards the payment of such sum of money as should be then due and owing for
principal and interest on foot of the aforesaid several bonds, and
the annuity of 4,000l. to Richard Earl Annesley, his executors,
administrators and assigns ; and to pay the residue thereof to
Viscount Glerawley, his executors, administrators and assigns.

And Viscount Glerawley covenanted to pay the annual premiums CAULFIELD
v.
MAGUIRE. on the several policies of insurance; and to pay the annuity of 4,000l. during the joint lives of himself and Earl Annesley; and also to pay the several annuities and outgoings, and the interest on the several charges and incumbrances mentioned in the schedule to the deed; and indemnify Earl Annesley, *his heirs, executors and [*147] administrators, against all such sums of money as should become due from the 1st of May, 1821, upon foot of the same: and Richard Earl Annesley granted and assigned to Viscount Glerawley, for his own use, all rents and arrears of rent, of the said manor, lands, tenements and hereditaments, which were due and owing thereout to him, on the 25th day of March, 1821; and also the household furniture, stock, &c., in the house or demesne of Castlewellan. By this deed Earl Annesley and Viscount Glerawley appointed certain persons to be receivers of the rents of the estates; and they were authorized and directed to apply the rents according to the trusts of the deed: and it was provided, that the provision thereby made for Viscount Glerawley should be in lieu and satisfaction of an annuity of 2,000l. provided for him by the settlement of 1808, and of certain other annuities therein mentioned: and further, that nothing in the deed contained should prejudice or affect the right of Richard Earl Annesley, as to any debt, charge or incumbrance, affecting the premises, then or theretofore vested in Richard Earl Annesley, his trustees, or assigns.

After the decree had been pronounced in *Salkeld's* suit, Richard Earl Annesley entered into an arrangement with Joseph Salkeld for the purchase of his rights under that decree; and by two indentures of assignment, of the 3rd of March, 1824, Joseph Salkeld, in consideration of 4,200l. paid to him by Richard Earl Annesley, assigned to a trustee for him the said two judgments; and by another indenture of equal date, Joseph Salkeld, in consideration of the sum of 1,500l., paid to him by Earl Annesley, assigned the benefit of the decree of May, 1823, to the same trustee, in trust for Earl Annesley.

Richard Earl Annesley died on the 9th of November, 1824. By [148] his will, dated the 24th of December, 1822, after reciting that he was entitled to a certain charge of 4,200l., affecting the settled estates, and to certain bond and judgment debts, due to him by his son-in-law, George Henry M'Dowell Johnston, he bequeathed the same to trustees, upon trust to raise and levy the amount thereof, in such manner, and at such times as his daughter, Lady

CAULFIELD
v.
MAGUIRE.

Anna Maria Johnston should direct ; and to pay and apply the same, and the interest thereof to and for her sole and separate use, free from the control of her husband : and he empowered his daughter, notwithstanding her coverture, to dispose of said sums of money, by deed or will (to be executed as therein mentioned), in such manner, and at such times, and to such persons as she should think fit ; and in default of appointment, in trust for his said daughter, her executors, &c. And after further reciting that his son, William Richard Viscount Glerawley had executed to him his bonds, conditioned for the payment of the sum of 25,040l. ; and that he himself had effected a policy of assurance upon his own life, for the sum of 5,000l., he directed that said two sums should constitute and be deemed part of the residue of his personal estate and effects ; and he gave and bequeathed the same respectively, and all interest due and to grow due thereon, and all the rest, residue and remainder of his personal estate and effects, which, at the time of his decease, he should be possessed of or entitled to, and not thereby specifically disposed of, to his executors after named, upon trust, to raise and collect the same, and from time to time to invest the same in the purchase of Government securities ; and to pay thereout his debts and legacies ; and, subject thereto, upon trust to pay and apply the

[*149]

interest or annual proceeds of one-third of such residue *to the use of his son, Charles Francis Annesley, for his life ; and from and after his decease, to pay and apply one-third part of the principal of said residue to the use of his children, as therein directed : and as to one other third part of such residue, upon trust to pay and apply the interest, or annual proceeds thereof, to and for the sole and separate use of his daughter, Lady Catherine O'Donel, free from the debts and engagements of her husband, and upon her receipt, during her life ; and from and after her decease, upon trust to pay and apply one-third part of the principal of said residue, to and for the use of all and every, or any child or children of Lady Catherine O'Donel, other than an eldest son, and to the exclusion of any one or more of them, in such shares, and at such times, as his said daughter, notwithstanding her coverture, should, by deed or will (to be executed in the manner therein mentioned) direct and appoint ; and in default of such appointment, or as to so much thereof as should be unappointed, to be equally divided between them, share and share alike, other than an eldest son : and as to the remaining third part of the said residue, upon trust to pay and apply the interest or annual proceeds thereof, to and for the

sole and separate use of his daughter, Lady Anna Maria Johnston,
for her life, free from the debts and engagements of her husband,
and upon her receipt; and from and after her decease, upon trust
to apply the remaining third part of the principal of such residue,
to and amongst her children, in such shares, and at such times, as
she should, by deed or will, appoint; and for want of such appointment, or as to so much thereof as should be unappointed, to be
equally divided between them: and in case his said daughter, Lady
Anna Maria, should die without leaving any child or children, then
upon trust to pay and apply the said remaining third part of such
*residue to and amongst all and every, or any one or more child or   [*150]
children, to the exclusion of any other or others of them, of Lady
Catherine O'Donel, in such shares, and at such times, as Lady
Anna Maria should, by deed or will (to be executed as therein
mentioned, and which, notwithstanding her coverture, she was
thereby empowered to execute), direct or appoint; and in default
of such appointment, or as to so much thereof as should be
unappointed, to be equally divided between such child or children,
other than an eldest son, share and share alike: and the testator
appointed Lady Anna Maria Johnston and the Rev. Arthur
Maguire, his executors; who, after his decease, proved his will.

By an indenture of the 13th of May, 1823, it was declared and
agreed upon by and between Earl Annesley, Viscount Glerawley,
and the trustees of the term of 200 years, created by the indenture
of 1821, that the securities given by Viscount Glerawley to the
Earl, for the sum of 25,040*l*. should not be payable with, or bear
any interest during the life of Richard Earl Annesley: and Earl
Annesley released and relinquished to Viscount Glerawley all
interest due, or which should become due on foot of the securities
for the 25,040*l*. during his life; such interest not to be raised or
paid for the benefit of any person, but to merge in the premises:
and Richard Earl Annesley, in consideration of Viscount Glerawley
paying a certain debt of 6,000*l*. and interest, by instalments of
2,000*l*. per annum, the same being the proper debt of Earl Annesley,
agreed to postpone the time of payment of the aforesaid sum of
25,040*l*., and the interest to accrue due thereon, until the end of
three years next after his decease: and it was further agreed, that
the Earl, *his executors, &c., should then accept payment of the   [*151]
said sum, and the interest which should have accrued thereon,
during the aforesaid period of three years, by half-yearly instalments of 1,000*l*., until the entire 25,040*l*. and interest should be

CAULFIELD
  v.
MAGUIRE.

paid off and discharged: and Viscount Glerawley covenanted that he would, from and after the expiration of three years next ensuing the decease of the Earl, pay to the executors, &c., of the Earl, the yearly sum of 2,000*l*., by half-yearly payments, until, by the application thereof, the principal sum of 25,040*l*., and the interest thereof, which should have accrued during the said period of three years, should be paid and discharged: and it was further agreed, that the 25,040*l*. should not be payable with, or bear interest after the expiration of the three years, provided and so long as the instalments of 1,000*l*. should be regularly paid; but if delay or default should be made in payment of the instalments, then, so often as same should happen, the 25,040*l*., or any balance due thereon, should be payable with interest, from the expiration of two months from the time when such instalment should become due, until the same, with such interest, should be paid.

Richard Earl Annesley executed three codicils to his will; by the second of which, dated the 1st of August, 1823, after reciting that, since the execution of his will and first codicil, a certain indenture of the 13th of May, 1823, had been executed by him, he declared that the execution of said deed should not revoke, prejudice or affect his said will or codicil: and by the third codicil to his will, dated the 24th of April, 1824, the testator, after reciting that Joseph Salkeld had then lately obtained a decree for payment of certain

[*152]

judgment debts affecting the Castlewellan *estates, and that he had paid off his demands, and taken an assignment of the judgments and decree, he directed that the money paid by him on foot of said decree and securities should be deemed to be part of the residue of his estate, and be paid and applied as by his will directed. And he directed, that in case his daughter, Lady Anna Maria, should not make any appointment of the 4,200*l*. mentioned in his will, the same should, after her decease, be paid to the children of Lady Catherine O'Donel, who should be then living, equally, share and share alike, except an eldest son.

The bill was filed by one of the children of Lady Catherine O'Donel, who was entitled to a portion of the residuary estate of the testator, against the several persons interested therein: and by a decretal order of the 16th of June, 1836, it was referred to the Master to take an account of the personal estate of Richard Earl Annesley, into whose hands the same came, and how applied and disposed of; and whether any, and what portion thereof remained still outstanding, or had been lost through the neglect or default of the executors of the testator; and to take an account of the debts, legacies, funeral and testamentary expenses of the testator; and further, that he do ascertain and report the clear surplus or residue of the testator's personal estate, and the rights of the plaintiffs and the other residuary legatees of the testator, in respect thereof; and whether the same had been applied or disposed of according to such rights or not.

On the 21st of November, 1844, the Master made his report, and found that, in addition to a sum of 14,494*l.* received by them, the executors of Richard Earl Annesley *were properly chargeable with the sum of 1,452*l.* portion of the sum of 5,700*l.*, charged by the decree of the COURT, made in *Salkeld's* cause, on the estates of which Viscount Glerawley was then seised, and which had been paid off by Richard Earl Annesley : and also with a further sum of 161*l.* 19*s.* 4*d.* for interest on the sum of 4,000*l.*, principal money, portion of the said sum of 5,700*l.*, which accrued from the 3rd of March, 1824, when the demand was so paid by Richard Earl Annesley, to the day of his death. He also reported, that the executors had misapplied the sum of 688*l.*, principal money, part of the sum of 14,494*l.*, by payment thereof to Lady Catherine O'Donel, the Hon. Francis Charles Annesley, and Lady Anna Maria Johnston, in equal shares; because that, according to the true construction of the will, the executors should have invested that sum in the purchase of Government securities, and paid the interest thereof, only, to the said residuary legatees.

The Master further reported, that the residuary personal estate of Richard Earl Annesley consisted, in part, of the sum of 5,700*l.* due on foot of Salkeld's securities, and of the sum of 25,040*l.* due by William Richard Viscount Glerawley, afterwards Earl Annesley, with interest thereon, at the rate of five per cent., for three years next after the decease of the testator ; said principal and interest amounting together to the sum of 28,796*l.*; and that, according to the true construction of the will, the executors ought to have invested, from time to time, the half-yearly instalments of 1,000*l.*, which were paid to them by William Richard Earl Annesley, in discharge of said sum of 28,796*l.* But that, instead of so doing, and although the executors had received 4,000*l.*, late currency, for instalments, up to *the 1st of November, 1829, paid to them by William Richard Earl Annesley, they paid 3,467*l.* 1*s.* 5*d.*, present currency, part thereof, to the Hon. Francis Charles Annesley, Lady Catherine O'Donel, and Lady Anna Maria Johnston, equally,

[*153]

[*154]

CAULFIELD
v.
MAGUIRE.

although they were only entitled to receive the interest of said sum ; and he therefore reported, that said sum of 3,467*l.* 1*s.* 5*d.*, was not paid by the executors according to the rights of the parties.

From the report and schedules, it appeared that the Master reported that the 5,700*l.* paid by Richard Earl Annesley, for the assignment of Salkeld's judgments and decree, and which was a charge upon the settled estates, together with the sum of 161*l.* 9*s.* 4*d.*, interest on the sum of 4,000*l.*, part of the said sum of 5,700*l.*, from the 3rd of March, 1824, to the death of the testator, and also the sum of 2,150*l.*, being the arrears of the fee-farm rent of 100*l.* per annum, due the testator out of the lands of Gibbstown, Troystown and Donaghpatrick, and which was received by his executors from John Gerrard, on the 9th of July, 1825, formed part of his residuary personal estate. And he charged the executors with the said sum of 2,150*l.*, received by them ; and with the sum of 1,452*l.*, being the balance of the sum of 1,700*l.* taxed costs and interest, charged on the family estates by the decree in *Salkeld's* cause, after giving credit for 248*l.*, paid on account of said costs and interest, by William Richard Earl Annesley, and which 1,452*l.* was lost by the default of the executors ; and also with the aforesaid sum of 161*l.* 19*s.* 4*d.*, lost by their default.

[*155]

The cause having come on to be heard upon report, exceptions and merits, the first question arose upon exceptions *taken by the personal representatives of the executors of Richard Earl Annesley, to that part of the report and schedules which charged the executors with the sums of 5,700*l.* and 161*l.* 19*s.* 4*d.* on foot of Salkeld's judgments, and 2,150*l.* for arrears of the fee-farm rent of Gibbstown, Troystown, and Donaghpatrick ; and they thereby insisted, (1), that the arrears of the fee-farm rent ought to have been applied by the Master in payment of the interest which accrued due on Salkeld's securities during the life of Richard Earl Annesley, and which interest formed part of the sum of 5,700*l.* and 161*l.* 19*s.* 4*d.* ; (2), that the executors ought not to be charged with any interest on the principal sum of 2,000*l.*, secured by Salkeld's judgments, as Richard Earl Annesley, being tenant for life of the lands, was bound to keep down the interest on the charges affecting the estates ; and that the executors ought only to be charged with the principal sums of 2,000*l.* and 1,500*l.* for costs ; (3), that the Master ought not to have charged the executors with the said sum of 2,150*l.*, but should have found upon the evidence, that same was properly applied in discharge of interest which accrued due on Salkeld's securities during the life of Richard Earl Annesley.

CAULFIELD
v.
MAGUIRE.

It was stated, that in 1826, the executors settled an account with William Richard Earl Annesley; and, having charged him with the sum due on foot of the money paid for the assignment of Salkeld's securities, they gave him credit for the 2,150*l.* received by them from Mr. Gerrard.

Mr. Moore, Mr. Brooke, Mr. J. S. Furlong, and *Mr. Maguire,* for the exceptants:

The executors ought not to have been charged both with the interest on the principal sum of 2,000*l.*, and with the *arrears of [*156] Gerrard's rent, which was the fund to pay it; for, having received the fund which was appropriated to the payment of the interest, they were not entitled to charge the estate a second time with the amount of that interest. Also, Richard Earl Annesley, being tenant for life of the estates, was bound to keep down the interest on the charges affecting the inheritance. * * The dealings between the parties in 1803 and 1821 render it impossible for Richard Earl Annesley, or his executors, ever to raise this interest out of the inheritance; for, in 1803, the father and son resettled the estates upon the assumption that the sum due on Salkeld's judgments was 2,000*l.* only; and in the arrangement of 1821 both the judgments and the lands held by Mr. Gerrard were omitted. These circum- stances show, that all parties agreed that, as between *themselves, [*157] the fee-farm rent should be the fund for payment of the interest.

The Solicitor-General (Mr. Greene), and *Mr. Monahan,* in support of the report:

The executors are properly charged with the arrears of rent, 2,150*l.*; it clearly formed part of the assets of the testator; it was an arrear which wholly became due in his lifetime. They are also properly charged with that portion of the 5,700*l.*, which consisted of interest on the 2,000*l.*, secured by Salkeld's judgments. That sum bore interest at six per cent.: and the entire amount of interest paid off by Earl Richard accrued due between 1786 and the death of Francis Charles Earl Annesley, in 1802. It was an arrear which became due during the tenancy of the prior tenant for life; and which the persons entitled to the inheritance had no right or equity to cast upon the succeeding tenant for life. * * The interest which becomes due during the time of each successive tenant for

CAULFIELD
v.
MAGUIRE.
[*158]

life is *properly payable by him; and the remainderman must look to his assets, and not to the assets of a subsequent tenant for life, for relief.

Mr. Brooke, in reply:

Lord Penrhyn v. *Hughes* (1) is an authority in point; for, in that case there were prior estates for life, during the existence of which part of the arrear probably accrued. And it is just and equitable that, as between a tenant for life and the remainderman, the tenant for life should be bound to pay off an arrear of interest which accrued due during the time of a prior tenant for life; for it is the duty of each succeeding tenant for life to see that the next preceding tenant for life does not permit an arrear of interest to accrue.

Upon this point the LORD CHANCELLOR reserved his judgment.

THE LORD CHANCELLOR:

This case was said to depend upon the mere question of law, viz., whether a second tenant for life of an estate charged with an incumbrance carrying interest, is not bound to discharge not only the interest which accrues in his own time, but also any arrears left unpaid by the previous tenant for life. For the affirmative of this position, the case of *Tracy* v. *Lady Hereford* (2) was relied on.

[*159]

In *Revel* v. *Watkinson* (3), the estate was devised to one for life, with remainders over, subject to a trust to raise his debts, in effect, by mortgage or sale. The estate was not *sold or mortgaged; and, during the continuance of a jointure under a prior settlement, the rents were insufficient to keep down the accruing payments and the interest of the debts. Lord HARDWICKE held that the whole life interest was liable to keep down the interest, (although, in effect, during the jointure, part of it was in reversion), so that when the jointure fell in, the tenant for life was bound to apply all the rents to the liquidation of the arrears of interest. But this only affected the time of the tenant for life. But Lord HARDWICKE said, that if there is a tenant for life, the remainder for life, and during the first estate for life, the whole profits are not sufficient to answer the interest of the debts, so that there is an arrear, he agreed that it should be a charge on the inheritance, when it is by the same settlement; a tenant for life being then only obliged to keep down the interest incurred during his own life.

(1) 5 Ves. 99.   (3) 1 Ves. Sen. 93.
(2) 2 Br. C. C. 128.

Tracy v. *Lady Hereford* was not, as it was insisted before me, the case of two successive tenants for life, in which the second was compelled to pay interest left unpaid by the prior tenant for life; but it was the case of a tenant for life of an interest under a will, subject to mortgages and charges, where part of the estate was in possession and part remained in the possession of a jointress for twelve years after the testator's death, under the limitations in a prior settlement. There was no attempt to charge the tenant for life beyond her own time: but during the life of the jointress, who was not bound to pay any part of the interest on the charges, the rents of the estate in possession were insufficient to pay the interest; and the tenant for life insisted that she was not liable to make good the arrear during her own time out of the additional rents when the jointress died: and it was decided that she was liable. *But this does not seem to me to touch the question between successive tenants for life and the remainderman.

[*160]

Lord Penrhyn v. *Hughes* (1) only decided that a mortgagee, buying the life estate, cannot charge any interest against the inheritance, which his vendor was bound to pay out of the rents, but which the mortgagee had permitted to remain unpaid before his purchase. I think this decision was quite right. But Lord ALVANLEY seems to have considered it as established by *Tracy* v. *Lady Hereford*, that the rents, during the estate for life, must be applied to the reduction of any interest accrued prior, as well as subsequent, to the commencement of that estate. It does not appear to me that the case established so wide a rule; nor was it necessary to lay down such a rule in order to decide the case of *Lord Penrhyn* v. *Hughes*. I am not prepared to fix the defaults of every previous tenant for life on the last taker for life. It is as incumbent on the reversioner in fee to look after the tenant for life in possession, as it is on a tenant for life in remainder. This may lead to some inconvenience, as to the manner in which an arrear shall be thrown upon the inheritance; but it is a duty from the labour of which a court of equity ought not to shrink. Upon the authorities now before me, I should be inclined to come to the conclusion, that every tenant for life is liable only for his own time; but that, to liquidate the arrears during his own time, he must furnish all the rents, if necessary, during the whole of his life. *Bulwer* v. *Astley* (2), is a remarkable instance of the anxiety of a court of equity to cast a burden rateably on the tenant for life and the reversioner.

(1) 5 Ves. 99. (2) 65 R. R. 416 (1 Ph. 122).

The case, however, before me is a peculiar one. The lands of
Gibbstown, producing 100l. a year, were, in the view of this Court,
made the particular fund for payment of the interest ; and were so
applied until 1786. It does not appear that the first tenant for life
ever received any part of the rents ; but in 1825 twenty-one and a
half years' arrears were paid to Richard Lord Annesley, the second
tenant for life. Now the interest had reached the amount of the
judgments in 1808, and Richard had only become tenant for life in
possession in 1802, and from that period he was, of course, liable
to the interest while it ran on. But it does not appear to me that
he was at liberty to retain the arrears, although accruing wholly
in his own time; for they were applicable specifically to the interest :
and even if, in an ordinary case, he could have retained them for
his own use, yet, after making the settlement of 1808, in which the
judgments are put down in the schedule at 2,000l., and the settlement of 1821, he was not, I think, entitled to claim the arrears of
the rent of 100l. for his own use, leaving the arrears of interest a
charge on the estate. That would be contrary to the true meaning
of the settlement, by which all the benefits of the estate were to go
to the eldest son, subject to the specific provisions for Earl Richard ;
and the arrears of rent, to which he was to be entitled, were regularly
secured to him by the settlement.

The exceptions were overruled ; but it was declared, on further
directions, that the exceptants were entitled to credit for the sum
of 2,150l. late currency.

The next objection, which also arose upon an exception taken by
the personal representatives of the surviving executor of Richard
Earl Annesley, had relation to the sum of *3,467l. 1s. 5d., which
the Master, by his report, found was not paid or applied by the
executors according to the rights of the residuary legatees ; the
executors insisting that the Master should have found that said
sum was duly paid pursuant to the trusts of the testator's will, it
being the amount of the interest which had accrued due on the
principal sum of 25,040l. after the testator's death.

Mr. Moore, Mr. Brooke, Mr. J. S. Furlong, and *Mr. Maguire,*
for the exceptants.

The *Solicitor-General* and *Mr. Monahan, contrà :*

According to the true construction of the will, the intention of
the testator was, that the three years' interest on the 25,040l.

should constitute part of the principal of the residue; and the CAULFIELD
interest only on it was properly payable to the tenants for life MAGUIRE.
of the residue.

Mr. Brooke, in reply.

THE LORD CHANCELLOR:

At the time when the will was made, the 25,040*l.* carried interest;
and it was distinctly given as part of the residue, in equal shares,
to three persons for their lives, and then to their children as they
should appoint. If the matter had rested there, no question could
have arisen: but the testator subsequently made a new arrangement with his son, whereby he released him from the payment
of interest upon the principal sum during his, the testator's, life,
and postponed the payment of the principal sum and interest for
three years after his death, at which period the interest was to
cease; and the three years' interest being added to *the principal   [*163]
sum, the whole was to be paid by half-yearly instalments of 1,000*l.*
each. The testator then added a codicil to his will; and thereby
reciting the deed by which the foregoing arrangement had been
made, he declared it to be his will, that the execution of that deed
should not revoke, prejudice, or affect his will in any respect.
Now, if that deed is not to revoke, prejudice, or affect the will, the
interests of the tenants for life of the residue must remain as they
were under the will, except so far as they are affected by the payment of the interest being postponed for three years. But that
interest was not relinquished, though the payment of it was postponed. How, then, can I execute the intention, if I do that which
the Master has done, viz., take from the tenants for life that which
was bequeathed as interest, and make it principal money? As
the three years' arrears of interest were to be paid off, together
with the principal money, by instalments, it was natural to form
them into one aggregate sum: but if the principal sum had borne
interest (as it was originally intended it should), the tenants for
life would have been entitled to this money; and the codicil declares
that the deed was not to revoke, prejudice, or affect their rights. The
interest is to remain in arrear for a certain period; but that is not
a reason why the residuary legatees should be deprived of it. It is
still interest. If the instalments are not paid regularly, then the
principal sum is to bear interest. To whom would that interest
belong? It would not form part of the capital, but belong to the

tenants for life. I cannot form a reasonable doubt upon this case.
I am not at liberty to read this will so as to make it applicable to
the subsequent change of circumstances ; but I am at liberty to
read it and the deed as connected together by the codicil ; and
to say that, so far as interest is payable, it *is to go to the tenant
for life. It would be a mere trap to catch executors, dealing
fairly in the execution of their trust, if I were to hold otherwise.
The persons entitled to the residuary estate are most unjustly
endeavouring to fix the executors with the payment of this sum.

Allow the exception ; and declare that the tenants for life are
entitled, according to the true construction of the will, to the three
years' interest, and that the sum mentioned in the exception was
properly paid to them by the executors, and ought to be allowed to
the executors in their account.

The next question arose under these circumstances, which were
stated in the report :

Sophia, formerly styled Countess Annesley, claimed to derive
certain charges on the real and personal estate of Francis Charles
Earl Annesley, under a deed of the 2nd July, 1798. To enforce
those claims she, in 1817, filed her bill against Richard Earl
Annesley and others ; and having obtained a decree to account
therein, Richard Earl Annesley entered into a consent with her,
in that cause, dated the 24th of January, 1820, whereby the Earl
agreed to secure her an annuity of 455*l.* for her life ; and she
agreed to give up to the Earl all money due to her on foot of the
deed of the 2nd of July, 1798. And, the better to carry that consent into effect, Richard Earl Annesley applied to his son William
Richard Viscount Glerawley, to join him in securing the said
annuity ; which he agreed to do : and, accordingly, by indenture
of the 27th of April, 1820, Richard Earl Annesley, and William
Richard Viscount Glerawley, granted to trustees, their executors, &c.,

an annuity of 455*l.*, late currency, equivalent to the sum of *420*l.*
present currency, for the natural life of Sophia Countess Annesley,
payable quarterly ; and also granted to the same trustees, their
executors, &c., the townland of Castlewellan, and other lands, for
the term of ninety-nine years, provided the Earl and Viscount, or
either of them, should so long live ; and Richard Earl Annesley
also assigned to the same trustees a policy of assurance, upon his
own life, for 5,000*l.*, and several charges affecting the Castlewellan
estates, therein mentioned : and it was declared that the lands and

securities were assigned to the trustees upon trust to permit Sophia
Countess Annesley, during her life, out of the rents of the lands,
and after the decease of Earl Richard, out of the said charges and
the said sum of 5,000*l.*, insured on the life of Earl Richard, or the
interest or proceeds thereof, to receive and take the said annuity.
And, by bond of equal date therewith, Richard Earl Annesley and
Viscount Glerawley jointly and severally became bound to the same
trustees in the sum of 3,000*l.* ; the condition of which was, that
if default should be made in payment of the annuity, for twenty-
one days after the same should become payable, then and so often
as the same should happen during the joint lives of the Earl and
Sophia Countess Annesley, it should be lawful for the trustees to
issue execution on any judgment to be obtained on the bond, against
the Earl, his executors or administrators; and to levy off his goods
and chattels, for the use of said Sophia, all arrears of said annuity :
and that if Sophia should survive the Earl, that it should be lawful
for her (1) to issue execution upon any judgment which should be
obtained against the Viscount Glerawley, his executors or administrators ; and, by virtue thereof, to levy off his goods and chattels
the said annuity, and all arrears thereof.

At the time when these securities were executed, Richard Earl   [166]
Annesley was tenant for life of the settled estates, with remainder
to William Richard Viscount Glerawley for his life, with remainder
to his first and other sons in tail ; and Viscount Glerawley joined
his father in executing them, merely as a surety, and without having
received any consideration for the same.

This annuity of 455*l.* was one of the annuities mentioned in the
schedule to the deed of the 1st of November, 1821, before mentioned,
and which, during the joint lives of Earl Annesley and Viscount
Glerawley, and the survivor of them, was to be paid and kept down
out of the rents of the estates.

William Richard Earl Annesley died in August, 1838, having
appointed J. R. Moore his executor ; and after his decease Sophia
Countess Annesley compelled J. R. Moore to pay her twenty-three
quarterly gales of the annuity, amounting to the sum of 2,415*l.*
present currency, the whole of which had accrued due after the
decease of William Richard Earl Annesley. And the Master
reported that J. R. Moore was entitled to claim and receive that
sum from the assets of Richard Earl Annesley; and that the
personal estate of the testator was also liable to such further sums

_____

(1) *Sic* in brief.

CAULFIELD
v.
MAGUIRE.

as J. R. Moore, as such executor, should be compelled to pay in keeping down and discharging said annuity.

To this report J. R. Moore excepted, because the Master had not allowed him interest on the sum of 2,415*l.* from the time he paid same.

Mr. W. Brooke and *Mr. Shaw* for the exception.

[167]   * * The executor of William Richard Earl Annesley is entitled to stand as an annuity creditor of Richard Earl Annesley, and to be paid the arrears of the annuity, with interest; for his executors, though in possession of funds to discharge the demand, have wilfully declined to do so.   Upon another ground also, the executor of William Richard is entitled to interest, viz., that one of the securities given for the. payment of the annuity was a policy of insurance on the life of Earl Richard for 5,000*l.*   That sum has been received by his executors, and has been invested in Government stock, where it has been fructifying.   The dividends ought to be applied in payment of the interest on the 2,415*l.*

The *Solicitor-General* and *Mr. Monahan* for the residuary legatees:

This case is not distinguishable from *Copis* v. *Middleton* (1).   * * *

[168]   THE LORD CHANCELLOR:

This appears to be an attempt to get rid of *Copis* v. *Middleton.* That case established that a surety in a bond, paying off the demand, does not become a specialty creditor of the principal, but only a creditor by simple contract.   But it was said that that simple contract debt carried interest.   I know of no authority for that. In an action for money paid, interest cannot be recovered unless there be some dealing between the parties to warrant it; something to show that it was part of the contract.   This is a mere simple contract demand, not carrying interest; and upon this point there can be no doubt.

The other point is of a different nature.   By the deed securing the annuity, for which the bond of the principal and surety was given, a policy of insurance, payable upon the death of Earl Richard, was assigned to trustees, as a collateral security, upon trust, after the decease of the Earl, to raise the annuity out of the monies secured thereby.   That fund became part of the assets of

(1) T. & R. 224. See note, 29 R. R. 73.—O. A. S.

Earl Richard, and was accordingly administered in this suit as a part of his estate; and the persons who now resist the demand of the surety, have received out of Court, as part of the residuary estate of the *testator, that very sum of 5,000l. which was pledged for the payment of the annuity, and also the interest which has accrued due on it since it was received by the executors. They, who now seek to throw this demand upon the surety, represent the principal debtor, and have got a portion of the very fund which, by the deed of 1820, was provided for the payment of the annuity itself. In this Court you cannot go against the surety whilst the fund primarily applicable remains; for he has a right to have that fund applied for his benefit : there is no doubt, therefore, that the surety would have a right to go against those parties for the whole amount of the 5,000l., and the interest on it, to be repaid thereout what he has lost. If that sum had been properly applied, he would not have lost anything; he never would have been called on to pay. Now, that 5,000l. has produced interest ; and I have no doubt that the surety is entitled to the benefit of that which it has produced. He is entitled to go against the interest, as far as it extends, to pay him what he has lost, and to go against the *corpus* of the fund for payment of the principal money. There is no doubt that the 5,000l. ought first to have been applied in payment of the annuity ; and, if necessary, the principal of the fund ought to have been sold for payment of the annuity. If that had been done, there would not have been a loss as to interest. This question ought, however, to come on upon further directions and merits; and then the relief would be to declare that the 5,000l. was the first fund for payment of the annuity ; and that the surety ought to be placed in the same situation as if that fund had been so applied. That can only be done by giving him interest, for the fund has been producing interest.

I think that the equity of the surety is, that he ought, *out of the interest which that sum would have produced, to be allowed interest on his several advances, from the times they were made to the present period ; and that then, out of the principal and interest, he is to be paid the principal sums he has advanced; and the remainder of that fund will still be liable to keep down the accruing gales of the annuity. I consider the 5,000l. as still bearing interest, though it has been paid over to the parties. I overrule the exception, and make this declaration upon further directions ; and refer it to the Master to ascertain what sum ought to be impounded to meet the demand of the surety on the estate.

CAULFIELD
v.
MAGUIRE.

[*169]

[*170]

Another question arose upon the execution of the power of
appointment given by the testator to Lady Catherine O'Donel, over
her one-third of the residuary personal estate.

By her will, dated the 26th of October, 1829, duly executed and
attested as required by the power, Lady Catherine O'Donel disposed
of her one-third of the sums of 25,040*l.* and 5,111*l.* 19*s.*, Government stock, therein particularly mentioned, being part of the
residuary personal estate of the testator, by giving certain sums
thereout to her daughters. The disposition in favour of her
daughter, Mary O'Donel, was in these terms: " And whereas my
daughter, Mary O'Donel, having declared her intention of becoming
a recluse or nun, and having already retired into a convent,
preparatory thereto, I deem her patrimony in that case sufficient
for her maintenance ; but should she change her mind, and return to
her family and friends, I leave and bequeath to my executors the
sum of 1,000*l.*, in trust for my said daughter Mary, to receive the
interest and produce of the same during her life, and, at her decease,
[*171] to be divided *to and amongst her children, if any ; or in either
case of her not leaving the convent, or not leaving any issue, the
said sum of 1,000*l.*, to be divided among my daughters aforesaid,
Margaret, Catherine, and Isabella," share and share alike ; and
she bequeathed to her daughters, Margaret, Catherine, and Isabella,
any residue or remainder of her one-third of the said sums of
25,040*l.* and 5,111*l.* 19*s.*, that might be after paying the several
legacies in her will mentioned, share and share alike. The testatrix
did not make any disposition of the remainder of her one-third of
the residuary personal estate of Richard Earl Annesley ; and died
in 1830, leaving Mary O'Donel and five other younger children
her surviving. The Master reported that Mary O'Donel ever since
continued, and still was, an occupant of the convent into which she
had retired, as in the will of the testatrix mentioned ; and that she
had declared her intention not to return to her family and friends ;
and that, following up her intention, she had become a professed
nun, or member of the religious community into which she had
retired in the life-time of Lady Catherine O'Donel : and he reported
that Mary O'Donel was entitled, for her life, to the interest or
dividends to arise on the sum of 1,000*l.*, so bequeathed by Lady
Catherine O'Donel, in trust for Mary O'Donel, in case she should
change her mind and return to her family and friends, and abandon
her intention of becoming a nun, and that she should leave the
convent into which she had retired preparatory thereto, as in the

will of Lady Catherine O'Donel in that behalf mentioned; and that, after the decease of Mary O'Donel, in the events aforesaid, the said sum of 1,000l. should go to be divided amongst her children, if any.

[*172]

The Master further reported that the principal sum of *1,000l., and the dividends and interest thereon, should be carried to the separate credit of Mary O'Donel, and should be impounded during her life-time; and that, after her decease, in the event of her not leaving the convent, certain persons mentioned in his report would be entitled to the principal sum of 1,000l. and the said interest and dividends thereon.

To this report Mary O'Donel excepted, on the ground that the Master ought to have reported that she was entitled to be paid the dividends and interest on the 1,000l. which should accrue during her life.

Mr. Deasy and *Mr. Graydon*, for the exception:

The appointment to Mary O'Donel is good, but the condition annexed to it is void, and separable from the gift; and, therefore, she takes a life interest in the 1,000l., discharged of the condition. In *Hay v. Watkins* (1), your Lordship observes: "The cases go to this extent: that where the intention to benefit the object of the power is clear, and that something is superadded, a condition not warranted by the power, there the gift is good; the Court will strike out what is excessive, and the appointee will take the fund absolutely." Here the fund was authorized to be paid "in such shares, and at such times" as the donor of the power should appoint; but these words do not authorize a conditional appointment. But if the condition be inseparable from the gift, then the whole gift is void: and the 1,000l. does not pass under the gift of the residue, for where there is a gift of portion of an ascertained fund to one person, and of the residue of it, after payment of the first gift, to another, and the first gift fails, the object of *the second gift does not take it, but it is undisposed of: *Easum* v. *Appleford* (2). In that view of the case, Mary O'Donel is entitled to a portion of the principal fund and interest, as being unappointed, and the report is incorrect. But if the condition be held to be operative, still Mary O'Donel is entitled to a portion of the interest which shall accrue during her life. For the gift over is, in the event of Mary O'Donel not leaving the convent, or leaving it and

[*173]

(1) 61 R. R. 62 (3 Dr. & War. 339).   (2) 51 R. R. 238 (10 Sim. 254; 5 My. & Cr. 56).

CAULFIELD
v.
MAGUIRE.

not leaving any issue; in either of which events, the principal sum of 1,000*l.*, but not the interest which shall accrue thereon during the life of Mary, is given over. That interest, therefore, goes as in default of appointment: *Henderson* v. *Constable* (1).

The *Solicitor-General* and *Mr. Monahan, contrà :*

In this case the donee had an exclusive power of appointment; she might give or not as she pleased; and consequently might annex a condition to her gift, excluding one of the objects of the power, unless certain terms were complied with. The gift, both of the interest and principal, is contingent upon Mary O'Donel leaving the convent. But if the appointment be invalid, the 1,000*l.* passes under the residuary gift in the will.

Mr. Graydon, in reply.

THE LORD CHANCELLOR :

I do not see where the difficulty is. Lady Catherine O'Donel had an exclusive power to appoint this fund among her younger children, in such shares and payable at such times, as she thought

[*174]

fit; therefore she might exclude any of *them, or provide for any of them as she pleased, within the limits allowed by law. She recites that her daughter, Mary, had declared her intention of becoming a nun, and had already retired into a convent preparatory thereto, and that her patrimony in that case would be sufficient for her maintenance; and then adds, that in case her daughter should change her mind, and return to her family, she gave to her executors 1,000*l.* in trust for her daughter to receive the interest and produce of the same during her life; and, at her decease, to be divided amongst her children (which was an excess in the execution of the power, and could not take effect); and in either case of her not leaving the convent, or not leaving any issue, the 1,000*l.* was to be divided among three of her daughters, whom she names, equally; and she then gives to the same three daughters any residue or remainder that may be after paying the several legacies before mentioned.

The question arises upon the validity of these gifts. The Master has found that the principal sum of 1,000*l.*, and the interest or accumulations thereon, are to remain impounded until the death of Mary O'Donel, who is still living. On the other hand it is insisted (1), that this is an absolute gift to Mary O'Donel for her life; that

(1) 59 R. R. 505 (5 Beav. 297).

the condition is void and separable; and, therefore, that the legatee CAULFIELD
v.
MAGUIRE. is entitled to the legacy, discharged of the condition : (2), or if not separable, that the entire appointment fails, and that the 1,000*l.* goes as in default of appointment, and does not pass under the gift of the residue : and (3), that, at all events, the interest of this sum, during her life, must go as in default of appointment. None of these points can, in my opinion, be maintained. This is not a gift with a condition annexed to it; but it is a gift which is to take effect *upon the happening of a contingency; and is clearly good [*175] as such, and warranted by the power. It is a gift, in case she shall leave the convent and come among her friends, to her for her life, and afterwards to her children. The gift to the children is void; and if the gift over had been made to depend upon the gift to the children, that gift also would have been void. But here the gift over depends upon the contingency of Mary O'Donel not leaving the convent, or dying without issue; and, according to the authorities, such a gift to the objects of the power is good. Then, as to the interest upon the 1,000*l.*, which shall accrue before the contingency happens,—there is no specific gift of that interest at all; the principal only of the fund is disposed of; and that upon a contingency which may never arise; but the Court will impound so much of the assets as is necessary to answer the contingency, if and when it arises. But the residuary gift is general; it is of whatever will remain after payment of the legacies before given out of the fund. It is said that this residuary gift would not carry the 1,000*l.*, if the 1,000*l.* had been badly appointed; but it is not necessary to discuss that question, for here there is no gift of this interest; and, therefore, the gift of the residue is a gift of the interest, which, from time to time shall accrue. It is nothing more than this : the testatrix gives to her three daughters the interest upon the 1,000*l.*, until her daughter, Mary, leaves the convent, and comes again into the world; and if she should leave the convent, then she gives the interest to her for her life, and the principal afterwards to her children (which is void) : and if she should not leave the convent, then she gives the principal to her three other daughters. The exception is wrong in point of form; but, upon further directions, I shall declare this to be a valid gift, to take effect in case Mary *O'Donel shall leave the convent and come again among [*176] her friends; and direct that a sufficient sum be appropriated to answer this 1,000*l.* when that event shall take place, or Mary shall die. And declare that so much of the funds in Court as have

CAULFIELD
v.
MAGUIRE.

arisen from the dividends upon this 1,000l. belong to the three residuary legatees, and that they are now entitled to have the same divided between them; and declare that the residuary legatees are entitled, under the residuary gift, to the interest and dividends which shall accrue whilst Mary O'Donel continues to reside in the convent; and, upon the death of Mary, reserve liberty for all parties to apply. I shall not, however, now declare that the gift to the children of Mary O'Donel is void, though it clearly is, because the event may never arise.

1845.
Jan. 30, 31.
Feb. 2.

SIR EDWARD
SUGDEN,
L.C.
[182]

THE COMMISSIONERS OF CHARITABLE DONATIONS AND BEQUESTS v. WYBRANTS.

(2 Jo. & Lat. 182—198; S. C. 7 Ir. Eq. R. 580.)

A testator devised lands to trustees and their heirs, upon trust to grant and convey the same to the use of J. W. for life, subject nevertheless to, and charged with four annuities, to commence upon the death of X.; three of which were to be paid to three different charitable institutions (two of them being corporate bodies), and the fourth to the poor of a parish: and after the death of J. W., subject to the annuities, to the use of his first and other sons in tail: and he directed said several annuities to be paid (not saying by whom) on the days therein mentioned; and expressly charged his estate with the same.

X. died more than twenty years before the filing of the bill to establish the charitable devises, and no payment or other satisfaction was ever made on foot of the annuities. No conveyance had been executed by the trustees; but J. W. had, since the death of the testator, been in possession of the estates; and he and his eldest son suffered a recovery and resettled them.

Held, that the right to recover the annuities was not barred by the Real Property Limitation Act, 1833 (3 & 4 Will. IV. c. 27); the trust for the charities being an express one, within the meaning of the twenty-fifth section of that Act.

Charities are, equally with other trusts, within the operation of the Real Property Limitation Act, 1833.

Every charge on an estate does not create a trust, although it imposes a burden; but it may create a trust depending on the nature of the charge. If the gift is an express one, and if the person taking the estate is bound to give effect to the gift as a trustee, then it is an express trust(1).

Where a testator gives an estate to one, subject to a charge, the person to pay the charge is the person who is liable to the burden; and this, in the case of a charity, impresses him with the character of trustee for the charity.

JOSEPH WRIGHT, being seised in fee of the lands of Rogerstown and Ballinlagh, in the King's County, and of other lands, made his will, dated the 19th of July, 1798, and thereby gave and bequeathed

---

(1) But see now 37 & 38 Vict. c. 57, s. 10, under which an express trust in aid of a charge is deprived of any operation in preventing the application of the statute; and see also the Trustee Act, 1888, s. 8, by which trustees are protected by the Statutes of Limitation in certain cases.—O. A. S.

all his messuages, houses, lands, tenements and hereditaments in
the kingdom of Ireland, and all his estate, right, title and interest,
in and to the same and every part thereof, whether the same be
lands of inheritance or leases for lives, with or without covenant
of renewal, unto Joshua Paul Meredyth and William Foster, their
heirs and assigns, according to such estate and interest as he had
therein respectively; in trust and to the intent that his said
trustees, and the survivor of them, and his heirs, should, in convenient time after his decease, by good and sufficient conveyances
and assurances in the law, grant, convey, assure and settle the
same, and every part thereof, so far as the law would allow and
the nature of his estates and titles would admit, to and for
such uses, upon such trusts, and to and for such intents and
purposes, *and under and subject to such powers and provisoes
as thereinafter expressed and declared, or as near thereto as the
deaths of parties and alteration of circumstances would admit
of. And after declaring the trusts upon which his Monaghan
estates were to be conveyed, the testator proceeded thus: "And
as to my estates and lands of Rogerstown and Ballinlagh, in
the King's County, in trust that my said trustees, and the survivor of them, and the heirs of such survivor, shall grant and
convey the same to the use and behoof of Joseph Henry Wybrants,
eldest son of John Wybrants, of, &c., by his present wife, Sarah
Wybrants, and his assigns, for and during his natural life; with
remainder to trustees and their heirs, during his life, to preserve
contingent remainders; subject, nevertheless, to, and charged and
chargeable with, one annuity of 20l. yearly to the said Sarah
Wybrants, wife of the above-mentioned John Wybrants, during
her natural life, in lieu of the like annuity of 20l. yearly, settled
upon her at her intermarriage with the said John Wybrants,
by a deed bearing date, &c.: and also subject to, and charged
and chargeable with, one other annuity of 30l. yearly, to be
paid out of the rents of the said lands of Rogerstown and
Ballinlagh to the said Sarah Wybrants during her natural life;
the said two annuities of 20l. and 30l. to be paid" to her
separate use, upon the days therein mentioned: "and from
and immediately after her decease, subject to, and charged and
chargeable with one annuity of 25l. yearly, to be paid to the
trustees or governors of the Lying-in Hospital, in Great Britain
Street, Dublin, for the use of the said charity; and also subject to,
and charged and chargeable with one other annuity of 25l. yearly,

to be paid out of the rents of the said lands of Rogerstown and Ballinlagh, to the governors of the Hibernian Marine Society in Dublin, for the use of *the said charity; and from and immediately after my decease, subject to, and charged and chargeable with one annuity of 20l. yearly, to be paid to John Bowers, my servant, during his natural life; and from and immediately after his decease, subject to, and charged and chargeable with, one annuity of 20l. yearly, to be paid to the governors or treasurer of the King's County Infirmary; and also subject to, and charged and chargeable with one other annuity of 5l. yearly to the poor of the parish in which said lands of Rogerstown and Ballinlagh are situated: and from and after the death of the said Joseph Henry Wybrants, subject to the said several annuities, to the use and behoof of" his first and other sons in tail male: "and for default of such issue, to the use and behoof of John Wybrants, second son of the aforesaid John Wybrants, for his life; with remainder to trustees and their heirs, during his life, to preserve contingent remainders; and from and after the death of John Wybrants, subject to the said several annuities, to the use of" his first and other sons in tail male: "and for default of such issue, subject to the said several annuities, to the use" of the third and other sons of John Wybrants, by his then present wife, Sarah Wybrants, in tail male: "and for default of such issue, to the use and behoof of my own right heirs, subject, nevertheless, and charged and chargeable with the said four annuities of 25l., 25l., 20l., and 5l., last mentioned: and I do hereby order and direct that the said several annuities shall, after my death, be paid half-yearly; the first payment of each to be made on the first day of January or first day of July after my death, that shall first happen: and I charge and encumber my said several estates, lands and premises, thereinbefore mentioned, with the said several annuities, for the purposes hereinbefore expressed concerning the *same." And he empowered his trustees, and the survivor of them, and his heirs, and the person who should be in possession of any of his estates, by virtue of any of the limitations aforesaid, to make leases thereof as therein mentioned.

Joseph Wright, the testator, died in January, 1796; and thereupon Joseph Henry Wybrants, by Joseph Wybrants, his father and guardian, entered into possession of the lands. He attained his age of twenty-one years in 1807, and thereupon personally entered into, and still was in possession of the lands. Sarah

Wybrants died in November, 1815, and John Bowers died in September, 1817.

Shortly after the decease of the testator, his will was proved in the Prerogative Court, Dublin; and in May, 1796, advertisements were inserted in the *Dublin Gazette*, stating the full particulars of the charitable bequests thereby made.

No payment was ever made on account of any of the before mentioned charitable bequests; nor was any application made for payment until shortly before the filing of the present bill. No conveyance of the legal estate had been executed by the trustees under the will.

The bill was filed on the 28th of October, 1843, against Joseph Henry Wybrants, Thomas Wybrants, his son, who was entitled, under family settlements and a recovery duly suffered, to the remainder in fee, expectant upon the life estate of his father, and against Joshua Colles Meredyth, the heir-at-law of the surviving trustee: and the plaintiffs thereby prayed that the said charitable devises and bequests *might be established, and the said respective [*186] annuities or rent-charges declared to be well charged on the said lands and premises: and that the trusts of the said will might be carried into execution, and all proper and necessary deeds and conveyances executed for the purposes aforesaid: and for an account of the sums due on foot of the several annuities or rent-charges so devised and bequeathed for the charitable purposes aforesaid; and that the same might be decreed to be well charged on the premises: and for a receiver: and that, if necessary, Joshua Colles Meredyth might be removed from the trusts, and new trustees appointed.

The defendants, Joseph Henry Wybrants and Thomas Wybrants, relied upon the length of time and the Statute of Limitations, as a bar to the entire relief sought by the bill in respect of the annuities; more than twenty years having elapsed since the deaths of Sarah Wybrants and John Bowers, without any payment or other satisfaction having been made or given during said period to any person whomsoever, on foot of such annuities, or any of them: and they insisted, that, supposing the said several annuities were not wholly barred by length of time, yet that the plaintiffs were not entitled to recover more than six years' arrears of said respective annuities: and they relied on the Statute of Limitations in bar to any further relief sought by the bill in relation to the arrears of the annuities.

The defendant, Meredyth, by his answer, stated that he believed that the legal estate in the lands was then vested in him.

The Lying-in Hospital and the Hibernian Marine Society *were corporate bodies; the other objects of the testator's charity were not.

Mr. *Robert Warren* and Mr. *Thomas Lefroy*, for the plaintiffs, [cited *The Incorporated Society* v. *Richards* (1) and *The Attorney-General* v. *Persse* (2)].

Mr. *Moore*, Mr. *Brooke*, and Mr. *Martley* for J. H. Wybrants and Thomas Wybrants:

There was no difficulty in the way of two of the charities suing in their own names for the annuities devised to them; for they are corporate bodies. * * *

[188]   The 3 & 4 Will. IV. c. 27, was one of a series of Acts passed for the limitation of actions; and the other statutes on that subject, the 2 & 3 Will. IV. c. 71, and 2 & 3 Will. IV. c. 100, apply to cor-

[189] porations sole and aggregate, temporal and spiritual. * * If this case be within the twenty-fifth section, then no annuity charged upon the estate of another person can be barred; for the owner of the estate would be a trustee for the person having the charge.

Mr. *Lefroy*, in reply:

[190]   * * But if charities are within the statute, then it is submitted that this is an express trust within the meaning of the twenty-fifth section, and is not barred by the operation of that section. Where the trust appears on the face of the instrument itself, it is an express trust within this statute: *Salter* v. *Cavanagh* (3). The charge of the annuity on the lands in itself created a trust. * *

[191] Here also the lands are devised to trustees, upon trust to convey them to the defendants, subject to the annuities. That trust has not as yet been executed: the legal estate still remains in the trustees: their right is not barred, for the possession of J. H. Wybrants is the possession of the trustee. * * *

[192]   Mr. *Martley*, by leave of the COURT, replied to the authorities cited by Mr. *Lefroy*, which were not referred to in opening the case.

(1) 58 R. R. 266 (1 Dr. & War. 258).   (3) 56 R. R. 222 (1 Dr. & Wal. 668).
(2) 59 R. R. 645 (2 Dr. & War. 67).

THE LORD CHANCELLOR :

The question in this case is, whether the annuities given by the will of Mr. Wright, in 1798, have been barred by the new Statute of Limitations. There was no concealment, as· the gifts were advertised three times in the *Dublin Gazette*, in May, 1796.

As to the general question ; before the late Statute of Limitations, time did not run against charities in this Court. Moore, in his reading on the statute of Elizabeth, in Duke, lays it down, "that if the heir of the disseisor be in by descent of lands given to a charitable use, yet he shall be bound by the decree ; for no *laches* of entry shall ever destroy a charitable use, nor any thing bar it but a conveyance to one upon good consideration, and without fraud or notice. Neither is a charitable use bound to the times expressed in the Statute of Limitations, made 32 Hen. VIII. c. 2, nor to that of 21 Jac." At law, the old Statute of Limitations operated against all claimants, although they held in trust for charities ; but in this Court, unless in the case of a purchaser for value without notice, they had no operation ; and, as we have seen, *laches* did not affect the *right to the charity funds. The rules, as stated by Moore, were the law of this Court down to the passing of the recent statute.

[*195]

This statute (3 & 4 Will. IV. c. 27) bars all legal rights, and does not contain any saving in favour of charities. No person is to make any entry or distress, except within the period there specified ; and this word "person" extends to a body politic, corporate, or collegiate, and to a class of creditors, or other persons, as well as an individual. The old Statutes of Limitations did not bar a legal rent-charge, and, therefore, there was no bar in equity of an equitable rent-charge or annuity out of land: *Stackhouse* v. *Barnston* (1) ; but such interests are expressly bound by the recent statute ; and I shall, therefore, assume that the right to the annuities in this case, if legal, is bound at law. Now the old statutes did not interfere with equitable rights ; but equity, in analogy to the legal provisions, held time to be a bar, except in some peculiar cases, of which charity was the leading one. The new statute no longer left courts of equity to act by analogy ; but expressly enacted that no person, claiming any land or rent in equity, should bring any suit to recover the same, but within the period during which, by virtue of the provisions in the Act, he might have made an entry or distress, or brought an action to

(1) 10 Ves. 467. See 28 R. R. 740, *n*.

recover the same, if he had been entitled at law to such estate, interest, or right, in or to the same, as he shall claim therein in equity. This, therefore, is quite as imperative as the enactment binding legal estates. No person can bring any suit but within the legal limitation. This leaves to equity no discretion. The statute deals generally with equitable rights, and treats them thus [*196] far on the *footing of legal interests. Then comes the exception in section twenty-five: That when any land or rent shall be vested in a trustee upon any express trust, the right of the cestui que trust to bring a suit against the trustees, or any person claiming through him, to recover such land or rent, shall be deemed to have first accrued at and not before the time at which such land or rent shall have been conveyed to a purchaser for valuable consideration, and then be deemed to have accrued only as against such purchaser, and any person claiming through him. And the statute then provides for the case of fraud. Now it appears to me that, unless the case can be brought within this saving, which operates between trustee and cestui que trust, it would fall within the general prohibition in section twenty-four. For charities were only saved in equity from the operation of the former statutes, as trusts, although highly favoured ones: and now all trusts are barred by section twenty-four, unless saved by twenty-five; and I am not at liberty to introduce an exception into the Act, which the Legislature, providing generally for all trusts, have not thought it proper to enact.

In the case of *Salter* v. *Cavanagh* (1), it seems to have been held that an implied trust is an express one within the Act, where it arises upon the face of the instrument itself, and is not to be made out by evidence; but upon this point I am not called upon to give any opinion. In *Phillipo* v. *Munnings* (2), the trust was an express one; and it was held that the trustee was bound by it, although he was an executor also, and appropriated the legacy as such.

[*197]   In this case the testator devised all his estates to trustees, *to grant, convey and settle the same to certain uses in strict settlement; subject to and charged and chargeable with some annuities for life to individuals, and to the annuities for charitable purposes; several to institutions of which there are governors, and one to the poor of a parish. It was considered throughout the argument, that the legal estate was still in the trustees, no legal conveyance

(1) 56 R. R. 222.   (2) 45 R. R. 63 (2 My. & Cr. 309).

ever having been executed. Is, then, the provision for the annuities to charities an express trust within section twenty-five? It certainly is so if the trust to convey is to be considered as still in existence: for the conveyance can only be properly made by securing the annuities; and the trustees have a power of leasing; and there is a direction to pay the annuities which would apply to the trustees. They are trustees for the trusts declared until they convey; and these are all express trusts.

If the case is now to be considered as if the devisees of the beneficial interest had acquired the legal estate subject to the charge, I should still be of opinion in favour of the charities. In the first place, the devisees must be considered to have acquired the legal estate from the trustees; and if not, yet the charge for the charities would, I think, create what in this Court must be deemed an express trust within section twenty-five. The gift is an express one; and if the person taking the estate is bound to give effect to the gift as a trustee, then it is an express trust. It certainly is not necessary to use the word "trust" in order to create an express trust. I do not intend to lay it down that every charge creates a trust, although it imposes a burden; but a charge may create a trust; depending on the nature of the charge. In *Bailey* v. *Ekins* (1) Lord ELDON said he was *confident Lord THURLOW's opinion was, that a charge (of debts) is a devise of the estate, in substance and effect, *pro tanto* upon trust to pay the debts: and this is supported by the current of authorities. The principle is no less powerful in the case of charities, particularly where the charity is to a fluctuating, uncertain body, like the poor of a parish. The testator gives the estate to one, subject to this charge. Who is to pay the annuities but the person who is liable to the burden: and this, in the case of a charity, impresses him with the character of a trustee for the charity. By the ancient rule of equity, no one could acquire an estate, with notice of a charitable use, without being liable to it. The statute has not altered the rule in equity; which must still prevail where the charity is not bound by section twenty-four, or is within the saving in section twenty-five. The doctrine in *Mills* v. *Farmer* (2) shows how much more favourably, in many respects, a legacy to a charity is to be construed than a legacy to an ordinary legatee. The distinctions taken by Lord ELDON, in *King* v. *Denison* (3), between a direct trust and

[*198]

(1) 7 Ves. 319, 323. See 48 R. R.   (2) 13 R. R. 247 (19 Ves. 483).
92, n.   (3) 12 R. R. 227 (1 V. & B. 260).

a charge, were, with reference to a resulting trust, in favour of the heir.

Upon the whole, therefore, I have satisfied myself that, even upon the strict construction of the statute, the plaintiffs are entitled to the relief which they pray. It is not a case in which the annuities were given to trustees for the charities, and the estate itself, subject to the annuities, was given to other persons beneficially. If that case should arise, it may be found more difficult to relieve the charities in this Court, where time has operated against the trustees of the annuities as a legal bar.

1845.
Jan. 18.
———
SIR EDWARD
SUGDEN,
L.C.
[199]

FOZIER *v.* ANDREWS.

(2 Jo. & Lat. 199—200; S. C. 7 Ir. Eq. R. 595.)

If a trustee has not misconducted himself, even though the Court punish him, as by making him pay interest on funds in his hands, yet he shall get the costs of the suit: but if his account be greatly reduced in the office, he shall not get the costs of passing it.

THE bill was filed by a cestui que trust against his trustee, for an account and a reconveyance. Upon taking the accounts, the sum claimed by the defendant was considerably reduced; but there still remained a balance due to him. The cause having come on to be heard on report and merits,

Mr. Dickson and *Mr. R. Fergusson*, for the plaintiff, asked for the costs of the suit against the defendant, on the ground that the plaintiff had succeeded in the suit, and had greatly reduced the sum claimed by the defendant.

Mr. Moore and *Mr. Darley*, for the defendant, stated, that his claim had been cut down in the office, because certain sums of money, which were advanced by him for the maintenance of the plaintiff, beyond the amount of his income, had not been allowed; and that no misconduct was imputable to him: and they cited *Trevor* v. *Townsend* (1) and *Tebbs* v. *Carpenter* (2).

THE LORD CHANCELLOR:

[*200]   It is said that the costs of this suit ought to abide the general rule, and be given to the successful party: but in *every case in which a cestui que trust files the bill for an account against his trustee, he must succeed in obtaining a decree; for as the relative

(1) 1 Moll. 496.   (2) 16 R. R. 224 (1 Madd. 290).

situations of the parties cannot be denied, the matter must go to
the Master. I believe the rule is general, that, if the trustee has
not misconducted himself, even though the Court punish him, as
by making him pay interest on funds in his hands, yet he shall get
the costs of the suit. Here the trustee cannot be said to have
misconducted himself; but he has made charges in his account
which cannot be maintained. As to some of those charges,
however, for instance those for maintenance, the demand of the
trustee has been disallowed, not by reason of its injustice, but
because of the limited amount of the fund to answer the demand:
the justice of the claim was established, although the amount of
the demand was reduced. This, therefore, is not a case for costs
against the trustee; on the contrary, I think that, according to the
general rule, he ought to have his costs: but as, in the office, he
has set up claims for large demands which he has not been able to
establish, and as the Master has, in my opinion, acted properly in
disallowing them, I shall in this case make the same distinction as
was made in *Tebbs* v. *Carpenter*, and give him the costs of the suit
generally, with the exception of the costs of the account in the
Master's office.

FOZIER
v.
ANDREWS.

In re CLARKES.

(2 Jo. & Lat. 212—222.)

1845.
Feb. 1, 4.

SIR EDWARD
SUGDEN,
L.C.

[212]

Four partners, and two sureties for them, entered into a joint and several
bond to trustees of a Banking Company, to secure the payment of all such
sums of money as, upon the balance of any account current between the
partners and the Bank, should from time to time be due by the partners, to
the extent of 1,000*l.* Separate judgments were entered against the obligors.

The trading firm having become bankrupt: Held, that the Banking Company might prove against the joint estate for a balance less than 1,000*l.*,
due on foot of an account current.

JOHN CLARKE, Archibald Clarke, Samuel Clarke, and Alexander
Clarke, co-partners, trading under the firm of John Clarke and
Brothers, and Hugh Barkley, and George B. Coulter, executed their
joint and several bond, payable immediately, to Sir Robert Campbell
and John Pretty Muspratt, two of the trustees of the Provincial
Bank of Ireland, in the penal sum of 2,000*l.* The condition of the
bond, after reciting, that the Clarkes (naming them) had opened an
account with the co-partnership called the Provincial Bank, and
were desirous of being accommodated by the Bank from time to
time in some or other of the various modes in which bankers are in
the habit of affording accommodation; and that in order to induce

the Bank to take the *said account, and to accommodate them from time to time in some one or other of the modes aforesaid, the obligors (naming them) had respectively agreed to enter into the above bond,—was, that if the Clarkes (naming them), or some or one of them, or their or some one of their heirs, executors, or administrators, did and should well and truly pay, or cause to be paid, to the said co-partnership, all and every such sum and sums of money as upon the balance of any account current which then was, or at any time or times thereafter should be open between the said Clarkes (naming them) and the said co-partnership, at any of the establishments of the co-partnership, should from time to time be due and owing from or by the said Clarkes (naming them), their executors, &c., together with all discount, postage of letters and commission, according to the usage and course of business ; but nevertheless to the extent only of 1,000l. principal money, exclusive of interest and costs, in case such balance should exceed that sum ; and so that the above bond should be a continuing security to the said co-partnership, to the amount of 1,000l. principal money, besides such interest and costs as aforesaid, notwithstanding any settlement of account, or other matter or thing whatsoever ; the bond was to be void.

Upon this bond separate judgments were entered up against the obligors.

John Clarke died in June, 1842; and in March, 1844, a commission of bankruptcy issued against Archibald, Samuel, and Alexander Clarke, under which they were, in April, 1844, found and declared bankrupts.

At the death of John Clarke, the firm of John Clarke *and Brothers was indebted to the Provincial Bank in the sum of 871l. 19s. 10d. principal money, on foot of advances made by the Bank to the firm, together with 18l. 5s. 9d. interest thereon: which sum, together with the further interest up to the date of the commission, was due to the Bank by the bankrupts, as the surviving partners of the firm, at the time of their bankruptcy. The bankrupts were also, at the date of the commission, indebted to the Bank in the sum of 77l. 0s. 6d., being the amount of three several bills of exchange, and interest thereon, which were endorsed to the Bank, by the bankrupts, after the death of John Clarke, and discounted by the Bank for the accommodation of the bankrupts in the course of their trade; and which bills were not paid when due. The several demands of the Bank amounted in the whole to 1,073l. 12s. 1d.

The proof of debts made by the public officer of the Provincial Bank, stated that the bankrupts were at the date of the commission jointly and severally indebted to the deponent, as such public officer, for and on behalf of the Bank, in the sum of 1,073*l.* 12*s.* 1*d.*, being the balance of principal and interest due thereon to the date of the commission, on foot of an account current; that for said sum the deponent had not, nor had any person or persons for his behoof, or who were authorized to receive same, received any payment, security or satisfaction whatever, save and except the securities specified in the schedule to the proof; viz., the joint and several bond of the 21st of September, 1840; the several judgments obtained thereon, in Michaelmas Term, 1840, against the several obligors; and a joint and several promissory note to Robert Murray by the said Hugh Barkley and George B. Coulter, dated *the 23rd of May, 1843, payable the 1st of January, 1844, 1,072*l.* 9*s.* 6*d.*

Upon this proof Mr. Commissioner MACAN adjudged, that the Bank was not entitled to prove for the amount claimed by the deposition against the joint estate of the bankrupts, but only against the separate estate of each of the bankrupts at foot of the separate judgments entered against them respectively. And from the minute of the order of the Court, it appeared that the Commissioner so adjudged upon these grounds: First, Because it appeared to him, that the Bank, by entering up separate judgments, determined their election, and fixed their status at the time of the bankruptcy. Secondly, Because, even if it were possible to obliterate the separate judgments, and go back to the bond, so as to treat the bankrupts as joint debtors, the claim of the Bank to prove on the joint estate would be encountered by the principle, that there were two other persons alive and solvent, bound jointly with the bankrupts, namely, the co-obligors (1).

The public officer of the Bank thereupon presented his petition to the Lord Chancellor, praying him to declare that the petitioner was entitled to prove against the joint estate of the bankrupts for the sum claimed by him in his deposition; and that the proof so exhibited by him, against the joint estate of the bankrupts, might be received.

Mr. Moore and *Mr. Rogers* for the petitioner:

The debt did not exist when the bond was executed; and a non-existing debt cannot merge in a collateral security: *Holmes* v.

(1) The case in the Bankrupt Court is reported in 7 Ir. Eq. R. 39.

Bell (1). The petitioner is clearly entitled to prove for the 97*l.*
advanced by the Bank on the bills of exchange after the death of
John Clarke; for the condition of the bond does not extend to a
liability incurred after the death of one of the partners.

Mr. Monahan and *Mr. Creighton* for the assignee :

The attention of the Commissioner was not directed to the fact,
that the 97*l.* was a debt incurred after the decease of John Clarke.
The petitioner is not entitled to prove as a simple contract creditor
against the joint estate, because, at the time of the bankruptcy, an
action of assumpsit for the balance of the account current could not
have been maintained; for the bond was an original, not a collateral
security, and the moment an advance was made, it became a specialty
debt by virtue of it: *Bulstrode* v. *Gilburn* (2). The case of *Holmes* v.
Bell is distinguishable; for there the bond was payable at a future
time, and therefore clearly only a collateral security. Here the bond
is payable immediately. The circumstance that other persons
joined in the bond as sureties does not demonstrate that the bond
is merely a collateral security: *Pudsey's* case, cited in *Hooper's*
case (3). Here the Bank, having entered separate judgments upon
the bond, have elected to treat their demand as a separate and not
a joint debt, and cannot fall back on the bond, which has merged in
the judgments: *Ex parte Christie* (4).

Mr. Rogers, in reply :

The Bank did not seek to prove their demand under the bond:
[*217] that distinguishes this case *from *Ex parte Christie*. The principle
of merger cannot apply to this case; for the bond was executed and
the judgment was confessed before any debt was contracted to the
Bank: *Ex parte Parnell* (5).

THE LORD CHANCELLOR :

I should be sorry if that which has been decided by the Court
below should turn out to be the law, for it would lead to great
inconvenience amongst traders. I will not finally part with this
case without looking into the authorities upon the subject, out of
respect to the learned Commissioner, who, in the exercise of his
duties, has taken so much pains in referring to, and commenting
upon the cases before him. It would not be acting with the respect

(1) 3 Scott, N. R. 479, 3 Man. & G.   (3) 2 Leon. 210.
213, 60 R. R. 492.   (4) 2 Dea. & Ch. 155.
(2) 2 Str. 1027.   (5) 2 Mon. Dea. & De Gex, 273.

which is due to him, if I decided without further consideration ; but I have so strong an opinion upon the subject, that I shall now express it, reserving to myself the power to change it, if I should ultimately agree with him. The facts of the case are these : There was a partnership consisting of four persons, who proposed to have certain dealings with the Provincial Bank ; and they, together with two sureties, entered into a joint and several bond in a penalty of 2,000*l.*, to secure the balances which at any time, if they chose to proceed on the bond, should be due to the Bank on any account current, with discount, interest, &c.; but the Bank was not to recover on foot of that security more than 1,000*l.*, exclusive of interest and discounts ; and it was to be at liberty to recover that sum, though accounts had been settled between the parties, and *the balances had been paid before the Bank proceeded on the security: and there was a warrant of attorney for entering up judgment upon that bond, in order the better to secure the advances which should be made. Accordingly the Bank entered up six separate judgments against the obligors in the bond ; and the traders having become bankrupts, the question is, whether, for the balance of the account as it stood between the Bank and the partnership at the date of the bankruptcy, the Bank is at liberty to prove against the joint estate of the traders as for a simple contract debt. The Bank would certainly be at liberty to do so, unless it can be made out that the bond and the separate judgments thereon constitute the only security,—I should rather say, the only contract,—between those two parties ; and thus prevent the Bank from maintaining a joint demand against the traders. I am not aware of any authority which bears directly upon this case; all those which have been cited by the learned Commissioner prove only, what is not disputed, that a bond taken for an existing simple contract debt merges the simple contract debt ; and that a bond debt will merge in the judgment entered up upon it. The case of *Ex parte Christie* (1) does not apply to the present, for there the original contract was a joint one, the creditors took a joint and separate bond from the debtors, and then entered a joint judgment upon that bond. There was, therefore, a merger of the bond, and there was no other contract to fall back upon than a joint contract. There could, therefore, be no right to prove against the separate estate. The case of *Bulstrode* v. *Gilburn*, is of a different nature, and does seem to bear somewhat more strongly on this point; but I apprehend that it turned upon *this: A prothonotary

(1) 2 Dea. & Ch. 155.

appointed a deputy, and it was arranged between them what the deputy was to have, and he covenanted to account for the rest. The deputy received fees, which were the subject of a dispute between him and the prothonotary, and the latter brought an action for money had and received against the deputy; and it was held, that, although he was entitled to what he demanded, he was not entitled to recover in assumpsit, because he had taken a covenant to account from the deputy, and therefore his remedy was by an action on the covenant. But that case, in fact, depended wholly on the covenant, whereby it was arranged how much each party was to have. Until the covenant was produced, it could not be ascertained what it was to which the plaintiff was entitled. Therefore he was obliged to resort to that security which constituted his only right to recover from his deputy. But this case is altogether different.

Put this case, that, ten hours before the bankruptcy, the bankers had advanced 3,000*l.* to these four traders. Now the moment after the expiration of the period for which the money was lent (laying aside, for the present, the consideration of the bond and judgment), an action of assumpsit might have been maintained. But then the bond is produced, and it is said that the bankers have lost their remedy as for a simple contract debt, for the amount which the bond would cover. But that is only as to one-third of the sum advanced, for they have not lost their remedy as to two-thirds of it; and therefore, in the case supposed, I should have to sever the contract, and consider it as two contracts; and say, that as to 1,000*l.*, the simple contract debt was merged in the bond and judgments, but that as to the remaining 2,000*l.*, it remained, as it originally

[*220]   was, a simple contract debt of all the partners. That is rather *a fanciful proposition. But how does the matter really stand? Upon every fresh transaction between the parties, a right of action of assumpsit accrued. Such right was of the essence of the transaction. How can that right be affected by a collateral security, such as this is, not covering an antecedent debt, or an ascertained balance, but any balance the creditor chooses, up to the sum of 1,000*l.*? Who shall say that every transaction is covered by this bond, which may not be sufficient to cover the whole of any one given transaction? I am not satisfied that such is the case. But if I hold this to be a continuing security for a fluctuating balance on an uncertain state of accounts, arising at any period of time, what injury do I do to any person; what rule of law do I contravene?

I leave the liability exactly as I find it, and I give the bond all
the force and efficiency it was intended to have. So far as the
party proceeds on the judgments, he must rely on them, and on
them alone; but if he proceed on foot of the original liability,
that liability is not barred or merged by the bond or judgments.
Observe the difficulty in which the learned Commissioner was
placed by his judgment. He says, that if he were to go back to
the bond, it is not the joint obligation of the bankrupts, but of the
bankrupts and two other persons who must be presumed to be alive;
and the rule is clearly established, that you cannot prove against
the bankrupt if the surety be alive and solvent. Does not that
show that the original demand is not merged in the judgments;
otherwise there could be no objection to the Bank proving against
some of the co-obligors. I entertain a strong opinion upon this
question, but I will not finally dispose of it without looking into the
authorities. In the meantime, if I do not alter my opinion, the
order appealed against stands reversed, with liberty to the petitioner
to prove against the joint estate.

THE LORD CHANCELLOR:

I have looked into the authorities, and I retain the opinion which
I expressed at the hearing, that this is a joint debt, proveable
against the joint estate of the bankrupts. The dealing was between
four parties and the Bank; and it would appear to have been
limited to a joint dealing. The security is not from the four
partners alone to the Bank, but from six persons, two of whom
were sureties for the other four, the partners; and it is given, not
to the Banking Company, but to two persons as trustees for the
Company. This, therefore, is a collateral security by six persons to
two persons; and the debt is from four persons to the Company
generally. The security, also, does not cover the debt which may
at any given time be due, but only a portion of that debt; neither
is it for the debt actually due at any given period, but it is to cover
that portion of the debt agreed on, which the party to whom the
security is given may at any given moment think fit to enforce on
foot of the security. It is a joint debt. What puts an end to all
doubt on the subject is, that the condition of the bond is not for any
payment to be made by the six to the two, from whom, and to whom
the security is given; but it is a bond from the six to the two, conditioned to be void upon payment by the four to the Company.
They considered, therefore, that the dealings would, as in fact they

did, continue with the four jointly with the Company; but the
security was by the six to the two trustees; it was, therefore, only
a further and collateral security.

I may observe that this point was not argued in the Court below.

As to the bills of exchange, they were *overlooked below. In fact,
part of the debt appears to have been covered by bills of exchange.
The demand on foot of them was not affected by the bond. I am
clearly of opinion that the security was collateral; therefore, the
petitioner must be permitted to prove against the joint estate for the
whole of the debt.

IN RE JOHNSTONS.

(2 Jo. & Lat. 222—228.)

Two out of three testamentary guardians declined to accept the trust.
They are not entitled, as of right, after the death of their co-guardian, to be
appointed guardians by the Court.

But the testamentary guardians (other circumstances being equal) will
be preferred to the person nominated in the will of the mother (the third
guardian), to be the guardians of the infants after her decease.

The solicitor for any of the persons who exercise a control over the
minors' estate, will not be appointed the guardian of their persons.

THIS was an appeal from an order of the MASTER OF THE ROLLS,
whereby he confirmed a report of the Master, approving of Messrs.
Graham and Collum to be the guardians of the persons of the
minors.

The father of the minors, by his will, appointed his wife and
Messrs. Graham and Collum to be guardians of his children. The
minors were made wards of Court, upon a petition presented by
their mother, stating that Messrs. Graham and Collum had declined
to act; and that she was willing to act as guardian of their persons;
and praying that she might be appointed guardian of their persons,
and the Master guardian of their fortunes. Upon this petition it
was referred to the Master to inquire, amongst other matters,
whether any guardians had been appointed by the will of the
testator; and if so, whether they, or any of them, were willing to
act. The Master reported, that Mrs. Johnston alone was willing
to act as guardian of their persons, and that Messrs. Graham and
Collum were not willing to act as guardians of their fortunes. Mr.
Collum, who was a solicitor, acted as the solicitor for Mrs. Johnston

*in the matter; and in her name presented a petition to have
that report confirmed. The other facts sufficiently appear in the
judgment of the LORD CHANCELLOR.

The *Solicitor-General* (*Mr. Greene*), *Mr. Brooke*, and *Mr. Sherlock*, for the petitioners.

In re
JOHNSTONS.

Mr. Moore, Mr. Monahan, and *Mr. Sproule*, for Messrs. Graham and Collum.

THE LORD CHANCELLOR:

As far as the question depends upon right, the case stands thus: the father of the minors, having by law the power to appoint a testamentary guardian, exercised that power by his will, and appointed his widow, Mr. Graham, and Mr. Collum, joint guardians; and the children being very young at the time of his death, the two gentlemen withdrew themselves from the guardianship, and left the entire management of the minors to the widow. A petition was presented by her, and the children were made wards of Court. The property, therefore, came under the direction of the Court itself; but that would not have deprived the testamentary guardians (who have both a power and a trust) of their control over the property and persons of the minors, if they had not themselves, in effect, relinquished the trust. The usual reference was made to the Master; and the widow was appointed sole guardian of the persons, and the Master was appointed guardian of the fortunes. Thus matters remained until the death of Mrs. Johnston. Some time before her decease she was desirous that another person should be appointed co-guardian with herself. It appears that at first she was willing that the children *should be placed with a clergyman of the Church of England, a maternal relative of their's, and that he should have the care of them, if the event of her illness required it; but she afterwards changed her mind, and became dissatisfied with her own relations, and desired that a relative of her husband should be joined with her in the guardianship; and accordingly she presented a petition, praying that Mr. Johnston, the paternal uncle of the minors, might be appointed co-guardian with her. Upon that petition being presented, Mr. Graham and Mr. Collum, who had in effect renounced the guardianship, presented a counter-petition, praying in effect that they might be permitted to resume their powers as testamentary guardians, along with her. Upon that petition coming before me, I struck out so much of it as prayed to that effect but I sent it to the Master to inquire who were fit and proper persons to be appointed guardians, having regard to the direction in the will of the father. That shows, that although I thought the Master

[*224]

In re
Johnstons.

ought to have regard to that direction, I did not consider that, after
their acts, the testamentary guardians had a right to be appointed.

Soon after, Mrs. Johnston died, and then the matter came to
be contested between the present litigants; and the Master, upon
the whole view of the case, has appointed the two testamentary
guardians to be the guardians of the persons of the minors. The
persons who opposed them had certainly a strong claim; for, by the
will of the mother, they were named as the persons to whose care
she wished the children to be confided ; and, so far as lay in her
power, she appointed them guardians of their persons. But she
had, by law, no power to appoint testamentary guardians. The
husband had the power, and exercised it; the wife had not the
[*225]   power, but attempted to exercise it. Her will was *a nullity in this
respect, except so far as the Court would look at it as a strong
expression of her confidence in the persons to whom she desired
that the guardianship of her children should be confided. Upon
the question of right, therefore, supposing that Messrs. Graham
and Collum had not relinquished their office, there could be no
contest, for the right would be in them : but I am of opinion that,
considering all the acts which have taken place, the testamentary
guardians have relinquished their trust; and, therefore, this
becomes a case in which neither party has an actual right; and
then it depends entirely upon what is expedient, and upon the discretion of the Court; but that discretion is to be ruled and governed
by the law of the Court. I shall therefore, in this case, have
regard to the fact of the appointment by the father, who had the
power to do so, and to the very strong desire expressed by the
mother : but if I must set the one against the other, I must give
the greater weight (the circumstances remaining the same) to the
desire of the parent who had the power to appoint. In determining
which of the applicants it is most expedient to appoint, I am only
to consider what will be for the benefit of the minors. It is a constant practice of the Court, and a wise one, not, upon light grounds,
to interfere with the decision of the Master in questions merely of
discretion, as in the appointment of receivers and guardians : and
if such be the rule in ordinary cases, it must apply much more
forcibly to the present case, in which the decision of the Master has
been confirmed by the MASTER OF THE ROLLS. Then how does this
matter stand in reference to the interest of the minors, putting
aside, for an instant, the questions upon the character and conduct
of Mr. Collum. I have not heard any thing which in the slightest

degree impeaches the character of Mr. Graham, or the moral character of Mr. Collum. With respect to the latter, *the objections are purely as to acts which he has done in his character of solicitor. I see no reason why, independently of the other circumstances to which I do not now advert, the persons appointed by the father should not resume the situation he meant to confer on them. If I affirm the Master's report, I shall place persons who have not changed their character, in the precise position in which the father meant to place them during the life of his widow: and, if he meant them to act in that character during her life, much more did he intend that they should act after her decease. I only give effect to what would have taken place, if these gentlemen had not given up their office. The other applicants have not a superior claim: they have been selected by the mother, who could only recommend their appointment; but I cannot place her recommendation above the appointment of her husband.

Looking at the other circumstances, I think the advantages are in favour of the appointment of the husband's nominees. It is said that they will not personally superintend the education of the children; no objection has been raised against Mr. Devereux, with whom it is proposed that the children should be placed, and who is their near relative: nothing can be more advantageous than that the children should be placed under his care. As to the persons with whom the mother wished them to be placed, one of them is a young man, a member of the Bar, who has, therefore, to follow his profession, and is not a person likely to look after young children. It is proposed that the care of the minors should devolve on the other, a lady, who has a large family of her own. I do not think that a recommendation, or that she is so likely to educate the minors properly as Mr. Devereux. It was then objected that Mr. Collum had acted as solicitor for the receiver, who is his *father; for the committee of the estate, the Master; for the minors themselves, in the minor matter; and for the trustees in the settlement; and that thereby considerable costs have been incurred,—I do not say improperly,—and that he now proposes to become the guardian of the persons of the minors: and that, if his application be granted, he will have power over every person (Mr. Graham being his client) who would, in any manner, have control over the estate. This having been brought under the consideration of the Master, Mr. Collum retired, of his own accord, from being solicitor for the minors, and is now willing to retire

In re
JOHNSTONS.
[*226]

[*227]

In re
JOHNSTONS.

from being solicitor for the receiver. It is said that he has appointed an attorney of his own nomination to be solicitor for the receiver. I give him full credit for the statement that he now comes forward simply for the benefit of the minors, and from friendship to the late Mr. Johnston; that he promised him to act as his trustee; and that, although he retired when his services were not wanted, he felt bound to come forward when they appeared to be wanted. But no man can serve two masters; and I cannot confirm his appointment, or permit him to act as guardian, unless he will relinquish all interest he may have in this matter as a solicitor. Therefore, without intending any reflexion on his character, he must, for the sake of the jurisdiction of the Court and the propriety of its proceedings, relinquish his office of solicitor to every person who has any control over the property. And I must direct the Master, having regard to the rule respecting the appointment of guardians and receivers, to take care that any solicitor who shall be appointed in his stead, shall not be under any obligation or agreement to give him any share of the profits; and he must not accept of such. I wish it to be understood that, in making this order, it is not my

[*228]

intention, in any manner, *to reflect upon the conduct of Mr. Collum. With that alteration, I shall affirm the order of the MASTER OF THE ROLLS.

I cannot give the applicants their costs, there having been already two decisions against them. But as they have come here to effectuate the wishes of Mrs. Johnston, I shall not make them pay the costs of the other side, which, according to the usual practice in such cases, must come out of the minors' estate.

1845.
April 18.

SIR EDWARD
SUGDEN,
L.C.

[295]

HAMILTON *v.* JACKSON.

(2 Jo. & Lat. 295—302; S. C. 8 Ir. Eq. R. 195.)

By marriage articles, the intended husband covenanted that in case he should die in the life-time of his intended wife, without issue by her, she should be entitled to one-half of what property, real or personal, he should die seised or possessed of; and that in preference to any creditor of his, or to any deed or will which he might make or execute in his life-time, contrary to the true intent and meaning of the articles. There was no issue of the marriage; and the husband died, leaving his wife surviving.

She is not entitled, in addition to the moiety of her husband's real and personal estate given to her by the articles, to dower out of the other moiety of his real estates of inheritance.

BY articles executed in contemplation of a marriage between William Hamilton, jun., and Anne M'Math, bearing date the

30th of April, 1794, and made between William Hamilton, the elder, of Lesquil, farmer, of the first part; William Hamilton, jun., his fourth son, of the second part; Anne M'Math, of the third part; and Andrew M'Math, of Aughdreena, farmer, her father, of the fourth part; William Hamilton, the elder, in order to make a provision for his son, William Hamilton, jun., in case the marriage should take effect, and in consideration of the marriage and of the marriage portion agreed to be paid, as after mentioned, assigned to William Hamilton, jun., certain leasehold lands and premises, subject to the payment of the rent reserved; and also, by his bond to his said son, secured to him the payment of the sum of 113l. 15s. on the day next after the solemnization of the marriage. And Andrew M'Math, in consideration of the intended marriage, and as a marriage portion with his daughter, agreed to give with her the sum of 200l. : that is to say, 100l. thereof, payable the day after the marriage; and the remaining sum of 100l. payable, with interest, one year after the birth of the first child of the intended marriage. And it was agreed that in case Anne M'Math should die in the lifetime of her intended husband, without issue, then the sum of 100l., part of the 200l., should go and revert back to Andrew M'Math. And William Hamilton, jun., covenanted with Andrew M'Math, that in case he should die in the life-time of Anne M'Math, his intended wife, without issue by her, *that then and in such case, the said   [*296] Anne M'Math should be entitled to one full half of what property, real or personal, of what kind soever, the said William should die seised or possessed of at the time of his death; and that in preference to any creditor or creditors of the said William, or to any deed or will which the said William might make or execute in his life-time, contrary to the true intent and meaning of the articles.

William Hamilton, jun., died in 1844, seised and possessed of several fee-simple, freehold and leasehold estates, and of personal property; and leaving his wife him surviving. There never had been any issue of the marriage. By his will, dated the 16th of December, 1843, he devised and bequeathed his real and personal property amongst his nephews and other relations, subject, as to part of it, to an annuity of 500l. per annum for his wife, during her life; and he also gave to her the use of his dwelling-house, furniture and plate, during her life.

Mrs. Hamilton elected to take against the will; and filed the present bill praying that she might be declared entitled to the benefit of the articles of 1794, and that same might be carried into

HAMILTON
*.
JACKSON.

execution; and for an account of the real and personal estate of
William Hamilton, jun., of which he died seised of, possessed or
entitled to; and that she might be declared entitled to a clear
moiety thereof, and to dower out of the other moiety of her
husband's real estate.

Mr. Serjt. Warren, Mr. W. Brooke, and Mr. Law, for the
plaintiff.

Mr. Bennett, Mr. Moore, Mr. Gayer, and Mr. Ross Moore, for
the several devisees of the real estate:

[297]   Though the provision made by the articles of 1794, for the
plaintiff, is not expressed to be for her jointure, it is manifest that
it was intended to be such; and it being apparent that the moiety
of the real and personal estate thereby given to her was intended
to be her only provision in case she should survive her husband, it
is a satisfaction of her claim to dower: Vizard v. Longdale (1).
[They also cited Gartshore v. Chalie (2), Wilcocks v. Wilcocks (3),
and other cases.]

[298]   Mr. W. Brooke, in reply:

* * Vizard v. Longdale was decided on the effect of the
words, "for her livelihood and maintenance," in the bond: but
in Couch v. Stratton (4) the wife was held to be entitled to
dower, notwithstanding a provision similar in its nature to the
present. * * *

THE LORD CHANCELLOR:

This case depends upon the construction of the marriage articles.
It is a mere question of intention, to be collected from the provisions
of the articles. I quite agree that Vizard v. Longdale is not
now to be disputed. It did not, however, decide a great deal: for
a jointure means a provision; and in that case it was declared,
that the bond to the wife was to be for her livelihood and maintenance. Now a jointure is a provision for the livelihood and
[*299]   maintenance *of the wife. The MASTER OF THE ROLLS thought
otherwise; but the CHANCELLOR reversed his decree, and held that
the wife took the bond in the nature of a jointure.
        In order to exclude the right of the wife to dower, there must be

(1) Cited in Tinney v. Tinney, 3   (3) 2 Vern. 558.
Atk. 8.   (4) 4 R. R. 230 (4 Ves. 391).
(2) 7 R. R. 311 (10 Ves. 1).

either an express declaration, or such a plain intention, to be collected from the whole instrument, as will satisfy the Court that, in excluding the claim to dower, it does not incur the danger of going contrary to the intention of the parties to the contract. It is very probable (though I cannot assume it as a fact), that at the time of the marriage, the husband had no real, and but a small personal estate. The parties were dealing about small properties; the husband was to have 100*l.* as the portion of his wife, and another 100*l.* if there should be issue of the marriage; and if the wife died in the life-time of her husband, without issue, then the second 100*l.* was to go to the wife's father. The parties contemplated both the case of the wife dying in the life-time of her husband, and of the husband dying in the life-time of the wife; but both events were contemplated under the same aspect, namely, the default of issue. No provision was made by the articles for the issue; they are left to be provided for by law. The framers of the articles assumed that, if there should be issue, they would be provided for out of the estates of their parents. The covenant by the husband is most naked in its form. He covenants with Andrew M'Math, that in case he should die in the life-time of Anne M'Math, his intended wife, without issue by her, in such case, Anne M'Math should be entitled to one full half of what property, real or personal, of what kind soever, he should die seised or possessed of at the time of his death; and that in preference to any creditor or creditors of his, or to any deed or will *which he might make or execute in his life-time, contrary to the true intent of the articles. [*300]

Now, independently of the question of dower, this is a provision, according to the authorities, which would leave the entire disposition of all the real and personal estate of the husband in his own power during his life-time, provided he disposed of it against himself. This, therefore, is a provision to operate in a contingent event only, and upon such property only as he *bonâ fide* should possess at the time of his death. There is no intention, apparent or to be inferred from the articles, to deprive the wife of her dower or thirds in the event not expressed, viz., of there being issue of the marriage. What then is the natural construction of these articles? Do they mean that there shall be, in the case provided for, an equal division of the property between the wife and the representatives of the husband: or that the wife shall have all the rights which the law, independently of the contract, would give her in that event; and in addition, that she shall take under the contract, the moiety of the

HAMILTON
  v.
JACKSON.

[*301]

[*302]

real and personal estate. The latter construction would be against
the meaning of the contract, which is, that, notwithstanding the
articles, the husband might dispose of any part of his real or personal
estate, during his life, as he thought proper ; for if the wife were to
have dower, the husband could not dispose of his real estate as
against her, discharged of her right to dower ; whereas it is plain
that the intention was, that the wife was to have nothing but one
moiety of what the husband was seised or possessed of at the time
of his death. Observe what would happen were this otherwise.
Suppose the husband had sold an estate of which he was seised in
fee, for its full value, and thereby increased the *amount of his
personal estate, the wife, on his decease, would, according to that
construction, be entitled to an equal moiety of the personal estate
under the contract ; and she would also be entitled to go against
the purchaser of the real estate, to recover her dower out of it ; the
consequence of which would be, that the purchaser would resort to
the personal estate for compensation. Was that the intention of
the parties ? I think it clearly was not. Again, the wife is dowable
of all the lands of which her husband was seised in fee ; and she is
entitled to have her one-third set out by metes and bounds. Was
it intended that she should take one-third of the fee simple lands
for her dower, and one-half of the residue under the contract? I
think it is impossible to hold that ; and yet that is the position
which is contended for. No one can be more unwilling than I am
to spell out an intention to exclude a woman of her right to dower :
the authorities do not permit it, and I do not desire to go one step
beyond what has been decided. I shall make the decree I am about
to pronounce, solely because it is my clear opinion that the whole
context of the covenant authorizes me to say that the provision made
thereby is, in the given event, a substitution for dower.

Again, there is no act remaining to be done : the covenant is only,
that she shall be entitled to a moiety of the real and personal estate
of which he shall die seised or possessed ; and therefore, though
Wilcocks v. *Wilcocks* (1), and that class of cases, does not directly
apply to the present, the case is open to this view, that she is entitled
to so much under the contract as, with the one-third which the law
gives her, will make up the one-half to which she *is entitled. Is
it not a performance of the covenant when she becomes entitled,
partly by operation of the rule of law and partly by contract, to
one-half of his real and personal estate? As to her claim to a

(1) 2 Vern. 558.

distributive share of the personalty, it is excluded; for by the articles   HAMILTON
she is to take the half, free from the debts of her husband.   r.
                                                                            JACKSON.

I think it is, upon the whole, plain, that in the event of there
being no children, the husband and wife were to divide the whole
of the property equally between them; and that was to be her
whole provision. I should be sorry if it were supposed that I
intend to go beyond the authorities upon this subject. I believe that
I am justified by them in making the declaration, that the plaintiff
is entitled to one-half of the real and personal estate of which her
husband died seised or possessed; but not to dower, or to a
distributive share of the personalty.

GREVILLE v. FLEMING.

(1 & 2 VICT. c. 109.)

(2 Jo. & Lat. 335—343.)

1845.
April 20, 21.

SIR EDWARD
SUGDEN,
L.C.

[335]

The Court would not, at the instance of a lay impropriator, appoint a
receiver for payment of tithe rent-charge, upon an affidavit merely stating
that he was the lay impropriator of the parish; where it appeared that his
title to the tithes had been and still was contested by the parishioners, and the
only payment he had obtained out of the lands of the respondent was by the
hands of a receiver of the Court, appointed in the suit of a third person.

THE petition prayed that a receiver might be appointed over the
lands of the respondent, for payment of tithe rent-charge due the
1st of May, 1844.

The affidavit of the land agent of the petitioner stated, that on
the 14th of January, 1837, William F. Greville, the lay impropriator of the parish of Scraby, died; and that the petitioner, his
eldest son, thereupon became, and had ever since continued, and
then was the lawful lay impropriator of the parish, and entitled to
all tithes or rent-charge in lieu of tithes in respect of the lands
situate in the parish, payable to the lay impropriator of the parish
for the time being. That in 1828 a composition in lieu of tithes
was duly effected, pursuant to the statute: and, that by certificate
of the 26th of October, 1828, the Commissioners certified that the
amount of the composition for all tithes within the parish was 171*l.*
per annum; of which the sum of 95*l.* per annum, being five-ninth
parts thereof, was due to the Rev. C. R., who was the vicar; and
76*l.*, being the remaining four-ninths, was due and payable to the
lay impropriator of the parish. The certificate did not name any
person as being the lay impropriator.

[*336]

The affidavit then stated the applotment, and the amount for which the respondent was liable, in respect of the lands in the petition mentioned, viz., 17*l*. 9*s*. 1¼*d*. per annum; and that said sum continued payable to William F. Greville, *as such lay impropriator, until his decease; and from the period of his decease, became and continued payable to the petitioner (as deponent believed), until the passing of the 1 & 2 Vict. c. 109, whereby a yearly rent-charge of 13*l*. 1*s*. 10*d*., equal to three-fourths of the sum of 17*l*. 9*s*. 1¼*d*. became chargeable on the lands, and was payable to the petitioner in lieu of such tithe composition.

That one J. S. Fleming was, at the time of the passing of the 1 & 2 Vict. c. 109, seised of the first estate of inheritance in the lands; and that the respondent then was seised and possessed thereof. That at the time of the passing of the 1 & 2 Vict. c. 109, and for some time after, a receiver of the Court of Chancery, in the cause of *Fleming* v. *Fleming* and *Browne* v. *Fleming*, was in the receipt of the rents of the lands; and that deponent, on applying to the receiver for payment of the rent-charge, was required by him to procure the approbation of the Master in the cause; that he accordingly filed a statement on behalf of the petitioner, and obtained a certificate of the Master's approbation, and was there-upon paid the amount of the rent-charge by the receiver up to the 1st of May, 1842; and that the rent-charge from that period was still due.

In answer to the application, affidavits were made by the solicitor and the land agent of the respondent, submitting that the petitioner had not shown any right or title in himself to the rent-charge. They stated that the claim of the petitioner to be lay impropriator of the parish had not been acquiesced in; but, on the contrary, had been the subject of opposition and dispute. That the petitioner had on several occasions attempted to establish his right to the impropriate

[*337]

tithes, and *had failed; and especially that at the time of making the composition, notice was given by the Commissioners to all claimants, to come forward and establish their claims to the tithes of the parish; and that one Slevin then claimed to derive title to the impropriate tithes under W. F. Greville, but that the Commis-sioners rejected his claim; and no claim whatever on behalf of W. F. Greville was then established before the Commissioners. That several of the landed proprietors throughout the parish had refused to pay; and that the petitioner had only lately obtained

some isolated payments: and that before the passing of the
1 & 2 Vict. c. 109, the tenants of the lands mentioned in the
petition had refused to pay the tithe composition to W. F. Greville;
and that no payments were made to him out of the lands. That
the respondent became entitled to the lands under a conveyance
from J. S. Fleming, dated the 20th of April, 1835; and submitted
that nothing afterwards done by J. S. Fleming or the receiver
could affect the rights of the respondent.

Upon these documents the MASTER OF THE ROLLS made an order for
the appointment of a receiver, pursuant to the prayer of the petition.

The respondent now moved, by way of appeal, that the order of
the MASTER OF THE ROLLS be set aside: and, in support of that
application, his solicitor made an additional affidavit, stating that
he had been informed and believed that William F. Greville, the
father of the petitioner, did not, nor did any person on his behalf,
receive any payment on account of the impropriate tithes, from the
year 1828 down to the year 1837, from J. S. Fleming, or any of
his tenants or other person, for the lands in the petition mentioned:
*and that the reason for non-payment was that Richard F. Greville   [*338]
was not able to show any title to the impropriate tithes : that
when the respondent became the purchaser of the lands, the annual
outgoings in respect of the charges affecting them, amounted nearly
to the entire rental; and that, under these circumstances, due
attention was not given to the proceedings in the cause of *Fleming*
v. *Fleming*, no person being much interested in contesting the
claim for tithe rent-charge. The agent for the respondent made
an affidavit in reply; but did not notice the statement, that W. F.
Greville never, from 1828 to 1837, received any payment on account
of the tithes, from J. S. Fleming, or the tenants on the lands.

Mr. *Butt* and Mr. *F. Walsh* for the respondent:

 * * The certificate is not evidence of title in the petitioner :
and, under the circumstances, no weight is to be given to the
payment of the rent-charge by the receiver of the Court.

Mr. *Moore* and Mr. *Sproule* for the petitioner :

 * * In support of the statement that the petitioner is entitled,   [339]
it appears from the certificate that there is a composition payable
to some lay impropriator ; it is not alleged that the lands are tithe
free ; nor does the respondent set up the title of any third person
as lay impropriator ; and tithe rent-charge has actually been paid

out of those lands to the petitioner. These facts combined establish the title of the petitioner.

Mr. F. Walsh, in reply :

The Court will not exercise its summary jurisdiction under this Act, unless the title of the petitioner is perfectly clear : but will leave him to his remedy by plenary suit or action at law.

THE LORD CHANCELLOR :

No doubt it is in the sound discretion of the Court whether it will appoint a receiver. This is a case of considerable difficulty. [*340] First, it is rather suggested than contended *that the certificate is void, because the name of the lay impropriator is not inserted in it. I should be slow to hold it void on that ground, for it would place parties in a great difficulty in cases in which the Commissioners had doubts as to the rights of the lay impropriator, and therefore, refused to insert his name : and though that may not have been the fact in this case, yet the question of title may have arisen in the investigation. It appears to me that no power was given to the Commissioners to settle questions of title ; and that their power was confined to the ascertainment of the amount of tithe composition, and the proportions into which it was divisible between the several owners of the tithe : and the words of the Act, with reference to the appeal given to the Lord-Lieutenant, or to the Judges of Assize, seem to point to the same conclusion.

But I am not called upon to decide that point ; for no person insists that the title in this case is concluded by the certificate, assuming it to be a valid one. I will, therefore, assume, first, that the certificate is valid, and secondly, that the title is not concluded by it ; for it cannot be held that the title of Mr. Greville is concluded by a certificate in which the name of the lay impropriator is not inserted. If Mr. Greville can show, *aliunde,* that he is the lay impropriator, the certificate has reference to him. It relates to the party, whoever he may be, who has the title.

It is stated in the affidavit of the agent of the respondent, no doubt upon information and belief merely, and at the distance of [*341] several years from the period to which the *matter relates, that the Commissioners refused to insert the name of Mr. Greville as the impropriator, because they were not satisfied he was entitled, as such, to the tithes. Now the Act of Parliament gave an appeal to any person aggrieved by anything improperly inserted or omitted

from the certificate. Here there was an omission: and Mr. Greville
might, if he had thought proper, have appealed to have his name
inserted in the certificate; but he did not do so. I must consider
that from 1823, when the certificate was made, omitting the name
of Mr. Greville as the person entitled, but stating that the lay
impropriator was entitled to a portion of the composition, no claim
whatever was made by Mr. Greville for tithe composition until
the year 1839. It is said, as some excuse for this delay, that
Mr. Greville first became entitled to the composition in 1837. His
succession to the possession fell in at that time, but his title commenced, perhaps, centuries before; and I am bound to consider
not merely what was done in 1837, or since, but on the question
whether I am to grant this summary relief, I must consider the
root of the title: how did the Grevilles acquire it; what enjoyment
had they under it; what is their proof of title; is it proved in the
ordinary way by a grant from the Crown, and a derivation under
the grant, or by mere transfers and conveyances between themselves, or by descents and actual receipt of the tithes? All that I
have on the face of this affidavit is a mere statement that the father
of Mr. Greville was entitled to these tithes, and that his son succeeded to his title in 1837. I have no doubt that if an attorney
tells his client that he is entitled to certain property, the client will
swear to it; but I cannot consider such swearing a proof of the
title. It is a circumstance, too, entitled to some weight, that the
*payments were made by a receiver of the Court, at a time when [*342]
the party who was entitled to the lands was involved in litigation.
It, therefore, is not like a payment by a party in possession of his
own property, with full notice of the nature of the claim made on
him. It can be easily imagined that, during the embarrassment
occasioned by the pendency of a litigation, a person may get a
payment of a small demand from a receiver, where he could not
have procured it from the party himself, if he had been in possession of his estate. The payment, however, is *primâ facie* evidence
of the title of the petitioner. But the facts, which have not been
denied by affidavit, that the Commissioners refused to insert
Mr. Greville's name in the certificate because of the doubt they
entertained as to the title, and that his title has been contested by
other persons in the parish, make it necessary that I should pause
before I appoint a receiver upon this summary application: for if
I grant this receiver, and there should hereafter be a default, I
must grant another; and so I should establish this title for ever.

GREVILLE
v.
FLEMING.

For how could the respondent relieve himself? I am not aware of any mode whereby he could ; for he could not try the title of the Grevilles to the tithes ; and he could not resist the order of the Court, and there is no appeal, I believe, against an order made in the case of a summary proceeding. But, however that may be, I should certainly conclude the question of title by granting this application ; whereas, by leaving the petitioner to his remedy, I shall do no} mischief : for if Mr. Greville has the title, he has the means of proving it, and can recover the rent-charge by other proceedings than by a receiver upon a petition. I should, therefore, feel much difficulty in affirming this order. I have great respect

[*343]

for the authority *by which it has been made ; but I cannot concur in it. There is quite sufficient to show that there is a doubt about the title. The respondent, no doubt, is fencing off the payment of this demand ; and, not denying that tithe rent-charge is really due, he is endeavouring to get rid of the petitioner's claim, in the hope that no other person can establish a title to the tithes. But, sitting here, I am not at liberty to take that into consideration. I must look to the title of the petitioner, and not to the object of the respondent. I think that title has not been reasonably established, so as to authorize me to exercise this jurisdiction ; and, therefore, upon the whole case, I must reverse the order.

1845.
May 8.

SIR EDWARD
SUGDEN,
L.C.

[358]

MOLESWORTH v. ROBBINS.

(2 Jo. & Lat. 358—374 ; S. C. 8 Ir. Eq. R. 1, 223.)

No one can give a lien on deeds to a solicitor of a higher nature than the interest he himself has in the deeds.

By settlement of 1780, D., seised *quasi* in fee, charged the lands with 2,500*l.* for his children. On his death, the inheritance descended upon his son R., who was also entitled to a portion of the charge. R. retained M. as his solicitor ; who, in the life-time of R., instituted a suit in his name to raise the charge. That suit having abated by the death of R., M., as the administrator of R., and the other persons entitled to the residue of the charge, instituted another suit, as co-plaintiffs, to raise its amount ; and M., as solicitor, conducted that suit for the co-plaintiffs. In the course of his professional employment, the title deeds relating to the estate and the charge came into his possession. A receiver was appointed in the suit, but no decree was obtained therein. The lands were afterwards sold under a decree in the suit of a puisne judgment creditor of D. ; and M. was ordered to bring in and lodge the title deeds, without prejudice to his lien ; which he did.

Held, that R., as owner of the inheritance, could not give M. a lien for costs on the title deeds of the estate, as against the persons entitled to the charge.

That R., as owner of a portion of the charge, could not give M. a lien on the deed creating the charge, as that deed belonged to him in common with the other persons entitled to the charge, and not to him solely.

That the lien of M. on the deeds evidencing the title of his clients to the charge, was not transferred to the sums decreed to them in respect thereof.

DONAGH M'CRAIGHT, being seised for lives renewable for ever of an undivided moiety of the lands of Loughloher, in the county of Tipperary, by indented articles of agreement, bearing date the 22nd of October, 1780, executed in contemplation of his marriage with Elizabeth Bunbury, and made between Donagh M'Craight, of the first part; Elizabeth Bunbury, of the second part; and trustees of the third part; covenanted with the trustees, that he would, immediately after the solemnization of the marriage, grant and convey unto the said trustees, their executors, *administrators, and assigns, for the term of 1,000 years, all his undivided moiety of the lands of Loughloher, to hold the same for the term of 1,000 years; upon trust, by sale or mortgage of the term, to raise the sum of 2,500*l.*, and place the same out at interest, and pay the interest thereof to Donagh M'Craight, for his life; and after his decease, in case he should leave children of the marriage, and Elizabeth Bunbury should survive him, in trust to pay her, out of the interest, a yearly sum of 60*l.*; and, subject thereto, in case Donagh M'Craight should die leaving one or more child or children of the marriage, to assign and pay over to such children, if more than one, the said sum of 2,500*l.*, in such shares and proportions as Donagh M'Craight should by deed or will appoint; and, for want of such appointment, in equal shares.

[*359]

The marriage was celebrated; and there was issue of it two children only, namely, Robert and Elizabeth M'Craight.

By settlement of the 11th of November, 1805, executed upon the marriage of Elizabeth M'Craight with William Percival, Donagh M'Craight, by virtue of the power contained in the articles of 1780 and with the consent of William Percival and Elizabeth M'Craight, appointed the sum of 1,500*l.*, part of the said sum of 2,500*l.*, to be paid to the trustees of the settlement on the day after the decease of Donagh M'Craight, with interest thereon from thenceforth; upon trust to lay out the same in the purchase of estates of inheritance, to be held to the use of Elizabeth for life, for her separate use; remainder to the use of William Percival for his life; and after his decease (in default of appointment by William Percival during *the joint lives of himself and Elizabeth M'Craight, or by Elizabeth M'Craight, if she survived him), to the

[*360]

use of the children of William Percival and his intended wife, equally to be divided between them as tenants in common, in tail general; with divers limitations over. And it was declared that, until the 1,500*l.* should be laid out in the purchase thereby directed to be made, the interest thereof should be received by such persons as should respectively be entitled to receive the rents of the lands to be purchased.

Elizabeth Percival afterwards died in the lifetime of Donagh M'Craight and of her husband, leaving one son, William B. Percival, and two daughters, the only issue of the marriage, her surviving. In 1821 William Percival obtained administration to her. He died in 1833, intestate, and without ever having exercised the power of appointment vested in him; and William B. Percival, his only son, obtained administration to him, and also administration *de bonis non* to his mother, Elizabeth Percival, otherwise M'Craight.

Donagh M'Craight died in May, 1816, without having made any further appointment of the said sum of 2,500*l.*, intestate, leaving his wife and Robert M'Craight, his only son and heir-at-law, him surviving. At the time of his decease he was much embarrassed in his circumstances, and was not possessed of any personal property, or of any real or freehold estate other than the moiety of the lands of Loughloher, which were then in possession of two creditors of his, named Robbins and Mansergh, under grants *in custodiam*. The custodees remained in possession thereof during [*361] the life of Robert M'Craight, and down to the year *1822, when they were dispossessed by the receiver of the Court, appointed in the cause of *Molesworth* v. *Robbins*.

In 1814 Robert M'Craight married Anne Bunbury, and shortly afterwards went to India, accompanied by his wife, where he died, on the 2nd of November, 1819, leaving his wife and one son, William B. Le Hunt M'Craight, his only child, him surviving. By his will, which was not executed so as to pass real estate, he gave all his property of every kind to his wife during her life; and after her decease to his son, William B. Le Hunt M'Craight. This will was not discovered until some time after the decease of Robert M'Craight.

Hickman B. Molesworth had been the agent and solicitor of Robert M'Craight; and on the 29th of June, 1821, he obtained administration to him, limited to continue and be in force only during the absence of Anne, the widow of Robert M'Craight. She died in India without having ever returned to Ireland; and the will of Robert M'Craight having been discovered and transmitted to this country, administration with the will annexed was granted to Edward Gill, a defendant in the second cause.

William B. Le Hunt M'Craight died in August, 1839, intestate, unmarried, and without issue: and upon his decease, the freehold interest in the lands of Loughloher descended upon William B. Percival, as his heir-at-law.

The cause of *Hodgens* v. *Percival* was a suit instituted by a judgment creditor of Donagh M'Craight, for an account of his real and personal assets, and for a sale. By a decree to account made in that cause, on the 3rd of February, *1835, it was, amongst other things, referred to the Master to inquire whether Robert M'Craight was, at the time of the death of Donagh M'Craight, entitled to any and what share of the sum of 2,500*l.* charged by the marriage settlement of October, 1780; and whether any and what sum remained due to the personal representative of Robert M'Craight on foot thereof. And it was further ordered, that the defendant, Hickman B. Molesworth, should bring in and lodge in the office of the Master, but without prejudice to whatever lien he might have thereon (if any he had), all such deeds, documents, and muniments of title, in his power or possession, relating to the lands and premises in the pleadings mentioned, and all such vouchers in his possession relating to the demands of the creditors of Donagh M'Craight, as the Master should direct or deem proper or necessary to have lodged for the purpose of taking the accounts or answering the inquiries directed by the decree. [*362]

The Master made his report, dated the 23rd of December, 1840, and thereby found that there was due to Edward Gill, as administrator of Robert M'Craight, on foot of one moiety of the unappointed sum of 1,000*l.*, part of the said sum of 2,500*l.*, the principal sum of 500*l.*, late currency, together with an arrear of interest thereon, amounting in the whole to 844*l.* 5*s.* 7*d.*; and that the same was so due to him in trust for the personal representative of William B. Le Hunt M'Craight, who, as sole next of kin of Robert M'Craight, was entitled thereto: and that there was due to William B. Percival, as administrator *de bonis non* of his mother, Elizabeth Percival, the like sum of 844*l.* 5*s.* 7*d.*, on foot of the other moiety of the said unappointed sum: and that the said sum of 2,500*l.* was the first charge on the lands.

The Master further reported, that Hickman B. Molesworth had, [363]

in obedience to the decree, lodged in his office the several title
deeds, documents, and vouchers specified in the schedule; amongst
which were the articles of the 22nd of October, 1780, and the
settlement of the 11th of November, 1805; and that he so lodged
them subject to the lien which he claimed to have on them, and on
the said charge of 2,500l., under the following circumstances, viz.:

Robert M'Craight in April, 1814, executed a general power of
attorney to Hickman B. Molesworth, authorizing him and empowering him to act for him in all matters; and shortly afterwards went
to India, where he died.

At the decease of Donagh M'Craight, Robbins was in possession
of the rents of part of the lands, as custodee; and the head rent
of the lands having been permitted to run into arrear, the head
landlord brought an ejectment for non-payment of rent; and also
served a notice requiring the tenants thereof to renew the lease,
some of the lives having dropped; and Hickman B. Molesworth,
as agent of Robert M'Craight, who, as heir-at-law of Donagh
M'Craight, was seised of one moiety of the lands of Loughloher,
procured from the occupying tenants of the lands, and from
Thomas M'Craight, the owner of the other moiety, the funds
necessary for the payment of the renewal fines and the arrears of
head rent; by means of which exertions the renewal was obtained,
and the interest of Robert M'Craight in the lands was preserved.

Hickman B. Molesworth also, as the agent and solicitor of Robert
M'Craight, and acting under the power of attorney, on the 19th of
[*364]   April, 1817, filed a bill in this *Court, in the name and on behalf
of Robert M'Craight, against Robbins, Mansergh, and others,
asserting and with the object of establishing the right of Robert
M'Craight to a portion of the said sum of 2,500l., and in order to
preserve his interest in the lands against Robbins and Mansergh;
and, accordingly, praying for a receiver over the lands.   A receiver
was appointed in that suit; but before any effectual proceeding was
had in the cause, Robert M'Craight died, and the suit abated.

After the decease of Robert M'Craight, Hickman B. Molesworth,
claiming as his administrator to be entitled to a share of the charge
of 2,500l., and William Percival, in his own right, and as the
administrator of his wife, Elizabeth, and their children, who were
then minors (being the several persons interested in the charge),
filed their bill in the year 1821, in this Court, against Robbins and
others, for the purpose of raising the said charge; and Hickman
B. Molesworth conducted that cause as solicitor on behalf of

himself and the other plaintiffs, until the 28th of November, 1828, when he ceased to act as solicitor therein; and from thenceforth William M'Dermott acted as solicitor for the plaintiffs in that suit. In that cause an order for the appointment of a receiver was made on the 30th of July, 1822; the receiver was subsequently appointed; and was, in 1833, extended to the second cause; and the rents brought in by him in the first cause, which were considerable, were transferred to the credit of both causes.

Under these circumstances, Hickman B. Molesworth claimed the several liens after mentioned, viz: (1) as against Edward Gill, as administrator of Robert M'Craight, to a *lien upon the several deeds and documents so lodged by him, and upon the sum reported to Edward Gill as such administrator, on foot of Robert M'Craight's share of the charge of 2,500*l.*, for the expenses incurred by him in obtaining the letters of limited administration of the estate and effects of Robert M'Craight; which amounted to 27*l.* 5*s.* 1*d.*: (2) and to a like lien for his costs incurred in the cause of *M'Craight* v. *Robbins*, instituted in the life-time of Robert M'Craight, as before mentioned; which amounted to 128*l.* 15*s.* 8*d.*: (3) and he further claimed to be entitled, not only as against Edward Gill, as such administrator, to a lien on the said several deeds and documents, and on the sum reported due to him, on foot of Robert M'Craight's share of the charge of 2,500*l.*, but also as against the defendant, William B. Percival, as administrator of his father, William Percival, and also as administrator *de bonis non* of his mother, Elizabeth, to a lien not only upon the said deeds and documents, but also upon the sum reported due to William B. Percival, as such administrator of his father, on foot of his father's interest in the charge of 2,500*l.*, and upon the sum reported due to William B. Percival, as administrator *de bonis non* of his mother, on foot of her interest in the said charge, for the costs incurred by him, Hickman B. Molesworth, and afterwards by William M'Dermott, in and about the prosecution and conduct of the suit instituted in the year 1821, by Hickman B. Molesworth, William Percival, and the minor children of William Percival; which costs amounted to 243*l.* 11*s.* 3*d.*

The Master reported that he had not taken on himself to decide, and submitted to the Court whether Hickman B. Molesworth was entitled either for the expenses incurred by him in obtaining the said limited administration to Robert *M'Craight, or for any part of the costs incurred by or on behalf of the plaintiffs in the said

[*365]

[*366]

several causes, to the several liens so claimed by him in respect
thereof, or any of said last-mentioned liens against the parties
against whom he so claimed the same, or against any of them:
and if so, in what proportions the parties liable to or bound by
such liens or any of them were so liable respectively.

By decree of the 22nd of February, 1841, the report was confirmed; and the consideration of the special points submitted by
the Master, as to the right of the defendant, Hickman B. Molesworth, to the several liens mentioned in the report, was reserved;
with liberty to apply.

The lands having been sold under the decree, it was, by an order
of the 12th of December, 1843, referred to the Master to allocate
the funds in Bank to the credit of these causes, according to the
rights of the parties under the decree of 1841; said order to be
without prejudice to the rights of Hickman B. Molesworth, as
reserved by that decree. The Master made his report, dated the
31st of January, 1845; and thereby allocated the funds in Court
in payment, *inter alia*, of the sums reported due to Edward Gill
and William B. Percival, and the several persons entitled to portions
of the charge of 2,500*l.*

The plaintiff in the second cause moved at the Rolls, that the
funds in Court should be paid out and transferred, pursuant to the
allocation report; and that the title deeds lodged in Court should
be handed over to the purchaser: and a cross-application was
made by Robert Molesworth, the executor of Hickman B. Molesworth, who had died, that so much of the stock as had been

[*367] allocated to Edward *Gill, as should be equivalent to the costs of
procuring the aforesaid renewal of the lands (which the Master had
reported that Hickman B. Molesworth was entitled to), and the
costs of procuring the limited administration to Robert M'Craight,
and the costs in the cause of *M'Craight* v. *Robbins*, amounting
together to the sum of 227*l.* 0*s.* 11*d.*; and also that so much of
the funds allocated to Edward Gill and to William B. Percival, as
administrator of his father and administrator *de bonis non* of his
mother, as should be equivalent to the sum of 243*l.* 11*s.* 3*d.*, the
costs in the cause of *Molesworth*, administrator of M'Craight and
Percival, v. *Robbins*, should be transferred to the said Robert
Molesworth.

The MASTER OF THE ROLLS made an order pursuant to the cross-
application of Robert Molesworth, as far as it related to the costs
of the renewal, and of obtaining the limited administration to

Robert M'Craight, but refused the rest of the application (1); and directed that the residue of the stock allocated to Edward Gill should be transferred to credit of the second cause, and *The matter of Calders*, minors; and that the stock allocated to William B. Percival should be transferred to the credit of the cause of *Atkins* v. *Percival*: and ordered that the title deeds should be delivered to the purchaser.

Robert Molesworth now moved, by way of appeal from the order of the MASTER OF THE ROLLS, that the Accountant-General should transfer to him so much of the Government stock allocated to Edward Gill, and by said order directed to be transferred to the credit of the second cause and *The matter of Calders*, minors, as would be equivalent to the *sum of 128*l*. 15*s*. 8*d*., the costs in *M'Craight* v. *Robbins*; and should also transfer to him so much of the Government stock allocated to Edward Gill and to William B. Percival, as administrator of his father and administrator *de bonis non* of his mother, and by said order directed to be transferred respectively to the credit of the second cause and *The matter of Calders*, minors, and the cause of *Atkins* v. *Percival*, as would be equivalent to the sum of 243*l*. 11*s*. 8*d*., the costs of the first cause; or that said order might be reversed so far as related to said transfers, and be varied by directing that Edward Gill and William B. Percival might be restrained from setting up the Statute of Limitations as a defence to any proceedings which might be taken by Robert Molesworth, or the solicitor for the plaintiffs in the first cause, for the recovery of the said demands, further than they might have done at the date of the final decree in the second cause: or that the proof of the demand of Hickman B. Molesworth, made in the second cause against William B. Percival, might be transferred to the cause of *Atkins* v. *Percival*.

[*368]

Mr. Francis Fitzgerald and *Mr. Monahan*, for Robert Molesworth, distinguished this case from *Bozon* v. *Bolland* (2) and *Blunden* v. *Desart* (3), as in those cases the solicitor voluntarily produced the deeds, and then actively sought to enforce his general lien against the fund realized thereby: whereas, in the present case, Mr. Molesworth produced the deeds under the compulsion of the decree of the Court, which expressly saved his lien on them, if any he had; and, therefore, the case was to be considered as if the deeds

(1) 8 Ir. Eq. Rep. 1.   (3) 54 R. R. 753 (2 Dr. & War. 405).
(2) 48 R. R. 121 (4 My. & Cr. 354).

were still in his possession, and the parties against whom he
claimed his lien were now seeking to *have them transferred to the
purchaser, which was resisted by him.   *   *   And they relied on
Worrall v. *Johnson* (1), as establishing that, under the circumstances
of the case, the lien on the deeds was transferred to the fund
recovered.

   Mr. Deasy for Edward Gill.

   Mr. Serjt. Warren and *Mr. Wall* for Atkins and wife.

   Mr. Hughes and *Mr. Mara* for the next of kin of William B. Le
Hunt M'Craight.

   Mr. Monahan, in reply, said, that, at all events, Mr. Molesworth,
as one of the co-plaintiffs in the cause of *Molesworth* v. *Robbins*, was
entitled to his costs in that cause out of the funds realized by the
receiver in it; which had been since transferred to the credit of
both causes, and paid out, pursuant to the decree of 1841, to the
parties, on account of their costs.

[370]   THE LORD CHANCELLOR:

   This case proves what I have always thought, that the question
of lien of a solicitor on deeds ought to be decided at the earliest
opportunity. As this case was opened before me, it was a mere
question of lien; not of the right of Mr. Molesworth, as one of the
plaintiffs in the first cause, to the costs in that cause, but a question
of his lien for those costs as the solicitor of Robert M'Craight. It
was not attempted to prove first that he had a lien upon the fund,
and therefore that the deeds could not be taken from him; but it
was argued that the deeds could not be taken from him, on the
ground that he had a lien on them. The nature of a solicitor's
lien is now well understood; and it does not appear to be of the
nature of a charge upon the fund. When Mr. Molesworth advanced
his money and saved the estate from being evicted by the landlord,
he obtained an actual right to a charge on the property to that
extent; not simply on the deeds, but upon the estate itself, and
against every person interested in it; and that right he might
enforce by suit in equity: whereas the solicitor's lien on deeds is
simply a right to withhold them. The solicitor could not file a bill
to enforce such a lien; he could only withhold the deeds, so as to

                    (1) 22 R. R. 106 (2 J. & W. 214).

prevent the party entitled from having the benefit of them. Now, observe what would be the consequence of allowing the claim of Mr. Molesworth in this case. Robert M'Craight was interested in the estate in two different rights : First, he was entitled to the *quasi* fee simple of the estate ; secondly, he was entitled to a portion of a sum of 2,500*l.*, which was the first charge on the estate : and there being a number of other incumbrances upon the estate, he elected to claim as an incumbrancer, the estate itself not being of sufficient value to pay the charges on it. But that *act could not divest him of his title as owner of the inheritance, holding the title deeds. Could he either withhold the estate itself, or the deeds, from the person entitled to the incumbrance, which had been charged on the property by those under whom he derived the estate ? The moment the charge was created, the covenant which created it and bound the estate, equally bound the deeds ; and the persons entitled to the charge had a right to enforce the payment of it against the inheritance and the inheritor holding the deeds, which were the evidence of the title to the estate so charged. Robert M'Craight had a common, not a superior right, with the persons entitled to the residue of the charge ; and those persons had altogether a right against himself as inheritor of the estate. The claim to the title deeds of the estate was by all the persons entitled to the charge against one of them, who was himself entitled to the estate charged. He could not, in his separate character of owner of the estate, withhold the deeds from the persons entitled to the charge ; then, could he, as being entitled to a portion of the charge, and also to the inheritance, withhold them ? How was the charge to be enforced but by sale and conveyance of the lands with the title deeds ? No man can give a lien to a solicitor, of a higher nature than the interest he himself has in the deeds ; and as he himsel must have delivered over the deeds to the persons entitled in common with himself to the charge, so must Mr. Molesworth. Therefore, I do not think that the decision of the MASTER OF THE ROLLS is faulty, as regards the rights of the claimants under the decree ; and I am of opinion that Mr. Molesworth had not the right which he claims. But then, it was said that Mr. Molesworth had a lien on the deeds, in respect of the right which Robert M'Craight had to deposit them, inasmuch as he was entitled to a portion of the charge of 2,500*l.* But that is the fallacy. He had no such right. *Robert M'Craight had a right to charge his portion of the 2,500*l.* ; but he had no right to charge the deeds, which did

not belong to him alone, but to himself in common with others,
and which he could not withhold from the class of persons entitled
to them.   Upon that simple ground, I think the decision is right.
The form of the notice is, in itself, fatal to this argument; for it
does not object to the deeds being handed over to the purchaser:
and Mr. Molesworth could not object to their being delivered to
him, for he was plaintiff as well as solicitor, engaged in a suit to
raise this charge, and for the sale of this very estate; and how
could he withhold those deeds from the purchaser in another cause,
in which he was a party defendant, and which was instituted
because he did not prosecute his suit, when he himself, by his own
bill, prayed such relief as would have compelled him to produce
these deeds? The form of the notice is, therefore, fatal to the
application; for I am not asked to reverse that part of the
order which directs the deeds to be given to the purchaser; but I
am required to transfer the lien from the deeds to the fund decreed
to be paid to Robert M'Craight.   Now, this Court will not wantonly
interfere with the lien of a solicitor, and if he really has a lien, it
will not compel him to part with the deeds, until the persons
wanting them pay him the money secured by the lien.   But the
circumstance of his being a plaintiff in the first cause relieves the
case of any difficulty in this respect.   It seems to me, therefore,
that the order of the MASTER OF THE ROLLS is right.

JOYCE *v.* DE MOLEYNS (1).

(2 Jo. & Lat. 374—379; S. C. 8 Ir. Eq. R. 215.)

A purchase for a valuable consideration, without notice, is a defence as
well against a legal as an equitable title.

THE Hon. Frederick Mullins, by his will, dated the 13th of June,
1825, devised all his right, title, and interest in the impropriate
tithes of Kilcolman, to his second son, William, for his life, with
divers limitations over to his issue; and died in 1832.

At the time of making his will, the testator was entitled to an
equitable estate in fee simple in the tithes of Kilcolman: the legal
estate in fee was conveyed to him by indenture of the 12th of
December, 1827.

Upon the decease of the Hon. Frederick Mullins, administration,

(1) *Ind Coope & Co.* v. *Emmerson* (1887) 12 App. Ca. 300, 56 L. J. Ch. 989, 56
L. T. 778.

with his will annexed, was granted to his eldest son and heir-at-law, JOYCE
v.
DE MOLEYNS. Frederick William Mullins ; who, with his brothers and sisters, afterwards, by Royal license, assumed the surname of De Moleyns. He obtained possession of the title deeds of several of the estates, the property of his father ; and, amongst others, of the conveyance *of the 12th of December, 1827; and in the month of October, 1840,   [*375] he applied to Sir E. Antrobus and Edward Majoribanks, bankers in London, to advance him a sum of 1,000*l.* ; which they accordingly did, upon the security of the promissory note of Frederick William De Moleyns, and upon his depositing with them the deed of the 12th of December, 1827, by way of equitable mortgage.   This deposit was made without the knowledge of William De Moleyns, who, from the decease of the testator, had been in possession of the impropriate tithes of Kilcolman, and who had frequently applied to Frederick William De Moleyns for the deed, but could not obtain it.

In 1842, Sir E. Antrobus and Edward Majoribanks filed their bill against Frederick William De Moleyns alone, for a sale of the impropriate tithes of Kilcolman, and for payment of the mortgage debt out of the produce of the sale.   A final decree for a sale was pronounced in that cause, in March, 1844.

The present bill was filed in 1843, by John Joyce, administrator of James Parker, a bond creditor of the Hon. Frederick Mullins, for an account and administration of his real and personal estate. He charged by his bill, that the deposit of the deed conveying the tithes to the Hon. Frederick Mullins could not give any title to Sir E. Antrobus and Edward Majoribanks as against the tithes or the deed, inasmuch as Frederick William De Moleyns had no title either to the tithes or the deed, and had no authority to deposit the same : and prayed that Sir E. Antrobus and Edward Majoribanks might be decreed to deliver up any deed in their possession, relating to the title to the impropriate tithes, discharged from any claim thereupon.

Sir E. Antrobus and Edward Majoribanks, by their answer, said,   [376] that at the time they made the advance to Frederick William De Moleyns, he represented that he was entitled to the impropriate tithes as the heir-at-law of his father ; and they insisted that they were purchasers for valuable consideration without notice of the will of the Hon. Frederick Mullins, or of the title of any person claiming thereunder the tithes in question, or of the demands of the plaintiff: and submitted that the bill should either be dismissed against them, or that the plaintiff should redeem them.

JOYCE
v.
DE MOLEYNS.

There was no evidence of notice.

Mr. Pigot, Mr. Deasy, and Mr. D. Lane, for the plaintiff.

Mr. Brooks and Mr. S. Miller for Sir E. Antrobus and Edward
    Majoribanks :

Although it appears that Frederick William De Moleyns had no
title to the tithes, and that the mortgagees have no defence, at law,
to an action for the deed, yet, being purchasers without notice, a
court of equity will not order them to deliver up the deeds : Jerrard
v. Saunders (1); Senhouse v. Earl (2) ; Hoare v. Parker (3); Sweet v.
Southcote (4); Plumb v. Fluitt (5). The bill ought, therefore, to be
dismissed.

Mr. Deasy, in reply :

[*377]

The bankers took the equitable mortgage from a person who was
not then nor ever had been in possession of the *tithes. But,
admitting that they are equitable mortgagees, the plaintiff is
entitled to keep them before the Court ; under the decree in the
cause they will get whatever they are entitled to.

THE LORD CHANCELLOR :

In this case, the question as to the right of a person claiming as
a purchaser without notice to hold title deeds, in respect of which
the person depositing them had no interest in the estate, seems
to arise. The heir-at-law of the person entitled to the tithes in
question acquired possession of the title deeds ; and he obtained an
advance of 1,000l. from certain bankers in London, upon a deposit
of the deeds with them. The bona fides of that transaction is not
impeached. The bankers have been made defendants in this suit ;
and they swear that they advanced their money without notice,
and claim to retain possession of the deeds as purchasers for value
without notice.

It is clear that the persons entitled to the tithes may maintain
trover for the deeds. There is no question as to their title to
recover at law ; but I apprehend that the defence of a purchase
for value without notice is a shield as well against a legal as an
equitable title. There has been a considerable difference of opinion

(1) 2 Ves. Jr. 454.   (4) 2 Br. C. C. 66.
(2) 2 Ves. 450.   (5) 3 R. R. 605 (2 Anst. 432).
(3) 1 Cox, 224.

upon the subject amongst Judges: I must decide the question for myself; and I have always considered the true rule to be that which I have stated. Therefore, I think that the mere circumstance that this is a legal right, is not a bar to the defence set up, if in other respects it is a good defence. That it is a good defence cannot be denied. Suppose a tenant for life under a will, with remainder over; and that the tenant for life, *being the heir-at-law of the [*378] testator, conveys the inheritance to a purchaser without notice, the remainder-man cannot have any relief in equity against the purchaser. He must establish his title, outside of this Court, as well as he can. It is the same with respect to title deeds. Deeds are chattels; and, where no adverse claimant interferes, the person entitled to the estate is entitled to the deeds. But the person who has possession of the deeds may deal with them as with any other chattels, subject to the rights of those who are interested in them. Here a person obtains the possession of title deeds, having no title to the estate; another person advances money to him upon the security of a deposit of the deeds. The rule, therefore, comes into operation (for it applies equally to real estate and to chattels), that if a man advance money, *bonâ fide* and without notice of the infirmity of the title of the seller, he will be protected in this Court, and the parties having title must seek relief elsewhere. It may be true that there is no case in terms applying that rule to the deposit of title deeds; but I think that Lord ELDON, in a case which came before him, expressed an opinion that the defence was a good one in such a case.

In answer to the objection made by the defendants, it is urged, that they are equitable mortgagees, and brought before the Court in that character; and that the Master will, under the decree, report on their title; and so they may, under the decree, have what is their right. That, however, is merely begging the question; for if their title as purchasers for value enables them to say that the bill must be dismissed as against them, then the plaintiff offers them nothing; for he says that the person who pledged the deeds had no interest of any kind in the estate: therefore, *though the plaintiff [*379] treats them as equitable mortgagees of the estate, yet at the hearing he denies them that character; and they cannot fill the character of equitable mortgagees of the deeds, for the person depositing them had no title. The defendants, therefore, use the possession of the deeds, as they have a right to do, as a shield to protect them against the plaintiffs: they can make no use of the deeds themselves; they

JOYCE
v.
DE MOLEYNS.

cannot maintain possession of them against the true owner; but in this Court they have a right to say that they ought not to be compelled to deliver them up, as they obtained them *bonâ fide* and without notice.   The bill must, therefore, be dismissed against them with costs.

April 25.

THE LORD CHANCELLOR:

I find that Lord ELDON decided the very point in this case, in *Wallwyn* v. *Lee* (1).   There the plaintiff was in possession of the estate, and filed his bill for the delivery of the title deeds, against the defendant, a mortgagee of a tenant for life of the estate, who pleaded that he was a purchaser for value, without notice.   There was a question in that case, whether the plea was available by a purchaser who had not been put into possession of the estate: but in this case possession could not be given, for tithes are an incorporeal hereditament.   I therefore think that the answer of the defendants contains sufficient averments.

In *Bernard* v. *Drought* (2), Sir A. HART extended the doctrine to the case of a solicitor's lien: but in *Smith* v. *Chichester* (3) I considered that he had carried it too far.   The decree I made is therefore to stand.

————

1845.
May 26.

SIR EDWARD
SUGDEN,
L.C.

[393]

HAMILTON *v.* KIRWAN.

(2 Jo. & Lat. 393—403; S. C. 8 Ir. Eq. R. 278.)

Strong suspicion that an appointment by a father to his son was for the benefit of the father, and a fraud upon the power of appointment, is not sufficient to avoid the transaction as against a mortgagee who was not shown to have any actual notice or ground for suspecting that the appointment was for the benefit of the father.

JAMES HAMILTON being seised and possessed of several houses and premises in the city of Dublin, held under leases for lives renewable for ever, and for terms of years, subject to rent, by indenture of the 21st of November, 1828, in consideration of love and affection, conveyed the same to his son, George Hamilton, his heirs, executors, &c., upon trust, in the first place, out of the rents and profits, to pay the head-rents and taxes, and other outgoings thereof; and then to pay an annuity of 52*l.* sterling to James Hamilton, the younger, the son of the grantor, during his life; and after his decease, in case he should leave lawful issue him

(1) 7 R. R. 142 (9 Ves. 24).   (3) 59 R. R. 746 (2 Dr. & War. 393).
(2) 1 Moll. 38.

surviving, to pay said annuity to such issue, as therein directed; and after payment of the head-rents and annuity and other out-goings, upon trust to pay and apply the surplus of the rents and profits to the support and maintenance of James Hamilton the elder, and for and towards the maintenance and education of his grandchildren, the children of his son, the said George Hamilton, until they should attain their respective ages of twenty-one years, or be married, when the same was to be divided and distributed between and amongst such of the said last-mentioned children as should live, in the manner thereinafter directed. And it was declared that in case James Hamilton, the younger, should die without lawful issue, then the annuity thereby provided for him should be added to the fund provided for the children of George Hamilton, who should live to attain the age of twenty-one years or be married: the entire of such fund as should be so created, to *be distributed and divided between and amongst them in such shares and proportions as George Hamilton should by deed or will appoint; and in default of such appointment, then upon trust for the issue of George Hamilton in equal shares and proportions.

[*394]

James Hamilton, the elder, died in 1842. The children of George Hamilton were the Rev. James Hamilton, George John Hamilton, and the plaintiffs, Charlotte, Frederick, and Mary Anne Hamilton.

The plaintiffs by their bill stated, that George Hamilton, in the year 1836, became involved in difficulties, and indebted to several persons, and, amongst others, to Messrs. Thomas and John Fottrell, in a sum of 284*l.*, which was secured by bills of exchange accepted by him; and being so indebted, he applied to John Fottrell to assist him in raising a sum of money by mortgage, to meet the pressing demands against him. That John Fottrell introduced him to his son, George Drevar Fottrell, a solicitor, who proposed to procure an advance of money for George Hamilton on a mortgage of the said lands and premises. That George Hamilton had been theretofore in the habit of consulting Joseph Maxwell as his solicitor, and went to him and told him of such proposal, when Maxwell informed him that he had no title to the premises, the same being vested in him solely as trustee; whereupon George Hamilton returned to George D. Fottrell, and having given him the deeds relating to the premises, Fottrell devised a plan for depriving the plaintiffs, who were then all under age, of their rights and shares of the said property, and for enabling George

Hamilton to raise money on it; and accordingly proposed that if George Hamilton would execute *an appointment under the deed of 1828, to one of his sons, and then procure such son to execute a mortgage of the property so appointed, purporting to be a mortgage in consideration of money paid to such son, he would procure Mrs. Bridget Fry, a relative of his own, to advance the money to George Hamilton on such security. That George John Hamilton, a son of George Hamilton, was then about twenty-seven years of age; and that Fottrell proposed that the intended appointment should be made to him, and that he should then execute the intended mortgage: and that George John Hamilton, who then was a clerk in his father's business, was induced to join in the plan solely for the purpose of getting the money for his father; he being wholly under his influence, and being assured by Fottrell that the intended plan for raising the money was perfectly legal.

By indenture of the 30th of July, 1836, after reciting the settlement of November, 1828, but not stating that the children of George Hamilton had any present beneficial interest thereunder for their maintenance and education, George Hamilton appointed to his son, George John Hamilton, certain parts of the settled property, which in fact constituted almost the entire of it. And by an indenture of mortgage of the 6th of August, 1836, made between George Hamilton, of the first part; George John Hamilton, of the second part; James Hamilton, the annuitant, of the third part; and Bridget Fry, of the fourth part; after reciting the deed of appointment of the 30th of July, 1836; that George John Hamilton had applied to Bridget Fry for a loan of 800*l.*, to be secured by mortgage on the premises so appointed to him; that Bridget Fry had consented to advance said sum on the terms aforesaid; and that James Hamilton had agreed to become an

executing party *thereto, in order that Bridget Fry should hold the premises discharged from the payment of his annuity; it was witnessed that, in consideration of the sum of five shillings paid to George Hamilton, and of 800*l.* paid to George John Hamilton, and of five shillings paid to James Hamilton, they, the said George Hamilton, George John Hamilton, and James Hamilton, according to their several estates and interests therein, conveyed the said lands to Bridget Fry, her heirs, executors, &c., subject to redemption upon payment of the sum of 800*l.* as therein mentioned.

It appeared that both these deeds were prepared by George D. Fottrell, and that they were perused by Mr. Maxwell. The execution

of the deed of appointment was attested by Mr. Fottrell and
Mr. Maxwell; that of the mortgage was attested by Mr. Maxwell.
It also appeared that the draft deed of mortgage, which had been
perused by Mr. Maxwell, was dated in July, 1836. Contempo-
raneously with the mortgage, George Hamilton and George John
Hamilton executed their joint and several bond to Mrs. Fry, conditioned for the payment of the sum of 800l., with interest; and
Mrs. Fry wrote a letter to George Hamilton, dated the 6th of
August, 1836, in these terms: " SIR, I acknowledge that it was
agreed between us, previous to you and your son, George John
Hamilton, executing the deed of mortgage to me for 800l., and
which is counter-secured by you and your son's bond to me for
that amount, that I would not call in the principal money for three
years, provided the interest shall be regularly paid every half-year,
or within ten days after each gale shall become due." No judgment was entered on the bond. The mortgage had a receipt for
the 800l. endorsed on it, signed by George John Hamilton, and
witnessed by Mr. Maxwell. There *was no direct evidence to
whom the money was paid. The bill charged that it was paid to
George Hamilton, and that he deposited 789l., part of it, in the
Hibernian Bank, in his own name; and evidence was given that
on the 12th of August, 1836, a sum of 789l. was paid (but by
whom, it did not appear) into the Hibernian Bank to the credit of
George Hamilton.

[*397]

In September, 1838, George Hamilton became a bankrupt; and
upon an application by George John Hamilton to prove for the
sum of 800l. under the commission, his Honour, the Bankrupt
Commissioner, expressed an opinion that the transaction of 1836
was a fraud upon the power; and he refused to allow the proof,
but directed the assignee to retain the amount of the dividend on
the 800l. until further order.

James Hamilton died in 1842, without issue; and Bridget Fry
died in June, 1840, and appointed James Kirwan and Edmond
Mooney her executors, who proved her will, and in November,
1842, filed their bill to foreclose the mortgage; upon which they,
in December, 1843, obtained a decree *pro confesso*.

George Hamilton had not executed any other appointment of
the trust property.

The bill, which was filed against James Kirwan and Edmond
Mooney, George Drevar Fottrell, George Hamilton, George John
Hamilton, and others, prayed that the deed of appointment of the

HAMILTON
v.
KIRWAN
[*398]

30th of July, 1836, might be declared null and void as to the plaintiffs; and that George Hamilton might be decreed to make an appointment to the plaintiffs *of three-fifth parts or shares of the premises comprised in the settlement of November, 1823, or that the Court might make distribution thereof, according to the rules of law and equity, and the rights of the parties; and that the mortgage of the 6th of August, 1836, might be declared null and void, so far as it purported to affect the shares of the plaintiffs; and that the executors of Bridget Fry might be restrained from proceeding to sell so much of the premises as the plaintiffs were entitled to; and that George D. Fottrell, and such other of the defendants as were liable thereto, might be decreed to pay all the costs of the suit.

The plaintiffs did not give any evidence in support of the statements in the bill, that the transaction was, in its inception, a loan to George Hamilton, or as to the plan thereby charged to have been devised by George D. Fottrell; and at the hearing they consented that the bill should be dismissed as against him. The defendants did not examine any witnesses.

Mr. Moore, Mr. Martley, and *Mr. Haig,* for the plaintiffs.

Mr. J. J. Murphy and *Mr. Wall* for the defendants, Kirwan and Mooney.

Mr. J. Plunkett for the Rev. J. Hamilton.

Mr. I. O'Callaghan for George D. Fottrell.

M'Queen v. *Farquhar* (1), *Palmer* v. *Wheeler* (2), and 2 Sugd. on Powers, 192, were referred to.

[399] THE LORD CHANCELLOR:

This bill is filed to impeach a mortgage granted to Mrs. Fry, on the ground that it arose out of an improper agreement between a father and his son. Upon the face of the instruments,—the deed of appointment and the mortgage,—there is nothing to convey to the mind that there was any improper dealing between the parties. It is a regular appointment by the father to his son, no doubt, of a considerable portion of the estate; but no question has been raised upon the doctrine of illusory appointments, nor

(1) 8 R. R. 212 (11 Ves. 467).   (2) 12 R. R. 60 (2 B. & Beat. 18).

could it be without reference to the provisions made for the other children. The execution of that appointment was witnessed by Mr. Maxwell, who, I must consider, was the solicitor of the family. So far the transaction appears to have been regular, and to have been entered into with the approbation of the family solicitor. The execution is also attested by Fottrell, the solicitor for Mrs Fry. The mortgage also is perfectly regular in its form and execution.

It is clear that the son might have effectually mortgaged the estate the day after the appointment, provided he raised the money *bonâ fide* for himself. Then as to the knowledge of the mortgagee in this respect: the mortgage recites an application by the son himself, for the money; and the whole of the money is stated to have been paid to him; and throughout the transaction it appears to be that of a mortgagee dealing with the son; and there is endorsed on the deed a receipt for 800*l.*, signed by the son, and witnessed by Maxwell. Therefore, Maxwell could not now be heard to say that this was an improper transaction. It is not asserted that Mrs. Fry herself knew of any underhand agreement *between the father and son; if she is to be visited with loss, it must be by the doctrine of constructive notice, upon the ground that Fottrell had notice of such an agreement. Before I examine it on that ground, I would observe, that Fottrell being charged with the fraud and made a defendant in the cause, and Mrs. Fry being charged with the consequences of that fraud, but no attempt being made to bring the fraud home to her except by the doctrine of constructive notice, the bill is, by consent of the plaintiffs, dismissed against Fottrell without costs. So that the person against whom the fraud is charged, is dismissed; and the other person, against whom it is not charged, is said to be still liable. If fraud had been proved against Fottrell, relief might have been had against him; and that relief would have afforded the strongest ground to visit Mrs. Fry with the consequence of notice of the fraud.

That there is a suspicion of fraud in this case, no person can deny who understands the nature of the transaction. The drafts of the appointment and mortgage are produced, both prepared by the mortgagee's solicitor. Unless the appointment was made for the purpose of the mortgage, that is not a probable transaction. But it cannot be argued, that because the appointment was made with the view of the son raising money by mortgage, therefore the

[*400]

HAMILTON
v.
KIRWAN.

[*401]

[402]

mortgage is invalid. The circumstance, in itself, amounts to nothing: it would have been important, if the parties had gone further and connected it with other matters: but when I find Maxwell attesting the execution of the mortgage, whatever little weight might be due to that circumstance is entirely done away with. In the draft of the mortgage the date is altered. That is not entitled to any weight, for I do not find any alteration in the date of the deed of appointment, which *must have been intended to be executed at an earlier date than the mortgage. Then it is objected that the father joined in the deed of mortgage. I think that was regular. The elder brother of the father, who had an annuity under the settlement charged on these lands, joined in the mortgage, and gave priority to it: the father had obtained a renewal of the lease under which the lands were held, and thereby became a trustee of the legal estate for the persons entitled: he was the proper person to take the renewal; it was, consequently, necessary that he should join in transferring the legal estate to the mortgagee. The way to try the matter is this: supposing this were a *bonâ fide* transaction, would the deed have been otherwise prepared? Clearly not. It would have been prepared just as it now stands. I cannot, therefore, attach any weight to these circumstances. It is then urged, that the father joined in the bond and warrant of attorney with the son, and that that circumstance casts great suspicion on the whole transaction. It certainly has more weight with me than any other circumstance in the case; for it is not noticed in the mortgage, which takes notice of the bond of the son, but not of that of the father, or that he was a co-obligor with his son. It looks as if the parties desired to keep out of view the fact of the father having joined in the bond. But it amounts to nothing more than a suspicion, although I think it is suspicious. So the letter addressed by the mortgagee to the father shows that the father was considered as more than a surety; but still that is consistent with this being a *bonâ fide* transaction; for, the son being a young man, nothing is more natural than that his father should take part in the transaction. Nevertheless, both those circumstances do constitute a shade of suspicion.

Then the case stands thus: the plaintiffs having undertaken to prove that there was a corrupt agreement between the father and son, have failed in doing so. They thought they should make their case stronger by showing that the father was in embarrassed circumstances; they have alleged it, but have failed to prove it.

They have not, therefore, laid a ground for imputing fraud; and they have wholly failed in proving payment of the money to the father. I must consider that the money reached the hands of the son alone; what was done afterwards with it I know not; and I am not at liberty, upon mere suspicion, to do so dangerous a thing as to impeach the title of a *bonâ fide* mortgagee without notice. In *M'Queen* v. *Farquhar* (1) the question did not arise between the immediate parties. Lord ELDON there observes: "I should very reluctantly lay down, that notice from opinions in an abstract, or anything that appears upon a deed, that there may by possibility be reason to suspect what I cannot know, and may not be true, that the title is bad, is such a notice as would affect a purchaser." He was there speaking of a transaction of a different nature; here the mortgagee was an actor; but the same doctrine, to a certain extent, must apply to this case. I may hold an actor more strongly to proof of the *bona fides*; but there is no ground shown why Mrs. Fry, with her money in her hand, should advance it except upon a good title. She was not a connexion of the family, and had no advantage beyond that of a common mortgagee. I must, therefore, dismiss the bill as against her; and the only question is, as to the costs.

If I were quite satisfied that there was no foundation for the bill, I should dismiss it with costs: but I am bound to *say, that there is so much of suspicion in the case as fairly justified the family in investigating the matter. It is better for persons with money not to mix themselves up with family transactions of this nature. I dismiss the bill without costs.

[*403]

WISE *v.* WISE.

(2 Jo. & Lat. 403—416.)

1845.
May 26.

SIR EDWARD
SUGDEN,
L.C.

[403]

Upon the admission of the heir-at-law, that the will of the testator, which was lost, was duly executed and attested, and that thereby certain lands were devised to him, subject to a perpetual rent-charge; and upon evidence of the contents of the will, by two witnesses, who heard it read, but could not state that it was executed and attested as by law required, further than that the person reading it read out the names of the testator and of certain persons as if they had executed and attested it; and upon proof of the payment of the rent-charge for thirty-five years up to the year before the filing of the bill, the COURT declared that the lands were well charged with the annuity; and that the heir-at-law, and the persons deriving with notice under a settlement of the lands executed by him, on

(1) 8 R. R. 212, 223 (11 Ves. 467, 482).

WISE
*.
WISE.

the marriage of his son, and duly registered, and also the judgment creditors of the heir-at-law, were bound to give effect to the devise of the rent-charge.

By marriage settlement, a rent-charge was granted to trustees and their heirs, upon trusts for the husband and the issue of the marriage; and the lands were granted to other trustees for a term of years, upon trust to secure the rent-charge. One of the trustees of the rent-charge admitted that, before the execution of the settlement, he had notice of a prior incumbrance on the lands; and one of the trustees of the term, denied that he had such notice. No evidence of notice was given: Held, that notice to the trustee of the rent-charge was sufficient: but, there being no issue of the marriage *in esse*, the Court would not declare that their interests were bound by the prior incumbrance, but declared that the trustee had notice of it.

Costs given against a party, who by his want of caution in settling an estate without giving notice that it was subject to a prior demand, rendered a suit by the prior incumbrancer necessary to establish his rights.

JAMES WISE being, in the year 1807, entitled to the lands of Bohernagore and Curragoosa, held under a lease for lives renewable for ever, made his will, whereby, as was alleged by the bill, he devised all his estate and interest therein to his eldest son, Thomas James Wise, subject to a perpetual annuity or yearly rent-charge of 600*l*. of the late currency, to the testator's second son, John Wise; provided, that in case Samuel Godsell and James Godsell should establish a claim or demand which they had upon the lands,

[*404]   then John Wise should have a rent-charge of 400*l*. *a year, for ever, chargeable upon all the property of the testator, in lieu of the rent-charge of 600*l*.

James Wise died in March, 1807, leaving Thomas James Wise and John Wise, his only sons, him surviving.

Upon the death of his father, Thomas James Wise entered into possession of the lands. The will was not proved: the bill suggested that it was not proved, because the devisees feared lest the knowledge of its contents might provoke the Godsells to assert any latent claim they might have to the lands; but Thomas James Wise regularly paid the rent-charge of 600*l*., from the death of the testator to the death of John Wise, which occurred in 1819, and from thence until the year 1842, as hereafter mentioned.

In 1812 the Godsells filed their bill in the Court of Exchequer, against Thomas James Wise, for the purpose of establishing their claim against the lands; and Thomas James Wise, in his answer to that bill, admitted that he claimed to be entitled to the lands under and by virtue of the will of James Wise: but before any further proceedings were had in that cause, the claim of the Godsells was compromised by the payment to them of the sum of 1,250*l*., by Thomas James Wise and John Wise, in equal shares.

John Wise, by his will dated the 22nd of October, 1819, after reciting that, by the will of his father, he was entitled to a rent-charge of 600*l.* per annum, charged upon the lands of Bohernagore and Curragoosa, devised the same to his son, James Laurence Wise, his heirs, executors, &c., and directed his executors thereout to appropriate certain annual sums therein mentioned, to the maintenance *and education of his said son, then a minor; and appointed Thomas James Wise and G. Brereton his executors.   [*405]

John Wise died, and his will was proved by his executors. G. Brereton died shortly afterwards, and Thomas James Wise applied the annual proceeds of the rent-charge according to the trusts of the will of John Wise.

James Laurence Wise attained his age of twenty-one years in September, 1837; and from thence up to the 1st of November, 1842, Thomas James Wise paid him the rent-charge of 600*l.* per annum.

By indenture of the 21st of June, 1841, being the settlement executed in contemplation of the marriage of the Rev. Henry Wise, second son of Thomas James Wise, with Miss Anne Gillman; after reciting that Thomas James Wise was then seised of the lands of Bohernagore and Curragoosa, by virtue of a renewed indenture of lease, dated the 11th of August, 1828, for the term of three lives therein named; he, Thomas James Wise, granted an annuity or rent-charge of 250*l.* per annum, charged upon and payable out of said lands, to James Wise and Thomas Gillman and their heirs, for the lives named in the then existing lease of the lands and to be named in every future renewal thereof, upon trust for the Rev. Henry Wise, for his life; and after his decease, for the benefit of the issue, if any, of the then intended marriage; and in default of such issue, upon trust for Thomas James Wise, his heirs and assigns; subject to a proviso therein contained for enabling Henry Wise to jointure any after-taken wife. And Thomas James Wise granted and demised the said lands unto Edward Wise and William Crooke, for the term of 500 years, upon trusts therein declared for *the purpose of further and better securing the payment of the   [*406]
annuity of 250*l.* And Thomas James Wise covenanted with Thomas Wise and Thomas Gillman, that he would, at all times, save harmless and keep indemnified the annuity of 250*l.*, and the lands charged therewith, from every charge and incumbrance whatever. There was no issue of this marriage.

The bill was filed by James Laurence Wise against Thomas

WISE
v.
WISE.

James Wise, the Rev. Henry Wise, James Wise, Thomas Gillman, Edward Wise, William Crooke, and the judgment creditors of Thomas James Wise. It charged that, immediately after the interment of James Wise, his will was opened and read in the presence of the two sons of the testator, and of several other persons ; and that it was then taken and accepted by all the persons present, as and for the last will and testament of James Wise, and as being duly executed and attested. It further charged that the will had been lost, and that no copy of it was to be found ; that the several parties to the settlement of the 21st of June, 1841, or having charges or incumbrances affecting the lands, created by Thomas James Wise, had notice of the will and of the devise of the rent-charge of 600l. per annum thereby made, at the respective times of the execution of the settlement, and of advancing the money secured to them by the judgments : and prayed that the said will of James Wise, as far as same regarded the devise of the perpetual rent-charge of 600l. per annum, late currency, to John Wise, might be established as against Thomas James Wise, the heir-at-law of James Wise; and that said rent-charge might be declared to be well charged upon the lands of Bohernagore and Curragoosa, in perpetuity, in priority to the several charges and incumbrances created by Thomas James Wise, affecting same lands ;

[*407]   and for an account of what *was due to the plaintiff on foot of same ; and for payment thereof.

Thomas James Wise, by his answer, admitted the will of James Wise as stated in the bill ; and that, immediately after the interment of James Wise, it was read in the presence of several persons, and was then taken and accepted by the persons present, as the last will of James Wise; and that it was duly executed and attested.

William Crooke said he never executed the settlement of 1841, or heard that he had been made a party to it, until he heard that he had been made a defendant in the suit; and he disclaimed all interest in the lands.

James Wise and Edward Wise said, that they heard and believed that James Wise duly made his will, of the import and effect in bill stated : but Edward Wise said that it was only since the execution of the settlement of 1841 he so heard, for that he was previously under the impression that James Wise had died intestate. They admitted that the will was duly attested; and submitted that, as the settlement of 1841 had been duly registered, the issue of the marriage were entitled, in respect of the estates and interests

limited to them, to priority over the rent-charge of 600l. per annum. WISE
v.
WISE.
And James Wise said, that before the execution of the settlement
of 1841 he had heard and believed, and Edward Wise said, that
since the execution thereof, he had heard and believed that the said
lands were charged with the rent-charge of 600l. per annum by the
will of James Wise.

Belinda Hornibrooke, a judgment creditor of Thomas James
Wise, said that she knew nothing of the will of *James Wise, or   [*408]
of the devise of the rent-charge to John Wise; and that she neither
admitted nor disputed, nor knew anything whatever about the
validity or priority of the rent-charge of 600l., or of the plaintiff's
title thereto; and referred to such proof as he should make in
respect thereof: and denied notice.

The cause was heard upon pleadings and proofs as against the
defendants, Thomas James Wise, James Wise, Edward Wise,
William Crooke, and Belinda Hornibrooke; and upon an order to
take the bill as confessed against the other defendants.

Henry Blakeney Wise and Thomas Wise, who alone, of the
persons present at the reading of the will of James Wise (except
the defendant, Thomas James Wise), were still living, were
examined.

Henry B. Wise deposed that, after the funeral, he went to the
house of James Wise, to hear his will read; that upon that occasion a will of James Wise was produced by one of his sons, and
was opened and read, but he could not say by whom, in the
presence of the sons of the testator and the other persons assembled;
that it was the last will of James Wise which was opened and read;
that he saw the will, but could not say that he took notice of its
being signed and executed; that the person who read out the will
read it as if it was duly signed, executed, and attested; that he
could not say by whom it was attested, but he took it for granted
and verily believed it was duly signed by the deceased, and attested
in due form; that he could not give any description of the will,
that is, he could not take it upon himself to say whether it was
written on paper or parchment, nor the names *of the witnesses   [*409]
thereto, nor in whose handwriting it was, nor if it was signed by
James Wise, further than that the person who read the will read
out the name of James Wise, as if signed thereto, as well as certain
names purporting to be witnesses thereto: that the will was received
by all persons present as the last will and testament of James Wise.
He then stated the purport of the will, which was as in the bill

mentioned : and in answer to another interrogatory said, that the person who read out the will read it as if it was duly signed by the testator, and duly witnessed by three or more persons.

The deposition of Thomas Wise was to the same effect.

A search for the will was proved.

Mr. Serjt. Warren and *Mr. Jenkins*, for the plaintiff, [cited *Doe* d. *Ashe* v. *Calvert* (1) ; *Villiers* v. *Villiers* (2) ; *Whitfield* v. *Faussett* (3), and other cases.]

Mr. Moore and *Mr. Herrick* for Thomas James Wise.

Mr. J. S. Townsend for Belinda Hornibrooke.

Mr. Leslie, for James Wise, one of the grantees of the rent-charge of 250*l.* per annum, and for Edward Wise and William Crooke, the trustees of the term of 500 years, to secure that rent-charge :

[*410]
No evidence of notice to the trustees before the execution of the settlement of 1841 has been given. James Wise, by *his answer, admits that he knew of the will before the execution of the settlement ; but that admission cannot be read against the issue of the marriage, if such should come *in esse*. Edward Wise denies that he had any notice of the will before the execution of the settlement. The issue claiming under the settlement of 1841 are, therefore, entitled to the annuity of 250*l.* in priority to the plaintiff's demand : *Eyre* v. *Dolphin* (4).

Mr. Serjt. Warren, in reply :

There was sufficient notice to the trustees. The settlement of 1841 recites that Thomas James Wise was entitled to the lands under a renewal of the original lease ; if, therefore, the trustees had traced back the title, they would have found that Thomas James Wise derived his title under the will of James Wise. One of the trustees admits he had notice ; which is sufficient.

THE LORD CHANCELLOR :

I think there is secondary evidence of the existence of the will of James Wise. It is true that it has not been proved that it was executed by the testator, or attested. If the will had been produced

(1) 11 R. R. 745 (2 Camp. 387).   (3) 1 Ves. Sen. 387.
(2) 2 Atk. 71.   (4) 12 R. R. 94 (2 B. & Beat. 290).

we should have seen whether, on the face of it, it purported to be
executed and attested, and there would have been no further evidence
required of those facts. There is clear proof that the will existed, that
it has been lost, and of its contents. The only question is, whether
I am to consider it as not sufficiently *proved, because the witnesses
do not say that they observed that it was attested by three witnesses.
The heir-at-law was present, and heard the will read; and it was
read as binding the real estate with the payment of this perpetual
rent-charge. He is still alive; and he has for thirty-five years
performed the obligation imposed on him by the will, paying the
rent-charge of 600*l.* per annum, which he was not bound to do
except by the will. If there were parties before me who were
really disputing the existence of the will, I might give them an
issue: but none of the parties before me can dispute it. Thomas
James Wise, the heir-at-law, is not at liberty to do so. Henry
Wise, his son, cannot dispute it; neither can the judgment creditors
or the trustees. I am of opinion that, for the purposes of this suit,
there is secondary evidence of the existence, loss, and contents of
the will; and that I am bound to establish it.

Then the question arises, how am I to bind the parties? All the
judgment creditors, save one, have allowed the bill to be taken *pro
confesso* against them. On behalf of the creditor who appears, the
objections made are principally those arising from defect of proof
of original title, which I have already dealt with. Can, then, the
judgment creditor object to the annuity being a charge on the lands
in priority to her demand? I think not; for if the will were now
produced I should hold that the party against whom the judgment
has been recovered, taking the estate subject to the legal rent-charge,
had no interest in the lands which could be bound by the judgment,
except the inheritance subject to the rent-charge; and his judgment creditor can have no greater interest. I therefore must
declare that the *plaintiff is entitled to the relief prayed as against
all the judgment creditors. The same declaration will be made
against Thomas James Wise, and Henry Wise, the tenant for life
of the annuity of 250*l.* The only question is, as to the unborn
children of Henry Wise, who are here represented by some of the
trustees. There were two trustees of the annuity of 250*l.* One of
them, James Wise, admits that he had notice of the plaintiff's title
before the execution of Henry Wise's settlement. I apprehend that
that admission of notice will bind not only the persons claiming
under him, but also his cestuis que trust. This is a case in which

WISE
v.
WISE.

[*411]

[*412]

the grantor of that annuity had notice; and Henry Wise, I must
assume, had notice, though not so as to bind other parties; and if
in addition, one of the trustees had notice, it would be very difficult
for the children of Henry Wise to get rid of it.   There were also
two trustees of a term for years to secure the annuity of 250*l.*, one
of whom did not execute the settlement.   That, however, is not
important; for where an estate is vested in trustees who do not
object at the time, they will not be allowed at a future time to say
that they never assented to the conveyance.   It would require some
strong act to induce the Court to hold that, in such a case, the
estate was divested.   I speak with respect to the effect which such
an act might have upon third parties.   Where an estate is regularly
conveyed to trustees, every Court and every jury will presume an
assent.   Here one of the trustees of the term disclaims; the other
says he had no notice of the plaintiff's title; and the question is,
what is the effect of that.   The want of notice to the trustees of
the term is of no consequence, if the trustees of the annuity had
notice.

[413]   But this suit, I apprehend, will not bind the issue of the marriage,
if any should come *in esse.*   I am not, therefore, disposed to make
any declaration purporting to bind the issue: that would be doing
more than I am called on to do.   I shall declare, according to the
precedents, that Thomas James Wise, Henry Wise, and the judgment creditors, are bound, according to their several interests in
the lands, to give effect to the will of James Wise; without prejudice to any question which may arise, after the death of Henry
Wise, between his issue and the plaintiff: and declare that James
Wise, the trustee, had notice of the plaintiff's title; and that Henry
Wise is not at liberty to exercise the power of jointuring given to
him by his settlement.

Then as to the costs.   If this were the simple case of the loss of
the will, I would not give costs, except to the trustees; but Thomas
James Wise, who has paid this annuity for thirty-five years, and
knew that the will had been lost, and that consequently there would
be a difficulty in establishing the title to the annuity, in 1841 made
a settlement and created the only difficulty in the case.   In that
settlement he did not disclose, as he ought to have done, the
circumstance that he was entitled to the lands subject to this
perpetual rent-charge of 600*l.* a year.   It was at least half the
value of the estate; and cannot be represented as a mere trifling
circumstance which it was unnecessary to notice.   He was not at

liberty to deal with the estate without apprizing the persons with
whom he was dealing, of the existence of this annuity.   And
though there is nothing special in the covenant of Thomas James
Wise against incumbrances, yet it appears to me that that covenant
has, in a great measure, led to this suit.   I therefore think that he
must pay all the costs of this suit.   *Without acting dishonestly,
he has acted with such a want of caution, that he has placed an
encumbrance on the estate, which has led to this suit.   The
plaintiff is to pay the costs of the other defendants, except Thomas
James Wise, and to have those costs over, together with his own,
against Thomas James Wise.

WISE
v.
WISE.

[*414]

MURPHY v. O'SHEA (1).

(2 Jo. & Lat. 422—431; S. C. 8 Ir. Eq. R. 329.)

If, in a transaction between principal and agent, it appears that there has
been any underhand dealing by the agent, ex. gr. that he has purchased the
estate of the principal in the name of another person, instead of his own,—
however fair the transaction may be in other respects, it has no validity in
a court of equity.

To set aside a sale from a principal to his agent, it is not necessary to
show that it was made at an undervalue.

An agent may purchase from his principal, provided he deals with him at
arm's length, and after a full disclosure of all that he knows with respect to
the property.

1845.
June 3.
—
SIR EDWARD
SUGDEN,
L.C.
[422]

MARGARET SHEE, being seised in fee, or otherwise well entitled to
several houses and premises in the city of Kilkenny, which were
let to tenants of the names of Laffan, Reynolds, Dollard, and
Kavanagh, for long terms of years, devised them, after the decease
of two persons named in her will, to her cousin, Gerard Murphy,
and his heirs; and died in 1794.   In 1814 Gerard Murphy became
entitled to the possession of the devised estates, the prior life
estates having determined.   He was at that time, and for many
years previously had been resident at Mahon, in the island of
Minorca, and afterwards resided at Cadiz, where he carried on
business as a wine merchant; and being unable personally to
attend to the management of the property so devised to him, or to
make himself acquainted with its circumstances, he appointed
Mr. Patrick Byrne to be his agent to receive the rents, and otherwise to manage the property for him.   Mr Byrne represented to
Mr. Murphy that the property was not satisfactorily circumstanced;

(1) *Dunne* v. *English* (1874) L. R. 18 Eq. 524, 31 L. T. 75.

MURPHY   that the rents were not well paid; that the houses were old and out
v.   of repair, and that it would be for his advantage to sell it; and the
O'SHEA.   latter, adopting that opinion, in November, 1820, executed a power
            of attorney, authorizing Mr. Byrne to sell all the houses in Kilkenny,
            and to execute conveyances to the purchaser; and Mr. Byrne after-
            wards became the purchaser of them under the circumstances
            mentioned by the LORD CHANCELLOR in giving judgment in this case.

[*423]   Gerard Murphy died in 1834, having, by his will, devised all his
            real estates to his two sons, the plaintiffs, and *his daughter, and
            their heirs, as tenants in common, in remainder after a life estate
            therein, which he gave to his widow.

                Patrick Byrne died in July, 1842; and by his will, he devised
            the lands in question to the Rev. Robert O'Shea and Richard
            Smithwick, upon trust for certain pious and charitable purposes
            therein expressed; and appointed them his executors. The Rev.
            Robert O'Shea alone proved his will.

                The bill was filed by the two sons of Gerard Murphy against the
            Rev. Robert O'Shea, James Bergin, and others, praying that the
            deeds of the 25th of May, 1829 (1), and 11th of July, 1833 (2), in
            the bill mentioned, might be set aside, having been obtained by
            fraud and imposition; and that [the] same might be delivered up
            to be cancelled; or that the same might be reformed, by omitting
            therefrom the premises called Kavanagh's holdings.

                Mr. Serjt. Warren, *Mr. Monahan*, and *Mr. Edward Pennefather*,
            for the plaintiffs.

                Mr. Moore, *Mr. Brewster*, and *Mr. Gibbon*, for the Rev. Robert
            O'Shea.

                Mr. O'Donnell for Richard Smithwick, who disclaimed.

                Mr. Kellet and *Mr. Lawson* for James Bergin.

                Mr. John Pennefather for Teresa Murphy, Thomas Valls, and
            Emilia Valls, otherwise Murphy, his wife.

[424]   *Whitcomb* v. *Minchin* (3), and *Morse* v. *Royal* (4), were referred to.

(1) Conveyance from Murphy to
Bergin.
(2) Conveyance from Bergin to
Byrne.
(3) 5 Madd. 91. "In this case the
VICE-CHANCELLOR (Sir JOHN LEACH)
held that as a trustee for the sale of an

estate could not purchase the estate for
himself, so the agent of the trustee
employed for the purpose of sale could
not purchase it." The report contains
nothing more upon the point for which
it is here cited.—O. A. S.

(4) 8 R. R. 338 (12 Ves. 355).

THE LORD CHANCELLOR:

An objection has been made to granting the relief sought, on the ground of the lapse of time which has occurred since the transaction in question ; but I am of opinion that the plaintiffs are not barred of relief by *laches*, if they be otherwise entitled to it. It is also said that there is no proof that the lands were sold at an undervalue ; but it is perfectly well settled, that it is not necessary to prove undervalue. A principal selling to his agent is entitled to set aside the sale upon equitable grounds, whatever may have been the price obtained for the property. Then it is said that the deed of sale has been registered : that amounts to nothing; and I may observe, that the Registry Act rather facilitates fraudulent transactions; for the registration of a fraudulent deed seems, in the eyes of the world, to give validity to it, which, if not registered, it would not have possessed.

This case, therefore, must depend on its merits, which are these. Murphy appears to have been the intimate friend of Byrne, who resided in this country. In his letters, Byrne constantly addressed him as "my dear friend." Murphy was resident in Spain; and having become entitled to some property in the city of Kilkenny, consisting of houses, which required to be looked after, he appointed his friend, Byrne, to be his agent, to collect his rents and manage the *property : and upon a representation that it would be for his advantage to dispose of his interest in these houses, he, in 1820, gave a power of attorney to Byrne, authorizing him to sell them in such manner as he should deem best. Byrne thereby obtained complete dominion over the property. He very soon began to depreciate it: he generally described it, in his letters to Murphy, as "them old houses ;" and he represented the title as being in hazard, for that the Marquis of Ormonde alleged that the property was held under him by lease for lives, and not by fee-farm grant. Under these circumstances, and as the tenants were very irregular in the payment of their rents, Murphy became desirous to dispose of the property. Byrne was equally anxious to become the purchaser of it; but he proceeded with great caution. He suggested that he should become the purchaser, and Murphy assented; but Byrne, in reply, said, that there was a rule of law which prevented him, as the agent, from becoming the purchaser. This, therefore, is a case, not merely of an agent who had his principal in his power, but one in which the agent had full knowledge of the rule of the Court; which, however, does not prevent an agent from

[*425]

22—2

MURPHY
v.
O'SHEA.

purchasing from his principal, but only requires that he shall deal with him at arm's length, and after a full disclosure of all that he knows with respect to the property.

At length, in December, 1826, Byrne wrote to his principal, stating, that he had been speaking to a Mr. Bergin, who, he said, had got a good fortune lately with his wife, and expressed a desire to lay out his money in purchasing land or houses; and that he proposed a sale of Laffan's, Reynolds', and Dollard's holdings to him : and added, "Let me know your inclination concerning them,

[*426]

as soon as you *can, and the lowest purchase you would let them go at. I will, at the same time, get as much for you over it as I can." That would be a fair question to ask, provided Bergin was really the purchaser ; but it turns out that Bergin was Byrne ; and, therefore, it was most unfair in Byrne to ask such a question of his principal. In April, 1828, the sale was agreed on ; and by indenture of the 25th of May, 1829, Byrne, as the attorney of Murphy, conveyed the property to Bergin, in consideration of 800l. of the late Irish currency. But what was the fact, as regards the circumstances of Bergin, the pretended purchaser ? He was in possession of a small farm of forty acres of land, of indifferent quality, held under Byrne himself at a rack rent ; and he had received a sum of 100l., which he got as a fortune with his wife. It was untrue, therefore, that Bergin had money to lay out in the purchase of lands, as was represented by Byrne. And then come these extraordinary circumstances. Bergin, in his answer, says that he had nothing to do with the purchase ; that he knew nothing about it ; but that Byrne came to him and told him this story : that when he, Bergin, was about nine years of age, his father had deposited with him, Byrne, a sum of between 300l. and 400l., a matter which he had never before disclosed ; and that he thought it would be beneficial for Bergin if he would lay out that money in the purchase of this property ; that it was a desirable property ; and that, as the purchase-money of it was double what Bergin had, he, Byrne, would advance the remainder, and enter into possession and repay himself. Bergin must have perfectly well understood what was the meaning of that transaction, and that the conveyance was executed to him as a trustee, his name being used merely for the purpose of defrauding Murphy. Without doubt, the purchase was made with

[*427]

Byrne's money ; and Bergin never received *the rents for his own use : Byrne received them ; but sometimes through the hands of Bergin. As soon as the matter was so far arranged, Byrne, the real purchaser, became desirous to have the title vested in himself; and he adopted this mode of obtaining his object. He put forward this allegation, and, I infer, did so fraudulently : I infer anything which the facts will warrant against a man in the situation of Byrne. The Court does not presume fraud; but it may be compelled to come to the belief that fraud does exist in one part of a transaction, where actual fraud is proved to exist in another part of the same transaction. He represented to Murphy that he had, by mistake, permitted him to convey to Bergin, under the description of the premises in the conveyance, another property of Murphy's, viz., Kavanagh's holdings, as part of the property sold; that Bergin was dissatisfied with his purchase, and desired to get back his money; that he was not aware of the mistake in the conveyance; that it was most important to obtain a re-conveyance of the property from him; and, in order to get rid of his complaints, he, Byrne, would take an assignment of the premises from him, provided Murphy particularly requested him to do so. The result was, that Murphy became alarmed, and gladly consented that Byrne should purchase the property. Byrne accordingly procured a conveyance of it to himself; and then, after that purchase had been made by Byrne, as Murphy believed, though it was all a sham, Murphy wrote to him, saying that he approved of his making it. But why did he approve of that purchase both before and after it was made? In one of his letters, written before the purchase was made, he requests Byrne to take a re-assignment of the premises on his own account, stating his belief that he was "highly worthy of his confidence:" and Byrne having written to him, that, agreeable to his desire *and request, he had "effected and purchased the assignment and conveyance of them old tenements in High Street, Kilkenny," from Bergin, and had thereby secured for him, free from litigation, whatever might be the fair value of Kavanagh's holdings; and offering to purchase them for 260*l.*, Murphy in reply says, "Your letter of the 17th last July, is highly satisfactory to me, for your having effected and purchased the assignment and conveyances, &c., from Mr. Bergin, as it secures for me, free from litigation, the fair value of the widow Kavanagh's house. I therefore very willingly accept your offer to pay me the sum of 260*l.* for said interest;" which offer, however, never was carried into effect. But if Murphy had been told that this was all a trick; that Bergin was Byrne; that the whole was but a contrivance to impose on him and cheat him; would he have written those letters, or addressed him

MURPHY
v.
O'SHEA.

[*428]

MURPHY
*.
O'SHEA.

as his "most dear friend?" It is now attempted to use those letters as a confirmation; but they are the strongest evidence of fraud, and show the want of knowledge in the principal, and the want of proper conduct in the agent.

Bergin, in his answer, swears, that he never executed any deed re-assigning the premises to Byrne; that the deed of July, 1833, is a fabricated instrument; and that no part of the consideration-money, mentioned in that deed, was ever paid to him. There are three witnesses to the execution of the deed by him, and to his receipt for the money endorsed on it; but no evidence has been given of the actual payment of the consideration-money. The only witness examined merely says, that the name subscribed is his handwriting, and that he is sure that no person paid any money to Bergin in his presence. The evidence, then, being all one way, I must believe that no money was paid on that occasion. *Whether the deed was executed by Bergin or not, I cannot say; this only is certain, that the whole transaction was a contrivance and a fraud on the part of the agent. Receipts by Bergin have been given in evidence, to show that possession went along with the title; but they prove something more; for one of them is for rent subsequent to the pretended re-conveyance: I am, therefore, inclined to think that the title may be still in Bergin. It is observable, looking at the pretence put forward by Byrne for getting the re-conveyance, that, after he had obtained it, he never executed a conveyance of Kavanagh's holdings to his principal as he ought to have done. The consequence is, that Byrne, having been brought to desire to set himself right in some measure in this dishonourable trans-action, devised this property to pious uses; and the persons entitled under his will find themselves compelled to insist on his title to Kavanagh's holdings. By his misconduct throughout, he has rendered this suit necessary; for which reason his assets will have to bear all the costs.

[*429]

One thing admits of no dispute: the moment it appears in a transaction between principal and agent, that there has been any underhand dealing by the agent,—that he has made use of another person's name as the purchaser, instead of his own,—however fair the transaction may be in other respects, from that moment it has no validity in this Court.

I have no hesitation in making a decree for the plaintiffs, setting aside the deeds, with costs to be borne by the defendant, O'Shea, the personal representative of Byrne. And though I do not desire

to give costs to any person connected with such a transaction, yet, MURPHY
as it appears that Bergin was a mere tool in the hands of Byrne, O'SHEA.
whose assets *are ample, I will direct his costs to be paid by the [*480]
plaintiffs; the plaintiffs to have them over against O'Shea.

BATTERSBY *v.* ROCHFORT.

(2 Jo. & Lat. 431—455; S. C. 9 Ir. Eq. R. 191.)

A. being entitled to lands in Ireland, was discharged in England as an
insolvent debtor, under the 1 Geo. IV. c. 119. The assignment of all his
estate and effects to the provisional assignee was filed in the Insolvent
Court, but was not registered. The sub-assignment to the general
assignees was registered. Afterwards A., by deed duly registered, conveyed his Irish estates, in mortgage, to B., who had no notice of the insolvency. The title of the mortgagee is to be preferred to that of the assignees
of the insolvent.

1845.
May 28, 29.
June 8.

1846.
Jan. 29.
Feb. 13.

SIR EDWARD
SUGDEN,
L.C.
[431]

UPON the marriage of William Rochfort with Elizabeth Sperling,
a settlement dated the 13th of May, 1788, was executed, whereby
William Rochfort conveyed the lands of Mallinstown and Belfield,
in the county of Westmeath, to the use of himself for his life; and,
after his decease, to the use, intent and purpose that Elizabeth
Sperling and her assigns, should receive and enjoy, out of the said
*lands, the clear yearly sum of 480*l*. for the term of her life, as and [*432]
for her jointure; the same to be paid quarterly; with power of
distress and entry for recovery thereof: and, subject thereto, and
to a term of ninety-nine years, vested in trustees upon trust to
secure the payment of the annuity, and to a further trust term of
500 years, the trusts of which did not arise, the lands were limited
to the use of the first son of the marriage and the heirs of his body,
with several limitations over.

There was issue of that marriage one child only, the defendant,
William Henry Rochfort.

William Rochfort died in 1798; and in 1801, Elizabeth Rochfort,
his widow, married the Rev. William Beville: and upon the occasion
of that marriage, a settlement dated the 5th of February, 1801, was
executed between the Rev. William Beville of the first part, Elizabeth
Rochfort of the second part, and trustees of the third part; whereby
[her annuity was charged with an annual payment of 100*l*., to
William Henry Rochfort on attaining 21].

In 1822 the Rev. William Beville died; and in 1827, Elizabeth [437]
Beville, his widow, married General Charles Brown, who died in
1836, leaving his wife surviving.

BATTERSBY
ᵥ.
ROCHFORT.

In 1821 William Henry Rochfort was discharged as an insolvent debtor in England. On the 21st of July, 1821, he executed an assignment of all his real and personal estate to the Provisional Assignee of Insolvents in England; who, by deed of the 17th of February, 1823, assigned same to William Gustard and Charles Smith, the assignees of the estate and effects of the insolvent.

By indenture of the 30th of March, 1841, William Henry Rochfort mortgaged the lands to Thomas Battersby, the plaintiff, to secure the repayment of a sum of 3,000l., then advanced by him to the mortgagor. This mortgage was duly registered on the 30th of March, 1841. The money lent was also secured by the bond and warrant of William Henry Rochfort, upon which judgment was entered, as of Hilary Term, 1841.

The bill was filed by Thomas Battersby against William Henry Rochfort, Elizabeth Brown, William Gustard, Charles Smith, and

[438]

others. It stated * * that the assignments by William Henry Rochfort to the provisional assignee, and by the latter to the general assignees, were not registered in the Office for Registering Deeds in Ireland; and that, at the time of the execution of the mortgage of 1841, and when he lent the 3,000l. on the security thereof, he had no notice of these assignments, or of the insol-

[*439]

vency of William *Henry Rochfort. The bill prayed a fore-closure and sale, subject to the annuity; and for the appointment of a receiver; and that the rents and profits might be applied, in the first instance, in payment of the accruing gales of the jointure of 480l. to Elizabeth Brown, and, subject thereto, to the liquidation of the plaintiff's debt and costs.

*   *   *   *   *

[441]

It appeared that the assignment from William Henry Rochfort to the provisional assignee had not been registered; but that on the 23rd of April, 1830, there had been filed, in the Office for Registering Deeds in Ireland, a document purporting to be a memorial to be registered pursuant to the Act, of an indenture bearing date the 17th of February, 1823, made between Henry Dance, the Provisional Assignee of the Estate and Effects of Insolvent Debtors in England, pursuant to the 1 Geo. IV. c. 119, of the one part, and William Gustard and Charles Smith of the other part; whereby, after reciting that by indenture dated the 21st of July, 1821, made between William Henry Rochfort, an insolvent debtor, then a prisoner in the King's Bench Prison, of the one part, and said Henry Dance, as such provisional assignee, of the other part,

all the estate, right, title, interest, and trust of the said insolvent,
in possession, reversion, remainder, or expectancy, except the
wearing apparel and necessaries therein mentioned, were conveyed
and assigned to Henry Dance, as such provisional assignee, his
successors and assigns; he, the said Henry Dance, did convey,
assign, transfer, and set over unto William Gustard and *Charles
Smith, their heirs, executors, &c., all the estate, title, interest, and
trust of, in, and to the real and personal estate, whatsoever and
wheresoever, which by virtue of the therein-recited indenture were
vested in Henry Dance; to hold to them, their heirs, executors, &c.,
according to the respective natures, properties, and tenures thereof.
The assignments from William Henry Rochfort to the provisional
assignee, and from the latter to the general assignees, were duly
filed as of record in the Court for the Relief of Insolvent Debtors in
England, pursuant to the 1 Geo. IV. c. 119, s. 7.

[*442]

Mr. Moore, Mr. Monahan, and *Mr. Hutton*, for the plaintiff:

[The mortgage has priority over the assignment to the provisional and general assignees, by virtue of its prior registration, for
the registration of the assignment from the provisional to the
general assignees does not operate as a registration of the assignment from the insolvent to the provisional assignee. Similar
assignments have been registered: *Sumpter* v. *Cooper* (1).] But if
the Court should be of opinion that the assignment to the provisional assignee did not require to be registered, to give it priority,
yet as the sub-assignment does require to be registered, and as the
memorial of it does not specify the names of the lands, or the
county, barony, parish, or townland in which they are situated,
the registration of it is invalid; and the plaintiff is entitled to
priority.

[443]

Mr. Serjt. Warren, Mr. Brooke, and *Mr. Hunt*, for Mrs.
Brown.

Mr. Battersby and *Mr. De Moleyns* for William Henry Rochfort.

Mr. Rolleston and *Mr. Graydon* for William Gustard and
Charles Smith.

[Their arguments sufficiently appear from the following judgment.]

(1) 36 R. R. 552 (2 B. & Ad. 23).

BATTERSBY
v.
ROCHFORT.

[444]

Mr. Monagan replied.

[There was another question as to the construction of the settlement of the 5th of February, 1801, which it is not thought necessary to retain in the Revised Reports.]

[445]   THE LORD CHANCELLOR:

I reserved the question upon the Registry Acts. It was properly admitted that if the assignment or conveyance from the insolvent to the provisional assignee ought to have been registered, the title of the plaintiff was to be preferred to that of the defendants, as the registry of the conveyance from the provisional assignee to the general assignees could not operate as a registration of the conveyance to the provisional assignee, or amount by itself to a sufficient registration. I have, therefore, only to decide the question, whether it was necessary to register the conveyance to the provisional assignee.

The Registry Act here is general in the permission which it gives to register all deeds and conveyances by which any hereditaments may be anyways affected; and priority is given to deeds according to the time of registering, over other registered documents; and any deed or conveyance, not registered, of any hereditaments comprised in a deed, a memorial whereof shall be registered, is made void against the registered deed and against judgment creditors. There is no exception of conveyances executed under the authority of Acts of Parliament, or required to be recorded elsewhere; and of course the Act, as several subsequent provisions show, was intended to comprise deeds executed out of Ireland. The opinion of the Judges in *Warburton* v. *Loveland* (1), as delivered in the House of Lords, after two arguments at the Bar, was, that the language of the Act throughout, and more particularly in the fifth

[*446]   section, seems to establish this to have been its leading *object; that, as far as deeds were concerned, the Act should give complete information, and that any necessity of looking further for deeds than into the register itself should be superseded. And it was manifest, they said, that no construction of the Act is so well calculated to carry into effect this its avowed object, as that which forces all transfers and dispositions of every kind, and by whomsoever made, to be put upon the face of the register, so as to be open to the inspection of all parties who may at any time claim an interest

1) 2 Dow & Cl. 496.

therein. These observations, which I willingly adopt, apply with as much force to this case as to that in which they are delivered. Any conveyance by William Henry Rochfort himself whilst solvent, although for his creditors, would have required registration to protect it against a subsequent registered deed. But it was argued that the provisions of the English Insolvent Act, which was in operation at the time of the conveyance (1 Geo. IV. c. 119), rendered a registration here unnecessary, not by express provision, but by implication. An insolvent was allowed by the Act to present a petition to the Court for his discharge, and he was required, at the time of subscribing such petition, to duly execute a conveyance and assignment in such manner and form as the Court should direct, of all his real and personal estate, so as to vest the same in the provisional assignee of the Court; which conveyance was to be void if the insolvent should not obtain his discharge; and if he should, proper persons were to be appointed as assignees, and the .provisional assignee is directed to assign to them the previous estate and effects; and every such assignment, whether to a provisional or other assignee, is to be entered on the proceedings of the Court, and an office copy is made evidence. The circumstance that, when the insolvent chose *to file a petition for his discharge, it was incumbent upon him to convey his estate to the provisional assignee, of course would not operate as a repeal of the Registering Acts in the county. Such a conveyance, unregistered, would be open to all the mischiefs intended to be guarded against by those Acts, if it were to have precedence over a subsequent registered deed. The like mischief continuing, therefore, the like remedy should still be operative. But it was contended that the assignments were to be recorded in the Court, and, therefore, could not be registered; and, consequently, registration must be considered no longer necessary. The Act does not prescribe the time within which the assignments are to be entered upon the proceedings of the Court. It does not appear to me that this provision is inconsistent with the prior registration here of the deed, nor indeed do I know how the entering of the assignment on the proceedings of the Court would prevent the subsequent registration of the deed with the permission of the Court, which would have been given as of course. The Acts of Parliament may well stand together; and the requisitions of both might have been complied with; the assignments might have been registered here and also entered on the proceedings of the Insolvent Court in England. It would be contrary to settled rules

[*447]

BATTERSBY
v.
ROCHFORT.

of interpretation, therefore, to hold the latter to be a repeal of the former Act. It was said that the late Act of 7 Geo. IV. enabled the assignees, by having two parts of the assignment to them from the provisional assignee, to register one part of it; but this, I think, does not affect the question. And the provision in the 1 & 2 Vict. c. 110, s. 46, copied into our Insolvent Act, I think clearly shows the impression of the Legislature, that, under the prior statutes,

[*448]

conveyances by *an insolvent debtor to the provisional assignee, and from the latter to the particular assignee, would be subject to registration ; and such was the anxiety of Parliament to further the object of these laws, that the vesting or other order, which came in lieu of a conveyance, is required to be registered just as the deed ought to have been. The evidence afforded by this provision, of the view taken of the former law by the Legislature when the late Act was passed, is not weakened by the criticism about the word Wales in the clause, if even that word was improperly introduced ; but although there is no general Registration Act in Wales, there may be laws requiring the registration of some particular deeds in certain localities. Upon the whole, I think it clear that the conveyance to the provisional assignee was subject to the general law as to registration in this country; and, therefore, that the claim of the plaintiff must prevail over the title of the assignees. The view which I have taken of the case renders it unnecessary to consider the other points upon the Registering Acts which were argued at the Bar.

1845.
June 9, 10, 14.

SIR EDWARD
SUGDEN,
L.C.

[460]

DYAS v. CRUISE (1).

(2 Jo. & Lat. 460—488; S. C. 8 Ir. Eq. R. 407.)

An estate was limited to L. for life, with power to lease at the best rent. L. demised the lands to a trustee for a term of years, to secure an annuity to G., and covenanted to exercise his power of leasing : and afterwards was discharged as an insolvent. L. and G. agreed to demise the lands, and accordingly executed the lease : Held, that the provisional assignee was bound to execute the lease, as he took the estate subject to all the equities and liabilities to which it was subject in the hands of the insolvent; and the exercise of the power was for benefit of the creditors.

An agent to let lands is bound to let them to the best advantage : but, upon the mere ground of undervalue, a *bona fide* letting, which would be binding on the principal himself, will be equally binding on him when he acts through an agent, if that agent has acted fairly and honestly.

Under a power to lease at the best rent, the highest rent need not be

(1) *Gaslight and Coke Co.* v. *Towse* (1887) 35 Ch. D. 519, 56 L. J. Ch. 889, 56 L. T. 602.

reserved. The question—What is the test that the best rent has been reserved? and the cases on the subject, considered.

An authority to let lands may be inferred from the letters and acts of the party.

Tenant for life, with power to lease at the best rent, agrees to make a demise for a term warranted by the power, but at a rent which afterwards appears not to be the best rent. There being no fraud in the transaction, the Court will decree a partial performance of the agreement, and direct the tenant for life to execute the agreement as far as his estate enables him to do so.

Harnett v. *Yeilding* (1) observed upon.

IN and previous to the year 1837, William Joseph Lynch and Patrick Russell Cruise were, under the will of their grandfather, P. Maguire, entitled, as tenants in common, for their respective lives, to undivided moieties of the lands *of Darvistown and Paris- [*461] town, in the county of Westmeath, containing about 246 acres; with a power to demise the same for the term of thirty-one years or three lives, but not for thirty-one years or three lives whichever should last longest, in possession, but not in reversion, and at the best rent. The lands were at that time held by John Hopkins, under a lease for a term of sixty-one years, which would expire on the 1st of May, 1843, at the rent of 209l., late currency, per annum.

[The material facts of this case are stated sufficiently for the purposes of this report by the LORD CHANCELLOR in the following judgment :]

Mr. Serjt. Warren, Mr. Moore, and Mr. Christian, for the [475] plaintiff.

Mr. Monahan, Mr. H. G. Hughes, Mr. D. Lynch, and Sir Colman O'Loghlen, for the defendant. * * *

THE LORD CHANCELLOR: [476]

This bill was filed for the specific performance of an agreement to grant a lease for thirty-one years, by Mr. Dyas, to whom the lease was to be granted, against Mr. Cruise, the tenant for life of an undivided moiety of the estate, which was settled in strict settlement, and against the provisional assignee of Mr. Lynch, an insolvent, tenant for life of the other moiety. The provisional assignee has allowed the bill to be taken *pro confesso* against him.

Mr. Lynch and Mr. Cruise were tenants in common, for their lives, of this estate, with remainders to their issue respectively, in

(1) 9 R. R. 98 (2 Sch. & Lef. 549).

strict settlement; with power to lease, in possession, at the best rent that could be obtained from a solvent tenant, for the term of thirty-one years. Previously to the agreement in question, the lands were held by a Mr. Hopkins, under an old lease, at rather a small rent. Mr. Cruise was resident in America; Mr. Lynch resides in this country. He had heavily incumbered his property, and had charged his life interest with an annuity to Mr. Galway, a solicitor; and had granted the lands to a trustee for Galway, for a term of years, dependent, of course, upon his life, upon trust to secure the annuity; and he had covenanted with Galway to exercise his power of leasing upon the expiration of Hopkins' lease. Lynch afterwards became an insolvent, and his provisional assignee has been made a party to the suit. Mr. Cruise appears to have been in straitened circumstances: the correspondence which has been read, shows that he was always pressing for the rent, I may say, before it was due. In fact, the rent of this property was all he had to depend on; it was therefore of the greatest importance to

[*477] him that the property should be let, and that not an hour *should be lost in transmitting the rent to him. He had an agent in this country, a solicitor and friend, named Smyth. Of course, his only duty, while the lease subsisted, was to receive the rent and transmit it to his principal in America. This he did regularly; and so matters stood until the period when the old lease was about to expire. It is obvious that, unless all the parties entitled to the property could agree in re-letting the estate to the same tenant, there could be no re-letting at all. Two husbandry tenants could not well manage a farm in common: such an occupation could not possibly be beneficial. Therefore, but two modes of proceeding were open; either that the parties should agree in the choice of one husbandry tenant, or that a bill for a partition should be filed: and in the circumstances in which Mr. Cruise was placed, nothing could have been more unfortunate for him than a bill of partition. Mr. Smyth went over the property in the autumn of 1842, to prepare for the re-letting; and he shortly afterwards wrote to Mr. Cruise, detailing its dilapidated condition, and stating that part of the lands had been exhausted, and that it would require much capital to restore them again to a good condition: and his description has been borne out by the evidence of every person examined in the cause. Mr. Smyth found the property to be in the possession of four persons, three of whom had been undertenants to Mr. Hopkins; one for a long period of time, the others for

shorter periods. The fourth was a person who had taken the grazing of part of the land; and whatever may be the notions of such persons as to tenant-right, it cannot be pretended that the claim of a man giving 10*l.* for the grass of the land, and thereby getting into possession, just at the expiration of the lease, is entitled to the smallest attention. On the contrary, it is to be looked upon with suspicion; for it has the appearance *of a party getting into possession in order that he may put forward an unfounded claim.   [*478]

Mr. Smyth and Mr. Galway prevailed on the undertenants to give up possession of the lands; that is, they gave up a formal possession, but they were immediately again put into possession, although the character of their holding was changed; they became caretakers and not tenants. It is plain that Smyth and Galway intended to act fairly towards the undertenants: for, when the property was re-let, they stipulated that Wheeler, an ancient tenant, should be provided for,—and he has been; and they also stipulated for fair terms for the other two tenants as to their growing crops. The undertenants had not a legal right to a lease; but they had a fair claim, if they acted properly. In the choice of a tenant I should always feel a desire to give a preference to the actual occupier of the soil, as far as it can be done with a due regard to the interests of the persons entitled to the property. In this case the claim of the undertenants is not entitled to much respect; for, not being amenable to the head landlord, they took advantage of their situation, and used the property in a way which would prevent any landlord from accepting them as tenants. I never would, as a Judge, or in my private capacity, accept a person as tenant who had exhausted and wasted the lands. But, though this was the case, I am satisfied that their conduct had no influence on the persons letting the estate.

Now, with regard to the re-letting, there is a circumstance which is entitled to some weight. Though Mr. Cruise was absent from the country, and had to depend on his agent, yet there were persons resident in this country, *Mr. Lynch and Mr. Galway, who   [*479] were equally interested with himself in seeing that the property was well managed. He had, therefore, an advantage from the state of the title, which he could not have enjoyed had he had an undivided possession of the lands. Under these circumstances, a printed notice was circulated, stating that this property was to be let; and referring persons, desirous of becoming tenants, to Mr. Galway, Mr. Lynch, and Mr. Smyth. The undertenants were

invited to send in proposals; and they did make offers, as did also
Mr. Dyas, a gentleman of capital and skill, who resided in the
neighbourhood and cultivated his own estate; and the result was,
that Lynch, Smyth, and Galway, accepted Mr. Dyas's offer in
preference to those of the undertenants; and agreed to let the
lands to him.

To this bill, filed for a specific execution of that agreement, it is
objected by Mr. Cruise, first, that Mr. Smyth had not any authority
from him to let the lands, and therefore that he is not now bound
to grant the lease: and secondly, that, if Smyth had authority to
let the lands, that authority was coupled with two conditions:
first, that it should be by a lease to be made by the owners of both
the moieties, and, consequently, that the plaintiff must now show
that he is entitled to a lease from the persons entitled to both
moieties; and secondly, that the lease should be made at the best
rent; and for that purpose, the power of leasing in the will, under
which both Cruise and Lynch derive, was referred to.

(His Lordship then commented on the evidence, and came to
the conclusion, that Mr. Smyth was authorized by Mr. Cruise to let
the lands.)

[480]   It was next objected, that if Mr. Smyth were authorized to let
the lands, his authority depended on the observance of two conditions: the first of which was, that the letting should be with the
concurrence of the co-owners of the estate: and it is said, but not
argued, that it is impossible to obtain that concurrence; for, though
both Lynch and Galway have executed the lease to Mr. Dyas, yet
the provisional assignee of Mr. Lynch has not been, nor can he be,
compelled to do so; and that the order to take the bill *pro confesso*
will not enable me to make a decree against him. The case stands
thus: the legal estate was in a trustee for Galway, for a term of
years, dependent on the life of Lynch; and he could make a legal
demise commensurate with his estate. Lynch had the reversion
expectant on the term for years vested in him; and he was capable
of exercising the power of leasing, subject, of course, to the term
granted to the trustee for Galway: he had covenanted with Galway
to execute that power upon the expiration of the lease to Hopkins;
and he and Galway, in whom the legal estate in the term was then
vested, joined in executing the lease to Dyas. This was not a legal
execution of the power; for the power was vested in the tenant for
life, subject to the incumbrance, and the estate for life in respect
of which only he could exercise it, had, upon his insolvency, passed

to the provisional assignee. But the provisional assignee took
the estate subject to all the equities and liabilities to which it was
subject in the hands of the insolvent: therefore, in this case, he
was bound, by the previous legal covenant of Lynch, to exercise
the power. The insolvent statutes give authority to assignees to
execute powers like these for the benefit of the creditors; and there
is no doubt that it is for their benefit that this power should be
exercised; for if they should become entitled in possession *to the   [*481]
estate, they will find a tenant paying a greater rent than could be
obtained, if the power were not exercised. Then, there being a
binding, *bonâ fide* contract entered into with the tenant for life, can
I enforce it against his assignee? There is an order to take this
bill *pro confesso* against him; and that amounts to an admission
by him of all the facts stated in the bill. He thus admits that he
has taken the life estate of the insolvent, bound by this covenant.
I shall therefore decree the provisional assignee to do all necessary
acts to give effect to the lease to Mr. Dyas, supposing I should be
of opinion that this contract ought to be enforced.   .

The next objection is this: it is said that in a letter from Mr.
Smyth to Mr. Cruise, asking for authority to let the lands, he said
that he would endeavour, with the aid of Lynch and Galway, to set
them to the best advantage: and his request being acceded to, it
was argued that these words were equivalent to similar words in a
power of attorney, and gave a conditional authority only to Mr.
Smyth. Even without such words, I think an agent is bound to let
the lands of his principal to the best advantage; and though I do
not agree that the rent is to be weighed in the same scales whether
a man is acting as owner or as agent, yet I agree that, if this be
not a contract for a lease at the best rent, it is not to be enforced.
But I do not desire to be understood, that, either in the case of a
purchase or lease, upon the ground of mere undervalue, a *bonâ fide*
letting or sale, which would be binding on the principal himself,
will not be equally binding on him where he acts through his agent,
if that agent has acted fairly and honestly. I could not do a more
mischievous thing than to avoid a contract, *bonâ fide* entered into
by an agent, because it is proved that the *property was worth a   [*482]
shilling or two more rent than he obtained for it.

(His Lordship then, after minutely going through the evidence
of value, came to the conclusion that the rent agreed to be paid by
Mr. Dyas was the best rent that could, under the circumstances,
have been obtained for the lands.)

I have examined the question of value with care, in order to show that what Mr. Dyas has given is fairly equal to the most that could have been obtained for the property; but it is worth while to consider what is the law upon this point, and whether there is anything in the objection, even supposing that this was a case where a higher offer had been made. In *Doe* v. *Radcliffe* (1) the defendant claimed under a lease made by a tenant for life under a power to lease at the best rent. The rent reserved was 48*l.* per annum. It was proved that the tenant for life, before he made the lease, had two offers from other persons, one at 50*l.* and the other at near 60*l.* a year; it was therefore said, that 48*l.* was not the best rent. The jury found that it was; and a motion for a new trial having been made, "the COURT refused the rule, there being no pretence to impeach the lease on the ground that the letting at 48*l.* a year was not done *bonâ fide* by the tenant for life at the time; he not having taken any fine or other consideration for the lease, and having a manifest interest to get the best rent, which, under all the circumstances, and due consideration of the ability and good management of the tenant, could reasonably be obtained. And they said that, where the transaction was fair, and no fine or other

[*483] collateral consideration was taken by the tenant *for life, leasing under the power, or injurious partiality manifestly shown by him in favour of the particular lessee, there ought to be something extravagantly wrong in the bargain, in order to set it aside on this ground; for in the choice of a tenant there were many things to be regarded besides the mere amount of the rent offered." I ask, is there anything extravagantly wrong in this bargain, which would call on me to withhold the aid of the Court to enforce the contract? In the case of *The Queensbury Leases* (2) Lord ELDON said, "There is but one criterion which our Courts always attend to as the leading criterion in discussing the question whether the best rent has been got or not; that is, whether the man who makes the lease has got as much for others as he had got for himself; for if he has got more for himself than for others, that is a decisive evidence against him. The Court must see that there is reasonable care and diligence exerted to get such rent as, care and diligence being exerted, circumstances mark out as the rent likely to be obtained." These authorities are conclusive as regards this question. The evidence as to value in this case is so clear, that it would seem extraordinary how the objection arose, were it not that Mr. Cruise was led to

(1) 10 R. R. 295 (10 East, 278).   (2) Cited 2 Sug. on Powers, 423.

suppose that there was some unfair dealing on the part of Mr. Smyth. It is seldom that a charge of fraud is put forward which is not grounded upon some fact proved in the cause; but here there is no foundation whatever for the allegations of Mr. Cruise. I should, therefore, feel no difficulty, upon that ground, of enforcing this contract against Mr. Cruise, even as a contract to bind the remainder-man, and leave him, if he thought proper, to impeach the lease; as was done in *Corry* v. *Corry* (1), in which a bill was filed against a tenant *for life, with power to lease at the best rent, for a specific execution of a contract to grant a lease; and the tenant for life objected that the rent reserved was not the best rent, and that the remainder-man ought to be a party to the suit. Lord LIFFORD overruled the second objection, and decreed a specific performance; but directed a clause to be inserted in the lease whereby the defendant should not be bound to warrant the title against the person in remainder.

If this had not been my opinion, I must have decreed a partial execution of the agreement against Cruise, for the term of his life. There are some authorities upon this subject; but none of them stand in the way of such a decree. In *Lawrenson* v. *Butler* (2) there was a power, with the consent of trustees of the settlement, to lease for lives renewable for ever, at the best rent, without fine. The tenant for life, without the consent of the trustees who refused to join, and the lessee colluded to have a lease granted in reality for a fine, though not apparently so: for it was agreed that the furniture, &c., was to be valued, and the lessee was to pay double the valuation to the tenant for life. Lord REDESDALE held, that he would not enforce an improper contract against the remainder-man, which no Judge in equity will ever do; but he also held, though he had not occasion to decide that point, that there could be no partial performance of the agreement; for that the parties did not mean to bind the interest, which the tenant for life had in the lands, but to commit a fraud on the power; and, therefore, that the Court would not assist either party. The state of the title, I may observe, was known to the parties, and they intended to execute the power illegally. *Ellard* v. *Lord Landaff* (3) was also the case of a power to lease at the best rent; and upon the making the agreement which the lessee sought to enforce, an old lease of the lands, one life in which was *in esse*, was surrendered. The surrender of the old

(1) Wallis' Rep. 278.
(2) 1 Sch. & Lef. 13.

(3) 12 R. R. 22 (1 B. & Beat. 241).

DYAR
r.
CRUISE.

lease was part of the consideration for granting the new; the best rent, therefore, was not reserved,—there was a great difference. Lord MANNERS dismissed the bill; for the lessee knew that, at the time he contracted for the new lease, the life in the old lease was at the point of death; which fact he concealed from his landlord. That case, therefore, is not an authority against decreeing a partial execution of the contract; it was a case of fraud. In *O'Rourke v. Perciral* (1) the lands were limited to the husband for life, with power to him and his wife, during their respective lives, to lease at the best rent, without fine. In 1779 the husband and wife demised the lands to the defendant for thirty-one years; and, fourteen years before the expiration of that lease, the husband alone agreed to grant another lease to the plaintiff, and took a fine. The bill was filed to enforce the agreement so far as the husband had power to carry it into effect; but Lord MANNERS refused to decree a partial performance. There again the agreement was a fraud on the power. The CHANCELLOR also relied on this, that there was no evidence to show that the rent reserved and the fine were, together, the full value of the lands. I do not understand that objection, or what weight is to be given to it; but I think the bill was properly dismissed in that case. *Harnett v. Yielding* (2) depended really upon the construction to be given to the memorandum, which Lord

[*486]

REDESDALE properly held did not *give the lessee a right to a renewed lease; but he certainly, in that case, laid down some rules which were not called for. In that case the lessor covenanted, by the old lease, to execute a further lease for twenty-one years, at any time during his life, at the old rent; and Lord REDESDALE thought that covenant was objectionable. I cannot entirely go along with him in that proposition; for though it would be an objection if, at the time when the contract is to be performed, it is not the best rent, I do not see how it is an objection, if, at that time, the old rent is the best rent. What harm is done in such a case, when the new lease is within the power? In *Doe d. Bromley v. Bettison* (3), a lease under a power was objected to, because the tenant for life covenanted that, during his life, he would, at the request of the lessee, every year renew the lease for the same term and at the same rent; but Lord ELLENBOROUGH, in pronouncing the judgment of the COURT overruling the objection, said, "Then, as to the covenant for renewal, it is said it has a tendency to induce the

(1) 12 R. R. 68 (2 B. & Beat. 58).   (3) 11 R. R. 385 (12 East, 304).
(2) 9 R. R. 98 (2 Sch. & Lef. 549).

DYAS
v.
CRUISE.

lessor to run the question on the *quantum* of rent reserved very closely; for if he renewed at the end of twenty years from the first granting of the lease, the remainder-man might have a lease fixed on him for twenty-one years from that time, reserving less than the best rent which then could have been reserved; but the answer is, that if the fact were so, the lease would be void, and the remainder-man might bring his ejectment and recover the premises." That does not quite agree with the position of Lord REDESDALE. There are other cases, which it is unnecessary to refer to more particularly, which do not support the doctrine of Lord REDESDALE on this subject; and my impression is, that if the best rent be reserved at the time, *the contract ought to be enforced. But then the question, whether the plaintiff was entitled to a partial performance of the agreement, arose. Lord REDESDALE refused it; for he said that the lessee knew the party had only a limited power of leasing, and intended to execute it; and that there was no mutuality. I doubt whether that can be maintained as the law of the Court, when there is no fraud in the transaction. If there be a *bonâ fide* intention to execute the power, and that contract cannot be carried into effect, I do not see why the interest of the tenant for life should not be bound, to the extent he is able to bind it, unless there be some inconvenience. In a late case, *Graham* v. *Oliver* (1), the MASTER OF THE ROLLS, alluding to the difficulties in these cases, observed, that the Court had thought it right, in many cases, to get over these difficulties, for the purpose of compelling parties to perform their agreements; and that it was right they should be compelled to do so, where it can be done without any great preponderance of inconvenience. If, therefore, it had appeared in this case, that Mr. Dyas was aware that the lease was to be made to him by means of the execution of a power, then, although the rent were not strictly the best, yet I should have been of opinion, this being a fair transaction, that Mr. Dyas would be entitled to a performance of the contract, to the extent of binding the life estate of Mr. Cruise: as in the case referred to, in the note to *Lawrenson* v. *Butler* (2), where an incumbent contracted with a tenant in tail in remainder for the purchase of the advowson, and, on the faith of that contract, built a better house on the glebe; afterwards, the person in whom the life estate was vested refused to join in making a tenant to the *præcipe* in order that *a recovery might be suffered; and consequently no sufficient conveyance could be made of the

[*487]

[*488]

(1) 52 R. R. 58 (3 Beav. 128). (2) 1 Sch. & Lef. 19.

advowson. But Lord THURLOW held that the purchaser was entitled
to a partial performance of the contract; for that, on the faith of
it, he had expended money on the glebe. So here, Mr. Dyas, on
the faith of this contract, has in the course of the first year of his
term expended upwards of 700*l.* in lasting improvements; and,
therefore, I should have held, if it had been necessary to decide
the point, that Mr. Dyas was entitled to a decree for a partial
performance of the contract.

I have gone into the consideration of this point, merely to show
Mr. Cruise that, in any view of the case, he could not have
succeeded to the extent he desired; but I hold without difficulty,
that this is a valid contract binding upon the inheritance, and that
the contract must be specifically performed by the grant of a lease
for the whole term mentioned in it; and Mr. Cruise must pay the
costs of the suit.

1845.
June 18.

SIR EDWARD
SUGDEN,
L.C.

[521]

BURROWES *v.* MOLLOY.

(2 Jo. & Lat. 521—529; S. C. 8 Ir. Eq. R. 482.)

Advances made by a mortgagee for the preservation of the estate (*ex. gr.*
head rent paid by him) follow the nature of the mortgage security: and if
the mortgagee is not entitled to foreclose the mortgage until after the
decease of mortgagor, neither is he entitled, during the life of the mortgagor, to a sale of the estate for payment of such advances: but if
necessary, a receiver will be appointed to keep down the interest on the
mortgage debt and advances.

The proviso for redemption in a mortgage of a leasehold for years was,
that upon payment of the principal, on a day mentioned, and interest
thereon, and the head rents in the mean time, the deed should be void. By
deed of equal date, reciting that the agreement of the parties was, that the
principal should not be called in until after the decease of the mortgagor,
but that, by mistake, it was stated in the mortgage deed that the principal
might be called in on a day certain, the mortgagee covenanted that the
principal money should not be called in until after the decease of the
mortgagor; anything in the deed of mortgage to the contrary notwithstanding.

Held, that the mortgagee could not foreclose the mortgage during the
life of the mortgagor, though the interest was in arrear, and the mortgagor
had not paid the head rent.

WILLIAM LOFTUS OTWAY, being possessed of several houses and
gardens under a lease thereof to him made by the Hon. S. Herbert,
for the term of sixty-one years, from the 25th March, 1832, at the
yearly rent of 120*l.*, by an indenture of the 27th of March, 1833, in
consideration of the sum of 250*l.*, charged them with an annuity
or rent-charge of 30*l.*, payable to Thomas O'Reilly during his life.
This deed contained a power to re-purchase the annuity upon

payment of the sum of 250*l.* and all arrears, and giving three months' notice.

In July, 1836, W. L. Otway assigned the premises demised to him to Arabella Lee, for the residue of his term therein, subject to redemption upon payment of the sum of 500*l.*

By a post-nuptial settlement of the 2nd of January, 1837, W. L. Otway assigned his interest in the lease to two trustees, upon certain trusts, for the benefit of his wife and children.

After the execution of this settlement, the plaintiff, Peter Burrowes, married Catherine, one of the children of W. L. Otway.

W. L. Otway being indebted to Peter Burrowes in the sum of 900*l.* for money lent, by indenture of mortgage of the 1st of June, 1841, made between himself of the one part, and Peter Burrowes of the other part, assigned the houses and premises demised by the lease of 1832, to him, for the residue of the term of sixty-one years; subject to a proviso, that if W. L. Otway, his executors, &c., should pay to Peter Burrowes, his executors, &c., the sum of 900*l.* on the 1st of May, 1842, together with interest thereon, in the mean time, at the rate of 8*l.* 10*s.* per cent. per annum, on every 1st of May and 1st of November in each year, and should, in the mean time, pay the yearly rent, and perform the covenants in the lease of the said lands, which were on the part of the lessee to be paid and performed, then the indenture and bond collateral therewith should be void.

By another indenture of equal date, and made between Peter Burrowes of the one part, and W. L. Otway of the *other part; after reciting the mortgage of equal date, and that upon the treaty for that mortgage it was stipulated and agreed on, that the principal sum secured by it should not be called in until after the decease of W. L. Otway, but that by mistake it was stated in the deed of mortgage, that the principal sum of 900*l.* might be called in after the 1st of May, 1842; and that Peter Burrowes, in order to correct that error, and to carry the original intention of the parties into execution, proposed to execute a deed of covenant, enlarging the time of redemption to the day of the decease of W. L. Otway, as originally agreed on; it was witnessed that, Peter Burrowes, for himself, his executors, administrators, and assigns, covenanted with W. L. Otway, his executors, &c., that the principal sum of 900*l.*, or any part thereof, should not be called in until after the decease of W. L. Otway, anything in the deed of mortgage or bond collateral therewith, to the contrary in anywise notwithstanding.

BURROWES
v.
MOLLOY.

In October, 1841, W. L. Otway granted an annuity of 31*l.* to Thomas Keller, his attorney, and charged the same on the premises demised by the lease: and on the 16th of May, 1843, he executed his bond and warrant of attorney to confess judgment thereon to the plaintiff, Peter Burrowes, in the penal sum of 480*l.*, conditioned for the payment of 240*l.*, with interest at 6*l.* per cent. per annum; on which bond judgment was entered as of Easter Term, 1843.

On the day after the execution of this bond, W. L. Otway was arrested for debt; and was afterwards discharged as an insolvent debtor, having previously executed an assignment of all his estate and effects to J. S. Molloy, the provisional assignee. At the time [*524] of his arrest, a large arrear *of the head rent of the mortgaged premises was due to the Hon. S. Herbert, who commenced legal proceedings for the recovery thereof. Peter Burrowes, in order to save the interest under the lease from eviction, on the 15th November, 1843, paid to the Hon. S. Herbert the sum of 387*l.* 10*s.* for rent up to the 29th September, 1843, and 3*l.* 3*s.* 6*d.* for costs. O'Reilly, the prior annuitant, also filed a bill to raise the arrears of his annuity ; and Peter Burrowes, to prevent further litigation and expenses to the estate, paid him 30*l.*, being the arrears due to him up to September, 1843, together with 17*l.* 16*s.* 10*d.* for costs.

The bill was filed by Peter Burrowes, praying that an account might be taken of the sum due to him on foot of his mortgage and judgments, and for his advances for arrears of head rent, annuity, and costs; and that the money so advanced by him in discharge of the arrears of head rent, with the interest thereof, might be declared to be a valid charge on the premises, in priority to all charges and incumbrances affecting the premises; and that he might be declared entitled to add the sums paid by him for the arrears of the annuity, and costs, to his other demands; and that the indenture of the 2nd January, 1837, might be declared fraudulent and void against the plaintiff; and for payment of the moneys to be found due to the plaintiff on the taking of such account; and in default, a foreclosure and sale; and that the plaintiff might be at liberty to redeem the mortgage of the 1st July, 1836, and, if necessary, to re-purchase the annuity of the 27th of March, 1833: and for a receiver.

At the time of filing this bill there was due to the plaintiff, on foot of the mortgage of 1841, the principal sum of 900*l.*, and a [*525] small arrear of interest on account of the half-year's *gale thereof, which became due next before the filing of the bill.

O'Reilly, by his answer, denied the right of the plaintiff to be paid the sum advanced by him for head rent, in priority to his annuity; as it had been paid without his privity or consent.

Keller insisted that, by reason of the deed of covenant, the plaintiff was not entitled to foreclose his mortgage until after the decease of W. L. Otway; and that his right to relief, on foot of the advances made by him, followed the nature of his title to the mortgage.

Mr. Serjt. Warren, *Mr. Brooke*, and *Mr. Bowen*, for the plaintiff: *Gladwyn* v. *Hitchman* (1); *Stanhope* v. *Manners* (2).

Mr. Pigot and *Mr. Maley* for the defendant, Keller, cited *Bonham* v. *Newcomb* (3); *Lawless* v. *Mansfield* (4); *Ramsbottom* v. *Wallis* (5).

Mr. Close for the defendant, O'Reilly.

Mr. R. Warren for other parties.

THE LORD CHANCELLOR: [526]

In this case, the mortgage under which the plaintiff claims bears date the 1st of June, 1841, and is in the common form, providing that upon the payment of the sum of 900*l.* on the 1st of May, 1842, with interest thereon, in the mean time, on every 1st of May and 1st of November, and upon payment in the mean time of the yearly rent, and performance of the covenants in the lease, the mortgage should be void; but by a deed of even date therewith, it appears that the agreement between the parties was, that the principal sum should not be called for until after the decease of the mortgagor. This deed recited, that by mistake it had been stated in the deed of mortgage that the principal sum might be called in upon the 1st of May, 1842; and that the parties to it were willing to correct that mistake, and to carry their original intention into execution; and that the mortgagee had proposed to execute a deed of covenant enlarging the time of redemption to the day of the decease of the mortgagor, as originally agreed upon: and then the mortgagee covenanted with the mortgagor, that the principal sum of 900*l.* should not be called in until after the decease of William Loftus Otway, the mortgagor, anything in the deed or bond to the contrary in anywise notwithstanding.

(1) 2 Vern. 135.
(2) 2 Eden, 197.
(3) 1 Vern. 232.
(4) 58 R. R. 303 (1 Dr. & War. 557).
(5) 42 R. R. 278 (5 L. J. (N. S.) Ch. 92).

BURROWES
v.
MOLLOY.

[*527]

[*528]

Supposing that the principal sum had been made payable on a given day, no matter whether it was one year or twenty years after the date of the mortgage, with interest thereon half-yearly in the mean time, and that, before the day of payment of the principal money, default had been made in the payment of the interest thereon, the mortgagee would, at any time after that event, have had a right to file his bill for a foreclosure ; because his right became absolute at law *by the nonpayment of the interest, the estate having been conveyed subject to a condition which had not been fulfilled.   But here the agreement was different; for although by the deed of mortgage it was stipulated that the principal sum was to be repaid on the 1st of May, 1842, in the ordinary form, yet from the deed of covenant it appears that the real agreement between the parties was, that the principal sum should not be called in until after the decease of the mortgagor ; and there is an actual covenant by the mortgagee that he will not call in the principal money during the life-time of the mortgagor, which is not qualified by any stipulation respecting the payment of the interest in the mean time, or of the rent reserved by the lease.   This transaction assumed a different shape with respect to the payment of the principal and the payment of the interest ; it was only upon the nonpayment of the principal sum, after the decease of the mortgagor, that the mortgagee was to have a right to foreclose.   Interest was to be paid half-yearly upon the principal sum ; and after the decease of the mortgagor any default in the payment of the interest would enable the mortgagee to file his bill of foreclosure, because the condition would then have been broken : but the covenant is independent of everything contained in the deed of mortgage ; and is, in point of fact, an absolute covenant, that, notwithstanding anything contained in the mortgage deed, the mortgagee will not call in the principal money during the life-time of the mortgagor.   I do not see how any default in the payment of the interest, during the life-time of the mortgagor, can enable the mortgagee to commit a breach of his covenant.   It was said that this was like a case where, although the money was by the proviso for redemption to be paid at a fixed period, yet the mortgagee covenants that he will not call in the principal for a longer period, unless default should be made in the payment of the interest in the mean *time ; but the parties here have not entered into such an arrangement.   I think, therefore, that under these instruments the plaintiff was not at liberty to file his bill for a foreclosure, as far as relates to the principal money; and therefore cannot do so in respect of the interest which accrued before the principal sum became payable.

Then comes the question, whether, on account of his salvage claims, the plaintiff is entitled to file this bill. No authority has been cited in support of this claim; and I am of opinion that he could not file such a bill as a mere salvage creditor: for, if claiming as a mortgagee, he cannot, during the life-time of the mortgagor file a bill to foreclose; neither can he, by making advances arising out of his character as a mortgagee, entitle himself to maintain a suit which he could not maintain in his original character of mortgagee. That is settled by the case of *Ramsbottom* v. *Wallis* (1), which has been referred to, where a second mortgagee, having covenanted not to foreclose his mortgage for ten years, purchased up the first mortgage, and then sought to foreclose; and it was held that he could not file his bill to foreclose that mortgage. Whatever might be the priority of his claim, he could not enforce that claim by reason of his covenant.

These observations refer to the defence set up by Mr. Keller: but as to Mr. O'Reilly, the plaintiff must submit to re-purchase the annuity granted to him, or have his bill dismissed as against him. A party has no right to file a bill against a person having an existing annuity, unless he have rights prior to the annuitant. If the plaintiff choose to re-purchase the annuity to O'Reilly, he is at liberty to do so. He may offer to re-purchase the annuity, but he cannot file *a bill against him without such an offer on his part. Instead of so doing, the plaintiff has filed this bill, and now declines to re-purchase the annuity.

[*529]

There is some difficulty in this case; but I think the plaintiff is entitled to a receiver. I do not see what right Mr. Keller has to prevent it; for he cannot contend that the plaintiff's interest on the principal sum ought not to be kept down. I regret that I cannot grant the relief sought, for this is a hard case, the deed of covenant having been prepared by Mr. Keller himself.

(1) 42 R. R. 278 (5 L. J. (N. S.) Ch. 92); Coote on Mortgages, App. 704.

1845.
June 18, 20.

SIR EDWARD
SUGDEN,
L.C.

[529]

GREEN *v.* GREEN (1).

(2 Jo. & Lat. 529—543 ; S. C. 8 Ir. Eq. R. 473.)

A testator devised lands to P., upon trust to convey them to his three sons, with remainders to their respective issue, in such shares as P. should appoint, and in default of appointment he gave the lands to them equally as tenants in common. In 1786 P., in execution of the trust, conveyed part of the lands to the use that in case S. (one of the sons) should marry with the consent of P. first obtained, but not otherwise, such woman or women as he should so marry, in case she should survive him, should, during her life, receive for jointure such annuity (not exceeding a certain sum), as S. should appoint; and to the further use, in case S. should marry with such consent, but not otherwise, that he might, by deed or will, charge the lands with 500*l.* for portions for his younger children, payable in such shares as he should appoint.

In 1788 S. married with consent; and, reciting his power, covenanted that the trustees of his settlement, in case there should be one or more younger children of the marriage living at his death, should raise 500*l.* out of the lands; said sum to be divided in such shares and proportions, amongst such younger children, as he should by will appoint; and for want of appointment, equally.

There was issue of this marriage three younger children.

S., after the death of P., married a second wife, and charged the lands with an annuity for her jointure; and died leaving his wife and four children of his second marriage, and the three younger children of his first marriage, surviving. By his will, in 1842, he appointed one shilling to each of the children of the first marriage, and the residue among the children of the second marriage.

Held, upon the construction of the settlement of 1786 and the circumstances, that the consent of P. was only requisite to any marriage of S. which should take place in his lifetime ; and that the children of the second marriage were objects of the power.

2. That the settlement of 1788 amounted to a contract, that so far as S. could bind his power, the children of the first marriage should take the fund equally between them, if he did not otherwise apportion it amongst them ; that upon there being issue of the second marriage, S.'s power of appointment was gone; and that the children of both marriages were entitled to the fund equally between them, as one class.

[*530] GODFREY GREEN, being seised of the lands of Green Hills, under a lease for three lives, with a covenant *for the perpetual renewal thereof, devised them by his will, which bore date in October, 1777, to Francis Green and Caleb Powel, and the survivor of them, and the heirs and assigns of such survivor, upon trust that they, or the survivor of them, should in his or their discretion convey them to his three sons, Godfrey Green, Samuel B. Green, and John Green, in such shares and proportions, for such estates, whether in fee, fee tail or for life, with remainder to their respective issues, and subject to such powers, conditions and limitations as the trustees,

(1) *Dawson* v. *Oliver-Massey* (1876) 2 Ch. D. 753, 45 L. J. Ch. 519, 34 L. T. 551.

or the survivor of them, should by deed or deeds limit or appoint;
and for want of such appointment, he directed that his said sons
should have, hold and enjoy the lands, share and share alike, to
them and their respective heirs, as tenants in common : and died
shortly afterwards.

Francis Green, one of the trustees, died in 1782; and disputes
having arisen relative to the mode in which the trusts of the will
should be carried into execution, a bill was filed by Caleb Powell
for the purpose : but all the parties being competent to compromise
the suit, an arrangement was entered into, which was carried into
effect by an indenture dated the 20th of November, 1786, and made
between Godfrey Green of the first part; John Green of the second
part ; Samuel Green of the third part; John O'Brien and Elizabeth,
his wife, and Edmund Prendergast and Mary, his wife, who were
annuitants named in the will of Godfrey Green, of the fourth part;
Caleb Powell of the fifth part ; Simon Purdon and Samuel Dixon
of the sixth part; and Robert Powell and Benjamin Friend of the
seventh part: whereby it was witnessed that, in pursuance and
execution of the trusts of the will, Caleb Powell, together with
Godfrey Green, John Green, and Samuel Green, according to their
several and respective estates and *interests therein, granted and   [*531]
released the said lands of Green Hills, and all their estates and
interests therein, unto Simon Purdon and Samuel Dixon, and the
survivor of them, his heirs and assigns, for the lives of the cestuis
que vie named in the existing lease of the lands, and the life of every
other person who should be added thereto, pursuant to the covenant
for perpetual renewal thereof : to hold that part of the lands called
the House Division, chargeable with the entire head rent payable
out of the entire of the lands, and subject to one-third part of the
renewal fines, to the use of the trustees for a term of 100 years ;
and, subject thereto, to the use of Samuel Green and his assigns
for his life ; and after the determination of that estate, to the use
of trustees and their heirs during his life, upon trust to preserve,
&c.; and from and after the decease of Samuel Green, then to the
use, intent, and purpose, in case he, the said Samuel Green, should
marry with the consent and approbation of the said Caleb Powell
first had and obtained in writing, but not otherwise, that such
woman or women as he should so marry, in case she should happen
to survive him, should, during her natural life, take and receive,
for and in the name of jointure, such annuity (not exceeding the
rate of 8l. by the 100l. for each 100l. as he, the said Samuel, should

GREEN
v.
GREEN.

[*532]

[*533]

actually receive as a portion with such woman or women) as he
should by deed appoint; with power to distrain for the same.
And to the further use, intent, and purpose, in case the said Samuel
Green should marry with such consent and approbation as aforesaid,
but not otherwise, that he should and might, by any deed to be by
him executed, or by his last will and testament, charge and
incumber the said part of said lands, so to him limited for life,
with any sum not exceeding the sum of 500*l.* as and for the portions
and provisions for his younger children lawfully to be begotten;
and *to be payable at such times and in such shares and proportions as he should by said deed or will limit and appoint: and
subject thereto, in case the said Samuel Green should marry with
such consent as aforesaid, then to the use of the first and other
sons of Samuel Green by his said wife, *quasi* in tail male; with
remainder to the daughters of the marriage in tail general; with
divers remainders over : and the deed contained similar limitations
of other parts of the lands to the other sons of the testator and
their issue. Upon the execution of this deed Samuel Green
entered into possession of the part of the lands limited to him.

In 1788 Samuel Green married Miss Anna Maria Young, having
previously obtained the written consent of Caleb Powell thereto;
and in contemplation of that marriage, a settlement of the 4th of
October, 1788, was made between Samuel Green of the first part;
Anna M. Young of the second part ; Caleb Powell of the third part;
and Robert Young of the fourth part; whereby, after reciting,
amongst other things, the will of Godfrey Green, and the indenture
of November, 1786, it was witnessed, that in consideration of 600*l.*,
the marriage portion of Anna Maria Young, and for the purpose of
settling and securing the sum of 500*l.* for the younger children of
him the said Samuel Green, on the body of Anna M. Young, out of
his the said Samuel Green's division or share of the lands of Green
Hills, under or by virtue of the several powers given unto him by
the will of Godfrey Green, and by the indenture of the 20th of
September, 1786; he the said Samuel Green, for himself, his heirs,
executors, and administrators, covenanted with Caleb Powell and
Robert Young, their heirs and assigns, that in case the said
intended marriage should take place, the share or division of the
lands of Green Hills, known by the name *of the House Division,
should be settled and assured, subject to a jointure of 48*l.* per
annum for Anna Maria Young, to the use of the first son of Samuel
Green on the body of Anna M. Young lawfully to be begotten, and

his heirs male ; with divers limitations over : and further, that they, the said Caleb Powell and Robert Young, [or the survivor of them, or the executors or administrators of such survivor (in case there should be one or more younger child or children of the body of Samuel Green on the body of Anna M. Young begotten, living at the time of the death of Samuel Green), should raise and levy the full sum of 500*l.* sterling, out of the rents, issues, and profits which should be issuing and payable out of the said House Division of the lands of Green Hills, over and above the jointure thereby provided for Anna Maria Young, and without prejudice to the same ; the said sum of 500*l.* to be divided in such shares and proportions amongst such younger children, if more than one, and in such manner, as Samuel Green should by his last will and testament appoint and direct; and in case there should be living but one younger child at the time of the death of Samuel Green, the said sum of 500*l.* to go and become the property of such younger child ; and for want of such appointment, that then and in such case the said sum of 500*l.*, if there were more than one younger child, should go in gavel amongst such younger children, to be paid to them at twenty-one or marriage : and in case there should be but one younger child by the then intended marriage, that then the said sum of 500*l.* should become the property of the said younger son or daughter, payable at the time therein mentioned.

There was issue of that marriage three children, viz.: Godfrey Green, and the defendants, Anna Maria Young, otherwise Green, and Sarah Young, otherwise Green.

Anna Maria Green having died, Samuel Green, in the year 1815 (Caleb Powell being then dead), married Frances Moffett ; and, upon that occasion, he received a fortune of 800*l.* with his wife. There was issue of that marriage five children, viz.: the plaintiffs, Samuel, John, Eliza, Alicia, and Frances Green. [534]

In 1839, Godfrey Green, the younger, died intestate, leaving Robert Young Green his eldest son and heir-at-law.

In 1841 Samuel Green executed a post-nuptial settlement, whereby, in consideration of her fortune of 800*l.*, he charged his portion of the lands with a jointure of 64*l.* per annum for his wife, Frances, during her life, in case she should survive him.

Samuel Green died in February, 1844, having made his will, dated the 2nd November, 1842, whereby, after reciting the indenture of the 20th of September, 1786, and his power to charge the lands with portions for his younger children, he charged and encumbered

GREEN
r.
GREEN.

that portion of the lands called the House Quarter with the sum of
500*l.* late currency, for portions and provisions for his younger
children; and he bequeathed the same to and amongst such
younger children in the manner following, that is to say, to his
eldest daughter, Anna Maria Young, one shilling; to his daughter,
Sarah Young, one shilling; to his son, Samuel Green, one shilling;
to his daughter, Eliza Green, 150*l.* sterling; to his daughter,
Alicia Green, 100*l.*; to his daughter, Frances Green, 200*l.*; and
to his son, John Green, 11*l.* 7*s.* 9*d.*

[535]

It was admitted that the defendants, Anna Maria Young and
Sarah Young (who had married in the life-time of their father),
had not received any portion or fortune on the occasion of their
respective marriages, and that they did not at any time receive
any sum of money by way of advancement in life, from their
father.

The bill was filed by the children of the second marriage against
Robert Young Green, the younger children of the first marriage,
and the widow of Samuel Green, for an account of the sum due on
foot of the charge of 500*l.* so bequeathed by the will; and that
whatever should be found due upon the taking of that account
might be paid to the parties entitled, by Robert Young Green; or,
in default, a sale.

Mr. Serjt. Warren, Mr. Moore, and *Mr. Billing,* for the
plaintiffs :

*   * The appointment by the settlement of 1788 is void,
having been executed in favour of some of the objects of the power
only. *   *   *

[536]

Mr. Moore, Mr. Brooke, Mr. E. Pennefather, and *Mr. R. P.
Lloyd,* for the younger children of the first marriage, [cited
West v. *Burney* (1)]:

In *Bradish* v. *Bradish* (2), a case like the present, it was held,
that the second settlement was a fraud upon the children of the
first marriage. We submit, however, that the children of the
second marriage are not the objects of the power; for that marriage
was had without the consent of the trustee. *   *   *

Mr. Martley and *Mr. Owen* for Robert Young Green.

(1) 32 R. R. 237 (1 Russ. & My. 431).   (2) 12 R. R. 109 (2 Ball & Bea. 479),

Mr. Monahan and *Mr. Charles Shaw* for the widow of Samuel Green.·

Mr. Moore, in reply.

[Other cases cited by counsel are referred to in the following judgment:]

THE LORD CHANCELLOR: [537]

The question in this case is as to the rights of the plaintiffs, the children of the second marriage. The case is one of some difficulty, and arises out of the will of Godfrey Green, by which the property was given to trustees, with the unusual power, at their discretion, to convey it to the three sons of the testator, in such shares and for such estates, and subject to such powers, conditions, and limitations, as they or the survivor of them should think proper; and in default of appointment to his sons in fee, as tenants in common.

In consequence of a dispute relative to the disposition of the estates, a suit was instituted by one of the trustees, to carry the trusts of the will into execution. That suit was compromised; and the property was divided into three portions; and the surviving trustee (the other having previously died), together with the three sons, conveyed the property to the use, as to each separate portion of it, of one of the sons for his life; and after his decease, in case he should marry with the consent of the trustee (Mr. Powell) first obtained in writing, but not otherwise, that such woman or women as he should marry, in case she should happen to survive him, should yearly during her life receive, in the name of jointure, such annuity, not exceeding the rate of 8*l.* by the 100*l.* for each 100*l.* as he should actually receive as a portion with such woman or women, as he should by deed appoint: and further, in case he should marry with such consent as aforesaid, but not otherwise, that he should and might, by deed or will, charge and incumber the part of the lands so to him limited for life, with any sum not exceeding 500*l.* as and for a provision for his younger children; and *to be   [*538] payable at such times, and in such shares and proportions, as he should by such deed or will limit and appoint: and, subject thereto, to the use of the first and other sons of the marriage in tail male; remainder to the daughters in tail general; and in default of such issue, then to the other two brothers and their issue, with precisely similar limitations. The same uses were declared respecting the shares of each of the other brothers, with the same condition requiring consent to marriage.

Upon the first marriage of Samuel, which was had with the consent of Mr. Powell, a settlement was executed, whereby he covenanted to settle a jointure upon his intended wife ; and also that the trustees, in case there should be one or more younger child or children of the marriage living at his death, should raise and levy the sum of 500l. sterling, out of the rents and profits which should be issuing out of the lands, over and above the jointure thereby provided; which sum of 500l. was to be divided in such shares and proportions, amongst such younger children, and in such manner, as he should by will appoint; and in default of appointment, the said sum of 500l. was to go in equal shares amongst such younger children.

Afterwards, the Act of Parliament for which I am responsible was passed; which did not give power to the appointor, in cases like the present, to exclude any of the children; but enabled him to give any sum which he might think proper to each of the objects of the power.

It is argued, first, that the execution of the power in favour of the children of the second marriage is bad; the appointor having married his second wife without the consent *of the trustee, who had died previously. The donee of the power has executed it by giving but one shilling to each of the children of his first marriage; and has appointed the bulk of the fund to the children of his second marriage.

[*539]

The first question which arises is, whether the obtaining the consent of the trustee to his first marriage was a sufficient compliance with the condition. I am of opinion that it would not be sufficient in this case, if the trustee had been living at the period of the second marriage : particularly as regards the widow; for it was expressly declared that in case he should marry with the consent of the trustee, but not otherwise, his wife should have the jointure. It is an express declaration, that none shall have the jointure but the woman whom he shall marry with the consent of the trustee. This altogether distinguishes the case from that of *Hutcheson* v. *Hammond* (1), and shows that the consent of the trustee to the first marriage did not render it unnecessary to obtain his consent to the second marriage. But here the question is different : Mr. Powell died before the second marriage; and the question is, whether

(1) 3 Br. C. C. 281.

his death, which rendered his consent unattainable, created an
insuperable bar to the exercise of the power in case Samuel should
marry again. *Mansell* v. *Mansell* (1) was relied upon as an authority
against this being held to be a good execution of the power: but
I am of opinion that that case is also distinguishable from the
present; for there the Court saw an intention that the power should
not be exercised without the consent required, and accordingly held
that there was a breach of the condition, because the consent might
have been obtained if the party had thought proper to give it.
*Upon the construction of the settlement I am of opinion, that all
that was intended by the clause was, that Mr. Powell personally,
during his life-time, should have control over the marriage of the
sons; and that consent having, by Mr. Powell's death, been
rendered unattainable, this marriage, although without the consent
of Mr. Powell, was such a marriage as to make the issue of it
objects of the power.

In coming to this conclusion, it is certainly very difficult to get
over the words of the settlement respecting the power of jointuring;
which limit the jointure "to such woman or women as he should
so marry," that is, marry with consent: but as I think the intention
of the parties was, that the obligation to obtain the consent should
be imposed only during the life-time of the party competent to give
such consent, I shall struggle with these technical terms, so as to
effectuate the intention of the parties. The limitations in the will
of Godfrey Green justify this view; for under it, in default of
appointment by the trustees, the three sons took the estate as
tenants in common in *quasi* fee: if, therefore, the trustees in the
settlement of 1786 had died before the marriage of any of the sons,
as their consent would in that case have been unattainable, the
settlement would have been defeated, and the sons must have fallen
back upon the limitations in their father's will. Upon the whole
case, therefore, I am of opinion, that the want of the consent of the
trustee did not, under the circumstances, prevent the exercise of
the power by the donee in favour of the children of the second
marriage; for I am bound to follow Lord ELDON in *Burrell* v.
Crutchley (2), and to hold that the power did include all the
children, as well those of the second as of the first marriage.

By the settlement executed upon the first marriage that *power
was exercised in favour of the younger children of that marriage
exclusively. This might have been a good execution of the power.

(1) Wilmot's Notes, 36.   (2) 15 Ves. 544.

GREEN
v.
GREEN.

[*540]

[*541]

GREEN
v.
GREEN.

It was not void upon the face of it; for the appointor might not have married again, or even if he did, he might not have had any children of the second marriage, who would be objects of the power. If he had not married again, the power would have been properly executed; for this settlement would, in that case, have included all his younger children. This, therefore, was not a bad execution of the power at the time when it was made; although it would become so, if there were any children of the second marriage; and such having been the case, it has become informal. Now, I quite agree in the proposition, that if a man execute a power imperfectly, and that there is nothing to prevent a further execution of the power by him, he may execute it again in a valid manner. The appointor, therefore, still possessed the ability to execute the power; and accordingly he executed it by his will. But then the question arises, could he execute it so as wholly to defeat the claims of the children of the first marriage under their settlement, and to let in the children of the second marriage exclusively.

There is no doubt upon the authorities, that a man having a power, may bind himself not to execute it, save subject to particular restrictions and conditions. He may release it altogether; or covenant to execute it in a particular manner; and the Court will give effect to such a covenant. Where the donee of the power restricts and limits himself in the execution of it, he must execute it accordingly, or not at all. In this case the donee of the power appointed the entire fund to the younger children of the first marriage, but reserved to himself the power of apportioning it [*542] amongst *them as he thought proper. The second marriage put an end to the power of apportionment. The money was to be raised as before, but the donee could not apportion the fund exclusively amongst the younger children of the first marriage; for the children of the second marriage had become entitled to a share of it. But in default of appointment the children of the first marriage were to take the fund equally. Is not that in effect a contract by him, that, so far as he can bind his power, the children of the first marriage shall take the fund equally between them; and is he at liberty, by his own voluntary act, to defeat the provision made for them? I am of opinion he had no such power: he bound himself to give effect to the provision in favour of the children of the first marriage, and could not, by a voluntary disposition, defeat the provision which by a solemn deed he had made for them.

I consider the execution of the power by the first settlement as still operative; and if operative, the donee could not defeat the interest of the children of the first marriage under it, as between themselves and the children of the second marriage, taking in default of any execution of the power. There is some difficulty in the matter; but the conclusion to which I have come is, that the children of the first and second marriages take the fund equally between them as children of one class. I think that, within the authorities (not meaning to strain the rule, but to carry into effect the intention of the parties), I am at liberty to hold that the 500*l*. belongs to the children of both marriages. I shall therefore declare that, in the events which have happened, all the children of both marriages are entitled, as the younger children of their father, in equal shares; and that the plaintiffs are entitled to their portion accordingly. The *costs of all parties must come out of the fund; and let the widow be at liberty to go before the Master to establish (if she can) her right to the annuity she claims; she must pay her own costs of that reference. The expense of raising the money must be borne by the estate.

[*543]

EXTRACT FROM THE DECREE.—Declare that the younger children of the first marriage, and all the children of the second marriage, take the sum of 500*l*. in the pleadings mentioned, between them, as one class; and that the plaintiffs in the cause are entitled, in the events which have happened, and under the instruments which have been executed, to their portions of the said sum of 500*l*. accordingly. Let the expense, if any, of raising said monies, be borne out of the estate, and let the costs of all parties to this cause be paid out of the fund. Declare that the defendant, Frances Green, otherwise Moffet, having married Samuel Green, deceased, in the pleadings mentioned, after the death of Caleb Powell, in the pleadings named, his consent to the said marriage was not necessary to enable the said Samuel Green to charge his portion of the lands in the pleadings mentioned with a jointure for the said Frances Green: and let the said Frances Green be at liberty to go before the Master and establish her right to the jointure in her answer in this cause mentioned; and if she should establish it, declare that she is entitled to have the same provided for her out of the lands.

1845.
Nov. 7, 8, 12,
25.

SIR EDWARD
SUGDEN,
L.C.

[720]

JENNINGS *v.* BOND (1).
BOND *v.* JENNINGS.

(2 Jo. & Lat. 720—746; S. C. 8 Ir. Eq. R. 755.)

A., being seised in fee of Ardgullen, confessed a judgment: and afterwards, upon the marriage of his son B., conveyed the lands to the use of B., for his life, remainder to the issue of the marriage; and covenanted that they were free from incumbrances. By his will he gave several legacies, and died, having appointed B. his executor, and leaving assets more than sufficient to pay all his debts and legacies. Upon the marriage of C., one of the legatees, a settlement was executed, whereby, after reciting the will of A., and that the legacy of C. was then in the hands of B., as executor, C. assigned the legacy to trustees, of whom B. was one, upon trust for C. for her life, and, after her decease without issue, upon trust for the benefit of the judgment creditor and his issue. In 1835 the judgment creditor instituted a suit for payment of his judgment out of the real and personal assets of the testator. In 1836 C. and her husband (there being no issue of their marriage) instituted another suit against B. and the persons entitled under their settlement in default of issue of their marriage, for the appointment of new trustees, and an account of the trust funds; and in that suit an order was made, on the consent of B., but without notice to the persons entitled in default of issue of C. and her husband, that B. should transfer to the credit of that cause, stock to the value of C.'s legacy, without prejudice to the rights of the parties; and it was ordered that the dividends thereof be paid to C. The stock was accordingly transferred by B., who purchased the same with the produce of the sale of part of the assets of the testator, which were outstanding in specie when the bill of 1835 was filed.

The assets having been wasted, the children of B., claiming as specialty creditors of A. under his covenant, filed a bill in 1840, to have the stock standing to the credit of C.'s cause applied in payment of the judgment debt.

Held, 1. That the stock had not been appropriated to the payment of C.'s legacy, either as against the specialty creditors or the other legatees of A., but that it still continued assets for payment of his debts and legacies.

2. That a purchaser for value of a legacy was but a purchaser of a chose in action; and that he was subject to the same equities, in respect of the legacy, as his vendor; and therefore to refund it if necessary for the payment of debts.

3. That a suit by a judgment creditor, for an account of the real and personal estate of his debtor and payment of his debts, is a sufficient *lis pendens* to affect an incumbrancer on the life estate of a defaulting executor in lands, the fee of which was subject to the judgment, with notice of an equity to have the life estate applied to answer the default of the executor.

4. Where the question is not between a registered and unregistered deed, notice by *lis pendens* is not affected by the registration of the title deed of the person sought to be affected thereby.

THE Rev. Wensley Bond was seised in fee of the lands of Ardgullen, in the county of Longford. In 1815, upon the marriage of his third daughter, the plaintiff Rebecca Jennings, then Rebecca Bond, spinster, with William Bond, the Rev. Wensley Bond and

(1) *Price* v. *Price* (1887) 35 Ch. D. 297, 56 L. J. Ch. 530, 56 L. T. 842.

William Bond respectively executed to trustees their several bonds, with warrants to confess *judgments thereon, each in the penal sum of 5,000*l*., conditioned for the payment of the principal sum of 2,500*l*. within three months after the decease of them respectively; upon trust, in the event of William Bond dying in the lifetime of Rebecca Bond, without leaving issue by her (which event happened), as to the sum of 1,500*l*., part of the sum of 2,500*l*., secured by the bond and warrant of the Rev. Wensley Bond, for the said Rev. Wensley Bond, his executors, &c.; and as to the sum of 1,000*l*., residue thereof, in trust for William Bond, his executors, &c. Judgment was, in Hilary Term, 1820, entered upon the bond of the Rev. Wensley Bond.

William Bond died in 1817; and by his will bequeathed to his wife, Rebecca, the interest on the 1,000*l*. for her life. Rebecca Bond afterwards married the Rev. William Jennings; and by settlement of the 29th of February, 1820, to which the trustees of the judgment and the personal representatives of William Bond were parties, after reciting that judgment had been entered upon the bond of the Rev. Wensley Bond, it was declared that said judgment should be held by the trustees thereof, upon trust that the Rev. William Jennings should receive the interest thereof during the joint lives of himself and his intended wife; and as to the sum of 1,500*l*., part of the principal sum of 2,500*l*., secured by the judgment, from and after the decease of the Rev. William Jennings, upon trust for the children of the marriage as the Rev. William Jennings should appoint.

There was issue of this marriage several children, who, with their parents, were plaintiffs in the first and defendants in the second cause.

In 1833, the executors of William Bond assigned to the *Rev. William Jennings the sum of 1,000*l*., parcel of the sum of 2,500*l*., secured by the judgment of Hilary Term, 1820, for his own use and benefit.

By indenture of settlement, bearing date the 1st of April, 1820, executed in contemplation of the marriage of Richard Wensley Bond, the youngest son of the Rev. Wensley Bond, with Miss Sophia Bond, the lands of Ardgullen were conveyed to James W. Little and George Little, and their heirs, upon trust (*inter alia*) to permit Richard W. Bond to receive the rents thereof during his life; and after his decease, subject to a jointure for his wife, to the use of the children of the marriage as Richard W. Bond should appoint; and in default of appointment, to the children equally as tenants in common in tail general. And the Rev. Wensley Bond thereby entered into absolute covenants with James W. Little and George Little for title; and for quiet enjoyment, free from all former and other gifts, grants, bargains, sales, mortgages, judgments, settlements, jointures, dowers, rights and title of dower, and all other charges and incumbrances whatsoever, a certain lease therein mentioned only excepted.

At the time of the execution of this settlement there was not any other incumbrance affecting the lands, save the judgment of Hilary Term, 1820.

The marriage was celebrated; and there was issue of it seven children, who were the plaintiffs in the second cause.

The Rev. Wensley Bond, previous to the execution of the settlement of the 1st of April, 1820, made his will and three codicils

[*723]

thereto. By his will he devised the *lands of Ardgullen to his son, Richard Wensley Bond, and his issue, in strict settlement. That devise was revoked by the settlement of the same lands in 1820. By his will he also gave to his son, the Reverend James Forward Bond, and Abraham H. Hutchinson, all his other estates, assets, and effects, of every nature and kind soever, in trust for payment of his just debts, funeral, and other incidental expenses; and bequeathed to his daughter Christiana the sum of 3,000*l.*, to his daughter Louisa 2,500*l.*, and to his daughter Catherine Tyrrell 1,000*l.*, and several other small legacies; and the remainder of his assets, if any, he bequeathed to his son, Richard Wensley Bond, his executors, administrators and assigns: and by his will he appointed his trustees and his son, Richard Wensley Bond, executors. The codicils did not affect the before-mentioned devises and bequests.

In October, 1820, the testator died, possessed of personal estate amounting to 15,527*l.* 5*s.* 4*d.*, late currency. His will was proved by his executors, but Richard Wensley Bond alone acted in execution of it.

Richard Wensley Bond, as such executor, received out of the assets several sums, amounting in the whole to 13,879*l.* 5*s.* 4*d.*, late currency; of which he had received, prior to the filing of the bill in the first cause, the sum of 10,027*l.* 0*s.* 4*d.*; and, subsequent to the institution of that suit, he assigned and disposed of two judgments, obtained by him as executor against the Earl of Courtown and Viscount Stopford, and an annuity granted to the testator by Sir James Bond, and applied same in manner hereinafter stated; and so possessed himself of the residue of the sum of 18,879*l.* 5*s.* 4*d.* Out of the sums so received by him he paid *the funeral and testamentary expenses of the testator, and all his debts, save the judgment of Hilary Term, 1820, amounting in the whole to the sum of 3,214*l.* 19*s.* 6*d.*, late currency. He also paid thereout several of the legacies bequeathed by the testator, amounting in the whole to the sum of 1,532*l.* 15*s.* late currency, leaving a sum of 9,132*l.* 10*s.* 10*d.*, late currency, in his hands, to be accounted for by him to the creditors and legatees of the testator at the time of the filing of the bill in the first cause.

In 1822 Louisa Bond married the Reverend Hugh Webb; and by indenture of settlement, bearing date the 16th of November in that year, and to which the trustees and executors of the Rev. Wensley Bond were parties, after reciting the will of the Rev. Wensley Bond and the intended marriage, and that the legacy of 2,500*l.* thereby bequeathed to Louisa Bond was in the hands of Richard Wensley Bond, as acting executor of the Rev. Wensley Bond, Louisa Bond assigned to James Forward Bond and Richard Wensley Bond the said legacy of 2,500*l.*, upon trust to pay the interest thereof to the separate use of Louisa Bond during her life; and, after her decease, to pay same to Hugh Webb, during his life; and, in default of issue of the marriage (which event happened) in trust for Christiana Bond and Catherine Tyrrell equally.

Louisa Webb died in July, 1824, without issue; Hugh Webb, who thereupon became entitled to a life interest in the legacy of 2,500*l.*, assigned same, on the 29th of October, 1835, to James W. Bond.

Christiana Bond, in 1826, married Thomas Golfin Young; and by indenture of settlement bearing date the 29th of May *in that year, to which the trustees and executors of the Rev. Wensley Bond were parties, after reciting the will of the Rev. Wensley Bond, and that the legacy of 3,000*l.* bequeathed to Christiana Bond was then in the hands of Richard Wensley Bond as such executor; and that, under the limitations of the settlement of Mr. and Mrs. Webb, Christiana Bond had become entitled to the sum of 1,250*l.*, one moiety of the legacy of 2,500*l.* to which Mrs. Webb had been entitled, subject to the life interest of Mr. Webb therein; Christiana Bond assigned to four trustees, of whom Richard Wensley Bond was one, the legacy of 3,000*l.*, and also the sum of 1,250*l.*, upon trust, as to the interest thereof, to the use of Christiana Bond

during her life ; and after her decease, to pay the interest of the
3,000*l.* to Thomas Golfin Young for his life ; and to pay and apply
the interest of the 1,250*l.* to the maintenance and education of the
issue of the marriage; but if no issue living at the death of Christiana
Bond, then to pay the whole of the interest to Thomas Golfin Young
during his life ; and after the decease of the survivor of them, to
pay the said principal sums to the children of the marriage, as
Christiana Bond should appoint ; and in default of appointment,
equally amongst them ; and if there should be no issue of the
marriage, then as to 500*l.*, part of the 3,000*l.*, for the sole use and
benefit of Thomas Golfin Young ; and as to the residue of the
3,000*l.* and the said sum of 1,250*l.* (subject to the life interest of
Mr. Webb therein), to pay the interest thereof to the separate use
of Rebecca Jennings during her life ; and, after her decease, to
pay the said principal sums of money to and amongst the children
of Rebecca Jennings, by her then present or any future husband, as
she should appoint ; and, in default of appointment, equally.

[726]   Mr. and Mrs. Young were living: there was no issue of their
marriage.

In 1824, Mary Tyrrell, a daughter of Catherine Tyrrell, married
George Vaughan ; and by indenture of settlement dated the 18th of
October, 1824, Catherine Tyrrell assigned to trustees the sum of
500*l.*, being one moiety of the legacy of 1,000*l.*, to which she was
entitled under the will of the Rev. Wensley Bond and also the sum
of 625*l.*, being one moiety of the sum of 1,250*l.*, to which she became
entitled on the death of her sister, Louisa Webb, expectant on the
death of Mr. Webb, upon trusts for the benefit of Catherine Tyrrell,
Mr. and Mrs. Vaughan and their issue.

There was issue of this marriage, several children. George
Vaughan died in January, 1840.

Richard Wensley Bond, up to the year 1835, paid the interest
on the sums of 3,000*l.* and 2,500*l.* to the persons entitled thereto.
The other trustees named in the settlements never acted in the
trusts thereof.

The bill in the first cause was filed on the 5th of November, 1835,
against the heir-at-law, personal representative, and devisees under
the will of the Rev. Wensley Bond: it set forth the title of the
plaintiffs to the judgment of 1820, and the will of the Rev. Wensley
Bond ; and charged that the Rev. Wensley Bond died seised and
possessed of very considerable real and personal property, much
more than sufficient, if properly applied, for the full payment of

all his debts and legacies; and that more than sufficient of said
personal property came to the hands of Richard Wensley Bond,
one of his executors, but that he had misapplied and *converted
same to his own use; and that no fund then remained available for
payment of the judgment, save the real estates of the Rev. Wensley
Bond. The bill further charged that Richard Wensley Bond had,
with the assets, paid off incumbrances affecting certain estates
which had been settled on himself, by his father-in-law, on his
marriage; and that the plaintiffs were entitled to pursue the assets
for payment of their demand: and prayed that the rights of all
parties under the will of the Rev. Wensley Bond might be declared;
and for an account of the real, freehold and personal estate of the
testator; and that the assets might be marshalled, and the trusts of
his will carried into execution; and if it should appear that any of
the assets of the testator had been applied by Richard Wensley
Bond in payment of any incumbrances affecting the estates settled
by his marriage settlement, that same might be declared to be part
of the assets of the testator; and for an account of the estates
comprised in such settlement, and sale thereof for payment of
their liabilities aforesaid.

On the 2nd of July, 1836, Thomas G. Young and Christiana, his
wife, filed their bill in this Court against Richard Wensley Bond
and others; and thereby prayed, *inter alia*, that Richard Wensley
Bond and the other trustees of their settlement might be restrained
from intermeddling with the trust monies, and might be removed
from the trusts of the settlement, and that new trustees might be
appointed in their place; and that the trust funds might be assigned
to such new trustees; and that Richard Wensley Bond might be
ordered to vest in Government Three and a-half per cent. stock, with
the privity of one of the Masters of the Court, the said two sums of
3,000*l.* and 1,250*l.*, late currency, and to transfer said stock to the
Accountant-General of the *Court, to the credit of the cause; or
otherwise might be ordered to lodge said sums of 3,000*l.* and
1,250*l.* in the Bank of Ireland, to the credit of the cause, with
the privity of the Accountant-General; and that all necessary
accounts might be taken.

Richard Wensley Bond, after the filing of the bill in the first
cause and shortly previous to the filing of the bill by Young and
wife, sold part of the personal estate of his testator, viz., the two
judgments obtained by him as executor, in Easter Term, 1835,
against the Earl of Courtown and Viscount Stopford, for the

JENNINGS
v.
BOND.

principal sum of 923*l.* 1*s.* 6½*d.*; and a judgment of same Term, obtained by him as executor, against the Earl of Courtown, for the principal sum of 461*l.* 10*s.* 9*d.*; and the annuity of 100*l.*, late currency, granted to the testator by Sir James Bond for an unexpired term of years. The judgments were assigned by him to Mr. Webb, by indenture of the 24th of December, 1835, in consideration of the sum of 1,000*l.*; and the annuity was assigned by him to Mr. E. Gibbon, by indenture of the 1st of May, 1836, in consideration of the sum of 1,400*l.*; and he applied the produce of these sales in the investment made by him to the credit of the cause of *Young* and wife v. *Bond*, hereinafter mentioned.

The Master, in the report hereinafter mentioned, found that Richard Wensley Bond was, at the time of the filing of the bill in the first cause, possessed, as executor of the Rev. Wensley Bond, of the said judgments and annuity; and that he sold and disposed of same to enable him to invest the trust fund mentioned in the settlement of Young and wife to his own credit, as trustee of said settlement; and that he so applied the produce thereof.

[729]

By an order of the 7th of July, 1836, made in the cause of *Young* and wife v. *Bond*, it was, on the consent of Richard Wensley Bond, ordered, that he should transfer to the credit of the cause the sum of 2,762*l.* 14*s.* 4*d.*, being equivalent, at the price of the day, to 3,000*l.*, late currency, in Government Three and a-half per cent. stock so invested to his credit with the produce of said assets, without prejudice to the rights of the parties at the hearing of the cause; and it was ordered that the Accountant-General should from time to time draw in favour of the defendant, Christiana Young, for the accruing dividends of said stock. Pursuant to this order, Richard Wensley Bond transferred the sum of 2,762*l.* 14*s.* 4*d.*, Three and a-half per cent. stock, to the credit of the cause; which transfer, the Master reported, was intended by him to be an appropriation, thereof, in payment of the legacy of 3,000*l.* in that suit.

The plaintiffs in the first cause, although named as parties defendants in the cause of *Young* and wife v. *Bond*, were never served with process therein: and immediately after the order of July, 1836, was made, they were, by amendment, struck out as parties defendants; and no further proceedings were had in that suit.

The bill in the second cause was filed on the 9th of June, 1840, by the children of Richard Wensley Bond, all of whom were minors, against the plaintiffs in the first cause, Richard Wensley Bond, Young and wife, and others; setting forth the marriage settlement of the 1st of April, 1820, and the covenant against incumbrances therein contained; and the proceedings in the first cause, and in the cause of *Young* and wife v. *Bond;* and charging that the personal assets of *the testator were the primary fund for payment of the judgment debt due to the plaintiffs in the first cause, and ought to be so applied; and that the investment of the 8,000*l.* by Richard Wensley Bond was made with the concurrence and at the instigation of Jennings and his wife, they and their children being entitled to the greater portion of that fund on the decease of Thomas Golfin Young and his wife: and they submitted that the investment was an improper application of the assets, and done in collusion with Jennings and wife by Richard Wensley Bond, in order to prevent a proper account being taken of the assets; and that the assets of the testator could not be properly administered in the suit of *Jennings* v. *Bond*, as Young and wife and the other persons interested in the assets, were not parties to that suit.

The bill prayed that the trusts of the settlement of the 1st of April, 1820, so far as same related to the lands of Ardgullen, might be carried into execution, and the rights of the plaintiffs declared; and that the covenant of the Rev. Wensley Bond therein contained might be specifically performed; an account of the sum due on foot of the judgment of 1820, and of all incumbrances prior to the settlement of 1820, affecting the lands of Ardgullen; an account of the personal estate of the testator, and of any real estate which descended upon his heir; an account of his debts and legacies, and that the personal estate might be applied in a due course of administration, and thereout the judgment debt of 2,500*l.* be paid; and, if necessary, that the said Government stock standing to the credit of the cause of *Young* and wife v. *Bond*, might be transferred to the credit of this cause, to be applied for the purposes aforesaid, under the directions of the Court; and that it might be declared that the plaintiffs were entitled to have the lands indemnified against the payment of any incumbrances thereon, out of the assets of the *testator: and for a receiver, and an injunction to restrain the defendants interfering with the assets.

By an order of the 10th of February, 1841, made in the second cause, it was ordered that the Government stock lodged to the credit of the cause of *Young* and wife v. *Bond* should be transferred to the credit of that cause and of the second cause; and that the defendant, Christiana Young, should continue to receive the half-yearly dividends thereon. The stock was transferred accordingly.

There were assets of the testator still outstanding, to the amount of 3,162*l.* 8*s.*, late currency; of which the sum of 300*l.* was irrecoverable.

By indenture of the 6th of September, 1838, between Richard Wensley Bond, of the one part, and James W. Bond, of the other part, after reciting, *inter alia*, that James W. Bond held the lands of Ardgullen, as tenant to Richard Wensley Bond, at the yearly rent of 212*l.* 15*s.* 10*d.*, Richard Wensley Bond, in order to secure the repayment to James W. Bond of the sum of 2,434*l.* 15*s.* 3*d.*, the amount of an old debt and a sum then advanced to him, assigned to James W. Bond certain policies of assurance; and it was thereby agreed upon between them that it should be lawful for James W. Bond, his executors, &c., and he and they were directed and empowered, every year, thenceforth, during the life of Richard Wensley Bond, to apply so much of the yearly rent of 212*l.* 15*s.* 10*d.* as should be necessary to pay the premiums on the policies of assurance ; and, after payment thereof, to retain and pay himself thereout the yearly interest on the sum of 2,434*l.* 15*s.* 3*d.*

[*732] The annual sums which James W. *Bond was so authorized to retain out of his rent, amounted to 211*l.* 19*s.* 9*d.* ; and James W. Bond and his executors accordingly retained that annual sum up to the 1st November, 1843 ; but a receiver having been appointed over the lands in April, 1844, they had not since retained same. The principal sum of 2,434*l.* 15*s.* 3*d.*, with interest, was still due to the executors of James W. Bond. By the same deed of the 6th of September, 1838, after further reciting that the assignment of the 29th of October, 1835, whereby Mr. Webb had assigned to James W. Bond the interest of the legacy of 2,500*l.*, to which he was entitled under his marriage settlement, had been executed to him in trust for Richard Wensley Bond, and that the sum of 750*l.*, thereby stated to have been paid to Mr. Webb, was the proper money of Richard Wensley Bond ; it was agreed that, in the events therein mentioned, the yearly interest of the 2,500*l.* should be a further security for the money due by Richard Wensley Bond to James W. Bond. This deed was registered shortly afterwards.

James W. Bond died in February, 1843 ; his executors were parties to both causes.

Under a decree to account, pronounced in the two causes of

Jennings v. *Bond* and *Bond* v. *Jennings*, on the 28th of April, 1843, the Master reported the before-mentioned matters; and further found, that the plaintiffs in the second cause were entitled, as specialty creditors of the Rev. Wensley Bond, on foot of the covenant contained in the settlement of April, 1820, to have the settled lands indemnified against all incumbrances out of the personal estate of the said Rev. Wensley Bond, to which said lands might be made liable, without prejudice to the rights of the plaintiffs in the first cause on foot of their judgment.

To this report, the plaintiff in the second cause took two exceptions: first, for that the Master by his report and the schedule thereto annexed, did not, in the account of the personal estate of the testator still outstanding, report that the sum of 2,762*l*. 14*s*. 4*d*., Government Three and a-quarter per cent. stock, invested to the credit of the second cause and of the cause of *Young* and wife v. *Bond*, formed a portion and was part of the personal estate of the testator: secondly, for that no account of the sum due on foot of the legacy of 8,000*l*. bequeathed to Christiana Young, was taken by the Master, pursuant to the decree; nor did the Master report whether any payment had been made on foot of that legacy out of the personal estate of the testator.

[783]

Mr. Moore, Mr. Brewster, and *Mr. Brereton,* for the plaintiffs in the second cause:

The Government stock which is now standing to the credit of the cause of *Young* and wife v. *Bond* and of the second cause, is the produce of the sale of part of the assets of the testator, which were in specie when the bill in the first cause was filed; and it has never been definitely appropriated to the payment of Mrs. Young's legacy, but is still under the control and disposition of the Court. It, therefore, is applicable to the payment of the debts of the testator; and ought to be so applied in priority to his real estate. The bill in the first cause prayed for an account of the personal assets of the testator; and after that suit was instituted, it was not competent for the executor to pay legacies. The order, also, under which the legacy was brought into Court in *Young's* cause, was made on the consent of the executor, and was without prejudice to the rights of the parties as they should appear at the hearing. The plaintiffs in the first cause were then parties to the suit of *Young* and wife *v. Bond;* that reservation in the order is therefore conclusive against its being considered as an appropriation

[*734]

JENNINGS
v.
BOND.

of the money in payment of Mrs. Young's legacy. *Gillespie* v. *Alexander* (1) is distinguishable; for there the appropriation was made by a decree ascertaining the rights of the parties.

[They also cited *March* v. *Russell* (2), *Hardwicke* v. *Mynd* (3), and other cases.]

> *Mr. Serjt. Warren* for the plaintiffs in the first cause, and *Mr. Brooke* for Mr. and Mrs. Young and their children:

The lodgment of the money in Court to the credit of the cause of *Young* and wife v. *Bond*, pursuant to the order, was a valid appropriation of the stock to the payment of Mrs. Young's legacy: *Gillespie* v. *Alexander* (1).

[They also cited *George* v. *Millbank* (4), *M'Leod* v. *Drummond* (5), and other cases upon the point. Their arguments are fully dealt with in the following judgment:]

[735]   THE LORD CHANCELLOR:

The question is whether this sum of money forms part of the assets of Wensley Bond, or whether it has been so appropriated to payment of the legacy to Mrs. Young, that it cannot now be resorted to as such. Wensley Bond by his will gave certain legacies to his younger children, and amongst them a sum of 8,000*l.* to his daughter, Christiana, afterwards married to Mr. Young; and appointed his son, Richard Wensley Bond, one of his executors. At the time of his decease he was indebted by judgment and otherwise; but although Richard Wensley Bond received sufficient assets to answer both debts and legacies, he neglected to pay, amongst other debts, the judgment to which Jennings was entitled, and the legacies to the younger children of the testator. The legacy to which Mrs. Young was entitled, was, by her marriage settlement of

[*736]   the 29th of May, 1826, assigned *by her to four trustees (of whom Richard Wensley Bond was one), upon trusts for Mrs. Young, her husband, and the issue of the marriage. That settlement recited the will of Wensley Bond and the title of Mrs. Young to the legacies, and that the amount thereof was, at that time, in the hands of Richard Wensley Bond, as executor of his father. No specific portion of the assets was assigned by the settlement; it was a mere transfer of the legacy for value; and the persons claiming under the settlement stood in the situation of the legatee; for,

(1) 27 R. R. 35 (3 Russ. 130).   (4) 7 R. R. 157 (9 Ves. 190).
(2) 45 R. R. 196 (3 My. & Cr. 31).   (5) 11 R. R. 41 (17 Ves. 152).
(3) 3 R. R. 562 (1 Anst. 109).

though purchasers, they were purchasers of a chose in action. Under the settlement, therefore, they had no right to say, that any specific portion of the assets had been appropriated to the payment of the legacy. Upon the 5th of November, 1835, a bill was filed by William Jennings, a judgment creditor, praying for an account, in the most general way, of the real and personal assets of Wensley Bond, and that provision might be made for payment of all his creditors of every degree; and perhaps it was necessary to pray for those accounts, considering the peculiar situation and liabilities of the assets. To that bill Richard Wensley Bond was a party. Nothing was done in that cause for some time; and in 1836, Young and wife filed their bill for their legacy, alleging that Richard Wensley Bond had sufficient assets to answer their demand; and to that suit they made Jennings, the plaintiff in the suit of 1835, a party. Now the executor, being a party to the suit of 1835, without resorting to the doctrine of *lis pendens*, was of course aware of its institution; but so also was every person in contemplation of this Court; for it was strictly a *lis pendens*, and, consequently, the parties who filed the bill of 1836 did so with full knowledge, in the view of this Court, of the existence of the suit of 1835. It has been said that, in the suit of 1835, there never could have *been a decree which would have embraced all the creditors; [*737] and therefore, that the suit of 1836, being instituted by a legatee, was properly constituted for the complete administration of the assets; and it has been urged, that no decree could be made in the suit of 1835 which would affect the rights of the parties to the suit of 1836. I do not think that is the case; for, whatever may be the value of the observations of Sir A. HART in *Bomford* v. *Wilme* (1), it appears that such decrees are made every day, and no doubts have been entertained as to the power of the Court to made a decree embracing all the assets and creditors in such a suit. But the answer to the objection is this: that, assuming that the Court ought not to make a decree beyond the rights of the judgment creditor, yet such a decree would be one affecting all the assets,—the personal, of course, before the real,—and for a distribution of such amongst that class of creditors. If, therefore, the suit of 1835 would not have authorized a decree embracing all the creditors, yet it is undeniable that it was so framed as to compel the Court to decree an account of all the assets. It is of course, in such decrees, to inquire as to the personal estate, and, if that be not

(1) Beatty, 253.

sufficient, then as to the real. Therefore, I am of opinion that the
suit of 1835 was properly constituted for the administration of the
personal as well as of the real assets of the testator, although,
with respect to creditors, it might not include any class beyond
judgment creditors.

Assuming that to be so, consider what was done in the suit of
1836. Richard Wensley Bond, who had incurred the liability to
the legatee, and was himself a trustee for Mr. and Mrs. Young

[*738] under the deed of 1826, was called on before *the suit to transfer
to the trustees of the settlement the amount of their legacies. He
had at that time in his possession, admitted assets, not then converted, consisting of certain judgment debts and an annuity, to
which the testator had been entitled in his lifetime. He refused,
however, to make the transfer; but ultimately, having converted
those assets into money, and invested the produce in Three and
a-half per cent. stock, he, pursuant to the order of the Court, transferred that stock to the name of the Accountant-General, to the
credit of the second cause; but the order directing that transfer to
be made was upon the terms that the transfer was to be made
without prejudice to the rights of the parties at the hearing of the
cause. I cannot doubt that Richard Wensley Bond did not mean
to commit himself by actually assuming power over the fund; but
he meant, as far as he could, to assist the Youngs, by bringing the
money into their suit, and thereby at the same time to indemnify
himself. I think it clear that there was some management by the
parties, so as best to support their own interests at the expense of
the creditors; for as soon as this order was pronounced, the Youngs
dismissed their bill against Jennings, the object of which was to
leave themselves unembarrassed in their suit. Without looking,
then, to the suit of 1840, consider whether at that moment there
was either payment or appropriation to the payment of this legacy.
It is clear that there was no payment, for the executor had refused
to pay the money to the trustees. Then was there an appropriation? I do not know how it can be so called; for appropriation
(in the sense in which the word is used at the present hearing)
means payment. In *Gillespie* v. *Alexander* (1) some of the legacies
had been paid to parties competent to give a discharge for them;

[*739] the other legacies were appropriated to the legatees who were *not
then competent to give discharges for them; and the reason for the
appropriation was, not that payment was not proper, but because

●   (1) 27 R. R. 35 (3 Russ. 130).

the legatees were not ready to receive payment and give discharges. In that case appropriation was equivalent to payment; and the moment the party was competent to receive the money, it would be paid to him as of course. Here the case is different. The dividends on the funds in Court, it is true, were directed to be paid to Mrs. Young, the tenant for life; but that order was made upon the non-appearance of the executor, who then was the only party to the suit. What is the value of such an order? Could the executor, after a suit had been instituted, more than a year before, for the administration of all the assets, appropriate any portion of them, in the face of the Court, without informing it of the real circumstances of the case? This Court would be powerless, if it were to suffer an executor to act in that manner. I cannot permit an executor to say that, because the fact of there being a demand of a higher nature outstanding against the assets has been concealed by him from the Court, he is at liberty to satisfy a demand of an inferior nature, by means of payment of the assets into Court in a suit instituted by the owner of the inferior demand. I am of opinion that there was only an appropriation *sub modo;* that is, if, at the hearing, the party appeared to be entitled to the assets, the money was in Court to answer his demand. Before, however, that cause came to a hearing, the parties entitled to the specialty, hearing of the proceedings, filed a bill in the year 1840; and then the money in Court, to the credit of the cause of 1836, was transferred to the credit of both causes. I do not consider that had the effect of displacing any right acquired by the parties claiming under the suit of 1836, to the money; but *primâ facie* it affords an inference *that the Court did not consider the payment into Court as an appropriation equivalent to an actual payment to the party. If there had been such an appropriation, the answer to the application to transfer the money to the credit of both causes, would have been, that the money already belonged to the parties in the suit of 1836, and that the plaintiffs in the suit of 1840 had no right to have it transferred to the credit of both causes. But it is plain that it was considered by the parties and the Court that that was a question to be decided at the hearing of the causes. I agree that, if it could be now established that there had been an appropriation, the parties would not be prejudiced by that order. The two suits came on together; and, so far from the persons claiming under the suit of 1836 thinking that the form of their suit gave them any peculiar claims, they allowed it to go to sleep; and

[*740]

with their permission a decree was made in the suits of 1835 and 1840. I do not say that that would damage them; but it shows that they did not consider that they had any peculiar claims under their suit.

It was argued that the parties stood on a higher footing, as purchasers for value under the deed of 1836. I have already answered that argument by stating the rule of the Court, that a purchaser of a chose in action stands exactly in the same position as the vendor: but I observed that the proposition was very cautiously laid down by the counsel who advanced it; for he said that, where a legacy was paid to a person who stood in the character of a purchaser for value, it could not be called back. As in the present case there has been no payment, I need not consider that proposition; it will be sufficient to do so when it arises: but I may observe that it will be difficult to maintain it where there is an [*741] existing *lis pendens*. The *case, therefore, lies in a very narrow compass, and is free from difficulty. This is a case in which I shall give to the creditors of the higher degree that right only to which by law they are entitled; and I give it to them over what were existing assets at the time when the bill of 1835 was filed, which now constitute the fund in Court, and over which the Court has never parted with its control.

There is some difficulty from the form in which this question comes on. I shall let the exception stand; and declare that the transfer did not amount to an appropriation in payment of Mr. and Mrs. Young's demand, as against the creditors of the testator: and that, under the circumstances, the money brought into Court remained as assets of Wensley Bond, to be administered in a due course of administration. The report must go back to the Master, and he will appropriate the assets according to this declaration.

After the foregoing judgment was delivered, *Mr. Brooke* submitted that there were still outstanding assets sufficient to pay the demands of the plaintiff in the second cause; and that the fund in Court was applicable to the payment of Mrs. Young's legacy in priority to the claims of the other legatees, though not as against the creditor: and further, that the life estate of Richard Wensley Bond in the lands of Ardgullen ought to be made answerable for his default as executor.

The LORD CHANCELLOR directed the case to be argued upon these points.

[The case was re-argued accordingly, and the arguments sufficiently appear from the following judgment :]

THE LORD CHANCELLOR :

Two points were reserved,—first, whether the funds in Court
were appropriated to the payment of the legacy to the Youngs,
as against the plaintiffs in the second cause before me; and,
secondly, whether any relief can be given against the purchaser.

Upon the first point *Walcot* v. *Hall* (1) was relied upon; but
there the residue was paid, and the particular legacy was properly
retained, as the executors were directed to invest it in their names.
Here there has been no actual payment of the fund; and it appears
to me that there has been no appropriation of it, binding as against
the persons having equal rights under the second cause.

Secondly: for the purchaser it was insisted, first, that the *lis
pendens* did not bind him, not relating specifically to the estate;
secondly, that it could not bind him, as he claimed under a
registered deed; and, thirdly, that his estate was saved by the recent
statute, which, to bind a purchaser, requires express notice or a
registration. As to the first point, the plaintiffs in the suit of 1835,
to recover the judgment, prayed the usual accounts of the real and
personal estates, and a receiver of the real estate; and the marriage
settlement is referred to upon the misapprehension that the estate
in it had been exonerated from debt out of the assets. I think
that this was a sufficient *lis pendens* to bind a purchaser of the
estate bound by the judgment, as real estate of the testator, and
which was also comprised in the marriage settlement. The
doctrine was laid down at large by two CHANCELLORS in *Culpepper*
v. *Austin* (2), and I am not *aware of any case in which it has been
laid down that such a suit as that of 1835 was not a sufficient *lis
pendens* to bind a purchaser. *Walker* v. *Flamstead*, in the second
part of the second volume of Lord Kenyon's Reports, only decided
that a creditor's suit does not stop the execution of the trusts of the
will. It had been decided in *Lord Oxford* v. *Darston* (3), that an
executor might pay a debt in equal degree with the plaintiffs after
he had appeared to the plaintiffs' bill; which was most reluctantly
followed by Sir JOHN LEACH in *Maltby* v. *Russell* (4): and there are
other authorities to the like effect. But the case before me is of a
different nature. The estate in question was vested in the testator

[*745]

(1) 2 Br. C. C. 305.   (3) Colles, P. C. 229.
(2) 2 Ch. Ca. 115, 221.   (4) 25 R. R. 191 (2 Sim. & St. 227).

at the time of the judgment recovered; his subsequent settlement of it did not affect the right of the judgment creditor. Mr. Richard Wensley Bond was tenant for life under the settlement, and there was a covenant from the settlor for quiet enjoyment free from incumbrances. The estate continued liable to the judgment; but the settlor's assets were liable to exonerate it from the burden. Richard Wensley Bond was the settlor's executor, and wasted more than sufficient assets to pay the judgment. The decree directs the judgment creditor to be paid out of the remaining personal assets: this was of course; but this payment would enure to the benefit of the defaulting executor, who ought to have paid off the charge. It is a plain equity against him, that the persons whose fund is applied to the payment of this demand should be recouped out of his life estate. But he made a security to James Wensley Bond, which, it is said, constitutes him a purchaser. This was in 1836. Besides the notice from the *lis pendens*, it is apparent from the deed

[*746]

of security, that James W. Bond knew that Richard *W. Bond was executor of his father. Now this security was not, like the mortgage in *Walker* v. *Flamstead*, a step which must be considered as taken in execution of the trust; but it was a charge for an old debt, and an additional loan to Richard W. Bond as owner of the life estate, and it transferred no estate to him. I think, therefore, that it is not protected by the authority of that case. James W. Bond says he had no notice of the judgment; but it bound the land although he had not notice; and as he came in *pendente lite*, he is bound by the same equity as the person under whom he claims. But then it is said that his deed is registered: to which I answer, that this is not a conflict between two deeds, one registered and the other not; but a claim to be relieved from the effect of the suit depending. The deed, in this case, would have been equally operative without registry, and derives no additional force from it. Lastly, the 7 & 8 of the Queen, c. 90, s. 10, was relied upon; but this case does not, I think, fall within that provision: for on the 1st of November, 1844, James W. Bond had express notice of the judgment; and this is not a case intended to be provided for by the Act. It appears to me, therefore, that this defence cannot prevail.

ANGELL v. BRYAN.

(2 Jo. & Lat. 763—765.)

1845.
Nov. 27.

SIR EDWARD
SUGDEN,
L.C.

[763]

The devisee of a leasehold estate for lives having suffered an arrear of rent to become due, the landlord brought an ejectment. A third person, at the request of the devisee, advanced money for the purpose of paying the rent, and it was applied accordingly, and the devisee mortgaged the lands to secure the repayment of it.

The mortgagee is not entitled to priority over the judgment creditors of the devisor.

THE bill was filed by the plaintiff, as assignee of a judgment obtained against Thomas Bryan, deceased, for an account of his real and personal estate and payment thereout. The freehold property of the testator consisted of a leasehold for lives renewable for ever, subject to the payment of a yearly rent and renewal fines. Jane Bryan, the devisee of Thomas Bryan, suffered an arrear of the rent to become due; and proceedings by ejectment were taken against her to enforce its payment. Under these circumstances, Charles French advanced her the sum of 425*l.*, to enable her to pay the rent and costs; and by indenture of the 17th of January, 1845, made between Jane Bryan of the one part, and Charles French of the other part, after reciting that a large arrear of rent having become due out of the premises, and an ejectment for non-payment thereof having been brought to evict the lease, Charles *French had advanced to Jane Bryan a sum of money sufficient to pay said rent and the costs of the ejectment, and that thereout the said rent and costs had been paid; Jane Bryan, in consideration of said sum of 425*l.*, so advanced for the purposes aforesaid, granted and released the demised premises, by way of mortgage, to Charles French and his heirs, to secure the repayment thereof, with interest. She also executed her bond collateral with the mortgage; on which judgment was afterwards entered.

[*764]

Charles French, being made a party defendant, submitted that as the sum of 425*l.* was advanced by him in order to pay the head rent and costs of the ejectment, and was applied by Jane Bryan to that purpose, whereby the original lease was prevented from being evicted, and thus the interests of all persons therein preserved, the said sum was a charge on the demised premises paramount to the plaintiff's judgment and all other charges.

Mr. Serjt. Warren for the plaintiff.

Mr. W. Brooke for Charles French.

ANGELL
v.
BRYAN.

THE LORD CHANCELLOR:

There is no doubt as to the law. I cannot establish in the mortgagee a right against third parties which did not exist in the person under whom he derives. The consequence of establishing such a right would be, that every tenant for life of a leasehold property would be enabled to give priority to his own mortgagees by simply suffering the rent to run in arrear, and then raising money by mortgage for payment of it. There are cases in which [*765] the Court *has properly given a salvage creditor priority over all other incumbrancers. I do not disturb those cases, but this is not within them.

IN THE COURT OF COMMON BENCH.

WILLIAM BARTON *v.* THOMAS ASHLEY (1).

(2 C. B. 4—12; S. C. 15 L. J. C. P. 36.)

A notice of objection delivered to the overseers under the Parliamentary Voters Registration Act, 1843 (6 & 7 Vict. c. 18), s. 17, sched. (B.) No. 10, where there are more lists than one made out by the overseers, must specify the particular list to which the objection refers.

WILLIAM BARTON objected to the name of Thomas Ashley being retained on the list of persons entitled to vote in the election of members for that city.   The objector gave in evidence, and duly proved the service of, a notice of objection upon the said Thomas Ashley, according to the form No. 11 in schedule (B.) of the statute 6 & 7 Vict. c. 18; and he also gave in evidence and proved the service of a notice of objection upon the overseers of the parish of St. Michael, in the list of *which parish, containing the names of persons entitled to vote in the election of members of Parliament for the said city, by virtue of the provisions of the statute 2 Will. IV. c. 45, the name of the said Thomas Ashley appeared as follows, that is to say :

[*5]

"The list of persons entitled to vote in the election of members for the city of Lichfield in respect of property occupied within the parish of St. Michael, by virtue of an Act passed in the second year of the reign of King William the Fourth, intituled, ' An Act to amend the Representation of the People in England and Wales.'

Christian Name and Surname of each Voter.	Place of Abode.	Nature of Qualification.	Street, Lane, or other like Place in this Parish, and Number of House where the Property is situated.
Ashley, Thomas.	Greenhill.	House.	Greenhill.

"

The last-mentioned notice of objection was in the following words :

"NOTICE OF OBJECTION.

"To the overseers of the parish of St. Michael, in the city of Lichfield.

"I hereby give you notice that I object to the name of Thomas

---

(1) Followed in *Hartley* v. *Halse* (1888) 22 Q. B. D. 200, 58 L. J. Q. B. 100 ; distinguished in *Aldridge* v. *Medwin* (1868) L. R. 4 C. P. 464, 38 L. J. C. P. 45.

BARTON
v.
ASHLEY.

Ashley being retained in the list of persons entitled to vote in the election of members for the city of Lichfield. Dated, this 25th of August, 1845.

> (Signed) " WILLIAM BARTON, of Stone Street,
> Lichfield, on the list of free-
> men for the city of Lichfield."

[*6]

In the city of Lichfield, it is the duty of the overseers of the several parishes, and, amongst the rest, of the said parish of St. Michael, to make out and publish two separate lists of persons entitled to vote in the election *of members for the said city; the one, in respect of persons entitled to vote in the election of members for the said city, in respect of property occupied within the said parish, by virtue of the provisions of the statute 2 Will. IV. c. 45; and the other, of persons, not being freemen, entitled to vote in the election of members for the said city, in respect of any right other than those conferred by the said last-mentioned statute.   The name of the said Thomas Ashley appeared on the first-mentioned list of voters only, namely, on the list of persons entitled to vote by reason of the provisions of the statute 2 Will. IV. c. 45, and did not appear on the other list made out and published by the overseers.

In the list of objections published by the overseers, the said Thomas Ashley was described as follows:

Christian Name and Surname.	Place of Abode.	Nature of Qualification.	Name of Street, &c., where situate.
Ashley, Thomas.	Greenhill.	House.	Greenhill.

agreeing with his description in the original list of persons entitled to vote in respect of property occupied within the said parish, by virtue of the said statute of 2 Will. IV. c. 45, as hereinbefore set forth.

It was objected, on the part of the said Thomas Ashley, that the said notice of objection served on the overseers, was informal and insufficient, inasmuch as it did not comply with the directions given in schedule (B.) No. 10, of the statute of 6 & 7 Vict. c. 18; there being two lists of voters made out by the overseers in that parish, and the notice not specifying, as it ought to have done, the particular list to which the objection referred.

The Revising Barrister held the notice to be informal and

insufficient for that reason: but, as the said Thomas Ashley was BARTON
present, and then consented that the proof of his qualification v.
should be gone into, subject to the *question of the validity of the ASHLEY.
said notice of objection, he proceeded to call evidence in support of [*7]
his right to have his name retained in the said list; but failed to
prove the same to the satisfaction of the Barrister.

The question for the opinion of the Court is, whether, upon the
facts stated, the above notice of objection to the overseers of the
said parish of St. Michael, was or was not sufficient in law to call
upon the said Thomas Ashley to prove his title to have his name
retained in the list of persons entitled to vote in the election of
members for the city of Lichfield, in respect of property occupied
within the said parish, by virtue of the said statute of 2 Will. IV.
c. 45.   If the Court shall be of opinion that the said notice was
sufficient, the name of the said Thomas Ashley is to be expunged
from the register of voters for the said city; otherwise, to be
retained thereon.

The cases of three other persons whose names appeared on the
list of voters for the parish of St. Michael, and two whose names
appeared on the list of voters for the parish of St. Mary, in the
same city, are consolidated with the principal case.

Kinglake, Serjt., for the appellant:

*   *   Under the 2 Will. IV. c. 45, s. 47, the only notice of objection   [8]
required was a general notice to the overseers, and the same lists
were then required to be made out as now: the seventeenth section
of the 6 & 7 Vict. c. 18, for the first time requires notice also to the
party objected to.   The notice to the party is a mere general notice.
To that required to be given to the overseers is appended a note
intimating, that, if there be "more than one list of voters, the
notice of objection should specify the list to which the objection
refers; and, if the list contains two or more persons of the same
name, the notice should distinguish the person intended to be
objected to."   The only object of that note is, to require that, in
cases where the voter's name appears on both lists, such information shall be conveyed to the overseers, as to enable them to
ascertain whether the objection applies to the qualification in both
lists, or to which of them—to point their attention to the particular
qualification intended to be objected to.   If the voter's name
appears only upon *one list, the information would be useless.   All   [*9]
the overseers can require is, such a degree of information as will

BARTON
v.
ASHLEY.

[10]

enable them to perform the duty imposed upon them by s. 18, of publishing a list of persons objected to, according to the form in schedule (B.) No. 12: and that is done here. A strict and rigid compliance with the form is not necessary. [It is enough if the direction is substantially complied with.] It may be admitted, that if the overseers' attention could have been distracted by the form of notice given, the decision of the Revising Barrister would have been correct. But this notice could not possibly have such an effect. At all events, the clause being directory only, and the overseer having acted upon the notice by publishing the name of the party objected to, as he would have done if the notice had been in the specific form required, no exception can be taken to it.

(MAULE, J.: You contend that there is no necessity for proving the notice before the Revising Barrister, provided the overseer has inserted the name of the party in the list of persons objected to.)

The object of the notice to the overseers is, to enable them to publish the list, which the parties objected to may see at the church door, and so ascertain the particular qualifications to which the objections apply. The list being published, the preliminary step is unimportant. Here, the overseers have received the notice, and have acted upon it as they would have done if the interpretation of the clause that is relied on by the respondent were the correct one.

Byles, Serjt., for the respondent, was not called upon.

TINDAL, Ch. J.:

[*11]

The fortieth section of the 6 & 7 Vict. c. 18, which provides that the objector shall prove before the Revising Barrister that he gave the notices *required by the Act, disposes of the argument last urged. As to the other point, the words of the direction, " if more than one list of voters, the notice of objection should specify the list to which the objection refers," are so clear that they admit of no doubt in their construction. Here, all that can be said is, that the omission to specify the particular list did not in fact create any confusion or difficulty (1). But I think it is much more convenient that the overseer should have his attention distinctly called to the list, and that it is safer to adhere to the words of the Act, and to hold that the notice must be in strict conformity with it in this respect.

(1) Upon every notice of objection in this form the overseer would have to examine two lists instead of one.

COLTMAN, J. :

Comparing the form (I), No. 5 in the 2 Will. IV. c. 45, with the form of notice given by the 6 & 7 Vict. c. 18, it would seem that the Legislature considered the former not stringent enough, and therefore required something more precise and specific.

MAULE, J. :

I agree with the Revising Barrister that the notice in question was not according to the form No. 10, or to the like effect. I also agree that, provided the effect is preserved, strict compliance with the form may not be material. If, however, the proper form had been adopted here, the overseers would have been saved some trouble. It is true, that, by a little additional labour, the overseers may come to the same result through an informal and imperfect notice, as they would through one strictly conformable to the statute. But the object of the note at the end of the form No. 10 is, to save them that additional labour. Suppose the statute required a reference to a volume and page, and the volume were given without the page ; could it be *said to be a virtual compliance, because, by a little additional labour, the party might find the page ?

[*12]

ERLE, J. :

It appears to me that the 6 & 7 Vict. c. 18, requires the notice to the overseers to be in a particular form, and that this particularity was intentionally prescribed, inasmuch as it departs from the form previously given by the 2 Will. IV. c. 45. It is suggested that the form need not be strictly followed, provided no inconvenience results in the particular case from a departure from it. To that doctrine, however, I cannot accede.

Decision affirmed, with costs.

WILLIAM HENRY WALKER *v.* JULIAN PAYNE.

(2 C. B. 12—14 ; S. C. 15 L. J. C. P. 38 ; 9 Jur. 1014.)

In a list of voters for a county, a voter was described in the column headed " Place of abode," as " travelling abroad : " Held, a sufficient description.

1845.
Nov. 17.
───
*County of
Middlesex.*
[12]

THE name, place of abode, and qualification of William Gibbs, as a voter in respect of property situate within the hamlet of Mile

WALKER
v.
PAYNE.

End Old Town, were described in the register of voters for the said county, in the following words :

Christian Name and Surname of each Voter at full Length.	Place of Abode.	Nature of Qualification.	Street, &c., where Property situate, &c.
Gibbs, William.	Travelling abroad.	Freehold house.	82, Heath St.

[*13]

This name was objected to by the appellant; and it was proved that the voter was, and for several years had been, travelling abroad, and had no fixed place of *abode: but it was contended by the appellant, that, as no place of abode was given, the name ought to be expunged.

The Revising Barrister was of opinion, that, as the voter had no fixed place of abode, but was travelling abroad, he was not at liberty to expunge the voter's name, and he therefore retained it.

If the Court of Common Pleas shall be of opinion that a better description of the voter's place of abode, under the circumstances above stated, ought to have been required, the name is to be expunged; else, to be retained.

G. Atkinson, for the appellant. * * *

[14]

Phipson, for the respondent, was not called upon.

TINDAL, Ch. J. :

The fortieth section of the 6 & 7 Vict. c. 18, enacts, that, wherever the christian name, or the place of abode, &c. of any person who shall be included in any list, shall be wholly omitted, in any case where the same is by the Act directed to be specified therein, or, if the place of abode, &c., shall in the judgment of the Revising Barrister be insufficiently described for the purpose of being identified, such Barrister shall expunge the name of every such person from such list, unless the matter or matters so omitted, or insufficiently described, be supplied to the satisfaction of such Barrister before he shall have completed the revision of such list. That direction means, that the place of abode of the party shall be inserted in the list if he has a place of abode. It was clearly not intended that he should lose his vote, because he happens to have no fixed place of abode at the time the lists are made out; otherwise every officer in the army or navy on foreign service, and every person abroad on public duty would be disfranchised.

COLTMAN, J. :

Nothing is omitted that could have been inserted. I think the
Act is sufficiently complied with, notwithstanding there may be a
difficulty in the service of notices.

MAULE, J. :

I also think that the place of abode is only required to be given
where the party has a place of abode. The Act likewise requires
the christian name *to be inserted : and yet no one would contend   [*15]
that a person who happens to have no christian name would be
thereby disqualified.

ERLE, J. :

The place of abode must be specified if the party has one.
Where he is travelling abroad, such a description as is here given,
is as near a compliance with the Act as the circumstances of the
case will admit of.

Decision affirmed.

JAMES HITCHINS v. THOMAS BROWN.

(2 C. B. 25—30 ; S. C. 15 L. J. C. P. 38.)

1845,
Nov. 20.

City of
Lincoln.
[25]

In a notice of claim to be inserted in a list of voters for a city or
borough, pursuant to the Parliamentary Voters Registration Act, 1843
(6 & 7 Vict. c. 18), s. 15, sched. (B.) No. 6, it is enough to describe the
nature of the qualification in the third column of the form as " house,"
notwithstanding the qualification in reality consists in the occupation of
two houses in immediate succession, provided the whole qualification is
accurately described in the fourth column.

And semble, that, at all events, the misdescription, if any, is amendable
under s. 40 (1).

WILLIAM UPTON appeared to have given due notice of his claim
to have his name inserted in the list of persons entitled to vote
in respect of property occupied within the parish of St. Peter-at-
Arches. The notice of his claim was as follows :

"NOTICE OF CLAIM.

" To the overseers of the parish of St. Peter-at-Arches, in the
city of Lincoln.

" I hereby give you notice that I claim to have my name inserted

<hr>

(1) As to amendment see now 41 &
42 Vict. c. 26, s. 28. This case was
discussed in Foskett v. Kaufman (1885)
16 Q. B. Div. 279, 55 L. J. Q. B. 1
(followed in Hurcum v. Hilleary [1894]

1 Q. B. 579, 63 L. J. Q. B. 306, C. A.,
and Mann v. Johnson [1893] W. N.
196) ; and was followed in Soutter v.
Roderick [1896] 1 Q. B. 91, 65 L. J.
Q. B. 145.—J. G. P.

HITCHINS
v.
BROWN.

in the list made by you of persons entitled to vote in the election of members for the city of Lincoln ; and that the particulars of my qualification and place of abode are stated in the columns below. Dated the 23rd day of August, 1845 :

Christian Name and Surname of the Claimant, at full length.	Place of Abode.	Nature of Qualification.	Street, Lane, &c., where the Property is situate, &c., where the Right depends on Property.
William Upton.	Muck Lane, Saint Peter-at-Arches, Lincoln.	House.	No. 5½, Muck Lane, Saint Peter-at-Arches, Lincoln ; and previously in the occupation of a house No. 21, Saint Mary Street, in the parish of Saint Mary le Wigford, Lincoln. "WILLIAM UPTON."

[26]   He proved that he had occupied the two houses described in the fourth column of his claim, in immediate succession, and had done all the things required by law to entitle him to have his name inserted.   The insertion of his name was duly objected to by James Hitchins, a registered voter for the said city, on the ground that the nature of his qualification was insufficiently described for the purpose of being identified.   On behalf of William Upton it was argued : first, that this description was sufficient ; secondly, that, if not, the Revising Barrister had power to correct the same.

The Barrister decided that the nature of the qualification was not sufficiently described for the purpose of being identified ; but, at his request, he altered the statement as follows :

Christian Name and Surname.	Place of Abode.	Nature of Qualification.	Street, &c., where Property situate, &c.
William Upton.	Muck Lane, St. Peter - at - Arches, Lincoln.	Houses occupied in immediate succession.	21, St. Mary Street, St. Mary le Wigford, and 5½, Muck Lane, St. Peter-at-Arches.

and inserted his name, with such alterations, in the list.

The claims of ten other persons whose right to have their names inserted in the list depended upon the same state of facts, were consolidated with the principal case.

Manning, Serjt., for the appellant:

The qualification was improperly described in the third column, as it originally stood; and the misdescription was one that the Revising Barrister had no power, under the Act, to correct. In *Bartlett* v. *Gibbs* (1) the description was *precisely the same as occurs here; and it was held insufficient and unamendable.

(TINDAL, Ch. J.: The two cases are not identical. This is the case of an objection to the claim; in *Bartlett* v. *Gibbs* the objection was to the description as it appeared on the list of voters: besides, here, the fact of the successive occupations appears in the fourth column, whereas there it was nowhere noticed.)

The first distinction pointed out makes the present objection stronger; for, here, the mistake is by the voter himself: and the second makes no substantial difference; the Act requires that the nature of the qualification be truly stated under the proper head. Any person looking at the third column, and knowing that the qualification there stated was not the true one, was not bound to look elsewhere to see if the misdescription was aided by any other part of the paper. If the mistake is to be helped out by the fourth column, why might not the claimant pray in aid a note sent to the overseers at the same time with the claim?

(ERLE, J.: Resort must be had to the fourth column to ascertain the locality of the qualification.)

The nature of the qualification is to be looked for in the third column; and it is no answer that the additional trouble to a party who is inquiring into one vote only, is inconsiderable. The question is, whether the requirements of the Act are to be complied with, or whether the party may substitute something which may or may not convey an equal amount of information.

(TINDAL, Ch. J.: The most you can insist on is, that "house" should have been "houses.")

That would not be enough: it should have been "houses occupied in succession," as was held in *Bartlett* v. *Gibbs*. A party might occupy two houses, each of the value of 10*l.*, simultaneously; a good qualification, but totally different from that now set up. By the 6 & 7 Vict. c. 18, s. 40, the Barrister is empowered in certain

(1) 63 R. R. 227 (5 Man. & G. 81; 7 Scott, N. R. 609).

HITCHINS
v.
BROWN.

[*28]

cases to amend mistakes, "provided *always, that, whether any person shall be objected to or not, no evidence shall be given of any other qualification than that which is described in the list of voters or claim, as the case may be, nor shall the Barrister be at liberty to change the description of the qualification as it appears in the list, except for the purpose of more clearly and accurately defining the same." The matter here in question is clearly within the prohibitory part of that section. The Barrister may correct mistakes and misdescriptions in the fourth column; but to the third column the prohibition applies. It is only upon that principle that the case of *Bartlett* v. *Gibbs* can be supported.

Clarke, Serjt., *contrà*, was stopped by the COURT.

TINDAL, Ch. J.:

It appears to me that the description of the qualification in this case was perfectly correct as it originally stood, and complied with all that the Act requires. The question turns upon the fifteenth section of the 6 & 7 Vict. c. 18, and also on the schedule (B), No. 6. Section 15 enacts, "that every person whose name shall have been omitted in any list of voters for any city or borough so to be made out as aforesaid, and who shall claim as having been entitled on the last day of July then next preceding to have his name inserted therein, and every person desirous of being registered for a different qualification than that for which his name appears in the said list, shall, on or before the 25th of August in that year, give or cause to be given a notice, according to the form numbered (6) in the said schedule (B), or to the like effect, to the overseers of that parish or township in the list whereof he shall claim to have his name inserted; or, if he shall claim as a freeman of any city or borough, or place sharing in the election therewith, then he shall, in like manner,

[*29]

*give or cause to be given to the town-clerk of such city, borough, or place, according to the form numbered 7 in the said schedule (B), or to the like effect; and the overseers and town-clerks respectively shall include the names of all persons so claiming as aforesaid in lists, according to the forms numbered 8 and 9 respectively in the said schedule (B)." The third column of the form No. 6 referred to is headed "Nature of qualification," and is intended to denote the general character of the qualification; and the fourth column is a mere exposition of the third, as appears from the heading—"Street, lane, or other place in the parish, or township, where

the property is situate, and number of the house (if any). (*When* HITCHINS
the right depends on property)." Evidently showing, by the words ᵗ·
in italics, that this is a list of persons claiming to be entitled to BROWN.
vote in respect of property, and that the whole application of the
fourth column is where the right depends on property, as contradistinguished from the claims to vote as freemen or in respect of
reserved rights. I therefore think the third column is satisfied by
showing a "house" qualification, and the fourth, by showing an
occupation of two houses in immediate succession. One cannot
suppose that the third column was intended to be as precise and
explicit as the fourth; otherwise the fourth would have been
unnecessary. In the case of *Bartlett* v. *Gibbs* the right of voting
depended on the successive occupation of two houses; and the
fourth column did not really describe the qualification of the voter
so as to be susceptible of identification. It seems to me that that
case was rightly decided, and that this case also will be well decided
by holding that the directions of the Act have been sufficiently
complied with in the framing of this notice.

COLTMAN, J.:

I am of the same opinion. This case is distinguishable from
Bartlett v. *Gibbs*. *There, the substantial qualification of the   [*30]
voter was not set out in the list: his real qualification was, the
occupation of two houses in succession; whereas the qualification
set out was, the occupation of one house only. I therefore think
the claim in this case was sufficient as it originally stood. I also
think the Revising Barrister was well warranted in amending the
description, and that this is precisely the sort of case that the
fortieth section contemplated. The Barrister is prohibited from
changing the qualification, except for the purpose of more clearly
and accurately defining the same. Here, the qualification remains
substantially the same as before the amendment; only it is a little
more clearly and accurately defined.

MAULE, J.:

I have not heard the whole of the argument; but, so far as I
have heard it, I see no reason to doubt the correctness of the
conclusion at which the rest of the Court have arrived.

ERLE, J.:

I also think the Barrister has done right in making the

HITCHINS
v.
BROWN.

amendment. The description of the qualification as it originally stood was, I think, sufficient. The nature of the qualification is "house," and it is that description of house qualification that is mentioned in the 2 Will. IV. c. 45, s. 28, viz. different premises occupied in immediate succession. It is to the fourth column that parties are referred for a more strict and accurate description of the property. In *Bartlett* v. *Gibbs* the qualification was insufficiently described: it was described as situate in " East Street ; " but, when the parties came before the Barrister, it was found the qualification consisted of the occupation of two houses in immediate succession, and not merely of a house situate in " East Street."

Decision affirmed, with costs.

1845.
Dec. 23.
—
*County of
Gloucester,
Eastern
Division.*
[45]

HENRY BISHOP *v.* RICHARD HELPS.

(2 C. B. 45—59 ; S. C. 15 L. J. C. P. 43.)

Sending a notice of objection to the party objected to by the post, pursuant to the directions of the Parliamentary Voters Registration Act, 1843 (6 & 7 Vict. c. 18), s. 100, is a sufficient substitute for giving the notice to the party, or leaving it at his place of abode, as required by s. 7.

Where, therefore, a notice was posted, under s. 100, in sufficient time to reach the party, according to the ordinary course of post, on the 25th of August : Held, that such service was sufficient notwithstanding that the actual delivery was accidentally delayed until the 27th.

And, held, that the provisions of s. 100 are equally applicable to notices to overseers, directed to their usual places of abode, as provided by s. 101 (1).

HENRY BISHOP objected to the name of John Cooke being retained upon the list of voters for the parish of Corse, in the county of Gloucester.

[*46]

The objector, who resided at Cheltenham, produced duplicates of notices of objection, in the proper form, to *the voter and overseers of the parish, bearing the Manchester post-mark of the 24th of August, 1845, and proved, that, in the ordinary course of post, those notices would have been delivered at the places to which they were respectively addressed, some time on the following day. The notices were not delivered at those places respectively until the 27th of August, and had the post-mark of the 27th at the places to which they were addressed also impressed upon them. It was contended, on the part of the voter, that the objector had not given

(1) *Hickton* v. *Antrobus*, 2 C. B. 82, is exactly the same point, and is therefore omitted.—J. G. P.

the notice required by the statute 6 & 7 Vict. c. 18, s. 7, in due time, either to the voter or the overseers.

The Revising Barrister retained the name upon the list, and also, upon a similar state of facts, the names of thirteen other persons, whose appeals are consolidated with the principal case.

If the Court is of opinion that both the notices were given in due time, as required by the statute, the names are to be expunged (1) ; but, if either of the notices was not so given, then the names are to be retained.

Talfourd, Serjt., for the appellant (2) :

This case raises the question, whether a party who complies with the provisions of the 6 & 7 Vict. c. 18, ss. 100, 101, by delivering a notice of objection, open and in duplicate, to the post-master, addressed to the voter, and also to the overseer, so that according to the ordinary course of the post such notices should reach the parties in due time, and produces before the Revising Barrister the stamped duplicate, has done enough to call upon the voter to prove his qualification ; or whether, assuming such stamped duplicates to be good *primâ facie* evidence of the service of the notices, it is competent to the voter to *show, that, by reason of some default on the part of the post-office authorities, the notices have failed to reach their destination in due time. * * The intention of the Legislature [in sect. 100] was, to simplify the proof before the Revising Barrister—to give the stamped duplicate an effect beyond what in ordinary cases such an instrument would have. * * The object of the proviso in sect. 100 was, to prevent the retention on the register of fictitious names, or *names with fictitious addresses. The question here is, not whether the Act dispenses with proof of the act of posting the notices; for, it may be assumed that the notices were duly posted, but that through some accident they did not reach the hands of the parties for whom they were intended.

(TINDAL, Ch. J.: From some cause that is unexplained, the notices did not arrive by the day on which, according to the ordinary course of the post, they should have arrived.

ERLE, J.: It appears from another case (3) that the delay arose

[*47]

[48]

[*49]

BISHOP
v.
HELPS.

---

(1) If the notice of objection had been held good, the respondent might have proved a qualification.

(2) The case was argued in Michael-

mas Term, before Tindal, Ch. J., and Coltman, Maule, and Erle, JJ.

(3) *Hickton* v. *Antrobus*, 2 C. B. 82

BISHOP
r.
HELPS.

from the great accumulation of letters at the Manchester post-office on the two or three days preceding.)

Are the consequences of that accident to be visited upon the objector?

(ERLE, J.: The question is, whether the mere posting of the notices, as directed by sect. 100, is sufficient proof of the sending and of the receipt.

TINDAL, Ch. J.: It may also be a question whether the provisions of the Act do not vary as to the two notices.)

It is submitted that the general words in sect. 101 incorporate all the provisions of sect. 100 as to the transmission of the notice and the effect of the stamped duplicate.

(MAULE, J.: I incline to think that is so.)

[50]

It is not necessary, however, to decide that question; for, here, both notices were duly posted. [He cited *Cooper* v. *Coates* (1), *Cuming* v. *Toms* (2).] The Court will put such a construction upon the Act as to carry into effect the obvious meaning of the words used.

(MAULE, J.: The objection is, that the proof on which you seek to rely is proof of something that is confessedly contrary to the fact. Now, the Act does allow of this in other cases. If the party to whom the notice is addressed has changed his abode or is abroad, and the post-office authorities have done all that their duty requires of them in endeavouring to effect a delivery, that will undoubtedly be a sufficient, or rather will be equivalent to, service.)

The stamped duplicate is put somewhat upon the footing of a record. General convenience requires that the service of the notices in this case should be held sufficient.

Byles, Serjt. (with whom was *W. R. Grove*), for the respondent:

The decision of the Revising Barrister was correct. The Barrister finds that the only evidence of the posting of the notices, was, the production of the stamped duplicates; and in both cases he finds, not that the notice did in fact ever reach the parties, but

(1) 63 R. R. 233 (5 Man. & G. 98).   (2) 66 R. R. 653 (7 Man. & G. 29; 8 Scott, N. R. 827).

that it did not arrive at the place to which it was addressed until   BISHOP
the 27th of August. The duplicate only is stamped at the place of   *v.*
posting.   HELPS.

(ERLE, J.: The question of law presented for our decision is
this : certain notices which, by the due course of post, would have
reached the parties on the 25th of August, did not in fact reach
them until the 27th; I, the Revising Barrister, decide that the
notices are too late, and retain the names; if the Court thinks my
decision wrong, the names are to be expunged from the list. That
is the only question we have to deal with.)

The Barrister reserves two questions for the Court—first, whether
the notice to the voter was given in time—secondly, whether the
notice to the overseers was in time.

1. As to the notice to the voter: that clearly was not given in   [51]
due time.   *   * Whether the notice arrives a day or two too late,
or fails to arrive at all, therefore, can make no difference : and the
case may be argued on the assumption that the notices here never
actually reached their destination. Taking it that the non-arrival
was the result of accident, upon whom is the inconvenience, if any,
to fall? Is it *to fall upon the objector, who had the choice of two   [*52]
modes of giving notice? or upon the voter, who has no such
election?

(MAULE, J.: The Legislature may have thought that no great
mischief could result from an accidental delay of a day or two.)

This may be likened to the case of a party who, having a remittance to make, has the option of doing it in either of three ways—
he may carry it himself, or send it by a servant or agent, or may
transmit it by post: if he adopts the latter course, unless at the
special request of the payee, and the money fails to reach its
destination, he alone must bear the loss.

(TINDAL, Ch. J.: Unless such a mode of remittance were authorized by an Act of Parliament.)

Suppose this notice had been sent by post directed to the voter's
actual place of abode, and it had never reached him?

(MAULE, J.: That clearly would not do: there is no provision
for that.

BISHOP
v.
HELPS.

TINDAL, Ch. J.: The difficulty that is cast upon the objector is, that he could not be aware of the way in which he was to be met, until he appeared before the Revising Barrister.)

A still greater difficulty is imposed upon the voter, if called upon to prove his qualification, when he has received no notice that it is objected to.

(MAULE, J.: You say that the Legislature, as to the evidence, only meant to substitute the stamped duplicate for the original, which it might be difficult to procure?)

Precisely so.

2. The notice to the overseers was not duly given. The only proof of notice was, the production of the stamped duplicate.

(ERLE, J.: You are assuming something contrary to the statement in the case.)

It is clear from the case that the notice was not received in due time: it may therefore be assumed that it never arrived at all.

[53]   *   *   Now, it does not appear upon the case, in what manner the notice in question was addressed.

(TINDAL, Ch. J.: We must assume that it was properly addressed; the case finds that both the notices were in the proper form. At all events, if any thing turned upon it, we would remit the case to the Revising Barrister to state the fact more specifically (1).)

In *Hinton* v. *The Town Clerk of Wenlock* (2) it was held that the Court will not remit a case for the insertion of a fact, which the Barrister considered to be immaterial.   This is not a notice within the Act at all.

(ERLE, J.: You are raising a question of fact, upon which the Revising Barrister has not exercised his judgment.   The only objection before him was, that the notices did not reach the hands of the persons to whom they were addressed in due time.)

The Court must see, upon the face of the case, that the notice was so directed to the overseers, as to let in the first objection.   *   *   *

(1) The Barrister, who was in Court,   (2) 66 R. R. 696, n. (1) (7 Man. & G.
stated that the notice was directed   166, n.; 8 Scott, N. R. 995).
"To the Overseers of Cheltenham."

Talfourd, Serjt., in reply:

* * The 100th section makes the delivery to the post-master, and the production of the stamped duplicate to the post-master, "sufficient" evidence of the notice having been given to the person at the place mentioned in such duplicate, on the day on which such notice would in the ordinary course of post have been delivered at such place: not evidence of the mere giving of the notice, but of its receipt also. In *Stocken* v. *Collin* (1), PARKE, B., said: "If a party puts a notice of dishonour into the post, so that in the due course of delivery it would arrive in time, he has done all that can be required of him; and it is no fault of his that delay occurs in the delivery."

(MAULE, J.: The law does not require the party to give notice; but to use due diligence to give notice.)

Enough is done if the notice *is posted, so that it would, according to the usual course of the post, arrive in due time. The statute means to give validity to the time as well as to the act of posting. There can be no distinction in this respect between the two notices. And it sufficiently appears upon the case that the notice sent to the overseers was properly addressed. The fact was not disputed before the Revising Barrister.

Cur. adv. vult.

TINDAL, Ch. J., now delivered the opinion of the COURT:

In this case, which was an appeal from the decision of the Revising Barrister for the eastern division of the county of Gloucester, the question reserved by him for the opinion of the Court was, whether the notices of objection to the party who claimed the right to vote, and to the overseers, were given in due time. The notices were proper in point of form, and were duly delivered to the post-master in such time as that by the ordinary course of the post they would have been delivered at the places to which they were respectively addressed, some time in the day of the 25th of August (2); but, in point of fact, they were not delivered at such places until after that day: so that the question is limited to the sufficiency of the notices in point of time.

Two questions were raised in the argument before us, one with

(1) 56 R. R. 785 (7 M. & W. 515).   sufficient if the notice is posted on the
(2) By sect. 100 it is declared to be   25th.

BISHOP
v.
HELPS.

[*56]

respect to the notice to the party objected to, the other with respect
to the notice to the overseers. We will first consider the case of
the notice to the party objected to.

The Act 6 & 7 Vict. c. 18, by the 7th section, requires a notice
of objection to be delivered on or before the *25th of August. The
100th section enacts, that, in case of notice to a person objected to,
it shall be " sufficient " if the notice shall be sent by the post, free
of postage, directed to the person to whom it is sent, at his place
of abode as described in the list of voters; and that, whenever any
person shall be desirous of sending such notice by the post, he
shall deliver the same, duly directed, open, and in duplicate, to the
post-master of a post-office where money orders are received or
paid, within such hours as shall have been given notice of, and
under such regulations with respect to the registration of such
letters as shall be made by the Postmaster-General. The Act then
directs the post-master, on payment of the fee for registration, to
compare the notice and duplicate, and to forward one, and to
return the other to the party bringing it. It then provides that
the production of a stamped duplicate by the party who posted
such notice, shall be evidence of the notice having been given
to the person mentioned in the duplicate, on the day in which
such notice would, by the ordinary course of post, have been
delivered to such place.

It was argued, on the part of the respondent, that the true
construction of this section was, that it should be sufficient if the
notice was effectually sent, that is, sent and delivered. And there
is no doubt that this would be sufficient: but it would, at the
same time, be unnecessary to have this provision, which is a
very special one, in order to make such a sending sufficient; for,
there is no doubt that any sending and delivery, by a servant or
otherwise, by which the notice came to the voter, would be sufficient by the ninth section. It is, therefore, evident that some
privilege is meant to be conferred by section 100 on a mode of
dealing with the notice which is so carefully provided for. The
notice must be posted at a select description of office; within

[*57]

*certain hours; the postage must be paid; it must be registered,
and the fee for registration must be paid; it must be delivered to
the post-master, open, and in duplicate; compared; stamped; and
the duplicate returned. And we think the meaning of the Act is
this—when all these conditions are complied with, such a sending
shall be a sufficient substitute for what the seventh section required

to be done, that is, a sufficient substitute for giving the notice to the person objected to, or leaving it at his place of abode.

It was probably considered that the public convenience would be promoted by the present provision, and that its advantages would greatly outweigh the inconvenience which, in some few cases, might possibly arise from it. Indeed, in the case of leaving notices at the place of abode, it may possibly happen, that, without any fault of the party objected to, the notice may be lost or destroyed, or simply not delivered, through the negligence of a servant, and so never come to his knowledge ; and yet there can be no doubt this would be a sufficient delivery. And perhaps such a miscarriage under section 7 may be of as probable occurrence as the non-delivery of a notice posted according to section 100 of the Act.

If this be the true construction of that part of the section which provides what sending is sufficient, it follows that the objector has done all that the Act requires him to do, to enable him to call on the voter to prove his right, whether the notice arrived or not, and whether it was prevented from arriving by insufficient description of the place of abode or by default of the post-office. So that, supposing, as it was insisted for the respondent, that the evidence of the stamped duplicate is not conclusive as to arrival, and was answered by proof of the contrary, as it was here, it makes no difference as to the right of the objector ; as the fact so *disproved, is not material to his right.   The stamp on the duplicate is clearly evidence of the posting on the 24th ; and there was no contradiction as to that fact ; so that, whatever might be the consequence if it had been shown in evidence that the notice was not really posted on the 24th, as the proof stood, all the facts constituting a sufficient sending were proved without contradiction.

[*58]

It was objected, secondly, with respect to the notice to the overseers, that such a notice was not within section 100, which applies only to notices to persons objected to ; and that section 101 did not help it, as that section says nothing of a duplicate being evidence : so that, as there was no proof of notice to the overseer, except the stamped duplicate, no notice was in effect proved.   But it appears to us that the clause in section 101, which provides, that, whenever by this Act notice is required to be given or sent to any person whatsoever, or public officer, it shall be sufficient if such notice shall be sent by the post, in the manner and subject to the regulations hereinbefore provided with respect to sending notices of objection by post, with a sufficient direction, addressed to the person

BISHOP
v.
HELPS.

[*59]

to whom the same ought to be sent, at his usual place of abode,
affords a sufficient answer to this objection. For, it seems to us,
that this clause applies the provisions in section 100 as to notices
to persons objected to (including that provision which requires the
notice to be delivered, open, and in duplicate, to the post-master,
and that the post-master shall stamp and return one part, and
its necessary consequence, that such stamped duplicate shall be
evidence of the time of posting and of delivery), to all notices to
overseers directed to them at their usual places of abode ; and, as
nothing appears upon the case stated, and no question was made,
respecting the address of the notice to the overseers, we *think the
notice to them falls within the same rule as the notice given to the
party objected to. It appears, therefore, to us that both of the
notices of objection were given in due time, and, consequently, that
the decision of the Revising Barrister must be reversed.

Decision reversed (1).

1846.
Jan. 15.

*City of
Rochester.*

[60]

GEORGE COLVILL *v.* LEWIS, TOWN CLERK OF
ROCHESTER.

(2 C. B. 60—62 ; S. C. 15 L. J. C. P. 70.)

A notice of objection sent by post, so that it would, in the ordinary
course of the post, be delivered on a Sunday, is nevertheless well served.
The Court cannot entertain an appeal in the absence of the respondent,
unless there be an affidavit of service upon him of notice of the appellant's
intention to prosecute the appeal under the Parliamentary Voters Registration Act, 1843 (6 & 7 Vict. c. 18), s. 64.

GEORGE COLVILL, on the list of freemen for the city of Rochester,
objected, in all respects duly (except as hereinafter mentioned), to
the name of John Barton Balcomb being retained on the list and
register of freemen voters for the said city, wherein the place of
abode of the said John Barton Balcomb was described as being
St. Nicholas, by posting a notice of such objection at the post-office
at Chatham, on Saturday, the 23rd of August, 1845 ; which notice
was in all respects in the form prescribed by schedule (B.), No. 11,
to the statute of 6 & 7 Vict. c. 18, and was directed to the said John
Barton Balcomb, at St. Nicholas.

The day on which such notice would, in the ordinary course of
post, have been delivered at St. Nicholas, was Sunday, the 24th of
August.

(1) In *Bishop* v. *Cox*, an appeal from
a decision of the same Revising
Barrister, upon precisely the same
state of facts as in the principal case,
the decision was reversed, on the same
ground.

Objection being duly made to the validity of such notice, on the COLVILL
v.
LEWIS.
ground that such notice was delivered and served on Sunday, the
Barrister decided that this objection ought to prevail, and that such
notice was invalid, by reason that the service of the same was
effected on Sunday, and was therefore void, as being within the
6th section of the statute 29 Car. II. c. 7, and within the mischiefs
thereby intended to be remedied ; and he retained the name of the
said John Barton Balcomb on the said list and register of voters.

If the Court shall decide that such service was good *and effectual,   [*61]
the name of the said John Barton Balcomb is to be expunged from
the list and register of freemen entitled to vote for the said city.

The cases of twenty-two other voters, similarly circumstanced,
were consolidated with the above.

* * *

C. Jones, Serjt., now appeared on behalf of the appellant :

The question is, whether the delivery of the notice of objection
by the post, at the house of the voter on a Sunday, renders the
service bad (1). The 6th section of the statute 29 Car. II. c. 7,
provides " that no person or persons upon the Lord's day shall
serve or execute, or cause to be served or executed, any writ, process, warrant, order, judgment, or decree (except in cases of treason,
felony, or breach of the peace), but that the service of every such
writ, process, &c. shall be void to all intents and purposes whatsoever ; and the person or persons so serving or executing the
same shall be as liable to the suit of the party grieved, and to
answer damages to him for doing thereof, as if he or they had done
the same without any writ, process, warrant, order, judgment, or
decree at all." This is not a writ, process, or other judicial proceeding. If the voter had abstained from opening the letter till
the Monday, the service clearly would have been unexceptionable.

(CRESSWELL, J.: If the notice is in the nature of process, the fact   [62]
of the recipient not looking at it until Monday would not render
good an illegal and void service on Sunday. You must contend
that a service of the notice on Sunday is good.)

Such a service is not within the prohibition of the statute.

No one appeared for the respondents. But, inasmuch as there
was no affidavit of service upon them of the notice required by

(1) The case does not expressly find that the notice reached the voter's
house on Sunday.

COLVILL
v.
LEWIS.

the 6 & 7 Vict. c. 18, s. 64, the COURT declined to pronounce any judgment.

C. Jones, Serjt., having on a subsequent day produced the requisite affidavit,

The COURT reversed the decision of the Revising Barrister.

Decision reversed.

1846.
Jan. 15.
——
*Lancashire,
Southern
Division.*
[72]

RAWLINS *v.* THE OVERSEERS OF WEST DERBY.

(2 C. B. 72—82 ; S. C. 15 L. J. C. P. 70.)

When the 20th of July falls on a Sunday, service of a notice of claim upon an overseer, under the Parliamentary Voters Registration Act, 1843 (6 & 7 Vict. c. 18), s. 4, by leaving it at his place of abode on that day, is good service.

Semble, that, where the respondent appears, he is precluded from objecting to the form of the service of the notice of appeal required by ss. 62, 64.

THE overseers of the township of West Derby, in the southern division of the county of Lancaster, objected to the names of George Atkinson, and of thirty-nine other persons, whose names and descriptions were set forth in a schedule annexed to the case, being retained on the list of claimants to vote in the said township.

The Barrister struck out the names of the said claimants from the said list, subject to the opinion of the Court of Common Pleas on the following case :

All the said claims were delivered at the dwelling-house of one of the overseers of the said township of West Derby, in his absence, about 9 o'clock of the evening of Sunday, the 20th of July last. The overseers, nevertheless, published such claims in the list of claimants, but inserted opposite to each name the word "objected;" and at the revision of the said list, they contended that such service of the said claims respectively was insufficient and invalid, having

[*73]

been made *on a Sunday, and the following day being too late by law for the service of such notices ; and that such claimants therefore were not entitled to have their names retained on the said list.

The Barrister allowed the objection, and consolidated the several cases.

[74]   *Crompton,* for the respondents.   *   *   *

[76]   *Arnold,* for the respondents.   *   *   *

[78]   *Crompton* was not called upon to reply.

TINDAL, Ch. J.:

It appears to me that this case may be determined by reference to the very plain language of the fourth section of the Act. That section directs that all persons who shall be desirous to have their names inserted *in the register, "shall, on or before the 20th day of July, deliver or send to the overseers a notice signed by him, of his claim, according to the form of notice set forth in that behalf in the form numbered 2, schedule (A), or to the like effect." The statute, therefore, in plain terms, gives the party power to send in a claim at any time on or before the 20th of July. The argument urged on the part of the respondent, is, that that direction is not obligatory in all cases; but that, when the 20th of July happens to be a Sunday, the day is to be excepted. The language being so plain, we must take the Act as we find it, unless there be some equal power requiring us to engraft upon it the proposed exception; especially as we see, that, where the Legislature have intended to except Sunday, they have done so in express terms. As to the statute 29 Car. II. c. 7, this clearly is not a matter within the prohibitory part of that Act, the first provision of which applies to things done by persons in the exercise of their ordinary callings, and the second to the service of writs or process of a judicial character, within neither of which can the present case be classed. Many things at common law were feasible and were held valid if done on a Sunday: an entry for condition broken, or to preserve an estate, was equally valid whether made on a Sunday or on any other day; so, a demand of possession, to support an ejectment, might well be made on that day; and all contracts, not made in the ordinary callings of the parties, are still valid though made on Sunday. I see no reason, therefore, why a notice of this sort may not be served on a Sunday. To make the argument drawn from the notice of dishonour of a bill of exchange at all favour the construction put forward on the part of the respondent, it must be contended that the notice would be void if forwarded on a Sunday, which is not the case, *although no doubt the party receiving a notice of dishonour on a Sunday might abstain from opening it until the following morning. I think, for these reasons, that the decision of the Barrister is wrong, and must be reversed.

[*79]

[*80]

MAULE, J.:

I am of the same opinion. The Act requires the notice of claim

RAWLINS
v.
THE
OVERSEERS
OF WEST
DERBY.

to be given or sent to the overseers on or before the 20th of July. If that be done, the overseers are enabled to perform the duty imposed upon them by sect. 5 of preparing lists of claimants before the last day of the month ; the object of sect. 4 being to give them for that purpose all the interval between the 20th and the 31st of July. They have had all that time here. If the 20th of July had not been Sunday, there is no doubt the claimant might have sent in his claim at any time on that day : and I must confess I find nothing in the Act to deprive him of that right because the 20th of July happened to fall on a Sunday. I do not think we ought to seek any other meaning than the words naturally bear, seeing that they are so clear and unequivocal. It may be conceded, that, if they comprehended something *contra bonos mores*, or against the common law, an exception might be implied. A party is not to commit a breach of the law of the land because he is required to do a certain act within a given time. But I know of no law that prevents these notices from being served on a Sunday. Certain things are by statute declared void if done on a Sunday : but *primâ facie* any act may be done on that day. In the case of bills of exchange, the custom of merchants has engrafted upon it the exception of Sunday from the days of grace, and a party is not called upon to take a notice of dishonour on that day. In the reign of Charles the Second an Act of Parliament passed providing that certain things

[*81]

that formerly might have *been done on Sunday should no longer be done on that day ; all other things being left to the freedom of the common law. There is therefore no ground for saying that the notices in question were not properly delivered. It may be remembered that we have already decided that a delivery by post may be made on a Sunday (1). The post-master is, by law, required to deliver letters on that day. For these reasons, I am of opinion that the decision of the Revising Barrister was wrong, and ought to be reversed.

CRESSWELL, J. :

I am entirely of the same opinion. The statute provides that the notices of claim shall be delivered " on or before the 20th of July." Upon that provision we are invited to engraft an exception, unless that day shall happen to be Sunday. How are we to follow that out? By saying, that, in that event, the last day shall be the 19th? Or by extending it to the 21st? How can we say what the

(1) *Colvill* v. *Lewis*, *ante*, p. 412.

Legislature would have done? (1). I agree with the LORD CHIEF JUSTICE and my brother MAULE, that there is no reason for departing from the plain words of the statute.

ERLE, J.:

I am of the same opinion. We should be disregarding the plain and express words of the statute, if we held that the delivery of these notices on a Sunday, is not valid. Such delivery is no violation of *any known rule of law. The overseer who receives the notice is not called upon to perform any duty that can interfere with the most scrupulous observance of the Lord's day.

[*82]

Decision reversed.

HOYLAND v. BREMNER.

(2 C. B. 84—89; S. C. 15 L. J. C. P. 133; 10 Jur. 36.)

1846.
Jan. 19.

Lancashire, Southern Division.

[84]

A conveyance from one vendor to several persons, who purchase with the intention of obtaining and multiplying votes by splitting and dividing the interest, the vendor not being cognizant of the purpose, is valid. Nor is such a conveyance brought within the 7 & 8 Will. III. c. 25, s. 7, by the mere knowledge, on the part of the vendor's solicitor or agent, of the object of the purchasers.

FRAZER WILLIAM HOYLAND, and seventeen other persons whose names appear in the first schedule annexed to this case, were objected to as not being entitled to have their names retained in the list of claimants for the township of Newton, in the southern division of the county of Lancaster, in respect of their several qualifications mentioned in such list.

The Barrister struck out the names of all the said *claimants from the said list, subject to the opinion of the Court of Common Pleas on the following case:

[*85]

It appeared in evidence, that, some time during the latter part of the year 1844, one Charles Duffield, a house-agent in Manchester,

---

(1) In general, where one branch of an alternative condition becomes impossible, the other branch stands as if the former had not been mentioned. If the statute of 29 Car. II. c. 7, s. 6, had prohibited the service of notices as well as the service or execution of "writs, process, warrant orders, judgments, or decrees upon the Lord's day," the words "on or before the 20th of July" in the Reform Act would probably have been read—on or before the 20th of July in those years in which the 20th of July shall not fall on a Sunday, and before the 20th of July when that day shall fall on a Sunday.

HOYLAND
v.
BREMNER.

was employed by the claimants, who were all members or supporters
of a certain political association called the Antimonopoly Association, to procure for them qualifications to vote for members of
Parliament for South Lancashire. Accordingly, Duffield, in the
month of January last, applied to one Worthington, a solicitor in
Manchester, who was known by Duffield to have property on sale
which would confer qualifications to vote for the division of South
Lancashire, to purchase such qualifications for Hoyland and the
other claimants. He agreed with Duffield to sell certain freehold
land and houses in the township of Newton, the property of one
Whittaker, who had employed Worthington to dispose of this and
other real estate. No contract in writing as to the purchase was
entered into between any of the purchasers, or Duffield as their
agent, and Whittaker. Duffield, as agent for the purchasers,
employed Worthington to draw the conveyance on their behalf;
and they did not personally consult him (Worthington) relative to
the purchase. Different portions of the above freehold premises
were conveyed to the claimants, in fee, by several separate deeds,
in all nine; such claimants, where more than one purchaser was
included in the conveyance, taking their respective shares as tenants
in common. All the conveyances were duly executed before the
31st of January last; and the purchase-money for each was handed
over to Worthington, at the time of execution, by Duffield, who
had previously received it from the purchasers. The price given
in respect of each purchase appeared to be the fair marketable
value of the property bought. The claimants have each received

[*86]

*the rents of their respective portions or shares, which are of a
sufficient value to confer a vote.

It did not appear that Whittaker knew of the object which the
claimants had in view in making their purchases.

The Barrister was of opinion that the object of the claimants
was to acquire for themselves votes, for the purpose of multiplying
voices for the election of members of Parliament for the southern
division of Lancashire, and for that purpose to split and divide
their interest in the houses and land so purchased by them. And
he was further of opinion that such object was known, and acquiesced
in, by the vendor's solicitor before the execution of the several
conveyances above referred to. He therefore thought all such conveyances void for the purpose of conferring such votes as aforesaid,
under the 7 & 8 Will. III. c. 25.

In the first schedule above referred to, the names, places of

abode, &c., of the several persons objected to, were stated in the   HOYLAND
following form :   *v.*
                                                                         BREMNER,

TOWNSHIP OF NEWTON.

Christian Name and Surname of each.	Place of Abode.	Nature of Qualification.	Street, Lane, &c., in this Township where Property situate, &c.
Hoyland, Frazer William.	Western Park, Moss Side, near Manchester.	Undivided share of freehold land and dwelling-houses.	Droylsden Road.

The appeal in the above cases was, by consent of the parties, consolidated with that of twenty-five other persons named in the schedule hereinafter contained, whose names the Barrister had struck out of the list of claimants in the township of Liverpool, the facts being similar with those above stated, except that, as to the claimants in the township of Liverpool, there were contracts in *writing entered into between the vendors and purchasers, and at   [*87] the time of signing such contracts the vendor's solicitor was not privy to the objects which the claimants had in view in making the purchase, although he was privy to such objects before the execution of the respective purchase-deeds.

TOWNSHIP OF LIVERPOOL.

Christian Name and Surname of each.	Place of Abode.	Nature of Qualification.	Street, &c., in this Township where Property situate, &c.
Bayliffe, William.	Princes Street, Woodside, Cheshire.	Freehold houses.	Lowther Street, G. D. and S. J. tenants.
Branker, John Houghton.	Field House, Wavertree, near Liverpool.	Do. (1)	Do. (1)

Cockburn (with whom was *Kinglake*, Serjt.), for the appellant :

This case is not distinguishable from *Marshall* v. *Bown* (2).   *   *
Here, the Revising Barrister decided that the case before him was   [88] not governed by that case, because the solicitor for the vendor was aware that the object of the purchasers was to acquire votes by

---

(1) The insertion of the · word   name immediately above it happened
"ditto" to avoid repetition is not   to be expunged.
warranted by the statute ; and it   (2) 66 R. R. 700 (7 Man. & G. 188 ;
might lead to great confusion if the   8 Scott, N. R. 889).

HOYLAND
v.
BREMNER.

[*89]

splitting and dividing the interest in the houses and land so purchased by them, and that he acquiesced therein. The grantor, however, not being cognizant of the supposed illegal purpose of the purchasers, the case is clearly not within either the statute of William, or the statute 10 Ann. c. 23 (1). The last-mentioned statute *pre-supposes a fraudulent intention on the part of the grantor personally.

Arnold, for the respondent :

The 53 Geo. III. c. 49, s. 2, shows that the statute of William was intended to operate on estates that could be beneficially enjoyed. Here, the knowledge of the vendor's agent is the knowledge of the vendor himself. Any representation or warranty made by the former would bind the latter : *Fitzherbert* v. *Mather* (2), *Irving* v. *Motly* (3).

(CRESSWELL, J. : Not, if beyond the scope of his authority (4).)

TINDAL, Ch. J. :

The agent's knowledge cannot affect the title. The Barrister not having found that the vendor had any illegal purpose in view, or any knowledge of any illegal object on the part of the purchasers, we think the case is within the principle of *Marshall* v. *Bown*, and that the decision is wrong.

Decision reversed.

1846.
Jan. 26.
—
*City of
Westminster.*

[90]

JAMES BISHOP v. FRANCIS SMEDLEY, HIGH BAILIFF OF WESTMINSTER.

(2 C. B. 90—96 ; S. C. 15 L. J. C. P. 73; 10 Jur. 269.)

A. claimed, under the Representation of the People Act, 1832 (2 Will. IV. c. 45), s. 30, to be rated in respect of premises occupied by him, and asked the overseer whether there were any rates due ; the overseer saying that he did not know, A. added, " If there are, I am prepared to pay them," but he did not produce or offer money : the overseer answered, " I'll see to it," and A. went away, and made no further inquiry on the subject : Held, not a sufficient tender to entitle A. to the benefit of that section.

JAMES BISHOP claimed to be registered as occupier of a house No. 213, Piccadilly, in the parish of St. James, Westminster.

(1) 10 Anne, c. 31, s. 1, in the Statutes of the Realm.—J. G. P.
(2) 1 R. R. 134 (1 T. R. 12, 16).
(3) 7 Bing. 543.
(4) For which see *Trusswell* v.

Middleton, 2 Roll. Rep. 269, 270 ; Cro. Jac. 653 ; *Strode* v. *Dyson*, 1 J. P. Smith, 400 ; *Alexander* v. *Gibson*, 11 R. R. 797 (2 Camp. 555) ; *Pickering* v. *Busk*, 13 R. R. 364 (15 East, 38, 45).

The Revising Barrister decided that the said James Bishop was not entitled to have his name inserted in the list of voters, in consequence of his not having been rated, in respect of the premises which he occupied as aforesaid, during the twelve months ending on the 31st of July, 1845, and of his not having paid on or before the 20th of July, all the rates which were due in respect of such premises, previously to the 6th of April preceding; subject, however, to the opinion of the Court of Common Pleas upon the following case:

Bishop had never been rated to the poor-rate for the house which he occupies. The only name that appears upon the rate-book is that of Edmund John Scott, the landlord. On the 20th of July there remained a sum of 3*l*. 2*s*. 6*d*. unpaid of rates due on the 6th of April last.

Bishop's evidence, in support of his claim, was to the following effect: "On the 19th of June last I called on Mr. James Catchpole, one of the overseers, at his shop in Regent Street. I there delivered to him a notice of claim to be rated for the house I occupy. I asked Catchpole whether there were any rates due. He said he did not know. I then said, 'If there are, I am prepared to pay them.' Catchpole replied, 'I'll see to it.' I never made any further inquiry; and I never heard again upon the subject. I am sure that, when I called *upon Mr. Catchpole, I had money in my pocket; because [*91] I remember having first gone home for a 10*l*. note. Nothing more than what I have stated passed between me and the overseer."

The Revising Barrister held, that the effect of the indulgence given by the 30th section of the 2 Will. IV. c. 45, to persons claiming to be rated, could not be to put them in a better position than those persons were in, who were actually rated; and that Bishop was bound to see that the rates due on the 6th of April, in respect of his premises, were paid on or before the 20th of July. He, also, decided, that there was not, according to Bishop's own evidence, sufficient proof, in this case, of such a tender of rates on the 19th of June, as is required by the statute.

If the Court of Common Pleas shall be of opinion that the decision was wrong, the name of the appellant is to be inserted in the register of voters.

Arnold, for the appellant:

The question arises upon the thirtieth section of the 2 Will. IV. c. 45. The *twenty-seventh section having required that the voter [*92] should be rated, and that he should have paid the rates that should have become payable from him in respect of the premises, previously to the 6th of April preceding; the thirtieth section enables him to acquire the same right by payment or tender of the rates, though not actually rated. Here, the claimant, having no better means of knowing what is due, in respect of the premises, than by applying to the overseer, whose duty it was to know the fact, inquires of him whether there were any rates due, saying that, if there are, he is prepared to pay them. The overseer not being able to inform him, no tender is actually made.

(MAULE, J.: The rate is a public thing; the party might, by inspecting it, ascertain the amount.)

He would not be able to ascertain, by inspecting the rate, whether his landlord had paid it or not. The facts clearly show a waiver or dispensation of a tender by the overseer.

(TINDAL, Ch. J.: How can the overseer dispense with a tender required by an Act of Parliament? The case of an ordinary tender is different; a man may well dispense with his own rights.)

Suppose the precise sum of 3l. 2s. 6d. had actually been tendered, the position of the overseer would not have been altered, inasmuch as he did not know the amount that was due.

(MAULE, J.: The overseer might have given him credit for accuracy, and have taken that sum.)

The Court will not require more strictness in a tender under an Act of Parliament than in a tender at common law.

(MAULE, J.: That may be so; and possibly this might have been sufficient, if the overseer had refused to ascertain the amount.)

[94] [He cited *Dickenson v. Shee* (1), *Douglas v. Patrick* (2), *Thomas v. Evans* (3), *Read v. Goldring* (4), and *Bevan v. Rees* (5).] Suppose the party claiming to be rated had produced a sum more than sufficient to pay the rate, and desired the overseer to take what was due, would not that have been a sufficient tender?

(1) 4 Esp. N. P. C. 68.   (4) 14 R. R. 594 (2 M. & S. 86).
(2) 1 R. R. 793 (3 T. R. 683).   (5) 5 M. & W. 306.
(3) 10 R. R. 229 (10 East, 101).

(MAULE, J.: Clearly not, under the circumstances. The overseer cannot be expected, at a moment's warning, to be able to tell each rate-payer the amount due from him.)

BISHOP
v.
SMEDLEY.

*   *   *

Merewether, for the respondent, was stopped by the COURT.

TINDAL, Ch. J.:

It appears to me that the decision of the Revising Barrister was proper under the circumstances *of this case. The thirtieth section of the 2 Will. IV. c. 45, provides that it shall be lawful for any person occupying certain premises, to claim to be rated to the relief of the poor, and that, upon the party so claiming, and actually paying or tendering the full amount of the rate or rates due in respect of the premises, the overseers shall put his name upon the rate for the time being; and that, in case the overseers shall neglect or refuse so to do, such occupier shall nevertheless be deemed to have been rated from the period at which the rate shall have been made. Now, it is perfectly clear that this party did not actually pay the rate in question; and it seems to me as clear that he did not actually tender the amount of the rate; for, when he called on the overseer, and inquired whether there were any rates due, upon the overseer saying he did not know, the claimant told him he was prepared to pay them, if any were due: to which the overseer replied, "I'll see to it:" and this was all that passed. The claimant seems to have left the overseer with a mutual understanding that he was to call again. Without, therefore, going into the two points raised by the case, it is enough to say that I think the Barrister has come to a right conclusion.

[*95]

MAULE, J.:

I also think the Revising Barrister came to a right conclusion in this case. The thirtieth section of the 2 Will. IV. c. 45, enables occupiers not named in the rate, to claim to be rated; and provides, that, upon their actually paying or tendering the full amount of the rate or rates due in respect of the premises, though not in fact rated, they are deemed to be so for the purposes of the Act. Here, there was no actual payment of the rate by the claimant: the only question is whether there was a tender within the meaning of the Act. Without saying whether or not the same degree of precision and nicety are required in a tender under this *Act as would be necessary to support a plea of tender, I think the claimant should

[*96]

at least show that he has done all that he reasonably could do towards payment. The claimant is to pay or to tender; and the overseer is to receive the rate. It seems to me that the overseer did all that he could reasonably be expected to do; but that the claimant did not conduct himself like one who was perfectly ready to pay. He went to the overseer, and he asked him whether there was any rate due; and received for answer, that which he might well have expected, viz. that the overseer did not know; for, it was very unlikely that he should recollect all the houses and the amount of rates, and whether they had been paid. The claimant then said, "If there are any, I am prepared to pay them." It was not absolutely necessary, perhaps, that he should actually exhibit the money. Upon the overseer replying, "I'll see to it," that is, "I will inquire as to the amount due," the claimant went away, and did not return. I think, under these circumstances, it is quite clear he did not do all that in him lay to pay the rate or to make a valid tender, and therefore that the Barrister has decided rightly.

CRESSWELL and ERLE, JJ., concurred.

*   *   *   *   *

Decision affirmed, with costs.

CROUCHER *v.* BROWNE.

(2 C. B. 97—111; S. C. 15 L. J. C. P. 74.)

Freemen and liverymen of London admitted freemen by purchase since the 1st of March, 1831, are entitled to be registered, notwithstanding the proviso in the Representation of the People Act, 1832 (2 Will. IV. c. 45), s. 32; such proviso applying not to liverymen of the city of London, but to freemen and burgesses of other cities and boroughs.

The Court will not give costs upon an appeal, though only one side is heard, where a question of law, the fair subject of a doubt, is involved.

JOHN HONOUR CROUCHER duly objected to the name of Edward Browne being retained in the list of such of the freemen of London as are liverymen of the Company of Bakers, entitled to vote in the election of members for the city of London.

The Revising Barrister retained the name of the said Edward Browne, subject to an appeal to the Court of Common Pleas upon the following case:

The respondent was admitted to the freedom of the Company of Bakers, and to the freedom of the city of London, by redemption or purchase, in the month of January, 1834, and to the livery of the

said Company in the month of March following.   His qualification   <small>CROUCHER</small>
was in other respects perfect.   <small>*v.*</small>
                                                                      <small>BROWNE.</small>

On behalf of the appellant, it was contended, that, by the
2 Will. IV. c. 45, s. 32, the respondent was disqualified, inasmuch
as, having been admitted a freeman since the 1st of March, 1831,
"otherwise than in respect of birth or servitude," he was not
entitled to vote "as such."

The Barrister decided that the words "as such" in the said
section were limited to persons who voted as "burgesses" or "as
freemen;" that the freemen and liverymen of London did not vote
as freemen, but as freemen and liverymen; and, therefore, that a
freeman and liveryman who had been admitted a freeman by
purchase after the 1st of March, 1831, was not disqualified by the
disfranchising proviso of that section.

If the Court shall be of opinion that the said decision was wrong,   [98]
the name of the respondent is to be expunged from the list of voters
for the said Company.

Kinglake, Serjt. (with whom was *Welsby*), for the appellant. * * *

Gurney (with whom was *Merewether*), for the respondent, was   [105]
not called upon.

TINDAL, Ch. J. :

The question in this case turns upon the proper construction to
be put upon the thirty-second section of the 2 Will. IV. c. 45, which
I think it is impossible to read without noticing the marked distinction therein between burgesses and freemen of boroughs or
cities generally, and freemen and liverymen of the city of London.
When speaking of boroughs or cities other than London, the
expression is "burgess *or* freeman," in the alternative : but when
speaking of London, it is in the conjunctive, "freeman *and* liveryman;" coupling the character of freeman with that of liveryman,
and making the right of voting depend upon the twofold qualification : and this distinction is maintained throughout the whole of
the section.   It begins with enacting "that every person who would
have been entitled to vote in the election of a member or members
to serve in any future Parliament for any city or borough not
included in the schedule marked (A.) to this Act annexed, either as
a burgess *or* freeman, or in the city of London, as a freeman *and*
liveryman, if this Act had not been passed, shall be entitled to vote

in such election, provided such person shall be duly registered
according to the provisions hereinafter contained ; " not meaning to
point to the proviso in this section, but to the general provisions
for registration *contained in the Act. The clause then goes on:
" but that no such person shall be so registered in any year, unless
he shall, on the last day of July in such year, be qualified in such
manner as would entitle him then to vote if such day were the day
of election, and this Act had not been passed, nor unless, where he
shall be a burgess *or* freeman or freeman *and* liveryman of any city
or borough, he shall have resided for six calendar months next
previous to the last day of July in such year within such city or
borough, or within seven statute miles from the place where the
poll for such city or borough shall heretofore have been taken."
Then follows a clause relating to places other than London, where
the expression burgess *or* freeman is again used : " nor unless,
where he shall be a burgess *or* freeman of any place sharing in the
election for any city or borough, he shall have resided for six
calendar months next previous to the last day of July in such year
within such respective place so sharing as aforesaid, or within seven
statute miles of the place mentioned in conjunction with such
respective place so sharing as aforesaid, and named in the second
column of the schedule marked (E. 2) to this Act annexed." We
now come to the proviso upon which the question mainly turns;
and there we find the same distinction prevailing : " Provided
always, that no person who shall have been elected, made, or
admitted a burgess or freeman since the first day of March, 1831,
otherwise than in respect of birth or servitude, or who shall hereafter be elected, made, or admitted a burgess or freeman, otherwise
than in respect of birth or servitude, shall be entitled to vote as
such in any such election for any city or borough as aforesaid, or to be so registered as aforesaid." Why are we to give
to this disfranchising exception a construction that would apply
it to the case of freemen and liverymen of the city of London,

*when that construction would be inconsistent with the distinc-
tion that pervades the earlier and enacting part of the section?
If we call in aid the forms given in schedule (K), we find the
same distinction there: see the forms Nos. 2 and 3. It appears
to me, therefore, that the Revising Barrister came to a sound
determination when he held that the words "as such" in the
proviso in question are limited to persons voting as " burgesses or
freemen," and do not extend to those claiming as " freemen *and*

liverymen " of the city of London. It certainly is not easy to say   CROUCHER
r.
BROWNE.
why such a distinction should be made in favour of London. It
may have been considered that the numerous and conflicting
interests of the chartered Companies in London would sufficiently
guard against the mischiefs the provisions was levelled at in other
corporations. But, be that as it may, I am of opinion that the
decision of the Revising Barrister was correct, and must be
affirmed.

MAULE, J.:

I also am of opinion that the Revising Barrister was right in the
construction he has put upon the thirty-second section of the
2 Will. IV. c. 45; and I cannot say that the very able and
ingenious argument of my brother *Kinglake* has, for a moment,
induced me to hesitate. It is impossible to handle the statutes
2 Will. IV. c. 45, and 6 & 7 Vict. c. 18, without turning up something to show the appellant's construction to be destitute of
foundation. Whether we look at the spirit of the Reform Act,
or at the words in which the spirit is embodied, there is no room
for doubt. The object was, to prevent the repetition of the corrupt
practices that had before existed in certain boroughs, of making,
on some particular occasion, a large number of new voters for the
purpose of swamping the old constituency. This provision was
therefore intended to apply to those cases where the corporation
who had to return the members, *had also the power to create   [*108]
voters. But, in the case of London, the corporation has not the
power of creating voters: the right to vote arises from the act of
the various Companies admitting freemen to be of their livery:
the statute did not intend to interfere with those rights. And the
way in which the intention of the Legislature has been carried out
is, by language that appears to me to be (reading the words in
their ordinary sense) perfectly plain and unequivocal. The general
scope of the thirty-second section seems to me to account sufficiently
for the omission, in the disfranchising proviso, of liverymen who are
mentioned in the earlier parts of the clause. It is done deliberately.
Taking the text of the Act of Parliament to be well established,
it comes simply to this: the earlier part of the section provides
"that every person who would have been entitled to vote in the
election of a member or members to serve in any future Parliament
for any city or borough not included in schedule (A), either as a
burgess or freeman, or, in the city of London, as a freeman *and*
liveryman, if this Act had not been passed, shall be entitled to vote

CROUCHER
v.
BROWNE.

[*109]

in such election, provided such person shall be duly registered according to the provisions hereinafter contained : " and the same distinction between those entitled to vote as burgesses or freemen of other cities or boroughs, and those entitled to vote as freemen *and* liverymen of London, pervades the whole Act. Then, it is said that that right is restricted by the proviso " that no person who shall have been elected, made, or admitted a burgess or free-man since the 1st of March, 1831, otherwise than in respect of birth or servitude, or who shall hereafter be elected, made, or admitted a burgess or freeman, otherwise than in respect of birth or servitude, shall be entitled to vote as such in any such election for any city or borough as aforesaid, or to be so registered as afore-said." The words "as *such* " evidently refer to "burgess or freeman," keeping up the distinction already adverted to. If, indeed, it could be said, that, in London, the voters could be strictly and properly described as voting as freemen only, there might be some foundation for the argument : but, throughout the Act, the Legislature has, deliberately and repeatedly, described the parties to vote in London, as "freemen *and* liverymen." I think, therefore, we should be doing the greatest violence to the Act, if we were to hold this proviso to be applicable to the city of London.

Then, it is contended, that, assuming the proviso not to have directly and immediately taken away the right of voting from persons circumstanced like the respondent in this case, it has done so indirectly and circuitously, by saying that they shall not be entitled to be registered. The words, however, are perfectly plain : the proviso says that certain parties shall not be entitled to vote or to be registered as burgesses or freemen. Upon the whole, I think there is no ground for saying that there is any obscurity in the clause, but, on the contrary, it appears to me that the Legislature has used words that are perfectly plain, and adequate to the purpose in view.

CRESSWELL, J.:

I am entirely of the same opinion. The thirty-second section begins with saying that every person (with certain exceptions) entitled, before the passing of the Act, to vote "either as a burgess or freeman, or, in the city of London, as a freeman and liveryman," shall vote "provided such person shall be duly registered according to the provisions hereinafter contained." Now, in order to be entitled

to vote as a burgess or freeman, or as a freeman and liveryman of   CROUCHER
the city of London, the party must be registered as entitled to vote   *v.*
in that particular capacity. Then it goes on: "but no such person   BROWNE.
shall be so registered in any year, unless he shall, on the last day
of July in such year, be *qualified in such manner as would entitle   [*110]
him then to vote, if such day were the day of election, and this Act
had not been passed ; nor unless, where he shall be a burgess or
freeman, or freeman and liveryman of any city or borough, he
shall have resided for six calendar months next previous to the last
day of July in such year within such city, or within seven statute
miles," &c., "nor unless, where he shall be a burgess or freeman
of any place sharing in the election for any city or borough, he
shall have resided," &c.   That provision does not touch the manner
in which parties may be entitled to become "burgesses or freemen"
or "freemen and liverymen."   Then comes the proviso that is
supposed to affect that question : " Provided always, that no person
who shall have been elected, made, or admitted a burgess or freeman since the 1st day of March, 1831, otherwise than in respect of
birth or servitude, or who shall hereafter be elected, made, or
admitted a burgess or freeman, otherwise than in respect of birth
or servitude, shall be entitled to vote as such in any such election
for any city or borough as aforesaid, or to be so registered as
aforesaid."   These words " as such " clearly refer to " burgesses
or freemen," and not to those claiming to vote as "freemen and
liverymen" of the city of London.   It is then said, that, at all
events, the party is not entitled to be registered.   That, however,
cannot be : he is not to vote or to be registered as a burgess or
freeman ; but that does not deprive him of the right to be registered
in respect of any other qualification.   I think there is no ground
whatever for contending that the decision of the Revising Barrister
was wrong.

ERLE, J. :

I am of the same opinion.   Throughout the Reform and Registration Acts, two species of qualification in respect of corporation
voters are recognized : *the one, consisting of the compound   [*111]
character of freeman and liveryman, in the city of London ;
the other, of that of burgess or freeman in any other city or
borough.   The Legislature imposes certain restrictions upon this
right upon both classes, and certain other restrictions that are
applicable to one class only.   The proviso, as well as to the right to

CROUCHER
v.
BROWNE.

vote, as to the right to be registered, clearly applies to persons claiming as " burgesses or freemen " only.

*   *   *   *   *

Decision affirmed.

———————◆———————

1846.
Jan. 26.
——
*City of
London.*
[111]

BUSHELL *v.* LUCKETT.

(2 C. B. 111—118; S. C. 15 L. J. C. P. 89 ; 10 Jur. 113.)

A rate is not a complete and valid rate until allowance and publication.

A rate was made on the 28th of September, 1844, and purported to be made " for thirteen weeks, from the 16th of September to the 16th of December." A new rate was made on the 23rd of December, 1844, allowed on the 3rd of January, 1845, and published on the 5th : Held, that a claim under the 2 Will. IV. c. 45, s. 30, made on the 27th of December, to be put upon " the rate for the time being," was a claim to be put on the rate made in September.

WILLIAM ENDELL LUCKETT duly objected to the name of William Bushell being retained on the list of persons entitled to vote in the election of members for the city of London, in respect of

[*112]

the occupation *of a house, No. 1, Still Alley, in the parish of St. Botolph, Bishopsgate.

The Barrister expunged the name of the said William Bushell from the said list, subject to an appeal to the Court of Common Pleas upon the following case :

The qualification of the appellant was duly proved in all respects, except as to the sufficiency of the rating. The poor-rates in the said parish are made under a local Act, 35 Geo. III. c. 61, by s. 16 of which, " the rector, churchwardens, overseers of the poor, and inhabitants of the said parish, are authorized and required to assemble and meet together in the vestry-room of the said parish, on the 25th of June, 1795, and from time to time for ever thereafter quarterly, or oftener, in every year, as occasion shall require, due notice having been given, &c. ; and they, or the major part of them so assembled, shall from time to time make such rate or rates, assessment or assessments, for paying the interest due on certain annuities, and for and towards the relief of the poor of the said parish, or for other the purposes of this Act, upon all and every person or persons who do or shall inhabit, &c. &c., as they the said rector, &c., at such meeting shall think necessary and proper to be rated and assessed," &c.

Four rates were made in the said parish, between the 31st of July, 1844, and the 31st of July, 1845. The first rate was made on the 28th of September, 1844, allowed on the 4th of October

following, and published on the 6th. That rate was headed as
follows :

"We, the rector, &c., being assembled and met together this
28th day of September, 1844, in the church of the said parish,
due notice having been given of such meeting, do hereby make the
following rate or assessment, being 10½d. in the pound, upon all and
every person or persons who do or shall inhabit, &c. &c. *(following   [*113]
the words of the Act), for thirteen weeks, from the 16th of September
to the 16th of December, 1844."

The second rate was made on the 23rd of December, 1844, was
allowed on the 3rd of January, 1845, and published on the 5th.
This last-mentioned rate had a heading similar in form to that of
the rate first mentioned, being made "for thirteen weeks, from the
16th of December, 1844, to the 17th of March, 1845."

The dates of the other two rates are not material: they were each
headed in a similar manner, and purported to be made for thirteen
weeks respectively.

Each rate, though it purported to be made on a particular day,
was not, in fact, made out as to the assessment of the different
parties included therein, till some days afterwards.

The appellant was not assessed to the first-mentioned rate, nor
did his name appear thereon ; but, at the end of the rate, after the
allowance thereof, there was a long list of names, including that of
the appellant ; which list was headed thus : " The following are the
names of persons who have made claim to be rated since the
completion of the foregoing rate."

It was not proved that any claim to be rated was made by the
appellant before the 27th of December, 1844 ; but, on that day, a
notice of claim was served, on his behalf, on one of the overseers.
The claim was in this form :

"To the overseers of the parish of St. Botolph, Bishopsgate.

"I hereby give you notice that I occupy a house at No. 1, Still
Alley, Bishopsgate Street, in your parish ; and I claim to have my
name inserted as occupier thereof, in the rates made to the relief
of the poor in your parish, pursuant to the 6 & 7 Will. IV. c. 96,
and to *the English Reform and Parliamentary Registration Acts.   [*114]
Dated &c.

(Signed)   " WILLIAM BUSHELL,
" residing at No. 1, Still Alley."

The said claim was served at the same time with several others ;

BUSHELL
v.
LUCKETT.

and, at the time of such service, the overseer was told that the names of the parties so claiming, ought to be put upon the September rate; in consequence whereof, the names were so inserted in the before-mentioned list, at the end of the September rate-book.

The appellant was duly rated to the rate made on the 23rd of December, 1844, and other subsequent rates.

On behalf of the appellant, it was contended, that, at the time the said claim to be rated was so made as aforesaid, the September rate was " the rate for the time being " within the thirtieth section of the 2 Will. IV. c. 45 ; and, therefore, that the appellant must be deemed to have been rated to that rate.

The Revising Barrister decided that the September rate was not the rate for the time being at the time when the said claim to be rated was so made as aforesaid.

If the Court shall be of opinion that the decision was wrong, the name of the appellant is to be re-inserted in the said list of voters.

The cases of thirteen other persons, the validity of the objections against whom depended upon the same point, were consolidated with the above.

   Welsby, for the appellant :

The rate made on the 28th of September, 1844, and allowed on the 4th of October following, and published on the 6th, was " the rate for the time being," within the 2 Will. IV. c. 45, s. 30. That

[*115]

section intended to give parties a right *to claim to be rated at any time, and contemplated the continued existence of poor-rates throughout the year. The rate has no legal existence until allowance and publication ; therefore, the thirteen weeks of its duration must be reckoned from the day of publication. The rate made on the 23rd of December, 1844, was not allowed until the 3rd of January, 1845. At the time the claim was made, therefore, that rate did not legally exist. " The rate for the time being " must mean the rate then in force, or those words must be relaxed, and be held to mean, the last rate made for the parish. The September rate (1) must, at all events, be in force, for the purpose of collecting the arrears.

   W. R. Grove, for the respondent :

The appellant has not brought himself within the thirtieth section

____

(1) This observation would apply to all preceding rates in respect of which any arrears remained to be levied.

of the Reform Act. In *Wansey* v. *Perkins* (1) it was held, that a
claim to be rated under this section, is good only for the single rate
at that time in force.

(MAULE, J.: That case assumes that there always is a rate for
the time being. A rate ceases to be the rate for the time being,
when a new one is made. The question here is, when did the
September rate cease to be "the rate for the time being.")

Where a rate is made generally, it will, of course, remain in force,
until superseded by a new one; but it is otherwise where, as here,
the rate is made for a specific time. The claim here was subsequent, in point of date, to the making of the rate of the 23rd of
December, and, therefore, it enured as a claim to be put upon the
last-mentioned rate.

(TINDAL, Ch. J.: The claim, though subsequent to the *making
of that rate, was before its allowance.)

[*116]

The rate of the 28th of September was a non-existing rate after the
23rd of December.

(TINDAL, Ch. J.: When the party made his claim, he could not
know of the making of the December rate.)

Welsby was heard in reply.

TINDAL, Ch. J.:

The rate in question was made on the 28th of September, allowed
on the 4th of October, and published on the 6th; and it professes
to be made "for thirteen weeks, from the 16th of September to the
16th of December;" the object being to make a provision to meet
the exigencies of one quarter. The question is, whether, after that
quarter is ended, and before a new rate is made and perfected
by allowance and publication, the rate so made was "the rate
for the time being" within the thirtieth section. It seems to me
that it does satisfy the words of the Act. If the parish officers had
to justify a distress for arrears, made in the interval, it must be
under that as the existing rate. It never was intended, in a case
like this, that, because the time had expired for which the rate was
made, the rate itself must be held to have expired.

(1) *Lockey's* case, 7 Man. & G. 145; 8 Scott, N. R. 970.

MAULE, J. :

I also am of opinion that " the rate for the time being " does not exclude the rate in question. The thirtieth section entitles the party occupying any house &c. in any parish or township in which there shall be a rate for the relief of the poor, to claim to be rated in respect thereof; and, upon his so claiming, and paying or tendering the amount of rates due, the overseers are required to put his name upon the rate for the time being; and it provides, that, in case of their refusal or neglect so to do, he shall be deemed *to have been rated to such rate. That assumes that there always is a rate for the time being in every parish. In fact there always is a rate existing. It has all the qualities of a rate at the time of its conclusion, as it had at its commencement. The words of the thirtieth section equally exclude the idea of there being two existing rates, as that of there being no rate existing. When a rate is once made, it exists until superseded by another duly made, allowed, and published. The party has always a right to be on some rate. It is said he should have claimed to be put on the rate made upon the 28rd of December, an incomplete rate, and not on that which was the last complete rate. I think, however, the rate inchoately made in December, was not " the rate for the time being " within the Act; and, consequently, that the demand was properly made, and the decision of the Revising Barrister was wrong.

[*117]

CRESSWELL, J. :

I also am of opinion that " the rate for the time being " means the last valid and binding rate. A rate once made continues to exist until quashed, or until superseded by a new rate duly made, allowed, and published, so as to be effectual and binding upon the parishioners. Here, the rate made on the 28th of September was the only complete and valid rate at the time the claim was made. A claim, therefore, to be put upon that rate was a claim to be put on " the rate for the time being."

ERLE, J. :

A rate expressed to be made for a specific time, merely means a rate that is calculated and intended to meet the exigencies of the parish for that period, not that it shall cease to be an existing rate when the time has elapsed. A rate is not a valid and complete rate

until it is allowed and published.   At the *time the claim in
question was made, the September rate was, in my opinion, the
rate for the time being.

Decision reversed (1).

EDWARD BAYLEY *v.* THE OVERSEERS OF THE TOWNSHIP OF NANTWICH.

(2 C. B. 118—122.)

1846.
Jan. 29.

*County of
Chester,
Southern
Division.*
[118]

The production of a stamped duplicate notice of claim, duly delivered
to the postmaster, and duly directed to the overseers, pursuant to the
Parliamentary Voters Registration Act, 1843 (6 & 7 Vict. c. 18), ss. 100, 101,
is sufficient evidence of the notice of claim having been given to the overseers at the place mentioned in such duplicate, on the day on which such
notice would, in the ordinary course of post, have been delivered at such
place, notwithstanding its actual delivery to the overseer is delayed until
after the time limited by the Act, in consequence of pressure of business at
the post-office.

EDWARD BAYLEY claimed to be entitled to vote in respect of
property situate within the township of Nantwich, in the southern
division of the county of Chester.

The claimant, as did also twenty-four other claimants (whose
cases were identical and were consolidated therewith), resided at
Nantwich. A notice of claim purporting to be signed by him, was
duly proved to have been posted at Manchester on the 19th of July.
This notice of claim, according to the ordinary course of post,
should have arrived at Nantwich, and been delivered to the overseers, on the 20th of July. It was not, in fact, delivered till the
22nd. The notice of claim, which was produced, bore the Nantwich
post-mark of the latter day.

The overseers of Nantwich published the names, with *this note:
"The whole of these claims, in consequence of negligence at the
post-office, were not delivered until after the specified time."

The Revising Barrister examined the postmaster of Nantwich,
who proved that the notices of claim only arrived from Manchester
on the 22nd of July, and that he had caused them to be delivered
immediately, and was free from all blame. It appeared that all the
twenty-five claimants might have delivered their notices of claim,
personally, in due time ; and that one of them denied all knowledge
of his claim having been made.

(1) If the rate had, by reason of the
words "to the 16th of December
following," ceased to exist as a rate on
that day, it would follow that no valid
claim to be put upon any rate could
have been made between that period
and the allowance of a succeeding
rate.

28—2

There was no proof of the cause of detention at Manchester. As the transmission of notices of objection had been proved to have been delayed several days by reason of their vast numbers, it was contended that the multiplicity of claims had also caused the delay; but of this, there was no legal evidence. None of the claimants were examined.

The Barrister held that the claims were not duly made or transmitted.

If the Court shall be of opinion that he was in error, the register is to be amended by adding the name of Edward Bayley, together with the names of the twenty-four other claimants, in the same situation with Bayley, according to an annexed list.

The case was argued on the 19th instant.

Cockburn (with whom was *Kinglake*, Serjt.), for the appellant:

The question raised in this case, is similar to that already decided in *Bishop* v. *Helps* (1), save that that was a notice of objection, this a notice of claim. * * *

[120]   (MAULE, J.: I suppose we are to assume, the case being silent on the subject, that these notices were properly addressed.)

The only question intended to be raised was, as to the period of delivery.

(MAULE, J.: At the common law, putting a letter into the post would be *primâ facie* evidence of its delivery in due course—subject to be rebutted. But s. 100 says, that, in certain cases, it shall be sufficient if the notice of objection be sent by the post, free of postage, or the sum chargeable as postage for the same being first paid, directed to the person to whom the same shall be sent, at his place of abode as described in the list of voters. The clause then goes on to prescribe the manner of sending by the post; and, these directions being complied with, the production of the stamped duplicate is to be evidence of the notice having been given. All that is incorporated into s. 100. In order to bring himself within that provision, it will be said to be necessary to show, not only that the notice was duly posted, but that all the other requisites of s. 100 have been properly complied with. As to all these, the case is silent.)

The Revising Barrister evidently intended it to be inferred, that all

(1) *Ante*, p. 404.

these provisions had been complied with. He finds that the
notice of claim was duly proved to have been posted at Manchester
on the 19th of July.

BAYLEY
v.
THE OVER-
SEERS OF
NANTWICH.

(CRESSWELL, J. : The word "duly" is put in the wrong place.)

Welsby, for the respondent :

[121]

The case is defective in other respects. It states, that a notice of
claim "purporting to be signed by the claimant," was duly proved
to have been posted.

(ERLE, J. : All that we have to deal with is, the question that the
Barrister intended to decide.)

He holds distinctly, that the claims were not duly made or transmitted. He does not find that the notices were posted post-free, or
that the provisions of s. 100 have, in any respect, been complied
with.

(TINDAL, Ch. J. : I think we ought to refer it back to the Revising
Barrister to state what was the particular question of law intended
to be raised for our decision.)

The case was accordingly remitted to the Barrister, who on a
subsequent day returned it with the following amended statement :

"The only question intended to be submitted to the Court was,
whether, taking the sections 100 and 101 of the 6 & 7 Vict. c. 18,
together, the production of the stamped duplicate of notice of
claim, duly delivered to the postmaster, and duly directed to the
overseers of Nantwich, was to be held conclusive evidence of the
notice of claim having been given to the overseers, at the place
mentioned in such duplicate, on the day on which such notice
would, in the ordinary course of post, have been delivered to such
place. It was admitted that all the provisions in sections 100 and
101, as to sending notices by the post, had been complied with.
The sole difficulty that presented itself to my mind was, whether,
under the circumstances, the duplicate notice of claim was conclusive evidence of the claim being in time : and this the Court of
Common Pleas has since decided in the affirmative " (1).

Cur. adv. vult.

(1) *Bishop* v. *Helps, ante,* p. 404.

TINDAL, Ch. J. :

This case has been referred back to the Revising Barrister to certify whether any objection was made before him as to the address of the notice of claim to the overseers of Nantwich being the proper address; and he has certified to us that no such objection was made—that it was admitted that all the provisions in ss. 100 and 101 of the Registration Act had been complied with, and that the sole point referred to us was, whether the duplicate notice of claim, properly stamped, was sufficient evidence of the claim being in time. This point was decided in the case of a notice of objection (1); and we think there is no distinction to be taken, in this respect, between a notice of objection and a notice of claim.

We therefore think the decision of the Revising Barrister is wrong, and that the same must be reversed, and the names of the twenty-five claimants placed on the register.

Decision reversed.

EDWARD NELSON ALEXANDER *v.* EDWARD NEWMAN.

(2 C. B. 122—146; S. C. 15 L. J. C. P. 134; 10 Jur. 313.)

A conveyance of land by one vendor to several purchasers for a *bonâ fide* consideration, is valid, although the avowed object of the vendor is to multiply, and that of the purchasers to acquire, the right of voting.

JOSEPH BOTTOMLEY and thirty-four other persons claimed to have their names inserted in the register of voters for the township of Lockwood, in the polling district of Huddersfield, in the West Riding of *the county of York, as the several owners, each respectively of one undivided thirty-fifth part, of freehold land and buildings there situated.

[*123]

The facts applicable to each case, were as follow :

Joseph Bottomley, being desirous of obtaining a qualification to vote in the election of members to serve in Parliament for the said riding, some time in the month of January, 1845, called upon J. R., the agent of a political association in the town of Huddersfield, and requested the said J. R. to obtain a vote for him the said Joseph Bottomley. Joseph Bottomley wished to obtain the qualification as cheaply as he could; but did not care about the nature or situation

(1) *Bishop* v. *Helps, ante,* p. 404.

of the property, provided it would confer the right of voting, and ALEXANDER
did not involve an outlay of money beyond what would give the NEWMAN.
qualification, and at the same time secure the ordinary rate of
interest. Joseph Bottomley's motive in applying to J. R. was not,
however, the investment of money in land or buildings, but only to
acquire the right of voting.

Some time in the same month of January, Messrs. C., being
wealthy manufacturers in the neighbourhood of Huddersfield,
authorized the said J. R. to sell for them certain lands and
cottages, their property, for the sum of 1,400*l.* The only object
of Messrs. C. in so authorizing the said J. R. to act for them, was,
to increase the number of voters for members to serve in Parliament for the said riding. They were not in want of money, and
would not have sold any portion of their real estate below its fair
and reasonable value. J. R. was not the attorney generally
employed, either by Messrs. C. or by Joseph Bottomley ; but,
as agent to the before-mentioned association, he had previously
caused advertisements to be inserted in the public papers inviting
parties either to sell or purchase small freeholds for the *purpose [*124]
of qualifying voters for the said riding, and referring to himself as
such agent.

In consequence of such authority from the said Messrs. C., and
of such instructions from Joseph Bottomley, and many other
parties similarly disposed, the said J. R. arranged the purchase
and sale of the said lands and cottages by the said Messrs. C. to
the said Joseph Bottomley and thirty-four other persons, as tenants
in common, for the sum of 1,400*l.* A deed conveying the said land
and cottages was accordingly prepared by the said J. R., and was
duly executed by the said Joseph Bottomley on the 22nd of January
last ; on which occasion the said Joseph Bottomley paid his
portion of the purchase-money, viz. 40*l.*, to the said J. R., for
and on behalf of Messrs. C., together with 1*l.* towards J. R.'s bill
of costs.

On the same 22nd of January, a lease of the land and cottages
in question was executed by Joseph Bottomley and the thirty-four
other tenants in common, to the said Messrs. C., for the period of
fifteen years, at the annual rent of 70*l.*, which rent has since been
duly paid. The land and cottages are within a very short distance of
Messrs. C.'s mill, and were before and at the time of the purchase,
and still are, in the occupation of persons employed by the said
Messrs. C. in the said mill.

ALEXANDER
v.
NEWMAN.

Joseph Bottomley has never seen the property in question ; and he stipulated, when he applied to J. R. on the subject, that he (Joseph Bottomley) was to have no trouble in the matter, but should receive 40s. per annum for his 40l., and secure the right of voting.

The conveyance was complete and *bonâ fide*, the purchase-money really paid by the said Joseph Bottomley and the several other purchasers, and there was no secret trust or reservation in favour of the sellers, nor any stipulation as to the mode in which the [*125] elective *franchise should be exercised by the said thirty-five purchasers, or any of them, nor had any of them any communication with Messrs. C., save through their common solicitor, J. R.

The said Messrs. C. and the thirty-five other persons entertain the same political opinions; and, though there was no immediate concert between them, the avowed and only object of the transactions on both sides was, to multiply voices in the election of members of Parliament for the said riding.

Upon these facts the claims of the said Joseph Bottomley and the thirty-four other persons to have their names inserted in the said list of voters, was opposed, on the ground that the case came within the statute 7 & 8 Will. III. c. 25, commonly called the Splitting Act, as being a conveyance made in order to multiply voices, or to split and divide the interest in houses or land among several persons, to enable them to vote at elections of members to serve in Parliament, and therefore void and of none effect.

The Revising Barrister decided that the statute did not apply to conveyances made under the circumstances disclosed in the foregoing statement of facts; that no conveyance of an estate for an adequate consideration, made *bonâ fide*, without reservation, ratified according to law, and accompanied by payment of the purchase-money on the one hand, and possession of the property or receipt of the rents, as in this case, on the other, can afterwards be nullified by an inquiry into the motives which may have actuated the contracting parties before or at the time of the transaction; and that the said Joseph Bottomley and the said thirty-four other claimants were entitled to have their names retained in the list of voters for the said riding in respect of their several and respective shares in the said freehold land and buildings.

[126]   The cases of sixteen other persons similarly circumstanced were consolidated with the principal case.

Annexed to the case is a copy of the list of claimants, the form ALEXANDER
v.
NEWMAN.
of which is as follows:

Christian Name and Surname &c.	Place of Abode.	Nature of the supposed Qualification.	Street &c. where Property situate &c.
Bottomley, Joseph.	No. 40, Westgate, Huddersfield.	Freehold land and buildings, one undivided thirty-fifth part thereof.	Cobden's Row, Crossland Moor, Lockwood, Nos. 5 to 16, inclusive.
Booth, Samuel.	No. 4, Queen Street, Huddersfield.	Freehold land and buildings, one undivided thirty-fifth part thereof.	Cobden's Row, Crossland Moor, Lockwood, Nos. 5 to 16, inclusive.
&c. &c.			

The case was argued in Michaelmas Term last (1).

Kinglake, Serjt., for the appellant.   *   *   *

S. Martin for the respondent.   *   *   *   [132]

Kinglake, Serjt., in reply.   *   *   *   [134]

Cur. adv. vult.

TINDAL, Ch. J., now delivered the opinion of the COURT:

This appeal against the decision of the Revising Barrister for the West Riding of the county of York raises the distinct question, whether a conveyance of land to a numerous body of purchasers, as tenants in common, is *void under the seventh section of the   [*135] statute 7 & 8 Will. III. c. 25; such conveyance being made, both on the part of the vendor and of the vendees, "for the avowed and only object of multiplying voices in the election of members to serve in Parliament," but, at the same time, being a *bonâ fide* conveyance made upon a contract of sale, where the purchase-money was really paid, and possession of the land really taken and kept, under the conveyance, and where there was no secret trust or reservation in favour of the sellers, nor any stipulation as to the mode in which the elective franchise should be exercised.

The question is, undoubtedly, one of considerable importance, not only as it involves a general principle of election law, but as it applies to a large number of the cases reserved for our determination. It has been argued before us both upon the present and upon another of the reserved cases; and we are of opinion, upon the proper construction of the statute above referred to, taking into

(1) Before Tindal, Ch. J., and Coltman, Maule, and Erle, JJ.

ALEXANDER
v.
NEWMAN.

consideration at the same time the statutes subsequently passed upon the same subject-matter, that the conveyance in question was not a void conveyance, and that the several persons claiming a right to vote under it were entitled to have their names retained on the list of voters for the West Riding of the county of York.

Even if the statute 7 & 8 Will. III. were the only statute passed upon the subject, and that statute were to be construed strictly by its very letter, we think its provisions could not be held to extend to the case of any conveyance made upon a real and *bonâ fide* contract for a sale and purchase of the land ; but that the statute was intended to apply to fictitious conveyances which had nothing more than the form and appearance of a conveyance, which consisted of the parchment and the seal only, the parties thereto having privately agreed *and intended that no interest should actually pass thereby.

[*186]

The first observation that arises upon the statute of Will. III. is, that the section now under discussion is declaratory only of the common law. The first branch of that section does, indeed, create a new law. It is thereby enacted that no person shall have a vote at elections, by reason of any trust-estate or mortgage, unless such trustee or mortgagee be in actual possession or receipt of the rents or profits of the same estate; but that the mortgagor, or cestui que trust, in possession, shall vote for the same estate. But the second branch of the section, which is that now under consideration, is framed very differently. By this latter branch, all conveyances in order to multiply voices and to split and divide the interest in any houses or lands among several persons, to enable them to vote, are thereby declared to be void and of none effect.

This marked distinction between the two parts of this section proves, incontestably, that the latter part was intended only to declare the law as it then stood, giving to such law the greater weight and sanction of a legislative declaration.

The first question, therefore, is, what conveyances made in order to multiply voices at elections would be void at common law.

The right of voting for knights of the shire did, by the common law, as regulated by the two statutes 8 Hen. VI. (1) and 10 Hen. VI. (2), belong to such people resident in each shire (3), whereof every one

(1) 8 Hen. VI. c. 7. See this statute in full, as it stands on the Parliament Roll, 4 Rot. Parl. 350 a. See also 66 R. R. 668, *n.*

(2) 10 Hen. VI. c. 2. See 4 Rot.

Parl. 402 b.

(3) This provision has since been repealed by the 14 Geo. III. c. 58, to the great increase of the expense of county elections.

had frank-tenement within the same county to the value of 40s. by ALEXANDER
the year, at *least, above all charges.   And there was no restriction
or prohibition, by the common law, against any man's purchasing
freehold within the county of sufficient amount to qualify him to
vote, nor, on the other hand, against any man's selling the same
to one or to any number of purchasers, although the object of
the seller and purchaser might be that the purchaser should acquire
a vote, and, consequently, that the number of voters should be
thereby increased.   By the common law, therefore, no conveyance
really and honestly made for the purpose of carrying such contract
into effect, was void.   But, by the common law, from the earliest
times, a conveyance, however perfect in point of form, being such
in form only, and intended, by the secret agreement or understanding between the parties, never to have any real effect as a
conveyance, was always held to be void, whatever the secret object
and purposes of the parties in making such conveyance might be.
The old text-writers lay it down as a maxim, that "the law abhors
covin, and therefore every covinous act shall be void."   And it is,
upon that principle, unquestionable, that a conveyance made in
order or for the purpose of giving a qualification to vote at an
election, or for any other purpose, if made with the secret intention
and design that it should appear to the world as a conveyance, but,
as between the parties themselves, should pass no interest, and
have no effect, would be fraudulent and void at common law.   Lord
Somers—and it is impossible to name an authority of greater
weight on a subject of this nature—is express to this point.   In
the observations made by him on the trial of the case of *Onslow* v.
The Bailiff of the Borough of Haslemere (1), for misconduct as a
returning officer, on which occasion it was proved that many of the
voters claimed *under conveyances of very minute and insignificant
parts of burgage lands, which had been lately made, and which
were fraudulently contrived to make votes against an election, he
lays it down thus : " This case should caution places having rights
to elect, against making votes by splitting burgage tenures by such
fraudulent conveyances ; all such conveyances as are not real,
and made *bonâ fide* upon good consideration, being in the case held
to be void by the common law."   He thus draws a very marked
distinction between conveyances made to give qualifications where
they are real and honest, and where they are fraudulent and
fictitious ; considering the latter only to be void at common law.

(1) Lord Somers's Tracts, vol. viii. p. 275,

ALEXANDER
    v.
NEWMAN.

[*187]

[*188]

ALEXANDER
v.
NEWMAN.

And, as this trial took place only about fifteen years before the passing of the statute of Will. III., the language of Lord Somers affords strong evidence how the common law stood at the time of the passing of that Act.

Again, the very language of the statute of William seems to point to the necessary distinction, that real and *bonâ fide* conveyances were not intended to be avoided, although the motive or purpose of the parties might be that of multiplying voices at elections, but such conveyances only made for that purpose as were pretended and fictitious. The statute says: "All conveyances in order to multiply voices" are declared to be void. The statute names the conveyance only: it makes no reference whatever to any contract for sale upon which a real conveyance was grounded, nor professes to deal in any manner with the estate or interest in the land which was affected by such contract of sale, nor provides for the revesting of the land which passed into the possession of the purchaser under the contract of sale, nor for the repayment of the purchase-money to the purchaser—all which provisions might reasonably be expected,

[*189]

if a conveyance upon a real *bonâ fide* contract of sale, and not a fictitious conveyance only, was intended to be avoided on account of the motive upon which it was entered into. And this is the more striking, as, in the very same-section, provision is made as to the estate of trustees and mortgagees; so that the mind of the Legislature must have been awake to the difference between a pretended conveyance, which conveyed no estate, and one which was the completion of a real contract between seller and purchaser —according to the distinction laid down by Lord THURLOW (1), " that, if the *jus disponendi* remains in any other person, it is in vain that the parchment conveys the right to the grantee; for, the real use of the estate remains in another." And, if the words of the statute do not in their strict and necessary construction compel us to hold a conveyance made for the completion of a *bonâ fide* contract of sale to be void, upon the ground that the object and purpose was to multiply voices at an election, there is no general principle upon which those words ought to be extended. The object of increasing the number of freeholders at a county election is not an object, in itself, against law or morality, or sound policy. There is nothing injurious to the community in one man selling and another buying land for the direct purpose of giving or acquiring such qualification. The object to be effected is neither *malum in se*

(1) 2 Lud. on Elections, p. 371.

nor *malum prohibitum*.   On the contrary, the increasing the number   ALEXANDER
of persons enjoying the elective franchise has been held by many   NEWMAN.
to be beneficial to the Constitution, and certainly appears to
have been the leading object of the Legislature in passing the late
Act for amending the representation of the people of England and
Wales.   What ground, therefore, can exist for extending to a real
and honest proceeding the words of a statute which may be
fully *satisfied by giving them the force of avoiding a fictitious   [*140]
conveyance only ?

It is further to be observed, that the holding the statute of
William to extend to a conveyance made upon a real sale, would
be productive of much inconvenience and injury to all claiming
under the purchaser.   The supposed object and purpose which the
sale was intended to effect, cannot be discovered upon the face of
the conveyance, but is altogether concealed in the breasts of the
parties themselves; so that, by means of the larger construction of
the statute contended for on the part of the appellant, at any future
time, and between other parties than those to the original conveyance, this secret motive for making the conveyance, if brought
to light by accident or otherwise, might destroy the title to the
estate, in whosesoever hands it might be.   The same rule of law
must apply, whether the purchasers are many or few: perhaps,
even, a conveyance of part of the seller's land to one single person,
with the object above mentioned, must be held to be void: so that,
upon such construction of the Act, a man of large landed estate
could not sell any part of it *bonâ fide*, for a full consideration in
money, to two different purchasers, or, perhaps, to one only, if the
object of such sale was to give the purchaser a vote for the county ;
for, the creation of two additional votes, or, perhaps, of one only,
would be equally within the principle, though not in equal degree
a multiplication of voices at an election, and a splitting and
dividing the interest in houses or lands among several persons.
The holding, therefore, the literal construction of the words of the
statute of William to make such *bonâ fide* conveyances absolutely
void, would very much fetter the full and free enjoyment of landed
property, and create insecurity in titles to estates.

Upon these various grounds, and for these considerations, *we   [*141]
think the sounder construction of the statute of William, taken by
itself, is, that, by the conveyances made in order to multiply voices
which are thereby declared to be void, are intended such conveyances only as at the time of passing the Act would have been

held to be void by the common law, that is, conveyances meant
by the parties not to transfer any real interest in the land, but
made for the purpose of multiplying voices at elections, and for
that purpose only. And, as to the observation made in the course
of the argument, that, if already void by the common law, there
was no necessity for avoiding them by the statute, it may be a
sufficient answer that it was thought useful, when such baneful
practices as those described by Lord Somers, in the passage before
cited, were in daily practice, to promulgate this doctrine of the
common law to sheriffs and other officers upon whom the duty of
conducting the election was cast, and to give it the additional
weight and solemnity of a legislative declaration.

If, however, any doubt existed upon the construction of the statute
of Will. III., when considered by itself, such doubt would be removed
when the subsequent statutes made upon the same subject, and to
effectuate more fully the same object, are taken into consideration.

The next statute in order of time is that of the 10 Ann. c. 23.
That statute, it is to be observed, is not so wide in its operation as
the statute of William ; for, whilst the earlier statute, by its general
terms, extends to all elections where the right of voting depended
on the ownership of land, whether in counties or boroughs, the
statute of Anne is confined exclusively to the multiplying of votes
upon the election of knights of the shire. This statute is intituled
" An Act for the more effectual preventing fraudulent conveyances
in order to multiply votes for electing knights of the shire to serve
[*142]   in Parliament;" the very title of the Act leading *to the inference
that it is directed, not against all conveyances for that purpose, but
against fraudulent conveyances only. The Act then begins by
reciting in terms the seventh section of the 7 & 8 Will. III., upon
which this question arises ; and it then further recites that many
fraudulent practices have been used of late " to create and multiply
votes, to the great injury (amongst others) of those persons who
have just right to elect." The recital, therefore, as well as the title,
equally point out the distinction between the creation of votes by
fraudulent and fictitious means, and the making of real votes ; the
latter of which could never be considered to fall within the language
of the recital, to be an injury to those persons who have just rights
to elect. And the first section then goes on to enact that all estates
and conveyances whatsoever made to any persons in any fraudulent
and collusive manner, on purpose to qualify them to give their votes
at such elections, subject, nevertheless, to conditions or agreements

to defeat or determine such estate, or to re-convey the same, shall   ALEXANDER
be deemed and taken, against the persons who executed the same,   v.
NEWMAN.
as free and absolute, and be holden and enjoyed by all such persons
to whom such conveyance shall be made as aforesaid, freely and
absolutely exonerated and discharged from all manner of trusts,
conditions, clauses of re-entry, &c., or other defeasances whatsoever:
and the Act then goes on to enact that all securities given for the
performance of such trusts, &c., shall be void; and imposes a
penalty of 40l. upon every person executing such conveyances, or
voting under them.

And we consider this latter statute to be a legislative exposition
of the clause of the statute of Will. III. therein set forth; that the
avoiding of conveyances made in order to multiply voices at elections
was meant by the original statute to be confined to such conveyances only *as were fraudulent and collusive— to conveyances which   [*143]
are such in form only, but never intended to pass the property; or
such as were accompanied with some secret trust or reservation for
the benefit of the grantors; and not to extend to a *bona fide* conveyance made in completion of an actual contract of sale and purchase
of land: for, the statute of Anne is expressly limited to fraudulent
conveyances; and it cannot be intended that the statute of Anne,
passed to render the former statute of William more efficacious,
should be, as to county elections, less comprehensive in its provisions than the former statute; or that the former should comprise
within it the avoidance of a *bona fide* conveyance, when the latter
is restricted to fraudulent conveyances only.

The statute of Anne, it is to be observed, meets the evil intended
to be put down, by a very different provision from that contained in
the statute of William: for, whereas the statute of William is con-
tented with simply declaring the fraudulent conveyance void, thus
leaving the grantor and the grantee as if the conveyance had never
been made, the statute of Anne, on the contrary, provides that the
fraudulent conveyance made for the purpose of giving a qualification, "shall be deemed and taken, against those persons who executed
the same, as free and absolute, discharged from any manner of trust
or condition for the benefit of the grantor," and, at the same time,
prohibits the grantee from voting under colour of the grant, by
making him liable to a penalty of 40l. to the common informer, the
Legislature, probably, thinking that the practice of granting fraudulent and collusive freeholds would be more effectually checked by
making such conveyances good against the grantor, and by frustrating

ALEXANDER
v.
NEWMAN.

[*144]

the object of the grantee. But this provision never could in reason or sense be meant to apply to a conveyance upon a real sale of the land, where the seller has already received the purchase-money, *and has always intended the grant to be good against himself; and, further, the oath directed by the statute of Anne appears quite conclusive as to the distinction between fraudulent and real conveyances made for the purpose of creating a vote, viz. "You shall swear that such freehold estate hath not been made or granted to you fraudulently, on purpose to qualify you to give your vote."

The next statute which touches this question, is, the 18 Geo. II. c. 18, s. 5, and the enactment contained therein confirms the distinction to which we have often recurred. That statute enacts "that no person shall vote in respect or in right of any freehold estate which was made or granted to him fraudulently, on purpose to qualify him to give his vote;" thereby, as in the statute of Anne, prohibiting the voting, not in every case where the estate is conveyed to him for the object of enabling him to vote, but in such case only where it is fraudulently made to him for that purpose; that is, where the grantee of the estate, although he appears on the face of the conveyance to take under it, does in reality, as between the parties themselves, take nothing, or where it is accompanied with a secret trust for the benefit of the grantor.

In the course of one of the arguments before us, some stress was laid by the counsel contending for the illegality of the vote, upon the statute 53 Geo. III. c. 49. That statute was passed to explain and amend the statute of Will. III.; and, after reciting that doubts had been entertained whether devises by will made in such cases and for such purposes as those mentioned in the former statute, were within the true intent and meaning of that Act, it enacts that all devises by will made in such cases and for such purposes as by the Act of William are described, are, and shall be taken to be, con-

[*145]

veyances within the true intent and meaning of the *Act, as if the same had been therein specially mentioned. And the argument was, that it was singular the 53 Geo. III. c. 49, should refer to the statute of William, not to the statute of Anne, unless the statute of William was in full operation, independently of the statute of Anne. But to this it may be answered, that the reference may well have been made to the statute of William, because the intention of the Legislature was, that the devise which gave a fraudulent qualification should be altogether void; whereas, if reference had been made to the statute of Anne, the devise would have been good against the

heirs of the devisor.   The whole object of the statute is, in fact, to
write the word "devises" into the statute of William; leaving
devises to be dealt with in the same manner and by the same rule
of law as applied to conveyances.   If the devise was fraudulent, if
it was never intended to pass the land, by means of a secret compact
with the devisor in his lifetime that the devisee would not take, or
that he would re-convey, then the statute of 53 Geo. III. would
bring the devise exactly into the same predicament as a fraudulent
conveyance under the statute of William.   But, on the other hand,
if the will even openly expressed that a father devised to his son an
estate of 40*s*. a year, intending thereby to qualify him to vote for
the county, yet, if the son entered into possession and held the land
without any secret understanding or reservation on his part, the
devise would then be in the same predicament as a conveyance for
the same purpose, and would be good.

Therefore, upon the whole state of the case, considering the statute
of William by itself, and with reference also to the later Acts, we
think a conveyance made in completion of a *bonâ fide* contract of
sale, where the money passes from the buyer to the seller, and the
possession also from the seller to the buyer, and where there is no
secret reservation or trust whatever for the *benefit of the seller, is
not avoided by reason of the object or motive of the purchaser and
seller being that of multiplying voices at an election: and, as the
Revising Barrister has by his finding brought the present case within
that description, we think his decision, by which he retained the
names of these purchasers on the list of voters, was right, and ought
to be affirmed.

Decision affirmed.

ALEXANDER
v.
NEWMAN.

[*146]

———————

JAMES NEWTON *v.* ROBERT HARGREAVES.

(2 C. B. 163—165; S. C. 15 L. J. C. P. 154; 10 Jur. 317.)

A deed of gift *bond fide* executed by a father to his sons, expressed to be
in consideration of natural love and affection, is not within the 7 & 8
Will. III. c. 25, s. 7, although the avowed object of the father was to
confer votes upon his sons.

JAMES NEWTON duly objected to the names of Robert Hargreaves
and Samuel Hargreaves being retained on the list of voters for the
township of Mobberley, in the northern division of the county of
Chester, in respect of certain freehold land called Holt's Farm.
The facts were as follow:

Robert Halstead Hargreaves, the father of the two claimants,

1846.
Jan. 29.
————
*County of
Chester,
Northern
Division.*

[163]

being seised in fee of a messuage and farm at Mobberley, in the
northern division of the county of Chester, and also of certain
hereditaments in the southern division of the county of Lancaster,
in December, 1844, proposed to the two claimants to execute a deed
of gift in their favour of sufficient property in both those counties
to entitle them to be registered as voters; and accordingly a deed
was executed on the 30th of January, 1845, by which the said
R. H. Hargreaves, in consideration of natural love and affection,
conveyed to the two claimants, and their assigns, for the life of the
grantor, two closes of land, part of Holt's Farm, in Mobberley
aforesaid, and a like estate in the said hereditaments in South
Lancashire. The deed was prepared by the solicitor of R. H. Hargreaves, the grantor, and was received by one of the claimants
from such solicitor a few days before it was produced at the Court
aforesaid. Before the execution of the conveyance, the claimants
had, by the permission of the grantor, depastured their horses on
the said closes in Mobberley, and had continued to do so subse-

[*164] quently to the date of *the deed; and the grantor had also continued
to depasture his cattle thereon since the date of the conveyance,
and had never paid, or agreed to pay, rent to his sons for the closes.
The yearly value of the closes in Mobberley was 36*l*.

The conveyance was made by the grantor to the two claimants
principally for the purpose of entitling them to be registered as
voters as aforesaid, but with a view also of making a provision for
them.

It was objected that this transaction was fraudulent, being for
the mere purpose of creating votes; and that the conveyance came
within the operation of the statute 7 & 8 Will. III. c. 25, s. 7, and
was void.

The Revising Barrister decided that the names of the claimants
should be retained upon the register: and his decision upon the
points of law in question was, first, that the deed was not void on
the ground of fraud, secondly, that it was not void under the 7 & 8
Will. III. c. 25, s. 7.

If the Court of Common Pleas shall be of opinion that the said
decisions, or either of them, were or was wrong, then the names of
the said Robert Hargreaves and Samuel Hargreaves are to be
expunged from the register. If otherwise, the appeal is to be
dismissed.

The case was argued on a former day in this Term (1).

(1) Jan. 19, before Tindal, Ch. J., and Maule, Cresswell, and Erle, JJ.

Cockburn (with whom was *Kinglake*, Serjt.), for the appellant, admitted that this case was in no respect distinguishable from *Alexander* v. *Newman* (1), save that the consideration for the conveyance was not a pecuniary one.

Granger, for the respondent, submitted, that the transaction in question did not fall within the 7 & 8 *Will. III. c. 25, s. 7; it being perfectly immaterial whether the consideration was pecuniary, or natural love and affection, so long as the conveyance was *bonâ fide* on the part of the grantor; and that the statute of 10 Ann. c. 23, was not the less to be considered as a legislative exposition of the statute of William, because its operation was limited to boroughs.

[*165]

Cur. adv. vult.

TINDAL, Ch. J., now delivered the opinion of the COURT:

This case also stood over to await the determination of that of *Alexander* v. *Newman* (1). We think the decision of the Revising Barrister, that the two names mentioned in the case should be retained on the register, is a right decision, and we affirm the same. This case is so far distinguishable from all the former, that, in this, the transaction is not that of purchase and sale, nor is the consideration that of money. But this is a conveyance by a father to his two sons, in consideration of natural love and affection. But, inasmuch as the law acknowledges the consideration of natural love and affection in the case of father and son to be as good a consideration to raise a use as a pecuniary consideration between strangers, and as no fraud in fact is found by the Barrister, and as we are not to infer it from any circumstances stated in the case, all we have to do is, to consider the question reserved for us, viz. whether the conveyance is void by reason of the statutes; and upon this point we come to the same conclusion as before.

Decision affirmed.

————•————

COOK v. LUCKETT (2).

(2 C. B. 168—176; S. C. 15 L. J. C. P. 78; 10 Jur. 116.)

1846.
Jan. 29.

*City of
London.*

[168]

A. was rated as the occupier of a house No. 3, Golden Lane, but by mistake inaccurately described as No. 4: the rates were paid, under an agreement, by the landlord; and A. had paid all his rent:

Semble, that this was not an "inaccurate description of the premises," within the Parliamentary Voters Registration Act, 1843 (6 & 7 Vict. c. 18),

(1) *Ante*, p. 638.   (1872) L. R. 7 C. P. 158, 41 L. J. C. P.
(2) Followed in *Moger* v. *Escott*   86.—J. G. P.

s. 75; but a sufficient rating of A. within the Representation of the People
Act, 1832 (2 Will. IV. c. 45), s. 27.

And, held, that the insertion of A. in the rate was a *bonâ fide* calling
upon him to pay, and the payment by the landlord a *bonâ fide* payment by
A., within the former statute.

WILLIAM ENDELL LUCKETT duly objected to the name of William
Cook being retained on the list of persons entitled to vote in the
election of members for the city of London in respect of the occupation of a " house, No. 4, Golden Lane," in the parish of St. Giles-
without-Cripplegate.

The said William Cook also duly claimed to have his name
inserted in the said list in respect of the occupation of a " house,
No. 3, Golden Lane," in the same parish.

[*169]   The Revising Barrister expunged the name of William *Cook
from the said list, and disallowed the claim, subject to an appeal to
the Court of Common Pleas upon the following case :

The qualification of the appellant was duly proved in respect of
the occupation of a house, No. 3, Golden Lane, except as to the
sufficiency of the rating. He was rated to all the poor-rates as the
occupier of No. 4, Golden Lane (but he did not occupy No. 4; and
he was inserted in the rate-book for No. 4 by a mistake of the
overseer (1)). He held the house No. 3 at an annual rent of 27*l.*,
and had an express agreement with his landlord that the latter
should pay all the rates and taxes in respect of the premises. His
landlord had called upon him to pay, and he had paid, all the rent
due in respect of the house. And the landlord had been called
upon to pay and had paid all poor-rates in respect of the house.

It was contended, on behalf of the appellant, that, though the
premises so occupied by him were inaccurately described in the
poor-rate, yet that he was the person liable to be rated for the
premises, and had (by his landlord specially constituted by his
agreement as his agent in that behalf) been *bonâ fide* called upon
to pay, and had *bonâ fide* paid, all the rates due in respect of such
premises, within the meaning of the seventy-fifth section of the
6 & 7 Vict. c. 18, and therefore that he was to be considered as
having been rated and as having paid all rates in respect of the
said premises, notwithstanding the inaccurate description in the
said rate of the said premises so occupied by him.

The Revising Barrister decided that this was an inaccurate
description, within the 6 & 7 Vict. c. 18, s. 75; but that the facts

(1) This was added, in Court, by the Revising Barrister, during the
argument.

proved did not show that the appellant had been *bonâ fide* called
upon to pay, and had *bonâ fide* paid, the rates due in respect of
such premises (1).

If the Court shall be of opinion that the said decision was wrong,
the name of the appellant is to be inserted in the said list of voters
as follows:

William Cook.	3, Golden Lane.	House.	3, Golden Lane.

Welsby, for the appellant:

Two questions were raised before the Revising Barrister: the
first, whether the rating of the appellant as the occupier of " No. 4,
Golden Lane," when in point of fact he was the occupier of No. 3,
was an inaccurate description of the premises occupied by him,
within the latter branch of the seventy-fifth section of the 6 & 7
Vict. c. 18 (2); the second, *whether, if it were so, the appellant
had been *bonâ fide* called upon to pay, and had *bonâ fide* paid, all
the rates due in respect of such premises, within the meaning of
the same section.   He was in fact rated, and did in fact occupy
premises of sufficient value to be entitled to vote; and by the
special agreement with his landlord, who had paid the rates, he
was to be looked upon as the person by or for whom the rates were

(1) This paragraph before amendment stood thus: "The Revising
Barrister decided that the appellant
had not been *bonâ fide* called upon to
pay, and had not *bonâ fide* paid, the
rates due in respect of such premises."

(2) Which, reciting that doubts had
arisen how far any misnomer or insufficient or inaccurate description in
a rate, of the person occupying any
such premises as in the recited Act
(2 Will. IV. c. 45, s. 27), are mentioned,
or any inaccurate description of the
premises so occupied, has the effect of
preventing any such person from being
registered and entitled to vote in
respect of such premises in any year,
declares and enacts, "that, where any
person shall have occupied such
premises as in the said recited Act are
mentioned, for twelve calendar months
next previous to the last day of July
in any year, and such person, being

the person liable to be rated for such
premises, shall have been *bonâ fide*
called upon to pay, in respect of such
premises, all rates made for the relief
of the poor in such parish or township
during the time of such his occupation so required as aforesaid, and such
person shall have *bonâ fide* paid, on or
before the 20th day of July in such
year, all sums of money which he shall
have been called upon to pay as rates
in respect of such premises for one
year previously to the 6th day of
April then next preceding, such person
shall be considered as having been
rated and paid all rates in respect of
such premises, within the meaning of
the said recited Act, and be entitled to
be registered in respect of the same in
any year, any misnomer or inaccurate
or insufficient description in any rate,
of the person so occupying, or of the
premises occupied, notwithstanding."

COOK
v.
LUCKETT.

paid: *Wright* v. *The Town Clerk of Stockport* (1) ; *Hughes* v. *The Overseers of Chatham* (2).

(MAULE, J.: No doubt, a payment by any person will enure as a payment by the person rated.)

* * As payment of the rates by the landlord is equivalent to payment by the tenant, it clearly must be sufficient that the landlord has been called upon to pay them.

W. R. Grove, for the respondent:

There is nothing on the face of the case to show that the rating of the appellant in respect of No. 4 was a mistake : and, if it was a mistake, it was one that the Barrister had no power to correct.

(The case was, by the direction of the COURT, handed over to the Revising Barrister, who was present, for amendment in this respect. Accordingly, the amendments before referred to were made by him.)

The amendments being made, the sole remaining question is, whether a calling on the landlord to pay is a calling upon the tenant within the meaning of the 6 & 7 Vict. c. 18, s. 75. * *

[172] In *Moss* v. *The Overseers of St. Michael, Lichfield* (3), A. occupied jointly with B. in the poor-rate. B. alone was assessed as occupier: A. *bonâ fide* paid the rates with his own hand, but without being called upon : and it was held that A. was not rated, and that the omission of his name was not cured by the 6 & 7 Vict. c. 18, s. 75.

(MAULE, J.: There, the party was not rated in any way: here, he is upon the rate. Is he not by the proclamation of the rate "called upon to pay" the rate ?)

He is thereby called upon in respect of No. 4.

(TINDAL, Ch. J.: By mistake for No. 3: that is mere matter of evidence.

MAULE, J.: Are not the words "called upon" satisfied by the name of the party being in the rate as a person who is to pay the money ?)

(1) 5 Man. & G. 33 ; 7 Scott, N. R.   581.
561.   (3) 7 Man. & G. 72 ; 8 Scott, N. R.
(2) 5 Man. & G. 54 ; 7 Scott, N. R.   832.

Clearly not. In *Cullen* v. *Morris* (1), a personal demand was held   COOK
necessary.   *v.*
                                                                          LUCKETT.

(MAULE, J.: That was the case of a scot and lot voter. No
doubt, under the 2 Will. IV. c. 45, s. 27, if the party is accurately
placed upon the rate, and pays it, he is entitled to vote. Here, he
has paid. The question is, whether he has been called upon to
pay, within the 6 & 7 Vict. c. 18, s. 75.)

That section *must mean something more than the twenty-seventh   [*173]
section of the former Act.

   Welsby, in reply, was stopped by the COURT.

TINDAL, Ch. J.:

   The alteration that has been made in the case, and in the
statement of the question for our opinion, has relieved us from all
difficulty. It appears that the Barrister thought the mistake of
the overseers in inserting the appellant as the occupier of No. 4
instead of No. 3, brought the case within the 6 & 7 Vict. c. 18,
s. 75, as being an inaccuracy of description that was amendable.
I almost doubt that any amendment was necessary at all. The
only question, however, remaining for us to deal with, is, whether
the appellant has been *bonâ fide* called upon to pay rates in respect
of the premises occupied by him, and whether he has *bonâ fide*
paid them. The facts of the case show that the tenant was rated;
that he held the premises under an express agreement with his
landlord, that the latter should pay all rates and taxes; that the
landlord had called upon him to pay, and that he had paid, all
the rent due; and that the landlord had been called upon to pay,
and had paid, all poor-rates due in respect of the house. It appears
to me, that, the tenant being rated, under these circumstances, the
calling upon the landlord to pay, and the payment by him, are
equivalent to a *bonâ fide* calling upon the tenant to pay, and a
bonâ fide payment of the rates by him. I cannot understand why
any formal call or personal demand should be necessary. The
tenant being on the rate, he was the only person who, by law,
could be called upon to pay. He was liable to a distress for it.
No greater notoriety could be given to the demand by calling at his
door. He is to pay either *in crumenâ* or *in personâ*. I think *the   [*174]
words of the seventy-fifth section are satisfied, and that the decision
of the Revising Barrister was wrong.

(1) 2 Stark. N. P. C. 577.

COOK
v.
LUCKETT.

MAULE, J. :

I think, also, that the appellant, in this case, was *bonâ fide* called upon to pay, and has *bonâ fide* paid the rates in respect of the premises occupied by him, within the 6 & 7 Vict. c. 18, s. 75. I also incline to think that the vote might properly be allowed upon the true construction of the 2 Will. IV. c. 45, s. 27, without the assistance of the seventy-fifth section of the subsequent Act. The twenty-seventh section confers the franchise upon the occupier of a 10*l.* house : it requires not merely that he shall hold himself out as an occupier, but that he shall submit himself to the parochial burthens ; and, to effect that purpose, the section requires that he shall be rated, and that he shall have actually paid rates. We have had several cases before us as to what is a sufficient payment of rates. It was, at first, contended that the payment must be by the party's own hand. Generally speaking, the payment of money is a thing that is, of all others, the least necessary to be done by the hand of the party himself. There cannot be the smallest doubt that, where one gets another person to pay the rate for him, and allows it in account, that is a good payment by the party rated. The Legislature, by *bonâ fide* payment, probably meant to exclude a gratuitous payment by a candidate. I am clearly of opinion that there has been here a complete payment by the party rated within the 2 Will. IV. c. 45, s. 27, as well as within the 6 & 7 Vict. c. 18, s. 75. The main question, however, is, whether the appellant has been *bonâ fide* "called upon to pay," within the latter clause, s. 75. That section is not necessarily introductory of new law. It may be, that it helps some cases to which the twenty-seventh section of the former Act would not apply. Its object was to remove the obscurity and obviate the

[*175]   *doubts that had been suggested upon the 2 Will. IV. c. 45, s. 27, to enable the Revising Barrister more easily to arrive at the same conclusion that he ought to have arrived at under the last-mentioned section. I apprehend the inaccuracy here is much the same as if a house were described as the "Black Lion," instead of the "Red Lion," which, I conceive, would have been within the twenty-seventh section of the Reform Act. The absence of the words "*bonâ fide*" throws some light upon the seventy-fifth section of the 6 & 7 Vict. c. 18 : it imports a substantial instead of a mere formal compliance with the requirements of the Act. The object of inserting a party's name in a rate, is, to warn him of the amount he is called upon to pay to the overseers. The seventy-fifth section

of the 6 & 7 Vict. c. 18, says, in effect, that any inaccuracy in the COOK
v.
LUCKETT. description of the premises or the person rated, is to be cured, not in all cases, but in those where the substance of the twenty-seventh section of the former Act has been complied with. It may be, and I incline to think it is so, that a rate so defective that it does not show who the party is that is rated, might be helped by something *dehors* the rate itself. If the insertion of the name of a party in a rate as liable to pay a certain sum, and the publication of such rate, be not a *bonâ fide* calling upon him to pay the rate, I am at a loss to conceive what would be. The Revising Barrister seems to have thought a visit at the house of the party necessary. In this he was clearly wrong. The amount of the rate has been disbursed by the appellant, and received by the persons entitled to receive it; and, therefore, he has *bonâ fide* paid, as well as been *bonâ fide* called upon to pay, the rate, within the meaning of the statute.

CRESSWELL, J.:

I also am of opinion that the appellant, in this case, was entitled to have his name *inserted in the register. I very much doubt [*176] whether it was necessary to introduce the seventy-fifth section of the 6 & 7 Vict. c. 18, into the present discussion. The facts are, that the party occupied No. 3, and was rated in respect of No. 3, though the house was inadvertently described as No. 4. He has, therefore, complied with the twenty-seventh section of the 2 Will. IV. c. 45, by being rated. The rates have been paid by his landlord, who, in consideration of his engagement to pay them, has received from him an increased rent. After the case of *Hughes* v. *The Overseers of Chatham*, it is impossible to contend that that is not a sufficient payment of rates by or on behalf of the tenant. But, assuming the matter to be at all doubtful, all doubt is removed by the 6 & 7 Vict. c. 18, s. 75. I incline to think, that, if the rating were such as to call upon the party to pay, that would be sufficient under the 2 Will. IV. c. 45, s. 27, and that the subsequent provision, which is declaratory as well as enacting, was unnecessary. If he was *bonâ fide* called upon to pay, and has *bonâ fide* paid the rates, he is to be considered as rated, notwithstanding any misnomer or inaccuracy of description: and, if rated, and the overseers intended (1) to call upon him to pay, and he submits by paying the amount, whether by his own hand, or by the hand of another, he is clearly within the seventy-fifth section.

(1) But see the next case, *post*, p. 458.

COOK
v.
LUCKETT.

ERLE, J.:

I also think that the Barrister erred in excluding the name of the appellant. It appears to me, that, if a party is put upon a rate with intent to make him liable, he is *bonâ fide* called upon to pay the rate, within the meaning of the 6 & 7 Vict. c. 18, s. 75. And I also think there has, in this case, been a sufficient payment of the rate by the appellant.

Decision reversed.

1846.
Jan. 29.

City of London.
[177]

PARIENTE *v.* LUCKETT.

(2 C. B. 177—182; S. C. 15 L. J. C. P. 83; 10 Jur. 115.)

In consequence of a claim made by A., an occupying tenant, his name was inserted in a rate, immediately after that of his landlord, who was duly rated in respect of the same premises. All the columns opposite A.'s name were left blank, and it was not otherwise connected with that of his landlord than by its juxtaposition:

Held, that A. was sufficiently rated.

And held that the Revising Barrister ought not to have been influenced by a statement of one of the overseers that A.'s name was so inserted without any intention to rate him; but should have decided upon the construction of the rate itself, irrespectively of any extraneous evidence.

WILLIAM ENDELL LUCKETT duly objected to the name of Joshua Pariente being retained on the list of persons entitled to vote in the election of members for the city of London, in respect of the occupation of a "house, No. 18, Coleman Street," in the parish of St. Stephen, Coleman Street.

The Revising Barrister expunged the name of the said Joshua Pariente from the said list, subject to an appeal to the Court of Common Pleas upon the following case:

The qualification of the appellant was duly proved in all respects, except as to the sufficiency of the rating.

Five poor-rates were made in the said parish in the year ending the 31st of July, 1845. The first rate was made on the 17th of October, 1844; the second rate, on the 17th of January, 1845; the third rate, on the 8th of April, 1845. The dates of the subsequent rates are not material. Thomas Haynes, the landlord of the house, was rated, and paid all the rates in respect thereof. The appellant was not rated to the said October rate, nor did his name in any way appear thereon.

On the 1st of January, 1845, a claim to be rated in respect of the house was served, on behalf of the appellant, upon the overseers

of the parish; and at that time no rate was due in respect of the
house.

At the time the assessment to the said January rate was made out, the appellant was not rated thereto, nor did his name appear upon such last-mentioned rate; but afterwards, and before the declaration at the foot of the said last-mentioned rate was signed by the churchwardens and overseers pursuant to the provisions of the 6 & 7 Will. IV. c. 96, the name of the appellant was inserted by interlineation upon the said rate between the name of the said Thomas Haynes and that of another party rated for other premises, but without any brace or other connecting mark, and without any particular premises or amount of rating being carried out in the several columns referring to such particulars.

The rate in this respect was in the following form:

				£	£	
2	Thomas Haynes. Joshua Pariente.	House.	18, Coleman Street.	67	50	&c.
3	A. B. (another party).	House.	&c. &c.	&c.	&c.	&c.

The name of the appellant was inserted in a similar manner upon the said April rate, and the subsequent rates; but upon a separate line, and not as an interlineation; and such last-mentioned insertions were made at the time the assessment was made out.

One of the parochial officers stated that the name had been so placed upon the rate in consequence of the claim so made by the appellant, but without any intention to rate him for anything.

The Revising Barrister decided that the appellant was not rated to the said January rate, and the subsequent rates.

If the Court shall be of opinion that the decision was wrong, the name of the appellant is to be re-inserted in the said list of voters, as follows:

Joshua Pariente.	Coleman Street.	House.	18, Coleman Street.

The cases of twenty-five other parties, which were decided upon
the same point of law, are consolidated with the principal case.

Welsby, for the appellant:

No question arises as to the rate made on the 17th of October, 1844, as to which there was clearly a sufficient claim within the

PARIENTE
v.
LUCKETT.

2 Will. IV. c. 45, s. 30. The only question presented for the opinion of the Court, is, upon the twenty-seventh section, as to which the case of *Wright* v. *The Town Clerk of Stockport* (1) is decisive.

The COURT called on :

W. R. Grove, for the respondent :

In the case cited the names of the landlord and of the various tenants were joined with a brace.

(TINDAL, Ch. J. : Though there is virtue sometimes, as Lord Coke observes, in an &c., I doubt whether you will find authority for saying there is any in a brace.)

The overseers never meant to rate the appellant.

(TINDAL, Ch. J. : Can they be permitted to say that? The party claims to be inserted in the rate, and they put his name upon it.

MAULE, J. : There can be no doubt that he might have been compelled to pay the rate.)

[He cited *Moss* v. *Overseers of Lichfield* (2).] If it had been the intention of the overseers to rate the appellant in respect of the house No. 18, Coleman Street, a "ditto," or something equivalent, [*180] would have been *added in each column, as in the form in the Parochial Assessment Act, 6 & 7 Will. IV. c. 96.

(MAULE, J. : Is not a blank equivalent to a ditto?

TINDAL, Ch. J. : The question is, whether this is not to be read as if all the particulars had been carried out in the same way as in the preceding line.)

The effect of the evidence on the Revising Barrister was, that the party was not properly rated. It is rather a question of fact than of law.

(CRESSWELL, J. : Not strictly so. In one sense, it is a question of fact whether or not an agreement has been executed : but, if it be admitted that the party did sign the instrument, then it is a question of law, whether it amounts to an agreement or not.)

(1) 5 Man. & G. 33; 7 Scott, N. R. 561.   (2) 7 Man. & G. 72; 8 Scott, N. R. 832.

At the most, it is an inaccurate description, which might have been   PARIENTE
amended under the 6 & 7 Vict. c. 18, s. 75; and that was never   LUCKETT.
suggested.

Welsby, in reply, was stopped by the COURT.

TINDAL, Ch. J.:

I think all the information derived by the Revising Barrister
from the overseer as to what the intention was, must be thrown
overboard; and that we are bound to give the rate a reasonable
construction, as we would do to any other instrument. In the
second column of the rate we find the name of Haynes, and opposite
to his name, in the other columns, we find the premises occupied
by him, their rateable value, and other particulars: then follows
immediately the name of the appellant, without those particulars,
all the columns opposite his name being left blank. Now, his
name must have been inserted in the second column with some
object: and I think we must read it as if all the particulars in the
preceding line had been repeated, or we must consider Haynes and
the appellant to be jointly rated in respect of the premises described.
That seems to me necessarily to follow from the numbers in *the   [*181]
margin, No. 2 applying to Haynes and the appellant, and No. 3 to
the party whose name immediately follows. It seems to me that
it is only in this way that we can give any sense to the rate; and
that therefore the decision of the Revising Barrister must be
reversed.

MAULE, J.:

I am of the same opinion. With respect to the first rate, it is
conceded that the party did enough to entitle himself to the benefit
of the 2 Will. IV. c. 45, s. 80 (1). With regard to the subsequent
rates, the question is whether or not he was actually rated; and
that is to be determined by looking at the rate itself. The Revising
Barrister seems to have been embarrassed by something said by
one of the overseers. The construction, however, of the rate is to
be ascertained quite irrespectively of the opinions or intentions of
the overseers. The intention of the overseers has as little to do
with the matter, as would a statement by a subscribing witness to
a bond, that the obligor signed and sealed it, but without any
intention to make himself liable to pay the money. The construction
I put upon this rate is the same as if all the columns opposite

(1) Except that he did not make "continual claim."

PARIENTE
v.
LUCKETT.

the name of the appellant had been filled up with the several particulars inserted opposite the preceding name. Leaving blanks is just as effective and good as inserting " ditto " (1) in each place.

CRESSWELL, J.:

Looking at the extract from the rate-book set out in the case, I think we are bound to hold that the appellant was properly rated. The figures in the first column denote the subject-matter of the rate. Placed as it is here, I think the name of the appellant could only have been intended to be inserted for the *purpose of connecting him with the preceding subject-matter of rate.

[*182]

ERLE, J.:

Finding an interlineation in the rate-book, the Revising Barrister was justified in requiring an explanation of the circumstances under which it was made. But he should not have allowed his judgment to be influenced by any thing that was said by the overseer as to his intention in placing the appellant's name on the rate. It was his duty to construe it as he would have done any other written instrument. Looking at the manner in which the name is placed, I have no doubt that it was intended to apply it to the subject-matter of rate in the preceding line. The effect unquestionably would be, to render the appellant liable to be called upon for the rate. I therefore agree with the rest of the Court in thinking that the decision of the Revising Barrister must be reversed.

Decision reversed.

———————

1846.
Jan. 29.

City of
London.

[182]

HENRY COOGAN *v.* WILLIAM ENDELL LUCKETT.

(2 C. B. 182—186; S. C. 15 L. J. C. P. 159; 10 Jur. 141.)

"The clear yearly value" of premises, under the Representation of the People Act, 1832 (2 Will. IV. c. 45), s. 27 (2), is matter of fact to be determined by the Revising Barrister upon the evidence before him.

The proper criterion of value seems to be, the amount for which the premises would fairly let, the tenant bearing the ordinary burthens incident to the occupation.

WILLIAM ENDELL LUCKETT duly objected to the name of Henry Coogan being retained on the list of persons entitled to vote in the election of members for the city of London, in respect of the occupation of a "house, 4, Red Cross Passage, in the parish of St. Giles-without-Cripplegate."

(1) *Vide ante*, p. 419, note (1).   (2) See note to *Colvill* v. *Wood*, p. 473, below.

The Revising Barrister expunged the name of the said Henry
Coogan from the said list, subject to an appeal to this Court upon
the following case :

The qualification of the appellant was duly proved in all respects,
except as to the value of the house occupied.

The rent paid by the appellant for the house in question was
4*s.* 9*d.* per week, amounting to 12*l.* 7*s.* per annum. The landlord
paid all the rates and taxes assessed upon the house. The landlord of the house (was also the owner or lessee of other houses in
the said passage, which houses were also let at weekly lettings ;
and he (1)) compounded for his poor-rates (for all such houses, and
also for the house so occupied by the appellant ; and the said landlord) was assessed in the poor-rate book in respect of the said
house, at 5*l.* per annum.

(It was not shown that there was any local Act authorising such
composition ; but it was assumed to have been made under the
59 Geo. III. c. 12, s. 19.)

The rates, commonly known as tenants' rates, payable in this
parish, amounted to 5*s.* 11*d.* in the pound per annum, viz. poor-rates
3*s.*, consolidated rate 1*s.* 4*d.*, police-rate 7*d.*, and church-rate 1*s.*

(It was proved that the said house, if the same were rated to
the tenant, would be assessed at the rate or value of 8*l.* per annum ;
on which assessment the tenants' rate would amount to 2*l.* 7*s.* 4*d.*
per annum.)

It was contended, on behalf of the appellant, that no other rates
or taxes, except the poor-rate and window-tax ought to be deducted
from the amount of rent actually paid, in order to ascertain what
was the "clear annual value" of the house within the meaning of
the *twenty-seventh section of the 2 Will. IV. c. 45 ; and, secondly,
that, if all the tenants' rates were to be deducted, yet that such
deduction should be made only for the amount for which the premises
were assessed to the landlord, viz. 5*l.*, and not upon the rent
actually paid by the tenant ; and that no greater amount than that
which the landlord was actually called upon to pay could legally
be deducted.

The Revising Barrister (was of opinion that the "clear annual
value" of premises must be taken to mean the rent at which they
might reasonably be expected to let for, from year to year, free of
all usual tenants' rates and taxes, at least, (see 6 & 7 Will. IV.

(1) The passages within brackets   rister, upon the case being remitted to
were inserted by the Revising Bar-   him for amendment.

c. 96, s. 1) that is, the rent which the landlord would, in such case, receive; but, inasmuch as there was no evidence before the Revising Barrister to enable him to ascertain what the house would let for, under such circumstances, he considered) that the proper principle of ascertaining the "clear annual value" of the house in question was, to deduct from the rent paid by the appellant, viz. 12*l.* 7*s.*, the amount of " tenants' rates and taxes " calculated upon (the rateable value of the said house, if assessed to a tenant), viz. 2*l.* 7*s.* 4*d.*, and, therefore, that the said house was not of the "clear yearly value " of 10*l.*

If the Court shall be of opinion that the decision was wrong, and that either of the principles of calculating the value contended for on behalf of the appellant was correct, the name of the appellant is to be re-inserted in the said list of voters, as follows :

| Henry Coogan. | Red Cross Passage. | House. | 4, Red Cross Passage. |

Welsby, for the appellant :

The principle upon which the Revising Barrister calculated the "clear yearly value" of the premises was erroneous. If it means the value *to the landlord, as was held in the *Woodstock* case (1), the value here was more than 10*l.* Whether any deduction is to be made on account of repairs or insurance, may be doubtful (2).

[*185]

(MAULE, J.: Are deductions on these accounts mentioned in the statute ?)

They are not.

(MAULE, J.: I should say the Legislature meant that the party should be entitled to vote, if he were of ability to occupy a house of the yearly value of 10*l.*, and to pay rates and taxes.)

The additional burthens to be borne by the tenant, are not to go in diminution of the value.

W. R. Grove, for the respondent :

" Clear yearly value" means value to the tenant. Whatever the amount of taxes, if paid by the landlord, they are to be deducted from the rent.

(1) *Prior's* case, Falc. & Fitz. 453.   where this point is decided in the
(2) See *Colvill* v. *Wood*, *post*, p. 473,   negative.

(ERLE, J.: The value is, what the tenement would fairly let for, the tenant paying the rates and taxes.)

[He cited *Rex* v. *Chaplin* (1).]

TINDAL, Ch. J., after referring to the 2 Will. IV. c. 45, s. 27, said:

What is the clear yearly value of the premises must be a question of fact to be determined by the Revising Barrister upon the evidence before him. Here, he has decided that the value is not sufficient to confer a vote; and, upon the facts stated, I am unable to discover that he has decided improperly.

MAULE, J.:   [186]

The case finds facts that have a bearing upon the question of value. The question is, what is the house worth by the year. That is to be ascertained by looking at the benefits to be enjoyed, and at the losses and burthens to be borne. The Revising Barrister has drawn a conclusion of fact from a statement of facts; and we cannot see that his conclusion is wrong. He talks about a principle; but it is not a principle of law, but a mere mode of ascertaining the fact. The only rule of law is, that, in order to ascertain the value, you must consider all the circumstances.

CRESSWELL, J.:

The clear yearly value is, what the house would let for, over and above the ordinary burthens to which a tenant would be liable who took it subject to such burthens.

ERLE, J.:

The value is entirely a question of fact. But I agree with the Revising Barrister, that the true test of annual value is, what would the premises fairly let for, under ordinary circumstances. The principle that obtains in the settlement cases is applicable here. In those cases, the rateable value has generally been considered the sum for which the premises would fairly let to a tenant bearing the public burthens cast by law upon him.

Decision affirmed.

(1) 1 B. & Ad. 926.

LUCKETT v. KNOWLES.

(2 C. B. 187—192; S. C. 15 L. J. C. P. 87; 10 Jur. 99.)

Held, that, where a voter's place of abode is untruly stated in the list, the Barrister has power to insert it correctly, under the Parliamentary Voters Registration Act, 1843 (6 & 7 Vict. c. 18), s. 40 (1).

And *semble*, per MAULE, J., that the place of abode is no part of the qualification.

WILLIAM ENDELL LUCKETT duly objected to the name of Philip Lionel Knowles being retained on the list of persons entitled to vote in the election of members for the city of London in respect of property occupied within the parish of St. Margaret, Lothbury.

The Revising Barrister retained the name of Philip Lionel Knowles upon the said list, subject to an appeal to this Court upon the following case:

The name of the respondent appeared upon the list as follows:

Name.	Place of Abode.	Nature of Qualification.	Street, &c., where Property situate, &c.
Philip Lionel Knowles.	Greenwich.	Counting-house.	1, Bank Chambers.

The only point in the case was, as to the power of the Revising Barrister to alter the place of abode of the respondent, as described in the list.

The respondent's place of abode was at Queen Square, Bloomsbury, and not at Greenwich. Both Greenwich and Queen Square are within seven miles of the city of London. The respondent required the Revising Barrister to alter the place of his abode as described in the said list; but it was contended, on behalf of the appellant, that the Revising Barrister had no power to do so, inasmuch as the place of abode was an essential part of *the description of the qualification of the respondent, which the Revising Barrister was not at liberty to change, under the fortieth section of the 6 & 7 Vict. c. 18.

[*188]

The Revising Barrister decided that the place of abode was no part of the description of the qualification of the respondent, and that the erroneous statement of the place of abode was a mistake in the list, which, under the said section, the Revising Barrister had power to correct; and he altered the place of abode accordingly.

(1) *Semble*, such an amendment is one which the Revising Barrister *must* now make under 41 & 42 Vict. c. 26, s. 28.—J. G. P.

If the Court shall be of opinion that the decision of the Revising
Barrister was wrong, the name of the respondent is to be expunged
from the list.

W. R. Grove, for the appellant :

The place of abode of the voter is part of his qualification ; and,
assuming that it is not, still it is a matter, the erroneous statement
of which is not amendable under the 6 & 7 Vict. c. 18, s. 40.   *   *
Accuracy of description is essential.   Here, the description is not
*merely insufficient ; it is wholly false.

[*189]

(MAULE, J. : When the place of abode is wholly omitted, or is
insufficiently described, the Barrister is to expunge the name of the
party from the list, unless the matter so omitted or insufficiently
described be supplied to his satisfaction, in which case he is to
insert the same in the list.   If the Barrister may amend in the
case of a total omission, surely he may amend in the case of a
misdescription.)

A total omission could not mislead : but the description of the
qualification cannot be altered.

(MAULE, J. : The place of abode is no part of the qualification.)

*   *   ^   ^   ^

Welsby, for the respondent, was not called upon.

TINDAL, Ch. J. :

It appears to me that the power of amendment given to the
Revising Barrister by the 6 & 7 Vict. c. 18, s. 40, is sufficiently
large to warrant the amendment made in this case.   That section,
so far as it relates to the voter's place of abode, applies to two cases
only, a case of total omission, and a case of insufficient description ;
in both of which the Barrister is required to expunge the name of
the party : but it goes on to provide, that, if, whilst the revision is
proceeding, the matter so omitted or insufficiently described is
supplied to his satisfaction, he shall insert the same in the list.   It
is conceded, that, in the case of a total omission, the *Barrister may
amend : but it is contended that insufficiency of description must
be limited to cases where the place of abode is inserted without
sufficient particularity, and does not extend to cases like the present,

[*190]

LUCKETT
v.
KNOWLES.

where it is altogether erroneous.   I think it is impossible for any
one to say that the description here is any other than an insufficient
one.   And I do not see why we should narrow the construction of
a clause, which was meant to be fairly and liberally interpreted,
and which seems to me to be reasonably adapted to comprehend
the present case.   I think the Revising Barrister's decision must be
affirmed.

MAULE, J.:

I also am of opinion that the name of the respondent was properly retained upon the list of voters.   The name was upon a list
on which the Revising Barrister was bound to retain it, unless the
circumstances rendered it his duty to expunge it.   Now, the only
ground upon which he was called on to expunge it, was, that the
respondent's place of abode was erroneously stated to be "Greenwich," when in fact it was "Queen Square, Bloomsbury."   The
party's name appearing regularly on the list, the Barrister could
not expunge it without sufficient cause.   It was necessary for the
respondent to prove his qualification as stated in the list.   He did
so.   Then it is said the place of abode is part and parcel of the
qualification.   That I do not admit.   The party may have resided
in several places : it clearly would not be necessary to insert them
all in the register.   The present case, therefore, does not fall within
that part of the fortieth section which empowers the Barrister to
expunge the name on the ground of the insufficiency of the description of the qualification.   If the voter's name is to be expunged at
all, it is not because no qualification is stated, or because the quali-

[*191]

fication is insufficient in *point of law ; but the power to expunge, if
it exist at all, arises under the subsequent part of the clause, which
imposes that duty upon the Revising Barrister, in cases where the
place of abode is wholly omitted or insufficiently described for the
purpose of being identified.   And then the power to expunge is conditional—" unless the matter or matters so omitted or insufficiently
described be supplied to the satisfaction of such Barrister before he
shall have completed the revision of such list, in which case he
shall then and there insert the same in such list."   Here, the
matter so omitted or insufficiently described was so supplied to and
inserted by the Barrister.   I therefore think the case clearly comes
within that part of the section ; though I very much doubt whether
there exists any other power to amend, if the matter be not supplied
to the satisfaction of the Barrister.

CRESSWELL, J. :

It is to be observed that the fortieth section begins with a power to the Barrister to correct mistakes. That may mean either a general power to correct mistakes, or it may be limited to those mistakes, omissions, and misdescriptions that are afterwards pointed out. It then goes on to provide, that, wherever the christian name, place of abode, &c., of the voter shall be wholly omitted, or insufficiently described for the purpose of identification, the name of the party shall be expunged from the list, unless the matter so omitted or insufficiently described is supplied pending the revision ; in which case the Barrister is to amend by inserting it. When a wrong place of abode is given, the case either is or is not within the latter part of the section. If it is not within it, the Barrister had no power to expunge the name of the voter; if it is, he had power to make the amendment he did. _Quâcunque *vid_, therefore, the Barrister did right in retaining the respondent's name on the list. I think it was a case of insufficient description.

[192]

EARLE, J. :

I also think the Revising Barrister was right. The principal object of the fortieth section was, to prevent a _bonâ fide_ qualification from being defeated by reason of a mere mistake. The section starts with a very general power to amend mistakes. Without deciding (though I am inclined to think we have already done so) that the Barrister had power to make an amendment like this under that part of the section, he clearly had that power under the subsequent part, which authorizes him to expunge the name of the party from the list, where his place of abode is either wholly omitted or insufficiently described for the purpose of identification. I see no reason why a misstatement of the party's place of abode should not be within the words, as it seems to me to be within the spirit of the section. The law is a remedial one, and ought therefore to receive a liberal construction.

Decision affirmed.

LUCKETT _v._ BRIGHT.

(2 C. B. 193—202; S. C. 15 L. J. C. P. 85; 10 Jur. 75.)

Six persons were joint lessees of a house, which they and others used for the purposes of a political association. The rent, and the wages of the servants who had charge of the premises, were paid out of a common fund to which the lessees and the other members of the association were

1846
Jan. 29.

City of London.
[193]

LUCKETT
BRIGHT.

subscribers.   Various members of the association transacted the business of
the association upon the premises; and the lessees, when in London,
frequented the premises, partly transacting the business of the association,
and partly transacting their own affairs.

The Revising Barrister having decided, upon these facts, that the lessees
occupied the premises as tenants within the Representation of the People
Act, 1832 (2 Will. IV. c. 45), s. 27; and that the same were not jointly
occupied by them and the other members of the association as tenants:

The COURT affirmed his decision (1).

WILLIAM ENDELL LUCKETT duly objected to the name of John
Bright being retained upon the list of persons entitled to vote for
members of Parliament for the city of London, in respect of the
occupation of "a house, No. 67, Fleet Street," in the parish of
St. Dunstan in the West.

The Revising Barrister retained the name of John Bright upon the
said list, subject to an appeal to this Court upon the following case:

The respondent, together with Richard Cobden, and four others,
were the joint lessees of the house, 67, Fleet Street, under a demise
for a term of three years from the 29th of September, 1843, in consideration of the payment of a premium of 150l., and a yearly rent
of 200l.   The said lessees were the only persons appearing as contracting parties with the lessor, or liable to him for the rent; and
there was no mention in the lease of any other parties, or of the
purposes for which the premises were taken.   But it appeared in
evidence that the whole of the premises were used for the purpose
of a voluntary association of persons styling themselves "The

[*194]   *National Anti-Corn-Law League."   More than twenty other
parties, members of the association, subscribed various sums of
money to a common fund, for the purpose of carrying out the
objects of the association.   The respondent and his said co-lessees
were also subscribers to the said common fund.   The rent of the
premises was paid out of the said fund, as were also the various
servants of the association who had charge of the premises.   Various
members of the association transacted the business of the association upon the premises; and the respondent and his co-lessees, when
in London, frequented the premises, partly transacting the business
of the association, and partly transacting their own affairs.

It was contended, on the part of the appellant, that the respondent and his co-lessees did not occupy the house as tenants within

(1) This case was decided on s. 27 of   repealed.   And see now, as to joint
the Reform Act, which is in part   occupation, 48 & 49 Vict. c. 3, s. 5,
repealed by 48 & 49 Vict. c. 3, s. 12,   and *Druitt* v. *Gosling* (1889) 58 L. J.
but s. 29 of the Reform Act is not   Q. B. 109.—J. G. P.

the meaning of the twenty-seventh section of the 2 Will. IV. c. 45 ;LUCKETT
or that, if they did, the same was jointly occupied by them and the   *v.*
other members of the association as tenants, and then that the   BRIGHT.
clear yearly value of the premises, divided by the number of the
said occupiers, would not give a sum of not less than 10*l.* for each
and every such occupier, within the meaning of the twenty-ninth
section of the statute.

The Revising Barrister decided that the respondent and his
co-lessees did occupy the premises " as tenants," and that the same
were not jointly occupied by them and the other members of the
association as tenants.

If the Court shall be of opinion that the said decision was wrong,
the name of the said John Bright is to be expunged from the list.

W. R. Grove, for the appellant:

The respondent and the other five joint-lessees did not occupy
the premises in question as tenants. A man cannot be said to
*occupy premises, unless he is personally resident there by himself   [*195]
or by some third person as his agent or servant: [*Rex* v. *The
Inhabitants of Ditcheat* (1) ; *Rex* v. *St. Nicholas, Rochester* (2). In
this case, if the co-lessees occupied at all, it was jointly with a
large number of persons members of the league.]

(CRESSWELL, J.: The case discloses no trust under which the
members of the association might, of right, come upon the
premises.)

It shows that the premises were used for the purposes of the
association, and that the rent was paid out of its funds. All the
cases that have hitherto been decided have gone upon the footing
of there having been something like an exclusive occupation.

(TINDAL, Ch. J.: I think there are sufficient *indicia* of occupation
found by the Barrister.)

Welsby, for the respondent, was not called upon.

TINDAL, Ch. J.:

The question here is, whether we can see that the Barrister was
wrong in the decision he has come to, or whether, upon the facts
found by him, we feel ourselves bound to come to a contrary

(1) 9 B. & C. 176; 4 Man. & Ry. 151.   (2) 5 B. & Ad. 219; 3 Nev. & M. 21.

conclusion. *The case finds that the respondent and his co-lessees were clothed with the character of tenants. The only question is, as to the mode of occupation. It appears that they were sometimes there; that they, when in London, "frequented the premises, partly transacting the business of the association, and partly transacting their own affairs." I cannot say that this was not such a user of the premises as to amount to an occupation by themselves or their agents. I therefore think the decision must be affirmed.

MAULE, J.:

I am of the same opinion. The Barrister has found that the voter occupied as tenant. It appears that the premises are let to six persons, of whom the voter is one; that the user of them was by these six persons and others associated with them; and that the persons who had charge of the premises were the servants of an association of which the lessees, and many others, were members. The rent and the servants' wages were paid out of the funds of the association. Upon this state of facts, the Barrister has come to the conclusion that the respondent and his co-lessees occupied the premises as tenants. I cannot say that he has drawn an unreasonable conclusion from the facts.

CRESSWELL, J.:

I also think the Barrister did right in retaining the names of the respondent and his co-lessees on the list of voters. The question is, whether the materials he had before him justified him in so deciding. It is clear the parties were tenants of the premises: the only question is, whether or not they occupied them. It does not appear that they have parted with the right they possessed as lessees, to turn out any one who came there, or that the other members of the association had any right to come upon the premises against their will. It is said that the rent and the servants' wages

were paid out of a common fund contributed by the lessees *and many other members of the association, and that the premises were occupied by those servants. But there is nothing in the case to show that these individuals were not there as the agents or servants of the respondent and his co-lessees. And it appears that the respondent and his co-lessees were in the habit of resorting to the house for their own private purposes, and of transacting their own business there. On these grounds, I think the decision was right.

ERLE, J. :

    I also think the decision of the Revising Barrister was right. I
am not aware of any definition of the term "occupation" which
would exclude the kind of user here found.

LUCKETT
v.
BRIGHT.

Decision affirmed.

GEORGE COLVILL *v.* CHARLES WOOD AND OTHERS(1).

(2 C. B. 210—217; S. C. 15 L. J. C. P. 160; 10 Jur. 336.)

The proper criterion of "clear yearly value," within the 2 Will. IV.
c. 45, s. 27, is the fair annual rent, without making any deduction on
account of repairs or insurance.

1846.
Feb. 23.
——
*Borough of
Chatham.*
[210]

GEORGE COLVILL, on the list of voters for the borough of
Chatham, duly objected to George Huben and William Jolley, on
the same list, as not being entitled to have their names retained
on such list.

    It appeared that each of them, the said Huben and Jolley,
claimed to be so entitled, in respect of a house in the parish of
Chatham, and that they had respectively occupied such houses
during the required period, at the yearly rent of 10*l.*, exclusive of
rates and taxes, and that there was no special agreement between
them and their respective landlords as to repairs and insurance. It
further appeared that the said rent of 10*l.* was, in each case, the
fair rent of the premises.

    In support of the objections, it was contended that the proper
measure of the "clear annual value" of a house, within the
meaning of the 2 Will. IV. c. 45, s. 27, was, not the rent for which
such house would let to a tenant, but the amount of such rent
after deducting therefrom the average annual expense of landlord's
repairs and insurance; and, consequently, that the houses in
question were not of the clear annual value of 10*l.*

    The Revising Barrister, however, was of opinion that the fair
annual rent was the proper criterion of value, without any such
deduction; and, the right of the said parties to be retained on the
list being established in all other respects, they were retained
accordingly.

[211]

(1) Explained in *Dobbs* v. *Grand
Junction Waterworks Co.* (1883) 9 App.
Cas. 49, 53 L. J. Q. B. 50. Sect. 27 of
the Reform Act, upon which this case
was decided, was repealed, with certain
reservations, by 48 & 49 Vict. c. 3,
s. 12, but the words "clear yearly
value of not less than 10*l.*" occur now
in s. 5 of the Representation of the
People Act, 1884 (48 & 49 Vict. c. 3).
—J. G. P.

COLVILL
v.
WOOD.

The names of fifteen other persons were, upon the same state of facts, inserted in the lists for the parishes of Chatham and Gillingham respectively, and their cases consolidated with the principal case.

The case was argued in Hilary Term last (1).

Kinglake, Serjt., for the appellant:

The decision of the Revising Barrister is erroneous. The rent is not the true criterion of value. "Clear yearly value" means that which comes to the hands of the landlord after deducting all reasonable disbursements, viz. for repairs and for insurance. * *

[212]   The subject-matter of the occupation must be of the clear yearly value of 10*l*. There is, obviously, a distinction between "yearly value" and "clear yearly value;" the latter expression indicates that some deduction is to be made. The value must diminish, unless money is expended in repairs; and the premises may be utterly lost to the landlord, unless he insures them from fire. * *

[213]   The rateable value would seem to be the fair criterion. It is difficult to lay down any other rule.

(TINDAL, Ch. J.: The Revising Barrister has not found the state of repair to be such as to affect the annual value.)

No counsel appeared on the part of the respondent.

TINDAL, Ch. J.:

We will suspend our decision until we have heard the argument in *Coogan* v. *Luckett* (2).

Cur. adv. vult.

TINDAL, Ch. J., now delivered the judgment of the COURT:

In this case the point of law reserved by the Revising Barrister for our determination was, whether, in the case of a person claiming the right to vote for a borough by reason of the occupation of a house as tenant, the fair annual rent was the proper criterion of value, without deducting therefrom the average annual expense of landlord's repairs; and we are of opinion that the Revising [*214]   *Barrister was right in holding the fair annual rent, without making such deduction, to be the clear yearly value within the meaning of the statute 2 Will. IV. c. 45, s. 27.

(1) Before Tindal, Ch. J., and   (2) *Ante*, p. 462.
Maule, Creswell, and Erle, JJ.

It was, indeed, contended before the Revising Barrister, not only that the average annual value of the landlord's repairs should be deducted from the rent paid by the occupier, but the landlord's expense of insurance also.   But this latter appears so plainly to be a voluntary charge on the part of the landlord, who, if he thinks right, may be, and very often is, his own insurer, that we declared our opinion in the course of the argument that the insurance never could be held a necessary deduction in order to ascertain the clear yearly value of the premises.   And we think the same as to the deduction of the landlord's repairs.

This is the case of the occupier of a house as tenant, who pays a rent of 10*l.* per annum exclusive of rates and taxes, that is, so far as the tenant is concerned, a clear yearly rent to the landlord of 10*l.* per annum.   But the statute requiring that the house must be of the clear yearly value of 10*l.* per annum, in order to confer a qualification, it is undoubtedly not enough to find that the tenant pays a rent of that amount; for, it is manifest, such rent is not necessarily the measure of the true value; the rent may be exorbitant, and such as no other tenant would give; or it may have been fraudulently fixed at that sum in order to acquire the vote.   It is necessary, therefore, in order to satisfy the statute, to show further that the house is of that clear yearly value, and for that purpose it is found in the case before us that 10*l.* per annum is the fair rent of the premises.   And whether this is proof of the clear yearly value, is the question before us.

There is some difficulty in ascertaining the true meaning of the Act in the use of this expression.   Where the right to vote depended, as it did formerly, on property *only, there was no difficulty in discovering the clear yearly value.   Thus, where the stat. 8 Hen. VI. c. 7, ordained that the knights of the shires should be chosen by people " whereof every one shall have free tenement to the value of 40*s.* by the year at the least, above all charges ; " and again, where the 18 Geo. II. c. 18, s. 5, has enacted that no person shall vote without having freehold " of the clear yearly value of 40*s.*, over and above all rents and charges payable out of or in respect of the same ; " it was easy to prove the yearly value to the owner, more especially when the sixth section of the latter Act had defined the nature of the charges intended to be deducted, by enacting that " no public or Parliamentary tax, nor any rate or assessment whatever, should be deemed to be any charge payable out of or in respect of any freehold estate within the

[*215]

COLVILL
*.
WOOD.

meaning of the Act." But, in the present case, the Legislature has created a new qualification for voting; namely, that of the occupier, as tenant, of a house of the clear yearly value of not less than 10*l.*; applying to the case of the tenant a description or definition, which, in strictness of language, and under former enactments, belonged exclusively to the owner of the property. For, in strict propriety of language, although the rent may be a fair criterion of the value to the landlord, it cannot be so to the tenant; the value in the case of the latter depending on the use to which he puts it, the profit he makes by his occupation, and other circumstances that exist in each case, quite independently of his paying 10*l.* a year rent to the landlord. But we think it obvious the Legislature could never have intended that the right of a tenant to vote should depend upon calculations so nice, artificial, and difficult of application. And although it may not be easy to give effect to all the words of the section,

[*216]

we think they may well bear the *meaning, that, where a house is occupied by a tenant at the clear annual rent of 10*l.*, if such house is fairly worth that rent to any one wanting to occupy it, if the house would generally fetch such rent, the occupation is that of a house of the clear yearly value of not less than 10*l.*, so far as the tenant is concerned. For, we think the Legislature intended that any person who is in such a condition, both as to credit and circumstances, as to be allowed by the owner of a house which is fairly worth the clear sum of 10*l.* to rent by the year, to become his tenant thereof, is a fit person also to have a vote in the election of a member of Parliament for a borough.

In the course of the argument we were referred to cases of rating under the Settlement Act, 13 & 14 Car. II. c. 12. But we think the appellant can derive no benefit from those cases. The rateable value of property has generally been considered that which it would fairly let for, the tenant bearing all such public burdens as by law attach to his occupation. And in consequence of disputes as to the principle upon which properties more or less perishable should be rated, the statute 6 & 7 Will. IV. c. 96, was passed, and that statute prescribed the mode of ascertaining the rateable value of all kinds of property, viz. that it should be the net annual value left, after making certain deductions specified in the Act from the rent that could be obtained for it; and, if we had found in the 2 Will. IV. c. 45, s. 27, the expression "rateable value," we must have ascertained such value by applying the rule laid down by the

6 & 7 Will. IV. c. 96. But the expression which we have to construe is "clear yearly value," without any direction as to the mode of ascertaining it. The consideration of these statutes, therefore, made entirely *diverso intuitu*, does not, as we conceive, militate against the principle we have laid *down as that which ought to govern the interpretation of the twenty-seventh section of the 2 Will. IV. c. 45. And, for these reasons, we think the decision of the Revising Barrister ought to be affirmed.

COLVILL v. WOOD.

[*217]

Decision affirmed.

JAMES MURRAY <i>v.</i> JOHN THORNILEY(1).

(2 C. B. 217—226; 15 L. J. C. P. 155; 10 Jur. 270.)

1846.
Feb. 23.

County of Chester, Northern Division.

[217]

The words " actual possession," in the Representation of the People Act, 1832 (2 Will. IV. c. 45), s. 26, mean a possession in fact, as contradistinguished from a possession in law.

Therefore, a grantee of a rent-charge is not entitled to be registered, unless he has been in the actual receipt of it for six months before the last day of July.

JOHN THORNILEY objected to the names of James Murray and William M'Connell being retained in the list of voters for the township of Stockport, in respect of the qualification following :

Name.	Place of Abode.	Nature of Qualification.	Where situate, &c.
James Murray.	Apsley Place, Ardwick, Manchester.	Undivided share of freehold rent-charge.	Giles Bury, Joseph Bury, and Thomas Speel, owners of the property out of which same is issuing: situation, No. 15, Higher Hillgate, Stockport.
William M'Connell.	The Polygon, Ardwick, near Manchester.	Undivided share of freehold rent-charge.	Giles Bury, Joseph Bury, and Thomas Speel, owners of the property out of which same is issuing: situation, No. 15, Higher Hillgate, Stockport.

A grant and conveyance to the said James Murray and William   [218]

---

(1) Followed in *Orme's* case (1872) L. R. 8 C. P. 281, 42 L. J. C. P. 38; distinguished in *Druitt* v. *Overseers of Christchurch* (1883) 12 Q. B. D. 365, 53 L. J. Q. B. 177; *Heelis* v. *Blain* (1864) 18 C. B. (N. S.) 90, 34 L. J. C. P. 88; and see *Hadfield's* case (1873) L. R. 8 C. P. 306, 42 L. J. C. P. 146; and *Lowcock* v. *Overseers of Broughton* (1883) 12 Q. B. D. 369.—J. G. P.

M'Connell, and their heirs, of a rent of 6l. 3s., issuing out of free-hold lands of adequate value, was produced, dated the 29th of January, 1845. This rent-charge had been created by a deed dated the 28th of January, 1845, by which it was granted as follows: "One clear yearly rent-charge or sum of 6l. 3s., on the 1st of January in every year, the first payment to become due and be made on the 1st of January then next ensuing."

It was objected, that a rent was an incorporeal hereditament, and as such was not capable of being possessed, except by the act of receiving; or that, at all events, the claimants could not be said to be possessed, or in the actual receipt of the rent until it became due; and that, inasmuch as the first payment of the said rent would not become due until the 1st of January, 1846, the claimants had not been possessed of the hereditaments in respect of which they claimed to be registered, for six calendar months previous to the last day of July, 1845, as required by the 2 Will. IV. c. 45, s. 26.

The decision upon the whole case was, that the names of the said James Murray and William M'Connell should be expunged from the list of claimants for the said township; and the decision upon the point of law in question was, that the said claimants had not been possessed, or in the actual receipt, of the said rent-charge in respect of which they claimed to be registered, for six calendar months next previous to the last day of July, 1845.

If the Court shall be of opinion that the said decisions were wrong, then the names of the said claimants are to be inserted in the list of voters for the said township: if otherwise, then the appeal is to be dismissed.

[219]   The case was argued in Hilary Term last (1).

Cockburn (with whom was *Kinglake*, Serjt.), for the appellant:

The question arises upon the 2 Will. IV. c. 45, s. 26. The rent-charge was created by a deed bearing date the 1st of January, 1845, though the grantee can receive no payment under it until the 1st of January, 1846. The grantee is possessed of the rent-charge from the moment he has an inchoate right. The object of the statute is sufficiently insured by such a possession; and the Court will not encourage any subtleties in its construction. * * *

Welsby, for the respondent:

The decision of the Revising Barrister is perfectly correct. There

(1) Before Tindal, Ch. J., and Cresswell and Erle, JJ.

was no rent *due, nor had there been any receipt of any thing in
the nature of rent under this deed, until after the registration.
The framers of the statute clearly had not at the time incorporeal
hereditaments in their minds : but the Court will construe possession
of a rent-charge to mean actual seisin ; and it is submitted there
can be no seisin of rent until the rent-day has arrived, or unless
some payment has been made in anticipation. [He cited Gilbert on
Rents, pages 88 and 106 *et seq.* ; Brooke's Abridgment, titles Assise
and Seisin ; Viner's Abridgment, title Seisin (A.), and Co. Litt. 14 b.]

(TINDAL, Ch. J. referred to Comyns's Digest (1), where the older
authorities are collected.)

* * The 3 & 4 Will. IV. c. 27, applies to incorporeal hereditaments : under that Act the period of limitation would commence
from the last legal rent-day, *or the last receipt of rent : and the
same construction must be put upon this Act. The Reform Act
does not recognise inchoate rights.

Cockburn, in reply :

Actual seisin is not necessary. A seisin in law is sufficient to
sustain a distress (2), and all that can be required to satisfy the
words of this Act : it is enough if the grantee has a complete title to
the rent-charge for a period of six months before the last day of
July. * * All that [the Act] intended to secure, was, that the
grant should have been in existence a given time.

Cur. adv. vult.

TINDAL, Ch. J., now delivered the opinion of the COURT :

In this case the claim to the right to vote was made in respect of
a freehold rent-charge. The rent-charge was created by deed,
bearing date the 28th of January, 1845, by which the same was
made payable on the 1st day of January in every year, the first
payment to become due and be made on the 1st day of January,
1846. The objection taken before the Revising Barrister was, that
the claimant had no title to be put *upon the register, inasmuch as
he had not been "in the actual possession, or in the receipt of the
rents and profits for his own use for six calendar months at least
next previous to the last day of July " next preceding the registration, as required by the 26th section of the 2 Will. IV. c. 45. The

MURRAY
v.
THORNILEY.

[*220]

[221]

[*222]

[*223]

(1) Title Seisin (O.).   (2) Com. Dig. Seisin (B.).

Revising Barrister allowed the objection, and directed the name of the claimant to be expunged; and, after the argument which has been heard, it appears to my brothers CRESSWELL and ERLE, and to myself, that the decision of the Revising Barrister is right. My brother MAULE, not having been present during the whole of the argument, declines giving any opinion.

It was contended on the part of the appellant, that he had the complete right to the rent-charge from the time of the execution of the deed by which it was granted, and that he had the actual possession also within the meaning of the statute, because he had all the possession of which the subject-matter is capable before the first day of payment had actually arrived. The question undoubtedly turns upon the meaning of the words "actual possession;" and we think those words mean a possession in fact, as contradistinguished from a possession in law; and that, as the possession in fact of a rent-charge must be the actual manual receipt of the rent itself, or some part of it, or of something in lieu of it, so there could be no such possession in fact in this case, where the first payment of the rent did not become due until after the expiration of the month of July, and where nothing whatever took place but the mere execution of the deed.   There is a long course of authorities fully establishing the distinction between a possession or seisin in fact of a rent-charge, and a possession or seisin in law. Littleton, § 235, is an authority in point: "And so it is, if a man grant by his deed a yearly rent issuing out of his land to another, &c., if the grantor thereafter pay to the grantee a penny *or a half-penny, in name of seisin of the rent, then, if after the next day of payment the rent be denied, the grantee may have an assize, or else not," &c.: and Lord Coke, in his commentary on this passage, is equally decisive: "By this &c., is implied, that the grant and delivery of the deed is no seisin of the rent; and that a seisin in law, which the grantee hath by the grant, is not sufficient to maintain an assize, or any other real action, but there must be an actual seisin"(1). And in Com. Dig. tit. Seisin, (C.) and (D.), the older authorities are brought together, establishing the distinction in this respect between a seisin in law and a seisin in fact, or, as it is called, an actual seisin. And this appears more distinctly in the commentary of Lord Coke on the eighth section of Littleton, which relates to the doctrine of *possessio fratris*, where Lord Coke says (2), "What then is the law of a rent, advowson, or such things that lie

(1) See Co. Litt. 160 a.   (2) See Co. Litt. 15 b.

in grant? If a rent or an advowson do descend to the elder son,   MURRAY
and he dieth before he hath seisin of the rent, or present to the   *v.*
church, the rent or adowson shall descend to the youngest son (that   THORNILEY.
is by the other venter), for that he must make himself heir to his
father." And, although Lord Coke there distinguishes the law as
to the case of tenant by the curtesy, where, in favour of that estate,
the husband shall have the rent, although his wife dies before the
rent day, it makes no difference as to the present argument. The
actual possession of rent being, therefore, a well-known legal phrase
or expression, the Legislature cannot be taken to have used it in any
other than such well-known sense, that is, as contradistinguished
from such possession in law, or right to the rent-charge, as the bare
delivery of the deed of grant would confer. And, when it is said
that the authorities only show that *such seisin in fact is necessary   [*225]
in order to maintain an assize, or make a *possessio fratris*, but that
it by no means follows that it is necessary to confer a vote, the
answer is, that it is a mere assumption on the part of the appellant
that the expression is used in the statute in a limited and restricted
sense ; and, at all events the burthen of proving this is cast upon
the appellant ; the statute having applied the expression to the
right of the claimant to be put upon the register. And, as it is
quite clear, that, in the case of land, there must be more than the
execution of the conveyance, that there must be actual possession
or receipt of the rents and profits, there seems no reason why, in
the case of an incorporeal hereditament, to which the provision
of the statute equally applies, there should not be such further
actual possession as the nature of the subject itself is capable of.
And, accordingly, by various statutes before the statute 2 Will. IV.,
the Legislature has made a similar provision, in the very same
terms, for the prevention of the occasional acquirements of freeholds for the purpose of voting. Such are the 18 Geo. II. c. 18, s. 5,
requiring such actual possession for twelve calendar months before
the election. Again, the 3 Geo. III. c. 24, which, after reciting that
annuities and rent-charges are of a private nature, and therefore
liable to fraudulent practices in elections, enacts that no person
shall vote in respect of any annuity or rent-charge, unless a
certificate upon oath shall be entered, twelve calendar months before
the first day of the election, with the clerk of the peace of the
county, and a memorial also of the grant registered with the clerk
of the peace for the same period of time. And, as this statute
is repealed by the statute 6 & 7 Vict. c. 18, s. 72, and no other

MURRAY
v.
THORNILEY.

[*226]

provision enacted in lieu of it, it may well be inferred, that, under the 2 Will. IV. c. 45, s. 26, the Legislature intended something more than the mere production of the deed, by requiring actual possession for *six calendar months.   We therefore think the decision is right, and affirm the same.

————————

Decision affirmed.

1845.
Nov. 7.

[258]

CAMPBELL *v.* WEBSTER.

(2 C. B. 258—268 ; S. C. 15 L. J. C. P. 4.)

Held, that any acknowledgment by the drawer of a bill, of his liability to pay, or any promise to pay the amount, though conditional as to the mode of payment, is evidence to be left to the jury, of due notice of dishonour, and, in the case of a foreign bill, of its having been duly protested.

Assumpsit, on a bill of exchange for 100*l.*, drawn, on the 1st of June, 1844, by the defendant, at Halifax, in Nova Scotia, upon Capron & Co., London, payable, at thirty days' sight, to the plaintiff or his order.   The declaration alleged a presentment to Capron & Co. for acceptance, a refusal by them, and a protest for non-acceptance, and also a presentment for payment at the end of the thirty days, and a protest for non-payment ; and that of all this the defendant had notice.   There were also the common money counts.

The defendant pleaded to the first count, that the bill was not duly protested for non-acceptance, and that he had no notice of the protest for non-acceptance, and, to the subsequent counts, he pleaded *non assumpsit.*

The cause was tried before Erle, J., at the second sitting at Westminster in Trinity Term last.   In support of the affirmative of the issue upon the protest for non-acceptance, a notary was called, who proved that he received the bill from Ransom & Co., the bankers in whose hands the bill had been placed for presentment, that he presented it, and afterwards noted and protested it for non-acceptance.   The protest was not produced : and, upon the objection being taken, and allowed by the learned Judge, a paper was put in, purporting to be a protest, drawn up since the com-

[*259]

mencement of the action.   *This the learned Judge rejected.   The following letters from the defendant to the plaintiff were then put in and relied on, either as a waiver of a protest, or as evidence that a protest had been duly made.   The first letter was not dated, but it bore a post-mark date of the 3rd of July, 1844.

"Sir,—I have accepted the bill for 200*l.*, and also the one for 180*l.*   There was another bill for 100*l.* presented, about which

there was some history attached, respecting its having been presented in place of another which has been cancelled. I do not
recollect any thing about that bill; and, as I have not yet received
the account you were to have sent me, I have no means of ascertaining any thing about it. I have deferred paying that bill until
such time as I should hear from you about it. If it should be all
right, draw on me again for the amount, and I will pay it as soon
as I know something of it. I do not intend to return to Halifax, as
I spend too much money there.

(Signed)   "Arthur Webster."

"August 30th, 1844.

" Sir,—I have at length received your letter, with the account
of the money transactions between us. I find it all correct, with
the exception that you have not credited me with a bill for 50l.
sterling I drew on the 17th of October, 1842. I consequently have
not given instructions to my agent to pay the bill for 100l. till that
matter is set right.

(Signed)   "Arthur Webster."

"Durham, October 12th, 1844.

" Sir,—I cannot conceive how you can say in your last letter
that you had explained to me about the 50l. bill, and that I was
quite satisfied about it. I remember that there was an impression
on your mind that I had had that money from you to buy a horse,
or something: but the impression is equally strong on my mind
that I *never had; and, what's more, I am confident I never
had. What could I have wanted it for ? I never bought a horse
from an artillery officer in my life ; and the first horse I bought in
Halifax, was on the 19th of November. I then, as you know, did
not pay Mayce for it for a year. As I said to you before, if you
will send home a cheque for 50l. sterling to England, I will cause
the 100l. bill to be paid immediately, and we shall then be square.

(Signed)   "Arthur Webster."

On the part of the defendant, it was insisted that these letters
were not evidence of actual protest, nor did they dispense with
proof of actual protest, inasmuch as they contained mere conditional promises to pay the bill ; and that, if intended to be relied
on as evidence of a waiver of protest, such waiver should have been
alleged in the declaration.

The learned Judge told the jury that the letters were evidence
whence they were at liberty to infer that the bill had been duly

CAMPBELL
v.
WEBSTER.

protested, and that the defendant had due notice of such protest. The jury thereupon returned a verdict for the plaintiff for the amount of the bill and interest.

Dowling, Serjt., in Trinity Term, obtained a rule *nisi* for a new trial, on the ground of misdirection. He cited *Burgh* v. *Legge* (1).

Byles, Serjt. (with whom was *Phinn*), now showed cause:

The ruling of the learned Judge was correct. Presentment for payment, protest, and notice of protest or of dishonour, may all be proved by admission: and the letters produced at the trial contain a sufficient admission of the defendant's liability on the bill, to be left to the jury as evidence, not conclusive, certainly, but as

[*261]

*evidence from which they might infer that the bill had been protested, and that the defendant had had due notice thereof. An absolute unconditional promise to pay is not necessary. [He cited *Croxon* v. *Worthen* (2), *Patterson* v. *Becher* (3), *Jones* v. *Morgan* (4), *Lundie* v. *Robertson* (5), *Rogers* v. *Stephens* (6), *Gibbon* v. *Coggan* (7), *Greenway* v. *Hindley* (8), *Booth* v. *Jacobs* (9), *Wilkins* v. *Jadis* (10), *Curlewis* v. *Corfield* (11), *Horford* v. *Wilson* (12), *Dixon* v. *Elliott* (13),

[264]

and *Brownell* v. *Bonney* (14).] These authorities show that an express promise to pay the bill, or an express admission of liability, is good evidence whence the jury may infer a presentment for payment, a protest, and notice of protest, or notice of dishonour; and that even equivocal expressions may suffice for the purpose. Here, the letters contain ample materials to justify the inference that the bill in question was regularly protested, and that the defendant had due notice of the fact, amounting as they do to a distinct admission by the defendant that he owes the plaintiff 100*l.* on this bill. *Burgh* v. *Legge*, cited on the motion, was strictly a case of dispensation, and therefore has no application.

Dowling, Serjt. (with whom was *Channell*, Serjt.), in support of the rule:

The learned Judge was clearly wrong in telling the jury that they might infer, from the letters produced, a regular protest, and notice

(1) 52 R. R. 788 (5 M. & W. 418).

(2) 5 M. & W. 5.

(3) 6 Moore, 319.

(4) 2 Camp. 474.

(5) 7 East, 231.

(6) 2 T. R. 713.

(7) 11 R. R. 692 (2 Camp. 188).

(8) 4 Camp. 52.

(9) 3 Nev. & M. 351.

(10) 36 R. R. 540 (1 Moo. & Rob. 41).

(11) 55 R. R. 436 (1 Q. B. 814; 1 G. & D. 489).

(12) 1 Taunt. 12.

(13) 5 Car. & P. 437.

(14) 1 Q. B. 39; 4 P. & D. 523.

thereof to the defendant. Those letters contain no admission of
the defendant's liability at all, but a mere conditional promise to
pay the bill when satisfied as to certain particulars; and there was
no evidence to show that that condition had been complied with by
the plaintiff. At the most, the letters can only amount to a waiver
of strict legal proof of presentment, protest, and notice; and,
according to the authority of *Burgh* v. *Legge* (1), *do not support   [*265]
an allegation of actual protest and notice.

TINDAL, Ch. J.:

It appears to me that this rule ought to be discharged. The
action is brought by the payee of a foreign bill of exchange, against
the drawer. The pleas that raise the point which has been argued
before us, are: first, that the defendant had no notice of protest;
secondly, that the bill was not duly protested for non-acceptance.
And the question is, whether the evidence given at the trial on
the part of the plaintiff, was properly received, the jury correctly
directed upon it, and the conclusion they came to right. The rule
seems to me to be properly laid down in the case of *Patterson* v.
Becher (2), which goes to the very foundation of the objection here.
The way in which RICHARDSON, J., there states the law upon the
subject, appears to me to be perfectly correct. "It has been
decided," he says, "in *Rogers* v. *Stephens*, that a promise to pay,
after a bill or note becomes due, will dispense with proof of notice
of dishonour. So, it will dispense with the proof of protest; as it
will amount to an admission, on the part of the defendant, that the
plaintiff had a right to resort to him upon the bill " (3). That is,
if, when payment is demanded, the party omits to avail himself
of the preliminary objection of want of protest, or of want of notice,
it is a question for the jury whether he does not thereby admit
that all the steps that are essential to create liability in him, have
been duly taken. The letters, then, *being admissible, do they   [*266]
warrant the conclusion the jury have come to? They seem to me

(1) 52 R. R. 788 (5 M. & W. 418).

(2) 6 Moore, 319.

(3) There, as well as in *Wilkins* v. *Jadis*, 36 R. R. 540 (1 Moo. & Rob. 41), it was immaterial, upon *non assumpsit*, whether the defendant had admitted notice, or had dispensed with notice. Since the new rules of pleading, if the defendant were to traverse the notice alleged in the declaration, and in another plea, to set up a dispensation, there would appear to be a difficulty in saying which plea the evidence established. In the principal case, such ambiguity, had it existed, might have been material; but, upon the correspondence, the question of waiver could hardly arise.

CAMPBELL *v.* WEBSTER.

to show that the defendant was conscious that there had been a protest, and that he had had notice ; otherwise he would not have put his non-liability to pay upon the ground he did. He is evidently struggling to avoid payment of the bill. If, instead of mentioning that which would have been a good answer, he sets up something foreign, that is an admission, according to all the cases, that the good ground of defence does not exist. And that is exactly what the defendant has done here. The letters are altogether silent as to the want of protest or notice : the objection to pay the bill is put upon the ground of some supposed inaccuracy in the accounts between the parties : in other respects, the defendant admits his liability ; and this, according to *Patterson* v. *Becher*, is sufficient.

The answer now attempted to be set up, is, that the letters contain a mere conditional promise to pay. But, when we are determining the point by reference to what is supposed to have been passing in the mind of the defendant, it is quite immaterial whether the promise is conditional or not. *Wilkins* v. *Jadis* (1) is a much stronger case than the present. There, proof that the drawer knew, two days after its maturity, that the bill was unpaid, and in the hands of a particular indorsee, and objected to pay it on the ground of fraud in the obtaining of it, was ruled by Lord TENTERDEN to be evidence to go to the jury that he had received regular notice of dishonour ; and this ruling was not questioned, though a new trial was moved for upon another ground. I am clearly of opinion that this case was properly submitted to the jury, and properly decided by them.

COLTMAN, J. :

I am of the same opinion. If a promise to pay were necessary to give the plaintiff a right *of action, the promise to be gathered from the letters in this case, being conditional only, might not have sufficed to entitle the plaintiff to recover. I do not apprehend, however, that a promise was necessary ; an admission of liability is enough to warrant the jury in inferring that all the steps necessary to create such liability, have been duly taken. The cases cited show that admissions much less strong than those contained in the defendant's letters, will suffice for that purpose.

[*267]

MAULE, J. :

am of the same opinion. This rule was obtained on the 11th

(1) 36 R. R. 540 (1 Moo. & Rob. 41).

of June. The defendant has, therefore, succeeded in obtaining a CAMPBELL
delay of five months, which evidently was his sole object. It WEBSTER.
appeared to me at the time, that there was no ground for the
motion. The only case that has been cited for the defendant is
Burgh v. *Legge*, which has nothing at all to do with the point now
before us. *Patterson* v. *Becher* and *Wilkins* v. *Jadis* are conclusive
in favour of the plaintiff. The defendant, in his letter of the 12th
of October, 1844, after referring to some former correspondence as
to a 50*l.* bill and the accounts between the plaintiff and himself,
as to the bill in question, says that he will cause it to be paid
immediately, but insists on a particular mode of payment. The
promise to pay is absolute, but conditional only as to the mode.
The letter is an express and distinct admission of his liability on
the bill. Now, he could not be liable to pay the bill, unless there
had been a regular protest, and due notice thereof given to him.
And no jury could possibly infer from the letters any other than
that the defendant had had such notice. The only question is,
whether the evidence was properly left to them. *Wilkins* v. *Jadis*
differs from the present case only in this, that there the evidence
was considerably weaker; and still it was held sufficient to go to
the jury. I think the jury would *clearly have done wrong had   [*268]
they come to any other conclusion than that at which they arrived.
I also think that they were properly directed.

ERLE, J.:

I also am of opinion that this rule must be discharged. An
admission by a party of his liability on a bill, is an admission that
all has been done which is requisite to constitute such liability.
I think the letters in question were evidence of a protest and of
notice thereof to the defendant, both of which were necessary (1) to
entitle the plaintiff to maintain his action.

Rule discharged.

HURRELL *v.* ELLIS (2).

(2 C. B. 295—299 ; S. C. 15 L. J. C. P. 18; 9 Jur. 1013.)

1845.
Nov. 19.

By the 6 & 7 Vict. c. 86, s. 21, the proprietor of a hackney carriage is [295]
required to retain in his possession the licence of every driver, &c.,
employed by him while such driver &c. remains in his service. A declaration in case stated, that the plaintiff obtained a driver's licence under the

(1) *Vide tamen, ante,* p. 485, n. (3).   *Norris* v. *Birch* [1895] 1 Q. B. 639,
(2) See *Rogers* v. *Macnamara* (1853)   64 L. J. M. C. 91.—J. G. P.
14 C. B. 27, 23 L. J. C. P. 1 ;· and

HURRELL
*.
ELLIS.

Act; that he was employed by the defendant, a proprietor of a hackney carriage, and, under the provisions of the Act, delivered the licence to him; and that, whilst the licence remained in the defendant's possession, the latter "wrongfully and unjustly wrote in ink upon the licence certain words purporting, and then being intended by the defendant, to give a character of the plaintiff as an unfit and improper person to act as a driver of hackney carriages, that is to say," &c. &c.; by reason whereof the licence became defaced and wholly useless to the plaintiff, and the plaintiff was thereby hindered and prevented from obtaining employment as a driver, &c.: Held, on motion in arrest of judgment, that the action was maintainable, that case was the proper form, and that the declaration was sufficient.

CASE. The declaration stated, that, before the committing of the grievances thereinafter mentioned, to wit, on &c., the plaintiff, under and by virtue of, and according to the provisions of, a certain statute made and passed in the seventh year of the reign of her Majesty Queen Victoria, "for regulating hackney and stage-carriages in and near London," obtained from the registrar of metropolitan public carriages, appointed under and by virtue of the said Act, and the said registrar then, under and by virtue of, and according to the provisions of the said Act, granted to the plaintiff a licence for him the plaintiff to act as driver of hackney carriages until the 1st of June, 1846, according to the provisions of the said Act. Averment, that, whilst the plaintiff was possessed of the said licence, and whilst the said licence continued in force, and before the committing of the grievance thereinafter mentioned, to wit, on &c., the defendant, then being a proprietor of a hackney carriage within the purview of the said Act, employed the plaintiff to act as driver of such hackney carriage; and the defendant then, under and by virtue of, and according to the provisions of the said statute, delivered the said licence to the defendant, to be by the
[*296] defendant retained in his *possession while he, the plaintiff, should remain in the service of the defendant as aforesaid, according to the provisions of the said statute : Breach, that the defendant, well knowing the premises, but contriving to injure the plaintiff, and to deprive him of the benefit and advantage of the said licence, and to hinder and prevent him from obtaining employment as a driver of hackney carriages under the said licence, whilst the said licence continued in force, and whilst the same was so retained in the possession of the defendant as aforesaid, and previously to the same being returned to the plaintiff by the defendant, on the plaintiff leaving the service of the defendant as thereinafter mentioned, to wit, on &c., wrongfully and unjustly wrote in ink in and upon the said licence certain words purporting to give, and being then

intended by the defendant to give, a character of the plaintiff as   HURRELL
an unfit and improper person to act as a driver of hackney carriages,   *v.*
that is to say, " Discharged ; having been guilty of the most care-   ELLIS.
less, reckless act, in attempting to get on the box, after letting in
a fare, without the reins in hand, whereby the horse's knees were
dreadfully lacerated, and other injuries sustained : in my opinion,
is not a fit and proper person to act as driver of a hackney carriage ;
the lives of the public are in jeopardy, and the property in his care
destroyed ; " the words so written on the said licence as aforesaid,
not being any entry which, according to the provisions of the said
Act, the defendant was authorized to make in or upon the said
licence ; and that the defendant afterwards, and whilst the said
licence continued in force, to wit, on &c., last aforesaid, on which
last-mentioned day the plaintiff left the said service of the defendant, returned the said licence to the plaintiff with the said words
so written thereon as aforesaid ; by reason of which premises, the
said licence became and was defaced and damaged, and wholly
useless *to the defendant, and the defendant [was] hindered from   [*297]
obtaining employment as a driver of a hackney carriage, by certain
persons named.

The defendant pleaded, first, Not guilty ; secondly, a justification,
which was traversed by the replication.

The cause was tried before Cresswell, J., at the first sitting in
London during the present Term, when a verdict was found for the
plaintiff, damages 7*l.*

Byles, Serjt., now moved to arrest the judgment :

The declaration, which is framed upon the eighth section of the
6 & 7 Vict. c. 86, " for regulating hackney and stage-carriages in
and near London," does not disclose any thing to entitle the plaintiff to maintain an action ; or, if there were any cause of action,
the proper remedy was trespass, and not case. * * The licence   [298]
is the property of the driver. The defendant was entitled to the
custody of it, until, by his wrongful act in defacing it, he determined the bailment. The property and the right of possession
thereupon immediately revesting in the plaintiff, *trespass was the   [*299]
proper remedy ; as in the case of a common bailee of goods
breaking bulk, or otherwise unlawfully dealing with the goods.

(ERLE, J. : The licence was lawfully in the defendant's possession
at the time he defaced it.)

HURRELL
v.
ELLIS.

Assuming that the form of action is well conceived, the declaration should, at all events, have alleged that the act complained of was done maliciously. Proof that the licence was defaced by accident or by negligence, would support this declaration.

TINDAL, Ch. J.:

Suppose the defendant had so blotted and blurred the document as to render the signature of the registrar invisible, and the licence had become wholly useless, would the plaintiff have had no remedy? The allegation is, that the licence was defaced wrongfully and unjustly, and the jury, by their verdict, affirm that the act was so done. It was not necessary to aver that it was maliciously done.

MAULE, J.:

It would be very hard indeed if the plaintiff were without remedy for such an injury as this, even in the absence of malice on the part of the defendant; and, if the plaintiff has any remedy, and I am clearly of opinion that he has, it is by an action upon the case, and not in trespass.

The rest of the COURT concurred.

Rule refused.

1845.
Dec. 23.

[412]

ROBERTSON v. G. L. JACKSON AND OTHERS.

(2 C. B. 412—429; S. C. 15 L. J. C. P. 28; 10 Jur. 98.)

By a charter-party, A., the owner, agreed that the ship should proceed to the Tyne, and there load a cargo of coals, and proceed therewith to Algiers, and deliver the same there, on payment of certain freight. B., the charterer, engaged that the vessel should be unloaded at a certain average rate per day; and that, if detained for a longer period, he would "pay for such detention at the rate of 5*l.* *per diem*, to reckon from the time of the vessel being ready to unload, and in turn to deliver."

According to the general regulations of the port of Algiers, vessels may commence unloading as soon as they enter within the mole: but, by a special regulation of the French Government, coals destined for the use of the marine department are required to be unladen at a particular spot, and in a given order:

Held, that evidence was admissible to show that the words "in turn to deliver" had by the usage of the particular trade acquired a known meaning in reference to this special regulation with respect to coals for the use of the French marine department, although A. was not cognizant of the fact of the coals having been shipped under a contract with the French Government; but that the testimony of three or four witnesses, speaking to a course of business that had only grown up within about five years, and with reference to charter-parties the language of which was not

identical with that of the charter-party in question, was insufficient to   ROBERTSON
establish such general usage.   *v.*
     Held, also, that the special regulation as to the unloading of coals for   JACKSON.
the French marine department, was to be considered one of the regulations
of the port, binding upon all vessels entering the port (1).

INDEBITATUS ASSUMPSIT, for the use of a certain vessel of the
plaintiff on demurrage.   Plea, *non assumpserunt.*

The cause was tried before Tindal, Ch. J., at the sittings at
Guildhall after last Hilary Term.   The plaintiff, it appeared, was
a merchant and ship-owner residing at Pembroke, in South Wales;
the defendants are ship and insurance brokers in London, carrying
on business under the firm of G. L. Jackson & Sons.   On the 10th
of December, 1841, the following memorandum of charter was
entered into between the parties:

"Memorandum of charter-party.   It is this day mutually agreed
between W. Robertson, owner of the good ship or vessel called the
Cambria, of the burthen of 347 tons register measurement, or
thereabouts, now in the port of London, and G. L. Jackson & Sons,
of London, *as agents, that the said vessel, being tight, staunch,   [*413]
and strong, and every way fitted for the voyage, shall, with all
possible dispatch, proceed direct to Carr's or West Hartley spout,
on the Tyne, and there receive on board, in the usual manner,
from the agents of the charterers, a full and complete cargo of
coals which they bind themselves to ship, not exceeding what she
can reasonably stow and carry over and above the tackle, provisions, and furniture; and, being so loaded, shall therewith
proceed to Malta or Algiers, at charterer's option, or so near
thereto as she may safely get, and deliver the same (2) there, on
being paid freight at and after the rate of 17*l.* sterling per keel, in
full; the coals to be taken alongside, free of expense to the ship;
(the act of God, the Queen's enemies, fire, restraint of princes, and
all and every dangers and accidents of the seas, rivers, and navigation, of what nature or kind soever during the said voyage, always
excepted).   The freight to be paid by an approved bill on London,
at three months from the delivery of a certificate to the charterers,
signed by the consignees, of the right and true delivery of the
whole cargo agreeably to bills of lading, less such cash as they may

(1) Compare *Hudson* v. *Ede* (1868)   form.   It originally contained the
L. R. 3 Q. B. 412, 37 L. J. Q. B. 166,   words "at the depôt," but these words
and see *Leidemann* v. *Schultz* (1853)   were objected to by the plaintiff, and
23 L. J. C. P. 17.—J. G. P.   were struck out.

(2) The charter-party was a printed

have advanced to the master, which he is at liberty to draw to the
extent of 100l., free of interest, and less the usual commission of
5 per cent. for procuring this charter.   The charterers engage that
the said vessel shall be loaded in regular turn as customary, also
that she shall be unloaded, weather permitting, at the average rate
of not less than twenty tons of coals *per diem*, Sundays excepted;
and, if detained, on their part, during a longer period, they engage
to pay for such detention at the rate of 5l. *per diem*, to reckon from

[*414]
the time of the vessel being ready *to unload, and in turn to
deliver.   The ship to be consigned to the charterers' agents at the
port of delivery, on the usual terms.   Penalty for non-performance
of this agreement, 500l.   It is further agreed, that, after the discharge of the coals, the ship shall proceed direct to Palermo for
orders whether to load there, or at any other usual loading place in
the Two Sicilies (Terra Nova excepted), a full and complete cargo of
wheat, or other lawful merchandize, for a safe port in the United
Kingdom, calling at Cork or Falmouth for orders, if required, for
the freight of 6s. per quarter of wheat, or 28s. per ton of 20 cwt. of
brimstone, net at the Queen's beam, and for all other goods in proportion to these rates, in full, an extra 6d. per quarter of wheat to be
paid should the vessel load wheat at any other place than Palermo.
Forty running days are allowed for loading and unloading the homeward cargo, from the vessel being in pratique, and ready to load
and unload.   The ship to be consigned to the charterers' agents,
who are to have the option of cancelling the charter-party, should
the vessel not reach Palermo on or before the 1st day of March
next.   Mats for the proper dunnage of the cargo, to be provided
at the charterer's expense.   It is agreed that no more than 5 per
cent. commission is to be charged on the homeward cargo, which is
to be sent alongside and taken from alongside free of expense to the
ship.   Cash to be advanced the master at his loading port abroad
for ship's use, not exceeding 100l., against his draft on his owner."

The following memorandum was indorsed on the charter-party:

"LONDON, 16th December, 1841.

"It is now mutually agreed that so much of this charter-party
as relates to the homeward voyage, shall be null and void in the
event of the ship being unable *to sail from Algiers or Malta, after

[*415]
the discharge of the coals, on or before the 24th of February next,
in which case the charterers are to receive 18l. in lieu of commission
on the homeward freight."

Under this charter-party, the *Cambria* proceeded to the river   ROBERTSON
Tyne, and there took in a cargo of coals, consisting of 198 chaldrons,   *v.*
with which she sailed, and arrived at Algiers on the 15th of March,   JACKSON.
1842. The captain, having cast anchor in the bay, went on shore,
and reported his arrival to Lacroutz, the consignee named in the
bill of lading, stating that he was ready to discharge. He was
then, for the first time, informed that the coals had been shipped
by the defendants, under a contract with the French Government,
for the service of the marine department, under, amongst others,
the following regulations as to unloading and delivery :

"Vessels bound for Algiers, Bona, and Bougie, shall proceed to
the roads of those three ports. The captains shall announce their
arrival to the senior naval officer, and shall conform themselves to
the instructions of this officer, with regard to placing the vessels to
unload. The discharge shall commence, at the latest, the third day
after the vessel shall have taken its assigned station. As in each
of the ports of delivery it will not be possible to appoint more
than one commission of receipt, the contractor should make his
arrangements that two vessels should not arrive at the same
port at the same time : but, if, notwithstanding this precaution,
one vessel shall arrive at the same time with another, or before the
discharge of the first shall be finished, it is then to be understood
that the delay (1) of three days before stipulated shall not run, but
shall date from the day when the discharge of the vessel or vessels
arriving before it, shall be completely finished."

The *Cambria* went into the harbour of Algiers, within the mole,   [416]
the general place of discharge, on the 19th of March, and there took
up a berth whence she might have been at once unloaded, but for
the special regulation above referred to. There being, however,
several other vessels at Algiers laden with coals consigned by the
defendants to Lacroutz for the use of the French Government, that
had arrived before the *Cambria*, her "turn to deliver," pursuant to
the defendants' contract with the French Government did not arrive
until the 27th of April, on which day Lacroutz required the captain
to proceed for that purpose to the Government inlet, in another
part of the harbour, which he did under protest. The unloading
commenced on the 29th of April.

On the part of the plaintiff it was insisted, that, according to the
true construction of the charter-party the unloading at Algiers was

———————————————

(1) " *Délai*," "appointed term" or "fixed period."

ROBERTSON
v.
JACKSON.

to commence as soon as the *Cambria* took up such a position in the port as to entitle her to begin to discharge her cargo according to the general regulations of the port.

On the other hand, it was contended that the language of the charter-party was such as to challenge inquiry, and that the plaintiff was bound to take notice that there was some particular "turn" or rotation for the discharge of the vessel, as to which he might have more specifically informed himself before he signed the charter-party.

In order to sustain their construction of the charter-party, the defendants attempted to show that there was a known, recognised course of trade in London with reference to the export of coals for the use of the French Government on the coast of Africa, such a general and universal practice, well known amongst all persons conversant with the trade, that the plaintiff might fairly be presumed to have been aware of it, and to have entered into the charter-party with reference to it. Four witnesses, ship-brokers and merchants,

[*417] were called to *speak to this custom. It was proposed, on the part of the defendants, to ask these witnesses whether there was any general understood meaning of the words " in turn to deliver," amongst ship-owners and merchants engaged in this particular trade. The question was objected to on the part of the plaintiff, but the objection was disallowed.

The witnesses stated, that, in the year 1836, the export of coals, under contracts, for the use of the British Government, had much increased; and that, since the year 1841, a considerable trade had been carried on, principally confined to three mercantile houses in London (of which the defendants' firm was one), in the export of coals to the coast of Africa for the use of the French Government.

Upon its being objected, on the part of the plaintiff, that this practice was of too recent date, and too limited in its character, to establish a course of dealing that would bind the plaintiff, a ship-owner wholly unconnected with the particular trade, and that there was no evidence to show the particular form of charter under which the shipments referred to took place, the defendants put in four charter-parties applicable to this particular description of trade. The first of these was produced by one Arnold, a ship-broker, who stated that it was a form that he had adopted for about two years: the stipulation for delivery of the coals was as follows: " To be delivered in her regular turn alongside craft, steamers, floating depôt, or pier, as the consignee may direct." The second and third ROBERTSON
v.
JACKSON. were produced by one Chapman: the one stipulated for a delivery "on the ship being in turn, ready to deliver into a steamer or a depôt at Constantinople:" the other stipulated that the vessel should "proceed to her Majesty's dock-yard, and deliver the cargo in her regular turn into store or the depôt ship there." The fourth was produced by one Day, and *stipulated that the ship should [*418] "proceed to a port indicated, and there deliver the cargo in her regular turn alongside craft, steamer, floating depôt, or pier."

There were no general regulations of the port of Algiers as to the turn of unloading coals or any other merchandize.

With regard to what took place at Algiers in reference to the unloading of the *Cambria*, the case, as well on the part of the plaintiff as on that of the defendants, rested mainly upon the examination and cross-examination of the captain upon interrogatories before one of the Masters, and upon the examination and cross-examination of Lacroutz and several other witnesses at Algiers under a commission. From these it appeared that the port of Algiers is governed by a director and officer of the Royal navy, appointed by the French Government; that no vessel laden with coals consigned for the use of the French marine department was permitted to unload except subject to the special regulation already mentioned; that several vessels laden with coals so consigned by other parties, which had arrived at Algiers since the *Cambria*, were unloaded at the Government inlet before that vessel, but that none of those consigned by the defendants, that had arrived subsequently to the *Cambria*, had been permitted to take precedence of her in discharging at that place; and that there had been no unnecessary delay on the part of the defendants' agent at Algiers in dispatching the vessel consistently with their contract with the French Government. It also appeared that vessels destined for the general trade at Algiers were incumbered with no such special regulations, and consequently were able to discharge coals and other merchandize at the mole without any difficulty or delay.

For the plaintiff, it was submitted that the evidence failed to establish the usage attempted to be set up; and *that the [*419] regulations of the marine department with reference to which the defendants' contract with the French Government had been entered into, were not to be taken into consideration in construing the charter-party, as if they had been general regulations of the port.

ROBERTSON
v.
JACKSON.

For the defendants it was insisted that the regulation in question in effect formed part of the general regulations of the port, and was binding upon all who entered it with coals for the use of the French marine department.

In presenting the case to the jury, the LORD CHIEF JUSTICE told them, that, if they considered it proved to their satisfaction that there was a course of trade in London relative to the export of coals to Algiers for the use of the French Government, so universally well known amongst all persons conversant with the trade that the plaintiff might fairly be presumed to have been cognizant of its particular regulations at the time he executed the charter-party, they must find for the defendants. But that, if, on the other hand, such course of trade was not made out to their satisfaction, the next question for their consideration was, what was the meaning of the expression " in turn to deliver " in the charter-party—whether the terms of the contract were such that they could only be satisfied by an unloading in turn at the Government inlet, as suggested by the defendants; or whether they might not be satisfied by an unloading in any other part of the harbour, in the same manner as vessels with coals, or other merchandize, not destined for the service of the marine department, were usually unloaded, as contended for on the part of the plaintiff.

The jury returned a verdict for the defendants.

[*420]

Sir T. Wilde, Serjt. (with whom was *J. P. Wilde*), in Easter Term last, obtained a rule *nisi* for a new trial, on *the ground that improper effect had been given to the evidence of usage, which, he submitted, was not admissible to control the charter-party, and that the verdict was against evidence. He cited *Randall* v. *Lynch* (1), *Hill* v. *Idle* (2), *Harman* v. *Clarke* (3), *Barret* v. *Dutton* (4), *Leer* v. *Yates* (5), *Brereton* v. *Chapman* (6), and *Bottomley* v. *Forbes* (7).

Channell and *Shee*, Serjts. (with whom was *Bovill*), in . Michaelmas Term, showed cause :

The expression in this charter-party, " in turn to deliver," being ambiguous, it clearly was competent to the defendants to show *aliundè* that these words had a known meaning amongst persons

---

(1) 11 R. R. 340, 727 (2 Camp. 352).

(2) 16 R. R. 797 (4 Camp. 327).

(3) 16 R. R. 768 (4 Camp. 159).

(4) 16 R. R. 798 (4 Camp. 333).

(5) 12 R. R. 671 (3 Taunt. 387).

(6) 33 R. R. 573 (7 Bing. 559 ; 5 Moo. & P. 526).

(7) 50 R. R. 629 (5 Bing. N. C. 121; 6 Scott, 816).

connected with the particular trade to which the contract in question ROBERTSON
related. [See *Robertson* v. *French* (1), *Hutton* v. *Warren* (2), and   v.
Cochran v. *Retberg* (3).]   In *Haynes* v. *Holliday* (4), the defendant,   JACKSON.
the master of a vessel, agreed in writing to take out to the Cape of   [421]
Good Hope a boat belonging to the plaintiff, not exceeding thirty
feet in length and ten in width; the plaintiff tendered a boat within
these dimensions, but it was a decked boat; the defendant refused
to take it on board unless the deck were removed; evidence was
given that it was the custom to remove the decks of such boats, as
they tended to impede the navigation of the vessel; and it was held
that such evidence was properly received.

(MAULE, J.: Suppose a party contracted to convey a lion, could
there be any doubt that evidence *would be admissible to show   [*422]
that it was customary to put animals of that description into
cages?)

* * None of the cases cited on the motion does more than recog-   [423]
nise the principle laid down in *Lewis* v. *Marshall* (5). The words " in
turn to deliver " were inserted in this charter-party for an obvious
purpose.   And the trade in question being in few hands, and
having grown up so recently, better evidence of usage could hardly
be expected. The words " in turn to deliver " can have no sensible
meaning, until explained by evidence as to the regulations and
practice of the port of delivery: and the regulation under which
the contractors here were bound to deliver in a particular order
coals shipped for the use of the French marine department,
was equally binding with the general regulations of the port of
Algiers.

Sir T. Wilde, Serjt. (with whom was *J. P. Wilde*), in support
of the rule :

There is nothing upon the face of this charter-party to show
that the contract between the plaintiff and the defendants, was
entered into with reference to any engagement by the latter for the
supply of coals to the French Government. And it would be
imposing a monstrous hardship upon a ship-owner who has let his
ship under a general charter like this, to hold him bound by the

(1) 7 R. R. 535, per Lord ELLEN-   (4) 33 R. R. 580 (7 Bing. 587; 5
BOROUGH, at p. 540 (4 East, 130, 135).   Moo. & P. 572).
(2) 46 R. R. 368, per PARKE, B. at   (5) 66 R. R. 777 (7 Man. & G. 729;
p. 377 (1 M. & W. 466, 475).   8 Scott, N. R. 477).
(3) 3 Esp. N. P. C. 121.

ROBERTSON
v.
JACKSON.
[*424]

terms of a contract entered into by the charterers with some third party, of which *he has no notice.   The ship-owner would, of course, be bound by any general regulations of the port to which his vessel is addressed, but not by particular stipulations contained in a private contract entered into by the charterers with any one else.   The evidence of usage was not admissible for the purpose for which it was offered ; and even if admissible it was not cogent.   It was much too limited in its character, and was too recent in point of date.   Evidence of custom or usage to control written contracts, is at all times most unsatisfactory, and difficult of application, and has always been admitted with reluctance and regret.   It is only upon the ground that it is so universal, and so well known that the parties must be supposed to have been dealing with reference to it, and to have intended to ingraft it upon their bargain.   [Custom or usage is binding only on those who are acquainted with it and have consented to be bound by it.   He cited and commented on *Bottomley* v. *Forbes, Gabay* v. *Lloyd* (1), *Bartlett* v. *Pentland* (2), and *Scott* v. *Irving* (3).]

[425]

(ERLE, J. : In those cases the evidence was offered for the purpose of modifying the contract ; to control the plain meaning of the words used.)

[426]

This is not like the case of *Smith* v. *Wilson* (4), where evidence was admitted to show, that, by the custom of the country, the word "thousand," as applied to rabbits, denoted "twelve hundred." The words "in turn to deliver" will be satisfied by a turn or rotation according to the general regulations of the port that bind all who enter it, without limiting their interpretation by the terms of some secret contract the charterers have entered into with strangers.   The evidence of usage, therefore, was not receivable, and, supposing the evidence to have been receivable, it failed to establish such a known and universal usage as the contracting parties might be presumed to have had in their minds when the charter-party was made.

Cur. adv. vult.

TINDAL, Ch. J., now delivered the judgment of the COURT :

This was an action brought by the owner of the ship *Cambria*

(1) 27 R. R. 486 (3 B. & C. 793; 5
Dowl. & Ry. 641).
(2) 34 R. R. 560 (10 B. & C. 760).

(3) 35 R. R. 396 (1 B. & Ad. 605).
(4) 37 R. R. 536 (3 B. & Ad. 728).

against the charterers of that ship, to recover damages under the charter, for her detention at Algiers from the 19th of March, when she was ready to deliver her cargo, until the 29th of April, when her discharge actually commenced. The jury found a verdict for the defendants; and the case comes before the Court upon a motion to set aside that verdict, and for a new trial, first, upon the ground that evidence was improperly received ; and, secondly, that the verdict itself was against the weight of the evidence.

The question upon the trial turned upon the clause in the charter-party which related to the delivery of the cargo, viz. that the vessel should be loaded in regular turn, as customary, and also that she should be unloaded, *weather permitting, at a certain rate *per diem*, and, if detained longer, " the charterers engage to pay for such detention, at the rate of 5l. *per diem*, to reckon from the time of the vessel being ready to unload, and in turn to deliver : " and the contest was, as to the meaning of the term " in turn to deliver."

The particular question to which an objection was taken at the trial, was, whether there was any general understood meaning of those words amongst ship-owners and merchants entering into charter-parties with respect to the commerce or business then under investigation. And we think, so far as the question is concerned, there could be no possible objection to it. The plaintiff had a right to prove his case, and the defendants an equal right to prove theirs, if the facts would allow them respectively to do so, by proving that the contract was entered into with reference to a known recognised use of the particular terms employed in, or amongst those persons conversant with, the line of commerce or business to which it relates. And, although the answers given by the witnesses failed altogether in establishing such usage, the inquiry itself was unobjectionable.

The cause, therefore, proceeded upon the investigation, by evidence, into the meaning of those words, with reference to the subject-matter of the contract.

The words, in themselves, bear no precise meaning, until they obtain their application by the evidence. No Judge or jury, looking only at the contract itself, can discover when it is that the ship *Cambria's* turn to deliver will arrive, or, consequently, from what day the demurrage is to be calculated. Evidence, therefore, is necessary to explain how those words apply themselves to the regulations and practice of the port of Algiers, where the delivery

ROBERTSON
v.
JACKSON

[*427]

ROBERTSON
v.
JACKSON.

[*428]

of the cargo was to be made. And, accordingly, at the trial, evidence was given by both *parties on this point; and the contention now before us is, whether the weight of such evidence was in favour of the plaintiff or the defendants; the plaintiff insisting, that, upon the evidence, the turn for delivery by the *Cambria* had, by those regulations which can be considered as properly the regulations of the port of Algiers, come to her long before the 29th of April, and that the delay in her delivery was occasioned solely by reason of some private regulations of the department of the French Royal marine, for the use of which these coals had been consigned.

But, upon looking at the evidence, we think there is no room for this distinction; but that the regulations of the French Royal marine form part of those regulations of the port by which this question is to be decided. There seems no principle upon which the regulations of the port are to be held strictly confined to those which have been declared by the Government itself; but that they may well include all such regulations as are made, and are actually enforced, with the sanction and approbation of the Government; under which latter description the regulations made by the department of the French Royal marine must be considered to fall.

Taking, therefore, the interpretation of the words to be, turn of delivery in conformity with the regulations of the port of Algiers, the question really becomes one of parcel or no parcel—was the regulation under which this delivery took place, a regulation of the port or not? And we think, upon the evidence, it was.

It was strongly pressed upon us, that a great hardship would be imposed upon the ship-owner who lets his ship by a general charter, if he is to be affected by the consequences of a contract by the charterer to which he is altogether a stranger. But we think the answer is, that he knew, generally, the purpose for which the ship was taken, and her destination, and might have *inquired as to the particular object of the charterers; the more particularly as the uncertainty of the expression "in turn to deliver" might fairly provoke such inquiry.

[*429]

We think, for these reasons, the rule *nisi* for a new trial should be discharged.

           Rule discharged.

IN THE EXCHEQUER CHAMBER.

ELLIOTT *v.* TURNER AND OTHERS.

(2 C. B. 446—462; S. C. 15 L. J. C. P. 49.)

1845.
Nov. 29.

The word " or " in its proper sense is a disjunctive particle and ought so
to be construed in a patent unless there is something in the context to give
it a different meaning or unless the facts properly in evidence, and with
reference to which the patent must be construed, show that a different
interpretation ought to be made.

[446]

[THIS was an action in covenant upon an indenture by which the
plaintiff granted to the defendants a licence to make and sell
buttons according to letters-patent granted to the plaintiff, and the
issue was whether certain buttons made by the defendants were
made according to the letters-patent and therefore under the
licence. The facts and the course of the proceedings sufficiently
appear from the judgment of PARKE, B.]

The jury having returned a verdict for the defendants, the case
came before this Court by writ of error, and was argued in Trinity
vacation last, before Parke, B., Patteson, J., Alderson, B.,
Williams, J., Coleridge, J., Wightman, J., Rolfe, B., and Platt, B.

[457]

M. Smith (with whom was *Webster*), for the plaintiff (1). * * *

Sir T. Wilde, Serjt. [(with whom were *Rotch* and *H. Hill*),
contrà. * * *

[458]

M. Smith, in reply. * * *

[459]

Cur. adv. vult.

PARKE, B., now delivered the judgment of the COURT:

The question in this case arises upon an exception to the
direction of my brother COLTMAN, in an action tried before him on
a covenant by the defendants to pay the plaintiff, the patentee, a
stipulated allowance for all buttons made by the defendants according to the plaintiff's patent, pursuant to a licence. The issue was,
whether certain buttons made by the defendants, called *Italian
twist dress buttons, were made under the licence to use the
plaintiff's patent.

[*460]

(1) The point marked for argument
on the part of the plaintiff, was as
follows :
  "That soft silk suitable for making
satins, and organzine silk suitable for
making satins, and any silk counter-
feiting, imitating, and resembling such
soft and organzine silk, are within the
licence and letters-patent, or one of
them."

The material parts of the specification are as follows: "The third part of my invention, being the application of such fabrics only wherein the ground or face of the ground thereof is produced by a warp of soft or organzine silk, such as is used in weaving satin, and the classes of fabrics produced therefrom." And again, "Thirdly, I claim the application of such figured woven fabrics to the covering of buttons with flexible shanks, made by pressure in dies, as have the ground or face of the ground woven with soft or organzine silk for the warp, when such fabrics have ornamental designs or figures for the centres of buttons."

On the trial, much evidence was given on both sides; the witnesses for the plaintiff stating that the buttons of the defendants were made with organzine silk; those for the defendants, that they were not; but the latter deposed that the buttons were made of a material called twist, which might be termed soft silk; organzine being a species of silk thread in which there is a spire or twist of each of the threads singly, before they are twisted together; and twist being a description of silk in which two or more threads are twisted together, each thread not having been previously twisted.

The learned Judge summed up the evidence to the jury on both sides, leaving to them the question whether the buttons made by the defendants were made of soft or organzine silk within the meaning of that part of the specification.

At the close of the summing up, the foreman of the jury said it would much assist the jury, if the learned Judge would tell them how they were to interpret the word "or" in the specification— whether it was disjunctive, or whether "organzine" was the construction of the word "soft;" and thereupon the learned [*461]   Judge *gave it as his opinion, that, unless the silk was organzine, it was not within the patent. The counsel for the plaintiff excepted to that opinion, and insisted that "soft silk," although not "organzine," was within the patent and licence.

We are all of opinion that the exception was well founded, and that the direction of the learned Judge was not correct.

The word "or," in its ordinary and proper sense, is a disjunctive particle; and the meaning of the term "soft or organzine," is, properly, either one or the other; and so it ought to be construed, unless there be something in the context to give it a different meaning, or unless the facts properly in evidence, and with reference to which the patent must be construed, should show that a different interpretation ought to be made.

There was nothing in the context to lead to a different construction of the words; but the facts might be such, that, applying the specification of the patent to them, the word " or " ought to be construed, not in its proper sense, but as giving another description of the same thing, and the words read as if they had been " soft, otherwise called organzine, silk: " and, if the fact was, that, at the date of the specification, organzine was the only species of soft silk in known use in weaving satin, that would be a sufficient ground for construing the specification, which applies to such soft or organzine silk as was then used, to mean to apply to " soft, *alias* organzine silk," and include organzine only. But, if there was soft silk, as well as organzine, used for the purpose at the time of the specification, then the words must be construed in their proper sense, and both species would be within the patent.

The interpretation, therefore, which the learned Judge put upon the specification was not correct, unless the facts were such as to lead to it; and those facts were *for the determination of the jury.   [*462]
The learned Judge should not have told the jury, absolutely, that soft and organzine silk were the same : he should have stated that the words were capable of being so construed, if the jury were satisfied, that, at the date of the specification, only one description of soft silk, and that, organzine, was used in satin weaving; but, otherwise, that the proper and ordinary sense of the words was to be adopted, and the patent held to apply to every species of soft silk, as well as to organzine silk. It was argued that the learned Judge's observations must be understood in connection with the facts proved at the trial, and that it proved the fact that organzine was the only known species of soft silk used in weaving satin at the date of the specification. But the answer is, that it is the bill of exceptions only that states the evidence : none of the other facts proved at the trial are found by the jury ; and none of them can be assumed to be true : and, as the construction of the specification depended on the facts, the question as to the truth of those facts should have been left to the jury.

There must therefore be a *venire de novo*.

Venire de novo (1).

(1) Upon the second trial, at the sittings at Westminster after Trinity Term, 1846, the jury returned a verdict for the plaintiff ; which verdict the defendants did not seek to disturb.

1846.
Jan. 12.

LEWIS v. LORD KENSINGTON.

(2 C. B. 463—475; S. C. 3 Dowl. & L. 637; 15 L. J. C. P. 100.)

[463]

In the attestation of the execution of a warrant of attorney or *cognovit*, under the 1 & 2 Vict. c. 110, s. 9 (1), it is not necessary that the precise words of the statute should be followed: it is enough if it appears by necessary inference, that the witness attended as the attorney for the party, at his request, and that he subscribed his name as such attorney.

[*464]

TALFOURD, Serjt., in Trinity Term last, moved for a rule *nisi* to set aside a warrant of attorney given by the defendant, and the judgment signed thereon, *upon the ground that it was not properly attested pursuant to the 1 & 2 Vict. c. 110, s. 9. The attestation was as follows : " Signed, sealed, and delivered in the presence of Henry Whittaker, 10, Lincoln's Inn, attorney for the said William Lord Kensington, and expressly named by him and attending at his request. And I hereby subscribe myself to be the attorney for him, having read over and explained to him the nature and effect of the above warrant of attorney, before the same was executed by him. And I hereby subscribe my name as a witness to the due execution thereof."

The attestation clause was a printed form, with a blank for the name of the attorney. There was no affidavit that the name " Henry Whittaker," at the end of the first sentence of it, was not the handwriting of that gentleman.

(CRESSWELL, J. : The statute requires that there shall be present an attorney on behalf of the defendant, and that he shall be expressly named by him, and shall attend at his request to inform him of the nature and effect of the instrument. It is not denied that all this has been done. The Act further requires the attorney to subscribe his name as a witness to the execution of the instrument. Here, he has done so. And he is to declare himself to be attorney for the defendant, and state that he subscribes as such attorney. Has he not done all that ?

MAULE, J. : The attesting witness has done all that the statute requires, and something more. This objection therefore fails.)

* The attestation clause is not subscribed at all. The witness does not pledge himself to a subscription as attorney for the party. He merely subscribes himself to be the attorney. * * *

(1) Repealed by 32 & 33 Vict. c. 83, s. 20. See now 32 & 33 Vict. c. 62, s. 24.—J. G. P.

A rule *nisi* having been granted,

Sir *T. Wilde*, and *Channell*, Serjts., in Michaelmas Term, showed cause. * * *

Talfourd, Serjt. (with whom was *Peacock*), in support of the rule. * * *

Cur. adv. vult.

TINDAL, Ch. J., now delivered the judgment of the COURT :

The question in this case is, whether a warrant of attorney executed by Lord Kensington was properly attested, within the meaning of the statute 1 & 2 Vict. c. 110, s. 9. By that Act it is provided that no warrant of attorney or *cognovit* shall be of any force, " unless there shall be present some attorney of one of the superior Courts on behalf of such person, expressly named by him, and attending at his request to inform him of the nature and effect of such warrant or *cognovit* before the same is executed ; which attorney shall subscribe his name as a witness to the due execution thereof, and thereby declare himself to be attorney for the person executing the same, and state that he subscribes as such attorney."

The Act, therefore, requires the attorney so named to be present and acting on behalf of the defendant, both before and at the time of the execution of the warrant of attorney and also afterwards, when he gives authenticity to the execution by signing his name as a witness ; and, in order to secure this, the Act directs that he shall, in the attestation, declare that he is the attorney of the defendant, and state that he subscribes as such attorney.

In the present case the attestation was as follows : " Signed, sealed, and delivered in the presence of H. *Whittaker, 10, Lincoln's Inn, attorney for the said Lord Kensington, expressly named by him, and attending at his request ; and I hereby subscribe myself to be the attorney for him, having read over and explained to him the nature and effect of the above warrant of attorney, before the same was executed by him ; and I hereby subscribe my name as a witness to the due execution thereof."

To this attestation two objections were taken. It was contended, first, that there was no proper subscription of his name by the attesting witness, the name appearing in the middle of the attestation, and not at the end of it, and that it is uncertain whether the words subsequent to the name " H. Whittaker " are to be considered as the words of Whittaker or not. But it must in all cases be a matter of extrinsic proof, whether the name of the attesting witness is in his handwriting; and, in the present case, it appears that the name "H. Whittaker" was in the proper handwriting of the witness: and it seems to us that the precise place where the name is written, is not material, so long as it appears upon the face of the attestation, that the attestation contains an assertion that all has been done by the witness which the Act requires; for, the Act does not require the witness to subscribe his name at the foot of the attestation, but only that he shall subscribe his name as a witness to the due execution thereof; and therefore the name seems to us not inaptly to be placed immediately after the words "signed, sealed, and delivered:" and, as there is no other subscribing witness than Whittaker, it is clear that the concluding words, "I hereby subscribe my name as a witness to the due execution thereof," must be taken to be the words of the witness, who is the only person speaking; and, consequently, in conformity to the ordinary rules of grammatical construction, the preceding words, "I *hereby subscribe myself to be the attorney," &c., must also be taken to be his words. This objection, therefore, we think, ought not to prevail.

[*473]

The second and principal objection was, that the attestation did comply literally with the Act of Parliament; as it was said that it neither contained a declaration by the witness that he was the attorney, nor a statement that he had subscribed it as such attorney. In support of this objection various cases were cited, all of which, however, may, we think, be distinguished from the present. The first was *Poole* v. *Hobbs* (1). In that case, the attestation was as follows: "Witness, George Edwards, defendant's attorney, named by him, and attending at his request." The attestation in that case contained no express statement that the witness subscribed as the attorney for the defendant, nor anything that could be considered as equivalent. The next case cited was *Potter* v. *Nicholson* (2). The attestation was as follows: "Joseph Bamford, one of the attorneys of her Majesty's Court of Exchequer of Pleas at Westminster, attending for the said William Nicholson, at his request, to, and did, inform him of the nature and effect of the above *cognovit* before the execution thereof by him." This attestation was also defective, as it did not state that he subscribed as such attorney. The next case cited was *Elkington* v. *Holland* (3). The

(1) 8 Dowl. P. C. 113.   (3) 9 M. & W. 659; 1 Dowl. N. S.
(2) 8 M. & W. 294.   643.

attestation in that case was as follows: " Signed, sealed, and
delivered by the said Joseph Ankers in my presence; and I subscribe myself as attorney for the said Joseph Ankers, expressly
named by him to attest the execution of these presents." This
attestation was held insufficient, by ALDERSON, B., because it did not
contain any express statement that Ankers was the attorney; the
statement that he subscribed as the *attorney not amounting to a
declaration that he was the attorney. The next case cited was
Ererard v. *Poppleton* (1). The attestation there was—" Signed,
sealed, and delivered by the above-named George Charles Poppleton
in the presence of us, of whom the said John Hope Shaw is the
attorney expressly named by him, and acting at his request, and by
whom the above-written warrant of attorney was read over, and the
nature and effect thereof explained to the said George Charles
Poppleton before the execution thereof by him. JOHN HOPE SHAW,
attorney, Leeds. JOHN RICHARDSON." This attestation was also
held defective, as not containing any statement that the witness
subscribed as such attorney. The last case, and the one most
relied upon, was *Hibbert* v. *Barton* (2). The attestation in that
case was as follows: " Witnessed by me, W. Pemberton, as the
attorney of the said William Barton, attending at the execution
hereof at his request, and expressly named by him. WILLIAM
PEMBERTON, Prescot, Lancashire." The objection urged (and which
the Court appears to have acceded to,) was, that the attestation did
not contain an express allegation that the witness was the attorney
employed in the transaction, but only a statement that he witnessed
it as the attorney.

The present case, however, is, we think, distinguishable from all
these cases; for, the attestation contains, first, the words " signed,
sealed, and delivered in the presence of H. Whittaker, attorney for
the said Lord Kensington, expressly named by him, and attending
at his request: " and this appears to us a sufficient allegation of
his being the attorney employed in the business by Lord Kensington; and for this the case of *Knight* v. *Hasty* (3) is an express
authority. And we think that *the words immediately following
the signature, " I hereby subscribe myself to be the attorney for
him," are equivalent to an allegation that he subscribes as such
attorney.

We think, therefore, that, in this case, there has been a

[*474]

[*475]

(1) 64 R. R. 461 (5 Q. B. 181).   434.
(2) 10 M. & W. 678; 2 Dowl. N. S.   (3) 12 L. J. Q. B. 293.

LEWIS
v.
LORD KEN-
SINGTON.

substantial compliance with the requisitions of the statute, and that
the rule ought to be discharged ; and, as there is no justice in the
defendant's complaint, that it should be discharged with costs.

Rule discharged with costs.

1846.
Jan. 13.
——
[476]

BURN *v.* BOULTON.
(2 C. B. 476—487 ; S. C. 15 L. J. C. P. 97.)

Where there is an admitted and ascertained debt due from the defendant
to the plaintiff and another debt which was always disputed by the
defendant and a payment of a small amount without any specific appropriation, there is evidence from which a jury may infer the payment was
made on account of the admitted debt so as to take the case out of the
Statute of Limitations.

DEBT. The first count was upon a promissory note, dated the
15th of August, 1827, made by the defendant in favour of the
plaintiff, for 130*l.*, with interest at 4½ per cent., payable on demand.
There were also counts for work and labour, money lent, and money
due upon an account stated.

The defendant pleaded : first, to the first count, that he did not
make the note ; secondly, to the subsequent counts, *nunquam
indebitatus ;* thirdly, to the whole declaration, the Statute of
Limitations.

[*477]

The cause was tried before Erle, J., at the sittings in *London
after Trinity Term last. It appeared that the action was brought
to recover 284*l.* 12*s.* 8*d.*, principal and interest, alleged to be due
upon the promissory note, and seventeen years' wages alleged to be
due from the defendant to the plaintiff as a domestic servant.

The facts of the case were these : The plaintiff, who had formerly
been a nurse in a lunatic asylum at Manchester, and was distantly
related to the defendant, some time in the year 1827 went to his
house to attend upon a relation who lived with him, and was of
unsound mind. The plaintiff, having 130*l.* in a Bank at Manchester,
drew out that sum, and deposited it with the defendant, receiving
from him the promissory note mentioned in the declaration. After
the decease of the person whom she originally came to attend, the
plaintiff continued to reside with the defendant, and remained with
him until October, 1844. There was no distinct evidence of the
character in which the plaintiff so remained in the defendant's
family : but it appeared that she made herself generally useful in
the house, and that she took her meals sometimes with him and

sometimes in the kitchen. It also appeared, that, in 1834, there had been a settlement between the plaintiff and the defendant of the amount due for interest on the note ; no claim being then made by the plaintiff in respect of wages.

To take the case out of the Statute of Limitations, the plaintiff relied upon the evidence of Anne Boulton, the defendant's daughter, who stated that the defendant was in the habit of giving the plaintiff small sums of money whenever she asked for it, and that, on the 11th of October, 1844, when the plaintiff was about to leave the defendant's house, the defendant offered her two sovereigns, of which she took only one. The defendant never on any occasion admitted that the plaintiff was entitled to wages, but, on the contrary, asserted that she resided with him merely as a friend, and that the *small services that a person of her advanced age was capable of rendering, were amply compensated by her board and lodging.

[*478]

On the part of the defendant it was insisted, upon the authority of *Tippets* v. *Heane* (1), that there was no evidence to take the case out of the statute, inasmuch as it was not shown that the payments spoken of, were made specifically on account of the note.

The learned Judge suggested that the plaintiff should have a verdict for the amount claimed for principal and interest on the note, subject to the opinion of the Court as to whether or not there was any evidence of a part-payment in respect of that debt. This suggestion being acceded to by the counsel on both sides, the learned Judge left it to the jury to say whether or not there had been any service on the part of the plaintiff upon a contract, or understanding, that she was to receive wages, and, if so, what, under the circumstances, would be a reasonable compensation for such services as she appeared to have rendered ; and whether or not there had been any part-payment on account of wages, within six years.

The jury returned a verdict for the plaintiff for 341l. 12s. 8d., being 234l. 12s. 8d. for principal and interest on the note, 77l. for wages for the first eleven years of the plaintiff's residence with the defendant, at 7l. per annum, and 30l. for the last six years, at 5l. per annum. And leave was reserved to the defendant to move to reduce the verdict to 30l.

Byles, Serjt., in Michaelmas Term last, accordingly obtained a

(1) 40 R. R. 549 (1 Cr. M. & R. 252 ; 4 Tyr. 772).

rule *nisi* to reduce the verdict by the amount of the note and interest, or by the eleven years' wages, or by both sums. The 30*l.* had already been paid *under an order for speedy execution. He cited *Tippets* v. *Heane, Mills* v. *Fowkes* (1), and *Waugh* v. *Cope* (2).

Shee, Serjt. (with whom was *Lush*), now showed cause:

After the cases of *Tippets* v. *Heane, Mills* v. *Fowkes*, and *Waugh* v. *Cope*, it is impossible to contend that there was evidence of any payment to take the case out of the statute, in respect of services rendered by the plaintiff beyond six years from the commencement of the action. But, as to the promissory note, the case is different. It was distinctly proved, that, when the plaintiff first went to reside with the defendant, she deposited with him 130*l.*, upon his promissory note, payable on demand, with interest at $4\frac{1}{2}$ per cent. ; that interest was paid upon the note down to the year 1834 ; that various small sums were from time to time paid by the defendant to the plaintiff; and that, in October, 1844, the last payment of 1*l.* was made. These payments would, in the absence of any specific appropriation by the parties, appropriate themselves to the older debt (3), viz. that upon the promissory note. The presumption, therefore, would be, that they were part-payments on account of the note. Besides, the defendant's whole case was based upon the assumption that there was no debt at all due for wages. It is, therefore, not competent to him now to suggest that the payments were made on account of a debt, the existence of which he denies, when there was a debt clearly and unequivocally due, to which they may be ascribed.

(ERLE, J.: If there was a *scintilla* of evidence from which the jury could find the 1*l.* given to the plaintiff on the 11th of October, 1844, to have been a part-payment on account *of the note, it is, by the agreement of the parties, to be taken that they have so found.)

There clearly was some evidence to warrant the jury in finding the payments made to have been on account of the note.

Byles, Serjt. (with whom was *R. Miller*), in support of the rule :

There was no evidence to go to the jury of any part-payment

(1) 50 R. R. 750 (5 Bing. N. C. 455 ; 7 Scott, 444).

(2) 55 R. R. 801 (6 M. & W. 824).

(3) See *Clayton's* case, 15 R. R. 161 (1 Mer. 604) ; *Biggs* v. *Dwight*, 1 Man. & Ry. 308 ; 4 Nev. & M. 17, *n.*

specifically made on account either of the promissory note, or of that
portion of the claim for wages that accrued more than six years
before the commencement of the action. * * *Willis* v. *Newham* (1)
and other cases have decided that a verbal acknowledgment of
payment of a part of a debt within six years, is not sufficient
(within the 9 Geo. IV. c. 14) to take the case out of the Statute of
Limitations.

(TINDAL, Ch. J.: You may prove the payment by the testimony of
a witness who saw the money handed over.)

To give a part-payment the effect of taking a case out of the statute,
it must be shown to have been expressly made in respect of the
particular debt which it is sought to take out of the statute, and
*in part-payment of that debt: *Tippets* v. *Heane*. * * The   [*481]
present case differs from *Tippets* v. *Heane*, in this, that, in the
latter, there was only one account.

(MAULE, J.: The payment there was only an admission of a debt
to the extent of the sum paid: there was no evidence that the
money was given as part-payment of a debt of a larger amount.
Here, there was a debt admitted once to exist, viz. for principal and
interest on a promissory note.   There was no plea of payment, no
evidence that that debt had ever been satisfied.   The debt on the
note was a specific and agreed debt.   A payment on an account not
ascertained and agreed, is no admission of the amount of the debt.
But, if a smaller sum be paid on account of a larger ascertained
debt, it admits that *something more is due.)   [*482]

[He cited *Mills* v. *Fowkes* (2), *Waugh* v. *Cope* (3), and *Waters* v.
Tompkins (4).]   In the present case, there was not such evidence as   [484]
the law requires to appropriate the payment in October, 1844, to
the debt due upon the note, even if that had been the only debt.
But it appeared that there was another debt, viz. the debt which
the jury have found to be due for wages.   There is nothing,
therefore, to justify the conclusion that the payment was made on
account of the note, rather than on account of the other debt.

(CRESSWELL, J.: How could the jury infer that the payment
might have been made on account of wages, when the party making
the payment denied the existence of any such debt?)

(1) 3 Y. & J. 518.   (3) 55 R. R. 801 (6 M. & W. 824).
(2) 50 R. R. 750 (5 Bing. N. C. 455;   (4) 41 R. R. 827 (2 Cr. M. & R. 723;
7 Scott, 444).   Tyr. & Gr. 137; 1 Gale, 323).

BURN
v.
BOULTON.

The jury have in effect found that the 1*l.* was paid on account of the first eleven years' wages.

(MAULE, J. : The finding of the jury cannot alter the effect of the compact you have entered into.)

TINDAL, Ch. J. :

The only question for our consideration in this case I take to be, whether or not there was any evidence to go to the jury of part-payments on account of the promissory note declared on. It appears to me that there was some evidence for them ; and, if so, we cannot inquire whether or not they came to a right conclusion. It is clear that there was at one time a debt due from the defendant to the plaintiff, for which the defendant gave his promissory note for 180*l.* and interest at 4½ per cent., payable on demand : and this debt never could have been lost sight of by the defendant. There being this clearly admitted and ascertained debt, the ground upon which it is insisted that the subsequent payments do not operate to take the case out of the Statute of Limitations, is, that there was

[*485]

then another debt due to the plaintiff for wages, and *therefore that [it] is at least uncertain to which of these debts the payments were intended to apply. I admit, that, if there was at the time a clearly ascertained debt for wages, and it was left in doubt on which of the two accounts the payments were made, such payments could not be applied to the promissory note, so as to take it out of the statute (1). But no payment was ever made specifically on account of wages ; and the jury would have been perfectly justified in finding that no wages were due at all. The defendant never admitted that any were due, and therefore was not likely to make a payment on account of wages. Then it appeared that, on the 11th of October, 1844, a sum of money was paid by the defendant to the plaintiff. It could not be said to have been a charitable donation. It does not at all bear the aspect of charity ; for, when offered two sovereigns, the plaintiff, it seems, took only one, which is quite inconsistent with all one's notions and experience on that subject. Upon the evidence, therefore, no debt was admitted by the defendant but the debt on this promissory note (2) : and there was a consistent course of testimony from which the jury were well warranted in inferring that the payment of 1*l.* on the 11th of October, and the

(1) But see *Walker* v. *Butler* (1856)   (2) This was the older debt : *vide*
6 E. & B. 506, 25 L. J. Q. B. 377.—   *Dawe* v. *Holdsworth*, 15 R. R. 595, *n.*
J. G. P.   (Peake, N. P. C. 64).

other payments subsequent to 1834, were made on account of the   BURN
note. I therefore think there is no ground for disturbing the verdict.   *v.*
                                                                    BOULTON.

MAULE, J.:

I am of the same opinion. There clearly was evidence for the
jury upon the question whether or not the debt due from the defendant to the plaintiff was barred by the Statute of Limitations.
That depended upon whether or not there had been part payment
within six years on account of a debt of a larger amount. It seems
to me that all the requisites *for establishing the right of the   [*486]
plaintiff to a verdict upon this issue, exist in the present case.
There was a debt of 180*l.* with interest at 4½ per cent. clearly
proved—one clear, definite, and undisputed debt. The jury have
found that there was also a sum due from the defendant to the
plaintiff for wages : but that has no bearing upon the question
whether or not there was evidence to go to them on the other point.
Not only was the alleged debt for wages disputed at the trial, but it
never had, in fact, been acknowledged. It was, at the least, an
equivocal debt, that never could have been the subject of any
expressly appropriated payment. The jury, therefore, found two
debts : the one, a clear and recognised debt on a promissory note ;
the other, in respect of a liability which the defendant had never
acknowledged. The defendant hands over money to the plaintiff,
under circumstances which the jury, correctly, I think, have decided
to be a payment in respect of a debt. The question is, whether
there was any evidence to warrant the jury in inferring the payment
to have been made on account of the note, rather than on account
of the unacknowledged demand for wages. I think there was abundant evidence for the jury that the payment was on account of the
debt which was not disputed. Then, was such payment an acknowledgment of a larger sum being due? Clearly it was. The evidence
was, that there was a debt of 180*l.* and interest due from the defendant to the plaintiff on the promissory note. The part-payment on
account was evidence of an admission of a specific debt, like a payment of money into Court upon a special contract. If applicable
to this debt at all, it is applicable to it as a debt of 180*l.* with
interest at 4½ per cent. There being, therefore, clearly evidence
to go to the jury, it is immaterial, for the purpose of the present
inquiry, whether they have or have not come to a right conclusion,
or whether *we individually, if on the jury, would have done as   [*487]
they have done.

CRESSWELL, J.:

I shall confine myself entirely to the consideration whether or not there was any evidence of a payment on account of the promissory note. Though, I have felt some doubt in the course of the argument, I cannot now say that there was not some evidence of a part-payment. It is said that the evidence leaves it ambiguous, whether the payment was made on account of the note or of some other debt. There being only one admitted debt, I think the jury might well infer that the payment had reference to that debt.

ERLE, J.:

If it had become necessary, I should have left it to the jury to say whether the payments were made in part-satisfaction of the principal or interest due upon the promissory note, severing the question on the wages from the demand on the note. The direction as to the wages would have been accompanied with the remark that the defendant had, throughout, denied the existence of any liability on that account.

The verdict, therefore, will be reduced by 77l., the amount assessed by the jury for wages in respect of the first eleven years.

Rule accordingly.

FIVAZ *v.* NICHOLLS (1).

(2 C. B. 501—515; S. C. 15 L. J. C. P. 125; 10 Jur. 50.)

One of two parties to an agreement to suppress a prosecution for felony, cannot maintain an action against the other, for an injury arising out of the transaction in which they have both been illegally engaged.

A declaration in case stated that B. (the defendant) had charged C. with embezzlement; that it was agreed between B. and A. (the plaintiff), that B. should abstain from prosecuting C., and that, in consideration thereof, C. should draw, and A. should accept, a bill of exchange, and that C. should indorse the same to the defendant. The declaration then went on to aver that a bill was drawn, accepted, and indorsed to B. pursuant to this corrupt and illegal agreement; that B., well knowing the illegal nature of the transaction, and that A. was not liable at law to pay the amount of the bill, and that there was no reasonable or probable cause for suing him thereon, conspired with D., a pauper, that the bill should be indorsed to D., and that D. should sue A. upon the bill, for the sole benefit of B.; and that an action was accordingly brought by D. against A. in which A. obtained a verdict, on the ground of the illegality of the consideration for

------

(1) See *Taylor* v. *Chester* (1869) L. R.
4 Q. B. 309, 38 L. J. Q. B. 225; *Whitmore* v. *Farley*, 43 L. T. N. S. 192
(S. C. 45 L. T. 99); *Begbie* v. *Phosphate Sewage Co.* (1875) L. R. 10 Q. B. 491,

1 Q. B. Div. 679, 44 L. J. Q. B. 233;
Scott v. *Brown, Doering, McNab & Co.*
[1892] 2 Q. B. 724, 61 L. J. Q. B.
738, C. A.—J. G. P.

the acceptance, but was unable to obtain his costs, in consequence of the
insolvency of D. :

Held, that, inasmuch as A. could not make out his case except through the
illegal transaction to which he himself was a party, the action would not lie.

CASE. The declaration stated, that, before the drawing and
accepting of the bill of exchange thereinafter mentioned, to wit, on
the 4th of November, *1840, the defendant had accused and charged
one J. A. Leeman with having committed a certain offence, that is
to say, that he, Leeman, being employed as the clerk of the defendant, did, by virtue of his said employment, and whilst he was so
employed, receive, and take into his possession, certain moneys
to a large amount, to wit, 400*l*., for and in the name of and on the
account of the defendant, his master, and that the said money
Leeman did fraudulently and feloniously embezzle, steal, take, and
carry away, against the form of the statute in such case made and
provided ; that the defendant had, on the day and year aforesaid,
charged Leeman with the said offences, upon the oath of the defendant, before J. T., Esq., one of the magistrates of the police courts
of the metropolis, sitting at the police court in Union Hall, within
the metropolitan police district, and Leeman was then in the custody
of the governor of, and a prisoner in, the county gaol at Newington,
in the county of Surrey, within the metropolitan police district, for,
and charged with, the said offence ; that the defendant had, before
and at the time of the accepting of the bill of exchange thereinafter
mentioned, threatened to prosecute, and was about to prosecute,
Leeman for the said offence; and thereupon, and before the making
and accepting of the said bill thereinafter mentioned, to wit, on the
20th of November, 1840, it was, amongst other things, agreed by
and between the defendant and the plaintiff, that the defendant
should not prosecute, and should desist from all further prosecution
of, Leeman for the said offence so charged against him as aforesaid,
and should procure Leeman to be discharged from the said custody;
and that, in consideration thereof, Leeman should, amongst other
considerations, draw, and that the plaintiff should accept, a bill of
exchange for the payment to the order of Leeman of the sum of
33*l*. 6*s*. 8*d*., six months after the date thereof, and that Leeman
should indorse the *same to the defendant: Averment, that, in
pursuance of the said agreement, Leeman did, on the 23rd of
November, 1840, draw his bill of exchange in writing, and directed
the same to the plaintiff, and thereby required the plaintiff to pay
him or his order 33*l*. 6*s*. 8*d*., for value received, six months after
the date thereof; and the plaintiff then accepted the said bill, as

[*502]

[*503]

and for the said bill to be so drawn, accepted, and indorsed as
aforesaid, and on no other account, and for no other consideration
whatsoever; and Leeman did then, in further pursuance of the said
corrupt and illegal agreement, indorse the said bill to the defendant,
and the defendant then took and received the said bill in pursuance
of the said agreement, and on no other account, and for no other
consideration whatsoever; and the defendant did then accordingly
forbear, and had from thence continually forborne, to prosecute,
and had desisted from all further prosecution of, Leeman for the
said offence so charged against him as aforesaid; and the defendant
then procured Leeman to be, and he was then accordingly, discharged from the said custody: that, after the accepting of the said
bill by the plaintiff as aforesaid, and after the discharge of Leeman
as aforesaid, and before the indorsement of the bill as thereinafter
mentioned, to wit, on the day and year aforesaid, the defendant well
knew and was acquainted with the fraudulent and illegal nature of
the transaction thereinbefore mentioned, and was well aware that
the plaintiff was not liable at law to pay the amount of the aforesaid bill of exchange, and that there was no reasonable or probable
cause whatsoever for suing him thereon; but the defendant, maliciously and unjustly contriving and intending to harass, oppress,
and injure the plaintiff, and to cause and procure him to be unjustly
and oppressively sued and harassed in respect thereof, fraudulently
and collusively combined and conspired with one George Rouse,

[*504]

who *then was, and from thence continually had been, a person in
poor and embarrassed circumstances, and unable to pay the costs
of the action thereinafter mentioned,—that, in order to make the
defence of the plaintiff to the payment of the said bill more difficult,
and to deprive the plaintiff of all effectual remedy for the costs of
such defence in case of his success, the said bill should be indorsed
by the defendant to Rouse, and that Rouse should, for enforcing
payment thereof, sue the plaintiff thereon, as thereinafter mentioned, for the sole benefit and advantage of the defendant; and the
defendant thereupon, for the purpose, and with the intent, and in
pursuance of the combination and conspiracy aforesaid, then and
after the bill became due, indorsed it to Rouse, in order that he,
Rouse, might sue the plaintiff for the amount thereof in his Rouse's
name, but for the sole benefit and advantage of the defendant:
that Rouse did accordingly, in furtherance of such purpose, intent,
and conspiracy as aforesaid, to wit, on the 18th of July, 1840,
before the Barons of her Majesty's Court of Exchequer of Pleas at

Westminster in the county of Middlesex, implead the plaintiff by FIVAZ
v.
NICHOLLS. writ of summons in an action on promises, and declared in the said action, and in the declaration therein alleged, as the fact was, that Leeman, on the 23rd of November, 1840, made the said bill of exchange in writing, and thereby required the plaintiff in this suit to pay to him, Leeman, or his order, 33*l.* 6*s.* 8*d.*, six months after the date thereof (which period, he alleged, had expired before the commencement of the said suit), and that the plaintiff then accepted the said bill, and that Leeman then indorsed the same to the defendant, being the indorsement thereinbefore mentioned, and that the defendant then indorsed the same to Rouse, being the indorsement in that behalf thereinbefore mentioned, of all which he Rouse further alleged in his said declaration that the plaintiff in this suit had notice, yet that the now plaintiff *had not paid the amount of   [*505] the said bill, to Rouse's damage of 50*l.*, and thereupon he brought suit &c.; to which declaration the now plaintiff pleaded several pleas, to wit, first, that he did not accept the said bill, and that thereof he put himself upon the country &c.: and for a further plea in that behalf, the now plaintiff secondly pleaded and averred, that, &c., &c. (setting forth the illegal agreement under which the acceptance was given, and its performance by the parties thereto respectively, and alleging that there was no consideration or value for the indorsement of the bill to Rouse, the plaintiff in the said action): and, for a further plea in that behalf in the said action, the now plaintiff lastly pleaded and averred the same facts and circumstances thereinbefore mentioned and alleged to have been by him pleaded and averred in the said second plea, save and except, that, instead of the said averment in the said second plea made, that there was no consideration or value for the said indorsement of the said bill to Rouse, the now plaintiff, in his said last plea, pleaded and averred that the said indorsement of the said bill to Rouse was after the same became due and payable, and not before, and that he did not become holder thereof until after the same became due and payable: that Rouse joined issue on the first plea, and as to the other two pleas replied *de injuriâ:* that such proceedings were had in the said Court in the said action, that, at the trial before Tindal, Ch. J., at the Summer Assizes for the county of Surrey, in 1841, a verdict was found for the plaintiff on the first issue, and for the defendant (the now plaintiff) on the issue upon *de injuriâ*, so far as related to the last plea, &c., and that the now plaintiff thereupon had judgment for his costs, &c.: that, after the pronouncing of the

FIVAZ
*.
NICHOLLS.
[*506]

said judgment, to wit, on the 1st of March, 1842, Rouse did depart,
and still was away, from this realm, to wit, in America, and had
left no property of any description to *which the now plaintiff
could resort for payment of his aforesaid costs : and that he, the
now plaintiff, had not been paid the amount of the said costs so
incurred, but the same, and every part thereof, still remained justly
due and owing to him. By means of which several premises the
now plaintiff had suffered great anxiety and pain of mind, and had
been put to great trouble and difficulty in making out and proving
his defence to the said action, and had been forced and obliged to
lay out and expend, and had laid out and expended, divers large
sums of money, in the whole amounting to 200l., in and about the
defending himself in the aforesaid action brought by Rouse as aforesaid, the same being greater and heavier costs and expenses than
if an action had been brought in the name of the now defendant ;
and that the now plaintiff had been and was otherwise greatly
injured in his circumstances, &c.

To this declaration the defendant demurred specially, assigning,
amongst others, the following causes : that, even if the declaration
disclosed any cause of action at all, which the defendant denied,
the cause of action was not shown with sufficient certainty or
precision ; that, as the declaration stood, the real cause of complaint, if it could be arrived at at all, could only be arrived at
through inference and deduction ; that, inasmuch as the plaintiff
admitted himself to have been a party to the agreement for con-
cocting the bill mentioned in the declaration, the plaintiff's consent
to its transfer was to be assumed until the contrary appeared, yet
it was nowhere stated upon the face of the declaration that the
alleged transfer was without the knowledge or against the consent
of the plaintiff, and, until the contrary appeared, it must be taken
that the alleged transfer was in furtherance of the now plaintiff's
original intention, and with his continued concurrence, so as to
rebut malice, and the plaintiff should have at least shown, in

[*507]

express *terms, that the alleged transfer of the bill was without
his knowledge or against his will ; that there was nothing stated in
the declaration from which the malicious and unjust intention and
contrivance in the declaration mentioned, was to be inferred, that
the law could not infer any malicious or unjust intention or contrivance from any thing apparent on the face of the declaration,
and it was therefore incumbent on the plaintiff to show affirma-
tively and with more precision wherein consisted such malicious

and unjust intention and contrivance; that the alleged illegality in the declaration mentioned should have been shown with more clearness, and by means of more positive averment, for that it was quite consistent with the declaration, that, at the time of the making of the alleged agreement and bill of exchange, the innocence and integrity of Leeman in the premises had been conclusively established, or that he had been pardoned; and that the only pretence for a cause of action, as disclosed on the face of the declaration, lay in the alleged transfer of the bill mentioned in the declaration to a party in embarrassed circumstances, whereas the law recognises no such evil consequences to the plaintiff as those upon which he had founded his action, and repudiates the same.

Joinder in demurrer.

Manning, Serjt. (with whom was *G. Hayes*), in support of the demurrer:

No cause of action can arise out of the transaction disclosed in this declaration. It has repeatedly been held, that a party cannot maintain an action in respect of a transaction directly arising out of an illegal contract to which he himself was a party. The facts set up here are, in effect, the same as those which were set up in answer to Rouse's action upon the bill. In *Simpson* v. *Bloss* (1), it was held that the test, *whether a demand connected with an illegal transaction is capable of being enforced at law, is, whether the plaintiff requires any aid from the illegal transaction to establish his case. * * No contribution will in general be allowed amongst wrong-doers: *Merryweather* v. *Nixan* (2). That doctrine, however, is subject to this qualification, that it does not apply where the act is not morally wrong (3).

[*508]

[509]

(MAULE, J.: Or, rather, where the party is ignorant that he is committing an offence (4).)

[He cited *Stephens* v. *Robinson* (5), *Colburn* v. *Patmore* (6), *Shackell* v. *Rossier* (7), *Harman* v. *Tappenden* (8), and *Ward* v. *Lloyd* (9).]

(1) 17 R. R. 509 (7 Taunt. 246).
(2) 16 R. R. 810 (8 T. R. 186). And see F. N. B. 162, C. D.; *Philips* v. *Biggs*, Hardr. 164; Bull. N. P. 146.
(3) *Betts* v. *Gibbins*, 41 R. R. 381 (2 Ad. & El. 57; 4 Nev. & M. 64). And see H. 34 Hen. VI. fo. 26, pl. 3; *Wilson* v. *Milner*, 2 Camp. 452.
(4) Acc. *Adamson* v. *Jarvis*, 29 R. R.

503 (4 Bing. 66; 12 Moore, 241).
(5) 2 Cr. & J. 209.
(6) 40 R. R. 493 (1 Cr. M. & R. 73; 4 Tyr. 677).
(7) 42 R. R. 666 (2 Bing. N. C. 634; 3 Scott, 59).
(8) 3 Esp. N. P. C. 278.
(9) 64 R. R. 847 (6 Man. & G. 785; 7 Scott, N. R. 499).

FIVAZ
v.
NICHOLLS.
[510]

Dowling, Serjt. (with whom was *Channell*, Serjt.), *contrà :*

This is not the case of one of several wrong-doers seeking to enforce by action against those who stand *in pari delicto* with him, a right arising out of the wrongful act. The plaintiff charges the defendant with having wrongfully conspired with a pauper to enforce against him a demand which he knew he could not enforce. The gist of the action is, the conspiracy to deprive the plaintiff of his remedy for his costs; and this is altogether collateral to, and independent of, the alleged illegal contract. *Gregory* v. *The Duke of Brunswick* (1) is an authority to show that an action upon the case will lie for a fraudulent conspiracy to do an act prejudicial to the plaintiff.

(MAULE, J.: Do you find any authority for an action for a conspiracy to bring a civil action?)

[*511]

In *Skinner* v. *Gunton* (2), an action was held to lie *against three persons, for that they *per conspirationem inter eos habitam,* maliciously procured the plaintiff to be held to bail. [He also referred to Fitzherbert's Natura Brevium (3), Com. Dig. Action upon the case for a conspiracy (A.) (4), and *Flight* v. *Leman* (5).]

[512]

Manning, Serjt., in reply, [cited *Scott* v. *Bye* (6).]

(MAULE, J.: That was not a case of conspiracy: the party of his own head sued out the writ.)

Here, no answer has been offered to the argument that the cause of action, if any, can only be made out by setting up the illegal agreement. Besides, in the action brought by Rouse upon the bill, the present plaintiff pleaded a false plea, viz. that he did not accept the bill: he therefore, in part at least, brought the difficulty upon himself.

TINDAL, Ch. J.:

I think that this case may be determined on the short ground that the plaintiff is unable to establish his claim as stated upon the record, without relying upon the illegal agreement originally

(1) 64 R. R. 759 (6 Man. & G. 205; 7 Scott, N. R. 972).

(2) 1 Wms. Saund. 228 c; 1 Ventr. 12, 18; Sir T. Ray. 176; 2 Keb. 473, 476, 497.

(3) P. 116, B. E. F. H.

(4) Citing F. N. B. 116 E., and Sir T. Ray. 176.

(5) 62 R. R. 495 (4 Q. B. 883). And see *Wade* v. *Simeon, post,* p. 523.

(6) 9 Moore, 649.

entered into between himself and the defendant. That is an
objection that goes to the very root of the action. Suppose,
instead of resisting the action brought against him by Rouse, the
plaintiff had paid the money, he could not have recovered it back :
had he attempted to do so, he would have been met by the maxim
of law, *ex dolo malo *non oritur actio*. If he could not succeed in
such an action, I do not see how he can recover damages in a court
of law for an injury incidentally resulting from the same state of
circumstances, inasmuch as he must put in the very front of his
declaration the illegal agreement to which he has been a party. The
case of *Simpson* v. *Bloss* seems to me in effect to decide the present.
I therefore think the defendant is entitled to our judgment.

MAULE, J.:

I am of the same opinion. The principle has been conceded,
that the plaintiff cannot recover, where, in order to maintain his
supposed claim, he must set up an illegal agreement to which he
himself has been a party. It has been contended, however, that
the present case does not fall within that rule, inasmuch as the
right of the plaintiff to recover does not depend upon the illegal
agreement with the defendant, to which he was a party, but upon
the subsequent fraudulent conspiracy between the defendant and
Rouse. I think that is not so. It was a necessary part of the
plaintiff's case to show that Rouse had no real cause of action
against him upon the bill. The absence of the cause of action in
Rouse arises out of the illegality of the consideration for which the
bill was given. The fraudulent transaction was a necessary part
of the plaintiff's case; in fact it is founded upon it; and that
enables the defendant to take advantage of the blot by demurring
to the declaration, which states that the defendant, well knowing
the fraudulent and illegal nature of the transaction therein-before
mentioned, and being well aware that the plaintiff was not liable
at law to pay the amount of the bill, and that there was no
reasonable or probable cause whatever for suing him thereon, but
maliciously and unjustly intending, &c., fraudulently and collusively combined and conspired with Rouse, a pauper, in order to
*deprive the plaintiff of all effectual remedy for the costs of his
defence, in case of his success, that the bill should be indorsed to
Rouse, for the purpose of enabling Rouse to sue thereon, for the
defendant's benefit. If the declaration had simply alleged the
conspiracy between the defendant and Rouse to impose upon the

FIVAZ
v.
NICHOLLS.

plaintiff an insolvent party, when the defendant was the person really interested in the result of the action, possibly it might have been good.   But that would only have postponed the plaintiff's difficulty to the next stage; for, as soon as it had been shown by plea that the transaction out of which the plaintiff's right to recover, if any, arose, was illegal, the action would have been answered.   I do not think the allegation as to the transaction out of which the bill arose could be struck out; it seems to me to be a material part of the declaration.   Where a party in pleading states the same thing generally as well as particularly, and the latter statement discloses some illegality in the transaction, I think the general allegation must be taken to have the same meaning.

I am by no means disposed to hold that an action can be sustained for inciting another to bring an action without reasonable or probable cause.   The cases seem to me to show the contrary. But it is not necessary to decide that on the present occasion; for, the case seems to me to fall within the general principle referred to.

CRESSWELL, J.:

I am of the same opinion.   It appears that the plaintiff's cause of action rests entirely upon the illegality of a transaction to which the plaintiff was himself a party.   The foundation of the plaintiff's claim is, the alleged conspiracy between the defendant and Rouse, that the latter should be put forward as plaintiff in an action upon a bill of exchange given in pursuance of an illegal contract.   But for the alleged illegality, Rouse had a good cause of action on the bill: *the illegality of the transaction, therefore, is the foundation of the plaintiff's cause of action.

[*515]

ERLE, J.:

I also am of opinion that the present action fails, inasmuch as the illegality of the original transaction is the very foundation of the plaintiff's claim.   The original transaction necessarily forms part of the statement upon which the plaintiff's right to complain of the fraudulent conspiracy rests; because, but for such illegality, Rouse had a *primâ facie* right to sue the plaintiff upon the bill. But for the illegal agreement disclosed by the declaration, I see nothing unlawful in that which is imputed to the defendant.

Judgment for the defendant.

Dowling, Serjt., for the plaintiff, prayed leave to amend.

TINDAL, Ch. J.:

We do not think that this is a case in which we ought to interfere. Both parties have been guilty of an infringement of the law.

WADE *v.* SIMEON.

(2 C. B. 548—568 ; S. C. 3 Dowl. & L. 587 ; 15 L. J. C. P. 114 ; 10 Jur. 412.)

A promise by a plaintiff in an action to forbear to proceed is no consideration for a promise to pay money, if the plaintiff knows and admits that he has no cause of action.

In assumpsit, the declaration stated that the plaintiff had brought an action against the defendant in the Exchequer, to recover certain moneys, that the defendant had pleaded various pleas, on which issues in fact had been joined, which were about to be tried, and that, in consideration that the plaintiff would forbear proceeding in that action until a certain day, the plaintiff promised on that day to pay the amount, but that he made default, &c.

Plea, that the plaintiff never had any cause of action against the defendant in respect of the subject-matter of the action in the Exchequer, which he, the plaintiff, at the time of the commencement of the said action, and thence until and at the time of the making of the promise, well knew :

Held, sufficient, on general demurrer (1).

ASSUMPSIT. The first count of the declaration stated, that, before and at the time of the making of the promise thereinafter next mentioned, an action on promises had been commenced and prosecuted by, and at the suit of, the plaintiff against the defendant, in the Court of Exchequer, that the plaintiff had declared in the said action against the defendant for the non-performance by the defendant of certain promises in the declaration alleged to have been made by the defendant to the plaintiff for the payment by the defendant to the plaintiff, of two sums, one amounting to 1,800*l.*, and the other amounting to 700*l.*, and the said action was so commenced and prosecuted, and the defendant declared therein as aforesaid, for the recovery of these sums and the damages by him sustained by the non-performance by the defendant of his promises in respect of the same, parcel of such damages being interest upon the said sum of 1,800*l.* from the 25th of May, 1840, until payment of *the said sum of 1,800*l.*, and other parcel of such damages being interest upon the said sum of 700*l.* from the 4th of July, 1840, until payment of the said sum of 700*l.* ; that, before and at the time of the making of the promise of the defendant

[*549]

(1) So much of the report as relates to the special demurrer to the seventh plea is omitted as being now of no importance. The lengthy arguments of counsel are omitted as the grounds of the decision appear fully from the judgments. See *Callisher* v. *Bischoffsheim* (1870) L. R. 5 Q. B. 449, 39 L. J. Q. B. 181.—J. G. P.

WADE
v.
SIMEON.

thereafter mentioned, the defendant had pleaded divers pleas to
the said declaration, and divers issues had been, and were, joined
between the plaintiff and the defendant in the said action, and the
plaintiff had given due notice for the trial of the same, and the
same were about to be tried at, &c., and the plaintiff had, according to the course and practice of the said Court, duly entered the
Nisi Prius record in the said action for the said trial, and the said
trial was duly appointed and fixed to take place on the 7th of
December, 1844, and the same would have taken place had it not
been for the promise of the defendant as thereinafter mentioned;
that, before and at the time of the making of the promise of
the defendant as thereinafter mentioned, the plaintiff had been
put to, and incurred, divers costs and charges amounting, to
wit, to 300l., in and about the said action; that, before and
at the time of the making of the defendant's promise thereafter
mentioned, the defendant had, to wit, on the 3rd of December,
1844, caused the plaintiff to be served with a notice that the
defendant would apply to and move her Majesty's High Court of
Chancery, for an injunction by that Court to restrain the plaintiff
from issuing execution in the said action on any judgment obtained
by him, in case the plaintiff should obtain such judgment; that
thereupon, to wit, on the 6th of December, 1844, being the day
next before the day when the said trial was so appointed and fixed
to take place as aforesaid, in consideration that the plaintiff would
forbear prosecuting and would stay all proceedings in the said
action until and upon the 14th of December, 1844, save and except
the taxation of the said costs and charges, and the obtaining and
drawing up of an order therein as thereinafter mentioned, he the

[*550]

defendant *promised the plaintiff that he the defendant would on
that day pay him the said sums of 1,800l. and 700l., and interest
thereon respectively as aforesaid, together with the said costs and
charges, to be taxed, and that, in the event of the defendant's not
paying the same, the defendant would suffer, and the plaintiff
should be at liberty to sign, judgment in the said action, and that
a Judge's order should and might be obtained and drawn up in the
said action, to secure such payment, and that the said notice and
the said application to, and motion in, the said Court of Chancery,
should be abandoned: Averment, that the plaintiff, confiding in the
said promise of the defendant, then, to wit, on the 6th of December,
1844, withdrew the said record, and forbore prosecuting, and stayed
all further proceedings in, the said action until and upon the said

14th of December, 1844, save and except the taxation of the said costs and charges, and the obtaining and drawing up of the said order to be so obtained and drawn up as aforesaid, and, save and except as aforesaid, the plaintiff had from thence continually forborne to prosecute, and had stayed all further proceedings in, the said action ; that, after the making of the said promise, and before the said 14th of December, 1844, to wit, on the 11th of December, 1844, the costs and charges of the plaintiff which he had been put to and incurred in and about the said action, and which the defendant promised to pay as aforesaid, were duly taxed at 81*l*. 1*s*. 10*d*., whereof the defendant then had notice ; and that, although the said 14th of December, 1844, had elapsed before the commencement of the suit, and although the said interest so promised to be paid as aforesaid on the said 14th of December, 1844, amounted to a large sum, to wit, 451*l*. 13*s*. 8*d*., yet the defendant, although often requested by the plaintiff so to do, had not as yet paid the plaintiff the said sum of 1,300*l*., and 700*l*., and the said interest amounting to 451*l*. 13*s*. 8*d*., and the said *costs and charges amounting to, and so taxed at, 81*l*. 13*s*. 10*d*. as aforesaid, or either of them, or any part thereof, and the same remained wholly due and unpaid to the plaintiff; that the defendant did not nor would suffer or permit the plaintiff to sign, and afterwards, and after the said 14th of December, 1844, to wit, on &c., and from thenceforward, wholly hindered and prevented the plaintiff from signing judgment in the said action ; that the defendant afterwards, to wit, on the 27th of January, 1845, obtained a rule and order of the said Court for setting aside a certain order before then, to wit, on the 6th of December, 1844, made by ALDERSON, B., and drawn up in pursuance of the said promise, and according to the same ; and that by means of the premises the plaintiff had been delayed in, and hindered and prevented from, recovering the said sums and moneys so promised by the defendant to be paid as aforesaid.

[*551]

There was also a count upon an account stated.

Fourth plea, to the first count, that the plaintiff never had any cause of action against the defendant in respect of the subject-matter of the action in the Court of Exchequer in that count mentioned ; which he, the plaintiff, at the time of the commencement of the action, and thence until and at the time of the making of the promise in the said first count mentioned, well knew.   Verification.

*   *   *   *   *

WADE
v.
SIMEON.
[555]

Special demurrer to the fourth plea, assigning for causes, that
it does not confess and avoid, or traverse, or deny, any of the
matters in the first count alleged ; that the matter pleaded affords
no defence to the cause of action in that count mentioned ; that the
plea sets up as a defence immaterial matter ; that the plea does not
allege or show that the defendant, before or at the time of the making
of the promise, was not aware that the plaintiff had no cause for the
said action, nor does it allege or show that the plaintiff concealed
any thing from the defendant ; that it is ambiguous and uncertain
what is meant by the allegation in the plea that the plaintiff never
had any cause of action against the defendant in respect of the
subject-matter of the said action ; that the plea does not exclude all
other consideration for the promise in the said count mentioned ;

[*556]

*that it is ambiguous, and uncertain from the plea, what is the
real defence the defendant intends setting up thereby ; and that
the plea should have concluded to the country. * * *

The defendant joined in demurrer.

[557]

Channell, Serjt., in support of the demurrers. * * *

[558]

Kinglake, Serjt. (with whom was *Barstow*), contrà. * * *

[561]

Channell, Serjt., in reply. * * *

[563]

(MAULE, J.: The better course, probably, will be to allow the
defendant to amend the fourth plea, by alleging that the plaintiff
never had any available cause of action ; upon which the plaintiff
may take issue. I incline to think the plea bad, but it is doubtful
whether the blot is hit by any of the causes of demurrer assigned.)

Kinglake, Serjt., for the defendant, declined to amend.

TINDAL, Ch. J. :

[*564]

The only question now remaining is upon the demurrer to the
fourth plea. I am of opinion *that the fourth plea is a good and
valid plea, on general demurrer. The declaration alleges that the
plaintiff had commenced an action against the defendant in the
Exchequer, to recover two sums of 1,300*l.* and 700*l.* respectively,
which action was about to be tried, and that, in consideration that
the plaintiff would forbear proceeding in that action, until the
14th of December then next, the defendant promised the plaintiff
that he would on that day pay the money, with interest, and costs ;
that the plaintiff, confiding in the defendant's promise, forbore

prosecuting the action, and stayed the proceedings until the day
named ; but that the defendant did not pay the money or the
costs. The fourth plea states that the plaintiff never had any
cause of action against the defendant in respect of the subject-
matter of the action in the Court of Exchequer, which he, the
plaintiff, at the time of the commencement of the said action, and
thence until the time of the making the promise in the first count
mentioned, well knew. By demurring to that plea, the plaintiff
admits that he had no cause of action against the defendant in the
action therein mentioned, and that he knew it. It appears to me,
therefore, that he is estopped from saying that there was any valid
consideration for the defendant's promise. It is almost *contrà bonos
mores*, and certainly contrary to all the principles of natural justice,
that a man should institute proceedings against another, when he
is conscious that he has no good cause of action. In order to
constitute a binding promise, the plaintiff must show a good consideration, something beneficial to the defendant, or detrimental to
the plaintiff. Detrimental to the plaintiff it cannot be, if he has
no cause of action : and beneficial to the defendant it cannot be ;
for, in contemplation of law, the defence upon such an admitted
state of facts must be successful, and the defendant will recover
costs, which must be assumed to be a full compensation for all
the legal damage he may sustain. The consideration, therefore,
*altogether fails. On the part of the plaintiff it has been urged,   [*565]
that the cases cited for the defendant were not cases where actions
had already been brought, but only cases of promises to forbear
commencing proceedings. I must, however, confess, that, if that
were so, I do not see that it would make any substantial difference.
The older cases, and some of the modern ones, too, do not afford
any countenance to that distinction. In *Tooley* v. *Windham* (1), it
is stated that the plaintiff had purchased a writ out of Chancery
against the defendant, to the intent to exhibit a bill against him :
upon the return of the writ, which was for the profits of certain
lands, which the father of the defendant had taken in his lifetime,
the defendant, in consideration he would surcease his suit, promised
to him, that, if he could prove that his father had taken the profits,
or had the possession of the land under the title of the father of
the plaintiff, he would pay him for the profits of the land : and
the Court held that the promise was without consideration, and
void. There the suit was in existence at the time of the making of

(1) Cro. Eliz. 206 (more fully reported, 2 Leon. 105).

WADE
v.
SIMEON.

the promise. So, in *Atkinson* v. *Settree* (1), an action had been commenced at the time the promise was made. These cases seem to me to establish the principle upon which our present judgment rests; and I am not aware that it is at all opposed by *Longridge* v. *Dorville*. It may be that the peculiar circumstances of that case took it out of the general rule (2). The ship was under detention by virtue of process from the Admiralty Court: the event of the suit in that Court was uncertain; neither party could foresee the result; and therefore the relinquishment by the plaintiff of his hold upon the ship, might well be a good consideration for the promise declared on. Here, however, there was no uncertainty: the defendant asserts, and the plaintiff admits, that there never

[*566]

was any cause of action in the *original suit, and that the plaintiff knew it. I therefore think the fourth plea affords a very good answer, and that the defendant is entitled to judgment thereon.

MAULE, J.:

I also am of opinion that the defendant is entitled to judgment on the fourth plea, though I think it extremely questionable whether that plea is not open to objection, provided it were rightly taken. Forbearance to prosecute a suit in which the plaintiff has no cause of action (and in which, as the LORD CHIEF JUSTICE properly adds, he must eventually fail), according to the authorities, is no consideration. It is no benefit to the defendant; and no detriment to the plaintiff. Costs are considered by the law a sufficient indemnification for a defendant who is sued, where there exists no cause of action: consequently, the defendant, in contemplation of law, derives no benefit from a stay of the proceedings. In *Smith* v. *Monteith*, it seems to have been considered that the allegation in the plea, that the plaintiff had not any claim or demand or cause of action against the original defendant, in respect whereof the plaintiff was entitled to recover the sum which the defendant promised to pay, did not sufficiently show that the plaintiff must necessarily have failed in the original action; and it may be doubted whether the fourth plea here does sufficiently show that there was no consideration for the defendant's promise, by reason of the plaintiff having no cause of action in the former suit, and

[*560, n.]

(1) Willes, 482.

(2) *There the matter in dispute was about to be decided in a tribunal governed by the *civil* law, with which

the Judges, *à fortiori* the parties to the compromise might be presumed to be unacquainted.

that, therefore, he must necessarily have failed in that suit. That objection would, I think, have shown the fourth plea pleaded in this case, to be bad, provided the objection had been properly pointed out as a cause of demurrer. But, on general demurrer, I think the plea must be taken impliedly to allege that the plaintiff must necessarily have failed, and is, therefore, sufficient, the absence of a direct allegation to that effect being only ground of special demurrer. It *has been contended that this objection is specially pointed out by that part of the demurrer which objects to the plea on the ground that it is ambiguous.   That, however, is not, in my opinion, a sufficient assignment of this cause of demurrer, within the statute.   Though I feel bound to state my opinion, I confess I should not be much surprised if a court of error should come to a different conclusion upon the doubt suggested.

CRESSWELL, J. :

The declaration in this case is founded upon a promise by the defendant to pay certain moneys in consideration of the plaintiff's forbearing to proceed with an action pending in the Court of Exchequer. The answer set up by the fourth plea, is, that the plaintiff never had any cause of action against the defendant in respect of the subject-matter of that suit, which the plaintiff well knew.   It has been surmised, in the course of the argument, that there is a distinction between abstaining from commencing an action, and forbearing to prosecute one already commenced.   In the older cases, I find no such distinction. Lord Coke lays it down broadly (1), that the staying of an action that has been unjustly brought, is no consideration for a promise to pay money. I cannot help thinking, on general principles, that the staying proceedings in an action brought without any cause, is no good consideration for a promise such as is relied on here. The plea, in plain terms, avers that the plaintiff never had any cause of action, and that he well knew it. Are we to assume that the defendant might, by some slip in plead- ing, have failed in his defence to that action, if it *had proceeded?

I think not. On general demurrer, the plea appears to me to be sufficient ; and none of the causes of demurrer specially assigned, in my judgment, hits the point made by my brother *Channell*.

(1) At common law, *ut videtur,* no reference appearing to be made to the 23 Hen. VIII. c. 15, which gave costs to defendants in certain actions, or to the 4 Jac. I. c. 3, which extended the remedy to all actions in which the defendant succeeded upon verdict, or the plaintiff was nonsuited after appearance (*i.e.* in which the plaintiff was non-prossed or nonsuited).

ERLE, J. :

It appears to me also that the fourth plea is sufficient. The declaration states that the plaintiff had commenced an action against the defendant in the Court of Exchequer to recover certain moneys, that the defendant had pleaded various pleas on which issues in fact had been joined, which were about to be tried, and that, in consideration that the plaintiff would forbear proceeding in that action until a certain day, the defendant promised to pay. The issues joined on that record, therefore, were perfectly well known and ascertained. The defendant pleads that the plaintiff never had any cause of action against him in respect of the subject-matter of the action in the Exchequer, which he the plaintiff, at the time of the commencement of the action, and thence until the time of the promise, well knew. I think the plea must be read as importing a distinct allegation, that, upon the issues joined in that action, whether of fact or of law, the plaintiff must have failed. Construing the plea in this way, I think it is a good plea, at least on general demurrer, and that the defendant is entitled to judgment thereon.

Judgment for the defendant on the fourth plea.

COXHEAD v. RICHARDS (1).

(2 C. B. 569—611; S. C. 15 L. J. C. P. 278; 10 Jur. 984.)

C., the mate of a ship, sends to B., a stranger, a letter charging A., the captain, with gross misconduct. B. shows this letter to D., the owner, who dismisses A. :

Held, by TINDAL, Ch. J., and ERLE, J., that the showing of the letter by B. to D. was a privileged communication.

Held, by COLTMAN and CRESSWELL, JJ., to be not privileged.

CASE, for a libel. The declaration stated, that, before the committing of the grievances by the defendant as thereinafter mentioned,

---

(1) Cited in *Davies* v. *Snead* (1870), L. R. 5 Q. B. 608, 39 L. J. Q. B. 202; *Robshaw* v. *Smith* (1878), 38 L. T. N. S. 423; and see *Blackham* v. *Pugh*, post, p. 555. WILLES, J., in *Amann* v. *Damm* (1860), 8 C. B. N. S. 597, at p. 602 (29 L. J. C. P. p. 314), says, "If it had been necessary I should have been fully prepared to go the whole length of the doctrine laid down by TINDAL, Ch. J. and ERLE, J., in

the case of *Coxhead* v. *Richards*." In *Stuart* v. *Bell* [1891] 2 Q. B. at p. 347 (60 L. J. Q. B. 577), LINDLEY, L.J., says, "Having carefully considered all the four judgments in that celebrated case, I have no hesitation in saying that the judgment of TINDAL, Ch. J., is the one which carries conviction to my mind, and is the one which I consider the most accurate and safe to take as a guide."—J. G. P.

the plaintiff had been and was a mariner and commander of vessels,   COXHEAD
and, as such mariner and commander, had always conducted him-   v.
self with care, skill, and propriety; that, before the time of the   RICHARDS.
committing of such grievances, to wit, on the 1st of December,
1838, he had been retained, employed, and appointed, for certain
reward to him the plaintiff, by one John Ward, to command, and
be master and captain of, and then was master, commander, and
captain of, a certain vessel of the said John Ward, called the
England, upon and for a certain voyage then about to be made by
the said vessel: that, before the committing of such grievances, to
wit, on the day and year aforesaid, he, the plaintiff, being such
master, captain, and commander as aforesaid, and, as such, being
on board of such vessel, and having the care and command thereof,
and divers, to wit, twenty persons, being on board of such vessel,
set sail and departed on her said voyage from London to and for
Llanelly, which last-mentioned place the said vessel went to in part
prosecution of her said voyage, with the plaintiff and the said crew;
that, in sailing and proceeding to the last-mentioned place, the said
vessel, the plaintiff being such master, captain, and commander as
aforesaid, passed by a certain island called the Isle of Wight, otherwise called the Wight, and also by part of a foreign coast, called the
French coast, and also by a certain rock in the ocean, called the
Runnelstone Rock; that, before the committing of such grievances,
the said vessel, after she *had so set sail and departed as aforesaid,   [*570]
to wit, on the 12th of December, 1838, arrived at Llanelly aforesaid;
that the plaintiff continued to be, and was, such master, captain,
and commander of the said vessel as aforesaid, and, as such, was
on board thereof, and had the care and command thereof, from the
time the said vessel departed and set sail as aforesaid, until and
upon her arrival at Llanelly aforesaid: yet that the defendant, well
knowing the premises, but contriving and intending to injure the
plaintiff, and to bring him into public scandal, infamy, and disgrace,
and cause it to be suspected and believed that he the plaintiff was
a drunkard, and unfit to be trusted with the command of the said
vessel, or any other vessel, and that the said vessel, while the
plaintiff was so on board and had the care and command thereof
as aforesaid, had been in danger by means of the drunkenness and
default of the plaintiff, and to deprive him of the means of supporting himself, theretofore to wit, on the 30th of December, 1838,
falsely &c., did publish &c., of and concerning the plaintiff, and of
and concerning him as such master, captain, and commander as

COXHEAD
v.
RICHARDS.
aforesaid, and of and concerning the said vessel, and of and concerning the same while under the care and command of the plaintiff,
and of and concerning the said persons on board the same, and of
and concerning the said voyage from London to Llanelly aforesaid,
and of and concerning the said John Ward, and of and concerning
the said island, and of and concerning the said part of the said
foreign coast, and of and concerning the said rock, a certain false,
scandalous, malicious, and defamatory libel, in a certain part of
which libel there was and is contained, amongst other things, the
false, scandalous, malicious, and defamatory matter following of
and concerning the plaintiff, &c., &c., that is to say, " LLANELLY,
December 12th, 1838. MY DEAR SIR,—I hasten to write to you,

[*571]   and beg your advice on a very important *affair, which I will endeavour to explain to you in as concise a manner as it will admit of.
You must know, then, that I have had to navigate the ship
(meaning the said vessel) much of the passage (meaning the said
voyage from London to Llanelly aforesaid) ; the captain (meaning
the plaintiff), from the time of our passing the Wight (meaning
the said island), having been in a state of intoxication. We (meaning
the said persons on board the said vessel) ran into great risk on the
French coast (meaning the said part of the said foreign coast),
before I actually found out what was the matter with him (meaning
the plaintiff). He (meaning the plaintiff) then kept to his cabin
night and day, without appearing at meals ; only occasionally
coming on deck when any thing was reported to him (meaning the
plaintiff). This was my most anxious time ; for, he (meaning the
plaintiff) vociferated orders, and captain's orders must be obeyed,
unless the mate will mutiny and take charge. I was compelled for
our safety to do this at last ; and only just saved the ship (meaning
the said vessel) from being dashed on the Runnelstone Rock (meaning
the said rock) by a rapid movement of the helm and sails, in the
performance of which I was promptly obeyed by the crew. He
(meaning the plaintiff) had just left the deck, happily, to which I
had summoned him (meaning the plaintiff) on sighting the Long-
ship's light, for which he (meaning the plaintiff) then shaped a
course. It was dark on Saturday morning. I suppose after that
he freshened the nip ; for, he (meaning the plaintiff) lay in bed
with his clothes on, insensible to what was passing, till I again
roused him (meaning the plaintiff) to say we were on the Welch
coast, whither I managed to get on Saturday and Sunday. Being
anxious, for his (meaning the plaintiff's) sake, that he (meaning

the plaintiff) should be in a fit state to receive the pilot, I by means of
the steward removed *all the liquor from his (meaning the plaintiff's)
cabin, and at last got him (meaning the plaintiff) sober, frequently
giving him (meaning the plaintiff) tea, &c. Sunday and yesterday
we were becalmed, so did not arrive till to-day. Now, how shall I
act? It is my duty to write to Mr. Ward (meaning the said John
Ward) ; but the captain (meaning the plaintiff), who I believe a
good man, has a wife and family. These, my doing so would ruin.
I would not for all the world do that. I would rather, much rather,
run all the risk of going to India with a drunkard, who would
drink in winter time, in the English Channel, and leave his mate
to take her across the Bristol Channel ; and that is running no
small risk. Yet better that than ruin him (meaning the plaintiff).
But my character is dear to me ; and I may be ruined by the ship
running on shore while I have charge of the deck, as might have
happened in the case of the Runnelstone Rock (meaning the said
rock), the breakers on which, Providence gave me a sight of, in time
to wheel her (meaning the said vessel) round. We may not always
be so fortunate. The sea foamed close under our quarter as we
(meaning the said vessel and the persons on board the same) passed
it (meaning the said rock) ; and we (meaning &c.) just shaved the
buoy upon it (meaning the said rock). We made the passage
between Scilly and the Land's End. Of course, nothing has trans-
pired between the captain (meaning the plaintiff) and me. Since
his (meaning the plaintiff's) recovery, we are as sociable as before.
He (meaning the plaintiff) wondered what could have made him
(meaning the plaintiff) so ill. He (meaning the plaintiff) fancied
it must be some new milk we got in the Downs : and I made no
reply. He (meaning the plaintiff) is excessively civil to me. But
he (meaning the plaintiff) need not fear ; though, as everybody on
board knows it, it is very likely sooner or *later to reach Mr. Ward's
(meaning the said John Ward's) ears. We had a contrary wind across
the Bristol Channel ; and at one time I had thoughts of bearing up
for the nearest port, and giving her (meaning the said vessel) in
charge of a pilot : but the above consideration, viz. his (meaning the
plaintiff's) wife and family, deterred me : and, as I received every
assistance from the second mate, who is a steady young man and
lives with us in the cabin, I determined on working her (meaning the
said vessel) over to Carmarthen. The captain (meaning the plaintiff)
also, in a lucid interval, now and then implored me to take care
of the ship (meaning the said vessel), like a good lad and dear boy.

COXHEAD
v.
RICHARDS.

[*572]

[*573]

COXHEAD
v.
RICHARDS.

I pitied him, so stood on. Pray write me soon your advice how to act. Shall I let all pass, and go through the voyage, or get my discharge and a written good character from the captain (meaning the plaintiff), saying that personal differences make it necessary that we part? Then, again, I shall offend Mr. Ward (meaning the said John Ward), for leaving his ship (meaning the said vessel) in the lurch ; for, the second will leave if I do. Your advice shall be my guide : only, pray keep the affair a secret from Mr. Ward (meaning the said John Ward). I could suffer any thing rather than that should be so." By means of the committing of which grievances the plaintiff had been and was greatly injured in his said good character, and brought into public scandal, &c., with divers good and worthy subjects of this realm, insomuch that divers of those subjects, and particularly the said John Ward, had, on occasion of the committing of the said grievances, from thence suspected and believed, and the said John Ward still did suspect and believe, the plaintiff to have been and to be a drunkard and a person unfit to be trusted with the command of the said vessel, or

[*574]

any other vessel, and also by *reason thereof the said John Ward afterwards, to wit, on the day and year last aforesaid, refused and declined to retain and continue the plaintiff to command and be master and captain of the said vessel, as he otherwise would have done, and then discharged and dismissed the plaintiff from the command of the said vessel, and from the retainer and employ of the said John Ward ; and by reason thereof he the plaintiff had not only lost and been deprived of the support, gains, &c., which might and would otherwise have arisen and accrued to him from and by reason of his being so retained and employed as aforesaid, but had from thence remained and continued and still was out of employ and deprived of the opportunity of supporting himself by honest and industrious means, and had been and was, by means of the premises, otherwise greatly injured and damnified, &c.

The defendant pleaded : First, Not guilty ; secondly, a justification, alleging all the material statements in the libel to be true ; thirdly, that the said John Ward did not, by reason of the publishing of the supposed libel by the defendant as in the declaration mentioned, refuse or decline to retain and continue the plaintiff to command and be master and captain of the said vessel, nor did he by reason thereof dismiss and discharge the plaintiff from the command of the said vessel, or from the retainer and employ of the said John Ward, in manner and form as in the declaration in that behalf alleged.

The plaintiff joined issue on the first and third pleas, and replied *de injuriâ* to the second.

COXHEAD
v.
RICHARDS.

The cause was tried before Tindal, Ch. J., at the sittings in London after Michaelmas Term, 1843. The plaintiff, a mariner, had been some years in the employ of Ward, the shipowner, and was commander of the *England* upon the voyage mentioned in the declaration. *Cass, who was an intimate friend of the defendant, was the first mate. On receipt of Cass's letter, the defendant showed it to a naval friend, one of the Elder Brethren of the Trinity House, and also to Soames, an extensive shipowner, and, in accordance with their advice, communicated it to Ward, who immediately sent another captain down to Llanelly to supersede the plaintiff in the command of the *England*, and thenceforth ceased to employ the plaintiff. It did not appear that Ward had instituted any inquiry into the truth of the charges against the plaintiff, contained in Cass's letter.

[*575]

Cass and the second mate were both called as witnesses on behalf of the defendant; but they failed to sustain the justification. It was, however, contended that the defendant was entitled to a verdict on the first issue, on the ground that the communication of the letter to Ward, was confidential and privileged.

On the other hand, it was insisted that the defendant was liable, notwithstanding the absence of proof of express malice; there being nothing in the circumstances to render the communication excusable —no relation between the parties, no interest in the defendant, and no moral duty rendering it incumbent on him to make it.

The LORD CHIEF JUSTICE told the jury, that the occasion and circumstances under which the communication of the letter took place were such, as, in his opinion, to furnish a legal excuse for making the communication; that the inference of malice, which the law, *primâ facie*, draws from the bare act of publishing any statement, false in fact, containing matter to the reproach and prejudice of another, was thereby rebutted; and that the plaintiff, to entitle himself to a verdict, must show malice in fact: concluding by telling them that they should find their verdict for the defendant, if they thought the communication was strictly honest on his *part, and made solely in the execution of what he believed to be a duty; but for the plaintiff, if they thought the communication was made from any indirect motive whatever, or from any malice against the plaintiff.

[576]

The jury returned a verdict for the plaintiff on the second and third issues, and for the defendant on the first.

COXHEAD
v.
RICHARDS.

Sir T. Wilde, Serjt., in Hilary Term, 1844, obtained a rule *nisi* for a new trial, on the ground of misdirection.

Talfourd, Serjt., in Easter Term, 1844 (1), showed cause:

The question was properly submitted to the jury. The defendant, having received from a person whom he had known for many years, a letter containing statements of vital importance to the interests of Mr. Ward, the owner of the vessel, respecting the conduct of his captain, and honestly believing those statements to be true, after having sought advice from persons who were peculiarly qualified to give it, communicated the contents to Mr. Ward. The circumstances clearly negative the inference of malice which the law ordinarily draws from the unauthorized publication of defamatory statements. It is true the defendant had no interest in the matter, and that he stood in no particular relation either to Ward or to Cass. This case, therefore, wants the ingredients that have in some of the cases been held to make the publication excusable. But the question is whether this was not a communication which, according to the exigencies of society, he was morally bound to make. * * *

[577]
[*578]

(CRESSWELL, J.: In *Cockayne* v. *Hodgkisson* (2), PARKE, B., lays it down, that every wilful *unauthorized publication, injurious to the character of another, is a libel; but that, where the writer is acting on any duty, legal or moral, towards the person to whom he writes, or where he has, by his situation, to protect the interest of that person, that which he writes under such circumstances is a privileged communication, and no action will lie for what is thus written, unless the writer be actuated by malice. If that be correct, the question here is, whether this defendant was bound, by any moral duty, to make the communication he did.)

He had a moral duty to protect the lives of the crew, and the property of the owner and charterers, which he had just grounds for believing to be in danger. [He cited Buller's Nisi Prius, 7th ed. p. 8, *Vanspike* v. *Cleyson* (3), *Wright* v. *Woodgate* (4), *Pattison* v. *Jones* (5), *Child* v. *Affleck* (6), *Todd* v. *Hawkins* (7), *Kine* v. *Sewell* (8), *Toogood*

(1) The Judges present being Tindal, Ch. J., and Coltman, Erskine, and Cresswell, JJ.

(2) 38 R. R. 845 (5 Car. & P. 543).

(3) Cro. Eliz. 541.

(4) 41 R. R. 788 (2 Cr., M. & R. 573).

(5) 32 R. R. 490 (8 B. & C. 578; 3 Man. & Ry. 101).

(6) 33 R. R. 216 (9 B. & C. 403; 4 Man. & Ry. 338).

(7) 2 Moo. & Rob. 20; 8 Car. & P. 88.

(8) 49 R. R. 603 (3 M. & W. 297).

v. *Spyring* (1), *Woodward* v. *Lander* (2), and *Shipley* v. *Todhunter* (3).]
The special damage alleged in the declaration in this case, is clearly
not a damage that is fairly and legitimately the result of the communication of the letter. It was the duty of Mr. Ward to make
inquiry into the truth of the aspersions cast upon the character of
the captain, before he acted upon the defendant's information.

>   *Sir T. Wilde*, Serjt. (with whom was *Bramwell*), in support of
>   the rule:

The publication of the letter by *the defendant was wholly
inexcusable. He had no interest in the ship or in the freight; he
stood in no such relation, either to the owner, the captain, or the
mate, as could impose upon him any duty, legal or moral, to act as
he did. The subject-matter of the communication was not so
pressing as to require him to act on the instant: there was ample
time for inquiry into the truth of the statement, seeing that the
ship was not to sail from Llanelly for at least three weeks (4), and
yet none was made. The writer of the letter expressly cautions his
friend (5) to abstain from doing the very act which has caused all
the injury of which the plaintiff complains, viz. showing the letter
to Mr. Ward. There is nothing in the law of England to justify a
party in thus becoming a volunteer in the propagation of slander.
Unless the circumstances rendered the occasion of the publication
lawful, there was no necessity to prove express malice : the act being
unauthorized, and injurious to the plaintiff, the law implies that it
is malicious. It is suggested on the part of the defendant, that, in
showing the letter to Mr. Ward, he acted in the honest and *bonâ fide*
execution of a moral duty. But, what is there to give rise to any
moral obligation on the defendant to repeat the slander? Did he
owe no moral duty to the plaintiff, to abstain from publishing
injurious statements until he had by inquiry satisfied himself that
they were founded in truth? There are various occasions upon
which, for the general convenience of society, communications
that would otherwise be unlawful, are held to be excusable. [He
cited *Rogers* v. *Clifton* (6), *Pattison* v. *Jones* (7), *Child* v. *Affleck* (8),

[*581]

(1) 40 R. R. 523 (1 Cr., M. & R.
181 ; 4 Tyr. 582).
(2) 40 R. R. 816 (6 Car. & P. 548).
(3) 7 Car. & P. 680.
(4) This appeared from a part of the
letter that was not set out in the
declaration.

(5) After saying "It is my duty to
write to Mr. Ward."
(6) 3 Bos. & P. 587.
(7) 32 R. R. 490 (8 B. & C. 578; 3
Man. & Ry. 101).
(8) 33 R. R. 216 (9 B. & C. 403 ; 4
Man. & Ry. 338).

COXHEAD
v.
RICHARDS.
[583]

M'Dougall v. *Claridge* (1), *Shipley* v. *Todhunter* (2), *Bromage* v. *Prosser* (3), and *Martin* v. *Strong* (4).] The present case, however, clearly does not fall within any of the classes of privileged communications allowed by law. There is a total absence of interest on the part of the defendant, as well as of that sort of relation between the writer of the letter and the shipowner, which could justify the exhibition of the letter to him. There was nothing to give rise to a semblance of duty, either legal or moral.

The COURT took time to consider their judgment: but, there being a difference of opinion amongst the Judges who heard the case argued, and ERSKINE, J. (5), having retired from the Bench, a second argument was directed.

The second argument took place in Easter Term, 1845, before Tindal, Ch. J., and Coltman, Cresswell, and Erle, JJ.

[584]

Talfourd and *Channell*, Serjts., for the defendant :

The question is, whether, in point of law, the communication complained of necessarily imported malice. The law *primâ facie* implies malice in the publisher of defamatory matter to the injury of another; but this presumption is liable to be rebutted by the circumstances of each particular case. That is shown by this, that the defence is admissible under Not guilty, and need not be specially pleaded; which, though the Court pronounced no opinion on the point in *Smith* v. *Thomas* (6), is now clear law. To sustain his action, the plaintiff must show that the publication was wrongful, and not justified by the occasion: *Lay* v. *Lawson* (7), *Hearne* v. *Stowell* (8). Formerly a greater latitude was allowed than can now be contended for: *Brooke* v. *Montague* (9), *Delany* v. *Jones* (10).

(CRESSWELL, J. : Is not the rule this—whether the occasion is such as to rebut the inference of malice, if the publication is *bonâ fide* is a question of law for the Judge; whether the *bona fides* existed, is a question of fact for the jury ?)

(1) 10 R. R. 679 (1 Camp. 267).
(2) 7 Car. & P. 680.
(3) 28 R. R. 241 (4 B. & C. 247; 6 Dowl. & Ry. 296).
(4) 44 R. R. 487 (5 Ad. & El. 535; 1 Nev. & P. 29).
(5) The opinion of that learned Judge is understood to have been in favour of the defendant.

(6) 42 R. R. 617 (2 Bing. N. C. 372; 2 Scott, 546; 4 Dowl. P. C. 333). And see Popham, 69.
(7) 43 R. R. 487 (4 Ad. & El. 795).
(8) 54 R. R. 663 (12 Ad. & El. 719).
(9) Cro. Jac. 90.
(10) 4 Esp. 191. See 43 R. R. 489, n.

Such undoubtedly is the rule.

COXHEAD
v.
RICHARDS.

(TINDAL, Ch. J. : The mode of publishing goes to the latter point; as where the publication is in a newspaper.)

Here, the defendant, who had been for some years on terms of intimacy with Cass, receives a letter from him, containing matters of a very alarming description relative to the conduct of the captain, which, though directly involving the safety of the ship, the cargo, and the crew, he is strictly enjoined not to communicate to Ward, the owner. Having no knowledge of the plaintiff, or of Ward, the defendant adopts the only course that an honest and discreet *person, under such circumstances, could pursue : he consults with one of the Elder Brethren of the Trinity House, and with an eminent shipowner ; under whose advice, he, without any comment, shows the letter to Ward. What, then, was the owner's duty ? Certainly not to dismiss the captain, without investigating the charges made against him. The dismissal was not the fair and legitimate consequence of the defendant's act (1). The information was of the utmost importance to the owner : the only doubt arises from there being no relation of any kind between him and the defendant, and no application by him for information. The definition of a privileged communication given by PARKE, B., in *Wright* v. *Woodgate*, is perhaps as accurate as any that can be found. That the rule is founded on a consideration of the importance of the information to the party to whom it is given, is evident from the cases. [They cited in addition to the cases cited on the first argument : *Padmore* v. *Lawrence* (2), *Blake* v. *Pilfold* (3), and *Warr* v. *Jolly* (4).] Here, the communication made by the defendant to Mr. Ward, was made in the honest and *bonâ fide* discharge of a moral duty towards that gentleman (5). If the defendant had had any interest in the matter, or was in any way connected with Mr. Ward, there could be no

[*585]

[587]

(1) Taking Ward to have been under contract to employ, he would appear to be alone responsible for the wrongful dismissal, notwithstanding legal, or even actual malice in the defendant : *Morris* v. *Langdale*, 2 Bos. & P. 284 ; *Vicars* v. *Wilcocks*, 9 R. R. 361 [but see note there, and Preface—F.P.] (8 East, 1). If there was no contract, Ward — whose interests might be endangered by delay, and who had incurred no responsibility as the propagator of an injurious report,—

would be under no legal obligation to investigate the truth of the charges made by Cass.

(2) 11 Ad. & El. 380 ; 3 P. & D. 209.

(3) 42 R. R. 776 (1 Moo. & Rob. 198).

(4) 6 Car. & P. 497.

(5) The jury must be taken to have negatived the apparent motive of the defendant, viz. a wish to obtain promotion for his friend Cass, the mate, at the expense of Coxhead, the master.

COXHEAD
v.
RICHARDS.

doubt that the legal inference of malice would be rebutted by the occasion : but the question is, whether the rule is to be so limited, and whether the defendant was not morally bound to communicate to Mr. Ward the information he had received from Cass.

[*588]

(COLTMAN, J.: Your argument would extend to the protection of a communication founded on mere *idle gossip.)

The communication would not be protected unless there were just grounds for believing the information to be true.

(CRESSWELL, J.: You would make the moral duty of communicating defamatory matter to one interested in the subject, to depend upon the source whence it comes, and upon whether the circumstances under which the communicating party received the information, made it reasonable for him to believe it to be true ?)

Precisely so.

(CRESSWELL, J.: That would lead to a very wide and inconvenient field of inquiry.

ERLE, J.: Suppose a conversation to take place in a public-house between very disreputable people, from which it appears that A. intends to commit a felony in the house of B. ; would not C., overhearing the conversation, be justified in communicating it to B.? The more disreputable the source of the information, the more ground for giving credence to it.)

The characters of the parties would certainly be one test. Here, the character and situation of the writer of the letter, as well as of the captain, were known to Mr. Ward. If the defendant was bound to disregard the communication, so was the owner (1). The letter clearly did not justify the captain's dismissal, and would have afforded no defence to an action for depriving him of the command (2).

Sir T. Wilde, Serjt., and *Bramwell* for the plaintiff :

The general point is of great importance, and the public are indebted to the Court for giving it further consideration. Every man is responsible for an intentional injury done to another, unless the circumstances are such as to justify or to excuse it. In the

(1) So, *e converso.*
(2) Whether such action would lie, would depend upon the existence, or non-existence, of a prospectively binding contract to employ, *supra,* p. 539, n. (1).

present case, to entitle the plaintiff to maintain the action, he was
not bound to show actual malice: it *was enough if the publication
of the libel took place under circumstances that deprived it of the
protection which the law affords to communications of a class to
which the term "privileged" is usually applied. * * The convenience of trade and commerce requires considerable freedom of
communication respecting the credit and responsibility of a trader:
and yet a distinction is taken between one who answers inquiries,
and one who volunteers information: *King* v. *Watts* (1).

(TINDAL, Ch. J.: Suppose the defendant had gone to Mr. Ward,
and told him he had received a communication that materially
affected his interest, and Mr. Ward had then asked him to show
the letter, would that have justified the production of it?)

Possibly it might. Here, however, nothing of the kind took place:
the defendant was a mere volunteer. The cases as to characters of
servants, are not in point. Judges may have been wrong in
supposing that a former master stands in a peculiar position. It
may be said that the servant authorises the master to libel him.
But, right or wrong, the cases proceed upon that distinction.

(ERLE, J.: In those cases, it is perfectly immaterial whether the
party was a volunteer: the sole question is, whether the information
was given honestly *and bonâ fide.*

CRESSWELL, J.: Mr. Justice BAYLEY deals much more clearly
with the principle upon which this class of cases proceeds than
Lord TENTERDEN does in *Pattison* v. *Jones.*)

[They cited *Mercer* v. *Sparks* (2), *Edmonson* v. *Stevenson* (3), *Getting*
v. *Foss* (4), *Humphreys* v. *Miller* (5), *Martin* v. *Strong* (6), *Fairman*
v. *Ives* (7), and *Brooks* v. *Blanshard* (8).]

                              Cur. adv. vult.

There being still a difference of opinion, the Judges now delivered
their opinions *seriatim*, as follows:

TINDAL, Ch. J.:

This was an action upon the case for the publication of a false

Marginal notes:
COXHEAD
v.
RICHARDS.
[*589]
[591]
[*592]
[593]

(1) 8 Car. & P. 614. And see
Bennett v. *Deacon*, *post*, p. 568.
(2) Owen, 51; Noy, 35.
(3) Bull. N. P. 8.
(4) 3 Car. & P. 160.
(5) 4 Car. & P. 7.

(6) 44 R. R. 487 (5 Ad. & El. 535;
1 Nev. & P. 29).
(7) 24 R. R. 514 (5 B. & Ald. 642;
1 Dowl. & Ry. 252; 1 Chitty, 85).
(8) 3 Tyr. 844.

and malicious libel, in the form of a letter written by one John Cass, the first mate of a ship called the *England*, to the defendant; the letter stating that the plaintiff, who was the captain of the ship, and then in command of her, had been in a state of constant drunkenness during part of the voyage, whereby the ship and crew had been exposed to continual danger: and the publication by the defendant was, the communication by him of this letter to the owner of the ship, by reason whereof, which was the special damage alleged in the declaration, the plaintiff was dismissed from the ship, and lost his employment.

The defendant pleaded: first, Not guilty; secondly, that the charges made by the mate against the plaintiff in his letter, were true; and, lastly, that the shipowner did not dismiss the captain by reason, and in consequence, of the communication of the letter to him.

Upon the last two issues a verdict was found for the plaintiff; but, upon the first issue, for the defendant.

I told the jury at the trial, that the occasion and the circumstances under which the communication of this *letter took place, were such, as, in my opinion, to furnish a legal excuse for making the communication; and that the inference of malice, which the law *primâ facie* draws from the bare act of publishing any statements false in fact, containing matter to the reproach and prejudice of another, was thereby rebutted; and that the plaintiff, to entitle himself to a verdict, must show malice in fact: concluding by telling them that they should find their verdict for the defendant, if they thought the communication was strictly honest on his part, and made solely in the execution of what he believed (1) to be a duty; but, for the plaintiff, if they thought the communication was made from any indirect motive whatever, or from any malice against the plaintiff. And the only question now before us is, whether, upon the evidence given at the trial, such direction was right.

There was no evidence whatever that the defendant was actuated by any sinister motive in communicating the letter to Mr. Ward, the shipowner: on the contrary, all the evidence went to prove that what he did he did under the full belief that he was performing a duty, however mistaken he might be as to the existence of such duty, or

[*594]

---

(1) A., a stranger, receives information respecting the misconduct of B.,
which he honestly misapplies to C. Is
   A. justified in causing the dismissal of
C. from the service of D. ?

in his mode of performing it. The writer of the letter was no COXHEAD
stranger to the defendant: on the contrary, both were proved to *v.*
have been on terms of friendship with each other for some years; RICHARDS.
and, from the tenor of the letter itself, it must be inferred the
defendant was a person upon whose judgment the writer of the
letter placed great reliance, the letter itself being written for the
professed purpose of obtaining his advice how to act, under a
very pressing difficulty. The letter was framed in very artful
terms, such as were calculated to induce the most wary and
prudent man (knowing the *writer) to place reliance on the truth   [*595]
of its details: and there can be no doubt but that the defendant
did in fact thoroughly believe the contents to be true, amongst
other things, that the ship, of which Mr. Ward was the owner,
and the crew and cargo on board the same, had been exposed
to very imminent risk, by the continued intoxication of the captain
on the voyage from the French coast to Llanelly, where the ship
then was, and that the voyage to the Eastern Seas, for which the
ship was chartered, would be continually exposed to the same
hazard, if the vessel should continue under his command. In
this state of facts, after the letter had been a few days in his hands,
the defendant considered it to be his duty to communicate its
contents to Mr. Ward, whose interests were so nearly concerned in
the information; not communicating it to the public, but to Mr.
Ward; and not accompanying such disclosure with any directions
or advice, but merely putting him in possession of the facts stated
in the letter, that he might be in a condition to investigate the
truth, and take such steps as prudence and justice to the parties
concerned required: in making which disclosure he did not act
hastily or unadvisedly, but consulted two persons well qualified to
give good advice on such an emergency, the one, an Elder Brother
of the Trinity House, the other, one of the most eminent ship-
owners in London: in conformity with whose advice he gave up
the letter to the owner of the ship. At the same time, if the
defendant took a course which was not justifiable in point of law,
although it proceeded from an error in judgment only, not of
intention, still it is undoubtedly he, and not the plaintiff, who
must suffer for such error.

The only question is, whether the case does or does not fall
within the principle, well recognized and established in the law,
relating to privileged or confidential *communications; and, in   [*596]
determining this question, two points may, as I conceive, be

COXHEAD
v.
RICHARDS.

considered as settled: first, that if the defendant had had any personal interest in the subject-matter to which the letter related, as, if he had been a part-owner of the ship, or an underwriter on the ship, or had had any property on board, the communication of such a letter to Mr. Ward would have fallen clearly within the rule relating to excusable publications; and, secondly, that if the danger disclosed by the letter, either to the ship or the cargo, or the ship's company, had been so immediate as that the disclosure to the shipowner was necessary to avert such danger, then, upon the ground of social duty, by which every man is bound to his neighbour, the defendant would have been not only justified in making the disclosure, but would have been bound to make it. A man who received a letter informing him that his neighbour's house would be plundered or burnt on the night following by A. and B., and which he himself believed, and had reason to believe, to be true, would be justified in showing that letter to the owner of the house, though it should turn out to be a false accusation of A. and B. The question before us appears, therefore, to be narrowed to the consideration of the facts which bear upon these two particular qualifications and restrictions of the general principle.

As to the first, I do not find the rule of law is so narrowed and restricted by any authority, that a person having information materially affecting the interests of another, and honestly communicating it, in the full belief, and with reasonable grounds for the belief, that it is true, will not be excused, though he has no personal interest in the subject-matter. Such a restriction would surely operate as a great restraint upon the performance of the various social duties by which men are bound to each other, and by which society is kept up. *In Pattison v. Jones* (1), the defendant, who had discharged the plaintiff from his service, wrote a letter to the person who was about to engage him, unsolicited; he was therefore a volunteer in the matter; and might be considered as a stranger, having no interest in the business; but, neither at the trial, nor on the motion before the Court, was it suggested that the letter was, on that account, an unprivileged communication; but it was left to the jury to say whether the communication was honest or malicious. Again, in *Child v. Affleck* and wife (2), the statement, by the former mistress, of the conduct of her servant, not only during her service, but after she had left it, was held to be

[*597]

(1) 32 R. R. 490 (8 B. & C. 578; 3 Man. & Ry. 101).

(2) 33 R. R. 216 (9 B. & C. 403; 4 Man. & Ry. 338).

privileged. The rule appears to have been correctly laid down by COXHEAD
the Court of Exchequer, that, " if fairly warranted by any reason-   *v.*
RICHARDS,
able occasion or exigency, and honestly made, such communications
are protected, for the common convenience and welfare of society ;
and the law has not restricted the right to make them, within any
narrow limits." In the present case, the defendant stood in a
different situation from any other person ; he was the only person
in the world who had received the letter, or was acquainted with
the information contained in it. He cannot, therefore, properly be
treated as a complete stranger to the subject-matter of inquiry (1),
even if the rule excluded strangers from the privilege (2).

Upon the second ground of qualification — was the danger
sufficiently imminent to justify the communication—it is true, that
the letter, which came to the defendant's *hands about the 14th of   [*598]
December, contains within it the information that the ship cannot
get out of harbour before the end of the month. It was urged that
the defendant, instead of communicating the letter to the owner,
might have instituted some inquiry himself. But it is to be observed
that every day the ship remained under the command of such a
person as the plaintiff was described to be, the ship and crew
continued exposed to hazard, though not so great hazard as when
at sea ; not to mention the immediate injury to the shipowner
which must necessarily follow from want of discipline of the crew,
and the bad example of such a master. And, after all, it would be
too much to say, that, even if the thing had been practicable, any
duty was cast upon the defendant, to lay out his time or money in
the investigation of the charge (3).

Upon the consideration of the case, I think it was the duty of the
defendant not to keep the knowledge he gained by this letter himself, and thereby make himself responsible, in conscience, if his
neglect of the warnings of the letter brought destruction upon the
ship or crew—that a prudent and reasonable man would have done
the same; that the disclosure was made, not publicly, but privately
to the owner, that is, to the person who of all the world was the
best qualified, both from his interest in the subject-matter, and his
knowledge of his own officers, to form the most just conclusion as
to its truth, and to adopt the most proper and effective measures

---

(1) He did not cease to be a stranger
in point of interest, by ceasing to be a
stranger in point of knowledge.

(2) In this view of the case, *quære,*
whether the defendant would have

once more become a stranger to the
subject-matter of inquiry upon ceasing
to be the sole depositary of the information ?

(3) *Vide supra,* 539, *n.* (1).

COXHEAD
v.
RICHARDS.

to avert the danger; after which disclosure, not the defendant, but the owner, became liable to the plaintiff, if the owner took steps which were not justifiable; as, by unjustly dismissing him from his employment, if the letter was untrue. And, as all this was done with entire honesty of purpose, and in the full belief of the truth

[*599]

of the information, *and that, a reasonable belief, I am still of the same opinion which I entertained at the trial, that this case ranges itself within the pale of privileged communication, and that the action is not maintainable.

I therefore think the rule for setting aside the verdict and for a new trial, should be discharged.

COLTMAN, J.:

I regret much that I am unable in this case to agree with the opinion of my LORD CHIEF JUSTICE, that it is a sufficient justification of the defendant's conduct, that he acted *bonâ fide*, and without malice.

The facts of the case, which I consider as material, are, that, on the 14th of December, the defendant received from the mate of a ship belonging to Mr. Ward, a letter containing imputations against the captain, of constant drunkenness and unfitness for command, asking for the defendant's advice, and informing him that the ship was then at Llanelly, and would not sail thence before the end of the month. There was no intimacy between the defendant and Mr. Ward, nor any relation in business between them. The defendant, after consulting with two friends, by their advice communicated the letter to Mr. Ward.

I apprehend the rule of law applicable to questions of this nature is laid down with accuracy by the Court of Exchequer in the case of *Toogood* v. *Spyring*, where it is said, " In general, an action lies for the malicious publication of statements which are false in fact, and injurious to the character of another (within the well-known limits as to verbal slander); and the law considers such publication as malicious, unless it is fairly made by a person in the discharge of some public or private duty, whether legal or moral, or in the conduct of his own affairs in matters where his interest is concerned. In such cases, the occasion prevents the inference of malice which

[*600]

the law draws from unauthorized *communications, and affords a qualified defence depending upon the absence of actual malice. If fairly warranted by any reasonable occasion or exigency, and honestly made, such communications are protected, for the common

convenience and welfare of society ; and the law has not restricted   COXHEAD
v.
RICHARDS.
the right to make them, within any narrow limits."

Communications of this nature have been commonly termed
privileged communications; and the term, if not strictly accurate,
is perhaps sufficiently so for practical purposes : and it has been
generally held, and, in my judgment, rightly held, that the question
whether a communication is privileged or not, is a question of law
for the Judge; but, in considering the question whether a communication is privileged or not, the condition necessary to make it
privileged, must be assumed.   What I mean by this remark, will
be more intelligible by referring to the line of argument used on
the discussion of the present motion.   In the first argument of this
case, many remarks were made on the mate's letter, tending to
show that a man at all experienced in the ways of the world,
could not have been duped by the statements in the letter, or have
believed them to be true.   But it appears to me that such a line
of argument is inapplicable to the question of law—whether the
communication was privileged; for, the question of law is, whether,
assuming that the defendant really and *bonâ fide* believed the contents of the letter to be true, the occasion was such as justified the
making the communication; in other words, according to the rule
laid down by the Court of Exchequer in *Toogood* v. *Spyring*, whether
there was any duty, public or private, legal or moral, calling on the
defendant to make the communication complained of.   It cannot, I
think, be said that there was any legal duty, was there any moral
duty, calling on him to make it ?

The necessity which exists in the transactions of society, for free   [601]
inquiry, and for facilities in obtaining information for the guidance
of persons engaged in important matters of business, has so far
prevailed, that it has been established as a rule, that, for words
spoken confidentially upon advice asked, no action lies, unless
express malice can be proved : *Bromage* v. *Prosser.*   The duty
which may be supposed to exist, to give advice faithfully to those
who are in want of it, has been allowed to prevail for the sake of
the general convenience of business, though with some disregard of
the equally important rule of morality, that a man should not speak
ill, falsely, of his neighbour.   Even though the statement be not
on advice asked, but is made voluntarily, that circumstance was
said, in *Pattison* v. *Jones*, not necessarily to prevent the statement
from being considered as privileged.   Assuming, then, upon the
authority of that case, that the circumstance of the communication

85—2

COXHEAD
v.
RICHARDS.

being voluntary, is no insuperable bar to its being regarded as a privileged communication, we return to the consideration of the question, whether there was any moral duty, binding on the defendant, to make the communication now in question. And, on the best consideration I can give the subject, I think the duty was plainly the other way. The duty of not slandering your neighbour on insufficient grounds, is so clear, that a violation of that duty ought not to be sanctioned in the case of voluntary communications, except under circumstances of great urgency and gravity.

It may be said, that it is very hard on a defendant to be subject to heavy damages where he has acted honestly, and where nothing more can be imputed to him than an error in judgment. It may be hard: but it is very hard, on the other hand, to be falsely accused. It is to be borne in mind that people are but too apt rashly to think ill of others: the propensity to tale-bearing and [*602] *slander is so strong amongst mankind, and, when suspicions are infused, men are so apt to entertain them without due examination, in cases where their interests are concerned, that it is necessary to hold the rule strictly as to any officious intermeddling by which the character of others is affected.

In the present case, the occasion was in no respect urgent. The vessel was not to sail till the end of the month. There was abundant time for the defendant to write to the mate, and for the mate to act as he should be advised; or for the defendant to take any other steps to ascertain the truth of the statement, before he communicated it in a quarter where it was likely to be productive of so much injury to the plaintiff. It appears to me, therefore, that the communication ought not to be considered as being privileged, and that its being made *bonâ fide* did not entitle the defendant to a verdict: and, with the greatest deference to those who differ from me, and whose opinions are entitled to much more weight than that which I have formed, I think it my duty to state my own.

CRESSWELL, J. :

I cannot, without much regret, express an opinion in this case at variance with that which is entertained by my Lord and one of my learned brothers. But, having given full consideration to the arguments urged at the Bar, and the cases cited, and not being able to shake off the impression which they made in favour of the plaintiff, I am bound to act upon the opinion that I have formed. I will not repeat the facts of the case, which have been already

stated, but proceed shortly to explain the grounds upon which my
opinion rests.

There is no doubt that the letter published by the defendant of
the plaintiff, was defamatory; and the truth of its contents could
not be proved.   The plaintiff was, *therefore, entitled to maintain
an action against the publisher of that letter, unless the occasion
on which it was published made the publication of such letter a
lawful act, as far as the plaintiff was concerned, if done in good
faith, and without actual malice.   To sustain an action for a libel
or slander, the plaintiff must show that it was malicious; but every
unauthorised publication of defamatory matter is, in point of law,
to be considered as malicious.   The law, however, on a principle of
policy and convenience, authorises many communications, although
they affect the characters of individuals; and I take it to be a
question of law, whether the communication is authorised or not.
If it be authorised, the legal presumption of malice arising from
the unauthorised publication of defamatory matter, fails, and the
plaintiff, to sustain his action, must prove actual malice, or, as it
is usually expressed, malice in fact.   In the present case, the
existence of malice in fact was negatived by the jury; and if my
Lord was right in telling them, that, in the absence of malice in
fact, the publication of the letter was privileged, this rule should
be discharged.   It therefore becomes necessary to inquire within
what limits and boundaries the law authorises the publication of
defamatory matter.   Perhaps the best description of those limits
and boundaries that can be given in few words, is to be found in
the judgment of PARKE, B., in *Toogood* v. *Spyring* : " The law considers such publication as malicious, unless it is fairly made by a
person in the discharge of some public or private duty, whether
legal or moral, or in the conduct of his own affairs in matters where
his interest is concerned."   It was not contended in this case that
any legal duty bound the defendant to communicate to the shipowner the contents of the letter he had received, nor was the
communication made in the conduct of his own affairs, nor was
his interest concerned: the *authority for the publication, if any,
must therefore be derived from some moral duty, public or private,
which it was incumbent upon him to discharge.   I think it impossible to say that the defendant was called upon by any public duty
to make the communication; neither his own situation nor that
of any of the parties concerned, nor the interests at stake, were
such as to affect the public weal. Was there then any private duty?

CoxHEAD
v.
RICHARDS.

There was no relation of principal and agent between the ship-owner and the defendant, nor was any trust or confidence reposed by the former in the latter; there was no relationship or intimacy between them; no inquiries had been made; they were, until the time in question, strangers: the duty, if it existed at all as between them, must, therefore, have arisen from the mere circumstance of their being fellow-subjects of the realm. But the same relation existed between the defendant and the plaintiff. If the property of the shipowner on the one hand was at stake, the character of the captain was at stake on the other; and I cannot but think that the moral duty not to publish of the latter defamatory matter which he did not know to be true, was quite as strong as the duty to communicate to the shipowner that which he believed to be true. Was, then, the defendant bound by any moral duty towards the writer of the letter, to make the communication? Surely not. If the captain had misconducted himself, the mate was capable of observing it, and was as capable of communicating it to the owner as to the defendant. The crew were, in like manner, capable of observing and acting for themselves. The mate (if he really believed that which he wrote to be true) might, indeed, be under a moral duty to communicate it to his owner: but the defendant had no right to take that vicarious duty upon himself: he was not requested by the mate to do so, but was, on the contrary, enjoined not to make the communication.

[605]   I will not attempt to comment upon the very numerous cases that were quoted at the Bar on the one side and on the other, but will advert to one or two which tend to explain the term "moral duty," and see whether it has ever been held to authorise the publication of defamatory matter under circumstances similar to those which exist in the present case. In *Bromage* v. *Prosser*, BAYLEY, J., in his very elaborate judgment, speaks of slander as "*primâ facie* excusable on account of the cause of speaking or writing it, in the case of servants' characters, confidential advice, or communications to those who ask it or have a right to expect it." With regard to the characters of servants and agents, it is so manifestly for the advantage of society that those who are about to employ them should be enabled to learn what their previous conduct has been, that it may be well deemed the moral duty of former employers to answer inquiries to the best of their belief. But, according to the opinion of the same learned Judge, intimated in *Pattison* v. *Jones*, it is necessary that inquiry should be made,

in order to render lawful the communication of defamatory matter,   COXHEAD
although he was also of opinion that such inquiry may be invited   RICHARDS.
by the former master. And in *Rogers* v. *Clifton*, CHAMBRE, J.,
quoted a similar opinion of Lord MANSFIELD'S, expressed in *Lowry*
v. *Aikenhead* (1).

It was contended during the argument of this case, that the
protection given to masters when speaking of the conduct of
servants, was more extensive, and applied also to communications
made to former employers; and *Child* v. *Affleck* was mentioned as
an instance. But the communication to the former master was
not made a ground of action in that case, and was introduced only
as evidence that the statement made in answer to the inquiry of
the new master was malicious. The *same observation applies to   [*606]
Rogers v. *Clifton;* and it may be collected from the report that
CHAMBRE, J., was of opinion, that, where statements are made
which are not in answer to inquiries, the defendant must plead,
and prove, a justification.

Again, where a party asks advice or information upon a subject
on which he is interested; or where the relative position of two
parties is such that the one has a right to expect confidential
information and advice from the other; it may be a moral duty to
answer such inquiries and give such information and advice; and
the statements made may be rendered lawful by the occasion,
although defamatory of some third person, as in *Dunman* v. *Bigg*(2)
and *Todd* v. *Hawkins* (3).

Two cases, *Herver* v. *Dowson* (4), and *Cleaver* v. *Sarraude*,
reported in *M'Dougall* v. *Claridge* (5), were quoted as authorities
for giving a more extended meaning to the term "moral duty,"
and making it include all cases where one man had information,
which, if true, it would be important for another to know. But
the notes of those cases are very short: in the former the precise
circumstances under which the statement was made—see *King* v.
Watts (6), that such a statement made without inquiry is not
lawful—and in the latter, the position of the defendant with
reference to the Bishop of Durham, to whom it was made, are left
unexplained. I cannot, therefore, consider them as satisfactory
authorities for the position to establish which they were quoted:
and, in the absence of any clear and precise authority in favour

(1) 3 Bos. & P. 594.   (4) Bull. N. P. 8.
(2) 10 R. R. 680, n. (1 Camp. 269). (5) 10 R. R. 680 (1 Camp. 268)
(3) 2 Moo. & Rob. 20; 8 Car. & P. 88. (6) 8 Car. & P. 614.

COXHEAD
v.
RICHARDS.
[*607]

of it, I cannot persuade myself that it is correct, as, if established at all, it must be at the expense of another moral duty, viz. not *to publish defamatory matter unless you know it to be true.

For these reasons, I am of opinion, that the rule for a new trial should be made absolute.

ERLE, J. :

In this case a rule *nisi* for a new trial was obtained on the ground of misdirection.

The plaintiff, who was the captain of a ship, brought his action for a publication of a libel in showing to the shipowner a letter from the mate to the defendant, imputing misconduct to the captain.

The defendant, who was a stranger to the plaintiff, and but little known to the shipowner, had reason to believe, from the contents of the letter, that the ship and crew were in danger of destruction if the letter was withheld, and that such danger would be averted if the letter was shown. The jury were directed to find for the defendant, if, in their judgment, the defendant acted *bonâ fide* in showing the letter; and this direction is the subject of objection.

The plaintiff contends that there was no evidence to rebut the presumption of malice arising from the publication of a libel; that there was no justifying occasion for the communication in question, because the defendant stood in no relation either to the shipowner or to the captain, and had no interest in the ship or crew.

But the principle upon which communications may be said to be protected, the presumption of malice being rebutted, appears to me to be not restricted in the manner so contended for. Among such protected communications, there are some in which the protection is derived from the subject-matter alone, without regard to any relation in which the author may stand, such as criticism and public comments: *Carr* v. *Hood* (1), *Parmeter* v. *Coupland* (2).

[608]

There are others in which the protection is derived from the relation in which the giver of the information stands to the person who is the subject of it; as in the case of a communication by a party in the conduct of his affairs where his interest is concerned: *Fairman* v. *Ives* (3), *M'Dougall* v. *Claridge* (4), *Toogood* v. *Spyring*.

There is also another class in which the protection appears to me to be derived from the relation in which the receiver of the information stands to the person who is the subject of it; as in

(1) 10 R. R. 701, n. (1 Camp. 355).   (3) 24 R. R. 514 (5 B. & Ald. 642).
(2) 55 R. R. 529 (6 M. & W. 105).   (4) 10 R. R. 680 (1 Camp. 267).

the case of information given to prevent damage from misconduct; and for this class I think it is not essential that the giver of the information should stand in any relation to the other parties.

It is clear that the rule is founded on a consideration of the importance of the information to the interest of the receiver. And this consideration has no reference to the source whence the information is derived.

Cases have been referred to in which such information was held to be justified, if the *bona fides* was found by the jury, and in which no mention is made of the defendant's being placed in any relation which made it a duty on his part to inform.

The notice to a vendor to beware of the plaintiff as purchaser, in *Herver* v. *Dowson*, also the notice to a landlord of the misconduct of the plaintiff, his steward, in *Cleaver* v. *Sarraude*, also the notice to a next friend of an infant plaintiff in a Chancery suit, to beware of the character of the plaintiff, as likely to create liability for costs, in *Wright* v. *Woodgate*, and the notice of a report of a run upon the Bank of the plaintiff to a person being in the neighbourhood, and liable to be affected thereby, in *Bromage* v. *Prosser*, may be taken as examples.

A common application of the principle is, in the giving of the characters of servants; and this occurs *most frequently in respect of a former master's answer to an inquiry; and the rule is often expressed as if it were essential that the giver of the information should stand in the relation of the former master. But, on considering the reason of the rule, and the authorities, that form of expression appears to me to be incorrect.   [*609]

It is clear that the rule is founded on the interest of the receiver to know the character of the servant. It is also clear, that, if the giver of the information indulges any selfish motive in giving a bad character, he loses the protection, on the ground of express malice.

In *Rogers* v. *Clifton*, *Pattison* v. *Jones*, and *Child* v. *Affleck*, it was considered by some Judges that a former master volunteering a character, would be justified if acting *bonâ fide*: but a former master so volunteering stands in no relation either to the servant or the new master; he is; in effect, a stranger, and is not called on by inquiry.

In *Blake* v. *Pilfold* (1), the defendant, who stood in no present or past relation to the plaintiff or his employers, was held justified in communicating the information he had received, on account of

(1) 42 R. R. 776 (1 Moo. & Rob. 198).

COXHEAD
v.
RICHARDS.

the interest which the employers of the plaintiff had in knowing his character.

One of the earliest cases on the protection to a former master in giving a character of a servant, is decided (1) as coming within the general principle respecting confidential communications, and not upon any consideration of the relation of master: *Edmondson* v. *Stevenson* (2).

In the present case, the defendant, having reason (3) to believe he was in possession of information important to the shipowner, in respect of his captain, gave it for the purpose of preventing a

[*610]

considerable damage to his *property from misconduct; and, on this ground, appears to me to be justified.

The defendant also had reason to believe, that, by giving this information, he should save the lives of the crew (4); and on this ground also, he appears to me to be justified in giving it, either to the crew, or to the shipowner on their behalf, supposing always that the jury found that he acted with good faith.

Some objection was made to the mode of communication. But it appears to me to have been as cautious as could be required under the circumstances; and, if the defendant acted incautiously, or went to some degree beyond what may be thought to have been strictly required for his purpose, these were matters for the jury, as evidence of malice.

The evil likely to arise from protecting information *bonâ fide* given to prevent damage from misconduct, appears to me much less than that which would result from putting a stop to such information, by rendering the giver of it liable in damages, unless he has legal proof of the truth: and the circumstance of the information being officious, or without reasonable grounds, or of slight importance, ought to be appreciated by the jury (5).

It follows, that, in my judgment, the rule should be discharged.

The COURT being thus divided in opinion,

The rule for a new trial fell to the ground, and the defendant retained his verdict (6).

(1) Or, at least, is so classed by the editor.

(2) Bull. N. P. 8.

(3) The finding was, that he did in fact believe.

(4) *Quære* whether this is an inference of law or a fact to be considered, if warranted by the circumstances, by the jury.

(5) The finding of the jury in this case, *supra*, p. 535, does not seem to be inconsistent with the information having been of slight importance, and communicated officiously, and without reasonable ground.

(6) See the next case.

BLACKHAM *v.* PUGH (1).

(2 C. B. 611—627; S. C. 15 L. J. C. P. 290.)

A., a trader, being indebted to B. upon an unexpired credit, employs C. to sell his goods by auction, and absents himself, under circumstances sufficient to induce B. to believe that an act of bankruptcy has been committed. B. gives notice to C. not to pay over the proceeds to A., "he having committed an act of bankruptcy." In an action by A. against B. charging this notice as a libel, it was held by TINDAL, Ch. J., and COLTMAN and ERLE, JJ., to be a privileged communication, *dissentiente* CRESSWELL, J.

CASE, for a libel upon the plaintiff in the way of his trade.

The first count of the declaration stated, that the plaintiff, before and at the time of the committing of the several grievances by the defendant thereinafter mentioned, was a trader within the meaning and intent of the laws and statutes in this realm relating to and concerning bankrupts, and carried on the trade of a currier &c., to wit, in London, and had always exercised and carried on his said trade with integrity and punctuality of dealing, and had always been able and willing to pay, and had in] fact always punctually paid, his just debts, and had never been in insolvent or bad circumstances, or committed an act of bankruptcy; and that by means of the premises the plaintiff, before and up to the time of the committing &c., had deservedly obtained the good opinion and credit of all his neighbours, and other good and worthy subjects of this realm to whom he was in anywise known, &c.; that, before, &c., the plaintiff, being desirous of retiring from his said trade, had advertised for sale, and caused to be sold, by public auction, by certain persons carrying on the business of auctioneers under the name, style, or title of Southey & Son, his, the plaintiff's, stock in trade and implements of his said trade, and other goods and chattels being in and upon the shop and premises where he, the plaintiff, so carried on his said trade as aforesaid, and the proceeds of the said sale, amounting to 500*l.*, had, after such sale as aforesaid, been received by, and at the time of the committing, &c. remained in the hands of, Southey & Son, as such auctioneers; that, before the *time of the committing, &c., and before the time of such sale as thereinbefore mentioned, the plaintiff had purchased divers goods of the defendant at or for the price or sum of 62*l.* 12*s.* 9*d.*, upon a certain credit, to wit, of two months; that such credit had not expired at the time of the committing, &c.; yet that the defendant

[*612]

(1) Approved in *Baker* v. *Carrick*   L. R. 5 Q. B. 608, 39 L. J. Q. B. 202,
[1894] 1 Q. B. 838, 63 L. J. Q. B. 399,   and *Robshaw* v. *Smith* (1878) 38 L. T.
C. A.   See also *Davies* v. *Snead* (1870)   (N. S.) 423.—J. G. P.

BLACKHAM well knowing the premises, but greatly envying, &c., and wickedly
v. and maliciously intending to injure the plaintiff in his good name,
PUGH. &c., and to cause it to be suspected and believed that the plaintiff
had been and was in bad and insolvent circumstances, and had
committed an act of bankruptcy, and was incapable of paying his
just and true debts, &c., and also maliciously to prevent the
plaintiff from receiving the proceeds of the said sale thereinbefore mentioned from Southey & Son (1), theretofore, to wit, on
the 27th of June, 1844, caused and procured to be written and
published of and concerning the plaintiff, and of and concerning
him in his said trade as aforesaid, a certain false, scandalous,
malicious, and defamatory libel, of and concerning the plaintiff,
and of and concerning him in his said trade, in the form of a notice
written by the direction, and at the request, and by the order of the
defendant, by certain persons then being the attorneys and solicitors
of the defendant, to wit, &c., and directed and sent by the last-
mentioned persons to Southey & Son, and containing, amongst other
things, the false, scandalous, malicious, and defamatory matter of
and concerning the plaintiff, and of and concerning him in his
said trade, following, to wit, "MESSRS. SOUTHEY & SON,—We hereby
[*613] *give you notice, and require you, not to part with the proceeds of
the sale of the stock in trade, goods, chattels, and effects of H. J.
Blackham, of, &c., (meaning the plaintiff), which have been lately
sold by you (meaning the said Southey & Son) by public auction
on the premises, the said H. J. Blackham (meaning the plaintiff)
having committed an act of bankruptcy; " that, by means of the
committing, &c. the plaintiff was greatly injured in his good name,
fame, and credit with and amongst all his neighbours and acquaintance, &c.; and that by means of the committing, &c., and in
consequence of the said notice so written and sent to Southey
& Son as aforesaid, Southey & Son confiding in, and believing
the truth of, the statement therein contained, detained the moneys
so remaining in their hands as aforesaid, being the moneys arising
from the said sale, and had wholly refused to pay the same to the
plaintiff; that the plaintiff had in consequence thereof lost and been
deprived of the use and benefit of the said moneys for a long space

(1) Both in this case and in *Coxhead* | which is laid as a special damage,
v. *Richards, supra*, p. 530, special | appears to be merely the wrongful
damage was laid; but this circum- | refusal, of a solvent debtor, to pay
stance was not treated as creating any | what is shown by the declaration, and
distinction between these and other | must be taken as against the plaintiff,
cases of libel. Here indeed, that | to be a clear legal debt.

of time, to wit, from the time of the committing, &c. until the com-   BLACKHAM
mencement of this suit; and that the plaintiff also by means of   *v.*
PUGH.
the premises had suffered and undergone great annoyance, trouble,
and pain of mind, &c.

To this count the defendant pleaded : First, Not guilty ; secondly,
to part of the declaration, that the plaintiff did not purchase any
goods of the defendant upon a credit which had not expired at the
time of the committing of the grievances, &c., *modo et formâ ;* concluding to the country ; thirdly, that, at the time of the committing
of the grievances in the first count mentioned, the plaintiff was
indebted to the defendant in 62*l.* 12*s.* 9*d.* for goods sold and
delivered (1) ; and that *this sum was then due, and that the plain-   [*614]
tiff, being so indebted and being a trader, had committed an act of
bankruptcy, by absenting himself from his place of business, with
intent to defeat and delay the defendant ; verification.

The plaintiff joined issue on the first and second pleas, and to the
third, replied *de injuriâ.*

The cause was tried before Parke, B., at the Summer Assizes for
the county of Surrey, in 1844. The facts were as follows : The
plaintiff was a currier and leather-seller, carrying on his trade in
Union Street, Southwark. The defendant was a tanner. In April,
1844, the plaintiff purchased goods of the defendant to the amount
of 62*l.* 12*s.* 9*d.*, upon the customary credit of two months. In
June, the plaintiff, intending to wind up his concerns and retire
from business, employed Messrs. Southey & Son, auctioneers, to
dispose of his stock by public sale. The sale was accordingly
advertised to take place on the premises on Wednesday, the
26th of June. On the following day, which was the customary
collecting day in the trade, the defendant's collector called for
payment of the account, when he found the goods all sold and in
course of being removed, no person being upon the premises to
explain the plaintiff's absence. The defendant immediately caused
the following notice to be served upon the auctioneers :

   "MESSRS. SOUTHEY & SON,—We hereby give you notice, and
require you, not to part with the proceeds of the sale of the

---

(2) A *debitum in præsenti solvendum
in futuro* would have justified the
notice to the auctioneers, supposing
an act of bankruptcy had been committed ; but the allegation of debt in
the third plea could be supported only
by proof of a debt actually due—
debitum solvendum in præsenti. The
third plea appears to be wholly unnecessary ; as the defendant could not
succeed upon that plea unless the
plaintiff failed to prove the fact
traversed by the second.

stock in trade, goods, chattels, and effects of Henry John Blackham, of No. 163, Union Street, Southwark, leather-seller, which
have been lately sold by you by public auction on the premises;
[*615] the said Henry John *Blackham having committed an act of
bankruptcy. Dated, this 27th of June, 1844.

(Signed)   "DIMMOCK AND BURBEY,

"12, Size Lane, solicitors for Mr. Edward Pugh, a
creditor of the said H. J. Blackham."

In consequence of this notice, Southey & Son refused to pay over
to the plaintiff the proceeds of the sale. On the 29th of June, the
defendant withdrew the notice; but the auctioneers declined to act
upon such withdrawal, unless the defendant's solicitors would assure
them that the notice that the plaintiff had committed an act of
bankruptcy had been given under a misapprehension. This the
defendants' solicitors refused to do; and the proceeds of the sale
were not paid over to the plaintiff until after the trial of this
cause.

A witness was called on the part of the defendant, to prove an
admission by the plaintiff that he had committed an act of bankruptcy, by absenting himself from his place of business for the
purpose of delaying his creditors. The attempt was held to have
failed.

It was then insisted on the defendant's behalf, that the notice to
Southey & Son was a privileged communication, inasmuch as it
was a statement made, *bonâ fide*, and in the full belief of its truth,
by a person having an interest in the subject-matter, and to a
person interested in receiving the information; and, consequently,
that the action was not maintainable without proof of express
malice.

The learned Baron told the jury that they must at all events find
for the plaintiff on the second issue, the period of credit not having
expired at the time the notice was served upon the auctioneers;
that the communication was not privileged, though made *bonâ fide*
and in the belief of its truth, and therefore that the plaintiff was
also entitled to a verdict on the first issue; and that he was
[*616] entitled likewise to a verdict upon the *third issue, unless they
thought the defendant had made out his third plea.

The jury returned a verdict for the plaintiff, damages 50*l.*

Shee, Serjt., in Michaelmas Term, 1844, on the part of the
defendant, obtained a rule *nisi* for a new trial, on the ground of

misdirection.   He cited *M'Dougall* v. *Claridge* (1), *Fairman* v.   BLACKHAM
Ives (2), *Woodward* v. *Lander* (3), and *Shipley* v. *Todhunter* (4).   *v.*
                                                                          PUGH.

Sir T. Wilde, and *Channell*, Serjts. (with whom was *Bramwell*),
     showed cause in Easter Term, 1845 (5) :

The notice in question, which falsely imputed to the plaintiff
the commission of an act of bankruptcy, was not a privileged
communication. The charge was wholly gratuitous and unfounded,
and was of a character most offensive and injurious. Is this within
the rule laid down by PARKE, B., in *Toogood* v. *Spyring* (6), a communication " fairly made by a person in the discharge of some
public or private duty, whether legal or moral, or in the conduct
of his own affairs in matters where his interest is concerned ? "
Here, the defendant had not the sort of interest that will afford an
excuse for a libel.   In *M'Dougall* v. *Claridge* (1), the letter was held
to be a privileged communication because written by a party to the
suit.   So, in *Dunman* v. *Bigg* (7), the communication was held to be
privileged because made by a creditor, to the surety of his debtor, in
a matter in which both are interested.   **Shipley* v. *Todhunter* (4) is   [*617]
also an authority to show that a man may lawfully communicate to
another any information he is possessed of in a matter in which
they have a mutual interest, though such communication may
convey reflections injurious to a third party.   *Fairman* v. *Ives*
and *Woodward* v. *Lander* have no application : they were cases
of complaints *bonâ fide* made to public offices, for the purpose of
obtaining redress of grievances. Here, the real question is, whether
this was a communication made by the defendant in a matter in
which his own interest was concerned, and made in the legitimate
conduct of his own affairs.   A man must not so conduct his own
affairs as altogether to overlook his neighbour's rights.

(ERLE, J. : Would the defendant have been justified, if it had
appeared that he had reasonable ground for supposing that the
plaintiff had committed an act of bankruptcy ?)

(1) 10 R. R. 679 (1 Camp. 267).

(2) 24 R. R. 514 (5 B. & Ald. 642;
1 Dowl. & Ry. 252; 1 Chitty, 85).

(3) 40 R. R. 816 (6 Car. & P. 548).

(4) 7 Car. & P. 680.

(5) The argument upon this rule,
which had been postponed until after
the second argument of *Coxhead* v.

Richards, *ante*, p. 530, took place
before Tindal, Ch. J., and Coltman,
Cresswell, and Erle, JJ.

(6) 40 R. R. 523 (1 Cr. M. & R. 193;
4 Tyr. 582).

(7) 10 R. R. 680, *n.* (1 Camp.
269, *n.*).

BLACKHAM
v.
PUGH.

Clearly not. But here the credit had not expired; the defendant must therefore have known that, as far as he was concerned, no act of bankruptcy could have been committed.

Shee, Serjt. (with whom was *Bovill*), in support of the rule :

The learned Judge ought to have told the jury that the circumstances under which the notice was given, afforded a legal justification. The case clearly falls within the principle of those authorities in which it has been held, that a communication *bonâ fide* made for the purpose of obtaining redress, to one who may fairly be supposed to have the means of affording it, is protected.

(CRESSWELL, J.: *Coxhead* v. *Richards*(1) turned upon the existence of a supposed moral duty on the part of the recipient of information, to convey it to one who has an interest in being possessed of it: this case turns on the ground of interest; there is no moral duty.)

[*618] Perhaps, *the defendant owed a moral duty to the auctioneers: they had an interest in the matter.

(CRESSWELL, J.: They could have had no interest, if they had had no notice.)

At all events, the defendant had such an interest in the matter, as to excuse any little excess of zeal on his part. In *Fairman* v. *Ives*, the letter was addressed to one who had no means of giving the redress that was sought. The present case falls precisely within the rule laid down by PARKE, B., in *Toogood* v. *Spyring* : and that rule is quite consistent with what is said by Lord DENMAN, Ch. J., in the subsequent case of *Tuson* v. *Evans*(2): "Any one, in the transaction of business with another, has a right to use language, *bonâ fide*, which is relevant to that business, and which a due regard to his own interest makes necessary, even if it should directly, or by its consequences, be injurious or painful to another; and this is the principle on which privileged communication rests." Here, the communication was made in the *bonâ fide* belief, that an act of bankruptcy had been committed; and in a manner as little injurious or offensive as the circumstances would admit of. Even if the credit had not expired, the defendant, assuming an act of bankruptcy to have been committed, would, for this purpose, have had all the rights of a present creditor.

Cur. adv. vult.

(1) *Ante*, p. 530.   (2) 54 R. R. 674 (12 Ad. & El. 733).

TINDAL, Ch. J.:

This was an action upon the case for a libel upon the plaintiff in the way of his trade.

The declaration stated that the plaintiff had sold his stock in trade by auction, and that the proceeds were then in the hands of his auctioneers; and that he, the plaintiff, had purchased of the defendant certain goods to the amount of 62*l.* and upwards, upon a credit which had not then expired; and that the defendant falsely *and maliciously published the libel complained of, in the form of a notice, which he procured his attorneys to send to his said auctioneers; by which notice they were desired not to part with the proceeds of the sale in their hands, the plaintiff having committed an act of bankruptcy.

Besides the general issue, there was a second plea, alleging that the goods were not bought upon a credit that had not expired at the time of the libel, and a third plea alleging that the plaintiff had committed an act of bankruptcy, both of which were found for the plaintiff; but upon neither of which any question now arises. Upon the general issue, the jury returned a verdict for the plaintiff, by the direction of the learned Judge, who told the jury this was not a case in which the defendant was justified under the general issue, although he made the communication *bonâ fide*, and believing it to be true at the time. And whether this direction of the learned Judge was right or not, is the question raised for our consideration, on a motion for a new trial.

This action, it is to be observed, is not an action against the defendant for maliciously, and without any reasonable or probable cause, directing his attorneys to give the notice to the auctioneers; under which form of action, the defendant would have been held liable in damages to the plaintiff, if, without any reasonable cause, but from over-precipitation, or unfounded suspicion, he had caused such notice to be given. But this is an action for a false and malicious libel. And the question is, whether such action is maintainable where there is altogether the absence of any malice in fact, and where the defendant, having a personal interest in preventing the money from being paid over to the plaintiff, did, with perfect good faith, and in the full belief that the plaintiff had committed an act of bankruptcy, direct his attorneys to give such notice to the auctioneers.

If the defendant had issued a *fiat* in bankruptcy against *the plaintiff, in pursuance of his notice(1), it is perfectly clear that the

(1) The notice under the statute.

BLACKHAM
v.
PUGH.

plaintiff could not have sued him in an action of slander or for a libel, but must have brought his action for maliciously, and without any reasonable or probable cause, issuing the *fiat*. And it does seem singular that a previous notice(1), which was absolutely necessary to protect the interest of the creditors of the plaintiff under such *fiat*, should be supposed to fall under a different construction of law from the issuing of the *fiat* itself. It does, indeed, seem to be part and parcel of the same transaction(2).

But, in any point of view, this case appears to me to fall within the range of that principle by which a communication made, by a person immediately concerned in interest, in the subject-matter to which it relates, for the purpose of protecting his own interest, in the full belief that the communication is true, and without any malicious motive, is held to be excused from responsibility in an action for a libel. *Delaney* v. *Jones*, *M'Dougall* v. *Claridge*, and *Toogood* v. *Spyring*, appear to me to be authorities which fully support this proposition. In the last of these cases, the judgment includes—under those cases in which the law considers the occasion to prevent the inference of malice which it draws from unauthorized communications injurious to the character of another,—such communications as are fairly and honestly made " by a person in the conduct of his own affairs, in matters where his interest is concerned."

It appears to me that the present case falls strictly within the principle so laid down, in the soundness and propriety of which principle I entirely agree; and, consequently, that the direction of the learned Judge was incorrect, and that the rule should be made absolute.

[621]   COLTMAN, J. :

The question of law which arises upon the facts reported by my brother PARKE in this case is, whether, assuming that the defendant acted *bonâ fide* and without malice, the occasion was such as justified him in making the imputation he has done on the plaintiff.

For the general rule which, in my humble opinion, ought to govern cases of this sort, I would refer to the case of *Coxhead* v. *Richards* (3), without repeating what I there said(4). In reference to the particular circumstances of the present case, I would remark

---

(1) The alleged libel.   (3) *Ante*, p. 530.
(2) *Secus*, where no *fiat*.   (4) *Ante*, p. 546.

that the defendant had the most direct interest in the matter with
reference to which the statement complained of, was made.   There
was, indeed, no debt then payable to him; but it was on the point
of becoming so.   He had a direct interest in preventing the money,
then in the hands of the auctioneers, from being paid over into the
hands of the bankrupt; as it was the fund out of which he might
hope to receive a dividend, if matters should come to a bankruptcy.
It was material to the defendant's interest,—at least, he might
reasonably suppose it to be material to his interest,—that he should
give notice of an act of bankruptcy having been committed (if one
had been committed), in order to prevent the auctioneers from
being discharged in case they should pay over the money to the
bankrupt before the issuing of a *fiat*.   Under these circumstances,
it appears to me that there was a sufficient justification for his
imputing bankruptcy to the plaintiff, if he *bonâ fide* believed that
an act of bankruptcy had been committed: and I am not prepared
to say that there were not such·reasonable grounds of suspicion as
might warrant a jury in thinking, that, in making the imputation
in question, he acted *bonâ fide* and without malice.   I think,
therefore, *though with that deference which I must feel for those
whose opinion is adverse to mine, that the question ought to have
been left to the jury, and that there should be a new trial.

CRESSWELL, J.:

This was an action for a libel contained in a letter written by the
defendant to a third person, in which he stated that the plaintiff, a
currier, had committed an act of bankruptcy.   Plea, Not guilty,
amongst others.   At the trial, before my brother PARKE, at the
Summer Assizes, 1844, for Surrey, it was contended for the defendant that the alleged libel was a privileged communication, having
been written on a lawful occasion, without any malicious motive.
The learned Judge ruled that it was not a privileged communication, and the plaintiff obtained a verdict.   In Michaelmas Term a
rule *nisi* for a new trial was granted, which was argued in Easter
Term; and it has stood over for consideration; and I now have the
misfortune to stand alone in the opinion that I have formed.

The facts upon which the question depends are very simple.   The
defendant had sold goods to the plaintiff, the time of payment for
which had not arrived, but was drawing near.   The plaintiff had
sold off great part of his goods by auction, and the auctioneers had
the proceeds in their hands, when the defendant wrote to them, and

BLACKHAM
*
PUGH.

[*622]

36—2

BLACKHAM
v.
PUGH.

gave them notice that the plaintiff had committed an act of bankruptcy, and desired them not to pay over the money to the plaintiff.
It was argued for the defendant that the publication of this letter
to the auctioneers was privileged, because it was written by the
defendant in good faith, and without malice, in the conduct of his
own affairs, in a matter where his interest was concerned, so as to
be within the description of privileged communications given by
PARKE, B., in *Toogood* v. *Spyring*. On the other hand, it was

[*623]

contended *that this letter was not written by the defendant in
the conduct of his own affairs, nor was his interest concerned,
within the meaning to be ascribed to those words as used in
Toogood v. *Spyring*, so as to constitute a lawful occasion for
publishing defamatory matter : and I am of opinion that the
occasion in question was not a lawful occasion, and that the
learned Judge was right in telling the jury, that, on the plea of
the general issue, the plaintiff was entitled to a verdict.

In determining this question, the cases depending upon the discharge of some legal or moral duty, may be laid out of consideration ; for the defendant, in giving notice to the auctioneers, was
acting solely for his own benefit ; and, if that which he did was
lawful, it must be so because it was an act done in the conduct of
his own affairs in a matter where his interest was concerned.

The cases bearing upon the point may be divided into two
classes : one, where the communication has been made by a person
having an interest in the very transaction to which it related, to
another person also interested or employed in conducting it ; the
other, where a party, having sustained a grievance, or that which
he thought a grievance, has addressed a complaint to a person
whom he supposed capable of redressing it, and, in so doing, has
used defamatory language. *M'Dougall* v. *Claridge* (1), *Wright* v.
Woodgate (2), *Spencer* v. *Amerton* (3), and *Shipley* v. *Todhunter* (4),
belong to the former class ; *Fairman* v. *Ives* (5), *Woodward* v.
Lander (6), *Coward* v. *Wellington* (7), to the latter.

In the present case, the defendant was not interested in the sale

[*624]

of the plaintiff's goods, nor was there any *connection between him
and the auctioneers in the transaction ; nor had the defendant,
at the time when the alleged libel was written, sustained any

(1) 10 R. R. 679 (1 Camp. 267).

(2) 41 R. R. 788 (2 C. M. & R. 573;
1 Tyr. & G. 12).

(3) 42 R. R. 814 (1 Moo. & Rob. 470).

(4) 7 Car. & P. 680.

(5) 24 R. R. 514 (5 B. & A 642).

(6) 40 R. R. 816 (6 Car. & P. 548).

(7) 7 Car. & P. 531.

grievance, nor had any thing really occurred which he considered   BLACKHAM
a grievance. The debt contracted by the plaintiff was not then   v.
payable; and, for any thing he knew, might be duly paid as soon   PUGH.
as he had a right to demand it; and he might never have any
interest at all in the proceeds of the goods that had been sold.
Now, there is nothing in the language of the Court, in deciding the
case of *Fairman* v. *Ives*, tending to show that the result would have
been the same had the defendant's letter been addressed to the
Secretary at War before the plaintiff's acceptances had been dishonoured. In *Woodward* v. *Lander*, the observations of the learned
Judge who tried the cause, were applied to the defamatory
language used by the defendant in representing to the Postmaster-
General things that had really occurred, and commenting upon
them. And in *Coward* v. *Wellington*, the letter complained of was
written by the defendant in his own vindication against a charge
of dishonesty. *Hargrave* v. *Le Breton* (1) and *Pitt* v. *Donovan* (2)
can hardly be treated as authorities for our guidance in deciding
this case. They were not actions for defamation, but for slander
of title, which are governed by different principles. In neither case
had the defendant published anything defamatory of the plaintiff;
but, claiming to be interested, had disputed the plaintiff's title to
an estate which he was about to sell. A publication of such a
nature is not an unauthorised publication which the law deems to
be malicious; and, in order to maintain the action, it is necessary
to prove actual malice, or, in Lord ELLENBOROUGH's words, "The
jury must arrive at their conclusion through the medium of malice
or no malice in the defendant."

It appears to me, then, that the present case does not fall within   [625]
any of the exceptions out of the general rule of law: that a man
must be responsible for publishing defamatory matter which he
cannot prove to be true; and that the rule for a new trial ought to
be discharged.

ERLE, J.:

In this case a rule *nisi* for a new trial has been obtained, on the
ground of misdirection.

The action, as far as this rule is concerned, was for a libel in
giving a notice that the plaintiff had committed an act of bankruptcy. The evidence showed that the defendant had sold goods
to the plaintiff upon credit; and, upon the day before the credit

(1) 4 Burr. 2422.   (2) 14 R. R. 535 (1 M. & S. 639).

expired, the defendant discovered that the plaintiff had apparently
sold off all his stock in trade, by auction, and had apparently
quitted his place of business without leaving his address. He,
therefore, believed that the plaintiff had committed an act of
bankruptcy, though in fact he had not.

If there had been an act of bankruptcy, the defendant and the
other creditors would have had a right to the proceeds of the sale
in the hands of the auctioneers; and a notice to them was essential
to prevent this right from being defeated. Accordingly, the notice,
which was the subject of the action, was given.

The learned Judge was of opinion, that these facts afforded no
evidence to rebut the presumption of malice from the publication
of libellous matter, and therefore directed a verdict for the plaintiff.
The correctness of this direction is now to be considered.

The defendant contends that he is within that class of the cases
where the presumption of malice is rebutted by the occasion, which
is grounded on consideration of the private interest of the party
publishing: and I think that he is, because he believed, with
[*626]   reasonable *cause, that the communication was required in prudence
to protect his rights.

There are numerous decisions that one kind of slander is justifiable, if made in asserting a claim of right, although the claim may
be entirely without foundation in fact: *Gerard* v. *Dickenson* (1),
Smith v. *Spooner* (2). And in *Pitt* v. *Donovan* (3) it was decided,
that if the defendant *bonâ fide* believed he had a claim to the plaintiff's land, he would be justified, although his belief was not only
contrary to the fact, but also without grounds sufficient for a man
of sense and experience.

Slander of title may be at the same time derogatory to the
plaintiff personally, as in the assertion of the bastardy of an heir
presumptive, by a younger brother, supposed in 4 Co. Rep. 17 a (4);
but the justification is not affected thereby.

In the present case, the notice of the defendant appears to me to
be, in substance, the assertion of a claim involving, of necessity,
that which the plaintiff complains of as a libel, and therefore
justified, if the jury found it was made in good faith, although the
plaintiff was mistaken in fact.

In *Hargrave* v. *Le Breton*, where the plaintiff lost the sale of his
estate at auction by a notice of the bankruptcy of the mortgagor,

(1) 4 Co. Rep. 18.   (3) 14 R. R. 535 (1 M. & S. 639).
(2) 12 R. R. 645 (3 Taunt. 246).   (4) *Gerard* v. *Dickenson*.

under whom he claimed, and which notice was partly true and partly not—the Court appear to have decided that the defendant was justified, on the ground that he believed the communication requisite to protect the right of a creditor over the estate of a debtor subject to the bankrupt law, although he asserted that a docket had been made out, when in fact no docket had been made out, either then, or when the rule for a new trial was made absolute.

In *Fairman* v. *Ives* the principle of the decision was, that a creditor who makes a statement that would be otherwise libellous, is justified if the occasion of his making it be an honest endeavour to obtain redress against his debtor. If, in this case, it was doubtful whether there was sufficient ground for making the assertion, or whether the publication in degree exceeded what was strictly necessary (1), these were matters from which the jury might find malice.

The objection that the plaintiff's debt was not payable when the notice was given, is answered; because, upon the supposition of a bankruptcy, on which the defendant acted, he had all the rights of a present creditor. And the objection that no act of bankruptcy existed in fact, is answered; because, in many of the cases of protection from the occasion, the defendant has been shown to have acted upon a mistake, but has been nevertheless held to be justified, if he acted on an honest belief.

The rule for a new trial, therefore, should, I think, be made absolute.

Rule absolute (2).

(1) *Vide Robertson* v. *M'Dougall*, 29 R. R. 684 (4 Bing. 670; 1 Moo. & P. 692; 3 Car. & P. 259) where such excess was held to constitute legal malice, independently of any inference of malice in fact, to be drawn from that excess by the jury.

(2) A second trial took place before Lord Denman, Ch. J., at the Summer Assizes for Surrey, in 1846, when that learned Judge, feeling himself bound by the opinion of the majority of this Court, directed the jury accordingly, at the same time intimating that he entertained considerable doubt as to the soundness of the direction. The jury returned a verdict for the defendant.

A bill of exceptions was tendered on the part of the plaintiff, and the errors assigned thereon now (in January, 1847), stand for argument in the Exchequer Chamber. [But the proceedings thereon do not appear to have been reported.—J. G. P.]

1846.
May 5.

[628]

BENNETT v. DEACON.

(2 C. B. 628—633; S. C. 15 L. J. C. P. 289.)

Quære, whether a caution *bonâ fide* given to a tradesman, without any
inquiry on his part, not to trust another, falls within the exception as to
privileged communications :
   Held, by TINDAL, Ch. J., and ERLE, J., that it does.
   Held, by COLTMAN and CRESSWELL, JJ., that it does not.

CASE, for slander of the plaintiff in his trade.

The declaration stated that the plaintiff, before and at the time
of the committing by the defendant of the grievances thereinafter
mentioned, used, exercised, and carried on, and still did use, exercise, and carry on the trade of a wheelwright, and had always
conducted the same with great punctuality of dealing, well and
faithfully observing and keeping his engagements and paying his
just debts, and that the plaintiff was not at the time of the speaking
and publishing of the several false, scandalous, and malicious words
thereinafter mentioned, nor at any time since, in insolvent circumstances or unable to pay his just debts; and, by reason of the
premises, the plaintiff, until the speaking of such slanderous words,
was deservedly held in great esteem and credit by his neighbours
and others, and particularly by those with whom he had any
dealings in his said trade, and enjoyed great reputation therein ;
whereby the plaintiff daily acquired divers great gains and profits
in his said trade, to the support and maintenance of himself and
his family, and the great increase of his fortune: and that the
plaintiff before the committing of the said grievances, had treated
with one William Clark, in the way of his, the plaintiff's, said
trade, for the purchase by the plaintiff from Clark of a certain
large quantity, to wit, 500 tons, of timber, at and for a certain
price or sum of money to be paid by the plaintiff to Clark in that
behalf ; yet the defendant, well knowing the premises, but contriving and wrongfully and maliciously intending to injure and
[*629]   destroy the good name and reputation of the plaintiff in his *said
trade, and to cause him to be regarded as a person of no credit,
worth, or substance, and in insolvent circumstances in his said
trade, and unable to pay his just debts, and thereby to injure and
prejudice him in his said trade and business, during the time the
plaintiff carried on his said trade as aforesaid, and before the commencement of this suit, to wit, on the 9th of October, 1845, in a
certain discourse which the defendant then had with Clark, of and
concerning the plaintiff, and of and concerning him in the way

of his aforesaid trade, and of and concerning the treaty for the BENNETT
v.
DEACON. said timber which Clark had so treated with the plaintiff to sell to the plaintiff as aforesaid, asked Clark a question in the words following: "Are you (meaning Clark) going to have ready money for it?" (meaning the said timber); and then, in reply to the following answer of Clark thereto to the defendant, "I (meaning Clark) am going to have about half ready money, and the other at a month's credit, and shall draw it (meaning the said timber) down to Bennett's yard, to get it from the station, or I shall have to pay demurrage," the defendant spoke to and in the hearing of Clark, of and concerning the plaintiff, and of and concerning him in the ways of his aforesaid trade, and of and concerning the said treaty for the said timber which Clark had so treated with the plaintiff to sell to the plaintiff, the false, scandalous, malicious, and defamatory words following, that is to say: "If you (meaning Clark) draw it (meaning the said timber) down to Bennett's (meaning the plaintiff's) yard, you'll lose it; for, he (meaning the plaintiff) owes me (meaning the defendant) about 25*l*., and I (meaning the defendant) am going to arrest him (meaning the plaintiff) next week, for my money, and the timber (meaning the said timber) will help to pay my debt;" thereby meaning that the plaintiff was in insolvent circumstances in his said trade, and unable to pay his just *debts; that, by means of the committing of [*630] such grievances by the defendant, the plaintiff had been, and was, greatly injured in his said good name, credit, and reputation in his said trade, and brought into public scandal and disgrace, and had been shunned and avoided by divers persons, and otherwise injured; and also the plaintiff, by reason of the premises, was prevented from completing the said treaty with Clark for the purchase of the said timber, and Clark, by reason of the premises, wholly refused to treat further with the plaintiff in respect thereof, &c.

The defendant pleaded Not guilty; whereupon issue was joined.

The cause was tried before Coltman, J., at the second sitting in London in Hilary Term, 1846. The facts were these: The plaintiff is a wheelwright, carrying on business in the Wandsworth Road, near the terminus of the South-Western Railway. The defendant is a timber-dealer and builder in the same neighbourhood. On the 8th of October last, one William Clark, a timber-dealer who resided at Chiddingfold, in Surrey, having brought up a quantity of ash timber by the railway, entered into a treaty for the sale of it to the plaintiff on the 9th of October. Before the sale had been finally agreed

BENNETT
v.
DEACON.

upon, the defendant, meeting Clark in the road, inquired of him if he had sold his timber yet ; to which Clark answered, " I believe I have : Bennett is going to have it." The defendant then asked, " Are you going to have ready money for it ?" To this Clark answered, " I am going to have half ready money, and the other at a month's credit ; " adding that he was going to get the timber drawn from the railway to Bennett's yard, in order to avoid demurrage. The defendant then remarked : " If you draw it down to Bennett's yard, you'll lose it ; for, he owes me about 25*l.*, and I

[*631]

am going to arrest him next week for my money, *and your timber will help to pay my debt." In consequence of this statement Clark declined to sell the timber in question to the plaintiff. It appeared that the plaintiff was really indebted to the defendant to the amount of about 23*l.* ; but it did not appear that the account had been sent in or the money demanded.

On the part of the defendant it was submitted that the circumstances under which the words were spoken, rendered the communication privileged, in the absence of any thing to warrant the jury in inferring that the defendant was influenced by any malicious or sinister motive.

The learned Judge, however, thought that, though the communication might have been privileged if *bonâ fide* made in answer to inquiries addressed to the defendant as to the credit and circumstances of the plaintiff, yet, inasmuch as he had volunteered the information, the case did not fall within the exception to the general rule.

The jury returned a verdict for the plaintiff, damages 40*s.*

Byles, Serjt., in the course of the Term, obtained a rule *nisi* for a new trial, on the ground of misdirection. He cited *Edmondson* v. *Stevenson* (1), *Bromage* v. *Prosser* (2), the judgment of BAYLEY, J., in *Pattison* v. *Jones* (3), and *Coxhead* v. *Richards* (4), *Blackham* v. *Pugh* (5).

Talfourd, Serjt., now showed cause :

The direction of the learned Judge was clearly right : it was precisely in accordance with that of Lord ABINGER, C. B., in *King* v.

[*632]

Watts (6), which has never been objected to. The *circumstance of the defendant being a volunteer has always been considered to have

(1) Bull. N. P. 8.
(2) 28 R. R. 241 (4 B. & C. 247 ; 6 Dowl. & Ry. 296).
(3) 32 R. R. 490 (8 B. & C. 584 ; 3

Man. & Ry. 101).
(4) *Ante,* p. 530.
(5) *Ante,* p. 555.
(6) 8 Car. & P. 615.

an important bearing upon the question of privilege. This appears BENNETT
v.
DEACON. from the observation of Lord LYNDHURST in *Brooks* v. *Blanshard* (1), that, " it is not merely because a communication is confidential that it is privileged, if it is volunteered by the party making it." All the authorities upon the subject having been so elaborately discussed and considered in the recent cases of *Coxhead* v. *Richards* (2) and *Blackham* v. *Pugh* (3), it is unnecessary to do more than refer to these cases. The communication cannot be privileged, without some evidence that the defendant *bonâ fide* believed the statement he made to be true.

Byles, Serjt., in support of the rule :

The communication in question clearly was privileged ; the defendant not being actuated by any malicious motive, but having given the information merely in kindness and friendship to Clark, who had an interest in the matter, even though the information was volunteered : *Edmondson* v. *Stevenson* (4), *Hervey* v. *Dowson* (4), *Wright* v. *Woodgate* (5), *Toogood* v. *Spyring* (6) ; and it is not necessary to his justification that the party making the communication should likewise be interested : *Peacock* v. *Reynall* (7).

(CRESSWELL, J. : We are all agreed as to the correctness of the rule laid down by PARKE, B., in *Toogood* v. *Spyring* (6).)

TINDAL, Ch. J. :

I am unable to distinguish the case in principle from *Coxhead* v. *Richards* (2) ; and I see no reason at present to alter the opinion I there expressed. It seems to me that the communication in question, *having been made *bonâ fide* to Clark in the ordinary   [*633] course of, and in relation to, his business, was privileged, and that the rule should be made absolute.

COLTMAN, J. :

I cannot accede to the argument of my brother *Byles*, that this was, under the circumstances, a privileged communication. I do not think that is the fair result of the authorities. I adhere to the opinion I expressed in *Coxhead* v. *Richards* and in *Blackham* v. *Pugh* (8), and, therefore, it appears to me that the present rule ought to be discharged.

(1) 3 Tyr. 849.
(2) *Ante*, p. 530,
(3) *Ante*, p. 555.
(4) Bull. N. P. 8.
(5) 41 R. R. 788 (2 Cr. M. & R. 573)

(6) 40 R. R. 523 (1 Cr. M. & R. 181 ; 4 Tyr. 582).
(7) Brownl. & G. 151.
(8) *Ante*, pp. 546 and 562.

CRESSWELL, J.: Nothing having since occurred to induce me to alter the opinion I expressed in the two cases referred to by my brother COLTMAN; and, conceiving the present case to fall within the same general principle, I think the rule should be discharged.

ERLE, J.:

I think this was entirely a matter for the jury: if they were satisfied that the communication was made *bonâ fide* and without malice (1), it was their duty to find for the defendant.

The COURT being thus equally divided in opinion,

> *The rule fell to the ground, and the plaintiff retained his verdict* (2).

ATKINS v. HUMPHREY AND W. SCRIVENER.

(2 C. B. 654—660; S. C. 3 Dowl. & L. 612; 15 L. J. C. P. 120.)

The plaintiff declared against A. and B. as executors, alleging that they as executors were indebted to him for the use and occupation of certain messuages held of him by them as executors under a demise to the testator, and that, in consideration of the premises, they as executors promised to pay.

Plea, by A., that B. never was executor, nor ever administered, &c.:

Held, that the declaration was good in substance; and that the plea was bad, as setting up a personal discharge, of which B. only could avail himself.

ASSUMPSIT against the defendants, charging them as executors of the last will and testament of J. Scrivener, deceased, alleging, in the second count, that the defendants, as executors as aforesaid, were indebted to the plaintiff in 100l. for the use and occupation of certain messuages, &c., of the plaintiff, by the defendants, as executors as aforesaid, held of the plaintiff for a long time before then elapsed, under and by virtue of a certain demise theretofore [*655] made to J. Scrivener; and *thereupon afterwards, to wit, on &c., in consideration of the last mentioned premises, the defendants, as executors as aforesaid, promised the plaintiff to pay him the last-

(1) The rule here laid down, would extend to every defamatory publication,—however unreasonable in itself and injurious to the party defamed,—the same degree of protection that was given in *Pitt* v. *Donovan*, 14 R. R. 535 (1 M. & S. 639); *Smith* v. *Spooner*, 12 R. R. 645 (3 Taunt. 246), to slander of title.

(2) The opinion of each of the learned Judges in this case was the same as that pronounced by them respectively in *Coxhead* v. *Richards*: the result to the parties was directly the reverse, the defaming party having succeeded in *Coxhead* v. *Richards*,—in *Bennett* v. *Deacon* (as also in a case, similarly circumstanced, of *Prowse* v. *Wilcox*, 3 Mod. 163), the party defamed.

mentioned sum ; yet the defendants, as executors as aforesaid, had
not paid the same, or any part thereof, &c.

Plea, by the defendant Humphrey, that W. Scrivener never was
executor of the last will and testament of J. Scrivener, nor ever
administered any of the goods or chattels which were of J. Scrivener
at the time of his death, as executor of the last will and testament
of J. Scrivener, *modo et formâ.* Verification

To this plea the plaintiff demurred generally.

Channell, Serjt., in support of the demurrer (1) :

It is not competent to one of two persons jointly sued as
executors, to plead that the other never was executor, that being a
plea of personal discharge. * * *

Talfourd, Serjt., *contrà :*

The plea is good in substance, though probably it would have
been held bad on special demurrer. The general principle, that
one of two persons sued as executors cannot plead that the other
never was executor, will not be impugned. But here, the defendants
are charged as joint-contractors ; and the plaintiff must prove his
case against both. * * If this had been an action in which it
was sought to charge the defendants, as executors, on promises by
the testator, one could not have pleaded that the other was not
executor ; because that is matter of personal discharge only. But
here the plea is in effect an informal *non assumpsit.*

[656]

(MAULE, J. : Would a plea of *plene administravit* be an answer to
this action ? The declaration alleges a demise of the premises to
the testator, an occupation by the defendants as executors, and a
promise by them, as executors, to pay the rent.)

The promise by the defendants as executors does not result from the
premises stated : they would be liable, if at all, *de bonis propriis.* The
declaration does not allege any entry or occupation by the defendants.

(TINDAL, Ch. J. : This is not debt on the demise ; but an action
for use and occupation under the statute 11 Geo. II. c. 19, s. 14,
the words of which are " held *or* enjoyed." I think the plea is
clearly bad : all it amounts to is, that the defendant W. Scrivener
is misdescribed as executor. The only question is, whether the
declaration is sufficient.)

(1) The point marked for argument
was, that the fact of W. Scrivener not
being an executor, is no defence to
the other defendant Humphrey.

Channell, Serjt., in reply :

In drawing this declaration, the pleader evidently intended to rely upon the case of *Wigley* v. *Ashton* (1), though he has not very well carried out that intention. * * That case shows that the right mode of declaring would be to charge the defendants personally ; and, in substance, this declaration does so treat the liability of the defendants ; it states a holding by them of the premises demised to the testator, and they are clearly responsible, though, in fact, they may never have entered.

TINDAL, Ch. J. :

In this case there is no special demurrer to the declaration, and therefore the objection, if any, arises as upon general demurrer ; and the question is, whether the declaration is bad in substance. I think it is not. I can conceive a state of facts to exist under which all that is stated here would be sustainable in point of law. The action is brought upon the statute 11 Geo. II. c. 19, s. 14, which provides that " it shall be lawful for the landlord and landlords, where the agreement is not by deed, to recover a reasonable satisfaction for the lands, tenements, or hereditaments held *or* occupied by the defendant or defendants, in an action on the case for the use and occupation of what was so held *and* enjoyed." As far, therefore, as the letter of the Act goes, the words being in the alternative " held *or* enjoyed," there is no necessity that the land should be occupied as well as held ; at least where the omission is *not pointed out as ground of special demurrer. One may conceive cases of land taken but not entered upon ; in such a case there is no reason why the party so taking, inasmuch as he keeps another from the occupation, should not be liable under this statute. The declaration in the present case alleges a demise to the testator of the messuages in question, and, without stating any entry by the defendants, alleges that they, as executors, promised to pay the rent. I can readily understand, that, if the testator originally entered under a demise, and the executors do not give up the premises, the assets of their testator may be made chargeable during such time as they virtually retain them in their possession. I therefore think this declaration is sufficient on general demurrer ; and, as the plea is bad, for the reason already pointed out, that the plaintiff is entitled to judgment.

[*658]

(1) 22 R. R. 316 (3 B. & Ald. 101).

MAULE, J.:

I also am of opinion that the declaration is good, and the plea, bad. The declaration states that the defendants were indebted to the plaintiff for the use and occupation of certain premises by the defendants, held of the plaintiff, and that they promised to pay. Now, the fourteenth section of the 11 Geo. II. c. 19, provides that "it shall be lawful for the landlord and landlords, where the agreement is not by deed, to recover a reasonable satisfaction for the lands, tenements, or hereditaments held or occupied by the defendant or defendants, in an action on the case for the use and occupation of what was so held and enjoyed." I therefore think this declaration shows a good cause of action. Further, I think it discloses a sufficient cause of action against the defendants in their representative capacity. It, in terms, so charges them; for, it means, unless it is impossible that the defendants could be liable in their representative character, that the plaintiff is seeking to charge them in respect of the assets of their testator. *It is probable that they may be so liable. If the testator held the premises, and if the defendants, since his decease, have not actually occupied, but have held only, and rent has accrued, they would not be personally liable, but the assets in their hands would be liable. Then, the declaration charging the two defendants as executors, one of them pleads that the other never was executor nor ever administered any of the goods of the deceased. That plea is addressed, not to the promise, but to the allegation at the commencement of the declaration, that the defendants and each of them were executors. That allegation is divisible, the matter of the plea being matter of personal exemption only. Just as, under a plea of *plene administraverunt* by two, there may be a verdict against one who has assets, and the other may be discharged. One cannot avail himself of a defence that is peculiar to his co-defendant.

[*659]

CRESSWELL, J.:

I am of the same opinion. The plaintiff in his declaration describes the two defendants as executors, and alleges that they, as executors, were indebted to him for the use and occupation of certain messuages of the plaintiff, by them as executors held of the plaintiff under and by virtue of a demise to the testator, and that, in consideration of the premises, they, as executors, promised to pay. The difficulty that at first presented itself to my mind was,

ATKINS   that, if the plaintiff is suing for use and occupation, it is not alleged
HUMPHREY.   that the defendants had occupied the premises; and, if for rent,
it is not alleged that rent was due. But the statute 11 Geo. II.
c. 19, s. 14, removes that difficulty. The case of *Pinero* v. *Judson* (1)
is a distinct authority to show that actual occupation is not
necessary to entitle the landlord to maintain the action.

[660]   As to the plea; where several persons are charged as executors,
and there is nothing here to show that these defendants did not
promise as executors, or that such a promise might not result in
law, they may deny their representative character, but then each
defendant must deny it for himself.

ERLE, J.:

For the reasons already stated, I think the declaration sufficient
on general demurrer, and the plea bad.

Judgment for the plaintiff.

1846.   REG. *v.* THE REV. RICHARD FOLEY.
Jan. 23.
———   (2 C. B. 664—698; S. C. 15 L. J. C. P. 108.)

[664]   A private Act of Parliament, after providing for a sale of glebe land.
and the erection of an additional church with part of the proceeds, directed
that the curate of the new church should, during the incumbency of A.
the then rector, be appointed by him; and that, after the death, avoidance,
or resignation of A., the new church should become the principal church,
with all the accustomed rights, immunities, and privileges appertaining to
a mother church, and the then church should become and be deemed a
chapel of ease thereto, to be served by a minister capable of having cure of
souls; and that " the patronage of or right of presentation to the chapel, as
well as the patronage of or right of presentation to the new church, should
be vested in the patron of the rectory, his heirs and assigns, so, nevertheless,
that the minister of the chapel should not be removable at pleasure : "
Held, that the chapel of ease thus created by the Act, was thereby made
presentative, and not donative. And
Semble, that, if it had been at first donative, it would have ceased to be
so, upon a presentation being once made by the patron to the ordinary,
followed by the institution and induction of the presentee.

QUARE IMPEDIT. The first count stated, that, by a certain Act
of Parliament made and passed in the 7 Geo. IV., A.D. 1826,
intituled " An Act for effecting a sale of part of the glebe lands
belonging to the rectory of Kingswinford, otherwise Swinford Regis,
in the county of Stafford, and the mines in and under the same, to
the Rt. Hon. John William, Viscount Dudley and Ward, and for
other purposes," after reciting (amongst other things), as the facts

(1) 31 R. R. 388 (6 Bing. 206).

were, that the Rev. Nathaniel Hinde, clerk, was the rector of the
said rectory of Kingswinford, in the county of Stafford, and that the
said rectory was and stood limited to such uses as the said Viscount
Dudley and Ward should by deed or will, to be executed and attested
in such manner as in and by a certain indenture of release of the
15th of June, 1804, was mentioned, direct, limit, and appoint, and
that the Bishop of Lichfield and Coventry was the ordinary of the
parish of Kingswinford aforesaid, and that there were certain glebe
lands belonging to the said rectory, and certain mines under the
same; and after also reciting, as the fact was, that the said
Nathaniel Hinde, *as such rector as aforesaid, had then lately
entered into an agreement, dated the 11th of March, 1826, with the
said Viscount Dudley and Ward, with the privity and consent of
the said Bishop of Lichfield and Coventry, and subject to the
approbation of Parliament, to the effect, amongst other things,
that the said Nathaniel Hinde, as such rector as aforesaid,
agreed to sell to the said Viscount Dudley and Ward a part of the
said glebe lands therein described, together with the mines there-
under, for the sum of 19,290l. 11s. 3d.; that certain expenses,
amounting to 193l., should be paid out of the said purchase money;
that the remainder of the purchase money should be considered
and taken as part of the said rectory; and that, after defraying
thereout the expenses of erecting a new rectory-house and out-
buildings, and setting apart a sum not exceeding 1,929l. 1s., being
10l. per cent. upon the amount of the purchase money, to be
applied in or towards the erection of a new church, as thereinafter
mentioned, the final residue thereof should be invested for the
benefit of the said rectory, in the manner therein mentioned; and
that a sum not exceeding the said sum of 1,929l. 1s. should be
applied by and out of the said residuary purchase money, in or
towards the erecting of a new church within the said parish of
Kingswinford, provided the parishioners thereof should, by rate,
subscription, or otherwise, and either with or without the aid of the
Commissioners for building additional churches in populous places,
within five years from the passing of the said Act agreed to be
applied for, raise so much money as, with the said sum not
exceeding 1,929l. 1s., would build a good and substantial church,
capable of holding one thousand persons at the least; and that, in
case such new church should be built, by the means, and within
the time, aforesaid, then, and in such case, the curate or officiating
minister thereof, who should, during *the life or incumbency of the

REG.
v.
FOLEY.

[*665]

[*666]

said Nathaniel Hinde, the then rector of Kingswinford, be appointed
by him, the said Nathaniel Hinde, to act during his life or incumbency, should be paid or allowed by the said rector such yearly
stipend or salary as, with the rents which might arise from the
letting of the pews of the proposed new church, would make up 150*l.*
per annum; and that, from and after the death, resignation, or
avoidance of or by the said Nathaniel Hinde, the said new church
should become the principal or mother church, and the then church
should become a chapel of ease thereto, and the patronage of, or
presentation to, the same chapel, as well as the patronage of, or
presentation to, the said new church, should be vested in Viscount
Dudley and Ward, his heirs and assigns, patron and patrons of the
said rectory of Kingswinford; and that, from thenceforth, the
interest of the purchase money, or so much thereof as should not
be applied and expended, or the rents and profits of the estates to
be purchased therewith, should be received and enjoyed by the
curate or minister for the time being of the said chapel of ease, for
ever: and, after reciting that it would be greatly for the advantage
of the said Nathaniel Hinde, and for the benefit of the said rectory
of Kingswinford, and also of the parishioners of the said parish of
Kingswinford, if the sale so agreed to be made to Viscount Dudley
and Ward, and the several other agreements thereinbefore mentioned, should be carried into effect—it was, on the petition of the
said Nathaniel Hinde, Viscount Dudley and Ward, and the Bishop
of Lichfield and Coventry, enacted, that it should and might be
lawful to and for Viscount Dudley and Ward, at any time within six
calendar months next after the passing of that Act, to pay or cause to
be paid the sum of 19,075*l.* 1*s.* 3*d.* sterling, being the residue of the
said purchase money or sum of 19,290*l.* 11*s.* 3*d.*, after deducting the

[*667]   expenses *incurred in boring the said lands, amounting to 193*l.*, and
the expense of making a certain valuation in the Act mentioned,
amounting to 22*l.* 10*s.*, into the Bank of England, in the name,
and with the privity, of the Accountant-General of the Court of
Chancery, to be placed to an account there " *Ex parte* the Rector of
Kingswinford, in the county of Stafford," pursuant to the method
prescribed by the Act of the 12 Geo. I. c. 32, and the general
orders of the said Court, and without fee or reward, according to
the 12 Geo. II. c. 24; and that, from and immediately after the
said sum of 19,075*l.* 1*s.* 3*d.* should be so paid into the Bank of
England as aforesaid, all and singular the pieces or parcels of land
situate, lying, and being in the parish of Kingswinford aforesaid,

particularly described and set forth in the schedule to that Act
annexed (being part of the glebe lands belonging to the said rectory
of Kingswinford, and containing in the whole, including the sites of
the present rectory-house and buildings, 38 a. 2 r. 3 p. (a little more
or less), together with all the mines, veins, layers, and strata of
coal and iron-stone, brick-clay, and other mines and minerals in
and under the same several pieces or parcels of land, and the rights,
members, and appurtenances thereto belonging; and the reversion
and reversions, remainder and remainders, yearly and other rents,
issues, and profits of all and singular the same pieces or parcels of
land and mines, should be freed and discharged and absolutely
acquitted and exonerated of and from all the estate, right, title,
interest, claim, and demand whatsoever of the said Nathaniel
Hinde and his successors, rector and rectors for the time being
of the said parish of Kingswinford, into and upon the same; and
that the same land and mines, so freed and discharged, acquitted,
and exonerated, should be vested in the said Viscount Dudley and
Ward, and his heirs, to the only use and *behoof of him the said
Viscount Dudley and Ward, his heirs and assigns, for ever: And it
was further enacted, that all the costs, charges, and expenses preparatory to, attending, or in any wise relating or incident to, the
applying for and obtaining that Act, should be paid out of the said
sum of 19,075l. 1s. 3d. so to be paid into the Bank of England as
aforesaid, and the residue of the said sum of 19,075l. 1s. 3d., after
payment of such costs, charges, and expenses as aforesaid, and
after setting apart the several sums of 3,000l. sterling, and 1,929l. 1s.
sterling, for the purposes thereinafter directed, should, when so paid
in, be laid out by the said Accountant-General in the purchase of
navy or victualling-bills, or exchequer-bills; and that, out of the
interest arising from the money so to be laid out in the purchase of
navy or victualling-bills, or exchequer-bills, as aforesaid, the annual
sum of 200l., to commence and take effect from the day whereon
the said sum of 19,075l. 1s. 3d. should be so paid in, or such less
annual sum as, with the rents and profits of the estates to be
actually purchased from time to time as thereinafter directed,
should amount to the annual sum of 200l. in the whole, should,
under the order and direction of the Court of Chancery, on a
petition to be preferred in a summary way by the rector of
Kingswinford aforesaid for the time being, be paid, by equal
half-yearly payments, to the said rector and his successors; and
the residue of such interest, and the money to be received for the

REG.
v.
FOLEY.

[*668]

87—2

navy or victualling-bills, or exchequer-bills, so to be purchased as they should be respectively paid off by Government, should be laid out by the said Accountant-General in the purchase of other navy or victualling-bills or exchequer-bills; provided that it should and might be lawful for the said Court to make such general order or orders, or special order or orders, as to the said Court should seem necessary, *&c. &c.; all which navy, victualling, and exchequer-bills, whether purchased or exchanged, should be deposited in the Bank of England, in the name of the said Accountant-General, and should there remain until a proper purchase or purchases of real estates wherein to invest the money to be laid out in the purchase of such bills, should be found, and approved by the said Court of Chancery, and until the same bills should, upon a petition to be preferred to the said Court in a summary way by the said rector or his successors, be ordered to be sold by the said Accountant-General, for the completing of such purchase or purchases as thereinafter authorized; and, if the money to be produced by the sale of such navy, victualling, or exchequer-bills, should exceed the amount of the money thereinbefore originally directed to be laid out in the purchase of such bills, then and in that case only the surplus or excess of the money to be produced by such sale, over and above the money so originally directed to be laid out as aforesaid, after discharging the expenses of the application thereby authorized to be made to the said Court, should be paid to such person or persons respectively as would have been entitled to receive the rents and profits of the estates thereinafter directed to be purchased, in case the same had been purchased pursuant to that Act, or to the personal representatives of such person or persons: And it was further enacted that it should be lawful for the said Court of Chancery, from time to time, upon a petition to be preferred to the said Court in a summary way, by or on the behalf of the said rector or his successors, to order and direct the sale of all or any of the navy, victualling, or exchequer-bills which should, for the time being, be standing in the name of the Accountant-General on the account aforesaid, and to order and direct all or any part of the moneys to arise by any such sale or sales, *not exceeding the amount of the money thereinbefore originally directed to be laid out in the purchase of such bills, to be laid out and applied in the purchase of freehold manors, messuages, farms, lands, tenements, or hereditaments of an estate of inheritance in fee-simple in possession, or of any copyhold lands or hereditaments convenient to be

[*669]

[*670]

held therewith, such copyhold lands or hereditaments not exceeding
in value one-sixth part of the whole estates to be so purchased, free
from all incumbrances, except quit rents, fee-farm rents, or other
usual outgoings or payments, to be situate somewhere within the
diocese of Lichfield and Coventry; and that all and singular the
freehold and copyhold manors, messuages, farms, lands, tenements,
and hereditaments which should be so purchased as aforesaid, should
be thereupon immediately conveyed, surrendered, and assured unto
and to the use of the said rector and his successors, for ever, and
should, from the time of such conveyance and surrender or assurance, be annexed to, and for ever thereafter continue to be part of,
the said rectory, but subject as thereinafter mentioned : And it was
further enacted, that, out of the said sum of 19,075l. 1s. 8d. so to
be paid into the Bank of England as aforesaid, the sum of 1,929l. 1s.
should be set apart for the purposes thereinafter directed, and should
be laid out by the Accountant-General in the purchase of navy or
victualling-bills, or exchequer-bills, and that the interest arising
from the money so to be laid out in navy or victualling-bills, or
exchequer-bills, as last mentioned, and the money to be received
for the same bills as they should respectively be paid off by Government, should be laid out by the Accountant-General in the purchase
of other navy or victualling-bills, or exchequer-bills, provided that
it should be lawful for the said Court to make such general order or
orders, or special order or orders, as to the said Court should seem
necessary ; that, *whensoever the exchequer-bills of the date of
those in the hands of the said Accountant-General should be in
the course of payment by Government, and new exchequer-bills
should be issued, such new exchequer-bills might be received in
exchange for those which were so in the course of payment, as
should be effectual for the enabling such receipt in exchange, and
in that event the interest of the old bills should be laid out as before
directed with respect to the interest where the bills were paid off;
all which navy, victualling, and exchequer-bills, whether purchased
or exchanged, should be deposited in the Bank of England in the
name of the Accountant-General, and should there remain until the
same should be ordered to be sold as thereinafter directed : And it
was further enacted, that, in case the parishioners of the parish of
Kingswinford aforesaid should, by rate, subscription, or otherwise,
and either with or without the aid and assistance of the Commissioners for building additional churches in populous parishes, raise
so much money as, with the money to be produced by the sale of

REG.
v.
FOLEY.

[*671]

the navy, victualling, or exchequer-bills last thereinbefore directed
to be purchased (including the bills to be purchased with the interest
of the said sum of 1,929*l.* 1*s.*), would be sufficient to defray the
costs, charges, and expenses of erecting and building a substantial
new church in the parish of Kingswinford, capable of holding one
thousand persons at the least, then and in such case, but not otherwise, it should be lawful for the Court of Chancery, and the said
Court was thereby directed, upon a petition to be preferred to the
said Court in a summary way, by or on behalf of the said rector or
his successors, or by or on behalf of the said Viscount Dudley and
Ward, or other the patron or patrons of the said rectory for the
time being, to order and direct the navy, victualling, or exchequer-
bills last thereinbefore directed to be purchased *with the said sum
of 1,929*l.* 1*s.*, to be sold, and the money to arise from the sale
thereof to be applied in or towards the erection of such new church :
and it was further enacted, that, in case a new church should be
built in the said parish of Kingswinford, partly by means of the
money to be produced by the sale of the last-mentioned navy,
victualling, or exchequer-bills, then and in such case the curate
or officiating minister thereof, who should, during the life or incumbency of the said Nathaniel Hinde, the then rector of Kingswinford
aforesaid, be appointed by him the said Nathaniel Hinde to act
during his life or incumbency, should be paid or allowed, out of the
interest of the money first thereinbefore directed to be laid out in
the purchase of navy, victualling, or exchequer-bills, or so much
thereof as should not, for the time being, be invested in the purchase of real estates as aforesaid, if such interest should be
sufficient for that purpose, but if not, then by the said Nathaniel
Hinde out of his own moneys, the sum of 100*l.* per annum, over
and above the rents which might arise from the letting the pews in
the said new church ; and then and in such case also, from and
after the death, avoidance, or resignation of the said Nathaniel
Hinde, the said new church should become the principal or mother
church of Kingswinford aforesaid, with all the accustomed rights,
immunities, and privileges appertaining to a mother church, and
the then church should become and be deemed a chapel of ease
thereto, to be served by a minister capable of having cure of souls ;
and the patronage of, or right of presentation to, the same chapel,
as well as the patronage of or right of presentation to the said new
church, should be vested in the said Viscount Dudley and Ward,
his heirs and assigns, patron and patrons of the said rectory

of Kingswinford, so, nevertheless, that the minister of the said
chapel should not be removable at pleasure; and the annual sum
*thereinbefore directed to be paid to such rector out of the interest
of the money to be invested in such navy, victualling, or exchequer-
bills as aforesaid, should belong and (under the order and direction
of the Court of Chancery, on a petition to be preferred in a summary way,) be payable to such minister of the said chapel and his
successors, and any hereditaments which might have been purchased pursuant to the direction thereinbefore contained, should
then forthwith, by virtue of that Act, become and be vested in such
minister and his successors for ever; and, in case any part of the
money thereinbefore directed to be invested in the purchase of
real estates as aforesaid, should remain undisposed of, any future
application by petition to the said Court to have the same or any
part thereof invested in the purchase of freehold or copyhold
hereditaments as aforesaid, should be made by the minister for the
time being, and not by the rector for the time being, with the consent and approbation of the ordinary for the time being; and the
hereditaments to be purchased in consequence of any such application, should, when so purchased, be conveyed or surrendered and
assured to and vested in the said minister for the time being and
his successors, for ever; and the said minister for the time being,
should be a sole corporation, capable of taking, holding, and enjoying
the hereditaments to be purchased pursuant to that Act—as by the
record of the said Act of Parliament, remaining among the Rolls of
Parliament, at Westminster, in the county of Middlesex, reference
being thereto had, would more fully and at large appear. The
count then alleged, that Viscount Dudley and Ward did, in pursuance of the Act, pay the sum of 19,075*l.* 1*s.* 8*d.* into the Bank of
England; that the costs and charges mentioned in the Act were
thereout duly paid; that the residue, after setting apart 3,000*l.*
and 1,929*l.* 1*s.*, was invested in manner required by the Act; that
the 1,929*l.* 1*s.* *so set apart, was laid out in the purchase of
exchequer-bills; that, on the 1st of January, 1828, the parishioners
of Kingswinford did, in the manner required by the Act, raise
2,000*l.*, which, with the money produced by the sale of the last-
mentioned exchequer-bills, and 4,000*l.* given by the Commissioners
for building additional churches in populous parishes, was sufficient
to defray the costs of erecting a substantial new church in the said
parish of Kingswinford, capable of holding one thousand persons;
that the Court of Chancery did, on the 1st of February, 1828, on

REG.
v.
FOLEY.

[*673]

[*674]

the petition of the said Nathaniel Hinde, order that the exchequer-
bills so purchased with the 1,929*l.* 1*s.* should be sold, and that the
money arising from the sale thereof, should be applied in the
erection of such new church as in the Act mentioned ; that the said
exchequer-bills were afterwards sold, and produced 2,200*l.* ; that,
within five years from the passing of the Act, such new church was
built in the said parish of Kingswinford, partly by means of the
sum of money so produced as aforesaid by the sale of the last-
mentioned exchequer-bills, and partly by the sum of money so
raised by the said parishioners of Kingswinford as aforesaid,
together with the sum so given by the said Commissioners for
building additional churches in populous parishes, and which new
church was duly consecrated by Henry, Bishop of Lichfield and
Coventry, then being the ordinary of the said parish ; that, after
the building of the said new church, to wit, on the 12th of November,
1831, to wit, at &c., the said Nathaniel Hinde died, without having
previously avoided or resigned his said living ; whereupon, and by
virtue of the provisions of the said Act of Parliament, the said new
church then became the principal or mother church of Kingswinford
aforesaid, and the then church became such a chapel as in the said
Act mentioned, and which same chapel then acquired and had from

[*675]   thenceforth continually *been called and known by, the name of,
and then was, the chapel of St. Mary's, Kingswinford, and the
patronage of and right of presentation to the same chapel, as well
as the patronage of and right of presentation to the said new
church, became and was then and there vested in the said Viscount
Dudley and Ward, and his heirs, he the said Viscount Dudley and
Ward then being the patron of the said rectory of Kingswinford,
and the said Viscount Dudley and Ward then and there became
and was seised as of fee of and in the same advowsons, rights of
patronage, and presentation ; that, being so seised thereof, he the
said Viscount Dudley and Ward, on the 1st of December, 1831,
presented one William Henry Cartwright, then being a minister
capable of having cure of souls, his clerk, to the said chapel, who,
upon the same presentment, afterwards, to wit, on the day and year
last aforesaid, was admitted, instituted, and inducted into the same
chapel ; that, on the 26th of July, 1831, to wit, at &c. aforesaid,
the said Viscount Dudley and Ward, who had then become and
then was Earl of Dudley, made and published his last will and
testament in writing, dated and attested &c., and thereby gave
and devised, amongst other things, the said advowsons and rights

of patronage and presentation of him the said Earl of Dudley, to
the said chapel, and to the said church, to certain trustees for the
term of ninety-nine years, to be computed from his the said Earl of
Dudley's decease, if one William Humble Ward, in the said will
mentioned, should so long live—upon trust, when and as each
or either of the said livings should first become vacant after his
decease, during the same term, to present thereto respectively such
several persons as he should nominate for that purpose by any
codicil or codicils to that his will; and, if he should make no such
appointment, or, having made one, the nominee should die or
refuse to accept such living, then *to present to each and every   [*676]
such last-mentioned living such person or persons as the said
W. H. Ward should nominate for that purpose; that, on the 6th
of March, 1833, the said Earl of Dudley died so seised of the said
advowsons and rights of patronage and presentation as aforesaid,
without having in anywise altered or revoked his said will, and
without having made any such nomination as therein mentioned by
any codicil to his said will; that the said trustees and W. H. Ward
(who by the death of the said Earl of Dudley became and was
William Humble, Lord Ward) survived him the said Earl of
Dudley, and thereby, and under and by virtue of the will of the
said Earl of Dudley, the said trustees became and were possessed
of the said advowsons and rights of patronage and presentation for
and during the said term of ninety-nine years from the death of
the said Earl of Dudley, if the said William Humble, Lord Ward,
should so long live; that, on the 9th of October, 1835, at &c. aforesaid, the said chapel of St. Mary's, Kingswinford, became vacant by
the free resignation of the said W. H. Cartwright to the ordinary of
the said chapel, to wit, the said Henry, Bishop of Lichfield and
Coventry, and by the acceptance by the said Bishop of the said
resignation; and that notice of such resignation was afterwards,
during the life of the said William Humble, Lord Ward, and before
the said term of ninety-nine years from the death of the said Earl
of Dudley thereinbefore mentioned had expired, to wit, on &c., at
&c., duly given by the said ordinary of the said chapel to the said
patrons thereof, and to the said William Humble, Lord Ward; and
the said patrons and the said William Humble, Lord Ward, then
and there had notice of the said resignation of the said W. H.
Cartwright; that the said chapel of St. Mary's, Kingswinford,
remained and was vacant and unprovided with a minister, for a
period of eighteen months and upwards after the resignation of

*the said W. H. Cartwright, and after the said patrons of the said chapel, and the said William Humble, Lord Ward, had notice of the said resignation of the said W. H. Cartwright, and of the said chapel being so vacant as aforesaid, and the said chapel still remained vacant and unprovided with a minister; and by reason thereof, no minister having been presented or collated to the said chapel during the time aforesaid, by the patron, ordinary, or metropolitan of the said chapel, the said right of presentation had devolved upon the Queen, and it then belonged to the Queen to present a fit minister to the said chapel of St. Mary's, Kingswinford, so vacant by the lapse of time as aforesaid, in manner aforesaid; and that the said John, Bishop of Lichfield, and Richard Foley, did unjustly disturb and hinder the Queen in presenting thereto.

The second count stated, that, before and at the time of the presentation next thereinafter mentioned, the Right Hon. John William, Earl of Dudley, was seised of the advowson and right of presentation to the chapel of St. Mary's, Kingswinford, as of fee, and, being so seised, on the 1st of September, 1831, at &c. aforesaid, presented one W. H. Cartwright, his clerk, to the said chapel, being vacant, who was afterwards, to wit, on the 2nd of September, 1831, duly admitted, instituted, and inducted into the same chapel on the said presentation of the said Earl of Dudley: that afterwards, to wit, on &c., the said Earl of Dudley made and published his last will and testament in writing, bearing date, &c., and thereby gave and devised, amongst other things, the said advowson and right of presentation of him the said Earl of Dudley to certain trustees for the term of ninety-nine years, to be computed from his the said Earl of Dudley's decease, if one W. H. Ward, in the said will mentioned, should so long live, upon trust, when and as the

[*678] said living should first become vacant after his *decease, during the said term, to present thereto such person as he should nominate for that purpose by any codicil or codicils to that his will, and, if he should make no such appointment, or, having made one, the nominee should die or refuse to accept such living, then to present to such living such person as the said W. H. Ward should nominate for that purpose; and that, afterwards, to wit, on the 6th of March, 1833, at &c. aforesaid, the said Earl of Dudley died so seised of the said advowson and right of presentation as aforesaid, without having in any wise altered or revoked his said will, and without having made any such nomination as therein mentioned by any codicil

thereto; and the said trustees and W. H. Ward, who, by the death
of the said Earl of Dudley, became and was William Humble,
Lord Ward, survived him the said Earl of Dudley; and thereby,
under and by virtue of the said will of the said Earl of Dudley, the
said trustees became and were possessed of the said advowson and
right of presentation for and during the said term of ninety-nine
years from the death of the said Earl of Dudley, if the said W. H.,
Lord Ward, should so long live: that, afterwards, to wit on the
9th of October, 1835, the said chapel of St. Mary's, Kingswinford,
became vacant by the free resignation of the said W. H. Cartwright
to the ordinary of the said chapel, to wit, the said Bishop of
Lichfield and Coventry, and by the acceptance of the said Bishop
of the said resignation; and that notice of the said resignation was
afterwards, during the life of the said W. H., Lord Ward, and
before the said term of ninety-nine years from the death of the said
Earl of Dudley had expired, to wit on &c. last aforesaid, at &c.
aforesaid, duly given by the said Bishop to the said patrons of the
said chapel, and to the said W. H., Lord Ward, and the said patrons
and the said W. H., Lord Ward, then and there had notice of the
said resignation of the said *W. H. Cartwright: that the said   [*679]
chapel of St. Mary's, Kingswinford, remained and was vacant and
unprovided with a parson for a period of eighteen months and
upwards after the resignation of the said W. H. Cartwright,
and after the said patrons of the said chapel and the said W. H.,
Lord Ward, had notice of the resignation of the said W. H.
Cartwright, and of the said chapel being so vacant as aforesaid,
and the said chapel still remained vacant and unprovided with a
parson; and by reason thereof, no parson having been presented
or collated during the time aforesaid, to the said chapel by the
patron, ordinary, or metropolitan of the said chapel, the said right
of presentation had devolved upon the Queen, and it then belonged
to the Queen to present a fit person to the said chapel of St. Mary's,
Kingswinford, so vacant by the lapse of time as aforesaid, in manner
aforesaid: and that the said John, Bishop of Lichfield, and Richard
Foley, did unjustly disturb and hinder the Queen in presenting
thereto.

Pleas: to the first count, that the said Earl of Dudley, by his
said last will and testament in the said first count of the declaration mentioned, so signed as therein mentioned, gave and devised
the said advowsons, rights of patronage and presentation comprised
in the said term of ninety-nine years, after the determination of the

said term, and after the decease of the said W. H. Ward, to
W. Ward, the eldest son of the said W. H. Ward, during his
natural life; that, after the said chapel of St. Mary's, Kingswinford, has so become vacant by the free resignation of the said
W. H. Cartwright as aforesaid, and within six months after the
said resignation, and the acceptance thereof as aforesaid, to wit,
on &c. aforesaid, the said W. H., Lord Ward, departed this life,
and thereupon the said term of ninety-nine years ended and
determined, and the patronage of and right of presentation to
[*680] the said chapel became and was vested in the said *W. Ward,
then William, Lord Ward, as devisee of the said Earl of Dudley;
that thereupon, afterwards, the said William, Lord Ward, after
the death of the said W. H., Lord Ward, and within six months
after the resignation of the said W. H. Cartwright, and the
acceptance thereof as aforesaid, to wit, on the 30th of January,
1836, duly nominated and appointed the defendant Richard Foley,
being then a clerk in orders, and in all respects qualified in that
behalf, to the said chapel of St. Mary's, Kingswinford, with all and
singular the rights, members, and appurtenances thereto belonging;
that thereupon, afterwards, to wit, on the 2nd of March, 1836,
the Hon. and Right Rev. Henry, Lord Bishop of Lichfield and
Coventry, being then the ordinary of the diocese in which the said
chapel was situate, did, in pursuance of the aforesaid nomination
of the said William, Lord Ward, by his certain licence in that
behalf then duly made and given, license the defendant Richard
Foley to read prayers, preach, officiate, and perform Divine offices as
curate or minister within the said chapel of St. Mary's, Kingswinford, according to law, and did invest him the said Richard Foley
with all and singular the rights, perquisites, salaries, members,
and appurtenances thereto belonging, and did by those presents
authorise him to preach the Word of God, and license him to be
curate or minister thereof; and that thereupon, to wit, on &c. last
aforesaid, the defendant Richard Foley became and had ever since
continued to be, and still was, minister of the chapel of St. Mary,
Kingswinford, aforesaid; verification, and prayer of judgment.

To the second count, the defendant pleaded that, before the said
Earl of Dudley became so seised of the advowson and right of presentation to the said chapel of St. Mary, Kingswinford, it was, by
the said Act made and passed in 1826, intituled, &c., after reciting
[*681] as in the first count mentioned, enacted in *manner and form as in
the said first count in that behalf alleged, as by the record, &c.:

that the said John William, Viscount Dudley and Ward, in the said Act mentioned, did, in pursuance of the said Act, within six months next after passing the said Act, to wit, on the 24th of November, 1826, aforesaid, pay the said sum of 19,025l. 1s. 3d., in the said Act mentioned, into the Bank of England, &c., according to the provisions of, and in the manner appointed by, the said Act of Parliament, and that the said costs, charges, and expenses in the said Act in that behalf mentioned were then thereout duly paid, and the residue thereof, after setting apart the said two sums of 3,000l. and 1,929l. 1s., was then duly invested in the manner required by the said Act; that the said sum of 1,929l. 1s. so set apart for the purposes in the said Act in that behalf directed as aforesaid, was, to wit, then and there, laid out in exchequer-bills, according to the provisions of the said Act of Parliament; and that, afterwards, to wit, on the 1st of January, 1828, to wit, at &c., the parishioners of the parish of Kingswinford aforesaid did, in the manner required by the said Act, raise a sum of money, to wit, 2,000l., which, together with the money produced by the sale of the bills last thereinbefore mentioned, and a certain other sum, to wit, 4,000l., then and there for that purpose given by the said Commissioners for building additional churches in populous parishes, was sufficient to defray the costs &c. of erecting and building a substantial new church in the said parish of Kingswinford, capable of holding one thousand persons; and that, thereupon, afterwards, to wit, on the 1st of February, 1828, the Court of Chancery directed a sale of the exchequer-bills; that, within five years from the passing of the Act of Parliament, to wit, on the 1st of March, 1830, such a new church as in the said Act mentioned was built in the said parish of Kingswinford, *partly by means of the money produced by the sale of the exchequer-bills, and partly by the money so raised by the parishioners of Kingswinford, together with the said sum so given by the said Commissioners, and which new church was then and there duly consecrated by the Bishop of Lichfield and Coventry, then being the ordinary of the said parish; that, after the said new church was so built as aforesaid, to wit, on the 12th of November, 1831, the said Nathaniel Hinde died, without having previously avoided or resigned his said living; whereupon, and by virtue of the provisions of the said Act of Parliament, the said new church then became the principal or mother church of Kingswinford aforesaid, and the then church became such chapel as in the said Act mentioned, and which same chapel then acquired, and

[*682]

from thenceforth and continually had been called and known by,
the name of the chapel of St. Mary, Kingswinford, and the
patronage of and right of presentation to the same chapel, as well
as the patronage of and right of presentation to the said new
church, then and there became and was vested in the said Viscount
Dudley and Ward, and his heirs, he the said Viscount Dudley and
Ward then being the patron of the said rectory of Kingswinford,
and he the said Viscount Dudley and Ward thereupon became and
was seised as of fee of and in the said advowson, right of patronage
and presentation, as in the second count of the declaration above
alleged; that the said Earl of Dudley, by his said last will and
testament in the second count of the declaration mentioned, so
signed &c. as therein mentioned, gave and devised the said
advowson and right of presentation to the chapel of St. Mary,
Kingswinford, aforesaid, after the determination of the said term
of ninety-nine years, and immediately after the decease of the said
W. H. Ward, to William Ward, the eldest son of the said W. H.

[*683] Ward, for his natural life. (The plea *then proceeded as in the
first plea, from the [third line on p. 588] to the end.)

To these pleas, the *Attorney-General*, on behalf of the Crown,
demurred generally. The objection relied on was, "that the
chapel of St. Mary's, Kingswinford, appeared by the declaration
to be presentative, and that, therefore, the right of presentation,
on the vacancy set out in the counts respectively, would lapse to
the Crown, notwithstanding the defendant Richard Foley might
have been nominated by the patron, and licensed by the ordinary."
The defendant joined in demurrer.

Talfourd, Serjt., for the Crown:

The question is, whether, upon the proper construction of the
Act of Parliament set out in the declaration (1), the chapel of
St. Mary's, Kingswinford, was donative or presentative; or whether,
supposing it to have been originally donative, it did not cease to be
so, and become presentative, by the presentation, institution, and
induction of Mr. Cartwright, upon the avoidance of Mr. Hinde.

That this is a chapel that might be presentative, is clear, upon all
the old authorities. In Co. Litt. 344 a, it is said: "A church
parochial may be donative and exempt from all ordinary jurisdiction, and the incumbent may resign to the patron, and not to
the ordinary; neither can the ordinary visit, but the patron, by

(1) 7 Geo. IV. c. xli. (private Act).

Commissioners to be appointed by him. And, by Littleton's rule,
the patron and incumbent may charge the glebe; and, albeit it be
donative by a layman, yet *merè laicus* is not capable of it, but an
able clerk *infra sacros ordines*, is; for, albeit he come in by lay
donation, and not by admission or institution, yet his function is
spiritual: and, if such a clerk donative be disturbed, the patron
shall have a *quare impedit* of this church *donative, and the writ   [*684]
shall say, *quod permittat ipsum præsentare ad ecclesiam*, &c., and
declare the special matter in his declaration (1). And so it is of a
prebend, chantry, chapel, donative, and the like; and no lapse
shall incur to the ordinary, except it be so specially provided in the
foundation. But, if the patron of such a church, chantry, chapel,
&c., donative, doth once present to the ordinary, and his clerk is
admitted and instituted, it is now become presentable, and never
shall be donative after, and then, lapse shall incur to the ordinary,
as it shall of other benefices presentable." So, in 2 Inst. 364, it is
said, "if a patron of a chapel present unto it by the name of a
church, and the clerk be instituted and inducted thereunto, &c., it
hath lost the name of a chapel." The distinction between donatives and presentatives is very clearly laid down in Gibson's
Codex, tit. 34, c. 10, s. 2 (2): "Donatives," it is there said, "are
so called, because they are given, and fully possessed, by the single
donation of the patron, in writing, without presentation, institution,
or induction. And the right in the donor (together with the exemption of the church from ecclesiastical jurisdiction) spring from the
consent of the Bishop to some particular Lords and great men, who
were desirous to erect places of worship for the convenience of
their families, and did obtain those privileges for them and their
heirs; in regard (as I suppose) that the places at first were considered only as private domestic chapels. And, as the families,
and by consequence the neighbourhood, increased or decayed, the
places, in process of time, became churches, and chapels with cure,
or *sine* cure. For, that a benefice with cure of souls, may be donative, appears from the rectory of St. Burien, in Cornwall, and the
church in the Tower of London, which are both cures, and both
*donatives. But, if these, and the like places, had been originally   [*685]
intended for distinct cures of souls, and not as places of private
worship only, it is not to be conceived that the Bishops should
grant them such privileges and exemptions: since the utmost
favour that was granted to the founders or endowers of churches

(1) *Vide post*, p. 601, *n*. (1).   (2) Vol. ii. p. 819.

(though intended only for their own tenants) was only the right of patronage. From whence it may be inferred that those grants of independence, made to the churches and chapels called donatives, were in consideration of their being at first of a merely private and domestic nature." In Blackstone's Commentaries (1) it is said: "An advowson donative is, when the King, or any subject by his licence, doth found a church or chapel, and ordains that it shall be merely in the gift or disposal of the patron; subject to his visitation only, and not to that of the ordinary; and vested absolutely in the clerk by the patron's deed of donation, without presentation, institution, or induction. This is said to have been antiently the only way of conferring ecclesiastical benefices in England; the method of institution by the Bishop not being established more early than the time of Archbishop Becket, in the reign of Henry II. And, therefore, though Pope Alexander III., in a letter to Becket, severely inveighs against the *prava consuetudo*, as he calls it, of investiture conferred by the patron only, this, however, shows what was the then common usage. Others contend that the claim of the Bishops to institution is as old as the first planting of Christianity in this island; and, in proof of it, they allege a letter from the English nobility to the Pope, in the reign of Henry III., recorded by Matthew Paris, which speaks of presentation to the Bishop as a thing immemorial. The truth seems to be, that, where the benefice was to be *conferred on a mere layman, he was first presented to the Bishop, in order to receive ordination, who was at liberty to examine and refuse him: but, where the clerk was already in orders, the living was usually vested in him by the sole donation of the patron, till about the middle of the twelfth century, when the Pope and his Bishops endeavoured to introduce a kind of feodal dominion over ecclesiastical benefices, and, in consequence of that, began to claim and exercise the right of institution universally, as a species of spiritual investiture. However this may be, if, as the law now stands, the true patron once waives this privilege of donation, and presents to the Bishop, and his clerk is admitted and instituted, the advowson is now become for ever presentative, and shall never be donative any more. For, these exceptions to general rules and common right, are ever looked upon by the law in an unfavourable view, and construed as strictly as possible. If, therefore, the patron in whom such peculiar right resides, does once give up that right,

[*686]

(1) Vol. ii. pp. 23, 24.

the law, which loves uniformity, will interpret it to be done with
an intention of giving it up for ever; and will thereupon reduce it
to the standard of other ecclesiastical livings." By the Act of
Parliament in question, the old parochial church of Kingswinford
is made a mere chapel of ease, the new church being created the
mother church. There is nothing on the face of the Act, nor can
any reason be assigned, why the new chapel should not be presentative, as the old church was, and as the newly built church is
to be for the future. The fair inference from the whole of the Act
is, that there should be uniformity in this respect.

(MAULE, J.: The Act, in the case of the old church, provides,
"that the minister shall not be removable at pleasure." That
probably was introduced from mere excess of caution.)

There are many authorities to show, that, where the patron
presents, and his clerk is instituted and inducted, *though the   [*687]
benefice was donative before, it, by the single act of presentment,
loses it donative character, and becomes for ever after presentative.
In *Farchild* v. *Gayre* (1), the whole COURT held that "admission
and institution is not requisite in case of a donative; but, if to
such a donative the patron presents to the ordinary, and suffers an
admission and institution thereupon, he thereby hath made it
always presentable."

(TINDAL, Ch. J.: The authority cited for that is Co. Litt. 344 a.
There is also a reference to F. N. B. 35 E.)

In Gibson (2) it is said: "If the patron of a chapel do present to
that chapel, it shall become a church, and be presentative. This
was affirmed by DODERIDGE, and assented to by COKE, in the Court
of King's Bench, 12 Jac. I., agreeably to what is said elsewhere of
donatives, that, if the patron present, and his clerk is admitted and
instituted, it is become presentable, and never shall be donative
after. But, on the other hand, if one is patron of two churches,
and presents to one only as the mother church, *cum capellâ de*
(naming the other); that other, having been originally a district
parish church, shall so remain, notwithstanding such presentment,
and that never so often repeated." Again (3): "If the patron of
a donative doth present to the ordinary, and suffer admission and

---

(1) Cro. Jac. 63; Yelv. 60; 1 Brownl.   (2) Tit. 9, c. 11, s. 4.
& G. 202.   (3) Tit. 34, c. 10, s. 5, p. 820.

institution thereupon, it is no longer donative, but for ever presentative, and liable to lapse, and subject to the jurisdiction of the ordinary. In this doctrine the books (1) are agreed, without exception even to the Crown; but with one other exception (in which they likewise agree), that such presentation must be made by the true patron; for, if it be by a stranger, it is so far from making [*688] the church *presentative, that it is in itself merely void. And there seems to be the same reason for a perpetual curacy's becoming for ever presentative, if the true patron, instead of nominating, shall present, and suffer admission and institution as aforesaid, because, if presentation in the case of a donative doth not only create a perpetual obligation to present, but also hath force enough to extinguish the original exemption from the ordinary, much more may it create such obligation in places that are, and always were, subject to the jurisdiction of the ordinary." Gibson then refers to a case of *Ladd* v. *Widdows* (2), which will probably be cited for the defendant; but he does not adopt it as an authority.

(TINDAL, Ch. J.: That, in all probability, was the case of a donative created by the Crown (3).)

In Watson's Clergyman's Law (4) it is laid down, that, "though generally these donatives be in themselves to be had only by the patron's collation, yet, if the true patron of such a donative doth once present to the ordinary of the respective diocese, and doth suffer admission and institution thereupon, he thereby hath made it always presentable (5); and hath made it also for ever to become a benefice with cure of souls (6). And this holds not only in the case of common patrons of donatives, but in the case of the King also " (7).

(1) Citing 1 Inst. 344 a; Cro. Jac. 63 (*Farchild* v. *Gayre*) ; Style, 272 (*Cremer* v. *Burnet*, 2 Style's Rep. 266). And see 8 Ass. fo. 18, pl. 29.

(2) 2 Salk. 541; *S. C.* Lord Holt, 259.

(3) In the two reports of this case, which are *verbatim* the same, except that in Holt the name of Serjt. *Selby* is omitted, HOLT, Ch. J., and POWELL, J., are stated to have held that a presentation could not destroy a donative " because its creation was by letters-patent, whereby land is settled to the parson and his successors, and he to come in by donation." In that case, as suggested, the benefice was perhaps a donative created by letters-patent. But the opinion may have been extra-judicial; the case stating that there was evidence of several pretended presentations, the new trial was probably moved for in respect of the insufficiency of that evidence.

(4) C. 15, p. 170.

(5) Citing *Farchild* v. *Gayre, ubi supra*, and Co. Litt. 344 a.

(6) *Clerk* v. *Heath*, Mich. 21 Car. II. B. R. 2 Keb. 556.

(7) By *Latch*, in his argument in *Cremer* and *Burnet's* case, Style, 272.

(TINDAL, Ch. J.: That is at variance with *Ladd* v. *Widdows*: and certainly there is nothing repugnant to good sense in holding that the character of the right may be thus changed.

MAULE, J.: *Ladd* v. *Widdows*, when closely looked at, will be found to be no authority at all. If there had been evidence given of presentation, institution, and induction, it would have been distinctly so alleged. Simple presentation will not do, without institution and induction : that is in accordance with all the authorities (1).)

Watson says (2) : " It has been generally held for law, that, if the patron of a donative doth once present to the ordinary, and suffer an admission and institution thereupon, the church, &c., is no longer donative, but shall be, for ever after, presentative, and liable to lapse, and in all things subject to the jurisdiction of the ordinary; in which doctrine the antient books seem to agree, without exception even to the Crown. Yet there are later authorities which say, though a presentation may destroy an impropriation, it cannot destroy a donative, because the creation thereof was by letters-patent, by which the land was settled to such a person and his successors, and he to come in by donation, which was the antient way of conferring benefices, and the institution to churches was not ordained by any temporal law, there being only a papal provision; and was not received in some places here in England, and where it was not received, they still went on in the old way and method of conferring benefices, which afterwards were called donatives.'

(TINDAL, Ch. J., referred to 3 Salk. 140 (3).)

These authorities clearly show that the *donative character of the living in question, if, upon the true construction of the Act, it ever was donative, was destroyed by the presentation of Mr. Cartwright, and his admission and institution, in December, 1831 ; and therefore the pleas, which allege not a presentation, but a mere nomination and appointment of the defendant Foley, afford no answer to the declaration.

[*690]

(1) In *Ladd* v. *Widdows* presentation is mentioned, and nothing is said of institution or induction. But the distinction taken in that case is, between an impropriation, destroyed by presentation, *i.e.*, u* *videtur*, by presenta-tion attended with its usual con-sequents, institution and induction, on the one hand, and a donative, not so destroyed, on the other.
(2) Page 173.
(3) Title Donative.

REG
v.
FOLEY.

Channell, Serjt. (with whom was *Byles*, Serjt.), for the defendant:

It may be that a donative, properly so called, becomes presentative if the patron once presents, and his clerk is thereupon instituted and inducted: but the case of *Ladd* v. *Widdows* is an authority to show, that, though a presentation may destroy an impropriation, yet it cannot destroy a donative, the creation of which is by letters-patent. The same rule will apply to a donative created by Act of Parliament. Watson, after referring to all the authorities, takes a distinction between donatives, properly so called, and others (1). " Some of the instances before mentioned," he says, " may rather be called *quasi* donations than properly donations: such are, 1. The collation of a Bishop without any presentation; 2. The grant of the King to prebends, &c., without institution; and, 3. The nomination to perpetual curacies, which is without either presentation, institution, or induction: for, these differ from donatives, properly so called, which are given and fully possessed by the sole donation of the patron in writing, inasmuch as collations and Royal grants are to be followed by induction and instalment; and persons nominated to curacies are to be authorised by a licence from the Bishop before they can legally officiate: whereas possession by donation is not subject to any of these consequents, but receives its full essence and *effect from the single act and sole authority of the donor, as aforesaid; and, if what is said in the case of *Clerk* v. *Heath* be true, that the King hath several donatives in Wales, which yet receive institution from the Bishop, it seems to be as true, that, by such institution, they have lost the proper nature of donatives (2); for, the grant of a donative, being once made, creates a right as full and lasting as presentation, admission, institution, and induction can, viz., a right not to be devested or taken away but by the resignation or deprivation of the donee, whereof the first must be made to, and the second by, the donor, for, both the church and the clerk are exempt from ordinary jurisdiction. And to this purpose is what we find in Sir John Davis's Reports, viz. that a donative cannot be granted for years,

[*691]

---

(1) Title Donation and Donative, O. 15, p. 172.

(2) The distinction possibly may be this: the King by presenting to the ordinary, does an act by which he releases his right of collating (or giving) without presentation; but where he collates (or gives) without presenting, his rights are not affected by mere *laches*, which cannot be imputed to the Crown in suffering the collatee (or donee) to receive institution and induction.

or at will only, because this great inconvenience would follow, that
the freehold (of the church, &c.) might be in perpetual abeyance,
which is an inconvenience that the law will not suffer.   The case
of those curacies called perpetual, in opposition to temporary
curates, who serve under other incumbents, was originally otherwise, being such churches the entire revenue whereof was united
and annexed *ad mensas monachorum*, and not (as other appropriations were) under the tie of having perpetual vicars appointed in
them, but left to be served by temporary curates belonging to their
own houses, and sent out as occasion required.   The like liberty
of not appointing a perpetual vicar, was sometimes granted, by
dispensation, in benefices not annexed to their tables, in consideration of the poverty of their *house, or the nearness of the church.

But, when such appropriations, together with the charge of providing for the cure, were transferred from spiritual societies to
single lay persons, who were not capable of serving them by themselves, and who, by consequence, were obliged to nominate some
particular person to the ordinary, for his licence to serve the cure,
the curates by this means became so far perpetual as not to be
wholly at the pleasure of the appropriator, nor removable but by
a due and legal revocation of the licence of the ordinary."   All the
authorities cited on the part of the Crown apply to donatives,
strictly and properly so called; and all rely on the passages cited
from Co. Litt. 344 a.   The old church having, by the plain words
of the Act, been converted into a mere chapel of ease without
cure of souls, the question is, whether the mere use of the word
" presentation " in the preamble and in the enacting part of the
Act of Parliament, takes this case out of the ordinary rule, that a
mere nomination is all that is necessary.   The word is evidently
not used in its strict legal sense, but merely to point out the person
by whom the patronage is to be exercised.   The Church-building
Acts, 58 Geo. III. c. 45, ss. 18, 19, and 59 Geo. III. c. 134, s. 18,
show that the Legislature knew how to express themselves, where
they intended to make benefices presentative.   The authorities
cited on the other side do not bear out the proposition that one
presentation, in the case of a donative, renders the benefice for
ever after presentative : when looked at, they will be found all to
apply to churches or chapels having cure of souls.   A mere chapel
of ease is scarcely recognised by the law.   The cases of *Rex*
v. *The Bishop of Chester* (1), *Bliss* v. *Woods* (2), and *William* v.

(1) 1 B. B. 237 (1 T. R. 396).   (2) 3 Hagg. 486.

Brown (1), may afford some assistance in the determination of this question.

[693]   *Talfourd*, Serjt., was heard in reply.

TINDAL, Ch. J.:

The real question in this case appears to me to be, whether, upon the true construction of the Act of Parliament, this chapel, which before was the old parochial church of Kingswinford, is a donative, to which the patron may appoint, without presenting his clerk to the ordinary, or whether it is presentative only, as is contended on the part of the Crown. Looking at the general scope and object of the Act, it appears to me that it is presentative only. The object of the Act appears to have been this: part of the glebe land having mines under it, which might be worked with advantage if in lay hands, it provided for the sale thereof if a purchaser could be found; and, accordingly, the patron enters into a contract with the incumbent, that a certain portion of the land shall be sold to the former for the sum of 19,290*l.* 11*s.* 3*d.*, and that, after payment of certain expenses, the remainder of the purchase-money shall be considered and taken as part of the rectory, that, after defraying thereout the expenses of erecting a new rectory-house and outbuildings, and setting apart a sum not exceeding 1,929*l.* 1*s.*, to be applied towards the erection of a new church, the final residue shall be invested for the benefit of the rectory. The Act then provides, that, in case such new church shall be built by the means and within the time specified, the curate or officiating minister thereof, who shall, during the life or incumbency of Mr. Hinde, the then rector, be appointed by him to act during his life or incumbency, shall be paid or allowed the sum of 100*l.* per annum, over and above the pew rents of the new church. The Act then goes on to provide for the enjoyment of the future patronage, in these words: "And from and

[*694]   after the death, avoidance, or resignation *of the said N. Hinde, the said new church shall become the principal or mother church of Kingswinford aforesaid, with all the accustomed rights, immunities, and privileges appertaining to a mother church, and the then church shall become and be deemed a chapel of ease thereto, to be served by a minister capable of having cure of souls; and the patronage of or right of presentation to the same chapel, as well as the patronage of or right of presentation to the said new church,

(1) 1 Curt. 54.

shall be vested in Lord Dudley and Ward, his heirs and assigns, patron and patrons of the said rectory of Kingswinford, so, nevertheless, that the minister of the said chapel shall not be removable at pleasure." These are the important words, to which we are now called upon to give a construction. What is the meaning of the words, "the patronage of or right of presentation to the same chapel, as well as the patronage of or right of presentation to the said new church, shall be vested in Lord Dudley and Ward, his heirs and assigns?" The same words are applied equally to the old church and to the new chapel of ease: and it seems to me to be very difficult to put a different construction upon them in the one case from that which is put upon them in the other. And this remark is the more striking when the earlier part of the clause, where it is provided that the curate or officiating minister of the newly built church shall during the life or incumbency of Mr. Hinde, the then rector, be appointed by him to act during his life or incumbency. If the Legislature had intended the creation of a donative, it would be somewhat singular that they should, when dealing with the future patronage, drop that word, and adopt a form of expression applicable to a totally different state of things, viz. "right of presentation" (1). This view is still further *confirmed by a consideration of the nature and the mode of creation of donatives. In Co. Litt. 344 a, it is said: "If the King doth found a church, hospital, or free chapel donative, he may exempt the same from ordinary jurisdiction," &c. Again, "As the King may create donatives, exempt from the visitation of the ordinary, so he may, by his charter, license any subject to found such a church or chapel, and to ordain that it shall be donative, and not presentable, and to be visited by the founder, and not by the ordinary; and thus began donations in England, whereof common persons were patrons." If, therefore, this were intended to be a donative, one would expect to find some words of special exemption. In the ordinary case of a donative, the original deed would be presumed to be lost; but then there would be the circumstance of the donee never having been presented to the Bishop. But here, we have the very Act creating the living, and, if it were exempted from ordinary jurisdiction, some words of exemption would undoubtedly be found. I was at first inclined to attach some importance, in favour of the defendant's argument, to the words that declare "that the minister of the said chapel shall not be removable at pleasure." But I think those

(1) *Vide post*, p. 601, n. (1).

REG.
v.
FOLEY.

[*695]

REG.
v.
FOLEY.

words were merely introduced *ex majori cautelâ*, lest the previous words should be construed to render the officiating minister appointed by Mr. Hinde during his incumbency, removable at his pleasure. Upon the whole, the true construction of the Act appears to me to be, that the chapel of ease is presentative by the patron of the living of the parish ; and this construction is in some degree fortified by the circumstance, that the only instance that has occurred since the avoidance of Mr. Hinde, is of a presentation. I therefore think there should be judgment for the Crown.

[696] MAULE, J. :

I am of the same opinion. It is not necessary to discuss whether a single instance of presentation by the patron, would have the effect of making a benefice presentative which before was donative. My own opinion is that it would have that effect. It is not necessary, however, nor is it possible, to decide that in the present case, because I think this benefice was originally presentative. That it was so, appears from indisputable evidence. The Act of Parliament provides in the same words for the future presentation to the new mother church and to the old church now made a chapel of ease ; and the same words in the same clause of an Act ought always to be construed in the same sense, when applied to the same or a similar subject-matter, unless any necessity exists for giving them a different construction. No such necessity exists here. In the present case, the living was presentative before the passing of the Act : and, although a considerable change has been effected in the parish, the presentative character of the living must remain, unless altered by the express words of the Act. I conceive ecclesiastical benefices generally are to be taken to be presentative, unless there be some evidence expressly showing them to be donative, and exempted from ordinary jurisdiction : and I can find nothing in this Act to show that this chapel is so exempted. On the contrary, I think there are circumstances to show that it falls within that description of benefices that are the proper subject of presentation. There is, at all events, nothing in the Act to exempt it from the characteristics that ordinarily belong to ecclesiastical benefices.

CRESSWELL, J. :

I also am of opinion that the benefice in question is to be considered as presentative ; and therefore that the church is not full,
[*697] there having *been no presentation. It cannot be contended that

the officiating minister of the church is to be considered as a mere curate. It might have been so contended, possibly, during the incumbency of Mr. Hinde ; for, he is so called in the Act (1). But, on the death of that gentleman, this change took place: A large sum of money had been produced by the sale of a portion of the glebe, which sum, by the terms of the Act, was to be, in part, appropriated to the building of a new rectory-house, and, in part, to the erection of a new church in the parish ; and the residue was to be invested by the patron and ordinary, in land for the benefit of the then rector during his life or incumbency, and, on his death or resignation, for the benefit of the minister of the old church, which was, by the Act, made a chapel of ease to the new church ; which latter then became the mother church. It is difficult to conceive how the ordinary could have any thing to do with the investing of this money, if the chapel of ease were to be a mere curacy, or even a donative. The new incumbent is to be a person " capable of having cure of souls."

The construction we put upon the Act of Parliament, relieves us from the necessity of considering, whether the older authorities are, in any degree, disturbed by the case of *Ladd* v. *Widdows*.

ERLE, J. :

As stated in the course of the argument, the Legislature have known how to express themselves, when it was thought desirable to make benefices presentative, and had it been intended that this living should be filled by appointment only, without presentation to the Bishop or ordinary, that intention would have appeared in this Act. For the reasons assigned by the rest of the *Court, I am of opinion that this was not a donative in its original creation.

[*698]

Judgment for the Crown (2).

(1) *Quære*, if, in the Act, the term "curate" is not used, as in the Liturgy, in its original and proper sense of "person having the cure of souls." *Curatus, curio, sacerdos ecclesiæ, curé.*

(2) In strict legal language all benefices are presentative, *præsentare ad ecclesiam*, or *ad capellam*, or *ad cantariam*, meaning nothing more than to nominate or appoint a minister or pastor to the vacant church, chapel, or chantry. Throughout the forms of writs of *quare impedit* in the Register

(Reg. Brev. Orig. 30, 31), the mandatory clause runs thus—*quod permittat prædictum* (querentem) *præsentare ad ecclesiam* (capellam or cantariam) without any special form for a donative : under this general writ, the plaintiff may count either upon an ordinary right of presentation, which is to, or rather through, the Bishop, or upon the exceptional right of direct absolute presentation, called a donation. F. N. B. 33 C.

In the reign of Mary, DYER, J , (afterwards Ch. J. of C. P.) is said to

1846.
Jan. 28.
—
[706]

MARTINDALE v. MARY FALKNER, AND
TWO OTHERS (1).

(2 C. B. 706—723 ; S. C. 3 Dowl. & L. 600 ; 15 L. J. C. P. 91 ; 10 Jur. 161.)

An attorney's bill must show the Court and the cause in which the
business referred to in it, or the greater part thereof, was done. These
particulars should be expressly stated, (held to be necessary by MAULE, J.),
or must be capable of being collected by fair and reasonable intendment
from the nature of the several items of charge.

Where costs are incurred in a suit the Statute of Limitations does not
begin to run against the earlier items until the suit is terminated.

DEBT, for work done as an attorney and solicitor, and for money
found due upon an account stated.

Pleas : First, never indebted ; secondly, that the several causes
of action in the declaration mentioned did not, nor did any of them,
or any part thereof, accrue to the plaintiff at any time within six
years next before the commencement of the suit, &c. ; thirdly, payment before action ; fourthly, that the plaintiff, before and at the
time of the doing of the said work, and of the providing of the said
materials, as in the first count mentioned, was an attorney and
solicitor, and the said work was done, and the said materials were
provided by him as such attorney and solicitor, and the said fees and
causes of action in the first count mentioned were and are for fees,
charges, and disbursements for business done by the plaintiff for
all the three defendants as such attorney and solicitor as aforesaid ;
and that the money so found to be due as in the last count mentioned,
was due, and found to be so, for and in respect of the said work and

have paid "an acceptable compliment
to the Queen's attachment to the
interests of the Church," by presenting
to, and thereby disappropriating, his
vicarage of Staplegrove near Taunton.
See Strype's Annals of the Reforma-
tion, vol. ii. p. 370 ; Life of Dyer,
prefixed to his Reports.

(1) This case has been frequently
cited upon the point first appearing in
the head-note. See *Ivimey* v. *Marks*
(1847) 16 M. & W. 843 ; *Sargent* v.
Gannon (1849) 7 C. B. 742 ; 18 L. J.
C. P. 220 ; *Dimes* v. *Wright* (1849) 8
C. B. 831 ; *Anderson* v. *Boynton* (1849)
13 Q. B. 308 ; 19 L. J. Q. B. 42 ; *Keene*
v. *Ward* (1849) 13 Q. B. 515 ; 19 L. J.
Q. B. 46 ; *Cook* v. *Gillard* (1352) 1 E.
& B. 26, 22 L. J. Q. B. 90. At the
present time it is worth preserving
mainly for the statement of MAULE, J.,

at pp. 719—720, as to the meaning of
the presumption that every one knows
the law. This passage was cited with
approval by BLACKBURN, J., in *The
Queen* v. *Mayor of Tewkesbury* (1868)
L. R. 3 Q. B. 629, 635, 37 L. J. Q. B.
288, 292. The Judicature Act, 1873,
has transferred to the High Court the
jurisdiction of the High Court of
Chancery and of the superior common
Law Courts, and it is probably not
necessary to show in what Division
of the High Court the business is
done, but solicitors' bills for proceedings in the County Courts are taxed
in those Courts, and no doubt a
solicitor's bill should show whether
the proceedings were taken in the
High Court or a County Court or any
other Inferior Court.—J. G. P.

materials, and for and in respect of the said fees, charges, and dis-   MARTIN-
DALE
v.
FALKNER.
bursements, and not otherwise, and that the said account was stated
as aforesaid of and concerning the same, and of and concerning no
other cause and matter; and that no bill of the said fees, charges,
or disbursements, or of any of them, or any part thereof, subscribed
with the proper hand of the plaintiff, or with the proper hand of
any assignee of the plaintiff, was, at any time before the commencement of the suit, delivered unto the defendants, or any of them, or
sent by the post to, or left for, the defendants, or any *of them, at   [*707]
their counting-house, office of business, dwelling-house, or last known
place of abode, or at the counting-house, &c. of any of them; nor
was any bill of the said fees, charges, and disbursements, or of any
of them, or any part thereof, at any time before the commencement
of the suit, delivered to the defendants, or to any of them, or sent
by the post to, or left for, them, or any of them, at their counting-
house, &c., or at the counting-house &c. of any of them, inclosed
in and accompanied by a letter subscribed with the proper hand of
the plaintiff, or with the proper hand of any assignee of the plaintiff,
referring to such bill, as required by, and according to, the statute
in such case made and provided.   Verification.

The plaintiff joined issue upon the first plea, and traversed the
others; upon which traverses respectively, the defendants joined issue.

The cause was tried before Maule, J., at the last Summer Assizes
at Northampton.   The plaintiff put in the retainer under which he
had acted as solicitor for the defendants, and which was in the handwriting of one of the defendants, and signed by the three, and was
addressed to the plaintiff in the following form:

"In Chancery.

"*Falkner* v. *Bolton* and others.

Falkner v. *Cambray* and others.

Falkner v. *Matthews.*

"SIR,—We retain you as our solicitor, and request you to take
such proceedings as will tend to a speedy and amicable arrangement
of these suits, as to you shall seem best, with our approbation, and
Mr. R. Ridgway's.   Dated, this 31st of December, 1835."

The bill, a signed copy of which was proved to have been duly
delivered, was then put in, &c.   It commenced without the mention
of any Court or cause, as follows:

£ s. d.   [708]

"1835, Dec. 22. Attending on you, conferring and
advising as to your suits in Chancery, and as to

MARTIN-
DALE
v.
FALKNER.

	£	*s.*	*d.*
the order for dismissal, &c., when you left me the papers to peruse, and promised to call to-morrow	0	6	8
23. Attending you, conferring and advising further on your affairs, and explaining to you the mode in which I thought you might be reinstated before the Court, when it was decided that you should bring me a retainer on Saturday next -	0	6	8
24. Perusing decrees and reports at Report Office, and sundry other papers intrusted by you to me, and paid - - - - - - -	1	7	6
29. Attending this morning on Mr. Ridgway, discussing your suits, and the best mode of proceeding with him, and again on you this evening, when it was decided that I was to see Mr. Ridgway again with you to-morrow - - -	0	6	8
30. Attending Mr. Ridgway, conferring and advising further on your affairs, and as to your wish to borrow 30*l.*, &c. - - - - -	0	6	8
1836, March 16. Attending at Six Clerks' Office, searching for record, and paid - - -	0	9	8"

Under the heading "Hilary Term, 1836. *Falkner* v. *Matthews*," which was the first mention of the name of any suit, were, amongst others, the following items :

	£	*s.*	*d.*
" Paid for minutes of decree - - - - -	0	5	0
Close copy - - - - - - -	0	2	6
Feb. 8. Attending registrar to settle minutes ; but he declined, in consequence of the insertion that rests were to be taken as a matter of course, not being authorised by the Court - - -	0	13	6
Copy title of cause, and prayer of bill - - -	0	2	6
Copy minutes as wished to be settled, for Lord Chancellor - - - - - - -	0	3	0
20. Attending Court, cause in paper ; ordered to stand over - - - - - - -	0	13	4
March 2. Paid for copy minutes as settled by the Court - - - - - - - -	0	5	0
Paid for decree - - - - - - -	4	16	8
Attending passing - - - - - -	0	13	4
Paid entering - - - - - - -	0	6	0

[709]

	£	s.	d.
Paid for reference to Master in rotation - -	0	1	0
Attending - - - - - - -	0	6	8
18. Instructions for interrogatories - -	0	13	4
Paid for Master's allowance, and attendance -	0	11	8"

Under the heading "Hilary Term, 1840," were the following:

	£	s.	d.
"Feb. 13. Warrant to sign report; copy and			
service - - - - - - -	0	4	6
Paid for report, and transcribing - -	5	10	0
Paid for Master's signature - - -	1	0	0
Copy draft report as finally settled, for use of			
Mr. Bull - - - - - -	2	15	0
Instructions for exceptions to Master's report -	0	13	4
Copy exceptions for Master of Rolls - -	0	6	8
Drawing and ingrossing petition for leave to set			
down cause for hearing on further directions -	0	6	8
Trinity Term, 1840.			
July 17. Attending Court on plaintiff's excep-			
tions - - - - - - -	0	13	4
Attending Court on defendant's exceptions - -	0	13	4
Attending Court on cause - - - -	0	13	4"

The like on the 18th, 20th, and three following days.   [710]

Michaelmas Term, 1840.

"Attending Mr. Bull, explaining to him the situation			
the parties were placed in by the decision of the			
Master of the Rolls - - - - -	0	6	8
Paid for order - - - - - -	3	10	0
Attending passing - - - - -	0	13	4
Trinity Term, 1841.			
Paid for report, and transcribing - -	1	9	6
Paid for Master's signature - - -	0	4	6
Drawing and ingrossing petition to set down cause			
for hearing on further directions - -	0	6	8
Copy order on further directions, for the Master			
of the Rolls - - - - - -	0	3	0
The like of report - - - - -	0	5	0
Attending to set down cause - - -	0	6	8
March 15. Attending Court - - -	0	13	4
Easter Term, 1842.			

	£	s.	d.
Paid for registrar's minutes - - - -	0	1	0
April 26. Instructions for petition of appeal -	0	6	8
Draft same, and copy- - - - - -	0	15	0
29. Making copy judgment pronounced by the			
Master of the Rolls - - - - -	1	6	8
Michaelmas Term, 1842.			
Attending on Mr. Walker, the registrar, altering			
title of order on further directions, &c. - -	0	7	2
Attending at the Master's office with order so			
altered, &c. - - - - - - -	0	6	8
Paid for report, and transcribing - - -	1	13	0
Paid for Master's signature- - - - -	1	0	0
Attending examining transcript - - - -	0	6	8
Paid filing, and for office copy report - - -	1	0	4
Paid for order and copy - - - - -	0	3	6
Instructions for drawing and ingrossing petition to			
set down cause for hearing on further directions	0	6	8
Paid presenting same - - - - -	0	19	0
Copy order - - - - - - -	0	3	6
Copy report - - - - - - -	0	6	0
Paid for order and entry - - - - -	0	6	0
Easter Term, 1843.			
Paid for minutes - - - - - -	0	2	0
Paid for order - - - - - - -	3	10	0
Attending passing - - - - - -	0	6	8
Paid entering - - - - - - -	0	3	0
Copy mandatory part, for taxing Master - -	0	2	6
Term fee, letters, &c. - - - - - -	0	15	0"

[711]

The total amount of the bill allowed on taxation, was 638*l.* 8*s.* 3*d.*
It appeared that the principal part of the business had been done,
in the suit mentioned in the early part of the bill, before the Master
of the Rolls.

It was insisted, on the part of the defendants, that the bill was
not duly delivered in compliance with the statutes, inasmuch as it
contained no sufficient intimation, on the face of it, of the Court,
or the cause, in which the business, or the greater part thereof,
had been done : and, further, that the earlier items, to the amount
of 41*l.*, were barred by the Statute of Limitations.

The learned Judge overruled the objections, and directed a verdict

for the plaintiff for the amount of the bill, reserving leave to the defen-   MARTIN-
dants to move to enter a verdict on the fourth issue, if the Court   DALE
should be of opinion that a proper signed bill had not been delivered;   FALKNER.
or to reduce the verdict, by the amount of the items accruing more
than six years before the commencement of the action.

Sir T. Wilde, Serjt., in Michaelmas Term last, accordingly   [712]
obtained a rule *nisi*.
He cited *Lewis* v. *Primrose* (1).

(ERLE, J., observed as to the second point, that, with reference to
costs incurred in one suit, the Statute of Limitations does not begin
to run until the suit is determined.)

Channell, Serjt. (with whom was *G. Hayes*), now showed cause:
The statute 8 Jac. I. c. 7, s. 1, enacts that "all attorneys and
solicitors shall give a true bill unto their masters or clients, or their
assigns, for all charges concerning the suits which they have for
them, subscribed with their hands and names, before such time as
they or any of them shall charge their clients with any the same
fees or charges." This clearly does not render necessary the mention of any Court or cause. Neither does the 2 Geo. II. c. 23, s. 23 (2),
in express terms require the Court or the title of the cause to be
mentioned: it enacts that "no attorney or solicitor, &c. shall commence or maintain any action or suit for the recovery of any fees,
charges, or disbursements, at law or in equity, until the expiration
of one month or more after such attorney or solicitor respectively
shall have delivered unto the party or parties to be charged therewith, or left for him, her, or them, at his, her, or their dwelling-
house or last place of abode a bill of such fees, charges, and disbursements, written in a common legible hand, and in the English
tongue, except law terms and names of writs, and in words at length
except times and sums: which bill shall be subscribed with the
proper hand of such attorney or solicitor respectively. And upon
application of the party or parties chargeable by such bill, or of any
other person in that behalf authorized, unto the said Lord High
Chancellor, *or the Master of the Rolls, or unto any of the Courts   [*713]
aforesaid, or unto a Judge or Baron of any of the said Courts
respectively in which the business contained in such bill, or
the greatest part thereof in amount or value, shall have been

(1) 6 Q. B. 265; 13 L. J. Q. B. 269.   s. 1. See now s. 37 of that Act.—
(2) Repealed by 6 & 7 Vict. c. 73,   J. G. P.

MARTIN-
DALE
v.
FALKNER.

transacted," &c., it shall be lawful for the Chancellor, &c., to refer the said bill to be taxed, &c. It is a sufficient compliance with this provision, if there be some fair reference to the title of the cause and the Court. [He cited *Lester* v. *Lazarus* (1) and *Lane* v. *Glenny* (2).] In *Lewis* v. *Primrose*, which will probably be relied on for the defendant, neither in the heading nor in any other part of the bill, was any mention *made of any Court or cause, nor was there any thing from which it could be inferred that the bill was for business done in any particular Court. Here, however, there is enough on the face of the bill to intimate that the principal part of the business was done in a suit of *Falkner* v. *Matthews* in the Court of Chancery.

[*714]

(MAULE, J.: To enable the defendants to ascertain that, it is necessary to assume that they have a knowledge of the practice of the Court of Chancery. For anything that appears on the face of the bill, the business may have been done in bankruptcy or lunacy, or in the House of Lords.)

The retainer, which may be referred to in order to aid the defect in the bill, *Taylor* v. *Hodgson* (3), is headed in Chancery, and contains the names of the several suits in which the business was for the most part done.

(TINDAL, Ch. J.: The question is, whether that which the statute requires, can be made out by fair intendment from the bill itself.

MAULE, J.: The retainer cannot help you. All that was decided in *Taylor* v. *Hodgson*, was, that, under the 6 & 7 Vict. c. 73, the want of a signature to the bill is supplied by the signature to a letter inclosing the bill.)

[715]

* * *Harris* v. *Osbourn* (4) and *Nicholls* v. *Wilson* (5) are distinct authorities to show, that, where an action is brought by an attorney in respect of business done in a suit, partly within and partly beyond six years from the commencement of the action, the Statute of Limitations does not attach upon any part of the demand.

Dowling, Serjt. (with whom was *R. Miller*), in support of the rule:

Since the case of *Lewis* v. *Primrose*, it is essential to the due

(1) 2 Cr. M. & R. 665; Tyr. & Gr. 129.
(2) 7 Ad. & El. 83; 2 Nev. & P. 258.
(3) 14 L. J. Q. B. 310.
(4) 39 R. R. 872 (2 Cr. & M. 629; 4 Tyr. 445).
(5) 63 R. R. 523 (11 M. & W. 106).

delivery of an attorney's bill, that the name of the cause and the   MARTIN-
title of the Court in which the business has been done, should   DALE
                                                                      v.
distinctly appear.   *   *   With respect to the Statute of Limita-   FALKNER.
tions, it may be that the case is taken out of the statute where the   [716]
bill consists of business done in the progress of one continuous
suit. But there was no evidence to show that that was so here.

(MAULE, J.: It was taken for granted throughout the cause.
Nobody disputed it.)

TINDAL, Ch. J.:

The objection as to the Statute of Limitations being disposed of,
the only remaining question is that which arises upon the statute
2 Geo. II. c. 23, s. 23 (1), which, it is said, requires that an attorney's
bill should, upon the face of it, show the name of the cause and the
title of the Court in which the business was done. I agree entirely
with the decision of the Court of Queen's Bench in *Lewis* v. *Primrose*, that, although the statute does not in express terms require
the Court and cause to be mentioned, yet it follows from the general
scope and object of the clause that such information is necessary,
in order to enable the client to *ascertain to what Court or Judge   [*717]
he is to apply for the taxation of the bill. We must assume, from
the language of the Judges in deciding that case, that they could
not by fair intendment from the bill discern either the name of the
Court or the parties to the suit. Here, however, the name of the
suit is given—*Falkner* v. *Matthews*: and I think it does appear, by
fair and reasonable intendment, that the suit is in the Court of
Chancery. The first item, under date the 22nd of December, 1835,
is, "Attending on you, conferring and advising as to your suits in
Chancery." Two days after occurs the following, "Perusing decrees
and reports at Report Office." Again, on the 6th of March,
"Attending at the Six Clerks' Office," an office that is peculiar to
the Court of Chancery. Then, Hilary Term, 1836, begins with the
title of the cause, *Falkner* v. *Matthews*, which seems to be continued
throughout; and many of the subsequent items of charge plainly
and unequivocally point to proceedings that could take place only
in a suit in Chancery, such as "Paid for minutes of decree,"
"Attending registrar, to settle minutes," "Copy minutes as wished
to be settled, for the Lord Chancellor," "Attending Court, cause in
the paper." Then follow charges for passing and entering a decree,

(1) Repealed by 6 & 7 Vict. c. 73, s. 1. See now s. 37 of that Act.—J. G. P.

"instructions for interrogatories," and many others of the like tendency. The bill contains no charge having reference to any proceeding in a court of common law. Upon the whole, the only inference I can draw from the bill itself is, that it was a bill for charges incurred in a suit carried on under the name of *Falkner* v. *Matthews*, and in the Court of Chancery.

MAULE, J.:

This is an action upon an attorney's bill; and the question arises upon a plea denying the delivery of a proper signed bill under the statute 2 Geo. II. c. 23, s. 23. At the trial I was of opinion that

[*718]

there *had been a sufficient compliance with the statute in this respect, and, accordingly, directed a verdict for the plaintiff for the amount of the bill; reserving leave to the defendants to move to enter a verdict for them on that issue, if the Court should be of opinion that I had come to a wrong conclusion. The LORD CHIEF JUSTICE has expressed an opinion that the view I took at the trial was correct; and I have reason to believe that my brothers CRESSWELL and ERLE agree with him in that opinion. I have the misfortune, however, to differ from them. I think I was wrong, and that I ought to have directed the jury to find for the defendants; and I form this opinion upon the best interpretation I am able to put upon the statute, as construed and explained by the authorities. The point certainly is not one that tends very much to the justice of the case. But I think it much more important that a statute should receive its proper construction, than that justice should be doled out to suit the circumstances of each particular case. The statute requires the attorney to deliver to his client a bill of his fees, charges, and disbursements, written in a common legible hand, and in the English tongue, except law terms and names of writs, and in words at length, except times and sums —a provision evidently calculated and intended to secure due information being given to simple people, to enable them at once to see, by a plain and intelligible statement, with what they are charged; and one that would have been unnecessary if the bill had been a document addressed to persons skilled in law and the practice of the Courts. The object of this provision appears, from the subsequent part of the clause, to be, to enable the client to apply to the Court, or to a Judge of the Court, in which the business, or the greatest part thereof, has been transacted, to have the bill taxed. The intent of the statute clearly was, to enable the

client conveniently to get the bill *taxed, and, for that purpose, to
inform him where he is to apply to obtain such taxation ; and that
object would not be conveniently effected, unless the bill showed
distinctly where the business had been done.   The case of *Lewis* v.
Primrose is, I think, substantially, in point.   In that case certainly
the name of the cause was not mentioned.   But the omission of
the name of the cause is a very slight inconvenience compared with
the omission of the Court.   We cannot, without distinctly overruling that decision, say that it is not essential that the name of
the Court should appear with reasonable distinctness.   Upon that
point there is no difference of opinion amongst us.   But the question is, what degree of certainty of information does the statute
require ?   And, connected with that inquiry, is another, what
degree of knowledge is the client bound to have ?   The LORD CHIEF
JUSTICE and my learned brothers think it does sufficiently appear
upon the face of this bill that the whole, or the greater part, of the
business contained in it, was done in the Court of Chancery, and
therefore that that Court only has jurisdiction to refer it to taxation.   This opinion is founded upon various items in the bill,
which, it is said, can alone have reference to proceedings in a suit
in Chancery.   That presupposes the client to possess a considerable knowledge of the law.   There is no presumption in this
country that every person knows the law : it would be contrary to
common sense and reason if it were so.   In *Jones* v. *Randall* (1),
Dunning, arguendo, says: "The laws of this country are clear,
evident, and certain : all the Judges know the laws, and, knowing
them, administer justice with uprightness and integrity."   But
Lord MANSFIELD, in delivering the judgment of the COURT, says :
"As to the certainty of the law mentioned by *Mr. Dunning,* it would
be very hard upon *the profession if the law was so certain that
every body knew it : the misfortune is, that it is so uncertain that
it costs much money to know what it is, even in the last resort."
It was a necessary ground of the decision in that case, that a party
may be ignorant of the law.   The rule is, that ignorance of the
law shall not excuse a man, or relieve him from the consequences
of a crime, or from liability upon a contract.   There are many
cases where the giving up a doubtful point of law has been held to
be a good consideration for a promise to pay money (2).   Numerous
other instances might be cited to show that there may be such
thing as a doubtful point of law.   If there were not, there would be

MARTIN-
DALE
v.
FALKNER.
[*719]

[*720]

_____

(1) Cowp. 37.   (2) *Vide Wade* v. *Simeon, ante,* 523.

no need of courts of appeal, the existence of which shows that
Judges may be ignorant of law. That being so, it would be too
much to hold that ordinary people are bound to know in what
particular Court such and such a practice does or does not prevail.
The question is, whether this bill conveys information enough to a
person as ignorant of the law as he may with propriety be. I
think the client is not to be presumed to know that the business
has been done in Chancery, because of the mention of warrants,
interrogatories, decrees, and the like. The first item of the bill
speaks of a conference and advice as to suits in Chancery. There
is, however, no heading, or any thing else, to show that this refers
to any business in Court. Afterwards there comes a charge for
"perusing decrees and reports at the Report Office," which, it is
said, the client must know could only be in Chancery. I do not
agree that the client is to be presumed to know any thing of the
kind. At the time to which these items relate—December, 1835—
the Court of Exchequer was a court in which decrees and reports
were familiar. Then, on the 16th of March, 1836, is a charge for
[*721]   "attending at the *Six Clerks' Office, searching for a record." This,
it is said, must be in the Court of Chancery. I really am unable
at the present moment to say whether there is or is not such an
office now existing as the Six Clerks' Office; and I do not see why
Miss Mary Falkner is bound to know it. That decrees may be,
and are, pronounced in other Courts besides the Court of Chancery,
we all know. In Doctors' Commons, for instance. Innumerable
items in this bill might be referred to whence it would be impossible
even for a person moderately skilled in law, to discover, with any
reasonable certainty, that it was a bill for business done in the
Court of Chancery. To my mind, it does not appear with sufficient
certainty that this business was done in a court having jurisdiction
to refer it for taxation; and, unless that does sufficiently appear,
the bill has not been properly delivered. On the 8th of February,
1836, I perceive a charge for "attending registrar to settle
minutes." That, however, by no means conclusively shows that
the business was in the Court of Chancery. It is true there is a
registrar in that Court; but there is also a registrar in Doctors'
Commons, and in the Court of Admiralty (1). The item under the
same date, "copy minutes, as wished to be settled, for the Lord
Chancellor," might have reference to an intended application for

(1) The defendants may have never heard of any other registrar than the
registrar of births, deaths, and marriages.

an injunction. "Instructions for interrogatories," might relate   MARTIN-
to proceedings in this, or any other common law, Court. The   DALE
                                                                 v.
items in which the Master of the Rolls is introduced, do not conclu-   FALKNER.
sively show that there were any proceedings in the Rolls Court (1);
still less, that the greater part of the proceedings took place there.
I *think I have done enough to show the grounds upon which my   [*722]
opinion of the insufficiency of this bill rests. I cannot, however,
regret the conclusion at which the rest of the Court have arrived,
seeing that justice will be more promptly attained than if I had
decided according to my present view at the trial.

CRESSWELL, J. :

    I am of opinion that the direction of my brother MAULE was
correct, and that the fourth plea afforded no answer to the action.
I quite agree with the remark of Lord TENTERDEN in *Frowd* v.
Stillard (2), that "the object of the Legislature is, that a client
shall have his bill delivered to him in such language as he can
understand." And I am not disposed to interfere with the decision
of the Court of Queen's Bench in *Lewis* v. *Primrose.* Lord DENMAN
says : "The object of giving the information is, to enable the client
to take steps to ascertain if the bill is a fair one." It appears to
me that there is enough on the face of this bill, to inform the client
of the Court and the name of the cause in which the business, or
the greatest part of it, was done. The earlier items, it is true, are
not for business done in any cause. But, in Hilary Term, 1886,
the name of a cause is introduced; and, construing it according to
ordinary intelligence and common sense, it would seem to me that
all the subsequent proceedings must be taken to have been in the
same suit. Several particulars have been pointed out by the LORD
CHIEF JUSTICE, which tend to show to any person who is competent
to read and to understand the natural meaning of words, that the
business was done in Chancery. By taking isolated instances, no
doubt, an ambiguity may be raised : but, looking at the whole
together, it seems to me to be intelligible enough. In Trinity Term,
1840, *there are charges for "attending Court on exceptions,"   [*723]
immediately following charges for "instructions for exceptions,"
and "copy exceptions, for Master of Rolls ; " and in the following
Term is an item, "Attending Mr. Bull, explaining to him the

---

(1) Proceedings before the Master   of *quare impedit,* pending in this
of the Rolls might relate to the amend-   Court.
ment of a writ of dower, or of a writ   (2) 4 Car. & P. 51.

MARTIN-
DALE
v.
FALKNER.

situation the parties were placed in by the decision of the Master of the Rolls." Any person reading that must conclude that these were charges for business done in the Rolls Court. Upon the whole, therefore, I think the information required by the statute is given with sufficient particularity, and therefore that the rule for entering a verdict for the defendants should be discharged.

ERLE, J.:

I also am of opinion that this rule should be discharged. The statute requires that a signed bill be delivered; and the Courts, looking at the intention of the Legislature, have superadded a requisition that it shall be shown, on the face of the bill, in what Court the business is done, as well as the name of the cause. Here, the bill is not headed in any Court; and there is no mention of the name of a cause until the third page. It seems to be agreed, that, if enough appears to convey to a person of ordinary understanding in what Court the business has been done, and in what cause, the requisitions of the statute have been complied with. I agree with the LORD CHIEF JUSTICE and my brother CRESSWELL that this bill does in these respects convey a reasonably sufficient amount of information. There is the title of a cause; and the subsequent items disclose the history of the proceedings, through the Masters' office, and the Rolls Court, down to the obtaining a judgment in the suit. I think the plaintiff has done all the law requires of him.

Rule discharged.

IN THE COURT OF EXCHEQUER CHAMBER.

1846.
Feb. 4.

IRVING *v.* MANNING AND ANOTHER (IN ERROR).

(2 C. B. 784—788.)

[RESERVED for 1 H. L. C. 287.]

IN THE COURT OF COMMON PLEAS.

1846.
April 21

[808]

SOUCH *v.* STRAWBRIDGE (1).

(2 C. B. 808—816; S. C. 15 L. J. C. P. 170; 10 Jur. 357.)

A contract for the maintenance of a child at the defendant's request, to enure "so long as the defendant shall think proper," is a contract upon a contingency, the performance of which is not necessarily to take place beyond the space of a year, and therefore not within the 4th section of the Statute of Frauds.

Semble, per TINDAL, Ch. J., that the statute does not apply where the action is brought upon an executed consideration.

ASSUMPSIT for board, lodgings, &c., supplied by the plaintiff to a child at the request of the defendant. Plea, *non assumpsit.*

The cause was tried before Erle, J., at the last Summer Assizes at Bristol. It appeared that the child, of which it was suggested that the defendant was the father, was placed by him under the care of the plaintiff shortly after its birth, in 1842, and that the defendant agreed to pay for its maintenance 5*s.* per week, or one guinea per month. At first it was proposed that the plaintiff should keep the child for one year ; but the defendant objected to that, on the ground that 5*s.* per week was too much for so young a child ; and ultimately it was settled that the child should remain with the plaintiff "until Strawbridge gave notice," or, in the language of another witness, "as long as Strawbridge should think proper." The child remained with the plaintiff until February, 1845. The defendant paid for one month himself, and afterwards gave or sent the money to the child's mother, that she might pay it. The action was brought to recover a balance of 15*l.*

On the part of the defendant, it was objected that the contract, not being in writing, nor to be performed within the space of one year from the making thereof, was void by the Statute of Frauds. The learned Judge nonsuited the plaintiff, reserving to him leave to move to enter a verdict for 15*l.*, if the Court should be of opinion that the contract was not within the statute.

---

(1) This case has been frequently cited with approval : see *Knowlman* v. *Bluett* (1873) L. R. 9 Ex. 1, 43 L. J. Ex. 29 ; *McGregor* v. *McGregor* (1888) 21 Q. B. Div. 424, 57 L. J. Q. B. 591. As to whether the statute applies when the action is brought on an executed consideration, see *Sanderson* v. *Graves* (1875) L. R. 10 Ex. 234, 238, 44 L. J. Ex. 210 ; *Pulbrook* v. *Lawes* (1876) 1 Q. B. D. 284, 45 L. J. Q. B. 178 ; *McGregor* v. *McGregor* (1888) 20 Q. B. D. 529, 57 L. J. Q. B. 268, and *Knowlman* v. *Bluett* (1874) L. R. 9 Ex. 307, 43 L. J. Ex. 151. See also *Giraud* v. *Richmond, post,* p. 620.—J. G. P.

SOUCH
v.
STRAW-
BRIDGE.

[809]

Sir T. Wilde, Serjt., in Michaelmas Term last, obtained a rule *nisi* accordingly.

Manning, Serjt., now showed cause:

The fourth section of the statute 29 Car. II. c. 3, enacts that no action shall be brought whereby to charge the defendant "upon any agreement that is not to be performed within the space of one year from the making thereof, unless the agreement upon which such action shall be brought, or some memorandum or note thereof, shall be in writing, and signed by the party to be charged therewith, or some other person thereunto by him lawfully authorized." And the cases have decided that the statute requires a complete performance within the year.

(TINDAL, Ch. J.: The child might have died within a year.)

So might an apprentice.

(MAULE, J.: An agreement to leave money by will need not be in writing, though uncertain as to the time of performance: *Fenton* v. *Emblers* (1).)

The parties clearly contemplated that this contract should not be completed within a year: [*Snelling* v. *Lord Huntingfield* (2), *Burch* v. *The Earl of Liverpool* (3), *Peter* v. *Compton* (4), *Boydell* v. *Drummond* (5).]

[810]

(CRESSWELL, J.: For how long a period beyond a year did the plaintiff contract to keep this child, and the defendant to pay for its maintenance?)

For no specific period.

(CRESSWELL, J.: How, then, can it be said to be a contract that is not to be performed within one year?)

In *Boydell* v. *Drummond*, no specific time beyond the year was agreed upon for the performance of the contract.

[*811]

(CRESSWELL, J.: The work was *to be supplied annually.)

* * In *Wells* v. *Horton* (6), it was held, that, where an agreement is to be performed on a contingency which may happen within the

---

(1) 3 Burr. 1278; 1 W. Bl. 353.   (4) Skinner, 353.
(2) 1 Cr. M. & R. 20; 4 Tyr. 606.   (5) 10 R. R. 450 (11 East, 142).
(3) 9 B. & C. 398; 4 Man. & Ry. 380.   (6) 4 Bing. 40; 12 J. B. Moore, 176.

year after it is made, and it does not appear on the face of the   SOUCH
agreement that it is to be performed after the year, it does not   *.
fall within the statute.   STRAW-
                                                                           BRIDGE.

(TINDAL, Ch. J.: That comes very near to this case.)

There was nothing in that case to show that the parties contemplated a performance of the contract after the year. In the present
case, however, the probability of the child being supported beyond
the year, was clearly in the minds of the parties at the time of
making the agreement.

(TINDAL, Ch. J.: You must bear in mind that this action is
brought upon an executed contract.)

The defendant is charged upon an express contract. If that be
rejected, what remains ? The action is then an action against a
stranger in respect of the maintenance of the child of a married
woman, not living separate from her husband, of which he is the
supposed father.

(CRESSWELL, J.: The child being supported by the plaintiff at
the defendant's request.)

There was no request, apart from the express contract, proved.

(TINDAL, Ch. J.: If a man enters into a contract to serve another
for two years, no action will lie for a non-performance of that
contract, unless it be *reduced into writing. But, if the service has   [*812]
been performed under it, an action for work and labour will lie.)

The acceptance of the service is an acknowledgment of the contract
binding the master. Here, there was no acquiescence in the service
performed either during its continuance or after its close, no
evidence whatever to affect the defendant, beyond the express
contract entered into at the time the child was first placed under
the plaintiff's care.

Sir T. *Wilde*, Serjt., in support of the rule :

The defendant, being under a moral obligation to support his
illegitimate child, engaged the plaintiff to take charge of it at a
certain price, upon an understanding that it was to continue under
the plaintiff's care as long as the defendant should think proper.
Something was said about continuing beyond a year ; but there

was nothing binding; either party might have given up the
engagement at the end of a month. Suppose the contract had
been for the keep of a horse for so long time as the defendant
might choose to keep it at the plaintiff's stables, would that have
been within the statute? The contract having been performed by
the plaintiff at the continued request of the defendant, the case is
wholly beside the authorities that have been cited. To bring the
case within the statute, it must appear that the contract is not to
be performed within the year, as in *Boydell* v. *Drummond*. [He
referred to *Wells* v. *Horton* (1) and *Burch* v. *The Earl of Liverpool* (2).]

[813]
Here, inasmuch as there was nothing to show that the contract
was not to be performed within a year, and as the defendant had
the option of determining it at any time, the case is not within the
statute. Besides, as the consideration is executed, and the defendant
has had the benefit of, and has acquiesced in the performance of the
contract on the plaintiff's part, he is liable in this form of action.

TINDAL, Ch. J. :

I am of opinion that the rule for entering a verdict for the
plaintiff in this case, must be made absolute. In the first place,
it appears to me that this is not an action which is within the pro-
[*814]
hibition of the *statute. It is brought for a by-gone or executed
consideration, viz. the support and maintenance of a child at the
request of the defendant. There was evidence enough to show
that the child was placed under the care of the plaintiff at the
charge of the defendant, with his assent, and that he had made
payments on account of its maintenance. That is equivalent to
the proof that is ordinarily given in an action for goods sold and
delivered, whence the law implies a promise on the defendant's
part to pay for them. The fourth section of the Statute of Frauds
enacts, that no action shall be brought whereby to charge the
defendant "upon any agreement that is not to be performed within
the space of one year from the making thereof, unless the agreement upon which such action shall be brought, or some memorandum or note thereof, shall be in writing, and signed by the
party to be charged therewith, or some other person thereunto
by him lawfully authorized." The meaning of that is, that no
action shall be brought to recover damages in respect of the non-
performance of such contracts as are therein referred to. The
statute was directed to a totally different object than the prevention

(1) 4 Bing. 40; 12 J. B. Moore 176.   (2) 33 R. R. 212 (4 Man. & Ry. 382).

of an action like the present: its design was, to prevent the setting
up, by means of fraud and perjury, of contracts or promises by
parol, upon which parties might otherwise have been charged for
their whole lives; and for that purpose it requires that certain
contracts shall be evidenced only by the solemnity of writing. It
has no application to an action in the present form, founded upon
an executed consideration. But, assuming that the fourth section
of the Statute of Frauds does apply to actions upon considerations
that are executed, it seems to me that the contract in the present
case is not within its terms. It speaks of " any agreement that
is not to be performed within the space of one year from the
making thereof; " *pointing to contracts the complete performance
of which is of necessity extended beyond the space of a year. That
appears clearly from the case of *Boydell* v. *Drummond*, the rule
to be extracted from which is, that, where the agreement distinctly
shows, upon the face of it, that the parties contemplated its performance to extend over a greater space of time than one year, the
case is within the statute; but that, where the contract is such
that the whole may be performed within a year, and there is no
express stipulation to the contrary, the statute does not apply.
Looking at the terms of the agreement here, I see nothing to show
that its performance was necessarily to extend beyond a year. A
contract to serve another for two years, would be within the
statute; but a contract to serve for an indefinite period, subject to
be put an end to at any time upon a reasonable notice, is not
within the statute, though it may extend beyond the year. Here,
there was no certain time stipulated for the duration of the contract. It seems to me, therefore, that, supposing the Statute of
Frauds to apply to executed contracts, the evidence excludes the
present case from its operation.

COLTMAN, J.:

I also think this case is not within the fourth section of the
Statute of Frauds. The contract was, that the child should be
maintained by the plaintiff at a charge of one guinea per month,
subject to be put an end to at any time at the option of the
defendant. That brings the case exactly within *Peter* v. *Compton*.
There, the defendant contracted, in consideration of one guinea,
to give the plaintiff a certain sum of money at his day of marriage:
the marriage did not happen until more than a year had expired;
but the Court was of opinion, that, as the contract was subject to

SOUCH
v.
STRAW-
BRIDGE.
[*816]

a contingency that might happen within a year, and there was no express agreement extending the performance beyond *the year, a note in writing was not necessary. So, here, there was an express contingency that might defeat the contract within a year, namely, the determination of the defendant's will. If it had been necessary to decide this case upon the other point, I should have wished to consider it; because, I feel some difficulty in saying that the plaintiff may rely on an executed consideration, where he is obliged to resort to the executory contract in order to make out his case. The case not being within the statute, however, we need not embarrass ourselves with the discussion of that point.

CRESSWELL, J. :

I also am of opinion that this rule should be made absolute. Upon the evidence reported to us, it is quite clear that this was not a contract within the fourth section of the Statute of Frauds, inasmuch as there was no stipulation or understanding that it was not to be performed within a year. In reality it was a contract at so much per month, determinable at any time at the defendant's pleasure.

ERLE, J. :

I also am of opinion that the rule should be absolute to enter a verdict for the plaintiff for 15*l.* The treaty certainly did contemplate the endurance of the contract for the child's maintenance beyond a year: but the ultimate contract was that the plaintiff should receive a guinea per month, and that the period should be, so long as the defendant should think proper. According to the case of *Peter* v. *Compton*, that is a contingency that prevents the application of the statute. Upon reconsideration, therefore, I am of opinion that I ought to have directed the jury to find for the plaintiff.

——————   *Rule absolute.*

1846.
April 23.
——
[835]

GIRAUD *v.* RICHMOND.

(2 C. B. 835—842 ; S. C. 15 L. J. C. P. 180 ; 10 Jur. 360.)

A. enters the service of B. under a written agreement, as follows : " I agree to receive you as clerk in my establishment, in consideration of your paying me a premium of 300*l.*, and to pay you a salary at the following rates, viz. for the first year, 70*l.* ; for the second, 90*l.*; for the third, 110*l.* ; for the fourth, 130*l.* ; and 150*l.* for the fifth and following years that you may remain in my employment : "

Held, that the agreement was one that by the Statute of Frauds was required to be in writing ; that, there being a precise stipulation for yearly payments, evidence was not admissible to show that at or after the time the letter containing it was sent by B. to A., it was verbally agreed that the salary should be paid quarterly; and that the fact of the payments having usually been made quarterly, did not vary the rights of the parties under the agreement.

ASSUMPSIT for wages and salary due to the plaintiff as clerk to the defendant. Plea, *non assumpsit*. At the trial before Coltman, J., at the sittings in Middlesex after Michaelmas Term last, it appeared that the plaintiff entered into the service of the defendant as clerk or book-keeper, under a memorandum of agreement bearing date the 2nd of May, 1842, signed by the defendant, and addressed to the plaintiff, of which the following is a copy:

"I agree to receive you as clerk or book-keeper in my establishment, in consideration of your paying me a premium of 300*l.*, and to pay you a salary at the following rates, viz. for the first year, 70*l.*; for the second, 90*l.*; for the third, 110*l.*; for the fourth, 130*l.*; and 150*l.* for the fifth and following years that you may remain in my employment; and I also agree, in case of the death of either of us, to return 150*l.*"

The action was brought to recover half a year's salary at the rate of 130*l.* per annum.

On the part of the plaintiff, it was proposed, upon the authority of *Ridgway* v. *The Hungerford Market Company* (1), to call a witness to prove, that, at or about the time the agreement was entered into, it was verbally *arranged between the plaintiff and defendant that the salary should be paid quarterly, and that, in consequence, the payments had in fact usually been quarterly payments.

[*836]

On the part of the defendant, it was insisted, that, under this agreement, the salary was payable yearly, and not otherwise, and consequently that this action was not maintainable.

The learned Judge thereupon nonsuited the plaintiff, reserving to him leave to move to enter a verdict for 46*l.*, the amount of half a year's salary, after allowing for certain payments made by the defendant on the plaintiff's account, if the Court should be of opinion that parol evidence, or the acts of the defendant, were admissible to explain the written contract.

Talfourd, Serjt., in Hilary Term last, obtained a rule *nisi* accordingly. He cited *Thomas* v. *Williams* (2), and *Ridgway* v. *The Hungerford Market Company*.

(1) 42 R. R. 352 (3 Ad. & El. 171; 4 Nev. & M. 797).

(2) 1 Ad. & El. 685; 3 Nev. & M. 545.

GIRAUD
v.
RICHMOND.

Byles, Serjt., now showed cause:

Parol evidence of what took place before, or at the time, or after the execution of the written contract, was altogether inadmissible for the purpose of varying its express terms. Where the agreement is, to pay so much a year, whether it be for rent or for services, nothing becomes due until the end of the year. In Bacon's Abridgment, Rent (F), it is said : "A lease reserving rent *pro quolibet anno,* is all one as if it had been made payable annually, and then it is paid at the end of every year (1). A rent, generally reserved, is payable at the end of the year (2) ; but, if rent be reserved *annuatim durante termino prædicto,* the first payment to

[*837]

begin two years *after, this controls the words of reservation (3). So, if a rent is made payable yearly during the time the lessee shall enjoy the land, the lessor cannot demand this rent half-yearly, but must wait to the end of the year" (4). So, in *Spain* v. *Arnott* (5), Lord ELLENBOROUGH says : "If the contract be for a year's service, the year must be completed, before the servant is entitled to be paid." [He cited *Turner* v. *Robinson* (6), *Snelling* v. *Lord Huntingfield* (7), and *Souch* v. *Strawbridge* (8).] Parol evidence clearly was not admissible to control or vary the terms of the written contract: *Goss* v. *Lord Nugent* (9) ; *Marshall* v. *Lynn* (10).

[838]
[839]

* * And the same rule obtains whether the contract is under seal or not: *Clifton* v. *Walmesley* (11). * * This question did not distinctly present itself for decision in *Ridgway* v. *The Hungerford Market Company :* the rule for a nonsuit was made absolute, on the ground that the plaintiff was properly dismissed from the service of the Company.

Talfourd, Serjt. (with whom was *G. Atkinson*), in support of the rule :

There is nothing in the language of the contract that necessarily leads to the inference that the plaintiff was to receive the stipulated salary only once a year.

(CRESSWELL, J.: Taking the agreement *per se,* when had the

(1) Citing 1 Lutw. 231.
(2) Citing Latch, 264.
(3) Citing 3 Bulstr. 329.
(4) Citing Litt. Rep. 61 ; Hetley, 53.
(5) 19 R. R. 715 (2 Stark. 256).
(6) 39 R. R. 650 (5 B. & Ad. 789 ;
2 Nev. & M. 829).

(7) 40 R. R. 484 (1 Cr. M. & R. 20;
4 Tyr. 606).
(8) *Ante,* p. 615.
(9) 39 R. R. 392 (5 B. & Ad. 58; 2
Nev. & M. 28).
(10) 6 M. & W. 109.
(11) 5 T. R. 564.

plaintiff a right to demand salary?   Could he claim to be paid at the end of each day or week?)

The argument certainly must go that length; otherwise, nothing would become due until the end of the five years.   If the times of payment be left uncertain, it is clearly competent to the parties to make a collateral agreement by parol to ascertain them.

(COLTMAN, J.: Then the difficulty arising from the Statute of Frauds presents itself: there is a material part of the contract that is not evidenced by writing.)

The case of *Ridgway* v. *The Hungerford Market Company* is strictly analogous.   * *   It is true there was no absolute decision upon [840] the point in this case; but the inclination of the Court was very distinctly expressed.   Here, the parol evidence was not offered for the purpose of adding to, or varying, the terms of the written contract.   The cases as to rent can have no application to a contract for personal services.

(CRESSWELL, J.: If the time of payment be a material part of the contract, then, inasmuch as the contract was one that was required by the Statute of Frauds to be in writing, and the whole agreement is not in writing, the plaintiff cannot sue upon it.)

If there is no binding contract, the plaintiff is entitled to recover upon a *quantum meruit*.

TINDAL, Ch. J.:

This appears to me to be a contract within the Statute of Frauds: it was not to be performed within a year.   The services were rendered by the plaintiff under this contract, and no other.   Looking at its terms, it appears to me that the salary thereby agreed to be paid, was payable at the end of every year, and not otherwise. This agreement must receive the same construction as would be put upon a lease reserving rent payable yearly.   The question, therefore, is, whether we can supply an alleged defect in the contract by parol evidence of a contemporaneous or subsequent agreement for the payment of the salary quarterly.   I think that would be a direct violation of the statute.   The plaintiff then desires it to be inferred from the subsequent acts of the parties, that the agreement was for quarterly payments.   *Goss* v. *Lord Nugent* is a distinct authority [*841]

GIRAUD   to show that a written contract cannot be so varied. *Ridgway* v.
v.   *The Hungerford Market Company* was decided upon a totally different
RICHMOND.   ground.

COLTMAN, J.:

It is clear that parol evidence was not admissible in this case to
vary the terms of the written contract: and the subsequent acts of
the parties stand upon the same footing. An agreement of this
nature must be wholly in writing.

CRESSWELL, J.:

I am of the same opinion. This is a case in which the Statute
of Frauds requires the contract to be in writing: and I think all
the material parts of this contract were in writing: it contained
quite enough to show what the parties respectively bound themselves
to do. The defendant engaged to pay the plaintiff the stipulated
amount of salary at the end of each year, and not at any intervening
periods. And I am clearly of opinion that no parol evidence was
admissible to vary the contract.

ERLE, J.:

I am of the same opinion, on the ground that the contract was
one which, by the Statute of Frauds, is required to be in writing.
The defendant was bound to keep the plaintiff in his service for the
space of five years at the least. If parol evidence was not admissible to explain, or vary, the terms of the written contract, the
salary clearly was payable yearly. The plaintiff, however, insisted
that he was at liberty to show a collateral parol agreement for
quarterly payments; or, at all events, that he might rely upon the
fact of the salary having always been paid quarterly. The terms of
the agreement being free from ambiguity, I think it was not competent to the plaintiff to give such evidence. The distinction
[*842]   between the present case and *Ridgway* *v. *The Hungerford Market
Company appears to me to be this: the contract there was not
necessarily one, the complete performance of which would extend
beyond one year; and therefore it might perhaps be varied by
subsequent acts or conversations.

                                        Rule discharged.

WALKER *v.* REMMETT.

(2 C. B. 850—860; S. C. 15 L. J. C. P. 174.)

A written authority in the following terms, "I authorize you to indorse my name to three several bills of exchange now in your possession" (describing them), was held to be a letter or power of attorney, requiring a 30*s.* stamp under 55 Geo. III. c. 184 (1).

So, although it goes on to say "and which indorsement I undertake shall be binding upon me; and I undertake to pay you the amount of the several bills as they respectively become due, should they not be duly honoured when mature."

ASSUMPSIT on a bill of exchange, by indorsee against acceptor. The declaration stated, that one Newman drew the bill upon the defendant, who accepted the same, and that Newman indorsed to one Harrison, Harrison to one Herbert, and Herbert to the plaintiff.

Plea, amongst others, that Harrison did not indorse the bill *modo et formâ ;* whereupon issue was joined.

At the trial, before Coltman, J., at the sittings in Middlesex after last Michaelmas Term, it appeared that the bill had been indorsed by Herbert, in the name of Harrison, under the following authority signed by Harrison, and which at the time it was offered in evidence was stamped with a 2*s.* 6*d.* agreement stamp:

"I do hereby authorize you to indorse, or cause to be indorsed, my name to three several bills of exchange now in your possession —Mr. Patten's account, 35*l.* 16*s.* 9*d.*, Mr. Edwards's do. 180*l.*, and Mr. Remmett's do. 250*l.*—and which indorsements I do hereby undertake shall be binding upon me; and I do further undertake to pay you the amount of the several bills as they respectively become due, should they not be duly honoured when mature."

On the part of the defendant, it was objected that this was a "letter, or power, of attorney," within the general Stamp Act, 55 Geo. III. c. 184, sched. part I.(1), or a "deed or other instrument of procuration," and liable, in either case, to a duty of 1*l.* 10*s.*

The learned Judge took a note of the objection, and received the document. The jury having returned a verdict for the plaintiff,

Dowling, Serjt., in Hilary Term, obtained a rule *nisi* for a new trial, on the ground that this evidence was improperly received. * * *

[851]

(1) See now the Stamp Act, 1891 (54 & 55 Vict. c. 39, sched.): "Letter or Power of Attorney . . . of any kind whatsoever not hereinbefore described."—J. G. P.

Byles, Serjt. (with whom was *F. V. Lee*), now showed cause:
* * If this letter requires either a power of attorney or a procuration stamp, every letter authorizing one man to act in any way for another, will be liable to be stamped with a 30s. stamp. This is, in truth, a mere agreement; the authority to indorse the bills being only ancillary to it.

(TINDAL, Ch. J.: The plaintiff is using it for the power contained in it, and not for the other purpose.)

If the Legislature had intended the charge to be so general, they would have added, " or written authority of any other kind," or words to that effect. Neither is this a " deed, or other instrument, of procuration," within the *Act. " Procuration " is a term well known to the Scottish law. See Bell's Commercial Index, vol. ii. title " Procuration;" Bell's Principles of the Law of Scotland, pp. 479—483; but it is unknown to the law of England, unless in the Ecclesiastical Court.

[*854]

(TINDAL, Ch. J.: The term " procuration " can hardly have been intended to be confined to Scotch law; for, that makes no distinction between deeds and other instruments in writing.

CRESSWELL, J.: Procuration is a well known term: we often hear of procuration (1) money.)

Dowling, Serjt. (with whom was *Temple*), in support of the rule. * * *

TINDAL, Ch. J.:

It appears to me that the instrument offered in evidence in this case falls within the words of the 55 Geo. III. c. 184, sched. part I., " Letter or power *of attorney of any other kind," which follow the mention of letters or powers of attorney of specific kinds; for, I cannot consider it in any other light than a delegation of authority or power in writing, to perform an act. The definition of an attorney given in Com. Dig., Attorney (A), is as follows: " An attorney is he who is appointed to do any thing in the place of another: and he has a general authority, or a special one for some particular purpose; as, to make livery, to deliver a deed," &c. So, in Co. Litt. 51 b, it is said that "attorney is an ancient English

[*855]

(1) There " procuration " seems to be used in the sense of " obtaining " not in the sense of " acting vicariously for another." The term is used in the latter sense, where instruments are said to be executed " by procuration."

word, and signifieth one that is set in the turn(1), stead, or place of WALKER
v.
BEMMETT.
another." And he may be appointed either by deed or by letter(2).
Here, the appointment is by letter (3). It has been contended that
this may be considered as an agreement only, because it contains an
undertaking to pay the amount of the several bills indorsed under
the authority or power, should they not be duly honoured. To that
it has very properly been answered, that the letter contains no
agreement to do anything more than the law would imply from the
indorsement itself. Again, Harrison's undertaking that the indorsements shall be binding upon him, imports no greater obligation
than the law would have imposed upon him without it. Another
answer to the argument, that this is an agreement only, is, that no
consideration is expressed in it: all is *to be done on one side(4).   [*856]
It seems to me that this letter falls within the description of instruments already adverted to, and that a 30s. stamp was necessary.

COLTMAN, J.:

I am of the same opinion. This case is governed by the decision
of the Court of Queen's Bench in *Reg.* v. *Kelk.* It is true,
that the Court there rely on the fact of the attorneys having a
discretion as to the parties they would vote for. I do not, however,
accede to the doctrine, that, in order to a valid appointment of an
attorney, he should have a discretion vested in him. The examples
given by Chief Baron Comyns, of an appointment of an attorney to
make livery, or to deliver a deed, show that it is not of the essence
of such an appointment that the attorney should have a discretion.
Where one is authorized in writing, on behalf of another, and in
his name, to do an act, that is an appointment of an attorney
within the meaning of the Stamp Act.

(1) "A tourner" is "to substitute,"
and an attorney is a person substituted,
"atourné," for his principal. The
appropriate form of appointing an
attorney in a suit is therefore "A. B.
ponit loco suo C. D. (or C. D. attornatum
suum) ad lucrandum ad perdendum.
So, the operation by which one lord is
substituted for another, is properly
"an attornment," though the term
has been latterly confined to the concluding act by which the substitution
is ratified and made complete, that by
which the vassal or tenant expresses
his assent to such substitution.

(2) Co. Litt. 52 a, b, *i.e.* a letter

under seal, a deed, as explained by
Coke himself.

(3) But the word "letter" is used
in one sense here (as *epistola*), and in
another by Lord Coke (as *literæ
sigillatæ*). *Vide post*, 628, *n.* (1).

(4) The contract would be unilateral,
the consideration, contingent. It is
not unusual to guarantee the repayment of advances which the banker
does not engage to make, or the price
of goods which the dealer does not
undertake to sell. Here, the contract
seems to be, to be responsible for the
bills, in case Harrison should raise a
consideration by indorsing them.

WALKER
v.
REMMETT.

CRESSWELL, J.:

I am of the same opinion. I quite agree with my brother *Byles* as to the principles on which the Stamp Acts are to be construed; and if I could have brought myself to think that it was fairly a matter of doubt, whether the instrument in question was within the words and meaning of the 55 Geo. III. c. 184, or not, I should have held that it was properly received in evidence without a stamp. But I entertain no doubt. It certainly is no part of the definition of an attorney, either in Comyns's Digest or in Co. Litt., that the party must be authorized to exercise a discretion. It is enough,

[*857]

*that he is authorized to do an act for, and in the name of, his principal. In the present case, the party is expressly authorized to do an act, viz. to indorse bills in the name of Harrison. And, lest there should be any doubt whether they were to be considered as indorsed for value, the principal goes on to say that he will be responsible to his agent or attorney for the due payment of the bills so indorsed. This stipulation cannot affect the construction of the former part of the instrument. I think we are bound to decide this case in accordance with *Reg.* v. *Kelk*, which appears to me to be directly in point.

ERLE, J.:

I feel compelled to concur with the rest of the Court, so far as saying that an authority in writing to indorse bills of exchange, is a letter or power of attorney within the 55 Geo. III. c. 184. The only difficulty I feel is, that the words of the schedule are so very wide, that our decision may be thought to extend beyond the particular case. But, limiting our judgment to the specific authority here given, I think the rule for a new trial should be made absolute.

Rule absolute (1).

(1) Lord Coke speaks of a " letter of attorney " as an instrument necessarily under seal, "for *letter d'attorney* is as much as a warrant of attorney by deed, as *literæ acquietanciæ* doe signifie a deed of acquittance," Co. Litt. 52 a. The Legislature, using the same term, impose upon "letters of attorney" an amount of stamp-duty, corresponding with that laid upon many other instruments under seal.

If it had been objected that the authority was void, not being by deed, the answer probably would have been, that, by the custom of merchants, a written authority without deed is sufficient; in other words, that a " letter of attorney " in the proper sense of the term, was not necessary. And see Statute of Merton, c. 10.

BROWN v. GILL.

(2 C. B. 861—877; S. C. 3 Dowl. & L. 823; 15 L. J. C. P. 187; 10 Jur. 666.)

1846,
April 29.

[861]

An omission to state in the plaint in a court-baron the nature of the action, is a mere irregularity, which may be waived.

In a suit in a court-baron, the proceedings were alleged to have been taken at a court held "before A., the steward of the said court, a free suitor thereof, and B. and C. and others, free suitors of the said court:"

Held, that the court was properly constituted, it being alleged that A. was a free suitor.

Held, also that A. was properly described as steward of the court, though it was not alleged that he was steward of the manor.

Held, also, that the court was properly described; and that it was sufficient to set forth the names of two only of the free suitors who attended.

UPON a writ of false judgment, directed to the Sheriff of Somersetshire, commanding him to cause to be recorded a certain plaint between James Gill and John Brown, in the court of the manor (1) of Taunton and Taunton-Deane (2), in that county, a record was returned as follows:

"Taunton-Deane, Somersetshire, to wit. The court-baron of Robert Mattock, Esq., lord of the manor of Taunton-Deane, in the county of Somerset, held on the 8th of November, 1843, at the Castle Hall, in and for the said manor, and within the jurisdiction of the said court, according to the custom of the said court and of the said manor, from time whereof the memory of man runneth not to the contrary there used and approved of in the same court and manor, before William Kinglake, Esq., the steward of the said court, a free suitor thereof, and W. Upham, and W. H. Mulford and others, free suitors of the said court.

" Be it remembered, that, at this court, comes James Gill, in his proper person, and now here, in the same court, levies his plaint against John Brown, in a plea of 39s. 11d. in the same court; and he finds pledges for *prosecuting his said plaint, to wit, John Doe and Richard Roe, and now in the same court here prays process of the same court here to be made to him thereon against the said John Brown in the plea of the said plaint: and it is granted to him, &c.   And hereupon it is commanded to the bailiffs of the said

[*862]

---

(1) *I.e.* the court-baron, the only court necessarily incident to a manor; as a manor may exist without a customary court, and the connection of a court-leet with it is merely accidental. The lord may sue for his own debt in his court-baron, for that the suitors are the judges: En temps Edw. I.; Fitz. Abr. tit. Dette, pl. 177.

(2) Formerly called the manor of Tawnton and Tawndeane, *i.e.* the manor of the town and of the dene (or valley) of the river Tawn or Tone.

manor, and ministers of the same court here, that they summon
the said John Brown, within the jurisdiction of the said court, so
that he be at the next court, to be held at the Castle Hall, in and
for the said manor, and within the jurisdiction of the said court, on
Wednesday, the 29th of November instant, at eleven o'clock in the
forenoon, to answer the said James Gill in his said plea of his said
plaint; and what the said bailiffs and ministers shall do thereon,
that they certify to the same next court. The same day is given to
the said James Gill, in and by the same court, to be there, &c.
At which same next court, to wit, at the court of the said manor,
held at the Castle Hall aforesaid, in and for the said manor, and
within the jurisdiction of the said court, on the 29th of November,
1848, before William Kinglake, Esq., steward of the said court,
W. Upham, and W. H. Mulford, and others, free suitors of the same
court, comes the said James Gill in his proper person, and offers
himself against the said John Brown in the plea of his said plaint;
upon which J. Hare, bailiff of the said manor, and minister of the
said court, now delivers to the same court the aforesaid precept to
him in form aforesaid directed, in all things served and executed,
to wit, that he, by virtue of that precept, to him in form aforesaid
directed by William Kinglake, clerk of the castle of Taunton, has
summoned the said John Brown, within the jurisdiction of the said
court, that he be and appear in the same next court, to answer the
said James Gill in the plea of the said plaint, as he was commanded:
Upon which, the said John Brown, being solemnly called, comes

[*863] into this *court here in his proper person to answer the said James
Gill in the plea of his plaint aforesaid: And thereupon the said
James Gill, in this same court, puts in his place J. D. Penny, his
attorney, against the said John Brown, in the plea of his said
plaint; and the said John Brown, in the same court here, puts in
his place J. Oxenham, his attorney, at the suit of the said James
Gill, in the plea of the said plaint: And thereupon, in the same
court here, the said James Gill prays a day to declare against the
said John Brown, in the said plea of the said plaint here, until the
next court of the said manor, to be held, at the place aforesaid, on
the 20th of December, 1848; and it is granted to him, &c.; and
the same day is given to the said John Brown, to be there &c.:
And at which same next court of the said manor, held at the place
aforesaid, and within the jurisdiction of the said court, on the 20th
of December, 1848, before William Kinglake, Esq., steward of the
said court, and W. Upham and W. H. Mulford, and others, free

suitors of the said court, come as well the said James Gill as the   BROWN
v.
GILL.
said John Brown, by their attorneys aforesaid ; and thereupon the
said James Gill, by his said attorney, now declares here in the same
court against the said John Brown in the said plea of the said
plaint, in form following, that is to say :

"At the manor court of Taunton-Deane, in the county of
Somerset, held at the castle of Taunton, on Wednesday, the 20th of
December, 1843. Somersetshire, to wit, James Gill, the plaintiff
in this suit, by J. D. Penny, his attorney, complains of John Brown,
the defendant in this suit, who has been summoned to answer the
plaintiff in an action of debt : for that whereas, &c. (The record
then set out the declaration, the defendant's pleas, the replications
thereto, a prayer of amendment by the plaintiff, a rule to declare,
an amended declaration, an imparlance, pleas to the amended
declaration, replications *thereto, a demurrer to the replications to   [*864]
certain of the pleas, a judgment for the plaintiff thereon, an award
of *unica taxatio*, and a *venire* to try the issues in fact—the whole
proceedings being alleged to have taken place at courts respectively
held " before William Kinglake, Esq., steward of the said court, and
W. Upham and W. H. Mulford, and others, free suitors of the said
court." The record then stated a trial, on the 13th of October,
1844, " before the said William Kinglake, Esq., steward of the said
court, and W. Upham and G. Matthews, and others, free suitors of
the said court," a verdict for the plaintiff with one farthing damages
and 12*d.* costs, and a prayer of judgment, the judgment being
entered as follows :)

"It is considered by the said court here, that the said James
Gill do recover against the said John Brown the said debt of
39*s.* 11*d.*, and his damages, costs, and charges aforesaid, by the
jurors (1) aforesaid in form aforesaid assessed, and also 10*l.* for his
costs and charges by him about his suit in this behalf expended, by
the court here adjudged of increase to the said James Gill, and
with his assent ; which said debt, damages, and costs amount in
the whole to 11*l.* 19*s.* 11*d.*"

The assignment of errors was as follows :

" And hereupon, on the 10th of November, 1845, comes the said
John Brown here, and says that the record aforesaid is vicious and
in many respects defective, and that false judgment is given against
him in and upon the plaint aforesaid, in this, to wit—that it does
not appear by the record aforesaid that the said court of the said

(1) No error assigned hereon.

[*865]

manor of Taunton-Deane, held on the 8th of November, 1843, or the several other courts of the said manor held on the several other days and times subsequent to the said 8th of November, 1843, in the said record mentioned, or any or either of them, was or *were held before any bailiff or steward of the said manor: and in this also, to wit, that, although it appears by the said record that the said court so held on the said 8th of November, 1843, and the said several other courts held on the several other days and times subsequent to the said 8th of November, 1843, in the said record mentioned, was and were the court-baron and courts-baron of the lord of the said manor of Taunton-Deane; yet it appears by the said record that the said court and courts were held before one William Kinglake, Esq., the steward of the said court and courts, as well as before the free suitors of the said court and courts, and not before the said free suitors alone, who are by the law of the land the only judges of courts-baron; nor does it appear by the said record that the said William Kinglake, at the times of holding any of the said courts after the holding of the said court on the said 8th of November, 1843, was even a free suitor of the said court, or a freeholder within (1) the said manor: and also in this, to wit, that it appears by the said record that the said court so held on the said 8th of November, 1843, was a customary court held according to the custom of the said manor of Taunton-Deane; yet the said court assumes to hold pleas of actions personal; and it does not appear by the said record that either the said James Gill or the said John Brown held any lands at the will of the lord, and according to the customs of the said manor: and in this, to wit, that it does not appear by the record aforesaid that the said James Gill levied any plaint in a plea of debt against the said John Brown: and in this, to wit, that it does not appear by the said record that it was, at the said court held on the said 8th of November, 1843,

[*866]

commanded by the free suitors of the *said court, or freeholders within the said manor, to the bailiffs and ministers of the said manor, that they should summon the said John Brown as in the said record mentioned; nor does it appear by the said record by

---

(1) I.e. of the manor, the lands of the freeholders being within the fee and seigniory of the lord but not within or parcel of the manor, though their services are parcel of the manor. On the trial of a case of *Knight* v. *Hardwill* in Q. B., at the Taunton Assizes, 3rd April, 1847, it was proved by the steward of the manor and clerk of the castle of Taunton, that no freeholders ever attended these courts. The parties here described as free suitors were copyholders, and the court a customary court.

whom it was so commanded: and also in this, to wit, that the
declaration set forth in that behalf in the said record, and the
matters therein contained, in manner and form as the same are
therein above stated and set forth, are not sufficient in law for the
said James Gill to have or maintain his aforesaid plea against the
said John Brown: and also in this, to wit, that it does not appear
by the said record, that, at the court of the said manor held on the
9th of October, 1844, it was considered by the free suitors of the
said court that the said replications of the said James Gill to the
said third and last pleas (1) were sufficient in law : and also in this,
to wit, that it does not appear by the said record, that, at the court
of the said manor held on the said 9th of October, 1844, it was
commanded by the free suitors of the said court, to the said J. Hare,
in the said record mentioned, in manner in the said record mentioned; nor does it appear by the said record by whom it was so
commanded: and also in this, to wit, that it appears by the said
record that the judgment on the demurrer of the said John Brown,
in form aforesaid given, was given for the said James Gill against
the said John Brown; whereas, by the law of the land, the said
judgment ought to have been given for the said John Brown against
the said James Gill: and also in this, that it does not appear by
the said record, that at the court of the said manor, held on the
30th of October, 1844, it was considered by the free suitors of the
said court, that the said James Gill should recover against the said
John Brown in manner and form as in the said record mentioned :
and also in this, to wit, that, although it appears by the said
*record that the several courts therein mentioned to be holden were   [*867]
holden before certain free suitors of the said court particularly
named in the said record, and also before other free suitors of the
said court, yet that the names or number of such other free suitors
before whom the said several courts were so holden, are nowhere
mentioned in the said record : and also in this, to wit, that it
appears by the said record that the judgment on the trial of the
plea aforesaid, in form aforesaid given, was given for the said
James Gill against the said John Brown; whereas, by the law of
the land, the said last-mentioned judgment ought to have been
given for the said John Brown against the said James Gill: and so
the said John Brown says, that, in the said court of the manor of
Taunton-Deane aforesaid, false judgment hath in divers instances
been given against him in the plaint aforesaid. And he prays that

(1) The replications that were demurred to.

BROWN
v.
GILL.

the said judgment, for the above and other defects in the record aforesaid, may be reversed, annulled, and altogether held for nothing, as being false and of no effect; and that he the said John Brown may be restored to all things which he has lost by occasion of the said judgment &c." Joinder in error.

The case now came on for argument.

Kinglake, Serjt., for the plaintiff in error (1) :

The proceedings in the court-baron are throughout described as having taken place before W. Kinglake, " steward of the said court," Upham, Mulford, and other free suitors of the same court. If Kinglake had a right to take any part in the proceedings, it could only be as steward of the manor of Taunton-Deane, which he is not alleged to be.

[*868]

(ERLE, J. : He is also *described as " a free suitor thereof." If qualified as a free suitor, he is not disqualified because he is steward also.)

The steward of the manor is a constituent part of the court.

(TINDAL, Ch. J. : The phrase used is common in these proceedings. Comyns speaks of a " grant of a stewardship of a court-baron " (2).)

Assuming, then, that the steward is correctly described, the judgment is the judgment of a court wrongly constituted. This is a common law court-baron, of which the suitors alone are the judges : it differs from the customary court-baron (3), of which the steward is the judge.

(COLTMAN, J. : Does not the averment that the judgment was pronounced by the court, amount to an averment that it was done by the persons who are properly the judges of the court ?

(1) The points marked for argument on the part of the plaintiff in error, were substantially those stated in the assignment of errors.

(2) Title Copyhold (R. 5), citing *Howard* v. *Wood*, T. Jones, 126; 2 Lev. 245, where the COURT held the grant of a stewardship, of the honour of Pomfret, in reversion, to be good as to the court-baron, but not as to the court-leet, the stewardship of the latter being a judicial office. It has been suggested that, as to matters in law, the steward is the judge of the court-baron. Kitchen's Jurisdiction of Courts, 81. *Tamen quære.*

(3) The customary court is not a court-baron, though usually held with the court-baron.

TINDAL, Ch. J. : How does Kinglake lose his character of free   BROWN
suitor by being steward also ?)   *v.*
                                                                 GILL.

He is alleged to have been a free suitor in November, 1843 : there
is no allegation in any of the subsequent proceedings that he still
continued to be a free suitor.

(TINDAL, Ch. J. : Is not the presumption of law that things
remain as they were, unless the contrary be alleged ?)

In these inferior jurisdictions, the Court will infer nothing in their
favour : every step must appear to have been properly taken.   In
Jones v. *Jones* (1), a declaration on a judgment in a county court,
stating the court to have been held before the sheriff and suitors,
was held bad on special demurrer.   Lord ABINGER there said :
" The words ' before such and such persons,' I think, necessarily
imply that the cause was heard before the persons who were the
lawfully constituted *judges of the court: the words ' before the   [*869]
sheriff and suitors,' therefore, imply that the sheriff is a judge
of the county court, which certainly is not the case.   If the suitors
were to differ in opinion, and the sheriff were to give a casting
vote, and thereby decide the question, the judgment would be bad.
Suppose a judgment recovered before the Court of Common Pleas
were pleaded as a judgment recovered ' before the justices of our
lady the Queen of the Bench, and the Lord High Chancellor,' it
would be error, and the latter part of the allegation could not be
rejected as surplusage."   And PARKE, B., said : " The old precedents all describe the court as the county court of the sheriff, held
before the suitors, and set out the names of the suitors."   That the
sheriff is a constituent part of the county court, and the steward, of
the court-baron, is clear ; but it is the suitors alone that are the
judges : *Tinsley* v. *Nassau* (2) ; *Tunno* v. *Morris* (3) ; *Holroyd* v.
Breare (4) ; *Jones* v. *Jones* (1) ; *Bradley* v. *Carr* (5).

(TINDAL, Ch. J. : The style of the county court is stated by
Comyns different from that of the court-baron (6).

CRESSWELL, J. : How can we say that the court is wrongly
described when we find an authority so old as the 4th Inst. p. 268,
which shows that it has been used for centuries ?)

(1) 5 M. & W. 523.   (5) 3 Man. & G. 221 ; 3 Scott, N. R.
(2) Moo. & Mal. 52.   521.
(3) 2 Cr. M. & R. 298.   (6) Com. Dig., tit. County (C. 1);
(4) 21 R. R. 361 (2 B. & Ald. 473).   tit. Copyhold (R. 8).

BROWN
v.
GILL.

The record states that the plaintiff below levied his plaint against the defendant below " in a plea of 39s. 11d." It is the plaint alone that gives the court jurisdiction; and, as the jurisdiction of the court is limited to particular descriptions of actions, the nature of the action should distinctly appear on the face of the plaint.

[*870]

(CRESSWELL, J.: That defect is cured by the declaration, and the defendant's plea. Suppose a writ *of summons were to omit to state the nature of the action, and the defendant were afterwards to appear and accept a declaration, plead thereto, and allow the cause to proceed to judgment; could he then be allowed to take advantage of the omission?)

The names of all the free suitors present on each occasion, though, perhaps, two would have sufficed, should appear in the proceedings: *Lewis* v. *Weeks* (1); *Rex* v. *Mein* (2). It might be that the judgment was pronounced by those who are not named.

Channell, Serjt., *contrà :*

The case of *Jones* v. *Jones* does not warrant the inference that is sought to be drawn from it. There, the declaration was held bad because the proper style of the court was not adopted. The style of the county court is thus given in 4 Inst. c. 55: "Buck. curia prima comitatus E. C. militis vicecomitis com' prædict' tent' apud B. &c. :" and that of the court-baron in c. 57 : " Curia baronis (3) E. C. militis manerii sui prædicti (having the manor's name written in the margin) tent' tali die, &c. Coram A. B. seneschallo ibidem." That of the hundred court is given in similar terms in c. 56. And of both these last-mentioned courts, the suitors are stated to be the judges. *Holroyd* v. *Breare* is a distinct authority that the steward of a court-baron is a member of the court. ABBOTT, Ch. J., there says: "It was contended, in argument, that the defendant, Breare, being the steward of a court-baron, was merely the minister of that court, to execute its process, and

(1) Carth. 85.
(2) 4 T. R. 480.
(3) Or rather *curia baronum*, the *barones* being the free tenants holding of the manor. It is the sheriff's *curia comitatûs*, the lord's *curia baronum*, in which the *comitatus* and the *barones* do

service as the judges *ratione tenuræ.* And see M. 6 Edw. IV. fo. 3, pl. 9; Gilbert's Tenures, by Watkins, 269 (210); Law Review, vol. v. p. 169.
[There is no foundation for this: Maitland, Introd. to Select Pleas in Manorial Courts, at p. xx.—F. P.]

was not clothed with any judicial character; and it was said that
his warrant to the other defendant *was analogous to that of the
sheriff to his bailiff, and rendered him, like the sheriff, civilly
responsible for the mis-execution of it. This was contended, on
the ground, that, in the court-baron, the free suitors are the
judges; and certainly they are so, for the purposes stated in the
authorities which have been cited. We are, however, of opinion
that the steward is not merely a minister of that court, but a
constituent and essential part of it. The court cannot be holden
without him." The case of *Tunno* v. *Morris* (1) seems to put the
sheriff in the same position with respect to the county court, though
he clearly is not a constituent part of the court in the same sense
that the steward of the court-baron or hundred court is. In Bacon's
Abridgment, title Courts, there is a case precisely in point (2):
" In an hundred court, the plea was laid to be *coram seneschallo et
sectatoribus:* Serjt. *Newdigate* took an exception to it, that it should
be laid to be held *coram seneschallo per sectatores:* but WYNDHAM,
ATKINS, and SCROGGS, thought it well enough; the CHIEF JUSTICE
contrà." With respect to the omission of the names of some of
the suitors, it is enough if the names of two free suitors present
be mentioned, two freeholders only being necessary to preserve
the manor (3). *Rex* v. *Mein* is wholly inapplicable: there the
election appeared to have been made by unqualified persons.

Kinglake, Serjt., in reply:

It is quite clear from the case of *Jones* v. *Jones,* that it is
improper to allege a county court to have been held before the
sheriff and suitors; and it is equally clear, according to *Tunno* v.
Morris, that the steward of a court-baron stands precisely upon
the same footing in this respect. No inference is to be drawn in
favour of the proceedings in these courts, which are not courts of
record. It must be shown that all has been done that is essential
to give them legal authority.

[*872]

TINDAL, Ch. J.:

It appears to me that the judgment of the court below in this
case ought to be affirmed. Four objections have been taken to the

(1) 2 Cr. M. & R. 298; 4 Dowl.
P. C. 224.
(2) *Clever* v. *Curteis,* 30 Car. II.
[*sub. nom.* "Of the Hundred Courts."
—J. G. P.]
(4) On the other hand, if the lord

alien or enfranchise all the demesnes,
although the manor is destroyed, the
court-baron remains, and must be
held by the lord in respect of that
which has now become a seigniory in
gross,—*un fief en l'air.*

regularity of the proceedings. The first was, that Mr. Kinglake, who is alleged to be the steward of the court, does not also appear to be the steward of the manor : and it was said (but for this no authority was cited) that it was not competent to him to preside in the court unless he was steward of the manor. In Comyns's Digest, tit. Copyhold (R. 8), it is said (1) : " The style of the court contains the time and place, and before what steward it is held." And then the style is given as follows: "Visus franc' pleg' (2) cum curiâ baron' J. B., militis, domini manerii prædict', ibidem tent' die Jovis, videlicet 12° die Octobris, anno regni, &c., fidei defensoris, &c., 19°, coram A. B., arm., seneschallo ibidem ; " not calling him steward of the manor. In Co. Litt. 61 b, it is said : " Every steward of courts is either by deed or without deed ; for, a man may be retained a steward to keep his court-baron and leet also belonging to the manor, without deed, and that retainer shall continue until he be discharged." And it is matter of daily experience that persons hold these courts by deputation, who are not stewards of the manor (3). This objection, therefore, fails.

[873]   The next objection, and that upon which the principal reliance was placed, was, that the proceedings appear to have taken place before an improperly constituted court. If that be so, then undoubtedly the jurisdiction fails. The style of the court, as set out in the return, is, " The court-baron of Robert Mattock, Esq., lord of the manor of Taunton and Taunton-Deane, in the county of Somerset, held on the 8th day of November, 1843, at the Castle Hall, in and for the said manor, and within the jurisdiction of the said court, according to the custom of the said court, and of the said manor, from time whereof the memory of man runneth not to the contrary, there used and approved of in the same court and manor, before William Kinglake, Esq., the steward of the said court, a free suitor thereof, and W. Upham and W. H. Mulford, and others, free suitors of the said court." If that be incorrect, then all the subsequent proceedings are tainted with the same irregularity. Upon reading this allegation, however, I do not conceive that it necessarily implies that Kinglake was present as judge of the court. I think it would be putting an erroneous interpretation upon the language employed, to say that he thereby places

(1) Citing Kitchen, 6 b, 53 b.

(2) This style is applicable only when the lord has a view of frank-pledge or leet, which he holds at the same time with his court-baron, the civil jurisdiction of the latter, and the criminal jurisdiction of the former, being frequently coextensive.

(3) Or stewards at all.

himself on the footing of a judge. The steward has a known definite duty to perform, viz. to collect and declare the opinions of the suitors. The suitors, also, have a known definite duty, viz. to adjudicate upon the matters presented to them. The case of *Jones* v. *Jones* (1), which has been mainly relied upon in support of this objection, came before the court on a special demurrer. That, too, was the case of a county court. There is a material difference between the style of the county court and that of the court-baron: and the decision in that case may be perfectly sound as to a county court, and yet not be applicable *to a court-baron. The style of the county court, as given in Comyns's Digest, County (C. 1), is: " Essex, to wit. *Curia prima comit'* A. B., *vic. com. præd. tent. apud.* D. &c." It may, therefore, be usurpation on the part of the sheriff, to call it his (2) court, or to say that it was held before him. In the Year Book, 21 Hen. VI. fo. 34 (3), it seems to have been thought sufficient to describe the county court as held before the sheriff. This second objection, therefore, for the reasons before given, in my opinion discloses no ground of error.

The third objection was, that the plaint does not specify the form of action. That only goes to the formality of the plaint: and the defendant having chosen to appear and plead, the time for taking advantage of the irregularity has gone by. It has been observed, that no intendment will be made in favour of the regularity of proceedings in a court not of record. But I believe the general rule is, that every intendment is to be made in favour of the regularity of the proceedings of an inferior court, where the matter appears to have been within its jurisdiction.

The last objection was, that the names of all the suitors present on the various occasions should have appeared. The first answer to that is, that no authority has been cited to show that it is necessary to name all. Certainly it must be shown that there were two free suitors present, otherwise there could be no court: *Chetwode* v. *Crew* (4). But, in the absence of any express *authority to show that more must be named, and seeing that the mention of an

[*874]

[*875]

---

(1) 5 M. & W. 523.

(2) The form does state the court to be the court of the sheriff; whereas the court baron is not the court of the steward, but of the lord; see F. N. B. 3.

(3) In that case (*The Abbot of Tavestocke* v. *Stourton*, P. 21 Hen. VI. fo. 34, pl. 22), the only question was, whether the under-sheriff might hold

plea upon a *justicies*, or whether it must be held by the sheriff himself: nothing was said as to before whom it was to be held, except that the plaintiff in false judgment complained that he was brought to answer (*mesne en respons*), *coram non judice.*

(4) Willes, 614.

BROWN
v.
GILL.

BROWN
v.
GILL.

indefinite number could only lead to mistake, I think we must hold that two alone will suffice, notwithstanding others may have been present.

Upon the whole, therefore, I am of opinion that our judgment must be for the plaintiff below.

COLTMAN, J.:

I am quite of the same opinion. The first objection rests on no solid foundation. The passage cited from Co. Litt. 61 b, which is also noticed in Comyns's Digest, title Copyhold (R. 5), and in Dyer, 248 a, shows that there is no objection to the officer being described as steward of the court. The next, which was the main objection, derives some colour from the case of *Jones* v. *Jones*. That, however, was the case of a county court; and it was decided upon a special demurrer for not using, in describing the court, the style consecrated by antient usage. The case cited from Bacon's Abridgment is a much closer authority. It was there held, by three Judges against one, that the hundred court was well described to have been held before "the steward and suitors." As to the third point, it sufficiently appears that the court had jurisdiction, and that the irregularity was waived. And as to the fourth point, the objection rests on no authority. I agree with the LORD CHIEF JUSTICE, that, the names of two suitors, which are required to constitute a court, being set out, it was not necessary to mention the names of any more.

CRESSWELL, J.:

I also am of opinion that our judgment must be for the defendant. I do not think it necessary to add any thing upon the first two objections. As to the third, I believe it is not necessary in the inferior courts to enter the plaint at length. *That appears from *Bishop* v. *Kaye* (1). All that the record there showed was, that, on the 22nd of October, 1817, Kaye levied a certain plaint against Bishop, whereupon a summons issued, returnable on the 5th of November, and a *capias* afterwards issued to arrest the defendant, returnable on the 19th November. If, however, it had been necessary to specify in the plaint the nature of the action, the omission so to do clearly could not be taken advantage of in this stage of the proceedings. The fourth objection was rested entirely upon the authority of *Rex* v. *Mein*. That was an information in the nature of a *quo warranto*, calling on the defendant to show cause

[*876]

(1) 3 B. & Ald. 605.

by what authority he claimed and exercised the office of port-reeve
of the borough and manor of Fowey, in Cornwall: the defendant
pleaded an immemorial custom for the homage of the free tenants
of the borough and manor to elect and present one of the free
tenants as a fit person to be port-reeve, &c., and that, at a certain
court, the homage of the free tenants, to wit, A. B., C. D., and
others elected and presented him, &c.: the replication, amongst
other things, denied that certain persons, twenty-three in number
(two of them being the persons named in the plea), were, at the
time of holding the court, free tenants of the borough and manor:
and the jury found that two only of the twenty-three persons
named in the replication were free tenants of the borough and
manor. ASHHURST, J. said: "When a defendant makes it a part
of his title, that a court at which he was elected was held before
twenty-three homagers, he cannot afterwards rely on this, that two
of them were of that description." I am at a loss to perceive what
bearing that case has upon the present. Upon the whole, I think
the judgment of the court below must be sustained.

ERLE, J. :   [877]

I concur with the rest of the Court, for the reasons already given
at sufficient length.

Judgment for the defendant.

IN THE COURT OF EXCHEQUER.

1845.
April 17.
———
[1]

HUMPHREYS *v.* JONES.

(14 Meeson & Welsby, 1—4; S. C. 14 L. J. Ex. 254; 9 Jur. 333.)

A. having signed, as surety for B., a joint and several promissory note made by A. and B., and being called upon after B.'s death for payment of the money due upon it, requested the holder to apply to B.'s executrix, stating (in writing), that "what she should be short he would assist to make up." The executrix having been applied to, but not paying anything: Held, that A.'s conditional promise of payment became thereby absolute, and rendered him liable in an action brought against him on the note more than six years after its date, and after a reasonable time for payment by the executrix had elapsed.

ASSUMPSIT on a joint and several promissory note for 400*l.* and interest, made by the defendant and one Robert Jones, since deceased, dated 6th June, 1833, payable to the plaintiff's intestate. Plea (*inter alia*) the Statute of Limitations. At the trial before Wightman, J., at the last Assizes at Liverpool, it appeared that the defendant signed the note as surety for his brother, Robert Jones, who had paid the interest up to the time of his death in 1835, and

[*2]

whose widow had also afterwards paid interest *on the note till 1839. The evidence to take the case out of the Statute of Limitations, as against the defendant, consisted of certain letters written by him in the years 1840 and 1841, in answer to applications from the plaintiff's attorney. On the 5th of December, 1840, the attorney applied to the defendant for payment of the note; and on the 8th the defendant wrote in answer, stating, that he had written to the executrix to come and arrange about it, and he would write again after he had seen her. On the 6th March, 1841, the plaintiff's attorney again wrote to the defendant as follows: "I beg to call your attention to my letter of the 5th December last, respecting the 400*l.* due on your note to Mr. Edward Humphreys. The money is wanted immediately, and I will therefore thank you to fix an early day for the payment thereof, in order that I may arrange with the parties." To this letter, on the 8th March, the defendant replied as follows: "I am in receipt of yours of the 6th, handed me this morning. I have forwarded it to Mrs. Jones, with a request that she will come over without delay to settle the business. May I beg you will write to her by the first post to press payment, and what she may be short, I will assist to make up. I send you her address." Application was accordingly made on the part of the plaintiff to

Mrs. Jones for payment, but without effect; and in 1844, this HUMPHREYS
action was brought against the defendant.
v.
JONES.

Upon this evidence the learned Judge directed a verdict for the
plaintiff, giving the defendant leave to move to enter a nonsuit or a
verdict for him, if the Court should be of opinion that these letters
did not constitute a sufficient acknowledgment to take the case out
of the Statute of Limitations.

Knowles now moved accordingly:

There is nothing in either of the defendant's letters which
amounts to such an *unconditional acknowledgment of the debt   [*3]
as that a promise to pay it can be implied therefrom.   There is no
admission of liability in himself, but merely an engagement to
assist the executrix of his co-maker, who was the person primarily
liable.

(PARKE, B.: That engagement was made with reference to a note
on which the defendant was originally liable; and it is such an
acknowledgment as imports a promise to pay the debt due upon
that note, in case the other party does not.   When she does
not pay, his promise becomes an absolute one, and admits the
declaration.)

The true construction of the letter is rather this: "She is the
party liable to pay; but if she do not, I will;" and there is no
authority that a promise by a party to pay the debt of another can
take a debt of his own, although upon the same security, out of the
Statute of Limitations.   The principle is thus stated by PARKE, B.,
in *Morrell* v. *Frith* (1): "According to the recent cases, the document, to take the case out of the statute, must either contain a
promise to pay the debt on request, or an acknowledgment from
which such promise is to be inferred.   Now the utmost that can be
made of the letter in this case is, that it acknowledges the existence
of the debt mentioned in the previous letters, but that the defendant
does not mean to express any promise to pay, but reserves it for
future consideration."

(PARKE, B.: There must, no doubt, be something proved which
fits the promise stated in the declaration, which is a promise to pay
on request.   But if the evidence be of a promise to pay upon a
condition, and the condition be performed, it becomes absolute, and

(1) 49 R. R. 659 (3 M. & W. 402).

41—2

HUMPHREYS
v.
JONES.

is a promise to pay on request. If the action had been brought immediately after the letter was written, so that there had been no time for the executrix to pay, the case might be different.

[*4]   POLLOCK, C. B.: The letter of the 8th of March must be *read with reference to all the previous letters. Now in that letter the defendant says in effect, "I am only a surety—Mrs. Jones is the person who ought to pay—and I renew my engagement as surety: apply to her, the principal, who ought to pay, and if she does not, I will pay."

PARKE, B.: It amounts to this: "I will pay whatever she does not, on application being made to her.")

Then should not that have been an application to her by means of legal process?

(PARKE, B.: No; the defendant promises to pay on non-payment by her when applied to for payment. It is not necessary to sue her, in order to make it an absolute promise by the defendant; when she fails to pay, it is absolute, and admits the declaration.

ALDERSON, B.: I doubt whether it even is a conditional promise at all.)

Per CURIAM (1) :
                                    Rule refused.

———————

1845.
April 18.
———
[28]

TANNER AND OTHERS v. SCOVELL AND OTHERS (2).

(14 Meeson & Welsby, 28—38; S. C. 14 L. J. Ex. 321.)

Goods were forwarded in bales by ship to London, deliverable to B. & Co., who were factors for sale, or their assigns; and were landed at the defendants' wharf. B. & Co. gave the defendants orders to "weigh and deliver" the goods to M., who had contracted with B. & Co. for the purchase of them. They were accordingly weighed, and an account of the weights sent to B. & Co., who made out invoices to M. accordingly. M. re-sold several bales of the goods, which were delivered by the defendants, upon his order, to his buyers: the rest remained on the defendants' wharf until they were stopped by B. & Co. as unpaid sellers. They were never transferred in the defendants' books from the names of B. & Co. to that of M., nor was any warehouse rent paid by him: Held, first, that, upon

(1) POLLOCK, C. B., PARKE, B.,   *McLaren* (1879) 11 Ch. Div. 68, 48
ALDERSON, B., and ROLFE, B.   L. J. Bk. 49, and 56 & 57 Vict. c. 71,
(2) See *Ex parte Cooper, In re*   s. 45 (7).—J. G. P.

these facts, the defendants never stood in the relation of wharfingers to M., so as to be liable to an action on the case by him for the non-delivery of the goods to his order.

Secondly, that, under these circumstances, B. & Co.'s right of stoppage *in transitu* was not determined by the part delivery to M.'s buyers.

CASE. The first count of the declaration stated, that the said E. M'Laughlin, before he became bankrupt, to wit, on the 1st January, 1844, and on divers days and times between that day and the 1st August, 1844, at the special instance and request of the defendants, left and continued in the care, custody, and keeping of the defendants, and the defendants, before the said E. M'Laughlin became bankrupt, to wit, on the 1st August, 1844, at their special instance and request, had in their care, custody, and keeping, divers goods and chattels of the said E. M'Laughlin by his permission, to wit, glue pieces, weighing a certain great weight, to wit, twenty tons, of great value &c., to be taken care of and safely and securely kept by the defendants, for certain reward and at certain charges, for the said E. M'Laughlin, and to be delivered by the defendants to the said E. M'Laughlin when the defendants should be thereunto requested, upon payment of such reward and charge as might be due to the defendants in respect of the said goods and chattels. The count then set forth the bankruptcy of M'Laughlin, the issuing of the *fiat*, the adjudication, and the appointment of the plaintiffs as assignees; and averred a request by the plaintiffs for the delivery of the said goods by the defendants to them as such assignees, and that they were ready and willing and tendered and offered to pay to the defendants such reward and charges, and whatever might be or was due to the defendants in respect of the said goods and chattels. Breach, in non-delivery of the said goods to the plaintiffs. There *were also counts in   [*29] trover, respectively alleging a property in the bankrupt before his bankruptcy, and in the plaintiffs as assignees since the bankruptcy.

The defendants pleaded, first, Not guilty. Secondly, to the first count, that the said E. M'Laughlin became bankrupt after the passing of the 2 & 3 Vict. c. 29, and that, after he had so left the said goods and chattels, and whilst the same were and continued, in the care, custody, and keeping of the defendants, and before the date or issuing of the *fiat*, to wit, on the 16th August, 1844, he the said E. M'Laughlin really and *bonâ fide* sold and transferred the said goods and chattels, and every part thereof, to certain persons, to wit, one John Walton and one James Walton, who then really and *bonâ fide* bought the said goods and chattels of and from the said E. M'Laughlin; and that afterwards, and before the date or issuing of the said *fiat*, the defendants really and *bonâ fide* delivered the said goods and chattels to the said John Walton and James Walton, by the direction and with the consent of the said E. M'Laughlin. Averments, that, at the time of the said sale and purchase of the said goods, the said John Walton and James Walton had not nor had either of them notice of any prior act of bankruptcy by the said E. M'Laughlin committed; and that, at the time of the delivery of the said goods and chattels to the said John Walton and James Walton, the defendants had not nor had either of them notice of any prior act of bankruptcy by the said E. M'Laughlin committed. Wherefore, and not otherwise, they refused and could not deliver the same or any part thereof to the plaintiffs. Verification.

Third plea, to the first count, that the said E. M'Laughlin became bankrupt after the passing of the 2 & 3 Vict. c. 29; and that, after he had so left the said goods and chattels, and whilst the same were and continued, in the care, custody, and keeping of the defendants as in the declaration mentioned, they the defendants, [*30] by the license, direction, *and authority of the said E. M'Laughlin, and before the date or issuing of the *fiat*, and before the defendants or either of them had notice of any prior act of bankruptcy by him committed, to wit, on &c., the said E. M'Laughlin ordered and directed the defendants to deliver the said goods and chattels to certain persons, to wit, to William Boutcher, William Mortimore, and Robert Vicary; and the defendants then, in pursuance of and obedience to such order and direction as aforesaid, and by the leave and license of the said E. M'Laughlin to them for that purpose then given, before the date or issuing of the said *fiat*, and before they the defendants or either of them had notice of any act of bankruptcy by the said E. M'Laughlin committed, really and *bonâ fide* delivered the said goods and chattels, and every part thereof, to the said William Boutcher, William Mortimore, and Robert Vicary, and have never since had the same or any part thereof in their custody, care, or keeping. Wherefore, and not otherwise, the defendants, at the said time when &c., omitted and refused to deliver the same to the plaintiffs, &c. Verification.

There were also two other pleas to the first count: the fourth plea denying the allegation that M'Laughlin left the goods in the care, &c. of the defendants as therein mentioned; and the fifth, the allegation that the plaintiffs tendered and offered to pay to the

defendants *modo et formâ :* and pleas to the second count, the sixth
denying the property of the bankrupt, the seventh setting up leave
and license; and lastly, a plea to the third count, denying the
property of the plaintiffs as assignees.

The plaintiffs joined issue on the first, fourth, fifth, sixth, and
last pleas ; and to the second, third, and seventh replied *de injuriâ*,
and issues were joined thereon.

At the trial, before Pollock, C. B., at the sittings in London after
Hilary Term, it appeared that the action was brought by the
plaintiffs as the assignees of E. M'Laughlin, who, before his bankruptcy, carried on the business of a *hair and glue merchant in   [*31]
Ivy Lane, Bermondsey, to recover from the defendants, who are
wharfingers at Topping's Wharf, damages for the non-delivery to
the plaintiffs of a quantity of glue pieces, in value about 1,500*l.*,
under the following circumstances :

The bankrupt had been in the habit of dealing largely for many
years with Messrs. Boutcher, Mortimore, and Vicary, who are leather
factors in Bermondsey, for glue pieces, which are portions of the
hides of oxen, dressed by tanners and fellmongers in a particular way,
and prepared for the purpose of being converted into glue. The
glue pieces were sent up from the country tanners who manufactured
them, to some of the river-side wharves in London, and on their
arrival orders were issued by Boutcher & Co. to the wharfingers to
weigh and deliver the goods to M'Laughlin, in the form hereinafter
stated. The weights were communicated to Boutcher & Co., who
made out invoices to M'Laughlin calculated thereon. M'Laughlin
used to allow the glue pieces to remain at the respective wharves
where they were landed until he required them, or until he sold
them to other parties, and they were then delivered to him or
his vendees upon his order, without any further authority from
Boutcher & Co.

In March, 1844, M'Laughlin entered into the following contract
with Boutcher & Co. :

"BERMONDSEY, March 15, 1844.

"I have this day bought of Messrs. Boutcher, Mortimore, & Co.
about 20 tons of hide pieces, at 34*l.* per ton, delivered alongside a
wharf in London; payment in cash on arrival, allowing two
months' discount, or by approved bill at two months' date, without
discount.

"EDWARD M'LAUGHLIN."

The pieces sold under this contract belonged to a Mr. Bucknell, of Bridgewater, for whom Boutcher & Co. were factors; and 48 bales of them were shipped thence *for London, under a bill of lading dated 23rd March, 1844, whereby they were made deliverable to Boutcher & Co., their assigns. The vessel arrived off Topping's Wharf on the 15th of April. On the 16th, Boutcher & Co. gave M'Laughlin the following order:

"To the Superintendent of Cotton's (1) Wharf.

"BERMONDSEY, April 16, 1844.

"Please weigh and deliver to Mr. M'Laughlin 48 bales glue pieces.

"For Boutcher, Mortimore, & Co.,

"RICHARD WELCH."

"Ship *William the Fourth*, Capt. Rees,
    from Bridgewater."

The defendants, on receipt of this order, weighed the 48 bales, and found the weight to be 98 cwt. 3 qrs. 13 lb., which was communicated to Boutcher & Co., who thereupon sent to M'Laughlin an invoice stating the weight and price, viz. 168*l.* 1*s.* 6*d.* On the 31st of May, five of these 48 bales, weighing 9 cwt. 2 qrs. 16 lb., were delivered by the defendants, on the order of M'Laughlin, to a Mr. Platt, to whom he had sold them. The other 43 remained at the wharf until they were stopped by Boutcher & Co. as hereinafter mentioned.

On the 11th of April, 64 more bales of the glue pieces were shipped from Taunton by the Taunton packet, and 38 by the *Benjamin*, consigned to Boutcher & Co. under similar bills of lading. The former arrived at Topping's Wharf on the 26th April, and on the 27th were weighed by the defendants at 127 cwt. 3 qrs. 10 lb. On the 2nd May, Boutcher & Co. sent a delivery order, in the same terms *as before, except that it did not specify the number of bales; and on the 4th of May they delivered to M'Laughlin an invoice thereof, stating the weight and price accordingly, viz. 217*l.* 6*s.* 6*d.* On the 30th of April 10 more bales (in addition to the 38 before shipped) were forwarded from Taunton by the *Benjamin*, and 35 by another vessel, the *Shamrock*. These

---

(1) Topping's Wharf having been destroyed by fire, the defendants, during its rebuilding, carried on the business at their other establishment of Cotton's Wharf. The glue pieces in question were the first goods landed at Topping's Wharf after its being rebuilt.

vessels arrived in London on the 18th and 27th of May respectively, and similar orders were given by Boutcher & Co. to the defendants, on the 15th of May and 12th of June, for the delivery of the bales brought by them to M'Laughlin, and similar invoices were made out, according to the weights taken at the wharf.

No transfer of any of these goods was made in the defendants' books from Boutcher & Co. to M'Laughlin, nor was any wharfage rent charged to him. There was evidence also that M'Laughlin claimed an allowance from the weights, in consequence of a portion of the goods being wet, and requested that they might be marked, in order that the question might remain open until they could be re-weighed; but M'Laughlin stated that he had afterwards given up this objection.

On the 27th of May, M'Laughlin sold to Mr. Platt 40 of the 48 bales which arrived by the *Benjamin*, and they were delivered to him by the defendants, on M'Laughlin's order, at various times between the 29th of May and 9th of July. The other 8 bales, and those also which came by the *Shamrock*, remained at the wharf until they were stopped by Boutcher & Co. as hereinafter mentioned.

On the 19th of July, Boutcher & Co., to whom M'Laughlin was then indebted on the balance of his account in upwards of 700*l.*, in consequence of his failure in making a payment to them according to his engagement, wrote a letter to the defendants, directing them not to deliver any more glue pieces to M'Laughlin. On the 18th of August, M'Laughlin committed an act of bankruptcy, on which a *fiat* issued on the 26th of September. On the 20th of December, the plaintiffs, as assignees, demanded from the *defendants the [*34] delivery of all the glue pieces at the wharf, (150 in all), offering to pay all rent, wharfage, and other charges which might be due to them in respect thereof. The defendants refused to deliver them, under an indemnity from Boutcher & Co., whereupon this action was brought. No evidence was given in support of the second plea.

The Lord Chief Baron, in summing up, left it to the jury to say, first, whether there was any difference between an order " to weigh and deliver," and an order to " weigh and transfer," and whether the former implied a complete delivery of the goods to the bankrupt; stating to them also, that, if the bankrupt never took the weights, objected to them, and desired that the goods might be marked that he might keep his objection open, in point of law he never acquiesced in that which was necessary to constitute it a perfect delivery; and that, if there was no complete delivery, inasmuch as the order to stop the goods was before the act of bankruptcy, the plaintiffs were not entitled to recover.

The jury found that the delivery was not complete, and the verdict was therefore entered for the defendants on the fourth, sixth, and eighth issues, and for the plaintiffs on the other issues.

In this Term (April 17)

Jervis moved for a new trial, on the ground of misdirection :

First, the plaintiffs were entitled to recover on the fourth issue, which raises the question, whether the goods were left and continued by the bankrupt in the custody of the defendants on the terms stated in the first count of the declaration. The order to " weigh and deliver " to the bankrupt implied a perfect delivery : *Hanson* v. *Meyer* (1), *Hammond* v. *Anderson* (2), *Lucas* v. *Dorrien* (3).

[*85]   (PARKE, B. : It may be that the property *passed to him ; but to sustain this issue, the plaintiffs must show that the defendants held the goods for him : there must be some evidence of a contract between the bankrupt and the defendants. Where is there any evidence of employment of them by him, they having been originally employed by Boutcher & Co. ?)

At all events, the plaintiffs are entitled to recover on the pleas of not possessed to the counts in trover. Those pleas put in issue the right of Boutcher & Co. to stop the goods ; and here there was no right of stoppage, for as against the vendors there was a perfect delivery to the bankrupt. With reference to the counts in trover, the delivery of part of the bulk was a delivery of the whole.

(PARKE, B. : That depends on the intention : if the intention was to separate the portion delivered from the bulk, it is not necessarily a delivery of the remainder.)

But here the separation is not by the deliverer, but by the receiver. There is certainly no intention on his part—who has bought the whole, and may take the whole if he pleases—to sever a portion from the remainder, and receive that portion only. His intention clearly is to take the whole, and at once to dispose of part, the rest remaining at his risk.

(1) 8 R. R. 572 (6 East, 614 ; 2   69).
Smith, 670).   (3) 18 R. R. 480 (7 Taunt. 278 ; 1
(2) 8 R. R. 763 (1 Bos. & P. (N. R.)   Moore, 29).

˹ (PARKE, B., referred to *Jones* v. *Jones* (1), *Wentworth* v. *Outhwaite* (2), and *Whitehead* v. *Anderson* (3).)

None of those were cases in which it was held that where the purchaser takes a portion of the goods, the *transitus* is not determined.

Again, it was wrongly put to the jury, that there was evidence of a dispute about the weight of the goods. There was no dispute about their weight, but merely a claim for an allowance because they were wet; and the bankrupt sells a part without any adjustment of that claim.

(PARKE, B. : It is a dispute about the real weight.)

Per CURIAM:

There will be no rule as to the failure on *the first count, because it is not made out that there was any relation of wharfingers to the bankrupt. As to the other point, we will take time to look into the authorities.

[*36]

Cur. adv. vult.

The judgment was now delivered by

POLLOCK, C. B.:

In this case, upon looking into the authorities, we are all agreed that the delivery of part of the goods was not intended to be, and did not operate as, a simple delivery of the whole, but was a separation for the purpose of that part only, leaving all the rest *in statu quo ;* and therefore, the only remaining point on which the Court had any doubt being cleared up to the satisfaction of my learned brothers, there will be no rule.

The first and leading case on this subject is that of *Slubey* v. *Heyward* (4), in which a part delivery was considered as putting an end to the right of stoppage *in transitu*. That was nothing else, in truth, than the delivery of the whole cargo : each part was taken away with the intention to take possession of the whole, not to separate the part that was delivered from the remainder. Lord TENTERDEN says, in the case of *Bunney* v. *Poyntz* (5), that that was "the delivery of part of the cargo, made in the progress of and with a view to the delivery of the whole ; " because you could not

(1) 58 R. R. 765 (8 M. & W. 431).   (4) 3 R. R. 486 (2 H. Bl. 504).
(2) 62 R. R. 664 (10 M. & W. 436).   (5) 38 R. R. 309 (4 B. & Ad. 571 ; 1
(3) 60 R. R. 819 (9 M. & W. 518).   Nev. & M. 229).

TANNER
v.
SCOVELL.

[*37]

take the whole of the cargo at one time, but must take hogshead by hogshead, or sack by sack, as the case may be. If there was no intention to separate the particular part delivered from the remainder, that incipient delivery, so to speak,—that inchoate delivery,—will amount to a determination of the right to stop *in transitu*. Before the time of the decision in *Slubey* v. *Heyward* (1), the subject of stoppage *in transitu* had not undergone the great consideration it has of late years: and hardly anything was held sufficient to determine the right, unless there was an actual taking possession by the purchaser himself, by going and weighing the commodity or otherwise, and so taking manual possession of it. In all the subsequent cases in which part deliveries have been held not to be sufficient to prevent the right of stoppage, (there are several of them), the vendee meant to separate the part delivered from the remainder, and to take possession of that part only, and in most of them the vendor concurred in that act. I may observe, that TAUNTON, J., in the case of *Betts* v. *Gibbins* (2), made an observation which is very justly questioned by Mr. Smith, in his book on Mercantile Law, viz. that " a partial delivery is a delivery of the whole, unless circumstances show that it is not so meant." Mr. Smith appends a *quære* to that *dictum*, and with very great reason. It will be found that the only two cases, so far as I have looked at them, which bear the semblance of an authority that a mere part delivery is sufficient to put an end to the right to stoppage *in transitu*, are these, *Slubey* v. *Heyward* and *Hammond* v. *Anderson* (3). In the case of *Bunney* v. *Poyntz*, part delivery of a portion of a haystack, with intent to separate that from the remainder, was held not to be sufficient. In *Jones* v. *Jones* (4), on the other hand, this Court held, that the vendee (who was assignee under a trust deed) took possession of part of the cargo, with the intention of obtaining possession of the whole, for the purposes of the trust, and therefore that such taking possession of part did put an end to the transit: but it was fully admitted in that case, that the mere delivery of part to the vendee, when he meant to separate that part from the remainder, did not put an end to the *right to stop *in transitu*. The same doctrine is laid down in *Miles* v. *Gorton* (5) and in *Dixon* v. *Yates* (6). There the vendee took samples,

[*38]

(1) 3 R. R. 486 (2 H. Bl. 504).

(2) 41 R. R. 381 (2 Ad. & El. 57; 4 Nev. & M. 64).

(3) 8 R. R. 763 (1 Bos. & P. (N. R.) 69).

(4) 58 R. R. 765 (8 M. & W. 431).

(5) 39 R. R. 820 (2 Cr. & M. 504).

(6) 39 R. R. 489 (5 B. & Ad. 313; 2 Nev. & M. 177).

coopered and marked the casks in which the goods were, and sold
them to different purchasers, one of whom obtained possession of a
part; and yet it was held that the lien of the unpaid vendor still
subsisted. Here, it is true, there is a general order to deliver to
the vendee's order the whole commodity, which means, either the
whole, or any part, if the vendee chooses to select a part, intending
to select that part only; and in such case, the delivery of that part
only does not operate as a delivery of the whole. If the vendee
takes possession of part, not meaning thereby to take possession of
the whole, but to separate that part, and to take possession of that
part only, it puts an end to the *transitus* only with respect to that
part, and no more: the right of lien and the right of stoppage *in
transitu* on the remainder still continue. Besides the cases I have
referred to, I have no doubt others may be found in which this
doctrine is clearly established. The whole, in truth, depends on
the intention of the vendee. We are of opinion, therefore, that
the verdict in this case is right, and that no rule should be
granted.

Rule refused.

TANNER
v.
SCOVELL.

DOE D. JUKES *v.* SUMNER.

(14 Meeson & Welsby, 39—42; S. C. 14 L. J. Ex. 337.)

Section 8 of the Real Property Limitation Act, 1833 (3 & 4 Will. IV. c. 27)
applies to tenancies from year to year created before and existing at the
passing of the Act.

1845.
April 19.

[39]

THIS was an ejectment to recover possession of a house and
premises in the parish of Walsall, in the county of Stafford. The
demise was laid on the 30th of July, 1844. At the trial, before
Pollock, C. B., at the last Staffordshire Assizes, the following facts
appeared :

By a settlement, made on the marriage of Gilbert Fownes and
Ann his intended wife, in the year 1788, and a recovery duly
suffered in pursuance thereof, the premises in question were limited
and settled (after the marriage) to such uses as the said Ann should
by deed appoint. The marriage took effect, and by a deed made on
the 27th of March, 1790, Ann Fownes appointed the property to the
use of John Finch and Joseph Jukes, and their heirs, upon trust,
after her decease, to sell the same, and apply the purchase-money
in such manner and for such purposes as she should by her will
direct and appoint; and in default of appointment, she directed
that it should form part of the remainder of her personal estate.

Doe d.
JUKES
v.
SUMNER.

Ann Fownes survived her husband, and by her will, dated 6th of October, 1808, disposed of her real and personal estate generally, but made no appointment as to the property in question, or the purchase-money to arise from the sale of it; and she appointed Peter Kempson and two other persons her executors, and died in 1811. Kempson survived his co-executors, and, in the year 1814, let the defendant's father into possession as tenant from year to year, without any lease or other writing of the premises in question, which (the deed of 1790 having been overlooked) were supposed to have passed under the general devise of real estate in the will. He continued in possession and paid rent to Kempson until the 25th of March, 1824, since which time no demand or payment of

[*40]

rent appeared to have been made, *Kempson having died in the month of May in the same year. The defendant's father died a few years ago, leaving the defendant in possession of the premises. Rent was demanded of him by the parties beneficially interested under the deed of 1790, and payment being refused, this ejectment was brought in the name of the heir-at-law of Joseph Jukes, who was the survivor of the trustees named in the deed of 1790.

It was objected for the defendant, that the right of action was barred by the stat. 3 & 4 Will. IV. c. 27, s. 8: and the LORD CHIEF BARON, being of that opinion, nonsuited the plaintiff, reserving him leave to move to enter a verdict.

Talfourd, Serjt., now moved accordingly:

The question in this case depends upon what is the true construction of the 8th section of the stat. 3 & 4 Will. IV. c. 27. * * The question is, whether that section is retrospective, and operates in cases where, at the time of its passing, there was a subsisting tenancy. If it does not, the lessor of the plaintiff was not barred

[41]

in this action. * * In *Doe* d. *Evans* v. *Page* (1) it appears to have been taken for granted that the seventh section of the statute, which applies to tenancies at will, had not a retrospective effect; and the terms of the two clauses are identical in effect. In *Doe* d. *Bennett* v. *Turner* (2) the point was not raised. Lord DENMAN, Ch. J., says, in *Doe* v. *Page*, that " the section (the seventh) is in terms only applicable to the case of a future, or at the most of an existing tenancy at will, and not to the case of a tenancy at will which had been determined, and not existing when the Act passed."

(1) 13 L. J. Q. B. 153.   (2) 56 R. R. 692 (7 M. & W. 226).

(PARKE, B. : Here the defendant was in possession, as tenant from year to year, after the passing of the Act.

ALDERSON, B.: Your argument would exclude three-fourths of England from the operation of the Act.

POLLOCK, C. B. : There are many cases in which lands have been held under an existing tenancy from year to year for fifty or a hundred years.   According to your argument, the statute is not to apply to any of them, but only to tenancies which begin and last for twenty years after the passing of the Act.

ALDERSON, B.: If a man allows his rent to remain unpaid for twenty years, the Act says he shall lose his land.

ROLFE, B. : It was necessary to draw an arbitrary line somewhere, and the Legislature fixed upon that.)

PARKE, B. :

I think no rule ought to be granted.   This case is clearly within the words of the 8th section, which are not the same as those of the 7th section, upon which *Doe* v. *Page* was decided.   The 8th section says, that " when any person shall be in possession or in receipt of the rents and profits of any land, or in the receipt of any rent, *as tenant from year to year, or other period, without any lease in writing, the right of the person entitled subject thereto, &c. shall be deemed to have accrued at the determination of the first of such years or other periods, or at the last time when any rent payable in respect of such tenancy shall have been received, which shall last happen."   Here the defendant's father was in possession of the land as tenant from year to year after the passing of the Act ; therefore the period of limitation is twenty years from the last receipt of rent from him, in April, 1824; it expired, therefore, in April, 1844, and this ejectment was consequently brought too late.   The effect of the Act is to make a Parliamentary convey- ance of the land to the person in possession after that period of twenty years has elapsed.

[*42]

The other Barons concurred.

Rule refused.

1845.
May 3.

[44]

BAILEY AND OTHERS *v.* PORTER.

(14 Meeson & Welsby, 44—46; S. C. 14 L. J. Ex. 244.)

Where a bill of exchange drawn by W. C. upon one J. C. was accepted
by the latter, payable at the plaintiffs' Bank, and the bill was subsequently
indorsed by W. C. to the plaintiffs, and on the day when it became due
there were no assets of J. C.'s in the Bank: Held, in an action by the
plaintiffs as the indorsees against the indorser, that it was not necessary to
show a presentment of the bill to the acceptor (1).

It was proved at the trial by the clerk of the plaintiffs, notice to produce
having been given, that on the day when the bill became due he wrote a
letter to the defendant informing him that "J. C.'s acceptance due that
day was unpaid, and requesting his immediate attention to it:" Held, a
sufficient notice of dishonour (2).

THIS was an action by the indorsees against the indorser of a
bill of exchange, dated the 14th of March, 1842, drawn by one
W. Court upon one James Court, payable three months after date
to the order of the said W. Court, and indorsed by the said
W. Court to the defendant, and by him to the plaintiffs.

The defendant pleaded, first, that the bill was not presented to
James Court on the day when it became due; secondly, that the
defendant had not due notice of presentment and dishonour, on
which issues were joined. At the trial, before Platt, B., at the
last Spring Assizes for the county of Monmouth, it appeared that
the plaintiffs were bankers; that the bill was accepted payable at
their Bank, and on the day it became due they were holders of the
bill; and their clerk on that day examined their books, and ascertained that there were no assets of James Court's in their hands to
meet the bill. No written notice of dishonour was produced, but
[*45]   (notice to produce having been *given) a clerk of the plaintiffs
proved, that, on the day the bill became due, he wrote a letter to
the defendant, informing him that "James Court's acceptance due
that day was unpaid, and requested his immediate attention to it."
For the defendant it was contended, first, that there was no
sufficient presentment proved; and, secondly, that the notice of
dishonour was insufficient; and the case of *Grugeon* v. *Smith* (3) was
cited. The learned Judge overruled the objections, and directed
a verdict to be entered for the plaintiffs, but gave liberty to move
to enter a verdict for the defendant on both or either of the issues.

Greaves moved accordingly, (April 21):

First, there was no sufficient evidence of presentment. Under

(1) See 45 & 46 Vict. c. 61, s. 45 (5).   (2) See *id*. s. 49 (5).—J. G. P.
—J. G. P.   (3) 6 Ad. & El. 499; 2 Nev. & P. 303.

the first issue, presentment to the acceptor ought to have been shown.   It is true that *Sanderson* v. *Judge* (1) may appear to the contrary, but that decision may be doubted.

(POLLOCK, C. B. : We think the case cited an express authority on this point, and we are not disposed to question it.)

Secondly, the notice of dishonour was not sufficient.   In *Furze* v. *Sharwood* (2), it was held that a notice of dishonour is insufficient, if it merely state that the bill has not been paid when due.   This letter amounts to no more than what was stated in the second and third letters in that case, which were held not to be sufficient notices of dishonour.   It is by no means clear here that the debt is demanded. And in *Hartley* v. *Case* (3) it was held, that the notice must contain an intimation that the payment of the bill has been refused by the acceptor ; but the utmost that can be said here is that it is matter of inference.   In *Messenger* v. *Southey* (4), the following letter from the plaintiff to the defendant was held not to be a sufficient notice of dishonour : " This is *to inform you, that the bill I took of you, 15*l.* 2*s.* 6*d.*, is not took up, and 4*s.* 6*d.*, expenses, and the money I must pay immediately.   My son will be in London on Friday morning."   That is a stronger case than the present.

[*46]

(ALDERSON, B. : The plaintiff does not say there that he looks to the defendant for payment.

POLLOCK, C. B. : In this case the writer " requests his immediate attention to it.")

The nearest case to the present is that of *Strange* v. *Price* (5).   That was an action by the indorsee against the indorser, and the letter was as follows : " Messrs. Strange & Co. inform Mr. James Price, that Mr. John Betterton's acceptance, 87*l.* 5*s.*, is not paid.   As indorser, Mr. Price is called upon to pay the money, which will be expected immediately."   That was held not to be a sufficient notice to Price of the dishonour of the bill.   If any inference is to be drawn from the circumstance of the letter calling upon the defendant for the money, the words in that case are stronger than those

(1) 2 H. Bl. 509.
(2) 2 Q. B. 388 ; 2 G. & D. 115.
(3) 4 B. & C. 339.
(4) 1 Man. & G. 70 ; 1 Scott, N. R.
180.
(5) 10 Ad. & El. 125 ; 2 P. & D. 287.

BAILEY
v.
PORTER.

in the present. He also cited *Solarte* v. *Palmer* (1), *Phillips* v. *Gould* (2), and *Boulton* v. *Welch* (3).

Cur. adv. vult.

POLLOCK, C. B., now said :

In the case of *Bailey* v. *Porter*, we are of opinion that there ought to be no rule. The notice in this case appears to us to be a distinct notice that the bill had been dishonoured ; and the expression in it, requesting his "immediate attention to it," must be understood by any person acquainted with business as directing the indorser's attention to the bill, and calling upon him to pay the amount of it. The terms of the notice were, I think, in compliance with the rules laid down in the various cases upon this subject.   *Rule refused.*

1845.
Feb. 15.
May 23.

[72]

MILLS *v.* GOFF.
(14 Meeson & Welsby, 72—75; S. C. 14 L. J. Ex. 249.)

A notice to quit a house held by the plaintiff as tenant from year to year, was given to him on the 17th June, 1840, which required him to quit the premises "on the 11th October now next ensuing, or such other day or time as his said tenancy might expire on." The tenancy had commenced on the 11th October in a former year: Held, that this was not a good notice for the year ending on the 11th October, 1841.

TRESPASS for breaking and entering the dwelling-house and premises of the plaintiff, and expelling him from the possession thereof. Plea, justifying the trespasses under the Small Tenements Act, 1 & 2 Vict. c. 74. The plea alleged, that the plaintiff was tenant of the premises from year to year, at a rent not exceeding 20*l.* ; and that "afterwards, and before the said time when &c., to wit, on the 11th October, 1841, all the term and interest of the plaintiff of and in the same premises ended and became duly determined by a legal notice to quit the same." The replication traversed this allegation in its terms, and issue was joined thereon. At the trial, before Williams, J., at the Summer Assizes for Suffolk, 1844, the defendant put in evidence a notice, dated and served upon the plaintiff on the 17th June, 1840, requiring him to quit the premises in question "on the 11th October now next ensuing, or such other day or time as your said tenancy may expire on." It appeared that the tenancy had commenced on the 11th of October in a previous year. It was objected, for the defendant, that this

(1) 37 R. R. 34 (7 Bing. 530; 1   (2) 8 Car. & P. 355.
Bing. N. C. 194).   (3) 3 Bing. N. C. 688 ; 4 Scott, 425.

notice, which clearly was insufficient for the 11th of the month of
October next ensuing its date, was bad also as a notice to quit in
any subsequent year, and that the issue ought therefore to be found
for the plaintiff.   The learned Judge thought that it was a good
notice to quit in October, 1841, and the jury accordingly, under his
direction, found for the *defendant.   A rule having been obtained   [*73]
for a new trial, on the ground of misdirection,

Byles, Serjt., showed cause in Hilary vacation, (Feb. 15) :

[He cited *Doe* d. *The Duke of Bedford* v. *Kightley* (1), *Doe* d.
Lord Huntingtower v. *Culliford* (2), and *Leech* v. *Bailey* (3).]

In this Term, (May 3),   [74]

Prendergast (*Palmer* with him) was heard in support of the
rule. * * *

POLLOCK, C. B. :

   The single question is, whether this is a good notice to quit for
Michaelmas, Old or New, in the year 1841.   I think it is not.   The
notice was served in June, 1840, and required the plaintiff to quit on
the 11th October then next ensuing, or such other day or time as his
tenancy might expire on.   The natural meaning of such a notice,
and that which every person reading it would understand it to
convey, is this : " You are to quit my premises on the 11th October
next ; but, as I am not certain whether that is the proper day or
not, I do not confine myself to that particular day, but add the
words ' or such other day or time as your tenancy may expire on.' "
If a three months' notice had been sufficient, this notice would have
been good.   It is argued for the defendant, that the notice is meant
to embrace the double alternative, of that not being the very day,
or that year not being the very year.   I think nothing in the notice
sufficiently appears to point to that conclusion, and that the tenant,
when reading it, could not so construe it, but might more *reason-   [*75]
ably infer that his landlord was in error as to the length of notice
necessary, and therefore that the notice was bad.   In the case of
Doe d. *Lord Huntingtower* v. *Culliford*, which has been referred to,
the notice was dated on the 27th, and served on the 28th September,
and required the tenant to quit " at Lady Day next, or at the end
of his current year."   The tenancy expired at Michaelmas ; and the

(1) 4 R. R. 375 (7 T. R. 63).   248).
(2) 44 R. R. 878 (4 Dowl. & By.   (3) 6 Price, 504.

MILLS
v.
GOFF.

COURT held, that it must reasonably be construed to mean a six months' notice, and not a two days' notice. BAYLEY, J., says, "We are to look to the intention of the landlord, when general language is used, which is open to doubt; the rule is to make it sensible, not insensible. The state of the defendant's holding shows it to be quite clear that the landlord did not mean the year ending Michaelmas Day. He could not intend to give a notice to quit in two days, because that would be no notice whatever." But here the notice is sensible and pertinent as a three months' notice, with reference to the subsequent Michaelmas; and if the landlord had intended it to operate as a notice for a subsequent year, he should have given the tenant more distinct information. The notice is therefore bad, and the rule for a new trial must be absolute.

ALDERSON, B., concurred.

ROLFE, B.:

I am of the same opinion. If it had been in these terms, "I give you notice to quit on the 11th October now next ensuing, or, if that be not long enough to make this notice good, then at the end of the next year of your tenancy," that would have been sufficient.

_____•_____   *Rule absolute.*

1845.
April 23.

[76]

THE CALDER AND HEBBLE NAVIGATION COMPANY v. PILLING AND OTHERS (1).

(14 Meeson & Welsby, 76—91; S. C. 14 L. J. Ex. 223; 9 Jur. 377; 3 Rail. Cas. 735.)

By a local Act, 6 Geo. IV. c. lxxi. the Company of Proprietors of a public navigation were empowered to make bye-laws for (*inter alia*) the good government of the Company, and the good and orderly using the navigation. The Company made a bye-law that the navigation should be closed on every Sunday throughout the year, and that no business should be transacted thereon during such time, (works of necessity only excepted), nor should any person during such time navigate any boat, &c., nor should any boat, &c. pass along any part of the said navigation on any Sunday, except for a reasonable distance for the purpose of mooring the same, and except on some extraordinary necessity, or for the purpose of going to, or returning from, any place of Divine worship: Held, that the Act did not authorize the Company to make the above bye-law, and that it was illegal and void.

TRESPASS for breaking and entering a close of the plaintiffs, being part of a certain canal called the Calder and Hebble Navigation,

(1) Distinguished in *Thomas* v. *Sutters* [1900] 1 Ch. 10, 69 L. J. Ch. 27, C. A.—J. G. P.

in the county of York, and then forcing and breaking a chain of the plaintiffs, then fastened across the said canal.

Plea, that, before and at the said time when &c., the said close was part of a public or common canal or navigation, that is to say, the Calder and Hebble Navigation, navigable for boats, barges, lighters, and other vessels, under certain Acts of Parliament, to wit, the 9 Geo. IV. c. lxxi. (and others, setting out the titles); and because the said chain, at the said time when &c., had been and was unlawfully and wrongfully placed, suspended, and fastened across the said canal, and obstructing the same, and the navigation thereof, at the said close in which &c., so that without removing the said obstruction, the liege subjects of our lady the Queen then could not navigate or pass upon and along the canal at the said close, &c., with their barges, &c., carrying therein goods, &c., as under and by virtue of the said statutes they otherwise ought to have done, and would have done; and because one John Wood, then being a liege subject of our lady the Queen, having, at the said time when &c., occasion to navigate on the said canal, at the said close, &c., with certain boats and other vessels of him the said John Wood, fit and proper &c., and not exceeding &c., for the purpose of carrying therein divers goods, wares, and merchandise, then loaded and being in and upon the said boats, &c., and being then so obstructed as *aforesaid, therefore the defendants, as servants of the said John Wood, and by his command, at the said time when &c., in order to remove the said obstruction, and that the said John Wood might be able to navigate on the said canal, &c., entered on the said close, and struck, forced, and broke the said chain, then being suspended and fastened, and obstructing as aforesaid, as they lawfully might for the cause aforesaid &c.

[*77]

Replication, that, after the passing of the said several statutes, and after the executing and completing of the several works thereby respectively authorized, and before the said time when &c., to wit, &c., at a general meeting of the Company of Proprietors of the said Calder and Hebble Navigation, held at &c., pursuant to the statute in such case made and provided, the said Company of Proprietors, in pursuance and by virtue of the powers and authorities to them given and granted by the said several statutes, &c., did make, constitute, and publish the following rule, bye-law, and constitution, in writing, under the common seal of the said Company, for the good government of the said Company, and for the good and orderly using the said navigation, and all such

warehouses, wharfs, passages, locks, and other things that were or
should be made for the same, and of and concerning all such
vessels, goods, and commodities as should be navigated and
conveyed thereon, and also for the well-governing of the bargemen,
watermen, and boatmen who should carry any goods, wares, or
merchandises upon any part of the said navigation, (that is to say),
"We, the Company of Proprietors of the Calder and Hebble
Navigation, in pursuance and by virtue of the powers and
authorities to us given and granted in and by the several statutes
in such case made and provided, some or one of them, do hereby
make and constitute the following rule, bye-law, and constitution,
for the good governing of the said Company, and for the good and

[*78]   orderly *using the said navigation, and all warehouses, wharfs,
and passages, locks, and other things that are or shall be made for
the same, and of and concerning all such vessels, goods, and
merchandise as shall be navigating and conveyed thereon, and also
for the well governing of the bargemen, watermen, and boatmen
who shall carry any goods, wares, or merchandise, upon any part
of the said navigation, (that is to say) ; that the said navigation,
and all such warehouses, &c., be closed on every Sunday throughout
the year, that is to say, from twelve o'clock each Saturday night
until twelve o'clock each Sunday night, and that no business shall
be transacted thereon or thereat during such time, (works of
necessity only excepted), nor shall any person during such time
navigate any boat, barge, or other vessel, whether empty or laden
with any goods, wares, or merchandise, nor shall any such boat,
barge, or other vessel be allowed to pass along any part of the said
navigation on any Sunday, on any pretence whatever, after twelve
o'clock on each Saturday night, except for such distance, not
exceeding 500 yards, as may be reasonable and necessary for the
safe mooring of such boat, &c., and except it be on some extraordinary necessity, or for the purpose of going to or returning from
any place of Divine worship; and if any bargeman, waterman, or
boatman, or other person having the charge of any boat, barge, or
other vessel navigating on any part of the said navigation, or any
person employed on the said navigation, or at any of the warehouses, wharfs, passages, locks, and other things that are or shall
be made for the same, belonging to the said Company, shall offend
in any of the premises, he, she, or they shall forfeit and pay for
every such offence the sum of 5l., to be recovered and employed as
directed by the said Acts." Of which said bye-law and constitution

the said John Wood and the defendants afterwards, and before the
said time when &c., viz. on the same day &c., year &c., had notice.
*The replication then went on to aver, that, after the making of
the bye-law, the Company, in pursuance thereof, and before the
said time when &c., suspended and fastened the said chain across
the cut in question, for the purpose of enforcing obedience to the
bye-law, &c., and for the good and orderly using the navigation,
but so as to afford the free use of the navigation on due compliance
with the rules and regulations thereof, such suspension and fastening
of the said chain, &c., being reasonable and necessary for that
purpose ; and that the said chain &c. remained and was so fastened
and suspended &c., until the defendants, well knowing the premises,
at the said time when &c., being on a Sunday, to wit, &c., of their
own wrong, entered on the said close in which &c., and struck,
forced, and broke the said chain, in manner and form as in the
declaration mentioned, for the purpose of enabling the said John
Wood to navigate upon and pass along the said canal, at the said
place &c., with his said boats &c., at the said time &c., and for a
distance exceeding 500 yards, and for purposes other than for going
to or returning from any place of Divine worship, and not on any
business of necessity, nor for any work of necessity, and there being
no extraordinary necessity for navigating upon or passing along
the said canal with the said boats &c. on that occasion, in violation
of and against the said bye-law and constitution, &c.

Demurrer, assigning for causes, amongst others, that the said
replication does not show with sufficient certainty, how the said
bye-law mentioned could be for the good government of the said
Company, and for the good or orderly using the said navigation,
and the warehouses, &c., and for the well governing of the bargemen, watermen, &c., or how the said Company were authorized, by
reason of the said statute or otherwise, to make the said bye-law.

The defendants' points were, that the replication did not *show,   [*80]
with sufficient certainty, how the bye-law was made in pursuance
of the alleged Acts of Parliament, and that it did not disclose a
valid bye-law, or such as rendered the defendants trespassers.

The plaintiffs' point was, that the bye-law was good and valid.

Cowling, in support of the demurrer :

The question in this case is, whether this bye-law, made under
the power given by the 37th section of the Act 9 Geo. III. c. lxxi.
(local and personal), is valid or not. The defendants contend that

CALDER
AND HEBBLE
NAVIGATION
COMPANY
v.
PILLING.

it is bad, for several reasons. By that section it is enacted, "that the Company of Proprietors, their successors and assigns for the time being, shall have power and authority, at any general meeting to be held &c., to make such new rules, bye-laws, and constitutions for the good government of the Company, and for the good and orderly using the said navigation, and all warehouses, wharfs, passages, locks, and other things that shall be made for the same, and all such vessels, goods, and commodities, as shall be navigated and conveyed thereon, and also for the well governing of the bargemen, watermen, and boatmen who shall carry any goods, wares, or merchandise upon any part of the said navigation, and from time to time to alter or repeal the said bye-laws and constitutions, and to impose and inflict such reasonable fines or forfeitures upon all persons offending against the same as to the major part of the said general meeting shall seem meet, not exceeding the sum of 5l. for any one offence," &c. And the 50th section makes it a public navigation, and gives the public liberty to use the navigation, subject to the bye-laws. The power of making bye-laws is an extraordinary one, and such a power ought to be construed strictly. First, this bye-law is in restraint of trade, and it is laid down as a principle that all bye-laws in restraint of trade

[*81]

must be reasonable and beneficial *to the public, or else they cannot be supported: *The Masters &c., of Gunmakers* v. *Fell* (1), *Bosworth* v. *Herne* (2). [Secondly, the Act only gives power to inflict fines upon persons offending : it gives no power to stop the canal by a chain : *Adley* v. *Reeves* (3) ; Com. Dig., tit. " Bye-law," (E. 1) and (E. 2).]

[82]

(POLLOCK, C. B.: Put this on the footing of a public road,—a canal is a public highway,—what right have they to put a chain across it ?

ALDERSON, B.: The extent of the general law is limited by the penalty, and, if so, so must this private Act.

[83]

This bye-law is altogether bad. [He cited *The Tailors of Ipswich* (4) and *Dodwell* v. *The University of Oxford* (5).] If persons offend by travelling on Sunday, they are punishable in the Ecclesiastical Court.

(1) Willes, 389.   (4) 11 Co. Rep. 53, 54 a.
2) Cas. temp. Hardw. 409.   (5) 2 Vent. 33, 34.
(3) 14 R. R. 582 (2 M. & S. 53).

(POLLOCK, C. B.: What do you say to the stat. 29 Car. II. c. 7, s. 2, which enacts, " that no person shall use, employ, or travel upon the Lord's Day with any boat, wherry, lighter, or barge, except it be on some extraordinary occasion, to be allowed by some justice of the peace of the county, or head officer, or some justice of the peace of the city, borough, or town corporate, where the fact shall be committed, upon pain that every person so offending shall forfeit the sum of 5s. for every such offence? ")

That Act has been repealed by the Thames Act, 7 & 8 Geo. IV. c. lxxv. s. 1, which, although enacted for a local object, viz. the regulation of the watermen on the Thames, has a clause which declares that it shall be deemed and taken to be a public Act. Besides, the 29 Car. II. c. 7, even if not repealed, does not apply to the case of canals, or other modes of travelling unknown at the time it was passed : *Sandiman* v. *Breach* (1). But even if it were applicable, this bye-law does not conform to that statute.

(ROLFE, B.: If the doing of the act be not prohibited by any public statute, can any private bye-law go further, and impose a penalty for doing it? Suppose, for instance, a bye-law were to impose a penalty for an assault, would not that be bad?)

Yes; that is borne out by the case of *The Tailors of Ipswich* (2) ; and *Rex* v. *Lord Grosvenor* (3) seems an authority to the same effect. All restraints imposed by bye-laws, until a satisfactory reason is shown for them, are invalid. (He cited also *Reg.* v. *The Governors of Darlington Free Grammar School* (4).)

Addison, contrà :

This is a reasonable bye-law, and in *every respect pursuant to [*84] the Act. It professes to be made for " the good governing of the Company, and for the good and orderly using of the navigation." The putting the chain across has nothing to do with the bye-law itself; but it is averred in the replication, that the chain was placed there for the purpose of enforcing obedience to the bye-law, and for the good and orderly using of the navigation ; and it is averred that the suspension and affixing of the chain was reasonable and necessary for that purpose, and that is admitted by the demurrer.

(1) 31 R. R. 169 (7 B. & C 96; 9 Dowl. & Ry. 659).

(2) 11 Co. Rep. 54 a.

(3) 20 R. R. 732 (2 Stark. N. P. C. 512).

(4) 66 R. R. 521 (6 Q. B. 682.)

(POLLOCK, C. B.: The defendant, by demurring to the replication, does not admit that. If it be a mere question of fact, then it
is conceded that the fact is admitted; but if in point of law it be
not justifiable, it is not admitted.

ALDERSON, B.: If a bye-law to prohibit navigation on the canal
on Sunday be justifiable, then you had a right to put up the chain.)

The sole question, therefore, is, whether the bye-law is a good and
reasonable one or not. [The stat. 29 Car. II. c. 7, s. 2, is still in
[85]   force.] It has been said it has been repealed by the Thames Act,
7 & 8 Geo. IV. c. lxxv.; but that Act was passed for purposes
purely local, and the general words of the first section are qualified
by subsequent sections, which show that the Legislature only
intended to repeal the 29 Car. II. c. 7, as to those limits within
which the Thames Act was to be in force.

(POLLOCK, C. B.: It is rather an anomaly to find the general
repeal of a public Act contained in a private one.)

* * Then, if the stat. 29 Car. II. c. 7, s. 2, be not repealed, it
is still penal to travel in barges on Sunday, and if so, it would
be impossible to call a bye-law unreasonable, which is in exact
accordance with the spirit of a public statute. * * *

[86]   (POLLOCK, C. B.: Suppose the 29 Car. II. c. 7, to be still in
force, the using a boat on Sunday is prohibited under a penalty
of 5s. How can it be said that 5l. is a reasonable sum, when the
general statute says 5s. is enough ? it is twenty times the amount.)

The plaintiffs have a right to use the Thames Act so far as to show
that there is a penalty of 5l. given by it, which shows that the
penalty imposed by the stat. 29 Car. II. c. 7, is not to govern the
case, and that the former is a reasonable penalty in the contemplation of the Legislature. By the 37th section of this Act, 9 Geo. III.
c. lxxi. the Company are empowered to make such new rules, bye-
laws, and constitutions for the good of the Company, and for the
good and orderly using the navigation, and to impose such reasonable fines upon all persons offending against the same, as to the
major part of the general meeting should seem meet, not exceeding
the sum of 5l.

(ALDERSON, B.: This is for not using it. An " orderly using " of
it must be when the person uses it.)

A good and orderly use of the navigation may mean the not using it on a Sunday. It is also "for the well governing of the bargemen, &c., who shall carry goods, wares, or merchandise upon any part of the said navigation." Surely that may apply to the well governing them in their general conduct.

(ALDERSON, B. : The well governing the bargemen, &c. must mean in the carriage of goods upon the navigation. The Act means to provide for the management of the canal ; why not leave the management of other matters to the higher law ? Would the corporation of London be justified in putting a chain across the Thames to prevent steamers going up it on a Sunday ?)

＊　＊　＊　＊　＊

Cowling, in reply, was stopped by the COURT.

[87]

ALDERSON, B. (1) :

The only question in this case is, whether this bye-law be good or not. For the purpose of determining that, we must look to the powers to make bye-laws given by the Legislature to this Company, in order to see whether this bye-law is within the scope of their authority, or whether it does not relate to matters which ought to be left to the general law of the land, by which the general conduct of the Queen's subjects is regulated. The power of making bye-laws is conferred upon the Company of Proprietors of this navigation by a local Act, 9 Geo. III. c. lxxi., s. 37, by which it is enacted, that "the Company of Proprietors, their successors and assigns, for the time being, shall have power and authority to make such new rules, bye-laws, and constitutions for the good government of the said Company, and for the good and orderly using the said navigation, and all warehouses, wharfs, passages, locks, and other things that shall be made for the same, and of and concerning all such vessels, goods, *and commodities as shall be navigated and conveyed thereon, and also for the well governing of the bargemen, watermen, and boatmen who shall carry any goods, wares, or merchandise upon any part of the said navigation." Now, looking at these words, it appears to me that all the power which the Legislature intended to give this company with respect to making laws for the government of this navigation, was solely for the orderly use of the navigation ; that is to say, to regulate in what manner and order the navigation should be used, so as to secure to the public the greatest convenience in the use of it. The rules

[*88]

(1) Pollock, C. B., had left the Court.

CALDER
AND HEBBLE
NAVIGATION
COMPANY
r.
PILLING.

which they are empowered to make have nothing to do with the regulation of moral or religious conduct, which are left to the general law of the land, and to the laws of God. The rules of the Company are to be solely for the purpose of convenience, and to advance the orderly use of the navigation; such, for instance, as that A. shall not go before B.; that vessels shall not pass during particular periods, and such like, in order that the greatest number of barges and other vessels may, with the greatest convenience, be able to pass along the navigation. That, it appears to me, is the power conferred on the Company relative to making rules "for the good and orderly using of the navigation." Then we come to the next clause, which empowers them also to make rules "concerning vessels, goods, and commodities which shall be navigated and conveyed thereon." Under this the Company may, for aught I know, have power to regulate the shape of the vessels to be used on the navigation, so as to render it most convenient for the greatest number; as, for instance, that no boats shall be employed except such as are of a certain width or length, &c., all which are matters very fit and proper to be regulated by the Company. So, again, they are empowered by this section to make bye-laws "for the well

[*89]

governing of the bargemen, watermen, and boatmen who *shall carry any goods, wares, and merchandise upon any part of the navigation." I do not apprehend that these words mean the government of those persons with the view of regulating their good conduct and character, but only of their conduct in their character of "bargemen, watermen, and boatmen who shall carry goods, wares, or merchandise along the navigation," that is to say, in their capacity of bargemen, watermen, and boatmen in so far as they carry goods on the navigation. The Company are to regulate the manner of carrying goods there; but as to the moral and religious conduct of those who carry them, that is a matter not left to the Company. If this be so, I have now gone through all the words of the section, and none of them say that these persons are to have any power to enforce the proper observance of religious duties. I am far from saying that the object which the framers of this rule had in view was not a proper one; but the course they have taken is not the proper one for carrying that object into effect, as I think they had no power under the statute to make such a bye-law. In doing so, they have exceeded their powers; and I am therefore of opinion, that the bye-law they have made is an illegal one, and that the demurrer must be allowed.

ROLFE, B. :

    I am of the same opinion. It has been contended by the defendants' counsel, that, by the Thames Act of 7 & 8 Geo. IV. c. 75, the stat. 29 Car. II. c. 7, s. 2, which prohibits all persons from using boats or barges on a Sunday, has been repealed. That I think is rather doubtful, but, in considering the subject before us, I do not think it is in the smallest degree material to determine that question. Supposing the 29 Car. II. c. 7, s. 2, is repealed, and that it is in general lawful to use barges or boats on a Sunday, then this bye-law is monstrous; for, if it be generally lawful to use barges on a Sunday, what *right have the proprietors of a particular navigation to prevent that, and say, that "We, acting *pro salute animarum* of the Queen's subjects, will not allow them to do what the law allows." But suppose, on the other hand, that the argument of the plaintiffs' counsel is right, and that the stat. 29 Car. II. c. 7, is still in force, then the Legislature by that Act have said, that it is not decorous and proper to use barges on a Sunday, and whoever does so shall pay a penalty of 5*s.*; and if so, what right has a Company to say there shall be a cumulative penalty, and the offender shall forfeit 5*l.*? It is perfectly clear, as pointed out by my brother ALDERSON, that the Company have done something quite beyond the power which the Legislature meant to repose in them. The Legislature says to the Company, "You may make bye-laws for the good and orderly navigation of the canal, and for the government of the boatmen and bargemen connected with it;" that is to say, in order that the navigation may be used with the utmost degree of convenience to every one. Now, the only point that occurred to me was this: whether, on a state of facts properly alleged, a bye-law like this might not, under peculiar circumstances, be held good. Suppose, for instance, the Company were to come to the conclusion that, in order to secure a due supply of water in the canal, it was necessary to have no navigation on it during one day out of seven, perhaps they would have power to close the canal for one day out of seven, in order to make the navigation good during the other six, and in that case to say, "If this must be done, we will take Sunday as the fittest day." But it is not contended that that was the object of the plaintiffs in this case; they only say that it was decorous that the canal should not be used on Sundays. That, I think, is a matter out of the cognisance of the Company, and consequently that their bye-law founded on that principle is void.

CALDER
AND HEBBLE
NAVIGATION
COMPANY
v.
PILLING.

[*90]

CALDER
AND HEBBLE
NAVIGATION
COMPANY
*.
PILLING.
[91]

ALDERSON, B., afterwards added, that POLLOCK, C. B., and PLATT, B., had, before they left the Court, expressed their full concurrence in the judgment given.

Judgment for the defendants.

1845.
May 6.
—
[112]

TURNER *v.* MASON.

(14 Meeson & Welsby, 112—118; S. C. 2 Dowl. & L. 898 ; 14 L. J. Ex. 311.)

Assumpsit for the wrongful dismissal of a domestic servant, without a month's notice or payment of a month's wages. Plea, that the plaintiff requested the defendant to give her leave to absent herself from his service during the night, that he refused such leave, and forbade her from so absenting herself, and that against his will she nevertheless absented herself for the night, and until the following day, whereupon he discharged her. Replication, that when the plaintiff requested the defendant to give her leave to absent herself from his service, her mother had been seized with sudden and violent sickness, and was in imminent danger of death, and believing herself likely to die, requested the plaintiff to visit her to see her before her death, whereupon the plaintiff requested the defendant to give her leave to absent herself for that purpose, she not being likely thereby to cause any injury or hindrance to his domestic affairs, and not intending to be thereby guilty of any improper omission or unreasonable delay of her duties; and because the defendant wrongfully and unjustly forbade her from so absenting herself for the purpose of visiting her mother, &c., she left his house and service, and absented herself for that purpose for the time mentioned in the plea, the same being a reasonable time in that behalf, and she not causing thereby any hindrance to his domestic affairs, nor being thereby guilty of any improper omission or unreasonable delay of her duties, as she lawfully might, &c.: Held, on demurrer, that the plea was good, as showing a dismissal for disobedience to a lawful order of the master, and that the replication was bad, as showing no sufficient excuse for such disobedience.

ASSUMPSIT. The declaration stated, that, in consideration that the plaintiff, at the request of the defendant, would become the servant of the defendant, to wit, in the capacity of housemaid, for certain wages, to wit, the wages of 7*l.* for the year, the defendant promised the plaintiff to employ her in that capacity, and for the wages aforesaid, and to continue her in such situation until the expiration of a month after notice or warning given by the plaintiff or defendant, or either of them, to put an end to such service ; and that, in case the defendant should put an end to such service without such notice or warning, he should pay to the plaintiff the said wages for a month. It then alleged that the plaintiff became the servant of the defendant upon the terms aforesaid, and that, although she was ready and willing to continue in such service, yet the defendant discharged her without such notice or warning as

aforesaid. Plea, that before the defendant discharged the plaintiff, as
in the declaration mentioned, to wit, on &c., the plaintiff requested
the defendant to give her leave to absent herself from his dwelling-
house, and from his said service and employ, during the then
ensuing night, and until the following day, and thereupon the
defendant then refused the said plaintiff such leave as aforesaid,
and forbade her from absenting herself from the said dwelling-
house, or from his said service or employ; and the said plaintiff
then, without the leave and license and against *the will of the
defendant, and disregarding her having been so forbidden as aforesaid, left the said defendant's dwelling-house, and his said service
and employ, and absented herself therefrom, from the day and year
last aforesaid, during the following night, and until the following
day, and therefore the defendant did then discharge the plaintiff
from his said service and employ. Verification.

Replication, that just before the said time when the plaintiff so
requested the defendant to give her leave to absent herself from his
said dwelling-house, and from his said service and employ, to wit,
on &c., one Hannah Turner, the mother of the plaintiff, had been
seized with sudden and violent sickness, and was then in imminent
peril of death, and by reason thereof the said H. Turner believed
herself likely to die, and being anxious to see the plaintiff before
her death, had then requested the plaintiff to visit her, whereupon
the plaintiff, at the said time when &c., requested the defendant to
give her leave to absent herself from his said dwelling-house, and
from his said service and employ, during the then ensuing night
and until the following day, (the same being a reasonable time in
that behalf), for the purpose of enabling the said plaintiff to visit
her said mother in her said sickness, and to see her before her
death; she the plaintiff not being thereby likely to cause any injury
or hindrance to the said defendant in his domestic affairs and
business, and not intending to be thereby guilty of any improper
omission, or of any unreasonable delay of her duties as such
servant; and because the defendant then wrongfully and unjustly
forbade her from so absenting herself from his said dwelling-house,
and from his said service and employ, she the plaintiff, for the
purpose of visiting her said mother in her said sickness, and seeing
her before her death, at the said time when, &c., left the defendant's said dwelling-house, and his said service and employ, and
*absented herself therefrom from the day and year, and for the
time in the said plea mentioned, (the same being a reasonable time

TURNER
v.
MASON.

[*113]

[*114]

TURNER
v.
MASON.

in that behalf), and for no other or longer period, or for no other
or different purpose, she the said plaintiff not thereby causing any
injury or hindrance to the defendant in his said domestic affairs or
business, nor being thereby guilty of any improper omission or
unreasonable delay of her duties as such servant of the said
defendant as aforesaid, as she lawfully might for the cause aforesaid.
Verification.

Special demurrer, assigning for causes, that the replication was
a departure from the declaration, which alleges that the plaintiff
was ready and willing to continue in the service of the defendant
until a month after notice or warning; and that the replication
admits a breach of contract, which justified the defendant in
discharging the plaintiff. Joinder in demurrer.

Gray, in support of the demurrer, was stopped by the COURT,
who called upon

Badeley, contrà :

The plea is bad in substance. The defendant thereby claims,
under all circumstances, and without any limitation, to retain the
plaintiff in his service, and not to permit her absence during the
term of it. There is no allegation that he had any need of her
services, or that her request to absent herself was unreasonable in
itself, or for an unreasonable time or purpose. It is setting up a
claim to slavery, instead of service. The contract of hiring and
service must be construed, like all other contracts, reasonably.
Suppose the plaintiff herself had been in peril of death, and had
requested a day's absence for medical advice, would the defendant
have been entitled to refuse that? Again, is she to forego in his
service all moral claims and obligations? He does not allege that
her excuse was false, or that her absence was *inconvenient.

[*115]

(PARKE, B.: This is wilful disobedience of orders.)

There may be a good reason for that.

(POLLOCK, C. B.: Then it should come by way of replication.)

But the master must show it to be a wilful disobedience of lawful
orders.

(ALDERSON, B.: Surely it is a lawful order not to stay out all
night.)

Fillieul v. *Armstrong* (1) is an authority for the plaintiff.

(POLLOCK, C. B. : That was not the case of a domestic servant.)

In *Jacquet* v. *Bower* (2), a plea, to an action for wrongfully discharging the plaintiff and his wife from the defendant's service, that the wife obstinately refused to work for the defendant, wherefore he discharged them, was held bad on general demurrer.

(ALDERSON, B.: That case only shows that obstinately does not necessarily mean unlawfully.

PARKE, B.: The obligation of a domestic servant is to obey all lawful commands. This plea sets out that which *primâ facie* is a lawful command, which you must answer by the replication. Now here the replication alleges the extreme illness of the plaintiff's mother, but does not say the plaintiff gave the defendant notice of that fact ; it only says that was the ground on which she applied for his permission, but not that she communicated it.

ALDERSON, B.: If the mother be very poor, is the daughter to absent herself from her service to work for her, to prevent her starving?

POLLOCK, C. B. : Or, if she has a right to go to the death-bed of her mother or father, why not of any other near friend ?)

The replication alleges expressly that the defendant had no need of her services.

(PARKE, B.: The master is to be the judge of the circumstances under which the servant's services are required, subject to this, that he is to give only lawful commands.)

Badeley cited also *Levison* v. *Bush* (3), and *Callo* v. *Brouncker* (4).

POLLOCK, C. B. :

I am of opinion that this plea is perfectly *good. It discloses an order, in itself perfectly lawful, by the master of a servant, that she shall not leave his house for the night; and alleges, that, notwithstanding that order, she did leave his house and his service, and stayed out all night. She had no right, against his will, to

[*116]

---

(1) 7 Ad. & El. 557.   (3) Lane, 65.
(2) 7 Dowl. P. C. 331.   (4) 4 Car. & P. 518.

TURNER
v.
MASON

leave his service at all. The plea is therefore a good plea. Then
the replication states, that the mother of the plaintiff was ill, and
in peril of death, and that, believing herself likely to die, and being
anxious to see the plaintiff before her death, she had requested the
plaintiff to visit her, whereupon the plaintiff requested the defendant
to give her leave to absent herself for that purpose; and because
he wrongfully refused it, she did absent herself for that purpose,
for the time mentioned in the plea. It does not state that she
gave the defendant any notice of the purpose for which she desired
to absent herself, or that her doing so was of advantage or use to
her mother, but merely that it was to visit her that she might see
her before her death. It is very questionable whether any service
to be rendered to any other person than the master would suffice as
an excuse : she might go, but it would be at the peril of being told
that she could not return. The plea being therefore good, and the
replication bad in form, our judgment must be for the defendant.

PARKE, B. :

I am of the same opinion. The contract between the master and
a domestic servant is a contract to serve for a year, the service to
be determined by a month's warning, or by payment of a month's
wages; subject to the implied condition, that the servant will obey
all lawful orders of the master. It was laid down by Lord
ELLENBOROUGH in *Spain* v. *Arnott* (1), and by me in *Callo* v
Brouncker, and confirmed by the Court of Queen's Bench in *Amor*

[*117]

v. *Fearon* (2), that the wilful disobedience of any *lawful order of
the master is a good cause of discharge. Here the plea discloses
a perfectly lawful order, namely, that the [plaintiff (3)] should not
absent herself from the service during a night, and the plaintiff's
disobedience thereto. Then the question is, whether the replication
discloses sufficient ground of excuse for such disobedience. *Primâ
facie*, the master is to regulate the times when his servant is to go
out from and return to his house. Even if the replication showed
that he had notice of the cause of her request to absent herself, I
do not think it would be sufficient to justify her in disobedience to
his order; there is not any imperative obligation on a daughter
to visit her mother under such circumstances, although it may be
unkind and uncharitable not to permit her. But the replication

(1) 19 R. R. 715 (2 Stark. 256).   (3) 14 M. & W. has "defendant,"
(2) 48 R. R. 584 (9 Ad. & El. 548; 1   which is obviously a slip for plaintiff.
P. & D. 398).   —J. G. P.

states nothing to show that the defendant had any notice or knowledge of the mother's illness. It is therefore clearly bad, and our judgment must be for the defendant.

TURNER
v.
MASON.

ALDERSON, B.:

I am of the same opinion. The plea is a good answer to the action, because it shows the discharge of the plaintiff to have been for wilful disobedience of the defendant's order to stay in his house all night. Then, is the replication a good answer to the plea? It is informal, because it does not show that the mother was likely to die that night, or that it was necessary to go that night to see her, or to stay all night. But if this were otherwise, these circumstances would amount only to a mere moral duty, and do not show any legal right. We are to decide according to the legal obligations of parties. Where is a decision founded upon mere moral obligation to stop? What degree of sickness, what nearness of relationship, is to be sufficient? It is the safest way, therefore, to adhere to the legal obligations arising out of the contract between the parties. There may, undoubtedly, be cases justifying *a wilful disobedience of such an order; as where the servant apprehends danger to her life, or violence to her person, from the master; or where, from an infectious disorder raging in the house, she must go out for the preservation of her life. But the general rule is obedience, and wilful disobedience is a sufficient ground of dismissal.

[*118]

ROLFE, B.:

In truth, the cases suggested by my brother ALDERSON are cases in which there is not legally any disobedience, because they are cases not of lawful orders. It is an unlawful order to direct a servant to continue where she is in danger of violence to her person, or of infectious disease.

Judgment for the defendant.

HINTON *v.* HEATHER.

(14 Meeson & Welsby, 131—135; S. C. 15 L. J. Ex. 39.)

1845.
May 6.

[131]

On the trial of an action for maliciously indicting the plaintiff for an assault, the facts proved were as follows: The defendant came to the house of the plaintiff (which was let out in sets of chambers) to inquire for a person who he said lived there, but being informed that no such person lived there, used abusive language, and on being required by the plaintiff to go away, laid hands upon him, upon which the plaintiff forced him out. There was contradictory evidence as to the degree of force used by the

HINTON
v.
HEATHER.

plaintiff in doing so. The defendant indicted the plaintiff for an assault;
the bill was found, and the indictment tried, and the plaintiff was acquitted.
On the trial of the action, the learned Judge directed the jury, that if the
defendant preferred the indictment with a consciousness that he was in the
wrong in the transaction, there was no reasonable or probable cause for
the indictment : Held, that this direction was substantially correct (1).

CASE for maliciously and without reasonable or probable cause
indicting the plaintiff for an assault on the defendant. Plea, Not
guilty. At the trial, before Pollock, C. B., at the sittings in Middlesex after Hilary Term, it appeared that the indictment which was
the subject of this action arose out of the following circumstances :

The defendant, in the afternoon of the 2nd November, 1844,
came up the staircase of a house in Leicester Square, which is let
out in chambers, and being met on the staircase by the housekeeper, who asked him whom he wanted, replied that he wanted
Mr. Smith. She told him that no person of that name lived in the
house : the defendant replied that he did ; and on the housekeeper's
repeating that no one of that name lived there, the defendant
(according to the housekeeper's evidence) called her a liar, and said
that a person down stairs had told him Mr. Smith occupied offices
at the top of the house, and therefore he should go and see. Some
further altercation took place between them, and at that moment
the plaintiff, who was the proprietor of the house, and had over-
heard the latter part of the conversation, came up stairs, and asked
the defendant whom he wanted. The defendant replied in an
abusive manner, and upon the plaintiff's requiring him to go down
stairs and leave the premises, seized the plaintiff with both hands,
as if to pull him down stairs ; upon which the plaintiff took him by
the collar and forced him out of the premises. According to the
plaintiff's evidence, this was done without any unnecessary violence;
but the defendant called witnesses who stated that he complained
[*132] of having been called a thief, and that his clothes were *torn, and
his hand and thumb bruised. The defendant indicted the plaintiff
and the housekeeper at the next Middlesex Sessions for an assault,
and upon the bill being found, a Bench warrant was, at the defendant's instance, issued for the apprehension of the plaintiff, upon
which he was taken into custody by a policeman and conveyed to a
police station, where he gave bail for his appearance at the following
Sessions. At those Sessions the indictment was tried, and after an
examination of witnesses on both sides, the plaintiff was acquitted.

It was objected for the defendant, at the close of the plaintiff's

(1) See *Hicks* v. *Faulkner*, 8 Q. B. D. 167, 51 L. J. Q. B. 268.—J. G. P.

case, that there was no evidence of want of reasonable and probable cause for the indictment, inasmuch as the plaintiff had
in fact committed an assault on the defendant; for which *Fish*
v. *Scott* (1) was cited as an authority.   The LORD CHIEF BARON ruled
that the case must go to the jury, but gave the defendant leave to
move to enter a nonsuit, if the Court should be of a contrary
opinion; and in summing up, his Lordship stated to the jury, that
if they thought the indictment was preferred by the defendant with
a consciousness that he was in the wrong in the transaction, it was,
in his opinion, without reasonable or probable cause; but that if
more violence was used by the plaintiff on the occasion than was
necessary to remove the defendant from the premises, there was
reasonable and probable cause for the prosecution.   The jury found
a verdict for the plaintiff, damages 20*l*.   In a former part of this
Term, (April 17 and May 3),

   Crowder moved to enter a nonsuit, pursuant to the leave
reserved, or for a new trial, on the ground of misdirection, [relying
on *Fish* v. *Scott* (1)], and he cited *Sutton* v. *Johnstone* (2), and   [133]
Blachford v. *Dod* (3).

   The COURT took time to consider whether a rule should be granted,
and now delivered their judgment.

POLLOCK, C. B. :

   In the case of *Hinton* v. *Heather*, which was moved by *Mr.
Crowder*, we are all of opinion, upon considering the evidence given
by the plaintiff, (who was the defendant in the indictment), that the
mere fact of an assault having been committed by the plaintiff was
not sufficient to constitute reasonable and probable cause for the
indictment, without reference to the other circumstances of the case.
Undoubtedly an assault may be committed under such circumstances as to afford no reasonable or probable cause whatever for an
indictment.   There is, therefore, no ground for a nonsuit in this
case, on the authority of the case referred to, of *Fish* v. *Scott* (1),
which (although probably very correctly decided, and perhaps not
very correctly reported) is apparently an authority for an indictment
whenever an assault has been committed of any kind.   The point I
left to the jury was, that if the indictment was preferred by the
defendant with the consciousness *that he was in the wrong, it was,   [*134]

(1) Peake, 135.   (3) 36 R. R. 532 (2 B. & Ad. 179).
(2) 1 R. R. 257 (1 T. R. 493).

HINTON
*.
HEATHER.

in my opinion, without reasonable or probable cause; and the Court concur in the correctness of that mode of presenting it to the jury. Then, if the matter was for the jury, I am not dissatisfied with the conclusion they came to, and therefore there will be no rule.

ALDERSON, B.:

Without doubt, reasonable and probable cause is a question for the Judge, the moment the facts are determined; but if the facts remain in dispute, the jury must ascertain them, and then the Judge is to direct them whether, in point of law, the facts so ascertained do or do not amount to want of reasonable or probable cause. In this case there are two contradictory statements, one of which seems sufficient to give the defendant a defence, on the ground that there was no want of reasonable and probable cause. On the other hand, the evidence on the part of the plaintiff is directly the reverse. The LORD CHIEF BARON then asks the jury, in substance, whether or not the assault upon the defendant, who first assaulted the plaintiff, was committed under such circumstances as that no reasonable man could have supposed that there was any excess in it. No doubt the plaintiff would be indictable for the assault committed by him in return, if it were excessive; and without doubt, also, the assault might not be excessive, and yet the defendant might have reasonable and probable cause for the indictment, because he may reasonably have supposed it to be excessive. The jury, therefore, are called upon to inquire whether or not the facts are such as that no reasonable man could have supposed the assault to be excessive. If that be the result of the facts, then it is clear there was no reasonable and probable cause for indicting the plaintiff. The question is, whether the defendant has been assaulted in such a manner as that the plaintiff is indictable for it. The substance of what the CHIEF BARON left to the jury was this,—*whether the defendant must have been conscious that he was in the wrong at the time of preferring the indictment; and the jury found for the plaintiff, because they thought that neither the defendant, nor any other reasonable man in his situation, could have believed that he had any reasonable or probable cause for indicting the plaintiff.

[*135]

ROLFE, B.:

I entirely concur, and I think we should not have had much difficulty in the case, if we had directed our attention specifically to the exact point left by the CHIEF BARON to the jury. Our doubt

arose from thinking it had been merely left to the jury to say which
side was right—whether there was excess or no excess: if that had
been the only point left to the jury, I should have thought, although
they found there was no excess, that that did not necessarily show
that there was not probable cause; but it appears that the jury were
not merely directed to say which side was right, but whether the
defendant instituted the prosecution with a consciousness that he
was in the wrong. Now, when that direction comes to be considered, it necessarily implies that there was no excess, and that the
defendant knew that there was no excess. The direction was
therefore right, and consequently there can be no rule.

HINTON
c.
HEATHER.

Rule refused.

WRIGHTSON *v.* MACAULAY (1).

(14 Meeson & Welsby, 214—232; S. C. 15 L. J. Ex. 121.)

1845.
June 4.

[214]

A testator devised real estates to his son and heir-at-law, Reginald H.,
for life, remainder to his first and other sons in tail, remainder to his
daughters in fee; and for default of such issue, to his nephew Reginald H.,
for life, remainder to Richard H., son of his said nephew, for life,
remainder to his first and other sons in tail; and in default of Richard's
being alive at his father's death, or in case of his being alive and taking an
estate under the will, and dying without issue male, then to the use of the
male heir who should be in possession of the ancient estate at M., belonging
to the H. family, for life, and to his first and other sons in tail; and, for
default of a male heir being in possession of the ancient estate at M., or in
default of issue male of such male heir, then to the use of the testator's
own right heirs, being of the name of Heber, in fee.

Reginald H., the son, enjoyed the estate for life, and died without issue;
then Reginald the nephew, and Richard, successively enjoyed it for life,
and the latter died without issue; and at his death there was no heir of the
testator existing of the name of Heber: Held, that the ultimate limitation
in fee vested on the death of the testator, in his son and heir-at-law,
Reginald H.

BY an order of his Honour the VICE-CHANCELLOR, Sir JAMES
WIGRAM, bearing date the 3rd day of August, 1844, the following
case was directed to be submitted for the opinion of the Barons of
her Majesty's Court of Exchequer:

The Rev. John Heber was, at the times of making his will and
of his decease, seised in fee simple of certain freehold estates of
inheritance, situate in the parish of Buckden, in the county of
York.

At the date of the will of the said John Heber, the manors
of East and West Marton, and divers estates in the parish of

---

(1) The subsequent proceedings
before Vice-Chancellor Sir James
Wigram are reported in 9 Hare, 487;
17 L. J. Ch. 54.—J. G. P.

Marton, which for a great number of years had been in the possession of the elder branch of the Heber family, were then vested in Elizabeth Heber for life, with remainder to the testator's nephew, Reginald Heber, (the father of the defendant, Mary Macaulay), for life, with remainder to his first and other sons successively in tail male, with divers remainders over; and this property is described by the Rev. John Heber, in his will, as the ancient estate at Marton, belonging to the Heber family.

The Rev. John Heber duly signed and published his last will and testament in writing, bearing date the 26th day of June, 1775, which was executed and attested in the manner then required by law for rendering valid devises of freehold estates; and thereby (amongst other things) he gave and devised all his freehold messuages, lands, tenements, and hereditaments, with their appur-

[*215] tenances, situate *and being at Marton, Buckden, and elsewhere, which he then was or thereafter should or might be seised of, with their appurtenances, to the Honourable Sir George Cayley, Bart., Reginald Heber, his nephew, and Cuthbert Allanson, and the survivors and survivor of them, and the heirs of such survivor, to the use of his son Reginald Heber, and his assigns, for and during the term of his natural life, without impeachment of or for any manner of waste; and from and after the determination of that estate, to the use of them the said Sir George Cayley, Reginald Heber his nephew, and Cuthbert Allanson, their heirs and assigns, for and during the natural life of his said son Reginald, (upon trust to support contingent remainders); and from and after the decease of his said son Reginald Heber, then to the use and behoof of the first son of the body of the said Reginald Heber his son, on the body of Mary his then wife, or any thereafter taken wife, to be begotten, and the heirs male of the body of such first son lawfully issuing; and for default of such issue, to the second, third, fourth, fifth, sixth, seventh, and all and every other son and sons of the body of his said son Reginald, on the body of his then present, or any other after-taken wife, to be begotten severally, successively, and in remainder, (in tail male); and for default of such issue, to the use and behoof of such of the daughter and daughters, if more than one, of the body of the said Reginald Heber on the body of the said Mary his then wife, or of any thereafter taken wife, to be begotten, as should be living at the time of his decease, or should be born in due time afterwards, and the heirs and assigns of such daughter and daughters respectively, if more than one, as tenants

in common; and in default of such issue, male and female, of the WRIGHTSON
body of his said son on the body of his then present or any there- MACAULAY.
after taken wife, begotten or to be begotten, then to the use and
behoof of his said *nephew Reginald Heber, and his assigns, for   [*216]
and during the term of his natural life, without impeachment of
or for any manner of waste; and from and after the determination
of that estate, to the use of them the said Sir George Cayley,
Reginald Heber his nephew, and Cuthbert Allanson, their heirs
and assigns, for and during the natural life of his said nephew
Reginald Heber, (upon trust to support contingent remainders);
and after the decease of his said nephew Reginald Heber, then to
the use and behoof of Richard Heber, son of the said Reginald
Heber, his nephew, if he should be living at his father's decease,
for and during the term of his natural life, without impeachment
of waste; and after the determination of that estate, to the use of
them the said Sir George Cayley, Reginald Heber his nephew, and
Cuthbert Allanson, their heirs and assigns, for and during the
natural life of the said Richard Heber, son of his said nephew,
(upon trust to support contingent remainders); and from and after
the decease of the said Richard Heber, the son of his said nephew
Reginald Heber, then to and for the use of the first son of the body
of the said Richard Heber lawfully to be begotten, and the heirs
male of the body of such first son lawfully issuing; and for default
of such issue, to the second, third, fourth, fifth, sixth, seventh, and
all and every son and sons of the body of the said Richard Heber,
to be lawfully begotten (successively in tail male); and in default
of the said Richard Heber being alive at the time of his father's
decease, or in case of his being alive, and taking an estate for life
by virtue of his said will, and dying without issue male of his body
as aforesaid, then to the use and behoof of the male heir of who
should be in possession of, and lawfully entitled for the time being
unto the ancient estate at Marton, belonging to the Heber family,
and the assigns of such male heir as last aforesaid, for and during
the term of his natural life, without impeachment of waste; and
from and after the *determination of that estate, to the use of them   [*217]
the said Sir George Cayley, Reginald Heber his nephew, and
Cuthbert Allanson, and their heirs, and the survivor of them and
his heirs, for and during the natural life of such male heir as last
aforesaid, (upon trust to support contingent remainders); and from
and after his decease, then to the use and behoof of the first son of
the body of such male heir as aforesaid lawfully begotten, and the

heirs male of the body of such first son lawfully issuing, (with
similar limitations as before, to the other sons successively in tail
male) ; and for default of a male heir being in possession of and
entitled unto the said ancient estate at Marton, at the times thereinbefore for that purpose respectively mentioned, or in default of
issue male of such male heir as aforesaid, then to the use of his
own right heirs, being of the name of Heber, and his, her, and
their heirs and assigns for ever.

The Rev. John Heber died in the year 1775, without having
revoked or altered his will, having had issue two children, and no
more ; namely, Reginald Heber, the first devisee for life, his eldest
son and heir-at-law, and John Heber, who died intestate and without issue, in the lifetime of his father. Reginald Heber entered
into possession or the receipt of the rents and profits of the estates
in Buckden devised to him for his life, and continued in such
possession or receipt up to the time of his death.

Reginald Heber, the son of the testator John Heber, made his
will, dated the 19th January, 1799, duly executed and attested to
pass freehold estates by devise ; but his will did not contain any
effectual devise of the estates in Buckden, mentioned in the will of
his father, as against his (the said Reginald Heber's) heir-at-law.
He died in the year 1799, without ever having had any issue ; and
Reginald Heber, the nephew of the Rev. John Heber, and the
second devisee for life mentioned in his will, and also the tenant
[*218] for life of the ancient family estates at Marton, *then entered into
the possession or the receipt of the rents and profits of the said
devised estates, and continued in such possession up to the time of
his death, which took place in the year 1804 ; and thereupon his
eldest son, Richard Heber, the third devisee for life mentioned in
the said will, and also the tenant in tail of the ancient family
estates at Marton, entered into the possession or the receipt of the
rents and profits of the said devised estates, and continued in such
possession or receipt up to the time of his death, which took place
on the 14th day of October, 1833. The said Richard Heber never
had any issue.

The said Richard Heber, in the year 1827, suffered a recovery of
the ancient family estate at Marton, and, by force of the recovery,
and the deed to declare the uses thereof, he became entitled thereto
as tenant in fee simple in possession, thereby barring the estate tail
which had existed in such estates in favour of his younger brother
Reginald Heber, the late Bishop of Calcutta. Richard Heber made

his will, dated the 1st day of September, 1827, executed and attested in the manner then required by law for rendering valid devises of freehold estates, whereby he gave and devised all his real estate, including, among other things, the ancient estate at Marton, to the defendant (his half-sister), a daughter of his father, Reginald Heber, by his second wife, then Mary Cholmondeley, widow, but now the wife of the defendant, Samuel Herrick Macaulay, who, upon his death in the year 1838, entered into and has ever since continued and is now in possession of that estate.

The eldest brother of the testator John Heber was Thomas Heber, who was tenant for life of the estate called by the testator John Heber, in his will, the ancient estate at Marton, belonging to the Heber family, with remainder to his first and other sons successively in tail male.

Thomas Heber died in 1752, in the life-time of John *Heber, leaving only two sons him surviving, namely, Richard Heber, his eldest son, and Reginald Heber, the second devisee for life mentioned in the will. Richard Heber, the eldest son of Thomas Heber, died in the year 1766, leaving his two children him surviving, namely, Mary Heber and Henrietta Heber. [*219]

Henrietta intermarried with William Wrightson, and had by him William Battie Wrightson, her eldest son and heir-at-law, and a daughter, Harriet Wrightson, who afterwards intermarried with and is now the wife of the Honourable Henry Hely Hutchinson. Mary Heber died in 1809, having by her will devised certain specific estates, not including any estate or interest she had or ought to have in the estates devised by will of the Rev. John Heber, to certain persons therein named; and she devised all the rest and residue of her real estate to her niece Harriet Hutchinson, and her heirs.

Henrietta Wrightson died in 1820, and her husband William Wrightson died in 1827, and, upon her death, William Battie Wrightson became, and is now, the heir-at-law of the Rev. John Heber, and of his son Reginald Heber.

Reginald Heber (the nephew of the Rev. John Heber, and tenant for life of the ancient family estate, with remainder to his first and other sons in tail male) had issue by his first marriage one son, namely, Richard Heber, the third devisee for life, and he had by a second marriage three children, and no more, namely, Reginald Heber, Thomas Cuthbert Heber, and Mary Heber, now the defendant Mary Macaulay, the devisee of the said ancient estate at Marton, under the will of Richard Heber.

The last-named Reginald Heber, afterwards Lord Bishop of

Calcutta, died in the year 1826, leaving two daughters, namely, Emily Heber and Harriet Sarah Heber, him surviving.

At the death of Richard Heber, the third devisee for life *under the will of the Rev. John Heber, and the then owner in fee of the ancient family estate at Marton, there was no male heir in possession of and lawfully entitled for the time being unto the said ancient estate at Marton ; but the defendant Mary Macaulay (formerly Mary Heber) became entitled to such estate. At that time, Emily Heber and Harriet Sarah Heber were the nearest relations of the Rev. John Heber then bearing the name of Heber, and would have been the co-heiresses-at-law of the Rev. John Heber, and of his son Reginald Heber, if the female line of Richard, the eldest son of Thomas Heber, had failed.

William Battie Wrightson, as the eldest son and heir-at-law of his mother, formerly Henrietta Heber, and the Honourable Henry Hely Hutchinson and Harriet his wife, in right of the said Harriet, as the devisee of Mary Heber, claim to be entitled to the said freehold estates at Buckden, in right of the said Mary and Henrietta Heber respectively, who were the co-heiresses of Reginald Heber, and also of the testator John Heber.

There being various equitable claims affecting the estates so devised by the Rev. John Heber, a suit has been instituted, among other purposes, to ascertain the rights and interests of the different parties in these estates.

The questions for the opinion of the Court are : 1st, Whether the ultimate limitation in the will of the Rev. John Heber, to the right heirs of the testator, being of the name of Heber, vested, at the testator's death, in his son Reginald Heber. 2nd, If it did not so vest, whether that ultimate limitation took effect at the death of Richard Heber, the third devisee for life. 3rd, Whether, at the death of the said Richard Heber, the said William Battie Wrightson, and the Honourable Henry Hely Hutchinson and Harriet his wife, or what other person or persons, became entitled to the possession of the estates and hereditaments so devised by the said Rev. John Heber.

[222]   *Malins*, for the plaintiff :

The plaintiff contends, either, 1st, that the ultimate limitation to the right heirs of John Heber, being of the name of Heber, vested at the testator's death in his son Reginald ; or, 2nd, that it was kept in suspense as a contingent reversion, until the determination of the

PEDIGREE OF THE HEBER FAMILY.

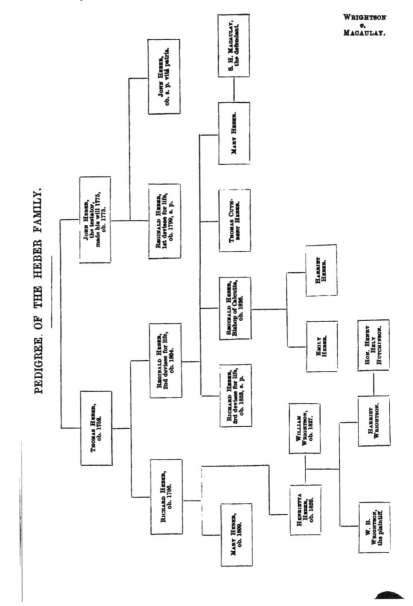

particular estates by the death of Richard Heber in 1888, and if so, that it failed altogether, because at that time there was no heir general who bore the name of Heber; and that the estate then vested in the person who then bore the character of heir-at-law of the testator.

1. It is an established rule of construction, that the Courts favour the vesting of estates at the earliest possible moment. And in this case there is nothing to show a contrary intention, to keep the estate in suspense, except in order that it might vest from time to time in the heir bearing a particular name. But the law of England knows of no such descent. In the case of an estate in fee simple, it is contrary to law that there should be a descent to a particular sex, still less to a particular name. It will be said, however, that the right heirs of the name of Heber take as purchasers. If these be words of purchase, the case is still stronger in favour of the plaintiff; because, in order to take as purchaser, the party must answer the whole description.

[He cited *Goodright* v. *Serle* (1), *Doe* d. *Andrew* v. *Hutton* (2), *Goodtitle* v. *White* (3), *Cownden* v. *Clerk* (4), Co. Litt. 27 a, *Doe* v. *Maxey* (5), *Doe* d. *Pilkington* v. *Spratt* (6), *Stert* v. *Platel* (7), *Doe* d. *Garner* v. *Lawson* (8), and *Boydell* v. *Golightly* (9).]

[225]   But, secondly, assuming that this was a contingent remainder, kept in suspense until the determination of the particular estates, it was a limitation to take effect by purchase, and has failed, because, upon the death of Richard Heber, there was nobody in existence who fulfilled the whole description, of right heir and being of the name of Heber. This rule of law has been relaxed in one instance only—as to the taking an estate tail by purchase, where the party is male or female, but not also heir, in order to effectuate the intention of the Statute de Donis; namely, that the estate tail may vest in the heir of a particular sex, although he be not heir general; that is, where he would take the estate tail by descent, he may also take by purchase: *Wills* v. *Palmer* (10), *Goodtitle* v. *Burtenshaw* (11).

On one or other of these grounds, then, the plaintiff contends, that the first question submitted to the Court by the VICE-CHANCELLOR

---

(1) 13 R. R. 441, n. (2 Wils. 29).
(2) 3 Bos. & P. 643.
(3) 13 R. R. 429 (15 East, 174).
(4) Moore, 860 ; Hob. 39.
(5) 12 East, 589.
(6) 39 R. R. 641 (5 B. & Ad. 731).
(7) 50 R. R. 738 (5 Bing. N. C. 434).

(8) 7 R. R. 454 (3 East, 278).
(9) 7 Jur. 53 [*S. C.*, upon further directions, 65 R. R. 597 (9 Jur. 2; 14 Sim. 32).]
(10) 5 Burr. 2615 ; 1 W. Bl. 687.
(11) Fearne, Cont. Rem., App., 570.

is to be answered in the affirmative, the second in the negative, and the third in the affirmative.

[226]

James Parker, contrà :

First, this estate did not vest on the death of the testator, but was suspended until the ultimate limitation took effect on the death of Richard Heber. Secondly, upon his death, the parties who became entitled were the *personæ designatæ*, the right heirs of the name of Heber ; not construing the will technically, but according to the intention of the testator. All the rules quoted on the other side are rules of construction, not of law; by which the Courts are not so strictly bound, as to be compelled to defeat a clear intention to the contrary expressed in the will.

[He cited *Minter* v. *Wraith* (1), *Loddington* v. *Kime* (2), *Periman* v. *Pierce* (3), *Jones* v. *Colbeck* (4), and *Butler* v. *Bushnell* (5).]

Secondly, assuming that this estate remained in suspense until it vested on the death of Richard Heber, it then vested in the person who filled, in the contemplation of the testator, the character of his "right heir being of the name of Heber ; " that is, in the persons who came nearest to the stock of the Heber family, viz. the daughters of Bishop Heber. The word " heir " is not used in its strict technical sense.

[229]

(ALDERSON, B. : You would say, if Bishop Heber had survived, and succeeded to the Marton estate, he would have taken as male heir.)

Yes; the testator meant, not the strict male heir, but the male representative of the family. It is a *designatio personæ*. The rule, that the heir taking by purchase must be very heir, is subject to great exceptions. In the previous limitation this testator uses the word in its more popular sense, as being the person who, by purchase or descent, had inherited the family property, although not very heir. In the ultimate limitation, he means to make the individual there designated a new *stirps*, to take the fee simple by purchase, and not by descent. If there had been two co-heirs, they would have taken in joint tenancy, not as coparceners : *Anon.,* Cro. Eliz. 431. In *Counden* v. *Clerke*, the party was excluded, not because he was not very heir, but because he did not fill the full character designated by the testator.

(1) 13 Sim. 52.
(2) 1 Salk. 224 ; 1 Ld. Ray. 203.
(3) Bridgman, 14 ; Co. Litt. 116, n.
(4) 6 R. R. 207 (8 Ves. 38).
(5) 41 R. R. 54 (3 My. & K. 232).

WRIGHTSON   (POLLOCK, C. B.: If these ladies had been married, would you
v.
MACAULAY.   say they would have taken?)

Probably they would; although it is not necessary to contend for that. *Goodtitle* v. *Burtenshaw*, *Wills* v. *Palmer*, and *Brown* v. *Barkham* (1), are all authorities to show that the special heir designated in the will may take, though he be not very heir; and if the rule is to be broken in upon thus far, why may it not as to the name, which has no more to do with the character of the heir than the sex. No

[*230]   absolute rule of law stands *in the way of carrying the intention of the testator into effect, if you can ascertain it. Here he has pointed out a particular character to be filled by the objects of his bounty at a remote period: the daughters of Bishop Heber fill that character, and thus the devise has not, as is contended, failed altogether.

(ALDERSON, B.: The testator's intention certainly was that both the estates should go together. By the events which have happened, they will do so if *Mr. Malins'* construction be right: we might, therefore, by adopting your view, be breaking his intention.)

If he had meant this estate to go along with the settlement, and according to the same limitations, he might have said so in very few words.

   Malins, in reply, was desired to confine himself to the first
   question, as to the period when the estate vested:

The intention of the testator is no doubt to be regarded, but so far only as is consistent with the rules of law, and the established principles of construction: and here, even if his intention were clearly shown to carry this estate down to the remotest posterity in the name of Heber, it cannot be carried into effect consistently with the rules of law. You are to ascertain at the death of the testator, if possible, when the fee simple is vested, in order that the rights of families may be ascertained, and property securely dealt with: per DAMPIER, J., in *Driver* v. *Frank* (2). Look at the consequences of the opposite construction. In this case, in consequence of the speedy failure of issue, the particular estates expired at the end of sixty years; but during that time the property would be useless for the purpose of sale, settlement, or devise. And there are no stronger words here than in every one of the cases, viz. that it is a limitation after the failure of certain issue.

(1) Prec. in Chan. 442, 461.   (2) 15 R. R. 385 (3 M. & S. 25).

(Parke, B.: There is nothing more, except the words "his, her, or *their heirs," showing that the person to take might be female.)

The testator could not tell, when he made his will, that his son would survive him; he might have died first, leaving a daughter or daughters.

(He was then stopped by the Court.)

Pollock, C. B.:

There is no doubt as to the rule of construction which is applicable to this case; and we are all of opinion that this estate vested at the death of the testator in his son Reginald Heber, and not at the death of Richard Heber, the third devisee for life. The rule of construction being as is laid down by Lord Coke (1), we shall not break in upon it further than has been already done. We shall certify our opinion to the Vice-Chancellor accordingly, and shall therefore answer the first question in the affirmative, the second in the negative, and the third in favour of the plaintiff.

Parke, B.:

I am of the same opinion, that the first question submitted to us ought to be answered in the affirmative, in accordance with the rule of law (which is a wise and beneficial rule), that we should construe estates to vest at the earliest possible period; and there is nothing in this case to show a clear intention to control that rule of law. To the second contingent question the answer will be, that the ultimate limitation did not take effect at the death of Richard Heber; because then there was no person to fill the double character of heir and being of the name of Heber: and we must construe this limitation in its strict sense. The rule laid down by Lord Coke has been broken in upon only with respect to estates tail; and there are no clear words in this will showing that the word "heir" is to be construed in any other than its strict legal sense. The established rule of construction can only be defeated by *that kind of evidence of intention which is said to amount to "demonstration plain." That is not so here, and therefore the rule of law prevails.

[*232]

Alderson, B.:

I am of the same opinion, that the first question ought to be

(1) Co. Litt. 27 a.

WRIGHTSON answered in the affirmative, and that we should proceed upon the
v.
MACAULAY. general rule of law, that the party to take should be determined, if
possible, at the death of the testator, and that the estate should
then vest in interest. That is a sound and wise rule: the incon-
veniences of departing from it have been properly pointed out by
Mr. Malins. The rule, therefore, is to be observed, unless there be
clear evidence of an intention to the contrary ; and there is none
such here: therefore we ought to abide by the rule. As to the
second question, we answer that this limitation did not take effect
at the death of Richard Heber, because there was at that time no
person who filled the double description in the will ; and if so, the
estate was undisposed of, and descended to the heir-at-law of the
testator, and from him to the plaintiff and Mrs. Hutchinson.

PLATT, B., concurred.

A certificate was afterwards sent to the Vice-Chancellor in
accordance with this judgment. .

1845.
May 27.
——
[239]
PLAYFAIR *v.* MUSGROVE AND ANOTHER.
(14 Meeson & Welsby, 239—249 ; S. C. 3 Dowl. & L. 72 ; 15 L. J. Ex. 26 ;
9 Jur. 783.)

> When a sheriff seizes and takes in execution a lease, the term does not
> vest in the sheriff, but remains in the debtor till the sheriff executes an
> assignment to the purchaser, and if, after selling the term, whether or not
> an assignment be executed, the sheriff remains in possession an unreason-
> able time, he is a trespasser.

TRESPASS for breaking and entering the plaintiff's dwelling-house,
and continuing therein for a long space of time, to wit, three months.

Pleas, 1st, Not guilty ; 2ndly, that the dwelling-house in which
&c. was not the dwelling-house of the plaintiff *modo et formâ :*
3rdly, a justification under a writ of *fieri facias* directed to the
defendants as Sheriff of Middlesex, under which they entered the
said dwelling-house, and seized and took in execution a certain
lease or instrument of demise in writing of the plaintiff of the said
dwelling-house in which &c., and then being therein, and of and
by which the plaintiff held and was then possessed, as in the
[*240] declaration mentioned, for a certain *term of years therein, that is
to say, of ten years and three-quarters wanting seven days, then
and at and after the time of the committing the said trespasses,
unexpired therein ; and afterwards, and before the return of the

said writ, sold the same, and the plaintiff's interest in the said term, and continued in possession of the said dwelling-house, as in the declaration mentioned, in and for the further execution of the said writ, and so committed the said supposed trespasses in the declaration mentioned.

The plaintiff joined issue on the 1st and 2nd pleas, and to the 3rd new assigned, that, after the defendants had seized and taken in execution and sold the said lease in the plea mentioned, and after the expiration of a reasonable time for such seizing, taking in execution, and selling, and for the completion of the purpose for which the defendants broke and entered the said dwelling-house of the said plaintiff, the defendants did not depart from and quit the dwelling-house of the plaintiff; but, on the contrary thereof, the defendants, on the several days and times in the declaration mentioned, the same being after the defendants had seized and taken in execution and sold as aforesaid, and after the expiration of such reasonable time as aforesaid, broke and entered the said dwelling-house, and stayed and continued therein for a long space of time, to wit, three months.

To this new assignment the defendants pleaded, 1st, Not guilty; 2ndly, that the dwelling-house in the new assignment mentioned was not, at the said times of the committing of the several alleged trespasses above newly assigned, or any of them, or any part thereof, the dwelling-house of the plaintiff, *modo et formâ:* upon which issue was joined.

At the trial before Pollock, C. B., at the Middlesex sittings after last Michaelmas Term, it appeared that the defendants had entered the plaintiff's dwelling-house under a writ of *fieri facias* for the purpose of executing the same, and seized, amongst other things, a lease for years of the *dwelling-house in question, and sold the plaintiff's interest therein by auction; but no assignment to the purchaser was made and executed by them. The jury found all the issues in favour of the plaintiff, except that on the second plea to the new assignment, on which, under the direction of the learned Judge, they found a verdict for the defendants, leave being reserved to the plaintiff to move to enter the verdict for him on that issue. *Humfrey* having, in Hilary Term last, obtained a rule accordingly,

Jervis and *Kennedy* now showed cause:

The question here is, whether a party who has ceased to have any legal interest in the house can be said to have possession so as to

PLAYFAIR
v.
MUSGROVE.

[*241]

PLAYFAIR
v.
MUSGROVE.

be entitled to maintain trespass, and whether he can treat the sheriff as a trespasser for continuing in the house afterwards. The seizure and sale of a term of years by the sheriff, under a writ of *fieri facias*, devests the right of the debtor and vests it in the sheriff, until he has executed an assignment to the purchaser and completed his title to the property, or until the execution is set aside, in which case the right of the execution debtor is revived. [He cited *Taylor* v. *Cole* (1), *Giles* v. *Grover* (2), *Taunton* v. *Costar* (3), *Butcher* v. *Butcher* (4), and *Doe* d. *Stevens* v. *Donston* (5).] In whom, from the time of the seizure and sale, is the property vested? It is not in the execution debtor, because it is taken from him. It is in the custody of the law—in the hands of the sheriff, until he executes the assignment.

[243]

(ALDERSON, B.: If, by the assignment of the sheriff, the property passes from the execution debtor to the vendee, it shows that the sheriff is a mere instrument to convey the property, and in that case the house remains the house of the execution debtor until it becomes the house of the sheriff's vendee, by virtue of the assignment. That was the opinion of PATTESON, J., as well as my own, in *Giles* v. *Grover*. If so, the issue on the second plea to the new assignment ought to be found for the plaintiff.

POLLOCK, C. B.: If the argument of the defendants' counsel be right, the new assignment was demurrable, and the defendants should have demurred instead of traversing it.)

In the allegation that the sheriff continued in possession an unreasonable time, there is involved a mixed question of law and fact, and it is by no means clear that the defendants could have demurred. The defendants had a right to show that the assignment had not been made, and the sheriff had a right to continue in possession until it was made.

(POLLOCK, C. B.: If that were so, a sheriff might continue in possession for any length of time, on the ground that he had not yet executed an assignment.)

He would be liable in an action on the case for remaining there improperly, and beyond a reasonable time for that purpose, or for

(1) 1 R. R. 706 (3 T. R. 292).
(2) 36 R. R. 27 (9 Bing. 128 ; 2 Moo. & Sc. 197).
(3) 4 R. R. 481 (7 T. R. 431).
(4) 31 R. R. 237 (7 B. & C. 399).
(5) 19 R. R. 300 (1 B. & Ald. 230).

any abuse of the power which the law vests in him; but trespass
is not maintainable.   Where the party is a mere wrong-doer, the
plaintiff is entitled to maintain trespass; but that cannot be so in
the case of a sheriff, who is justified under the execution.   He is
obliged to enter the house, and to sell the property he finds there.
It is clear he is not *functus *officio* at the end of the sale, as he has
a further duty to perform, viz. to assign the property.

PLAYFAIR
v.
MUSGROVE.

[*244]

(ALDERSON, B.: Where is the necessity for his remaining in the
house to sell the term?

PLATT, B.: In *Rex* v. *Deane* (1), it was held that if a sheriff, on a
fi. fa., sell a lease or term of a house, he cannot and must not put
the person out of possession, and the vendee in; but the vendee
must bring his ejectment.)

It has been held that that applies only to a forcible expulsion.
That case decided no more than *Newton* v. *Harland* (2), in which it
was held, that where a tenant remains in possession after the expiration of his term, a landlord is not justified in expelling him by force,
in order to regain possession.   And even there BOSANQUET, J., says,
" If a tenant hold over the land after the expiration of his term, he
cannot treat the lessor, who enters peaceably, as a trespasser."

Humfrey and *Peacock, contrà,* were stopped by the COURT.

POLLOCK, C. B.:

I am of opinion that this rule ought to be made absolute, and
that the plaintiff is entitled to the verdict on the second plea to the
new assignment.   The declaration is, in trespass for breaking and
entering the plaintiff's dwelling house, and continuing therein for
the space of three months; and the third plea to that was, a justification by the defendants as Sheriff of Middlesex under a *fi. fa.*,
under which the defendants entered the dwelling-house, and seized
and took in execution a lease under which the plaintiff held and
possessed the house for a term of years; and it alleged, that afterwards, and before the return of the writ, the defendants sold the
term, and the plaintiff's interest in it, and continued in possession
of the dwelling-house, as in the declaration mentioned, for the
*further execution of the writ.   To that plea there was a new
assignment, that the defendants stayed in the house an unreasonable

[*245]

(1) 2 Show. 85.   (2) 56 R. R. 488 (1 Man. & G. 644;
                                        1 Scott, N. R. 474).

PLAYFAIR
v.
MUSGROVE.

time after they had seized and taken in execution and sold the said lease. The second plea to that new assignment is, that, at the time of the committing of the trespasses newly assigned, the said dwelling-house was not the dwelling-house of the plaintiff. The question now is, whether the plaintiff or the defendants be entitled to the verdict on that plea ; the fact being, that the lease was seized under the execution and sold by auction, but no assignment executed to the purchaser. Now it appears to me that the verdict ought to be entered for the plaintiff, whether the word "sold" means an actual assignment to the purchaser, or a mere inchoate act towards a transfer, to be afterwards perfected by an assignment. If it means an actual assignment, the sheriff was *functus officio* as soon as the assignment was made, and had no right on the premises afterwards, and by continuing there became a trespasser ; and if, on the other hand, it is not to be understood as meaning an assignment, but as a mere inchoate act towards one, then beyond doubt the house was the house of the plaintiff, for the property remained in him. I think it is quite clear, that the term remains in the original lessee until an actual assignment by the sheriff; and I cannot at all accede to the suggestion in argument, that, on the seizure of a term of years, the term becomes vested in the sheriff until he executes an assignment of it to the purchaser. It may be, that things which pass by delivery are, for some purposes, vested in the sheriff by the act of seizure ; but in the case of chattels real it is not so. I think, therefore, the rule ought to be made absolute.

ALDERSON, B. :

[*246]

I am of the same opinion. The plaintiff's complaint against the sheriff is, that having entered his dwelling-house under a writ of *fieri facias*, and seized *and sold the lease, he remained an unreasonable time afterwards in the house. The sheriff says, "The house the plaintiff speaks of is not the house of the plaintiff." The question, therefore, comes to this : was it, as against the sheriff, who, having remained an unreasonable time, had no right to be there, the plaintiff's house ? If the sheriff had any property in the house, why did he say he did not remain an unreasonable time : why raise that question ? The sheriff has a right to enter the house for the purpose of executing the writ, but he has no business there beyond a reasonable time for the execution of it. He has a right to seize the debtor's property, and to sell and assign it, but he is only the conduit-pipe to transfer the right of the debtor

to the purchaser ; and if so, the house remained the house of the
plaintiff until it was legally transferred.   And that is so in the case
of goods ; for in *Giles* v. *Grover*, my brother PATTESON says :
" That the general property in goods, even after seizure, remains in
the debtor, is clear from this, that the debtor may, after seizure,
by payment suspend the sale and execution."   Perhaps the sheriff
might, in this case, have justified remaining in possession as
against the purchaser ; but, supposing that by the word " sold " it
is meant that he assigned the term, and that he had no right to
remain as against the purchaser, it is clear he had no right to
remain as against the plaintiff, who was in actual possession.   I
am disposed, however, to think that the word " sold " does not
mean an actual assignment, and that the possession was still in the
plaintiff.   I therefore agree, that this issue should have been found
for the plaintiff, and that the rule must be absolute.

ROLFE, B. :

The sheriff has pleaded that he was justified in entering the
plaintiff's dwelling-house by the writ of *fieri facias ;* and that, before
the return, he sold the lease, and the plaintiff's interest in the
term, and continued *in possession of the dwelling-house for the   [*247]
further execution of the writ.   Now, the word " sold " seems to me
to mean " bargained and sold ; " for the law knows nothing of the
sale of a chattel real, except by an instrument under seal ; and the
mere knocking it down at an auction is nothing more than making
a contract to sell it.   To that extent I go with the defendants'
counsel.   The plea is open to the objection that it does not show to
whom the premises were sold, and a special demurrer might have
been had on that ground ; but it is unnecessary to consider that
point now.   The sheriff, therefore, having sold and assigned the
term (for that seems to me to be the meaning of the plea), the
plaintiff says, that, after he had so done, he remained on the
premises an unreasonable time.   The sheriff then says, in answer,
that the house was not the house of the plaintiff.   That, however,
is not at all made out ; for it is admitted on the pleadings, that the
house was the plaintiff's until the sheriff commenced the execution
of the writ.   If there had been no goods in the house, the sheriff
had only to sell the debtor's interest in the lease, and had no right
to continue in the house beyond a reasonable time.   The *dictum* of
BULLER, J., in *Taylor* v. *Cole,* was unnecessary to the decision of
that case ; and it is not stated with much confidence.   It is said it

PLAYFAIR   has never been overruled; but has it ever been acted on? It
*.
MUSGROVE.   seems strange that, under a *fieri facias*, a sheriff should be able to
execute an *habere facias possessionem*. I think the word "; sold"
must be understood to mean "bargained and sold;" that is, such
an act as gives the purchaser a right to come into possession, and
to enforce his right by ejectment.

PLATT, B.:

I concur in thinking that the plaintiff was entitled to the verdict
on this issue, and that the rule should be absolute.

_____   *Rule absolute.*

1845.   UDAL AND OTHERS *v.* WALTON AND OTHERS (1).
June 9.
_____   (14 Meeson & Welsby, 254—260; S. C. 14 L. J. Ex. 262; 9 Jur. 515.)
[254]
A notice by a bankrupt to an execution creditor, that "he had
committed several acts of bankruptcy," is a sufficient notice of a prior act
of bankruptcy, within the 2 & 3 Vict. c. 29 (2): the notice need not state
the nature or particulars of any act of bankruptcy.

THIS was an interpleader issue, directed to try the question
whether certain goods belonged to the plaintiffs as assignees, as
against and free from the defendants' execution. The declaration
averred that they were the goods of the plaintiffs as assignees,
which averment was traversed by the plea: and thereupon issue
was joined. At the trial, before Pollock, C. B., at the last
[255]   Gloucester Assizes, * * it appeared that the defendants' execution had gone in just before the issuing of the *fiat*, and the question
arose whether, at the time of the execution, they had notice of a
prior act of bankruptcy committed by the bankrupt Innes, within
the meaning of the statute 2 & 3 Vict. c. 29. A copy of a letter was
proved by the bankrupt, which had been written by him to the
defendants before the levying of the execution, and in which he
informed them that "he had committed several acts of bankruptcy." The act of bankruptcy and the petitioning creditor's debt
were subsequently proved by other evidence. The defendants'
counsel contended that the bankrupt's letter was not a notice
sufficiently specific to satisfy the statute, and that some particular
act of bankruptcy ought to have been specified. The LORD CHIEF
BARON thought the notice sufficient, and under his direction the

_____
(1) Cited and followed by LINDLEY,   (2) Repealed by 12 & 13 Vict. c. 106,
J., in *Lucas* v. *Dicker* (1880) 5 C. P. D.   s. 31. See now 46 & 47 Vict. c. 52,
150.—J. G. P.   s. 45.—J. G. P.

plaintiffs had a verdict, leave being reserved to the defendants to move to enter a nonsuit.

Talfourd, Serjt., in Easter Term, obtained a rule *nisi* pursuant to the leave reserved. * * *

Keating and *Dowdeswell* now showed cause :

* * The letter was a sufficient notice of the act of bankruptcy. [257]

(POLLOCK, C. B.: If that be not sufficient, it is difficult to see where we are to stop. If a general notice be not sufficient, what is? Must it state all the circumstances, as where the bankrupt was denied, and to whom?)

If so, a pleader must be employed to draw it. [He cited *Hawkins* v. *Whitten* (1), *Spratt* v. *Hobhouse* (2), *Ramsey* v. *Eaton* (3) *Rothwell* v. *Timbrell* (4), *Arthur* v. *Whitworth* (5), and *Hocking* v. *Acraman* (6).]

Talfourd, Serjt., and *Lush, contrà :* [258]

* * The notice of the act of bankruptcy was not sufficiently specific to satisfy the statute. This question was considered in a very recent case, of *Conway* v. *Nall* (7), in the Court of Common Pleas. * * *

(POLLOCK, C. B.: That case was decided on the ground that the particulars communicated only amounted to an act of bankruptcy *in fieri.* It was merely a statement of facts, out of which an act of bankruptcy might perhaps grow.)

The words of the statute, " any prior act of bankruptcy," appear to point to the communication of some definite specified act. * * *

POLLOCK, C. B. : [259]

I am of opinion that this rule ought to be discharged. * * I think the notice of the act of bankruptcy was sufficient. In the case of *Conway* v. *Nall,* which has been referred to, there was merely a statement of circumstances, which in themselves did not amount to an act of bankruptcy; it was not a mere general notice that the party had actually committed an act of bankruptcy. The case of *Hocking* v. *Acraman* is not at all opposed to this view of the case. Notice of a docket having been struck merely informs

(1) 10 B. & C. 217.
(2) 4 Bing. 173 ; 12 Moore, 395.
(3) 10 M. & W. 22.
(4) 1 Dowl. P. C. N. S. 778.

(5) 6 Jur. 323.
(6) 12 M. & W. 170.
(7) 14 L. J. C. P. 165; (S. C. 1 C. B. 643).

UDAL
v.
WALTON.

the party that another person has taken a certain step which is adverse to the debtor ; the commercial world gather nothing from that fact, except that some person has made a certain affidavit. But here there is direct notice that acts of bankruptcy have been committed, and such a notice is, on general principles, sufficient to satisfy the Act of Parliament. There would be great inconvenience in putting any other construction upon it, for there are twenty different kinds of acts of bankruptcy, and it would be almost impossible to state with accuracy what ought to be the form of notice adapted to each act of bankruptcy. Some light is thrown upon this point by the former statute, of the 48 Geo. III. c. 135, s. 3, which makes the issuing of a commission and the striking of a docket notice of an act of bankruptcy. Now, when a docket is struck, the act of bankruptcy is not stated ; it is merely stated that the party is a bankrupt ; and the commission itself gives no more information on that subject : nor is the specific act of bankruptcy made known until the examination takes *place. I think, therefore, on principle, that there has been in this case sufficient notice of an act of bankruptcy.

[*260]

ALDERSON, B., ROLFE, B., and PLATT, B., concurred.

Rule discharged.

1845.
June 12.

[303]

CHAPPELL *v.* PURDAY (1).

(14 Meeson & Welsby, 303—322; S. C. 14 L. J. Ex. 258; 9 Jur. 495.)

A foreign author, residing abroad, who composes and publishes his work abroad, has not, at common law, or under the stats. 8 Anne, c. 19, and 54 Geo. III. c. 156 (2), any copyright in this country.

Therefore, a person to whom he transfers abroad, by an instrument, not under seal, but which is valid according to the law of that country, the copyright of the work in England has no right of action against a British subject who afterwards publishes the work in England.

Where depositions in a suit in equity are given in evidence at law, and the bill and answer are also put in to show that the depositions are admissible in evidence, the opposite counsel has no right to refer to the bill and answer in his address to the jury.

CASE for the infringement of the plaintiff's copyright in a musical composition, being the overture to an opera called "Fra Diavolo."

(1) Other proceedings in connection with this case are reported as follows : *Chappell* v. *Purday* (1841) 4 Y. & C. 485 ; *Chappell* v. *Purday* (1843) 67 R. R. 357 (12 M. & W. 303); and *Chappell* v. *Purday* (1847) 2 Ph. 227. See *Jefferys* v. *Boosey* (1854) 4 H. L. C. 815 ; and

cp. *Routledge* v. *Low* (1868) L. R. 3 H. L. 100, a decision on 5 & 6 Vict. c. 45.— J. G. P.

(2) Repealed by 5 & 6 Vict. c. 45, s. 1, and see now the International Copyright Act, 1886 (49 & 50 Vict. c. 33).—J. G. P.

There were pleas denying the existence of the copyright claimed, CHAPPELL
v.
PURDAY. and that the plaintiff was the proprietor thereof.

At the trial, before Pollock, C. B., at the Middlesex sittings after Trinity Term, 1844, the following facts were proved:

In the year 1829, M. Auber, being a subject of France, and residing at Paris, composed there the overture to " Fra Diavolo," and shortly afterwards assigned it to a M. Troupenas, who, by an instrument in writing, dated the 28th of January, 1830, assigned it to M. Latour, a denizen in England. The opera was represented and the overture played, at the Opéra Comique in Paris, before such assignment to Latour. On or about the 9th of February, 1830, the overture was entered at Stationers' Hall, in the name of Messrs. D'Almaine & Co., who were in correspondence with Troupenas. On the 13th of February, 1830, Latour, in Paris, sold the copyright of the overture in England to the plaintiff, Mrs. Chappell, by a memorandum in writing, not under seal, but which was by the French law a valid and perfect assignment. On the 5th of March, 1830, the overture was printed and published in Paris. On the 2nd of June, 1836, Latour, Auber, and Troupenas, joined in an indenture whereby they assigned to the plaintiff the copyright in England; and on the 14th May, 1840, the plaintiff published the music in England. The defendant afterwards, without the license of the plaintiff, published copies of the overture in England, for which publication this action was brought.

The plaintiff tendered in evidence certain depositions *taken in [*304] a suit in equity relating to the same matter. The reading of these depositions was objected to, unless the bill and answer, which also were put in by the plaintiff, were allowed to be read by the defendant's counsel, and to be referred to by him in his address to the jury. The learned Judge received the depositions in evidence, but would not allow the defendant's counsel to make use of the bill and answer in his address to the jury.

It was contended on behalf of the defendant, that the plaintiff had no right of action; for that a foreign author, residing abroad, composing a work there, and first publishing it there, could not communicate to another person any exclusive copyright in such work in England; and that even if he could, the assignment of the 13th of February, 1830, to the plaintiff was invalid, not being by deed, nor being attested by two witnesses, pursuant to the 8 Ann. c. 19. The LORD CHIEF BARON reserved these points for the consideration of the Court, and the plaintiff had a verdict,

CHAPPELL
v.
PURDAY.
leave being reserved to the defendant to move to enter a nonsuit, or a verdict for him on the issues denying the copyright and the proprietorship.   In last Michaelmas Term,

Jervis moved for a rule upon the points reserved, and also for a new trial, on the alleged ground of the improper reception of the depositions in evidence.   He contended, with respect to the latter point, that he ought to have been permitted to refer to the bill and answer in his address to the jury at the trial, and cited *Edwards* v. *The Earl of Glengall* (1).

Per CURIAM :

There will be no rule on this point.   The learned counsel was not entitled to read and make use of the bill and answer in his
[*305]   address to the jury; the Judge *only is to look at them, for the purpose of determining whether the depositions are evidence, by seeing what was in issue in the suit.

On the other points a rule was granted, against which, in the same Term (Nov. 15 and 16),

Martin, Byles, Serjt., and E. James showed cause:

The question is, whether, under the circumstances of this case, the plaintiff had any title to this copyright as against a person who has pirated the composition and published it in England : and it is contended that she clearly has.   It was proved that, by the law of France, this copyright exists; and it was also proved that the assignment made by Latour to the plaintiff was a valid assignment
[306]   according to the law of that country.   *   *   On this case coming before the Lord Chief Baron, sitting in equity (2), this question arose, whether, after a foreigner has published his work in a foreign country, he can, at common law, assign his copyright, limited to Great Britain, to a British subject, so as to give the assignee the benefit of the statute relating to copyright; and his Lordship came to the conclusion that Mrs. Chappell had that right.   It is quite indifferent to the plaintiff, whether she takes the right under the statute of Anne or at common law.   There is, at all events,
[307]   nothing, *in that statute which takes away her right.   The true view of this subject appears to be, that a British subject has a complete and perfect copyright in his own production; that a

(1) 9 L. J. (N. S.) Ex. 65.   (2) 4 Y. & C. 485.

foreigner has an imperfect right, defeasible by prior publication in this country by another person ; and that a pirate has no right at all.   All, therefore, that M. Auber had to do, in order to secure his right, was to take care that he was not anticipated by a prior publication here.   Then, *Bentley* v. *Foster* (1), and the former decision in *Chappell* v. *Purday*, are direct authorities to show that he may assign his right to a British subject.   Did he then assign it to the plaintiff by a valid instrument of assignment?   It is said that this instrument amounts, not to an assignment, but to a mere license.

(POLLOCK, C. B. : They say, because it professes to be an assignment of a limited interest only in the copyright, namely, in the United Kingdom, it therefore can operate only as a license to publish the work within those limits.)

The answer is, that wherever the common-law right exists, the statute fastens on and applies to it ; and therefore, where there is the common-law right abroad, the statutable right may be created here.   * * *

Then as to the supposed necessity for two witnesses to the assignment, it is sufficient to say that there are no words in the Acts of Parliament requiring it.   [They cited *Donaldson* v. *Beckett* (2), *Delandre* v. *Shaw* (3), *D'Almaine* v. *Boosey* (4), *Page* v. *Townsend* (5), *Clementi* v. *Walker* (6), *Millar* v. *Taylor* (7), and *Power* v. *Walker* (8).]

In the same Term (Nov. 16 and 17), and in Hilary Term (Jan. 23),

   Jervis, Godson, and *Crompton* were heard in support of the
      rule.   [They discussed the cases cited for the plaintiff and
      cited *Guichard* v. *Mori* (9), and continued :]

The authorities, therefore, being thus meagre on the subject, it becomes necessary to consider the question how far there can exist, in a foreigner residing abroad, any common-law right such as is now claimed.   In considering it, the distinction between patents

CHAPPELL
v.
PURDAY.

[309]

[311]

(1) 10 Sim. 320.

(2) 4 Burr. 2408.

(3) 2 Sim. 237.

(4) 41 R. R. 273 (1 Y. & C. 288).

(5) 35 R. R. 174 (5 Sim. 395).

(6) 26 R. R. 569 (2 B. & C. 861).

(7) 4 Burr. 2325.

(8) 15 R. R. 378 (3 M. & S. 9).

(9) 9 L. J. (O. S.) Ch. 227.

CHAPPELL
v.
PURDAY.

[*312]

and copyrights must not be forgotten. The statute of Anne has been said to apply to a person who brings from abroad the fruits of his study and invention: *Edgeberry* v. *Stephens* (1); because, *quoad* this country, he is deemed the first and true inventor. *Can, then, a foreigner restrain a British subject from publishing here a work which he brings from France? Could Auber, who composed and published abroad, have sued a person who bought the composition in France, and published it here? No; because the municipal law of this country recognises this country only.

(POLLOCK, C. B.: They say it was originally published in this country by Auber.)

It was not so, but by the plaintiff as the mere agent of Latour. But can the foreign composer do indirectly that which he cannot do directly? If he cannot restrain the free publication of the work here, can his assignee? He cannot stand higher than the original composer who assigned to him. The common law of England affixes, as incident to the composition, a perpetual right of copy; the law of France affixes to it a different right: how can the composer clothe a publisher in England with that foreign right? The French law, with all its incidents, can be in force only in that country. The incident exists only by the application of the common law of the country, which can avail only in that country, and within the ambit of the jurisdiction of that law.

(PARKE, B.: The French law of copyright surely cannot give a Frenchman any copyright here, or any right of action for its infringement here; whether it be by common law or statute, it cannot have any extraterritorial power. Then does the English law give him any such right?)

In truth, the question comes to this, whether, by the English law, a foreigner, publishing abroad, has any copyright here; and upon general principles, it would seem to be clear that he has not. It is a mere municipal right, which the law of the country attaches to the composition, namely, the right of multiplying it; which may vary in every country. The obvious argument to be drawn from the International Copyright Act, 1 & 2 Vict. c. 59, is that, independently of it, the foreign author had no copyright. It is admitted, that, if there had been a previous publication in France,

(1) 2 Salk. 447.

the composer *of this work would have no copyright in England.
But how can he have a common-law English right, which an act
done abroad can destroy?   M. Auber publishes his MS. in France;
a British subject brings a copy to England, and multiplies it,
which it is admitted he may do; then Auber makes an assignment
to another British subject, out of what is called his British right:
so that, according to the plaintiff's argument, there may be two
sets of copies running together, both legal, in altogether different
rights.   Again, suppose Auber never printed the MS., but only
played the music at the theatre; and an Englishman present took
down the notes, and brought the music to England: he has a
right to multiply copies for his own use; can he then afterwards
be made liable as for an infringement, by a subsequent assignment
by Auber to an Englishman?

(PARKE, B.: How can the common law of France—which is only
like an old statute—give a Frenchman a right of publishing a
book in England, and excluding all Englishmen from publishing
it in England?   How can the French municipal law have an
extraterritorial power?)

Nor can the plaintiff assert any right under the statute of Anne,
which is expressly confined to authors of books printed or to be
printed in this country, and accordingly makes provision for the
deposit of copies in certain English libraries.   And the 7th section
expressly enacts, that nothing in the Act contained shall extend to
prohibit the importation, vending, or selling of any books, in any
foreign language, printed beyond the seas.   Yet it is now said this
very statute gives to a foreigner the exclusive right of selling such
a book in England.   Thus the same law expressly allows the
importation of works from abroad, by which it is now said in effect
to be prohibited.

(PARKE, B.: It would seem that, to bring himself within the
statute of Anne, it must be the author who first publishes in
England, or the assignee of that author.)

Clementi v. *Walker* *is an express decision, that a publication by a   [*314]
third party prevents the right of the foreigner here.
Next, as to the validity of the assignment of 1830.   This is a
right which, at common law, could pass only by deed.   *   *   Lastly,   [315]

in order to transfer the right, there must be an actual sale,—the property must pass ; whereas this is a mere contract to sell, giving merely an equitable right to a specific performance ; and before it was carried into effect by the legal assignment in 1836, there was a publication in France, and by the plaintiff (who was then legally unauthorized) in England; and in this state of circumstances, the doctrine of *Clementi* v. *Walker* strictly applies, and is decisive of the present case.

Cur. adv. vult.

The judgment of the COURT was now pronounced by

POLLOCK, C. B. :

This was an action for the infringement of the copyright of the music of the opera of " Fra Diavolo," claimed by the plaintiff. The pleas denied the copyright claimed, and denied that the plaintiff was proprietor of it.   The material facts, as they appeared in evidence at the trial, are, that in 1829, Auber, a Frenchman, composed at Paris the overture to " Fra Diavolo," which is the subject of the present action.   Soon after, Auber assigned it to Troupenas ; and Troupenas, on the 12th of January, 1830, sold it to Latour, a denizen of England, by an instrument in writing, dated the 28th of January, 1830.   There was a representation of the piece, and the overture was played, at the Opéra Comique in Paris.   About the 9th of February, 1830, there was an entry at Stationers' Hall, in the name of D'Almaine & Co., who were in connexion with Troupenas.   On the 10th of February, 1830, Latour, in Paris, sold to the plaintiff, by memorandum in writing, not under seal (which was proved at the trial to be good and valid by the French law), the copyright in England.   On the 5th of March, the overture was printed and published at Paris.   On the [*316] *2nd of June, 1836, Latour, Auber, and Troupenas, by indenture, assigned to the plaintiff the copyright in England, and on the 14th of May, 1840, the plaintiff published the music in England ; subsequently to which the defendant published copies in England, for which this action was brought.

Two questions of importance were raised in the course of the argument.   The first is, whether, at common law, a foreigner, residing abroad, and composing a work, has a copyright in England. The second is, whether such foreign author, or his assignee, has such a right by virtue of the English statutes.

Upon the first question we do not feel any difficulty; and we are
of opinion that a foreign author, residing abroad, and publishing a
work there, has not by the common law of England any copyright
here.

A copyright is the exclusive right of multiplying copies of an
original work or composition, and consequently preventing others
from so doing. The general question, whether there was such a
right at common law, was elaborately discussed in the great cases
of *Millar* v. *Taylor* (1) and *Donaldson* v. *Beckett* (2). In *Millar* v.
Taylor, it was decided by Lord MANSFIELD, Mr. Justice ASTON, and
Mr. Justice WILLES, that at common law such a copyright existed,
and the judgment was given for the plaintiff; and in *Donaldson* v.
Beckett, which was an injunction founded upon the judgment in
Millar v. *Taylor*, the majority of the Judges held that such a
common-law right existed; but the majority also held that it was
taken away by the statute of Anne. We are, however, all of
opinion that no such right exists in a foreigner at the common law,
but that it is the creature of the municipal law of each country,
and that in England it is altogether governed by the statutes which
have been passed to create and regulate it, as in France it must be
*governed by the law of that country, but such a law has no
extraterritorial power, and cannot be enforced beyond the limits of
the State. Admitting, therefore, that by the law of France no one
can, against or without the consent of the author, make or print
any copy of his work, at any time or in any place, no right can be
claimed in this country as founded upon such a law, nor can any
right be claimed here, except what can be supported by the law of
this country. The subjects of this country are not bound to obey
such a law of France, nor the Courts of this country to enforce it.
It follows, that a British subject may, at the common law, freely
print and publish in Great Britain any number of copies of a
French work, without being exposed to an action at the suit of the
French author, whose exclusive privilege, founded upon the French
law, is limited by the French territory: and indeed, if this were not
so, the attempt to establish international copyright by treaty would
have been altogether unnecessary.

A foreign author having, therefore, by the common law, no
exclusive right in this country, the only remaining question is,
whether he has such a right by the statute law: and this depends
on the construction of the statutes relating to literary copyright

CHAPPELL
v.
PURDAY.

[*317]

(1) 4 Burr. 2303.   (2) *Id.* 2408; 2 Br. P. C. 129.

CHAPPELL
v.
PURDAY,

which were in force at the time of the transaction in question,
namely, the 8 Anne, c. 19, and 54 Geo. III. c. 136 (1).

If a judicial construction had been put upon these statutes by a
direct and deliberate decision of any Court, we should feel bound
by it ; but supposing for the present that there is no such decision,
and that the question comes now to be considered for the first time,
we should feel no difficulty as to the proper construction to be put
upon these statutes.   They were passed for the encouragement of
learning and the arts, by ensuring to authors, artists, and inventors,
the reward of their labours.   In their language the Acts are general ;
but *primâ facie* it must be intended that a British Legislature

[*318]

means only *to protect British subjects, and to foster and encourage
British industry and talent ; and therefore, when statutes of the
United Kingdom speak of authors and inventors, they mean authors
and inventors, being subjects of and residents in the United Kingdom, or at least subjects by birth or residence, and do not apply
to foreigners resident abroad : and, adverting principally to the
statutes of the 8 Anne, and 54 Geo. III., their provisions clearly
refer to such works as are first published in Great Britain or the
United Kingdom, from which first publication the time begins to
run within which an entry is (under the 2nd section of the former
statute, and under the 5th section of the latter) to be made at
Stationers' Hall, in order to the recovery of penalties, and within
twelve months after which publication copies are to be delivered by
the publisher to the British Museum and other libraries.   We
should therefore conclude, upon the construction of the statutes
alone, that a foreign author, or the assignee of a foreign author,
whether a British subject or not, had no copyright in England,
and no right of action on the ground of any piracy of his work
committed in the British territories.

It remains to consider what have been the decisions of our
Courts upon the construction of these and other similar Acts of
Parliament.

Under the stat. 21 Jac. I. c. 3, against monopolies, the 6th
section, which leaves as they stood at common law all the letters-
patent, for fourteen years, of new manufactures granted to the
first inventors, it has been decided that an importer is within the
clause, and if the manufacture be new in the realm, he is an
inventor, and may have a patent, though he is not the assignee of
he foreign inventor, and though he may be a foreigner himself, if

(1) This should be 54 Geo. III. c. 156.—J. G. P.

the Crown chooses to grant him a patent. The authority for this is to be found in *Edgeberry* v. *Stephens* (1). The principle of this decision is, *that the common law authorizes the part of a monopoly in this case, it being for the public benefit to introduce new inventions from abroad. Under the Copyright Acts there is, we believe, no decision precisely in point, but the result of the *dicta* and the authorities is, that a foreign author, or his assignee, may have the benefit of the statute, if his publication be in England, but otherwise not; and that the mere importer, without title, is not the author within the meaning of these Acts.

CHAPPELL
v.
PURDAY.

[*319]

The first case on the subject is *Clementi* v. *Walker* (2), which occurred in 1824; in which the opinion of the Court was strongly expressed in favour of what I have stated to be *primâ facie* the construction of these Acts. The points actually decided in that case were, first, that the plaintiff, who was not the author, nor then the assignee of the author, gained no right by a mere first publication in England; and, secondly, that the assignee had no right here, if another had first published in this country. Whether, if the foreigner had first published in this country, he would have had the right under the statutes, or would have been deprived of it if he had first published abroad, are points undecided by that case; but there is a strong opinion expressed, that if the foreign author does not publish here promptly, he loses any right he might otherwise have. The next case on the subject was in 1828, of *Delandre* v. *Shaw* (3), before the Vice-Chancellor of England. It certainly does not decide the question now before us; but there is a *dictum*, that the Court does not protect the copyright of a foreigner, which is quite true, if there be nothing more than a foreign work, not published here on account of the author or his assignee. In 1831, there was the case of *Guichard* v. *Mori* (4), in which Lord Chancellor BROUGHAM decided, that if a book were written by a foreigner, and published in a foreign country, the person *who purchased the right to publish it here could not support any claim to the copyright in this country, either at law or in equity. This case was followed by one on a similar subject, the copyright of an engraving, *Page* v. *Townsend* (5), in which the VICE-CHANCELLOR OF ENGLAND expressed an opinion, that the object of the Legislature, in the statutes as to engravings, was to protect those works which

[*320]

(1) 2 Salk. 447.
(2) 26 R. R. 569 (2 B. & C. 861).
(3) 2 Sim. 237.

(4) 9 L. J. (O. S.) Ch. 227.
(5) 35 R. R. 174 (5 Sim. 395).

CHAPPELL
v.
PURDAY.

were designed, engraved, etched, or worked, in Great Britain, and not those which were designed, engraved, etched, or worked abroad, and only published in Great Britain. In 1839, another case came before the Vice-Chancellor of England, *Bentley* v. *Foster* (1), in which the learned Judge decided, that the stats. 8 Anne, and 54 Geo. III., did not extend to a foreign author and his assignees, if he or they first published in England. There is an ambiguity in the judgment, as reported, for it may mean, if he is the first who published in England, or if the first publication anywhere be in England; and the context does not enable us to determine with certainty in which sense the words were used, though more probably the latter. An action was directed to be brought, but the defendants submitted, and no further investigation took place. In the meantime, in 1835, the case of *D'Almaine* v. *Boosey* (2) was decided by Lord ABINGER. His Lordship granted an injunction to restrain the piracy of music composed by Auber at Paris, but not published there, and first published in England, not by the composer, but by his assignee, a native British subject. The decision puts the assignee on the footing of the author or composer, and holds him entitled to the copyright by virtue of such first publication, whether at common law or under the statutes.

[*321]

These are the cases on the subject : and the result seems to be, that if a foreign author, not having published *abroad, first publishes in England, he may have the benefit of the statutes; but that no case has decided, that if the author first published abroad, he can afterwards have the benefit of it by first publishing here. The 7th section of the 4 Geo. III. c. 107, favours this construction; for it protects against piracy, by importation from abroad, those works only which are first composed, written, printed, or published in "this kingdom;" probably it would include the whole of the United Kingdom; and this protection would seem to be co-extensive with the right to be thereby secured. A further argument may be derived, though perhaps not a very cogent one, from the International Copyright Act, 1 & 2 Vict. c. 89, which empowers her Majesty, by Order in Council, to give to the authors of works published abroad the sole power and liberty of printing in the British dominions, for a term not exceeding that which authors, being British subjects, were then by the law entitled to, in respect of books first published within the United Kingdom. This shows the opinion of the Legislature, which may assist us in interpreting

(1) 10 Sim. 329.   (2) 41 R. R. 273 (1 Y. & C. 298).

the law, and it shows that, by the former statutes, a foreigner, who
first published abroad, was not entitled to the protection of the Act,
and probably was not entitled under any circumstances. Upon the
whole, then, we think it doubtful whether a foreigner not resident
here can have an English copyright at all; and we think he certainly cannot, if he has first published his work abroad before any
publication in England.

It remains to be considered whether the plaintiff is in the situation of a foreigner who has first published abroad. At the time of
the assignment to her, no publication had taken place; but before
she published in England, a publication had taken place by the
assignor in France; therefore the work had been published abroad
before the plaintiff published it in England, and such publication
was not by a wrongdoer, but by a person who was lawfully entitled
to *publish. It seems to us, therefore, that for this purpose the
plaintiff and Auber and Troupenas must be considered the same
person; and we therefore think, that as the publication in Paris,
by the composer or his assignee there, prevents a copyright from
being acquired under the statutes, and there being no right at
common law, or under the statutes, the rule for a nonsuit must
be made absolute.

[*322]

Rule absolute.

CHOLMELEY, Bart., and Another *v.* DARLEY.

(14 Meeson & Welsby, 344—347; S. C. 14 L. J. Ex. 328.)

> A., B., and C. made a joint and several promissory note for 100*l.*,
> payable to the plaintiffs, trustees of a Banking Company, or their order, on
> demand. A memorandum, indorsed on the note at the same time, signed
> by A., B., and C., stated that the note was given to secure floating advances
> made by the Company to A., from the respective times when such advances
> had been or might be made, together with commission, &c., not exceeding
> in the whole, at any one time, the sum of 100*l.* In an action by the
> payees of the note against C., to which he pleaded the Statute of
> Limitations, the plaintiffs proved payments by A., in reduction of the
> floating balance, within six years, and sought to use the memorandum
> indorsed on the note to show that such payments had reference to the
> note: Held, that it could not be read in evidence without an agree-
> ment stamp.

Assumpsit on a promissory note for 100*l.*, dated 1st July, 1836,
made by the defendant, payable to the plaintiffs, or their order, on
demand, with lawful interest. Pleas, first, that the defendant did
not make the note; second, the Statute of Limitations: on which
issue was joined. At the trial, before Parke, B., at the last

Assizes at Norwich, the note was produced, and was in the following form :

" MARKET RASEN, July 1, 1836.

" Borrowed and received of the Lincoln and Lindsey Banking Company the sum of 100*l.*, which we jointly and severally promise to pay to Sir Montague Cholmeley, Bart., and William Wriglesworth (trustees of the said Banking Company), or their order, on demand, with lawful interest for the same.

"THOMAS SMITH, sen.
"THOMAS SMITH, jun.
"THOMAS DARLEY."

On the back of the note the following memorandum was indorsed :

" The within note is given for securing floating advances from the Lincoln and Lindsey Banking Company to the within-named Thomas Smith, sen., with lawful interest for the same, from the respective times when such advances have been or may be made, together with commission, stamps, postages, &c., and all usual charges and disbursements, not exceeding in the whole, at any one time, the sum of 100*l.* within mentioned.

"THOMAS SMITH, sen.
"THOMAS SMITH, jun.
"THOMAS DARLEY."

[345]   It was proved that the note and indorsement were written at the same time, and before any of the signatures were affixed to them. Payments were shown to have been made by Thomas Smith, sen., in reduction of the balance due on the banking account, within six years before the commencement of this action.   It was objected, for the defendant, that the whole instrument taken together amounted, not to a promissory note, but to a special agreement, and ought to have been stamped accordingly, and declared upon as such ; and therefore that the plaintiffs must be nonsuited. The learned Judge declined to nonsuit, and under his direction a verdict passed for the plaintiffs, leave being reserved to the defendant to move to enter a nonsuit or a verdict for him. In last Easter Term, a rule *nisi* was obtained for that purpose ; against which

Byles, Serjt., and *Gunning* now showed cause :

This instrument was rightly received, and supported the declaration. The note, and the indorsement upon it, together make but

one instrument, and amount to a promissory note. The indorse- CHOLMELEY
ment is, in truth, nothing more than an amplification and explanation v.
of the words " value received." There is no doubt that a floating DARLEY.
balance on a banking account may consitute a good consideration
for a promissory note or a bond: *Pease* v. *Hirst* (1). And there is
nothing in the memorandum indorsed to make the note payable on
a contingency. *Leeds* v. *Lancashire* (2) will probably be relied on
for the defendants. There the note, which was, as here, in the
common form of a joint and several note, signed by three persons,
was indorsed with a memorandum made at the time of its signature,
which stated, that it was taken as a security for all the balances to
the amount of the sum within specified, which one of the three
might happen to owe to the payee; that it should be *in force for   [*346]
six months, and that no money should be liable to be called for
sooner in any case. There Lord ELLENBOROUGH ruled, that the
payee could not declare upon this instrument, against one of the
sureties, as a promissory note, for that between those parties it was
an agreement, and must be stamped and declared on as such. But
that case is distinguishable, on the ground that the indorsed memorandum there introduced a condition or contingency into the contract.
Here it is merely descriptive of the consideration. *Brill* v. *Crick* (3)
is in point. There the note had an indorsement, stating that it was
given on the conditions mentioned in the memorandum of agreement annexed, (which was an agreement to postpone the trial of a
cause on the defendant's undertaking to give the plaintiff a promissory note, by way of security, in case the plaintiff should recover a
verdict, but to be given up in case he should fail in the action): and
the COURT held, that this was an agreement collateral to the note,
not intended to alter its legal effect, but made only for the purpose
of ear-marking it, and to show that it was the note referred to in
the agreement.

   Whitehurst (with whom was *O'Malley*), *contrà :*

   This instrument, taken altogether, is clearly not a promissory
note, but an agreement, and ought to have been stamped and
declared upon as such. This is not, as it pretends to be, a promissory note for value received, but is in the nature of a guarantee
by the defendant to repay the plaintiffs so much money as they may
thereafter advance to Thomas Smith, sen., not exceeding 100*l.* If

   (1) 10 B. & C. 122.   (3) 1 M. & W. 232.
   (2) 2 Camp. 205.

CHOLMELEY
v.
DARLEY.

[*347]

nothing had been proved to be due from him, nothing would have been payable upon this instrument. In the case of *Brill* v. *Crick*, the COURT adopted the distinction taken in *Stone* v. *Metcalfe* (1), that if an indorsement of this kind be contemporaneous *with the note itself, it is part of the agreement between the parties.

(ALDERSON, B.: If this note were indorsed over, what would the indorsee recover ?)

That is wholly uncertain: he would recover according to the state of the banking account. *Hartley* v. *Wilkinson* (2) was a stronger case than the present; and *Leeds* v. *Lancashire* is also precisely in point.

(PARKE, B.: Suppose the indorsement be not part of the note, but an independent agreement; it is nevertheless a material part of the plaintiffs' case, in order to enable them to ascribe the payments to the note, so as to defeat the plea of the Statute of Limitations. The case cannot be taken out of the statute, except by part payment of principal or interest on the note. For that purpose the plaintiffs must connect the floating balance with the note, to show that it was intended to be a security for the floating balance. Then, for that purpose, this is an agreement the matter of which is above the value of 20*l.*; because it refers to a note of the value of 100*l.*: it ought, therefore, to have borne an agreement stamp.

ALDERSON, B.: My brother *Byles* says it is only an amplification of the "value received ;" still it is an agreed amplification of it.)

The learned counsel was then stopped by the COURT, who made the

Rule absolute to enter a nonsuit.

————•————

1845.
June 21.

[408]

CHANTER v. JOHNSON AND ANOTHER.

(14 Meeson & Welsby, 408—411 ; S. C. 14 L. J. Ex. 289.)

Semble, a license, under seal, to use a patented article, does not require a stamp (3).

ASSUMPSIT. The declaration stated, that the defendants were indebted to the plaintiff in 33*l.*, for the license, consent, and

(1) 4 Camp. 217.
(2) 4 Camp. 127.
(3) Under 55 Geo. III. c. 189, as a "deed not otherwise charged." Cf.

the Stamp Act, 1891, "Deed of any kind whatsoever not described in this schedule."—J. G. P.

permission of the plaintiff, granted to the defendants, to use upon   CHANTER
the defendants' premises a Chanter & Co.'s patent furnace, accord-   *JOHNSON.*
ing to certain patent inventions whereof the plaintiff was then the
owner and proprietor. The defendants pleaded *non assumpserunt*,
and several other pleas, which it is not necessary to refer to. At
the trial, before Wightman, J., at the last Assizes at Liverpool,
plaintiff tendered in evidence the following license (given in the
pursuance of the defendant's order for a license in writing), which
was under seal, but not stamped :

"I, John Chanter, on behalf of myself and Company, of Wine   [409]
Office Court, Fleet Street, in the city of London, county of
Middlesex, patentee and proprietor of the inventions known as
Chanter and Company's, and other patents for improvements in
furnaces, boilers, moveable fire-bars, condensers, &c., &c., by virtue
of the King's letters patent, under the Great Seal of Great Britain,
bearing date, &c., do hereby, in consideration of the sum of 33*l.*,
to be paid by Messrs. Johnson & Co. (as by receipt hereunto
annexed), give and grant to the said William Johnson & Co. full
and free license, consent, and permission to erect and use, upon or
at the premises situate at Wood Street Mill, Wigan, but not
elsewhere, say one patent furnace to a thirty-horse steam boiler,
one set of moveable bars of the same or similar construction with
the said inventions referred to above, for which the said letters
patent have been granted. As witness my hand, at London, this
19th day of February, 1844.
                                                    "JOHN CHANTER (L. s.)."
"Registered, G. E. STUBBS."

It was objected for the defendants, that this document was a deed,
and was inadmissible without a stamp: and the learned Judge,
being of that opinion, rejected it. The defendants' counsel then
contended, that as the plaintiff was bound by his contract to give
the defendants a license in writing, and no such writing was in
evidence, he must be nonsuited. The learned Judge, however,
refused to nonsuit, on the plaintiff's counsel contending that a
verbal license was sufficient, and referring to *Chanter* v. *Dewhurst* (1),
but reserved leave to the defendants to move to enter a nonsuit;
and proof having been given of the supply of the furnace to and
its use by the defendants, the plaintiff had a verdict, damages 33*l.*

In Easter Term, *Martin* obtained a rule *nisi* to enter a nonsuit,   [410]
or for a new trial, on the ground of misdirection; against which

(1) 67 R. R. 481 (12 M. & W. 823).

CHANTER *C. Saunders* and *Aspinall* (with whom was *Knowles*), now
r.
JOHNSON. appeared to show cause, but the COURT called upon

> *Cowling* (with whom was *Martin*), in support of the rule:

The defendant was entitled to a nonsuit, upon the evidence given
at the trial. His order to the plaintiff was for a license in writing;
and inasmuch as the plaintiff, by reason of the document being
unstamped, and therefore not receivable in evidence, was unable to
prove the giving of a license in writing, in pursuance of the order,
he was not entitled to recover.

(PARKE, B.: Does the Stamp Act require a stamp to such a
document as this ? Can it be considered as a deed, so that, if the
licensee had been interrupted in the enjoyment of the license,
he could have sued the plaintiff?)

It is under seal, and appears to fall within the description of
a "deed not otherwise charged," within the meaning of the
55 Geo. III. c. 189, sched., pt. 1, title "Deed." At all events,
this document having been rejected, the plaintiff proved no written
notice, and consequently the defendants are at least entitled to a
new trial. He then contended that the acts of the defendants did
not amount to an acceptance of the license, and also said that he
should contend that the license should be a deed, in order to be
valid.

The COURT then called on

C. Saunders and *Aspinall*, *contrà*, who contended, first, that
there was evidence to go to the jury of the defendants having
waived the necessity of showing a license in writing, and of their
actual enjoyment of such a license as stated in the declaration;
[*411]   and secondly, that the document in question *was not a deed,
and did not require a stamp as such: as to which they cited
Taylor v. *Walters* (1).

PARKE, B.:

The contract of the defendants was to pay the plaintiff a certain
sum for a license in writing, and I do not see any evidence of that
contract having been waived or altered, and another substituted for
it. But then the license was rejected at the trial, for want of a
stamp, and the question, therefore, arises whether any stamp was

(1) 18 R. R. 499 (7 Taunt. 374).

necessary. The defendants say the instrument is a deed, and   CHANTER
ought to be stamped as such: but that is not so; it does not   *v.*
purport to be sealed and delivered as a deed; it rather resembles   JOHNSON.
an award, or a warrant of a magistrate, which, though under seal,
are not deeds. There seems to be some doubt whether leave was
reserved to enter a verdict for the plaintiff, if the document
was receivable in evidence. We will refer to my brother
Wightman.

On a subsequent day (June 25),

PARKE, B., said, that they had ascertained from the learned Judge
that he had not reserved the point, and therefore the rule would be
absolute for a new trial.

Rule absolute accordingly.

PALMER *v.* EARITH.

(14 Meeson & Welsby, 428—432; S. C. 14 L. J. Ex. 256.)

A sewers' rate, not being imposed directly by Act of Parliament, is not
a "Parliamentary tax."

1845.
June 27.

[428]

TRESPASS for breaking and entering the plaintiff's house and
shop, and seizing his goods.

Plea, Not guilty, by statute.

At the trial, before Rolfe, B., at the Middlesex sittings in Hilary
Term last, a verdict was found for the plaintiff, damages 15*s.*,
subject to a special case, which stated the following facts: The
plaintiff, in 1843, became tenant to the defendant of a house
in Goswell Street, situate within the limits of the Commissioners of
Sewers for the Holborn and Finsbury district, under an agreement
which contained the following stipulation: "All taxes, parochial
and Parliamentary, to be paid by the said tenant." The plaintiff,
during his tenancy, was assessed to the sewers-rate in the sum
of 15*s.*, which he paid in December, 1844; after which, on the
defendant demanding his rent, due at the previous Michaelmas, the
plaintiff tendered the same, deducting the 15*s.* for sewers-rate.
The defendant refused the amount tendered, and distrained upon
the plaintiff's goods, whereupon the present action was brought.
The *question for the opinion of the Court was, whether the
plaintiff was entitled to deduct the sewers-rate from the defendant's
rent.

[*429]

Peacock, for the plaintiff:

A sewers-rate, not being a tax imposed directly by Act of Parliament, is not a Parliamentary tax, and is therefore not a tax, within the stipulation in this agreement, to be paid by the tenant. In *Brewster* v. *Kitchel* (1), it is stated, that, in the debate of that case, it was laid down by HOLT, Ch. J., "that the word ' taxes,' generally spoken with reference to a freehold, or where the subject-matter will bear it, shall be intended Parliamentary taxes *propter excellentiam*. But there be other taxes not Parliamentary, as repair of churches, commission of sewers." That shows that a tax imposed by Commissioners of Sewers is not a Parliamentary tax. It is imposed by them under a power to make a rate; and in this respect it is like a paving-rate. In *Waller* v. *Andrews* (2), where, by the agreement, the tenant was to pay "all outgoings whatsoever, rates, taxes, scots, &c., whether parochial or Parliamentary," it was held, that an extraordinary assessment, made by Commissioners of Sewers upon the lands, was within the agreement; but that was on the ground of its being a scot, and not a Parliamentary tax.

(PARKE, B. : Yes; and in that case there were the other words in the agreement, "all outgoings whatsoever."

ALDERSON, B. : Is a poor-rate a Parliamentary tax ?)

It is apprehended not. In *Baker* v. *Greenhill* (3), a landowner, liable with others to repair a bridge, *ratione tenuræ*, demised the land, and the lessee covenanted to pay the rent clear of the land-tax and all other taxes and deductions whatever, either Parliamentary or parochial, taxed or imposed upon the premises, or upon the lessor in respect *thereof, the landlord's property-tax only excepted; and by stat. 25 Geo. III. c. 124, reciting the liability to repair *ratione tenuræ*, it was enacted, that the landowners, liable as above, should repair and keep in repair the bridge during the continuance of the Act, and on their default road trustees were empowered to do the repairs and recover against the owners ; and for raising the sums required, power was given to the landowners to call meetings and to make rates according to the value of the chargeable lands, such rates to be levied, if necessary, by distress : it was held, that the original liability for contributions to repairs did not, by these

[*430]

(1) 2 Salk. 616.   (3) 61 R. R. 173 (3 Q. B. 148 ; 2
(2) 3 M. & W. 312.   G. & D. 435).

enactments, become a Parliamentary tax or deduction within the PALMER
v.
EARITH. lessee's covenant, and that he, having been compelled to pay a rate made and charged upon him as lessee and occupier, might (in the manner pointed out by the statute) recover the amount from the lessor.   There, although it was clear the rate could not have been made except by virtue of the Act, yet it was held that it was not a Parliamentary tax, and that the lessee was not liable to pay it.

(ALDERSON, B. : A county rate is not a Parliamentary tax, although it is, in one sense, made by Parliament ; but the rate is not fixed or assessed by Act of Parliament.)

A sewers-rate is not imposed directly by Act of Parliament, in the same manner that the income and window taxes are imposed ; the amount of which is fixed by the Act.   In the case of a sewers-rate, it is not a tax when the Act is made.   (He was then stopped by the COURT.)

Barstow, for the defendant :

The question here is as to the meaning of the parties to this particular agreement, taking into consideration the local liabilities of the parties.   If the landlord be held chargeable, it will be in consequence of the parties putting in a redundancy of words.   If the parties had used the term " all taxes " only, and the word " Parliamentary " had been excluded, it is clear this rate would have fallen on the tenant. But the word " Parliamentary " *means only a tax imposed by authority of Parliament. [*431]

(ALDERSON, B. : According to that view, a poor-rate would be a Parliamentary tax, and would fall on the landlord.)

A sewers-rate is by the Acts made payable by the tenant ; and in Callis on Sewers, a sewers-rate is stated to be a tax which, in the first instance, is chargeable on the tenant.   The cases as to the land-tax are applicable to the present case.   In *Amfield* v. *White* (1), where a tenant verbally agreed to pay " all taxes," it was held, that, under that agreement, he was bound to pay the land-tax, although it was not specifically mentioned.   And in *The Governors of Christ's Hospital* v. *Harrild* (2), where the lessee covenanted " at his own charge, to pay all Parliamentary, parochial, and other taxes, tithes, and assessments then or thereafter to be issuing out

(1) 27 R. R. 745 (Ry. & Moo.   (2) 58 R. R. 546 (3 Scott, N. R. 126 ;
246).   2 Man. & G. 707).

PALMER
v.
EARITH.

of all or any of the thereby demised premises, or chargeable upon the landlords or tenants thereof for the time being in respect thereof," it was held, that land-tax, which had been redeemed or purchased by a former lessee of part of the premises, under the provisions of 42 Geo. III. c. 116, was a Parliamentary assessment within the meaning of the covenant.

(PARKE, B. : There is a provision in the Land-Tax Acts, that if the tax is redeemed, the party redeeming shall have a remedy against the tenant ; so that the tenant is to pay the tax at all events.)

PARKE, B. :

It is quite clear, on the authority of Lord HOLT in *Brewster* v. *Kitchel*, that sewers-rates are not to be considered as Parliamentary taxes. A Parliamentary tax is one that is imposed directly by Act of Parliament. The case of *Waller* v. *Andrews* is distinguishable from the present, as there the tenant agreed to pay "all outgoings whatsoever ;" but here the words are much less extensive. The

[*432]

tenant was under no obligation to pay the whole rent *without deduction, and at the time of distress he tendered enough.

ALDERSON, B., ROLFE, B., and PLATT, B. concurred.

Judgment for the plaintiff.

1845.
June 27.

[437]

HARVEY v. BRYDGES AND OTHERS.

(14 Meeson & Welsby, 437—443; S. C. 3 Dowl. & L. 35; 14 L. J. Ex. 272;
9 Jur. 759.)

Trespass. The declaration stated, that the defendants, with force and arms, broke and entered a certain messuage, cottage, and dwelling-house, situate in Nova Scotia Gardens, in the parish of St. Martin, Bethnal Green, and then expelled the plaintiff from the possession and occupation of the same. Plea, that the messuage, cottage, &c., were the soil and freehold of the defendants, wherefore they committed the said trespasses in the said messuage, &c., as they lawfully might for the cause aforesaid : Held, first, that the plea of *lib. ten.* was a good plea to this declaration, although the close was particularly described in the declaration ; secondly, that it was not to be inferred from the declaration that there was any breach of the peace or forcible entry, the averment of *vi et armis* being a mere formal allegation that the defendants entered with some force, sufficient to enable them to get into possession (1).

TRESPASS. The declaration stated, that the defendants, with force and arms, &c., broke and entered a certain messuage, cottage,

(1) See *Lows* v. *Telford* (1876) 1
App. Cas. 414, 426, 45 L. J. Ex. 613;

Beddall v. *Maitland* (1881) 17 Ch. D.
174, 50 L. J. Ch. 401.—J. G. P.

and dwelling-house of the plaintiff, situate, lying, and being in a
certain place called or known as Nova Scotia Gardens, in the parish
of St. Martin, Bethnal Green, in the county of Middlesex, and
which were in the actual possession and occupation of the plaintiff,
and then with force and arms evicted, ejected, expelled, *put out,
and amoved the plaintiff and his family from the possession,
occupation, and enjoyment of the same.

HARVEY
v.
BRYDGES.

[*438]

Plea, that the said messuages, cottage, &c., were the soil and
freehold of the defendants, wherefore they committed the said
alleged trespasses in the said messuage, cottage, &c., as they
lawfully might for the cause aforesaid.

General demurrer, and joinder in demurrer.

The plaintiff's point was, that the common bar was not admissible
in an action for a trespass in the plaintiff's dwelling-house, and
that it afforded no justification for a forcible entry into it.

Lush, in support of the demurrer :

The question is, whether the plea of *liberum tenementum* is a good
answer to this declaration. That plea is never good, when the
place is particularly described and defined in the declaration; it is
only allowed when the declaration is general, in order to compel
the plaintiff to describe the abuttals of the property.   *   *   *

(PARKE, B. : How many thousand cases have there been in which
this plea has been pleaded, and always been allowed? Though
considered as an anomaly, nobody in modern times has ever
doubted about its being a good plea. All you can say is, that,
upwards of a hundred years ago, WILLES, Ch. J., doubted whether
the plea was good; but since that time it has been pleaded a
thousand times without objection.)

[439]

It has never been expressly held to be good, where the place has
been named in the declaration. It is not a good plea in justification, and if the usage does not allow it as such, it ought not to be
permitted. The cases only show that it has been pleaded as a
means of compelling the plaintiff to new assign where the declaration
is general. (He referred to *Cooke* v. *Jackson* (1) and *Whittington* v.
Boxall (2).)

(PARKE, B. : You will have great difficulty in *persuading us that

[*440]

(1) 9 Dowl. & By. 495.   (2) 5 Q. B. 139; 1 Dav. & M. 184.

this is a bad plea, after it has been allowed for such a length of time. We cannot overturn what has been the constant practice so long.)

Then, secondly, if it be a good plea to an action of trespass *quare clausum fregit*, it is not a good plea to this declaration, which states a forcible entry, and expulsion of the plaintiff from the house. The plea justifies it on the ground that the defendants are owners of the freehold ; but their being so will not justify a breach of the peace. The plea puts forward this proposition,—that a party who can show himself to be the owner of the freehold, may enter upon the possession of the occupier of a house, night or day, and violently turn him out of it.

(PARKE, B.: You assume a breach of the peace, which is really assuming too much.)

This point arose, but was not decided, in *Newton* v. *Harland* (1).

(PARKE, B.: It does not arise here, as there may have been a legal possession only. The declaration does not necessarily mean that the plaintiff was actually in possession. All the plaintiff would be bound to prove would be an entry on the land.)

The defendants justify the whole of the trespasses alleged, and they thereby undertake to justify all the force that the plaintiff can prove under his declaration.

(PARKE, B.: No. They undertake to justify, not all the force that the plaintiff can prove, but all that he must prove to support the action. The plea justifies an entry with some force—as much as would amount to legal force.)

The defendants ought to have pleaded that they used no more force than was necessary, and then the plaintiff would have been at liberty to have replied and put in issue the excess.

(PARKE, B.: Is there no force whatever that a party may use to get into possession ?)

Not any amounting to a breach of the peace.

(PARKE, B.: That is not alleged in this declaration. It in truth

(1) 56 R. R. 488 (1 Man. & G. 644 ; 1 Scott, N. R. 474).

alleges no force at all, and if issue had been taken on the allegation   HARVEY
of *vi et armis*, the plaintiff *would not be bound to prove any force.   *v.*
If you had replied that the defendants used more force than   BRYDGES.
necessary, you would have raised the question in *Newton* v. *Harland*.   [*441]
You might have averred that the defendants entered in a violent
manner, and with a breach of the peace; but not having done so,
you can claim no advantage from that illegal act, if it existed.)

The averment of *vi et armis* is equivalent to an allegation of a
breach of the peace and forcible expulsion : *Rex* v. *Storr* (1), and
Rex v. *Bathurst*, there cited. The declaration here uses words
which amount to the statement of a breach of the peace, and the
plea does not aver that the defendants entered using no more force
than necessary : *Leeward* v. *Basilee* (2).

(PARKE, B. : That is no objection to the plea on general
demurrer.

ALDERSON, B. : If the defendants might lawfully enter with any
force, you admit it by your demurrer. In *Rex* v. *Wilson* (3), the
allegation of *vi et armis* is expressly distinguished from that of
manu forti.)

Hugh Hill, *contrà*, referred to Reeves's History of the Common
Law, Vol. 2, pp. 340—343, and was then stopped by the COURT.

.PARKE, B. :

We think our judgment must be for the defendants.   The plea
of *liberum tenementum* was originally invented for the purpose of
driving the plaintiff to prove his title to the disputed close; and
there can be no doubt, that, in order to free himself from the
necessity of doing that, the plea would have been demurred to long
ago, if any one had thought such a demurrer would be successful.
This is the use of that plea ; and indeed, in one case, the Court of
Queen's Bench held that you cannot go into evidence of title under
a plea of not possessed.   But then it is argued, that the plea of
liberum tenementum *is not good when the place of the supposed   [*442]
trespass is described in the declaration; but the only effect of
describing the close in the declaration is, as appears from the case
of *Cocker* v. *Crompton* (4), that the defendant then knows the precise

(1) 3 Burr. 1698.   (3) 4 R. R. 694 (8 T. R. 357).
(2) 1 Salk. 407.   (4) 1 B. & C. 489; 2 Dowl. & Ry. 719.

spot in which the trespass is charged to have been committed, and
must therefore make out his title to the freehold on that very spot;
and, on his proving a *primâ facie* right to enter the close, because
it is his freehold, it will be competent to the plaintiff to prove that
it has been demised to him, and to show his lease if he have one.
The next point was that raised in *Newton* v. *Harland* (1); and if it
were necessary to decide it, I should have no difficulty in saying,
that where a breach of the peace is committed by a freeholder,
who, in order to get into possession of his land, assaults a person
wrongfully holding possession of it against his will, although the
freeholder may be responsible to the public in the shape of an
indictment for a forcible entry, he is not liable to the other party.
I cannot see how it is possible to doubt, that it is a perfectly good
justification to say that the plaintiff was in possession of the land
against the will of the defendant, who was owner, and that he
entered upon it accordingly; even though, in so doing, a breach of
the peace was committed (2). But the point does not arise in this
case; for we cannot intend on these pleadings that there was any
breach of the peace or forcible entry by the defendants. The
expression in the declaration, "that they entered the premises
vi et armis," is a mere formal allegation, implying that they entered
with some kind of force, with a degree of force sufficient to enable
them to get into possession, and which might or might not amount
to a breach of the peace. In *Lawe* v. *King* (3), it was held, that the
words "*vi et armis*" in a declaration in trespass are mere matter
[*443]   *of form, the omission of which is aided, on general demurrer,
by the stat. 27 Eliz. c. 5, and which call for no answer from the
defendant. It is true, that the words "using no more force than
necessary" are usually inserted in pleas in trespass, but many
precedents omit them; and, even supposing this improper, the
plaintiff could not take advantage of the defect on general demurrer.
Under the words "*vi et armis*," the plaintiff need not have proved
anything; neither was he bound to prove the eviction; proof of the
trespass would have been enough: and the defendants must only be
taken as answering what the plaintiff would be bound to prove.

ALDERSON, B.:

I agree with my brother PARKE upon both points. The plea of

(1) 56 R. R. 488 (1 Man. & G. 644 ;   29 Ch. D. 174.—J. G. P.
1 Scott, N. R. 3, 474, 502).   (3) 1 Saund. 81.
(2) See *Beddall* v. *Maitland* (1881)

liberum tenementum is equally applicable, whether the place is mentioned in the declaration or not. In the one case, the defendant says, "I suppose you are going for such a close, and I tell you it is mine: " in the other, when the place is described, he says, " I know you are going for such a close, and I tell you it is mine." The other point comes to this : may a freeholder lawfully enter on his own premises with any degree of force—for the distinction is very plainly taken in *Rex* v. *Wilson* (1), between entering, even a dwelling-house, *vi et armis* simply, and entering it *manu forti*? I have still the misfortune to retain the opinion that I expressed in *Newton* v. *Harland* (2), although the majority of the Court of Common Pleas have held the contrary; but as the plaintiff in this case has not new assigned, so as to raise that point, we need not decide it at present.

PLATT, B., concurred.

Judgment for the defendants.

IN THE EXCHEQUER CHAMBER.

(IN ERROR FROM THE COURT OF EXCHEQUER.)

HARVEY *v.* BRYDGES.

[1 Exchequer, 261—263.]

[THE plaintiff having brought a writ of error on the judgment of the Court of Exchequer (3)] the case was now argued by *Miller*, for the plaintiff :

* * [The plea of *liberum tenementum*] *affords no justification for the forcible expulsion of the plaintiff and his family from the premises. The declaration states, that the plaintiff was in the actual possession and occupation of the premises, which must be taken to mean the legal occupation, and though the defendant might be tenant at will or by sufferance, and the plaintiff could determine such tenancy by entry, yet he has no right to expel the plaintiff by force.

(PATTESON, J. : It was formerly the practice to plead "as to the

----
(1) 4 R. R. 694 (8 T. R. 357).   —J. G. P.
(2) See per FRY, J., in *Beddall* v.   (3) *Supra*, p. 718.
Maitland (1881) 29 Ch. D. at p. 189.

46—2

Margin notes:
HARVEY
v.
BRYDGES.

1847.
June 18.

[1 Ex. 261.]

[*262]

HARVEY
v.
BRYDGES,

force and arms, and against the peace, &c." Not guilty, and as to the other part of the declaration a justification (1).)

[He cited *Perry* v. *Fitzhowe* (2).]

Martin, for the defendant, was not called upon.

LORD DENMAN, Ch. J. :

*263]   We have no doubt whatever that *the plea is good. I may observe that in the case of *Perry* v. *Fitzhowe* great pains were taken to distinguish the case of a peculiar and articulate justification of all the acts charged to have been committed, from a case like that of *Taylor* v. *Cole* (3), where it was evident from the plea that there were no acts of violence, but the words used in the declaration were only those of the ordinary language of the law, stating a trespass committed with so much force as was necessary to change the possession.

Judgment affirmed.

IN THE COURT OF EXCHEQUER.

1845,
June 26.

[14 M. & W.
452]

SMITH AND OTHERS *v.* MAWHOOD.

(14 Meeson & Welsby, 452—464; S. C. 15 L. J. Ex. 149.)

The 25th and 26th sections of the Excise License Act, 6 Geo. IV. c. 81 (4), which subject to penalties any manufacturer of or dealer in or seller of tobacco, who shall not have his name painted on his entered premises in manner therein mentioned; or who shall manufacture, deal in, retail, or sell tobacco without taking out the license required for that purpose, do not avoid a contract of sale of tobacco made by a manufacturer or dealer who has not complied with the requisites of these sections; their effect is merely to impose a penalty on the offending party for the benefit of the revenue.

But where it appears that the intention of the Legislature was to prohibit the contract itself, although that be only for purposes of revenue, the contract is illegal and void, and no action can be maintained upon it (5).

DEBT for goods sold and delivered, and on an account stated.

Second plea, that the goods in the first count mentioned were divers quantities of tobacco, and the same, and each and every of them, were sold and delivered by the plaintiffs, as manufacturers of

---

(1) See Lev. Ent. 175, 178, 181; Pl. Ass. 485.
(2) (1846) 8 Q. B. 757.
(3) 1 R. R. 706 (3 T. R. 292).
(4) See 30 & 31 Vict. c. 90, ss. 8 and 9.—J. G. P.
(5) Cited by COTTON, L. J., in *Melliss* v. *Shirley Local Board* (1885) 16 Q. B. Div. 446; 55 L. J. Q. B. 143.—J. G. P.

tobacco, after the 5th July, 1835, to wit, on &c., and that the account
in the last count mentioned was stated between the plaintiffs and the defendant of and concerning the monies claimed to be due from the defendant to the plaintiffs, in respect of the said sale and delivery of the said goods, and of and concerning no other monies or debts, and the money in the last count mentioned as found to be due upon the said account, was and is the money claimed to be due in respect of the said sale and delivery of the said goods, and no other money ; and that the plaintiffs had not, at any time before, or at the time of the sale and delivery of the said goods, or any or either of them, taken out or obtained any excise license, required by the statute in such case made to be taken out by every manufacturer of tobacco or snuff, or any excise license required to be taken out by every dealer in or seller of tobacco or snuff, and containing or setting forth the purpose, trade, or business of the plaintiffs, and the true names and places of abode of the plaintiffs, and the place at which their business was carried on, and authorizing them to sell the said tobacco ; but, on the contrary thereof, the plaintiffs sold and delivered the said tobacco, and every part thereof, without having taken out any excise license authorizing them to manufacture or sell *the said tobacco, [*453] contrary to the form of the statute in such case made.   Verification.

Third plea, that the plaintiffs, before and at the time of contracting the several supposed debts in the declaration mentioned, were manufacturers of and dealers in tobacco, and were and are, as such manufacturers and dealers, required by the laws of the excise to make entry of their premises, in order to exercise and carry on therein their trade and business as such manufacturers and dealers in tobacco ; and that the plaintiffs, before and at the time of the sale and delivery of all the goods in the first count mentioned, had taken out such excise license as by the statute in such case made is required to be taken out by every manufacturer of tobacco or snuff, and had duly entered the premises in which they exercised and carried on their said trade and business, to wit, premises situate and being No. 57, Red Cross Street, Cripplegate, in the city of London; and that the goods in the first count mentioned, and every of them and every part thereof, were tobacco sold and delivered at the said premises to the defendant by the plaintiffs, as such manufacturers, so exercising and carrying on business at and in the said premises, and in the course of the said trade and business of manufacturers and dealers in tobacco, carried on by them in and upon the said premises, and after the fifth day of July in the year of our Lord

SMITH
v.
MAWHOOD.

[*454]

[*455]

1825, to wit, on the 15th March, 1845 ; and that the account in the last count mentioned was stated of and concerning the price of such goods so sold and delivered as in this plea aforesaid, and of and concerning no other monies or debts ; and the money in the last count mentioned, as found to be due upon the said account, was and is the price of such goods so sold and delivered as in this plea aforesaid, and no other money. And the defendant further says, that the plaintiffs had not, before or at the time of the said sale, painted, placed, or fixed, or caused to be painted, placed, or fixed, in letters *publicly visible and legible, and at least one inch long, in or upon their said entered premises, their names respectively, at full length, or the name or style of the firm or partnership under which the plaintiffs carried on the said trade and business, and after each name or names the word " licensed," with any word or words added thereto necessary to express the purpose, or trade or business, for which such license had been and was granted, in some conspicuous place on the outside of the front of the said premises, over the principal outward door or gate or entrance door thereto, and not more than three feet from the top of such outward door or gate or entrance door ; but on the contrary thereof, the plaintiffs wholly neglected so to do, and therein wholly failed and made default, contrary to the form of the statute in such case made : and the plaintiffs sold and delivered the said goods to the defendant, and each and every of them, at and from the said premises, contrary to the form of the statute in such case made.   Verification.

The plaintiffs demurred specially to each of these pleas ; and assigned (*inter alia*) the following causes of demurrer to the second plea : That the said second plea confesses the matter and substance of the said declaration, but does not avoid the same : That the want of such license or licenses as in the said second plea mentioned does not invalidate the contracts confessed in and by the said plea, or bar the plaintiffs from recovering upon the same : That the said second plea does not state or show any cause or reason why the plaintiffs were bound to take out a license to manufacture tobacco, or a license as dealers in or sellers of tobacco : That it is not stated in or by the second plea, that the plaintiffs were at any time manufacturers of tobacco, and that if it be meant by the allegation in the plea contained, to the effect that the said goods were sold by the plaintiffs as manufacturers of tobacco, to imply that the plaintiffs were such manufacturers, the said allegation *is indirect and argumentative, and presents and offers no certain, decisive, or pertinent

issue; whereas the defendant ought to have directly and positively
stated that the plaintiffs were manufacturers of tobacco at the time
of the said sale : That it is not averred in or by the said second
plea, that the plaintiffs were at any time dealers in or sellers of
tobacco, and that the same cannot be properly inferred from the
fact in the said plea mentioned, that the plaintiffs have sold tobacco
to the defendant ; and that even if it could be so inferred, the said
plea is insufficient, uncertain, and informal, in not directly and
positively alleging that the plaintiffs were dealers in or sellers of
tobacco at the time of the said sale to the defendant : That it is not
stated or shown in or by the said second plea, that the said tobacco
so sold and delivered by the plaintiffs to the defendant was tobacco
manufactured by the plaintiffs, nor does it even appear by the said
second plea that the said tobacco was manufactured and not raw
tobacco : That for aught that appears in or by the said second plea,
the said tobacco might have been foreign tobacco, remaining
deposited and secured in the import warehouses, before payment
of the import duty thereon, and legally saleable without a license,
according to the provisions of the said statute : That it is not stated
in or by the said second plea, that the plaintiffs were not duly
licensed at the time of their manufacturing the said tobacco, (if it
be intended to allege that they did manufacture the same), but on
the contrary thereof, it is quite consistent with the said second plea,
that the plaintiffs, being duly licensed, manufactured the said
tobacco and sold the same to the defendant at some subsequent
time, when the plaintiffs had ceased to be manufacturers of tobacco,
and yet were not dealers in the same : That it does not appear in or
by the said second plea, that the said sale or manufacture of the
said tobacco was made or took place in the United Kingdom of Great
*Britain and Ireland, or that the plaintiffs or the defendant were
resident in the said kingdom, or subject to the laws thereof : That
it does not distinctly appear in or by the said second plea, that the
plaintiffs did not take out proper licenses at some time after the said
sale and delivery, but during the same year, computed as in the
said statute mentioned, authorizing them by relation to manufacture
and sell the said tobacco in the said plea mentioned : That it does
not appear in or by the said second plea that the plaintiffs were
not properly licensed at the time of the stating of the said account
as in the said plea mentioned : That as to the last count of the
declaration, the said plea amounts to the general issue, &c.

The causes of demurrer to the third plea were: That the

SMITH
v.
MAWHOOD.

[*456]

SMITH
v.
MAWHOOD.

facts in that plea mentioned do not constitute a defence to this action, the same being directly collateral to the contracts in the declaration mentioned: That it does not appear in or by the said third plea, that the tobacco therein mentioned was tobacco manufactured by the plaintiffs, nor is it even shown that it was manufactured tobacco, and not raw tobacco: That if it can be implied from any averments in the said third plea that the said tobacco was manufactured by the plaintiffs, such averments are indirect and argumentative: That the plea ought to have shown, and does not show, that the particular sale therein mentioned was one requiring a manufacturer's or a dealer's license to authorize it: That it is not directly and positively stated that the names of the plaintiffs, or the name or style of the firm or partnership under which they carried on their business, were not painted, placed, or fixed in or upon the said premises, but only that the plaintiffs had not painted, placed, or fixed, or caused to be painted, &c., the said names as aforesaid: That it is not stated or shown in or by the said third plea that the said last-mentioned

[*457] tobacco was upon the said premises at the time of *the said sale: That so far as it relates to the last count of the declaration, the said third plea amounts to the general issue, &c.

Joinder in demurrer.

Fish, in support of the demurrer:

Both these pleas are bad in substance. The substantial question in the case depends on the construction to be put upon the 25th and 26th sections of the Excise License Act, 6 Geo. IV. c. 81.

[*458] On the part of the plaintiffs it is contended, *first, that no license is required on the sale of tobacco, unless when sold by a person exercising or carrying on the trade or business of "a dealer in or seller of tobacco;" and secondly, that even if such license be required to be taken out by a party not being "a dealer in or seller of tobacco," the omission to take out such license merely exposes the party to the penalty imposed by the Act, and does not vitiate the contract of sale, so as to estop him from maintaining an action for the price of the tobacco sold. [He cited *Wetherell* v. *Jones* (1), *The Gas Light and Coke Company* v. *Turner* (2), *Brown* v.

[460] *Duncan* (3), *Bensley* v. *Bignold* (4), and *Foster* v. *Taylor* (5).] As to

(1) 3 B. & Ad. 226.   698, 707.
(2) 5 Bing. N. C. 666; *S. C.* 6   (4) 24 R. R. 401 (5 B. & Ald. 335).
Bing. N. C. 324.   (5) 39 R. R. 698 (5 B. & Ad. 887).
(3) 10 B. & C. 93. Stated 39 R. R.

the third plea, * * the same objection applies to it as to the former
plea, namely, that the contract is not vitiated by non-compliance with the statute, and therefore the action is maintainable.

Pearson, contrà :

* * With respect to the general question, it is laid down by Lord HOLT, in *Bartlett* v. *Vinor* (1), that "a penalty implies a prohibition." This is a contract with reference to a thing prohibited, and therefore void. The case of *Brown* v. *Duncan* is strongly questioned by PARKE, B., in *Cope* v. *Rowlands.* The Court ought to step in wherever they *see that the disallowing of the contract will aid the object of the Legislature in securing the revenue. Every subject has an interest to assist in protecting the revenue from frauds; and the Court will not inquire into the amount of this interest. *Tyson* v. *Thomas* (2) is an authority for the defendant.

[461]

[*462]

(ROLFE, B. : There the parties were prohibited from contracting except by the weight mentioned in the Act.)

In *Little* v. *Poole* (3), and *Law* v. *Hodson* (4), there was no express prohibition of the contract.

(ROLFE, B. : Those were cases of regulations to protect one party to a contract from fraud by the other party.)

So here the object is to protect that in which all the subjects of the realm have an interest—the revenue. What interest has the party for whom printing is done, that the printer's name should be at the bottom of the page ? That provision is not directed against fraud between the parties; yet, if it be violated, the price of the work cannot be recovered : *Bensley* v. *Bignold* (5), *Stephens* v. *Robinson* (6).

(ALDERSON, B. : But there the Legislature has prohibited the act itself. If you can show that the Legislature has here prohibited the act of selling, the case falls within those authorities.)

They have prohibited it, by saying that the sale shall, under such circumstances, be subject to a penalty.

(1) Carth. 252.
(2) M'Clel. & Y. 119.
(3) 32 R. R. 630 (9 B. & C. 192).
(4) 10 R. R. 513 (11 East, 300).
(5) 24 R. R. 401 (5 B. & Ald. 335).
(6) 2 Cr. & J. 209,

SMITH
v.
MAWHOOD.

(PARKE, B. : You must show that the object of the Legislature was to prevent the contract from being entered into. The argument on the other side is, that the only effect of its being entered into is that the party shall pay a certain sum by way of penalty, in aid of the revenue. As to the third plea, it is quite idle to say that an enactment, which requires the party to put his name of a certain length over the door of his house, amounts to a prohibition of a contract in that house unless this be done.)

[*463]   It is submitted *that the Act of Parliament in effect prohibits a contract of sale made by the manufacturer or dealer in such a house, by the imposition of the penalty.

Fish was not called upon to reply.

PARKE, B. :

With respect to the second plea, that is clearly defective for want of an allegation that the sale of this tobacco was a dealing in tobacco, so as to require a license. But, even if it were good on that ground, I think the object of the Legislature was not to prohibit a contract of sale by dealers who have not taken out a license pursuant to the Act of Parliament. If it was, they certainly could not recover, although the prohibition were merely for the purpose of revenue. But, looking at. the Act of Parliament, I think its object was not to vitiate the contract itself, but only to impose a penalty on the party offending, for the purpose of the revenue. The plaintiffs, therefore, would be entitled to recover upon their contract, according to the principle laid down in *Johnson* v. *Hudson*.

The third plea is not bad in form, because it alleges that the plaintiffs are dealers in and manufacturers of tobacco : but it is bad upon the other ground, that the Legislature did not intend to vitiate the contract by reason of a non-compliance with the requisites of the 26th section, but only to render the party carrying on trade upon such premises liable to a penalty. I quite agree, that if it be shown that the Legislature intended to prohibit any contract, then, whether this were for the purpose of revenue or not, the contract is illegal and void, and no right of action can arise out of it.

ALDERSON, B. :

With respect to the second. plea, that is clearly defective, on the special ground assigned as cause of demurrer, namely, that it does SMITH
v.
MAWHOOD. not show that the plaintiffs were dealers in or manufacturers of tobacco; and I *shall therefore say nothing further upon it. [*464] With respect to the question arising on the third plea, I think the true principle of law is that which has been stated by my brother PARKE. The question is, does the Legislature mean to prohibit the act done or not? If it does, whether it be for the purposes of revenue or otherwise, then the doing of the act is a breach of the law, and no right of action can arise out of it. But here the Legislature has merely said, that where a party carries on the trade or business of a dealer in or seller of tobacco, he shall be liable to a certain penalty, if the house in which he carries on the business shall not have his name, &c. painted on it, in letters publicly visible and legible, and at least an inch long, and so forth. He is liable to the penalty, therefore, by carrying on the trade in a house in which these requisites are not complied with; and there is no addition to his criminality if he makes fifty contracts for the sale of tobacco in such a house. It seems to me, therefore, that there is nothing in the Act of Parliament to prohibit every act of sale, but that its only effect is to impose a penalty, for the purpose of the revenue, on the carrying on of the trade without complying with its requisites. I am of opinion, therefore, that both the pleas are bad, and that our judgment should be for the plaintiff.

ROLFE, B., concurred.

PLATT, B.:

I am of the same opinion, for the reasons which have been stated by my learned brothers. The case of *Johnson* v. *Hudson* appears to me to lay down the correct principle of law, and I am unable to distinguish that case from the present.

Judgment for the plaintiffs.

BAKER v. WALKER.

(14 Meeson & Welsby, 465—468; S. C. 3 Dowl. & L. 46; 14 L. J. Ex. 371.)

1845.
June 27.

[465]

To an action against the maker of a promissory note payable three months after date, the defendant pleaded, that the promissory note was made and delivered by him to the plaintiff for and on account of a judgment debt recovered by the plaintiff against him, and that except as aforesaid, there never was any consideration or value for the making or delivery of

the said note to the plaintiff: Held, that the plea was bad, inasmuch as it
showed there was an existing debt on account of which the note was made,
and the giving of the note was evidence of an agreement by the plaintiff to
suspend his remedy upon the judgment, which was a sufficient consideration
for the note.

DEBT. The first count of the declaration stated, that the
defendant was indebted to the plaintiff in the sums of 13*l.* 2*s.* 6*d.*
and 7*l.* 13*s.*, upon a judgment recovered against the defendant.
The second alleged that, on the 21st of March, 1844, the defendant made his promissory note, and thereby promised to pay the
plaintiff 26*l.* 5*s.* three months after the date thereof.

Plea to the second count, as far as the same relates to the sum
of 20*l.* 15*s.* 6*d.*, parcel of the said sum of 26*l.* 5*s.*, that the said
promissory note was made and delivered by him the defendant
to the plaintiff for and on account of a certain judgment debt
of 20*l.* 15*s.* 6*d.* recovered by the plaintiff against the defendant,
and that, except as aforesaid, there never was any consideration or value for the making or delivery of the said note to
the plaintiff.

Replication, *de injuriâ.*

Special demurrer, assigning for causes, that the general replication *de injuriâ* is inapplicable to this case, inasmuch as the plea to
which it is pleaded involves matter of record, which is not triable
by the country.

Joinder in demurrer.

The point marked for argument on the part of the plaintiff was,
that the plea was bad, as it showed on the face of it a good and
sufficient consideration for making the promissory note.

Hugh Hill, in support of the demurrer:

The replication is clearly bad, as it puts in issue the matter of
record alleged in the plea.

(PARKE, B.: No doubt the replication is bad, but what do you
say to the plea?)

Secondly, the plea is good. The promissory note is not stated to
be payable to order; and as it was given without consideration,
the party making it was not bound to pay it. It appears *by the
plea that it was given on account of the judgment debt, and
probably on the supposition that it would suspend the remedy
upon the judgment until the note became due and was dishonoured;
but it would not suspend the judgment debt, or the remedy to

[*466]

recover it, for a single moment, more especially as it was not made negotiable, and it was therefore no consideration whatever for the defendant's promise. In *Green* v. *Harrington* (1), which was assumpsit for rent of a house and land upon a demise, on motion in arrest of judgment, it was urged " that no action lay upon this promise, but it is debt for the rent of land, and the assumpsit is of a less nature; as if one be indebted upon an obligation, and that being forfeited he promised to pay it, no action lies, for the debt is due upon the obligation ; " which the Court agreed to.

(PARKE, B. : That case is distinguishable from the present, as that is the case of a mere promise, without any security. Would not the plaintiff, by accepting this promissory note, suspend his remedy upon the judgment for three months ?)

No, not in the present case, as the note was not made payable to order. It amounts to nothing more than a mere naked promise. In an *Anonymous* case (2), it was held, that a promise by a defendant to pay a judgment debt, in consideration that the plaintiff would stay execution thereon, would not support an action of assumpsit. Lord MANSFIELD, Ch. J., there says : "If the undertaking had been by a third person in consequence of the forbearance, it would have been a good ground of assumpsit against such third person. But here the promise is by the defendant himself, to pay a debt to which he was before liable upon record ; and therefore I am of opinion that such promise is no ground upon which to raise an assumpsit." A mere parol agreement to give time to the principal does not discharge the surety at law.

(PARKE, B. : This is something more than a parol agreement— it is a security.)   [467]

In *Davis* v. *Gyde* (3), it was held that a promissory note given by the tenant to his landlord for rent does not extinguish the claim for such rent, which is a debt of a higher nature than that arising upon the note ; and that the receipt of such note did not of itself suspend the right of distress until the note was due.

(PARKE, B. : There was no averment there of any express agreement.)

(1) Hutton, 34, 35.   (3) 41 R. R. 489 (2 Ad. & El. 623;
(2) 1 Cowp. 128.   4 Nev. & M. 462).

BAKER
v.
WALKER.

Nor is there here; and it is distinctly alleged in the plea that there was no other consideration for the making or delivery of the note.

(PARKE, B.: A promissory note given for the debt of a third person suspends the right of action, although no new consideration be given. His Lordship referred to *Lechmere v. Fletcher* (1).)

In *Davis* v. *Gyde*, LITTLEDALE, J., says: " *Mease* v. *Mease* (2), and other cases which are there cited, serve to show that you cannot plead a parol agreement to extend the time for the payment of a specialty debt: " and à *fortiori* a debt of record.

(PARKE, B.: But that does not show the converse, that it being a debt due on a specialty, it is an answer to an action on a promissory note given for it. If I give a promissory note for the debt of a third person, I am bound to pay it when due. If that be so, I do not see why it is not a suspension of the remedy in the case of a specialty debt. The *Anonymous* case cited from Cowper was that of a simple promise, without any security: but a promissory note is a security.)

In this case the note was not negotiable, and was therefore no suspension of the action upon the judgment. In *Popplewell* v. *Wilson* (3), where it was held that a promissory note for the debt of another was within the stat. 3 Anne, c. 9, the note was evidently payable to order; but where it is not, it will not suspend the [*468] time of payment; and therefore *the party giving the note gets no benefit from it, and there is no consideration for it. The plea is therefore a good answer to the action.

Hance, contrà, was stopped by the COURT.

PARKE, B.:

I am of opinion that the plea is bad, for it shows there was a debt in existence on account of which the note was made, and that is sufficient to make the note good. It is like the case of a note given for a debt of a third party, which has been held to be a sufficient consideration. It was so held in *Popplewell* v. *Wilson*, and that principle has been acted upon in many other cases. A promissory note, although not a specialty, resembles a specialty, and at all events it is a security. Where a man who has a judgment

(1) 38 R. R. 688 (1 Cr. & M. 623).   (3) 1 Stra. 264.
(2) 1 Salk. 325.

debt takes from his debtor a promissory note for the amount, pay-able at a certain time, it must be inferred that he thereby enters into an agreement to suspend his remedy for that period, and if so, that is a good consideration for the giving of the note. Here, there being a judgment debt, a promissory note is given for the amount of it, and that is evidence of an agreement to suspend the judgment until the note is due, which is a sufficient consideration to support an action on the note. This distinguishes the case from *Serle* v. *Waterworth* (1). I am therefore of opinion that the plea is bad, and that the plaintiff is entitled to judgment.

ALDERSON, B., ROLFE, B., and PLATT, B., concurred.

Judgment for the plaintiff.

EX PARTE BUCKLEY, IN RE CLARKE (2).

(14 Meeson & Welsby, 467—474 ; S. C. 14 L. J. Ex. 341.)

1845.
July 2.

[469]

Messrs. J. C., R. M., J. P., and T. S., carrying on business as bankers, a promissory note in the following form was signed by R. M.: "I promise to pay the bearer, on demand, five pounds, value received." "For J. C., R. M., J. P., and T. S." "R. M.": Held, that the holder of this note had not a separate right of action against the party so signing, but that the firm were liable.

THE following case was sent by the LORD CHANCELLOR for the opinion of the Court of Exchequer:

On the 31st of May, 1843, a *fiat* in bankruptcy was issued against John Clarke, Richard Mitchell, Joseph Phillips, and Thomas Smith, all of Leicester, in the county of Leicester, bankers and co-partners, carrying on business at Leicester aforesaid, and also at Lutterworth, in the said county of Leicester, and at Melton Mowbray, in the same county, and at Uppingham and Oakham, both in the county of Rutland, under the style or firm of Clarke, Mitchell, Phillips, and Smith : the said Richard Mitchell also carrying on, in his individual capacity, the business of a hosier at Leicester aforesaid.

On the 2nd of June, 1843, the said *fiat* was opened in the Birmingham District Court of Bankruptcy, before Mr. Commissioner Balguy, when the said J. Clarke, R. Mitchell, J. Phillips, and

---

(1) 4 M. & W. 9. The judgment in that case was reversed on error, in *Nelson* v. *Serle*, Id. 795, but the allegation that "there never was any other consideration for the note," had been omitted by mistake in the briefs of the case in the Court below, and the latter COURT gave judgment on the assumption that there was no such averment.

(2) See the Bills of Exchange Act, 1882 (45 & 46 Vict. c. 61), s. 85.— J. G. P.

T. Smith, were declared and adjudged bankrupts; and on the same day, James Christie was duly appointed official assignee; and on the 22nd of June, 1843, Thomas Edward Dicey, Esq., Edward Allen, bookseller, John Sidney Crossley, bookseller, Robert Hawley, farmer and grazier, and Thomas Ward, were duly chosen creditors' assignees of the estate and effects of the said bankrupts, and the said *fiat* is now in course of prosecution.

Before and at the date and issuing of the said *fiat*, R. Buckley, of Thurlaston, in the county of Leicester, was the *bonâ fide* holder for value of ten promissory notes (amounting in value to 65*l*.), of them the said bankrupts, issued by them from their banking house at Leicester aforesaid.

[*470]   Three of the said notes, being for 5*l*. each, were (omitting *the date, number, and name of the entering clerk) in the following form:

"LEICESTER AND LEICESTERSHIRE BANK.   £5

"I promise to pay the bearer, on demand, five pounds, value received.

> For John Clarke,   Joseph Phillips, and
> Richard Mitchell,   Thomas Smith,
>   RICHARD MITCHELL."

The other seven notes (with the like exception of date, number, and name of entering clerk) were in the following form:

"LEICESTER AND LEICESTERSHIRE BANK.   £5

"I promise to pay the bearer, on demand, five pounds here, or at Messrs. Williams, Deacon, Labouchere, Thornton & Co., bankers, London, value received.

> For John Clarke,   Joseph Phillips, and
> Richard Mitchell,   Thomas Smith,
>   RICHARD MITCHELL."

On the 17th of July, 1843, the said Robert Buckley exhibited a proof under the said *fiat*, and was admitted a creditor against the joint estate of the said bankrupt for the sum of 65*l*., the amount of the said notes.

On the 22nd of June, 1844, the said Robert Buckley, presented a petition to the Court of Review, thereby offering to withdraw his said proof against the joint estate, and praying to be at liberty to tender a proof under the said *fiat*, for the said debt of 65*l*., against

the separate estate of the said Richard Mitchell, and an order was
made on the said petition, dated the 9th of July, 1844, by the said
Court of Review, that the said Robert Buckley should be at liberty
to withdraw his said proof against the said joint *estate, and be at   [*471]
liberty to tender such proof (if any) as he could establish against
the said separate estate of the said Richard Mitchell, but the order
was to be without prejudice to the question, whether he had any
right of proof against the said separate estate of the said Richard
Mitchell.

On the 12th of July, 1844, the said Robert Buckley exhibited a
proof under the said *fiat*, and was admitted a creditor for the said
debt of 65*l*. against the said separate estate of the said Richard
Mitchell.

On the 20th of July, 1844, the assignees under the said *fiat* presented their petition to the said Court of Review, alleging that,
having regard to the form of the notes, the said bankrupts became
jointly bound to pay the sums mentioned therein, but that the said
Richard Mitchell did not become separately bound to pay the same,
and praying that the said proof against the said separate estate
might be expunged: and by an order of the said Court of Review,
made upon the said petition, on the 30th day of July, 1844, the
said Court ordered the said proof to be expunged accordingly.
The said Robert Buckley alleging himself to be aggrieved by the
last-mentioned order, a special case was, at his instance, stated
under the provision of the Bankrupt Act, 1 & 2 Will. IV. c. 56, s. 3,
by way of appeal to the Lord High Chancellor against the said
order, and on the hearing of the said appeal, on the 11th of April,
1845, the LORD HIGH CHANCELLOR ordered that a case be stated for
the opinion of the Barons of her Majesty's Court of Exchequer, upon
the following questions:

First, whether, if an action at law had, previously to the said
fiat, been brought against the said Richard Mitchell separately,
upon the three above-mentioned notes, by the said Robert Buckley,
as the holder of the said notes, the said R. Mitchell would, upon
the form of the said notes, have had a valid defence.

Secondly, whether, if an action at law had, previously to the said   [472]
fiat, been brought against the said Richard Mitchell separately upon
the seven above-mentioned notes, by the said Robert Buckley, as
the holder of the said notes, the said Richard Mitchell would, upon
the form of the said notes, have had a valid defence.

The case was now argued by

W. T. S. Daniel, on behalf of Buckley:

The two questions in this case resolve themselves substantially into one, whether Mitchell is liable separately upon the form of these notes. That point has been in effect decided by *Hall* v. *Smith* (1); in which case it was held that, where a promissory note, beginning, "I promise to pay," was signed by one member of a firm for himself and his partners, the party signing was severally liable to be sued upon the note. Bayley, J., there says, " The words used are, 'I promise to pay ; ' and it is signed by the defendant. What then is the import of those words? Surely that W. Smith promises. It is true that he promises for himself and others, but he alone promises. Now there are many cases where a party, entering into a contract in his own name on behalf of others, may be sued, or those for whom he contracts may be sued ; and *e converso*, an agent may sue, or the parties beneficially interested may sue." [He cited *March* v. *Ward* (2), *Clark* v. *Blackstock* (3), *Doty* v. *Smith* (4), and *Galway* v. *Matthew* (5)].

[473]   (Parke, B. : The question is, what is the meaning of the words, "I, for myself and three others (naming them), promise to pay?" Does it not mean that he intends to bind all the persons named? Here he makes but one promise, and you cannot make two promises out of one. He makes the promise as agent for the others, and for himself as principal. If he really had authority to subscribe the promise for all, they all are liable; but if not, then he is personally liable,—at all events for misrepresentation. There is a clear distinction between this case and that of a person signing for a firm of which he is not a member. The difficulty in supporting *Hall* v. *Smith* is, that they there make one contract into two. The meaning of it is, I make this promise for the firm.)

The question depends upon the form of the note, and it must be
[*474]   *decided on the general law applicable to contracts. It is found as a fact in the case that Mitchell carried on a separate trade. The words, "I promise to pay," constitute a several liability. A party signing a note, though a partner in a firm, may make himself personally liable, and Mitchell has done so here.

(Parke, B. : I think the instrument must either bind himself or

(1) 1 B. & C. 407; 2 Dowl. & Ry. 504.   474).
(2) 3 R. R. 667 (1 Peake, 177).   (4) 11 Johnson's American Rep. 543.
(3) 17 R. R. 667 (Holt's N. P. Rep.   (5) 10 R. R. 289 (1 Camp. 403).

the firm ; not both. It imports an agency for the firm, in making
a joint contract for them and himself. Suppose he had said, " I,
as agent for the firm, make this contract ; " would not they all be
jointly liable? The partner is only the agent of the firm in making
the note. Here the firm are liable, and you cannot make it out
that they are liable jointly and Mitchell separately.)

* * Suppose, in this case, Mitchell had been the clerk of the
firm, *Leadbitter* v. *Farrow* (1) shows he would be personally liable.

(PARKE, B. : I think you would be told not; because he states
himself to be undertaking for the firm. Your argument must go
this length, that notwithstanding he uses the name of the firm, he
is liable only.)

The general principle of law is *that the instrument is to be con-   [*475]
strued most strongly against the party subscribing it, and here he
says, " I promise to pay."

(PARKE, B. : His using the words, " For John Clarke," &c.,
shows that he makes the act of signature for the firm. It seems
to me that it is difficult to say we are to make two contracts out
of one. It comes to this,—is this the act of the firm or the act of
the individual ?)

Shipton v. *Thornton* (2) is important, as bearing on the question of
the two contracts. * * *

(PARKE, B. : That is not like the present case, because here he
says, " I promise, &c. for John Clarke, &c.")

M. D. Hill, contrà (Chapman and *Macaulay* with him) :

The object of this case was to inquire into the validity of the
decision in *Hall* v. *Smith*. (He was then stopped by the COURT.)

PARKE, B. :

This is *primâ facie* a promise by one partner, for himself and the
other three partners, and it amounts to one promise of the four
persons constituting the firm ; and if Mitchell had authority, the
firm is bound. I really must say that I think *Hall* v. *Smith* cannot
be *supported. The partner, in making the promise, is only an   [*476]

(1) 17 R. R. 345 (5 M. & S. 345).   (2) 48 R. R. 507 (9 Ad. & El. 314;
                                              1 P. & D. 216).

agent for the firm. Then does it bind him personally, or does it bind the firm? No doubt the instrument was intended to bind the firm; and as he had authority as a partner to do it, it had that effect. I think we must certify our opinion to the Lord Chancellor, that there was no separate right of action against Mitchell upon any of these notes.

ALDERSON, B., concurred.

PLATT, B.:

I have no doubt that *Hall* v. *Smith* cannot be supported.

A certificate in accordance with the above decision was afterwards sent.

REDMAN *v.* WILSON.
SAME *v.* HAY.

(14 Meeson & Welsby, 476—484; S. C. 14 L. J. Ex. 333; 9 Jur. 714.)

Where a ship, insured against the perils of the sea, was injured by the negligent loading of her cargo by the natives on the coast of Africa, and in consequence shortly afterwards became leaky, and, being pronounced unseaworthy, was run ashore in order to prevent her from sinking, and to save the cargo: Held, that the insurers were liable for a constructive total loss, the immediate cause of the loss being the perils of the sea, although the cause of the unseaworthiness was the negligence in the loading.

ASSUMPSIT on a policy of insurance, dated the 7th July, 1841, upon a ship called the *Lord Wellington*, on a voyage from London to Sierra Leone, while there, and back to her port of discharge in the United Kingdom; and by the contract the assurance was to commence at and from London, and was to continue during the ship's abode there, and until she should have arrived at or as aforesaid, and there moored at anchor; and the perils insured against were, amongst others, "perils of the seas, men-of-war, fire, enemies,
pirates, &c., barratry of the master and mariners, *and all other perils, losses, and misfortunes" that had or should come to the hurt, detriment, or damage of the said ship. The loss was averred to be, that whilst the said ship was proceeding and was on her said voyage, and was protected by the said policy, to wit, on &c., the said ship was by the perils and dangers of the seas, and stormy and tempestuous weather, strained, broken, and damaged, and afterwards and whilst she was upon her said voyage, to wit, on the day and year last aforesaid, by reason of the shipment and loading of

certain goods and chattels in and on board the said ship, to be
carried and conveyed therein on and for freight, and in the course
and consequence thereof, the said ship or vessel accidentally, and
without any personal negligence whatever of the plaintiff, became
and was further strained, broken, and damaged, and the said
straining, breakage, and damage first-aforesaid thereby became
and was aggravated and increased.   And, by reason of the premises,
the said ship, after the shipment and loading of the said goods
and chattels as aforesaid, and during the continuance of the said
voyage, became and was broken, leaky, and unseaworthy, and unfit
further to proceed on her said voyage; and the said ship afterwards,
to wit, on the day and year last aforesaid, was by perils and
dangers of the seas, and other perils, losses, and misfortunes
insured against by the said policy, wholly lost, and never did
arrive at London aforesaid; of all which premises the defendants,
to wit, on &c., had notice.   Breach.

Pleas: first, that the said policy of insurance was obtained from
the defendants, and they were induced to make the same, by and
through the fraud, covin, and misrepresentation of the plaintiff;
secondly, that at the time when the said vessel departed and set
sail from London, she was not seaworthy; and thirdly, that the
said vessel was not by the perils of the seas, or other perils or
losses *insured against by the policy, strained, broken, damaged,   [*478]
or lost, *modo et formâ*.

Issue was taken upon the above pleas.

At the trial, before Pollock, C. B., at the London sittings after
Trinity Term, 1844, it appeared that the vessel arrived on her
voyage outwards on the 2nd of September, 1841, and went up the
river at Sierra Leone to an island called Tassel, where she began
to load her homeward cargo on the 13th of September.   It appeared,
also, that it is usual for the natives to be employed in loading
vessels; and it was suggested, and the fact probably was, that the
vessel was injured in loading her cargo of timber on board.   She
came down the river to Freetown on the 7th of November, fully
loaded.   It was then found that she was leaking.   A survey took
place, and the opinion of the persons who examined her was that
she could not prosecute her voyage.   Part of her cargo was ordered
to be discharged.   On the following day there was a slight tornado;
two anchors were out, but the vessel drifted two miles down the
river.   She was afterwards brought back, and part of her cargo
was discharged; but the leak increased, and on a second examination

REDMAN
v.
WILSON.

she was pronounced unseaworthy, and she was run on shore to preserve the cargo, and to prevent her sinking in the river. She was ultimately sold as not being fit to repair, and the assured now claimed damages for a constructive total loss. The jury found, that the ship was seaworthy when she sailed from London; that there was no fraud in effecting the policy: and that the vessel was lost by perils of the sea; and they thereupon returned a verdict for the plaintiff on all the issues.

A rule was obtained in Michaelmas Term, 1844, calling upon the plaintiff to show cause why there should not be a new trial, on the ground that the loss proved at the trial was not, in point of fact, a loss by the perils of the sea, but was the consequence

[*479]

of negligence or want of skill in the *loading the cargo on board the vessel; and that the attention of the jury ought to have been directed to the negligent mode of loading, and they should have been told, that, if they thought the loss was the result of such negligence, the defendant was entitled to their verdict. Against this rule,

Jervis, *Martin*, and *Hoggins* showed cause, in the vacation sittings after last Hilary Term (Feb. 12):

In this case the underwriter was clearly liable. Even if the injury to the vessel were occasioned by the loading of it, and on being brought out in the smoothest water she went down, the underwriter would be liable, for it would be a peril insured against. The insurance on this vessel was from London to Sierra Leone, while there, and back to her port of discharge in the United Kingdom; and she was therefore under the protection of the policy during the whole time. The rule is, that you must look at the proximate cause of the loss. Now it was proved in this case that the vessel had sustained severe weather whilst in the river, and that although two of her anchors were out, she drifted two miles down the river; and it was after that, upon a second examination, that she was pronounced to be unseaworthy, and she was obliged to be run on shore to prevent her from sinking. The proximate cause of the loss was therefore a peril of the sea. The vessel was totally lost when she was lying on the shore at Freetown, in a state in which it was impossible to repair her. But even if the loss were occasioned by the act of the natives employed in loading her, the underwriter would still be liable. It is perfectly clear that an injury occurring to a ship without the personal neglect of the

assured, but occasioned by persons ordinarily employed in loading   REDMAN
her, would be a peril insured against. The owners are bound to   WILSON.
provide a sufficient crew and a captain of competent skill for the
voyage, *and, having done that, they are not responsible for the   [*480]
performance of their duties, or for any neglect or misconduct of the
master or crew. Here the losses insured against are perils of the
sea, &c., barratry of the master and mariners, and all other perils,
losses, and misfortunes. [They cited *Dixon* v. *Sadler* (1), *Cullen* v.
Butler (2), and *Devaux* v. *J'Anson* (3).]

Watson, *Tomlinson*, and *Forsyth*, in support of the rule :   [481]

Assuming that the injury happened in the loading of the vessel,
that was not a loss within the meaning of the policy. The words
" other perils, losses, and misfortunes," mean matters *ejusdem
generis* with the other words in the clause—such as fire, enemies,
pirates, jettisons, surprisals, takings at sea, arrests, restraints and
detainments of all kings, princes, and people, barratry of the master
and mariners, &c. But no liability was insured against for any
accident or damage arising from the negligent conduct of the master
or mariners, or persons whom they employed in loading the vessel,
and the underwriters are not responsible for their acts. In *Dixon* v.
Sadler, it was decided that the underwriters were liable, not for the
negligence, but for the consequences of the wilful act of the master
and crew, not amounting to barratry. There is nothing to show
that the underwriters are liable for the negligent act, even of the
mariners.

(POLLOCK, C. B. : They may not be liable, unless it ends in a loss
by the perils of the sea.)

The insurance is against perils of the sea and losses *ejusdem generis*
with perils of the sea. It has been said, that a loss by perils of the
sea is *ejusdem generis* with barratry ; but that is not so. The
vessel remained a vessel in specie, with a *partial loss, and the   [*482]
captain sells her as such. This is something clearly distinct from
perils of the sea, and was not one of the perils insured against.

(POLLOCK, C. B. : Do you admit, that, if the ship were rendered
unsafe by the injury she sustained in loading her, and she

(1) 52 R. R. 784 (5 M. & W. 405;   (3) 50 R. R. 786 (5 Bing. N. C. 519;
8 M. & W. 895).   7 Scott, 507).
(2) 17 R. R. 400 (5 M. & S. 461)·

afterwards put to sea and was lost, the underwriters would be liable?)

That admits of another question, whether, sending the vessel to sea in such a state, she would be seaworthy.

Cur. adv. vult.

The judgment of the COURT was now delivered by

PARKE, B.:

This was an action on a policy of insurance dated 7th July, 1841, on the ship *Lord Wellington*, on a voyage from London to Sierra Leone and back. The pleas were, first, fraud; secondly, that the vessel was not seaworthy; and thirdly, that she was not lost by the perils of the sea.

At the trial, the jury found all the issues in favour of the plaintiff; but a rule was granted in Michaelmas Term last, to show cause why the verdict should not be set aside, and a new trial be had, on the ground that the loss which was proved on the trial was not, in point of fact, a loss by the perils of the sea, but was the consequence of negligence or want of skill in the loading the cargo on board the vessel. Cause was afterwards shown, when the facts appeared to be shortly these. The vessel arrived on her voyage outwards the 2nd of September, and went up the river to Tassel (an island); she began to load her homeward cargo on the 13th of September. It is usual for the natives to be employed in loading, and it was suggested, and probably the fact was, that the vessel was in some degree injured, by loading her cargo of timber on board. She came down the river to Freetown on the 7th November, fully loaded. It was then found that she was leaking and was deep in the water. At this time she made *four feet and a half water in twenty-four hours. A survey was held, and the opinion of those who examined her was, that she could not prosecute her voyage. They ordered part of the cargo to be discharged. The following day there was a slight tornado; two anchors were out, but she drifted two miles down the river. She was brought back and part of the cargo was discharged, but the leak increased, and on a second examination she was pronounced unseaworthy, and she was run ashore to preserve the cargo, and to prevent her from sinking in the river; ultimately she was sold, as not being fit to repair, and the assured claimed for a constructive total loss.

[*483]

The jury having found that the ship was seaworthy when she

sailed from London, and that there was no fraud in effecting the
policy, the only question discussed on the argument was, whether
the loss was occasioned by the perils of the sea ; and it was contended, on behalf of the defendant, that the attention of the jury
ought to have been directed to the negligent mode of loading the
cargo, and that if they thought the loss was the result of such
negligence, the defendant was entitled to a verdict.   But it appears
to us that the rule " *causa proxima non remota spectatur* " applies
to this case, and that the immediate cause of loss was a peril of the
sea, for the stranding was a loss by a peril of the sea : and if it be
said that it was voluntary, it was only to avoid the sinking of the
vessel, which would have been a peril of the same sort.   In
Walker v. *Maitland* (1) (recognised and acted on in *Bishop* v.
Pentland (2), it was decided that the underwriters on a policy of
insurance are liable for a loss arising immediately from a peril
insured against, but remotely arising from the negligence of the
master and mariners ; and we cannot distinguish between the
negligence of the master and mariners, and the negligence of the
natives (if they were *negligent, and remotely gave occasion to the   [*484]
loss) who were employed to put the cargo on board.

It appears to us, therefore, that the rule for a new trial must be
discharged : and the same with the other case, of *Redman* v. *Hay*.

Rule discharged.

GILBERT *v.* SCHWENCK AND WIFE.

(14 Meeson & Welsby, 488—493 ; S. C. 14 L. J. Ex. 317 ; 9 Jur. 693.)

1845,
July 9.

[488]

Where two persons are appointed joint testamentary guardians of an
infant, under 12 Car. II. c. 24, s. 8, trespass lies by one of them against
the other, for forcibly removing the infant from the lawful service of the
former, against his consent.

TRESPASS.   The declaration stated, that the defendants, on &c.,
assaulted one F. S. Gilbert and one J. Gilbert, then being the sons
and servants of the plaintiff, and forcibly and with violence took
away and removed them from the plaintiff, and kept them so
removed for a long space of time, to wit, from thence hitherto ; *per
quod servitia amisit*, &c.

The defendants pleaded, that long before the said time when &c.,
the plaintiff married one J. M. Gilbert, since deceased, and that
the said F. S. Gilbert and J. Gilbert were the lawful issue of that

----

(1) 24 R. R. 320 (5 B. & Ald. 171).   (2) 7 B. & C. 219 ; 1 Man. & Ry. 49.

marriage. The plea then stated, that, by a codicil to the will of J. M. Gilbert, he willed and directed that William Gilbert should be a guardian *of the said F. S. Gilbert and J. Gilbert, " with a certain person therein in that behalf named," and did thereby dispose of the custody, governance, and tuition of the said F. S. Gilbert and J. Gilbert, to the said William Gilbert and the said other person, in possession, &c. The plea then alleged the death of J. M. Gilbert, without revoking his will, and the acceptance of the trust by William Gilbert, whereby he became lawful guardian, with the said other person, of the said children ; and it then stated, that the children were under the age of eight years and above the age of four, and were in the custody of the plaintiff as such servants as in the declaration mentioned, and that she had them in her custody without the licence or consent and against the will of the said William Gilbert, who was desirous of having the care, custody, &c. of them. The plea then averred a request by the defendants, as servants of William Gilbert, to the plaintiff, to deliver up the children to William Gilbert, the refusal of the plaintiff, and the removal by the defendants of the children, by command of William Gilbert, that he might have the care, custody, &c. of them. Verification.

Replication, that, by the said codicil, the said William Gilbert was appointed joint guardian with the plaintiff during her life or widowhood, the plaintiff being the said " other person " in the said codicil named ; and that the plaintiff accepted the said trust, and had continued unmarried, &c. Verification.

Special demurrer, and joinder in demurrer.

In Trinity Term (May 28),

Jervis argued in support of the demurrer:

This replication is bad, both on the ground of departure from the declaration, and also for not alleging that which is necessary to found the right of the plaintiff to complain of the trespass as the testamentary guardian of the infant. But, in the first place, no action will lie by the testamentary guardian *against the defendants, for taking out of her custody a child, in which the party by whose authority they acted had, as co-guardian with her, a joint interest. It is like the case of joint tenants of a chattel. *Donaldson* v. *Williams* (1) is in point. * * But further, here the declaration is founded upon the fact of the children being the servants of the

[*490]

(1) 38 R. R. 613 (1 Cr. & M. 345).

plaintiff, and upon a trespass *per quod servitium amisit.* The   Gilbert
defendants justify the trespass under their testamentary guardian;   Schwenck.
to which the plaintiff replies, that she is so also. That is a
departure from the declaration : her being their guardian does not
make her their mistress. There is no question here as to her
right to have the custody of them for the purpose of nurture, or of
any parental right.

(PLATT, B.: Is not the plea bad?)

No; for the stat. 12 Car. II. c. 24, s. 8, gives to the testamentary
guardian a positive control over the infant after the father's death,
although the Courts, in their discretion, have said that they will
not remove it out of the custody of the mother within a certain
age. Upon the plea, it must be taken as if the plaintiff were not
named as a guardian in the will at all. The plea in effect says,
the infants were in the service of the plaintiff without the licence
of William Gilbert as their testamentary guardian, and the defendants took them away by his authority. Then the plaintiff, in her
replication, claims them in the same character: and it does not
even say that she had the possession of them as her wards; but
merely that she also is testamentary guardian. The action under
the statute, as guardian, is quite different from the present; and
there the damages go to increase the estate of the *child. But   [*491]
when she comes into conflict with the co-guardian, she cannot, as
against him, assume the character of mother, and therefore mistress.
Littleton says expressly (s. 323), "Where two be possessed of the
wardship of the body of an infant within age, if the one taketh the
infant out of the possession of the other, the other hath no remedy
by an action by the law, but to take the infant out of the possession
of the other when he sees his time."

Peacock, contrà :

The plea is bad in substance. This action is brought in right of
the plaintiff's character as mistress of servants—not merely as
mother, nor as guardian. It is only on this ground that the
mother can sue for an injury to her child; the declaration therefore alleges a loss of service. The plea admits they were her
servants; but if so, the testamentary guardian cannot take an
infant out of the custody of its master or mistress, and so destroy
the contract of service. Suppose the case of an infant of the age
of eighteen or nineteen, with no provision under his father's will,

GILBERT
*.
SCHWENCK.

who has bound himself apprentice to a trade: can his uncle, who may have been appointed his testamentary guardian, take him out of his master's custody, and prevent his earning his wages?

(POLLOCK, C. B.: The question is, whether an infant can make a contract of service which shall prevent the right of custody of the guardian under the Act of Parliament.)

Suppose the co-guardian seduced the infant daughter while living with her mother, surely she might sue him for the seduction; yet she cannot, unless the infant could make a good contract of service with her. [He cited *Rex* v. *The Inhabitants of Chillesford* (1).]

[492]   *Jervis*, in reply:

It is admitted on the other side that this declaration is not founded upon any right of guardianship, but upon a supposed contract of service. Then the plea is, that that contract was entered into without the consent of the testamentary guardian. That is a sufficient answer; for an infant cannot disentitle his guardian to his statutory right, by making a private contract of service with a third party. He may, indeed, as in *Rex* v. *Chillesford*, contract for his own benefit, and so acquire a settlement, and the assent thereto of the father will be presumed till the contrary appears. But such a contract is not valid to prevent the dissenting testamentary guardian from intervening. The two stand *in loco parentis*. The remedy of the master, if any, must be against the one who consented to the contract. If one guardian can, as is expressly said by Littleton, take the infant out of the possession of the other, and no action lies, no action also can lie by the party who is the master with consent of the other guardian. But here, in her replication, the plaintiff assumes a new character.

(ROLFE, B.: No; she is not going on her title as guardian, but only showing why the facts alleged in the plea do not destroy her title as mistress, because she says the contract of service was made with the consent of the co-guardian.)

                                                       Cur. adv. vult.

The judgment of the COURT was now delivered by

[493]   PLATT, B. [His Lordship stated the pleadings, and continued:]

The question raised upon this demurrer is, whether William

                    (1) 4 B. & C. 94.

Gilbert, by reason of his having been united with the testator's widow in the testamentary guardianship of infant children, the issue of her marriage with her deceased husband, could legally remove, against her will and during her widowhood, those children from her custody and service. The solution of this question depends upon the nature of the power which, at the time of the alleged trespass, vested in William Gilbert by virtue of his appointment of joint guardian.

Guardians appointed by will, according to the statute of 12 Car. II. c. 24, have no more power than guardians in socage, and are but trustees. This doctrine is recognized in *The Duke of Beaufort* v. *Berty* (1) and *Frederick* v. *Frederick* (2). But one of two joint trustees cannot act in the trust in defiance of the will of the other; each has an equal power. It seems to follow, that as the children were in the custody of the plaintiff, and in a service which, upon these pleadings, must be taken to have been in its nature lawful, the defendants, as the servants of William Gilbert, were not justified in removing them against the plaintiff's will.

It is unnecessary to discuss the effect of the plaintiff's being, in the absence of any appointment of testamentary guardian, the natural guardian of the infants. We think that, upon the pleadings, the plaintiff is entitled to judgment.

Judgment for the plaintiff.

BRADBURNE v. BOTFIELD (3).

(14 Meeson & Welsby, 559—574; S. C. 14 L. J. Ex. 330.)

1845.
July 9.

[559]

A declaration in covenant stated, that, by indenture of lease, Sir E. W. and J. A. A., (who were seised in fee of an undivided fourth part of the premises in trust for E. M. F.), E. F. and E. M. F. his wife (the cestui que trusts), M. W., who was seised in fee of another undivided fourth part, W. T. who was seised in fee of half, and G. T. and S. T., who had equitable interests in that half, jointly demised, according to their several estates, rights, and interests in certain coal-mines, to the defendant and two others, yielding and paying certain rents to the said E. F., E. M. F., Sir E. W., J. A. A., M. W., S. T., G. T., and W. T. respectively, and to their respective heirs and assigns, according to their several and respective estates, rights, and interests in the premises; that the defendant and the two other lessees covenanted with all the above parties, and each and every of them, their and each and every of their heirs, executors, administrators, and assigns, to repair the premises, and to surrender them in good

(1) 1 P. Wms. 703.
(2) *Id.* 721.
(3) Cited as a leading authority by Bowen, L. J., in *Pulmer* v. *Mallet*

(1887) 36 Ch. Div. 422, 57 L. J. Ch. 226; and see *Sorsbie* v. *Park* (1848) 67 R. R. 283 (12 M. & W. 146). —J. G. P.

BRADBURNE
v.
BOTFIELD.

repair to the lessors, their heirs and assigns, respectively, at the end of the term, and to work the mines properly. The declaration then deduced to the plaintiff a title to the moiety of the said W. T., and alleged as breaches the non-repair of the premises, and the improper working of the mines. Plea, that J. A. A. was the survivor of all the covenantees: Held, that the covenants were joint, and not several, and that the surviving covenantee ought to have brought the action.

COVENANT. The declaration stated, that, at the time of the demise thereinafter mentioned, Sir E. Winnington and J. A. Addenbrooke were seised in their demesne as of fee of one undivided fourth part of the demised premises ; that Mary Whitby was seised of one other undivided fourth part, and that W. Townsend was seised of two other undivided fourth parts; and thereupon, by an indenture of lease, of the 1st of October, 1801, made between the Honourable E. Foley and Eliza Maria his wife, of the first part; the said Sir E. Winnington and J. A. Addenbrooke, of the second part; Mary Whitby, of the third part ; Sarah Townsend, widow, relict of Gilbert Townsend, deceased, of the fourth part ; George Townsend, only son and heir-at-law of the said Gilbert Townsend, of the fifth part; the defendant and Thomas Botfield and Beriah Botfield, of the sixth part; after reciting, that, by virtue of an indenture of bargain and sale, dated the 13th of August, 1793, and made between the said Edward Foley and Eliza Maria his wife, one of the three co-heirs of Thomas Hoo, Esq., deceased, of the one part, and Sir E. Winnington and J. A. Addenbrooke, of the other part, and also by virtue of a fine levied in pursuance thereof, one fourth part or share of the premises thereinafter stated to be demised stood limited unto and to the use of the said Sir E. Winnington and J. A. Addenbrooke, their heirs and assigns for ever, in trust (inter *alia) for such persons and for such estates, &c., as the said Eliza Maria Foley should by deed or will appoint; and also reciting that the said Mary Whitby was seised in fee of one other undivided fourth part of the same premises; and further that, by indenture dated the 23rd of January, 1784, and a fine levied pursuant thereto, one undivided moiety of the same premises were limited unto and to the use of Gilbert Townsend and William Townsend, their heirs and assigns for ever, in trust, as to the estate of the said William Townsend, for the said Gilbert Townsend, his heirs and assigns for ever: it was witnessed, that the said Sir E. Winnington, J. A. Addenbrooke, E. Foley, Eliza Maria Foley, Mary Whitby, William Townsend, Sarah Townsend, and George Townsend, according to their several and respective estates,

[*560]

rights, and interests in the tenements thereby demised, did demise
to the defendant, and to the said Thomas Botfield and B. Botfield,
a certain messuage, buildings, and several closes of land, with all
and every the mines and veins of coal and iron-stone lying and
being under the said several closes, with full power for the defendant
and the said T. Botfield and B. Botfield, their and each of their
executors, administrators, and assigns, their and each of their
agents, &c., to work the said mines and veins of coal and iron-
stone, &c.: to hold the said messuage and buildings and closes of
land, and to hold, use, exercise, and fully enjoy all and every the
said mines, &c., unto the defendant and the said Thomas Botfield
and Beriah Botfield, their executors, &c., for the term of sixty
years, yielding and paying unto the said Edward Foley and Eliza
Maria Foley his wife, Sir E. Winnington, J. A. Addenbrooke,
Mary Whitby, Sarah Townsend, George Townsend, and William
Townsend respectively, and to their respective heirs and assigns,
according to their said several and respective estates, rights, and
interests in and to the said premises, the yearly rents and reservations therein mentioned.   And it was by the said indenture further
witnessed, *that, in consideration of the said demise, the defendant   [*561]
and the said T. Botfield and Beriah Botfield, and every of them,
did thereby for themselves and himself, and their and his joint
and several heirs, executors, &c., covenant and agree to and with
the said E. Foley and E. M. Foley his wife, Sir E. Winnington,
J. A. Addenbrooke, Mary Whitby, Sarah Townsend, George Townsend, and William Townsend, and each and every of them, their
and each and every of their heirs, executors, administrators, and
assigns, in manner following, viz., to keep the said messuage and
buildings, and also all and every the furnaces, fire-engines, iron-
works, dwelling-houses, and other erections and buildings, in good
and sufficient repair, and the same, so repaired, to deliver up at
the end or other determination of the said lease to the said lessors
(naming them), and their heirs and assigns respectively.   There
were also covenants to work the mines, &c., in a proper and
workmanlike manner.   There was also a proviso, that if the
defendant and the said T. Botfield and B. Botfield should be
desirous of determining the lease at the expiration of any one year,
and should signify such their intention by notice at least one year
before the expiration of any one year of the said term, then the
said lease should cease and determine.   The declaration then
stated the entry of the defendant and the said T. Botfield and

BRADBURNE
v.
BOTFIELD.

Beriah Botfield into the demised premises, and that they became and were possessed thereof for the said term, and so continued until the 25th of March, 1842, when the said term of sixty years was determined by a notice to quit, given by the lessees pursuant to the power to them given by the lease. The declaration then stated the death of Gilbert Townsend, and deduced a title to the plaintiff as assignee of the moiety of the said William Townsend. It then assigned for breaches, that the defendant and the said T. Botfield and B. Botfield did not keep the premises in repair, nor so yield them up at the determination of the lease, and did not work the mines in a proper and workmanlike manner.

[562]

To this declaration the defendant pleaded, and alleged the death of all the covenantees *seriatim*, except the said J. A. Addenbrooke, who was left them surviving.

General demurrer, and joinder.

The plaintiff's points marked for argument were, that the plaintiff, being the assignee of the reversion of one tenant in common, is entitled to sue alone, without joining the other tenants in common; that the covenants declared on are not only joint with all the covenantees, but also several with each covenantee, and that on the several covenants the plaintiff may sue alone; that the objection of the non-joinder of the other covenantees ought to be raised by a plea in abatement; that the order of time in which the lessors and covenantees died, and the survivorship of John A. Addenbrooke, as stated in the last plea, do not affect the right of the plaintiff to sue for breaches after the conveyance of the reversion to him.

The defendant's points were, that the plea is good, as it shows the right to sue upon the covenants to be out of the plaintiff; and that the declaration is bad, as it does not show any right to sue upon them in the plaintiff. That the covenants are joint, and could only be put in suit by all the covenantees, or the survivors or survivor, or the representative of the survivor. That the plaintiff, not being the original covenantee, can have no right of action, except by virtue of the stat. 32 Hen. VIII. c. 34; but that that statute does not apply to this case. That the reversion in one-fourth of the premises is not shown to have been ever vested in George Townsend, through whom the plaintiff claims; but is stated to have been granted by William to uses, without specifying the grantees, who may, therefore, have been living at the time of the breaches of covenant alleged in the declaration.

On the 27th of June and 2nd of July,

Unthank argued in support of the demurrer :

The declaration shows that the parties demising were tenants in
*common, and the demising power was, therefore, separate, and a   [*563]
lease by tenants in common operates as a separate demise by each :
Doe d. Poole v. *Errington* (1). The plaintiff was, therefore, entitled
to sue alone, for, his interest being several, the covenants are in
fact made with each and every of the lessors. The rule laid down
in *Windham's* case (2), and in the notes to *Eccleston* v. *Clipsham* (3),
is, that though a man covenant with two or more jointly, yet if the
interest and cause of action of the covenantees be several and not
joint, the covenant shall be taken to be several, and each of the
covenantees may bring an action for his particular damage, notwithstanding the words of the covenant are joint. That rule is
somewhat qualified by *Sorsbie* v. *Park* (4), where it was held, that
where the words of a covenant are expressly joint, it will be so
construed, although the interest may be several, and *vice versâ ;*
but where the words are ambiguous, they may be construed to be
joint or several, according to the interest. That decision, although
somewhat questioned by the Court of Queen's Bench in *Hopkinson*
v. *Lee* (5), is in accordance with the doctrine laid down in
Anderson v. *Martindale* (6).

(PARKE, B. : Perhaps the Court of Queen's Bench misunderstood
what I said in *Sorsbie* v. *Park.* When I used the word "joint," I
meant expressly joint.)

It is admitted that, if the interest were joint, it might have been
necessary for all the covenantees to join in the action ; but here the
recitals show that the interest was several, and that some of the
parties, namely, Mr. and Mrs. Foley, had no legal estate whatever.
Slingsby's case (7) shows that, the interest being several, and the
covenants being made with the lessors, and each and every of them,
they may sue separately. *There it was agreed, that "when it   [*564]
appears by the declaration that every of the covenantees hath or is
to have a several interest or estate, there when the covenant is

(1) 40 R. R. 415 (1 Ad. & El. 750;   146).
3 Nev. & M. 646).   (5) 66 R. R. 617 (6 Q. B. 964).
(2) 5 Co. Rep. 18 a.   (6) 6 R. R. 334 (1 East, 497).
(3) 1 Saund. 154.   (7) 5 Co. Rep. 18 b.
(4) 67 R. R. 283 (12 M. & W.

BRADBURNE
v.
BOTFIELD

made with the covenantees *et cum quolibet eorum,* these words make *cum quolibet eorum* the covenant several in respect of their several interests. As if a man by indenture demises to A. Black-acre, to B. White-acre, to C. Green-acre, and covenants with them and *quolibet eorum* that he is lawful owner of all the said acres, &c., in this case, in respect of the several interests by the words *et cum quolibet eorum,* the covenant in the deed is several. But if he demises to them the acres jointly, then these words *cum quolibet eorum* are void, for a man, by his covenant, (if not in respect of several interests), cannot make it first joint, and then make it several by the same or the like words, *cum quolibet eorum.*"

(PARKE, B.: The difficulty is, how are the Foleys to sue ?—the introduction of their names makes the difficulty. If all may sue, all must sue.)

The words "*cum quolibet eorum*" make it a separate cause of action.

(PARKE, B.: It may be so as to all of them except those who have no interest at all. *Slingsby's* case appears to be against you there.)

All the parties to the indenture might sue, or Winnington and Addenbrooke might sue separately for the Foleys.

(PARKE, B.: *Hopkinson* v. *Lee* is precisely in point, and I think is good law. Lord DENMAN there appears to have mistaken what I said in *Sorsbie* v. *Park.* I meant to say, where the covenant was positively joint. If you covenant with A., B., and C. jointly, and the survivor of them, they must sue jointly on the covenant. It follows from that, that if you join parties to the deed who have no interest, you cannot sever and sue separately.)

The covenant, as far as it is joint, is a covenant in gross; then the adding the words "*cum quolibet eorum*" makes it also several. The interest of the Foleys is a several interest as cestui que trusts.

(ALDERSON, B.: Then you get to this vicious argument, that the whole is not equal to its parts.)

[*565]   If this is *a covenant in gross, and all the parties be dead, who is to sue ?

(PARKE, B. : The executor of the survivor, who represents the testator. Every covenant is a personal matter, and goes to the executor : *Rennell* v. *Bishop of Lincoln* (1). This might have done very well if the Foleys had not been covenantees.)

In *Slingsby's* case it is also said, " So, if a man make a feoffment in fee by deed to three, and warrant the land to them *et quolibet eorum*, the warranty is joint and not several ; but in such case, if their estates were several, their warranty would be several accordingly." And in this case, the interest of the covenantees being several, the words "*et quolibet eorum*" make them separate covenants.

(ALDERSON, B.: You must sue in the names of all jointly, or of each separately, in respect of their several interests. The covenants cannot be joint with all, and separate with all, except A. B.

PARKE, B.: You must construe the deed at the time it is dated, and then there is nothing in which Mr. and Mrs. Foley are jointly interested with the rest of the covenantees.)

If the whole deed were set out, it would appear that they had a several interest for the rent.

(PARKE, B. : We adopted that course in *Sorsbie* v. *Park*, to see if there were a separate interest, which would make the covenant several. And if you can amend your case by showing that there is such an interest, you may do so.)

(The case was then postponed till Wednesday, July 2nd, when, the learned Barons having been furnished with a copy of the lease, the argument proceeded.)

Unthank, for the plaintiff :

(PARKE, B.: I do not see any separate covenants in the lease, which give the parties a separate interest, except the covenant as to the rent : all the rest are joint. With regard to the covenant for getting coal, all are equally interested in that covenant. *The covenant here declared upon is to do one thing, namely, to repair the premises. Suppose there were a covenant with four tenants in common to repair, could each sue separately ?)

BRADBURNE
v.
BOTFIELD.

[*566]

(1) 36 R. R. 139 (7 B. & C. 113; 9 Dowl. & Ry. 810).

BRADBURNE
v.
BOTFIELD.

It is submitted that they could. In *Wilkinson* v. *Hall* (1), it was held that tenants in common cannot sue jointly for double value for holding over, where there has been no joint demise. There TINDAL, Ch. J., after quoting Littleton, ss. 316 and 317, says, " So, if there be no joint demise, there must be several actions of debt for rent, for a joint action is not maintainable except upon a joint demise. Here, upon the face of the declaration, it appears that the defendants held a moiety of the premises under one of the tenants in common, and another moiety under the other." And he afterwards adds, " How can two tenants in common have a joint interest in the proceeds of several demises ? "

(PARKE, B. : If there is a demise by one tenant in common as to his moiety, and a demise by the other tenant in common as to the other moiety, by the same instrument, and there is a covenant to repair, I want you to show that each may sue separately.)

The difficulty in the cases has been, whether they may join. In *Midgley* v. *Lovelace* (2) and *Kitchen* v. *Buckly* (3), it was held that they may join. And in *Wentworth* v. *Russell* (4), it was held that an action for pound breach brought by two tenants in common was maintainable, or that one only might have sued. So, in *Johnson* v. *Wilson* (5), it was held that tenants in common might recover in an action for not performing an award. All the cases, except *Foley* v. *Addenbrooke* (6), are in favour of the plaintiff. There, however, there was a distinct statement of a joint demise by both.

(PARKE, B. : The joint words, you say, were satisfied, because there was a joint demise.)

[*567]

Yes; but in this case there is a separate demise *by each, and a reservation according to the several interests of the parties ; and according to TINDAL, Ch. J., in *Wilkinson* v. *Hall*, where the demises are several, the actions must be several.

(PARKE, B. : Littleton says, in s. 316, that, if two tenants in common make a lease to another, rendering to them a certain rent during the term, " the tenants in common shall have an action of debt against the lessee, and not divers actions, for that the action is in the personalty.")

(1) 1 Bing. N. C. 713; 1 Scott, 675.
(2) Carthew, 289.
(3) 1 Lev. 109.
(4) 1 Moore, 452.
(5) Willes, 248.
(6) 62 R. R. 326 (4 Q. B. 197; 3 G. & D. 64).

That is where there is a joint demise. There is another point, BRADBURNE
which was not taken in *Foley* v. *Addenbrooke*, that, if four persons BOTFIELD.
make a joint lease, and afterwards one part is conveyed away, the
others may sever, and, if one sues alone, it can be taken advantage
of by plea in abatement only ; that is, because there is no variance.
That has always been the ground of the decision in these cases.
(He cited Serjeant Williams's note to *Cabbell* v. *Vaughan* (1),
Mountstephen v. *Brooke* (2), *Jell* v. *Douglas* (3), *Whelpdale's* case (4),
and *Addison* v. *Overend* (5).)

J. W. Smith, contrà :

There is no pretence for saying that this is anything but a joint
demise. The demise is joint, and so are the covenants also. But
it is said that there are covenants in the other part of the lease
which are several, and which may be imported into the case
in order to construe those declared upon. They must, however, be construed by themselves, unless there are words of
reference to the other covenants. One may be joint, and the
other several : *James* v. *Emery* (6) is an express authority for
that. It is impossible that covenants in one part of a deed can be
used to render covenants in another part of it several, which would
be otherwise joint. The covenants here are made with four persons
who had no interest, and four who had an interest; but, even if
they had been all tenants in common, *the covenants would have   [*568]
been joint, according to *Foley* v. *Addenbrooke* (7). [He cited
Littleton, s. 316, *Powis* v. *Smith* (8), and *Wallace* v. *M'Laren* (9),
and discussed the cases cited for the plaintiff, and continued :]
The plaintiff cannot deny that this is a joint covenant, in respect   [570]
of which all the covenantees might sue, but he says, that because
there are four tenants in common amongst them, the moment one
assigns his interest, it becomes a joint and several covenant, so that
the assignee may sue separately. According to that, the assignees
of each of the four who had an interest are to have a remedy by
action, in which they will recover damages for the whole breach of
covenant, and it would be impossible for the other four to maintain
any action at all. But covenants do not become joint or several by

(1) 1 Saund. 291 c.
(2) 1 B. & Ald. 224.
(3) 23 R. R. 310 (4 B. & Ald. 374).
(4) 5 Co. Rep. 119.
(5) 6 T. R. 766.
(6) 19 R. R. 503 (8 Taunt. 245; 2
Moore, 195).
(7) 62 R. R. 326 (4 Q. B. 197 ; 3 G.
& D. 64).
(8) 24 R. R. 587 (5 B. & Ald. 851).
(9) 31 R. R. 334 (1 Man. & Ry. 516).

BRADBURNE matter *ex post facto* : they must be either the one or the other at
v.
BOTFIELD. the time of the execution of the deed.

(PARKE, B. : I think the right to sue cannot be altered by the
circumstance of one of the covenantees assigning his interest. The
question is reduced to this, whether there is any several interest,
which compels us to construe the covenant to be several. That will
depend upon the lease, which we will take time to look through, as
well as into the authorities which have been cited.)

Unthank replied.

Cur. adv. vult.

The judgment of the COURT was now delivered by

PARKE, B. :

In this case, a lease had been made of certain coal and iron
mines to the defendant and others. By the indenture of demise,
Sir E. Winnington and J. A. Addenbrooke, who appeared by the
recital to be seised in fee of an undivided fourth part of the
demised property, in trust for Mrs. Foley; Edward and E. M.
Foley; Mary Whitby, who was seised in fee of another undivided
fourth part; W. Townsend, who was seised in fee of one half;
and George Townsend and Sarah Townsend, who had equitable
interests in that half, all joined in demising, according to their
[*571] several *and respective existing estates, rights, and interests in the
tenements, to the defendant and others, yielding and paying certain
rents to Edward Foley, E. M. Foley, Sir E. Winnington, J. A.
Addenbrooke, Mary Whitby, S. Townsend, G. Townsend, and W.
Townsend, respectively, and to their respective heirs and assigns,
according to their several and respective estates, rights, and
interests in the premises; and the defendant and others did
thereby covenant to and with E. Foley, E. M. Foley, &c., and
each and every of them, their and each and every of their heirs,
executors, administrators, and assigns, in manner following. And
the declaration proceeded to state covenants to repair the premises,
the furnaces, and buildings, and to surrender in good repair to the
lessors, their heirs and assigns respectively, at the end of the
term, and to work the mines properly, &c. : it then deduces
a title to William Townsend's moiety to the plaintiff, and alleges
breaches.

There is a plea stating John A. Addenbrooke to be the survivor

of all the covenantees, and a demurrer, which raises the question, BRADBURNE
whether the covenants declared upon are covenants with all the $\qquad$ v.
parties demising, or are or may be treated as several covenants BOTFIELD.
with the legal owners of each undivided part.

On the argument of the demurrer, we expressed our opinion that
upon the face of the declaration the covenants were such as all the
covenantees must have jointly sued upon, for the name of no one
covenantee could be rejected. There must be some covenant on
which all could sue, and all stated in the declaration were of the
same character. If they related to the separate legal interest of
each tenant in common, still the other covenantees must join, on
the principle of the case of *Anderson* v. *Martindale* (1). But it was
suggested that the lease ought to *have been set out on *oyer*, and if   [*572]
it had been, that it would have appeared that there were other
covenants, covenants in gross, in which all must join, and then the
covenants running with the land, those declared upon, might be
construed to be several covenants with each legal tenant in common ;
and the case stood over that we might be furnished with a copy of
the lease. On this being done, *Mr. Unthank* cited several authorities,
which he contended established the proposition, that the covenants
declared upon might be treated as several covenants, and the Court
took time to look into those authorities.

There is no occasion to refer to the cases relating to the rule of
construction as to covenants being joint or several according to the
interest of the parties, which is perfectly well established. In the
case of *Sorsbie* v. *Park* (2), Lord ABINGER and myself, on referring to
the established rule, as laid down by Lord Chief Justice GIBBS in the
case of *James* v. *Emery* (3), approved of Mr. Preston's qualification
and explanation of it in his edition of the Touchstone, 166, namely,
that, if the language of the covenant was capable of being so construed,
it was to be taken to be joint or several, according to the interest of
the parties to it. Mr. Preston adds, that the general rule proposed
by Sir VICARY GIBBS, and to be found in several books, would
establish that there was a rule of law too powerful to be controlled
by any intention, however express ; and I consider such qualification
to be perfectly correct, and at variance with no decided case, as it
is surely as competent for a person, by express joint words, strong
enough to make a joint covenant, to do one thing for the benefit of
one of the covenantees, and another for the benefit of another, as it

(1) 6 R. R. 334 (1 East, 497).   (3) 19 R. R. 503 (2 Moore, 195).
(2) 67 R. R. 283 (12 M. & W. 146).

BRADBURNE
v.
BOTFIELD.
[*573]

is to make a joint demise where it is for the benefit of one. I mention this, because the Court of Queen's Bench, in the case of *Hopkinson* v. *Lee* (1), have supposed, that Lord ABINGER and *myself had sanctioned some doctrine at variance with the case of *Anderson* v. *Martindale*, and *Slingsby's* case, which it was far from my intention, and I have no doubt from Lord ABINGER's, to do; it being fully established, I conceive, by those cases, that one and the same covenant cannot be made both joint and several with the covenantees. It may be fit to observe, that a part of Mr. Preston's explanation, that, by express words, a covenant may be joint and several with the covenantors or covenantees, notwithstanding the interests are several, is inaccurately expressed : it is true only of covenantors, and the case cited from Salkeld, p. 898, relates to them ; probably Mr. Preston intended no more, and I never meant to assent to the doctrine that the same covenant might be made, by any words, however strong, joint and several, where the interest was joint ; and it is this part, I apprehend, of Mr. Preston's doctrine to which the Court of Queen's Bench objects. I think it right to give this explanation, that it may not be supposed that there is any difference on this point with the Court of Queen's Bench.

We have looked, since the argument, into the lease now set out on *oyer*, and into all the authorities cited for the plaintiff, and are still of opinion that he cannot recover upon the covenants stated in the declaration.

It is impossible to strike out the name of any covenantee, and all the covenantees must therefore necessarily sue upon some covenant ; and there appear to us to be no covenants in the lease which are of a joint nature, if those declared upon are not, or which would be in gross, if the persons entitled to the legal estate had alone demised ; for all relate to and affect the quality of the subject of the demise, or the mode of enjoying it, and could have been sued upon by the assignee of the reversion on such a lease, before breach.   The covenant relied upon as being in gross, viz. that the lessors should be at liberty to use the ropes, &c. to descend into the mines, is a

[*574]

special covenant, relating to *the entry to view, and would, we think, go to the assignee of the reversion on such lease. If all the covenantees could not sue on the covenants declared upon, they could sue upon none.   All, therefore, in their lives, and after the death of any, the survivors, are the proper plaintiffs.   It becomes, therefore, unnecessary to decide whether one of several tenants in

(1) 66 R. R. 617 (6 Q. B. 964).

common, lessors, could sue on a covenant with all to repair, as to   Bradburne
which there is no decisive authority either way (1).   That all could   Botfield.
sue is perfectly clear : *Kitchen* v. *Buckly* (2).

Our judgment must be for the defendant.

Judgment for the defendant.

RUSSELL *v.* LEDSAM.

1845.

(14 Meeson & Welsby, 574; S. C. 14 L. J. Ex. 353; 9 Jur. 557; in Ex. Ch.
16 M. & W. 633; in H. L., 1 H. L. C. 687.)

[THE reports of this case in the Court of Exchequer and the
Exchequer Chamber will be consolidated with the report in the
House of Lords in a future volume of the Revised Reports.]

PHILLIPPS *v.* SMITH.

1845.
July 9.

(14 Meeson & Welsby, 589—595; S. C. 15 L. J. Ex. 201.)

[589]

Lessee for years cutting down willows, and leaving the stools or butts,
from which they will shoot afresh, is not waste, unless they are a shelter
to the house, or a support to the bank of a stream against the water (3).

THIS was an action of assumpsit, brought by the plaintiff against
the defendant, who had been his tenant from year to year of a farm
in the county of Leicester, for managing and cultivating it contrary
to the course of good husbandry, and in a bad and untenant-like
manner.   The defendant pleaded *non assumpsit*, and also that he
managed and cultivated the farm in a good and tenant-like manner ;
on which issues were joined.

At the trial, before Maule, J., at the last Leicester Assizes, the
only acts provided against the defendant were, the cutting down,
for the purpose of sale, of a number of pollard willow trees, of considerable size, which grew on the side of a brook, but were not
shown to be of any service *as a support of the bank against the   [*590]
water, nor to be any protection to the farm-house ; and also some
trivial injuries to the fences.   The willows were cut down close to
the ground, leaving the stools or butts, from which fresh shoots
grow again.   It was contended for the defendant, that such cutting
down of these trees was not a breach of the implied agreement to
cultivate according to good husbandry and in a tenant-like manner :

(1) See *Thompson* v. *Hakewill* (1865)   (2) Sir T. Ray. 80 ; 1 Keb. 565 ; 1
19 C. B. (N. S.) 713, 35 L. J. C. P. 18 ;   Sid. 157 ; 1 Lev. 109.
and *Roberts* v. *Holland* [1893] 1 Q. B.   (3) See *Dashwood* v. *Magniac* [1891]
665, 62 L. J. Q. B. 621.—J. G. P.   3 Ch. 306, 60 L. J. Ch. 809.—J. G. P.

PHILLIPPS
v.
SMITH.

for the plaintiff it was answered, that it was so, inasmuch as this amounted to positive waste. The learned Judge reserved the point, and the jury having assessed the value of the willows cut down at 64l., he gave the defendant leave to move to reduce the damages (which in the whole were 66l. 4s. 6d.) by that sum.

In Easter Term, *Humfrey* moved pursuant to the leave reserved, and having cited the Year Book, 12 Hen. VIII. 1, b (1), as an authority that the cutting down of these willow trees was not waste, obtained a rule *nisi*, against which, on a former day of the present sittings (June 19),

Whitehurst (with whom were *Hill* and *Willmore*) showed cause:

The question here is not whether the cutting of these willows was waste or not, but whether it was managing the farm in a good and tenant-like manner.

(PARKE, B.: No custom of the country is alleged; what, then, is untenant-like management but waste? There can be no obligation on the tenant, except to farm according to the custom of the country or special agreement—both of which are excluded here,—or according to the common law.)

Then the plaintiff will contend that the cutting of these trees was destruction of the inheritance, and so waste at common law. The common law must be founded *on reason. Now, in flat and marshy districts, the only timber for the use of the farm, for house-bote, &c., may be willows, which are most valuable for that purpose; and can a tenant not merely take their toppings, but wholly destroy them, without being guilty of waste?

[*591]

(PARKE, B.: It is laid down in Co. Litt. 53 a, that "waste properly is in timber trees (viz. oak, ash, and elm, and these be timber in all places), either by cutting of them down, or topping of them, or doing any act whereby the timber may decay. Also, in countries where timber is scant, and beeches or the like are converted to buildings for the habitation of man, or the like, they are all accounted timber:" and that "cutting down of willows, beech, birch, ash, maple, or the like, standing in the defence and safeguard of the house, is destruction.")

(1) "Unô si le lessee doit reparer ô, donq ô seroit wast, côe willows ne sont wast, si sont cressāts in ascū lieu; mes si sont in view d'un manoir p̄ defendr̄ le vēt, ou sōt in un banc pur sustenir le banc, dōq sōt wast." [Corrected with Y. B.—J. G. P.

At common law, the tenant cannot use the stocks of trees except **PHILLIPPS**
for the purposes of the farm; if he sells or otherwise uses them, it   *v.*
is waste. The authorities on this subject are collected in Vin. Abr.,   **SMITH.**
Waste (E.). It is there said, " Of whitethorns waste may be
by cutting down ; " citing 46 Edw. III. 17, and 9 Hen. VI. 67.
" If a termor cuts down underwood of hazel, willows, maple, or
oak, which is seasonable, it is not waste : M. 11 Jac. B." (1) Again,
" Waste may be committed by cutting down of certain pear-trees :
7 Hen. VI. 38. So it may be committed in cutting down certain
apple-trees : 7 Hen. VI. 38." In Bro. Abr., Waste, pl. 44, it is also
said to have been agreed that cutting down whitethorns was waste.
So, in Dyer, 35 b, *n.* 33, it is said, that eradicating or unseasonably
cutting them is waste. So, in Cro. Jac. 126, pl. 15, " Stubbing up
a whitethorn hedge, or felling timber, or any kind of trees standing
for the safeguard of the house or cattle, is destruction." It seems,
therefore, from these authorities, that if the tenant destroys the
tree so as to prevent the crop, that is waste as to other than timber
trees. Lessee may cut a hedge, but may not grub it up: so he
might lop or cut these trees, but he could not destroy *them to the   [*592]
bottom. The passage from the Year Book, 12 Hen. VIII., mentioned on moving for this rule, was a mere *obiter dictum* of
BRUDNEL, J., and no authority is cited ; and whether he refers to
mere pruning, or cutting down altogether, does not appear.

(ROLFE, B. : A hedge may stand on a different footing ; because
it is important as marking the boundaries of the land.)

This was not a cutting as a crop, or for the use of the farm, but for
sale, and amounted, according to the authorities, to waste at the
common law.

Humfrey and *Macaulay, contrà :*

This was not waste. Every exposition given in Co. Litt. 53 a,
of what is waste, excludes this. When it is said that " cutting down
of willows, &c., standing in the defence and safeguard of the house,
is destruction," that is *exclusio alterius.* Nor is there any authority
which says that the mere cutting down of trees, not timber trees,
is waste. Thus in Cro. Jac. 127, the case is thus: " Note, it was
held by all the COURT, that eradicating of whitethorns is waste ;

(1) The quotation from Viner has   Smith's Case (Mich. 11 Jac. I. in the
been corrected. The reference " M.   Common Pleas), reported in Godbolt,
11 Jac. B." is to Sir John Gage and   p. 209.—J. G. P.

PHILLIPPS
v.
SMITH.

but *succidendo* (*i.e.* felling) *et vendendo* is no waste, unless it be laid that they grew in pasture for defence of cattle, and were of the greatness of timber." In Com. Dig., Biens (H.), the rule of law is stated to be, that "lessee for life or years has only a special interest and property in the fruit and shade of timber-trees, so long as they are annexed to the land; and he has a general property in hedges, bushes, trees, &c., which are not timber; and therefore, if the lessee cuts down hedges or trees not timber, the lessee shall have them." That rule is adopted by TINDAL, Ch. J., in *Berriman* v. *Peacock* (1), where he says, that, "according to the old authorities, the general property in trees (*i.e.*, timber trees) is in the landlord, and the general property in bushes is in the tenant; although, if

[*593]

he exceeds his right, *as by grubbing up or destroying fences, he may be liable to an action of waste." The tenant undoubtedly cannot eradicate a tree not timber, because that is necessarily a damage to the inheritance; but the cutting down of trees which spring again from the stools, like willows, is not so.

(ROLFE, B. : In the case of a fir tree, I should say the cutting it down to the ground would be waste, because it will not grow again.)

Cur. adv. vult.

The judgment of the COURT was now delivered by

ALDERSON, B. :

The only point upon which the Court reserved its judgment in this case was, whether the cutting down of the willow trees, in respect of which the jury have assessed the damages at 64*l.*, amounted to waste at the common law. And, upon full consideration, we think it did not; and that the verdict found by the jury should be reduced to the sum of 2*l.* 4*s.* 6*d.*, according to the reservation of the learned Judge.

These willow trees were of considerable size, and were standing by the side of a brook, but were not serviceable either as a defence or support of the bank against the water, nor were they standing so as to be a protection to the house demised.

The principle upon which waste depends is well stated in the case of *Lord Darcy* v. *Askwith* (2), thus : "It is generally true that the lessee hath no power to change the nature of the thing demised ; he cannot turn meadow into arable, nor stub a wood to make it pasture, nor dry up an ancient pool or piscary, nor suffer ground

(1) 35 R. R. 568 (9 Bing. 384).   (2) Hob. 234.

to be surrounded, nor destroy the pale of park, for then it ceaseth
to be a park; nor he may not destroy the stock or breed of anything, because it disherits and takes away the perpetuity of succession,
as villains, fish, deer, young spring of woods, or *the like." Thus,
the destruction of germens, or young plants destined to become
trees, Co. Litt. 53 a, which destroys the future timber, is waste;
the cutting of apple-trees in a garden or orchard, or the cutting
down a hedge of thorns, Co. Litt. 53 a, which changes the nature
of the thing demised ; or the eradicating or unseasonable cutting
of whitethorns, Vin. Abr., Waste (E.), which destroys the future
growth, are all acts of waste.   On the other hand, those acts are
not waste which, as RICHARDSON, Ch. J., in *Barrett* v. *Barrett* (1),
says, are not prejudicial to the inheritance, as, in that case, the
cutting of sallows, maples, beeches, and thorns, there alleged to be
of the age of thirty-three years, but which were not timber either
by general law or particular local custom.   So, likewise, cutting
even of oaks or ashes, where they are of seasonable wood, *i.e.* where
they are cut usually as underwood, and in due course are to grow
up again from the stumps, is not waste.   Now if we apply the
principles to be extracted from all these authorities to the present
case, we have no difficulty in saying that the cutting of these willows
does not amount to waste.   They are not timber trees, and when
cut down they are not, so far as appears by the evidence, destroyed,
but grow up again from their stumps, and produce again their
ordinary and usual profit by such growth ; therefore neither is the
thing demised destroyed, nor is the thing demised changed as to
the inheritance, for profit remains, as before, derivable from the
reproduction of the wood from the stump of the willow cut down.
Nor are the trees in such a situation as to make the cutting of them
waste, by reason of what is called collateral respect ; as where trees
not timber are situated so as to be useful for protection of a house,
Co. Litt. 53, and so become, as it were, a part of the house ; as in
Hob. 219, willows growing within the site of the house.   Nor are
they willows within view of the manor-house, which defend it from
the wind, *or in a bank to sustain the bank, 12 Hen. VIII. 1; or like
whitethorns used for the like purpose, or where they stand in a field
depastured, and are used for the shade of the beasts depasturing, and
so are intended permanently to remain in that particular form, for
the advantage of those to whom the inheritance may thereafter come.
   We therefore think that the cutting of them by the defendant

(1) Hetley, 35.

was not an act of waste at the common law; and as he is not liable, either by agreement or by the custom of the country, for having cut them, we think the verdict should be reduced, and the rule made absolute for that purpose.

Rule absolute.

WIGGINS AND JAMESON *v.* JOHNSTON.

(14 Meeson & Welsby, 609—623; S. C. 15 L. J. Ex. 202.)

The defendant chartered a vessel for a voyage from London to Bombay, at which port she was addressed to G. & Co., the defendant's agents there; and by another charter-party of the same date, it was agreed that the ship should, after discharging her cargo at Bombay, take in a homeward cargo, for which the defendant agreed to pay freight, as to one-half the cargo, at 3*l.* per ton, and as to the rest, at the current rate of freight when the ship should be loading. In this latter charter-party there was also a stipulation, that the master of the vessel (who was a part owner) and G. & Co., the agents at Bombay, were at liberty to make such alterations in the charter-party as they might mutually think proper, without prejudice to that agreement. Soon after the arrival of the ship at Bombay, the master and G. & Co. entered into a written agreement (which was indorsed on the second charter-party) that the ship might proceed to Aden with Government coals and stores (her outward cargo), and return to Bombay with all possible despatch, without prejudice to the charter-party. She accordingly, in the month of February, sailed to Aden, and there discharged her cargo, and returned to Bombay, where she arrived in May. The owners received a large sum as freight for this voyage to Aden: Held, that the defendant was bound by the alteration made in the charter-party by G. & Co. permitting the voyage to Aden, which was within the scope of the authority given to them by the stipulation above mentioned; and therefore that he was bound to pay the charter-rate of 3*l.* per ton for half the cargo, although that exceeded the current rate of freight at the time of the loading, and although the alteration might be prejudicial to his interests; and that he was not entitled to have the freight earned by the owners on the voyage to Aden brought into the account.

THIS was an action of assumpsit, stated in the particulars of demand to be brought to recover 968*l.* 11*s.* 4*d.*, balance of freight per ship *Harmony*, due from the defendant to the plaintiffs.

The declaration stated, that the defendant was indebted to the plaintiffs in 3,000*l.*, for freight and reward due and payable from the defendant to the plaintiffs for and in respect of the carriage and conveyance of divers goods, merchandizes, and chattels, by the plaintiffs before that time carried and conveyed for the defendant, and at his request, in and on board of a certain ship or vessel, from divers ports and places to divers other ports and places, and there, to wit, at the last-mentioned ports and places, delivered by the plaintiffs for the defendant, at his request, and in 3,000*l.* for money due from the defendant to the plaintiffs on an account stated

between them ; and that the defendant promised to pay the said   WIGGINS
sums on request ; and concluded with the usual breach.   *v.*
                                                                   JOHNSTON.

The defendant pleaded to the whole of the declaration, that he
did not promise as alleged ; and further pleaded, as to 701*l.* 4*s.* 9*d.*,
parcel of the sum of 3,000*l.* in the first count of the declaration
mentioned, payment to the plaintiffs and acceptance by them of
the sum of 701*l.* 4*s.* 9*d.* in satisfaction.

The plaintiffs joined issue on the first plea, and traversed *the   [*610]
second, on which the defendant has joined issue.

By the consent of the parties, and by the order of ALDERSON, B.,
the following case has been stated for the opinion of the Court
since issue was joined :

On the 1st day of August, 1842, the plaintiffs (by Mr. Wiggins,
their agent mentioned in the following charter-parties) and the
defendant entered into and signed the two charter-parties, of which
the following are copies :

"LONDON, 1st August, 1842.—It is this day mutually agreed
between Mr. Wiggins, for the owners of the good ship or vessel
called the *Harmony*, of the measurement of 830 tons or thereabouts,
now in the port of Liverpool, and Mr. Robert Johnston, merchant,
that the said ship, being tight, staunch, and strong, and every way
fitted for the voyage, shall with all possible despatch proceed direct
to Clyde, to be loaded at Greenock, free of lighterage to the ship,
and there load, in the usual and customary manner, in regular
turn, at any one of the collieries freighters may name, a full and
complete cargo of coals, not less then 750 nor more than 1,000 tons,
which said freighter binds himself to ship, with liberty to take any
light freight which may offer, not exceeding what she can reasonably
stow and carry over and above her tackle, apparel, provisions, and
furniture, and, being so loaded, shall therewith proceed to Bombay,
to sail in fifteen days after the coals are on board, or so near thereunto as she may safely get, and deliver the same into craft which
will be sent alongside for that purpose : notice to be given to the
agents of the vessel being ready to discharge, (the act of God, the
Queen's enemies, fire, and all and every other dangers and accidents
of the seas, rivers, and navigation during the said voyage always
mutually excepted) : the freight to be paid at and after the rate of
20*s.* per ton of 20 cwt. on the quantity delivered in full ; and such
freight is to be paid, say one-third by *bill at two months from the   [*611]
final sailing of the vessel from her last port in Great Britain, or in
cash under discount, the same to be returned if the vessel be lost,

the freighter having power to insure the amount and deduct it from the first payment of freight; and the remainder in rupees to the master, at the exchange of 2s. 2d. per rupee, on right delivery of the cargo. The vessel to take turn to delivery as customary, not less than twenty-one tons per day. If the vessel return to London, she is to be addressed to and reported at the Custom-house by Henry and Calvert Toulmin, of No. 8, George Yard, Lombard Street, to whom the commission on this charter-party is due, ship lost or not lost. Penalty for non-performance of this contract, 1,000l. The vessel to be addressed to freighter's agents at Bombay."

"LONDON, 1st August, 1842.—It is this day mutually agreed between Mr. Wiggins, for the owner of the good ship or vessel called the *Harmony*, of the measurement of 830 tons or thereabouts, now at Liverpool, and Mr. Robert Johnston, of London, merchant, that the said ship, being tight, staunch, and strong, and every way fitted for the voyage, shall with all convenient speed sail and proceed to Bombay with coals from Clyde, or so near thereunto as she may safely get, and there load from the factors of the said merchant a full and complete cargo of cotton, or other legal merchandize, not exceeding what she can reasonably stow and carry over and above her tackle, apparel, provisions, and furniture, and, being so loaded, shall therewith proceed to London, Liverpool, or Clyde, as may be determined at Bombay—if London, in any dock the said freighter may appoint, or so near thereunto as she may safely get—and deliver the same on being paid freight at and after the rate of 3l. per ton for half of the cargo; the remainder of the cargo to be procured at the current rate of freight at the time

[*612]

the ship be loading; upon which freighter's agents are to be *paid by the owners the usual commission for procuring the same, and the tonnage of the whole to be computed according to the new schedule of tonnage now in use at Bombay, (the act of God, the Queen's enemies, fire, and all and every other dangers and accidents of the seas, rivers, and navigation, of whatever nature and kind soever, during the said voyage, always excepted): the freight to be paid on unloading and right delivery of the cargo, in cash, two months after the report of the ship inwards at the Custom-house, or under discount: eighty running days are to be allowed the said merchant (if the ship is not sooner despatched) for loading the said ship at Bombay, to commence from the period of the vessel being ready to load, the master giving freighter's agents written notice to that effect, and ten days on demurrage over and above the said

laying days, at 10l. per day: the vessel to be consigned to Henry   WIGGINS
and Calvert Toulmin on her return to London, with whom the   JOHNSTON.
original charter-party is deposited. Penalty for non-performance
of this agreement, 3,500l. The master to sign bills of lading for
half of the cargo, at any rate of freight not less than the current
rates, without prejudice to the charter-party, and for the remaining
half at the current rates of freight at which the cargo is procurable.
It is also further understood and agreed, that the master of the
vessel, and the agents at Bombay, are at liberty to make such
alterations in this charter-party as they may mutually think
proper, without prejudice to this agreement."

The above charters were both made and entered into at the same
time, and in pursuance of them the vessel sailed from Greenock
with coals for Bombay, in September, 1842, addressed (on the
nomination of the defendant) to Messrs. Grey & Co., at Bombay,
as the agents of the defendant, and arrived at Bombay on the 31st
January, 1843. Meantime, namely, on the 6th December, 1842,
in London, the defendant entered into an agreement in writing
*with Messrs. Grey, Coles & Co., who carried on business under   [*613]
that name in London, and under the said firm of Grey & Co. at
Bombay, as merchants, of which the following is a copy:

"Dec. 6th, 1842.—MESSRS. GREY, COLES & Co., London.—It is
this day mutually agreed between Messrs. Grey, Coles & Co.,
London, and Robert Johnston, charterer of the ship *Harmony*,
bound from the Clyde to Bombay, that the said ship shall be
addressed at Bombay to Messrs. Grey & Co. ; in consideration thereof
the said Messrs. Grey & Co. hereby engage to furnish her with a full
and complete cargo of legal merchandize for London, Liverpool, or
the Clyde, at the current rates of freight; and the said Robert
Johnston hereby agrees to allow unto the said Messrs. Grey & Co.,
of Bombay, a commission of 5l., say 5l. per cent. upon amount of
freight the ship may make. The cargo to be furnished within
eighty days from the date she is ready to receive it, or Messrs. Grey,
Coles & Co. to pay demurrage according to Mr. J.'s charter-party
with the owners annexed.

(Signed)   "GREY & Co., London.
"R. JOHNSTON, London."

A copy of the charter-party secondly above set forth was annexed
to this agreement.

Such agreement was entered into without the knowledge of the

WIGGINS
.
JOHNSTON

plaintiffs, nor was any notice thereof given to them. Messrs. Grey & Co. had not any authority or instructions to enter into the agreement hereinafter mentioned for the intermediate voyage to Aden, except so far as such authority or instructions were conferred by or contained in, or may reasonably be inferred from, the charter-party secondly above mentioned, and the agreement of the 6th of December, 1842, and the facts and other documents stated in this case, or any of them.

[614]

Shortly after the arrival of the vessel at Bombay, namely, on the 13th of February, 1843, the said Messrs. Grey & Co., being such agents as aforesaid for the defendant at Bombay, and the plaintiff James Jameson, the master of the vessel, agreed, that, before loading her homeward cargo, the said vessel might proceed on an intermediate voyage to Aden, and the following memorandum was accordingly indorsed on the charter-party secondly above set forth, and signed by the said Messrs. Grey & Co. and the plaintiff James Jameson respectively : " It is hereby agreed that the ship *Harmony* may proceed to Aden with the Government coals and stores, &c., and return to Bombay with all possible despatch, without prejudice to charter-party, as per annexed copy." In pursuance of this agreement the plaintiffs entered into a charter-party with the East India Company, for the ship to proceed to Aden with the Government coals and stores (being the cargo laden at Greenock as aforesaid), and return to Bombay as agreed upon as above mentioned ; and in pursuance of this charter, the ship sailed with the cargo last above mentioned, from Bombay, on the 16th of February, for Aden, and after discharging there, returned with all possible despatch to Bombay, which she reached on the 11th of May, 1843. The freight earned by the voyage under the said charter with the East India Company was 1,100*l.*, which the plaintiffs received of the East India Company.

Messrs. Grey & Co., at Bombay, by letter written at that place on the 28th of February, 1843, communicated to Messrs. H. and C. Toulmin, in London, they being the ship-brokers of the defendant in London, the fact of their having made the above alteration in the second charter, and arrangement for the vessel to make the intermediate voyage to Aden and back. This letter reached Messrs. Toulmin in London in April, and by the next mail they, by the

[*615]

defendant's authority, wrote and sent to Messrs. Grey & *Co. a letter, dated 1st of May, 1843, of which the following is a copy :

(The case then set out this letter, which expressed the defendant's

disapprobation of the arrangement for the voyage to Aden, and his   WIGGINS
belief that it was detrimental to his interests, but contained no $\overset{v.}{\text{JOHNSTON.}}$
express affirmance or repudiation of it.)

This letter reached Grey & Co., at Bombay, in the middle of June,
1843. This period, including the months of March, April, and
May, is usually the best period of the year for procuring cargoes
and high rates of freight from Bombay to ports in Great Britain;
and the period from the beginning of June to the end of July, being
the rainy season, is usually in each year a bad time for procuring
cargoes or good rates of freight from Bombay to the said ports.

The rates of freight from Bombay to ports in Great Britain were
higher when the *Harmony* first arrived at Bombay, as aforesaid,
than when Messrs. Grey & Co. procured her a cargo for London, as
hereinafter mentioned.

In the ordinary course of things, a ship sailing in the middle of
February from Bombay would perform the voyage to Aden,
discharge there, and return to and reach Bombay by the middle of
May, and before the commencement of the rainy season; and the
time of performing such a voyage was generally known to merchants
and shipowners when the above charter-parties were entered into.

A ship at Bombay is sometimes unable, or it is found difficult, to
procure a cargo or good rates of freight for London, Liverpool, or
the Clyde, when a cargo or good rate of freight for some other port
in Great Britain, or in Holland, may be obtained; and this fact
was generally known to merchants and ship-owners when the above
charter-parties were entered into.

Shortly after the vessel's return to Bombay, the said Messrs.
Grey & Co. proceeded to procure a cargo for *her, and obtained   [*616]
one, amounting to 1,110 tons, for London, at rates averaging
25*s.* 4*d.* per ton, which were the then current rates of freight.
With this cargo she sailed from Bombay on the 31st of July, 1843,
and reached London on the 11th of November, 1843, where her
cargo was duly delivered; and the plaintiffs received the freight
arising from this home voyage, amounting to 1,402*l.* 9*s.* 6*d.*, of
one-half of the amount of which, namely 701*l.* 4*s.* 9*d.*, the defendant
is to be at liberty to avail himself under the plea of payment: but
the plaintiffs claim of the defendant the difference between the said
sum of 701*l.* 4*s.* 9*d.*, being the amount of the current rates of freight
on half the cargo, and 1,664*l.* 16*s.*, being the chartered rate of 3*l.*
per ton on half the cargo, which difference amounts to 963*l.* 11*s.* 3*d.*,
and is the sum for which this action is brought.

WIGGINS
v.
JOHNSTON.

It is agreed that the Court may draw such inferences from the facts above stated as a jury would be warranted in doing.

The question for the opinion of the Court is, whether the defendant is bound by the said alteration made in the said charter-party by the said Messrs. Grey & Co. and the plaintiff James Jameson; and if so, whether the defendant is entitled to be allowed for the said freight produced by the voyage to Aden and back, or any and what part thereof.

If the Court shall be of opinion that the defendant is bound by the alteration, then the defendant agrees that a judgment shall be entered against him, by confession, for 968l. 11s. 3d., or so much thereof as the Court may adjudge to be recoverable, (subject to such deduction, if any, as the Court may think him entitled to in respect of the freight of the intermediate voyage), besides costs, immediately after the decision of this case, or otherwise as the Court may think fit; but if the Court shall be of opinion that the defendant is not so

[*617]   bound, then the plaintiffs agree *that a judgment shall and may be entered against them of *nolle prosequi* immediately after the decision of this case, or otherwise as the Court may think fit.

The case was argued in last Trinity Term (May 28th) by

> *Crompton*, for the plaintiffs :

The defendant is bound by the alteration made in the charter-party by Grey & Co., who were his agents at Bombay; and he has, therefore, no claim for an allowance in respect of the freight produced by the voyage to Aden. The terms of the second charter-party, by which the master and the agents at Bombay were at liberty to make such alterations in it as they might mutually think proper, clearly authorized that which was done by Grey & Co.; and the subsequent correspondence amounts in effect to an adoption of their act by the defendant. [He cited *Galloway* v. *Jackson* (1) and *Clipsham* v. *Vertue* (2).]

[618]   > *Peacock, contrà :*

The alteration made in this charter-party is in fact a new contract, and therefore justice requires that the defendant should only pay according to the current rate of freight which would have been earned by the vessel at that time. If the agents had no authority (as they certainly had not) to enter into a new charter-party, the

_____

(1) 3 Man. & G. 960; 3 Scott, N. R.   (2) 64 R. R. 484 (5 Q. B. 265).
753.

owner is not bound by such an agreement. The questions are, first, whether the alteration was authorized; secondly, whether the correspondence shows a ratification of it by the defendant.

(POLLOCK, C. B.: I think nothing turns upon the correspondence; the defendant's letter neither adopts nor rejects it.)

The only question therefore is, whether the agents at Bombay had authority, on behalf of the owners, to enter into an intermediate contract of charter-party with the Government there. [He cited *Rex* v. *Peto* (1).]

This is not adding to the contract, but altering the scheme of it altogether. It matters not that Grey & Co. might think this alteration was for the benefit of the freighter; the question is, whether, under this stipulation, they had the power to direct it. Could they have sent the vessel home, and let her come out again a year afterwards? The meaning of this clause clearly was only to authorize them to make some small addition to or deviation from the homeward voyage, such as that the ship might call at intermediate ports, but not to empower them to enter into an intermediate contract, which must endure for months, even though that contract might possibly be beneficial to the freighter. This alteration clearly would have avoided a policy of insurance on the ship as being a deviation: it is a change of the whole scheme of the contract.

[619]

(POLLOCK, C. B.: Might not the agents have bargained for a greater number of lay days at a stipulated price?)

No doubt; but there it remains the same contract.

(POLLOCK, C. B.: Then is it not the same contract if they say, "We see we shall not want the ship for a certain time, and, instead of her lying idle, you shall use her for a short intermediate voyage?" If that voyage were of an unreasonable extent or duration, as to the North Pole, it would be a different case; but this is merely postponing the commencement of the charter-party until after the performance of a short intermediate voyage.)

It comes back to the same question, whether it is not a different voyage from that stipulated for by the charter-party.

(1) 1 Y. & J. 37.

WIGGINS   (POLLOCK, C. B.: No; it is merely postponing the commence-
v.
JOHNSTON.   ment of the second charter-party, and allowing the owners to use
            the ship in the meantime.   No doubt it would discharge a policy of
            insurance ; as to that it is a different voyage ; but as to the charter-
[*620]   party, it is a mere postponement of *the voyage.   Could not the
            agents have altered the *terminus ad quem*, and added a port of
            destination ?)

The defendant contends they could not.   The question is not
whether the agents have acted to the best of their discretion ;
but what is the discretion vested in them.   Here, however,
probably, the alteration was injurious to the defendant, because the
intermediate voyage was during the period when high freights were
obtainable at Bombay.   At all events, the freight earned by the
voyage to Aden ought to be brought into account between the
plaintiffs and the defendant.

    Crompton, in reply.   *   *   *

                                   Cur. adv. vult.

[621]   The judgment of the COURT was now delivered by

ROLFE, B. :

The question in this case turns on the construction of a clause
contained in a charter-party.   The plaintiffs were owners of the
ship *Harmony*, of which the plaintiff Jameson was also the master.
The plaintiffs, on the 1st day of August, 1842, entered into a
charter-party with the defendant, whereby they agreed to charter
the ship to him for a voyage to Bombay, at which port she was
to be addressed to the defendant's agents.   On the same day they
also entered into another charter-party with him, whereby they
agreed that the ship should, after discharging her cargo at Bombay,
take in a homeward cargo, for which the defendant agreed to pay
freight, as to one-half the cargo, at 3*l.* per ton, and as to the rest,
at the current rate of freight when the ship should be loading.   At
the end of this second charter-party is the following clause : " It is
also further understood and agreed, that the master of the vessel,
and the agents at Bombay, are at liberty to make such alterations
in this charter-party as they may mutually think proper, without
prejudice to this agreement."

The ship sailed from Great Britain pursuant to the first charter-
party, and reached Bombay on the 31st of January, 1843, and, on

the nomination of the defendant, she was addressed to Messrs.   WIGGINS
Grey & Co. as his agents there.   Soon after her arrival, the plaintiff   *v.*
Jameson (the master), and Messrs. Grey & Co., as agents of the   JOHNSTON.
defendant, entered into a written agreement, which was indorsed
on the second charter-party, and whereby they agreed that the
ship might proceed to Aden with the Government coals and stores,
and return to Bombay with all dispatch, without prejudice to the
charter-party.

In pursuance of this arrangement, the ship sailed to Aden, and
there discharged her coals, &c., and returned to Bombay, where
she arrived on the 11th of May.   The owners received above 1,100*l.*
as freight for this voyage to *Aden.   On the return of the ship to   [*622]
Bombay, the defendant's agents procured her a cargo at the rate of
1*l.* 5*s.* 4*d.* per ton, being the then current rate of freight.   With
this cargo she sailed from Bombay, and reached London on the
11th of November, 1843.   The plaintiffs received the whole of the
freight (1,402*l.*); and this action was brought to recover, as to one-
half of the freight, the difference between the charter-rate of 3*l.*
per ton and the sum actually received, namely 701*l.*; and it was
agreed that the difference amounts to 963*l.* 11*s.* 3*d.*

The point therefore is, whether the plaintiffs are entitled to claim
from the defendant the charter-rate of 3*l.* per ton ; and that depends
on the question, whether the voyage from Bombay to London was
the voyage in respect of which the defendant, by his contract, agreed
to pay freight at that rate.   The defendant contends that it was
not, for that, by the two contracts taken together, the ship was to
proceed to Bombay, and then, after discharging the cargo, return
forthwith to London ; whereas, after her arrival at Bombay, the
plaintiff Jameson and the defendant's agents agreed, for the exclusive profit of the owners, to allow the ship to make a new voyage,
intermediate between her voyage out and her voyage home, whereby
the defendant contends that his obligation under the charter-party
was at an end.   But it must be observed, that the charter-party
contained an express clause enabling the plaintiff Jameson and the
defendant's agents at Bombay to make any alteration in the charter-
party which they might deem expedient ; and we think this clearly
authorized the defendant's agents to accede to the proposed voyage
to Aden.   It was said by the defendant's counsel, that the meaning
of the clause was merely to enable the parties to make further
stipulations at Bombay as to the homeward voyage, to authorize
the touching at other ports, and to make trifling changes of that

nature. But we are unable to fix any limits as to the extent of authority given—certainly none that can enable us to say *that what was done was beyond the scope of the authority. Several facts are stated in the case, strongly tending to show that the delay occasioned by the voyage to Aden was likely to cause, and that it did in fact cause, great injury to the defendant's interest. This may give him a good ground of action against his agents, but cannot at all show that the agents had not authority to take the course they did take. They had authority to make any alterations in the charter-party which they should think proper. They did think proper to alter it, by stipulating, that, instead of unloading at Bombay, and there forthwith taking in a homeward cargo, the ship should go and discharge at Aden, and then return to Bombay for her cargo. This was to be done expressly without prejudice to the charter-party, which means, was to be done without affecting the charter-party, otherwise than by interposing the intermediate voyage to Aden. Under these circumstances, it appears to us clear that the obligation of the defendant to pay the 3*l.* per ton remained unaffected. It was contended, that, at all events, the freight earned by the voyage to Aden ought to be brought into account; but we see no ground whatever for this. The meaning of the parties obviously was, that the owners should have the vessel for their own benefit on the interposed voyage. This it was which formed the subject of complaint on the part of the defendant: and the case states, that, as soon as the new agreement was entered into at Bombay, the plaintiffs entered into a charter-party with the Indian Government for the voyage to Aden. If the defendant had been intended to participate in any way in the benefit of this voyage, it would have been so stipulated. Nothing of the sort appears; and we are therefore of opinion that he can have no abatement on this account.

The result is, that the plaintiffs will be entitled to our judgment for the full amount of 963*l.* 11*s.* 3*d.*, for which the action is brought.

Judgment for the plaintiffs.

LOCKHART v. BARNARD (1).

1845.
Nov. 3.

[674]

(14 Meeson & Welsby, 674—680; S. C. 15 L. J. Ex. 1.)

A hand-bill relating to a stolen parcel offered a reward of 100*l*. to "whoever should give such information as should lead to the early apprehension of the guilty parties:" Held, that the information must be given, not in mere conversation, but with a view to its being acted on, either to the person offering the reward or to his agent, or to some person having authority by law to apprehend the criminal. And where the communication was first made by the plaintiff to C. in conversation, but the information was afterwards communicated to a constable jointly by the plaintiff and C., it was held that they both ought to have joined in the action.

ASSUMPSIT. The declaration stated, that heretofore, to wit, on &c., the defendant caused to be printed and published a certain advertisement, stating that a certain parcel, directed to Messrs. Sir Charles Price & Co., bankers, King William Street, London, containing certain bank notes, together with sundry bills of exchange, specially indorsed, payable to the order of the said Sir Charles Price & Co., had been lost or stolen in London on the afternoon of Monday the 25th then instant; and the defendant did thereby promise, that whoever would give such information as might lead to the immediate recovery of the above parcel if lost, or to the early apprehension of the guilty parties if stolen, should receive a reward of 100*l*. And the plaintiff saith, that the said *parcel was stolen, and that he, confiding in the said promise of the defendant, afterwards, and before the commencement of this suit, to wit, on &c., did give such information as did then lead to the early apprehension of the guilty party, to wit, one J. Richards, who was afterwards, to wit, on the day and year last aforesaid, tried and convicted as such guilty party as aforesaid, whereof the defendant afterwards, and before the commencement of this suit, to wit, on the day and year last aforesaid, had notice; whereby and by reason of the premises, the defendant became and was liable to pay the said sum of 100*l*. to the plaintiff, when he the defendant should be thereunto requested. Breach, the non-payment of the said sum of 100*l*., or any part thereof.

[*675]

The defendant pleaded, first, *non assumpsit*; secondly, that the plaintiff did not give such information as did lead to the early apprehension of the said J. R. in the declaration named, *modo et formâ*; thirdly, that J. R. was not the only guilty party, *modo et formâ*.

(1) See *Carlill* v. *Carbolic Smoke Ball Company* [1893] 1 Q. B. 256, 62 L. J. Q. B. 257, C. A.—J. G. P.

LOCKHART
v.
BARNARD.

At the trial, before Alderson, B., at the last Assizes for the county of Bedford, it appeared that this action was brought to recover a reward offered by the defendant for the recovery of a lost parcel, containing bank notes and bills of exchange, sent from Bedford to London by coach. A hand-bill was admitted and read, which, so far as it related to this case, was as follows: "100l. Reward.—Lost or stolen, in London, on the afternoon of Monday the 25th inst., a parcel directed to Messrs. Sir Charles Price & Co., bankers, King William Street, London, containing the following bank notes, together with sundry bills of exchange, specially indorsed payable to the order of Messrs. Sir Charles Price & Co., payment of all which has been stopped." (Here followed a list of the notes.) "Whoever will give such information as will lead to the immediate recovery of the above parcel, with its contents safe, if lost, or the early apprehension of the guilty parties if stolen, shall

[*676]

receive the above reward. Measures are *taken for discovery, if the above notes or bills are attempted to be fraudulently circulated. —27th September, 1843." It was proved, that Richards, who was afterwards convicted of the felony, came on the 22nd of May, 1844, to the plaintiff's shop, and, in payment for three pairs of stockings, tendered a 10l. bank note. The plaintiff desired him to write his name on the note, and afterwards gave him the change for it. After making inquiries as to the address which Richards had written on the note, the plaintiff suspected it to be a forgery, and communicated his suspicions to a person named Cheshire, who thereupon informed the plaintiff that Richards had also passed notes to himself and others. Having afterwards heard of the robbery, the plaintiff and Cheshire related the above circumstances to several of their neighbours, and in the course of conversation, the plaintiff proposed to go for a constable; but a groom named Robinson, who was present, said he had better go, and accordingly went and brought back the constable, who, upon the information he received, was enabled to find out and apprehend Richards. The plaintiff was the only person who could identify him as having had any part of the stolen property in his possession. Richards was afterwards convicted and transported. Two objections were made on behalf of the defendant: first, that the communication made by the plaintiff to Cheshire was not such information as entitled the plaintiff to recover, it not having been made either to the party offering the reward or any agent of his, or to any person authorized by law to apprehend the criminal; secondly, that the information

to the constable, being made jointly by the plaintiff and Cheshire, LOCKHART
was not such information by the plaintiff alone as led to the BARNARD.
apprehension of J. R., and that Cheshire should have been joined
in the action as a co-plaintiff. On the first issue, the learned Judge
directed the jury to find for the plaintiff, which they accordingly
did; on the second, he desired them to consider, whether, in their
opinion, the plaintiff communicated his information to the constable
in *the first instance; and if they thought he had not, then   [*677]
whether the communication to Cheshire was made with a view to
its being communicated by him to the constable, or whether it was
not made to him merely with a view to further inquiry, and that
both afterwards gave joint information to the constable. The jury
found, that the information given to the constable by Robinson,
and which led to the apprehension of the criminal, was the joint
information of the plaintiff and Cheshire. The second issue was
thereupon entered for the defendant, leave being reserved to the
plaintiff to move to enter a verdict for himself, if the Court should
be of opinion that the plaintiff was entitled to succeed upon the
finding of the jury.

Byles, Serjt., now moved accordingly :

First, the information given by the plaintiff to Cheshire in the
first instance, and which led to the apprehension of the felon, was
sufficient information within the meaning of this advertisement.
It is sufficient if the information be given to the defendant or to his
agent, or to a peace officer, or to any other person, provided it
actually leads to the apprehension of the offender. * * The   [678]
person who first gave the information in consequence of which the
felon was brought to justice is entitled to the reward, and that was
the plaintiff. If it were otherwise, the real informer might be
deprived of his reward by any person to whom he accidentally
mentioned his information going to the advertiser and giving the
information in his own name.

(PARKE, B.: You say it is sufficient if a person tells the matter to
another, and he gives the information to a constable.)

Yes, if he does it, not in idle conversation, but with a view to the
apprehension of the felon. [He cited Lancaster v. Walsh (1) and
Williams v. Carwardine (2).]

(1) 4 M. & W. 16.   (2) 38 R. R. 328 (4 B. & Ad. 621; 1
                                      Nev. & M. 418).

LOCKHART
v.
BARNARD.

POLLOCK, C. B. :

I am of opinion that the direction of my brother ALDERSON was correct, and I think the jury have come to a proper verdict on the second issue. The question is, what is the meaning of the expression " such information as may lead to the early apprehension of the guilty party." In the case of *Lancaster* v. *Walsh*, the words were, " information by which the same may be traced ; " and it was there decided, that a communication to a constable, whose duty it is to search for the offender, was within the terms of the hand-bill. I do not mean to say that there might not be circumstances under which *the doctrine of that case might be properly extended to other persons than constables ; but I think, in this case, it ought not to be so extended. Here the plaintiff communicates certain information to Cheshire, who, in return, makes a communication to him ; and then, deeming their joint knowledge sufficiently important to call for further inquiry, they jointly communicate it to Robinson and others, and he, as the agent of both, communicates it to a constable. I therefore think, that the finding of the jury, that the information which led to the detection of the felon was given, not by Lockhart alone, but by him jointly with Cheshire, and the entry of the verdict upon that finding, were perfectly right, and that no rule ought to be granted.

[*679]

PARKE, B. :

I am of the same opinion. According to the true construction of this advertisement, the information must be given, with a view to its being acted on, either to the person offering the reward, or his agent, or some person having authority by law to apprehend the criminal ; and therefore I think my brother ALDERSON was correct in leaving to the jury the nature of the first communication from the plaintiff to Cheshire, viz. whether it was made with a view to its being acted on, or merely in the course of conversation, and afterwards communicated, through Robinson, to the constable by both of them. Then, assuming that the information was communicated to the constable jointly by the plaintiff and Cheshire, ought they not both to have joined in the action? I think they ought, seeing there is but one reward offered for certain information, and that both of them concurred in giving it. The second issue was, therefore, rightly found for the defendant ; and, indeed, the jury would have been justified in finding for the defendant on *non*

assumpsit; but, there being no motion before us as to that issue, it   LOCKHART
is unnecessary to give any opinion on it.   *v.*
                                                                          BARNARD.

ALDERSON, B. :   [680]

I have no doubt I was wrong in directing the jury to find for the
plaintiff on *non assumpsit.*

ROLFE, B., concurred.

                                                        Rule refused.

————————

DOE D. HULL *v.* WOOD.

(14 Meeson & Welsby, 682—687; S. C. 15 L. J. Ex. 41.)

W. H., being tenant from year to year to Lady H., died, leaving his
widow in possession. J. H. some time afterwards took out administration
to the deceased; but the widow continued in possession, paying rent to
Lady H., with the knowledge of J. H., who never objected to such
payment, or made any demand of rent: Held, first, that there was no
evidence of a surrender by operation of law, so as to create the relation of
landlord and tenant between Lady H. and the widow; secondly, that there
were no circumstances from which a tenancy from year to year to the
administrator could be presumed.

1845.
Nov. 5.
———
[682]

EJECTMENT upon a demise by one John Hull, dated the 26th of
February, 1845.

At the trial, before Tindal, Ch. J., at the last Surrey Assizes, it
appeared that the premises in question were formerly occupied by
one William Hull, as tenant to Lady Hotham, under a lease which
terminated in the year 1831; but he continued in possession,
paying rent to Lady Hotham, until his decease in August, 1842.
His widow had since remained in possession, paying rent to Lady
Hotham up to Christmas last. Letters of administration were
granted to the lessor of the plaintiff, who was the father of William
Hull, on the 15th of March, 1844; but he never received or
demanded any rent for the premises. In October, 1844, the
deceased's widow married Henry Wood, the defendant, who had
paid rent to Lady Hotham since his marriage. The demise was
laid on the 26th of February, *1845, two days after a demand of   [*683]
possession had been made. It was proved that the plaintiff knew
the rent was paid to Lady Hotham, and that he had never made
any objection to such payment, or required it to be paid to himself.

It was contended for the defendant, at the trial, that the lessor
of the plaintiff had not made out any title: first, because the
evidence showed that, at the time of the demise, there was no term
in existence, and nothing to show that the lessor of the plaintiff

had any interest in the premises; secondly, that if the facts
established any tenancy at all, it was a tenancy to Lady Hotham;
or, even assuming that they showed a tenancy to the administrator,
it was a tenancy from year to year, and a six months' notice to quit
was necessary. The learned Judge directed the jury to find for the
plaintiff, but gave leave to the defendant to move to enter a nonsuit
on the above points.

Montagu Chambers now moved accordingly:

The widow of William Hull having continued in possession, and
paid the rent to Lady Hotham, with the privity of John Hull, the
administrator, it must be inferred that she became tenant to Lady
Hotham with his consent, and that tenancy must be assumed to be
a tenancy from year to year. If that be so, then the lessor of the
plaintiff, the administrator, ceased to have any interest in the
premises, and had therefore no title to sue.

(PARKE, B.: The tenancy from year to year, which belonged to
William, passed to John as administrator; and that tenancy was
never determined, either by surrender or otherwise.)

The circumstances are such from which a surrender by operation
of law may be implied: *Thomas* v. *Cook* (1). The possession was
lawful, and the administrator never demanded the rent; and, at
[*684]   the time that the letters of administration were taken *out, a two
years' tenancy by the widow had existed.

(ROLFE, B.: It cannot be contended that the administrator loses
his right, because he does not take out administration for eighteen
months or two years.)

The facts are sufficient to imply a surrender in law.

(PARKE, B.: I think not.)

Then, secondly, assuming that there was no such surrender, and
that the relation of landlord and tenant between Lady Hotham and
the widow did not exist, the payment of rent to Lady Hotham, with
the consent of the administrator, was virtually a payment to him,
and might create a tenancy from year to year to him.

(PARKE, B.: If it amounts to anything, it is that of a mere

(1) 20 R. R. 374 (2 B. & Ald. 119).

agreement that she shall pay the rent to Lady Hotham ; but that does not create any tenancy to him.   Here the plaintiff proved a clear *primâ facie* case, as there was a tenancy from year to year, which passed to the administrator.   Then you say there was evidence of something which, according to *Thomas* v. *Cook*, amounts to a surrender.   If it had been shown that Lady Hotham had accepted the widow as tenant, and the administrator had assented to it, then the case would have been brought within the decision in *Thomas* v. *Cook*.)

The administrator's having a full knowledge that the widow was in possession and paying rent to Lady Hotham, virtually amounts to an assent to her doing so, so as to make her tenant to him.   There ought therefore to have been a six months' notice to quit, to entitle the plaintiff to recover : *Right* d. *Flower* v. *Darby* (1).

(PARKE, B. : That case was cited in *Richardson* v. *Langridge* (2), and commented upon by the Judges, and particularly by CHAMBRE, J., who "denied the proposition, that, at this day, there is no such thing as a tenancy at will ; the taking of the dung by the landlord gave the tenant no interest in the premises.   Surely the distinction has been a thousand times taken ; a mere general letting is a letting at will : if *the lessor accepts yearly rent, or rent measured by any aliquot part of a year, the Courts have said that is evidence of a taking for a year.")

Here a quarterly rent was paid.

(PARKE, B. : Not by the widow to the lessor of the plaintiff.)

POLLOCK, C. B. :

I am of opinion that no rule ought to be granted in this case. This is an ejectment brought by the administrator of William Hull against John Wood ; and it has been contended, that, from the circumstances of the case, it must be presumed that the defendant was tenant from year to year under the administrator, or that the facts proved amount to a surrender or an assignment, and that he became tenant to Lady Hotham.   The facts of the case appear to be, that William Hull, who was tenant from year to year, died in August, 1842 ; that his widow continued in possession of the

(1) 1 R. R. 169 (1 T. R. 159).   (2) 13 R. R. 570 (4 Taunt. 128).

Doe d.
HULL
v.
WOOD.

[*685]

Don d.
HULL
v.
WOOD.

premises, and might, if she had thought proper, have taken out administration to her husband, in which case the term from year to year would have vested in her. She, however, remained in possession without taking out administration, and continued to occupy the premises, paying rent to Lady Hotham, (who, no doubt, had a right to go on the premises and demand rent of any person she found in possession) ; and, having married the defendant, it afterwards appears that, on the 15th of March, 1844, John Hull took out administration to the deceased. At that time it seems quite clear that he had a right to demand possession of the premises. The term might be a valuable one or it might not ; but the principles of law are the same in the one case as in the other. It is perfectly clear, that, on taking out administration, John Hull might have recovered possession of these premises for the benefit of creditors, or any other legal purpose : the question then is, has he done anything since to divest himself of that right? He has done nothing, but simply

[*686]

permitted matters to go on as before ; and are we *or the jury to presume from that an agreement for an under-tenancy from year to year between the administrator and the occupier ? How can we presume such a tenancy from the fact that the rent was paid, not to the administrator, but to the owner of the property, Lady Hotham ? I think there is no foundation for it. The only legitimate presumption appears to me to be, that the occupier, knowing she had no title to the premises, continued therein, paying rent to Lady Hotham, and liable at any time to be required to give up possession.

PARKE, B. :

I am entirely of the same opinion. The lessor of the plaintiff has proved a tenancy from year to year in William Hull, the decease of William Hull, and letters of administration granted to himself in March, 1844. The term (for a tenancy from year to year is a term) therefore vests in him until there is some legal determination of it ; and thus he has made out a good *primâ facie* case, because the *onus* of showing a legal determination of the term rests on the defendant. In this case I think there was no evidence that this tenancy from year to year had been determined by operation of law, as suggested, viz., by surrender, according to the authority of *Thomas* v. *Cook*, either by the administrator allowing the widow to occupy the premises under Lady Hotham, or by a virtual assignment of them. In order to make out that, it must be shown that there was the relation of landlord and tenant, with the assent of the administrator, between Lady Hotham and the defendant. But it is further contended, that the widow, if not tenant to Lady Hotham, was tenant from year to year to the administrator, and was entitled to six months' notice to quit ; but there is no evidence at all to show an agreement for a tenancy from year to year to the administrator : it only amounts to this,—that he allowed her to pay the rent for him to the head landlord instead of to himself.   We cannot infer *a tenancy from year to year from a simple payment by the occupier.   *Richardson* v. *Langridge* correctly lays down the law on this subject, viz. that a simple permission to occupy creates a tenancy at will, unless there are circumstances to show an intention to create a tenancy from year to year ; as, for instance, an agreement to pay rent by the quarter, or some other aliquot part of a year.   That was not so here, and I think there should be no rule.

ALDERSON, B., and ROLFE, B., concurred.

Rule refused.

DOE D. HUTCHINSON *v.* THE MANCHESTER, BURY, AND ROSSENDALE RAILWAY.

(14 Meeson & Welsby, 687—695 ; 15 L. J. Ex. 208 ; 9 Jur. 949.)

A Railway Act gave the Company power to agree with the owners of lands which they were empowered to take for the purposes of the railway, for the absolute purchase of their interest therein ; and provided, that if any difference should arise between them as to the value of the lands, or the compensation to be made in respect of them ; or if by reason of absence the owner should be prevented from treating ; or if he should fail to disclose or prove his title to the lands, &c., the amount of compensation should be settled by a jury, in the manner mentioned in the Act. Another clause (§ 153) provided, that if the owner of any lands, on tender of the purchase-money or compensation agreed for or awarded to be paid in respect thereof, should refuse to accept it ; or if he should fail to make out a title to the lands in respect whereof such purchase-money or compensation should be payable, to the satisfaction of the Company ; or if he should be gone out of the kingdom, or could not be found, or should refuse to convey, it should be lawful for the Company to deposit the purchase-money or compensation payable in respect of such lands in the Bank of England, in the name of the Accountant-General, and thereupon all the interest in such lands, in respect whereof such purchase-money or compensation should have been so deposited, should vest absolutely in the Company : Held, that this latter clause applied prospectively to the period after the purchase-money was agreed upon, or the amount of compensation was settled by the jury ; and therefore that the Company could not, immediately upon the finding of

DOE d.
HULL
v.
WOOD.

[*687]

1845.
Nov. 6.

[687]

DOE d.
HUTCHINSON
v.
MANCHES-
TER, BURY,
AND
ROSSENDALE
RAILWAY CO.

[*688]

the jury, pay the amount awarded by them into the Court of Chancery, and take possession of the land, but must first call upon the owner to make out a title to their satisfaction, although before the assessment by the jury he had failed to disclose or prove his title (1).

THIS was an action of ejectment, brought by the plaintiff to recover from the defendants the possession of certain pieces of land, which the plaintiff held by a lease for years under the Earl of Derby, and which had been taken by the defendants for the purposes of the railway, under *the 153rd section of their Act of Parliament, 8 Vict. c. lx. (2).   At the trial, before Cresswell, J., at the last

(1) Section 153 of the Railway Act upon which this case turned is similar to s. 76 of the Lands Clauses Consolidation Act, 1845 (8 & 9 Vict. c. 18). With this case compare *Douglass* v. *L. & N. W. Ry. Co.* (1856) 3 K. & J. 173, and *Wells* v. *Chelmsford Local Board* (1880) 15 Ch. D. 108, 49 L. J. Ch. 827.—J. G. P.

(2) By sect. 136 of this Act, power was given to the Company to agree with the owners of the lands which they were authorized by the Act to enter into and take for the purposes of the railway, for the absolute purchase, for a consideration in money, of any such lands, or such parts thereof as they should think proper, and of all subsisting leases therein, and all rent-charges and incumbrances affecting such lands, and all commonable and other rights to which such lands might be subject, and all other estates or interests in such lands, of what kind soever.

Sect. 153, for the purpose of providing for the payment and application in certain cases of the purchase-money or compensation to be paid in respect of any lands not belonging to parties under disability, enacted, "that, in the following cases, that is to say, if the owner of any such lands, or of any interest therein, on tender of the purchase-money or compensation either agreed or awarded to be paid, refuse to accept the same; or if any such person fail to make out a title to the lands in respect whereof such purchase - money or compensation should be payable, or to the interest therein claimed by him, to the satisfaction of the Company; or if such

owner shall be gone out of the kingdom, or cannot be found, or be not known, or shall refuse to convey or release such lands as directed by the Company, it shall be lawful for the Company to deposit the purchase-money or compensation payable in respect of such lands, or any interest therein, in the Bank of England, in the name and with the privity of the Accountant-General of the Court of Chancery, to be placed to his account therein, to the credit of the parties interested in such lands, &c.; and thereupon all the interest in such lands, in respect whereof such purchase-money or compensation shall have been deposited, shall vest absolutely in the said Company."

Sect. 161 requires the Company to give notice to the parties interested, in manner therein mentioned, of their intention to treat for any lands; and by sect. 162, the parties are to state their claim within one month after such notice.

Sect. 169 provides, that if any difference shall arise, or if no agreement can be come to between the Company and the owner of any lands, or of any interest in such lands, taken or required for, or injuriously affected by, the execution of the said railway, &c., as to the value of such lands or any interest therein, or as to the compensation to be made in respect thereof; or if, by reason of absence, any such owner be prevented from treating; or if any such owner fail to disclose or prove his title to any such lands, or any interest therein; or if, by reason of any impediment or disability, any such owner be incapable

Assizes at *Liverpool, it appeared that the Company, having purchased from Lord Derby the reversion of the lands in dispute, sent
the plaintiff notice, in July, 1844, of their intention to treat with him
for his interest in them : and in the November following they made
him an offer of 3,500l., with notice of their intention to summon a
jury to assess the amount of compensation to which he was entitled.
On the 13th January, 1845 (the plaintiff not having in the mean-*
time given the Company any information as to his title or interest,
nor made any communication to them), an inquisition was held
accordingly, and the jury made their assessment, awarding the
plaintiff the sum of 4,000l. After the delivery of their verdict, the
plaintiff's attorney said to the defendant's agent, " You shall never
construct your railway, unless you come to some arrangement
satisfactory to Mr. Hutchinson." The Company, however, without
afterwards calling upon the plaintiff to make out his title to the
land, paid the amount of the compensation-money into the Court
of Chancery, in the manner directed by the statute, and began to
construct their railway over the land, upon which the plaintiff
brought this ejectment. Upon these facts, the learned Judge stated
to the jury, that, in order to entitle the Company to pay the compensation-money into the Court of Chancery, and take possession of the
land, they were bound to call upon *the lessor of the plaintiff, after
the assessment of the compensation, to make out his title to the
land ; and therefore that their possession was wrongful, and the
plaintiff was entitled to recover. A verdict was accordingly taken for
the plaintiff, leave being reserved to the defendants to move to enter
the verdict for them, if the Court should be of the contrary opinion.

Baines now moved accordingly :

The defendants have complied with the requisitions of the Act of
Parliament.   Taking all its enactments together, it sufficiently

of making any agreement, conveyance, or release necessary *for enabling the Company to take such lands, or to proceed in making the railway or works, &c.; or if any such difference arise as to the amount of the damage occasioned to any lands by the temporary occupation thereof in making the railway, &c., or otherwise in the execution of the power given by the Act, and for which any party may be entitled to demand compensation according to the provisions of this Act, in all such cases the amount of the compensation to be paid by the Company is to be settled by a jury.

By sect. 166, the Company are to give notice of their intention to summon a jury, and to state in such notice how much they are willing to give for the lands.

By sect. 223, parties claiming compensation for lands held by leases may be required by the Company to produce the leases, &c.

Doe d.
HUTCHINSON
v.
MANCHES-
TER, BURY,
AND
ROSSENDALE
RAILWAY Co.

[*689]

[*690]

[*689, n.]

Doe d.
Hutchinson
v.
Manches-
ter, Bury,
and
Rossendale
Railway Co.

appears that there has been such a failure on the part of the plaintiff to make out a title to the land as entitled the Company to pay the compensation-money into Court, and take possession of the land. The Legislature appear to have intended to vest a complete title in the Railway Company, without any conveyance, where the owner of the land refuses to state the nature of his rights. Here he refused to do so in the first instance; and the declaration of his attorney at the time of the taking of the inquisition showed a determination to persist in that refusal.

(Alderson, B.: The words of the 153rd section are: "If any such person fail to make a title to the lands in respect whereof such purchase-money or compensation shall be payable." No purchase-money or compensation was payable in respect of these lands until after January, 1845.)

It is sufficient that they are the same lands in respect of which the compensation is afterwards awarded.

(Pollock, C.B.: All the provisions of the 153rd section have reference to the period after the purchase-money is agreed for as assessed by the jury.

Alderson, B.: It is clear that, if the plaintiff were out of the country at the time mentioned in the 164th section, it would not dispense with your calling upon him, under sect. 153, after the taking of the inquisition. That shows that the two sections are to be construed distinctly and separately, with respect to the different periods of *time.)

[*691]

It is submitted that the latter section is a key to the former, and shows what is the failure of title meant in sect. 153. The Company having commenced their works on this land, are in a difficult and embarrassing position; and if a rule be granted, it may lead to some arrangement between the parties.

Pollock, C.B.:

I am of opinion that no rule ought to be granted in this case. It appears to me that the language of the 153rd section of the Act, on which the question turns, is perfectly clear; and we certainly ought not, merely in order to give parties an opportunity of coming to some arrangement, to raise doubts in the minds of others, where we entertain none ourselves. The only part of the 153rd section which is applicable to the question before us is that which enacts, "that if the owner of any lands, &c. shall fail to make out

a title to the lands in respect of which such purchase-money or
compensation shall be payable, or to the interest therein claimed by
him, to the satisfaction of the Company ; or if such owner cannot be
found, or be not known, or refuse to convey or release such land
as directed by the Company, it shall be lawful for the Company
to deposit the purchase-money or compensation payable in respect
of such lands, or any interest therein, in the Bank of England, in
the name and with the privity of the Accountant-General of the
Court of Chancery."   Now, the various alternatives mentioned in
this clause appear to me to be all of them alternatives arising after
the assessment of the damages, and after the compensation-money
has been ascertained.   Indeed, the words appear to me, when perfectly construed, to be as plain as if these words were introduced—
" if any such person shall, after the amount of compensation-money
has been ascertained, fail to make out a title," &c. ; in which case
it clearly would be the duty of the Company, after the amount of
the compensation-money had been ascertained by the verdict of the
jury, to call *upon the party to make out a title to the land, if he
were willing to accept that amount; on his failing to do which,
and then only, they would be entitled to pay the money into the
Court of Chancery.   I observe, indeed, that the clause is worded
very favourably to the Company; for the provision is, " if he shall
fail to make out a title to their satisfaction."   It is said that the
Company are placed in a difficulty, in consequence of their having
begun to construct their works upon this land : but they need never
have placed themselves in that position ; for unless there had been
some feeling of hostility, such as that which displayed itself in the
expressions used after the finding of the jury, why did not the
Company, when they found that the plaintiff was proceeding with
an ejectment, call upon him to make out a good title ?   Even now
they are not too late to do so ; it is still open to them, indeed, to
tender the amount of the compensation assessed by the jury, and, if
the plaintiff refuses to accept it, to pay to his account the money
which is already in Chancery.   I agree with the learned counsel
that this case is an important one, for it is in substance this : Is a
Railway Company, or any other Company, entitled to say to a
person whose land they require, " Because you would not render
us any assistance before we went before the compensation jury, we
will take your land without any further communication ? "   And,
called upon as we are to say whether the title of this Company was
perfect, we are bound to say that it was not ; that no absolute

DOE d.
HUTCHINSON
v.
MANCHES-
TER, BURY,
AND
ROSSENDALE
RAILWAY CO.

[*692]

DOE d.
HUTCHINSON
v.
MANCHES-
TER, BURY,
AND
ROSSENDALE
RAILWAY Co.

interest has yet vested in them ; and therefore that the lessor of the plaintiff was entitled to recover in this ejectment.

PARKE, B. :

I am of the same opinion. It seems to me that the true construction of the 153rd section, and of the conditions contained in it, is, that the provision empowering the Company to pay the purchase or compensation-money into the Court of Chancery is prospective,

[*693] applying *to the case where the party fails to make out his title to the land, after the inquisition has been executed, and the money has been ascertained and become payable. But admitting, for argument's sake, that it were otherwise, and that if the plaintiff had previously refused to make out a title, the Company would be justified in taking the course they have done, still the facts before us do not support their case ; for here there does not appear to have been any such refusal on the part of the plaintiff to disclose or make out his title. The Company are entitled, by the 164th section, to proceed to an inquisition on the non-compliance by the parties with certain conditions ; one of which is, if the owner of the land fail to disclose his title, or, having disclosed it, fail to prove a good title, that is, if he cannot make it out to the satisfaction of the Company. And I concur with the LORD CHIEF BARON, that the 153rd section is to be construed prospectively, with reference to acts to be done after the inquisition ; and there is this very good reason for it, that a party who was unable in the first instance to make out a title might find the means of doing so after the inquisition, and ought to have the means afforded him of remedying the defect, before he is compelled to apply to the Court of Chancery. I think, therefore, that the ruling of my brother CRESSWELL was perfectly right, and that there ought to be no rule.

ALDERSON, B. :

I am of the same opinion. The 164th section of the Act no doubt provides, that if the owner of lands fail to disclose or prove his title, the Company may go before a jury to assess the compensation which is to be paid to him for them : for which provision there is this obvious reason, that the failing to disclose his title prevents any offer from being satisfactorily made to him, and the failing to prove it prevents any valid agreement from being come to ; and therefore they have the right, in that case, of resorting to

[*694] the compulsory clause. But when we turn to *the 153rd section,

and see what it requires to be done in failure of making out a good title, it is obvious that the party ought to have an opportunity afforded him to remedy that defect, which before arose from his inability or his want of inclination to prove his title. He is then in a very different situation, after the decision of the jury, and ought to have that *locus pœnitentiæ* allowed him: if, after all that information has been given him, and this change of circumstances has taken place, he still refuses to proceed, the Company may go on without him. Why should not this clause be so construed? It is clear that some of its words are to be construed prospectively; as, for instance, the case of the owner of the land being out of the kingdom; for it is clear that, if the owner were abroad at the time of the first offer, but in the way when the compensation was assessed, the Company would have no right at once to pay the money into Chancery. It must therefore be future as to that, and why not also as to the other cases, when we thereby give the best effect to it, in favour of a party whose land is to be taken from him compulsorily, and by a very stringent process? The statute gives this Company power to take a man's land without any conveyance at all; for if they cannot find out who can make a conveyance to them, or if he refuse to convey, or if he fail to make out a title, they may pay their money into Chancery, and the land is at once vested in them by a Parliamentary title. But, in order to enable them to exercise this power, they must follow the words of the Act strictly, and they have not done so here. This clause therefore fails them as a defence; and the consequence is, that the plaintiff is still entitled to the land.

ROLFE, B.:

I am clearly of the same opinion. The clear object of this Act was to enable parties claiming compensation for their lands to make out a good title, after they should have ascertained what was the amount of compensation *they were to receive. Here an offer is made by the Company, which the plaintiff treats as a nullity; upon which the Company, who want the land for their works, apply to a jury to assess the compensation, and it is assessed accordingly. After that was done, they were bound to call upon him to show his title; and until they had done so, they had no right to take possession of his land, and pay the compensation-money into Chancery. Neither the letter nor the spirit of the Act bears such a construction, and it would be most unjust if it did.

Rule refused.

[*695]

DOE d.
HUTCHINSON
v.
MANCHES-
TER, BURY,
AND
ROSSENDALE
RAILWAY CO.

1845.
Nov. 10.

[698]

DOE d. SAMS v. GARLICK.

(14 Meeson & Welsby, 698—710; S. C. 15 L. J. Ex. 54.)

A testator, after charging certain lands with an annuity to his wife for her life, and giving them successively to several persons for life, devised them as follows: "And, from and after &c., I give and devise the same (but subject and charged as aforesaid) to such person or persons as at the time of my decease shall be the heir or heirs-at-law of William Hull, formerly of Pisford, Esq., who was formerly the owner of the said messuages, &c., and who devised the same to my first wife Lydia, and which estate and premises descended to and became vested in my late son, W. G., as the only son and heir-at-law of my said late wife Lydia, and which said premises, &c. my said son W. G. devised to me in fee simple:" Held, that the words "such person or persons as at the time of my decease shall be the heir or heirs-at-law of W. H.," were merely a *designatio personæ;* and that the person answering that description took an estate for life only in the devised premises.

A devise of an indefinite estate, without words of limitation, *primâ facie* is a devise for life only; and a previous charge on the estate, without any charge on the devisee in respect of it, will not enlarge it into a devise of an estate in fee.

EJECTMENT for lands, houses, &c. at Pisford, in the county of Northampton. The facts were, by consent of the parties, stated for the opinion of the Court, under a Judge's order, in the following case:

The question in this case arises under the will of Thomas Garlick, of Toddington, in Bedfordshire, who died in the year 1824, in possession of the estate in question, which came into his family under the will of William Hull of Pisford, who died in 1782. William Hull of Pisford had a brother named Jonas, and a sister named Elizabeth, who married one Jonathan Balls. Jonas Hull had a son and heir, named William, afterwards known as William Hull of Fakenham, who was the heir-at-law of his uncle, William Hull of Pisford, at the time of the death of the testator, Thomas Garlick. William Hull of Fakenham died in 1840, leaving several children, of whom the lessor of the plaintiff became the sole trustee. Elizabeth Balls, the sister of William Hull of Pisford, had a daughter, Lydia Balls, who afterwards became the first wife of the testator, Thomas Garlick. William Hull of Pisford, by his will, of the 30th of July, 1776, devised the Pisford estate to his niece, Lydia Balls, (afterwards the wife of Thomas Garlick), for life, with remainder to her first and other sons in tail, with other remainders over, with ultimate remainder to his own right heir. Thomas Garlick, of Barnsley, who died in 1793, had, among other children, two sons, the elder of whom, and his heir-at-law, was one Anthony Garlick, of Pogmore, who died in 1808; and the younger of whom

was the testator, *Thomas Garlick of Toddington.   Anthony   Doe d.
Garlick of Pogmore had nine children, his eldest surviving son and   Sams
                                                                         v.
heir being Anthony Garlick of Greetham, (the testator's nephew,   Garlick.
and devisee for life of the Pisford estate), who died in 1840, without   [*699]
issue; and the second surviving son of Anthony Garlick of Pogmore
was another Thomas Garlick, who died in America about 1835,
leaving several children, his eldest son and heir-at-law being
William Garlick, the defendant.   Thomas Garlick had by his wife
Lydia (the first tenant for life under the uncle's will) two children,
namely, William Hull Garlick, and Edith, afterwards the wife of
Matthew Berry.   On the death of Lydia Garlick, her son entered
into possession of the estate, of which he suffered a recovery, and
afterwards, by his will, devised the same to his father, the testator,
Thomas Garlick of Toddington, who thus became owner of the
estate in fee simple on the death of his son, in 1807.   Edith Berry
had but two children, one of which was still-born, and the other
lived but a few hours.

The testator Thomas Garlick died in the year 1824, having by
his will, which bore date the 24th May, 1821, devised as follows:
"I give and devise all my messuages, &c. to the use of the said
John Slade and David Lee Willis, their executors &c., during the
natural life of my said daughter, Edith Berry, but upon the trusts
hereinafter mentioned, and subject and chargeable in the meantime
to and with the payment of a clear annuity or yearly sum of 100*l.*
unto my said wife, Elizabeth Garlick; and, from and after the
decease of my said daughter, I give and devise all my said
messuages, cottages, farms, and hereditaments in the said county
of Northampton, subject as aforesaid, unto and to the use of all and
every the sons and daughters of my said daughter, Edith Berry,
lawfully to be begotten, as tenants in common, and not as joint-
tenants, and to their respective heirs and assigns for ever; and, in
case my said daughter shall have but one child, then I give and
devise the same messuages, cottages, farms, lands, tenements, and
hereditaments *in the said county of Northampton (but subject and   [*700]
charged as aforesaid) unto such only child, his or her heirs and
assigns, for ever; and, in case my said daughter shall have no
children, then I give and devise the same messuages, subject and
charged as aforesaid, to Anthony Garlick of Greetham, in the
county of Lincoln, farmer, son of my late brother, Anthony
Garlick, deceased, and his assigns, for and during the term of his
natural life; and, from and after his decease, I give and devise the

Doe d.
SAMS
v.
GARLICK.

same (but subject and charged as aforesaid) to such person or persons who at the time of my decease shall be heir or heirs-at-law of William Hull, formerly of Pisford, Esq., deceased, who was formerly owner of the said messuages, cottages, farms, lands, tenements, and hereditaments at Pisford aforesaid, and who, by his last will and testament, devised the same to my first wife Lydia, formerly Lydia Balls, spinster, who was the mother of my daughter, Edith Berry, and which estate and premises descended to and became vested in my late son, William Garlick, as the only son and heir-at-law of my said late wife Lydia, and which said premises he my said son William Garlick, devised to me in fee simple."

On the death of Anthony Garlick of Greetham, in 1840, William Hull of Fakenham became entitled to the estate in question, as heir-at-law of William Hull of Pisford, and died a few months afterwards.

The question for the opinion of the Court is, whether the said William Hull, of Fakenham, under the devise of Thomas Garlick, took an estate in fee, or for his own life only. If the Court should think that he took an estate in fee, judgment is to be entered for the plaintiff; but if the Court should be of opinion that he took an estate for life only, judgment is to be entered for the defendant.

The case was argued in Hilary Term last (Jan. 27), by

Chilton, for the plaintiff:

[*701]

It is impossible to doubt that the intention of the testator was to give an estate in fee to *William Hull of Fakenham; the only question is, whether he has used words which enable the Court to carry that intention into effect. [He cited Sir James Wigram, on the Interpretation of Wills (Proposition 5), *Doe* v. *Allen* (1), *Right* v. *Sidebotham* (2), *Bowen* v. *Scowcroft* (3), *Smith* v. *Coffin* (4), *Wilce* v. *Wilce* (5).]

(PARKE, B.: These difficulties have arisen from confounding the testator's intention with his meaning. Intention may mean what the testator intended to have done; whereas the only question, in the construction of wills, is on the meaning of the *words.)

[*702]

In this case it is clear, that if the words had been " to the heir or heirs-at-law of William Hull," instead of " to such .person or

(1) 8 T. R. 497.
(2) Doug. 759.
(3) 2 Y. & C. 654.

(4) 3 R. R. 435 (2 H. Bl. 444).
(5) 33 R. R. 606 (7 Bing. 664).

persons as at the time of my decease shall be the heir or heirs-at-law of William Hull," that would have been sufficient to carry the fee. It is important, also, to consider, that in the introductory clause of the will the testator shows a clear intention to dispose of the whole of his property ; for he says, " As to my estate, both real and personal, I dispose thereof in manner following," indicating plainly his intention not to die intestate as to any part : *Ibbotson* v. *Beckwith* (1) ; *Cole* v. *Rawlinson* (2). Further, he appears to have known how to limit an estate for life by express words, when he intended to give no more : *e.g.* to Anthony Garlick, who would be his heir-at-law in failure of issue of his daughter. And, with respect to the terms of this particular devise, Mr. Powell observes (3) : " It seems, according to the early authorities, that a devise to the heir of a person, as purchaser, (the ancestor taking no estate of freehold), vests in such heir an estate in fee simple, without any words of limitation, inasmuch as the term ' heir ' includes all the heirs of such heir :" for which he cites *Durdant* v. *Burchet* (4), where POLLEXFEN, Ch. J., assigns as the reason for this opinion, that " ' heir ' is *nomen collectivum ;* and it is all one to say ' heirs of J. S.,' as to say ' heir of J. S., and heirs of that heir,' for every particular heir is in the loins of the ancestor, and parcel of him."

(ALDERSON, B. : It does not appear here that the ancestor is dead.

PARKE, B. : The demise here is to the person who shall fill the character of heir of William Hull at the testator's death. It is just the same as if, having ascertained who he is, you were to write his name in the will.)

Secondly, this devise may be read as if the words in the *latter clause of the will, beginning " who was formerly the owner," down to the words " devised to me," were included in a parenthesis ; and then there is an absolute devise of the fee simple.

[*703]

Lastly, the devise being indefinite, and the lands being charged with an annuity to the testator's widow, the devise ought therefore to be construed to give an estate in fee. *Peppercorn* v. *Peacock* (5) is strongly in point on this part of the case, and appears not to be distinguishable.   *   *   *Andrew* v. *Southouse* (6), *Doe* d. *Palmer* v.

(1) Cas. temp. Talbot, 157.
(2) 1 Salk. 234.
(3) 2 Powell on Devises, 595.
(4) Skin. 205.

(5) 3 Man. & G. 356 ; 3 Scott, N. R. 651.
(6) 5 T. R. 292.

DOE d.
SAMS
v.
GARLICK.

Richards (1), *Doe* d. *Stevens* v. *Snelling* (2), and *Gully* v. *Bishop of Exeter* (3) are also authorities in support of this view of the case.

(PARKE, B. : The ground on which an estate for life is enlarged by implication to an estate in fee, is, that where there is a charge on the person of the devisee, it is presumed that it was intended that he should recoup himself, for which purpose he is to have the estate. It must be a charge on the person in respect of the estate. Here there is no charge on the person, but only on the estate.

ALDERSON, B. : If the testator means the devisee to pay, of course he must have the estate to pay it out of. But here the estate is first charged, into whosesoever hands it may come.

POLLOCK, C. B., referred to *Doe* d. *Hanson* v. *Fyldes* (4).)

[*704] *Mr. Jarman cites as authorities for his proposition the case of *Denn* d. *Miller* v. *Moor* (5) and *Fairfax* v. *Heron* (6). In the former case, there were no words charging the estate in the hands of the devisee. In the latter, the personal estate was sufficient to pay all the charges. The case of *Doe* d. *Clarke* v. *Clarke* (7) has been cited as overruling *Gully* v. *Bishop of Exeter*, but such is not the case.

(PARKE, B. : The reasons for the decision are not given in *Peppercorn* v. *Peacock ;* probably the Court thought that the testator meant the devisee to pay, whether he were in funds or not, construing the words " subject to " as being that the devisee is subject to the charge, as similar words were construed in *Andrew* v. *Southouse*.)

The words in *Andrew* v. *Southouse* were " charged and chargeable," which can hardly be applied to the person of the devisee.

(ALDERSON, B. : How can you say the devise is enlarged by the charge, when it is only given out of the charged lands ? Where the devise is to a person, if he will subject himself to a charge, I can understand how that may enlarge the estate. It is on the ground of an understood condition that the principle rests. But this is an unconditional devise of the estate, charged with the annuity in whosesoever hands it may be.)

(1) 3 T. R. 356.
(2) 5 East, 87. See 8 R. R. 450, n.
(3) 29 R. R. 565 (4 Bing. 290 ; 12 Moore, 591).
(4) Cowp. 833.

(5) 5 T. R. 558 ; 6 T. R. 175 ; 1 Bos. & P. 558 ; 2 Bos. & P. 247.
(6) Prec. in Ch. 67.
(7) 1 Cr. & M. 39.

The case was adjourned, that the COURT might consider whether it was necessary to hear *Crompton*, who appeared to argue for the defendant; and now, without calling upon him, the COURT gave judgment.

DOE d.
SAMS
v.
GARLICK.

POLLOCK, C. B.:

The question in this ejectment turns upon a devise in the will of Thomas Garlick. [His Lordship read the material parts of the will, and proceeded:] Unless the words, "in fee simple," at the close of the devise, *can be considered as applicable to the estate given by the testator to "the person or persons who shall be the heir or heirs-at-law of William Hull," the case is that of a devise in general terms, without any words of limitation at all. It was contended, for the lessor of the plaintiff, that those words might be applied, as words of limitation, to the estate given to the heir or heirs-at-law of William Hull; and if by any reasonable construction we could have seen that they were meant so to be used, we should have had no reluctance in giving effect to that which we can hardly doubt was the intention of the testator, and in applying these words in order to carry that intention into effect. But it seems to me to be perfectly clear that a parenthesis ought not to be inserted in the manner suggested by *Mr. Chilton;* but that the words at the close of the devise, "in fee simple," belong entirely to the description of the estate given by the son, William Garlick, to his father, "which he devised to me in fee simple." The case is one, therefore, where the language used with reference to the immediate devise is without any words of limitation whatever. And the argument of *Mr. Chilton* was, first, that the words "such person or persons as, at the time of my decease, shall be the heir or heirs-at-law of William Hull," imported that the heir or heirs-at-law of William Hull were to take in fee simple. But it appears to me that these words are nothing but the *designatio personæ;* and that, as soon as you have discovered the person answering that description, you are to insert his name, and then read the devise as if the name had been there originally.

The next question is, whether there is anything in this devise that will enable the Court to enlarge the estate beyond an estate for the life of the devise. Our attention was called to the circumstance that this is a devise charged with and subject to an annuity for life. But it is perfectly established that a charge upon the estate, and not upon the person of the devisee, will not enlarge the estate to a fee simple. *The case of *Gully* v. *The Bishop of Exeter* was relied upon

[*705]

[*706]

in the argument; but since that decision there is the case of *Doe* d. *Clarke* v. *Clarke*, decided by Lord LYNDHURST in this Court, and by which the case before Lord Chief Justice Best must be considered as overruled. It has been well observed, with reference to these cases, by the editor of a very learned work, Mr. Jarman, that although, undoubtedly, there are two cases which may be adduced, in which devises seeming to belong to this class were held to carry the fee, yet one of these cases professedly recognised, although it actually departed from, the principle which distinguishes between charges on the land merely, and charges on the devisee in respect of the land; and the other case, as I have said, must be considered as overruled. It appears most distinctly in the present case, that the charge is upon the estate, and therefore the devise is in fact a devise of the residue of the estate after the satisfaction of that charge. There are no words by which the Court can enlarge the estate, according to any case which was cited at the time of the argument, or any which we were able to find relating to the subject. It was pressed upon us, that there could be no doubt whatever what this testator intended; and, in order to satisfy the Court that he intended to give an estate in fee simple, it was suggested that he had himself mentioned, in the history of the estate coming into his family, a reason for giving it back again into the family of William Hull. But it is clear, both upon authority and principle, that the circumstance of the apparent motive by which a party is actuated, cannot be used to enlarge the sense of his words beyond the legal construction which is to be put upon them in the instrument. And I quite agree with what is said by Mr. Jarman, that if no one of these matters standing alone could enlarge that which would otherwise be an estate for life into an estate in fee, so neither can two or more of them, concurring together in the same instrument. Mr. Jarman

[*707] truly remarks, that the rule of construction *with respect to this matter is entirely technical, and that in many instances the Courts of law, while giving their judgment, have expressed an intimation that they were probably deviating from the real intention of the testator. But the object of all these rules is to create certainty, and to prevent litigation; to enable those who are conversant with these subjects to give such advice as may save the expense of litigation, by rendering the law certain, and not liable to fluctuation in each particular case. Acting upon these rules, and in accordance with the decided cases, it appears to me that the judgment of the Court, on the present occasion, ought to be for the defendant.

PARKE, B.:

I agree with the LORD CHIEF BARON, that the defendant is entitled
to the judgment of the Court. The question arises on the will of
the testator Thomas Garlick, and it is this—whether William Hull
of Fakenham, who answered the description of the person who was
at the time of the decease of the testator the heir-at-law of William
Hull formerly of Pisford, took under that will an estate in fee simple
or for life only. I am clearly of opinion that he took an estate for
life only. The devise is—after subjecting the estate to the charge
of an annuity in favour of the wife of the testator, and after certain
life estates—a devise of the lands in question, " subject and charged
as aforesaid," that is, with the annuity, " to such person or persons
as at the time of my decease shall be the heir or heirs-at-law of
William Hull, formerly of Pisford aforesaid." Now the question
upon this part of the will simply is, whether or not there is anything
to enlarge this indefinite estate, which must *primâ facie* be considered to be an estate for life, into a fee simple. *Mr. Chilton's*
main argument was, that it was enlarged into a fee, because the
estate was charged with an annuity. But I apprehend that the rule
on that subject is settled beyond all question : it is laid down in very
distinct terms by LE BLANC, J., in *Doe* d. *Stevens* v. **Snelling*, and   [*708]
has been recognized ever since. Whether it has in all cases been
fully acted on, with reference to wills, is certainly a matter of doubt ;
there appear to be some cases, of which the case of *Gully* v. *The
Bishop of Exeter* is one, in which the Court, while professing to act
upon the rule of law, had perhaps in some degree departed from
it. The rule itself, however, seems to be manifestly clear and
settled beyond all doubt. LE BLANC, J., states it in these terms :
" According to all the determinations, the question whether the
devisee takes a fee or not, in respect of charges," (that is, where
there is a devise of an indefinite estate), " must depend on this,
whether he personally, or the estate given to him, be charged with
the payment of debts." It is the same with respect to any other
charge. If the devisee be personally charged with payment of debts
or legacies, or if they be charged upon the *quantum* of estate given
to the devisee, he must take the fee ; because, if he take for life only,
he may be a loser, or the estate may be insufficient. Therefore the
question in all the cases is, whether it is a charge upon the devisee
personally, and he is directed to pay it, or it is charged upon the
quantum of the estate given to him personally, in which case it is
enlarged by the operation of that rule of law into a fee ; or whether

he merely takes an estate in the land already charged. Now I think
it is clear beyond all question in this case, that the estate itself—
the *corpus* of the estate—is charged with this annuity before it
comes into the hands of the devisee, and therefore that this charge
has no operation, according to that rule of law, to give an estate in
fee to the heir-at-law of William Hull of Pisford.

But *Mr. Chilton* contended, that under the words of this devise,
independently of the rule of law to which I have adverted, an estate
in fee is given to William Hull of Fakenham, because he says there
is authority that a devise to the heirs-at-law of A. will give a fee;
and he refers to certain passages in Jarman on Wills, and to Powell
on Devises, *p. 595, for that doctrine. Admitting that to be so, I
quite agree that the observation is inapplicable to the present case,
because this is manifestly a devise to a person or persons who, at
the time of the testator's death, shall be the heir or heirs-at-law.
Then it was suggested by *Mr. Chilton* (who did not, however, place
much reliance on that argument), that, by reading the last sentence
in a parenthesis, and treating the words " in fee simple " as applicable to this devise of the estate to William Hull of Fakenham, he
would take in fee simple. That really is merely a question of
grammatical construction ; and I own it appears to me to be perfectly clear that this last clause is a mere recital of the estate which
had previously been given to the testator by the will of his son ;
which " became vested in my late son, William Garlick, as the only
son and heir-at-law of my said wife Lydia, and which premises he
my said son, William Garlick, devised to me in fee simple." It
seems to me to be quite clear that this is merely a recital of the
estate that he had, and that it cannot be considered that he intended
the words " in fee simple " to apply to the former part of the will,
and therefore that they should be read parenthetically.

I am, therefore, clearly of opinion, upon the whole case, that an
estate for life only passed to William Hull, and that our judgment
must be in favour of the defendant.

ALDERSON, B. :

I am of the same opinion. All that the testator bequeaths is the
estate charged. Now, if the bequest be of an estate charged, the
authorities which have been referred to by the LORD CHIEF BARON
and my brother PARKE show that that of itself will not carry the
fee. Then the next question is, to whom does the testator devise
the estate charged ? He devises it, after the death of his daughter,

who died without leaving any issue, and after the death of his
nephew, to whom it had been given for *life, "subject as aforesaid," that is, to the same charges, "to such person or persons
who at the time of my decease shall be the heir or heirs-at-law
of William Hull, formerly of Pisford." Now, undoubtedly, if the
bequest had been merely "to the heir or heirs-at-law of William
Hull, formerly of Pisford," the authorities to which we were
referred would have been strong to show that the word "heirs"
would not only designate the person to whom the estate was to go,
but would also contain a limitation to them in fee; being to be
construed in the double sense, according to the rule given in the
case in Skinner, 205, which was cited in the course of the argument. But here the testator speaks of the person who, at the time
of his decease, shall be the heir; the word "heir" being merely
the description of the individual, and not extending to a limitation
of the estate. It seems to me, therefore, that the person who was
thus designated took the estate without any words of inheritance,
and consequently had only an estate for life. Then the only
remaining question is, whether we can add to this devise the concluding words, "in fee simple." That would be to act entirely
upon the supposed idea of the testator's intention, and for that
purpose to do very great violence to the words: and I think it
would be very wrong so to construe these words, which I have
no doubt were not meant in that sense, in order to effectuate
a supposed intention of the testator with respect to another part
of the will.

Judgment for the defendant.

DOE d.
SAMS
v.
GARLICK
[*710]

In re BARBER, Gent.

(14 Meeson & Welsby, 720—727; S. C. 3 Dowl. & L. 244; 15 L. J. Ex. 9.)

> Where a surveyor of highways within a parish employed an attorney to
> conduct an indictment for an obstruction of one of the highways, and to
> transact other business, and paid his bill out of the monies raised by the
> highway rate: Held, that the rate-payers were not persons "liable to pay,"
> within the meaning of the Solicitors Act, 1843 (6 & 7 Vict. c. 73), s. 38, and
> could not, therefore, apply for a reference of the bill to taxation.

1845.
Nov. 18.

[720]

THIS was a rule calling upon Mr. Barber, an attorney of this
Court, to show cause why his bill of costs should not be referred to
the Master for taxation. Mr. Barber had been employed by the
surveyor of the highways of the township of Rastrick, to prefer and
conduct an indictment for an obstruction of one of the highways,
and to transact other business (not in this Court), his charges for

which amounted *in the whole to 760*l*. 8*s*. 4*d*., of which 525*l*. 14*s*. 8*d*.
had been paid to him. The present application was made on behalf
of the Railway Company and the major part of the other rate-payers
of the township of Rastrick; a rate having been made therein,
under the stat. 5 Will. IV. c. 50, s. 27, for the payment (*inter alia*)
of the bill in question. A similar application had been first made
to COLERIDGE, J., at chambers, and refused on the ground that the
rate-payers were not persons "liable to pay" the bill, within the
meaning of the stat. 6 & 7 Vict. c. 73, s. 38, and therefore
not competent to make application for a reference of the bill to
taxation.

Martin and *Addison* now showed cause against the rule :

There are two answers to this application. In the first place,
this Court has no authority to refer to taxation an attorney's
bill for business done on the Crown side of the Court of Queen's
Bench (1). * * *

[722]   The rate-payers are not persons "liable to pay" the bill, within
the meaning of this section. The surveyor is the client of the
attorney, and they levy a rate for the payment of it. It is a
personal contract of the surveyor, although he is, by the concurrence
of the majority of the rate-payers, to be reimbursed by a rate levied
on the whole of them.

[*723]   (ROLFE, B.: The rate-payers are to *contribute by a rate to a
fund, which, in the hands of another person, is to be applied to the
payment of the bill.)

Or rather, to contribute to a fund for his reimbursement. The
39th section expressly provides for the case of a cestui que trust,
thereby excluding other cases, such as the present. These parties
are liable to pay the rate, but not to pay the attorney's bill; and,
under the 105th section of the Highway Act (5 & 6 Will. IV. c. 50),
there is an appeal to the justices in Sessions against the allowance
of the surveyor's accounts, so that there is an adequate check
against improper expenditure of this nature.

Knowles and *Hoggins*, in support of the rule, were desired to
address themselves to the latter point :

The rate-payers are persons "liable to pay" the bill, within the

(1) As to this point see now Judica-   s. 16, and *In re Pollard* (1888) 20 Q. B.
ture Act, 1873 (36 & 37 Vict. c. 66,   Div. 656, 57 L. J. Q. B. 273.—J. G. P.

meaning of the 88th section. The object of this Act undoubtedly In re
BARBER.
was to render the taxation of attornies' bills more easy and general.
The 87th section gives the right of applying for a taxation to the
persons chargeable by the bill, and their representatives and
assignees, meaning thereby the parties legally liable to pay it.
Then the 38th section, for the protection of parties not directly
chargeable, extends the same right to all persons who shall be
liable to pay or shall have paid the bill; that is, construing the
clause reasonably, to all persons who are ultimately to be charged
for the purpose of paying it. Here the rate-payers are bound to
contribute to form a fund, out of which the party legally chargeable
is to pay the bill. It is their money which pays it, and they are
the persons who have really an interest in the taxation.

(ROLFE, B. : Is each of them to tax *toties quoties ?*)

No; a taxation at the instance of one would enure for the benefit
of all.

(POLLOCK, C. B. : Then a single rate-payer might, by collusion,
procure a taxation of the bill, although all the others might be
willing to pay it.)

On the other hand, there may be collusion between the surveyor
and the attorney, *to the great prejudice of the rate-payers. A   [*724]
mortgagor has been held entitled to tax a bill of costs supplied to
his mortgagee : *In re Carew* (1).

POLLOCK, C. B. :

I think this rule ought to be discharged. The question, whether
this bill is the subject of taxation in this Court, does not necessarily
arise, and I give no opinion upon it. But it is contended that,
under the 38th or 39th section of this Act of Parliament, the
6 & 7 Vict. c. 73, a taxation of this bill ought to be directed. The
38th section is in these terms: (His Lordship read it.) The
case of *In re Carew*, which has been cited, where an attorney's
bill of costs was taxed on the application of a mortgagor, shows
that that is one instance (and no doubt there are several others) to
which that section applies. The 39th section applies only to the

(1) 14 L. J. Ch. 100.

case of trustees and their cestuis que trust. The question, therefore, really is, whether a person, who contributes as a rate-payer to
a fund out of which an attorney's bill is to be paid, is within the
provisions of the 38th section, as being a person not the party
chargeable with the bill, but liable to pay the same to the attorney
or to the party chargeable with it. It appears to me, that such a
case cannot be said to be within either the language or the spirit of
this enactment. It is certainly not within the words; for the rate-
payer is not liable to pay the bill, but only to pay a rate out of
which the bill may by possibility be paid. And with respect to the
spirit of the Act, I cannot think that it could have been intended
to give persons who have only such a species of interest in the
payment of the bill as this, a right to have it taxed, in the absence
of any special provision for that purpose, and of any mode of
carrying it out. In truth, there are other means provided by law,
by which the rate-payers may be protected against misconduct in
the *persons entrusted with the administration of the affairs of the
parish; namely, by application to the magistrates, who have to
settle and allow the accounts of the surveyors. The violation
of their duty by those whose business it is to take care of the
interests of the rate-payers is not to be presumed; but, if they do so
violate their duty, their default cannot be supplied by this Court,
where the Act of Parliament contains no words that enable it to
do so.

[*725]

For these reasons, I concur in the view of this case which was
taken by my brother COLERIDGE, and think this rule ought to
be discharged.

PARKE, B. :

I entirely agree in the view of this case which has been taken by
the LORD CHIEF BARON. It is not necessary on the present occasion
to say whether this Court has the power, under the 37th section of
this Act, to order a taxation of this bill; though I am strongly of
opinion that it has, and that a common jurisdiction is given by
that section to all the common law Courts. But, upon the other
point, I think my brother COLERIDGE has put a right construction
on the 38th section. This is a mixed fund in the hands of the
surveyor, consisting partly of the contributions of the rate-payers
already in his hands, and partly of the rates which he is empowered
to make under the 5 & 6 Will. IV. c. 50, s. 27, and out of which he
is to pay, not only the attorney's bill, but also other expenses,

penalties, and forfeitures which may be payable out of it. He is,
however, the party liable to the attorney for his bill, and the rate-
payers are not in any sense persons liable to pay it, within the
meaning of sect. 38.

ALDERSON, B. :

I am of the same opinion. I think a rate-payer is not one of
those persons who either has paid or is liable to pay the bill, either
to the attorney or the surveyor. That he is not liable to pay the
attorney is too clear for argument. Neither is he liable to pay it to
the *surveyor, until it has been allowed in his accounts by the
justices. Nor is the rate-payer without remedy in case of any
abuse; for it is his duty to apply to the justices when the surveyor
is passing his accounts, and if a proper case be made out, the
justices will no doubt discharge their duty, and call upon the
surveyor either to show that he has taxed the attorney's bill, or to
satisfy them that it did not require taxation. No difficulty can
arise if the magistrates do their duty, and we will not presume the
contrary.

ROLFE, B. :

I am of the same opinion. It struck me at first sight that this
Court had no authority to order the taxation of a bill for business
done in another of the common-law Courts; but, upon further
consideration, and after hearing what has been thrown out by my
brother PARKE, I am disposed to concur with him on that point.
But I am clearly of opinion that this bill cannot be taxed on the
application of these parties. The 27th section of the 5 & 6 Will. IV.
c. 50, is that which enables the surveyor to make a rate, which is
the fund wherewith he is to discharge his duties. Then it is said
that the rate-payers are interested in the whole of this fund. But
how is their interest provided for? By the 44th section, which
provides that, " within fourteen days after the election or appointment of the surveyor, the accounts made in writing, and signed by
the surveyor, district surveyor, or assistant surveyor for the year
preceding, of all monies received or disbursed by virtue of this Act,
ending on the day of the election or appointment of surveyor, shall
be made up, balanced, and laid before the parishioners in vestry
assembled, who may, if they think fit, order an abstract thereof to
be printed and published; and within one calendar month after the
election or appointment of surveyor as herein directed, the said

In re
BARBER.

[*726]

accounts shall be signed by the surveyor, &c. for the year preceding,
and laid before the justices of the peace at a special Sessions for the
highways, holden at the place *nearest to the parish or district for
which such surveyor shall have been appointed, and such justices
are hereby authorized and required to examine him as to the truth
of the said accounts, or of any charge contained therein : provided
always, that, if any person chargeable to the rate authorized to be
made by this Act, has any complaint against such accounts, or the
application of the monies received by the said surveyor, it shall be
lawful for any such inhabitant to make his complaint thereof to
such justices at the time of the verification of such accounts as
aforesaid, and the said justices are hereby required to hear such
complaint, and, if they shall think fit, to examine such surveyor
upon oath, and to make such order thereon as to them shall seem
meet." Now, if a proper case be made out, showing that the
surveyor has paid, or is about to pay an attorney's bill without
submitting it to the proper taxation, the magistrates might say to
the surveyor that they would not pass it unless it were taxed, and
some person were present on the part of the rate-payers to see that
justice were done. That course would prevent any difficulty ; but
the doctrine contended for to-day would lead to difficulties insur-
mountable. Besides that suggested by my brother PARKE, that this
is a mixed fund in the hands of the surveyor, applicable to various
purposes, it is also composed partly of the balance of the preceding
year, and, for aught we know, that balance might be sufficient for
the payment of the bill.

Rule discharged, with costs.

HART v. PRENDERGAST.

(14 Meeson & Welsby, 741—746 ; S. C. 15 L. J. Ex. 223.)

The following letter, written by the defendant to a clerk of the plaintiff,
in answer to an application for payment of the debt : Held not sufficient to
defeat a plea of the Statute of Limitations : " I will not fail to meet Mr. H.
(the plaintiff) on fair terms, and have now a hope that before perhaps a
week from this date I shall have it in my power to pay him, at all events,
a portion of the debt, when we shall settle about the liquidation of the
balance " (1).

DEBT for goods sold and delivered. Pleas, *nunquam indebitatus*,
and the Statute of Limitations. At the trial, before Pollock, C. B.,

---

(1) Cited in *Chasemore* v. *Turner* (1875) L. R. 10 Q. B. 500, 45 L. J. Q. B. 66,
Ex. Ch.—J. G. P.

at the Middlesex sittings after Trinity Term, it appeared that the debt was contracted above six years before action brought, while the defendant was a clerk in the Excise Office. In order to take the case out of the Statute of Limitations, the plaintiff gave in evidence the following letter, written by the defendant in answer to an application by a clerk of the plaintiff for payment of the debt :

"Jan. 8, 1841.

"SIR,—Having no longer any connexion with the Excise, I only this day received your obliging note of the 6th instant, which will account for any apparent remissness on my part, in not either calling on you or earlier replying. I assure you I will not fail to meet Mr. Hart on fair terms, and have now a hope that before perhaps a week from this date I shall have it in my power to pay him, at all events, a portion of the debt, when we shall settle about the liquidation of the balance."

It was contended for the defendant, that this was not a sufficient acknowledgment to satisfy Lord Tenterden's Act, 9 Geo. IV. c. 14. The LORD CHIEF BARON reserved the point for the opinion of the Court, and a verdict was found for the plaintiff for the amount claimed, the defendant having *leave to move to enter a verdict for him on the second issue.

[*742]

On a former day in this Term, *Lush* obtained a rule *nisi* accordingly ; against which

Hugh Hill now showed cause :

It is now fully established that the construction of documents of this kind is for the Court, and not for the jury : and, upon an examination of the cases, the Court will find that acknowledgments much less unequivocal than is contained in this letter have been held sufficient to satisfy the statute. The defendant fully admits the subsistence of the debt, and no condition is annexed to that admission. * * *

(PARKE, B. : There must be an acknowledgment of the debt, from which we may infer a promise to pay. If the defendant says in writing, " I admit the debt," that is enough ; but if he says, " I admit the debt, but I have not *made up my mind how or by what means to pay," how can you from that infer a promise to pay ?)

[*743]

* * There can be no doubt that this document contains a distinct

admission of the debt, and the only question is whether the other words of it negative the inference of a promise to pay the debt.

(PARKE, B.: No; whether it implies a promise to pay taken altogether. The substance of it is, "I owe you the debt, but I really cannot tell when or how I am to pay you, and I refrain from making any promise.")

Rather that he admits the debt, adding that he thinks he shall pay part of it in a week. [He cited *Dabbs* v. *Humphries* (1), *Bird* v. *Gammon* (2), and *Dobson* v. *Mackey* (3).]

Lush, contrà :

The present case differs from some of those which have been cited.

(PARKE, B.: This evidence is to prove a promise to pay on request. An unconditional acknowledgment is good evidence for that purpose, because you would infer from it that the party meant to pay on request. But if he annexes any qualification or condition, that is not a sufficient acknowledgment, without proof of the performance of it. The principle is correctly laid down in *Tanner* v. *Smart* (4).)

And also in *Cripps* v. *Davis* (5): The questions therefore are, first, does this letter taken altogether, amount to a promise to pay? secondly, does it support the promise laid in the declaration, to pay on request? It is, at most, only the expression of a hope that in a

[*744]

week he shall be able to pay; and that applies *only to an undefined part of the debt, and at all events would not support the declaration for the whole. As to the residue, he says merely that he will then settle about the liquidation of the balance. No evidence was given of the defendant's ability to pay. How, then, can this prove a promise to pay on request? *Morrell* v. *Frith* (6) is an express authority for the defendant. * * *

POLLOCK, C. B.:

I am of opinion that this rule ought to be made absolute. I gave no opinion upon the point at the trial; but when the cases

(1) 10 Bing. 446; 4 Moo. & Sc. 285).   (4) 30 R. R. 461 (6 B. & C. 603; 9
(2) 43 R. R. 839 (3 Bing. N. C. 883;   Dowl. & Ry. 549).
5 Scott, 213).   (5) 67 R. R. 292 (12 M. & W. 159).
(3) 8 Ad. & El. 225, n.; 4 Nev. & M.   (6) 49 R. R. 659 (3 M. & W. 402).
327.

are looked at, there are some which furnish very strong ground
for this application ; and it is better to adhere to the principle
of some decision, instead of reasoning on the terms of the particular
document in each case.   Now the case of *Tanner* v. *Smart* lays
down the principle very clearly, on a review of all the authorities ;
namely, that, " under the ordinary issue on the Statute of Limitations, an acknowledgment is only evidence of a promise to pay ;
and unless it is conformable to and maintains the promises in the
declaration, although it may show to demonstration that the debt
has never been paid, and *is still subsisting, it has no effect."   It
is not sufficient that the document contains a promise by the defendant to pay when he is able, or by bill, or a mere expectation that
he shall pay at some future time : it should contain either an
unqualified promise to pay,—that is, a promise to pay on request,—
or, if it be a conditional promise, or a promise to pay on the arrival
of a certain period, the performance of the condition, or the arrival
of that period, should be proved by the plaintiff.   The only question
in the present case is, whether this letter contains a promise to pay
the debt on request.   Now certainly it does not in terms contain
such a promise ; all that the writer says is, that " he will not fail
to meet the plaintiff on fair terms "—what those " terms " may be
I cannot say ;—and that " he has now a hope that before perhaps
a week he shall have it in his power to pay him, at all events,
a portion of the debt, when they shall settle about the liquidation
of the balance."   That liquidation might be by his then asking for
further time, with or without security.   What are the terms to
which the defendant alludes it is impossible to speculate ; but there
is no promise to pay the whole debt at all, nor to pay a single
shilling of it on request, but a mere expression of a hope that he
may be able to pay part, and then that they may settle—in what
manner does not appear—as to the liquidation of the balance.   I
am of opinion, therefore, that this letter does not contain a sufficient
acknowledgment or promise to satisfy the Act of Parliament, and
therefore that this rule must be made absolute.

PARKE, B. :

I am of the same opinion.   There is no doubt of the principle of
law applicable to these cases, since the decision in *Tanner* v.
Smart ; namely, that the plaintiff must either show an unqualified
acknowledgment of the debt, or, if he show a promise to pay coupled
with a condition, he must show performance of the condition ;

HART
e.
PRENDER-
GAST.
[*746]

so as *in either case to fit the promise laid in the declaration, which is a promise to pay on request. The case of *Tanner* v. *Smart* put an end to a series of decisions which were a disgrace to the law, and I trust we shall be in no danger of falling into the same course again. In the present case I agree with the LORD CHIEF BARON, that, taking the whole document together, it contains no promise to pay any part of the debt on request, but a mere expression of the defendant's hope that in a week he may be able to pay a part of it, and that then the parties may be able to make some settlement for the liquidation of the balance.

ALDERSON, B. :

I am of the same opinion. We must look to the principle of the cases, although there are some with which it may be difficult to agree upon the particular facts ; as in *Gardner* v. *M'Mahon* (1). Different minds came to different conclusions of fact upon such documents. But the principle is clear, that the plaintiff must prove an acknowledgment conformable to the promise laid in the declaration, viz., either an unconditional acknowledgment, from which a promise to pay on request is inferred, or an acknowledgment subject to a condition which has been performed, and which then becomes absolute, and so equally maintains the promise laid in the declaration. This document contains neither the one nor the other.

ROLFE, B. :

I am of the same opinion. The principle is said to be, that the document must contain either a promise to pay the debt, or an acknowledgment from which such a promise is to be inferred. Perhaps it would be more correct to say, that it must in all cases contain a promise to pay, but that from a simple acknowledgment the law implies a promise ; but there must, in all cases, be a promise, in order to support the declaration.

Rule absolute.

1845.
Nov. 20.
——
[747]

WILLIAMS *v.* NEWTON.

(14 Meeson & Welsby, 747—757 ; S. C. 15 L. J. Ex. 11.)

The 62nd section of the Pilotage Act, 1825 (6 Geo. IV. c. 125), provides, "that nothing in this Act contained shall extend, or be construed to extend, to subject to any penalty the master or mate of any ship or vessel, being the owner or a part owner of such ship or vessel, and residing at Dover, Deal, or the Isle of Thanet, for conducting or piloting such his own ship or vessel

(1) 61 R. R. 314 (3 Q. B. 561 ; 2 G. & D. 593).

WILLIAMS
v.
NEWTON.

from any of the places aforesaid, up or down the rivers Thames or Medway, or into or out of any port or place within the jurisdiction of the Cinque Ports:" Held, that the "places aforesaid," in this section, mean Dover, Deal, and the Isle of Thanet; that, therefore, the clause exempts from penalties such masters only as navigate their vessels from Dover, Deal, or the Isle of Thanet; and, consequently, that the penalties imposed by section 58 were recoverable from a master piloting his own vessel on a foreign voyage commencing in the port of London, although he was a part owner, and resident in the Isle of Thanet.

DEBT by the plaintiff, as secretary of the Society of Licensed Trinity House Pilots, for penalties under the Pilot Act, 6 Geo. IV. c. 125, s. 58 (1). The declaration stated, that whereas heretofore, and after the passing the said Act, to wit, on &c., a certain vessel called the *Dart*, of divers, to wit, 242 tons burthen, and drawing divers, to wit, ten feet water, and of which said vessel the defendant was then master, was navigating and passing in and upon a certain navigable river called the Thames, within the limits of the jurisdiction of the said corporation, that is to say, between London Bridge and the Downs, to wit, at the Lower *Pool in the said river, the said vessel being then navigating and passing in and upon the said river on a certain voyage, to wit, from the port of London to a certain other place beyond the Downs, to wit, to the island of Madeira, in the Atlantic Sea. And the plaintiff further says, that whilst the said vessel was so navigating and passing as aforesaid, within the limits aforesaid, between London Bridge and the Downs, in and upon the said river, to wit, on the day aforesaid, one Henry Beer Mumford, at the time of the offer hereinafter mentioned to have been made by the said Henry Beer Mumford to take charge

[*748]

(1) Which enacts, "That every master of any ship or vessel who shall act himself as a pilot, or shall employ or continue employed as a pilot any unlicensed person, or any licensed person, acting out of the limits for which he is qualified, or beyond the extent of his qualification, after any pilot, licensed and qualified to act within the limits in which such ship or vessel shall then actually be, shall have offered to take charge of such ship or vessel, or have made a signal for that purpose, shall forfeit for every such offence double the amount of the sum which would have been legally demandable for the pilotage of such ship or vessel, and shall likewise forfeit for every such offence an additional penalty of 5*l.* for every fifty tons burden of such

ship or vessel, if the corporation of Trinity House of Deptford Strond, as to cases in which pilots licensed by or under the said corporation shall be concerned, or the said lord warden for the time being, or his lieutenant for the time being, as to cases in which the Cinque Port pilots shall be concerned, shall think it proper that the person prosecuting should be at liberty to proceed for the recovery of such additional penalty, and certify the same in writing." [This section was repealed by 17 & 18 Vict. c. 120, s. 4, and is now replaced by 57 & 58 Vict. c. 60, s. 598; but section 62 of the Act is still in force by virtue of 17 & 18 Vict. c. 104, s. 353, and 57 & 58 Vict. c. 60, s. 603. —J. G. P.]

WILLIAMS
v.
NEWTON.

of the said vessel, being a pilot under the jurisdiction of the said corporation, was duly licensed by the said corporation, and qualified to act as such pilot, and to have taken charge of such vessel as such pilot, within the limits aforesaid, in which the said vessel then was; and the plaintiff avers, that, at the time of the offer and refusal hereinafter mentioned, the said vessel was not in charge of any pilot licensed to act within the said limits; of which said several premises the defendant, at the time of the making of the offer hereinafter mentioned, to wit, on the day aforesaid, had notice. And the plaintiff avers, that afterwards, and within twelve calendar months next before the commencement of this suit, to wit, on the day aforesaid, the said Henry Beer Mumford then and there duly tendered himself to the defendant (he the defendant being and acting as master of the said vessel, then on her voyage aforesaid) to take charge of the said vessel as pilot, for the purpose of conducting the said ship within the said limits of her said voyage; and the plaintiff avers, that, at the time of the said offer, the license of the said Henry Beer Mumford as such pilot as aforesaid had been duly registered, according to the statute in such case made and provided, by the principal officers of the Custom-house of the place at which the said Henry Beer Mumford did reside, to wit, at the Custom-house in the city of London; and that he the said Henry Beer Mumford, *at the time of such offer, had his license in his personal custody, and then produced the same to the defendant; but the plaintiff says, that the defendant then altogether refused to allow the said Henry Beer Mumford to take charge of the said vessel as such pilot as aforesaid, and then and there, after the said offer and tender as aforesaid, and within the limits aforesaid, he the defendant, not being a licensed pilot in that behalf, acted and continued to act as a pilot on board the said ship, within the limits aforesaid, against the form of the statute, &c. And the plaintiff avers, that the sum that would have been legally demandable for the pilotage of the said vessel was the sum, to wit, of 7l. 17s. 8d., whereby and by virtue of the statute the defendant hath forfeited for his said offence a large sum of money, to wit, the sum of 15l. 14s. 6d., being double the amount of the sum which would have been legally demandable by the said Henry Beer Mumford for the pilotage of the said vessel. And the plaintiff further avers, that afterwards, to wit, on the day aforesaid, the case hereinbefore mentioned was a case in which pilots licensed by the corporation were concerned, and that thereupon, to wit, on

[*749]

the day aforesaid, the said corporation did think it proper that WILLIAMS
the person proceeding, to wit, the plaintiff, should be at liberty to NEWTON.
proceed for the recovery of the additional penalty incurred by the
defendant for such offence, to wit, the sum of 5*l.* for every fifty
tons burthen of the said vessel; and the said corporation did then,
to wit, on the day aforesaid, certify the same in writing, whereby
and by virtue of the said statute the defendant hath forfeited a
further large sum of money, to wit, 20*l.*, the same being the amount
of the four several sums of 5*l.* for every fifty tons burthen of the
said vessel; and thereby and by virtue of the said statute, and of
the said certificate of the said corporation, an action hath accrued
to the plaintiff to demand and have of and from the defendant the
said several sums of 15*l.* 14*s.* 6*d.* and 20*l.*, respectively, &c.

Plea, Not guilty, by statute.   [750]

The cause was tried, before Pollock, C. B., at the London sittings
after last Trinity Term, upon the following admissions, signed by
the attornies in the cause; and a verdict was taken for the defendant,
subject to a motion to enter a verdict for the plaintiff, damages
35*l.* 14*s.* 6*d.*, if the Court should be of opinion that the defendant
was not, under the circumstances stated in the admissions, exempt
from taking a pilot at the time when he offered himself.

" The defendant was the master and part owner of the brig *Dart*,
of and belonging to the port of London, in the pleadings mentioned,
on the occasion of the voyage hereinafter mentioned. At the time
and on the occasion hereinafter mentioned, the defendant was
residing at and in the Isle of Thanet. The *Dart*, on the 2nd of
January, 1844, sailed from the London Dock down the river
Thames, from London, under the defendant's command, bound for
the island of Madeira. Her burthen was 242 tons, and she drew
ten feet water. She had not, at any time during the voyage, a
licensed pilot on board, or any pilot but the defendant; and she
was conducted and piloted by him without the aid or assistance of
any licensed pilot, or other person or persons than the ordinary
crew of the said ship or vessel. On the said 2nd of January, 1844,
upon her leaving the London Dock to proceed on her voyage out,
and whilst she was in the river Thames, and before she reached
Greenwich, Henry Beer Mumford, a licensed pilot, as in the declaration mentioned, offered to the defendant, who was then acting as
master, to take charge of her as in the declaration mentioned. His
license had been registered as in the declaration mentioned, and
he then had it in his custody, and produced it to the defendant.

The defendant refused to allow him to take charge of the vessel. The vessel proceeded on her voyage to Madeira, but she stopped at Gravesend, where she brought up for the night, and pursued her said voyage in the morning; and the defendant *acted and continued to act as pilot for the purpose of the voyage. The pilotage, if Mumford had acted as pilot, would have amounted to 7*l.* 17*s.* 3*d.*

"The pilot has leave to sue under the authority of the Trinity House, as in the declaration mentioned.

" That the port of London extends as far as Gravesend; that the geographical positions of the several places, &c. above named, and referred to in the statute 6 Geo. IV. c. 125, may be taken and noticed at the trial, and afterwards on the motion, from any maps or charts in ordinary use."

On a former day in this Term, *Jervis* moved pursuant to the leave reserved at the trial, and obtained a rule *nisi* to enter the verdict for the plaintiff.

Shee, Serjt., and *Bovill* now showed cause. * * *

[754]   *Jervis* and *Barstow*, contrà. * * *

[755]   POLLOCK, C. B.:

It appears to me that this rule ought to be made absolute. The question turns mainly on the construction of the 62nd section of this Act (6 Geo. IV. c. 125); I think the 59th section has no bearing on the point. The question is, what is the meaning of the expression in the 62nd section, "places aforesaid?" Now Lord TENTERDEN, in the case of *Hammond* v. *Tremayne*, has already put a construction upon those words; and it appears that, in a recent case, the Court of Queen's Bench, adopting that construction, have held those words to refer to the places mentioned in the same section; so that we have the opinion of an eminent Judge, of itself entitled to

[*756]   great respect, especially on a matter relating to navigation, *and also a recent confirmation of that opinion by a decision of the full Court of Queen's Bench. But apart from authority, upon the history of this Act, and looking to the words in the recital, " that whereas there hath been time out of mind, and now is, a society of pilots of the Trinity House of Dover, Deal, and the Isle of Thanet, who have had the pilotage of all ships from the said places up the river Thames," where it is clear that those words refer to Dover, Deal, and the Isle of Thanet, I have no doubt that, by the expression

in this section, "places aforesaid," the Legislature only meant to
include Dover, Deal, and the Isle of Thanet. If so, we must substitute them for the expression we find, "places aforesaid," and
read the clause thus: "That nothing in this Act shall extend to
subject to any penalty any master of any vessel, being the owner or
part owner of such vessel, and residing at Dover, Deal, or the Isle
of Thanet, for conducting or piloting such his own vessel on any
voyage from any of those places up or down the river Thames,"
&c. It is quite clear, therefore, that the exemption in the 62nd
section does not extend to the case of such person piloting his own
vessel on a foreign voyage, commencing in the port of London.
The verdict for the defendant must therefore be set aside, and a
verdict entered for the plaintiff for 35*l.* 11*s.* 6*d.*

PARKE, B.:

I agree with my LORD CHIEF BARON in the construction of this
clause of the Act of Parliament. In that construction we are
supported by the opinion of Lord TENTERDEN, and by the recent
decision of the Court of Queen's Bench. But, independently of
authority, it seems to me that it is the true construction of this
section; and the reason is pretty obvious, on looking to the history
of these statutes. The 8 Geo. I. c. 13, s. 2, exempted the master
of any vessel, or part owner, residing at Dover, Deal, or the Isle of
Thanet, from penalties for piloting his own vessel from any of the
places aforesaid up the said rivers. Then the *52 Geo. III. c. 39,   [*757]
gave a much more extended privilege, without the same limit that
existed under the 8 Geo. I. But afterwards, the Legislature, considering that they had given thereby too extensive a privilege, read
the two Acts together, and by the present Act limited it thus: viz.
" to masters or mates, being also owners, of vessels sailing from
the places aforesaid, that is, Dover, Deal, or the Isle of Thanet, up
or down the rivers Thames or Medway," &c. With respect to the
meaning of the words " up or down," the reasonable construction
is, that the owner of a vessel having liberty to go up the river from
those places, should also be at liberty to go down again when he
has so gone up. As to the subsequent words, " or into or out of
any port or place within the jurisdiction of the Cinque Ports," we
do not pronounce any opinion whether they are limited to a voyage
from Dover, Deal, or the Isle of Thanet, or not; it is unnecessary
on the present occasion to do so, although I have a strong opinion
on the subject. But, both on authority and on the just construction

WILLIAMS
v.
NEWTON.

of the statute, it appears to me that there was no exemption in the present case, and therefore that this rule must be made absolute.

ROLFE, B.:

I am of the same opinion. The difficulty arises from the vague manner in which the Legislature has expressed its meaning; and, therefore, when once a construction has been put upon such a clause by a judicial decision, that ought of itself to be a sufficient authority for our adopting the same construction. But if I had now for the first time to put a construction upon this clause, I should say that the meaning of the Legislature is not difficult to discover; viz. that from Dover, Deal, and the Isle of Thanet,—taking those places as being, for this purpose, the extremity of the river Thames,—the masters of vessels residing at those places may lawfully conduct their vessels up and down the river without a pilot.

Rule absolute.

1845.
Nov. 21.

[762]

BRITTAIN *v.* LLOYD.

(14 Meeson & Welsby, 762—774; S. C. 15 L. J. Ex. 43.)

Where a person acting at the request of and in pursuance of an authority given by another has incurred a liability, and has in consequence been, before action, obliged to pay money in discharge of that liability, he is entitled to have that money repaid to him; and the count for money paid is a proper count under which to recover it (1).

THIS was an action of assumpsit for money paid by the plaintiff, an auctioneer, for the use of the defendant, and on an account stated.

The defendant pleaded *non assumpsit*, on which issue was joined; and the cause was tried, before Tindal, Ch. J., at the Derbyshire Spring Assizes, 1844, when it was agreed that a verdict should be found for the plaintiff for 107*l.* 3*s.* 9*d.* damages, the sum claimed by the plaintiff, and 40*s.* costs, subject to the opinion of this Court on a special case; the Court to have power to draw all inferences from the facts which a jury could or might draw.

The defendant, being the owner of a freehold estate, consisting of a farm-house, out-buildings, and lands, situate at Woolow, near Buxton, in Derbyshire, employed the plaintiff, who long before and at the time of the auction hereinafter mentioned, and ever since,

---

(1) The head-note as above is taken from the judgment of BLACKBURN, J., in *Mollett* v. *Robinson* (1872) L. R. 7 C. P. 84, 102 (*S. C.* (1874–5) L. R. 7 H. L. 802, 44 L. J. C. P. 362), who cited *Brittain* v. *Lloyd* therefor.

has been an auctioneer duly licensed, to sell the said estate by an *auction, to be holden at the "Bull's Head Inn," at Fairfield, near Buxton aforesaid, on the 25th of January, 1843. Previous to the commencement, and on the day of the auction, the defendant delivered to the plaintiff the following authority to bid for her, signed by herself and John Poundall: "To Mr. John Brittain, auctioneer, Green, Fairfield. Take notice, that Mr. John Poundall is appointed by Mrs. Charlotte Lloyd, the real owner of the estate intended to be by you put up to sale by way of auction, at the 'Bull's Head Inn,' Fairfield, on the 25th day of January instant; the said Mr. Poundall being actually employed by the vendor of such estate to bid at the said sale for the use and behoof of the said Charlotte Lloyd. And take notice, also, that the said Mr. John Poundall hath agreed and doth intend accordingly to bid at the said sale for the use and behoof of the said Charlotte Lloyd. As witness the hands of the said Charlotte Lloyd and John Poundall, the 25th day of January, 1845. CHARLOTTE LLOYD, JOHN POUNDALL. Witness, SAMUEL WOOD." Which notice, duly signed by the defendant and the said John Poundall, being the person intended to make the bidding, was duly given to the plaintiff before the commencement of the sale, and before the bidding by the said John Poundall hereinafter mentioned.

The estate was put up for sale by auction by the plaintiff on the said 25th of January, 1843, and several persons attended and bid, and Poundall attended in the sale-room during the auction, and bid as hereinafter mentioned. The estate was put up for sale by the plaintiff, subject to the following (amongst others) conditions of sale, which were prepared by the plaintiff in the course of his employment as such auctioneer, and read by the plaintiff at the commencement of the auction, viz.: "That the highest bidder should be the purchaser. That no bidding should be retracted. That the vendor or her agent should have the right of bidding once for the property. That a deposit *should be paid on the fall of the hammer, as also the whole of the auction duty, to the auctioneer by the purchaser. That the residue of the purchase-money should be paid at a future day, when the estate should be conveyed. All fixtures, articles, and things, timber and timber-like trees growing on the premises, down to and including those of the value of 1*s.* each, were not to be included in the purchase-money of the premises, but to be paid for in addition to such purchase-money, at a fair valuation, at the time of completing the purchase."

BRITTAIN
v.
LLOYD.

The biddings then commenced, the defendant being in a room in the inn adjoining to that in which the auction was held, and having a servant in attendance in the room, to give her information respecting the biddings, &c. Among the bidders were the names of two persons of the name of Barker and Shaw, the latter of whom ultimately became the purchaser of the estate, as hereinafter mentioned. After several biddings, including several by Shaw, Barker bid 3,150*l.*, and Shaw shortly afterwards bid 3,300*l.* : this was communicated to the defendant by her aforesaid servant, and she immediately sent him to desire Mr. Barker to come to her in the private room, and there was a suspension of the auction for a few minutes ; Mr. Barker went to the defendant, who inquired of him whether he was bidding for any one in the room, and offered to let him bid a time or two, if he liked ; and stated that he might go up to 3,800*l.*, and he should not be charged with the auction duty ; and that if he bid she would not take any advantage of it. He objected, that it was more than the estate was worth ; she then requested him to bid for her, to which he acceded, and returned to the auction-room, and the sale was resumed by Barker bidding 3,350*l.* for the defendant. Shaw then bid 3,400*l.*, which was communicated by her said servant to the defendant, and who was immediately sent to fetch Shaw to the defendant out of the auction-room.

[*765] Shaw was taken to the room where *defendant was, when she asked him if he would give her the auction duty over his last bidding ? Shaw replied, he did not know what the auction duty was, but he would wait upon her the following day. It was agreed upon between them that Shaw would wait on her at her residence, at Woolow, the following day, and the hour of two o'clock in the afternoon was fixed. She then told Poundall, in Shaw's presence, to go and bid the reserved bidding, which he did, and bought in the estate at 3,800*l.*, and the plaintiff knocked down the estate to Poundall, observing, that all the parties attending the sale were then at liberty, according to the usual practice, to bid by private contract ; but Shaw would, according to the usage, have the first option. There had been no bidding after Shaw's, of 3,400*l.*, before Poundall bid the reserved bidding.

The next morning, Shaw met Poundall (who acted for the defendant) at her residence at Woolow, and there saw the defendant. Poundall and Shaw looked over the estate, and Poundall named 3,550*l.* or 3,560*l.* for the estate, including timber, fixtures, &c., which were estimated in a lump at the sum of 45*l.* : he had not received any previous instructions so to do. Shaw then offered 3,500*l.* for the estate, and 40*l.* for the fixtures, &c., and said, if he could not have it at that price, he would not have it at all. Poundall then consulted the defendant, and they agreed to split the difference, and that the purchase-money should be 3,545*l.* The bargain was made, according to the testimony of Shaw, without any reference to the sale by auction at all.

The defendant then sent for the plaintiff to come to the defendant's house, on the 27th of January, 1843, being two days after the sale, to prepare the agreement between the defendant and Shaw; and the plaintiff and Shaw, on the 27th of January, 1843, came to the defendant's house, when an agreement, to which the plaintiff was an attesting *witness, of which the following is a copy, was copied by the defendant's daughter, at the request of plaintiff, from a book of the plaintiff's.

"Memorandum.—That Mr. William Shaw is declared the highest bidder and purchaser of the Woolow estate, situate in the parish of Hope and township of Fairfield, in the county of Derby, at the sum of 3,545*l.*, including the timber plantations and fixtures on the premises; at which sum the said Mr. William Shaw doth agree to become the purchaser thereof accordingly, and doth also agree, on his part, to perform the before-written conditions of sale; and, in consideration thereof, Charlotte Lloyd, the vendor, doth agree to sell and convey the said estate and premises unto the said Mr. William Shaw, his heirs and assigns, or as he or they shall direct, according to the said before-written conditions of sale. And it is also agreed, that the sum of 350*l.* shall be paid as a deposit, which sum is to be considered as part of the purchase-money. Dated this 27th day of January, 1843.

(Signed)	"CHARLOTTE LLOYD,
	"WILLIAM SHAW.

"JOHN POUNDALL,
"RICHARD SHAW, } Witnesses."
"JOHN BRITTAIN,

There are no other conditions than those set out in the early part of this case.

In March, 1843, the plaintiff duly made the return of the sale to the proper officers of Excise, and that the estate was bought in by defendant for 3,800*l.*, and duly verified and produced, and left, as

BRITTAIN
v.
LLOYD.

[*767]

required by the Act of Parliament, the notice of the said appointment of Poundall, &c.; and also verified the fairness and reality of
the transactions to the best of his knowledge and belief, and did all
other acts required by law by him to be done, to get the duty on
the said auction and sale allowed and *remitted to the defendant;
but the Commissioners of Excise refused to allow or remit the same.

On the 22nd of March, 1843, the plaintiff had an interview with
the defendant, in order to settle his account against the defendant
for the sale of the estate hereinbefore mentioned, and also for
another sale the plaintiff had had for the defendant.   Some
unpleasantness took place between the plaintiff and defendant, in
consequence of the defendant complaining of the exorbitancy of the
plaintiff's bill, alleging that the plaintiff had charged her too much.
The defendant said to the plaintiff, " You had thought to have
thrown the auction duty away; but I would not let you."   The
plaintiff told the defendant that he had not yet settled the sale
account with the Excise, and that when he did settle it, if the
auction duty (1) was demanded of him, he should demand it of
defendant; to which the defendant replied, " Then you must get it,
and take it."

Ultimately, in September, 1844, the Commissioners of Excise, or
the persons duly authorised in that behalf, required the plaintiff to
pay the said auction duty, amounting to 107l. 8s. 9d., in respect of
the said sale of the said estate above-mentioned, being the amount
of duty on 8,500l., and formally demanded the same of the plaintiff,
which requisition and demand was duly communicated to the
defendant by the plaintiff, and she was required to pay the amount,
or to indemnify the plaintiff against proceedings for the recovery of
the duty, which was refused by the defendant.   Correspondence
then took place between the plaintiff and defendant, and the defendant and the Commissioners of Excise; and ultimately the plaintiff
was compelled by the Commissioners of Excise to pay the above
duty of 107l. 8s. 9d. to the Commissioners of Excise, of which
payment due notice was given to the defendant, and she was
required to pay the same to the plaintiff, but which she refused;
and this action was brought to recover that amount.

[768]

The question for the opinion of the Court is, whether the plaintiff
is entitled to recover the amount of the said auction duty.

(1) An auction duty was imposed
on sales by auction by 19 Geo. III.
c. 56, repealed by S. L. R. Act, 1861.

The effect of the Act is stated by
Whitehurst in his argument below.—
J. G. P.

The case was argued on the 17th of November, by

Whitehurst, for the plaintiff:

The plaintiff is clearly entitled to recover. The duty imposed on sales by auction by the stat. 19 Geo. III. c. 56, is, by sect. 6, made payable on the knocking down of the hammer, and is thereby declared to be chargeable on the auctioneer; and the 7th section empowers the auctioneer to recover the same by action of debt or on the case, against his employer or the party on whose account the sale was made. Then comes the 12th section, on which the question in this case mainly depends, which enacts, that, where owners of estates bid for themselves, or employ others to bid for them, an allowance of duties is to be made to them, provided notice be given to the auctioneer thereof; and in case of collusion or unfair practice, the allowance is not to be made. Now, the facts of this case show clearly that this was not such a transaction as was contemplated by that section, and in which it was intended to give the vendor relief; for this was a mere covert proceeding by the vendor, in order to screen her from the payment of the duty. The plaintiff, therefore, having paid the duties under these circumstances, is entitled to recover back the amount from his employer. Moreover, the defendant has litigated this matter before the Commissioners of Excise, who are the parties to determine whether a fraud was committed or not, and they having decided the matter, it is no longer open to discussion.

Humfrey, contrà:

This action for money paid is not maintainable. The auction duty is nowhere made *chargeable upon the vendor; but, on the [*769] contrary, is expressly charged by the Act of Parliament upon the auctioneer. The defendant, therefore, was not liable to the Crown for the auction duty, and therefore the money paid by the plaintiff to discharge it was not money paid to the use of the defendant. [He cited *Spencer* v. *Parry* (1), *Grissell* v. *Robinson* (2), and *Lubbock* v. *Tribe* (3).]

But, further, is the defendant liable to the plaintiff at all? The [771] auctioneer must look to the purchaser for the duty, and has no right to charge the vendor with it.

_____

(1) 3 Ad. & El. 331; 4 Nev. & M. 3 Scott, 329).
770.   (3) 3 M. & W. 607.
(2) 43 R. R. 574 (3 Bing. N. C. 10;

BRITTAIN
v.
LLOYD.

(POLLOCK, C. B. : The defendant is clearly liable in some form or other.)

Whitehurst, in reply :

The defendant is liable in this form of action, for she was ultimately liable to pay this money, inasmuch as the auctioneer, by the 7th section of the Act of Parliament, is entitled to recover back the amount from her as his employer ; and it makes no difference that she was not liable directly to the Crown. In effect and substance, the principal, not the agent, is the party chargeable.

[*772]

(PARKE, B. : The auctioneer sued the vendor for *money paid in *Cruso* v. *Crisp* (1), and this objection was never taken.)

So also in *Capp* v. *Topham* (2).   *   *   *

Cur. adv. rult.

The judgment of the COURT was now delivered by

POLLOCK, C. B. :

This case was argued on Monday last. It was an action by an auctioneer against the defendant, his employer, for the duty which he had been obliged to pay to the Crown on a sale of her estate ; and the form of action was for money paid. The Court intimated its opinion, that it was clear that the defendant was liable, but took time to consider whether this was the proper form of action.

It was argued by *Mr. Humfrey*, that this form of action could not be maintained, unless the effect of the payment was to relieve the defendant from some liability for the amount to the party to whom payment was made, and that otherwise it could not be paid for the defendant's use ; and he relied on the case of *Spencer* v.

[*773]

Parry (3) as an authority *for that proposition ; and contended, that, as the defendant in this case was not made liable to the Crown by the Act of Parliament, the money was paid to one who had no claim upon her, and therefore not to her use.

This proposition, however, is not warranted by the decision of *Spencer* v. *Parry*, though some expressions in the report of the judgment give a countenance to the argument of the learned counsel ; nor can the proposition be maintained ; for it is clear, that, if one requests another to pay money for him to a stranger, with an express or implied undertaking to repay it, the amount,

(1) 3 East, 337.   (3) 3 Ad. & El. 331.
(2) 6 East, 392.

when paid, is a debt due to the party paying from him at whose request it is paid, and may be recovered on a count for money paid; and it is wholly immaterial whether the money is paid in discharge of a debt due to the stranger, or as a loan or gift to him ; on which two latter suppositions the defendant is relieved from no liability by the payment. The request to pay, and the payment according to it, constitute the debt; and whether the request be direct, as where the party is expressly desired by the defendant to pay, or indirect, where he is placed by him under a liability to pay, and does pay, makes no difference. If one ask another, instead of paying money for him, to lend him his acceptance for his accommodation, and the acceptor is obliged to pay it, the amount is money paid for the borrower, although the borrower be no party to the bill, nor in any way liable to the person who ultimately receives the amount. The borrower, by requesting the acceptor to assume that character which ultimately obliges him to pay, impliedly requests him to pay, and is as much liable to repay, as he would be on a direct request to pay money for him with a promise to repay it. In every case, therefore, in which there has been a payment of money by a plaintiff to a third party, at the request of the defendant, express or implied, on a promise, express or implied, to repay the amount, this form of action is maintainable.

In the case of *Spencer* v. *Parry*, there was no such implied [774] request. In the case of *Grissell* v. *Robinson*, referred to in the argument, it was considered, and we think rightly, that there was; and the Court of Queen's Bench thought the decision of *Brown* v. *Hodgson* was to be supported on the same ground. We have now to apply this doctrine to the facts of the present case ; and we all think that the plaintiff, having been placed by the defendant in the situation of being obliged to pay the auction duty to the Crown, under circumstances in which the defendant was bound to repay him, may be considered as having paid money to the Crown at her request, and consequently may maintain this action.

Judgment for the plaintiff.

1845.
Nov. 19.
———
[789]

HALE *v.* OLDROYD.

(14 Meeson & Welsby, 789—793; S. C. 15 L. J. Ex. 4.)

In case for the diversion of water, the plaintiff alleged in his declaration
a reversionary interest in three closes of land, to wit, three ponds filled
with water, one pond being upon each of the said closes, and a right to the
flow of the water into the said closes, for supplying the said ponds in the
said closes with water for the watering of cattle. The defendant traversed
the right to the flow of the water as alleged.

It appeared in evidence at the trial, that the plaintiff had enjoyed an
immemorial right to the flow of this water into an ancient pond in one of
his closes, but that, above thirty years ago, he made a new pond in each of
the three closes, and turned the water so as to supply them, and thenceforth
disused the old pond, which was gradually filled with rubbish and overgrown with grass. The plaintiff's right in respect of the three ponds
having been defeated by proof of an outstanding life estate, under the
Prescription Act, 1832 (2 & 3 Will. IV. c. 71), s. 7: Held, that he was
entitled, under this declaration, to recover in respect of his right to the
flow of water to the old pond.

CASE. The declaration stated, that, before and at the time of
the committing of the grievances by the defendant as thereinafter mentioned, divers, to wit, three closes of land, situate &c.,
and certain, to wit, three, ponds filled with water, one pond
thereof being in and upon each of the said closes respectively,
were in the possession of one J. Bromley, as tenant thereof to
the plaintiff, the reversion thereof being in the plaintiff; and that
a certain other close, adjoining and near to the said three closes of
the plaintiff, was in the possession of the defendant. It then
stated, that the several tenants of the said three closes were and
are entitled, from time whereof the memory of man was not to the
contrary to the overflow of a certain stream of water, from the said
close of the defendant into the said closes of the plaintiff, for
supplying the said ponds in the said closes with water for
watering the cattle of the said tenants, &c. The declaration
then alleged a diversion of the water of the said stream by the
defendant, by means whereof the reversionary estate of the plaintiff
was injured, &c.

Pleas, first, Not guilty; secondly, a traverse of the right of the
tenant to the overflow of the water, *modo et formâ*. Issues thereon.

At the trial, before Coltman, J., at the last York Assizes, the
following facts appeared in evidence:

The defendant was the owner of a close called the Well Close,
on the east side of which was an ancient public well, this close
being separated by a hedge and ditch from the three closes of the
plaintiff. The water from this well, which occasionally overflowed,

had, from time immemorial, *run down to the ditch and fence, and
plaintiff's closes, where it was used for the watering of cattle.   In
the year 1811 or 1812, one John Collinson, the then occupier of the
Well Close, made a new drain from the well to the ditch, whereby
he diverted the stream that had supplied his well, and brought the
water from the east to the west end of the Well Close, where it was
received in a cistern, and used by the public.   Shortly after this,
the then occupier of the plaintiff's three closes made a new pond
in each of them, and supplied them with water by a cut from the
ditch into each of them.   The ponds so supplied were used by the
successive tenants of the plaintiff's three closes, from that time
until the diversion complained of, being more than twenty and less
than forty years.   After the making of the new ponds, the plaintiff's
old pond was disused, and was gradually filled with rubbish and
overgrown with grass.   In 1843, the defendant, by a new drain,
again turned the water in the well away from the ditch and the
plaintiff's three ponds, upon which this action was brought.   Under
these circumstances, it was contended for the plaintiff, that he had
acquired a title to the flow of water into his three new ponds by
twenty years' enjoyment; but that, at all events, he had established
a right to a flow of water into his old pond by immemorial user.
The defendant's counsel contended, that the three new ponds were
alone claimed in the declarations, and, in answer to the plaintiff's
case as to them, gave evidence that John Collinson was devisee for
his life of the defendant's close, up to his death in the year 1826,
and, therefore, that, under the exception in the 7th section of the
Prescription Act, 2 & 3 Will. IV. c. 71, the time of his life estate
being excluded from the computation, no right was gained by the
plaintiff under that statute.   The learned Judge, however, thought
that, under the terms of the devise, John Collinson was tenant in
tail of the Well Close, and, the jury having found that the plaintiff
and his predecessors had used the *water in the old pond from time
immemorial, he directed the verdict to be entered for the plaintiff,
reserving leave to the defendant to move to enter a verdict for him
as to the right to the overflow to the three new ponds.

On a former day in this Term, *Martin* obtained a rule *nisi*
accordingly ; against which

Bains, Crompton, and *Hoggins* now showed cause, and contended,
first, that the plaintiff was entitled, under this declaration, to show

HALE
v.
OLDROYD.

his right, by reason of immemorial user, to have the flow of the water into his old pond, and that it was no answer to that claim of right to say that the pond had been filled up and disused. There was no proof of his having released or expressly abandoned his claim ; and this declaration did not confine him to proof of his title to the flow of water into the three new ponds. The allegation of title to three ponds was clearly divisible. Secondly, they argued that John Collinson was tenant in tail, and therefore the statute did not prevent a right being acquired to the flow of water into the three new ponds : but the COURT intimating a clear opinion, that, under the terms of the devise, John Collinson was tenant for life only, this point was given up.

Martin, Tomlinson, and *Hugh Hill,* in support of the rule:

It is obvious that this declaration has been framed with reference to the plaintiff's claim to the three new ponds, and that it is adapted to that claim only. * * The whole of this declaration, and the whole conduct of the cause, show that the plaintiff ought to be limited to that which alone was his real claim, namely, the right to the water for the use of his three existing ponds.

[792]

(PARKE, B., referred to *Bower* v. *Hill* (1).)

POLLOCK, C. B. :

I am of opinion that the plaintiff is entitled to retain his verdict in respect of the old pond, and that the verdict should be entered for the defendant as to two ponds. (His Lordship stated the pleadings and facts, and continued :) The plaintiff, in bringing his action and declaring for an infringement of his right to a flow of water to the three ponds, meant, no doubt, to recover in respect of the three new ponds. At the trial, however, he was met by an objection of an outstanding tenancy for life in the *party from whom the right to the flow of water to these three ponds was derived. He then fell back upon his claim to recover in respect of the old pond; his argument being, that the three ponds were merely a substitution for the old one, and that, by disusing the latter, he had not lost his legal right to it altogether. And it seems to me that he is right in this argument, and that, having been defeated as to the three ponds, he was entitled to resort to the other ; and that it is no objection to his doing so, that that pond was not, at the time of the diversion,

[*793]

(1) 2 Bing. N. C. 339. See 41 R. R. 636.

in a fit state to be actually used by him.   The verdict will therefore
stand as to one pond, and the rule will be absolute to enter a verdict
for the defendant as to the two others.

PARKE, B.:

I am of the same opinion.   The use of the old pond was discontinued only because the plaintiff obtained the same or a greater advantage from the use of the three new ones.   He did not thereby abandon his right, he only exercised it in a different spot; and a substitution of that nature is not an abandonment.   He has a right, therefore, under this declaration, to recover in respect of the old pond.   The right alleged is a right to have the uninterrupted flow of certain surplus water into a pond; and that right is equally proved, whether it be by prescription or lost grant, or under Lord Tenterden's Act.   The declaration means no more than this, that the plaintiff has a right to the overflow of water, either in one pond or in three ponds.

ALDERSON, B., concurred.

ROLFE, B.:

I am of the same opinion.   The declaration means only that the plaintiff has a right to have certain land covered with water; and no abandonment of that right has been proved.   If the plaintiff had even filled up the pond, that would not in itself amount to an abandonment, although, no doubt, it would be evidence of it.

Rule absolute accordingly.

ALSAGER AND OTHERS *v.* THE ST. KATHERINE'S DOCK COMPANY (1).

(14 Meeson & Welsby, 794—800; S. C. 15 L. J. Ex. 34.)

A charter-party stipulated that the ship should proceed from London to Bombay, and, being there loaded, should proceed to London, and discharge in any dock the freighters might appoint, and deliver her cargo, "on being paid freight at and after the rate of 4*l*. per ton," &c.   By a subsequent clause it was stipulated, that the freight was to be paid " on unloading and

1) Cited by CHARLES, J., in *Baumvoll Manufactur von Scheibler* . v. *Gilchrist* [1891] 2 Q. B. at p. 317 *(S. C.* [1893] A. C. 8, 62 L. J. Q. B. 201), as establishing that in construing a charter-party no greater effect can be given to writing than to print, *sed quære.*   See the judgments below.— J. G. P.

right delivery of the cargo, in cash, two months after the vessel's inward
report at the Custom-house :" Held, that, upon the construction of these
stipulations taken together, the freight was not payable until two months
after the inward report ; and the shipowner had not, after the cargo was
discharged pursuant to the charter-party, any lien thereon for the freight.

ASSUMPSIT to recover the sum of 1,852*l.* 6*s.* 8*d.*, as money had and
received by the defendants, to the use of the plaintiffs. An interpleader summons having been taken out by the defendants, the
following case was, by consent of the parties, ordered to be stated
for the opinion of this Court :

The plaintiffs are the assignees of Messrs. Evans, Foster, and
Langton, bankrupts.   On the 23rd of August, 1841, a charter-
party, being partly printed and partly written, was entered into
between the bankrupts and William Mitcheson, who was the
owner of the ship called the *East London.* The charter-party was
to the following effect : "That it was agreed between William
Mitcheson, owner of the ship called the *East London*, then
lying in the river Thames, and Messrs. Evans, Foster, and
Langton, of London, merchants, that the said ship shall proceed
to Bombay, and there load from the factors of the freighters a full
and complete cargo of legal merchandize, and, being so loaded, shall
therewith proceed to London, and discharge in any dock freighters
may appoint, *or so near thereto as she may safely get and deliver the
same, on being paid freight* at and after the rate of 4*l.* per ton, such
ton to be computed according to the new schedule of tonnage now
in use in Bombay, and those goods not in the schedule to be computed by fifty cubic feet measurement ; sufficient money to be
advanced the master, not exceeding 250*l.*, free of interest and
commission, for ordinary ship's disbursements, against his draft
upon the owners for the same, drawn at usance, (*the act of God, the
Queen's enemies, and all and every other dangers and accidents of the
seas, rivers, and navigations, of whatever nature and kind soever,
during the said voyage, always excepted*), *the freight to be paid on
unloading *and right delivery of the cargo*, in cash, two months after
the vessel's inward report at the Custom-house, London," &c. (1).

[*795]

Pursuant to the terms of this charter-party, the vessel sailed
upon her intended voyage, and, having arrived in safety in Bombay,
was there, during the months of July and August, loaded by the
bankrupts with merchandize, belonging in part to themselves and
in part to general shippers.   After the loading and sailing of the
vessel, and previous to the completion of the homeward voyage

(1) In the original, the words in italics were printed ; the rest was written.

and the arrival of the ship in the Thames, Messrs. Evans, Foster, and Langton committed acts of bankruptcy; and previous to such completion of the homeward voyage, namely, on the 24th of October, 1842, a *fiat* in bankruptcy was issued against them, under which the plaintiffs were appointed assignees. On the 25th of January, 1843, the ship arrived, with her cargo on board, in the St. Katherine's Docks, and the cargo was landed in the said docks, and lodged in the custody of the defendants, the proprietors of the docks, under the provisions of the 3 & 4 Will. IV. c. 57, s. 47. The ship was reported at the Custom-house on the 25th of January, 1843, and the cargo was landed and lodged on or about the 26th of January. Notice was given of the claim of the freight, both on the goods of the bankrupt and of the general shippers, by the said William Mitcheson, the owner of the said ship; and the plaintiffs, the assignees of the bankrupts, also claimed, in due form, to have the goods belonging to the bankrupts delivered to them without paying freight to the shipowner, and also claimed the freight due from the general shippers, amounting to 130*l.* 19*s.* 11*d.*   The sum of 1,521*l.* 6*s.* 9*d.* was claimed by the owner of the said ship for the freight of the goods shipped by the bankrupts on their own account; and *that sum was deposited with the defendants, under the provisions of the 3 & 4 Will. IV. c. 57, s. 47, by the plaintiffs, under protest, in order that they might obtain possession of the goods belonging to the bankrupt's estate; and that sum remained in the hands of the said Company, until it was afterwards brought into Court for the use of the parties entitled thereto.

[*796]

The question for the opinion of the Court is, whether the plaintiffs, as assignees of the said Messrs. Evans, Foster, and Langton, are entitled, or whether the said William Mitcheson is entitled, to the sums of 1,521*l.* 6*s.* 9*d.·* and 130*l.* 19*s.* 11*d.*, deposited with the defendants; and the said sums so paid into Court are to be paid to such of the said parties as in the opinion of the Court are entitled to the same; the Court to be at liberty, if they shall please, to draw any inference as to the matters of fact which they shall think a jury ought to have drawn.

Martin, for the plaintiffs :

Upon the true construction of this charter-party, the plaintiffs, as assignees of the bankrupt charterers, are entitled to the possession of the goods without payment of the freight. The general rule is, that the right to freight arises on the true delivery of the cargo;

ALSAGER
v.
THE
ST. KATHE-
RINE'S DOCK
Co.

but the time for payment of it is a matter of contract between the parties; and here they have expressly postponed the time of payment until the expiration of two months after the inward report. There are two clauses of the charter-party on which the question turns, and they appear to be somewhat inconsistent with each other. The first is, that the vessel shall deliver her cargo " on being paid freight at and after the rate of 4*l.* per ton ; " the other, that the freight is " to be paid on unloading and right delivery of the cargo, in cash, two months after the vessel's inward report at the Custom-house." The latter clause was plainly inserted in this charter-party for the very purpose of fixing the time of payment.

[*797]

And where *effect is to be given to two parts of such an agreement, which are apparently inconsistent, the Court will look at the written part of the contract as expressing the intention of the parties.

(PARKE, B.: That rule of construction is certainly laid down by Lord ELLENBOROUGH in *Robertson* v. *French* (1).)

The expressions introduced by the parties in the particular case must be considered as conveying their real intention.

Jervis, contrà :

In considering this question, the language of the Warehousing Act, 3 & 4 Will. IV. c. 57 (2), must be looked at in conjunction with the terms of the charter-party. That Act enacts, by s. 47, that goods landed in docks, and lodged in the custody of the proprietors of the docks, shall, when so landed, be subject to such and the same claim of freight in favour of the masters or owners, as they were liable to when on board the ship. The question then is, whether the defendants are not entitled to a lien for the freight, or whether that lien is prevented from attaching by the agreement that payment shall be made in cash at two months after the inward report. Now there are undoubtedly cases in which the Courts, in construing policies of insurance and bills of lading, which are mercantile instruments that have acquired a settled form, have given greater effect to written words inserted in them, than to the printed part of the instrument; but no such rule is established with respect to charter-parties, in which the Courts endeavour, if possible, to give effect to all the words of the instrument : *Saville* v. *Campion* (3).

(1) 7 R. R. 535 (4 East, 130).   s. 2.—J. G. P.
(2) Repealed by 8 & 9 Vict. c. 84,   (3) 21 R. R. 376 (2 B. & Ald. 503).

Now here the meaning of the first clause is plain —that the vessel
is to deliver the cargo "on being paid freight for the same;" that
is, on delivery.   Then the other stipulation is, that "freight is to
be paid on unloading and right delivery of the cargo, in cash, two
months after the vessel's inward report." The *word "delivery"
there means delivery free, and the only effect of this clause is to
fix the time within which delivery shall be made.   On the other
side, the clause is read as if the payment were to be made two
months after delivery, whereas it is two months after the inward
report.   The owner ought not to be deprived of his right to the
payment of the freight when earned, except upon the clearest
declaration of an intention to the contrary.   (He cited *Stevenson
v. Blakelock* (1) and *Hutton* v. *Bragg* (2).)

ALSAGER
v.
THE
ST. KATHE-
RINE'S DOCK
CO.

[*798]

Martin, in reply:

Looking to the whole of this contract, and particularly to the
specific stipulation which the parties have themselves inserted in
it, it is clear this is *debitum in præsenti, solvendum in futuro*—a
debt due on the unloading of the vessel, but to be paid at a future
day.   The expression, "on being paid freight," qualified, as it
must be, by the subsequent clause, cannot mean that the payment
is a condition precedent to the unloading, but only that the freight
then becomes a debt, to be paid at the time and in the manner
afterwards provided for.

POLLOCK, C. B.:

I am of opinion that the plaintiffs are entitled to the judgment
of the Court.   The question turns upon the construction to be
given to this charter-party.   Did the owner intend to abandon his
lien, and receive payment of the freight two months after the inward
report, or did he mean to retain his lien, and keep his right to
refuse delivery of the cargo until the freight was paid?   If the
shipowner could not have refused to deliver the goods, provided
the charterer had continued solvent, he cannot maintain that claim
now.   It has been contended that there is no difference in the
construction to be given to the printed and the written words of
an instrument of this nature, and that both are to be considered
of equal force.   I cannot assent to that argument.   I have always
understood, *that, in the case of policies of insurance partly printed   [*799]

(1) 14 R. R. 525 (1 M. & S. 535).   (2) 17 R. R. 431 (2 Marsh. 339).

ALSAGER
v.
THE
ST. KATHE-
RINE'S DOCK
CO.

and partly written, if there was any variance or inconsistency
between the two parts, most regard was to be paid to the written
part. We ought, no doubt, if possible, to give effect to both. Now
I think the fair construction of the whole of this instrument is,
that the shipowner is to be paid at a certain rate, and at a certain
time, namely, 4l. per ton, on right delivery of the cargo, two months
after the inward report.

PARKE, B.:

The question in this case turns entirely upon the construction
of this charter-party. I give no opinion as to the different weight
to be attributed to the written or printed words of the instrument;
that would depend upon the usage of trade, and we have no evidence of such usage in this special case; and if the whole instrument
were set out on the record, there would be no distinction between
the written and the printed words, unless a statement to that effect
were introduced. I may observe, however, that policies of insurance
are instruments to which mercantile usage has assigned a certain
meaning, and in their case the written part may reasonably be
entitled to more weight than the printed. I come, therefore, to
consider the language of this charter-party taken altogether; on
which the question is, whether payment of the freight is to be
contemporaneous with the delivery of the goods, or independent
of it. Now the terms of the two clauses which have been referred
to are clearly at variance, and therefore they must be qualified and
explained to some extent. The first clause is, that the vessel may
discharge in any dock, and deliver her cargo "on being paid freight"
at 4l. per ton. Primâ facie, then, the delivery and payment of
freight are contemporaneous acts. But then, when we look at the
context, and find that "freight is to be paid on unloading and right
delivery of the cargo, two months after the vessel's inward report,"

[*800]

it becomes impossible to *reconcile the clauses, and therefore the
expression, "on being paid freight," &c., must be qualified, and
must be read as if it had been "on payment of freight as hereinafter mentioned." The payment of freight is therefore irrespective
of the delivery of the goods, as the payment is not to take place
until two months after the inward report. The primâ facie meaning
of the words "on unloading and right delivery of the cargo" must
also be qualified, and then the whole is made consistent, and the
meaning of the charter-party is, that the payment of freight is
irrespective of the delivery of the goods. No lien, therefore, existed

in this case, and the plaintiffs are consequently entitled to the judgment of the Court.

ALDERSON, B., and ROLFE, B., concurred.

Judgment for the plaintiffs.

ALSAGER
v.
THE
ST. KATHE-
RINE'S DOCK
CO.

GIBBS v. RALPH.

(14 Meeson & Welsby, 804—806; S. C. 15 L. J. Ex. 7.)

Where, upon the trial of a cause, a juror is withdrawn by consent of counsel, if the plaintiff afterwards bring another action for the same cause, the Court will stay the proceedings (1).

1845.
Nov. 24.

[804]

SHEE, Serjt., had obtained a rule, calling upon the plaintiff to show cause why the proceedings in this action should not be stayed, with costs to be paid by the plaintiff, on the ground that it was brought contrary to good faith, a former action for the same cause having been terminated by the withdrawal of a juror at the trial. It was stated in the affidavit of the defendant's attorney, that a juror was withdrawn by the consent of the counsel on each side, and that there was a distinct understanding that all further proceedings should cease. The affidavit of the plaintiff's attorney, on the other hand, stated, that no such understanding existed, and that he was not aware that the withdrawal would preclude him from bringing a fresh action; that he was induced to consent to the withdrawal in consequence of the absence of his senior counsel; and that the defendant's attorney, on being subsequently informed by him that he intended to take the cause to trial again, expressed no surprise thereat, but *merely recommended him to be provided with a better witness. Against the above rule

[*805]

Horn now showed cause:

The authorities show that the withdrawal of a juror is no bar to a future action for the same cause, unless it be clear from all the circumstances of the case that both the parties intended it should have that effect: *Sanderson* v. *Nestor* (2), *Moscati* v. *Lawson* (3). Now here it is plain, from the statements in these affidavits, that neither of the attorneys thought there was any legal impediment in the way of bringing a second action. There was no understanding

---

(1) See, however, *Thomas* v. *Exeter Flying Post Company, Limited* (1887) 18 Q. B. D. 822, 56 L. J. Q. B. 313. —J. G. P.

(2) Ry. & M. 402.
(3) 43 R. R. 350 (4 Ad. & El. 350; 1 Harr. & Wol. 572).

that the withdrawal of a juror should be a final end of the cause; each attorney had his own reasons for withdrawing the case from the consideration of that particular jury.

Shee, Serjt., *contrà*, was stopped by the COURT.

POLLOCK, C. B.:

This is a very plain case. It must be taken as a positive rule of practice, that, when the parties to a cause agree to withdraw a juror, that puts a final end to the litigation between them, and no future action can be brought for the same cause. The counsel on both sides were of course aware of the consequences of that proceeding, and the understanding of the attorneys as to its effect is quite immaterial. All that the case of *Sanderson* v. *Nestor* decides is, that, if a second action be brought for the same cause, and the defendant, instead of applying to the Court to stay the proceedings, chooses to allow the action to proceed, he cannot avail himself of the withdrawal of a juror as a defence at the trial.

ALDERSON, B.:

I have always understood it to be perfectly clear, that the withdrawal of a juror put an end to the cause. The parties are in [*806] the hands of their counsel, *and when, by the concurrence of the counsel, that course is adopted, the parties are bound by it.

ROLFE, B., concurred.

Rule absolute.

────────

PERKINS *v.* ADCOCK.

1845.
Nov. 25.

[808]

(14 Meeson & Welsby, 808—810; S. C. 3 Dowl. & L. 270; 15 L. J. Ex. 7.)

Where a plaintiff is bankrupt or insolvent, and has assigned the debt for which the action is brought, and is suing for the benefit of the assignee, the Court will require security for costs (1).

THIS was a rule calling on the plaintiff to give security for costs. It appeared from the affidavits in support of the rule, that the plaintiff was in insolvent circumstances; that in June last he assigned all his property, debts, and effects, including the debt for which this action was brought, to two trustees for the benefit

(1) Cited and distinguished in *Denston* v. *Ashton* (1869) L. R. 4 Q. B. 590, 38 L. J. Q. B. 254; and *Cowell* v. *Taylor* (1885) 31 Ch. Div. 34, 55 L. J. Ch. 92; and see *Lloyd* v. *Hathern Station Brick Co.*, 85 L. T. 158.—J. G. P.

of the general body of his creditors; that in July his attorney PERKINS
wrote a letter to the defendant, stating that such assignment had ADCOCK.
*been made by deed, and demanding payment of the debt to [*809]
the trustees, and threatening proceedings if it were not paid to
them by a day mentioned; and finally, that the present action
was brought solely and entirely for the benefit of the trustees. The
plaintiff's affidavit, in opposition to the rule, stated, that the deed
of assignment did not convey all his property to the trustees, but
that furniture and effects to the value of 200*l.* had been expressly
excepted out of it; that he had obtained a release from his creditors;
that he had since set up in business for himself, and made some
property; and that he was now solvent, and able to pay the defendant's costs, if the verdict in this action should go against him;
and that the action was brought with his knowledge and consent.

Ogle showed cause:

The Court will not compel the plaintiff to give security for costs,
unless they see clearly that the defendant is in danger of not
obtaining them in the ordinary course. Now here the plaintiff
shows that he has not assigned away all his property, and he
swears that he is solvent, and able to pay the costs, if the defendant
succeeds in the action. [He cited *Morgan* v. *Evans* (1), *Wray* v.
Brown (2), and *Day* v. *Smith* (3).]

(POLLOCK, C. B.: In *Morgan* v. *Evans*, the Court seem to have
considered that the action was really *brought for the benefit of   [*810]
the plaintiff.

ALDERSON, B.: And in *Wray* v. *Brown*, the judgment proceeded
on the ground that the assignees were not really suing.)

P. M'Mahon, contrà, having cited *Hearsey* v. *Pechell* (4), was
stopped by the COURT.

POLLOCK, C. B.:

We think the rule must be absolute. I apprehend the principle
is, that, where the nominal plaintiff is bankrupt or insolvent, or
has assigned the debt, and is suing for the benefit of the assignee,
he ought to give security for the costs.

(1) 7 Moore, 344.   (4) 50 R. R. 757 (7 Dowl. P. C.
(2) 6 Bing. N. C. 271; 8 Scott, 557.   437).
(3) 1 Dowl. P. C. 460.

ALDERSON, B.:

In none of the cases cited by *Mr. Ogle* was the plaintiff shown to be suing for the benefit of his assignee.

ROLFE, B., concurred.

Rule absolute.

RIGBY AND ANOTHER *v.* THE GREAT WESTERN RAILWAY COMPANY.

(14 Meeson & Welsby, 811—819; S. C. 15 L. J. Ex. 60.)

In covenant, the declaration alleged, that the defendants, the Great Western Railway Company, demised to the plaintiffs certain refreshment-rooms at Swindon for ninety-nine years, at the annual rent of 1*d.*; that the plaintiffs covenanted (*inter alia*) to keep the premises in repair, and not to carry on there any other business than that of the refreshment-rooms; and that the defendants covenanted with the plaintiffs, that, in case the Swindon station should be disused as the regular and general place of stoppage for refreshment of passengers, they would purchase the buildings of the plaintiffs on the terms therein mentioned; that it was by the said indenture declared to be the intention of the defendants, and the understanding of the plaintiffs, that, in consequence of the outlay to be incurred by the plaintiffs in erecting the refreshment-rooms, the defendants should give every facility to the plaintiffs for enabling them to obtain an adequate return by the profits of the rooms; and that all trains carrying passengers, not goods trains or to be sent express for special purposes, which should pass the Swindon station, should, save in case of emergency or unusual delay arising from accident, stop there for refreshment of passengers for a reasonable period of about ten minutes; and that the defendants covenanted with the plaintiffs not to do any act which should have an effect contrary to the above intention. The breach alleged was, that the defendants, whilst the Swindon station was used as the regular and general place of stoppage for the refreshment of passengers, did divers acts which had an effect and were contrary to the intention of the defendants in the said indenture; that is to say, they caused divers trains containing passengers, not being trains sent express, &c., to pass the Swindon station without stopping there for refreshment of the passengers for a reasonable period of ten minutes; and the defendants caused several trains to stop, and the same did stop, at Swindon, for a short and unreasonable time, to wit, for one minute and no more, the said period of time not being sufficient to enable the said passengers to obtain refreshment.

The defendants set out the deed on *oyer*, which corresponded with the statement of it in the declaration, except that the terms of the covenant declared on were, that the defendants engaged not to do any act which should have an effect contrary to the above intention.

Held, on demurrer, that this amounted to a covenant on the part of the Company not to do any act to prevent the trains from stopping at Swindon, so long as it was used as the regular refreshment station; and, secondly, that a good breach of that covenant was alleged in the declaration.

COVENANT. The declaration stated, that heretofore, to wit, on &c., by a certain indenture then made between the defendants and the plaintiffs, the defendants demised to the plaintiffs certain refreshment-rooms, &c., situate at Swindon, in the county of Wilts, for ninety-nine years, at *the annual rent of 1*d.*; that the plaintiffs thereby covenanted with the defendants to complete the said refreshment-rooms, and that the business should be conducted in an orderly manner; and that the charges to passengers by the Great Western Railway for using the said refreshment-rooms should be fixed by the directors of the said Company; that the plaintiffs would keep the premises in repair, and not carry on there any other than the business of the refreshment-rooms, and would insure the premises, &c.; and that the defendants covenanted with the plaintiffs, that, in case the Swindon station should be disused as the regular and general place of stoppage for refreshment of passengers, they would purchase the buildings of the plaintiffs at the full cost, in case the disuse should take place within five years from the date of the lease, but if afterwards, then at a fair price, to be settled by arbitration.   The declaration then alleged, that it was in and by the said indenture declared to be the intention of the defendants, and the understanding of the plaintiffs, that, in conse-quence of the outlay to be incurred by them the plaintiffs in erecting the said refreshment-rooms at Swindon, &c., the defendants should give every facility to the said plaintiffs for enabling them to obtain an adequate return by means of the rents and profits to be derived from the said refreshment-rooms; and that all trains carrying passengers, not goods trains or trains to be sent express or for special purposes, and except trains not under the control of the said defendants, which should pass the Swindon station, either up or down, should, save in case of emergency or unusual delay arising from accidents, stop there for refreshment of passengers for a reasonable period of about ten minutes: and that the defendants covenanted with the plaintiffs not to do any act which should have an effect contrary to the above intention.   The declaration then stated general performance by the plaintiffs of their covenants, &c., and alleged as a breach, that the defendants, *whilst the said Swindon station continued to be used by the defendants as the regular and general place of stoppage for the refreshment of passengers, to wit, on &c., did divers acts which had an effect and were contrary to the intention of the defendants in the said inden-ture; that is to say, that the defendants, on divers days and times &c., caused divers trains containing passengers, not being trains to be sent express, &c., to pass the Swindon station, without stopping there for the refreshment of the said passengers for a reasonable

RIGBY
c.
THE GREAT
WESTERN
RAILWAY CO

[*812]

[*813]

period of ten minutes, contrary to the tenor and effect, intent and meaning of the said indenture; and the defendants, on the days and times aforesaid, did cause several trains to stop, and the same did stop, at Swindon for a short and unreasonable time, to wit, for the space of one minute, and no more; the said period of time not being sufficient to enable the said passengers to obtain any refreshment from the said refreshment-rooms, contrary &c.

The defendants set out the indenture on *oyer*, which corresponded with the statement of it in the declaration; except that it appeared that the terms of the covenant declared on were, that the defendants thereby engaged not to do any act which should have an effect contrary to the above intention, &c. The defendants then demurred generally, and the plaintiffs joined in demurrer.

The point stated for argument by the defendants was, that the declaration did not disclose the breach of any covenant in the indenture, and was therefore insufficient in law.

Sir T. Wilde, Serjt., in support of the demurrer. * * *

[815]   *Watson*, *contrà*, was stopped by the COURT.

PARKE, B. :

The questions in this case are, first, whether in this deed there is a covenant on the part of the Company that the trains shall stop at the Swindon station; and, secondly, if there is, whether a good breach of that covenant is assigned in the declaration. I am of opinion that there is a covenant, and that the declaration assigns a good breach of it. With respect to what is a covenant in point of law, *Sir Thomas Wilde* has properly admitted that no particular form of words is necessary to constitute a covenant; wherever a party by deed obliges himself to do an act, that amounts in law to a covenant. Then the question here is, whether the Company have by this deed obliged themselves to do or not to do a particular thing, *and what is the nature and amount of that obligation. The deed no doubt is, in this part of it, inartificially drawn. It is declared to be the intention of the defendants, and the understanding of the plaintiffs, that, " in consequence of the outlay to be incurred by them in erecting the refreshment-rooms at Swindon, &c., the defendants should give every facility to the plaintiffs for enabling them to obtain an adequate return by means of the rents and profits to be derived from the said refreshment-rooms; and that

[*816]

all trains carrying passengers, not being goods trains or trains to be
sent express or for special purposes, and except trains not under
the control of the defendants, which should pass the Swindon
station, either up or down, should, save in the case of emergency
or unusual delay arising from accidents, stop there for the refreshment of passengers for a reasonable period of about ten minutes."
If there had been no other words than these, it might have been
doubtful whether this was anything more than a declaration of
intention on the part of the Company, that certain things should be
done; although, in some cases, a declaration of intention is quite
enough to create a covenant: there are cases in the books of a
declaration of an intention to levy a fine, which is said to amount
to a covenant to levy a fine.   But this particular part of the
indenture does not stop here; there is an express engagement on
the part of the Company to do something; they "engage" (which
has the same force as the word "covenant") "not to do any act
which should have an effect contrary to the above intention," that
is, they are not to do anything which shall have the effect of causing
the trains carrying passengers not to stop at Swindon for a reasonable period for refreshment.   That is the effect of this covenant
taken by itself.   They have not covenanted absolutely that all the
trains shall stop; if they had made an absolute engagement to that
extent, they would be liable, even though the trains did not stop in
consequence of any *act of third persons, or if their own servants,
although unintentionally, carried the trains by without stopping;
but they protect themselves from that liability by these words, and
the engagement on their part is, that they will not do anything to
cause the trains not to stop at the appointed place, and wait there
a reasonable time.   But it is said that this construction is at
variance with other covenants in the deed, particularly with that
by which the Company bind themselves, in case at any time
Swindon should cease to be the general place of stoppage for
refreshment, to buy out the plaintiffs on certain terms; and there
is at first sight an apparent incongruity between these two covenants: but it is our duty so to construe this indenture, as, if
possible, to give effect to all the stipulations in it; and I think we
may do so by construing the covenant in question to be a covenant
not to prevent the stopping of the trains at Swindon, so long as the
Company think fit to continue Swindon as the general place of
stoppage for refreshment.   The covenant does not oblige the
Company to cause all the trains, or any particular trains, to stop

RIGBY
v.
THE GREAT
WESTERN
RAILWAY Co.

[*817]

there, if they have determined that Swindon shall cease to be the place of stoppage; but, so long as they make that the general place of stoppage for refreshment, they are obliged to do nothing which may prevent the stopping of every train there, except those which come within the particular exceptions specified in the deed. By thus construing the covenant, we make both parts of the deed consistent. Then, in order to allege a proper breach of this covenant, it should be shown in the declaration that the act of the Company in stopping the trains took place while Swindon was continued as the general place of refreshment, and that is expressly averred. But then, it is said, there is no good breach, unless it is shown that there were passengers in the trains who required refreshments. But I think it cannot be said that this is a covenant only to stop in case the passengers require refreshment, and give notice of it; that [*818] *would be a very inconvenient arrangement. It seems to me that the covenant is an absolute covenant that the trains shall stop for ten minutes, to enable the passengers to obtain refreshment, if they choose to have it; and, therefore, that a good breach of that covenant has been assigned. The plaintiffs are therefore entitled to our judgment.

ALDERSON, B.:

I am of the same opinion; and, as the case has been so fully gone into by my brother PARKE, I shall add only a few words. I think the intention of the covenant was, that the great bulk of the trains should stop, so long as Swindon continued to be the general place of stoppage; and that they were not merely to stop for the purpose of ascertaining whether the passengers required refreshments, or on those occasions only when the passengers expressed their desire to stop. I think the meaning of the covenant is, that the defendants have undertaken to stop the trains, with a view to tender to the passengers the temptation of the plaintiff's refreshments. Then, with regard to the disuser, that is provided for by the previous clause. So soon as the Company disused Swindon as the general place of refreshment, they would be liable, under their covenant with the plaintiffs, either to buy them out at what they had expended, if that event took place before five years, or, if not, by making a reasonable compensation.

ROLFE, B.:

I am of the same opinion. With regard to the argument, that

the parties ought not to be bound to have the trains stopped in the
event of their buying up the interest of the plaintiffs in the Swindon
station, I think my brother PARKE has explained that by showing,
that, by construing the clauses together, a qualified meaning is to
be given to this covenant. But, even if it could not be construed
consistently with the previous provision, the *parties have here
entered into an absolute covenant ; and though they did not contemplate the inconvenience that might arise from a change of
circumstances, they must be bound by that covenant.

RIGBY
v.
THE GREAT
WESTERN
RAILWAY CO.

[*819]

PLATT, B. :

I think, when the parties use the word "intention," they must
be understood to have entered into a covenant, the effect of which
is, that all trains carrying passengers, with certain exceptions, shall
stop at Swindon for the refreshment of passengers "for the reasonable time of ten minutes ; " and then, where the Company go on to
engage "not to do any act which shall have an effect contrary to
the above intention," that is, contrary to the meaning of the covenant, it must be considered that to compel the trains, or any of
them, to pass by the station after that, is doing an act contrary to
the meaning of the covenant. I think the part of the deed I have
alluded to has been introduced to meet an intermediate case between
the entire disuser of the place as a general refreshment-room, and a
partial infringement of the use of it. Anything that would amount
to a total disuser is provided for by the previous clause, and would
enable the plaintiffs to demand the value of the buildings, &c. ; but
anything short of that was intended, as it seems to me, to be met
by this covenant. I therefore think there is an intelligible engagement on the part of the Company, that it has been infringed, and
that the breach of it is properly stated upon the record.

Judgment for the plaintiffs.

EARL OF ROSSE <i>v.</i> WAINMAN (1).

(14 Meeson & Welsby, 859—873 ; S. C. 15 L. J. Ex. 67.)

1845
Dec. 5.

[859]

Certain waste lands in the manor of Shipley, to the soil of which, and
everything constituting the soil, the lord of the manor was entitled, were,
by an Inclosure Act, 55 Geo. III. c. xviii. (which recited the lord's title),
taken away from the lord and allotted to commoners, except as saved by

---

(1) See <i>A.-G. for Isle of Man</i> v.
Mylchreest (1879) 4 App. Cas. 294, 48
L. J. P. C. 36 ; <i>Midland Ry. Co.</i> v.

Haunchwood Brick and Tile Co. (1882)
20 Ch. D. 552, 51 L. J. Ch. 778 ; <i>Earl
of Jersey</i> v. <i>Neath Poor Law Union</i>

the 32nd clause. That clause reserved to the lord all mines and minerals, of what nature or kind soever, lying and being within or under the said commons and waste grounds, in as full, ample, and beneficial a manner, to all intents and purposes, as he could or might have held and enjoyed the same in case the said Act had not been made; and enacted, that he should and might at all times thereafter have, hold, win, work, and enjoy exclusively all mines and minerals, of what nature or kind soever, within and under the said commons and waste grounds, with full liberty of digging, sinking, searching for, winning and working the said mines and minerals, and carrying away the lead ore, lead, coals, iron-stone and fossils, to be gotten thereout: provided that the lord, in the searching for and working the said mines and minerals, should keep the first layer or stratum of earth separate and apart by itself, without mixing the same with the lower strata. The 33rd section provided for reimbursement to the owners of allotments, for injury done by searching for or working the mines and minerals: Held, that the reservation clause must be construed with reference to the title of the lord to the whole of the soil; and, inasmuch as the object of the Act was to give to the commoners the surface for cultivation, and leave in the lord what it did not take away for that purpose, the word "minerals" must be understood, not in its general sense, signifying substances containing metals, but in its proper sense, as including all fossil bodies or matters dug out of mines, that is, quarries or places where anything is dug; and this notwithstanding the provision in the latter part of the clause, authorising the carrying away the "lead ore, lead, coal, iron-stone, and fossils," as fossils may apply to stones dug in quarries: therefore, that the clause reserved to the lord the right to the stratum of stone in the inclosed lands.

TROVER, charging the defendant with the conversion of fossils, stones, flagstones, and other minerals, to which the defendant pleaded Not guilty, and a denial of the plaintiff's property.

Issue having been joined, a case was stated by consent of the parties for the opinion of this Court, as follows:

For many years previous to and at the time of the passing of the Act of Parliament hereinafter next mentioned, the Reverend Cyril Jackson, D.D., was seised in fee of the manor of Shipley, in the county of York.

By an Act of Parliament passed in the 55th year of the reign of his late Majesty King George the Third, intituled "An Act for inclosing Lands within the Manor and Township of Shipley, in the Parish of Bradford, in the West Riding of the county of York," after reciting, that there were, within the manor and township of Shipley) in the parish of Bradford, in the West Riding of the county of York, several commons or parcels of waste ground called *High Bank and Low Moor, and several other parcels of waste ground,

[*860]

(1889) 22 Q. B. D. 555, 58 L. J. Q. B. 573; *Hext* v. *Gill* (1872) L. R. 7 Ch. 699, 41 L. J. Ch. 761; *Lord Provost of Glasgow* v. *Fairie* (1887) 13 App. Cas. 657, 58 L. J. P. C. 33; *Midland Ry. Co.* v. *Robinson* (1889) 15 App. Cas. 19, 59 L. J. Ch. 442.

containing in the whole, by estimation, 280 acres, or thereabouts; and also reciting, that the Reverend Cyril Jackson, D.D., was lord of the manor of Shipley, and as such was owner of the soil of the said commons and waste grounds, and entitled to all mines and minerals within and under the said commons and waste grounds; and reciting, that the said Cyril Jackson, and several other persons, were owners and proprietors of estates within the manor and township of Shipley aforesaid, and in respect thereof were entitled to right of common and other rights and interests in and upon the said commons and waste grounds; it was (amongst other things) enacted (1), that the Commissioner appointed for carrying the said Act into execution should, after setting out and appointing the public carriage roads and highways through and over the said commons and waste grounds intended to be divided, allotted, and inclosed as aforesaid, set out, allot, and award unto and for the said Cyril Jackson, as lord of the said manor, and to such person or persons as should then be entitled to the said manor, his, her, or their heirs and assigns, such part and parcel of the residue and remainder of the said commons and waste grounds as should, in the judgment of the said Commissioner, be equal in value to one full sixteenth part of the said residue of the said commons and waste grounds, in lieu of, and as a full recompense for, all such right and interest in and to the soil of the said commons and waste grounds as was not thereinafter expressly saved and reserved.

And it was further enacted (2), that the said Commissioner should, in the next place, set out such part or parts of the said commons and waste grounds as he should think proper, not exceeding two acres in the whole, to be used and enjoyed by the respective proprietors of land within the said manor and township of Shipley for the purposes of common *watering-places for cattle, and getting stones and other minerals for erecting and repairing buildings, bridges, walls, fences, and other works, and for the reparation of public and private roads within the said manor and township.   [*861]

And it was further enacted, that the said Commissioner for the time being should set out, assign, and allot the residue of the said commons and waste grounds unto and amongst the said Cyril Jackson and the said several other persons entitled to right of common or other rights and interests in and upon the said commons and waste grounds, their respective heirs, executors, administrators, and assigns, according to the value of the messuages,

(1) By section 17.   (2) By section 18.

cottages, mills, old inclosed lands, tenements, and hereditaments in respect whereof they were so respectively entitled to such right of common as aforesaid, and according to the value of such other rights or interests as aforesaid.

And it was thereby further provided and enacted (1), that nothing therein contained should extend or be construed to extend to defeat, lessen, or prejudice the right, title, or interest of the said Cyril Jackson, or any future lord or lords, lady or ladies of the manor of Shipley aforesaid, in or to the seigniories and royalties incident or belonging to the said manor of Shipley, but that the said Cyril Jackson, and such other person or persons as aforesaid, should and might from time to time for ever thereafter hold and enjoy all rents and services, courts, perquisites, and profits of courts, goods and chattels of felons and fugitives, felons of themselves, parsons outlawed and put in exigent, deodands, waifs, estrays, forfeitures, and all other jurisdictions whatsoever in and upon the said commons and waste grounds, thereby directed to be divided and inclosed as aforesaid, and all mines and minerals, of what nature or kind soever, lying and being within or under the said commons and [*862] waste grounds, in as full, ample, and beneficial a *manner, to all intents and purposes, as they could or might respectively have held and enjoyed the same in case the said Act had not been made: and that the said Cyril Jackson, and such other person or persons as aforesaid, should and might, from time to time and at all times thereafter, have, hold, win, work, and enjoy exclusively all mines and minerals, of what nature or kind soever, within and under the said commons and waste grounds, and within and under every part thereof, together with all convenient and necessary ways, and full liberty of laying, making, and repairing waggon ways and other ways in, through, over, and along the said commons and waste grounds, or any part thereof, and with full and free liberty, power, and authority of digging, sinking, searching for, winning, and working the said mines and minerals, and leading and carrying away the lead ore, lead, coals, iron-stone, and fossils to be gotten thereout, and of making pits, shafts, and pumps, pit-rooms, drifts, levels, and watercourses, and of repairing, amending, and uphold-ing the same, and of erecting, building, and using houses, kilns, fire-engines and other engines, mills, and other erections and buildings, and of altering, changing, pulling, and carrying away the same or all or any of the materials thereof at their free will and

(1) By section 32.

pleasure, and to do, execute, and perform all such other works,
matters, and things, either then in use or thereafter to be invented,
as should or might be necessary or convenient for the full and
complete working, use, and enjoyment of the said mines and
minerals thereby reserved, in as full, ample, and beneficial a
manner, to all intents and purposes, as they might or could have
done in case the said Act had not been made, without any interruption, disturbance, claim, or demand whatsoever : provided nevertheless, that the said Cyril Jackson,' his heirs and assigns, and his
and their tenants and lessees, should, and they were thereby required,
in the searching for and working the said mines *and minerals, to   [*863]
keep the first layer or stratum of earth separate and apart by itself,
without mixing the same with the lower stratum.

And it was thereby further enacted (1), that all and every such
damage and injury as should or might be occasioned in any allotment or allotments which should be set out under that Act, by
means of the searching for or working the aforesaid mines and
minerals, or any of them, or on account of any works, buildings, or
concerns relating thereto, upon or within the said allotments, should
be reimbursed to the owner and owners, occupier and occupiers of
the same allotments respectively, and should be borne and paid by
the several owners of the allotments to be made in pursuance of the
said Act.

The Commissioner appointed by the said Act of Parliament, in
due manner, on the 30th of May, 1825, made his award, and did
thereby, amongst other things, allot and award unto the heirs or
devisees of William Wainman, Esq., in lieu of his rights in the
commons or waste lands of the manor of Shipley, as owner of
certain freehold land within the said manor, four several allotments
or inclosures of land.

By indenture of lease and release, dated the 28th and 29th of
February, 1820, the said manor of Shipley, with the manorial
rights thereto belonging, by the description of all that the manor
or lordship of Shipley, with the rights, members, and appurtenances
thereof, situate, lying, and being in the parish of Bradford aforesaid, and also all and every the mines and minerals, of what nature
or kind soever, lying and being within or under all and every the
lands and grounds theretofore divided and inclosed under or by
virtue of the said Act of Parliament, with all such liberties, privileges, powers, and authorities of digging, sinking, searching for,

(1) By section 33.

winning, working, and enjoying, taking and carrying away the said
mines and minerals as were reserved, granted, and limited in and
by the said Act, *unto the said Cyril Jackson, or any future lord or
lady of the said manor, were, together with a considerable estate in
the same township, conveyed and assured by the devisees in trust
of the said Cyril Jackson, unto John Wilmer Field, late of Heaton,
in the county of York, Esq., deceased, and his heirs and assigns.

The said manor and estate continued vested in the said John
William [sic] Field down to the year 1837, when he died intestate,
leaving two daughters (of whom Mary, Countess of Rosse, the wife
of the plaintiff, is one) his co-heiresses-at-law him surviving ; and,
by virtue of certain settlements since executed, the said manor and
estate of Shipley, before the taking of the stone by the defendant's
authority, as hereinafter mentioned, became and were, and now are
legally vested in the plaintiff, as tenant for life thereof, without
impeachment of waste.

Beneath the common lands inclosed under the provisions of the
before-mentioned Act of Parliament are several valuable beds of
coal and iron-stone, and nearer the surface there is also in some
places the stone common in the district.

The defendant, before the taking of the stone hereinafter
mentioned, became seised of a life estate in the said pieces of land
so allotted by the award of the said Commissioner to the heirs or
devisees of the said William Wainman, as aforesaid, subject to the
provisions of the said Act.

The defendant, having ascertained that there was some stone fit
for building under one of the said allotments to which he is entitled
for life as aforesaid, agreed to sell such stone to Messrs. Nathan
Atkinson, William Hill, Thomas Hillary, David Hillary, and
George Hillary, all of Bradford aforesaid, stone merchants, who
forthwith commenced getting it, and by the authority of the
defendant, previously to the commencement of this action, raised,
severed, took and carried away 296 superficial square yards of the
said stone, the same being of the value of 44*l.* 8*s.*   The plaintiff

*claimed from the defendant, that, as lord of the said manor, he
was entitled to the said stone so found and raised in the said
allotment; but the defendant denied that the plaintiff had such
right; whereupon the plaintiff caused this action to be brought.

The question for the opinion of the Court is, whether the plaintiff
is entitled to the said stone so gotten and raised under the said
allotment.   If the Court shall be of that opinion, then the parties

consent that judgment shall be entered for the plaintiff by confession, for 44*l*. 8*s*. damages; but if the Court shall be of the contrary opinion, then the parties consent that judgment of *nolle prosequi* shall be entered for the defendant, but with liberty to either party to take the case down to trial, for the purpose of turning it into a special verdict.   Copies of the Inclosure Act, and of the award of the Commissioner, accompany this case, and form part of it.

The point marked for argument on the part of the plaintiff was, that he contended he was entitled to the stone in question as lord of the manor of Shipley, according to the true construction of the Shipley Inclosure Act, and especially of the reservation therein contained to the lord of all mines and minerals under the several allotments to be set out under the provisions of the Act.

The case was argued (Nov. 17 and 19) by

Hugh Hill, for the plaintiff:

The question here depends on the construction to be put on the meaning of the words "mines and minerals, of what nature or kind soever," contained in the clause of reservation in the 32nd section of the Shipley Inclosure Act (1).   *   *   The word "minerals" must [867] be understood to mean, not only metallic substances, but all fossil matter obtained from mines or pits; and in the 32nd clause, the word "fossils" is expressly used, and that would surely include stone.   The definition of "mines, minerals," *&c., in Tomlins' [*868] Law Dictionary, is "quarries or places where any thing is digged." Dr. Johnson defines a mine to be "a place or cavern in the earth which contains metals or minerals:" and he defines a mineral to be a "fossile body ; matter dug out of mines : all metals are minerals, but all minerals are not metals."   He defines stone thus : "Stones are bodies insipid, hard, not ductile or malleable, nor soluble in water."

(ALDERSON, B. : The 18th section provides, that the Commissioner shall set out such parts of the commons as he shall think fit, not exceeding two acres, to be used and enjoyed by the proprietors of land, for the purposes of common watering-places for cattle, and getting stones and other minerals for erecting and repairing buildings, &c., and for the reparation of the public roads.)

That shows that the stones would otherwise be vested in the lord,

(1) See above, p. 844.

EARL OF
ROSSE
v.
WAINMAN.

or there would have been no necessity for excepting them out of the Act.

Cowling, contrà :

Stones are not included within the terms "mines and minerals" in the 32nd section. * * A mine is a subterraneous working, [*869] and clay, if got low in the earth, *may be called a mine, but not if near the surface : *Rex* v. *Brettell* (1). A reservation of this stone would be contrary to the spirit of the Act, the object of which was to promote the improvement of the land. There is no such reservation in the general Inclosure Act; and the 14th and 10th sections of that Act will be found to be at variance with it. This reservation must be construed strictly against the lord : the words are, " mines and minerals 'within and under' the waste." Whether or not a place is a mine, depends on the mode of working it, and it must be subterraneous : *Rex* v. *Dunsford* (2) and *Rex* v. *Sedgeley* (3).

(PARKE, B. : Is the lord's right to a mineral to depend on the mode of working it ?)

A mineral is something which comes out of a mine. All stone is part of the mineral kingdom, and if the lord's construction of this reservation is right, he might take gravel and clay. [He cited *Townley* v. *Gibson* (4).]

Hugh Hill, in reply. * * *

Cur. adv. vult.

[870]   PARKE, B. :

The question in this case is, whether the plaintiff, Lord Rosse, is entitled to the stratum of stone under the allotments of the waste of the manor of Shipley, inclosed by virtue of the Act of 55 Geo. III. c. 18.

Lord Rosse is the assignee of Dr. Cyril Jackson, who was lord at the time of the inclosure, and has all the rights reserved to him by the Inclosure Act.

What these rights are depends upon the construction of the Act, which is not very clearly expressed, and is open to much doubt; but the result of our consideration of the whole of its provisions is, that, in our opinion, the right to the stratum of stone was reserved to the lord, and consequently the plaintiff is entitled to recover.

(1) 3 B. & Ad. 424.   (3) 36 R. R. 475 (2 B. & Ad. 65).
(2) 2 Ad. & El. 565.   (4) 1 R. R. 600 (2 T. R. 701).

It is clear from the recital, that, before the passing of the Act, the lord was entitled to the soil of the waste, and to everything constituting that soil, including every stratum of stone; and the question is, how much of this right is taken away and transferred under the Inclosure Act to those to whom allotments are made?

All is taken away except that which is reserved by the saving clause (the 82nd), which is to be construed with reference to the original title of the lord to the whole of the soil. That section provides, that "nothing in the Act *contained is to be construed to [*871] extend to defeat, lessen, or prejudice the right, title, or interest of Cyril Jackson, or any future lord or lords of the manor of Shipley aforesaid, in or to the seigniories and royalties belonging to the said manor of Shipley, but that Dr. Jackson may from time to time enjoy all rents, services, courts, &c., and all mines and minerals, of what nature or kind soever, lying and being within or under the said commons and waste grounds, in as full, ample, and beneficial a manner, to all intents and purposes, as they could or might respectively have held and enjoyed the same in case this Act had not been made." Then it goes on to make a provision for the working of the mines and minerals: "And that the said Cyril Jackson, and such other person or persons as aforesaid, shall and may, from time to time and at all times thereafter, have, hold, win, work, and enjoy exclusively all mines and minerals, of what nature or kind soever, within and under the said commons and waste grounds, and within and under every part thereof, together with all convenient and necessary ways, and full liberty of laying, working, and repairing waggon ways and other ways in, through, over, and along the said commons and waste grounds, or any part thereof, with full and free liberty, power, and authority of digging, sinking, searching for, winning and working the said mines and minerals, and leading and carrying away the lead ore and coal, iron-stone, and fossils, to be gotten thereout, and of making pits, shafts, and pumps, &c., and of erecting, building, and using houses, kilns, fire-engines, and other engines, &c. at their free will and pleasure, and to do, execute, and perform all such other works, acts, matters, and things, either now in use or thereafter to be invented, as shall or may be necessary or convenient for the full and complete working, use, and enjoyment of the said mines and minerals thereby reserved, in as full, ample, and beneficial a manner, to all intents and purposes, as *they might or could have done in case this Act had not [*872] been made, without any interruption, disturbance, claim, or demand

EARL OF
ROSSE
v.
WAINMAN.

whatsoever : Provided, nevertheless, that the said Cyril Jackson, his heirs and assigns, and his and their tenants and lessees, shall, and they are hereby required, in the searching for and working the said mines and minerals, to keep the first layer or stratum of earth separate and apart by itself, without mixing the same with the lower strata."

The term "minerals," here used, though more frequently applied to substances containing metals, in its proper sense includes all fossil bodies or matters dug out of mines ; and Dr. Johnson says, that, " all metals are minerals, but all minerals are not metals ;" and mines, according to Jacob's Law Dictionary, are " quarries or places where anything is digged ;" and in the Year Book, 17 Edw. III. c. 7, "mineræ de pierre " and "de charbon " are spoken of. Beds of stone, which may be dug by winning or quarrying, are therefore properly minerals, and so we think they must be held to be in the clause in question, bearing in mind that the object of the Act was to give the surface for cultivation to the commoners, and to leave in the lord what it did not take away for that purpose ; and this construction is greatly favoured by the last clause, which provides that the surface soil, " the first layer or stratum of earth, is to be kept separate, without mixing with the lower strata ;" a provision which clearly indicates that the removal of the surface soil to a great extent may take place, and be subsequently restored, so that the getting strata of stone by quarrying must have been contemplated.

It must, however, be admitted, that the provision authorising the working of mines and minerals, and leading and carrying away the lead ore, lead, coals, iron-stone, and fossils, leads to the supposition that the Legislature intended to reserve metallic minerals only, and creates much doubt about the true construction of the word in this Act. But *the word "fossils," in a strict sense, may apply to stones dug or quarried ; at any rate, we do not think that this provision so clearly indicates the intention of the Legislature to limit the proper meaning of the word, as to call upon us to do so.

[*873]

We place no reliance on the word "minerals " being connected with stone in the 18th section, and treated as *ejusdem generis*, as the word is probably introduced by mistake for the word " materials."

We are, therefore, of opinion that the plaintiff is entitled to recover.

Judgment for the plaintiff.

IN THE EXCHEQUER CHAMBER.

(In Error from the Court of Exchequer.)

WAINMAN *v.* The EARL of ROSSE.

(2 Ex. 800.)

The judgment of the Court of Exchequer in *Earl of Rosse* v. *Wainman* affirmed.

1848.
June 6.

[800]

In pursuance of the power reserved to the parties by the special case stated in this cause, it was, after the judgment of the Court of Exchequer for the plaintiff below thereon, taken down to trial and turned into a special verdict, upon which a writ of error was brought into this Court. The case was argued in Hilary Vacation, 1847 (February 7), by

Cowling (with whom was *Addison*), for the plaintiff in error (defendant below) ; and by *Knowles* (with whom was *Hugh Hill*), for the defendant in error.

The Court (1) took time to consider, and their judgment was pronounced by

WILDE, Ch. J. :

This Court has fully considered the case of *Wainman* v. *The Earl of Rosse*, which is certainly one attended with considerable difficulty ; but the result of the consideration of the Court is, that the judgment below must be affirmed.

Judgment affirmed.

(1) Lord DENMAN, Ch. J., WILDE, MAULE, J., CRESSWELL, J., and Ch. J., PATTESON, J., COLERIDGE, J., WILLIAMS, J.

PRACTICE CASES.

1844.

[33]

In re PEACH (1).

(2 Dowl. & L. 33—37; S. C. 13 L. J. Q. B. 249.)

An attorney had delivered a bill in 1840, and continued to act as attorney afterwards. In 1842, the client being pressed for payment, demanded a statement of his account, and gave two joint notes of hand, which the attorney swore he received "in lieu of cash." The attorney, after these notes became due and were paid, delivered two other bills, comprising some of the items, and extending over a portion of the time, included in the first: Held, on motion to refer the bills for taxation, that the three bills together, constituting, in point of fact, but one bill; "the payment of any such bill," within the 41st section of the Solicitors Act, 1843 (6 & 7 Vict. c. 73), so as to preclude taxation after the lapse of twelve months, must be a payment after the delivery of the whole of such bills.

Semble, the mere delivery of a bill of exchange or promissory note is not a payment within that section, where, if the bill of exchange or promissory note were dishonoured at maturity, the client would remain liable on the attorney's bill.

THIS was an application on the part of one Benjamin Hutchings, to tax the bills of an attorney of the name of Peach, under the following circumstances. Peach had acted as attorney for the applicant from the year 1835 down to the year 1841, and had raised money for him on certain securities, and the charges were chiefly, for items connected with these transactions. In 1840, Peach had delivered to the applicant a bill of costs appended to the affidavits, and marked number (1), amounting to 186*l.* 9*s.* 5*d.*, which, he swore in his affidavit, had been looked over and approved

[*34] of by the applicant; and also a *cash statement of account, marked (A.), on which a balance of 132*l.* 3*s.* was due to him. The account, however, still ran on. In consequence of the embarrassed state of applicant's affairs, Peach repeatedly pressed for payment of it, and also of a large sum of money, which had been advanced by Peach's father as a loan to the applicant, and for which applicant had executed a mortgage, and afterwards given a *cognovit* in an action of ejectment brought upon a foreclosure of that mortgage. The applicant being pressed for payment, gave, on the 10th of June, 1842, two joint notes of hand, of himself and his brother-in-law, one T. B. Trotter, which Peach, in his affidavit, swore "he took in full of the balance then remaining due to him, and received such notes in lieu of cash, well knowing the said T. B. Trotter to be a responsible individual." These notes respectively became due and

(1) *In re Romer* and *Haslam* [1893] 2 Q. B. 286, 290, 62 L. J. Q. B. 610, 69 L. T. 547, C.A.

were paid, on the 18th of February, 1848, and on the 18th of June,
in the same year. In consequence of repeated demands both before
and after the giving of the promissory notes on the part of the
applicant, to be furnished with Peach's account as against him,
that gentleman, on the 22nd of June, 1848, gave in two bills, which
were appended to the affidavits, and marked numbers (2) and (8),
and in the August following, a cash account, marked (B.), on the
face of which it appeared, that the sum of 116*l.* had been discharged by the two notes of hand, which had been paid, leaving a
balance due against the applicant of 2*l.* 18*s.* 8*d.* Bill, No. (2), consisted of various charges connected with the mortgage transaction,
amounting to 98*l.*, which, as the mortgage was only for 500*l.*, and
the original loan only for 800*l.*, it was contended by applicant, was
a most exorbitant sum. Bill, No. (8), consisted of items of general
business, his liability to some of which applicant denied, and
amounted to 68*l.* 8*s.* 4*d.* On the part of the applicant, it was alleged
that various items in bill, No. (2), were also to be found included
in bill, No. (1). Peach, in his affidavit, met this by showing that
the sum had been deducted, so as *only to be charged once against
the applicant in the cash statement, on which the balance was
found to be due.

[*85]

E. V. Williams showed cause :

In this case, the bill marked No. (1), has been paid more than
twelve months ago and this application comes too late now to refer
it to taxation. *In re Wilton* (1), shows that the 6 & 7 Vict. c. 78,
s. 41, applies to bills delivered before the passing of the Act. It
has been paid more than twelve months before the application ; for
the payment must date from the time of giving the notes of hand.
The MASTER OF THE ROLLS, in a late case (2), expressed an opinion,
that the mere delivery of a promissory note was not payment,
unless expressly accepted as such. In the present case it is sworn,
that "the notes were taken and received in lieu of cash."

(COLERIDGE, J. : You do not mean " taken as cash," in the sense
that if the notes were not paid, the attorney would not have held
the client liable ?)

As respects bills, No. (2) and (8), they are for conveyancing items

(1) See the note to the case of *Binns*   (2) *Sayer* v. *Wagstaffe*, 59 R. R. 540
and others v. *Hey*, 1 D. & L. p. 666,   (5 Beav. 415).
note (*a*).

only, and, therefore, according to section 37 of the late statute, the application should be made to an equity Judge.   *   *   *

Hoggins, in support of the rule:

These bills which Mr. Peach has chosen to divide into three, are in truth but one bill. If so, at the time the notes were given, there was no delivery of a bill within the 41st section of the 6 & 7 Vict. c. 73.

Cur. adv. vult.

[36]   Afterwards (1),

COLERIDGE, J., delivered judgment:

This was an application to tax an attorney's bill. I took time to consider, because I wished to read the affidavits and look at the accounts which are somewhat complicated ; and also, because the construction of the 41st section of the 6 & 7 Vict. c. 73 was brought in question, which, it was said, was at present before the Court of Exchequer (2). Upon the facts, I have satisfied myself that all the three bills delivered at several times should be considered as one entire bill, and that in itself taxable, and that no such settlement has taken place as in justice ought to preclude a taxation. But it appears that more than a year before this application, two promissory notes were given at eight and twelve months for the amount claimed, and that these were paid at maturity within a year before the application. This was contended to be payment from the time of giving the notes.

It appears to me, that I need not decide this as a general question, and, therefore, need not suspend my judgment till the decision of the Court of Exchequer ; though I may observe, that there would be some difficulty in holding the giving of a bill of exchange or promissory note to be a payment, in any case in which a right of action remained on the original bill, if the note or bill were dishonoured at maturity ; otherwise this inconsistency might occur,— a bill at a longer date than a year might be given, the application to tax might be made more than a year after the giving of it, and refused, on the ground of payment ; yet at maturity the bill might be dishonoured, and the attorney might then sue on his original bill as unpaid.

However, I need not decide this point, because at all events it is clear, that the attorney must have made out and delivered his bill

(1) In Trinity Term.   See the case reported, 1 Dowl. & L.
(2) *In re Harries*, since decided.   1018.

of costs before the bills or notes were given, on the giving of which
he relies as payment of it.   *Now here it is sworn on the one side,
and not denied on the other, that the two latter bills were not
delivered till some days after the latest note was paid ; but if these
two bills should have been delivered with the first, they are to be
considered as parts of it, and then not having been delivered, no bill
had been delivered.   The rule, therefore, will be absolute.

Rule absolute.

BRUN *v.* HUTCHINSON (1).

(2 Dowl. & L. 43—45; S. C. 13 L. J. Q. B. 244.)

A. being informed that a writ of *fi. fa.* was in the sheriff's hands against
him, sent a party to the house of the sheriff's officer, to whom the warrant
had been delivered, with a Bank post bill, and some country notes to an
amount sufficient, as he thought, to discharge the execution.   On inquiry,
however, the amount not being sufficient, the party returned to fetch the
balance, leaving the bill and notes on the table ; and in his absence, the
sheriff's officer levied on the money so left in his hands, and claimed
poundage thereon, which was paid under protest: Held, that this was a
colourable levy ; that the sheriff was not entitled to poundage ; and that the
Court would order him to refund the sum he had so received.

A RULE had been obtained, calling on the Sheriff of Durham to
refund the sum of 7*l.* 10*s.* which he had demanded and *received
by way of poundage on a levy, which he had professed to make,
under a *fieri facias*, against the defendant in the above action.   It
appeared, that the defendant expected that a writ of *fieri facias*
against him would be lodged in the sheriff's hands, had sent a
message to his officer, desiring that he might be informed when it
arrived, as he would then at once settle it.   Accordingly, upon the
officer's informing him of its arrival, the defendant sent a person
with a Bank post bill for 55*l.* 5*s.*, payable at four days' sight, and
eight country bank notes of 5*l.* each, which he expected would cover
the amount of the warrant.   The warrant, however, was indorsed
to levy 97*l.* 11*s.*, including the costs of the mandate and warrant.
The party entrusted with the money, after some conversation, left
it with the sheriff's officer, lying on his table, and went to fetch the
balance.   On his return, he gave the officer the balance, namely,
2*l.* 11*s.* ; but the officer then claimed a further sum of 7*l.* 10*s.*, as
due for poundage, he having, in the mean time, as he stated, levied
upon the money so left in his hands.   The defendant refusing to

(1) *Mortimore* v. *Cragg* (1878) 3 C. P.   poundage, see now the Sheriffs Act,
Div. 216.   As to sheriffs' fees and   1887, s. 20.

BRUN
v.
HUTCHIN-
SON.

pay this further sum, the officer levied upon some sheep belonging
to the defendant, who then paid the 7*l.* 10*s.*, under protest.   No
objection was made by the officer, at the time, to the money being
in a Bank post bill, or country notes.

Raines showed cause :

The sheriff's officer acted rightly in levying upon the bill and
notes. He would not have been justified in taking them as cash.
He was, therefore, bound to make a levy, and so was entitled to
poundage.

Lush, in support of the rule :

The levy was merely colourable ; and not being *bonâ fide,* the
Court will not consider the sheriff as entitled to poundage. The
officer made no objection to the bill or notes, as not being equivalent
to cash ; and, it is clear, that he received them at the time, as
part payment. It is even questionable, whether he is entitled to

[*45] poundage, when he levies upon *money under the late Act.

(COLERIDGE, J. : Have you any authority to show that the Court
can interfere in this summary way ?)

Colls and others v. *Coates* (1), shows, that where there is no levy,
the sheriff is not entitled to poundage : and that where he has
received it, the Court will, on motion, order him to refund it.

COLERIDGE, J. :

I am of opinion, that in this case, the sheriff had no right to
poundage unless there was a levy ; and, I think, that no levy was
made. It is true, that it is sworn that there was an actual levy ;
but in order to determine whether this is so, we must look at all
the facts of the case. Here, a party, who is a limited agent, comes
for the purpose of paying the amount of the warrant ; but finding
he has not enough, returns to fetch the balance, leaving the money
on the table. When he so left it, he had no authority to part with
it, except as payment. The sheriff's officer then, with a view, no
doubt, of obtaining the poundage fees, upon his return, informs
him, that the bill and notes which he had left, had been levied
upon. This I take to be a colourable levy, and as such, I think
the sheriff was not entitled to any poundage fees upon it. I had
some doubt as to the jurisdiction of the Court to interfere in this

(1) 11 Ad. & El. 826 ; 3 P. & D. 511.

summary manner; but the case of *Colls* v. *Coates*, which has been
cited, although the objection was not raised there, is, I think, a
sufficient authority for entertaining the present application. The
rule will, therefore, be absolute.

Rule absolute, with costs.

ELLEMAN *v.* WILLIAMS.

(2 Dowl. & L. 46—49; S. C. 13 L. J. Q. B. 219.)

Where a cause, with all matters in difference, was referred to arbitration,
the costs of the cause and of the reference to abide the result, and the costs
of a cross action between the parties, to be also in the discretion of the
arbitrator, but no power was given to enter up judgment for the amount
awarded; and the arbitrator found that a sum of 17*l.* 3*s.* was due to the
plaintiff, and that nothing was due with regard to any other matters in
difference between them, and that the costs of the cross action should be
borne equally between the parties; and it appeared that the defendant had
successfully resisted an application to try the cross action before the
sheriff: Held, the Master having taxed the plaintiff's costs on the higher
scale, that the Court would order a review of his taxation.

JERVIS had obtained a rule, calling on the plaintiff to show
cause why the Master should not review his taxation herein. The
plaintiff and defendant, it appeared, had brought cross actions
against each other, in which the particulars of demand in the one
action were the same as those of the set-off in the other. In the
action by the present defendant against the present plaintiff, which
was that first brought, a summons had been obtained to try before
the sheriff. This application had been successfully resisted by the
present defendant, on the ground that the debt sought to be
recovered was above 20*l.* On the present action coming on to
be tried at the Hereford Summer Assizes of 1843, the cause, with
all matters in difference, was referred, the costs of the cause and of
the reference to abide the result, and the costs of the cross action
commenced by the present defendant, to be in the discretion of the
arbitrator. There was no power given to enter up judgment for the
amount awarded. The arbitrator found that a sum of 17*l.* 3*s.* was
due to the plaintiff, and that nothing was due with regard to any
other matters in difference between them; and ordered that the
costs of the cross action should be borne equally between the
parties. The Master had taxed the costs upon the higher scale.
It was submitted, that in so doing he had acted wrongly. In
Wallen v. *Smith* (1), the sum awarded by the arbitrator under an

(1) 3 M. & W. 138; see S. C. 6 Dowl. 103.

ELLEMAN
v.
WILLIAMS.

order of reference, was less than 20*l*., and it was held, that the Master should have taxed the costs upon the lower scale.

Huddlestone now showed cause:

[*47]

The directions to taxing officers, Hil. Vac., 4 Will. IV., are in the nature of "directions" only, and not rules depriving them of a discretionary *power. * * The Master, in the present case, has properly exercised his discretion; for in the cross action brought by the defendant, the defendant resisted the application to try before the sheriff.   And the fair inference to be gathered from the terms of the submission to reference is, that the parties intended that the costs, which had been incurred up to the time of the reference, should be a part of the sum to be found due by the arbitrator's award. * * *

[48]

Jervis, in support of the rule. * * *

COLERIDGE, J.:

This rule must be made absolute. In the case of *Wallen* v. *Smith*, the remarks of Lord ABINGER, C. B., and PARKE, B., clearly show that the term " recovery " is to be taken in its popular, and not in its strictly legal sense; and means that if a party does not recover more than 20*l*. as the fruits of his process, he is to be allowed costs only according to the lower scale.   It has been contended, that as this was a reference, and as such, an agreement to take whatever sum the arbitrator should think fit to award, the amount found by him to be due to the plaintiff, is the amount of the debt and costs taken together.   But looking at the terms of the rule, I think it cannot fail to be seen, that it was the intention of the parties to make a distinction between the debt and costs, and that the latter

[*49]

were to attend upon the disposal of the former.   I, *therefore, think that this case falls under the rule of Hilary Vacation, and the Master should consequently have taxed the costs on the lower scale.   I by no means agree with what has been said as to the discretion of the Master, as to taxing the costs on the lower scale. I conceive that when the sum recovered is less than 20*l*., he is bound to do so, and has no discretion, and if he does not, this Court will direct a reviewal of his taxation.

Rule absolute.

IN THE MATTER OF A. S. WARNER AND OTHERS.

(2 Dowl. & L. 148—161; S. C. 13 L. J. Q. B. 370; 8 Jur. 1097.)

A submission made between the executors of a deceased partner, and the
surviving partner and others, recited a partnership as existing under an
agreement from the 1st of January, 1837, and that it was alleged by N.,
the surviving partner, that a partnership had existed between him and the
deceased, previous to the date mentioned, and that differences had arisen
between the parties touching the accuracy of certain statements of accounts
delivered by N., showing the amount to which the deceased partner was
entitled in respect of the said partnership, &c., and also touching several
other matters and things touching the said account, and touching the
administration of the estate of the deceased partner; and witnessed that
the parties accordingly agreed to refer the same, and also all other matters
and things in difference between the said parties. The arbitrator found
that a partnership had existed between the said parties from the 18th day
of December, 1835, up to the time of the death of the deceased partner,
and that a certain sum was due as the balance upon the account: Held,
sufficiently specific and certain, and that he was not bound to find
separately how much was due under the partnership, under the agreement
in 1837.

On motion by an executor and trustee under a will to set aside an award
under a submission entered into by himself and other trustees and legatees
for the purpose of ascertaining the assets and settling the accounts under
the will : Held, that it was no objection that certain married women who took
interests under the will, which were affected by the award, were parties to
the submission : Nor that there were certain infant legatees who were not
bound thereby, who were also interested : Nor that the matters submitted
affected the trust estate of married women and infants.

By the deed of submission, it was covenanted that the parties thereto
should execute all such deeds, &c., as might be requisite for putting an end
to the differences, and administering the estate and effects, &c., and carrying into execution, the trusts, &c., as the arbitrator should direct; even if
such deed were to be between them and a stranger to the submission :
Held, no excess of authority that the arbitrator had directed that in
consideration of certain sums paid and to be paid, conveyances should be
executed of certain freehold and leasehold property of the deceased;
although one of the conveyances was to be to a stranger to the submission ;
the affidavits showing that the question of these conveyances had been
discussed before the arbitrator, with the assent of all parties, and that it
was one of the matters in dispute between the parties, and intended to be
referred by the deed of submission.

Nor was it held any objection, that the award directed one of the parties
thereto to pay the amount of the legacy duty on certain shares of the
assets, of which he had become the owner.

A RULE *nisi* had been obtained in Michaelmas Term last, on
behalf of a Mr. Farnel, to set aside an award, under the following
circumstances :

One Sarah Mason, a widow, had made a will; whereby she
appointed the Rev. A. S. Warner and Mr. Farnel, her executors;
and devised and bequeathed to them, her freehold, copyhold, and
leasehold estates, and personal property ; upon trust to sell and

convert the same into money, and to pay her debts and certain legacies in the first instance, and to divide the residue into nine parts. She then bequeathed a ninth part to each of her children, Henry John, Robert, William, Mary Ann the wife of James Norris, Hannah, and Sarah, absolutely. She bequeathed another ninth for the use of the children of her son John Leeds Mason, to be paid, applied, and disposed of, as he or his representatives should think fit, for their maintenance *and education until the youngest attained twenty-one years of age; and upon his death, or upon the youngest child attaining the age of twenty-one, whichever should last happen, then to be divided equally amongst the children. She directed, that in case John Leeds Mason should be willing to take the bequest on these trusts, it should be paid to him, and his receipt be a sufficient discharge to her executors. Another ninth share, was to be laid out in Government or real securities, with power to vary the securities, and the interest thereof to be paid to her daughter Elizabeth, the wife of J. Thurston, to her separate use, without power of anticipation, and after her death, to be divided equally among her children. The remaining ninth share was afterwards by a codicil directed to be divided into eight parts of which one was to be added to each of the foregoing shares. There were the usual trustee clauses in the will. On the 12th of December, 1836, she entered into an agreement of partnership with her son-in-law James Norris, for a period of ten years, from the 1st of January, 1837; with a proviso, that he should be at liberty in the event of her death, to purchase her moiety of the partnership effects at a valuation, and to continue in possession of the premises in which the business was carried on, and which belonged to her, for the remainder of the term. By a codicil to her will, she directed that he should have the right of pre-emption with respect to these premises for a sum fixed. In November, 1840, she died. Up to the time of her death, Norris remained on the premises, carrying on the business of the partnership; and after that event, he elected to buy her share, and to purchase the premises at the price named. The money, however, was never paid. The executors afterwards entered into an agreement, with the sanction of several of the children, for the sale of a part of the testatrix's leasehold estate to H. J. Mason, for 160l.

The executors being unable to get what they considered a satisfactory account of the partnership effects from Norris, agreed to refer the matter to arbitration. Accordingly a *deed was executed

[*149]

[*150]

between the Rev. A. S. Warner and J. Farnell, as executors and
trustees, of the first part, and R. Thurston and Elizabeth his wife,
of the second part, and J. Norris and Ann his wife, of the third
part. It recited that it was alleged by J. Norris, that previously to
1837 there were certain partnership dealings between the said
Sarah Mason and J. Norris; and recited the agreement of partnership of the 12th December, 1836, and that the partnership had
subsisted from the 1st January, 1837, to the day of her death. It
also recited her will, and that Henry John Mason, William Mason,
Robert Mason, Hannah Mason, and Sarah Mason, the wife of
H. King, had sold their shares; and that the said John Leeds
Mason had sold his share or interest of his children under the will,
to the said James Norris and wife; and that therefore R. Thurston
and wife, and James Norris and wife were the only persons beneficially interested in the proper distribution of the said trust funds
and property: and that "differences had arisen between the parties
thereto, touching the accuracy of certain statements of account
which had been delivered by the said James Norris purporting to
show the amount to which the said testatrix was entitled in respect
of the said partnership at the time of her decease, and the value of
her share in the stock and capital thereof; and also touching
several other matters and things in regard to the said account, and
touching the said account, and touching the administration and
carrying into due execution the trusts of the will of the said Sarah
Mason; and that in order to put an end to the said differences, all
the said parties had agreed to refer the same, and also all other
matters and things whatsoever in difference between the parties."
It therefore witnessed that A. S. Warner and J. Farnell as executors
and trustees, and R. Thurston and wife, and J. Norris and wife,
did covenant and agree to abide by, observe, and perform, the award
of J. N. "of and concerning the premises so as aforesaid referred, or
any thing in anywise relating thereto, *and also of and concerning
all actions, causes of action, suits, bills, bonds, contracts, accounts,
reckonings, sums of money, controversies, and demands whatsoever,
both at law and in equity—commenced or depending between the
said parties." It was also covenanted that each of the said parties
should make out, prepare, sign, and execute "all such accounts,
statements, deeds, instruments, and writings, and fulfil and perform
all such contracts, as may be requisite for putting an end to the
said differences, and for duly administering the estates and effects
late of the said Sarah Mason, and carrying into execution the trusts

In re
WARNER.

[*151]

of her said will and codicil, as the said arbitrator shall direct; and
that, whether any of such deeds or instruments be between the
parties to these presents, or between them or any of them and any
other person or persons not a party or parties hereto." A power
was also given to the arbitrator to award concerning costs. The
deed was duly executed by the respective parties thereto.

On the 1st of June, 1843, the arbitrator made his award, finding
that "a partnership subsisted between the said Sarah Mason and
J. Norris, as, &c., from the 18th of December, 1835, up to the
time of the decease of the said Sarah Mason;" and that "in taking
the account between the said executors and the said J. Norris as to
the testatrix's share of the partnership assets, the sum of 994*l*. 13*s*. 9*d*.
was the balance upon the said account, and is now in the hands of
the said J. Norris to be accounted for by him," &c. The award then
stated that the executors had contracted to sell to Henry John
Mason, certain leasehold premises, part of the estate of the said
Sarah Mason, at the price of 160*l*.; and that James Norris had
agreed to purchase the freehold premises on which the business
was carried on, with respect to which by the will of the testatrix
he was to have the right of pre-emption, for the stipulated sum of
1,400*l*.; and that he had also purchased the share of H. J. Mason

[*152] to the residue of the testatrix's estate *for 250*l*., 90*l*. of which he
had paid to H. J. Mason, and for the remainder was to account to
the estate, as the purchase money of the leasehold premises, which
H. J. Mason had agreed to purchase of the executors. It also
stated that the executors were only entitled to the equity of redemption in the freehold premises subject to a mortgage of 1,000*l*.; and
therefore awarded that J. Norris should be accountable to the estate
for 400*l*. only, in addition to the 160*l*. The arbitrator then found
that the estate consisted of certain property which he specified.
He awarded certain costs to be paid out of the estate; and directed
that the said A. S. Warner and J. Farnell, as such executors and
trustees as aforesaid, should before, &c. duly execute to H. J. Mason
the assignment of the leasehold premises, &c., and to J. Norris the
conveyance of the equity of redemption of the freehold premises, &c.
That J. Norris was to pay out of the money in his hands for which
he was accountable, 39*l*. 16*s*. 10*d*., to A. S. Warner for his costs,
and that J. Farnell might retain a similar sum, but was to pay
three-fourths of the costs of the arbitration. He also awarded that
J. Norris should pay to the executors one-eighth part of the balance
of the assets remaining in his hands; which eighth part, after

paying thereout the legacy duty, and the expenses of the legacy discharge, was to be invested by the said executors " pursuant to the direction of the aforesaid will and codicil for the share of the wife and children of the said Richard Thurston, in manner following," &c. He then directed it to be invested, and limited the trust with regard to it, in exact conformity with the terms of the will. And he further ordered that James Norris should pay the legacy duty on the seven shares of residue, to the receipt of which he was entitled as above recited.

The affidavits also stated that Farnell had objected when he found the arbitrator was entering into the question of the general distribution of the estate, and had thereupon *revoked the power of the arbitrator. As the deed, however, contained the usual clause for making it a rule of Court, this was inoperative. The children of John Leeds Mason were minors, as were also those of Thurston.

[*153]

The award was now sought to be set aside on the following grounds :

First, That the award was not made in pursuance of the submission, the terms of which specify a partnership therein mentioned, with reference to a certain settlement of accounts therein, and all matters in difference; whereas the award bore reference to "a certain partnership from December, 1835, to the death of Sarah Mason, and takes an account of such partnership."

Secondly, That the award was not final, inasmuch as the children of one John Leeds Mason who were minors, the wives of Norris and Thurston, and the children of Thurston also minors, and all interested parties, were not bound by its terms.

Thirdly, That the award as to the purchase of Henry John Mason, and the conveyance awarded, and payment of 160l. was beyond the submission, and is not final.

Fourthly, That the award was beyond the submission, and uncertain, and not final in awarding James Norris to pay or account for 400l. in payment of the estate, and leaving the mortgage, 1,000l. unpaid.

Fifthly, That the arbitrator had no power to make an award with reference to the estate of Sarah Mason.

Sixthly, That the award was bad, and beyond the submission, and not final, and was uncertain in awarding that James Norris should pay the legacy duty.

The affidavits in answer, showed that there had existed a

In re
WARNER.

partnership between Norris and Sarah Mason, ever since December,
1835, and that the accounts of that partnership were one of
the matters in difference, and that it was much discussed on
both sides before the arbitrator.   They also showed that the

[*154]

mode of disposing of and conveying the *freehold property purchased by Norris, and the leasehold purchased by H. J. Mason,
and the payment of the purchase money, were likewise discussed, and that Norris had agreed, on purchasing the different
shares, to pay the legacy duty, which was also a matter discussed
before the arbitrator ; and that Mrs. Mason had only the equity
of redemption in the freehold premises in which the business
was carried on, and which had been purchased by Norris, and
that she had never made herself personally liable for the mortgage
thereon.

Cowling and *Palmer* showed cause (1) :

As to the first objection,   *   *   there is, no excess of authority
here ; the subject is *primâ facie* included in the terms of the submission, and the opposite side should have shown by affidavit,
which they have not done, that it was not intended to be included.
The second objection seems to be, that the executors could not
refer disputes between themselves as executors and others ; because
they were trustees for married women as well as for infants.   Even
were this a good objection to the award, it is not one on which this
Court would grant the present motion, but leave the parties to
make it in case the award should be attempted to be enforced :
Wrightson v. *Bywater* and others (2).   With respect to married

[*155]

women, it is by no means clear *that they could not give a consent
to a reference.   *   *   As to the objection that the children of
J. L. Mason, and of Thurston, who are minors, cannot be bound
by the award, the case of *Jones* v. *Powell* (3) shows that that is no
objection, when made as in the present instance by a party, who
was aware of the fact at the time of entering into the deed of
reference.   The same doctrine is held in *Wrightson* v. *Bywater* and
others (2).   Besides here, there is nothing ordered to be done by
the award with respect to the children.   As respects the third
objection, the arbitrator had power to award with regard to matters
and things " touching the administration and carrying into due
execution the trusts of the will " of Mrs. Mason, and he accordingly

(1) In Easter Term.   Dowl. 359).
(2) 49 R. R. 570 (3 M. & W. 199 ; 6   (3) 49 R. R. 728 (6 Dowl. 483).

has ordered the trustees to fulfil the contract which they had
entered into. * * The fourth objection is met by our affidavits,
which show that Mrs. Mason had nothing whatever to do with the
mortgage of 1,000*l.*, having purchased only the equity of redemption,
and never having made herself personally liable for the mortgage.
The fifth objection is already answered by what has been said with
respect to the second. The sixth objection is met by our affidavits,
which distinctly show that it was a matter in dispute, and discussed
before the arbitrator.

Watson, in support of the rule:

As respects the first objection, there should have been an award
of how much was due in respect of the alleged partnership up to
1837, and how much since. The award should have been specific
*on these points, *Randall* v. *Randall* (1), 1 Roll. Abr. 256, tit.   [*156]
" Arbitration," and *Pope* v. *Brett* (2), and not being so, is bad
altogether. Indeed, it is not clear that the arbitrator has awarded
at all in respect of the partnership mentioned in the agreement;
and, therefore, the award is defective: *In the Matter of Rider* and
Fisher (3). The second objection is an important one, namely, the
want of mutuality between the parties. It is said, that a party
aware of the objection at the time of signing the deed of reference,
cannot avail himself of it. But to hold this doctrine is to overrule
the case of *Biddell* v. *Dowse* (4). * * So also in *Thorp* v. *Cole* (5),
the party must have been aware, at the time of the submission, of
the want of power on the part of the parish officers referring; but
that circumstance was not held to bar him from afterwards raising
the objection. * * The third objection is, that the award has   [157]
reference to Henry John Mason, who is no party to the submission.
It directs the executors to convey the estate to him, and he sells to
Norris, who is to be accountable to the estate for the purchase
money. The case of *Fisher* v. *Pimbley* (6) shows that the award is
bad on this ground. * * *

Cur. adv. vult.

COLERIDGE, J. now delivered judgment:

This was a rule to set aside an award on several grounds. It

(1) 8 R. R. 601 (7 East, 81 ; see   (4) 28 R. R. 574 (6 B. & C. 255;
S. C. 3 Smith, 90).   see S. C. 9 Dowl. & Ry. 404).
(2) 2 Saund. 292; see S. C. 2   (5) 41 R. R. 733 (2 Cr. M. & R. 367;
Keble, 736.   see S. C. 4 Dowl. 457).
(3) 43 R. R. 836 (3 Bing. N. C. 874;   (6) 11 East, 188. See 52 R. R. 630,
see S. C. 5 Scott, 86).   631.

appears that one Sarah Mason, a widow with many children, had carried on business in Norwich; and for some years previously, and up to the time of her death, in partnership with James Norris, who had married one of her daughters. She died in November, 1840, leaving a will, by which she in effect devised her property in equal ninth shares amongst her children, and the issue of those who had died before her. These shares, by purchase, had all come either to James Norris and his wife, or Richard Thurston and his wife, another daughter. Disputes had arisen between them respectively and the executors, and these had led to the submission and arbitration, of which the award in question was the result. The submission
[*158]
and award are long and *complicated, and many affidavits were filed; but when the facts are understood, the case seems free from difficulty.

The first objection is, that the award is not in pursuance of the submission, in this, " that the latter relates to a partnership therein mentioned, with reference to a certain settlement of accounts therein, and all matters in difference; whereas the award refers to a certain partnership from December, 1835, to the death of Sarah Mason, and takes an account of such partnership." I collect, however, on reference to the submission, that although there was certainly an agreement for a partnership commencing in December, 1836, yet James Norris had contended, that partnership dealings had taken place between the deceased and himself at some certain period not precisely fixed; that the accuracy of his account generally was disputed, and that for want of more satisfactory accounts, it was alleged that the affairs of the executorship could not be properly wound up. I find, also, that not only the partnership from the admitted date, and the accounts relating thereto, and the differences respecting the same; but also all other matters and things in difference between the parties, were referred in the largest terms. It seems to me, therefore, no excess of jurisdiction in the arbitrator, to inquire into the date of the commencement of any partnership, and if he found one to have existed previously to the agreement of 1836, he might very probably also find that the accounts were so blended with those of the partnership after the agreement, as to make it impossible to award on the latter separately. With a view to the real object of the arbitration, namely, the determining the share of the testatrix, and how her account alternately stood with her partner, for the purpose of distribution under the will, it would have been manifestly useless so to do. This ground of objection, therefore, fails on the facts.

Secondly, it is objected that it is not final, because the children of one John Leeds Mason, who are minors, the *wives respectively of Norris and Thurston, and the children of Thurston, also minors, who are interested parties, are not bound thereby. With regard to the children of John Leeds Mason, they were to take a share under the will, which was left during their minority in the management of their father, and it appears that before the submission, their father had sold that share to Norris; whether such sale was authorized by the will or not, is immaterial for the present question; they were in no way made parties to the reference, nor are their rights affected by the award; the arbitrator could not inquire into the legality of any conveyance or purchase by which Norris had become the owner *de facto* of one or more shares; he could only deal with the parties before him, according to the shares and interests, which they admitted each other to have, as the basis of distribution. The same answer does not apply to the wives of Norris and Thurston, and the children of the latter; Norris and Thurston as to certain parts of the property, being interested under the will, only in respect of their respective wives and children. But as to the wives, they are made parties to the reference; of this all the other parties are cognisant, and I am opinion, that I ought not to yield to the objection of their coverture, now put forward by one of the executors, and set aside the award on this ground at his prayer. He never should have consented to refer the matter in dispute and allowed them to become parties, if he intended to make this objection. An award is only to be set aside for some miscarriage of the arbitrator; but he has been guilty of none in dealing between the parties referring and on the matters referred. As to Thurston's children, I cannot see that the award in any way affects them—the executors had clearly a right to ascertain the assets in any way they chose—at least they have elected to do so under this arbitration, and one of them cannot now disannul that election—and when the sum to be divided is thus found, the award only directs as to the Thurston's share, that it is *to be invested, and limits the trust with regard to it in exact conformity with the will. This may have been wholly unnecessary; but it cannot prejudice the rest of the award.

[*160]

The third and fourth objections relate to parts of the testatrix's estate other than the partnership, a leasehold property and a freehold estate; and it is objected, that there is excess in the award in dealing with these at all; and also that the manner of dealing with

of her said will and codicil, as the said arbitrator shall direct; and
that, whether any of such deeds or instruments be between the
parties to these presents, or between them or any of them and any
other person or persons not a party or parties hereto." A power
was also given to the arbitrator to award concerning costs. The
deed was duly executed by the respective parties thereto.

On the 1st of June, 1843, the arbitrator made his award, finding
that "a partnership subsisted between the said Sarah Mason and
J. Norris, as, &c., from the 18th of December, 1835, up to the
time of the decease of the said Sarah Mason;" and that "in taking
the account between the said executors and the said J. Norris as to
the testatrix's share of the partnership assets, the sum of 994*l.*18*s.*9*d.*
was the balance upon the said account, and is now in the hands of
the said J. Norris to be accounted for by him," &c. The award then
stated that the executors had contracted to sell to Henry John
Mason, certain leasehold premises, part of the estate of the said
Sarah Mason, at the price of 160*l.*; and that James Norris had
agreed to purchase the freehold premises on which the business
was carried on, with respect to which by the will of the testatrix
he was to have the right of pre-emption, for the stipulated sum of
1,400*l.*; and that he had also purchased the share of H. J. Mason

[*152] to the residue of the testatrix's estate *for 250*l.*, 90*l.* of which he
had paid to H. J. Mason, and for the remainder was to account to
the estate, as the purchase money of the leasehold premises, which
H. J. Mason had agreed to purchase of the executors. It also
stated that the executors were only entitled to the equity of redemption in the freehold premises subject to a mortgage of 1,000*l.*; and
therefore awarded that J. Norris should be accountable to the estate
for 400*l.* only, in addition to the 160*l.* The arbitrator then found
that the estate consisted of certain property which he specified.
He awarded certain costs to be paid out of the estate; and directed
that the said A. S. Warner and J. Farnell, as such executors and
trustees as aforesaid, should before, &c. duly execute to H. J. Mason
the assignment of the leasehold premises, &c., and to J. Norris the
conveyance of the equity of redemption of the freehold premises, &c.
That J. Norris was to pay out of the money in his hands for which
he was accountable, 39*l.* 16*s.* 10*d.*, to A. S. Warner for his costs,
and that J. Farnell might retain a similar sum, but was to pay
three-fourths of the costs of the arbitration. He also awarded that
J. Norris should pay to the executors one-eighth part of the balance
of the assets remaining in his hands; which eighth part, after

paying thereout the legacy duty, and the expenses of the legacy discharge, was to be invested by the said executors " pursuant to the direction of the aforesaid will and codicil for the share of the wife and children of the said Richard Thurston, in manner following," &c. He then directed it to be invested, and limited the trust with regard to it, in exact conformity with the terms of the will. And he further ordered that James Norris should pay the legacy duty on the seven shares of residue, to the receipt of which he was entitled as above recited.

The affidavits also stated that Farnell had objected when he found the arbitrator was entering into the question of the general distribution of the estate, and had thereupon *revoked the power of the arbitrator. As the deed, however, contained the usual clause for making it a rule of Court, this was inoperative. The children of John Leeds Mason were minors, as were also those of Thurston.

[*153]

The award was now sought to be set aside on the following grounds :

First, That the award was not made in pursuance of the submission, the terms of which specify a partnership therein mentioned, with reference to a certain settlement of accounts therein, and all matters in difference; whereas the award bore reference to "a certain partnership from December, 1835, to the death of Sarah Mason, and takes an account of such partnership."

Secondly, That the award was not final, inasmuch as the children of one John Leeds Mason who were minors, the wives of Norris and Thurston, and the children of Thurston also minors, and all interested parties, were not bound by its terms.

Thirdly, That the award as to the purchase of Henry John Mason, and the conveyance awarded, and payment of 160*l.* was beyond the submission, and is not final.

Fourthly, That the award was beyond the submission, and uncertain, and not final in awarding James Norris to pay or account for 400*l.* in payment of the estate, and leaving the mortgage, 1,000*l.* unpaid.

Fifthly, That the arbitrator had no power to make an award with reference to the estate of Sarah Mason.

Sixthly, That the award was bad, and beyond the submission, and not final, and was uncertain in awarding that James Norris should pay the legacy duty.

The affidavits in answer, showed that there had existed a

SCOTT
v.
ENGLAND.

Udall, in support of the rule:

The argument is not that no action can be brought; but that the present cannot be maintained. The defendant does not deny that the property in a specific chattel passes by a contract of sale; what he contends for is, that it does not pass unless the seller is himself the owner. The case of *Hinde* v. *Whitehouse* (1), is quite distinguishable; for in that case, by the express terms of the contract, the goods were to remain at the risk of the buyer. It is assumed by the other side, as universally true, that this action can be maintained, because the property passed; that is not so. [He cited *Simmons* v. *Swift* (2), *Tempest* v. *Fitzgerald* (3), *Dixon* v. *Yates* (4), and *Bloxam* v. *Sanders* (5). He contended that a purchaser under the conditions of sale at this auction did not acquire [524] property before paying the auctioneer.] If this action will lie, the plaintiff will get the price of the goods, although he may have never been in a condition to deliver; for if the action is now maintainable, it was equally so immediately after the contract, as no subsequent assent to the contract was given. The reason that this action cannot be maintained on a contract for making an article not *in esse* at the time, is because the subject of the contract cannot then be appropriated or delivered; so here, this, although a specific chattel, could not be delivered by the plaintiff, or appropriated by him, because it was not his to deliver or appropriate. It is, therefore, submitted, that the plaintiff not having the property in him at the time of the contract, or if having the property, not having the right of possession, both of which must concur to make a complete bargain and sale, this action cannot be maintained.

Cur. adv. vult.

PATTESON, J.:

I am of opinion that this rule must be discharged. All that is necessary to enable a party to maintain an action for goods bargained and sold is, that the property in the specific goods should have passed. In the case of *Atkinson* v. *Bell* (6), which has been cited, the property had never passed, as the plaintiff might have delivered the machines to any third person; in *Simmons* v. *Swift* (7),

(1) 8 R. R. 676 (7 East, 558; S. C. 3 Smith, 528).

(2) 29 R. R. 438 (5 B. & C. 857, 865; S. C. 8 Dowl. & Ry. 693).

(3) 22 R. R. 526 (3 B. & Ad. 680).

(4) 39 R. R. 489, 497 (5 B. & Ad. 313, 340; S. C. 2 Nev. & M. 177).

(5) 28 R. R. 519 (4 B. & C. 948; 7 Dowl. & Ry. 396).

(6) 32 R. R. 382 (8 B. & C. 277; 2 M. & R. 292).

(7) 29 R. R. 438 (5 B. & C. 857; 8 Dowl. & Ry. 693).

the bark had never been weighed; and in *Dixon* v. *Yates* (1), the
original vendor never intended to part with the property.   In the
present case, there is no doubt that an action would have lain
against the present plaintiff at the suit of the original vendor, and
that the property became vested in him.   That property, by his
bargain with the defendant, vested in the defendant; and he may,
*therefore, maintain the same action against the defendant, as he   [*525]
would have been liable to at the suit of the original vendor.   The
rule will, therefore, be discharged.

Rule discharged.

Ex parte LE CREN.

(2 Dowl. & L. 571—576; S. C. nom. *R.* v. *Churchwardens of St. Stephen's,*   [571]
Coleman Street, 14 L. J. Q. B. 34; 9 Jur. 255.)

A *mandamus* will not lie to compel the vicar, churchwardens, and
parishioners of a parish, to meet for the purpose of electing an organist
to the parish church; although within the time of living memory, there
has always been an organist who has been paid a stipend out of the
Church rates.

At a vestry meeting convened for the purpose of electing an organist, it
was unanimously agreed that the course pursued on a former vacancy
should be followed, namely, that a committee of the vestry should select
six out of the candidates, who should perform in the parish church each on
a separate Sunday, and that one of those six should be elected to the office;
but that no vote given for any other than one of the six candidates should
be received : Held, that this mode of proceeding was not unreasonable, and
that the Court would not grant a *mandamus* to admit to the office a person
in whose favour the greatest number of votes had been tendered, but who
was not one of the six candidates.

PASHLEY moved for a rule *nisi* for a *mandamus* to the vicar,
churchwardens, and parishioners of St. Stephen, Coleman Street,
in the city of London, commanding them to hold a vestry meeting
for the purpose of electing a proper person as organist, or to admit
Miss Le Cren into that office.

It appeared by the affidavits in support of the motion, *that from   [*572]
a time beyond living memory, there had been an organist for the
parish of St. Stephen, who had been regularly paid a fixed salary
out of the Church rates : that in the event of a vacancy occurring,
the candidate for the office was elected by the rated inhabitants of
the parish in public vestry, by a show of hands, or by a poll, if
demanded : that in the month of April, 1844, a vacancy having
occurred, a vestry meeting was held on the 19th; at which it was
agreed, in pursuance of the precedent of the course held upon a

(1) 39 R. R. 489 (5 B. & Ad. 313; 2 Nev. & M. 177).

former vacancy in 1827, that a committee should be appointed, who should reduce the number of candidates to six; and that then each of those six should perform once on a separate Sunday, and then be elected by show of hands, or poll, if demanded. The minutes of this vestry were confirmed at a subsequent meeting duly convened and held on the 20th of June, and the names of the six candidates were there stated, among whom Miss Le Cren was not included. It was then moved that she be included; but on a show of hands, the motion was lost by a majority of fifty-three against twenty-one. A written demand for a poll on her behalf was then made. A poll was then taken for the other five candidates (one having with-drawn); but the votes offered for Miss Le Cren were refused to be recorded, and marked only as tendered. On the close of the poll, the candidate who had the greatest number of votes, and was declared to be duly elected, had only seventy-six votes; whilst Miss Le Cren, the votes in whose favour were only marked as tendered, had eighty-three. Miss Le Cren had since offered to perform the duties of organist, but had been denied; and a demand of a quarter's salary on her behalf (a sum having been voted by the vestry for the payment of the organist) had been made to the churchwardens and refused.

Under these circumstances it was submitted, that if the Court should hesitate to grant a *mandamus*, calling upon the vicar, churchwardens, and parishioners, to admit Miss Le Cren to the office of organist; yet that the writ might *properly issue, calling on the vicar, churchwardens, and parishioners, to proceed to the election of an organist. Organs are not of very ancient date, and, therefore, authorities are not likely to be found in the books upon the subject; but analogous decisions are found, and, it is sub-mitted, that the major part of the inhabitants may clearly lay a rate to defray the expenses incident to maintaining the organ and paying the organist. It is laid down in 2 Roll. Abr. tit. "Prohi-bition," (K), pl. 4, " Si le pluis part del parishioners d'un parish [la ou](1) sont 4 bells agree que la serra fait un fifth bell, et ceo font accordant, et font un rate pur payment pur luy ; ceo liera le meinder parte del parishioners coment que ils ne agree al ceo, car auterment ascun obstinate persons poient hinder ascun chose intend et que est fit pur le ornament del Esglise : " and, in the case of *The Churchwardens of St. John Margate* v. *The Parishioners,*

[*573]

(1) *Cou la* in Ro. Ab., *ou la* in this report, neither of which will make sense even in " law-French."—F. P.

Vicar, and Inhabitants of the Same (1), a faculty for erecting an
organ was held to be good. In the present case, the organ has
been erected beyond the time of living memory. * * A poll has
been substantially refused to Miss Le Cren; for, although the votes
in her favour were taken, they were not received and treated as
actual votes, but marked merely as votes tendered.   Miss Le Cren
had the majority of votes in her favour on that occasion; and it
cannot be denied that the majority of the inhabitants have the
right to bind the rest, and that a poll is an incident to the election
of every parish office: *Campbell* v. *Maund* (2). * * Here the   [*574]
will of the majority of the electors, who were in favour of Miss
Le Cren, has been disregarded, and the election is consequently void.

(PATTESON, J : The difficulty that I feel is, whether the office of
an organist be an office known to the common law. Whether, even
if it be conceded that the expenses may be paid out of a rate, the
parishioners may not, if they choose, refuse to have an organist
at all.)

At all events those, who by the existing arrangements are liable to
pay the salary, are entitled to vote in the election. Although the
place of organist be not in strictness what Lord Coke would have
termed an office; yet the Court will not, on that account, refuse to
grant a *mandamus.* * * *

                                                Cur. adv. vult.

PATTESON, J. :

This was an application for a *mandamus* to the vicar, churchwardens, and parishioners of St. Stephen, Coleman Street, to
proceed to the election of an organist, or to admit Miss Le Cren
into that office.

On looking at the authorities, I cannot find any which go the
length of saying that I can issue such a writ for the election of an
organist.   The utmost that Lord STOWELL decided in the case of
The Churchwardens of St. John's Margate v. *The Parishioners, Vicar,
and Inhabitants of the *Same* (1) was, that he would grant a faculty   [*575]
for erecting an organ, because the majority of the parishioners
might direct a rate for keeping it up, and paying the organist.
That is the utmost extent to which that case goes, and I cannot find
that the other authorities carry it any further.   I therefore think it
is impossible that a *mandamus* should go to the inhabitants generally,

(1) 1 Hagg. C. R. 198.   (2) 44 R. R. 619 (5 Ad. & El. 865;
                                      see S. C, 1 N. & P. 558).

to elect an organist. The only case I have found in which a writ
was issued to the inhabitants at large is *Rex* v. *Wix* (1). There the
parishioners were commanded to meet and elect churchwardens, but
that is a very different matter, and I can find no case which says
that the Court can issue a *mandamus* for a purpose like the present.

In this case, it is true, that there has been from time to time a
vote for the expenses of the organist out of the Church rate; but
I see nothing to prevent the parishioners from rescinding their
appointment of organist, and determining for the future to have
none.

With respect to the other alternative of the motion, I do not think
this is a case in which, even if I had the power, I ought to interfere.
The facts appear to be, that at the first vestry meeting a committee
was appointed to reduce the number of candidates to six, and that
each of those six should perform the service on a separate Sunday.
Sixty candidates offered themselves, and they were reduced by the
committee to six. Miss Le Cren was not amongst the six. It
appears that one afterwards retired. At a subsequent meeting of
the vestry, the minutes of the former meeting at which this resolution was carried unanimously, were confirmed without objection;
and then an election took place, confined, it is true, to those five;
and the successful candidate declared duly elected. I collect from
the affidavits that this was the mode of proceeding adopted on
the occasion of the last vacancy. I cannot see that this was an
unreasonable mode of conducting the election; or that it was not
[*576]   competent, under such an *arrangement, to say that no votes should
be given for any but the six selected candidates, and to declare that
the votes given for any other person were thrown away.

Rule refused.

———————

COX v. BALNE (2).

(2 Dowl. & L. 718—721; S. C. 14 L. J. Q. B. 95; 9 Jur. 182.)

Where an under-sheriff, who was acting as attorney for certain creditors
of the defendant, informed them of a writ of *fieri facias* at the suit of the
plaintiff, having been placed in his hands to execute, by which means the
issuing of a *fiat* in bankruptcy against the defendant was accelerated, and
the plaintiff's execution thereby defeated; the Court refused to grant the
sheriff relief under the Interpleader Act.

This was an application on behalf of the Sheriff of Dorsetshire
for an interpleader rule, under the following circumstances. It
appeared that a writ of *fieri facias* on a judgment entered up by the

(1) 36 R. R. 545 (2 B. & Ad. 197).   (2) R. S. C. Ord. LVII. r. 2 (b).

plaintiff against the above defendant on a warrant of attorney, was delivered to the Under-sheriff of Dorsetshire on the 5th of December, 1844, and on the same day the goods of the defendant were seized in execution. On the following day, the under-sheriff received a notice of a claim to the goods in question from certain parties, claiming under a deed of settlement. On the 7th of December, a *fiat* in bankruptcy issued against the defendant. An interpleader summons had been obtained on behalf of the sheriff, on the 9th of December, which was heard before Mr. Justice Wightman, at Chambers, and discharged. That application was opposed on behalf of the plaintiff, on an affidavit of the plaintiff's attorney, stating that he was informed, and believed that at the time of the issuing of the writ of *fieri facias* at the suit of the plaintiff, the under-sheriff was acting as agent to the petitioning creditor under the *fiat* against the defendant; and that after the writ had reached his hands, and before the *fiat* was issued, the under-sheriff had made a communication to the parties prosecuting the *fiat*, by which the issuing of such *fiat* had been accelerated, and the plaintiff's execution frustrated. The affidavit also *stated that on delivering the writ of *fieri facias* to the under-sheriff on the 5th December, he looked at the amount indorsed, and then observed, that it would be of no use to execute the writ, as a docket would be immediately struck against the defendant; that the deponent thereupon requested him to execute a bill of sale to the execution creditor; but that he refused to do so, notwithstanding there was ample time for that purpose. The affidavit of the under-sheriff in answer, denied collusion; and stated that before the writ of *fi. fa.* in question reached his hands, he had been concerned for certain creditors of the defendant; but it did not negative the fact, that he had made a communication, by which the issuing of the *fiat* had been accelerated.

[*719]

> *Barstow* now applied, on behalf of the sheriff, for an inter-
> pleader rule:

He submitted, that under these circumstances, the under-sheriff was justified in the course he had pursued. The Act 6 & 7 Vict. c. 73, having repealed the 22 Geo. II. c. 46, by the 14th section of which Act it was provided, that no under-sheriff or his deputy, should act as a solicitor, attorney, or agent, or set out any process at any place where he should execute the office of under-sheriff, under a penalty of 50*l.*; he was bound, both with a view to the interests of those clients, for whom he had been previously concerned, and also for

Cox
v.
BALNE.

the protection of the general creditors, when a *fiat* was about to issue, to make the communication in question.   *   *   *   The case is altogether different from that of *Dudden* v. *Long* (1), which at first sight might appear an authority against the present application.   *   *   *

[720]   WILLIAMS, J. :

There is no doubt that the facts in the case of *Dudden* v. *Long*, which has been referred to, were much stronger than in the present instance; but that case is important, as recognizing the principle on which an under-sheriff ought to act; namely, that of entire impartiality between the contending parties.   Though it is, no doubt, competent to the under-sheriff, under the statute referred to, to act as an attorney during his under-shrievalty; still he is not at liberty to take any steps which may have the effect of defeating a writ of execution which has been delivered into his hands.   *Mr. Barstow* admitted, and indeed it must be assumed, that the under-sheriff did, in fact, make the communication complained of; and in referring to the case of *Dudden* v. *Long*, which he very properly brought to my notice, attempted to distinguish it from the present. I think he has not done so successfully.   The under-sheriff had no right to make a communication, of which the effect might be to hasten, more or less, the issuing of the *fiat*, and he ought to have refrained from giving assistance to either party.   The rule on which

[*721]   the Courts act in cases of *laches*, shows how strictly they hold the sheriff to his duty before they consent to interpose in the manner now prayed for; and the reason on which that rule is founded, applies much more strongly to proceedings which may essentially affect the rights of parties who come to the sheriff for assistance. While the execution is pending, the under-sheriff's mouth ought to be closed : that has not been the case here.   The sheriff may resort to any other remedy which may be open to him, but he has not entitled himself to the one he now seeks.

Rule refused.

Barstow then applied for and obtained four days' time for the sheriff to make his return to the writ.

(1) 1 Bing. N. C. 299 ; 1 Scott, 281 ; 3 Dowl. 139.

TUNLEY AND HODSON v. EVANS.

(2 Dowl. & L. 747—752; S. C. 14 L. J. Q. B. 116.)

In an action for work and labour by A. and B., who were partners at the time that the cause of action accrued, the defendant put in evidence a letter written by C., who had since the transaction become a partner with B. in the room of A., admitting that the plaintiffs had given credit to another party : Held inadmissible, without proof that C. had authority from B. to make the statement.

THIS was an action of debt, to recover the value of work done and materials provided for the defendant, and for the carriage of the goods of the defendant, and for money due on an account stated : to which the defendant had pleaded the general issue. At the trial, which took place in October, at the Sheriff's Court in London, it appeared, on the case for the plaintiffs, that the plaintiffs were carriers by water, and the defendant a manufacturer of earthenware, who was in the habit of sending his goods by the plaintiff's boats. That the sum for which the action was brought, was a sum of 18*l.* 18*s.*, for the carriage of certain goods consigned by the defendant to his agent, Mr. Floyd : that on the arrival of those goods, the plaintiffs refused to deliver them to Mr. Floyd, unless he would give a guarantee for the amount of the freight; and that Mr. Floyd accordingly gave the following guarantee :

" To MESSRS. TUNLEY AND HODSON,

"GENTLEMEN,—I hold myself responsible for the boat load of bottles from Mr. Evans, of Ilkeston, which arrived at your wharf, May 22nd, 1843.

(Signed) " CHAS. FLOYD.

" May 25, 1843."

That at the time in question, the plaintiffs, Tunley and Hodson, were in partnership; that Hodson had since retired ; *and that the plaintiff, Tunley, and one Simpson, were now in partnership. On the part of the defendant, a letter written by Simpson to the defendant was put in, to the following effect :

[*748]

" LONDON, January 24, 1844.

" MR. EVANS,

"SIR,—Mr. Floyd informs me, you had arranged with Mr. Tunley to settle your account with him. I beg to say, that Mr. Tunley has said nothing to me on the subject ; if he had, it would make no difference, as we shall not look to you for the 18*l.* 18*s.* 0*d.*, for which Mr. Floyd is accountable. To oblige him I have renewed his bill with expenses, 19*l.* 7*s.* 2*d.*, for one month, due February 26th,

TUNLEY   1844.   Your claims upon us (you say) are 22*l*. 13*s*. 1*d*.   After
v.   making inquiries, I find there is not less than 15*l*. 17*s*. 2*d*. which
EVANS.   we shall not allow.   Your's, &c.

"   " JOHN SIMPSON.

"P.S.—I shall furnish Mr. Tunley with particulars of your account
in a few days."

The reception of this letter in evidence was objected to by the
plaintiffs, on the ground that it could not be evidence against the
plaintiffs, Simpson not being a partner at the time, and no authority
being shown to him to write it.   The learned Commissioner overruled the objection.   An invoice was then put in, signed by
Simpson, charging Floyd with an account of 18*l*. 18*s*. due to the
plaintiffs; and a bill of exchange, dated 13th November, 1843,
drawn by plaintiffs on Floyd, and accepted by Floyd, due 16th Jan.,
1844.   The plaintiffs then proved that the invoice had been made
out in Floyd's name, after he had given the above guarantee.   The
learned Commissioners left it to the jury to say, " to whom did the
plaintiffs originally look for payment, and to whom was the credit
given.   *Primâ facie*, the consignor was liable.   Did the mode of
proceeding here vary the *primâ facie* case?   If the plaintiffs held

[*749]   *the defendant liable originally, no subsequent substitution of
another would exempt him under his present plea and the issue
thereon; but if not originally liable, the defendant was entitled to
the verdict.   The jury having returned a verdict for the defendant,

Lush obtained a rule (1), calling on the defendant to show
cause why the verdict entered for the defendant should not be set
aside, and a verdict entered instead for the plaintiffs; or for a
new trial, on the ground of misdirection (2), and that the verdict
was against evidence (3).

Humfrey now showed cause:

It may be conceded that the defendant cannot put his case
higher, than by treating the admission of Simpson as the admission
of the managing clerk of the plaintiffs.   As such, it is submitted,
it was properly receivable in evidence.   A managing clerk must
have authority to make any admissions which would naturally

---

(1) In Michaelmas Term.
(2) This point was virtually given
up on the argument; as upon production of the sheriff's notes the

alleged misdirection did not appear in
his summing up.
(3) This point depended on the
success of the first.

occur in the course of carrying on the business.   An admission by TUNLEY *v.* EVANS. him of payment, or of the value or quantity of the goods furnished, would unquestionably be evidence against his employers ; because, payment to him would be sufficient, and because he has the care of conducting the business.   •   •   •

Lush, in support of the rule :

This was not such an admission, as it was within the province of a clerk, although managing the business, to make.   Even were it clear that a managing clerk could make an admission, with reference to whom credit was given by him in the course of managing the business, he could not, it is submitted, make an admission as to whom credit had been given, before he entered the business, as in the present case.   There may be an implied authority by a partner who retires to the remaining partner, to collect the debts and wind up the general affairs of the concern ; but there can be no authority presumed to make admissions destructive of his right to recover. The admission here is not strictly in the necessary conduct of the business : *Garth* v. *Howard* (1).   A recognition of the admission by Tunley might possibly render it binding : *Wood* v. *Braddick* (2) ; *Catt* v. *Howard* (3) : but here no evidence of any recognition has been given.   The renewal of the bill of Floyd may have been quite independent of any agreement of Simpson's.

Cur. adv. vult.

WIGHTMAN, J. :

This was a motion for a new trial, in a case tried at the Sheriff's Court in London, and in which •a verdict had passed for the defendant.   The grounds upon which the application was made were : first, that a certain letter, written by a person of the name of Simpson, had been improperly received in evidence ; secondly, that the Judge had misdirected the jury ; and thirdly, that the verdict was against evidence.   With respect to the second objection, I do not see upon the Judge's notes any foundation for it.   As regards the third ground, it depends upon the validity of the first objection ; for if the letter of Simpson were properly receivable in evidence, it is impossible to say that there was not sufficient evidence to warrant the jury in finding a verdict for the defendant.   The case will, therefore, resolve itself into a consideration of the first ground of

(1) 34 R. R. 753 (1 Moo. & Sc. 628;   (2) 9 R. R. 711 (1 Taunt. 104).
8 Bing. 451).   (3) 23 R. R. 751 (3 Stark. 3).

TUNLEY
v.
EVANS.

objection, which I am of opinion must prevail.   It appears that the letter in question was written by Simpson, who at the time of writing it was a partner of the plaintiff Tunley; but it has been conceded upon the argument, and I think rightly, that the case cannot be put higher than by treating him as the clerk of Tunley, and that the fact of his being a partner may be wholly rejected, as not affecting the present question.   Now when the cause of action accrued, Simpson was not the partner of the plaintiffs, nor is there any evidence that he was in any way connected with them; and the only question is, whether he can bind them by an admission made after his entry into partnership with Tunley, regarding a transaction which took place prior to that time.   In order to make a declaration by one party binding on another, it is necessary to show that the person was authorized, either generally in carrying on the business, or with reference to the particular transaction.   In the present instance, however, I do not find any evidence of such authority from Tunley to Simpson, with regard to this particular transaction, or any evidence by which such an implication should necessarily arise from the situation of clerk or partner; and no case has been cited which would show that he could bind the plaintiffs,

[*752]

either as clerk or partner, without such proof *being given.   It therefore appears to me, that the letter in question was not properly received in evidence, and the rule for a new trial must consequently be made absolute.

Rule absolute.

———◆———

1845.

[919]

In re HILLIARD(1).

(2 Dowl. & L. 919—921; S. C. 14 L. J. Q. B. 225; 9 Jur. 664.)

Where the attorney of the defendant had given an undertaking to pay the debt, in consequence of which the plaintiff stayed proceedings; the Court enforced the undertaking; although it was void under the 4th section of the Statute of Frauds.

A RULE had been obtained in last Term, calling upon an attorney of the name of Hilliard to show cause why he should not pay a sum of 29l., in pursuance of his undertaking.   It appeared that Hilliard had acted as attorney for the defendant in a cause of *Wennington* v. *Forrester;* and that on notice of trial being given the defendant consented to execute a *cognovit,* which Hilliard attested as his attorney.   It was asserted in the affidavits in support of the rule, and not contradicted, that Hilliard was aware, at the

(1) *In re Woodfin* and *Wray* (1882) 51 L. J. Ch. 427.

time of the execution of the *cognovit*, that the attestation was invalid for not following the form required by the 1 & 2 Vict. c. 110, s. 9. The plaintiff afterwards discovering that the attestation had been informal, obtained a Judge's order to set aside the *cognovit* and execution which had issued, without costs; which being done, he proceeded in the action. Negotiations were then entered into; by which the plaintiff agreed to stay proceedings, on Hilliard's giving a personal undertaking; which he did in the following form :

" I agree to pay to Mr. Samuel Smith within one calendar month from this day, the sum of twenty-nine pounds. Witness my hand, this thirtieth day of October, 1844.

" J. H. HILLIARD

The money having been demanded and not paid, the present rule had been obtained.

Martin now showed cause :

This is a promise to pay the debt of a third party, and is, there-fore, void under the 4th section of the Statute of Frauds. The meaning of that section is not that a contract, coming within its terms, shall stand for all purposes, except that of being enforced by action; but that the contract shall be altogether void: *Carrington* *v. Roots* (1). The Court will not, it is presumed, exercise a summary jurisdiction, to enforce a contract, which is void in law. * * *

[*920]

Gray, in support of the rule :

The Court may force an attorney in this way to do justice, independent of any binding contract in law. The case of *In re Greaves* (2) is precisely in point, and has been acted on in the two subsequent decisions which have been cited.

It was also acted on in the case of *In re Hayward* (3) in this Court.

Cur. adv. vult.

COLERIDGE, J. :

This was a rule to enforce the performance by an attorney of an undertaking to pay the sum of 29*l.* for his client; and the ground taken on the argument was that the contract was void by the

(1) 46 R. R. 583 (2 M. & W. 248).　　(3) H. T. 1841, not reported.
(2) 1 Cr. & J. 374, *n.*

In re
HILLIARD.

4th section of the Statute of Frauds, for want of a consideration appearing on the face of it. It was admitted, that in the case of *In re Greaves* (1), the same objection was made and overruled by the COURT; and that in two other cases, rules had been granted on the authority of that case, with some remark on it by the learned Judges, and made absolute without cause shown. And I have since been furnished with a case, not I believe reported, in which my brother WILLIAMS acted upon it in this Court, in Hilary Term, 1841 : *In re Hayward.*

Against this authority none was cited, and the argument used was founded entirely on considerations of contract. It seems to me

[*921]

that the Court does not interfere merely with *a view of enforcing contracts, on which actions might be brought, in a more speedy and less expensive mode; but with a view to securing honesty in the conduct of its officers, in all such matters as they undertake to perform or see performed, when employed as such, or because they are such officers. The Court acts on the same principle, whether the undertaking be to appear, to accept declaration, or other proceedings in the course of the cause, or to pay the debt and costs. It does not interfere so much as between party and party to settle disputed rights; as criminally to punish by attachment, misconduct, or disobedience in its officers. In this view, the objection relied on does not apply. I have no desire to narrow the jurisdiction of the Court as to these undertakings on any such ground as the present; they are very often most beneficially made for both parties in a cause, and there would be great injustice in letting the attorney loose from them, after the party has foregone the advantage or paid the price which was the consideration; while there is no hardship on the attorney in enforcing them; he is never compelled to enter into them; if he does, he should secure himself by his arrangement with his client, and he must be taken to know the legal consequences of his own act.

Rule absolute.

(1) 1 Cr. & J. 374, *n.*

NEWPORT *v.* HARDY.

(2 Dowl. & L. 921—924; S. C. 14 L. J. Q. B. 242.)

In an action of debt for use and occupation, the defendant may show, under the general issue, that J. S. had recovered a judgment in ejectment for the premises, and that to avoid being turned out of possession, he had attorned and paid the rent subsequently accruing due to J. S.: but he cannot, with respect to the rent previously due, set up as a defence under this plea, that he has paid it to J. S.

THIS was an action of debt for use and occupation, to which the defendant had pleaded the general issue. At the trial, which took place at the Sheriff's Court in London, the plaintiff proved a *primâ facie* case of rent due to the amount of 18*l.* 1*s.*, of which it was agreed that 2*l.* 14*s.* were due on the 27th May, 1844. The defence was, that one *Joshua Clark had in 1837 recovered judgment in ejectment for the premises against the casual ejector; which judgment was revived by *scire facias* on the 8th of May, 1844. On the 27th of May, the defendant had notice of these proceedings from Clark's solicitor, and was told that a writ of possession would be executed, and he would be turned out, unless he attorned and paid rent to him; whereupon he accordingly paid the sum of 2*l.* 14*s.*, being the rent then due, deducting taxes, and had continued since that time to pay the rent to Clark. It was objected that this defence was not available under the plea of the general issue; but the learned Commissioner directed the jury to find a verdict for the plaintiff, reserving to the defendant the liberty to move to enter a nonsuit, or to reduce the verdict to 2*l.* 14*s.*

[*922]

Tomlinson, having obtained a rule *nisi* accordingly;

Humfrey showed cause:

If a recoverer in ejectment stand in the same light as the mortgagee of the premises, it cannot be denied that the case of *Waddilove* v. *Barnett* (1) is an authority to show that as respects the rent accruing due subsequent to the notice to the defendant, the defence is open under the general issue. But that case is also an authority expressly in point, that with respect to the rent which had previously accrued, the defence should have been specially pleaded. The plaintiff, therefore, is entitled, at any rate, to the verdict for 2*l.* 14*s.*

Tomlinson, in support of the rule:

A mortgagee is entitled to by-gone rents, as well as such as

(1) 2 Bing. N. C. 538; 2 Scott, 763; 4 Dowl. 347.

subsequently accrue due: *Pope* v. *Biggs* (1) ; and a recoverer in ejectment stands upon the same footing.

(COLERIDGE, J. : *Pope* v. *Biggs* is only an authority that a mortgagee can recover *by-gone rents that remain unpaid.).

The present is even a stronger case than that of payment to a mortgagee ; for here there could be no election. The case of *Hodgson* v. *Gascoigne* (2) shows that the recovery in ejectment relates back to the date of the demise as laid in the declaration, and that the relation between landlord and tenant ceases from that time.

Cur. adr. rult.

COLERIDGE, J. (after stating the facts of the case as above):

Upon the argument it was not, I think, seriously contended that the judgment with notice, and the *bonâ fide* threat of a writ of possession followed by an attornment thereon to the recoverer in the ejectment, were not equivalent to an eviction ; so that the subsequent occupation was by his permission, and not by that of the plaintiff, the former landlord. And it was admitted, if that were so, that *Waddilove* v. *Barnett* (3) had decided that this might be given in evidence under *nunquam indebitatus ;* and that the action was answered as to the subsequently accruing rent. But the same case was relied on, to show that, with regard to the rent due before the notice, the defendant could only be discharged, if at all, by a special plea ; for that *de facto* the previous occupation had been by permission of the original landlord, the plaintiff, and that its character was not altered by the subsequent notice and attornment.

And unless there be some distinction, material to the present purpose, between the relation of the mortgagor and his tenant before notice, and that of the recoveree in a judgment in ejectment and his tenant before notice, this argument will be just. For the defendant it was contended that there was such a distinction ; and *Hodgson* v. *Gascoigne* (2) was relied on as showing, that from the day of the demise in the ejectment the defendant was a mere

*trespasser, and of course not liable to the payment of any rent as an occupier under contract, or by permission. That case decided, that where the landlord recovered in ejectment for a forfeiture against his tenant, the tenancy ceased from the day of the demise :

(1) 32 R. R. 665 (9 B. & C. 245;   (3) 2 Bing. N. C. 538 ; see *S. C.* 2
see *S. C.* 4 Man. & Ry. 193).   Scott, 763 ; 4 Dowl. 347.
(2) 24 R. R. 295 (5 B. & Ald. 88).

the landlord had treated the tenant as a trespasser from that day, and the judgment showed that he was so: consequently, the growing crops were his, not the tenant's, and he could not claim a year's rent, to be paid to him by the sheriff, under the statute of Anne, out of the goods seized under an execution at the suit of a third person, for that right was only given to a landlord in the case of an existing tenancy. This is a sound decision, but it concludes nothing as between the tenant, and a person, the apparent owner, under whom he has taken possession, and by whose permission *de facto*, he has occupied land. However infirm or merely colourable the title of Newport, he, in fact, gave possession to Hardy, and Hardy has occupied by his permission. And no consequences in law follow from the judgment in ejectment affecting these facts; whether it be considered as a judgment against Newport, or against Hardy, it leaves their relation to each other untouched. Now these two facts of possession had from Newport, and occupation by his permission, are all that are denied by the plea : the promise to pay is implied by law. If the defendant had intended to rely on the notice and eviction as furnishing a reason why he should not pay in spite of the occupation by plaintiff's permission, he should have pleaded them in confession and avoidance. *Waddilove* v. *Barnett* (1), therefore, seems to me to govern this case on both points. The rule, therefore, will be absolute to reduce the damages to 2*l.* 14*s.*, and discharged as to the remainder.

Rule accordingly.

HAWKYARD AND ANOTHER *v.* STOCKS AND OTHERS (2).

(2 Dowl. & L. 936—939; S. C. 14 L. J. Q. B. 236.)

A cause, after issue joined, having been referred to arbitration, but no power given to award a verdict; the arbitrator awarded a verdict to be entered for the defendants, and directed the plaintiffs and defendants respectively to execute mutual releases of all manner of actions, &c.: Held, that the award was bad for excess of authority, and that that portion of it ordering a verdict to be entered could not be rejected as redundant; since, if struck out, the meaning of the award would be altered.

An affidavit verifying a copy of the award to be a true copy, need not state that the copy has been compared with the original award.

Parties are not bound to take office copies of exhibits attached to affidavits.

THIS cause after issue joined, was referred by a Judge's order to arbitration, "the costs of the cause to abide the event, and the

(1) 2 Bing. N. C. 538; see S. C. 2 Scott, 763; 4 Dowl. 347.

(2) *Everest* v. *Ritchie* (1862) 7 H. & N. 698, 31 L. J. Ex. 350, 351.

HAWKYARD
v.
STOCKS.

[*937]

costs of the reference and award to be in the *discretion of the arbitrator;" but no power was given to direct a verdict to be entered.   The award, which was made "of and concerning the premises," directed that a verdict should be entered for the defendants on all the issues joined between the parties in the cause; and that the plaintiffs and the defendants should respectively bear and sustain the costs incurred by them respectively in and about this reference, and should respectively pay a moiety of the costs of the award; and that the plaintiffs and defendants should, respectively, on the request and at the costs and charges of the party requiring the same, sign and seal, and as their respective act and deed deliver, each unto the others of them, mutual general releases in writing, of all and all manner of action and actions, cause and causes of action, bills, bonds, covenants, debts, suits, specialties, controversies, claims and demands whatsoever.

A rule had been obtained in last Michaelmas Term, &c., to set aside the award on the following grounds:

1. That the arbitrator had not awarded on all the matters in difference between the parties, and that the award was not final.

2. That the arbitrator had exceeded his authority in awarding a verdict to be entered for the defendants.

The rule was drawn up on reading the affidavit of W. P. Dickson, clerk to the plaintiffs' agents, and the copy award, or umpirage thereto annexed.   Dickson deposed "that the paper writing hereunto annexed marked D, is a true copy of the award or umpirage of George Thompson Lister, of Bradford, in the county of York," &c., "as this deponent has been informed and believes:" and that he received the said paper writing from the plaintiffs' attorney in the country.

Addison now showed cause, and took a preliminary objection that, although, the affidavit of Dickson referred to a paper annexed, there was no such paper attached to the affidavit; and, therefore, the award was not before the Court; and *that another affidavit to which a copy was annexed, was not properly entitled in the cause, and, therefore, could not be used.   He cited *Sherry* v. *Oke* (1).   He also contended that the affidavit of Dickson, even had a copy of the award been annexed, was informal; as it should have stated that the copy of the award had been compared with the original.

[*938]

(1) 3 Dowl. 349.

Cowling, contrà :

This is only an office copy of the affidavit, and the practice now is not to take office copies of papers annexed to the affidavits. It is clear the award must have been attached to the original affidavit when sworn, or the rule could not have referred to it. The affidavit is sufficient in terms, as the party seeking to set aside the award, may have no opportunity of seeing the original.

COLERIDGE, J. :

The Master informs me that parties are not bound to take office copies of papers annexed to an affidavit. With respect to the objection, that the affidavit should have stated that the copy was compared with the original, it is a sufficient answer, that cases may frequently occur, where a party may never see the original award, but only have a copy furnished him.

Addison :

With regard to the award, it must be admitted that the arbitrator has exceeded his authority in directing a verdict to be entered for the defendants. But that portion of it may be treated as surplusage, and the award is sufficiently final without it; for the award of mutual releases would settle the costs in the action, and amounts to a *stet processus.* He referred to *Birks* v. *Trippet* (1), *Wharton* v. *King* (2), and *Wynne* v. *Edwards* (3).

Cowling, in support of the rule, was not called upon.

COLERIDGE, J. :

[939]

The costs of the cause were to abide the event of the award. By the award of a verdict for the defendants, the arbitrator must clearly have meant to give the defendants the costs; and the argument against the present rule is, that that intention is not inconsistent with the other parts of the award, if standing alone. But if I am to take no notice of that part of the award which directs the verdict to be entered for the defendants; then they will have to execute a release, and so lose the costs of the action which the arbitrator meant to give to them. The rule as to redundancy not vitiating an award, only applies where the redundant matter being struck out, the sense of the award remains the same. Here

(1) 1 Wms. Saund. 32.　　　　(3) 12 M. & W. 708; 1 Dowl. & L.
(2) 36 R. R. 643 (2 B. & Ad. 528).　　976.

HAWKYARD
v.
STOCKS.

the words in the release "all manner of actions," mean all manner of actions excepting this one; and, therefore, would not be final, if so much of the award as relates to the finding a verdict for the defendants were to be struck out. The arbitrator, it is admitted, has exceeded his authority in awarding a verdict to be entered; and, as that part cannot be rejected without altering the sense of the rest of the award, this rule must be made absolute.

Rule absolute.

1845.

[967]

In re GEORGE MORPHETT, JOHN MORPHETT, and WILLIAM WITHERDEN, and Others.

(2 Dowl. & L. 967—980; S. C. 14 L. J. Q. B. 259; 10 Jur. 546.)

By a deed of submission dated the 25th of August, 1840, between G. M., J. M., and W. W., as trustees and executors of G. M. deceased, &c., and also as trustees, &c., and R. M.; after reciting that disputes had arisen between the parties touching the estate and effects of G. M., deceased, and touching several other matters and things, the parties referred the same to the award of T. S. and J. J., and such third person as umpire as they should appoint, and agreed to abide by their award touching the premises or "any thing in any wise relating thereto." The arbitrators made an award directing that R. M. should pay a certain sum to G. M., J. M., and W. W., but not stating whether it was payable to them in their character of trustees and executors, &c. or of trustees, &c. They also directed that it should be payable with interest up to a day subsequent to the date of the award; and if not paid by that day, G. M., J. M. and W. W. were authorised to withhold the payment of a certain annuity, by the same award directed to be paid by them to R. M.; until out of the arrears of such annuity, the said sum should be liquidated: Held, that the arbitrators had exceeded their authority, and that the award was bad.

On the same day that the deed was executed, the arbitrators indorsed the following memorandum at the foot of it, in the presence of the parties: "Memorandum, that before proceeding with the within-mentioned arbitration, we appoint W. L. to be umpire in case we cannot agree about making our award; and that the said award is to be delivered on or before the 3rd day of November next:" Held, that they had no authority to limit the time, as the deed did not do so, so as to vitiate an award made subsequently to the time limited.

One of the parties to the deed had no notice of a meeting of the arbitrators, at which, however, no business was transacted beyond adjourning the meeting. He afterwards attended at a subsequent meeting, and delivered in a protest against the proceedings; but on another and distinct ground, than that of want of notice to attend the former meeting: Held, that the want of notice was, under the circumstances, no ground for setting aside the award.

BY a deed of submission, bearing date the 25th day of August, 1842, and made between George Morphett, John Morphett, and William Witherden, trustees and executors under the will of George Morphett, deceased, father of the said George Morphett, party thereto, of the first part; and George Morphett, John Morphett, and William Witherden, trustees of the estate and effects of Robert Morphett, one of the sons of the said George Morphett, deceased, of the second part; and the said Robert Morphett, of the third part; after reciting that differences had arisen and were depending between the said George Morphett, John Morphett, *and William [*968] Witherden, as trustees and executors as aforesaid, and the said Robert Morphett; and also between the said George Morphett, John Morphett, and William Witherden, as trustees as aforesaid, and the said Robert Morphett; touching the estate and effects of the said George Morphett, deceased, and also touching several other matters and things; and that, in order to put an end to the said differences, the said parties had agreed to refer the same to the award and determination of Thomas Smallfield and James Jenner; and that in case the said Thomas Smallfield and James Jenner should take upon themselves such arbitration, but should not agree in making an award, then the said Thomas Smallfield and James Jenner should mutually choose some third person to join with them in determining the said matters in dispute: The said George Morphett, John Morphett, and William Witherden, as trustees and executors as aforesaid, and the said George Morphett, John Morphett, and William Witherden, as trustees as aforesaid, and the said Robert Morphett, did, each for himself, severally and respectively, and for his several and respective heirs, executors and administrators, covenant and agree, &c., to observe and perform the award and determination of the said Thomas Smallfield and James Jenner, of and concerning the premises aforesaid, or any-thing in anywise relating thereto; and also of and concerning all actions, causes of action, suits, bills, bonds, specialties, covenants, contracts, promises, accounts, reckonings, sums of money, judg-ments, executions, extents, controversies, trespasses, damages, and demands whatsoever, both at law and in equity, at any time theretofore had, made, moved, brought, commenced, sued, prose-cuted, committed, or depending by or between the said parties, or any of them; so as the said award of the said arbitrators be made in writing, under their hands: or in case the said arbitrators should not agree in their award, then to observe and perform the award and determination of the said Thomas Smallfield and James Jenner, and of such third person so to be chosen as aforesaid, or any two of them; but so as such last-mentioned award *be made in writing, [*969] under the hands of the parties making the same.   The deed

contained the usual clause for making it a rule of Court. The costs
of the arbitration were to be in the discretion of the arbitrators, or
any two of them. And, for the full performance of the award so
to be made as aforesaid, the said parties bound themselves severally
and respectively, their several and respective heirs, executors, and
administrators, each to the other of them respectively, in the penal
sum of 500*l*.

On the same day that this deed was executed, the following
memorandum was indorsed on the deed, and signed by the
arbitrators in the presence of the parties : " Memorandum : that
before proceeding with the within-mentioned arbitration, we appoint
William Lansdell, of Benenden in the county of Kent, farmer, to
be umpire, in case we cannot agree about making our award ; and
that the said award is to be delivered on or before the third day
of November next."

It appeared from the affidavit of Thomas Smallfield, one of the
arbitrators, in support of the present application, that a meeting
was held on the same day that the deed was executed, and that
J. Jenner, the other arbitrator, raised a question as to a claim for
interest on certain monies alleged to be due from the said Robert
Morphett to the said executors and trustees ; and that it was on
such occasion stated, by all the several parties to the submission,
and by all of them admitted, that no claim was intended to be made
against the said Robert Morphett, for interest upon any sum or
sums which might be found to be due from, or to have been
advanced to him ; and that the question of interest was not
therefore a matter in dispute, or one to which the attention or
adjudication of the said arbitrators was required. That a further
meeting took place on the 3rd of November, at which Lansdell was
present, when Jenner again renewed the question of interest, and
that a very partial investigation of this matter took place, because
Smallfield refused to enter on that question. Another meeting
took place on *the 10th of April, which was adjourned, as Smallfield did not attend. That a lengthened correspondence took place
between the parties, and that Smallfield had had no notice of any
meeting for the purpose of considering the award, after one which
was fixed for the 24th of August, and at which he did not attend.
From the affidavit of Robert Morphett, it also appeared that the
question of interest was not in dispute, or intended to be referred
by the parties to the deed. That he had no notice of, nor attended
at any meeting after that of the 3rd of November, 1842, except the

[*970]

one on the 24th of August, 1843, when he delivered in a protest to the following effect: "To MR. WILLIAM LANSDELL. SIR, I do hereby deny the right or power of Mr. James Jenner as one of the arbitrators in a case of reference between me and the executors of my late father, to put or refer to you for your decision any question or matter relating to interest on the account between the said executors and me, and also deny your right or power in any way to decide or give your opinion thereon, as it is not within his or your jurisdiction, the matters relating thereto having long since been agreed on by me and them that no interest should be paid, and the parties acknowledged the same to be true at the time of our signing the submission, and giving power to Messrs. Jenner and Smallfield as the arbitrators; and I protest against the proceedings. I am, Sir, yours obediently, ROBERT MORPHETT. August, 24, 1843." There was no protest, however, on the ground that the time for making the award had elapsed.

It was distinctly denied in the affidavits filed in opposition to this rule, that there was any understanding or agreement that the question of interest, due from Robert Morphett to the trustees and executors, should not be gone into. It was distinctly asserted, that Robert Morphett had notice of all the meetings except that of the 10th of April, 1843, at which, however, nothing was done, and no matter discussed but the question of adjournment.

In consequence of Smallfield's refusal to join in making *the award, Lansdell and Jenner, on the 15th of April, 1844, made the following award:

After reciting the deed of submission, it continued thus: "And whereas we the said Thomas Smallfield and James Jenner, by virtue of the authority given by the said recited indenture, did nominate and appoint the said William Lansdell to act with them (1) in the said reference, before they (1) proceeded with the same; and whereas the said Thomas Smallfield having acted with us, the said William Lansdell and James Jenner, in the said reference, and having proceeded with the same, did decline to agree with us or either of us, in making an award, and left us to proceed alone to determine the said matters. Now know ye, that we, the said William Lansdell and James Jenner, having taken upon ourselves the charge of the said award, and having heard and considered the several allegations, accounts, vouchers, and proofs brought before us, by and on behalf of the said parties respectively, do find that

[*971]

(1) *Sic.*

the said Robert Morphett, on the 10th day of December, 1842, duly
passed, allowed, and signed an account relating to the estate and
effects of the said George Morphett, deceased, and admitted that
the principal sum to which the children of the said Robert Morphett
are entitled on his decease, and in respect of which the said trustees
and executors are, by the will of the said George Morphett, deceased,
proved in the Prerogative Court of Canterbury, on the 10th day of
December, 1818, required to pay the interest arising therefrom to
the said Robert Morphett, during the term of his life, amounted to
the sum of 380*l.* 17*s.* 10*d.*   And (subject as hereinafter mentioned),
we do award that the said Robert Morphett is entitled to the sum
of 304*l.* 13*s.* 4*d.* for sixteen years' interest on the said principal
sum of 380*l.* 17*s.* 10*d.*, calculated up to Michaelmas, 1842; and
that there is due to the said Robert Morphett the further sum of

[*972]

130*l.* 4*s.*, as a compensation in the nature of sixteen *years' interest,
also calculated up to Michaelmas, 1842, in respect of the said sum
of 304*l.* 13*s.* 4*d.*, which has not been paid to the said Robert
Morphett, and that the total sum due to the said Robert Morphett,
from the said trustees and executors, up to the period last aforesaid, amounts to 434*l.* 17*s.* 4*d.*   And we do award, order, and direct
that the said sum of 434*l.* 17*s.* 4*d.*, shall be applied and retained by
the said trustees and executors, for the purpose and in the manner
hereinafter mentioned.   And we do also find, that on the 15th day
of February, 1823, the said Robert Morphett duly passed, allowed,
and signed an account between himself and the said trustees and
executors, whereby he acknowledged to be due from him to the said
trustees and executors, for money lent and advanced by them to
him up to Michaelmas, 1822, the sum of 330*l.* 2*s.* 11*d.*   And we do
accordingly award such last-mentioned sum to be due from the said
Robert Morphett to the said trustees and executors, together with
the further sum of 330*l.* 2*s.* 11*d.* for twenty years' interest thereon,
calculated up to Michaelmas, 1842, and making together the full
sum of 660*l.* 5*s.* 10*d.*   And we do further award that there is
due from the said Robert Morphett to the said George Morphett,
J. Morphett, and William Witherden, in respect of the matters
relating to the trust estate and effects of him the said Robert
Morphett, the sum of 50*l.* 3*s.* 11¾*d.*, and also the further sum of
40*l.* 2*s.* 8*d.*, for sixteen years' interest thereon, calculated up to
Michaelmas, 1842, and making together the full sum of 90*l.* 6*s.* 7¾*d.*,
which last-mentioned sum being added to the before-mentioned
sum of 660*l.* 5*s.* 10*d.*, makes the sum of 750*l.* 12*s.* 5¾*d.*   And we do

award that the total amount due up to Michaelmas, 1842, from the
said Robert Morphett to the said George Morphett, John Morphett,
and William Witherden, in their respective characters of trustees
and executors, and trustees as aforesaid, is the said sum of
750*l*. 12*s*. 5¾*d*. And we do further award, order, and direct that
the said sum of 434*l*. 17*s*. 4*d*. hereinbefore awarded to be due to
the said Robert Morphett, *shall be retained by the said George
Morphett, John Morphett, and William Witherden, and applied by
them in part payment to them of the said sum of 750*l*. 12*s*. 5¾*d*.,
hereinafter awarded to be due to the said George Morphett, John
Morphett, and William Witherden. And, accordingly, we do hereby
award, that upon the whole of the said accounts to Michaelmas,
1842, there is a balance in favour of, and to the said George
Morphett, John Morphett, and William Witherden, from the said
Robert Morphett, amounting to 315*l*. 15*s*. 1¾*d*. And we do award,
order, and direct, that the said Robert Morphett shall pay the said
sum of 315*l*. 15*s*. 1¾*d*., with interest thereon, to be computed from
Michaelmas, 1842, to the said George Morphett, John Morphett,
and William Witherden, or the survivors or survivor of them, or
the executors or administrators of such survivor, on or before the
1st day of June next. And upon such last-mentioned payment
being duly made at the time last aforesaid, we do likewise award,
order, and direct that the said George Morphett, John Morphett,
and William Witherden, shall immediately thereupon pay to the
said Robert Morphett, one year's interest, from Michaelmas, 1842,
to Michaelmas, 1843, on the before-mentioned sum of 380*l*. 17*s*. 10*d*.,
with a further compensation in the nature of interest, upon the
amount of such one year's interest, from Michaelmas, 1843, to the
time of such payment being made. And we do likewise award,
order, and direct that if the said Robert Morphett shall make
default in such payment as he is awarded, ordered, and directed to
make on the said 1st day of June next, the said George Morphett,
John Morphett, and William Witherden, or the survivors or survivor of them, or the executors or administrators of such survivor,
shall withhold and retain the amount of the interest payable to the
said Robert Morphett in respect of the aforesaid principal sum of
380*l*. 17*s*. 10*d*., in each and every year, from Michaelmas, 1842,
during the life of the said Robert Morphett, until, so far as can be,
the said balance of 315*l*. 15*s*. 1¾*d*., with *interest thereon, from
Michaelmas, 1842, to the time of payment or satisfaction shall have
been fully paid and satisfied ; the said Robert Morphett being also

*In re
MORPHETT.*

[*973]

[*974]

allowed credit for interest upon every such annual payment from Michaelmas last, so to be withheld and retained for the purpose and in manner aforesaid. And we also find there is a balance in the hands of the said trustees and executors forming part of the residuary estate of the said George Morphett, deceased, of 168*l*. 16*s*. 9½*d*., which, with interest thereon, amounting to 79*l*. 14*s*. 5*d*., amounts in the whole to 248*l*. 11*s*. 2½*d*., and is to be applied according to the trusts relating to such residuary estate, contained in the will of the said George Morphett, deceased." It then awarded mutual releases between the parties, " for the said sum of 434*l*. 17*s*. 4*d*., hereinbefore awarded to be due, and to be retained and applied as aforesaid ; " and directed that the costs of the award should be borne by the parties in equal moieties; and that upon performance of this award all differences and disputes in anywise subsisting by and between the said parties, or any of them, previous to the day of the date of the said indenture touching the premises should ultimately cease and determine.

In Trinity Term, 1844, a rule was obtained on behalf of Robert Morphett, to set aside the above award, on the following grounds :

First. That the award was not made within the time limited by the parties for the arbitrators to make their award.

Secondly. That the award embraced matters, namely, an award of interest, which the parties agreed not to be a matter in dispute in the arbitration, and which in fact was not a matter in dispute in the arbitration.

Thirdly. That the award is bad in embracing matters beyond the submission, namely, on the arbitrators awarding interest up to Michaelmas, 1842, and interest to Michaelmas, 1843, being for a period after the submission, and in stating the amount up to Michaelmas, 1842.

[975]   Fourthly. That Robert Morphett had no notice of the meeting.

Fifthly. That Thomas Smallfield had not notice of the several meetings between the other two arbitrators, Jenner and Lansdell ; particularly subsequent to August, 1843, and an opportunity of discussing the matters before the arbitrators.

Bramwell now showed cause :

[He argued that there was no time limited by the submission within which the award was to be made ; that the award might therefore be made at any time; and that the submission was sufficiently wide to include the question of interest. He cited *In re Hick* (1) and other cases.]

W. H. Watson, in support of the rule :

It was not necessary to notice the limitation of time in the rule. If it had been by parol, it clearly could not have been done.

(COLERIDGE, J. : That brings it to the question whether the parties could limit the terms of a submission by deed, by any agreement of a less formal character.)

The parties here acquiesced in the arrangement, as may be inferred from their silence at the time, and their subsequently attending such of the meetings as were held within the time limited. The award is, however, clearly bad for awarding interest up to a date subsequent to that of the award. * * It is not asserted that Smallfield had any notice of the meeting at which the award was signed, and it must be taken that there was a meeting for that purpose.

(COLERIDGE, J.: That ground of objection is not stated in the *rule.)

It is stated in the last ground of objection that he had no "opportunity of discussing the matters before the arbitrators."

COLERIDGE, J. :

As to the first and fourth grounds of objection, I see no reason for setting aside this award. Whether Robert Morphett had notice of the meeting on the 10th of April, 1843, or not, is perhaps immaterial ; for nothing was done at that meeting beyond adjourning the inquiry into the matters to a future day. I should not be inclined to accede to this objection, even if the party had protested expressly on this ground ; but when we find that he attended at a subsequent meeting on the 24th of August, and handed in a protest on a totally different ground, I think he must be taken to have waived the objection. With respect to the objection that the award is beyond the time limited by the parties, the answer is that no time was limited by the parties in the deed. It appears that, at the first meeting that was held, the two arbitrators agreed to appoint a third arbitrator, and that he was accordingly appointed,

(1) 21 R. R. 511 (8 Taunt. 694).

and took his authority under the deed of submission. If that be
so, the two arbitrators had no authority without his concurrence
to limit a time, so as to render an award made after that time
invalid. But independently of this, I think that even the three
together could not, in the absence of some power so to do, limit
the time for making their award. It is said, however, that the
parties to the deed have by their silence acquiesced in this arrangement. But the answer is that their intentions are expressed by
the deed, which limits no time, and that the deed cannot be altered
by a parol agreement. It is clear that this was a mere arrangement by the arbitrators amongst themselves as to the time of
making their award, and was not intended to limit their authority.
Certainly no point would have been made of it, if other objections
had not arisen.

[978]   With respect to the other grounds of objection, I will take time
to consider them.

Cur. adv. vult.

COLERIDGE, J. :

This was a rule for setting aside an award. Some of the
grounds on which it was moved, I disposed of when argued; it
will only be necessary for me to consider one of those which
remain, because I have been unable to overcome the difficulty
which it presents to the sustaining the award.

The rule states it thus : "the award is bad in embracing matters
beyond the submission, viz., in the arbitrators awarding interest
up to Michaelmas, 1842, and interest to Michaelmas, 1843, being
for a period after the submission, and in stating the amount to
Michaelmas, 1842."

The submission is dated in August, 1842, and is of all existing
differences, and "anything in anywise relating thereto." These
last words were relied on, as extending the power of the arbitrators
to matters arising after the submission ; but they clearly have no
such effect, the matters relating to the existing differences must
themselves exist at the same time with the existing differences.

The objection is very weakly stated in the rule. It would seem
to be a very slight excess, if any, to calculate the accounts between
the parties to the next quarter day beyond the submission ; and to
direct the payment of the interest on the principal so calculated,
on the Michaelmas of that and the following year, would seem to
be no excess, or, at all events, one that might be rejected without

prejudice to the rest of the award. But in order to understand the force of the objection, the circumstances must be stated, and then the scheme of the award considered, from which it will appear that the arbitrators have misunderstood entirely, and therefore exceeded the limits of their power.

Robert Morphett, the party applying, is the son of George Morphett, deceased, of whose will the three persons, parties *on the other side are executors and trustees. Robert Morphett appears to have become embarrassed, and the same three persons are the trustees of his affairs under some deed. Under the father's will, a sum of money was bequeathed to the trustees, the interest of which was to be annually paid to Robert Morphett, for his life, the principal to go to his children on his death. This sum appears to have been agreed to amount to 380l. 17s. 10d.; it further appears, that many years ago the trustees and executors advanced to him, out of the testator's estates, the sum of 330l.; no interest appears to have been paid to him for sixteen years before the submission, nor any by him for twenty years.

[*979]

This account was the first subject of difference between the parties—collateral to this was a difference respecting a sum many years since advanced to him by the trustees, of 50l. 8s. 11¾d., on which no interest had been paid for sixteen years, nor is it said out of what fund it was advanced, but I presume out of that which his own effects had created.

These are the facts found by the arbitrators in their award, and, under the terms of the submission, the utmost limit of their power would be to ascertain the respective principal sums due from Robert Morphett, and whether they were to carry any and what interest, and from what period; to ascertain the principal sum to the interest of which he was entitled; for how many years his claim to that interest was to be carried back, and at what rate; and whether he was entitled to consider each year's interest withheld as a principal loan, bearing interest, to be set off against that which he was to pay. Having ascertained all these particulars up to the date of the submission, their duty would have been to direct the payment by him of the balance forthwith, or at a future time or times.

This would have made a final end, as far as in them lay, of the differences referred; but the arbitrators appear to have considered that they had a right to deal with all these *respective accounts without reference to the date of the submission, and to regulate

[*980]

the future dealings of the parties with regard to them, as if those had been expressly placed within their power. The consequence has been that the award having ascertained balances due from Robert Morphett, on both accounts, down to Michaelmas, 1842, consolidates them into one sum, directs that on that Michaelmas Day and the following, interest shall be paid upon it, without distinguishing between the two characters in which the same persons were entitled to it, nor the funds to which it was properly to be referred. It further directs, that this consolidated sum shall be paid on the 1st of June, 1844, and then makes the payment by the executors of the interest on the legacy to Robert Morphett, indefinitely, during his whole life, dependent, first, on his paying the specified interest at Michaelmas, 1842, and 1843, and, secondly, on his paying off the principal consolidated sum on the 1st of June, 1844. No provision is made for dividing this sum between the two funds to which it belongs, nor any for the payment of interest after Michaelmas, 1843, if it remains unpaid after June, 1844.

It is quite obvious that this complicated, and yet imperfect arrangement, made to commence from a period beyond the submission, and carried on, it may be, through the whole life of one of the parties, and with regard to the others, extending to survivors, and the executors of the survivor, is beyond the powers conferred by the submission. My doubt has been, whether the objection has been properly stated in the rule—imperfectly it certainly has been—but the stating the amount at a period beyond the submission, is in itself, an excess, which forms a part of the whole, a part which I am unable to separate from it—the same may be said of the award of the interest, made up as that is of a sum improperly consolidated from two sources.

I am of opinion, therefore, that this objection must prevail, and the rule will be absolute.

Rule absolute.

CASAMAJOR *v.* STRODE (1).

1843.
Nov. 17, 18.
—
Chancery.
SHADWELL,
V.-C.
[14]

(8 Jurist, 14—15.)

Will—Construction—Vested legacy.

Bequest to trustees, upon trust for the six children (by name) of L. F., deceased, for their respective lives, and the capital equally among the children of each tenant for life, *per stirpes*, to be paid at twenty-one or marriage; and if any of said six children should die without leaving any children or child, then over: Held, a vested indefeasible interest in each child of a tenant for life, on attaining twenty-one.

W. STRODE, having, by his will, bequeathed three-fourths of his stocks, funds, and securities, upon certain trusts, proceeded in the following terms: "And as to such remaining fourth part or share of the said stocks, funds, or securities, and the dividends, interest, or annual proceeds thereof, I will and direct that my said trustees, and the survivor of them, and the executors, administrators, and assigns of such survivor, shall stand possessed thereof, upon trust to divide such remaining fourth share into six equal parts, for the benefit of John Fowler, Esq., Levine, the wife of John Perkins, Esq., Robert Fowler, Elizabeth, then the wife of William Desborough, William Fowler, and Henry Fowler, the six children of Levine Fowler, deceased, the other of the said four nieces of the said John Leman and the children or issue of such six children, in manner following: that is to say, to pay the interest or dividends, or one of such six shares, to each of them the said six children during their respective lives; but I direct that the interest or dividends on the said two sixth shares of the said William Fowler and Henry Fowler shall accumulate and increase the capital until they respectively attain the age of twenty-five years, at which period I direct that such interest or dividends, as well of the accumulation as of the original capital, shall begin to be paid to them; and I will and direct that the interest of the shares of the said Levine Perkins and Elizabeth Desborough shall be for their sole and separate use, independent of the debts, control, or engagements of their husbands; and that in case the said John Perkins should survive the said Levine, his wife, the interest or dividends of the said sixth part of the said Levine shall be paid to the said John Perkins during his life; and I direct that the capital of the said sixth parts shall, upon the respective deaths of the persons entitled to the dividends thereon, become divisible equally among the children of each such person, (such children taking *per stirpes*), the shares of sons to be paid at the age of twenty-one years, and the shares of daughters at

(1) *In re Ball* (1888) 40 Ch. Div. 11, 14, 57 L. J. Ch. 493.

57—2

that age or marriage, with benefit of survivorship and accruer in the meantime, and with power for his said trustees to advance such sums of money as they should think proper for maintenance, education, and advancement in the world. And I further will and direct, that, in case any or either of the said six children shall die without leaving any children or child, that the share or shares of them, him, or her so dying shall survive and go over to the survivors or survivor of them, for their, his, and her lives and life, and the child or [*15] children of such of them as should be then dead *leaving issue, and the capital of the share or shares of such survivor or survivors shall, upon his, her, or their death or deaths, become divisible among their children equally, in the same manner as their own original shares, the children in all cases taking according to the share of their parents."   One of the tenants for life had died without issue; another had died leaving children who had attained twenty-one, and who had received their parent's share.   The other tenants for life were still living and having children, some of which children had attained twenty-one, and others not.   The shares in the funds had been carried over to the separate account of the various tenants for life, and a petition in the cause was now presented by one of the tenants for life, who was a widow and of the age of sixty-one, and one of her children who had attained twenty-one, praying an immediate transfer to that child of his portion of his mother's share, or that his portion should be transferred from the separate account of the mother to the joint account of himself and his mother, with liberty for him to apply for payment of the same upon the death of his mother.

Stuart and Parry, for petitioners:

The vested interest expressly given to the children in the first part of the will cannot be taken away by implication. We submit that the words " without leaving " must be construed as " without having had " : Powis v. Burdett (1), Maitland v. Chalie (2). The power to trustees for advancement would enable them entirely to defeat the limitation over, even if valid.

James Parker and Gipps, for children of a deceased tenant for life, whose interest it was to contend that the shares of the children did not vest until the death of their respective parents:

Maitland v. Chalie is not in point, and Powis v. Burdett was a case

(1) 7 R. R. 259 (9 Ves. 428).   (2) 23 R. R. 209 (6 Madd. 243, and cases there cited).

of portions where the rule is different. It "leaving" is to be construed as "having," then, if a tenant for life dies having children,
who afterwards die under twenty-one, there would be an intestacy,
(which the Court does not favour), unless "children" be construed
as "such children." To do all this, would be making, not expounding,
the will. The very power of advancement relied on by the other
side shows the testator's intention that the children's shares should
not be vested in the lifetime of the parents.

Paton, for other parties, took no other part in the argument
than submitting, that, if the Court could not construe the words
"without leaving" as "without having had," then, in case any
tenant for life died leaving no children, but leaving grandchildren,
it might be a question whether the limitation over took effect, and
whether the word children would not be held to mean issue: Wythe
v. Thurlston (1), Gale v. Bennett (2), Wyth v. Blackman (3).

THE VICE-CHANCELLOR:

The difficulty upon this will has been created by the bequest
being in a lump to the six children. If the testator had made a
limitation to one of the six, and then said he gave the remaining
five-sixths, each in the same manner, to the other five children, it
would have been a different thing; but, for the sake of brevity, he
has introduced an obscurity, for the clause is, "And I direct that
the capital of the said six parts shall, upon the respective deaths of
the persons entitled to the dividends thereon, become divisible
equally among the children of each such person, (such children
taking per stirpes)," &c. It is plain that that is an absolute gift, to
the children of each child, of a sixth of the fourth; and the words
"per stirpes" are just as applicable to children attaining twenty-one
in the lifetime of the parent, as to children who survive the parent.
Nothing can be more clear than that this gives a vested interest to
the children upon their attaining twenty-one or marriage. The
testator then goes on, "And I further will and direct, that, in case
any or either of the said six children of the said Levine Fowler
shall die without leaving any children or child, that the share or
shares of them, him, or her, so dying, shall survive and go over to
the survivors or survivor of them, for their, his, and her lives and
life, and the child or children of such of them as should be then

(1) Amb. 555.   (3) 1 Ves. 197.
(2) Id. 681.

CASAMAJOR
v.
STRODE.

dead leaving issue," &c. Now, *Mr. Parker* says that that clause prevents an absolute indefeasible interest from vesting in any child until it survives the parent. But that is begging the question ; and I think, that that is not the meaning of the testator is clear from the subsequent words, "And the capital of the share or shares of such survivor or survivors shall, upon their, his, or her death or deaths, become divisible among their children equally, in the same manner as their own single shares," &c., which lets in all the previous provisions which he had used with reference to the original shares. It seems to me that this case is not distinguishable from the case of *Maitland* v. *Chalie*, and that it requires very strong words to take away the effect of a prior clear vested gift.

Declare, that the children of tenants for life take vested inde-feasible interests on attaining twenty-one, whether in the lifetime of parent or not.

———

1843.
Dec. 11.
———

Chancery.
SHADWELL,
V.-C.
[92]

BOWES *v.* STRATHMORE (1).

(8 Jurist, 92—94.)

Trustees—Implied power.

Trustees under a will of real estates, the surplus rents and profits of which, during minority, &c., were to be invested in the purchase of other real estates, to go as the devised estates, expended very large sums of the surplus rents and profits in repairing houses, building houses, draining and fencing farms, and other similar improvements: Held, that they were entitled to be allowed those sums in their discharge; the will containing this general direction, during minority, &c., " that the said trustees or trustee, for the time being, of the same term, do and shall, generally, superintend the management of the same manors, hereditaments, and premises, and appoint such stewards, bailiffs, agents, and collectors, and with such salaries as they shall think proper," &c.

THE question upon this petition arose upon the will of the Right Hon. John Bowes, late Earl of Strathmore, dated the 3rd July, 1817 ; and the question was, whether the trustees of the will were to be allowed, in their discharge, various large sums of money expended by them in building and repairing farm-houses, draining, fencing, liming, sinking wells, and other expenditures, not of a permanent nature. The testator, by his will, limited a term of 1,000 years in all his real estates to the trustees, preceding the limitations to his son, the present petitioner, in strict settlement. The will directed the surplus rents and profits, after the payment of various annual charges therein mentioned, to be invested by the

(1) See now Settled Land Acts, 1882, s. 21, and 1890, s. 13.

trustees in the purchase of other real estates, to be settled upon the
same trusts as the devised estates.   The will contained a direction
to the trustees to cut all such timber as should be in a state of
decay, or which ought to be cut down for the improvement of other
timber and trees, and to apply so much of such timber as should be
required for the rebuilding or repairs of all or any of the houses or
buildings upon any part of the manors and premises, and to sell
the rest of such timber; the proceeds to be invested in the same
manner as the surplus rents and profits above mentioned.   The will
did not give any express authority to the trustees to expend any
part of the rents and profits upon repairs and improvements, except
as contained in the following passage of the will : "And, upon this
further trust, that the said trustees or trustee, for the time being,
of the said term of 1,000 years, do and shall, during the minority
of my said son or reputed son, John Bowes, with and out of the
annual rents and profits of the said manors, &c., in the first place
keep and preserve in good repair, order, and condition, my said
castle, capital messuage or mansion-house, called Streatlam Castle,
and also my capital messuage or mansion-house called *Gibside,   [93]
and the offices, park, chapel, ornamental buildings, gardens,
pleasure-grounds, and appurtenances thereto respectively belonging,
and such of the adjacent lands now in my own occupation as the
said trustees or trustee shall think proper to be held therewith
respectively," &c.   In a subsequent part, the will contained the
following clause, in reference to the trust of the 1,000 years:
"Upon this further trust, that, during the minority of my said son
or reputed son, John Bowes, and also during such time or respective
times as, in consequence of the trusts of the said term or (1) 1,000
years, the person for the time being entitled, under the limitations
hereinbefore contained, to the first estate for life, or in tail male,
immediately expectant upon the said term, shall not be entitled to
the rents and profits of the manors, hereditaments, and premises
comprised in the same term, or any part thereof, other than or
besides the annual sum hereinafter provided, the said trustees or
trustee for the time being of the same term do and shall, generally,
superintend the management of the same manors, hereditaments,
and premises, and appoint such stewards, bailiffs, agents, and
collectors, and with such salaries and allowances, as they, the said
trustees or trustee, shall think proper."   The testator died on the
3rd July, 1820.   In the course of the cause, which was instituted

(1) *Sic.*

for the purpose of having the direction of the Court in carrying out
the trusts of the will, various references were made at different
periods to the Master, to inquire into the quantity and value of the
timber trees which ought to be cut, and into the state of the property with respect to repairs of houses, buildings, &c., and, generally,
as to the state of the entire property.   Much evidence was produced
before the Master, showing the very bad state of the property, and
the impossibility of the tenants' dwelling on or occupying their
farms, in consequence of the bad state in which the farm-houses
were, and also in consequence of the want of draining and fencing,
&c. upon their farms.   And it appeared that the value of the timber
which was proper to be cut was altogether insufficient for the
purpose of defraying the expense of the repairs and improvements
which the estate required.   Amongst other things, it had been
referred to the Master to inquire whether it would be proper that
the trustees should apply for an Act of Parliament to enable them
to raise money for the purposes of the repairs ; but the Master
reported that he did not consider it necessary for them to do so.
No order had been made by the Court, authorising the trustees to
expend rents and profits of the estate in draining, fencing, liming,
or certain other particulars mentioned in the Master's report ; but
they, of their own accord, expended large sums of the surplus rents
and profits for those purposes and the other particulars mentioned
in the Master's report, dated 28th March, 1848, whereby he found,
amongst other things, that several sums of money had been laid
out and expended by the orders of the trustees, or some of them, in
erecting farm-houses and other buildings, and in the repairs of
farm-houses and other buildings upon the testator's estate called
the Streatlam and Highland estate, and that the same, as far as it
was practicable, had been laid out and expended upon such farm
buildings and erections, and repairs of old farm-houses and other
buildings, in the manner mentioned in, and according to the directions of, the said order, dated the 12th day of February, 1824, and
that the several sums of money mentioned and set forth in the first
schedule to his said report, amounting to the sum of 19,785l. 14s. 5d.
had been properly laid out and expended in such erections and
repairs.   And the Master further found, that several sums of money
had been laid out and expended by the order of the trustees, or
some of them, in draining and fencing the said Streatlam and
Highland estate, and also in sinking wells at Streatlam Castle
aforesaid, and in making and sinking wells and pumps on the same

estate, and in cutting Sudburn and Alwent Bicks, and erecting the
bridge, and forming, repairing, and altering the roads; and that
the said several sums of money which had been so properly laid out
and expended in the several matters last mentioned and referred to
were contained in the second schedule to his said report, amounting
to the sum of 7,255l. 9s. 9d., and which had been carried to the
discharge of the trustees. This petition was presented by the
plaintiff, John Bowes, the tenant for life, and it prayed that the
Master's report might be confirmed.

Koe and *Kinglake*, for the petition.

Chandless and *Roundell Palmer*, for some of the trustees:

The question here is analogous to a tenant for life granting leases
under a power. Where a tenant for life has power to grant leases,
he may do so upon the terms of the tenant repairing: *Shannon* v.
Bradstreet (1). Indeed, that case goes further than the present, for
that was the case of a tenant for life, with power to let at the best
rent, and no doubt the tenant would have given a better rent, if he
had not been bound to repair; but the present is the case of trustees,
who have no beneficial interest whatever; they might have let the
land to tenants who were bound to repair, in which case they would
have paid so much less, and the rents and profits would have been
proportionably less. They cited also *Hibbert* v. *Cooke* (2).

Cole, for another of the trustees. ✱ ✱ ✱

Calvert, for Lord Glamis, the first tenant in tail:

There is nothing in any of the orders to sanction the order which
is now asked. The orders were without prejudice to Lord Glamis.
The petition omits stating that the surplus rents and profits were
to be invested, and that Lord Glamis is interested in them. Sums
amounting to 27,000l. have been already allowed to the trustees for
permanent repairs, &c.; but the question now is, whether these
other sums, assuming the character of present improvements, are
to be allowed, the whole of the expense having come out of the
rents and profits: draining is only good for twenty years, and
liming not for so long a period. The only fund that the testator
pointed out to be applied for repairs was the proceeds of timber
which should be cut; and the inference from that is, that no other
money was to be applied in repairs. The orders of reference only

(1) 9 R. R. 4 (1 Sch. & Lef. 52).　　(2) 24 R. R. 225 (1 Sim. & St. 552).

BOWES
v.
STRATH-
MORE.

related to the question of cutting timber for that purpose ; and if
the proceeds of the timber should be insufficient for the repairs,
then, as to the propriety of applying to Parliament to enable the
trustees to raise money for the repairs. The report, therefore, of the
Master was not warranted by the orders which have been made in the
cause. He cited *Bostock* v. *Blakeney* (1), as showing that the trustees
had no right to be allowed the sums for the repairs in question.

THE VICE-CHANCELLOR :

I entirely agree, *Mr. Calvert*, with what you say as to the effect
of the orders. I do not think that what has been done can be
sanctioned merely by the form of the orders ; that is to say, the
orders were not made in such a form prospectively to sanction, or
by retrospection to approve of, what had been done. The question
is, whether, under the general direction to superintend and manage,
which is a direction given by the will, the trustees have not general
authority to do that which, I cannot but myself collect from the
will, must have been the testator's intention. You see the will is
framed in such a manner as to show the testator was, first of all,
looking at the improved state of certain buildings, which, together
with certain lands, were in his possession. The expression is,
"and with and out of the annual rents and profits of the said
premises, in the first place, keep and preserve in good repair, order,
and condition, my said castle, capital messuage, or mansion-house,

[*94]

*called Streatlam Castle, and also my capital messuage or
mansion-house called Gibside, and the offices, park, chapel, ornamental buildings, gardens, pleasure-grounds, and appurtenances
thereto belonging, and such of the adjacent lands now in my own
occupation as the trustees or trustee shall think proper to be held
therewith." It is quite plain, therefore, the first object he had was
the improvement of what I would call the demesne lands. But
then, if those improvements were to take place out of the rents and
profits, there must be rents and profits to improve with ; and when
you find the testator has in that part of the will not set forth in the
petition, after those directions to which I have alluded, and after
the direction to keep up the establishment and to make certain
annual payments therein directed, added, "and, upon trust, that,
during the minority of my said son, and also during such time or
times as, in consequence of the trust," and so on, "the said
trustees or trustee of the same term, for the time being, do and

(1) 2 Br. C. C. 653.

shall generally superintend the management of the same manors, hereditaments, and premises, and appoint stewards, bailiffs, agents, and collectors, with such salaries and allowances, as they, the said trustees or trustee, shall think proper;" which is a very large and extensive power. I cannot but myself think, that the testator, when he gives a general power to superintend and manage, he gives a general power without a limit, that is, according to the discretion of the trustees; and unless it appears that what they did in the exercise of the power to superintend and manage was really not a fair exercise of the discretion, it appears to me, of necessity, the Court must uphold what they have done, so far as I understand it. Though it may be said that some of the drainings that were done would not last twenty years, I do not see, upon the report, that the draining which has been made has become defective. With respect to sinking wells and erecting pumps, and so on, it appears to me, it is one of the most beneficial things that can be done; because, if you are to have a responsible tenantry, who are to remain upon the estate, not to be shifted from time to time, it is your duty, if you can, to make those tenants comfortable in their farm-houses. I cannot but, myself, think, that what has been done has been done for the general improvement of the estate, for the general improvement of the estate, for this reason, that it appears, as a matter of fact, that the rent-roll has increased in a very large amount, as stated in the Master's report. I do not want any particular cases upon this point. I am to put a construction upon these large and general words " superintend " and " manage." It appears to me that what the trustees have done is sanctioned by those words. Therefore, the report will be confirmed.

SHIPPERDSON v. TOWER (1).

(8 Jurist, 485—486.)

1844.
May 25.

Chancery.
KNIGHT
BRUCE, V.-C.
[485]

Apportionment of rents—The Apportionment Act, 1834 (4 & 5 Will. IV. c. 22).

A testator, after devising his real estates in strict settlement, gave a general power to his trustees, at the request of the tenant for life, to sell or exchange, with a direction that the lands purchased or taken in exchange should be settled upon the same trusts as those sold or given in exchange; and he declared, that, if, at any time thereafter, any person thereby made tenant for life of his said real estates should, when he or she should become

(1) *Donaldson* v. *Donaldson* (1870) L. R. 10 Eq. 635, 639, 40 L. J. Ch. 64 ; *Clive* v. *Clive* (1872) L. R. 7 Ch. 433, 437, 41 L. J. Ch. 386.

beneficially entitled to the possession or to the receipt of the rents of his
real estates, be under the age of twenty-one years, then it should be lawful
for his trustees, during the minority of such tenant for life, to hold
possession of his real estates, and receive the rents, &c. thereof, and out of
the same apply any annual sum, as they should think proper, towards the
maintenance of such minor, and, subject thereto, to lay out and invest the
surplus rents in their names in the funds, or at interest upon Government
or real securities, so that such rents might accumulate in the way of
compound interest, and to stand possessed of and interested in the said
trust monies, upon the same trusts therein declared concerning the money
to arise from the sale by that his will authorised to be made of his said real
estates. At the time of the testator's death, the tenant for life was a
minor, but had since, on the 29th June, attained twenty-one years of age.
A sum of stock had accumulated from the investment of the surplus rents
during his minority, the dividends on which were payable in January and
July. The rents of the estates were due in May and November: Held,
that the case came within the provisions of 4 & 5 Will. IV. c. 22 (1), and
that both the half-yearly dividends and rents payable in the July and
November next following the day on which the tenant for life attained
twenty-one must be apportioned.

GEORGE BABER, by his will, dated the 5th July, 1833, gave and
devised all and singular his freehold and copyhold messuages, lands,
and tenements, and all his real estates whatsoever and wheresoever
which he had power to dispose of by his will, (except such as were
vested in him by any trusts or by way of mortgage), with their and
every of their appurtenants, unto and to the use of John Dalton,
Thomas Richard Shipperdson, and Thomas Forster, their heirs and
assigns, upon the trusts thereinafter declared or referred to, (that
is to say), subject to the charges thereinbefore made upon his real
estate, in trust for his grandson Henry John Tower, the eldest son
of his daughter Isabella Judith, during the term of his natural life,
with remainder in trust for the only son, or, in case there should
be more than one son, for the first and other sons of the said Henry
John Tower, severally and successively in tail male, with divers
remainders over. And the testator gave a general power to the
trustees, at the request of the tenants for life or tenants in tail, to
dispose of, either by way of sale, or in exchange for other hereditaments in England or Wales, all or any part of the devised estates;
and he directed, that the estates so to be purchased or taken in
exchange should be settled upon the trusts, and subject to the
powers, provisions, and declarations, as were thereinbefore expressed
and contained of and concerning the hereditaments so to be sold
or given in exchange, or as near thereto as the nature and quality
of the said estates and other circumstances would admit of. The
testator then declared as follows: " Provided always, and I hereby

(1) See Apportionment Act, 1870 (33 & 34 Vict. c. 35).

further declare, that, if, at any time hereafter, any person hereby SHIPPERD-
SON
v.
TOWER. made tenant for life of my said real estates hereinbefore devised, shall, when he or she shall become beneficially entitled to the possession or to the receipt of the rents and profits of my real estates, or any part thereof, be under the age of twenty-one years, or if any person hereby made tenant in tail male or in tail of my real estates, shall be, when he or she shall become beneficially entitled to the possession, or the rents and profits thereof, under the age of twenty-one years, provided such last-mentioned event shall happen within the period of twenty-one years from my decease, then and in either of the cases it shall be lawful for the trustees or trustee for the time being of this my will, during the minority of such tenant for life, and during such proportionable part or period of the minority of such tenant in tail as shall arise within twenty-one years from my decease, to enter into and hold possession of my real estates, or any part thereof, and receive and take the rents and profits thereof, and by and out of the same receive and apply any sum or sums of money, according to the age of such minor, as they my said trustees or trustee for the time being shall think proper, for and towards the maintenance of such minor, and (subject thereto) to lay out and invest the surplus of the said yearly rents and profits in the names or name of my said trustees or trustee, in the Parliamentary stocks or public funds of Great Britain, or at interest upon Government or real securities in England, to be from time to time varied as occasion shall require, and also to receive the interest, dividends, and annual produce thereof, and from time to time to make similar and repeated investments thereof, so that the said rents and profits may accumulate in the way of compound interest. And I do hereby declare, that, at the end of each such respective period of accumulation, or sooner, if the said trustees or trustee shall think proper, they or he shall call in and convert the accumulated fund into money, and apply the same in satisfaction and discharge of any principal sums of money which shall then affect my said real estates hereinbefore devised, or any part thereof, together with the interest thereof, whether such incumbrances shall be subsisting thereon at my decease, or shall have been created in pursuance of any trusts or powers herein contained, and whether such trust-monies and accumulated funds shall have proceeded from the parts so encumbered or not, and do and shall stand possessed of and interested in the rest of the said trust-monies, (if any), upon the same trusts

herein declared or referred to concerning the money to arise from
the sale by this my will authorised to be made of my said real
estates." At a former hearing of the cause (1), the COURT held,
that the accumulations of the surplus rents were intended by
the testator to go in the same way as the body of the estate.
At the time of the testator's death, Henry John Tower, the tenant
for life, was a minor, and consequently a considerable amount of
stock had accrued from the investment of the surplus rents, the
dividends on which became due in the months of January and
July. The rents of the estates were payable on the 11th May
and the 11th November. Henry John Tower attained his age of
twenty-one years on the 29th June. The only question now raised

[*486] *was, whether he was entitled to the whole of the half-yearly
dividends which had become payable in July, and to the whole
of the half-year's rents which had become payable on the 11th
November following his attaining twenty-one years of age, or
whether such dividends and rents ought not to be apportioned
pursuant to 4 & 5 Will. IV. c. 22, s. 2 (2), which enacts, " That,
from and after the passing of this Act, all rents-service reserved
in any lease by a tenant in fee, or for any life-interest, or by any
lease granted under any power, (and which leases shall have been
granted after the passing of this Act), and all rents-charge and
other rents, annuities, pensions, dividends, moduses, compositions,
and all other payments of any description, in the United Kingdom
of Great Britain and Ireland, made payable or coming due at fixed
periods under any instrument that shall be executed after the
passing of this Act, or (being a will or testamentary instrument)
that shall come into operation after the passing of this Act, shall
be apportioned, so and in such manner, that, on the death of any
person interested in such rents, annuities, pensions, dividends,
moduses, compositions, or other payments as aforesaid, or in the
estate, fund, office, or benefice from or in respect of which the same
shall be issuing or derived, or on the determination by any other
means whatsoever of the interest of any such person, he or she,
and his or her executors, administrators, or assigns, shall be entitled
to a proportion of such rents, annuities, pensions, dividends,
moduses, compositions, and other payments, according to the time
which shall have elapsed from the commencement or last period
of payment thereof respectively, (as the case may be), including

(1) *Vide* 6 Jur. 658.   in Ireland, 23 & 24 Vict. c. 154, s.
(2) Rep. as to landlord and tenant   104.

the day of the death of such person, or of the determination of his SHIPPERD-
or her interest, all just allowances and deductions in respect of SON
charges on such rents, &c., and other payments, being made." TOWER.

Wigram and *Freeling*, for Henry John Tower, the tenant for life :

We submit that the tenant for life is entitled to the whole of the
dividends and rents payable on the respective quarter-days next
after his attaining twenty-one, inasmuch as the present case does
not come within the 2nd section of the Act. There is no determination of an interest, but merely of an office, for the legal estate
still remains vested in the trustees.

KNIGHT BRUCE, V.-C. :

I am of opinion, that, on the true construction of the Act, there
must be an apportionment of rents. The estates are left to trustees
to hold possession and receive the rents and profits thereof, and,
after applying a portion towards his maintenance, to accumulate
the surplus until the tenant for life attain twenty-one. It is clearly
a case of an interest determinable on the tenant for life attaining
twenty-one. The same rule must be applied to the dividends as
to the rents. There must be an apportionment of each.

Russell and *De Gex* appeared for the several parties entitled in
remainder, but were not called upon to address the Court.

Simpkinson and *Toller* appeared for the plaintiffs, the trustees.

BRAHAM v. STRATHMORE.

(8 Jurist, 567.)

1844.
July 1.

Chancery.
SHADWELL,
V.-C.

[567]

Receiver.

A receiver had been appointed upon bill filed by an annuitant on the
estate. All arrears having been paid off, under the circumstances, the
order appointing the receiver was discharged.

THE original bill in this suit was filed in 1814, by Philip Braham, to
whom the Earl of Strathmore had granted an annuity of 1,307l. 10s.,
on behalf of himself and all other the annuitant creditors of the
said Earl of Strathmore. The bill prayed for the payment of the
arrears of the plaintiff's annuity, and for the appointment of a
receiver. Eight several annuities were proved amounting in the
whole to 7,732l., and receivers were duly appointed. By indentures
of 22nd and 23rd December, 1823, and 29th February and 1st March,

1824, the estates on which these annuities were charged were conveyed to trustees, on trust to receive the rents, and apply them in manner therein mentioned. It appeared that, at the present time, no arrears were due upon the annuities, and that the estates now in the hands of the receivers produced a surplus of 2,500*l.* a year, beyond the said annuities. It was stated at the Bar, that, under the receiver, considerable expense was occasioned in granting leases, and in other matters; and this was a motion to discharge the order, appointing the receiver, the trustees undertaking to pay the annuities.

Bethell and *Lovat*, for the motion:

There has been no arrear for a long period; and the only question is, whether, if an order for a receiver has once been made, the Court will continue it as long as the annuity continues: [*Jenkins* v. *Milford* (1) and *Sankey* v. *O'Maley* (2).]

L. Lowndes and *Goldsmid*, contrà:

In *Sankey* v. *O'Maley*, there was a legal power to distrain; here, we have none. As a proof that the appointment of the receiver is beneficial, it appears, that, since he has been appointed, the annuity has never been in arrear. It does not appear that the expense of granting leases is greater.

Stuart, for other parties.

Bethell, in reply.

THE VICE-CHANCELLOR:

It appears to me, that this is a question only for the discretion of the Court, because I do not recollect an instance having occurred before me like this, that when an estate cannot pay interest at first, it can at last. But here, either by the improvement of rents, or for some other reasons, it does appear that the rental is 10,000*l.* a year, at least. Then the annuitants say they must have the consent of all parties to the leases; and it will only perhaps be a shifting in form, and the leases will have to be settled in the usual way by the concurrence of all parties, out of the Master's office. But it appears to me, that, with these offers, there is no sufficient reason why the application should not be granted. It appears to me, that it will not prejudice other parties; and if any prejudice occur, it will be competent to the parties to apply to the Court.

(1) 21 R. R. 262 (1 J. & W. 629).   (2) 2 Molloy, 291.

QUARRILL *v.* BINMORE.

(8 Jurist, 1113.)

1844.
Dec. 18.

Chancery.
KNIGHT
BRUCE, V.-C.

[1118]

Infant—Guardian, appointment of.

A. and B., infants, intermarry; A.'s father and natural guardian is living; but B.'s mother, who was also her testamentary guardian, is dead. The Court will appoint A.'s father to be B.'s guardian, without a reference to the Master.

IN this case, two infant parties had intermarried. The father and natural guardian of the husband was still living, but the mother, who was also the testamentary guardian, of the wife was dead. There was also another infant, party to the suit, who was illegitimate. One of the questions was, who was to be appointed guardian of the wife.

Terrell appeared for the plaintiffs.

Elwin, for the defendants.

KNIGHT BRUCE, V.-C. :

His Honour said that he would have appointed the husband's father to be guardian of the wife without a reference to the Master ; but that, as there must be a reference as to the appointment of a guardian for the infant who was illegitimate, they had better take a reference in respect of both, with a direction to the Master to prefer the husband's father as a guardian for the wife, provided there appeared no objection to him.

INDEX.

END OF VOL. LXIX.

BRADBURY, AGNEW & CO. LD., PRINTERS LONDON AND TONBRIDGE

Lightning Source UK Ltd.
Milton Keynes UK
UKHW010813110119
335238UK00010B/1059/P